D0330961

Pan Am's World Guide

The Encyclopedia of Travel

McGraw-Hill Company

*New York   St. Louis   San Francisco
Hamburg   Mexico   Toronto   Sydney*

Copyright © 1976, 1978, 1980, 1982 by Pan American World Airways, Inc. Published by arrangement with the DR Group, Inc. and McGraw-Hill Book Company, New York. All rights reserved. Printed in the United States of America. Except as permitted under the United States Copyright Act of 1976, no part of this publication may be reproduced or distributed in any form or by any means, or stored in a data base or retrieval system, without the prior written permission of Pan American World Airways, Inc.

26th Edition

13 14 15 16 17 DOC/DOC 9 9 8 7 6 5 4 3 2 1 0

Library of Congress Cataloging in Publication Data

Main entry under title:
Pan Am's world guide.
    Includes index.
    1. Voyages and travels—1951-   —Guide-
books. I. Pan American World Airways, Inc.
G153.4.P36 1982   910'.2'02   81-17231
ISBN 0-07-048433-3   AACR2

Contents

CONTENTS

Acknowledgments

We wish to acknowledge the supervision and project coordination by The DR Group, Inc. and the work of McGraw-Hill World News bureaus and correspondents throughout the world in updating and assembling the information for this Guide. We also wish to acknowledge the assistance of the Tourist Boards, Embassies and Consulates who cooperated in providing accurate up-to-date facts and figures.

Editorial Supervision for Pan Am: Maureen A. Hickey

Photo Credits: Austrian National Tourist Office; Belgian National Tourist Office; Italian Government Travel Office; Netherlands National Tourist Office; Norwegian National Tourist Office; Spanish National Tourist Office; Swiss National Tourist Office; Yugoslav National Tourist Office; Moroccan National Tourist Office; Tunisian National Tourist Office; Israel Government Tourist Office; National Council of Tourism in Lebanon; Pacific Area Travel Association; Hawaii Visitors Bureau; Hong Kong Tourist Office; Philippine Tourist Office; New York Convention and Visitors Bureau; United States Travel Service; South Dakota Tourism; Mexican Tourist Office; Venezuelan Government Tourist & Information Center; Barbados Tourist Board; Bermuda News Bureau; Mr. Charles R. Meyer; French West Indies Tourist Board; Puerto Rico Tourism Development Company: St. Lucia Tourist Board; St. Maarten Tourist Office; Caribbean Tourism Association; United Nations; and Pan Am's Photo Library.

Introduction

As the World's Most Experienced Airline, we've amassed a wealth of knowledge about travel. This encyclopedia is the authoritative compendium of that knowledge and experience, reaching back more than 50 years and covering 131 different countries in detail.

We make every effort to keep this best-selling travel guide accurate. Perfection is impossible, when so many changes occur on such short notice. But through our on-the-spot reports from many lands, we've gathered the kind of information that can only be obtained locally—about countries all around the globe. We want to share our experience with you, to help ensure that wherever you may go around Pan Am's world, your trip will live up to your every expectation.

WHAT'S IN IT FOR YOU?

The encyclopedia of travel is really what its title implies—*the* book of information a traveler needs about every country. And you can use the World Guide just as you'd use any encyclopedia. Begin by looking up the name of the country you want to know about. Within "area" sections (see Table of Contents), the countries are listed in alphabetical sequence. You'll find an outline map showing surrounding countries or bodies of water, plus many major cities and a special indication for the capital. Each country section begins with "general" background information about the country, its character, size, population, and other basic data, including holidays and currency, how to get there, the difference between local time and Greenwich Mean Time (the world's standard), entry requirements, and airport information. Then there's the "working information" section: accommodations, banks, tipping, electricity, transportation within the country, etc. After that, the latest available data on what to do and see—food and restaurants, drinking tips, entertainment, shopping, and so on—in the major cities and outlying areas. And finally, a list of sources of further information, in the event the encyclopedia doesn't answer all your questions.

The information in this guide is as accurate and up to date as we could make it, as of the date of issue. However, because of changing conditions and the possibility of typographic and other human error, the publisher disclaims responsibility for absolute accuracy.

SIMPLIFIED CUSTOMS/EXCISE LAW

This brief "recap" of US and international laws affecting travel, including Customs regulations, should cover almost everything you need to know. However, there are always exceptions and there are occasional changes in regulations during the year. So it's best if you have any questions to check with the appropriate agency first. (Note that each country's section also contains localized "Requirements for Entry and Customs Regulations.")

Papers US Citizens Will Need: A valid US passport is the most commonly required document. To get one, you will need to present proof of citizenship, 2 passport photos, and a modest fee.

If you were born in the US you must present a certified birth certificate, 2 identical passport photos (front view, full face, $2'' \times 2''$, in front of a light background), a form of identification with a physical description on it such as a driver's license, and $15.00. If you cannot obtain a proper birth certificate, a notarized affadivit of your birth vouched for by a relative or someone who has known you for a long time is sometimes accepted, so you should call the nearest passport agency first to make sure. If you are a naturalized citizen, instead of the birth certificate you must present your naturalization certificate.

If you have an expired passport that is within 8 years of issue you need only present that along with 2 passport photos and $10. (If it expired more than 8 years ago you must pay $15.)

Bearing the necessary documents, you should apply in person to the Passport Division of the Department of State or a Passport Agency of the Department of State (in Washington, D.C., Boston, Chicago, Honolulu, Houston, Los Angeles, Miami, New Orleans, New York, Philadelphia, San Francisco, Seattle, or Stamford). In other cities, apply to the clerk of a federal court or at selected post offices. Some agencies accept cash—otherwise a check or money order. A passport will no longer be issued for a whole family—only for individuals, and it will remain valid for a five-year period.

Requirements for non-US Citizens: The basic requirements for international travel are the same for practically all nationalities, although the procedures for application vary from country to country, as do the validity and cost of passports and visas. World Health Organization requirements apply irrespective of nationality. Your nearest Pan Am office will be glad to answer any questions about travel requirements.

IMPORTANT: When traveling, carry your passport *on your person*. Do not pack it in your baggage. Also, do not surrender it to anyone except authorized immigration officials or police officers (and, in some countries, hotel reception desks).

Some countries also require that your passport carry a visa before you may enter. Visas are issued for a small fee by the embassies and consulates of the countries concerned. When your itinerary is set, check with your travel agent or Pan Am office to find out whether any visas are required. You will also find this information in this publication.

Vaccination Requirements: Under World Health Organization (WHO) regulations, some countries require visitors to be vaccinated against smallpox, cholera, and/or yellow fever. Currently, only two countries require smallpox vaccinations: Chad, plus Sao Tome and Principe. (Vaccination certificate requirements are listed under the respective country headings.) A smallpox vaccination certificate is valid for three years; cholera, six months; and yellow fever, ten years. These official WHO certificates are recognized around the world and can be obtained from most local boards of health, travel agencies, physicians, etc.

Typhoid inoculations are not required, but in some countries they may be advisable—as well as gamma globulin, tetanus, and malaria shots. In fact, well before your trip—three months if possible—you should consult the US Public Health Service to find out just what precautions and vaccinations should be taken. Or if you prefer, consult with your travel agent or Pan Am. Either has the necessary forms and can direct you to an approved doctor or clinic. Furthermore, you'll be glad to learn that vaccination techniques have so improved that most people suffer never a twinge.

We suggest that you check with your local Passport Office, Pan Am travel agent, or other authorities for travel advisories if there is a possibility of recent changes related to health and safety conditions in areas you plan to visit.

Bringing It Back to the US: This section covers what US citizens will be allowed to bring back into the United States. The duty-free allowances for each country are dealt with in the country listings.

Shopping abroad is one of the pleasures of international travel. US Customs officials are generally lenient with travelers from abroad provided the goods they have bought are clearly intended for the traveler's own use or for gifts, and are declared on arrival in the US.

Provided your stay outside the US exceeds 48 hours and you have not used any part of this exemption within the preceding 30 days, you may bring in goods purchased abroad up to $300 in value without paying duty. If you are arriving from the US Virgin Islands, Guam, or American Samoa, you may bring in goods worth up to $600, but only items totaling $300 in value may be from areas other than these. Such goods must accompany you on the flight, and it is a good idea to have receipts to prove the value of your purchases. You may also mail gifts to the United States from abroad without duty, although the value of such gifts must not exceed $25 each. Original works of art and antiques (articles 100 years old or older) may also be brought into the US duty free, provided each is accompanied by a document attesting its authenticity.

Entering the US, up to 100 cigars, 200 cigarettes, and one quart of wine or liquor may be included in your exemption. (Liquor and tobacco may be subject to state and/or local taxes.) Returning from the US Virgin Islands, Guam, or American Samoa, you may bring in one gallon of wine or other liquor. Remember, the cost is included in your duty allowance. You must be 21 years of age or older to include alcoholic beverages in your exemption.

When you bring in articles worth more than your personal exemption, the first $600 worth of goods in excess of your exemption will be assessed at a flat rate of duty of 10%. That's based on fair retail value of the goods in the country where you acquired the articles. (There's a 5% rate of duty on goods brought in from the US Virgin Islands, Guam, and American Samoa.) However, the flat rate of duty only applies to articles for your own personal use or for gifts, but not if they're for sale.

The head of a family may make a joint declaration for all members residing in the same household and returning together to the US, including children. Thus, while one family member may have articles that exceed his or her exemption, when combined together with the articles of the whole family, they may not be subject to any duty. What's more, the flat rate of duty for the first $600 of duty in excess of the exemption is also computed for families.

If you have been outside the US less than 48 hours, or have already used your $300 or $600 exemption during the past 30-day period, you may bring in, without duty, goods to the value of $25—including a maximum of 50 cigarettes, 10 cigars, 4 ounces of alcoholic beverages, and 4 ounces of alcohol-based perfume.

The US "Generalized System of Preferences" allows many articles from "beneficiary developing countries" to be brought into the US duty free in addition to your basic Customs exemption. The nearest US Customs Office can give you a copy of "GSP and the Traveler," containing details of the GSP program.

Unless accompanied by an import license from a US government agency, most meat, fruit, vegetables, plants, and plant products will be impounded and destroyed by US Customs. Similar rules apply to furs and pelts of "endangered species," such as leopard skins. Contact the US Fish and Wildlife Service or the US Department of Agriculture for detailed information.

Although vaccination against rabies is not required for your dog or cat if you are bringing them in from a rabies-free country, they still must be free of any evidence of diseases communicable to man. Also, you might check with your state, county, or municipal officials to make sure they have no restrictions on importing a pet. The leaflet "Pets, Wildlife, US Customs" gives specific regulations if you are planning to take your pet abroad, or import one on your return. For animals requiring quarantine, boarding kennels are available at ports of entry.

The importation of anything originating in North Korea, Vietnam, Iran, Cambodia, or Cuba is prohibited without a US Treasury license (which tourists will find almost impossible to obtain).

If you can anticipate your purchases it's best to consult with Customs before you go. The US Customs Service also publishes an informative handbook entitled *Know Before You Go—Customs Hints for Returning Residents*. It may be able to answer most of your questions. And remember, US Customs is one of the most rigorous and thorough operations in the world.

Bringing Things Back to Other Countries: Each country has its own set of rules for travelers returning home, most being somewhat similar to the US regulations covered here. There are considerable variations in some instances, however. If you are in doubt about what goods you may bring back duty free, check with any Pan Am office or travel agent.

TRAVEL IN HEALTH

While there was a time when travel in the tropics and/or certain nondeveloped areas was considered a health hazard, modern medicine and hygiene control have reduced the risk almost to zero. Provided you adhere strictly to common-sense personal hygiene rules, little harm can come to your health almost anywhere you choose to travel. Minor internal upsets are the most common cause for complaint, more often than not caused by a change in drinking water and an inevitable change in diet. To play it safe, drink bottled water (available almost everywhere) and avoid fruit with cut or damaged skin. In the tropics, doctors recommend that you drink at least four pints of liquid a day to guard against dehydration. And, particularly if you're sensitive to sunburn, accustom yourself gradually to sunlight in the tropics, where you can sunburn very quickly even on overcast days.

POUNDS, PENCE, PESETAS, ETC.

The most variable of all subjects covered in this guide are official currency exchange rates. One or another currency relationship may change almost hourly, and on occasion, the fluctuation over a period of a week or more can be drastic. So you are advised to check exchange rates and currency regulations with your travel agent or bank before starting on a trip.

The soundest way to carry money when traveling is in travelers' checks. They can be cashed almost anywhere in the world, at almost any time, in the currency of the place. By tearing out the check record and keeping it separate from the checks themselves, you can quickly report any loss for refund. It is also sensible to carry a few small-denomination bills, so as to avoid breaking larger bills for exchange into currencies you really do not want (as during a stopover, for example). It is also helpful to arrive at any destination with a small amount in local currency for tipping porters, paying taxi drivers, etc.

Widely known credit cards, such as American Express, Diners Club, Visa, or MasterCard, are quite generally accepted around the world (at least in major cities), but of course there is always a possibility that a credit card will not be accepted by a particular establishment.

WHERE TO STAY

We have researched every hotel mentioned in the *World Guide,* although we cannot guarantee that prices will remain as quoted indefinitely or that services will still warrant mention in the book. As a rule, service does not decline drastically overnight, but prices have been moving upward in many areas. You may check with your nearest Pan Am office or your travel agent for up-to-date prices at the time you plan to depart. We have indicated, for your convenience, the location of the hotels as they relate to the center of a city or town.

Throughout the book, peak season rates are given in US$ for a double room with bath or shower, unless other wise indicated. In many areas, you may find that less expensive accommodations are available. When meals are included in quoted prices, the following abbreviations have been used:

> CP (Continental Plan) includes room and Continental breakfast; BB indicates room and full breakfast; AP (American Plan) includes three meals a day; MAP (Modified American Plan) includes breakfast and either lunch or dinner.

OTHER

Insurance: Personal effects insurance policies are well worth the few extra dollars. The unpleasant feeling that accompanies having luggage lost or stolen is greatly compounded by your being unable to file a claim for its replacement. "Trip Insurance" policies are available at reasonable cost. But if you do a reasonable amount of traveling during the year, you may find the annual travel accident policies offered by some leading companies to be even more of a bargain.

Driving Overseas: If you enjoy motor trips in familiar territory, you'll find there are many places overseas that are well suited to a leisurely driving tour—and some places that may be *best* seen and appreciated with the freedom afforded by a car. We suggest, however, that you check with your local Automobile Club about areas you may be planning to tour by car. There are countries where only the truly adventurous would be advised to drive themselves, perhaps because the laws of that country do not offer adequate protection to a visitor in case of a mishap. Your automobile association can tell you how to acquire an International Driver's License, valid in almost all countries, and can also put you in touch with an affiliated motoring organization in the country you're planning to visit—usually on a reciprocal service basis which costs you nothing extra.

Climatic Changes: Although the idea of flying from one climate extreme to another in a few hours may sound traumatic, it's usually not upsetting. Central heating is common in cold climates, and air conditioning has permeated even the less sophisticated areas of the tropics. Remember that the seasons are reversed in the Northern and Southern hemispheres—December is midsummer in Argentina and Australia, midwinter in China and Canada. As a general rule, the closer to the equator, the hotter and more humid the climate, although altitude is also a significant factor. (Temperature drops approximately 1°F for each 1,000 feet of altitude gained.) The quoted climatic statistics in each chapter of this book are accurate averages, but of course conditions on any specific day will vary from the average.

International Dateline: If you travel all the way across the Pacific, you will cross the International Dateline and will either lose or gain a full day (depending on the direction of flight). Heading west, for example, you might depart Honolulu at 2pm on Monday and land in Tokyo at 5:55pm on what seems to be the same day. But it will be Tuesday in Tokyo, because the dateline has been crossed. Flying in the other direction, if you leave Tokyo at 10pm, you'll arrive in Honolulu at 9:30 of the same morning.

Photography: Each chapter of this book contains a paragraph headed "Photography," in which you'll find a brief run-down of available photographic services, plus any local restrictions on the use of cameras (such as photographing religious services, places of strategic or military importance, etc.). If you will be carrying a really expensive camera or any new equipment, it is advisable to have the original purchase invoice or sales slip in your possession. This could save a lot of annoyance at Customs checkpoints. 35mm or 2¼" × 2¼" color film is available almost everywhere, but prices do vary considerably and you may find places where only 64 ASA is available. If you want really fast film or infra-red, it's a good idea to carry it with you, although some countries restrict the number of rolls you may bring in. Kodak's international processing labs operate in some improbable places, usually with efficiency. But unless you are on an extended trip or have a strong reason for wanting immediate development, it's probably wisest to wait until you get home to have your film developed.

If you are visiting remote tribal villages or other unsophisticated areas, do not expect the people to ignore your picture-taking activity. In some places, you may discover all backs turned until you have come up with the obligatory coin, cigarette, or whatever. And you may come across persons who have a serious objection to being photographed for reasons which are very real to them. In such cases, it is only good taste—and sometimes avoids unpleasantness—to point your camera in another direction. Occasionally, what looks like a charming rural bridge may be considered a military installation by authorities. Remember the old rule: When in Rome . . .

Another warning: Some electronic devices used for baggage checking may damage exposed but undeveloped film. When possible, it is safest to carry such film in your hand luggage. Or better yet, consider purchasing a lead-lined pouch to keep your film in to protect it from harmful radiation.

Electricity: There are many different "travel" appliances—shavers, travel irons, hair driers, and other electrical items—designed to make life easier for the international traveler. Most come equipped with adapter plugs to fit the many different types of outlet sockets in hotels around the world. Some, however, do not have the built-in transformer to adapt the local power supply to that which your appliance requires. And while it is true that most countries provide a 120-volt, 60-cycle alternating current, some still adhere to the 200/400-volt, 50-cycle supply. There are a few places, the more remote areas, which still offer a direct-current power supply, but AC has become almost standard. In any event, there *are* places where appliances may be burned out if operated without proper adapters.

If you feel the need to carry electrical appliances, a lightweight all-purpose transformer costing under $20 will cope with just about any eccentricities in power supply you may encounter. Where a hotel prohibits the use of electrical appliances, there is undoubtedly a good reason, and it is probably in your own best interest not to try. Electric shaver owners might note that using your shaver on 50-cycle AC will not damage the shaver, but it will mean slower, less efficient operation.

Your Pan Am Travel Agent: Even this comprehensive and detailed encyclopedia of world travel will leave you with some questions, and reservations must be made somewhere. We suggest your local Pan Am travel agent, a real authority on travel who has the full range of Pan Am's worldwide services instantly available through our Panamac Reservations System. He or she knows everything there is to know about itineraries, reservations, passports, and inoculations and can make *all* your arrangements, for air, land, or sea travel, for sightseeing, for accommodations . . . wherever in the world you plan to travel. If you like, your travel agent can help you with *that* decision, too. His or her advice and services can take a lot off your mind—and since agents are paid by commission on the various travel services they arrange, their help usually costs you nothing. Also important to you, the agent's best interest is obviously served by having you back for another trip, so you can be sure he or she will see that you enjoy the very best your money will afford.

GETTING READY TO GO

As your departure date draws close, you may feel there are a thousand and one things to be done (which is an excellent reason for having your travel agent handle the detailed arrangements). Stopping the milk, the mail, and the newspapers, arranging for pet care . . . most of the things are simple enough, but they must be done.

Glasses and Medications: If you wear glasses and are headed for places with bright sunshine (or even brighter snowy slopes), you may want to get clip-on or prescription sunglasses. It's also wise to carry a spare pair of your regular glasses, so an accidental loss or breakage won't deprive you of seeing all there is to be seen. Similarly, if you regularly take a prescription medication, either take enough to last the duration of your trip or make sure the medication you need is available where you're headed. Have your doctor write out a clear list of any prescriptions you might need to have refilled en route.

Baggage Rules: On flights between the United States and most countries two methods for determining free baggage allowances are now in effect. The method used is dependent upon the carrier(s) involved and the origination and/or destination points of your flight. So check with your travel agent or with Pan Am for details.

The weight method, which applies to most flights that do not arrive or depart from the US and Canada, has the following free weight allowances: for First/Business Class, 66 pounds (30 kilograms); for Tourist/Economy Class, 44 pounds (20 kilograms).

The piece method, which applies to flights in and out of the US and Canada, calculates the free baggage allowance by the number of pieces of checked and/or unchecked baggage and the size of the pieces. For First/Business Class passengers, you're allowed 2 pieces of checked luggage with a combined height, depth, and width that doesn't exceed 62 inches (158 centimeters) and one unchecked piece of 45 inches (115 centimeters) so that it can fit under the seat in front of you. For Economy Class the total dimensions of the checked baggage must not exceed 106 inches (270 cm) and for one or more unchecked pieces the sum of linear measurements must not exceed 45 inches (115 cm). (Total weight for each checked bag should not exceed 70 pounds or 32 kg.)

In all cases there is a charge—it could be substantial—for excess baggage. So you should consult with your travel agent or with Pan Am to find out how much this would be.

What to Take: Depending on destination, a man should normally be able to get by with one dark suit and a sportcoat, a woman with a couple of cocktail dresses—as far as dress-up occasions are concerned. Washable, drip-dry shirts and blouses are always a boon; but inquire about the artificial fabrics you choose—some don't "breathe" too freely and can be uncomfortable in warm, humid climates.

A sweater is nearly always desirable, even in hot climates, for evenings or excursions to higher altitudes. For cooler climates, a sturdy topcoat, waterproof shoes or boots, and perhaps even a collapsible umbrella may be handy, as are sandals and light clothing for warmer climates.

Take your bathing suit (if you swim) wherever you're headed, but excess jewelry is apt to be more nuisance than benefit. A needle and thread for emergencies is advisable—as is weighing your packed luggage well before departure, in case you may need time to decide which items are more important than others. Modern luggage is quite lightweight—and of course the less your luggage weighs, the more you can carry inside it.

Dressing for the Trip: The weather where you *are* is of little concern when dressing for the trip. Be sure to consider what you're wearing as part of your travel wardrobe. And as far as your comfort en route is concerned, plan on a comfortable Pan Am Clipper cabin temperature of 70-75°F and dress accordingly.

Checking In: While there is seldom any problem, officially passengers cannot be guaranteed a seat on a flight when they arrive after the stated check-in time. So it's wise to arrive at the airport at least an hour before take-off time—as much as two hours, if you're leaving from a city terminal.

Patience, Patience: Of course travelers arriving at a strange and exciting destination are eager to get "into it." But it is only common sense to think about the time you've spent traveling, however comfortably, when planning activities immediately after arrival overseas. After a long flight, a hot bath and a catnap—or even a night's rest—will make all that follows more of a pleasure.

Tour Travel: Preplanned group travel, either escorted or independent, is a major form of economy. And, of course, the better the tour arrangements, the greater the economy and the value.

WE'RE ALL EARS!

Despite the almost continuous checking and revision through which we try to keep this guide up to the minute, we'd appreciate knowing how you, the reader, evaluate our encyclopedia of travel. We'd like very much to know where you found it helpful . . . and where not. Tell us where you find it to be either correct or in error. Address any comments to: Sales Promotion Department, Pan American World Airways, Pan Am Building, New York, NY 10166.

Comparative Table of Clothing Sizes

All over the world there are different ways of sizing things up. If in doubt, it is always best to try on a garment before purchase.

MEN'S CLOTHING

Suits

UK	34	35	36	37	38	39	40	41	42
USA	34	35	36	37	38	39	40	41	42
European	44	46	48	49½	51	52½	54	55½	57

Shirts

UK	14½	15	15½	16	16½	17	17½	18
USA	14½	15	15½	16	16½	17	17½	18
European	37	38	39	41	42	43	44	45

Shoes

UK	6	7	8	9	10	11	12
USA	7	8	9	10	11	12	13
European	39½	41	42	43	44½	46	47

WOMEN'S CLOTHING

Dresses

UK	10	12	14	16	18	20
USA	8	10	12	14	16	18
European	38	40	42	44	46	48

Cardigans, Sweaters, Blouses

UK	32	34	36	38	40	42
USA	8	10	12	14	16	18
European	38	40	42	44	46	48

Shoes

UK	3	3½	4	4½	5	5½	6	6½	7
USA	4½	5	5½	6	6½	7	7½	8	8½
European	35½	36	36½	37	37½	38	38½	39	39½

CHILDREN'S CLOTHING CHART

Dresses and Coats (knitwear one size larger)

UK	18	20	22	24	26
USA	3	4	5	6	6X
European	98	104	110	116	122

For older children, sizes generally correspond with their age.

Shoes

UK	7	8	9	10	11	12	13	1	2	3	4	5½
USA	8	9	10	11	12	13	1	2	3	4½	5½	6½
European	24	25	27	28	29	30	32	33	34	36	37	38½

Weights, Measures, Temperatures

WEIGHT

(1 pound = 0.454 kilogram)

Kilograms	1	2	3	4	5	6	7	8
Pounds	2.2046	4.4	6.6	8.8	11.0	13.2	15.43	17.64

LIQUID MEASURES

(1 Imperial gallon = 1.2 US gallons or 4.5 liters.)

Liters	1	2	3	4	5	6
US Gal	0.264	0.53	0.79	1.06	1.32	1.58

Liters	7	8	9	10	50	100
US Gal	1.85	2.11	2.38	2.64	13.20	26.40

LENGTHS AND DISTANCES

(1 foot = 0.3048 meter; 1 meter = 39 inches)
(1 mile = 1.609 kilometers. Roughly speaking 1 kilometer = ⅗ mile)

Meters	1	2	3	4	5	6
Feet	3.3	6.6	9.8	13.1	16.4	19.7

Meters	7	8	9	10	50
Feet	23.0	26.2	29.5	32.8	164.0

Kilometers	1	2	3	4	5	6
Miles	0.62	1.24	1.86	2.48	3.11	3.73

Kilometers	7	8	9	10	20
Miles	4.35	4.97	5.58	6.20	12.40

TEMPERATURE

Centigrade	40	39	38	37	36	35
Fahrenheit	104.0	102.2	100.4	98.6	96.8	95

Centigrade	34	33	32	31	30	29
Fahrenheit	93.2	91.4	89.6	87.8	86.0	84.2

Centigrade	28	27	26	25	24	23
Fahrenheit	82.4	80.6	78.8	77.0	75.2	73.4

Centigrade	22	21	20	19	18	17
Fahrenheit	71.6	69.8	68.0	66.2	64.4	62.6

Centigrade	16	15	14	13	12	11
Fahrenheit	60.8	59.0	57.2	55.4	53.6	51.8

Centigrade	10	9	8	7	6	5
Fahrenheit	50.0	48.2	46.4	44.6	42.8	41.0

Centigrade	4	3	2	1	0	−1
Fahrenheit	39.2	37.4	35.6	33.8	32.0	30.2

Centigrade	−2	−3	−4	−5	−6	−7
Fahrenheit	28.4	26.6	24.8	23.0	21.2	19.4

EUROPE

FINLAND

Helsinki

● Moscow

U.S.S.R.

ROMANIA

Bucharest

BLACK SEA

BULGARIA

Istanbul

CASPIAN SEA

TURKEY

ECE

Cyprus

SYRIA

N SEA

LEBANON

ISRAEL

EGYPT

RED SEA

EUROPE CURRENCY CONVERSION

Country	United States $				United Kingdom £			
	5¢	10¢	50¢	$1	5p	10p	50p	£1
Andorra								
pesetas • centimos	4.55	9.09	45.45	90.90	9.51	19.00	94.99	189.98
fancs • centimes	.27	.55	2.75	5.49	.56	1.15	5.75	11.47
Austria								
schillings • groschen	.81	1.62	8.10	16.20	1.69	3.39	16.93	33.86
Balearic Islands								
pesetas • centimos	4.55	9.09	45.45	90.90	9.51	19.00	94.99	189.98
Belgium								
francs • centimes	1.86	3.72	18.59	37.17	3.89	7.77	38.85	77.69
Bulgaria								
leva • stotinki	.04	.09	.44	.88	.08	.19	.92	1.84
Canary Islands								
pesetas • centimos	4.55	9.09	45.45	90.90	9.51	19.00	94.99	189.98
Cyprus								
pounds • mils	.02	.04	.20	.39	.04	.08	.42	.82
Czechoslovakia								
korunas • hellers	.47	.93	4.67	9.35	.98	1.94	9.76	19.54
Denmark								
kroner • ore	.36	.72	3.60	7.19	.75	1.50	7.52	15.03
Finland								
finmarks • pennia	.22	.43	2.16	4.31	.46	.90	4.51	9.01
France								
francs • centimes	.27	.55	2.75	5.49	.56	1.15	5.75	11.47
Germany								
deutsche marks • pfennigs	.11	.23	1.15	2.29	.23	.48	2.40	4.79
Gibralter								
pounds • pence	.02	.05	.24	.48	.05	.10	.50	1.00
Great Britain								
pounds • pence	.02	.05	.24	.48	.05	.10	.50	1.00
Greece								
drachmas • leptas	2.81	5.62	28.09	56.18	5.87	11.75	58.71	117.42
Hungary								
forints • fillers	1.37	2.74	13.70	27.40	2.86	5.73	28.63	57.27
Iceland								
kronas • aurar	.33	.66	3.29	6.57	.69	1.38	6.88	13.73
Ireland								
pounds • pence	.03	.06	.31	.63	.06	.13	.65	1.32
Italy								
lire • centesimi	57.08	114.16	570.77	1141.55	119.30	238.59	1192.91	2385.84

EUROPE CURRENCY CONVERSION

Country	United States $				United Kingdom £			
	5¢	10¢	50¢	$1	5p	10p	50p	£1
Liechtenstein francs • centimes	.10	.20	1.02	2.04	.21	.42	2.13	4.26
Luxembourg francs • centimes	1.74	3.47	17.36	34.72	3.64	7.25	36.28	72.56
Malta pounds • cents	.02	.04	.19	.38	.04	.08	.40	.79
Monaco francs • centimes	.27	.55	2.75	5.49	.56	1.15	5.75	11.47
Netherlands guilders • cents	.13	.26	1.28	2.56	.27	.54	2.68	5.35
Norway krone • ore	.28	.56	2.78	5.56	.59	1.17	5.81	11.62
Poland zloty • groszy	1.56	3.13	15.62	31.25	3.26	6.54	32.65	65.31
Portugal escudos • centavos	3.05	6.10	30.49	60.98	6.37	12.75	63.72	127.45
Romania lei • bani	.75	1.49	7.46	14.93	1.57	3.11	15.59	31.20
Spain pesetas • centimos	4.55	9.09	45.45	90.90	9.51	19.00	94.99	189.98
Sweden kroner • ore	.25	.49	2.45	4.90	.52	1.02	5.12	10.24
Switzerland francs • centimes	.10	.20	1.02	2.04	.21	.42	2.13	4.26
USSR roubles • kopeks	.04	.07	.37	.74	.08	.15	.77	1.55
Yugoslavia dinars • paras	1.52	3.05	15.24	30.48	3.18	6.37	31.85	63.70

Andorra

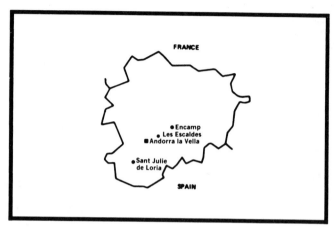

WHAT'S SPECIAL

Perched high in the Pyrenees between France and Spain, Andorra is so small that you can drive across it in less than an hour, although during the peak season it can take up to four times as long due to heavy traffic. It has mountain peaks, valleys and forests, lakes and rivers, medieval buildings, and the lowest-priced shopping in Europe.

COUNTRY BRIEFING

Andorra covers an area of 188 square miles, with an entirely Roman Catholic **population** of 35,000—approximately one-third of whom live in the **capital**, Andorra la Vella. It is an autonomous co-principality with France and Spain. **Currency:** There is no local currency; both the French franc (5.1F = US$1) and the Spanish peseta (90ptas = US$1) are in circulation. **Language:** Catalan; French and Spanish are spoken; very little English. **Climate:** Delightful, warm summer days from May to September, although the mountain air is always cool, and the evenings can be cold. Cold winter weather with snow from mid-November to mid-May. The national **holiday,** the Gowning of the Holy Virgin of Mezitxell, takes place on 8 Sept.

HOW TO GET THERE

Andorra can be reached by road from either Barcelona or Toulouse. Time in Andorra: GMT+1.

REQUIREMENTS FOR ENTRY AND CUSTOMS REGULATIONS

Passport. Customs formalities and restrictions are same as for France and Spain. Andorra is accessible only through one of these two countries.

ACCOMMODATIONS

More than 250 hotels, about a dozen summer camping sites, and private apartments for rent. Hotel reservations are advisable during peak summer season—July to September. Some reduction is often available off-season. Hotels in Andorra la Vella:

Rates are in US$ for double/twin room with bath or shower

Andorra Palace, Prat de la Creu (from $21)

Andorra Park, Plana de Guillemó (from $23)

Eden Roc, 1 Avinguda Dr Mitjavila (from $40)

Flora, Antic Carrer Major 23 (from $30)

President, 40 Avinguda Santa Coloma (from $35)

Pyrénées, 20 Avinguda Princep Benlloch (from $15)

All hotels listed above are centrally located.

USEFUL INFORMATION

There are six main **banks** in the capital, with branches in main villages. Currency and travelers' checks can also be exchanged at various Bureaus of Exchange, or at hotels. Banks open 9-1 and 3-6 Mon-Fri, 9-12 Sat. **Postage stamps** obtainable at post offices and hotels. Local correspondence between Andorran villages is free. Post offices are either French or Spanish—French mailboxes are yellow and square, Spanish boxes silver cylinders with red and yellow stripes. **Telephones:** there are a few booths; calls can also be made from restaurants and cafés. Useful numbers: **Tourist Office & Information,** 20 2 14; **Operator** and **Emergencies,** 11 or 15; **Ambulance** and **Fire Service,** 20 0 20. English-language **newspapers** and magazines available. **Tipping:** a service charge of 10-15% is generally included in bills, but about 10% extra is appreciated. When a service charge is not included, you may leave 10-20% extra, but there is no compulsion to do so in Andorra. As a general rule, give porters 10ptas per piece of luggage; taxi drivers and hairdressers 10%; cloakroom attendants, 10ptas. Hotel porters and chambermaids do not generally receive tips unless a special service has been given. **Electricity** is 125 volts 50 cycles AC throughout the country. **Laundry:** good services; laundromats in main villages. **Hairdressing:** salons charge from 200ptas. **Photography:** good selection of equipment available, and film costs substantially less than in Spain or France. **Babysitting** can be arranged through your hotel concierge. **Rest Rooms:** women, *senyores* or *Dones;* men, *senyors* or *Homes.* **Health:** imported pharmaceuticals and toiletries inexpensive.

TRANSPORTATION

Unscheduled minibus services between main villages. Jeep trips can be arranged through your hotel or local travel agencies in the capital. Local taxis can be hailed at stands on the street or telephoned; fares are not fixed and depend on the distance traveled. Rented cars average US$20-25 a day. Trains, long-distance bus services, and taxis link Andorra with France and Spain.

FOOD AND RESTAURANTS

International cuisine is available; cooking is usually French, Catalan, or Spanish style. Breakfast is 7-10, lunch 1-3, and dinner 8-11. Good restaurants at about US$7-10 per person: **Celler d'En Toni** (tel: 21 2 52), **La Borda** (tel: 21 7 21), and **Els Fanals** (tel: 21 3 81), all in Andorra la Vella. Less expensive meals can be enjoyed at **La Graella** (tel: 21 0 88) and **El Club,** also in Andorra la Vella; and **L'Entrecọte** in Les Escaldes.

ENTERTAINMENT

Movie houses in the capital and a number of villages show films dubbed in French and Spanish and some in English. There are two radio and television stations, one Spanish and one French. The nightlife includes discothèques and nightclubs. In Andorra la Vella, there are discothèques at the **Andorra Palace** and **President** hotels. Other nightspots are: in Les Escaldes, **El Refugio** (tel: 21 4 35) and **La Bodega;** in Encamp, the **Rosaleda Hotel** (tel: 21 2 04), and in Pas de la Casa, **Le Georgia, 1001 Club, Bay-Bay,** and **Adam's Club.**

SHOPPING

Purchases are tax-free, and international merchandise costs less than anywhere else in Europe. Best buys include liquor, suede, furs, cameras, jewelry, tobacco, and locally made wooden objects. Major shops are **Almacenes Pirines** in Andorra la Vella and **Forum** in Les Escaldes. Stores open 9-8 daily and Sundays until 7.

SPORTS

Skiing from November to May; the main resort is **Pas de la Casa.** Ski information from **Esqui Club d'Andorra** (Babor Camp). Trout fishing in mountain streams from 15 March-late August—permits from the Sindicat d'Iniciative. Swimming pools at several hotels and camping sites; horseback riding stables at the **Aldosa.** Tennis can be played except between December and February. Spectator sports are soccer and rugby. Bullfights are banned.

WHAT TO SEE

In **Andorra la Vella** the most important feature is the **House of the Valleys** (seat of the General Council), built in 1580, which contrasts sharply with the modern **Broadcasting House and Studios.** The lakes and mountains are the principal attractions. Especially beautiful are **Pessons Lake** near **Grau Roig** and **Engolasters Lake,** accessible by cable car from Encamp. An antiquities museum is under construction.

SOURCES OF FURTHER INFORMATION

Any **Pan Am** office around the world; **Sindicat d'Iniciative de les Valls d'Andorra**, Plaça Príncep Benlloch 1, Andorra la Vella (tel: 20 2 14); **Andorra National Tourist Board**, PO Box 69617, Hollywood CA 90069; **Andorra Official Information Office**, 63 Wesover Road, London, SW18 2RF.

Austria

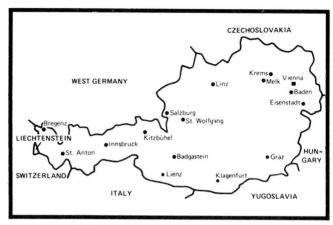

WHAT'S SPECIAL
Austria is geographically a small country, and yet for elegance and sheer joy of living, Vienna is the equal of any capital in the world. Small wonder that Austria attracts a record number of visitors. Music and art play an extremely important part in the cultural life of Austria, and the visitor will have unrivaled opportunities to enjoy them.

COUNTRY BRIEFING
Size: 32,374 square miles   **Population:** 7,456,745
Capital: Vienna   **Capital Population:** 1,614,841
   Climate: Cold winters and delightful summers. June-September are the best months for warm-weather touring. December-April is an ideal time for a winter sports vacation.

Weather in Vienna: Lat N48°15'; Alt 664 ft.

Temp (°F)	Jan	Feb	Mar	Apr	May	Jun	Jul	Aug	Sep	Oct	Nov	Dec
Av Low	26°	28°	34°	41°	50°	56°	59°	58°	52°	44°	36°	30°
Av High	34°	38°	47°	57°	66°	71°	75°	73°	66°	55°	44°	37°
Days no rain	23	21	24	21	22	21	22	21	23	23	22	22

Government: Austria is a republic.
Language: German. English understood and spoken by many.
Religion: Approximately 88% Roman Catholic, 12% Protestant.

Currency: Schilling. 100 groschen = AS1 (in German, OS—Öster-reichische Schilling).

	AS 1	AS 5	AS 10	AS 20	AS 50	AS 100	AS 500	AS 1,000
US (dollars, cents)	.06	.31	.62	1.23	3.09	6.17	30.85	61.70
UK (pounds, pence)	.03	.14	.30	.59	1.48	2.95	14.74	29.49

Public Holidays:

New Year's Day, 1 Jan

Epiphany, 6 Jan

Easter Monday

Labor Day, 1 May

Ascension Day

Whit Monday

Corpus Christi

Assumption Day, 15 Aug

National Holiday, 26 Oct

All Saints Day, 1 Nov

Immaculate Conception, 8 Dec

Christmas Day, 25 Dec

Boxing Day, 26 Dec

HOW TO GET THERE

Flying time to Vienna, Schwechat Airport from New York is 8½ hours, from London, 3 hours, from Frankfurt, 1¾ hours, from Tokyo, 17 hours. Time in Austria: GMT+1, GMT+2 summer.

REQUIREMENTS FOR ENTRY AND CUSTOMS REGULATIONS

Valid passport required, but no visa for stays of up to three months. No restrictions on currency. Duty-free allowance: 400 cigarettes or 100 cigars or 500 grams tobacco (200 if arriving from another European country); 1 liter liquor; 2 liters wine. Various personal effects including two sporting guns and 200 cartridges.

AIRPORT INFORMATION

Schwechat Airport is 11 miles from the center of Vienna. Buses to and from the City Air Terminal at the Hilton Hotel run daily every 30 minutes between 6:30-10:30am and 6-7pm, otherwise every 20 minutes during the day. The fare is AS42 for adults, AS17 for children, luggage free. Taxis charge about AS280 for the ride to town. There is a bus service between the main hotels and the airport for AS150 per person. No arrival or departure tax at Schwechat. The airport has a duty-free shop, a nursery, a hotel reservation counter, and various car rental desks.

ACCOMMODATIONS

Comfort, along with a love of the past, reigns supreme in the Austrian hotel scene. On the luxury level, there are large and well-appointed hotels, with excellent and most courteous service. The same is true of many of the smaller hotels and pensions in the city and, indeed, throughout the country. Good examples of this are the castles or *Schloss* hotels, built inside the walls of medieval, Renaissance, and baroque landmarks. The **Austrian National Tourist Office** publishes up-to-date hotel and pension lists as well as a brochure *Castle Hotels & Mansions in Austria.*

  Inexpensive accommodations are not hard to find. The under-30 travelers on a budget can stay at hostels organized by the **Austrian Youth Hostels Association.** Go to their office at Gonzagagasse 22, A-1010 Vienna 1, (tel: 63 52-53 or main office at Mariahilferstrasse 24, A-1070, Wien 7—tel: 93 7158) for information. Guests over 30 must apply at the hostels in person after 7:00pm and are admitted only on a space-available basis. There are many modest pensions and bed-and-breakfasts—look for the *Zimmer frei* signs or *Gasthaus.* Hotels in Vienna:

Rates are in US$ for a double/twin room with bath or shower

Ambassador, Neuer Markt 5 (from $100)

Am Parkring, Parkring 12 (from $76)

Am Stephansplatz, Stephansplatz 9 (from $68)

Astoria, Kärntnerstrasse 32 (from $80)

Atlanta (Pension), Wahringerstrasse 33 (from $48)

Bellevue, Althanstrasse 5 (from $60)

Bristol, Kärntnerring 1 (from $100)

De France, Schottenring 3 (from $90)

Europa, Neuer Markt 3 (from $83)

Hotel Alba, Margaretenstrasse 53 (from $85)

Imperial, Kärntnerring 16 (from $100)

INTER·CONTINENTAL VIENNA, Johannesgasse 28 (from $100)

Kummer, Mariahilferstrasse 71a (from $77)

Palais Schwarzenberg, Schwarzenbergplatz 9 (from $100)

Parkhotel, Schönbrunn, Hietzinger Hauptstrasse 12 (from $90), 30 minutes from center city

Prinz Eugen, Wiedner Gürtel 14 (from $83), 10 minutes from center city by trolley

Sacher Hotel, 4 Philharmonikerstrasse (from $100)

Savoy, Lindengasse 12 (from $40)

All hotels centrally located unless otherwise indicated.

USEFUL INFORMATION

Banks: Open Mon-Wed and Friday 8-12:30 and 1:30-3:30. Thurs 8-12:30, 1:30-5:30, closed weekends. Money exchange bureaus in large towns, in hotels, and railroad stations. Many stores and boutiques accept travelers' checks. Among the American banks with branches in Vienna are the Bank of America, Chase Manhattan, the Chemical Bank, First National of Boston, Citibank, European-American Bank, and American Express.

Mail: Stamps *(Briefmarken)* at post offices, tobacco shops, cigarette kiosks, shops, and hotels.

Telephone Tips: For public phones use a schilling piece. Useful numbers in Vienna:

Pan Am 52 66 46	**Weather** 1566
City Tourist Information 43 1608	**Police** 133
Operator 08	**Ambulance** 144
Information 16	**Doctor** 63 16 61
Time 1503	**Automobile Club** 72 9 79

Newspapers: English-language newspapers, magazines, and the Paris edition of the *Herald Tribune* are sold in Vienna and most large Austrian cities.

Tipping: Widespread and usually expected. Service charge of 10% to 15% is generally added to hotel and restaurant bills, but in cafés and restaurants it is customary to leave a little extra (5% or the loose change). Taxis—10% of the fare, 15% for extra-courteous service; luggage porters—AS8 per piece of luggage; hotel porters—AS20 minimum; chambermaids—AS5 minimum for each night spent in the hotel; cloakroom attendants—AS5; museum guides—AS10 minimum.

Electricity: 220 volts 50 cycles AC.

Laundry: Quick and relatively inexpensive; dry-cleaning is good in the capital, of varying quality in the provinces (dry-cleaning a suit from AS60; laundering a shirt from AS15).

Hairdressing: Salons in most first-class hotels (shampoo and set from AS165; man's haircut from AS55; tip 10%).

Photography: Film and equipment of excellent quality in large cities. Color film developed in 4 or 5 days, black and white rolls in 2 or 3 days. Film prices: black and white from AS40; color from AS64.

Clubs: Lions, Kiwanis, and Rotary Club meet in Vienna.

Babysitting: In Vienna contact The Babysitter Center, 1040 Vienna, Belvedere Gasse 32 (tel: 65 28 93) and the Austrian Student Society or Osterreichischer Akademischer Gästedienst (tel: 57 57 39 and 56 23 74).

Rest Rooms: Called *Toiletten* or *Klosett;* women, *Damen;* men, *Herren.*

Health: A good many doctors and dentists speak English. Imported pharmaceuticals in the drugstores (called *Apotheken*). The drinking water is safe.

TRANSPORTATION

Getting around Vienna on buses, streetcars, and the *Stadtbahn* is reasonably priced and relatively simple. Buses are plentiful, and the Ring and outer districts teem with streetcars. The *Stadtbahn* is a form of streetcar that travels above and below as well as at ground level. Metered taxis can be obtained by phone, hailed on the street, or boarded at any of the numerous stands. Charge is AS22 for the first kilometer and AS8 for each additional kilometer. A charge of AS10 is made for luggage. Taxis may also be rented at fixed, prearranged rates for excursions out of town, about AS125 per hour. The trains are punctual and clean. The Eurailpass is accepted in Austria. Also notable is the Europabus, the Continent-wide bus service which offers sightseeing bargains. The Tourist Office and American Express in Vienna have full schedules and price lists for the popular Vienna-Salzburg and Vienna-Innsbruck routes, as well as for the international runs to Italy, Hungary, and Czechoslovakia. Danube steamers operate between Passau and Vienna. In conjunction with Soviet, Czech, and Hungarian lines, there is service to the Black Sea,

Bratislava, and Budapest respectively. The run between Vienna-Linz is one of the more scenic river routes in the world.

FOOD AND RESTAURANTS

Austrian cooking has been influenced by the Hungarians, Czechs, Germans, Croats, Turks, and Italians and is as distinct as it is distinguished. In general terms, three categories are especially distinctive: the soups, the *Schnitzel*, and the world-famous pastries. Dumpling-garnished broths are a universal first course. Especially delicious is a steaming bowl of *Rindsuppe* decked with *Leberknödl*—a combination of meat stock and liver puffballs. Many other dishes feature dumplings *(Knödl)* made of flour and bacon, breadcrumbs, onion, and *Speck* (smoked lard), or minced ham, egg, and parsley, all in a variety of broths. Veal ranks highest and is the basis for the renowned *Wiener Schnitzel*—a filet pounded thin, breaded, and sautéed to crispness. Other main dishes worth trying are the *Backhendl,* which resembles Southern fried chicken, spicy stuffed peppers and cabbage, and the boiled beef dish known as *Tafelspitz* and served with horseradish and a number of other sauces.

Austria's pastries have to be seen to be believed. Cakes, cream puffs, fruit tarts of every type are in the nation's bakeries or *Konditoreien. Sachertorte,* chocolate sponge cake coated with chocolate icing, is one masterpiece.

Lunch or dinner for one in a luxury restaurant will cost from US$25 to 30; at a medium-priced restaurant it will come to approximately US$13 to 15; in an inexpensive bistro about US$8 to 10.

Among Vienna's first-class restaurants are the dining room of the **Hotel Sacher** (famous for its *Sachertorte*) (tel: 52 55 75); the **Drei Husaren** or Three Hussars (Weihburggasse 4—tel: 52 11 92); the **Stadtkrug** (Weihburggasse 3—tel: 52 79 55); the **Rotisserie** at the **Inter·Continental Hotel** (tel: 56 36 11); the **Prinz Eugen Room** of the Vienna Hilton (tel: 75 26 52); the restaurant at the **Palais Schwarzenberg** (tel: 72 51 25); the **Bristol** (tel: 52 95 52); the **Sirk** (tel: 52 74 82); and the restaurants at the **Ambassador** (tel: 52 75 11) and **Astoria** (tel: 52 65 85) hotels.

In the medium-price bracket are **Griechenbeisl** (Fleischmarkt 11—tel: 63 19 41); **The Rathauskeller** (Rathausplatz 1—tel: 42 12 19); **Hausboot,** by the Danube on Schwedenplatz (tel: 63 44 94); **D'Rauchkuchl** (Schweglergasse 37—tel: 92 13 81); **Zum Weissen Rauchfangkehrer** (Weihburggasse 4—tel: 52 34 71); **Das Altes Haus** (Himmelstrasse 35—tel: 32 23 21); and the **Grotta Azzurra** (tel: 56 11 44) and **Coq d'Or** (52 12 85).

For quick service you might try the **Wienerwald** chain, whose prices are not the lowest but who offer their fried chicken, hamburgers, and other light meals really fast.

At the budget level there is the **Gösser Bierklinik** (Strindlgase 4); **Figh-Mueller** (Wollzeile); and **McDonald's** (Schwarzenbergplatz 17), with at least 3 other locations.

The staple for quick eating in this part of the world is the sausage in a wide range of flavors. It may be had at street stalls and in most eating places.

DRINKING TIPS

Austria has excellent wines. Among the best are the whites from Grinzing and Krems, the reds from Klosterneuberg and Baden and from the "Wine District," or *Weinviertel*, above Vienna, and from the vineyards of Burgenland and Steiermark. The Austrian beer, of course, is memorable.

A Viennese custom is the casual winefest, a *Heuriger*, which denotes both the newly pressed wine and the locale where it is served—usually the tavern of a private vineyard in whose garden the tasting goes on. **Grinzing** and **Sievering** are famous for their *Heuriger*, and in summer many guided tours of the **Vienna Woods** will include a stop at such a gathering.

Prices are reasonable, and there are no restrictions on the sale of liquor; drinks are served from 12 noon-2pm and 6-11 or 12 in restaurants and up to 4am in nightclubs.

No review of Vienna's eating and drinking places would be complete without mention of its cafés, the favorite meeting places of a gregarious and witty people. They offer pastries and up to half-a-dozen different coffee concoctions—with or without whipped cream. Among the more famous are the coffee house in the Imperial Hotel; the **Café Mozart**, on Albertinaplatz; the **Sacher; Demel's** (Kohlmarkt 18), the pastry palace to end them all; and the more than 20 of the **Aida** chain.

ENTERTAINMENT

Vienna is one of the great musical capitals of the world, and music is everywhere: in summer from park bandstands, in cold weather from zither players in the cafés, during the winter season from the great concert halls and the opera houses.

Getting tickets in a town where half the population seems to spend much of its time listening to the other half can be difficult. Porters at luxury hotels will often do their best to get tickets for orchestral performances at the **Musikverein** and **Konzerthaus**—the two main halls—and the **State Opera** and **Volksoper.** Lovers of lighter fare will find musicals and operettas at the **Theater an der Wien** and, in summer, open-air band concerts in the **Prater** and **Stadtpark.** The **Vienna Festival** takes place during the last week of May and the first three weeks of June. Tickets are best obtained in advance through the Austrian Travel Agency in Wien.

For those who understand German, Vienna's theaters will prove a treat, from the famous **Burgtheater** and the old **Josefstadt** house to small groups scattered about the city.

There is plenty of nightlife in the city's numerous bars, nightclubs, and casinos. For a sophisticated nightclub atmosphere, try the **Eve Nachcabaret** (Führichgasse 3—corner Kärntnerstrasse) or the **Eden Bar** (Liliengasse 2). **The New Splendid** (Jasomirgottgasse—Stephansplatz) is another popular beat; **Chez Nous** (Kärntnerstrasse 10) is small and has a cozy atmosphere. The **Club Take Five** (Annagasse 3a) is in the discothèque category, which in Vienna is called Disc-Dancing; others include **Voom-**

Voom (Daungasse 1), **Tiffany Club** (Goethegasse 2), the **Steckenpferd Bar** (Dorotheergasse 7), **Fatty George Jazz Salon** (Petersplatz), and **Atrium Club** (Schwarzenbergplatz, 10).

SHOPPING

Austria is renowned for its porcelain, *petit point,* knitwear, leather goods, ski equipment, and handicrafts, and Vienna is the place to find them. The boutique reigns supreme, as a promenade down the main shopping streets will make very clear. Vienna has a good selection of the country's handicrafts, from Tyrolean wood carvings to enamel and wrought-iron work. For antiques, take a look inside the **Dorotheum** (Dorotheergasse 17), a unique clearinghouse for *objets d'art* which has been holding auctions for over two centuries. A little further down Dorotheergasse, music lovers will enjoy browsing through the records and books on music at **Doblinger's.**

For souvenirs, try the group of shops in the underground passage on the **Opernring,** and for everyday necessities (inexpensive toiletries, etc.) try two department stores—**Gerngross** and **Herzmansky**—on the busy Mariahilferstrasse, also **Steffl's** in the Kärntnerstrasse.

Maria Stransky at the Hofburgpassage has a wide selection of *petit point* work. Evening bags and other articles covered in this Renaissance-inspired embroidery are not inexpensive, but considering the painstaking needlework they require, the prices are quite reasonable. For **Augarten** porcelain, go to the shop of this name at Stock-im-Eisen-Platz 3-4, and also to **Rasper & Söhne** (Graben 15). Leather goods can be found on all three shopping streets mentioned above, as well as quality stationery, desk articles, and exquisite wall calendars, which make useful gifts. **Lanz** (Kärntnerstrasse 10) and **J. Jolles Studios** (Andreasgasse 6, 1070 Wien) have charming folkdresses of small-print cottons with solid-color aprons and, for evening, brocade versions with velvet trim. Socks and sweaters that rival Scotland's best can be found at **Lodenplankl** (Michaelerplatz). Austria's fine outdoor-goods shops are **Johann Springer** (Graben, Vienna) and **Dschnulnigg** in Salzburg.

SPORTS

The provinces of **Tyrol** and **Salzburg** are filled with skiers in winter. **Kitzbühel** and **St Anton, Badgastein** and **Zell-am-See** are typical of the highly developed winter sports facilities offered by these regions. But there is also powdery snow on the slopes of **Vorarlberg, Carynthia, Steiermark,** and **Upper** and **Lower Austria.** There are no less than some 800 towns and villages where winter sports can be enjoyed.

In spring and summer, golf and tennis can be played all over the country, and you can swim, sail, and water-ski in the many Alpine lakes. Mountaineering figures prominently among the Austrians' favorite sports, and fishing in the lakes and mountain streams is also popular. Horse lovers can go for cross-country rides. Over 150 resorts have stables and a range of amenities from riding instruction to dressage courses.

WHAT TO SEE

Vienna: Narrow streets lined with splendid mansions; spacious parks; a wide, curving thoroughfare leading to some of the world's smartest shops; palaces and churches and museums which seem to tumble over one another—such is a visitor's first impression of Vienna. The ever-curving promenade is the **Ring,** and it follows part of the old city wall. Within it is **St Stephen's Cathedral.**

The **Cathedral** is famous for carvings and vaults, and from its single spire—known affectionately as *Alter Steffl* or Old Stevie—there is an incomparable view of the city. Next should come the **Augustinerkirche** on Augustinerstrasse, in whose vaults lie the hearts of the great Maria Theresa and many other sovereigns of the Hapsburg Empire; their bodies are in the **Imperial Vault** at the Capuchine Monastery at Neuer Markt.

The Hapsburgs' enormous palace, the **Hofburg,** is a symbol of the power they once exercised over Europe. The Hofburg is an imperial compound with private apartments, office suites, and gardens. It is also here, in the heart of this complex of ancient buildings, that the famous white Lipizzaner stallions of the **Spanish Riding School** perform from fall to spring. In the Chapel, the **Vienna Boys Choir** sings the high mass every Sunday except in summer. In the treasure chamber, perhaps the most precious object is the Crown of the Holy Roman Empire, almost 1,000 years old. Outside lie two of Vienna's most beautiful small parks, the **Burggarten** and the **Volksgarten.**

Of the city's baroque palaces, **Belvedere** is the most resplendent. The **Peterkirche** is in the Inner City, and the **Karlskirche** is just outside the Ring on Karlsplatz.

The **Vienna State Opera** is on the corner of the Ring named in its honor; there are tours of its interior. Farther down the Ring are the **Museum of Natural History** and the **Fine Arts Museum.** In the picture gallery of the latter hang canvases by Breughel, Holbein, Dürer, Rembrandt, Titian, Velasquez, Rubens, and Tintoretto. The array of prints and drawings at the **Albertina,** on Augustinerstrasse, is one of the richest and greatest in the world.

Parliament and Vienna's big *Rathaus,* or **City Hall,** complete the buildings on the periphery of the **Old Town.** Follow the Ring as it curves back clear across the city to the **Stadtpark,** with its monument to Johann Strauss, violin in hand. Here in summer there are band concerts by the open-air restaurant. **The Prater,** Vienna's most romantic park, is on the far side of the Danube and incorporates an amusement center complete with ferris wheel.

On the outskirts of the city stands **Schönbrunn,** summer home of the Imperial Family and one of the most colorful palaces in Europe. Its rooms, with walls painted, porcelained, and lacquered in sunny pastels, are not to be missed.

Make an excursion to the **Vienna Woods,** beech-covered hills overlooking the city and the people's favorite playground. There are guided tours to the most picturesque spots, especially to **Kahlenberg** and **Kobenzl,** the two main vantage points.

Salzburg: From its fort high on a hill to the narrowest alley in the town below, Salzburg is overwhelming. To take it all in you must stand on the east bank of the Salzach and look across to one of the most beautiful sights in the world: a medieval city pierced by the spires of a dozen or so baroque churches, the whole topped by a fortress.

On the left bank many of the houses still bear on their facades the 13th-, 14th-, and 15th-century dates of their erection. Tunneling across entire blocks are the narrow alleyways of the Middle Ages which give on to patios with porticoed galleries at second- and third-story level. There are miniature shops, restaurants, and shoebox-like hotels.

The five-story dwelling on **Getreidegasse,** once the property of a grocer named Hagenauer, is open to the public. In one of its rooms Wolfgang Amadeus Mozart was born in 1756. There are mementoes of his life, early editions of his works, and scale models of sets of *The Magic Flute, Don Giovanni,* and other operas.

The great Italianate **Cathedral,** with its light, airy nave, is a masterpiece of early baroque. Nearby is **St Peter's Monastery** and the **Franziskaner-kirche,** with a high altar by the great Fischer von Erlach, architect extraordinary of the Austrian baroque.

There are two residences facing each other across the square of this name. One was used as the Archbishop's See in the 12th century and enlarged in the 17th and 18th centuries. Its courtyard is the scene of orchestral concerts during the Summer Festival. The other, the **Neugebäude** or "New Building," dates from the 17th century. A small square on the other side is, appropriately enough, **Mozartplatz,** with a statue of the city's favorite son in the middle.

Opera performances take place in two theaters, the **Large** and the **Small,** which form a solid bastion at the top end of the Old Town, having been carved out of the old royal mews. For those visiting the city outside Festival time, the famous **Marionettes** stage their own version of Mozart operas and Strauss operettas in their delightful theater on **Schwarzstrasse.**

The **Hohensalzburg Fortress,** once a medieval stronghold so big that its inner courtyard is like the square of a good-sized village, merits a visit for the view it affords over the entire city.

The right bank of the city is more modern, though it does contain one of Salzburg's most admirable house-and-garden ensembles—the **Mirabell Palace,** built by Archbishop Wolf Dietrich von Raitenau for his mistress, Salome Alt. In spring and summer Mirabell is more like a mirage, with symmetrical flowerbeds, manicured hedges, and smooth lawns framing an unforgettable view of the old fortress and the city's spires.

Also on the right bank is the **Mozarteum,** the city's music school, where the Festival recitals take place. There are tours of the building with a special stop in the garden, where the little wooden hut in which Mozart composed *The Magic Flute* has been installed.

If you plan to attend the **Salzburg Festival,** you should make reservations for hotels and tickets no less than a year in advance and confirm them with care. Austrian tourist offices and travel agents will be of assistance in securing such plans.

Excursions out of Salzburg should include **St Gilgen** and **St Wolfgang** and their respective lakes; **Mondsee,** another beautiful body of water; **Hellbrunn,** the name of the "Fun Palace" built by an archbishop, Markus Sittikus, whose favorite pastime was drenching his guests from concealed spouts and fountains as they sat at table or promenaded about the house. Visitors are warned to step lively when they hear what seems to be the patter of rain. The nozzles have deadly aim, and though the guides who work them usually go for the younger members of a party, ladies' hairdos and makeup have been known to come apart under an unexpected shower or two.

There are also all-day trips along the **Grossglockner Highway** between May and October, although, even then, sporadic snowstorms may block this spectacular Alpine road which climbs through panoramas of bare rocky splendor to heights of over 6,000 feet. At the **Edelweissspitze** (8,500 feet) there is a restaurant with an incomparable view of over 30 snow-clad peaks and innumerable glaciers. Hotels in Salzburg:

Rates are in US$ for a double/twin room with bath or shower

> **Europa,** Rainerstrasse 31 (from $100)
>
> **Fondachhof,** Gaisbergstrasse 46 (from $71)
>
> **Goldener Hirsch,** Getreidegasse 37 (from $100)
>
> **Johann Strauss,** Makartkai 37 (from $53)
>
> **Osterreichischer Hof,** Schwarzstrasse 5-7 (from $100)
>
> **Schlosshotel Klessheim,** Wals-Siezenheim, Klessheim (from $100), 20 minutes outside of town

All of the above-listed hotels are in the city center unless otherwise indicated.

To the south of Salzburg, 2 hours drive from the city, is the spa of **Badgastein.** Its waters have been famous since they reportedly healed the wounded Duke Frederick of Styria in the late Middle Ages. The town is picturesque, and its Kur hotels have that turn-of-the-century charm typical of so many European spas. In winter, Badgastein's skiing facilities are enjoyed by hundreds.

Zell-am-See, beside the Zeller Lake in the shadow of 3,000- to 9,000-foot mountains, is one of the province of Salzburg's most famous tourist attractions. The 13th-century **parish church** and **Rosenburg Castle** are its principal sights. You should not miss the cable car ride to the top of Schmittenhohe, where another Alpine view awaits the tourist. Stay at the **Grand Hotel Am See** (from US$45), the **St Georg Hotel** and the **Grand Hotel** (from US$42), or the **Seehotel Zauner** (from US$30).

Vorarlberg, Tyrol, and **East Tyrol: Bregenz** is the capital of tiny Vorarlberg, Austria's westernmost province and the center of its textile industry. The town rises by the Bodensee, or **Lake Constance,** which borders on Switzerland and Germany as well. The ancient **St Martin's Chapel** (14th century), the Gothic church of **St Gallus,** and the 1511 **Town Hall** are among the landmarks of the old quarter, which is built on a rise away from the lakeside. Modern Bregenz stretches along the shore of the Bodensee; the city stages its **Summer Music Festival** on floats moored in the lake. Accommodations include the **Central,** Kaiserstrasse 24-26 (from

US$43), **Messmer,** Kornmarkt 16 (from US$50), **Schwaerzler,** Landstrasse 9 (from US$50), and **Weisses Kreuz,** Römerstrasse 5 (from US$55).

Little **Feldkirch,** directly south of Bregenz, has arcaded streets dating from the Middle Ages. The **Schattenburg Castle,** dating from the 12th century (there is a restaurant within), is open to the public, and there is also a late gothic **Cathedral.**

East of Vorarlberg is the province of **Tyrol,** with flower-decked chalets from one end to the other and a ski run, it would seem, on every mountain. One of its most famous and lively winter resorts is **Kitzbühel,** with a network of cable cars and chairlifts so intricate that it is known as the Ski Circus. There are excellent restaurants and shops with Tyrolean handicrafts and, for summer visitors, tennis courts and a golf course as well as sailing and swimming in the **Schwarzsee.** Accommodations include **Schlöss Lebenburg,** (from US$53), **Goldener Greif** (from US$53), **Romantic Tennerhof** (from US$53), **Schweizerhof** (from US$37), **Weisses Roessl** (from US$55), and **Zum Jaegerwirt Hotel,** Jochbergerstrasse 12 (from US$53).

Innsbruck, the provincial capital, is worth a visit, for here one can speak of the "Golden Age of the Gothic." Among the city's landmarks is the famous **Goldenes Dachl,** which crowns a third-story balcony on a gothic building. The Dachl, or roof, is made of gilded copper but shines like gold. It dates from 1500 and crowns the royal box from which Emperor Maximilian I watched performances on the square below.

In 1563 work was completed on a sarcophagus which would contain the Emperor's remains. Though the tomb in the **Hofkirche** is empty (the body is buried at the Austrian Military Academy in Wiener Neustadt), the **Cenotaph** is the most impressive monument of its type in the German-speaking world. Sculptured in marble and bronze, it has statues of Maximilian and 28 of his royal relatives.

The old **Hofburg,** built in the 15th century, was remodeled by order of Maria Theresa after it was damaged by fire; it is a showcase of rococo ornamentation. The **Cathedral of St Jakob** is another of the country's great baroque churches, with a painted ceiling and a famous Madonna by Lucas Cranach. Outside the city is **Ambras Castle,** built in the 11th century and remodeled along Renaissance lines in the 16th. It has a collection of medieval art treasures and weapons and a park surrounding it. Innsbruck hotels include the **Europa,** Sudtiroler Platz 2 (from US$70); **Goldener Adler,** Herzog-Friedrich-Strasse 6 (from US$45); and the **Holiday Inn** (from US$100).

Halfway between the provinces of Tyrol and Salzburg, on the southern extreme of the country, is **East Tyrol** with its capital, **Lienz,** at the foot of the Dolomites. Lienz is popular as both a skiing and summer resort. Its parish church dates from the 15th century, and on its main square is the 16th-century **Liebburg Palace.** Outside the town is magnificent **Bruck Castle,** solidly gothic with Renaissance additions. Accommodations include **Hotel Traube** (from US$78), **Sonne** (from US$70), and **Gloeckl-turm** (from US$41).

Lower and Upper Austria: Lower Austria is readily accessible from

Vienna, and most Viennese travel bureaus have excursions to the **Vienna Woods, Baden, Heiligenkreuz,** and **Klosterneuburg.** There are steamer trips up the Danube to **Krems** and **Melk** through the valley known as the **Wachau,** a most attractive and scenically beautiful area.

Baden, on the southern outskirts of Vienna, is a little spa which was once the watering place of royalty. In summer, its bandstands come alive with music, the outdoor cafés do a brisk business, and visitors flock to the house where Beethoven spent several working vacations. In summer there are operetta performances in the town's **Arena Theater.**

Heiligenkreuz and **Klosterneuburg** are two of the best-known monasteries of the region. The first is west of Baden and dates back to the 12th century. Its great church and cloister are romanesque. **Klosterneuburg Abbey,** with its imposing church, rises north of Vienna. The enameled altar by Nikolaus von Verdun (1181) is perhaps its greatest jewel, but the Abbey museum, its vast library, and the treasury also merit attention.

The wine produced by the monks at Klosterneuburg was always famous. This is vineyard country, as a trip down the Danube will show. It is also castle country, and the excursion will afford glimpses of ancient fortresses on hilltops overlooking the river. Farther upstream is the majestic silhouette of **Melk,** the country's most beautiful abbey and its most perfect baroque structure. The church has elaborate paintings, the library is another reminder of the part played by the monasteries in the cultural and scientific life of past centuries, and, even today, the monastery produces an excellent wine which visitors may taste.

Upper Austria is mountainous and studded with blue lakes. Its southern portion, the **Salzkammergut,** contains such well-known resorts as **St Wolfgang** and **St Gilgen,** usually approached from Salzburg. The provincial capital, **Linz,** is on the Danube. On a rise just outside the city stands the oldest church of the nation, a tiny place of worship called the **Martinskirche,** which was last rebuilt in the 8th century and has been in continuous use since the time of Charlemagne.

The baroque **Cathedral,** the Renaissance **Landhaus** (seat of the provincial government), and the old **Castle** of Emperor Friedrich III are some of its other attractions. The castle is of interest, not only for its late 16th-century architecture, but for its **Museum** of Upper Austrian art history and folklore.

Among the province's abbeys, the baroque **St Florian** must be singled out. It is built over the tomb of a saint who was martyred by the Romans. The composer Anton Bruckner, who was born in the nearby village of **Ansfelden,** is buried in the Abbey church, not far from the organ which he so often played.

Carinthia, Styria, and **Burgenland:** Sunny Carinthia is for the tourist who wants a relaxed, unhurried lakeside vacation. The province has lakes in abundance and mountains. It is one of the most popular summer resorts in Austria, with the **Wörthersee** as its main attraction. This large and beautiful lake has the city of **Klagenfurt** on one end, the resort of **Velden** on the other. Velden has plenty of hotels and gambling casinos.

Less fashionable and quieter is another lakeside village, **Pörtschach,** though here, too, the visitor will find a lively program of sporting activities and folklore evenings.

Klagenfurt, the capital, has a dragon as its symbol and has **Dragon Square** as its heart. The **Cathedral,** the 16th-century **Landhaus,** and the **Bishop's Palace** (the latter housing a collection of medieval art) should be on every sightseer's list.

Northeast of Carinthia lies **Styria.** Its capital, **Graz,** is the nation's second-largest city. The province is proverbial for its greenness, and Graz is well provided with parks and squares. Its Renaissance **Landhaus,** 16th-century **parish church,** and 15th-century **Cathedral** are among its landmarks. Accommodations include **Hotels Daniel** (from US$60), **Weitzer** (from US$60), **Parkhotel** (from US$60), **Wiesler** (from US$60), **Erzehog Johann** (from US$48), and **Steirerhof** (from US$65), among numerous others.

The mountainous side of Styria can be seen at its most spectacular in the **Tauern Range** of the Alps. Such villages as **Schladming**—to be the site of the **1982 World Ski Championships**—and **Gröbming** double as ski and summer sports centers. Near the former is **Ramsau,** a resort with a great view of the Dachstein peaks. A new cable car takes you to the top of the Dachstein.

For greenness and mountains all in one, the visitor could choose **Bad Aussee,** with the neighboring lakes of **Altaussee** and **Grundlsee.** The performances of folk singing and dancing arranged for visitors are said to be among the best in the country.

With the province of **Burgenland** the Austrian landscape undergoes a radical change. This is the beginning of the Central European plain, with flat, fertile country that stretches into Hungary. Burgenland's historical and ethnic links with this country are evident everywhere, from the *puszta* or "steppe" look of the countryside to the splendors of the **Esterhazy Palace** in its capital city, **Eisenstadt.**

The **Neusiedlersee** is Burgenland's prime vacation spot; it is an extremely shallow lake—some say no deeper than seven feet from one end to the other—and windstorms have a way of piling the water off to one side, leaving the other bare. The reeds and marshes on its shores shelter such a variety of birds that the place is an ornithologist's paradise. **St Andrä** and **Frauenkirchen,** two villages on its banks, are famous for their basketweaving.

SOURCES OF FURTHER INFORMATION

Pan Am, Kaerntnerring 5, A-1010 Vienna, and any Pan Am office around the world; **Austrian National Tourist Office,** Österreichische Fremdenverkehrswerbung, Margarentstrasse 5, 1050 Wien 5, and 545 Fifth Avenue, New York, NY 10017; with branches at 1007 NW 24th Avenue, Portland, OR 97210; 3440 Wilshire Boulevard, Los Angeles, CA 90010, and 200 East Randolph Drive, Chicago, IL 60601. Austrian National Tourist Office, 30 St. George Street, London WIR 9FA.

Balearic Islands

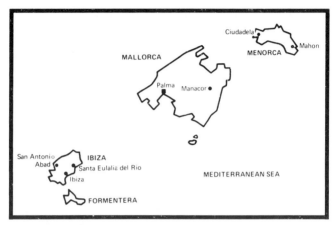

WHAT'S SPECIAL

The charm of the Balearic Islands, set in the blue and sunny Mediterranean, lies in their cosmopolitan atmosphere and outstanding beauty. For centuries they were invaded by every nation whose ships sailed by. Phoenicians, Romans, Moors, and Spaniards all left their mark on the culture of these islands. Now it is tourists—a multinational invasion on a larger scale than ever before—and there are hotels galore, sophisticated nightclubs, colorful bars, and every conceivable provision for visitors. But there is still room to escape through miles of fig and almond groves into the peaceful green mountains, or to some deserted cove along the coast where no one disturbs your communion with sun, sand, and sea.

COUNTRY BRIEFING

Size: Mallorca—1,350 square miles; Ibiza—230 square miles; Menorca—293 square miles; Formentera—38 square miles
Population: 652,487
Capital: Palma, Mallorca   **Capital Population:** 291,078
   Climate: Mallorca has a peak season from June to August, though fall and spring are balmy and beautiful and winters are mild. The mountainous section in the north of Mallorca tends to be cooler and wetter and occasionally has snow in winter. Menorca is a windy island, making it cool in summer and wet in winter. Ibiza and Formentera are the driest and warmest islands.

Weather in Mallorca: Lat N39°34'; Alt max 4,740 ft

Temp (°F)	Jan	Feb	Mar	Apr	May	Jun	Jul	Aug	Sep	Oct	Nov	Dec
Av Low	42°	43°	45°	49°	55°	61°	66°	67°	64°	57°	50°	44°
Av High	57°	59°	62°	66°	73°	80°	84°	86°	81°	74°	65°	59°
Days no rain	23	20	23	25	26	27	30	29	24	23	21	21

Government: The islands are a province of Spain.

Language: The official language is Spanish; Mallorquines also speak a local dialect of Càtalan.

Religion: Predominantly Roman Catholic.

Currency: The Spanish peseta—96ptas to US$1 (see currency chart for Spain).

Public Holidays:

New Year's Day, 1 Jan
Epiphany, 6 Jan
St Joseph's Day, 19 Mar
Maundy Thursday
Good Friday
May Day, 1 May
Corpus Christi

King's Day, 24 June
St James' Day, 25 July
Assumption Day, 15 Aug
Columbus Day, 12 Oct
Immaculate Conception,
    8 Dec
Christmas Day, 25 Dec

HOW TO GET THERE

Flying time to Palma from New York is 7 hours; from London, 2 hours; from Madrid, 1 hour; from Tokyo, 19 hours. Time in the Balearic Islands: GMT+1.

REQUIREMENTS FOR ENTRY AND CUSTOMS REGULATIONS

Passport, but no visa for up to six months' stay. Vaccination certificate required only if coming from an infected area. Currency regulations allow you to take in up to 50,000ptas in Spanish currency, and up to 3,000ptas out. Duty-free allowance: 200 cigarettes or 50 cigars or 250 grams tobacco; 1 bottle liquor and 1 bottle wine; small amount of perfume for personal use.

AIRPORT INFORMATION

San Juan Airport is eight miles from Palma, 350ptas by taxi, plus a 10% tip. Porters display a badge; tip 25ptas per bag. No departure tax. San Luis Airport, Menorca, is just outside Mahón; Ibiza airport is 6 miles from town center.

ACCOMMODATIONS

The islands have one of the highest concentrations of hotels, villas, and pensions per capita of any popular resort area in the world. Despite this, it is still necessary to make reservations well in advance. Hotels in Palma, Mallorca:

Rates are in US$ for a double/twin room with bath or shower
Alcina, Paseo Marítimo (from $24)
Arenal Park, Calle Padre Bartolome Salva, El Arenal (from $19), 8½ miles from center
De Mar Sol, Illetas Beach (from $86), 5 miles from center
Fenix, Paseo Marítimo (from $68)
La Cala, Cala Mayor (from $22), 2½ miles from center
Maricel, Ca's Catalá, Carretera Andraitx (from $38), 4 miles from center
Melia Mallorca, Monseñor Palmer 2 (from $61)
Nixe Palace, Playa Cala Mayor (from $49), 2½ miles from center
San Carolos, Calle can Morro 16 (from $20)
Son Vida Castle, Castillo de Son Vida (from $64), 3 miles from center
Valparaiso, Francisco Vidal (from $88)
Victoria Sol, Calvo Sotelo 21 (from $78)
All hotels in center city unless otherwise indicated.

USEFUL INFORMATION

Banks: Open 9-2, Mon-Fri; 9-1 Sat. Money can also be changed at hotels and travel agencies.

Mail: You can buy stamps at tobacconists and put your mail in the yellow mailboxes.

Telephone Tips: Local call costs 5ptas for 3 minutes.

Airport Information 264624	**Directories** 003
Tourist Office 212216	**Emergencies** 222179

Newspapers: *La Semana Mallorquina* is partly in English. Other useful publications: *Majorca General Information* and the *Daily Bulletin.*

Tipping: A well-established custom. A service charge of 15% is usually included in hotel and restaurant bills, additional 10-15% tip expected. Tip taxi drivers 10%; hairdresser 50-75ptas; hotel porters 50ptas a day, 200ptas a week; chambermaids, 20 ptas a day, or 100ptas a week; cloakroom attendants, 25ptas.

Electricity: 110-120 volts 50 cycles AC; 220 volts in some buildings.

Laundry: Service fast, efficient, and 24-hour in most places in Palma (to dry-clean a suit, from 175ptas; to launder a shirt, from 50ptas).

Hairdressing: There are many first-rate hairdressers in Palma. Shampoo and set from 400ptas; man's haircut from 250ptas.

Photography: Good selection of equipment available; a roll of color film with 20 exposures is expensive and would cost about 1,000ptas to develop. Processing of both black and white and color takes only a day or two.

Clubs: Kiwanis. The Spanish Tourist Office in Palma will supply you with all information on clubs.

Babysitting: Hotels will arrange this.

Rest Rooms: For women, *Señoras;* for men, *Caballeros* or *Hombres.* There is generally a 5ptas charge.

Health: Many doctors speak English. Most brands of cosmetics and toiletries are available. Drink mineral water rather than fresh water.

TRANSPORTATION

Taxis are the easiest means of transportation. Fares are at fixed rates. Car rental and chauffeur-driven transport are available. A train service links Palma to Sóller, Inca, Manacor, and other centers. There are bus services linking the main towns and popular tourist spots. You can sail to Ibiza and Menorca, or fly with the Spanish airlines. The boat to Ibiza takes 4 hours, and in summer there are daily sailings. Boat trips to Menorca (Mahón) take 10 hours and are less frequent. There are several flights daily to both islands, taking ½ hour.

FOOD AND RESTAURANTS

There are plenty of restaurants and lunch bars in Palma and around Mallorca. Catalan dishes predominate in local cooking and tend to be more highly seasoned than on the Spanish mainland. *Ensaimada,* a fluffy pastry bread, is a local specialty, as is *caldera de peix,* a fish soup. Mayonnaise was reputedly invented at Mahón on Menorca. In the center of Palma, **Mesón Carlos I** (Apuntadores 49—tel: 22 60 29) has excellent food in an authentic 16th-century setting. For real French cuisine, there is **Cana Sophie** (Apuntadores 62—tel: 22 60 86). **Antonio** (Paseo Generalísimo Franco 21—tel: 22 26 13) is good and moderately priced. On the seafront on the western side of the bay is **La Caleta** (Marqués de la Cenia 147—tel: 23 27 51)—expensive but first-class. At Terreno, about 1 mile west of Palma, you will find **El Patio** (Consignatario Schembri 5, Plaza del Mediterráneo—tel: 23 24 41), one of the top restaurants, **Bora Bora** (Plaza Gomila 6—tel: 23 58 84), Polynesian in decor but with an international menu, and the **Pizzeria Terreno** (Bellver 22), for French and Italian dishes.

DRINKING TIPS

Local drinks to try are *Palo,* a bitter-sweet liqueur; sherry; *Anis* (try the local brand called *Tunel*); and *Firgola,* an herb liqueur from Ibiza. Bars open from 9am to 12:30am or later.

ENTERTAINMENT

The islands have a busy nightlife. **Tito's,** in Palma, is one of the most spectacular clubs in Europe. Others are **My Own Place, Jack El Negro, Tago Mago,** and **Trocadero** (in the Porto Pi area); **Barbarela, Sgt Peppar** (Plaza Mediterráneo, Terreno), **Zhivago, Rodeito,** and the **Lord Nelson** are others. For really good flamenco, try either **Los Rumbas** (Ca'an Pastula) or **The Nightclub** (Pueblo Español). Concerts are held throughout the year in the **Palma Auditorium** and are popular with visitors. English films are shown at the **Cine Regina** (Teniente Mulet, Terreno).

SHOPPING

Mallorca has many fine stores. Its pearls are famous, and the genuine product is sold under the name "Perlas Majorica"; you can buy them at Avenida Jaime III 65, Palma. You can also visit the Manacor pearl factory (Via Roma 52, Manacor). Intricate wrought-iron work from **La**

Casa del Hierro (Calle Victoria 22) and beautiful needlework and hand-embroidered linen from **Casa Bonet** (San Nicolás 15) are good buys too. Spanish antiques from **Linares** and shoes made in Mallorca (try **Calzados Majorica,** Avenida Jaime II 74) are excellent souvenirs. Original paintings done on the island can also be a bargain.

SPORTS

There is much to offer the sporting enthusiast. Water sports are very popular; good facilities for swimming, yachting, skin-diving, skiing, and fishing. Also tennis, golf, and horseback riding. You can go mountain climbing in the northern section of Mallorca, especially around Sóller. Spectator sports are boxing, wrestling, and soccer. Bullfights are held every Saturday and Sunday at the **Palma Plaza.** Bloodless bullfights (from September to June) are on Tuesday, Thursday, and Saturday at 6pm in Palma's **Cortijo Vista Verde.** The Basque sport of *pelota* is a fast and furious ball game.

WHAT TO SEE

Mallorca is a sophisticated, lively island, with colorful, elegant restaurants and bars, luxury hotels, swinging clubs, and glorious sunny beaches. You will enjoy the simple pleasure of promenading and drinking amid the colorful atmosphere of the **Paseo Borne** promenade.

The town of **Palma** is dominated by its golden **Cathedral** dating from 1230 and the time of Jaime I of Aragon, with an exquisite rose window and simple graceful interior. Above the altar hangs what is said to be the original "crown of thorns." Down on the bay is the medieval complex of the **Lonja** or exchange, among twisting narrow streets and white-washed buildings. Go up to the hilltop castle of **Bellver,** also dating from the 13th century, for its panoramic views. The castle houses the **Municipal Museum.** At the **Gordillo Furnaces** you can watch glass being made in a factory that has been operating since the 17th century. Take a short taxi ride and visit the **Pueblo Español,** a Spanish village where over 100 palaces have been built to represent various types of Spanish architecture.

There are many day excursions to make out of Palma by bus or car. Visit the **Caves of Drach** at Porto Cristo, and take a boat ride on the underground lake amidst a forest of stalactites and stalagmites. On the subterranean **Lake Martel,** you can sit in a shadowy amphitheater and enjoy concerts performed from illuminated barges. The **Royal Carthusian Monastery** at **Valldemosa** is where George Sand and Chopin lived and worked. Californians especially will be interested in visiting **Petra,** the birthplace of Friar Junípero Serra, the Franciscan missionary who built a chain of missions along the California coast. You can visit the old monasteries at the top of **Monte Cura, San Salvador, Galitea,** and **Lluch,** and stay the night if you like. Lovely little villages to visit are **Miramar,** the garden estate of a former Austrian archduke; **Deva;** and **Puerto Sóller,** with its lovely crescent port. There are beautiful beaches at **Formentor, Magaluf, Paguera, Cala d'Or,** and **San Vincente;** the drive along the coast from Paguera to Palma and from Palma to Formentor offers spectacular views.

Ibiza: The "white island" has a warmer, drier climate than the other islands. Ibiza has become the haunt of many artists, writers, and sunworshippers, who came for a visit and stayed. Many of them have opened arts and crafts shops or little restaurants. There is a cosmopolitan feeling on the island that makes it very appealing. Ibiza was first discovered by the Phoenicians, but the town was founded by the Carthaginians in 654 BC. It was later occupied by the Arabs, of whom the white medieval Moorish buildings are a picturesque reminder. The quarter of the town known as **La Peña,** with its tortuous winding streets, has an oriental flavor. The **Cathedral,** dating from the 13th century, is worth a visit. The town is encircled by a wall built to repel the Barbary pirates, and from its ramparts there are beautiful views of the town, sea, and bay. The **Archeological Museum** in Ibiza contains the most important Punic remains in Europe: Phoenician, Carthaginian, and Roman relics tell of days when these three powers contested their strength in the Mediterranean.

Restaurants to try in the town of Ibiza are **El Corsario** (Poniente 5), at the top of the hill, with superb food and a panoramic view, and the **Dalt Vila** (Plaza Luis Tur), one of the island's top gourmet delights. Buy a copy of *Ibiza Insight* for more information.

The main resorts on the island, aside from the town of Ibiza itself, are **San Antonio Abad,** with its beautiful beaches, and **Santa Eulalia del Rio,** on the banks of the only river in the Balearics. Two good hotels in San Antonio Abad are **Calla Gracio** (from US$23 double) and the **Palmyra** (from US$60 double); listen to guitar music at **El Refugio, Ses Guitares,** and **El Coto,** or dance at the **Playboy, Capri,** and **Copacabana.** **Cap Nono** (from US$22 double) is in the smaller resort town of San José. In Santa Eulalia del Rio stay at the **Fenicia** (from US$46 double) or the **S'Argamassa** (from US$27 double) and do your nightclubbing at **La Cala** or **Ses Parres.**

Formentera: Under 2 hours by boat from Ibiza, Formentera is a dry, windswept little island. Its capital is San Francisco Javier.

Menorca was occupied by the British in the 18th century, and the mark of occupancy is still evident in the architecture and way of life. **Mahón,** the main town, is built on one of Europe's finest harbors and is an old and hilly town of narrow streets and quiet days. For the archaeologist, Menorca poses many interesting problems. There are mysterious conical stones called *Talayots* dotted all over the island; some appear to be part of a village formation. There is also a series of strange monuments in the form of upside-down boats, which possibly were tombs. One of them was dedicated to Isis, the goddess of sailors. There are a number of caves dating back to the Iron and Bronze Ages, many decorated with engravings and paintings. The best can be seen at **Cala Coyas.** The island is blessed with innumerable beaches. Recommended restaurant is the **Triton** (Norte 15, Mahón). At **San Clemente,** near Mahón, you can have a drink in the **Cueva d'en Xorio,** a caveman's dwelling now transformed into an unusual bar. The best hotel in Mahón is the **Port-Mahón Hotel** (from US$39 double).

SOURCES OF FURTHER INFORMATION

Pan Am, Madrid: Edificio España, Plaza España, and any Pan Am office around the world; **Information and Tourist Office,** Avenida Jaime III 10, Palma; the **Spanish National Tourist Office,** 665 Fifth Avenue, New York, NY 10017, and 67 Jermyn Street, London SW1.

Belgium

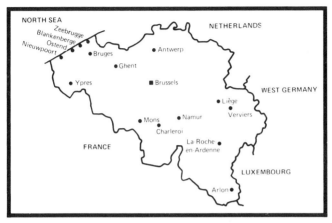

WHAT'S SPECIAL

Belgium is a small patchwork country with a high population density, though the Ardennes region is still a beautifully forested and romantic rural area. The people are very much part of the 20th century, and yet Bruges is one of the few places in the world where a medieval city remains intact and unspoiled. The two contrasting cultures of the Flemish and the French sections of Belgium provide a variety of architecture, language, and cuisine for the visitor to enjoy, and they come together in Brussels, the bilingual capital.

COUNTRY BRIEFING

Size: 11,775 square miles   **Population:** 9,800,000
Capital: Brussels   **Capital Population:** 1,050,000
   Climate: Temperate if somewhat unreliable, with frequent rain showers. May-September is the best time to visit.

Weather in Brussels: Lat N50° 48'; Alt 328 ft.

Temp (°F)	Jan	Feb	Mar	Apr	May	Jun	Jul	Aug	Sep	Oct	Nov	Dec
Av Low	31°	31°	35°	39°	46°	50°	54°	54°	50°	44°	36°	33°
Av High	42°	43°	49°	56°	65°	70°	73°	72°	67°	58°	47°	42°
Days no rain	19	18	20	18	21	19	20	20	19	19	18	18

Government: A constitutional monarchy with nine provinces.
   Language: Both French and Flemish are official languages, with Flemish spoken in the north and French in the south. German is spoken by a small minority in the east of the country. Some English is spoken

in hotels, restaurants, and shops. Brussels is bilingual in French and Flemish.

Religion: The predominant religion is Roman Catholic.

Currency: Belgian franc. 100 centimes = 1 Belgian franc.

	F	F	F	F	F	F	F	F
	1	10	20	50	100	500	1,000	2,000
US (dollars, cents)	.03	.27	.54	1.35	2.69	13.45	26.91	53.82
UK (pounds, pence)	.01	.13	.26	.65	1.29	6.43	12.86	25.72

Public Holidays:

New Year's Day, 1 Jan	National Holiday, 21 July
Easter Monday	Assumption Day, 15 Aug
Labor Day, 1 May	All Saints Day, 1 Nov
Ascension Day	Armistice Day, 11 Nov
Whit Monday	Dynasty Day, 15 Nov
	Christmas Day, 25 Dec

HOW TO GET THERE

Flying time to Brussels National Airport from New York is 7½ hours; from London, ¾ hour; from Caracas, 12 hours; from Tokyo, 17½ hours. Time in Belgium: GMT+1.

REQUIREMENTS FOR ENTRY AND CUSTOMS REGULATIONS

Valid passport; smallpox vaccination certificate not required for those traveling from European countries, US, and Canada. Cholera and yellow-fever vaccination certificates required if arriving from an infected area. No visa necessary for stays less than three months. There are no currency regulations. Visitors from European countries may export articles totaling not more than 5,000F in value, while non-Europeans can export articles totaling no more than 25,000F. Duty-free allowances for Europeans: 300 cigarettes or 75 cigars or 400 grams tobacco; 4 liters wine, 1½ liters liquor; 75 grams perfume. Non-Europeans may bring in 400 cigarettes or 100 cigars or 500 grams tobacco; 2 liters wine, 1 liter liquor; 50 grams perfume.

AIRPORT INFORMATION

The major airport is Brussels National Airport, about 8 miles from the city center. There is a frequent train service from the airport operating between 6:30am and 8pm in the Central Station in Brussels. The train fare is 52F for adults, 26F for children. Taxis always available, the cost from airport to city center being about 700F, inclusive of tip. The airport has a duty-free shop, a nursery, and hotel reservations counters. There is no departure tax.

ACCOMMODATIONS

There are accommodations bureaus in all major cities: Antwerp (Suikerrui 19—tel: 32 01 03); Brussels (rue Marché aux Herbes 61-63—tel: 513 89 40/513 90 90); Ghent (Borluutstraat 9—tel: 25 36 41); and Bruges (Markt

7—tel: 33 07 13). The tourist season runs from June-September, plus Easter, Whitsun, Christmas, and the New Year. At other times, off season rates are in effect. Some provision for student accommodations in Brussels; information from the **Tourist Office** or **Infor Jeunes** (rue Marché aux Herbes 27—tel: 512 96 02). Brussels hotels:

Rates are in US$ for a double/twin room with bath or shower
(Note: All addresses given in French followed by Flemish.)

Amigo, rue de l'Amigo 1-3, Vruntstraat (from $85)

Astoria, rue Royale 103, Koningstraat (from $91), 5 minutes from city center

Atlanta, Boulevard Adolphe Max 7, Ad. Maxlaan (from $93)

Bedford, rue du Midi 135, Zuidstraat (from $60)

Brussels Europa, rue de la Loi 107, Wetstraat (from $95), 15 minutes from city center

Brussels Hilton, Boulevard de Waterloo 38, Waterloolaan (from $104), 10 minutes from city center

Holiday Inn, Holidaystraat 1920 (from $88), near airport

Hyatt Regency, rue Royale 250, Koningstraat (from $85), 10 minutes from city center

MacDonald, Avenue Louise 321-325, Louizalaan (from $54), in uptown residential area

Mayfair, Avenue Louise 318-383, Louizalaan (from $115), in uptown residential area

Metropole, Place de Brouckere 31, de Brouckereplein (from $66)

Novotel, Brussels Airport (from $62), near airport

Ramada, Chaussée de Charleroi 36, Steenweg (from $81)

Sheraton, Place Rogier, Rogierplein (from $98), near Gare du Nord railway station

Siru, Place Rogier, Rogierplein (from $46), near Gare du Nord

Royal Windsor, rue Duquesnoy 5-7, Duquesnoystraat (from $112)

Van Belle, Chaussée de Mons 39-43, Bergensesteenweg (from $37), 10 minutes from city center

Windsor, Place Rouppe 13, Rouppeplein (from $33)

All hotels listed above centrally located unless otherwise indicated.

USEFUL INFORMATION

Banks: Most open 9-3:30 or 4, and closed 12:30-2:30, Mon-Fri.

Mail: Stamps can be bought at some souvenir shops selling postcards as well as at post offices. Mailboxes are red.

Telephone Tips: Telephones found in cafés, restaurants, hotels, etc. Booths are coin-operated. Local calls cost 5F. Useful numbers in Brussels:

Pan Am 511 64 05	**Time** 992
Tourist Information and	**Police** 906
Accommodations Offices	**Ambulance** 900
513 89 40/	**Weather** 991
513 90 90	

Newspapers: English-language newspapers and magazines available. Local English-language publication: *The Bulletin.*

Tipping: Customary. Generally 15% unless service charge already included. Porter, 20F per piece of luggage; cloakroom attendant, 10-20F; cinema usher, 5F per person; taxi driver, meter price includes tip.

Electricity: Most areas have 220 volts 50 cycles AC, but a few country areas still have 130 volts.

Laundry: There are good laundry and dry-cleaning services (dry-cleaning a suit, from 250F; laundering a shirt, 30F).

Hairdressing: First-class hotels have salons (shampoo and set 600-700F; man's haircut and shampoo, from 400-500F; tip 10% for both).

Photography: Good selection of equipment; black and white and color film available throughout the country (black and white, about 80F, color about 125F).

Clubs: Lions, Rotary, Kiwanis.

Babysitting: Services can be obtained through major hotels.

Rest Rooms: In cafés, hotels, and stores and some public places. Women, *Damen* or *Dames;* men, *Herren* or *Messieurs.*

Health: Many doctors and dentists speak English. Imported pharmaceuticals available. Water is safe to drink.

TRANSPORTATION

There are bus, streetcar, and taxi services available throughout the cities in Belgium. Brussels and Antwerp have subways. Metered taxis are readily available and can be hailed on the street or found at taxi stands. Rental cars are available. Traffic is lively, so be careful. Drive on the right. Automatic priority is given to traffic coming from the right. Wearing of seat belts is compulsory in front seat. Train services good. The Eurailpass is accepted in Belgium.

FOOD AND RESTAURANTS

Food in Belgium tends to be very rich, and the variety of specialties is endless. Belgian endive or *witloof,* shoots of chicory grown totally in the dark and in heated earth, is a vegetable specialty. Waffles and french fries are served just about everywhere. Stews are also notable in Belgium, and among the many available you should try the *Hochepot* (made with pork and mutton); the *Carbonnade flamande* (beef cooked in beer); *Waterzooi* (creamed chicken and finely shredded vegetables); and *Choesels au Madère* (oxtail joints, breast of veal, and lamb kidneys and feet, in Madeira wine with mushrooms, herbs, spices, and Belgian beer). The best of the highly individual regional dishes are available in Brussels—try the *Lièvre aux pruneaux,* which is prepared with Flemish beer and prunes. If you visit Belgium in the spring you can eat fresh asparagus *à la Flamande* (dipped in a sauce of mashed hard-boiled eggs, melted butter, and parsley), or have some *moules* (mussels) when they are in season (any month with an R in it). Standard meal times are 6-9:30 breakfast; 12-2 lunch; 6-10 dinner. One of the best restaurants in Brussels is the **Comme Chez Soi** (Place Rouppe 23—tel: 512 29 21 or 512 36 74); specialties here are the woodcock pâté, *mousse de saison,* the *sole mousse-*

line au Riesling, and the *sole cardinale.* **La Cravache d'Or** (Place A. Leemans 10—tel: 538 37 46) is famous for having the freshest fish in Brussels, and you should also try the *oeufs à la moelle* (eggs cooked in red wine). **Chez Adrienne** (Avenue Louise 124—tel: 649 54 41) is famous for its hors d'oeuvres; at **Le Coq au Vin** (rue du Marché au Charbon 62—tel: 513 23 68) reserve in advance. **Au Vieux Saint-Martin** (Place du Grand Sablon 38—tel: 512 64 76) serves good *waterzooi.* **Rugbyman** (Quai aux Brigues 4—tel: 512 56 40) is great for lobster, and the food is excellent at **Vincent** (rue des Dominicains 8-10—tel: 511 23 03).

DRINKING TIPS

Belgians are fond of *Gueuze* beer, drunk either by itself or with grenadine. Other beers are *Trappist, Westmalle,* and *Leffe.* French and German wines are available. *Faro* is wheat-based beer; and one of the oldest beers of Brussels, but it is difficult to find. *Lambic* is another local beer, wheat- and barley-based, and *Kriek* is a lambic beer in which cherries have been macerated. There are a number of English-style pubs in the major cities.

ENTERTAINMENT

There is a wide variety, especially in Brussels. Go to one of the oldest puppet theaters in Europe—"The Marionettes de Toone," at Petite rue des Bouchers 6, Impasse du Schuddeveld. Opera and ballet can be seen at the **Théâtre Royal de la Monnaie** and **Palais des Beaux Arts;** Brussels is also the home of Bejart's **Ballet du XXme Siècle.** Most theatrical productions are in French, except at the **Flemish Theater.** Local Flemish-language productions can also be seen in some of the Flemish towns. The **Parc, Théâtre Royal des Galeries,** and **Théâtre National** provide good theatrical entertainment, and for the more avant-garde, there are the **Théâtre Cent-Quarante** and the **Théâtre de Poche.** There are a number of nightclubs, those in Brussels including **Le Crazy** (rue Capitaine Crespel 15); **Chez Paul** (rue Fosse-aux-Loups 16); **Maxim** (rue Capitaine Crespel 22); and **Le Grand Escalier** (rue au Beurre 25). Jazz may be heard at the **Bloomdido Jazz Café** (rue Borgval 14) and the **Brussels Jazz Club** (Grand' Place 13). Belgium also has an enormous number of religious and folkloric festivals, beer festivals, fairs, and pageants on its annual calendar (copies available at the Belgian National Tourist Office). The **Festival of Flanders** is a music festival in two parts: a spring section from April through June and a summer section from August through mid or late September. Concerts—by foreign and Belgian ensembles— are held principally in Brussels, Ghent, and Leuven, but also in other towns. Brussels and Antwerp cinemas show English-language films.

SHOPPING

There is great variation in store hours, but all remain open during lunch; closing times vary from 6-8pm. Best buys are pralines (chocolates filled with nut cream); ginger cookies; Bruges lace; brassware; copperware; tapestries; diamonds; leatherwork; and linen. There are two major shopping districts in Brussels, the first in the lower city around the **Boulevard Adolphe Max** and the **rue Neuve;** the other between **Porte de Namur** and the **Place Stephanie** (Avenue Louise, Avenue de la Toison d'Or, Chaussée d'Ixelles). There are also a number of galleries, or shopping arcades, throughout the city. Bargaining is not the custom in stores. Some of the major shops in Brussels are: for chocolate; **Godiva** (Grand' Place 22 and many other locations) and **Leonidas** (many central locations) for pralines; lace, **Manufacture Belge de Dentelles SA (1810)** (Galerie de la Reine 6-8) and **Maria Loix** (rue d'Arenberg 52); leathergoods from **Kent** (Avenue Louise 36); linen from **Tissages Réunis de Courtrai** (rue Royale 107). Major department stores are **Au Bon Marché, Innovation, Galeries Anspach,** and stores in the **Sarma** and **GB** chains. There are elegant antique shops around the Grand Sablon.

SPORTS
Spectator sports include soccer, horse shows, basketball, horse racing, Grand Prix auto racing at **Francorchamps** and **Zolder,** and tennis. There are golf courses near most of Belgium's main cities, tennis courts and clubs, and good horseback riding in many parts of the country. There is good swimming all along the coast and yachting at **Ostend, Blankenberge, Zeebrugge,** and **Nieuwpoort.** Freshwater fishing is good in the rivers of the **Ardennes,** and there is also a hunting season in the Ardennes, from October through February. There is skiing in the **province of Liège** (if weather conditions permit) and land-yachting on the beaches along the west coast.

WHAT TO SEE
Brussels: In the center of Brussels is the **Grand' Place,** which is the city's first marketplace and dates from the 12th century. It was destroyed and rebuilt during the 17th century and has been described as an "architectural jewel." Victor Hugo called it the "most beautiful square in the world." The **Town Hall** in the Grand' Place was completed in 1449 and has a collection of Brussels tapestries. Also in the Grand' Place are the **Maison du Roi** and the many **Guild Houses** which serve as reminders of the city's past. Not far from the Grand' Place is the statue of *Mannekin-Pis,* much loved by the Belgians and often regarded as the personification of Belgian ribaldry. There are a number of lovely churches scattered throughout the city, among them the **Church of St Nicholas, Church of Notre-Dame du Sablon, Church of Notre Dame aux Riches-Claires,** the **Church of St John the Baptist** *"Au Béguinage,"* the **Finistère Church,** the **Chapel de la Madeleine,** and **St Michael's Cathedral.** Also worth seeing are the **Bourse,** the **Palais de la Nation,** and the **Place Royal.** The **Théâtre de la Monnaie** is a reputable opera house, and the **Hotel Ravenstein** is the last remaining mansion of the Burgundian Court here. Of the museums, one of the best and most justifiably popular is **Erasmus House** (rue de Chapitre 31—tel: 521 13 83). The **Brueghel Museum** (rue Haute 132) is also well worth a visit. Other museums include the **Musical Instruments Museum** (Place du Petit Sablon 17), the **Ixelles Fine Arts**

Gallery (rue Jean Van Volsem 71), and the **Musée Horta** (rue Americaine 25). Outside Brussels visit the site of the Battle of Waterloo and the **Royal Central African Museum** in Tervuren.

Ostend is perhaps the most famous of the seaside towns, with a promenade 100 feet wide and 5 miles long. The city has an **Aquarium,** casinos, and the **Royal Theater.** Hotels include the **Europe,** Kapucijuestraat 52 (from US$30 double); the **Imperial,** Van Iseghemlaan 74-76 (from US$49 double); and the **Andromeda,** Albert I Promenade 60 (from US$57 double).

Other spots worth visiting on the coast are **Knokke-le-Zoute**—stay either at **La Réserve** (Elisabethlaan 132) or **Majestic** (Zeedijk 129). To the south are **Oost-Duinkerke** and **Le Coq** with a largely unspoiled coastline and less expensive places to stay.

Antwerp, the second city of Belgium, has at its center the **Cathedral of Notre Dame,** which contains three major Rubens paintings: *The Elevation of the Cross,* the *Deposition,* and the *Assumption.* The house Rubens occupied for the last 25 years of his life is off the Meir (Rubensstraat 9) and open to the public. The **Gallery of Fine Arts** (Leopold de Waelplaats) has over 1,000 works by Old Masters. Antwerp has its own **Grand' Place** with the **Stadhuis,** a Renaissance Town Hall. The port and the diamond district are also main attractions. Some hotels to stay at are **Antwerp Docks,** Noorderlaan 100 (from US$38 double); the **Tourist,** Pelikaanstraat 20 (from US$32 double); the **Theater,** Arenbergstraat 30 (from US$63 double); and the **Waldorf,** Belgiëlei 36 (from US$59 double).

There are a number of theaters, mostly Flemish, and the **Royal Flemish Opera** (Frankrijklei 3). **Ancienne Belgique** (Kipdorpvest 26) and **Billard Palace** (Koningin Astridplein 40) are both music halls, and symphony concerts are held at the **Queen Elizabeth** concert hall. Restaurants in Antwerp include **La Pérouse** (Steenplein—tel: 32 35 28), the best, open September through May; **La Rade** (Van Dijckkaai 8—tel: 33 49 63); **Criterium** (De Keyserlei 25—tel: 32 21 80); **Le Gourmet sans Chiqué** (Vestingstraat 3—tel: 32 90 02); and **Sir Anthony Van Dijck** (16 Oude Koornmarkt—tel: 31 61 70).

Bruges is a beautiful, quiet, and intact medieval town surrounded by stretches of original town wall and interlaced with winding canals. There are more than 50 bridges over the canals. Behind the Grote Markt and the Belfry is the two-storied **Chapel of the Holy Blood** (lower church 12th-century Romanesque, upper chapel 15th-century Gothic). The city is known primarily for its collection of Van Eycks at the **Groeninge Museum** and Memlings at the **St John's Hospital.** Hotels are the **Holiday Inn,** Boeveriestraat 2, built in a converted 17th-century abbey (from US$66 double); **Europ,** Augustijnenrei 18 (from US$41 double); **Portinari,** Garenmarkt 15 (from US$42 double); and the **Duc de Bourgogne,** Huidevettersplein 12 (from US$48 double). Restaurants include **Civière d'Or** (Markt 33—tel: 33 17 93) and **Panier d'Or** (Markt 28—tel: 33 39 85), both terrace restaurants on the Markt; **Central** (Markt 30—tel: 33 18 05); and the dining room of the **Duc de Bourgogne.**

Within easy traveling distance of Bruges are three interesting towns, **Damme, Furnes,** and **Ypres,** almost totally destroyed in the First World War but now largely rebuilt. The **Cloth Hall** and **Cathedral** in Ypres are notable. Damme was originally a fore-port of Bruges, dating from the 13th to 15th centuries. Furnes is another ancient town which, like Ypres, survived the First World War.

Ghent is well known for its canals and for the late-August Begonia Festival in the nearby village of Lochristi. It is built around three rivers: the Lys, the Live, and the Scheldt. There are some fine Van Eycks in this city: the *Adoration of the Lamb* in **St Bavos Cathedral** is perhaps the city's greatest treasure. The **Fine Arts Museum** in Citadel Park (with paintings by Brueghel, Rubens, Tintoretto, etc.), the **Museum of Decorative Arts** (7 Breydelstraat), and the **Folklore Museum** (Kraanlei) are all notable. Hotels are the **Carlton,** Koningin Astridlaan 62 (from US$39 double); **Europa,** Gordunakaai 59 (from US$46 double); **Holiday Inn,** Ottergemsesteenweg 600, on city outskirts (from US$50 double); and **Terminus,** Kon. Maria Hendrikalaan 6-7 (from US$33 double).

West of Brussels: In the Tournai Region, **Mons** and the city of **Tournai** itself deserve a visit. Mons is an industrial town with First World War associations, and in its **Collegiate Church** it has one of the best examples of late-Gothic architecture in Belgium. Tournai, on the Scheldt, has a magnificent cathedral and is otherwise noted for its tapestries, porcelain, gilt, and bronzes and sculptures.

The Meuse Valley, which begins in France and ends in the Netherlands, makes its way through important tourist centers; **Liège** and **Namur** are the chief towns of the province. **Dinant** is the most picturesque.

Liège has a large number of museums and a surprising number of churches. The city's treasure is the **Church of St Barthélémy,** which dates from 1108. Hotels in Liège are **De la Couronne,** Place des Guillemins 11-13 (from US$54 double), **Ramada,** Boulevard de la Sauvenière 100 (from US$76 double), and the **Holiday Inn Liège,** Palais des Congrès, Esplanade de l'Europe (from US$70 double). Good restaurants include **Chez Septime** (rue St Paul 12—tel: 23 22 55); **Vieux Liège** (Quai de la Goffe 41—tel: 23 77 48); **Au Rouet** (rue des Mineurs 13—tel: 32 07 25); **Le Seigneur d'Amay** (rue d'Amay 12—tel: 32 00 44); **Pont d'Avroy** (rue Pont d'Avroy 32—tel: 23 28 95).

The Ardennes are the Belgians' playground and provide a wide variety of vacation diversions, from camping to taking the waters at a spa, just as was done in the 18th and 19th centuries at the original **Spa,** from which all others take their name. In Spa stay at the **Hostellerie Ardennaise,** rue de la Poste 13-15 (from US$38 double). In the **Lesse Valley** you can visit the **Han Grottos,** first discovered in 1814. Alternatively, visit **La-Roche-en-Ardenne,** beautifully situated in a loop of the river Ourthe, where the ruined castle of Henri, Count de la Rouche, still stands. Two hotels to stay at are **De l'Air Pur,** Route de Houffalize 11 (from US$52 double), and **Des Ardennes,** rue de Beausaint 2 (from US$35 double).

SOURCES OF FURTHER INFORMATION

Pan Am, Cantersteen 55, Brussels, and any other Pan Am office around the world; **Commissariat Général au Tourisme,** rue Marché aux Herbes 61, Brussels; **Belgian National Tourist Office,** 745 Fifth Avenue, New York, NY 10022; 66 Haymarket, London SW1Y 4RB.

Bulgaria

WHAT'S SPECIAL

Bulgaria stands on the old overland route from Europe to Asia. There are high, snowy mountains, the fertile Danube valley, the Thracian plain, and the Mediterranean-like playground on the Black Sea. Sofia, the capital, was a settlement 5,000 years ago.

COUNTRY BRIEFING

Size: 42,823 square miles   **Population:** 8,500,000
Capital: Sofia   **Capital Population:** 1,100,000

Weather in Sofia: Lat N42°42′; Alt 1805 ft

Temp (°F)	Jan	Feb	Mar	Apr	May	Jun	Jul	Aug	Sep	Oct	Nov	Dec
Av Low	22°	25°	32°	41°	49°	54°	57°	56°	50°	42°	35°	26°
Av High	34°	39°	51°	62°	70°	76°	82°	82°	74°	63°	50°	37°
Days no rain	25	22	23	22	20	21	24	25	24	24	23	24

Government: A socialist people's republic.
Language: Bulgarian. Russian widely spoken. German, French, and English spoken in tourist hotels, public offices, etc.
Religion: Eastern Orthodox Church; many churches and monasteries have become museums. Roman Catholic churches in Sofia, Plovdiv, Burgas, and Varna; Methodist and Congregational churches in Sofia.

Currency: Leva. 100 stotinki = 1 lev.

	10 st	20 st	50 st	1 Lv	10 Lv	20 Lv	50 Lv	100 Lv
US (dollars, cents)	.11	.23	.55	1.14	11.40	22.80	57.00	114.00
UK (pounds, pence)	.05	.11	.27	.54	5.44	10.88	27.19	54.38

Tourists get 50% more above the official exchange rate.

Public Holidays:

New Year's Day, 1 Jan
Women's Day, 8 Mar
Labor Days, 1 & 2 May
Day of Bulgarian Culture, 24 May

National Holiday, 9 & 10 Sept
Day of the Russian Revolution, 7 Nov

HOW TO GET THERE

Flying time to Sofia's Sofia Airport from New York is 10 hours; from Rome, 2 hours; from Istanbul, 1 hour. Time in Bulgaria: GMT+2. Daylight Saving Time observed.

REQUIREMENTS FOR ENTRY AND CUSTOMS REGULATIONS

Passport. Bulgaria has declared a non-visa policy for all foreign tourists provided they stay not less than 48 hours and not more than 2 months and have prepaid a minimum of 3 days tourist services through travel agents representing Balkantourist in the US and major European capitals, or have bought the same minimum services at Balkantourist border office. Tourists can also buy prepaid services for the length of their stay or, after the minimum 3 days, can pay for services in cash or by traveler's check. Persons who do not prepay services (those visiting relatives, for instance) can obtain a visa from any Bulgarian diplomatic mission abroad. A fee of US$14 is charged for the visa; no photographs required. Upon arrival, visitors are requested to fill out basic personal data on yellow information cards, a copy of which they retain during their stay. This card should not be thrown away. It is handed back at departure and failure to do so can cause delay or missed flight connections.

There are no restrictions on the amount of foreign currency a tourist can bring into Bulgaria, although one is not permitted to bring in Bulgarian leva. Foreign currency can be exchanged at the Bulgarian National Bank, at points of entry, or at hotels and offices of Balkantourist. Any surplus Bulgarian leva may be reconverted into Western currency upon departure provided all original exchange receipts are presented. Exports exceeding in value the amount of levas received by legal exchange will be subject to Bulgarian duty.

Customs formalities upon entrance and exit are minimal, although import of personal goods intended for resale is forbidden. Two liters of wine, 1 liter of alcohol, and 350 grams of cigarettes, cigars, or tobacco may be imported.

AIRPORT INFORMATION

The major airport is Sofia Airport, 7½ miles from the capital. Buses run from 4:30am-midnight to the city center, leaving about every 15 minutes between 5:30am and 10:30pm; fare is 6 stotinki. The taxi fare is about 3 leva. Arriving tourists should allow at least 30 minutes for the drive into the city. There is a duty-free shop and a room for mothers with young children. The information desk will help with accommodations.

ACCOMMODATIONS

All travel plans, including accommodations, sightseeing tours, and car rentals with or without driver, can be coordinated through the national travel bureau **Balkantourist** in Bulgaria or through travel agencies representing Balkantourist abroad. If you have prepaid services through a travel agent well enough in advance, you will receive hotel and meal vouchers before departure; otherwise you will be supplied a receipt confirming prepayment and can pick up the vouchers on arrival. Vouchers are honored at all Balkantourist facilities—at least 95% of the hotels and restaurants in Bulgaria. Sofia has luxury and first-class hotels and there are good hotels throughout the country, including the mountain areas. The great resort complex on the Black Sea has extensive accommodations of all kinds. In resort areas, there are price reductions of 25% at the beginning and end of the season in June and September, and 40% reductions out of season from October to the end of May. Inexpensive accommodations can also be arranged through Balkantourist in private houses.

More than 100 camp sites throughout the country provide electricity, water, and all services for campers, from 2-2.70 leva per person per night within a resort and 1.50-2.10 outside a resort. Tents, cars, and trailers are extra. Many of these sites also have bungalows available. There are motels along the major highways. It is strongly recommended that reservations be secured in advance; never arrive in Sofia without a hotel reservation. Hotels in Sofia:

Rates are in US$ for a double/twin room with bath or shower
  Grand Hotel Balkan, Lenin Square (from $54 BB)
  Grand Hotel Sofia, Naradno Sobranie Square (from $56 BB)
  Novotel Evropa, 131 Georgii Dimitrov Boulevard (from $52 BB), ½ mile from center city
  Park-Hotel Moskva, Nezabravka 9 (from $48 BB), 1 mile from center city
  Pliska, 87 Boulevard Lenin (from $30 BB)
  Serdica, 2 Vladimir Zaimov Boulevard (from $30 BB)
  Slavia, 2 Sofiiski Geroi Street (from $30 BB)
  Vitosha New Otani, 100 Anton Ivanov Boulevard (from $68 BB), 1 mile from center city
All hotels centrally located unless otherwise indicated.

USEFUL INFORMATION

Helpful Hints: With the help of a phrase book try out *molya* for please, *bluggodurryer* for thank you, *dobar den* for good-day, and *zdravej* for a less formal hello.

Banks: Opening hours 8-11:45am. Uniform banking system, Bulgarian National Bank, all over the country. Exchange bureaus at border crossing points, the airport, and in towns. Remember to keep the exchange receipts.

Mail: Street mailboxes are red for Express, yellow for ordinary mail.

Telephone Tips: There are public telephone booths, coin-operated (2 stotinki is initial charge), and larger restaurants and cafés also have public phones. A 3-minute long-distance call costs 9 to 54 stotinki depending on distance, and there is a surcharge for urgent calls. Useful numbers in Sofia:

Balkantourist 84 131	International Calls 123
Airport 71 201 (Balkan Airlines)	Information 144 (state
Taxi 142	agencies)
	145 (private listings)

Newspapers: Foreign newspapers in all languages on sale at kiosks in the towns. Bulgarian publications in English: *Bulgaria Today, Film News, Resorts,* and *Bulgarian Foreign Trade,* but no Western periodicals. *Sofia News* is full of useful information.

Tipping: Not officially expected. Service charge is included in restaurants and hotels, but an added 10-15% is useful if staying longer in one place.

Electricity: 220 volts 50 cycles AC throughout the country.

Laundry: Laundry and dry-cleaning services in main cities and major hotels. Laundromats in principal cities.

Hairdressers: Main hotels have salons.

Photography: Bring your own film. Only Soviet and East German films (ORWO) sold in the country. Black and white film can be developed locally anywhere; color film takes 10 days. Corecom (hard-currency) stores sell West German films but won't develop.

Babysitting: This can be arranged at major hotels. Sunny Beach, on the Black Sea, is an international family resort with special facilities for children, including swimming pools and playgrounds, kindergartens and babysitters, restaurants with special menus for children, and pediatricians.

Rest Rooms: Women, *zhenny;* men, *muzhay.* Unless you know the Cyrillic alphabet, watch for the symbols.

Health: There is a national health service, with free emergency treatment, hospital care, and doctors' visits, but any prescription medicines must be paid for. Bulgarian medicines differ from Western ones, so it is best to take pharmaceuticals with you. Water in cities and towns safe for drinking.

TRANSPORTATION

In Sofia and large towns there is a public transportation network of buses, streetcars, and trolley buses. Tickets can be bought at kiosks near the stops. Metered taxis are inexpensive and in fairly good supply. Regular long-distance bus services connect the towns. There is an internal train service with sleeping and restaurant cars. Balkan Airlines (Narodno Sobranie Square—tel: 88 44 93 or 88 44 33 for international flights, 88 44 36 or 88 13 94 for domestic flights) links all the major towns, with flights taking from 30 to 50 minutes. Boats connect the Black Sea ports of Varna and Burgas, and there are regular cruises to the Soviet Black Sea Coast and Istanbul. There are steamship services on the Danube within Bulgaria.

The highways are good and well maintained, especially the main highways from Sofia to Plovdiv or the Black Sea resorts. In more remote areas night driving is discouraged, particularly where unlit agricultural vehicles are on the roads. Cars can be rented in the main cities and resorts through Balkantourists. Avis operates in Sofia, Albena, Burgas, and Varna. The charge is about US$11-18 per day depending on model and US11-19¢ per kilometer; chauffeur-driven cars are about US$8 per hour plus US30¢ per kilometer. Gas can be paid for in leva or in foreign currency, but it is advisable to consult Balkantourist, as there are concessions and reductions. Super is 1 leva per liter, normal 80 stotinki per liter, and diesel 40 stotinki per liter.

FOOD AND RESTAURANTS

The Bulgarians say they owe long life and happiness to eating yogurt, their national food, which figures in many recipes. Dishes are Eastern Mediterranean in character, spicy and pungent with a basis of rice and excellent vegetables. Favorite meat dishes include *kebabches,* which are broiled meat rolls on skewers. Fruit is abundant. Meals tend to be eaten early, though in hotels they serve breakfast 7-9, lunch 12-3, dinner 7-9. Restaurant prices with wine, through Balkantourist, are about US$9 deluxe and US$7 for a first-class meal. Recommended restaurants in Sofia include **Krim** (17 Slavyanska Street—tel: 87 01 31); **Opera** (116 Rakovski Street); **Budapest** (145 Rakovski Street—tel: 87 27 50); **Berlin** (4 Vassil Levski Square—tel: 44 12 58); the **Czech Restaurant** (15 D. Polyanov Street); the restaurant at the **Journalist's Club** (4 Graf Ignatiev Street); and **Ropotamo** (Lenin Housing Estate). Restaurants in the Vitosha New Otani, Novotel Evropa, Park-Hotel Moskva, Grand Hotel Sofia, and the Grand Hotel Balkan are all excellent.

DRINKING TIPS

Bulgarian grapes and fruit provide attractive wines and brandies; the plum brandy, *slivova,* is the most popular. Imported drinks are available; a whisky and soda (100 grams) costs from 6.60 leva at the **Novotel** bar, 11-17 leva at the **Vitosha New Otani.** Beer is also available. There are no restrictions on the sale of alcohol. Women are welcome in bars.

ENTERTAINMENT

There are 50 theaters and opera companies in Bulgaria, mostly in the capital and the larger towns. A dozen symphony orchestras tour extensively, to factories and villages as well as to the big cities. The Bulgarian circus is popular; Sofia has a zoo. There are more than 3,000 movie houses in Bulgaria, mostly showing foreign, including Western and US films with the original soundtracks and subtitles. Nightclubs, such as the **Astoria Bar** (16 Rousski Boulevard) and the **Orient Bar** (2 Stamboliiski Boulevard), are often open from 10pm-4am, and occasionally feature modest striptease. There is a gambling casino in the **Vitosha New Otani Hotel.**

SHOPPING

Bulgaria is renowned for its folk art and crafts—ceramics, wood carvings, hats and gloves, coats, and belts in skins and furs and vivid embroideries. Visitors from abroad can buy Bulgarian goods at reduced rates if they pay in foreign currency. The state-run **Corecom** has special departments in centrally located stores. **Stamboliiski Boulevard** has a number of interesting stores.

SPORTS

Soccer is the great Bulgarian game. Wrestling is popular too, as are basketball and volleyball. Yachting, angling, and fishing on the Danube and the Black Sea are available all the year round, with no closed season. Hunting (shooting) is available in game reserves throughout Bulgaria. Balkantourist organizes mountain excursions, and there are skiing and winter sports. The **Rhodopa Cup International Ski Competition** takes place in February.

WHAT TO SEE

Balkantourist arranges trips and excursions to all parts of the country from every major center.

Sofia, a pleasant open city, is 5,000 years old. The **Alexander Nevsky Cathedral** was built 1904-1912, but go there to hear the choir and to see the exhibition of ancient icons in the crypt. The remains of the 4th-century **Church of St George** are in the courtyard of the Balkan Hotel. Many mosques survive as reminders of Turkish rule including the **Big Mosque,** the **Black Mosque** and the **Banya Baski Mosque.** The pride of the **Archeological Museum,** Deveti Septemvri Square, is the **Vulchi Trun** treasure, 8th century BC. The museum is open 3-8 Tuesday to Saturday, 10-1 Sunday; closed Monday. The **National Gallery,** in the former royal palace, is open 10:30-6:30 daily.

Ancient and medieval Bulgaria is preserved in "Museum towns"—complete villages, or the old quarters of larger towns. **Koprivshtitsa** is a museum town in the district of Sofia and **Veliko Turnovo** is another, about halfway between Sofia and Varna. **The Black Sea Coast** is an up-to-date vacation area where new holiday towns appear among the ports and fishing villages. The main centers are Varna, Drouzhba, Golden Sands, Sunny Beach, and Albena, Bulgaria's newest Black Sea resort. Among the better of the many motels are (prices are for doubles with full board): **Varna**—the **Cherno More** (from US$66) and the **Odessa** (from US$30). **Drouzhba**—the **Grand Hotel Varna** (from US$100), **Tchaika** (from US$72). **Prostor** and **Rubin** (both from US$52), and **Lebed** (from US$38). **Golden Sands**—the **International** (from US$88), the **Astoria, Shipka,** and **Zlatna**

Kotva (all from US$48 double AP), and the **Metropol** (from US$50). **Sunny Beach**—the **Cuban** (from US$72), the **Bourgas** (from US$74), and the **Globus, Europa,** and **Olymp** (all from US$50).

SOURCES OF FURTHER INFORMATION

Any **Pan Am** office around the world. **Balkantourist,** 1 Lenin Square, Sofia. **Bulgarian Tourist Office,** 50 East 42nd Street, Suite 1508, New York, NY 10017; 126 Regent Street, London WI.

Canary Islands

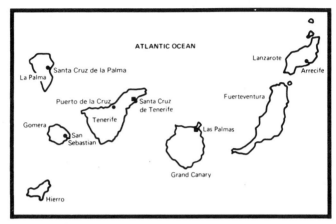

WHAT'S SPECIAL

These seven islands are the result of a series of volcanic eruptions from the sea and are known as "The Fortunate Isles" because of their year-round spring climate. They are known in legend as the highest peaks of the lost continent of Atlantis. The Canaries form two provinces of Spain: Las Palmas, consisting of the islands of Grand Canary (Gran Canaria), Lanzarote, and Fuerteventura; and Santa Cruz de Tenerife, comprising the islands of Tenerife, La Palma, Gomera, and Hierro.

COUNTRY BRIEFING

The Canary Isles cover an **area** of 2,807 square miles with a **population** of 362,706 on Grand Canary and 191,286 on Tenerife. The **capital** of Grand Canary is Las Palmas; of Tenerife, Santa Cruz. **Climate:** only slight variation in temperature throughout the year; average for January is 64°F and for August 76°F. Very little rain. **Government** as in Spain, and the **language** is Spanish. **Religion**—Roman Catholic. **Currency** is the Spanish peseta—96ptas to US$1. **Public Holidays** are as for Spain.

HOW TO GET THERE

Flying time to Las Palmas de Gran Canaria from New York is 8½ hours; from London, 3½ hours; from Madrid, 2½ hours; from Frankfurt, 4½ hours. Time in the Canary Islands: GMT.

REQUIREMENTS FOR ENTRY AND CUSTOMS REGULATIONS

Passport; no vaccination certificate is required unless coming from an infected area. Currency regulations are the same as for the rest of Spain. A duty-free port.

AIRPORT INFORMATION

Buses or taxis to city centers; airport coach service to Las Palmas is 30ptas (limousine 800ptas) to cover the 10-mile distance to town; Tenerife bus service is also available from Los Rodeos for 50ptas and limousine for 450ptas. Bus from Reina Sofia—Tenerife Sur Airport, across the island from Santa Cruz, is 230ptas; taxi, 1,920ptas. No arrival or departure tax.

ACCOMMODATIONS

Hotels are generally reasonable (as in Spain), and range from first-class to modest pension guesthouses. There are at present five *Paradores* (government-sponsored inns) on Grand Canary, Tenerife, Fuerteventura, La Palma, and Gomera. There are tourist bureaus at Triana 70, Las Palmas, and Rambla de General Franco 59, Santa Cruz. Hotels are:

Rates are in US$ for a double/twin room with bath or shower

Botanico, Avenida Richard J. Yeoward, Puerto de la Cruz, Tenerife (from $73)

Don Juan, Eduardo Benot 3, Las Palmas, Grand Canary (from $43)

Guajara, 15 Avenida Generalisimo, Puerto de la Cruz (from $24)

Reina Isabel, Paseo de las Canteras, Las Palmas (from $59)

Santa Catalina, Parque Doramus, Las Palmas (from $53)

Tagor, La Virtud 3, Puerto de la Cruz (from $20)

Tigaiga, Parque del Taoro, Puerto de la Cruz (from $62)

Tenerife Playa, Avenida de Colon 12, Puerto de la Cruz (from $40)

Ybarra Valle Mar, Avenida de Colon 2, Puerto de la Cruz (from $70)

USEFUL INFORMATION

Banks: Open 9-2, Mon-Fri; 9-1 Sat; few outside main cities. Currency and travelers' checks can be changed at hotels, shops, and travel agencies. **Mail:** stamps can be bought at post offices and authorized tobacco booths known as *Estancos*. Mailboxes are yellow. Coin-operated public **telephone** booths are plentiful—local calls cost 5ptas. Phones also in cafés, restaurants, bars, hotels. Useful numbers:

Tourist Information, 21 87 65; **Tourist Offices,** 26 46 23 or 24 35 93; **Airport Information,** 22 39 40; **Directories,** 003; **Time,** 093; **International Trunk Calls,** 008.

Newspapers of many nationalities available. **Tipping** customary; restaurants do not generally include service charge, so tip 10%; porters, 25ptas per piece of luggage; taxi drivers, 10% of fare or minimum of 10ptas; hotel porters, 100ptas for week's stay. **Electricity** is 125 volts (220 in modern building) 50 cycles AC. Major hotels have express **laundry** service, but dry-cleaning is usually slow (from 150ptas to dry-clean a suit; 50ptas to launder a shirt). **Hairdressing** salons in first-class hotels (shampoo and set from 400ptas; man's haircut from 250ptas. Tip 25-50ptas). Inexpensive **photographic** equipment and films available; allow 2-3 days to develop color and black and white film. **Babysitting** available through hotels. **Rest Rooms** in bars, hotels, restaurants; women, *Señoras;* men, *Caballeros.* **Health:** some doctors speak English; pharmaceuticals available and inexpensive. Safest to drink bottled water.

TRANSPORTATION
Bus service (standard fare 12ptas) in towns and the fare increases long distance. Plenty of taxis. Car rentals available (extra charge for English-speaking drivers). There are additional boat services between islands.

FOOD AND RESTAURANTS
Fish (octopus, squid, sardines, mussels, prawns, and shrimps) is the islanders' staple diet, especially delicious served with *mojo picon,* a hot spicy sauce made with herbs and peppers. Another specialty is *potaje de berros,* a watercress and herb soup. *Sancocho Canario* is salt fish in a piquant sauce. For dessert there are locally-grown bananas, melons, and almonds.

For international cuisine in Las Palmas try the grill at the **Hotel Reina Isabel** (Paseo de las Canteras—tel: 26 01 00) and the **Pampa Grill** (Colombia 6—tel: 26 10 51), well-known for fine steaks. For Spanish *paella,* try the **Liberia** or **El Cortijo,** both at Puerto de la Cruz, Tenerife. Another restaurant there, **Patio Canario,** is good for shellfish. In Las Palmas the **Restaurante Ikea** (Joaquin Costa 26) has a Basque kitchen, and good medium-priced meals can be found at **Juan Perez,** on a restaurant-studded street of the same name in Santa Cruz de Tenerife; **Juan Perez** also located in Puerto de la Cruz, Tenerife; other good restaurants around Santa Catalina Square in Las Palmas.

DRINKING TIPS
Drinks are inexpensive, and there are no licensing restrictions. Single women welcome in most bars. In Las Palmas you can drink in Santa Catalina Square and at **Paseo de las Canteras** on the beach. In Tenerife try **Plaza del Charco** in Puerto de la Cruz and **Las Paraguitas** in Santa Cruz. Local wines are good. Beer and rum are made locally.

ENTERTAINMENT
In spring there is a short international theater and concert season. Nightclubs and discothèques abound, and many hotels have dancing during dinner hours, as well as cabarets. Try to find your way to **Los Jameos del Agua,** a most unusual and little-known nightspot which is built in an underground gallery near the **Verdes cave** on the coast of Lanzarote. Other nightspots are **Mirador Vista Bella, Rosaleda,** and **Rega,** Santa Cruz de Tenerife. An excellent discothèque is **Monte del Moro** in San Augustin, Grand Canary.

The Canaries calendar has many purely Spanish fiestas: the **Cavalcade of the Three Wise Men,** on 5 January in both Santa Cruz de Tenerife and Las Palmas; the **Holy Week festivals** on all islands; and the celebration of **Corpus Christi** in March. **Carnival** in Tenerife (one week before Ash Wednesday) is well worth seeing.

SHOPPING

Stores are open 9-1:30 and 4:30-8; closed Saturday afternoon and Sunday. Watches, cameras, transistor radios, tape recorders, and record players are inexpensive in the **Triana Street** and port areas of Las Palmas. You should bargain, but not in department stores such as **Galerias Preciados** and **Almacenes Cuadrado,** both on Leon y Castillo, Las Palmas. Good buys are pottery, wood carvings, basket work, drawnwork, and embroidery.

SPORTS

Lucha canaria, a unique form of wrestling, is a star attraction at many fiestas. There is also single-stick fighting, soccer, *jai alai* or *pelota,* bullfighting, cockfighting, and greyhound racing. Conditions are ideal for water sports. There are several excellent golf courses and tennis clubs which admit visitors.

WHAT TO SEE

The **Canary Museum,** Las Palmas, with a collection of Canary aboriginal relics, and also **Columbus House** are worth a visit. Las Palmas has a Gothic **Cathedral,** and there is a striking Gothic church at Arucas, Grand Canary.

In **Tenerife** see the **Botanical Gardens** of La Orotava near Puerto de la Cruz. The **Church of the Conception** in Santa Cruz has interesting examples of the baroque and houses the banners taken from Admiral Lord Nelson during his attack on the city in the Peninsular Wars of the early 19th century. The **Santa Cruz Museum of Painting and Sculpture** has canvases by Breughel, Ribera, Mardrazo, and Van Loo.

Towering over Tenerife is the 12,250-foot-high mountain of **Teide,** the highest peak of Spain, which is snow-covered in winter. Below is the volcanic crater of **Las Canadas del Teide,** which is now a national park. **La Palma** boasts one of the largest volcanic craters known—the **Caldera de Taburiente.** Volcanic eruptions in the 18th and 19th centuries have given **Lanzarote** an eerie lunar landscape. The **Verdes cave** is an immense volcanic tunnel. Don't miss **Los Jameos del Agua** nightclub, uniquely set inside a giant volcano bubble.

On **Arrecife,** stay at the **Hotel Los Fariones,** which overlooks the mountain at **Playa Blanca.** For children, in addition to the beaches at Playa Blanca de Tenerife and Grand Canary, there is in **San Augustin,** Grand Canary, a "Wild West" cowboy town.

SOURCES OF FURTHER INFORMATION

Pan Am, Edificio España, Plaza España, Madrid; and any other Pan Am office around the world; **Spanish National Tourist Office:** Parque de Santa Catalina, Las Palmas; Palacio Insular, Santa Cruz de Tenerife; 665 Fifth Avenue, New York, NY 10022; 67 Jermyn Street, London SW1.

Cyprus

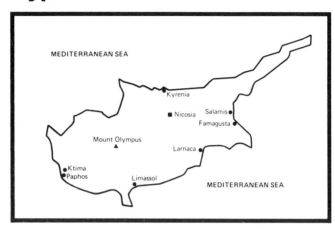

WHAT'S SPECIAL

Cyprus is in the eastern Mediterranean, 44 miles south of Turkey and 64 miles west of Syria. Aphrodite (or Venus) was said to have been born here, coming ashore, as in Botticelli's painting, in a huge seashell; the beach where she landed is still a popular bathing spot on the south coast of the island between Paphos and Limassol. Excellent bathing beaches stretch for miles and can be enjoyed most of the year. Cyprus' beauty and its 8,000 years of culture make the island unique. The third-largest island in the Mediterranean, Cyprus has been a crossroad for Europe, Asia, and Africa.

COUNTRY BRIEFING

Size: 3,572 square miles   **Population:** 650,000
Capital: Nicosia   **Capital Population:** 120,000
   Climate: A good sunny climate from April to December with summer day temperature over 90°F, but cooler at night. In the Troödos mountains enough snow falls to make skiing possible.

Weather in Nicosia: Lat N35°09'; Alt 716 ft

Temp (°F)	Jan	Feb	Mar	Apr	May	Jun	Jul	Aug	Sep	Oct	Nov	Dec
Av Low	42°	42°	44°	50°	60°	65°	69°	69°	65°	58°	51°	45°
Av High	58°	59°	65°	74°	83°	91°	97°	97°	91°	81°	72°	62°
Days no rain	21	20	25	27	28	29	31	31	29	29	25	23

Government: An independent republic, member of the British Commonwealth.

Language: Greek and Turkish. English widely spoken.

Religion: Independent branch of Greek Orthodox church. The Turkish population is Muslim.

Currency: Pound. 1,000 mil = 1 Cyprus pound.

	25 mil	50 mil	100 mil	500 mil	£C 1	£C 5	£C 10	£C 20
US (dollars, cents)	.06	.13	.26	1.28	2.55	12.76	25.52	51.03
UK (pounds, pence)	.03	.06	.12	.61	1.22	6.09	12.17	24.34

Public Holidays:

New Year's Day, 1 Jan	Good Friday
Epiphany, 6 Jan	Easter Saturday
Green Monday	Easter Monday
Greek Independence Day, 25 Mar	Greek Resistance Day, 28 Oct
Independence Day, 1 Apr	Christmas Day, 25 Dec
	Boxing Day, 26 Dec

HOW TO GET THERE

Fly direct to Athens, then by connecting flight to Larnaca International Airport. Flying time from Athens is about 1½ hours. Frankfurt 3½ hours, and from Rome 3 hours. Time in Cyprus: GMT+2.

REQUIREMENTS FOR ENTRY AND CUSTOMS REGULATIONS

Citizens of the US, UK, most Western European countries, Yugoslavia, Kuwait, and Japan need a valid passport but no visa. All others need both. No health certificates unless traveling from an infected area. Virtually no limit on currency brought in; on leaving only £C10 may be taken out. You are allowed to take in duty-free 200 cigarettes, ½ pound tobacco; ¾ liter liquor (1 bottle); 2 fluid ounces perfume per adult. Because of Turkish military control, travel to the northern part of the island is generally impossible except by leaving the country and entering the north at Ercan International Airport, served by Turkish or Cypriot airlines; a 3-month visa must be obtained.

AIRPORT INFORMATION

Larnaca International Airport is 2 miles from Larnaca and 30 miles from Nicosia. Limassol is 1-hour drive from Larnae Airport (40 miles). A taxi to Nicosia takes about 1 hour and costs £C5-6. Taxis can be shared; there is no airport bus to Nicosia. There is an airport departure tax of £C1.500. The airport has a duty-free shop and Tourist Information desk.

ACCOMMODATIONS

There is a good range of hotels on the coast, including some new first-class ones in the Limassol, Larnaca, and Paphos areas. Prices below include service charges and taxes. Reductions are often available at seaside hotels from 1 November to 31 March and at mountain hotels from 1 October to 30 June.

Rates are in US$ for a double/twin room with bath or shower

Aloe, St Antonios Street, Paphos (from $39 CP)

Amathus Beach, Amathus, 6 miles from Limassol (from $76 CP)

Apollonia Beach, Yermassoyia, 4 miles from Limassol (from $63 CP)

Churchill, 1 Achaeans Street, Nicosia (from $41 CP)

Churchill Limassol, 28th October Avenue, 3 miles from Limassol (from $38 CP)

Cleopatra, 8-12 Florina Street, Nicosia (from $39 CP)

Curium Palace, Byron Street, Limassol (from $39 CP)

Cyprus Hilton, Archbishop Makarios Avenue, Nicosia (from $75 CP)

Dionysos, 1 Poseidon Street, Paphos (from $39 CP)

Excelsior, 4 Photios Stavrou Pitta Street, Nicosia (from $35 CP)

Forest Park, Platres (from $45 CP)

Four Lanterns, 19 Athens Avenue, Larnaca (from $39 CP)

Kennedy, 70 Regaena Street, Nicosia (from $39 CP)

Miramare, Potamos tis Yermassoyias, 2 miles from Limassol (from $45 CP)

Paphos Beach, St Antonios Street, Paphos (from $45 CP)

Philoxenia, Eylenja Avenue, Nicosia (from $43 CP)

Posidonia Beach, 4 miles east of Limassol (from $46 CP)

Regina Palace, 8-12 Regaena Street, Nicosia (from $25 CP)

Splendid, Platres (from $21 CP)

Sun Hall, Athens Avenue, Larnaca (from $47 CP)

Tröodos, Tröodos (from $25 CP)

The Nicosia hotels listed above are all either in the city center or within 10 minutes' walking distance of the center. Limassol hotels are on the seafront out of town with the exception of the Curium Palace, in town. The Four Lanterns Hotel and Sun Hall in Larnaca are on the seafront. The Aloe and Paphos Beach hotels are both on the seafront in Paphos. The Forest Park and the Splendid in Platres are both close to the town center, and the Tröodos is close to the center of Tröodos.

USEFUL INFORMATION

Banks: Open 8:30-12:00 Mon-Sat. Money can be changed in hotels and some travel agencies.

Mail: Stamps at street kiosks, post offices. Mailboxes yellow.

Telephone Tips: Booths in the streets and coin-operated phones in restaurants and cafés. Cost of a local call—15mil. Useful numbers:

Operator, Directories, Information 192	Hospital 403311
	Nicosia Tourist Office 44264
Emergencies 999	Larnaca Tourist Office 54322
Long-distance Calls 190	Paphos Tourist Office 32841
Overseas Calls 198	Limassol Tourist Office 62756

Newspapers: Foreign and English-language newspapers available. Local English-language publications: *Cyprus Mail; The Cyprus Weekly.*

Tipping: Customary. In restaurants 10% for service is added to the check. Porter, 300-400mil; taxi drivers not usually tipped; hotel porter, 250-300mil; chambermaid, 400-500mil; hairdressers, 300-400mil.

Electricity: 240 volts 50 cycles AC, throughout the island.

Laundry: Major hotels have express service (from £C1 to dry-clean a suit; from 250mil to have a shirt laundered).

Hairdressing: First-class hotels have salons (shampoo and set about £C7; man's haircut, from £C2).

Photography: Black and white and color film available. About 5-10 days to have color film developed, about 2-3 days for black and white.

Clubs: The Rotary Club meets Thursdays, Hilton Hotel.

Babysitting: Services organized through hotel porter.

Rest Rooms: In certain squares and public gardens. Ladies' room, *ouritiria yinekon;* men, *ouritiria andron.*

Health: All doctors and dentists speak English. Imported pharmaceuticals available and reasonably priced. Local water safe.

TRANSPORTATION

No railroads, but 2,332 miles of serviced roads. Driving is on the left. Bus services around the island stop around 8pm. A shared taxi system runs between the main centers regularly until around 7pm. The cost is 400mil for approximately 25 miles (reserve through hotels). Taxis can be hailed in the street or phoned for in the cities. Minimum charge around £C1. Car rentals cost from £C7. Boat services available to Lebanon, Egypt, Greece, and Italy.

FOOD AND RESTAURANTS

Food is mainly Greek. Lamb kebabs are roasted on spits in every town and village and served in a bread "envelope" called *pita.* Restaurants are Greek style, mostly out of doors under vine awnings within walled gardens, as at **Charlie's** (Lemonias) (5 Themistocles Dervis Street, Nicosia—tel:45339), probably the best on the island; you eat sitting on high-backed chairs under lemon trees. Another good Nicosia restaurant is the **Greek Tavern** (46 Grivas Dhigenis Avenue—tel: 45556). **The Date Club** (2 Themistocles Deris Street—tel:43843) has very good pizzas; **Makedonitissa** (Airport Road—tel: 43099) has excellent local food—try *souvla* (lamb cooked in charcoal); the **Cosmopolitan** (121 Prodromos Street—tel: 43186) is a nightclub with very good cuisine. In Limassol, try the **Avenida** and **Monastiraki,** both restaurants on Nicosia Road, and **Neon Phaleron** (135 Glasstonos) and **Sundowner Restaurant** (28 October Street); in Larnaca, **Dionysos,** near Larnaca Castle.

DRINKING TIPS

Cyprus has an ancient wine industry based around the Limassol area, where there is a yearly wine festival, usually during September. *Commandaria,* a sweet fortified wine, was adopted by the Knights Hospitaller during the Crusades. Sweet and dry sherries and white rosé, and some red wines are produced. *Ouzo,* an aniseed drink, is the favorite local apéritif, and *filfar* is a local orange-based liqueur. Beers are Keo and Carlsberg. Women are welcome in bars.

ENTERTAINMENT

Movies are shown with original soundtracks. Theatrical performances are given in the setting of the ancient theater of **Curium,** and festivals are numerous. Nightclubs in Nicosia include **Cosmopolitan** (121 Prodromos Street—tel: 43186), **Archontissa** (48D, Grivas Dhigenis Avenue—tel: 43404), and **Crazy Horse** (18c, Homer Avenue—tel: 73569). Some discothèques: **Altamira** (Makarios III Avenue—tel: 43931) and **Spider** (48 Grivas Dhigenis Avenue—tel: 43404) in Nicosia, and **C'Est La Vie** in Limassol.

SHOPPING

Stores are open 8-1 and 2-6, closed Saturday afternoons and Sunday. Best local crafts are lace from Leftkara, rugs and carpets, weaving and Turkish embroidery, wood carvings, Turkish delight from Paphos, pottery, shepherd bags, wickerwork, sheepskin items, silver filigree jewelry, and metal ware.

SPORTS

The **Nicosia Tennis Club, Larnaca Tennis Club, Nicosia Field Club, Cyprus Ski Club,** and **Cyprus Turf Club** all welcome visitors. Try the horseback riding at **Episkopi** or the fine swimming at all the resorts. There is also yachting in the major coastal towns; good fishing all round the coast; hunting in season; skiing after Christmas; and mountaineering. Other sports include horse racing on Sundays, soccer, and sailing regattas.

WHAT TO SEE

Nicosia, the capital of Cyprus, is located on the site of ancient Ledra. Outstanding is **Selimiye Mosque,** formerly the Cathedral of St Sophia. An imposing building is the Byzantine-style **Palace** of the Archbishop of Cyprus. Visit the **National Museum,** the **Folk Art Museum,** and the **Venetian walls.**

Larnaca, on the southeast coast, was the birthplace of Zeno, the philosopher who pronounced the doctrine of stoicism. It is also the place in which St Lazarus is said to have lived up to the time of his second death.

Limassol is a thriving port town. Here Richard Coeur de Lion married Princess Berengaria of Navarre in 1191. The 12th-century **Limassol Castle** houses a museum.

Paphos in the west of Cyprus is the ultimate Greek-Cypriot resort. Visit also the quaint little town of **Ktima** nearby. According to Greek mythology, it was here that Aphrodite emerged from the sea before her ascent to Mount Olympus.

The **Tröodos** mountains, culminating in **Mount Olympus** (6,400 feet), are very popular for skiing; this is an area of great scenic beauty.

SOURCES OF FURTHER INFORMATION

Pan Am agent, R A Travelmasters Ltd, 82a Makarios Avenue, Nicosia, and any Pan Am office around the world; **Cyprus Tourism Organization,** 5 Princess de Tyras Street, Nicosia; **Cyprus Consulate General of the Republic,** 13 East 40th Street, New York, NY 10016; **Cyprus Tourist Office,** 213 Regent Street, London W1R 8DA.

Czechoslovakia

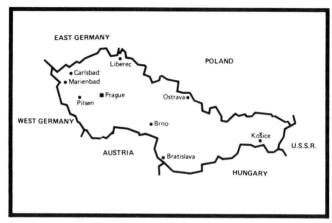

WHAT'S SPECIAL

Czechoslovakia lies across the heart of central Europe and is really two nations—Bohemia and Moravia in the west, and Slovakia in the east. The languages are different, though related. Although at the moment the majority of tourists are from other East European countries, Cedok, the national travel bureau, works hard to organize tourist arrangements for Westerners.

COUNTRY BRIEFING

Size: 49,371 **Population:** 15,239,000
Capital: Prague **Capital Population:** 1,250,000
   Climate: Very cold (average 25°F) and dry in winter, mild in spring and fall, with some rain; summers usually sunny, with temperatures averaging 73°F. Best to go May-September, or December-March for winter sports.

Weather in Prague: Lat N50°5′; Alt 662 ft

Temp (°F)	Jan	Feb	Mar	Apr	May	Jun	Jul	Aug	Sep	Oct	Nov	Dec
Av Low	25°	28°	33°	40°	49°	55°	58°	57°	52°	44°	35°	29°
Av High	34°	38°	45°	55°	65°	72°	74°	73°	65°	54°	41°	34°
Days no rain	19	17	18	18	18	16	17	19	19	20	18	18

Government: Socialist federal republic.
Language: Czech and Slovak. English and German widely spoken in main towns and most hotels, also French and Russian.

Religion: There are both Roman Catholic and Protestant churches.
Currency: Koruna. 100 hellers = 1 koruna.
Rate of exchange is official exchange rate for tourists.

	1 Kčs	2 Kčs	5 Kčs	10 Kčs	20 Kčs	50 Kčs	100 Kčs	500 Kčs
US (dollars, cents)	.11	.21	.54	1.07	2.14	5.35	10.70	53.50
UK (pounds, pence)	.05	.10	.26	.51	1.02	2.55	5.10	25.52

Public Holidays:

New Year's Day, 1 Jan   Labor Day, 1 May
Easter Monday   Christmas Day, 25 Dec

HOW TO GET THERE

Flying time to Ruzyně Airport, Czechoslovakia from New York is 10 hours; from London, 2½ hours; from Frankfurt, 1 hour. Time in Czechoslovakia: GMT+1.

REQUIREMENTS FOR ENTRY AND CUSTOMS REGULATIONS

Passport and visa required. The latter is obtainable from Czechoslovak embassies (submit two photographs); it allows a stay of up to 5 months for overseas visitors, 3 months for Europeans. Children under 15 accompanied by and entered on their parents' passports require no separate visa. Health certificates not required for entry, except for visitors from Asia and Africa. No import or export of Czechoslovak currency allowed. Any amount of foreign currency or travelers' checks may be brought in, but all transactions must be entered on visa form to be shown to customs on leaving. Special bonus rate of exchange for tourists. Each visitor must exchange the equivalent of DM25 for each day of their stay (children ages 6 to 15 half this amount, under 6, nothing). It is, therefore, advisable to buy prepayment vouchers for hotel accommodations and meals to cover this amount. They can be obtained in advance from Cedok, the national tourist bureau, in New York or major European capitals or through its accredited travel agents. Personal belongings come in duty-free, but duty must be paid on gifts worth more than US$30. Duty-free allowance: 250 cigarettes or a corresponding amount of other tobacco; 1 quart liquor plus 2 quarts wine; 3 kilos foodstuffs; ½ liter cologne; 3 rolls film, 100 meters of 8mm or 16mm movie film; 1,000 shots for sporting guns and 50 rifle cartridges. A special permit is required for the importation of firearms. This permit may be obtained at any Czechoslovak Consulate. On leaving the country, surplus korunas (beyond the obligatory minimum to be exchanged daily) can be changed into foreign currency at border crossings and at Prague and Bratislava airports. Certain kinds of food, clothing, and footwear cannot be exported, and a list of such goods is available from customs authorities at all border crossings. Antiques and works of art may be bought only at Tuzex shops or Artia Publishing House. These and other items bought at Tuzex shops can be exported duty-free on showing the invoice to customs.

AIRPORT INFORMATION

Ruzyně Airport is 11 miles from Prague. Airport bus to city terminal, fare Kčs6 (children up to 10 years, Kčs3). Prague public transport bus runs at 10-minute intervals during the day, fare Kčl. Taxi fare is about Kčs124 plus 10% tip. Luggage porters expect Kčs2 per bag. There is no departure tax. There is a duty-free shop, a bank, and a Cedok office.

ACCOMMODATIONS

Visitors can travel anywhere in Czechoslovakia; reserve in advance through Cedok, whose subsidiary, Interhotels, runs the majority of hotels. Wide selection of accommodations from deluxe hotels and three floating boatels on Prague's Vltava River, to family boarding houses and mountain cabins. During July and August visitors can stay inexpensively in students' hostels in Prague. Hotels in Prague:

Rates are in ·US$ for a double/twin room with bath or shower

Alcron, Stěpánská 40 (from $114 MAP)

Ambassador, Václavské náměstí 5 (from $59 MAP)

Esplanade, Washingtonova 19 (from $114 MAP)

INTER · CONTINENTAL PRAGUE, náměstí Curievých 110 (from $114 MAP)

International, náměstí Družby (from $59 MAP)

Jalta, Václavské náměstí 45 (from $114 MAP)

Olympik, Na Invalidovně (from $59 MAP)

Olimpik II, Na Invalidovně (from $46 MAP)

Palace, Panská 12 (from $43 MAP)

Park, Veletržní 20 (from $59 MAP)

All hotels listed above are in city center or within 3-mile radius.

USEFUL INFORMATION

Helpful Hints: Handshakes all around upon arrival or departure mark any meeting, formal or informal, business or private. Invitations to homes are rare, but on such occasions a bouquet of flowers or a bottle of good wine will be appreciated. There is a certain formality to social events and at a festive occasion a dress or dark suit for men and an evening gown for women are preferred.

Banks: Open 8-4 weekdays, until noon Sat. Money and travelers' checks can be changed at Cedok offices and hotels.

Mail: Stamps can be bought at post offices and tobacconists.

Telephone Tips: Street phone booths are usually red and yellow. You can also telephone from hotels and restaurants. Useful numbers in Prague:

Pan Am 26 67 47-9	Operator 128
Prague Airport 334	Directories 120
Flight Information 26 96 08	Medical First Aid 155
Cedok 22 42 51-9	

Newspapers: Some foreign newspapers are available at hotels and newspaper stands. Some Interhotels have non-communist western newspapers available.

Tipping: Officially discouraged but privately welcomed. Tip waiter 3-5%. Give taxi drivers 5-10%, porters Kčs2 per piece of luggage.

Electricity: 220 volts 50 cycles AC.

Laundry: Main hotels have laundry services, and dry-cleaning is available (dry-cleaning a suit, from Kčs57; laundering a shirt, from Kčs15). Laundromats in main cities.

Hairdressing: Some big hotels have salons. Average cost of shampoo and set from Kčs75 (tip Kčs10); man's haircut, from Kčs10 (tip Kčs2).

Photography: Local stores sell East German and Agfa film; Kodak available at Tuzex. Developing services slow; black and white from Kčs5, color from Kčs35, but safest to have it done at home. Do not take pictures near military or frontier zones or as marked.

Babysitting: Arrange with hotel or try the student service—Studentsky Podnik (tel: 29 45 22).

Rest Rooms: Public ones charge 50 hellers. Also in hotels and restaurants; women, *Dámy* or *Ženy;* men, *Páni* or *Muži.*

Health: Health services are first-class. There is a clinic for foreigners at Karlovo náměstí, Prague (English spoken). First aid for accidents available at any hospital or health counter. Some doctors and dentists speak English. Pharmaceuticals available by prescription only.

TRANSPORTATION

You can travel by streetcar, bus, or trolley anywhere in Prague for Kčl, but it is necessary to buy tickets in advance at hotel reception desks, restaurants, or tobacconists. Prague also has a two-line 21-kilometer subway system; fare is Kčl, but one must have the coin to get through the turnstile. Taxis are expensive but available (Kčs18.40 per mile, no extra charge for luggage).

It is possible to arrange through Cedok to rent chauffeur-driven or U-drive cars. Motorists need an international driving license. Fines are high for speeding and driving when intoxicated. Speed limits are 62 mph on highways and 56 mph on main routes. A 37-mph speed limit is enforced in built-up areas except between 10pm and 5am. Seat belts must be worn outside towns and cars parked in no-parking zones may be towed away. For cheaper gas, purchase petrol vouchers with foreign currency at either Tuzex shops or banks.

Czechoslovakia has a good rail system, though trains tend to be crowded. Long-distance bus services are good, and the internal airline (Czechoslovak Airlines, known as CSA) flies between Prague, Bratislava, Brno, and holiday centers.

FOOD AND RESTAURANTS

This is not a country for people on diets. The Czechs are hearty eaters and enjoy dumplings with nearly everything—in soups, stews, and again as a dessert. The national dish is roast pork *(vepřová)*, or goose *(husa)*, with sauerkraut *(zeli)* and dumplings *(knedliky)*. Vegetables are scarce, but meat *(maso)* is usually served with a salad.

Restaurants and hotels offer both international cuisine and local specialties. For a meal with a view go to **Praha Expo** or to **Zlata Praha** at the Inter • Continental. Chinese (Vodicková 19, tel: 262697) and Indian foods (Stěpanská 61, tel: 245601) are available. Other restaurants are the **Oživlé Dřevo** (Living Wood) in the Strahov Monastery and the **Opera Grill** at Divadelní 24. In the Lesser Town across the river try the **U labuti** (Swans, Hradčanské náměstí 11—tel: 539476), **Valdsteinská Hospoda** (Tomášská 16—tel: 536195), and **U tří pstřosu** (Ostriches, Dražického náměstí 12—tel: 532238). Food is good at inexpensive restaurants such as the **Pelikán** (Na Prikope 7—tel: 220782) or the **Vysočína** (Národní 28—tel: 225773). There are a number of lunch bars and self-service automats. For fish, try the **Rybi Grill** (Václavské náměstí). A meal in an expensive restaurant will come to about US$7 per person, not including wine; in a medium-priced one US$3.50-4; in an inexpensive one, about US$2.50.

DRINKING TIPS

Czechoslovakia is famous for its Pilsner beer. You'll find several beer gardens in former monasteries where sturdy dark beer is served, for example, **U Fleku** (Krémencova 9) and **U Tomaše** (Letenská 12). Prague also has a number of interesting wine cellars, among them **U Zlaté Konvice** and **U Zlatého Jelena.** From Moravia comes the fiery *Slivovice* (plum brandy). Imported wines and liquor are available, but a whisky and soda will cost you about US$4.

ENTERTAINMENT

There are sophisticated nightclubs and cabarets at, for example, the **Jalta Hotel Club, Lucerna** (Stěpanská 61), and **EST-bar** (Washingtonova 19, Prague). The **Alhambra,** in the basement of the Ambassador Hotel, and the **Club-Bar,** on top of the Inter • Continental, both have floor shows. Prague has a profusion of theaters at which opera, ballet, plays, and puppet and mime shows are performed, and there are five symphony orchestras. The **Prague Spring International Music Festival** is held from mid-May to the first week in June. The **Laterna Magika** show combines opera, ballet, theater, and cinema. Tickets to cultural performances generally cost about US$5. All larger towns have movie houses showing domestic and foreign films. Some of the foreign films are in the original version, but they are usually dubbed. Larger towns also have theaters and discos.

SHOPPING

Shop at the country-wide network of **Tuzex** state stores, where you can buy local or imported goods for Tuzex vouchers (obtainable at banks for foreign currency) or for foreign currency at advantageous rates, duty and tax free. Keep the invoices for exit customs. **Úva** (Na-Príkope 25) and **Uluv** (Wenceslas Square) are good for handicrafts; **Bijoux de Bohéme** (Star-omestské náměstí 6) for jewelry; and **Ceské Sklo a Keramika** (Národni 43) for glass and ceramics. The **Moser** shop (Na Príkope 12) specializes in crystalware. Other stores include **Dum Mody** (fashions and textiles), **Dum Obuvi** (shoes), and **Detsky Dum** (children's goods). Prague also boasts three department stores: **Bila Labut** (Na porici 23), **Kotva** (náměstí Republiky), and **Maj** (Národni 29). Prices are stabilized, so there is no bargaining. Stores are open from 8 or 9am-6pm weekdays, until noon Saturdays.

SPORTS

Soccer is the main spectator sport, but there is also world-class ice-hockey as well as skating, tennis, and horseback riding. Winter sports are a big tourist attraction; good snow conditions are found December to April in the **High Tatra** mountains. Hunting is popular; arrangements are handled by Cedok. There is angling in the rivers, lakes, and dams. Prague, Carlsbad, and Marienbad have 18-hole golf courses; Prague and Bratislava, mini-golf courses.

WHAT TO SEE

Golden **Prague**, the city of a hundred spires, is built on seven hills and spans the river Vltava. It is small enough for the walker to see many of the major sights. **Hradcany Castle** is the former home of Czech kings. The **National Museum** is in Wenceslas Square. About 20 miles southwest of Prague lies the magnificent castle of **Karlstein**, built in the 14th century. **Slapy Dam Lake**, 25 miles long, is a recreation center for Prague. It can be reached by bus or by excursion steamer.

Brno, capital of Moravia, is the country's second largest city and industrial center. Two good hotels are the **Continental**, Leninova 20 (from US$65 double MAP) and the **International**, Husova 16 (from US$65 double MAP). The 13th-century **Spilberk Castle** has spine-chilling torture chambers and dungeons; the **Capuchin Monastery** has mummified monks. At the top of the square is **Dietrichstein Palace**, now the Moravian Museum. Thirteen miles east of Brno is **Slavkov**, site of the Battle of Austerlitz in 1805. The town of **Telc**, 50 miles west of Brno, is a gem of Renaissance architecture.

Bratislava, the capital of Slovakia, was at one time the capital of Hungary. Stay at the **Kyjev**, Safařikovo náměstié 7 (from US$59 double MAP) or the **Devin**, Riečná Ulicé 4 (from US$114 double MAP). The **Primate's Palace** has the ornate Hall of Mirrors where Napoleon signed the Peace of Pressburg after his victory at Austerlitz.

Spa Towns: Czechoslovakia has more than 50 spa resorts. **Carlsbad** (Karlovy Vary) has long been one of Europe's most fashionable health resorts. Stay at the **Grand Hotel Moskva-Pupp**, Mirové náměstí 2 (from US$114 double MAP). **Marienbad** (Mariánske Lázne) has more than 40 mineral springs. The waters of **Piešťany**, 50 miles from Bratislava, are said to relieve arthritis and rheumatism. Try the **Magnolia Hotel**, Ulice Kpt Nalepku (from US$65 double MAP).

SOURCES OF FURTHER INFORMATION

Pan Am, Parizska Street 11, Prague, and any Pan Am office around the world; **Cedok**, Na Prikope 18, Prague; **Czechoslovak Travel Bureau**, 10 East 40th Street, New York, NY 10016; 17-18 Old Bond St, London W1.

Denmark

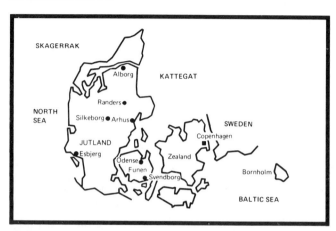

WHAT'S SPECIAL
Denmark is a land of farms, light industry, and fishermen. But it is for Copenhagen, the capital, which hums with almost Mediterranean gaiety, that most people come to Denmark. It has rococo palaces, high green spires, fine restaurants, pleasure gardens—and spontaneous, friendly people.

COUNTRY BRIEFING
Size: 16,611 square miles   **Population:** 5,188,000
Capital: Copenhagen   **Capital Population:** 699,300

Weather in Copenhagen: Lat N55°41'; Alt 43 ft

Temp (°F)	Jan	Feb	Mar	Apr	May	Jun	Jul	Aug	Sep	Oct	Nov	Dec
Av Low	29°	28°	31°	37°	44°	51°	55°	54°	49°	42°	35°	32°
Av High	36°	36°	41°	50°	61°	67°	72°	69°	63°	53°	43°	38°
Days no rain	22	21	21	23	21	23	22	22	19	22	20	20

Government: Constitutional monarchy.
Language: Danish. German and other Scandinavian languages are widely understood. English is spoken by most people.
Religion: Lutheran, but other faiths represented.
Currency: Krone. 100 ore = 1 krone.

	10 ore	50 ore	1 Kr	5 Kr	10 Kr	50 Kr	100 Kr	500 Kr
US (dollars, cents)	.01	.07	.14	.69	1.39	6.93	13.86	69.30
UK (pounds, pence)	—	.03	.07	.33	.66	3.31	6.62	33.12

Public Holidays:

New Year's Day, 1 Jan

Easter

Whit Monday

Constitution Day, 5 Jun

Christmas Day, 25 Dec

Boxing Day, 26 Dec

HOW TO GET THERE

Flying time to Kastrup Airport, Copenhagen, from New York is 8 hours; from London, 1½ hours, from Frankfurt, 1¼ hours. Time in Denmark: GMT+1.

REQUIREMENTS FOR ENTRY AND CUSTOMS REGULATIONS

Passport. Visitors from European countries and North America need no other documents for a stay of up to three months. Visas required of some visitors; check with your travel agent. A valid international smallpox vaccination certificate required if arriving within two weeks of having left or crossed through a country reporting smallpox. Currency regulations: no limits except that exports of a value over Kr5,000 in Danish currency allowed only if amount was brought into Denmark with you. Duty-free allowance for non-Europeans: 1 bottle liquor or 2 liters wine if arriving via a non-EEC country, also 400 cigarettes or 500 grams tobacco. Two bottles liquor or 3 liters wine and same tobacco allowance if arriving via an EEC country. EEC residents permitted 2 bottles liquor or 3 liters wine, 300 cigarettes, if staying over 24 hours. Non-EEC Europeans allowed 1 bottle liquor or 2 liters wine plus 200 cigarettes if staying over 24 hours.

AIRPORT INFORMATION

Kastrup Airport is 6 miles from Copenhagen. Frequent buses at all hours to the SAS terminal in the Central Railway Station; fare Kr12. Taxi fare about Kr55. No airport tax. Duty-free shop, hotel reservations counter, several car rental services.

ACCOMMODATIONS

The full range of hotels is available and, in addition, the typically Scandinavian "Mission Hotels." These offer good, clean (but strictly non-alcoholic) accommodations at moderate prices. The Danish Tourist Board issues a complete list of all accommodations, with prices and description. Most local tourist boards also have a list of private houses that welcome guests. In summer, farmhouse vacations can be arranged from about Kr105 per day with full board. The **Accommodations Bureau** at Kiosk P, Central Railway Station, is open daily in season, 9am–midnight. Off-season discounts of about 30% can be had by arrangement with individual hotels. For students there is a wide range of hotels. Prices include 20.25% VAT and 15% service. Copenhagen hotels:

Rates are in US$ for a double/twin room with bath or shower

Arthur Frommer, Nørre Søgade 11 (from $65), near downtown

D'Angleterre, Kongens Nytorv 34 (from $85), downtown

Bel Air, Løjtegårdsvej 99 (from $60), near airport

Copenhagen Admiral, Toldbodgade 24 (from $70), overlooking harbor
Grand, Vesterbrogade 9 (from $65), near Central Station
Imperial, Vester Farimagsgade 9 (from $75), near downtown terminal
Kong Frederik, Vester Voldgade 25 (from $80), near City Hall
Mercur, Vester Farimagsgade 17 (from $70), near downtown terminal
Missionshotellet, Løngangsstraede 27 (from $52), downtown
Østerport, Oslo Plads 5 (from $50), near Langelinie Promenade
Palace, Rådhuspladsen 57 (from $85), on City Hall Square
Richmond, Vester Farimagsgade 33 (from $70), near downtown
Royal, Hammerichsgade 1 (from $85), near Central Station
Scandinavia, Amager Boulevard 70 (from $85), near downtown
71 Nyhavn, Nyhavn 71 (from $73), near harbor
Sheraton-Copenhagen, Vester Søgade 6 (from $90), near downtown
    air terminal

3 Falke, Falkoner Allé 9 (from $81), near zoo

Triton, Helgolandsgade 7-9-11 (from $55), near Central Station
Webers, Vesterbrogade 11 (from $65), near Central Station

USEFUL INFORMATION

Helpful Hints: Danes are on the whole friendly and informal. Women may go into bars and cafés, except in the Nyhavn district. If you are invited to a Danish home for the evening do not assume it means dinner; very often the family meal will be over by 7, and entertaining takes place later.

Banks: Open 9:30-4 Mon-Fri, Thur until 6pm. Currency can also be changed at the airport, the SAS terminal, and the railway station (open until 10pm).

Mail: Mailboxes red. Stamps from machines or kiosks.

Telephone Tips: Public telephones in cafés, bars, and booths. Useful numbers in Copenhagen:

Pan Am (01) 24 15 55

Information 0030

Tourist Office (01) 11 14 15

Directories 0034

Operator 0038

Calls to US 0016

Emergency 000

Information for Copenhagen
    numbers 0034

Information for rest of
    Denmark 0038

Newspapers: English-language newspapers and periodicals sold in Copenhagen.

Tipping: Hotel tips are included in the 15% service charge. Taxi fares also inclusive of tip. Baggage porters, about Kr3 per item; Kr2 usual in cloakrooms. Ask for tipping information before visiting smaller towns.

Electricity: 220 volts 50 cycles AC.

Laundry: Plenty of good laundries (dry-cleaning a suit, from Kr50; laundering a shirt from Kr10).

Hairdressing: Excellent salons in cities and at good hotels (shampoo and set from Kr55-60; man's haircut from Kr55).

Photography: Equipment plentiful, prices reasonable. 24-hour processing available.

Clubs: Kiwanis; Rotary (tel: 11 00 46) meets Wed, 12 noon at Hotel d'Angleterre; Inner Wheel (tel: 11 00 46 for information); Lions International (tel: (02) 27 47 67).

Babysitting: Studenternes Babysitters (Åkrogen 20, 2600 Glostrup—tel: (02) 45 90 45). Glostrup is about 8 miles from downtown Copenhagen but bus service is frequent.

Rest Rooms: In bars and cafés some public facilities. Women, *Damer* or *Kvinder;* men, *Herrer* or *Maend.*

Health: Many doctors and dentists speak English. Imported pharmaceuticals available, but fairly expensive.

TRANSPORTATION

The mainstay of Copenhagen's system is the municipal bus and S-train system, with many bus routes and frequent trains. A single ticket for Kr4 is good for an hour's travel by bus, train, or both in the central area. If you will be traveling frequently, you can buy a punchcard on the bus or in stations. There are several types of cards depending on where in the city you travel. Taxis are metered; call one at 35 35 35. Car rentals from **Pitzner Auto,** Trommesalen, 4 DK 1615 (tel: 11 12 34). Bicycles can also be rented. There is excellent train service throughout the country, with a wide range of discount fares. The Eurailpass is valid in Denmark as is the Scandinavian Rail Pass, which is also valid on ferry crossings between Denmark and southern Sweden. Internal air services are run by SAS/Danair (tel: 58 58 11); ticket sales at the downtown air terminal, or in New York, London, or Scandinavian capitals.

FOOD AND RESTAURANTS

Internationally famous is the *smørrebrød* (meaning literally bread and butter)—hundreds of different and imaginative ways of serving an open sandwich. Shrimps, herring, cheese, eggs, lettuce, bacon, roast beef, and sausage are just some of the ingredients used to make *smørrebrød.* You might have it as a first course with a glass of *akvavit,* or take a selection for a summer lunch. As a main course, you could have ground pork served as *frikadeller* (meatballs), or *hakkebøf* (like large hamburgers). Roast pork (*flaeskesteg*) is a delicacy usually served with red cabbage; another local specialty is freshly caught plaice (*rødspaetter*). Dinner prices generally run from Kr75-100, excluding coffee and dessert. Hotdog stands have the sign *pølser,* and there are sandwich shops in the Vesterbrogade, near the Central Station. Two famous fish restaurants are side by side in Gammel Strand: **Krogs** at No. 38 (tel: 15 89 15)—try the dish called *Tout de Paris*—and the delightfully Victorian **Fiskehuset** at No. 34 (tel: 14 79 16), which is closed Sundays. Just down the street is **Fiskekaelderen** (Ved Stranden 18—tel: 12 20 11), also excellent for seafood. **La Cocotte** (Ved Farimagsgade 33—tel: 14 04 07) adds French sophistication to Danish produce. Other recommended top-class restaurants are at the D'Angleterre (tel: 12 00 95), Royal (tel: 14 14 12), Sheraton-Copenhagen (tel: 11 35 35), Scandinavia (tel: 11 23 24), and Plaza (Bernstorffsgade—tel: 14 92 62) hotels. **Krinsen,** a little lunch spot also in the Hotel D'Angleterre, is good. Other good food buys are **Den Gyldne Fortun** (Ved Stranden 18—tel: 12 20 11), closed Sundays; **Restaurant Heering** (Pilestraede 19—tel: 15 22 40); **Østerport** (Oslo Plads 5—tel: 11 22 66) for its smørgåsbord; **Queen's Grill** (King Frederik Hotel, V. Volgade 25-27—tel: 12 59 02); **St Gertruds Kloster** (Hauser Plads 32—tel: 14 66 30); **Jan Hurtigkarl** (Dronningens Tvaergade 43—tel: 15 05 54); **Den Sorte Ravn** (Nyhavn 14—tel: 13 12 33); **Ostehjørnet** (Store Kongensgade 56—tel: 15 85 77); **DSB Grill and Buffet** in the Central Railway Station (tel: 14 12 32). For character, if not eccentricity, there is **Tokanten** (Vandkunsten 1), where the artists eat. The perfect example of a traditional Danish restaurant is **Bjornekaelderen** (Frederiksberggade 55—tel: 31 62 52). Danish home cooking, 17th-century style, is available at **Abelone**, a tiny restaurant located at Magstraede 16 (tel: 15 27 35), near the waterfront. Also typically Danish is the **Axelborg Bodega** (Axeltorv 1—tel: 11 00 96), where a mug of beer and a day's sandwich plate constitutes a cheap lunch. At **Ida Davidsen** (St Kongensgade 70—tel: 11 36 55), try a Hans Christian Andersen sandwich—liverpaste, bacon, tomato, and horse-radish. Copenhagen has lots of beefsteak restaurants, including **Peder Oxe** on Gråbrødre Square in the old city (tel: 11 00 77) and **A Hereford Beefstouw** at Åbenrå 6-8 (tel: 11 91 90). There are also Chinese, Japanese, Balkan, and other ethnic restaurants. A 20-minute drive out of town takes you to **Søllerød Kro** (Søllerødvej 35—tel: 02-80 25 05) for excellent food at reasonable prices.

DRINKING TIPS

Among Scandinavian countries, Denmark is the most liberal about drinking. The Danes also make two of the world's most famous beers: *Carlsberg* and *Tuborg*—you can visit the breweries (Carlsberg, 9am, 11am, and 2:30pm weekdays only; Tuborg, between 8:30am and 2:30pm weekdays only). Normally Danes drink an ice-cold glass of *akvavit* (snaps) to start lunch, accompanied by a fishy snack. With the main course they drink wine or beer. That other famous local product, *Peter Heering* (cherry liqueur), goes with coffee. Taxes are high, so that a glass of good *akvavit* (say Aalborg) at the **Grand Café** in Kongens Nytorv will cost you the equivalent of about US$2. A Tuborg would be about the same, but whisky at least double. Good places to spend an evening are around the Nikolaj Kirke, such as the inner room of the **Cafe Royal**. Also good is **Københavnerkroen**, near Central Station. **Hviid's Vinstue** in Kongens Nytorv has considerable character. Single people get together at the **Wonder Bar** or the **Kakadu Bar**, and there are numerous pubs and bars tucked away in the Tivoli Gardens, open summer only.

ENTERTAINMENT

Copenhagen is famous for its nightlife. A jolly evening of laughter can be had at **Puk's Pub** or **Tokanten**, while there's music and group singing at **Vin & Olgod** (Skindergade 47)—all good spots to meet a new friend. The friendly family place is the **Lorry** (Allegade 7), which has relaxing prices. For a little more *luxe* (wear a tie) try the **Valencia** (Vesterbrogade

32), which features a floor show or **Tiffany** (Pilestraede 14—tel: 12 39 12). Other nightspots are the **Artilleri Bar** at the Scandinavia Hotel or the **Penthouse Club** at the Sheraton. There are a number of lively discothèques in Copenhagen; check your hotel for names and addresses. For hard rock, **Daddy's Dance Hall** at Axeltorv 5, **Tordenskjold** (Kongens Nytorv 19), or **Bonaparte** (Gothersgade 15). Jazz lovers go to the **Montmartre** (Norregade 41). Movies are shown with original soundtracks, and you can reserve seats by phone. Performances are at 2, 4, 7, and 9:15pm. Live theater is in Danish. Internationally famous is the **Royal Ballet**, in the Royal Theater. The season starts in the fall, and it is best to make reservations well in advance. Concerts are held year round in the **Tivoli Gardens** concert hall, the only part of Tivoli to remain open all year. The circus, **Benneweis,** is open from April to September.

SHOPPING

Generations of craftsmen have made Danish furniture and silver among the best in the world. There is a wide choice in the main department stores: **Daell's Varehus** (Nørregade 12); **Magasin du Nord** (Kongens Nytorv 13); and **Illum** is at Ostergade 52. This last street is one of the five that, joined together, are known as **Strøget,** which leads from the City Hall Square (Rådhuspladsen) to Kongens Nytorv. It is a pedestrian precinct, and has antiques and modern furniture side by side (visit **Form og Farve** and **Illums Bolighus,** which is the most famous furniture and home furnishings store in Copenhagen); bold, bright textiles; exclusive fur shops (**A C Bang, Birger Christensen**); and a wide range of clothes for both sexes. Do not miss the **Georg Jensen** modern silver and **Bing & Grondahl** and the **Royal Porcelain Factory's** top quality china. For antiques, take a stroll down **Fiolstraede** (running into Strøget at Nygade) or stroll along **Kompagnistraede** that runs parallel to Strøget. Visit the **H. Skjalm P.** shop (Nikolajplads 7-ll) for interior decoration cleverly mixing old and new. Turn off Strøget for a stroll up **Kobmagergade** towards the Round Tower for other interesting shops. Along the **Gammel Strand** are several art galleries selling attractive and reasonably priced prints by modern artists. Stores open 9-5:30 weekdays, some until 7pm on Fridays, but close generally at 1pm on Saturdays. To avoid paying the 22% VAT tax, ask about personal export plans run by the better stores.

SPORTS

Yachting can be enjoyed all summer along the lovely isles and inlets of the southern Baltic. For information call the **Royal Danish Yacht Club** (tel: 14 87 87) or the **Amateur Sailing Club** (Svanemøllehavnen—tel: 20 71 72); boats may be rented from **Danish Boat Charter** (Strandvejen 327, Klampenborg—tel: 63 08 00), **CBC Boat Charter** (Kalkbraenderihavn 22—tel: 18 31 22), and **Holiday Boat Charter** (Falkoner Centret—tel: 19 09 00). Swimming can be enjoyed from hundreds of beaches north of the capital, such as **Charlottenlund** or **Bellevue** (train to Klampenborg). Golf is gaining popularity in Denmark and there are now over

30 courses: **Copenhagen Golf Club** is at Eremitagesletten in the Klampenborg Deer Park (20 minutes by train or car), where you can also ride horses. **Østerbro Stadium** has soccer on Sundays, skating in winter, and next door is the **B93** tennis club, which accepts temporary members. There are ample fishing possibilities in rivers and on the coast; fishing vacations are easy to arrange. Other sports include horse racing, trotting, auto racing, archery, bicycle racing, and canoeing.

WHAT TO SEE

There are many tours of Copenhagen organized by Copenhagen Excursions, some by water, others to enable you to see something of modern Danish life. The **Glyptotek** near the Tivoli Gardens is full of exceptionally good sculpture, a selection of paintings by the French Impressionists, and a collection of classical pieces, Greek, Roman, and especially Egyptian. **Den Permanente**, in the Vesterport buildings, houses the best of Denmark's present crafts. Along Strøget are the finest shops in Scandinavia. The **National Museum** shows a visual history of Denmark, and across a bridge from the museum is **Slotsholm Island,** where several important buildings are conveniently gathered. First is **Christiansborg Palace,** home of kings for three and a half centuries and now the seat of Parliament. Nearby is **Tøjhusmuseet** with its huge collection of medieval weapons and armor. **Thorvaldsen's Museum** is a monument to the great sculptor, and the **Børsen** is the oldest stock exchange in the world. On the other side of Frederiksholm Canal, **Vor Frelser's Kirke** (Our Saviour's Church), with an outside spiral staircase, provides a vantage point for viewing the city. Nearby is the 17th-century **Holmens Church** with its carved altar-piece and pulpit. In Kongens Nytorv are the **Royal Theater** and **Charlottenborg,** which houses the Fine Arts Academy.

Further out is **Amalienborg Palace,** fine rococo buildings which are the homes of the Danish royal family and are guarded by soldiers in bearskin hats. Two other notable buildings in this quarter are the neoclassical **Marble Church** and the **Museum of Decorative Arts.** Then there is the **Museum of the Resistance** on Esplanaden and the moated 17th-century fortress called the **Citadel.** Take a look at Copenhagen's famous **Little Mermaid** by the harbor. Another morning go to the gardens called **Kongens Have** and look at **Rosenborg Palace,** containing the Crown Jewels and personal effects of generations of kings. Close by is the **Royal Museum of Fine Art,** with Cranachs and Rembrandts and a room full of fine paintings by Matisse. On the same excursion you might visit the **Round Tower,** built in 1640 by Christian IV as an astronomical observatory. Inside is the famous spiral ramp up which Peter the Great is said to have driven his carriage. Nearby are the **University** with its hall of Gobelin tapestries, and Copenhagen's own **Cathedral,** with Thorvaldsen's sculpture of Christ and the Apostles. A remarkable building well worth seeing is **Grundtvig Church** at Bispebjerg, designed this century in a modern idiom influenced by medieval Danish architecture. The **City Museum** is out at Vesterbrogade 59. At the **Tivoli Gardens,** open all day long from 1 May to mid-September, there is all the fun of several fairs, eating, drinking, pantomime, a children's playground, and the parade of Tivoli's Boys' Guard (weekends 6:30pm-8pm).

Out of town: To the south **Dragor,** an unspoiled fishing village where geese still wander the streets, has a museum. **Frilandsmuseet,** a more extensive museum, lies to the north at **Sorgenfri,** near Lyngby. An open-air museum, it covers over 40 acres, dotted with old farmhouses brought from all over Denmark. Take the S-train to **Klampenborg** and stroll through the **Deer Park** (open year round), or visit **Bakken,** a festive amusement park open spring and summer at the south end of Deer Park. Farther out is the modern art gallery of **Louisiana.** From the tall windows of a low white building you look out across the lawns at modern sculpture (Moore, Brancusi) set against trees and sparkling water. Inside are exhibitions by Scandinavian artists and an interesting permanent collection of modern paintings (Albers, Kline, Francis, and many more). Take bus No. 188 from Klampenborg to **Humlebaek.** While you are here you could go on to **Elsinore** to look across at Sweden and visit the later version of Hamlet's castle. There is also a **Maritime Museum.** An even more interesting castle for the tourist is **Frederiksborg** at Hillerød. Built by Christian IV and reconstructed in the last century, it is now the **National Historical Museum.** Six miles away is **Fredensborg Palace,** the summer home of the Royal Family and once a gathering-place for royalty of five nations. There is a famous old inn here, the **Store Kro,** where comfort and food are as good as any in Denmark (from US$65 double). Still within easy reach of Copenhagen in this northern part of Zealand is the cathedral town of **Roskilde,** once the capital. Here Danish monarchs have been buried since the 10th century. Nearby is the **Viking Ship Museum** (open until 8pm in summer, 6pm in spring and fall, 4pm in winter). In Roskilde stay at the **Prindsen,** Algade 13 (from US$50 double). Five miles to the west is a unique experiment in history, the **Iron Age Village,** where students and their professors live as our primitive ancestors did. It is open only in summer. Twenty-five miles to the south of Copenhagen lies the attractive old town of **Køge,** with its museum and church of St Nicolaj, and the **Hvide Hus Hotel,** Strandvejen 111 (from US$55 double).

Odense is the birthplace of Hans Christian Andersen. Several of the old homes are memorials to him now; his reputed birthplace, his childhood home, with his desk, his famous umbrella, his hat, and his manuscripts. Two miles from Odense is another of Denmark's showplaces, **Den Fynske Landsby,** an open-air museum where old buildings have been gathered to form a village. To the south lies the place that sailing men have made their capital: the beautiful old town of **Svendborg.**

Jutland is Denmark's piece of mainland Europe, reached by ferry, train (5-6 hours from Copenhagen), by direct flight, or by bridge from Funen. It has fjords, moors, dunes, and forests. Denmark's oldest city is here too, **Ribe,** a medieval port, now landlocked and famous for its dwindling stork population. The capital of Jutland is the port of **Arhus.** A 100-year-old steamer takes you down river to **Silkeborg** to see the remarkable remains of "Tollund Man," preserved in a bog for 2,000 years.

SOURCES OF FURTHER INFORMATION

Pan Am, Gl Kongevej 3, DK-1610, Copenhagen V, and any Pan Am office around the world; **The Danish National Tourist Office,** Banegårdspladsen 2, DK-1570, Copenhagen V; 75 Rockefeller Plaza, New York, NY 10019; Britannia Building, 151 Bloor Street West, Toronto M5S1S4, Ontario, Canada; Australia Square, Suite 3912, George Street, Sydney 2000, NSW, Australia.

Finland

WHAT'S SPECIAL

Finland (Suomi) lies northwest of the USSR and east of Norway and Sweden. It is a land of 60,000 lakes, a large part of it, Lapland, above the Arctic Circle. At its northernmost reaches, this "Land of the Midnight Sun" has daylight at midnight for nearly two months of the summer, but also darkness at noon during nearly two months of the winter "Polar Night." From a central forested plateau of 500 feet, the land rises in the north where certain peaks reach 3,000 feet, making for good skiing in the spring and beautiful scenery throughout the year. In the south and southwest are the 30,000 islands of the Finnish Archipelago, and most of the population.

COUNTRY BRIEFING

Size: 130,165 square miles **Population:** 4,771,000
Capital: Helsinki **Capital Population:** 483,000
   Climate: Summer is warm. During June-August, temperatures range from 66°F to 71°F. July is the warmest month. The fall comes suddenly, in early September; in southern Finland the snow starts in December; in the north it is falling in October. The duration of the "midnight sun" varies. At Rovaniemi, just a few miles below the Arctic Circle, it is light enough to read at night from 6 June-5 July; at Utsjoki, from 18 May-25 July. The duration of the "polar night" varies also, starting above the Arctic Circle and increasing until its maximum duration at Utsjoki, 26 Nov-16 Jan.

Weather in Helsinki: Lat N60°10′; Alt 30 ft

Temp (°F)	Jan	Feb	Mar	Apr	May	Jun	Jul	Aug	Sep	Oct	Nov	Dec
Av Low	17°	15°	22°	31°	41°	49°	57°	55°	46°	37°	30°	22°
Av High	27°	26°	32°	43°	55°	63°	71°	66°	57°	45°	37°	31°
Days no rain	20	20	23	22	23	21	23	19	19	19	19	20

Government: A republic.

Language: Official language Finnish, second language Swedish, English widely taught in schools.

Religion: Lutheran and Orthodox.

Currency: Finmarks and penniä. 100 penniä = 1 finmark.

	25	50	1	5	10	50	100	200
	p	p	Fmk	Fmk	Fmk	Fmk	Fmk	Fmk
US (dollars, cents)	.06	.12	.23	1.16	2.31	11.55	23.10	46.20
UK (pounds, pence)	.03	.06	.11	.55	1.10	5.52	11.04	22.08

Public Holidays:

New Year's Day, 1 Jan
Good Friday
Easter Monday
May Day, 1 May
   (preceded by all-night parties)
Midsummer Day, nearest
   Fri and Sat to 24 June

All Saints Day, nearest
   Sat to end Oct or
   beginning Nov
Independence Day,
   6 Dec
Christmas Day, 25 Dec
Boxing Day, 26 Dec

HOW TO GET THERE

Flying time to Helsinki Airport from New York is 8 hours; from London, 3¼; from Hamburg, 1¾ hours. Time in Finland: GMT+2.

REQUIREMENTS FOR ENTRY AND CUSTOMS REGULATIONS

Passport for all except Danish, Icelandic, Swedish, and Norwegian visitors. No vaccination certificates, providing previous 14 days have been spent in North America or Europe. You may take out the same amount of foreign currency as you bring in, but without permission of the Bank of Finland, the import or export of Fmk500 or more is forbidden. It is better to change your Finnish currency before you leave the country. On entry, special permits needed for pets, firearms, and ammunition. Duty-free allowance for non-Europeans: 400 cigarettes or 1 pound tobacco; 2 liters beer, 1 liter other mild alcoholic drink, 1 liter liquor; or 2 liters beer and 2 liters other mild alcoholic drink. For Europeans: 200 cigarettes or ½ pound tobacco; liquor allowance the same as for non-Europeans.

AIRLINE INFORMATION

Helsinki Airport is 12 miles from the city center. Bus service to the center (Fmk8) or taxis are always available (Fmk50). At the airport there is a duty-free shop, children's nursery, and a hotel reservation service. Airport tax is included in the price of the ticket.

ACCOMMODATIONS

A wide range of accommodations is available in Finland; there are hotels, motels, and nearly 200 "holiday villages" which have self-contained cottages, sometimes also hotels and restaurants, and are almost always located near one of Finland's many lakes. There are also individual summer cottages to rent throughout Finland, located near lakes, rivers, or the sea. Or the tourist can stay in country farmhouses, renting rooms with or without meals. Information about these accommodations is available from tourist board offices. There is a good network of motels located along Finland's highways. There are 120 youth hostels for travelers of all ages, listed in *Camping Sites and Youth Hostels in Finland.* Inexpensive accommodations are also available in Summer Hotels—student dormitories during the rest of the year. The central sources for help in finding hotel or private accommodations in Helsinki are the **Hotel Booking Center** (Railway Station-tel: 171 133) and travel agents. Hotels in Helsinki:

Rates are in US$ for double/twin room with bath or shower

Helsinki, Hallituskatu 12 (from $55)

HELSINKI INTER · CONTINENTAL, Mannerheimintie 46-48 (from $75), near Olympic Stadium and Parliament

Hesperia, Mannerheimintie 50 (from $90), near Olympic Stadium and Parliament

Kalastajatorppa, Kalastajatorpantie 1 (from $70), about 15 minutes from center

Klaus Kurki, Bulevardi 2-4 (from $70)

Marski, Mannerheimintie 10 (from $70)

Merihotelli, Hakaniemenranta 4 (from $75)

Olympia, Läntinen Brahenkatu 2 (from $65)

Palace, Eteläranta 13 (from $65)

Presidentti, Et. Tautatiekatu 4 (from $80)

Torni, Yrjönkatu 26 (from $90) .

Vaakuna, Asema-aukio 2 (from $68)

All above-mentioned hotels located in central Helsinki unless otherwise indicated.

USEFUL INFORMATION

Helpful Hints: When invited anywhere in Finland, promptness is expected. Mention your surname whenever introduced as a guest, and remember that men, women, and children shake hands when they meet. Don't take a drink until your host has toasted you. The **sauna,** the world-famous Finnish bath, is part of every Finnish home, and to be invited to a sauna party is to meet the Finn at his most hospitable. Most hotels in Finland have saunas as well.

Banks: Open 9:30-4 Mon-Fri (may vary locally). Travelers' checks and currency can also be changed at hotels and shops. Branches of the major banks in main cities.

Mail: Stamps can be purchased at post offices, bookstores, train or bus stations, and hotels. Mailboxes are yellow with posthorn sign.

Telephone Tips: Public telephones (coin operated)—in restaurants and cafés. Local call, 50 penniä. Useful numbers in Helsinki:

Pan Am 694 2422	**Tourist Office** 169 3757 & 174 088
Airport Information 829 2451	**General Alarm** 000
Emergencies, Police 002/003	**Weather** 038
Doctor Service 008	**Events in Helsinki** 058
News in English 018	

Newspapers: English-language newspapers and magazines available. Local English publication is *Helsinki This Week*. Many newspapers carry English news sections during the summer.

Tipping: Service charge (15% on hotel bill, 14% on weekdays and 15% on Sundays in restaurants) is always included so there is little tipping, and none at all to taxi drivers, hairdressers, or guides. Hotel porters, cloakroom attendants, and luggage porters receive Fmk2-3. For special service in restaurants, leave a few extra coins.

Electricity: 220 volts 60 cycles AC.

Laundry: Laundry and dry-cleaning services good and efficient, 24-hour service. Laundromats in principal cities.

Hairdressing: Salons in all first-class hotels. Shampoo and set about Fmk50; man's haircut Fmk30 or more. No tip.

Photography: Black and white and color film available in all major cities. Film developed in 1-7 days.

Clubs: Rotary, Lions, Jaycees.

Babysitting: Most hotels have a service. Telephone directories give local services, or ask at the local Tourist Office. Good supply of student help.

Rest Rooms: In all stores, restaurants, cafés, and stations. Street ones carry a WC sign; Women, *Naiset* (or a hen symbol); Men, *Miehet* (or a cockerel sign).

Health: Many doctors speak English. Pharmaceuticals in drugstores or pharmacies *(apteekki)*; chemists *(kemikalikauppa)* sell only cosmetics.

TRANSPORTATION

Finland has one of the densest and least expensive air networks in Europe, with 20 airports. There are reduced-fare tourist tickets for some short routes combined with train, bus, or boat tickets (summer season only). Conducted tours (all expenses included) are reasonably priced. There are special "Midnight Sun Flights" from Helsinki to Rovaniemi. A good and reliable railway network links with lake steamers and boats. A Finnrail pass gives unlimited travel from any railway station. The Eurailpass and the Nordic Tourist Ticket by Train are also accepted. The lakes are divided into three areas, each served by its own shipping line: the Silver Line between Hämeenlinna and Tampere; the Poet's Way between Tampere and Virrat; and the Saimaa Lake routes between Lappeenranta and Kuopio. Cars can be rented in Helsinki and in other cities. Drive on the right. Helsinki has a good bus service (books of tickets from the City Transport Bureau). A 24-hour tourist ticket (Fmk18) gives unlimited travel on the city's streetcars and buses. There are plenty of metered taxis (taxi stands are listed in the telephone book under **Autoasemat**). After 11pm and on Sundays, Fmk2 is added to the basic fare. No tipping.

FOOD AND RESTAURANTS

Finnish cooking is a combination of French, Swedish, and Russian, and standards are high. Meat is generally broiled or roasted. As well as famous smoked fish, you can also enjoy your fish broiled, or sautéed in butter. Salmon and reindeer are the special dishes of the country, and a favorite Finnish dessert is *Kiisseli* (a thickened fruit dish), pancakes, and ice cream. There is also a Finnish *Smörgåsbord* called *Voileipäpöyta*, usually eaten for lunch. Two regional dishes are *Kalakukko,* a type of fish and pork pie, and *Karjalan Piirakka,* a pastry of rye flour, stuffed with rice and potato and eaten with egg butter. The greatest Finnish delicacy is crayfish *(Rapuja);* the season is between 21 July and 31 October. Breakfast is from 7:30-9, lunch 11-2, and dinner 7-9. Some inexpensive eating places are licensed to serve light beer. Good places to dine and, in many cases, to dance in Helsinki hotels (but remember to make reservations) are the Helsinki (tel: 630 701); the Marski (tel: 641 717), which is very convenient and has smart modern furnishings; Vaakuna, beside the railway station (tel: 171 811), which is a top-floor restaurant with panoramic views; the **Seurahuone,** known for its good food (Kaivokatu 12—tel: 170 441); the Palace (tel: 171 114), which overlooks the harbor; the Hesperia (tel: 441 311); the Inter•Continental (tel: 441 331); the **Merihotelli** (tel: 711 455), very modern with fine views; the Torni (tel: 644 611), with diversified restaurants; the Presidentti (tel: 6911); and the Klaus Kurki (tel: 602 322). They do wonderful things with fish at the **Havis Amanda** (Unioninkatu 23—tel: 639 610). The **Savoy** (Eteläesplanadi 14—tel: 176 571) overlooks the Esplanade—designed by Alvar Aalto; it serves mostly French and Russian dishes. The **Motti** (Töölöntorinkatu 2—tel: 494 418) has fine continental food. Old-time atmosphere redolent of Finland's heroes and vast portions of local dishes are at the **Karl König** (Mikonkatu 4—tel: 171 271). The **Happy Days** (Pohj. Esplanadi 2—tel: 624 023) and **Adlon** are two more midtown restaurants to try. Time your visit to **Tapiola** so you can have lunch or dinner in the watertower restaurant **Haikaranpesa,** overlooking this model suburb and the pine forests and bays between it and the Helsinki skyline 6 miles away. Two of the staunchly fortified islets in Helsinki harbor now have delightful restaurants. From June to September boats leave the tip of Kaïvopuisto every half hour from 4pm for the excellent and reasonably priced summer restaurant Särkänlinna (tel: 667 381). Small local restaurants worth trying are **Lehtovaara** (Mechelininkatu 39—tel: 440 833) and **Bellevue** (Rahapajankatu 3—tel: 179 560).

DRINKING TIPS

Finnish beer comes in light or stronger grades. Next to beer, the national drink is Finnish vodka, drunk as *Schnapps;* like the Finnish berry liqueurs *Mesimarja* (Arctic bramble) and *Lakka* (Cloudberry), it is usually served ice-cold with meals. Scotch and bourbons are expensive. Restaurants and bars open until 1 or 2am; nightclubs open until 3am.

ENTERTAINMENT

Apart from a lively winter theater season, many towns also have their own theaters. **Tampere** has a famous revolving open-air theater which moves the audience rather than the sets. **Helsinki** has several summer theaters. In summer there are open-air concerts with special festivals of folk music and dance. There are more than 40 movie houses in Helsinki, showing films with original soundtrack. Performance times are 7 and 9pm. Lively nightspots centrally located include the **Safari** (Eerikinkatu 14—tel: 90 648 877), the **Helsinki Club** in the Helsinki Hotel, the **M Club** in the Marski Hotel, the **Adlon** (Fabianinkatu 14—tel: 90 664 661), **Fennia** (Mikonkatu 17—tel: 90 175 433), and **Kaivohuone** (Kaivopuisto—tel: 90 177 881), all the latter four with floor shows. **The Casino** (Hopeasalmenpolkul, Kulosaari—tel: 90 688 202), with dining, dancing, and roulette, is 15 minutes by taxi from the center of town. For a very special evening, take a 15-minute taxi ride to **Kalastajatorppa** (Munkkiniemi, Kalastajatorpantie 1—tel: 90 488 011), set in woods beside a bay; good floor shows and dancing.

The Finland festivals of the summer months are: **Ilmajoki Music Festival,** folk opera; **Kuopio Dance and Music Festival,** classical ballet, modern dance, folk dancing, ballroom dancing; **Naantali Music Festival,** picnic concerts and chamber music; **Jyväskylä Arts Festival,** seminars, concerts, and soloist recitals; **Savonlinna Opera Festival,** opera, soloist recitals, exhibitions; **Pori Jazz,** jazz performances, jam sessions, seminars, exhibitions, movies; **Folk Music Festival Kaustinen,** folk music, songs and dances, cavalcades, exhibitions; **Kuhmo Chamber Music Festival,** internationally known, chamber music in country setting; **Lahti International Organ Festival,** organists and choirs; **Turku Music Festival,** concerts, opera, rock music; **Tampere Theatre Summer,** national review of Finnish theater; **Helsinki Festival,** opera, theater, ballet, jazz, rock music, exhibitions. For further information contact Finland Festivals, Simonkatu 12 B 12, Helsinki 10—tel: 694 3972.

SHOPPING

Stores are open 9-8 Mon and Fri; 9-5 Tues-Thurs; 9-2 Saturday. Stores may deduct a purchase tax of 14% from goods sent directly out of the country (i.e. to an address outside Finland, or to a ship). Most larger stores do this, and it is worth asking about. Personal checks are not normally accepted. Finnish glass and ceramics are both beautiful and practical. The best-known name in Finnish china is **Arabia.** Jewelry is outstanding in its combination of traditional design and craftsmanship; modern pieces made from silver and Lapp gold, for instance, are lovely. Finnish furs include mink, fox, Finn racoon, and fitch. Deadly accurate Finnish hunting weapons are on sale, and *puukko* knives are a good buy. There is also everything for the salmon fisher. Finnish handicrafts can be bought at **Vokki-Virkki** (Merikannontie 3); hand-woven Ryijy rugs and textiles of all kinds would make special reminders of your visit. The major department stores in Helsinki are **Stockmann's** (Aleksanterinkatu); **Centrum** (corner of Aleksanterinkatu & Kluuvikatu); **Sokos** (Mannerheimintie 9); and **Rake** (Bulevardi 2). Specialist shops are **Marimekko** (Pohjoisesplanadi 31) and **Vuokko Design** (Pohjoisesplanadi 25), both for fashions and textiles. For furniture, **Artek** (Keskuskatu 3); **Asko** (Mannerheimintie 18-20); and **Isku-Kaluste** (Kalevankatu 4). For jewelry try **Aarikka** (Pohjoisesplanadi 27); **Kalevala Koru** (Keskuskatu 4); **Kaunis Koru** (Annankatu 31-33G); and **Björn Weckstrom** (Frederikinkatu 24). There is a **Finnish Design Center** (Kasarmikafu 19). Finland's first underground shopping precinct is at **Helsinki Railway Station,** with shops open until 10pm seven days a week.

SPORTS

Spectator sports are racing, yachting regattas, log rolling, auto and motorcycle races, track meets, Finnish baseball (which is called *pesäpallo*), international canoeing competitions, cycling championships, tennis, soccer in the winter, and, most important of all, the **International Winter Games.** The best time to ski in south and central Finland is January-March; in Lapland you can still ski at the end of April. Inclusive tours to ski centers are available, and there are over 40 modern ski resort hotels where double room, including meals, sauna, ski tows or lifts, and even rented boots and skis, costs from Fmk80-90 a day. There are special walking tours (information from the **Finnish Tourist Board,** Kluuvikatu 8, POB 625, Helsinki) throughout Finland, and aspiring frontiersmen can travel into Lapland in the far north and pan for gold in the **Lemmenjoki** river or shoot the rapids on the **Tornio** river. You can swim or waterski on the lakes or from the best-known beaches at **Hanko** on the south coast and on the west coast at **Pori** and **Kalajoki.** Play golf or tennis, ride, sail, or fish. The best fishing season is from the beginning of June to the end of August. You need a general fishing license obtainable from post offices and valid for one year plus a fishing permit from the owner of the waters in which you will fish. This could be a local fishing association formed by owners of water areas or a hotel, holiday village, or campsite with its own fishing area. Local National Board of Forestry offices and local tourist boards can also sell permits.

WHAT TO SEE

Helsinki, known as the "white city of the north" because of its strikingly modern light-colored buildings, is, however, over 400 years old. Parks and squares are filled with some of Finland's most magnificent sculpture; on the **Market Square** the statue of the *Maid of Helsinki Rising from the Sea;* in **Sibelius Park** a monument to Sibelius made in steel; on **Observatory Hill** one of Finland's most symbolic statues, *Shipwrecked;* and in front of Stockmann's store the statue of the *Three Smiths.* All are by outstanding Finnish sculptors. Places to see include the **Stadium Tower, Senate Square,** the **Cathedral, Parliament House, Market Square,** the **City Gardens** at Eläintarha Park; the extraordinary **Temppeliaukio**

Church, blasted from solid rock; the beautiful **Finlandia Concert Hall and Congress Center,** designed by Alvar Aalto; and the old town, **Vanha-kaupunki,** the original city site begun in 1550. Visit **Suomenlinna Fortress,** which has never been captured, or take a ferry from the North Harbor at the lower end of Aleksanterinkatu to **Korkeasaari Island** for a visit to Finland's only zoo. On **Seurasaari Island** there is an open-air museum.

Turku, in the southwest, 25 minutes by air from Helsinki, is Finland's former capital and the most ancient city in the country, having been founded in the 13th century. The **Cathedral** and the **Castle** date from this time. There is a **Sibelius Museum** and a **Handicraft Museum,** at which you can try your hand at weaving, printing, or pottery. The **Modern Museum** and **Resurrection Chapel** are masterpieces of modern Finnish architecture. Hotels in Turku: **Seurahuone,** Humalistonkatu 2 (from US$50 double CP); **Ruissalo,** Ruissalo (from US$50 double CP); **Hamburger Börs,** Kauppiaskatu 6 (from US$60 double); and the **Ikituurin,** Pispalantie 7 (from US$60 double).

Tampere is a city on the isthmus, two lakes with the **Tammerkoski Rapids** flowing through. From **Pyynikki Ridge** you get a total view of the city. The **Provincial Museum** is also on top of a hill. There are two art museums. If you are a summer visitor, try the **Rosendahl** summer restaurant, and do not forget to visit the **Pyynikki Theater,** in which the auditorium rotates in the middle of the scene settings. Among hotels are **Grand Hotel Tammer,** Satakunnankatu 13 (from US$58 double); **Kaupunginhotelli,** Hämeenkatu 11 (from US$49 double); **Domus,** Pellervon-katu 9 (from US$25 double); **Cumulus,** Kyttälänkatu 2 (from US$58 double); **Victoria,** Itsenäisydenkatu 1 (from US$45 double); and **Rosendahl,** Pyynikintie 13 (from US$60 double).

Hämeenlinna, in Finland's lake district, is where Sibelius was born. Visit the 13th-century castle, and stay at the **Hotel Aulanko,** with double rooms from US$65. **Lahti,** the center for the modern Finnish furniture industry, is also a favorite ski resort.

Finnish Lapland, deep in the Arctic Circle, is the most astonishing part of the country. **Rovaniemi** is the only major town and is the provincial capital, almost exactly on the Arctic Circle. At the **Arctic Circle Lodge** you can get a certificate to show that you have crossed the circle. Rovaniemi is 70 minutes by air or 11 hours by train from Helsinki. There are good hotels including the **Polar Rovaniemi,** Valtakatu 23 (from US$55 double); **Polar Ousnavaara,** Ousnavaara Hill (from US$35 double); **Pohjanhovi,** Pohjanpuisto 2 (from US$60 double CP); **Lapinportti,** Kairatie 2 (from US$40 double); and the **City-Hotelli,** Pekankatu 9 (from US$35 double). **Domus Arctica,** Ratakatu 8 (from US$22) is open summers only. In Lapland, skiing goes on far into the spring, but the special sport is **reindeer** *joring.* This means climbing into a one-seat *pulkka* and driving it skimming across the snow following the leader.

SOURCES OF FURTHER INFORMATION
Pan Am, Salomonkatu 17 A, 2nd floor, Helsinki, and any Pan Am office round the world; **Finnish Tourist Board,** Kluuvikatu 8, POB 625, Helsinki;

FINLAND

City Tourist Office, Pohjoisesplanadi 19, Helsinki; **Finland National Tourist Office,** 75 Rockefeller Plaza, New York, NY 10019; **Finnish Tourist Board,** Finland House, Annexe, 53-54 Haymarket, London SW1Y 4RP.

France

WHAT'S SPECIAL

Almost everything is "special" about France. It is the home of *haute couture* and *haute cuisine*, of great writers, artists, and philosophers. At its heart is Paris, an exciting, romantic, and beautiful city. But the capital city is not the whole of France any more than New York is the whole of the United States. France includes the industrial northeast, the valleys and peaks of the Massif Central, the rocky Atlantic coast of Brittany, the châteaux of the Loire, the French Alps, and the sun and brightness of Provence and the Mediterranean Coast.

COUNTRY BRIEFING

Size: 212,841 square miles
Capital: Paris

Population: 53,373,000
Capital Population: Paris—city: 2,300,000 approx.
metro: 9,800,000 approx.

Climate: Paris is generally mild, with average temperatures of 43° in January and 76° in midsummer. The Riviera is sunny throughout the year, with average temperatures in Nice of 55° in January and 80° in midsummer.

Weather in Paris: Lat N48°45'; Alt 164 ft

Temp (°F)	Jan	Feb	Mar	Apr	May	Jun	Jul	Aug	Sep	Oct	Nov	Dec
Av Low	34°	34°	38°	43°	49°	55°	58°	58°	53°	46°	40°	36°
Av High	43°	45°	54°	60°	67°	73°	76°	75°	70°	60°	50°	44°
Days no rain	14	14	19	17	19	18	19	18	17	18	15	15

Government: A republic with 95 departments. The parliament consists of a national assembly and a senate.
Language: French.
Religion: Roman Catholic.
Currency: Franc. 100 centimes = 1 franc.

	10c	50c	1F	5F	10F	50F	100F	250F
US (dollars, cents)	.02	.09	.18	.91	1.81	9.06	18.12	45.30
UK (pounds, pence)	.01	.04	.09	.43	.86	4.33	8.66	21.65

Public Holidays:

New Year's Day, 1 Jan
Labor Day, 1 May
Ascension Day
Bastille Day, 14 July

Assumption, 15 Aug
All Saints Day, 1 Nov
Armistice Day, 11 Nov
Christmas Day, 25 Dec

HOW TO GET THERE

Flying time to Paris, Charles de Gaulle Airport from New York is 7 hours; from Miami, 8½ hours; from Rome, 2½ hours. Convenient connections can be made from Charles de Gaulle Airport to Côte d'Azur Airport in Nice. Flying time from Paris to Nice is 1¼ hours. Time in France: GMT+2 in summer; GMT+1 in winter.

REQUIREMENTS FOR ENTRY AND CUSTOMS REGULATIONS

Valid passport; vaccination certificates needed if arriving from an infected area. No visa required for stays of 3 months or less. If you wish to stay longer a visa is required, obtainable from a French Consulate abroad or from the Police Préfecture in Paris—or in the *chef-lieu* (county town) of the department in which you are staying. Duty-free allowances of tobacco and liquor (for visitors over 15 only) must be carried in your hand luggage; if coming from a Common Market country, you may bring in 300 cigarettes, 50 cigars or 350 grams of tobacco, 2 liters of wine plus 1½ liters of alcohol of more than 22-proof, 75 grams of perfume and ⅜ liter of toilet water. If arriving from a non–Common Market country, you will be allowed 400 cigarettes, 125 cigars, or 500 grams of tobacco. Also permitted: 1 liter alcohol more than 22-proof, 2 liters under 22-proof, 50 grams of perfume, and ¼ liter toilet water. Anyone may bring in two still cameras, with 10 rolls of black and white or color film for each camera; one movie camera, with 10 reels of color or black and white film. Drugs (except medication for personal use), narcotics, pornographic material, guns, and ammunition (except two hunting guns with 100 cartridges for each) may not be brought into the country. Visitors are allowed to take out F5,000 in French currency or its equivalent in other currencies without any formalities, but regulations may alter, so check current legislation before departure. There is no departure tax.

AIRPORT INFORMATION

The international airports for Paris are Charles de Gaulle (Roissy), 20 miles from the city; Orly, 11 miles; and Le Bourget, just over 15 miles from the city center and mostly used for charter flights. Buses leave the airports for the terminals at Porte Maillot (for Charles de Gaulle) and Les Invalides (for Orly) every 15 minutes. The fare is F20 from Charles de Gaulle and from Orly. There is a connecting service between the three airports, with departures every 20 minutes; the fare is F35, free to connecting airline passengers. A rail link is available at Orly as part of the new suburban high-speed train system. Departures every 15 minutes at F14 for several Paris stops. Taxis are also available: fares to the city center are around F100 during the day, F120-150 at night, from Charles de Gaulle and F80 from Orly. Tip porters F1 for every piece of luggage. All airports have duty-free shop and hotel reservations counter. Car rental counters are at all the airports. If you are flying to the Riviera, you will land either at Marignane Airport, 18 miles from Marseilles, or at Nice-Côte d'Azur Airport, 3 miles from town.

ACCOMMODATIONS

Provided you reserve early, you will find accommodations to suit your taste and pocket, from the luxury of the Parisian hotels to country inns, vacation villages, private villas, or deluxe apartments on the Riviera. There are more than 300 youth hostels and over 3,600 camping sites. Some hotels charge up to 25% additional on bills for service and extras, but you can ask for the *prix forfaitaire*, a rate including extras. Prices can be lower by as much as 20% in some hotels in Paris and on the Riviera from 20 December to 1 March. In Paris there are six Welcome Information Bureaus, located in the train stations and air terminals, with multilingual hostesses who will make on-the-spot reservations by Telex. The central bureau is at 127 avenue des Champs-Elysées, 8e (tel: 723 6173). The government is also buying and converting old farms and country houses to make them suitable for reasonably priced vacations. Latest details from France Informations Loisirs, 8 avenue de l'Opéra in Paris (tel: 296 6363) and at other cities around France. This type of vacation has been deliberately created for the overseas visitor. Note that Paris is usually crowded during July and August, and it may be worth considering a visit to the more rural areas at these times. Paris hotels: *Rates are in US$ for a double/twin room with bath or shower*

    Angleterre, 44 rue Jacob (from $37) near St-Germain des Prés.

    Baltimore, 88 bis, avenue Kléber (from $100), near Arc de Triomphe

    Bedford, 17 rue de l'Arcade (from $50), near Arc de Triomphe

    Bristol Hotel, 112 Faubourg St Honoré (from $150)

    California, 16 rue de Berri (from $95)

    Claridge Bellman, 37 rue François Ier (from $77)

    Commodore, 12 boulevard Haussmann (from $83), near Arc de Triomphe

    Concorde Lafayette, place Porte des Ternes (from $100), near Arc de Triomphe

    Concorde St-Lazare, 108 rue St-Lazare (from $85), near Opéra

    Crillon, 10 place de la Concorde (from $143), near Tuileries

    François, 3 boulevard Montmartre (from $52), near Opéra

George V, 31 avenue George V (from $162), near Arc de Triomphe

Grand, 5 Place de l'Opéra (from $114) near Opéra

INTER · CONTINENTAL PARIS, 3 rue de Castiglione (from $140), near Tuileries

Littré, 9 rue Littré (from $60), near Montparnasse

Lotti, 7 rue de Castiglione (from $95), near Tuileries

Meurice, 228 rue de Rivoli (from $100), near Tuileries

Napoléon, 40 avenue de Friedland (from $83), near Arc de Triomphe

Orly Hilton, 94 Aéroport d'Orly (from $73), at Orly Airport

Paris Hilton, 18 avenue de Suffren (from $123), near Eiffel Tower

Pas de Calais, 59 rue des Saints-Péres (from $50), near St-Germain des Prés

Plaza Athénée, 23-27 avenue Montaigne (from $175), off Champs-Elysées

PLM-St. Jacques, 17 boulevard St. Jacques (from $93), in Montparnasse

Ritz, 15 place Vendôme (from $190), near Tuileries

Saint-Sulpice, 7 rue C. Delavigne (from $36) near Odéon.

Sofitel Bourbon, 32 rue St Dominique (from $110), near St Germain des Prés

Sofitel Roissy (from $57) near Charles de Gaulle airport

USEFUL INFORMATION

Helpful Hints: In August many Parisians are on vacation, and a number of theaters, nightclubs, and restaurants close down. Best time for Paris is late spring or early fall.

Banks: Open 9-4 Mon-Fri.

Mail: Stamps from post offices, hotels, *bureaux de tabac* (tobacconists), and machines. Mailboxes are yellow. Post offices (P.T.T), where you can also send telegrams and cables, open 8am-7pm, and to noon Sat. PTT in Paris on rue du Louvre open 24 hrs, 7 days a week.

Telephone Tips: Telephone booths on streets and in restaurants, cafés, and subway stations. Automatic phones are token or coin operated—tokens *(jetons)* available from post offices at 50 centimes. Useful numbers in Paris:

Pan Am 266 45 45	**Operator** 10
Airport Information	**Directories** 12
Charles de Gaulle 862 12 12	**Time** 463 84 00
Orly 687 12 34	**Weather** 555 95 90 (Paris)
Le Bourget 862 12 12	555 91 09 (France)
Tourist Offices 723 61 72	**Police** 12 or 17
Tourist Information 720 16 78	**Fire** 18
Accommodations Office 723 61 73	**Check "S.O.S." numbers in**
Traffic and Road Condition 858 33	**telephone directory for**
33	**many emergency services.**

Newspapers: Newspapers and magazines in English easily available; the *International Herald Tribune* appears in English, daily; *A Touch of Paris,* an English feature oriented paper appears five times each year, always including an interesting Paris guide with each issue.

Tipping: A way of life. In a movie theater tip the usher at least F1. Hotels usually have a service charge of up to 25% but you should still give the porter or *concierge* about F2 for every day you are at the hotel; give the bellboy F2-3; the room-service waiter F1 every time he brings something to your room; the doorman F1 every time he gets you a taxi; and the chambermaid F5 if you stay longer than three days. Many restaurants include a service charge on the check, but you should still leave a little extra. The *sommelier* (wine waiter) found in luxury restaurants gets a minimum of F10. Hatcheck and washroom attendants get F1; theater ushers F1; tour guides F1 for a short tour. At the hairdresser, 15% is sometimes included in the bill, but give the person who washes your hair F3 and the stylist F8-10. Taxi drivers are tipped 15% of the meter reading, minimum F2.

Electricity: 220 volts 50 cycles AC; some hotels have converters.

Laundry: Dry-cleaning and laundry service available in hotels and all major towns (dry-cleaning a suit, from F28; laundering a shirt, from F8).

Hairdressers: Salons are available in first-class hotels. There are many superb hairstylists and beauticians in Paris. Prices vary; a coiffure in a medium-range salon will cost from F90—much more in a top salon. A man's haircut costs from F40.

Photography: Equipment and film are available almost everywhere. Black and white film, about F6 and about 24 hours to develop; color film, F10-12 and 6-10 days to be processed. Same-day Ektachrome service is now available in a number of shops.

Clubs: Kiwanis, Lions, Rotary (Paris, Nice, and some other cities).

Babysitting: Ring the Institut Catholique (tel: 548 31 70), the Alliance Française (tel: 544.38.28), or Copar (tel: 329.12.43) in Paris; in Nice, Europnurses Express (tel: 80 10 30). Any Bureau d'Accueil will also be able to help. Fees around F12-16 per hour. At family resorts on the Channel and Atlantic coasts, there are Clubs de Plage for children from 4-13 with sessions mornings and afternoons at about F20 per diem.

Rest Rooms: In subway stations, cafés, museums, restaurants, larger stores, and at some fast disappearing street locations. Women, *Dames;* men, *Hommes.*

Health: Should you need medical help, your hotel porter or embassy will put you in touch with an English-speaking doctor. British and American pharmaceuticals are available but they can be expensive. Every *arrondissement* has at least one druggist open on Sundays and public holidays. By law, any water supply not safe to drink is marked *Eau Non Potable,* including that on trains and buses. The **American Hospital,** Neuilly (63 blvd Victor Hugo—tel: 747.53.00) is excellent but expensive.

American Express: office at 11 rue Scribe (tel: 266.09.99, but 732.30.80 to report a stolen credit card, travelers' checks) is frequently used as a message center, and besides usual services offers some duty-free shopping.

TRANSPORTATION

All French towns have bus services, but the quickest and least expensive way to get about Paris is on the subway—the *Métro*. Métro lines are identified by the name of the terminus in each direction; if you have to change trains, follow the yellow signs marked *Correspondance*. *Billets de tourisme,* valid for 7 days' unlimited travel on either subway or buses, are available at F35 valid 2 days, F53 valid 4 days, or F88 valid for 7 days of first-class travel on subways or buses at several locations listed on the rapid transit brochure available from Métro ticket windows or at 53 quai des Grands-Augustins, from the RTAP office at place de la Madeleine, or at official French Tourist Offices in the USA or Canada, and from the French Railways Ltd, 179 Piccadilly, London W1. A carnet of 10 one-time tickets for Métro or bus costs F17.50. Monthly "Carte Orange" ticket is reusable on buses and subways and costs F85. Metered taxis are plentiful, except during rush hours. You can hail one in the street, pick one up from a taxi stand called a *tête de station,* or phone. Minimum fare is F5.50. There is an extra charge of 50 centimes for each piece of luggage over 5 kilos, although not all drivers charge the fee.

Europcar is at 42 avenue de Saxe (tel: 273 3520), and also has offices in the airports. Traffic in Paris is undisciplined, to say the least. There is cut-throat competition for parking space; *zones bleues* (blue zones) need a parking disc *(disque),* which you can get from your hotel or garage. Parking meters are well policed by meter maids. Europcar desk in Nice is at 89 rue de Saxe (tel: 87 08 53) and for reservations anywhere in France, tel: 645.21.25.

Probably the best way to travel outside of Paris during the summer and to ski resorts in winter is by the French National Railway (SNCF). The Eurailpass is accepted in France. There are also car-sleeper expresses which will convey you overnight in a sleeping berth, with your car traveling on the same train. Air Inter has an extensive service to many cities within France, including Strasbourg, Lyons, Marseilles, Nice, and Bordeaux. Visitors to France can get 25% reductions on air fares round-trip tickets within France for cities if tickets are purchased at the time they buy their international flight and stay at least one Sunday night in the city of destination. There are ferry and hovercraft services' across the English Channel, and the SNCM (Société Nationale Corse Mediterrannée) runs regular car and passenger ferry services from Nice and Marseilles to Bastia, Ajaccio, and Calvi in Corsica.

FOOD AND RESTAURANTS

Paris alone has more than 8,000 restaurants and bistros, each with its own *spécialité de la maison.* All over France are restaurants which serve a special tourist menu, including *hors d'oeuvres,* a main dish chosen from the day's *à la carte* menu, cheese, and dessert. Do not miss *escargots,* snails in garlic, butter, and parsley; *pâté de foie gras,* rich gooseliver paté; *soupe à l'oignon,* onion soup usually served in china tureens. In Provence you must certainly try *ratatouille,* eggplant, red peppers, tomatoes, and zucchini stewed in olive oil; and the famous *bouillabaisse* of Marseilles, a stew of fish, mussels, and other shellfish. Also try *soufflé au saumon frais,* fresh salmon soufflé; *langouste grillée aux herbes,* broiled crayfish seasoned with herbs; *cuisses de grenouilles,* tender frog's legs; *filet de sole au champagne;* or simply a medium-rare Chateaubriand steak with french fries. Sauces, of course, are the secret of French cooking. The main course is usually followed by salad, an inviting cheese platter, then a dessert. When a restaurant does not have a menu posted outside, it is very expensive. A meal in an expensive restaurant will cost you F350 (US$70-75) per person, or more. A meal in a medium-priced restaurant will cost roughly F100 (US$20) and one in an inexpensive restaurant F60 (about US$12). There are also over 50 self-service restaurants in Paris where a three-course meal will cost you about F22 (about US$5.35).

You will rarely go wrong in choosing a restaurant in Paris, but reserve your table in advance. Recommended restaurants are **Lasserre** (17 avenue Franklin D. Roosevelt, 8e—tel: 359 53 43), with its sliding roof; **Tour d'Argent** (15 quai Tournelle 5e—tel: 354 23 31), one of the very best in Paris, with a spectacular selection of wines, and known for its duck (the number of yours will be given on a souvenir card, and by all means, see all floors of this building); **Prunier-Madeleine** (9 rue Duphot, ler—tel: 260 36 04), where you should order the *filet de turbot V'erilhac;* **Aux Lyonnais** (37 rue St Marc, 2e—tel: 297 42 95), which specializes in Lyonnais cooking, reputedly the best in France; **Les Belles Gourmandes** (5 rue Paul-Louis Courier, 73—tel: 548 47 08), a bistro with an imaginative menu; **Le Soufflé** (36 rue du Mont-Thaboz, ler—tel: 260 27 19), for light, delicate soufflés; **Lamazère** (23 rue de Ponthieu, 8e—tel: 359 66 66) for truffles and lobsters; **Allard** (41 rue St André des Arts—tel: 326 48 23), where you should try the *poissons au beurre blanc* or *canard aux olives;* **Chiberta** (3 rue Arsène-Houssaye, 8e—tel: 563 77 90), for nouvelle cuisine; **Brasserie Flo** (7 cour des Petites Ecuries, 10e—tel: 770 13 59), the oldest brasserie in Paris; **Vivarois** (192 avenue Victor Hugo, 16e—tel: 504 04 31), an excellent restaurant with a dazzling menu. These are just a few of the good restaurants in Paris. You will have no trouble in finding snack bars serving enormous sandwiches, cheese, modest patés, hamburgers, boiled eggs, and tempting *pâtisseries.* Some restaurants, such as the **Brasserie Lipp** in St-Germain (and where you may have to wait for a seat) or **Pied de Cochon** (6 rue Coquillière, ler—tel: 236 11 75), stay open late. There are plenty of moderately priced restaurants all over Paris where one can dine well without the price tag of the better known places. For a tender steak and excellent *pommes frites,* the **Cour St-Germain** is an example. Then there are the numerous Vietnamese restaurants, where this style of oriental *cuisine* may be found to near perfection. For those in a hurry, there are a number of **McDonald's** and **Burger Kings,** including such premier locations as the Champs-Elysées. **Le Drugstore**—at both ends of the Champs-Elysées, Place de l'Opéra, and several other locations—stays open late for light meals, snacks, newspapers, magazines, cigarettes, souvenirs, and numerous other items, including pharmaceuticals.

DRINKING TIPS

Imported beer is easily available, but *bière pression* (on tap, from barrels) is much cheaper—a "demi," half a pint, from about F4. Some pubs now specialize in beers from all over the world. Also very popular is the delicious aniseed-flavored pernod; sip it slowly in one of the sidewalk cafés, preferably **Café de Flore** or **Café des Deux Magots** on the boulevard St Germain in Paris. You may prefer a Dubonnet, a Martini—but if you do, be sure to order an American martini (martini americain) if that's what you want—or a Bartissol before your meal, or even an English pint at one of the several, typically English pubs. With your meal you can have a carafe (or a demi-carafe) of white, red, or rosé wine for about F15. One successful New York transplant is the **Joe Allen** establishment at 30 rue Pierre Lescot, near to the Beaubourg Musée, with some of the best hamburgers and chili in town. After dinner you might like a brandy; ask for a *Fine,* a bar-brandy, probably better than the more famous names you get at home, or a cognac (the best ones are made by Hennessy, Martell, and Bisquit). Gin and whisky are usually served as doubles. If you want a single, ask for a "baby." A whisky and soda can cost you F15-18. Bars, bistros, and cafés are usually open from 7am-12pm or later. Popular drinking spots in Paris are **Harry's Bar,** 5 rue Daunou; **La Closerie des Lilas,** 171 boulevard Montparnasse; **La Coupole,** 102 boulevard Montparnasse; **Le Café de la Paix,** avenue de l'Opéra; **Le Sélect,** 99 boulevard Montparnasse; and of course, Café de Flore and Café des Deux Magots, on boulevard St Germain. Young people under 18 cannot be served alcoholic drinks.

ENTERTAINMENT

Paris is the home of the two great **Comédie Française** establishments—at the **Salle Richelieu,** 2 rue de Richelieu and at the **Théâtre National de l'Odéon,** Place de l'Odéon; here too you will find the famous **Théâtre de la Ville,** in the place du Châtelet. There are many other avant-garde theaters, but the most adventurous work in Paris is now being done by the **Théâtre de Soleil,** in an old warehouse at Vincennes, avenue de la Pyramide. Grand opera can be heard throughout the year (except during the August holidays) at the **Opéra,** where ballet performances also take place. See light opera at the **Opéra Comique,** concerts and recitals at the **Salle Gaveau, Salle Pleyel, Théâtre des Champs-Elysées,** the **Palais des Congrès,** and **Maison de Radio France.** In summer there are special performances out of town at **Chartres Cathedral,** the **Abbey of Royaumont, Sceaux,** and **Versailles.** An excellent historical *son et lumiére* (sound and light) show can be seen outdoors—except in winter—at **Les Invalides.** You might also enjoy a musical or a variety show at the **Châtelet** or the **Mogador,** or at one of Paris' three great music halls, **Olympia** (28 boulevard des Capucines), the **Bobino** (20 rue de la Gaité), and the **Palais des Sports** (place Porte de Versailles). Tickets can be bought at box offices, through theater ticket offices, at larger hotels and at **FNAC**—a discount book, record, camera, and appliance chain with its newest outlet at the **Forum des Halles.** Evening performances usually start between 8:30 and 9pm, matinées on Thursdays and Sundays at 3pm. Every theater is closed on one day of the week. For current programs see *Pariscope* (F1.80) or *Officiel des Spectacles* (F1.50) at all newsstands.

Movies are shown either with original soundtrack *(version originale)* or dubbed *(version française)*. Seats for movie theaters in Paris cost F20-25, except for *art et essai* movie houses showing older films at prices from F15. Many show poor prints, and it is occasionally wise to ask the state of the *pellicule;* demand a refund if the print is poor. The **Cinémathèques** in Paris, where you can see experimental movies and classics—usually good prints—are at the **Pompidou** (Beaubourg) **Center** and at Palais de Chaillot. Nightclub tours in several price ranges are offered by hotels and travel agencies. Of course you should see the spectacular shows at the **Lido** (avenue des Champs-Elysées), the **Folies Bergère** (32 rue Richer), the **Alcazar de Paris** (62 rue Mazarine), the **Moulin Rouge** (place Blanche, Montmartre), or the **Casino de Paris** (16 rue de Clichy, 9e), near la Trinité. Other popular nightspots are **L'Eléphant Bleu** (12 rue de Marignan), **Le Paradis Latin** (28 rue de Cardinal-Lemoine) and **Raspoutine** (58 rue de Bassano). The **Crazy Horse Saloon** (12 avenue George V) packs people in for its sophisticated strip shows, **Le Chat Qui Pêche** in the Latin Quarter for its excellent modern jazz. Or squeeze into **Les Trois Mailletz** (56 rue Galande), where the jazz is classical. **Le Lapin Agile** (22 rue des Saules) has the authentic atmosphere of old Montmartre, and is equally bohemian. **Le Bilboquet** (13 rue Saint-Benoît) and **Tour Eiffel** (Champs de Mars) are very popular with young people, who also throng to the **Open One** (21 rue du Vieux Colombier). At **L'Abbaye** (6 rue de l'Abbaye), which is always crowded, you must not clap when the excellent folk singers finish a number; snap your fingers instead.

SHOPPING

Stores are open 9-12 and 2, 6:30 or 7pm Tues-Sat. However, many large department stores are now open on Mondays and remain open throughout the lunch hour. Paris is the place for *haute couture,* of course, but ready-to-wear clothes are still the best buys. There are many boutiques, including **Yves Saint Laurent** at Faubourg Saint Honoré, 46 avenue Victor Hugo, and 21 rue de Tournon, and **Pierre Cardin** at 186 boulevard Saint Germain, 59 Faubourg St Honoré, and the Forum des Halles—Paris' newest shopping and architectural attraction underground on the Les Halles site which is to become a park. For lingerie go to **Dior's** lingerie department; **Pache** (6 rue de Castiglione); or **Gribiche** (49 rue de Rennes). Women's accessories, gloves, handbags, belts, scarves, and umbrellas, classical and elegant, make superb gifts. Try **Morabito** (1 place Vendôme) for the loveliest custom-made bags; **Hermès** (24 Faubourg Saint Honoré) for purses and the most beautiful gloves and scarves; and **Vendrenne** (9 rue St Roch) for umbrellas. For men, **Pierre Cardin** has a *boutique monsieur* at 29 avenue Marigny; **Ted Lapidus** is at 37 ave Pierre-ler-de-Serbie, 1 Place St-Germain des Prés, and at 6 place Victor Hugo.

For Lalique glass and Daum crystal, go to the rue de Paradis; **Baccarat** is at 30 bis, **Daum** at 41, and **Saint-Louis** at number 30. Or you might prefer to do your shopping at one of the larger department stores— **Galeries Lafayette** (40 boulevard Haussmann), **Au Printemps** (64 boulevard Haussmann and also 25 Cours de Vincennes), **Le Bon Marché** (22 rue de Sèvres), or **Trois-Quartier** (17 boulevard de la Madeleine). **Monopriv** and **Prisuic** are budget Parisian chain stores. Many large stores will also pack and ship purchases for you, and some shops have an export plan. **Dehillerhin** (18 rue Coquilliére) has exceptional kitchen equipment. Many of the larger towns such as Lyons, Marseilles, and Nice have a branch of the department store **Galeries Lafayette** and **Au Printemps** and there are plenty of good regional buys, such as china from Limoges and pottery and printed provençal cottons from the south.

No visitor to Paris should miss **Le Marché aux Puces,** the famous Flea Market (Métro: Porte de Clignancourt) open on Saturday, Sunday, and Monday. Every neighborhood has its food market. Two of the most colorful are situated on the **rue Mouffetard** (métro Monge) and **rue de Buci** (métro Odéon).

SPORTS

There is horse racing every day of the week throughout the year at one of Paris' eight racetracks—the biggest event is the Prix de l'Arc de Triomphe at **Longchamps.** Soccer is played every Sunday at the **Parc des Princes** and at **Colombes Stadium.** The French are also great rugby players. Extremely popular too is cycling, culminating in the famous **Tour de France,** finishing after a month's circuit of France on the Champs Elysées in late July. There are tennis tournaments at the **Stade Roland-Garros** in the Bois de Boulogne, and if you want to play yourself, get in touch with the **Fédération Française de Lawn Tennis** (2 avenue Gordon Bennett, tel: 743 96 81). Golf courses in Paris are usually crowded, especially on weekends, and to play you must be a member of a club in your own country; information from **Fédération Française de Golf** (69 ave Victor Hugo). Skiing is superb, and there are resorts in the French Alps, the **Pyrenees,** the **Vosges,** and the **Massif Central.** There are ski schools everywhere. You might also like to explore the caves in the Pyrenees, in Provence, and at Grande Chartreuse—information from the **Fédération Française de Spéléologie** (130 rue St Maur). Hunting for wild boar is excellent in the Vosges and Ardennes—get in touch with the **St Hubert Club de France** (10 rue de Lisbonne, Paris)—and there is superb fishing for trout and salmon in the streams of Brittany, the Pyrenees, the Alps, Auvergne, and Corsica. Yachting, swimming, deep-sea diving, water-skiing, and surfing are available along the coasts, where there are also horseback riding clubs, golf courses, and mini-golf. For sports in France contact the **Touring Club de France,** who can give you a great deal of information: 65 avenue de la Grande Armée, Paris 16e (tel: 500 19 87).

WHAT TO SEE

Paris: Towering over Paris is the **Tour Eiffel,** over 1,000 feet high, inaugurated in 1889 by Edward VII, then Prince of Wales. On the Place Charles de Gaulle, formerly the Place de l'Etoile, stands the **Arc de Triomphe,** erected by Napoleon; stretching away from it is the avenue des Champs-Elysées, which leads down to **Place de la Concorde,** where Louis XVI and Marie Antoinette were guillotined. See the **Place de la Madeleine** and the **Opéra;** the massive towers of **Notre Dame Cathedral** and the golden spire of **Sainte-Chapelle,** on the Ile de la Cité; **Montmartre** with its bohemian cafés, winding streets, and basilica of the **Sacré Coeur** at its summit. You can take the funicular to the top of Montmartre from Place d'Anvers. You must also visit **Les Invalides,** where Napoleon is buried under the highest dome in Paris, the **Louvre Museum,** where you can see the *Mona Lisa* and *Venus de Milo,* the **Musée de l'Art Moderne,** the **Rodin Museum,** the **Orangerie,** the **Musée de l'Homme,** the **Musée de Cluny,** where there are medieval tapestries, sculptures, and other exhibits, and the **Musée du Jeu de Paume,** with its striking collection of Impressionist art. The new **Georges Pompidou National Center for Art and Culture,** housed in an ultramodern building on rue St Martin on the Plateau de Beaubourg, features all the arts in changing exhibitions. (Most museums are closed on Tuesdays.) In any national museum you have to pay F5 to use a tripod-mounted camera, but hand-held shots are free. Go to the **Quartier Latin,** where you will find the **Sorbonne** and the **Panthéon** as well as the colorful boulevard St Michel and Saint Germain-des-Prés, with their famous sidewalk cafés (the Greenwich Village or Soho of Paris). Nearby are the famous **Jardins** and **Palais du Luxembourg.** Browse through the bookstalls along the Seine; take a boat trip down the river on the colorful *Bateaux Mouches,* or drive through the **Bois de Boulogne,** playground of Paris. Stroll through the **Marais,** starting from the place de la Bastille; go along the rue Saint-Antoine to the place des Vosges (former residence of Victor Hugo is at number 6), to the **Musée Carnavalet** on the rue de Sévigné—a museum recreating the history of Paris and the Revolution—then along the rue Francs-Bourgeois to the **Archives Nationales.** If you want to explore the sinister underground corridors of the **Catacombs,** tours start from 2 place Denfert-Rochereau at 2pm during the summer; or you might like to spend the afternoon watching a demonstration of French cooking at **Le Cordon Bleu,** 24 rue du Champ-de-Mars (for information call 555 02 77). Very popular too are the excursions through the **sewers of Paris** by barge—the meeting place is under the statue of Lillie, place de la Concorde, every Thursday from 1 July to 15 October from 2-5, unless there have been heavy rains.

For the children there are the beautiful woods in the **Bois de Vincennes,** with a zoo and an aquarium. Take them too to the **Jardin d'Acclimatation** in the Bois de Boulogne or the beautiful garden in the **Tuileries,** and let them see the Punch and Judy show in the Jardins du Luxembourg. They will love the **wax museums** of **Musée Grévin** (10 boulevard Montmartre) and **La Butte Montmartre,** on rue Poulbot. If they are getting hot and sticky, take them to the swimming pools of Deligny (25 quai Anatole France). In winter you should take them to see the famous *Cirque d'Hiver* (winter circus).

Ile de France: Within a few hours' drive from Paris lie some of France's most beautiful monuments, notably **Versailles,** palace of Louis XIV, with its beautiful landscaped gardens, the chapel, royal bedrooms and *petits appartements,* the Grand and Petit Trianon; and **Fontainebleau,** with the famous forest covering 42,000 acres and the dazzling Renaissance château, a favorite residence of the Emperor Napoleon. During the summer the gardens and fountains of Versailles and Fontainebleau are brilliantly illuminated, and there are evening festivals and *son et lumière* spectacles. The cathedral of **Chartres** is an awe-inspiring masterpiece, with its stained-glass windows and Gothic sculptures. You should also visit four châteaux: **Chantilly,** with its art museum, **St Germain-en-Laye,** which has a 1½-mile-long terrace, **Vaux-le-Vicomte,** richly baroque, and **Thoiry,** where there is an African animal reserve. Near Compiègne is the **Clairière de l'Armistice,** where Hitler insisted the surrender of France should be signed in 1940—on the same spot and in the same railway coach where the Armistice of 1918 was signed. There are several day-long trips and guided tours of the historic region. You can also cruise down the Marne and Yonne rivers on the air-conditioned **Lazy Dolphin** (book trips from SNCF, 18 avenue de l'Opéra, and from 81 New Bond Street, London, W1) or in a rented boat.

Loire Valley: The river Loire flows through the Château Country—five centuries of the history of France beautifully preserved in magnificent castles, fortresses, and abbeys. Kings and queens and the nobility, partisans and revolutionaries come to life again in the gorgeous *son et lumière* spectacles. Traveling south by car along the N10 highway, you will come to the fortress castle of **Châteaudun;** follow the same route and you will reach the Loire and the city of **Tours,** the center of this region. To the east, along the valley (upstream) you will find **Amboise,** in whose château Charles VIII died and where 1,500 Huguenot conspirators were massacred in 1560; **Blois,** where you will be shown the death chamber of Catherine de Medici; **Chambord,** with its château of 440 rooms, walled-in gardens, and the largest estate in France. Westward along the valley toward the Atlantic, you will come to **Azay-le-Rideau,** with one of the most beautiful châteaux of the early Renaissance; **Saumur,** renowned for the Cavalry School and its *Cadre Noir* (Black Squadron); **Angers,** whose château with 190-foot-high towers is surrounded with 30-foot-deep moats, and where you should see the **Cathédrale Saint-Maurice** and the **Museum of Tapestry.** There are 120 castles to visit. If you are in France on 7 and 8 May, go to Orléans for the annual **Festival of Joan of Arc.**

Normandy: With beaches of fine sand and rocky coves, Normandy has many delightful vacation resorts. **Rouen,** a busy modernized medieval city with fine museums and lovely churches, should be the starting point of your visit; see the **Place du Vieux-Marché,** where **Joan of Arc** was burned at the stake, the remarkable **Cathédrale de Notre Dame,** and the **Renaissance Clock,** both in the old section of town. **Deauville** is where the millionaires, film stars, princes, and diplomats go. There is a luxurious casino, polo, horse racing, deep-sea fishing, tennis, and golf. August is the month to go, but Deauville is smart all the year round. You should not miss the extraordinary cliffs at **Etretat.** The 235-foot **Bayeux Tapestry,** depicting the conquest of England by William the Conqueror, and a lovely Norman church should be seen in **Bayeux;** the 11th-century **Abbaye aux Dames** and the **Abbaye aux Hommes** in **Caen** are worth a visit. See the **D-Day Beaches** of Omaha, Utah, and Arromanches. Above all in Normandy, see the grandeur of **Mont-St-Michel;** the towering abbey was founded in the 8th century—you reach it by a single cobblestoned street lined with little shops and restaurants. In Mont-St-Michel stay at the **Hôtel de la Mère Poulard** (from US$38), well known for its "Mère Poulard" omelettes.

Brittany stands where the English Channel and the Atlantic meet. Near **Carnac** are the **menhirs,** gigantic monuments in granite erected more than 4,000 years ago—and don't miss the mysterious dolmens of **Locmariaquer. Saint Malo en l'Isle,** the "City of Corsairs," is a walled city with massive medieval ramparts; it was burnt by the occupying Germans in 1944 and later scrupulously rebuilt. The **Pointe du Raz,** the most western point of France, juts out into the Atlantic. **Quimper** is the main Breton tourist center, where on market days (Wednesday and Saturday) thousands of Bretons, many in provincial costume, flock to the square in front of the ancient **Cathedral.** One of the main tourist attractions of the region is the **Pardons,** religious pilgrimages with chanting and candlelit processions through the open meadows and woods, celebrated all over Brittany, from February to October. **Nantes** is a bustling city with a 15th-century ducal castle, superbly illuminated at night. **Dinard** is the most popular resort by the sea, with splendid villas, beautiful beaches, and a great casino. Stay at **Le Grand Hotel,** 46 avenue George V (from US$71 high season/$35 low season) or the **Roche Corneille,** 4 rue Georges Clemenceau (from US$50 high season/$27 low season).

Alsace-Lorraine is separated from Germany only by the Rhine. **Strasbourg,** with 257,000 inhabitants, is one of the largest cities in France, an important river port on the Rhine in the shadow of the 470-foot spire of the **Gothic Cathedral.** This is the site of the famous astronomical clock. Visit the **Château de Rohan,** with its exciting museums, the **Alsatian Museum,** lively **Place Kléber,** and the attractive "la Petite France" quarter. Hotels in Strasbourg include the **Sofitel,** place St Pierre-le-Jeune (from US$62); **Le Grand,** 12 place de la Gare (from US$40); the **Monopole-Metropole Mapotel,** 14-16 rue Kuhn (from US$31); and the **Terminus Gruber,** 10 place de la Gare (from US$50). From Strasbourg you can go to **Colmar,** where the famous **Musée d'Unterlinden** is, and to the medieval village of **Riquewitz** in the heart of the Alsatian vineyards.

Metz has the oldest church in France, the 4th-century church of **Saint-Pierre-aux-Nonnains,** while the **Cathédrale de St-Etienne** is a Gothic masterpiece. From its 300-foot tower, the view is sublime. Hotels in Metz include **Hotel Central,** 3 bis rue Vauban (from US$29); the **Royal Concorde,** 23 avenue Foch (from US$50); **Frantel Metz,** 29 Place St-Thiebault (from US$49). **Nancy** is full of architectural gems and harmonious squares, such as the beautiful **Place Stanislas** opposite the Arc de Triomphe and the **Place de la Carrière.** Accommodations in Nancy include **Hotel Americain,** 3 Place Andre Maginot (from US$28); **Astoria,** 3 rue Armée-Patton (from US$35); **Frantel Nancy,** 11 rue Raymond-Poincare (from US$41); **Grand Hotel Concorde,** Place Stanislaus 54 (from US$48); **Europe,** 5 rue des Carmes (from US$25).

The Atlantic Coast and Massif Central: In this area are the vineyards of **Bordeaux,** the trout streams of **Auvergne,** the Gallo-Roman remains of **Périgueux,** the canals of the "Green Venice" near **Niort,** the subterranean river of the **Gouffre de Padirac,** the caves and grottoes of the **Périgord,** and the **Dordogne** valley, where the bones of the Cro-Magnon man were discovered. Bordeaux is the wine capital of France and the country's fifth-largest city. Here you should climb the 288 steps of the **Tour Saint Michel** and then go on to visit the crypt, which is full of mummies. See the **Grand Théâtre,** the **Cathédrale Saint André,** the **Musée des Beaux-Arts.** An excursion through the vineyards is a must. There are a number of good hotels in Bordeaux including **Frantel Bordeaux** (from US$56), **Terminus** (from US$40), **Novotel Bordeaux le Lac** (from US$38), **PLM Aquitania** (from US$50), among several others. **Limoges** is famous for its china and porcelain, made from the pure white clay found in nearby Saint Yrieix. Périgueux is the most important town in the Dordogne valley; go on an excursion to the **Château de Périgord,** on the subterranean river of Gouffre de Padirac. It is 300 feet deep, and you reach it by elevator and stairs and then explore it on foot or by boat; it is one of the most extraordinary sights in Europe, with its vast chambers, stalactites, and stalagmites, and grotesque rock formations.

The French Alps: One of the most spectacular regions in Europe, stretching from Lake Geneva to the Riviera, the French Alps are a paradise for skiers. Resorts are equipped with ski schools, snow nurseries, skating rinks, and the most modern ski lifts and cableways. Popular resorts are **Val d'Isère, Les Houches, St Gervais,** and **Mégève.** Stay at the **Mont Blanc Hotel** in Mégève (place de L'Eglise). From **Chamonix,** which is linked to Mégève by cableway, you can take a trip by railway to the **Mer de Glace** glacier, or ride up the highest cableway in the world (12,605 feet) to the **Aiguille du Midi. Grenoble,** headquarters for the 1968 Winter Olympics, is famous for its university and for its art museum, with an excellent collection of modern art.

The Rhône Valley: Lyon is a thriving city with a wealth of historic sights—Roman monuments (it was through the Rhône Valley that the Romans penetrated deep into Europe), medieval churches, and Renaissance houses. Lyon also has many fine museums. There are a number of excellent hotels in Lyon, and good places to stay include **Sofitel,** 20 quai Gailleton (from US$75); **Carlton,** Place de la République (from US$32); **des Beaux Arts,** 75 rue de President Herriot (from US$39); **Le Grand,** 11 rue Grolee (from US$47); **Royal,** 20 Place Bellecour (from

US$48); or the **PLM Terminus,** 12 cours de Verdun (from US$36). The countryside around the city of Lyon abounds in fine inns and restaurants, and if you have the time—and the money—a visit to the world renowned **Paul Bocuse** restaurant could create the memory of the fine *haute cuisine de France* that you'll savor all your life. **Avignon** is famous nowadays for its summer drama festival held in the **Palais des Papes**—reserve your seats well in advance.

Provence: The southern region of the Rhône Valley contains many classical and medieval monuments. **Nimes** is an important industrial and wine center, with its magnificent **Roman Amphitheater** and the **Pont du Gard,** an aqueduct constructed in three stories of arches in 19 BC. **Arles** is where, on Sundays during the summer, the Provençal bullfights, known as *courses à la cocarde,* are held in the ancient **Roman Amphitheater;** you must also see the **Roman Obelisk** on the place de la République and the **Museon Arlaten,** illustrating Provençal folklore. **Aix-en-Provence,** the "City of Fountains," has spacious avenues, including the famous **Cours Mirabeau,** and 17th- and 18th-century houses—don't miss the **Studio of Cézanne** and **Tapestry Museum.**

Pyrenees—Basque Region: Between France and Spain run the Pyrenees, with spas and winter sports centers, seaside resorts, mountain amphitheaters, subterranean grottoes, and caves rich in prehistoric finds. **Biarritz** is the smartest of Atlantic seaside resorts. There is an 18-hole golf course, a casino, restaurants (while here you must try *cargolade,* broiled snails with peppers, or fried eels *à la bordelaise*), and several deluxe hotels. Far more picturesque and intimate is the fishing port of **Saint-Jean-de-Luz.** Eastward along the mountain range is **Pau,** the starting point for tours of the Pyrenees. Every year two million visitors come to the pilgrimage city of **Lourdes** to see the grotto where, in 1858, St Bernadette had visions of the Virgin Mary. The most important pilgrimage takes place from 18 to 26 August. **Luchon,** overlooking Spain, has excellent ski runs and thermal baths. You must see the **Grotte de Gargas,** near **Saint Bertrand,** whose vault is covered with the prehistoric imprints of mutilated hands, and the **Caves de Mas-d'Azil,** near **Saint Girons,** with fascinating rock-drawings of horses, bison, reindeer, and cats—the *Caverne Merveilleuse* extends for 2½ miles. These caves were used during World War II as aircraft factories.

Côte d'Azur (Riviera): Extending from Toulon to Menton, this is France's international playground. Sophisticated resorts, yacht marinas, picturesque little harbors, long sweeping beaches, and the warm clear Mediterranean invite a throng of visitors.

Marseilles: The second-largest city in France and the country's busiest Mediterranean port, boasts a famous street, **la Canebière;** the **Promenade of the Corniche;** the **Château d'If,** from where the legendary Count of Monte Cristo is supposed to have escaped; the **Museum of Fine Art;** and Le Corbusier's modern **Cité Radieuse.** If you want to stroll in beautiful gardens, go to the **Parc Borely,** which is near the residential quarter surrounding the lovely Avenue du Prado. A visit to the **Saint-Victor Abbey** near the vivid and picturesque Vieux Port is also a must. There are many fine hotels in the city, among them the **Concorde Palm Beach,** Promenade de la Plage (from US$60); **Concorde-Prado,** 11 avenue de Mazargues (from US$50); **Grand Hotel Noailles,** 66 La Canebière (from US$43); **Sofitel Vieux-Port,** 36 boulevard Livon (from US$60); and the **Rome et St Pierre,** 7-11 cours Saint Louis (from US$32). A superb, if expensive, restaurant is the **Calypso** (3 rue Catalems), which specializes in seafood dishes. To the west of Marseilles lie the wild and marshy plains of the **Camargue,** a nature reserve inhabited by pink flamingoes and wild birds, fighting bulls, and herds of small white horses said to have been brought to France by the Saracens. This is the land of the French cowboys in their lonely *mas* or ranches. Tours are organized from **Saintes-Maries-de-la-Mer,** and horseback riding can be arranged. In May and October there are gypsy processions.

To the east of Marseilles lie many attractive resorts, some small and intimate, where you can get away from it all (**Cassis, Bandol, Sanary, Cavalaire, St Raphael,** and others). **St Tropez** is very popular with the young set, with its cafés, boutiques, nightclubs, and discos; drop in at the **Caves du Roy.**

Cannes: Stroll along **Boulevard la Croisette,** or have a *pastis* in a *café terrasse.* Along the **rue d'Antibes** you will find branches of Paris shops; there are two casinos and three golf courses. The beaches are superb, of course, and you must see the harbor, dotted with luxurious yachts. There are over 160 hotels, including **Le Grand** (from US$110), the **Majestic** (from US$105), and the **Carlton** (from US$103), all on the boulevard de la Croisette. Dine on *filet d'agneau* at **La Reine Pédauque** (4 rue Maréchal Joffre) or on *rognons de veau* at **Le Chapon** (26 rue J Jamès). **La Coquille** (65 rue Félix Fauré) is excellent for shellfish, while **Mère Besson** (13 rue Frères-Pradignac) provides the best Provençal food in town. **Juan-les-Pins** (12 miles from Cannes) is popular, loud, and flashy; the sandy beach is magnificent and the nightlife uninhibited. Try the **Hotel du Parc,** avenue Guy de Maupassant (from US$59) or **Belles Rives,** boulevard Baudoin (from US$90). **Antibes** (15 miles from Cannes) is a picturesque resort founded as long ago as the 5th century; try **La Bonne Augberge** there for excellent seafood in a typical Provençal setting; don't miss the Picasso exhibition at the **Grimaldi Museum** on the ramparts of the old city.

Nice is the undisputed Queen of the Riviera, with sumptuous waterside hotels, rich secluded villas, the **Promenade des Anglais,** the **Flower Market,** several fine museums (**Matisse, Beaux Arts Masséna**), the **Palais de la Méditerranée,** the **Opera House,** and the **Théâtre de Verdure,** where there are open-air variety shows in summer. There is also a drive-in movie house. You must try *langouste grillée aux herbes* at **La Poularde Chez Lucullus** (9 rue Deloye), the *soufflé brioche à l'Emmenthal* at St **Moritz** (5 rue Congrès), or the *courgette aux truffes* at **Chantecler** (37 promenade des Anglais). In the evenings, go to the casino at the **Palais de la Méditerranée,** to **Brummel's Discothèque** (in downtown Nice), or **Chez Les Ecossais,** a very pleasant nightclub and cocktail lounge. The start of the **Nice Carnival** is 12 days before Shrove Tuesday. In the hills behind Nice visit the **Maeght Foundation of Modern Art** at Saint-Paul-de-Vence.

Corsica is the Mediterranean island (under 40 minutes by air from Nice) where Napoleon was born in 1769. This "scented isle" is full of rugged grandeur, with an unspoiled harbor and coves far from the noisy crowds of the fashionable Riviera. **Ajaccio,** the main town (hardly more than 50,000 inhabitants), is worth a full day of sightseeing. Pine and chestnut woods, myrtle, sandy beaches, and waters ideal for skin-diving and underwater fishing make Corsica the perfect spot for a vacation. The best and most tranquil period for sightseeing is from April through June.

SOURCES OF FURTHER INFORMATION

Pan Am in Paris, 1 Rue Scribe; and any Pan Am office around the world. **The National Bureau of Tourist Information** in Paris, 127 Champs-Elysées, Paris 8e; **The French Government Tourist Office,** 610 Fifth Avenue, New York, NY 10020; 178 Piccadilly, London W1V 0AL.

Germany

WHAT'S SPECIAL

West Germany has a variety of natural beauty that is scarcely to be matched around the world, ranging from mountains and mountain lakes in the south, forests and fine pastures, and a series of bracing seaside resorts to the north. Extensive industrialization has for the most part been contained without the ugliness associated with it elsewhere, though pollution is becoming a problem. Meanwhile, the nation enjoys some of the best modern communications in the form of railroads, internal air services, and highways. And for the gourmet, there is a range of fare running from freshwater crustacea and seafood to an incredible variety of fresh meat and game, plus the many fine wines of the land.

Perhaps the nicest fact about Germany is that while its people are industrious and hard-working, they also know how to relax and enjoy themselves—and that can range from fine opera and concerts, to the popular floorshows at nightclubs which abound in almost every city, to the friendly conviviality of a local *Bierstube*.

COUNTRY BRIEFING

Size: 95,965 square miles (excluding West Berlin)

Capital: Bonn

Population: 61,600,000

Capital Population: 287,000

Climate: Sunny summers often lasting through October. Winters are generally cold, especially in the Alpine districts. January is the coldest month. Best time to visit is April-September.

Weather in Frankfurt: Lat N50°07'; Alt 338 ft

Temp (°F)	Jan	Feb	Mar	Apr	May	Jun	Jul	Aug	Sep	Oct	Nov	Dec
Av Low	29°	31°	35°	41°	48°	53°	56°	55°	51°	43°	36°	31°
Av High	37°	42°	49°	58°	67°	72°	75°	74°	67°	56°	45°	39°
Days no rain	22	19	22	21	22	21	21	21	21	22	21	20

Government: Federal republic.

Language: German.

Religion: Christian, mainly Lutheran in the north; Roman Catholic in the south.

Currency: Deutsche mark. 100 pfennigs = 1 DM

	5 Pf	10 Pf	50 Pf	1 DM	10 DM	20 DM	100 DM	200 DM
US (dollars, cents)	.02	.04	.22	.44	4.36	8.72	43.59	87.18
UK (pounds, pence)	.01	.02	.10	.21	2.08	4.16	20.79	41.58

Public Holidays:

New Year's Day, 1 Jan
Good Friday
Easter Monday
Labor Day, 1 May
Ascension Day
Whit Monday

Corpus Christi
Day of Unity, 17 Jun
Repentance Day, 22 Nov
Christmas Days, 25 and 26 Dec

HOW TO GET THERE

Flying time to Frankfurt-am-Main Airport from New York is 7½ hours; from London, 1½ hours; from Munich, 50 minutes. There is frequent local service between Hamburg, Stuttgart, Frankfurt, Nuremberg, and Munich. Time in Germany: GMT+1.

REQUIREMENTS FOR ENTRY AND CUSTOMS REGULATIONS

A passport is the only requirement. There are no currency restrictions. Duty-free allowance: 200 cigarettes if arriving from a European country, 300 cigarettes if arriving from a Common Market country, 400 cigarettes if from elsewhere; 1 liter liquor, 1.5 liters liquor if arriving from a Common Market country; 2 liters wine, 3 liters wine if arriving from a Common Market country; 50 grams perfume; gifts worth up to DM100, or DM460 if purchased in a Common Market country.

AIRPORT INFORMATION

Porters for luggage are rarely available at airports, but there are luggage carts that are free of charge except in Munich where the charge is DM1. When there are porters, they charge DM2 for the first bag and DM1 for each additional bag. If you wish, give them a tip of DM1-2. For detailed information about airports, see sectional headings.

ACCOMMODATIONS

Every city and town has a *Verkehrsamt* or *Verkehrsverein* to assist tourists in finding accommodations. Inexpensive accommodations may be found in pensions and guesthouses. A room and breakfast at a simple inn costs from US$20. For luxury try a "Castle Hotel," US$40.

USEFUL INFORMATION

Banks: Hours are 8:30-12:30 and 2-4, with the following exceptions: Thursdays until 6pm; Friday afternoons 1:30-3:30pm. Exchange offices at main railway stations are open daily until late at night. There are also exchange offices at airports and in many post offices.

Mail: Stamps can be bought from post offices, vending machines, and stations. Mailboxes are yellow.

Telephone Tips: There is direct self-dial service within Germany and to many cities in the US and Europe. Public booths at post offices, cafés, and restaurants. Insert two 10-pfennig coins, dial, and speak. Hotel calls are much more expensive and should be avoided, particularly when calling overseas. Useful numbers:

Pan Am:	Tourist Information:
Frankfurt 250591	Frankfurt (0611)231108
Berlin 881011	Bonn (022221)830215
Hamburg 5009281	Munich (089)23911
Munich 558171	Berlin (030)21234
Stuttgart 799001	Hamburg (040)326917
Operator 010	Nürnberg (0911)204256
Directory 118	Düsseldorf (0211)350505
Time 119	Cologne (0221)2213311
Weather 1164	Stuttgart (0711)299411
Emergencies 110	

Newspapers: Many foreign newspapers are available and may almost always be found at the **International Zeitungskiosk.** All airports and main railway stations contain one.

Tipping: Restaurants: service charge of 10% included in checks, and DM1-3 can be left in addition; taxis 5%; porters, DM2 per bag; hotel porters DM1.50; chambermaids, nothing except for exceptional service; cloakroom attendants, 50 pfennigs.

Electricity: 220 volts 50 cycles AC.

Laundry: Quick and efficient, usually takes 2 days, but 24-hour services are available. Major hotels have an express service (laundering a shirt from DM6; dry-cleaning a suit DM25-30).

Hairdressing: Major hotels have salons (cost of a shampoo and set, from DM30; man's haircut from DM20; tip 10%).

Photography: All film and excellent equipment is readily available. Black and white film costs from DM4.95 and takes 24 hours to be developed; color film costs from DM10.95 and takes 2-5 days.

Clubs: Kiwanis, Lions, American Chamber of Commerce in many cities.

Babysitting: Some hotels have services.

Rest Rooms: Public facilities are available costing 30 pfennigs. Women, *Damen;* men, *Herren.*

Health: Many doctors and dentists speak English. Imported pharmaceutical goods and toiletries are available.

TRANSPORTATION

All towns have good bus services. Frankfurt and Munich also have streetcars. There are subways *(U-Bahn)* in Berlin, Frankfurt, Munich, Hamburg, Düsseldorf, Cologne, Bonn, and Hanover, and suburban lines *(S-Bahn)* in Berlin, Hamburg, Munich, and Düsseldorf. Payment is by cash and ticket. Taxis are readily available at designated areas or by phone, and they all have meters. Luggage is charged at 50 pfennigs per bag, and there is an additional light fare. City peak traffic hours are 7-9am and 4-7pm. Long-distance trains, with sleepers and restaurant cars, are excellent, particularly the express and the deluxe Trans Europe trains. The Eurailpass is accepted in Germany. *Netzkarten* (for the whole railroad network) and regional *Bezirkskarten* offer travel within a regional district at discount prices up to one week or one month. The railroad's *Tourenkarten* can be used in connection with another railroad ticket (issued for more than 124 miles only). The *Tourenkarten* allows 10 days' unlimited travel at DM30 for one person, DM40 for two, and DM50 for a family. There is also a good long-distance express bus linking all cities. Roads are excellent, and the extensive freeway network *(Autobahnen)* is well equipped with rest facilities, hotels, restaurants, and garages. Germany's national airline Lufthansa links major cities, and Pan Am's Inter-German service flies between Hamburg, Stuttgart, Frankfurt, Berlin, Nuremberg, and Munich.

FOOD AND RESTAURANTS

Germans are enthusiastic eaters, and the variety of dishes to be found in each part of the country is vast. The northern areas have a wide range of seafoods and poultry. Some of the better known dishes include stuffed turbot *(Gefüllte Steinbuttschnitte)* and turbot dumplings in sorrel sauce *(Steinbuttklösschen in Sauerampfersauce),* Helgoland fish platter *(Fischgericht Helgoländer Art),* pike in raisin sauce *(Hecht in Rosinensauce),* charcoal-grilled Baltic salmon *(Ostseelachs in Silberfolie vom Holzkohlengrill),* Hamburg eel soup—which contrary to popular theory is made with dried fruit, a smoked ham bone, vegetables, herbs, and eel *(Hamburger Aalsuppe),* pickled salmon in puff pastry *(Hausgebeizter Lachs in Blätterteig),* famous Hamburg baked oysters *(Gebackene Austern Hamburger Art),* and tender baked or grilled young poultry *(Hamburger Stubenküken).* Wild duck *Junge Vierländer Mastente* or *Wildente in Wacholderrahm,* where it's served with a juniper berry cream. Then there's *Mastkalbsteak*—literally, fatted calf steak—the northern answer to the southern (also Austrian, Swiss, and Liechtenstein) *Tafelspitz*—rump steak. Mention must be made of *Labskaus*—a fisherfolk dish of meat, potatoes, beet, and herring, with finely chopped onion, served with sour pickle and a fried egg on top. And then there's *Rote Grütze mit Sahne,* a mouth-watering dessert of red fruit, topped off with whipped cream.

The great plain of Westphalia, along which runs the ridge of the Teutoburg Forest, produces much fine livestock and the incredibly delicious Westphalian ham—Germany's answer to Italian prosciutto. There's plenty of venison in season, for Germany has a number of species of deer and so *Wildgerichte* (venison dishes) are plentiful. Partridge, pheasant, guinea fowl, blackcock, grouse, and quail plus wild mushrooms provide the basis of many a dish. Further south, the Black Forest adds its own particular cured hams, plus delicious pastries and the fabled Black Forest trout, often smoked *(Geräucherte Schwarzwälder Forelle)*. Bavaria adds its own gastronomic touch with *Gefülltes Lendchen badisch*—stuffed loin of pork, or the delectable crayfish—*Krebse in Weissbier,* and spit-roasted leg of lamb with an anchovy butter *(Lammkeule am Spiess in Sardellenbutter)*, plus *Kalbsfilet in Morchelrahm* (fillet of veal served with a morel sauce).

Then there are the dishes for which Germany is known internationally, including the ubiquitous hamburger—known locally as *Deutsches Beefsteak* and often made with a mix of beef with pork, beef with veal, or equal parts of all three; the dozens of different types of sausage ranging from salami type *(Wurst)* to the famous frankfurters (including *Bockwurst, Bratwurst, Bauernwurst*); the various smoked meats of the Black Forest *(Schwarzwälder Rauchfleisch);* hot liver pâté *(Leberkäse); Sauerbraten* (marinated pot roast, cooked in various styles); *Eisbein* (pigs' hocks, served—in Berlin especially—with split peas and sauerkraut); *Kasseler Rippchen* (smoked loin of pork); *Lachsschinken* (smoked round of ham, resembling smoked salmon from which it takes its name); *Spätzle* (noodles also of Switzerland and Austria); *Schwäbische Maultaschen* (known elsewhere in Germany as *Krapfen*—meat-filled pockets of dough); *Rollmops* (marinated pickled salt herring); *Kohlrabi* and *Blaukraut*—as red cabbage is properly called when cooked to a deep purple hue. Then there are numerous pastries, cakes, and tarts, not least of which are *Apfelstrudel* and *Schwarzwälder Kirschtorte*—Black Forest Cherry Torte, plus numerous nourishing breads including the chewy *bauernbrot* (farmers' bread). The best cheese comes from Mainz, Munster, Lüneburg, and the Harz mountains. Around Würzburg, bakers' shops sell small fried fish with bread and wine. Breakfast is eaten from 7-10; lunch 12-3; and dinner from 6-10. Dinner for one without wine in an expensive restaurant costs from US$50, in a moderate one US$25, and in an inexpensive one US$6-10. Contact the tourist office in any city or town for a list of restaurants and their prices.

DRINKING TIPS

Imported liquor is available, but with the exception of whisky (average price US$5-7 per glass) the local brews are hard to beat. Germany's many fine wines include the famous Rhine and Moselle, and there are excellent beers (light and dark) ranging from Spaten (Munich), Beck's (Bremen), several Ruhr beers (including Dortmunder Union), Hamburg, and Berlin. In Berlin *Weisse mit Schuss* is a light beer with raspberry syrup. Liquor can be cherry- *(Kirsch),* raspberry-*(Himbeer),* or juniper-based *(Steinhäger). Schnapps* is a potent liquor. The minimum drinking age is 18, but otherwise there are no restrictions. Beer is popularly drunk in beer-cellars or beer restaurants *(Bierstuben)*, and local wines taste their best in wine-restaurants, inns, and taverns. Town halls generally have *Ratskeller* (town hall cellars) where councilmen in the Middle Ages did their eating and drinking. These cellars serve special brews and good food, and remain old fashioned or even medieval in decor today.

ENTERTAINMENT

Germans are among the most actively culture-conscious people in the world, and even small towns have their own repertory theaters and orchestras. All major cities have permanent opera companies, most with ballet companies attached. Among the most important musical events are the **Wagner Festival** at Bayreuth in July and August, and the **Wiesbaden International Festival** in May. June brings the **Mozart Festival** at Würzburg and the beginning of the **Augsburg** season of open-air opera and operetta, which runs through July. For a month from early July there is the **Munich Opera Festival.**

SHOPPING

Best buys are cameras (Zeiss, Leica, Rollei); binoculars; Dresden, Meissen, and Rosenthal porcelain; cuckoo clocks, wood carvings, and handmade crystal from Bavaria; silver and steelware, toys, dolls, and antiques. An inexpensive gift is a beer *Stein,* made of pewter or clay. Shopping hours are 8 or 8:30-6:30 Mon-Fri, until 2pm on Sat, except until 6pm the first Saturday of every month. Some shops close for lunch. Major stores pack and ship, and foreign visitors will not be charged the 13% VAT (value-added-tax) on goods sent directly out of the country.

SPORTS

Soccer is the most popular spectator sport, but others include field hockey, ice hockey, cycling, polo, boxing, and wrestling. **Derby Week** in Hamburg is the major horse-racing event (June), and in July there is a **Horse-racing Week** at Bad Harzburg. The motor-racing **Grand Prix** is in July. **Kiel Week** (June) attracts yachting enthusiasts. With more than 300 winter resorts in the **German Alps,** the **Harz Mountains,** the **Black Forest,** and the **Bavarian Forest,** winter sports are popular.

FRANKFURT

AIRPORT INFORMATION

The Frankfurt-am-Main Airport (tel: 6901), which has a duty-free shop and children's nursery, is 8 miles away from the city terminal and reached by taxi (about DM25-30) or a fast train service operating about every 20 minutes (DM3).

ACCOMMODATIONS

Hotels in Frankfurt:
Rates are in US$ for a double/twin room with bath or shower
    Arabella-Hotel, Lyoner Strasse 44-48 (from $78), 3 miles southwest
      of center of town

CP Frankfurt Plaza, Hamburger Allee 2 (from $99)
Excelsior, Mannheimer Strasse 7-9 (from $43)
FRANKFURT INTER · CONTINENTAL, Wilhelm-Leuschner Strasse
43 (from $110)
Frankfurt Savoy, Wiesenhuttenstrasse 42 (from $80)
Hessischer Hof, Friedrich-Ebert-Anlage 40 (from $108)
Parkhotel, Wiesenhüttenplatz 26-36 (from $106)
Sheraton, Flughafen (from $98), at airport
Steigenberger Airport, Flughafenstrasse (from $94), at airport
Steigenberger Hotel Frankfurter Hof, Kaiserplatz 17 (from $95)
All hotels listed above located in central Frankfurt unless otherwise indicated.

EATING AND ENTERTAINMENT
Best restaurants are to be found at the Steigenberger Hotel Frankfurter
Hof and Parkhotel, also the **Dell'Arte, Brasserie,** and **Silhouette Supper
Club,** all in the Inter · Continental Hotel (tel: 230561); the **Grill Room**
(tel: 26970) of the Parkhotel; the old **Weinhaus Brückenkeller** (Schützenstrasse 6—tel: 284238); **da Bruno** (Elbestrasse 15—tel: 233416, Italian
cuisine); the **Schloss Hotel Kronberg** (Kronberg/Taunus, Hain Strasse
25—tel: 06173/7011); **Alter Haferkasten** (Neu-Isenburg, Löwengasse 23—
tel: 06102/36059); **Heyland Weinstuben** (Kaiserhofstrasse 7—tel: 284840);
also good, just a little way out of town, is the **Jahrhunderthalle** (tel:
300166), Frankfurt-Höchst, the **Plaza Exquisit** in the Main-Taunus shopping center (tel: 06196-300001), the **Waldrestaurant Unterscheinstiege**
(tel: 69851) toward the airport, and in Sachsenhausen the **Henninger
Turm** and **Zum Grauen Bock** (Grosse Rittergasse 30—tel: 618026). A
favorite drink in Frankfurt is *Apfelwein* (apple cider—*ebbelwoi* in the
local dialect), which can be sampled at taverns in the Alt-Sachsenhausen
district.

Good bars include the **Prolog Bar** at the Inter · Continental Hotel;
Frankfurter Stubb and **Lipizzaner Bar** (with dancing) at the Frankfurter
Hof; **Jimmy's Bar** at the Hotel Hessischer Hof. For dancing, try the rooftop
of the Inter · Continental and the **Tourbillon** at the Frankfurt Savoy.
Nightclubs include the **Imperial** (Moselstrasse 46) and, for Jazz, the **Jazz-
Haus** and the **Jazzkeller,** both on Kleine Bockenheimer Strasse and **Sink-
kasten** (Brönnerstrasse 5—tel: 280385). For typical Bavarian atmosphere
try the **Maier Gustl's Bayrisch** (Münchener Strasse 57). The weekly *Frankfurter Wochenschau* gives current theater, sports, and tourist news (in
English).

WHAT TO SEE
Frankfurt is equally proud of its international trade fairs and of Goethe,
whose birthplace is now a museum (Grosser Hirschgraben 23). The high-
lights of the old part of town are the steeply gabled gothic buildings
on Römerberg Square, including the **Town Hall** with the Emperor's
Coronation Hall, the **Cathedral** with its tall 15th-century bell tower, **St
Leonhard's** and **St Nicholas'** churches, and the **Carmelite Monastery,**

which houses a museum. **Frankfurt Zoo** is one of the world's greatest: afternoon concerts and plays are presented here.

Wiesbaden, an international spa in beautiful natural surroundings, has an active social life and lively casino. The major event is the **May festival,** when first-rate opera, ballet, and drama are performed. The baroque castle of the Dukes of Nassau stands on the shores of the Rhine. On the opposite bank of the Rhine is 2,000-year-old **Mainz,** the largest wine market in Germany. **Wine Festival,** last weekend in August to first weekend in September. Johann Gutenberg, the inventor of movable type, was born here, and the **Museum of Printing** contains his 42-line Bible. The **Mardi Gras** carnival is nationally famous.

Heidelberg, 50 miles south of Frankfurt, is a romantic university town at the head of the Neckar Valley. The old quarter is clustered around a Gothic church. The famous castle (reached by cable railway) and old bridge are illuminated in summer. In the town museum, partly housed in a baroque palace, is the *Twelve Apostles* altar piece by the 16th-century wood-carver Riemenschneider. **Mannheim,** farther west along the Neckar River, is the second-largest inland port in Europe. The 17th-century town center is laid out like a chessboard: the streets are numbered and the blocks are lettered. The **Elector's Palace** is a large baroque building with a lovely library. The **Fine Arts Museum** has a good collection of 19th- and 20th-century European paintings. The first bicycle and the first automobile (Benz) were built in Mannheim. **Karlsruhe,** about 40 miles south, is an elegant city with a **Ducal Palace** and an excellent collection of German primitive paintings in its **Art Museum.** About 80 miles east of Frankfurt lies **Würzburg.** The baroque **Residenz** has a splendidly decorated Great Hall. In the **Imperial Fortress** *(Marienberg Festung)* is a superb collection of the religious wood-carvings of Riemenschneider.

MUNICH

AIRPORT INFORMATION
Riem Airport (tel: 92110), with a duty-free shop and children's nursery, is 6 miles out of town. Airport buses, every 20 minutes to train station, charge DM4. Taxis charge from DM20, depending on destination. There is a charge of DM1 for baggage carts.

ACCOMMODATIONS
Hotels in Munich are:
Rates are in US$ for a double/twin room with bath or shower
    Ambassador, Mozartstrasse 4 (from $65)
    Bayerischer Hof, Promenadenplatz 2-6 (from $82)
    Bundesbahnhotel, Bahnhofplatz 2 (from $38)
    Der Königshof, Karlsplatz 25 (from $74)
    Deutscher Kaiser, Arnulfstrasse 2 (from $78)
    Drei Löwen, Schillerstrasse 8 (from $55)
    Eden Hotel Wolff, Arnulfstrasse 4-8 (from $69)

Excelsior, Schützenstrasse 11 (from $69)
Grand Hotel Continental, Max-Joseph-Strasse 5 (from $69)
Hilton International, Am Tucherpark 7 (from $91)
Holiday Inn-Olympic, Schleissheimerstrasse 188-192 (from $77), near
    Olympic area
Metropol, Bayerstrasse 43 (from $46)
Munich Penta, Hochstrasse 3 (from $74)
Olympiapark, Helene-Mayer-Ring 12 (from $57)
Preysing, Preysingstrasse 1 (from $63)
Reinbold, Adolf-Kopling-Strasse 11 (from $51)
Residence, Artur Kutscher Platz 4 (from $71)
Sheraton, Arabellastrasse 6 (from $87)
VIER JAHRESZEITEN Maximilianstrasse 17 (from $104)
All hotels listed above in central Munich unless otherwise indicated.

EATING AND ENTERTAINMENT

The **Walterspiel** restaurant in the Vier Jahreszeiten Hotel is probably the best known in the area, though Der Königshof Hotel restaurant is also excellent. The **Aubergine** (2 Maximilianplatz 5—tel: 598171) has become the first German restaurant to receive the fabled Michelin 3-star rating. Of French restaurants, possibly **Tantris** (Johann-Fichte-Strasse 7—tel: 362061) is best known, while for fish the **Boettner** (Theatinerstrasse 8—tel: 221210) is popular. The **König** in Promenadeplatz is noted for its nouvelle cuisine. Other notable restaurants include **Maximilianstuben** (Maximilianstrasse 27—tel: 229044) and **Käfer-Schänke** (Schumannstrasse 1—tel: 476011). Other good restaurants include the **Schwarzwälders Weinhaus** (Hartmannstrasse 8—tel: 227216); for Italian food **El Toula** (Sparkassenstrasse 5—tel: 292869), **Il Tartufo** (Prinzregenten Platz 11); and **St Hubertus Stuben** (Grünwalderstrasse 9—tel: 6516623), specializing in game. Less expensive are two by the cathedral: **Nürnberger Bratwurstglöckl** (Am Frauenplatz 9—tel: 220385) and **Schwäbinger Weinschatulle** (Theresienstrasse 72—tel: 287160). Do not miss eating at **Dallmayr's** (Dienerstrasse 14), the world-famous delicatessen. Wine taverns with reasonably priced food include **Pfälzer Weinprobierstube**, in the Residenz (entrance Residenzstrasse 1—tel: 225628), and the 16th-century **Weinstadl** (Burgstrasse 5). Many restaurants have Bavarian music in the evening, and lusty singing is the traditional accompaniment to drinking in the large cellar-like beerhalls, the most famous of which are the **Augustiner Keller** (Arnulfstrasse 52—tel: 594393) with a huge beer garden, and **Hofbrauhaus** (Platzl), with a restaurant, dancehall, and summer garden. Well-known bands perform at the nightclub at the Bayerischer Hof Hotel, and the **Yellow Submarine** at the Holiday Inn features live sharks. Yodeling and *Schuhplattler* dancing are attractions at **Platzl Restaurant**. The **Boccaccio** (Briennerstrasse) is a popular nightclub. Munich has a **State Opera House**, several concert halls, and 22 theaters. The **Marionettentheater** and **Puppentheater** have puppet shows. The **Cuvilliés Theater** stages ballet, concerts, and plays. The **Oktoberfest Fair** begins in September with a big parade. **Fasching,** the annual pre-Lenten Bavarian Carnival, starts with the New Year and lasts until Lent.

WHAT TO SEE

Marienplatz is the heart of town, and the nearby **Neuhauserstrasse, Theatinerstrasse,** and **Sonnenstrasse** are the main shopping areas. Antique shops are centered around **Ottostrasse,** by Maximilianplatz. The most famous of Munich's many museums and art galleries is the **Alte Pinakothek,** with an outstanding collection of European paintings. Other museums include the **German Museum, National Museum of Bavaria,** the **City Museum** with puppets and musical instruments, and the **German Brewery Museum.** The **Residenz** has fine displays of porcelain and a remarkable chapel treasury. **Leopoldstrasse,** lined with terraced cafés, leads into **Schwabing,** the students' and artists' quarter, where it becomes an open-air market. The best buildings in the city are the **Rathaus** in Marienplatz, where the Glockenspiel figures perform daily at 11am, and the gothic **Frauenkirche,** a block away, with two onion-shaped domes. The **Hofbräuhaus,** which is about 100 years old, is the latest in a succession of brewery taverns that goes back to 1589. **Nymphenburg,** the baroque summer palace of Bavarian kings, is a streetcar ride from the city center. Its splendid apartments are open to the public, and concerts are given here in summer. Among the lakes and streams of the magnificent park are set small castles and pavilions, and the small 200-year-old **Nymphenburg Porcelain** factory is here. Just out of town is **Hellabrunn Zoo,** the largest in Europe, and to the north is **Schleissheim Castle,** with regal rooms and galleries and a large selection of paintings.

The **German Alps** extend some 150 miles from **Lake Constance** in the west to **Berchtesgaden** near the southeast border with Austria. Skiing begins at **Garmisch-Partenkirchen** in November with the ice-hockey season, and **International Winter Sports Week** is held in early January. The **Posthotel Partenkirchen** (from US$48) was founded in 1542 and is a good example of a South Bavarian hotel. Also pleasant are the **Partenkirchen Hof** (from US$39) and its excellent **Reindl Grill Room** and **Hotel Alpina** (from US$60). Communications are excellent despite the high mountains—**Zugspitze** near Garmisch is nearly 10,000 feet, with cogwheel-railway and cableway services and good mountain roads. The German Alps have many health and thermal spas, such as **Oberstdorf, Bad Tölz** (a picturesque old Bavarian town), **Bad Wiessee, Tegernsee, Schliersee, Ruhpolding,** and **Berchtesgaden** near the beautiful **Königssee,** and are also the realm of fairytale castles and palaces built by King Ludwig II—**Linderhof, Herrenchiemsee,** and **Neuschwanstein.** Masterpieces of baroque building are the Bavarian churches of **Schliersee, Ottobeuren, Wieskirchen,** and **Ettal. Oberammergau,** with its painted houses and woodcarving workshops, is most famous for its **Passion Play,** first performed in 1634 as thanks for having been spared the plague and performed at 10-year intervals (except in time of war) ever since.

Nuremberg, 125 miles north of Munich, is a fine medieval city retaining its double fortifications (with 125 towers) and ancient castle. Hans Sachs and the Meistersinger lived in Nuremberg, and in 1526 the first science university in Germany was founded here. Albrecht Dürer's 15th-century gabled house is now a museum. **St Sebald's Church** is rich in 14th- and 15th-century art, and **St Lawrence's** has a lovely *Annunciation* by Veit Stoss. The **National Museum** has superb collections of fine arts and crafts, including works by Dürer. One local culinary specialty here is *Lebkuchen*, gingerbread. Good restaurants include **Goldenes Posthorn** (established 1498); **Nassauer Keller**, in the 13th-century cellar of Nassau House (art collection); and **Bohm's Herrenkeller** (Theatergasse 19), with medieval decor. Sausage-houses are **Bratwurst-Herzle** (Brunnengasse 1) and **Bratwurst Häusle** (Rathausplatz 1). One of the best places to sample local fare is at **Zum Waffenschmied** (Obere Schmiedgasse 22—tel: 225859). Beer restaurants: **Fischküche Luftsprung** (founded 1516—Unterer Bergauerplatz 10) and **Mautkeller** (Königsstrasse 60).

Places of interest around Nuremberg included **Bamberg** with a beautiful cathedral, medieval **Altdorf Heilbronn** with a gothic Minster (lovely stained glass), rococo **Ansbach** with its Margrave's Palace, **Coburg** with a large fortress, **Regensburg** (Ratisbon) on the Danube with its cathedral, and the forested **Fichtel** mountains. At **Bayreuth** the annual **Wagner Festival** is held in July and August, in a theater designed by the composer himself.

BERLIN

AIRPORT INFORMATION
Tegel Airport (tel: 41011) is served by city buses for DM1.50. Taxis charge from DM12 depending on destination in the city. Tegel has a duty-free shop and nursery. Departure tax is DM5 (only for international flights).

ACCOMMODATIONS
Hotels in Berlin:
Rates are in US$ for a double/twin room with bath or shower
  Am Zoo, Kurfürstendamm 25 (from $74)
  Arosa, Lietzenburger Strasse 79 (from $63)
  Berlin, Kurfürstenstrasse 27 (from $61)
  Berlin Ambassador, Bayreuther Strasse 42-43 (from $69)
  Bristol, Kurfürstendamm 27 (from $97)
  Europäischer Hof, Messedamm 10 (from $56)
  Excelsior, Hardenbergstrasse 14 (from $68)
  Hamburg, Landgrafenstrasse 4 (from $57)
  INTER · CONTINENTAL BERLIN, Budapesterstrasse 2 (from $80)
  Palace, Europa Center (from $66)
  Parkhotel Zellermayer, Meinekestrasse 15 (from $71)
  Plaza, Knesebeckstrasse 63 (from $50)
  Savoy, Fasanenstrasse 9-10 (from $56)
  Schweizerhof, Budapester Strasse 21-31 (from $74)
  Seehof, Lietzensee Ufer 11 (from $67)

Sylter Hof, Kurfürstenstrasse 114-116 (from $56)
All hotels listed above are in central West Berlin.

TRANSPORTATION

Ticket cards are available for five one-way or four transfer rides on bus or subway. A BVG tourist card permits 4 days unlimited travel on public tranport in West Berlin, except the surface train *(S-Bahn),* and costs DM17.

EATING AND ENTERTAINMENT

Local food specialties are *Bockwurst,* a thick frankfurter sold at street stalls; *Aal grün mit Gurkensalat,* boiled eel with dill sauce and cucumber salad; *Kartoffelpuffer,* fried potato pancake, and *Königsberger Klops,* meatballs, herring, and capers. Restaurants are located mainly around Kurfürstendamm and side streets; good hotel restaurants are the Berlin, Palace, and Bristol. The **Funkturm** (Messedamm 11) in the radio tower at the fair gardens and **I-Punkt Berlin** on the 20th floor of the Europa-Center have marvelous views. The first-class **Ritz** (Rankestrasse 26) serves local Berlin specialties and international dishes, **Anselmo** (Damaschke-strasse 17) has Italian food, and the **Conti-Fischstuben** (Sybelstrasse 14) specializes in seafood. Excellent French cuisine can be found at the **Maitre** (Meinekestrasse 10), and **Chapeau Claque** (Damaschkestrasse 21) is also good. The restaurant in the **Jüdisches Gemeindehaus** (Fasanenstrasse 79/80) has kosher food. Other good restaurants include the **Tessiner Stuben** (Bleibtreustrasse 33), **Logenhaus** (Emserstrasse 12), **Altberliner Schneckenhaus** (Kurfürstendamm 37), and the **Alexander** (Kurfürstendamm 46). The **Altberliner Biersalon** (Kurfürstendamm 225) has rustic charm. Berlin, with its famous **Philharmonic Orchestra,** is an excellent music center, with three main concert halls and two opera houses. The **Schiller Theater** presents classical drama, and there are a number of smaller theaters. Popular nightclubs are the two **Edens** (New and Big Eden) on Kurfürstendamm and Damaschkestrasse; **Coupé 77** (Kurfürstendamm 177), a lively disco; **Kesse** (Ernst-Reuter-Platz) and **Palais Madame** (Nürnberger Strasse), where ladies ask gentlemen to dance; and the **Rheinische Winzerstuben** (Hardenbergstrasse 29a), with a Rhine panorama show. The **Berlin Festival** begins in September and in January there is the **Press Ball.** The **Berlin Film Festival** is held June-July and **Berliner Jazz Days** in November.

WHAT TO SEE

West Berlin is notable for its greenery (only one-third of its area is built up; one-fifth of the remainder is devoted to agriculture and there are more than 100 farms in and around the villages of Gatow, Lubars, and Mariendorf), while East Berlin is known for its old historic center and museums. **Kurfürstendamm** (Ku'damm), with its Kaiser Wilhelm memorial church, is the main thoroughfare of **West Berlin,** lined with luxury hotels, shops, cafés, and cinemas. Near the church are the **Zoo** and **Tiergarten,** a great park extending as far as the Berlin Wall. Of the few surviving old buildings, the most notable are **Charlottenburg Castle,** the 18th-century **Brandenburg Gate** (just inside the Eastern sector), the reconstructed **Reichstag,** and the **Rathaus Schöneberg,** seat of the Senate, where the Liberty Bell is rung at noon. Important museums include the **Egyptian Museum,** with the famous bust of Nefertiti; **Museum Dahlem,** with 13th- to 16th-century paintings including famous Rembrandts and Vermeers; the **Berlin Museum,** where the collection depicts the development of the city; and the **New National Gallery** designed by Mies van der Rohe. The **Olympic Stadium,** constructed for the 1936 games, holds 100,000 people. In the western suburbs are the forest and lake areas of the **Grunewald,** one of the largest of the Berlin forests where the 16th-century Prince Electors used to hunt. Deer and wild boar still roam freely. The scenic **Havelchaussee** runs to the south along the **Wannsee,** and the Wannsee beach is very popular during the summer. Sightseeing tours of West and East Berlin and along the sector border are organized by Severin und Kühn (Berlin 15, Kurfürstendamm 215-216) and Berolina (Berlin 15, Kurfürstendamm 25). Excursion parties go to **Potsdam** in the German Democratic Republic to visit Frederick the Great's **Palace of Sans Souci,** with its great art treasures, and to the ancient **Cecilienhof Palace,** once the residence of the Crown Prince, where the Four-Power Agreement was signed in 1945.

DÜSSELDORF

AIRPORT INFORMATION

Düsseldorf-Lohausen Airport (tel: 4211) is 5 miles from Friedrich-Ebert-Strasse and is served by the S-Bahn train (DM1.50). A taxi costs about DM15.

ACCOMMODATIONS

Hotels in Düsseldorf:

Rates are in US$ for a double/twin room with bath or shower
  Breidenbacher Hof, Heinrich-Heine-Allee 34 (from $117)
  Düsseldorf Hilton, George-Glock-Strasse 20 (from $108), near airport
  Eden, Adersstrasse 29-31 (from $71)
  Esplanade, Fürstenplatz 17 (from $65)
  Excelsior, Kapellstrasse 1 (from $69)
  INTER · CONTINENTAL DÜSSELDORF, Karl-Arnold-Platz 5 (from $93), near fair ground
  Parkhotel Steigenberger, Corneliusplatz 1 (from $93)
  Stuttgarter Hof, Bismarckstrasse 39 (from $48)
  Uebachs, Leopoldstrasse 5 (from $78)
All hotels listed above are in central Düsseldorf unless otherwise indicated.

EATING AND ENTERTAINMENT

In addition to the first-rate restaurants in the Breidenbacher Hof and Parkhotel, other restaurants are excellent, though expensive: **Orangerie**

(Bilkerstrasse 30—tel: 373733); **Frickhöfer** (Stromstrasse 47—tel: 393931); **Bateau Ivre** (Kurze Strasse 11—tel: 328688), with French cuisine; **Müllers und Fest** (Königsallee 14—tel: 326001), renowned for their steamed turbot with fennel; **KD (Müllers und Fest)**—(Königsallee 12—tel: 326001); **Naschkörbchen** (Wilhelm-Marx-Haus—tel: 327301), **Victorian** (Königstrasse 3—tel: 372361); **Rheinterrasse** (Hofgartenufer 7—tel: 446951); and **Le Petit Four** (Achenbachstrasse 132—tel: 661204). Less expensive are the **Grand'Italia** (Huttenstrasse 30—tel: 376097) and the **Balkin-Grill** (Hunsrückenstrasse 42—tel: 80983). Popular regional dishes can be sampled in the beer taverns of the old town, the best of which are **Zum Schlüssel** (Bolkerstrasse 45); **Zum Schiffchen** (Hafenstrasse 5); and **Zum Uerige** (Bergerstrasse). There is dinner-dancing at the Breidenbacher Hof and Parkhotel and night-spots include: **Pferdestall** and the bohemian **Fatty's Atelier** (Hunsrückenstrasse 13).

WHAT TO SEE

A fashion-conscious city, Düsseldorf's most elegant shops are on the **Königsallee (KO)**, the **Berliner Allee**, and **Schadowstrasse**. In the **Old Town** *(Altstadt)* overlooking the Rhine are the tower, the solitary survival from the 13th-century castle, and the twisted belfry of the gothic **St Lambert's Church**. The poet Heine's birthplace is Bolkerstrasse 53, and the picturesque **Schneider-Wibbel-Gasse** has a Glockenspiel which performs at 11, 3, 6, and 9pm. The city is dotted with small lakes, and the most attractive garden is the **Hofgarten**, where the **Goethe Museum** has a collection of the writer's manuscripts and first editions. **Jägerhof Castle**, a former hunting lodge, has superb collections of Meissen porcelain and 20th-century paintings (Klee, Picasso, Chagall, Ernst). The **Fine Arts Museum** displays sculpture and German Expressionist paintings, and the adjoining **Hetjens Museum** covers 7,000 years of world ceramic art. **Benrath Castle**, 6 miles outside town, is a beautiful rococo building in a fine park.

COLOGNE (KÖLN)

There is a bus (DM5 one way, DM7 round trip) from Köln-Wahn Airport which takes you to the center of town. A taxi costs DM30. This is the capital of the Rhineland, 30 miles south of Düsseldorf. It is noted for remnants of antiquity such as a 3rd-century tower, the ruins of a palace (beneath the new town hall), the Dionysus mosaic floor, a mausoleum (in suburban Weiden), a gate, and a precious collection of glass housed in the **Roman Museum**. Eau de Cologne was first made here in the 18th century. The city is also renowned for its "Beautiful Madonnas," medieval sculptures in the gothic **Cathedral**, with its 14th-century stained-glass windows, in **St Mary of the Lily Church**, and in the **Schnütgen Museum**. Medieval German painting can be seen in the **Wallraf-Richartz Museum**. Even older than the Cathedral are Cologne's Romanesque churches, including **St Severinus**, with a 4th-century shrine, and **St Pantaleon**, with a fine roodscreen. The **Gürzenich**, a 15th-century gothic dance-hall, still performs the same function. The **Hohe Strasse** and **Schildergasse** are pedestrian shopping districts, and the **Ring** is an elegant boulevard of shops, cafés, cinemas, and nightclubs. An attractive view of the spires and belfries fronting the Rhine is seen from the **Severinus Bridge,** and there is a good view over the old town from the **Rhine Park** (concerts and dancing). In Cologne stay at the **INTER · CONTINENTAL COLOGNE,** Helenenstrasse 14 (from US$102 double); the **Ambassador,** Barbarossaplatz 4a (from US$71); the **Dom Hotel,** Dom Kloster 2a (from US$113); the **Excelsior Hotel Ernst,** Domplatz (from US$117); or **Hotel Consul,** Belfortstrasse 9 (from US$59). Excellent restaurants are **Die Bastei** (Konrad Aden auer Ufer 80—tel: 122825), on the river; **Chez Alex** (Mühlengasse 1—tel: 230560); **Poêle d'Or** (Komödienstrasse 52—tel: 134100); **Weinhaus in Walfisch** (Salzgasse 13—tel: 219575); **Zum Roten Ochsen** (Thurnmarkt 7—tel: 237573); and the **Hanse-Stube** in the Excelsior Hotel; and the **Schultheiss am Ring** (Theodor-Heuss-Ring 23). Regionally typical and less expensive are the **Mohr-Baedorf; Früh am Dom;** and **Brauhaus Sion.** There are wine restaurants in the **Alter Markt** and **Heumarkt** areas.

Aachen (Aix-la-Chapelle), less than 50 miles from Cologne, is a noted spa. The hot springs were popular in pre-Roman times. Charlemagne made Aachen an imperial city, and 30 princes were crowned in the cathedral, which still houses his marble throne. Do not miss the superb treasury. Hotels in Aachen are: **Parkhotel Quellenhof** (Monheimsallee 52), double rooms from US$78, and the **Kurhotel Schwertbad** (Burtscheider Markt), double rooms from US$43. South of Aachen are **Monschau,** a well-preserved town of half-timbered, steep-roofed houses, and **Trier** (also known as **Treves**), former capital of the Roman Empire in the west, with its famous **Porta Nigra.** The Rhine flows down from the Swiss Alps into a great plain and then beyond **Mainz** twists between high, vine-covered hills. Along its 820 miles, every islet, rock, and castle has a romantic legend attached to it, the most famous being those of the *Lorelei* and the *Nibelungen.* There are daily river cruises (3-10 hours) between **Bingen** and **Rüdesheim** to **Koblenz,** and longer cruises down the Rhine to Basle, lasting up to 5 days.

BONN

There is a bus (DM5 one way, DM7 round trip) from Köln-Wahn Airport which takes you to Bonn. A taxi costs DM45. Gateway to the Rhine Valley, Bonn was until 1949 a quiet university city. It is rapidly adjusting to its new role as capital of Federal Germany. Parliament and the Federal Council meet in the **Bundeshaus,** overlooking the Rhine. The suburb of **Bad Godesberg,** an 18th-century spa, is the government and diplomatic quarter. Beethoven was born in Bonn in 1730. His birthplace at **Bonngasse 20** is now a museum, and an annual **Beethoven Festival** is held in modern **Beethovenhalle.** The university occupies the baroque **Elector's Palace,** which is linked by the tree-lined Poppelsdorfer Allee to **Poppelsdorf Castle.** The **Collegiate Church** has 12th-century towers and beautiful cloisters of the same period. Beneath the towering **Alter Zoll** bastion is an attractive promenade along the Rhine to the Bundeshaus. Good restaurants are **Wirtshaus St Michael** (Brunnenallee 26—tel: 364765), and **Weinhaus Maternus** (Bad Godesberg, Post-strasse 3), **Ambassador** at the Steigenberger, and the restaurants at the Bris in Bonn proper. The restaurants at the Steigenberger, Bristol, and Schlosspark are popular. Across the Rhine are the **Siebengebirge** (Seven Mountains), the most famous of which is **Drachenfels**, where Siegfried supposedly killed the dragon. Hotels in Bonn are:

Rates are in US$ for a double/twin room with bath or shower

    Am Tulpenfeld, Heussallee 2-10 (from $69)

    Bristol, Poppelsdorfer Allee (from $91)

    Godesburg Hotel, Auf dem Godesberg 5 (from $56), in Bad Godesberg

    Königshof, Adenauerallee 9-11 (from $56)

    Rheinhotel Dreesen, Rheinaustrasse 1-3 (from $62), in Bad Godesberg

    Schlosspark-Hotel, Venusbergweg 27-31 (from $50)

    Steigenberger, Am Bundeskanzlerplatz (from $100)

    Zum Adler, Koblenzerstrasse 60 (from $50), in Bad Godesberg

All hotels listed above are in central Bonn unless otherwise indicated.

STUTTGART

Although this is an industrial center (Mercedes cars, printing, and publishing houses), wine grapes are harvested within 300 yards of Stuttgart's main station.

AIRPORT INFORMATION

Stuttgart Airport (Pan Am tel: 7901341) has a duty-free shop open daily and is 9 miles from the city. Bus fare is DM3.50, taxi about DM25 depending on destination in the city.

ACCOMMODATIONS

Hotels in Stuttgart:

Rates are in US$ for a double/twin room with bath or shower

    Am Schlossgarten, Schillerstrasse 23 (from $77)

    Parkhotel, Villastrasse 21 (from $74)

    Royal, Sophienstrasse 35 (from $84)

    Steigenberger Hotel Graf Zeppelin, Arnulf-Klett-Platz 7 (from $87)

    Stuttgart International, Plieninger Strasse 100 (from $80), near airport

All hotels listed above are in central Stuttgart unless otherwise indicated.

EATING AND ENTERTAINMENT

For gourmet cuisine, try **Alte Post** (Friedrichstrasse 43); **Scheffelstuben** (Hausmannstrasse 5); **Alte Kanzlei** (Schillerplatz 5A); the **Mövenpick-Rotisserie Baron de la Mouette** (Kleiner Schlossplatz 11); the **Walliser Stuben** (Langestrasse 35); **Breuninger Exquisit** (Karlstrasse); **Lotos**—for Chinese fare (Königstrasse 17); and the **Höhenrestaurant Schönblick** (Hölzelweg 2). Swabian specialties at the **Zeppelin Stüble** in the Hotel Graf Zeppelin are excellent. Opera and ballet companies in Stuttgart have international reputations.

WHAT TO SEE

Located among hills near the Black Forest, Stuttgart is the gateway to an atttactive countryside dotted with spas and recreational areas. In the Old Town square, the **Schillerplatz,** are the **Altes Schloss** (old castle), housing an interesting local museum, and the gothic **Collegiate Church.** The Schillerplatz, also flanked by a former princely residence and **Royal Chancellery,** is used as a vegetable and flower market Tuesdays, Thursdays, and Saturdays. In the Schlossgarten park are the baroque **Neues Schloss** (new castle), the modern **State Parliament House,** a theater, and an opera house. Stuttgart has a tradition of avant-garde architectural design, and the **Liederhalle,** a concert-hall complex, is one of its best. Daimler-Benz, the oldest automobile factory in the world, is in the **Untertürkheim** suburb and has an interesting museum.

The **Black Forest,** extending 40-60 miles west of Stuttgart to Karlsruhe, Freiburg, and Basel, and so called because of its dense coniferous woodlands, is really a mountain massif with valleys. Many of its sparkling streams have curative value, and it is a delightful area of wide-roofed houses, colorful costumes peculiar to each valley, and colorful festivals. The most important of the many spa resorts is luxurious **Baden-Baden,** also a popular starting-off point for scenic drives through the Black Forest. The **Baden Wine Road** and the **Black Forest High Road** leading through picturesque small villages are both well marked.

HAMBURG

This city came to prominence in the 13th century as a member of the Hanseatic league and is today a major European port with an unusual degree of sophistication.

AIRPORT INFORMATION

Fuhlsbüttel Airport (tel: 5081), with a duty-free shop and hotel reservations counter, is 7½ miles from the Central Bus Station. From the airport into the town center is DM5 by the Jasper limousine-bus service, DM2.50 by public bus No 31, DM1.80 by public bus No 109, or DM18-20 by taxi.

ACCOMMODATIONS

Hotels in Hamburg:
Rates are in US$ for a double/twin room with bath or shower
   Alster Hof, Esplanade 12 (from $52)
   Ambassador, Heidenkampsweg 34 (from $70)
   Atlantic, An der Alster 72 (from $100), on Alster Lake
   Berlin, Borgfelder Strasse 1-9 (from $65)
   Central Hotel Smolka, Isestrasse 98 (from $71)
   CP Hamburg Plaza, Marseiller Strasse 2 (from $108)
   Europäischer Hof, Kirchenallee 45 (from $70)
   INTER · CONTINENTAL HAMBURG, Fontenay 10 (from $100), on
      Alster Lake

Norge, Schäferkampsallee 49 (from $66)
Prem, An der Alster 9 (from $67), on Alster Lake
Reichshof, Kirchenallee 34-36 (from $70)
Vier Jahreszeiten, Neuer Jungfernstieg 9-14 (from $141), on Alster Lake
All hotels listed above are in central Hamburg unless otherwise indicated.

EATING AND ENTERTAINMENT

There are an incredible number of restaurants and cafés (covering most price ranges) at which one can eat well in this former Hansastadt. The best restaurants are the **Haerlin Restaurant** at the Vier Jahreszeiten and the **Atlantic Grill** at the Hotel Atlantic. Both produce prodigiously good examples of local specialties in addition to normal items from French and international cuisine. They're closely followed by the **Mühlenkamper Fährhaus**—one of the two former ferry houses now transformed into restaurants in the city—at Hans-Henny-Jahnn-Weg 1 (tel: 2206934). Then there's **W. Schümanns Austernkeller** (Jungfernstieg 34—tel: 346265) for seafood, and those especially delicious Hamburg oysters, the **Kranzler Grill** at the new Congress Center (tel: 3592452), the venerable **Ratsweinkeller** (Gr Johannisstrasse 2—tel: 364153), and the **Restaurant im Finnlandhaus** (Esplanade 41—tel: 344133) on the 12th floor. Out in the riverside suburb of Blankenese are **Op'n Bulln** (55 Blankeneser Landungssteg—tel: 869962) and the other ferry house restaurants, the **Sagebiels Fährhaus** (Blankeneser Hauptstrasse 107—tel: 861514) in an attractive, old-fashioned setting, and the **Süllberg** (auf dem Süllberg—tel: 861686), both delightful in summer and warmly cozy in winter. Down in St Pauli are the **Bavaria Blick** (Bernhard-Nocht-Strasse 99—tel: 314800) and **Überseebrüke** (Vorsetzen—tel: 313333), both with an excellent view of the port and the latter with outstanding seafood, and **Provence** (Millerntorplatz 1—tel: 310641); while nearby are **Fischereihafen Restaurant** (Gr Elbstrasse 143—tel: 3898212) and **Landhaus Dill** (Elbchaussee 404—tel: 828443), and just a little further is the pleasant **Rittscher** (Elbchaussee 221—tel: 8803178) with garden terrace and attractive view. The revolving restaurant on the television tower, **Fernsehturm Restaurant** (Lagerstrasse 2—tel: 441641), gives magnificent scenes of Hamburg on a clear day and the food is good. Just a little way out in Hamburg Bergstedt is **Zum Lindenkrug** (Bergstedter Chaussee 128—tel: 6049171) which has rooms for those who don't wish to return to town for the night. Out near the airport in Hamburg Wellingsbüttel is the **Restaurant Randel** (Poppenbütteler Landstrasse 1—tel: 6956425).

Other pleasant places to eat include the fashionable **Alsterpavillon** (Jungfernstieg 54—tel: 345052), **Collins Austernstuben** (Brodschrangen 1—tel: 3247), **Peter Lemboke** (Holzdamm 49—tel: 243292), and **Ehmke im Cremon** (Cremon 36—tel: 36). For a good view over the Alster and nice dining there's the **Panorama** (Ferdinandstor 1—tel: 337936).

In part because of its long history as a free trading port, Hamburg's nightlife is extraordinarily varied. For solid elegance, there are the bars at the Atlantic and the Vier Jahreszeiten, where one may drink and dance. On the Alster itself is **die insel** (Alsterufer 34—tel: 446651), a fashionable nightclub in a converted villa with dinner-dancing. For more action and an informal atmosphere, try the port area of **St Pauli** where **Reeperbahn, Grosse Freiheit,** and **Spielbudenplatz.** Tickets for night tours of St Pauli are available from the tourist information office or from your hotel porter.

SHOPPING

Mönckebergstrasse has popular department stores. A more fashionable area is around the **Binnenalster.** Antique shops are concentrated in the district behind the **Gänsemarkt** and in the arty **Pöseldorf** quarter. Every Sunday morning in St Pauli there is a colorful **Fish Market.**

WHAT TO SEE

Hamburg, situated on the Elbe river estuary, is (like Venice) built on piles over water and has more bridges than Venice and Amsterdam together. Of its 288 square-mile area, some 80% is covered by water, resulting in more than 60 dock basins with 40 miles of quays, and one of the busiest ports in the world. Take a boat trip from the **St Pauli Landungsbrücken** for an hour's ride around the port (60 dock basins). In the city center a broad stretch of water called **Aussenalster** is also popular for boat trips, sailing, and canoeing and affords a fine view of the spires of the town hall and five principal churches.

North from Hamburg is **Lübeck,** former capital of the Hanseatic League; its famous **Holstentor** (which may still be seen) decorates the 50 DM bill. Lübek is still the busiest West German port on the Baltic, and the heart of the city, the **Altstadt** or Old Town, is well worth the visit. Of particular interest is the **Marienkirche,** with its twin towers, begun in 1250. The **Haus der Schiffergesellschaft** (Seamen's Guild House) now houses a restaurant, but maintains the air of earlier times with aged refectory tables, pews and benches, numerous ships' models, copper lamps and lanterns. The food is also good. The distinguished German author Thomas Mann originally came from Lübeck. Also north of Hamburg are **Travemünde,** the most popular of the Baltic coastal resorts, and **Kiel,** on the canal linking the Baltic to the North Sea.

Hanover, seat of the Royal House of Hanover (related to the British throne) until 1886, is today a center of commerce and industry. The important **International Trade Fair** is held in April. The **Old Town Hall,** the gothic **Marktkirche,** the 17th-century **Ballhof** (where the first opera was performed in Hanover in 1672), and a row of half-timbered houses are all that remains of the old part of town.

Bremen, the oldest German maritime city, had market rights granted to it in 965. It is the third of the Hanseatic cities, and it began trading with America in 1783. The best of its old buildings are grouped around the **Marktplatz,** which has an enormous 15th-century statue of Roland in front of the town hall.

SOURCES OF FURTHER INFORMATION

Pan Am: Frankfurt—Am Hauptbahnhof 12; Berlin—Europa-Center; Hamburg—Colonnaden 1; Nuremberg—Nuremburg Airport; Munich—

3 Lenbachplatz; Stuttgart—Lautenschlagerstrasse 2 (and any Pan Am office around the world). Local Tourist Offices: **German National Tourist Association,** Beethovenstrasse 61, D 6000 Frankfurt/Main 1; **German National Tourist Office,** 630 Fifth Avenue, New York, NY 10020; 61 Conduit Street, London WIR OEN.

Gibraltar

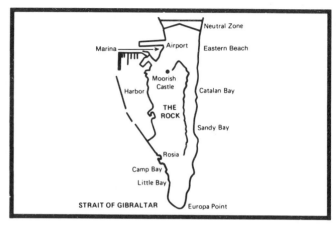

Neutral Zone
Marina — Airport
Eastern Beach
Moorish Castle
Harbor
Catalan Bay
THE ROCK
Sandy Bay
Rosia
Camp Bay
Little Bay
STRAIT OF GIBRALTAR
Europa Point

WHAT'S SPECIAL

Gibraltar—the famous British rock fortress rising perpendicularly out of the Mediterranean to a height of 1,396 feet—is connected to the southern tip of Spain by a flat and narrow isthmus. It is one of the few places in the world where you can see two continents at once. You will find beautiful beaches, lively nightspots, and excellent duty-free shopping.

COUNTRY BRIEFING

Gibraltar is 2¼ square miles in area, with a **population** of 29,800. The **climate** is temperate, with hot, dry summers cooled by sea breezes. Winters are mild. Gibraltar is a self-governing British colony, and the official **language** is English, though Spanish is widely spoken. The predominant **religion** is Roman Catholic. **Currency:** sterling (100 pence = £1); there is also the Gibraltar pound of equivalent value (£1 = US$2.09). **Public Holidays:** New Year's Day, 1 Jan; Good Friday; Easter Monday; Commonwealth Day; Queen's Birthday; Late Summer Bank Holiday; 25 Dec Christmas; 26 Dec Boxing Day.

HOW TO GET THERE

Flying time to North Front Airport from New York is 7½ hours; from London, 2½ hours; from Madrid, 1 hour. Time in Gibraltar: GMT+1.

REQUIREMENTS FOR ENTRY AND CUSTOMS REGULATIONS

Valid passport; visas not required of citizens of most Western nations; smallpox vaccination certificate only if arriving from an infected area.

Gibraltar is part of the Sterling Area, so at present there are no foreign currency restrictions. It is beneficial to convert all local currency before leaving. Declare all dutiable articles on entry. Duty-free allowance: 200 cigarettes or 50 cigars or 250 grams tobacco; 1 liter alcohol over 38.8 proof or 2 liters wine; 2 fluid ounces perfume; gifts (total value £10). No firearms may be imported; cats and dogs allowed only directly from the UK and then only in compliance with strict inoculation procedures.

AIRPORT INFORMATION

North Front Airport is ¾ mile from the city center. Buses operate for each incoming and outgoing flight. Taxis to the city center no more than £1, plus 10p extra per person and 10p per suitcase. Airport tax is £1. Airport has a duty-free shop.

ACCOMMODATIONS

There is an excellent range of hotel accommodations and bed and breakfast establishments. The **Tourist Offices** at the airport and in the Piazza, Main Street, offer help in finding accommodations.

Rates are in US$ for a double/twin room with bath or shower

Both Worlds Holiday Apartments, Sandy Bay (from $30.50)
Bristol, Cathedral Square (from $26.30)
Caleta Palace, Catalan Bay (from $31)
Cannon, Cannon Lane (from $13)
Holiday Inn, Governor's Parade (from $80)
Montarik, Bedlam Court, Main Street (from $35)
Ocean Heights Holiday Apartments, Montagu Place (from $24)
Queen's, Boyd Street (from $24)
Rock, Europa Road (from $54)

USEFUL INFORMATION

Banks open 9-3:30 Mon-Fri, also 4:30-6 on Fridays. Money can be exchanged only through a bank. Stores, hotels, and restaurants accept foreign currency. **Mailboxes** are red. **Telephone** booths are coin operated; local call, 5p. Facilities for international calls are available at City Hall, John Mackintosh Square. International calls must be booked through the operator. Useful numbers: **Tourist Office,** 4623; **Tourist Information,** 5555; **Airport Information,** 2996; **Operator,** 00; **Directories,** 95. **English-language newspapers** and magazines available. Local English publications—*Gibraltar Chronicle,* daily; *Calpe News, Gibraltar Evening Post, Panorama,* and *The Vox,* weeklies in English and Spanish. **Tipping:** a service charge of 10-12% generally included in restaurant checks, otherwise leave 10%; tip porters 20p per piece of luggage and taxi drivers 10% of fare, minimum 10p. **Electricity** is 240/250 volts 50 cycles AC. **Laundry:** major hotels offer good express laundry and dry-cleaning services; cost of dry-cleaning a suit, £2; laundering a shirt, from 70p. Hotels have **hairdressing** salons—average price for shampoo and set, from £5 plus 10% tip; man's haircut from 70p, tip from 10p. Good selection of **photographic** equipment; black and white film developed in 1 day, color in 2 days. **Health:** imported pharmaceuticals and toiletries relatively inexpensive. Water safe to drink.

TRANSPORTATION

There is a bus service (standard fare 17p) and fixed-rate taxis obtained by phone or from a taxi stand. A taxi tour of the *Rock* costs a fixed £10 per car. Traffic drives on the right. Frequent car-ferry and passenger boats to Tangier, Morocco, take 2½ hours (20 minutes by air); cost of a day excursion, £12. Due to restrictions, it is not possible to cross over to or from Spain (by passenger boat or car ferry), but there is a once daily (except Sunday) hydrofoil Gibraltar-Tangier-Algeciras, Spain, and a once daily return trip. Fare Gibraltar to Tangier £13, fare Gibraltar to Algeciras £20. Round-trip fares double.

FOOD AND RESTAURANTS

Top restaurants include the **Casino Royale** (7 Europa Road—tel: 2815) with Continental cuisine; **Winston's Restaurant** (4 Cornwall's Parade—tel: 2655), English food; and **Romano's** (tel: 70544), at the Ocean Heights, for Italian cooking. Both Worlds' **Terrace Restaurant** (Sandy Bay—tel: 6191) and the Rock Hotel (3 Europa Road—tel: 73000) are famous for their Angus beef. Cordon Bleu enthusiasts should visit **Harry's** (1A Rosia Road—tel: 2550). Good English food is sold at the popular **Country Cottage** (Giro's Passage—tel: 70084), **The English Eating House** (13 Market Lane—tel: 2313), and **The Copper Kettle** (la Convent Place—tel: 5654). **La Bayuca** (21 Turnbull's Lane—tel: 5119) specializes in Spanish cuisine, the **Lotus House** (292 Main Street—tel: 5153) in barbecued spareribs, and the **Mermaid** (Catalan Bay—tel: 2677), by the bay, in paella. For good, inexpensive food, **La Trattoria del Pescatore** (79 Irish Town—tel: 5566), for seafood specialties, and the **Copacabana** (242 Main Street—tel: 2596) are worth trying.

There are both typically English pubs and Continental bars. Drinks are generally inexpensive—a bottle of beer or 1 ounce of whisky about 40p. A bottle of wine at the table averages about £3.50. High tea is served on Sundays at the Casino Royale.

ENTERTAINMENT

Gibraltar at night is lively, and you can dance the evening away at **Goggles** (Europea Point), the **Canes** (under Queen's Hotel), the **Gimcrack** (at the Rock Hotel), **Oasis** (at Holiday Inn), and the **Penelope** (Corals Road). The magnificent **Casino** of the International Sporting Club, on Europa Road, has a nightclub, cabaret, restaurant, and gaming rooms. For 20p per pair, play match-point duplicate bridge at the **Garrison Library** (tel: 4529). This starts at 8:30pm, but entries should be in by noon. There are four English-language cinemas.

SHOPPING

Stores are open 9-1 and 3-7 Mon-Fri, 9-1 Sat. The principal shopping area is **Main Street,** and prices are among the lowest in Europe. Best buys include cosmetics, perfume, wines, liquor, cigarettes, cameras, radios, watches, and jewelry.

SPORTS

There are endless opportunities for water sports. Some of the attractions are underwater exploring, water-skiing, five good beaches for swimming (**Catalan Bay, Camp Bay, Rosia Bay, Sandy Bay,** and **Little Bay**), a yacht marina, boats to rent, and, for the keen angler, a great variety of marine life and an annual **International Shark Angling Festival** in April. Tennis courts are available at **Sandpits.** Visitors are welcomed at **The Gibraltar Yacht Club,** Queensway, and **The Mediterranean Rowing Club,** 6 Bayside.

WHAT TO SEE

For a great view take a cable car to the top of the **Rock** and see the famous colony of wild Barbary apes. Other points of interest include the **Moorish Castle;** the **Upper Galleries,** miles of passages hollowed out of the solid rock during the Great Siege (1779-1783) and World War II, and the impressive **St Michael's Cave,** 1,000 feet above sea level, with its fine stalagmites and stalactites (the largest of the numerous caverns in the heart of the rock is used for concerts and *Sound and Light* performances). Visit the **Gibraltar Museum,** the lighthouse on **Europa Point,** and the luxuriant **Alameda Gardens** on the western side.

SOURCES OF FURTHER INFORMATION

Any **Pan Am** office around the world; **Gibraltar Tourist Office,** Cathedral Square, Gibraltar; Arundel Great Court, 179 The Strand, London WC 2R 1EH.

Great Britain

WHAT'S SPECIAL

Until the arrival of the Romans, no serious attempt had been made to colonize the British Isles, which had been peopled by Celtic tribes since as early as 3,000 BC. It was a series of bardic nations who lived here, whose heroism was dedicated to the art of song and poem rather than that of sword. No serious decision was ever made without prior consultation with the Druids, whose name means "oak-men." To this day, as the winter solstice approaches, the people of Britain gather mistletoe—sacred to the Druids—and holly with which to decorate their homes at Yuletide.

It was partly on account of the Druids' schools that Rome decided to attempt the colonization of Britain by Julius Caesar. Leaders of continental European tribes were being educated in Britain and causing casualties to the armies of Rome. Then, too, there was the desire on the part of Rome to extend the benefits of citizenship ever further afield, and under Claudius—43 AD—colonization began.

Today, Great Britain means England, Northern Ireland, Scotland, and Wales, though strictly speaking the proper term is the United Kingdom. In the west, this United Kingdom combines a past unequalled in its political, economic, and cultural greatness that is matched only by that of the Chinese in the east. For the visitor from any part of the world there is an incredibly diverse variety of attractions and modes of living to be experienced. This densely populated and amazingly compact country provides a feast of history and beauty in its monuments, cathedrals, artistic treasures, and ceremonial grandeur; but Britain is not only a museum of the past, there is a viable and lively present-day culture, which still offers the best in drama, art, and music.

The joys of the British countryside are world-famous for the sheer beauty of the natural landscape and for the charm of the villages sprinkling it, as well as for the majestic public monuments to be found throughout the country. It is a place where the North American traveler, especially, will feel at home; the common language and the cultural and social heritage derived from the mother country will provide a basis for the visitor to see the real difference between the cultures. Britain is today seeking a new world role for itself, and perhaps the key to its success will be in its traditional sense of the importance of human rights and tolerance, its diplomatic skills, inventive genius, and dry, self-effacing sense of humor.

COUNTRY BRIEFING

Size: 94,500 square miles **Population:** 55,883,100
Capital: London **Capital Population:** 6,877,100
Climate: Temperate, but unpredictable; don't forget your umbrella!

Weather in London: Lat N51°29'; Alt 149 ft

Temp (°F)	Jan	Feb	Mar	Apr	May	Jun	Jul	Aug	Sep	Oct	Nov	Dec
Av Low	35°	35°	36°	40°	45°	51°	54°	54°	49°	44°	39°	36°
Av High	43°	45°	49°	55°	62°	68°	71°	70°	65°	56°	49°	45°
Days no rain	16	13	17	17	19	18	18	18	18	15	14	15

Government: A constitutional monarchy with Queen Elizabeth II at its head.

Language: English; Gaelic in parts of Scotland and Northern Ireland, Welsh in parts of Wales.

Religion: Church of England (Protestant); but also all other sects respected.

Currency: Pound. 100 pence = £1.

	1p	5p	10p	50p	£1	£5	£10	£20
US (dollars, cents)	.02	.10	.21	1.05	2.09	10.46	20.93	41.85

Public Holidays:

New Year's Day, 1 Jan
Good Friday
Easter Monday
May Day, first Mon in May
Spring Bank Holiday, last Mon in May
Summer Bank Holiday, last Mon in Aug

Christmas Day, 25 Dec
Boxing Day, 26 Dec
In Northern Ireland only, 17 Mar and 13 July
In Scotland only, 2 Jan, 1st Mon in Aug

HOW TO GET THERE

Fly direct to London, Heathrow Airport, from the following cities: Flying time to Heathrow Airport, London from New York is 6¾ hours; from Frankfurt 1 hour, from Berlin 2 hours, from Tokyo 21¾ hours.
Time in Great Britain is GMT; from March to October, GMT+1.

REQUIREMENTS FOR ENTRY AND CUSTOMS REGULATIONS

A valid passport; visas not required for US or Canadian citizens, all others should check with the British consulate in their country. Smallpox and cholera vaccinations required if coming from an infected area. Duty-free allowance: 1 pound tobacco in any form (¾ pound if coming from a European country); 1 bottle liquor and 2 bottles of wine; ¼ pint perfume. You can bring in an unlimited amount of foreign currency. Note: British customs checkpoints offer a choice of two entry gates—green, "nothing to declare" (subject to spot checks), and red for those wishing to make declarations. Don't forget your driver's license—as a visitor, you may use it for car rentals throughout Britain. When you leave Britain take what you like but certain works of art and antiques are subject to export licensing control. Pets brought in are subject to 6 months' quarantine.

AIRPORT INFORMATION

Britain's major international airport is Heathrow, 15 miles west of London. A subway connects airport with city. Fare to Piccadilly Circus is £1.80 one way. The No A1 London Transport bus goes to Victoria, leaving every 20 minutes; one-way fare £2. Pan Am's city terminal is in Semley Place, Victoria. One-way fare is £2 (children £1); no charge for luggage; and the journey takes about 45 minutes to 1 hour depending on traffic. Taxis are also available, but take a metered cab from the taxi stand and insist on a metered fare; it should cost about £11 (depending on destination) to the city center. British Rail trains shuttle between Gatwick and Victoria every 20 minutes, one-way fare £2.60 (children £1.30).

Facilities in the terminal buildings at Heathrow include three duty-free shops, as well as restaurants, banks, bars, and cafeterias (snack bar). Also in the airport concourse you'll find a London Hotel Reservation Desk. There is no arrival or departure tax.

ACCOMMODATIONS

In London alone there is a tremendous variety of accommodations for visitors. Room rates are generally lower in the off-peak season, from October to March but excluding Christmas, New Year, and Easter. Accommodations in guesthouses, private hotels, and bed-and-breakfast establishments start around US$10 for the most modest accommodations. A good source for short-notice bookings is the **Hotel Reservation Centre** at Victoria (tel: 01-828-1027). **Trust Houses Forte,** Britain's largest hotel chain, offers a central booking service for all their hotels (tel: 01-567-3444). For complete listings of available accommodations in Britain, contact any bureau of the **British Tourist Authority** with offices in almost every country of the world. In addition to country inns and bed-and-breakfast arrangements, stays can be arranged at guesthouses, country homes and manors, farmhouses, and varieties of self-catering arrangements, including camping, caravaning, and aboard sailboats. Many hotels, especially during out-of-season, offer packages that are much cheaper than the standard prices quoted here. For accommodations in London, contact **London Tourist Board,** 26 Grosvenor Gardens, London SW1 (tel: 01-730-0791). Check hotel prices before you make a reservation. And it cannot be overstressed that accommodations in London are sometimes difficult to find at short notice. Hotels in London:

Rates are in US$ for double/twin room with bath or shower

Carlton Tower, Cadogan Place, SW1 (from $189), near Victoria Station and Pan Am Terminal

Cavendish, Jermyn Street, SW1 (from $155), in Mayfair

Churchill, 30 Portman Square, W1 (from $173), in Mayfair

Connaught, Carlos Place, W1 (from $150), in Mayfair

Cumberland, Marble Arch, W1 (from $118), in Mayfair

Dorchester, Park Lane, W1 (from $173), in Mayfair

Gloucester, 4-18 Harrington Gardens, SW7 (from $123), in South Kensington

Grosvenor House, Park Lane, W1 (from $167), in Mayfair

Heathrow, Hounslow, Middlesex (from $123), near airport

Hilton International, Park Lane, W1 (from $171), in Mayfair

Inn on the Park, Park Lane, W1 (from $184), in Mayfair

INTER·CONTINENTAL LONDON, One Hamilton Place, W1 (from $155), at Hyde Park Corner

Kensington Close, Wrights Lane, W8 (from $78), in Kensington

Kensington Hilton, Holland Park Ave (from $107), in Kensington

Little Mayfair, 7 Down Street (from $67), in Mayfair

London International, Cromwell Road, SW5 (from $84), in South Kensington

Montcalm, Gt Cumberland Pl (from $120), in Mayfair

PORTMAN INTER·CONTINENTAL, 22 Portman Square, W1 (from $144), in Mayfair

Royal Garden, Kensington High Street, W8 (from $117), near Kensington Gardens

Royal Lancaster, Lancaster Terrace, Hyde Park, W2 (from $129), 10 minutes from Mayfair by cab

Russell, Russell Square, WC1 (from $93), in Bloomsbury

Savoy, Victoria Embankment Gardens, WC2 (from $173), near Trafalgar Square

Selfridge, Orchard St, W1 (from $151), north Mayfair

Sherlock Holmes, Baker St, W1 (from $75), north Mayfair near Bond St

Stafford, St James' Pl (from $156), SW1, central London West End

Strand Palace, Strand, WC2 (from $78), near Trafalgar Square

Tavistock, Tavistock Square, WC1 (from $56), in Bloomsbury

Tower, St Katharine's Way, E1 (from $93), near Tower of London

Waldorf, Aldwych, WC2 (from $122), near Covent Garden

Westbury, Conduit Street, W1 (from $122), near Covent Garden

Note that hotels vary as to the inclusion of service, tax, and breakfast in the prices quoted, and these details should be checked in advance. While inflation in Britain has lessened, it is still a factor for tourists to consider since prices often rise at least once a year.

USEFUL INFORMATION

Banks: Open 9:30-3:30 Mon-Fri. Most of leading American banks have branches in London and reciprocal agreements with British joint stock banks. You can cash travelers' checks at any bank, restaurant, at Thomas Cook and American Express offices, and at almost all hotels. There is also a 24-hour bank at West London Air Terminal and at Heathrow.

Mail: You can buy stamps from post offices, open 9-5:30 Mon-Sat though early closing Sat is observed by many, but stamp machines are provided on post office walls. Mailboxes are red. There is one 24-hour post office at Trafalgar Square. The office also has excellent facilities for making long-distance calls—known to the British as "trunk calls."

Telephone Tips: Phones are automatic, and coin-operated phones can be found in street booths, subway stations, post offices, railroad stations, air terminals, pubs, and restaurants. Local calls cost 5p for about 2 minutes; machines take only 5p or 10p coins. Read the directions carefully before dialing (01 is the London prefix, omit when calling from there). New electronic booths with blue "Intercontinental" logos facilitate overseas dialing. There is an International Telephone Bureau on Victoria Street, near Parliament. Useful numbers in London:

Pan Am	**Time** 123
01-734-7292	**London Weather** 01-246-8091
Teletourist (The main events	**American Express** 01-930-4411
of the day in London):	**Directory Enquiries** 142
English 01-246-8041	(London), 192 (elsewhere)
French 01-246-8043	**Automobile Association**
German 01-246-8045	(breakdowns, road information):
Operator 100	01-954-7373
British Tourist Authority	**London Transport Information:**
01-499-9325	01-222-1234
Fire, Police Ambulance 999	**All London Taxis:** 01-286-6010
International Telegrams 193	

Newspapers: Britain is one of the few nations to have a truly national press. Late editions of the London dailies reach most northern areas by noon. Quality dailies include the *Times*, the *Guardian*, the *Daily Telegraph*, in London, while the *Yorkshire Post, Birmingham Post*, the *Scotsman* are read elsewhere. The leading weekend newspapers are *The Sunday Times* and *The Observer*. Britain is possibly the most literate nation in the world, producing the *Economist*—for the most in-depth coverage on world politics, current affairs, business, economics, and science—*Punch* (a typically British lowbrow humorous magazine), and *Private Eye*, for British-style iconoclastic wit and satire. Nearly all the world's leading newspapers and magazines are available at London newsstands. To discover the whereabouts of royalty, read the Court Circular in the *Times*.

Tipping: Standard rates are 12-15% in hotels and restaurants, which may or may not be added to the bill; 10-15% for hairdresser; minimum 20p for porters and 5p for every piece of baggage above two. Minimum for taxi drivers is 15p for a £1 bill. In large hotels, a special service from the head porter will require at least 50p. Getting clothes pressed in a hurry will cost 10-20p. Cloakroom and rest-room attendants, 10p. You needn't tip barmen and theater ushers.

Electricity: 220 volts 50 cycles AC. Some hotels have 120-volt shaver plugs.

Laundry: Laundry and dry-cleaning services are good throughout Britain, and are usually available at hotels. Dry-cleaning a suit, from £2.50, laundering a shirt, about £1. There are also laundromats in most cities.

Hairdressing: First-class hotels have hairdressing salons. Shampoo and set, from £7; man's haircut from £4.

Photography: Photographic supplies and services are available everywhere and British-made Ilford black and white film is recognized as the finest available in the world. Film prices are highly variable depending upon quality. Black and white, from about £1.20 for 20 exposures (£1.60 for 36); color from about £1.50 for 20 exposures (£2 for 36). Film processing takes 5-8 days (some places, 24 hours) and is expensive.

Clubs: Many international clubs hold regular meetings in London. Contact: Kiwanis; Lions International (4 The Drive, Hove, Sussex—tel: 0273-723-611); Rotary International (Sheen Lane House, Sheen Lane, London SW14—tel: 01-878-0931).

Rest Rooms: Most railway and some subway stations, stores and restaurants, and public conveniences are to be found in every town.

Health: Charge is made for anything other than immediate first-aid service; your hotel can put you in touch with a doctor or hospital.

TRANSPORTATION

Transportation in and around London consists of buses, the subway (officially called the "Underground," unofficially "the tube"), and taxis.

Buses: The red, double-decker buses go just about everywhere in the central London area; fares depend on how far you travel, beginning at 12p, and are paid after you get on to a conductor who will tell you the stop for your destination. Riding on the top of a double-decker is a highly recommended, inexpensive way of seeing London. Every hour from 10am to 9pm (summer) or 4pm (winter) buses leave Victoria, Piccadilly Circus, and Marble Arch for 2-hour tours of the City and West End; cost £2.40 (£1.50 for children under 16). Extra buses are put on in the summer. For details of other tours, and for free bus maps, call London Transport Enquiries, 01-222-1234.

The Underground: Travel by subway is usually the fastest way to get around town: fares depend on how far you are going, and start at 30p. There are several special-rate tickets available for extensive travel on Underground trains and/or London Transport buses. For example, a 3-day "go as you please" ticket will give unlimited travel on the tube and on red buses for £10.50 (£3.50 for children under 14). A 4-day ticket costs £13 (£4.50 for children under 14), while a 7-day ticket costs £18.50 (£6.50 for children under 14). Ask at a ticket office in the Underground for a free pocket guide, which makes getting where you want to go a lot easier. Destinations and directions are well marked, but get a general idea of the direction you want before going down or up a stairway.

Taxis: London taxis are metered and are for hire when the roof sign is illuminated. You can hail one in the street. There is a small additional charge for luggage and travel after 8pm.

Travel around Britain: Great Britain was responsible for the invention of the railroad, and although matters might be said to have peaked about 100 years ago in terms of speed and comfort, modern technology and an appreciation of the responsibilities that nationalization brings with it have been making their appearance in recent times. If Switzerland is number one in Europe in terms of modern utilization of railroads, there is something close to a deadheat today between France, Germany, and Great Britain for the second spot. With the gradual substitution of the Inter-City 125 for the Pullman service during the early 70s—and improvement of the roadbed (or track)—point to point journeys are now increasingly operated by frequent, fast, comfortable, high-speed trains, with speeds of up to 125 mph common and journey time averages of better than 75 mph city center to city center. Some examples: from London to York (188 miles) in little more than 2 hours, and faster than airplane; from London to the Birmingham International Convention Centre (104 miles) just 77 minutes; while London to Edinburgh (almost 400 miles) takes a bare 5 hours. Sleepers are available for long journeys and should be booked in advance. An **All-Line Rail Rover** pass gives unlimited travel on the network for £85 (1 week) or £130 (2 weeks). Cheaper passes are also available for each region. Ask at any British Rail station. British Rail will have a car waiting for you at most main rail stations, returnable to any other rental point. Typical cost for 1 week: £40 per person, including insurance but not gas, 4 days with car or cars at separate points, and 7 days of rail pass.

Internal Airlines: British Airways "Inter-Britain" service brings the extremities of the country within 90 minutes of Heathrow. Call 01-370-5411 for flight information and reservations.

FOOD AND RESTAURANTS

Postwar English cooking earned a poor reputation, but the cooking itself has improved immeasurably. London particularly has more good restaurants, of more varied ethnic types, than most other large cities in Europe. French, Italian, Greek, Chinese, Indian, and even American restaurants are numerous. The great old English dishes, such as game pie or venison, do not feature in day-to-day life the way they used to, but the standard English dishes today, though simple, can be very good due to the high quality of the ingredients. Eating out, especially in London, is not a cheap way of passing the time.

Mass catering is not inspired, so if you want a good but inexpensive meal and don't know where to go—choose a pub. Pub lunches are simple and tend to be much the same everywhere—shepherd's pie, veal and ham pie, steak and kidney pudding, or "bangers and mash" (sausages and mashed potatoes)—but they are also of dependable quality every-where and are not expensive. Fast food addicts will be relieved to know that several of the better US chains have homes in the city center.

Best restaurants in London for English food are **Wilton's** in St James's, **Stones Chop House**, off the Haymarket, **Simpson's-in-the-Strand**, **Rules** in Covent Garden, **Lockets**, Westminster, and the **Hungry Horse**, Fulham. The English love fish, and good fish restaurants include **Wheeler's** chain, **Overtons** in St James's, and **Bill Bentley's** in the City, best known for oysters. Try a dozen oysters and a pint of Guinness as a counter lunch. Tea at **Browns** (Dover Street, W1) or the **Ritz** will give you the feel of old England, cucumber sandwiches and all.

Other good restaurants include the **Connaught Grill** at Connaught Hotel (if you can get a reservation); also **Robert Carrier's** in Islington; **Inigo Jones** in Covent Garden; **Porter's**, Henrietta St (near the Opera/Covent Garden); **Tutton's**, Covent Garden, good for inexpensive food, including breakfast, and a view of the market; **Leith's** in North Kensington; the **Café Royal** on Regent St; the **Savoy** and **Langan's Brasserie**, where a meal is regarded as an "interesting experience" and the cuisine is excellent. And there's also **Prunier's**, St James's Street (French); the **White House**, Albany Street (a longtime favorite with gastronomes); the **White Tower**, Percy Street; **Bentley's**, Swallow Street; and **Trattoria da Otello**, Dean Street, Soho. Medium-priced English restaurants include **Busby's**, Chelsea; the **Baker & Oven**, Marylebone; **Aunties**, Mayfair; **Samuel Pepys** at Brooks Wharf, EC4. Restaurants featuring international menus: French—**Le Poulbot**, Cheapside; **Le Gavroche**, Lower Sloane Street, **L'Artiste Assoiffe**, Westbourne Grove, and **Le Francais**, Kensington, are expensive, while **Le Cellier du Midi** in Hampstead is a bit less so. Indian—one of the best is **Tandoori**, Fulham; or try **Shezan** in Knightsbridge. Italian—expensive and fashionable are the **Tiberio**, Mayfair, and the **Terrazza** in Soho; less expensive are **San Lorenzo**, Knightsbridge, and **Trattoo**, Kensington. Japanese—the **Mikado**, Mayfair, is well established and fairly expensive. Hungarian—London's most famous Hungarian restaurant is the **Gay Hussar**, Soho. Lunch, supper, and dinner cruises on the Thames may be enjoyed May to September (tel—01-839-2349). Inexpensive meals can be had in branches of the **Bistingo** chain, in the **Rendezvous** at the Swiss Centre in Leicester Square, branches of the **Stockpot**, the **Ark** at Notting Hill Gate, the **Twin Brothers** in Kensington Church Street, **South of the Border** near the Old Vic, or the **Chelsea Kitchen** in the King's Road. If you just can't survive without a hamburger, try the **Great American Disaster** in Fulham Road or the **Hard Rock Café** in Piccadilly. A classier American restaurant is **Joe Allen's**, Exeter Street, near Covent Garden. For vegetarian food try **The Raw Deal** in York Street (not licensed to serve alcohol but they do not charge corkage) or **Cranks**, Soho, for daytime eating.

DRINKING TIPS

In addition to being renowned for their skills with harp and poesy and song, the early British were also equipped with the arts of brewing and distillation, making ale, mead, and a drink known variously as "water of the gods" or "spirit of life," known to us as whisky. This last they made from grain.

Over the years a renaissance of sorts has taken place in the production of ales, and today numerous small companies make products of increasing excellence. By applying the same mix of science and know-how that the Swiss apply to their wines, the British produce wholesome beverages that satisfy when ingested but which leave few (if any) residual aftereffects. Sample these beers (look for a "Real Ale" sign) at any of the numerous public houses, or pubs, as the British call them. Bitter is drunk at room temperature or just slightly chilled, and is an acquired taste—three half-pints will usually do it. If you prefer a lighter beer, ask for lager, which is available bottled and occasionally on draught. Then there are the various types of black beers, stouts, and porters, of which Guinness from Ireland is the best known; again, bottled or draught. Scotch whisky comes in various blends of which *Dewars White Label* and *Teachers* are the best known, while there are an increasing number of single malt whiskies available, including *Talisker*.

Most pubs are tied to a brewery and they are unique institutions. The licensing laws vary from place to place but are normally 10:30 or 11am to 3pm and 5 or 5:30 to 11, Mon-Sat and 12-2 and 7-10:30 Sun. Even the humblest of pubs offers some form of food, ranging from a "ploughman's lunch" of bread and cheese in the country, to some very sophisticated fare in market towns. Two riverside pubs that are well worth a visit are the **Dove** at 19 Upper Mall, Hammersmith, and the **City Barge** at 27 Strand-on-the-Green, Chiswick, both of which date back to Elizabethan times. In the West End near Covent Garden is the ancient **Lamb and Flag**. It has a literary clientele and serves a delicious game pie when in season. One of the oldest pubs in town is the **Prospect of Whitby** on the Thames at Wapping in the East End. It's a fascinating place but hard to find, so take a taxi. There are thousands of pubs in London, almost as many as there are opinions about which is best.

ENTERTAINMENT

London's artistic attractions are many and varied; there is good theater, ballet, opera, concerts of all types of music, films, nightclubs, and every other form of entertainment, including a few music hall events.

Cultural events: London's theater is perhaps the most active in the world. Every night some of the best and most famous actors can be seen on the stage—at the **Theatre Royal** in Drury Lane, the **Aldwych** (London home of the Royal Shakespeare Company), and the modern **National Theatre** (home of the National Theatre Company) on London's South Bank by the River. Plays, musicals, and revues are presented at the **Prince Charles, Her Majesty's,** and the **London Palladium,** to name only a very few. Shows usually start at 7:30 or 8, later on Saturday. Current productions are listed in the daily *New Standard,* and the weekly *Time Out,* and at theater-booking agencies. Daily newspapers also carry listings.

A ticket booth in **Leicester Square**, open 2:30-6:30pm Mon-Sat, sells same-day, half-price tickets to most theaters.

There are frequent orchestral concerts at the **Royal Festival Hall**, the **Royal Albert Hall**, and other smaller concert halls. The **Royal Opera House**, Covent Garden, is the home of the **Royal Opera Company**, which stages operas in their original languages with visiting stars, and the **Royal Ballet**, one of the world's leading classical ballet companies. Tickets are costly and sell out fast. The **English National Opera** gives excellent performances of opera in English at the **London Coliseum**, St Martin's Lane. There are also a number of modern dance and opera groups performing regularly throughout London.

Films: The cinema business is booming in Britain, and London has many first-rate movie houses. West End cinema prices around £3. Out of the center of town, more like £1.50.

Nightclubs: There are many nightclubs in London that offer atmosphere, first-class international cabaret acts, reasonably priced food, and dancing. One of the most famous nightspots is **Ronnie Scotts** jazz club at 47 Frith Street (tel: 439-0747); admission costs £8, depending on the calibre of the artist, to hear some of the best jazz musicians. In the grand tradition of extravaganzas are the shows at **Talk of the Town** at the Hippodrome Corner near Leicester Square. Admission, which includes dinner and cabaret, comes to £18.45 weekdays, and £21.75 on Fridays and Saturdays.

Discothèques: Some of the most fashionable and popular are **Samantha's**, 3 New Burlington Street (tel: 734-6249)—"private," though temporary membership arranged if you bring your passport; the **Marquee**, 90 Wardour Street, W1, one of London's oldest discothèques; and **La Valbonne** in Regent Street, upstairs at **Ronnie Scott's**; **Thursday's** in Kensington High Street and **Gullivers** in Down Street.

SHOPPING

Most stores in London open 9-5:30, Mon-Sat; some close on Saturday afternoons, others stay open until 7:30 on Wednesday or Thursday. Most notable among London's top department stores are **Harrods** in Knightsbridge (it would be simpler to list what it doesn't sell than what it does); **Selfridges** in Oxford Street; **Fortnum and Mason's** on Piccadilly (mainly food); and **John Lewis**. London is a shopper's paradise. For the latest fashion in furniture, fabrics, and toys try **Habitat** or **Heals** on Tottenham Court Road. **Bond Street** and **South Molton Street** are where the fashionable people shop, and the revamped and fashionable **Covent Garden** is worth a visit. For antiques explore shops along **Camden Passage** in Islington, **Portobello Road** market on Saturday mornings, or **Mount Street** in Mayfair, or take a look in at **Sotheby's** or **Christies**—London's top auction houses. You shouldn't miss **The Scotch House** in Knightsbridge, which sells tartans and traditional Scottish regalia. **Foyle's** on Charing Cross Road and **Hatchards** on Piccadilly are well-known bookshops. For records try the **Virgin Megastore** on Oxford Street. **HMV**, at the other end of Oxford Street, stocks music for all tastes.

SPORTS

The national sports of Britain are soccer and, in the summer, cricket. Rugby football also has a vociferous following. In London you can attend a league football game on Saturday afternoons from mid-August to April. During the summer months county cricket and "test" (international) matches are played at **Lord's Cricket Ground** near Regent's Park and at the **Oval**, not far from Waterloo Station. There are excellent golf courses near London, and if you bring a letter of introduction from your club secretary you will be able to play at the **Sunningdale** course in Berkshire, Selsdon Park, Surrey, and the **Wentworth Club** in Surrey.

WHAT TO SEE

London

No visit to London would be complete without a glimpse of **Westminster Abbey**, where the Kings and Queens of England are crowned. It is also a national shrine to the artists, poets, heroes, and statesmen of Britain. The Abbey is open to the public every day until sunset, except during state occasions. You can combine a visit to the Abbey with a look at the adjacent **Houses of Parliament**, but to see the inside you will have to stand in line to enter the Strangers' Galley in the **House of Commons; the House of Lords** admits no visitors. **Big Ben**, the world's most famous bell in a beautiful clock face, stands in the tower at the east end of the Parliament building. Nearby is **Downing Street**, with the Prime Minister's house at No 10 and the Chancellor of the Exchequer next door at No 11. A mile or so down river is the **Tower of London** (you can go by boat from Westminster pier). Things to look for are the Crown Jewels, Traitor's Gate, and the ravens—whose departure, legend has it, would herald the fall of England. Nearby is the magnificent **Tower Bridge**. In the City is **St Paul's Cathedral**, the magnificent work of Sir Christopher Wren, who reconstructed London after the Great Fire of 1666. If you feel like a long climb, ascend to the "whispering gallery" in the dome.

At 11:30 every morning during summer, alternative days in winter, the famous ceremony of **Changing the Guard** takes place in the forecourt of **Buckingham Palace**, the Queen's London residence. Get there early for a good view. Queen Elizabeth II has an official birthday celebration each year on the first or the second Saturday in June, and it is the occasion for **Trooping the Colour**, when the Queen takes the salute at a march past the regiments of the Brigade of Guards, accompanied by music from the Brigade bands. Contact any British Tourist Authority office for current details.

London houses great beauty, history, and riches in its many museums and galleries. The **British Museum** alone has under its roof the Rosetta Stone, the Portland Vase, the magnificent Elgin Marbles, two copies of the *Magna Carta*, an amusing collection of clocks, and one of the most important libraries in the world. The **Victoria and Albert Museum** is a world in itself, containing the fine and applied arts of all periods. The

National Gallery, Trafalgar Square, has a representative collection of European painting; next door at the National Portrait Gallery is a collection of portraits of famous Britons through the ages. The Tate Gallery houses modern and British art. Apsley House is now a museum recording the adventures of the Duke of Wellington, whose London residence it was. The Science Museum and Imperial War Museum are also of interest, especially to children.

London's extensive system of parks and gardens provides the visitor with an opportunity to walk and enjoy rural surroundings right in the middle of the city. Hyde Park has a lovely, winding body of water, the Serpentine, and there are flowers and ponds in the adjoining Kensington Gardens. Regent's Park is immense (470 acres), and contains the London Zoological Gardens within its bounds. St James's Park leads from White-hall to the Palace, and is famous for its variety of birds.

A trip well worth taking while in London is a riverboat ride down to Greenwich for a look over the splendid tea clipper, the Cutty Sark. Nearby is Gipsy Moth IV, the boat in which the late Sir Francis Chichester sailed around the world single-handed, the National Maritime Museum, and Greenwich Park, the original site of the Royal Observatory through which passes the Prime Meridian. The second recommended trip is up river to the Royal Botanical Gardens, at Kew, where almost every species of plant on earth is cultivated; admission is only 2p.

Further out of London, a half-hour train ride from Waterloo Station, is Hampton Court, expropriated by King Henry VIII from Cardinal Wolsey in the 16th century and a royal residence for over 200 years. The magnificent tapestries and paintings make splendid viewing, and the gardens contain a private maze. Further west and within 10 minutes' drive of Heathrow Airport is Runnymede, a meadow bordering the Thames, where King John is said to have signed the *Magna Carta,* a charter of rights that laid the foundations for British democracy. There is a stone memorial to John F. Kennedy on a hill nearby.

Chartwell, the home of the late Sir Winston Churchill, is 21 miles south of London and can be reached by Green Line bus. Its setting gives it lovely views over the surrounding Kent countryside. The garden is especially interesting; Sir Winston built several of the walls himself.

The South of England

Canterbury: This ancient city is dominated by the splendid Canterbury Cathedral, the spiritual center of the worldwide Anglican community, the place where Thomas á Becket was murdered, and the destination of Geoffrey Chaucer's pilgrims. The city retains many of its medieval features and much of its charm.

Dover: One hour's drive from Canterbury, Dover is the site of the famous white cliffs that have inspired poets and songwriters over the years. It is also a principal gateway to Europe with ferries and hovercraft services to the continent. (The hovercraft make the channel crossing in a bare 35 minutes as they skim over the waves). The Pharos, a Phoenician lighthouse, that once marked the headland, is now little more than a pile of stones. But the Castle is still worth the visit, and it was in these grounds that Louis Bleriot made his landing following the first cross-channel flight on July 25, 1909.

Brighton: A busy, often crowded resort since the 18th century, Brighton has two piers, lots of antique shops in its many alleys, the "Lanes," and the extraordinary **Royal Pavilion.** It is the essence of any English seaside resort town. Hotels in Brighton: **Old Ship,** Kings Road (from US$89 double BB), and **Royal Albion,** Old Steine (from US$98 double BB).

Southampton: This ancient and historic port is now a busy commercial and industrial center and still has part of its old town walls. Adjacent to the harbor is the **New Forest,** one of Britain's best preserved woodland areas, which has wild ponies and an incredible variety of birds. It was originally set aside as a royal hunting ground by William the Conqueror in the 11th century.

Winchester: North of Southampton, Winchester is a beautiful cathedral town; it was the capital of England during the reign of King Alfred the Great. It is one of England's most unspoiled and graceful cities. **Winchester Cathedral** has the longest Gothic nave in Europe.

Salisbury: The plateau called **Salisbury Plain** is dominated by the magnificent **Salisbury Cathedral,** whose 404-foot spire is visible for many miles; it has been immortalized by the paintings of John Constable. Near Salisbury is **Stonehenge,** the most famous of the country's prehistoric monuments.

The West Country

Bath: Since Roman times Bath has been known for its mineral waters; visit the **Roman Baths** and the **Pump Room,** an elegant place where you can taste the supposedly health-giving waters. The city's elegant appearance is the result of 18th-century planning and architecture; the lovely Georgian crescents of houses make walks around the city rewarding. The **Abbey** has a lovely interior with very fine fan vaulting. The annual **Bath Music Festival** is held every summer. Hotels in Bath: **Beaufort,** Walcot Street (from US$84) and the **Francis,** Queen Square (from US$93).

Bristol: An inland port of some importance, Bristol has the lovely perpendicular-style **Church of St Mary Redcliffe.** John Cabot sailed from Bristol in 1497 to discover the American continent, and the city was the original home of William Penn, developer of Pennsylvania. Try to see a performance of the **Bristol Old Vic** theater company, which performs at the **Theatre Royal.** Hotels in Bristol: **Grand,** Broad Street (from US$84). Nearby is the town of **Wells,** with its harmonious 12th-century **Cathedral. Glastonbury** is also near, a town associated with the Arthurian legends; the remains of **Glastonbury Abbey** are well worth a visit.

Plymouth: On the southwest coast of Britain, Plymouth is one of the principal towns in the county of Devonshire. Major celebrations are planned to commemorate the 400th anniversary of Sir Francis Drake's epic circumnavigation which started and finished here. And it was on

Plymouth Hoe that Drake was said to have finished his game of bowls before setting out to vanquish the Spanish Armada. It was from Plymouth, too, that the Pilgrim Fathers set out for the New World aboard the *Mayflower* in 1620. Today Plymouth is a blend of ancient and modern and makes a good base for exploring **Devon,** the **Cornish Peninsula,** and the bleak, dramatic landscape of **Dartmoor** and **Exmoor.** Hotels in Plymouth: **Holiday Inn,** Armada Way (from US$94) and the **Mayflower Post House,** Cliffe Road, The Hoe (from US$90).

Oxford and the Cotswolds

Oxford: The spires of Britain's oldest university present a magnificent spectacle from the low-lying hills that surround the city, looking much as they did hundreds of years ago. Some time during the 12th century, Oxford became a center of erudition and scholarship. Throughout the ensuing centuries, right up to the present day, colleges have been built through royal and private patronage, and the visitor would do well to spend some time walking through the grounds of at least some of the university's 28 colleges. Especially notable are the grounds of **Magdalen** and **Christ Church,** and the blend of new and old architecture at **Brasenose College.** The city has other treasures, including Wren's **Sheldonian Theatre,** the **Bodleian Library,** and the **Ashmolean Museum.**

Henley and Windsor: Southeast of Oxford in the Thames valley, Henley is the site of the annual **Henley Royal Regatta; Windsor Castle** is an official residence of the reigning monarch; nearby are the lovely grounds of **Windsor Great Park,** and across the Thames are the playing fields of **Eton College,** the famous "public" school.

The Cotswolds: The Cotswolds are a range of hills in the west Midlands of Britain. The characteristic limestone and thatched-roof cottages that are to be found in the area's many charming villages provide a picture of English village life which has looked the same for centuries. **Broadway,** at the foot of a steep hill, is a perfect example and provides a good base for exploring surrounding countryside. Stay at the **Lygon Arms,** High Street (from US$128). **Chipping Campden** is perhaps one of the most beautiful nearby villages; it was a prosperous wool town and its 17th- and 18th-century buildings are dominated by its lovely church. **Cirencester** was the site of a Roman villa; it has an extremely large collection of 15th- and 16th-century monumental brasses in its large Norman church. **Cirencester Park** covers an area of 3,000 acres and is a beautiful spot for walks. Nearer Oxford is the town of **Woodstock,** site of the beautiful **Blenheim Palace,** gift of Queen Anne to the Duke of Marlborough; it was designed by Vanbrugh, and its grounds were laid out by Capability Brown. Sir Winston Churchill was born in an unpretentious bedroom in the palace.

Gloucestershire: West of the Cotswold hills is the county of Gloucestershire, with unspoiled countryside and the elegant Georgian spa town of **Cheltenham.** Stay at **Queen's,** The Promenade (from US$90). The country town of Gloucester has a splendid medieval cathedral.

Shakespeare Country

Stratford-upon-Avon: Shakespeare's birthplace has kept its character intact, in spite of the many tourists that visit there each year. The buildings, mainly Elizabethan and Jacobean, with some Georgian additions, are worth a close look. The visitor will want to attend a performance in the **Royal Shakespeare Theatre** on the banks of the River Avon (performances March-January, tickets from £2.50). There are several other properties of interest, including Shakespeare's birthplace and **Anne Hathaway's Cottage,** a lovely thatched-roof house in a pleasant walk away from the center of town. Hotels in Stratford-upon-Avon:

Falcon, Chapel Street (from US$85)

Shakespeare, Chapel Street (from US$99)

Stratford Hilton, Bridgefoot (from US$105)

Swan's Nest, Bridgefoot (from US$91)

White Swan, Rother Street (from US$79)

Warwick: North of Stratford, the **Forest of Arden** leads you to Warwick, the east and west gates of which date back to the 12th century. There are some interesting half-timbered buildings, notably **Lord Leycester Hospital,** the **Church of St Mary,** and the great **Warwick Castle,** situated above the River Avon.

Kenilworth: The Castle here is one of the grandest ruined fortresses in Britain; it was used by the Saxons, Normans, and Elizabethans, and it is a fascinating place to wander around.

East Anglia

The expanses of flat and marshy, sometimes black-earthed countryside that make up most of Cambridgeshire and Lincolnshire have given East Anglia its characteristic fen landscape. But East Anglia, once the Saxon Kingdom on the east coast of England, also includes the Norfolk Broads, a perfect place for a waterborne summer vacation, and the rolling, lovely countryside of Suffolk, with its charming villages and magnificent churches that have become familiar through the paintings of John Constable.

Norwich: This, the provincial capital of East Anglia, is a beautiful city, unspoiled by the modern world, and has a fine Norman **Cathedral,** a **Castle** with a museum and art gallery, and medieval houses placed along winding streets. It also boasts the **Maddermarket Theatre,** a replica of an Elizabethan theater, with an apron stage. Stay at **Maid's Head,** Tombland (from US$81); **Castle,** Castle Meadow (from US$63).

Bury St Edmunds: This attractive and lively market town blends modern planning with ancient beauty. It has a lovely little Regency **Theatre Royal,** recently restored. The area to the south of Bury is the heart of "Constable Country"; the painter was born in East Bergholt, Suffolk.

Newmarket: Situated on open heathland, Newmarket has been the historic home of horse racing in Britain since the time of King James I in the early 1600s. There are two tracks, the **Rowley Mile Course** used for racing in May, and the **July Course,** used from June through September. Newmarket continues as the center of the thoroughbred world with its famous bloodstock sales in October and December. The rest of the year you will see the best of Britain's equine population and their trainers at work on the 4,000-acre heath.

Ely: Built on high ground and visible for miles from the fens, **Ely Cathedral** is one of the most beautiful in East Anglia; its eight-sided lantern tower is one of special interest and great structural ingenuity. Ely was for centuries a place of refuge, accessible only by boat until the 17th- and 18th-century fen drainage was completed; it remains a focal point for visitors to East Anglia.

Cambridge: The name of the town comes from the fact that here was one of the few places solid enough for a bridge to be built over the Cam, or Granta River. The city's loveliness is a combination of its setting and the graciousness of the buildings of the **University of Cambridge.** The peaceful green lawns of the colleges, many of which extend down to the river, are called "The Backs," and every visitor should take a boat along the river to get the best view. The college buildings of most interest include **King's College Chapel,** with magnificent fan vaulting, Wren's **Trinity College Library,** and the 15th-century **Cloister Court** at Queens College; the gate, bridge, gardens, and main building of **Clare College** are best seen from the river. The city also has the **Fitzwilliam Museum,** a treasure house of paintings and crafts of all ages. A visitor to Cambridge should also explore the **Market Square** and climb to the top of **Great St Mary's Church** for a magnificent view of the city. Stay at the **University Arms Hotel,** Regent Street (from US$72).

Peterborough: This thriving city and market town has a lovely Market Place and 17th-century Guildhall. Its stone **Cathedral** is one of the finest Romanesque structures in the country, with a unique screened west front displaying arched recesses.

The Midlands

This industrial heart of Britain includes not only the factories that produce much of the nation's wealth but some beautiful countryside; the area stretches from the North Sea shore on the east all the way to the uplands on the border of Wales. With its thriving rail and road network, **Birmingham** is a center, both industrial and cultural. The city has a magnificent city **Library** and a leading **Repertory Theatre. Coventry,** east of Birmingham, is rich in history; rebuilt since the massive bombing in World War II, the new **Cathedral** is well worth a visit. **Nottingham** has a beautiful **Council House,** a **Castle** overlooking the city, and an ancient inn. The modern **Nottingham Playhouse** is interesting, as is the older **Theatre Royal.** The 12th- and 13th-century **Lincoln Cathedral,** on a steep limestone hill dominating the town of **Lincoln,** has the highest central tower in England, and a fantastic 13th-century Angel Choir. In Lincoln stay at **White Hart,** Bailgate (from US$63). North of Nottingham is **Sherwood Forest,** of Robin Hood fame, which has magnificent oaks and is great walking country. **Sulgrave Manor,** Sulgrave, Nottinghamshire, is the ancestral home of George Washington.

The North and the Lake District

The north of England has some of the most magnificent scenery and interesting towns in Britain. Dividing it right down the middle is the Pennine chain of hills, called the "backbone" of the country; at the southern end of the area there is the Peak District, where rivers have created vast underground caverns and holes in the soft limestone.

Manchester: A thriving port because of its connection with the Mersey River by the Manchester Ship Canal. Manchester is an industrial city and the heart of the cotton industry in Britain. It is a city with great Victorian buildings, a marvelous **Public Library,** a large university, and the famous **Halle Orchestra.**

York: Dominated by its cathedral, **York Minster,** which has some of the finest stained-glass windows in Europe. York has stretches of its medieval city walls along which the visitor can still walk. The **Shambles,** a cluster of narrow streets where the second floors overhang the streets and nearly touch each other, gives the city its characteristic ancient appearance. Stay at **Royal Station,** Station Road (from US$85) or the **Viking,** North Street (from US$89). Southwest of York is the old spa town of **Harrogate** and the old market town of **Ripon.** Visit the ruin of **Fountains Abbey** and the gardens of **Studley Royal.**

The Moors: North of Manchester and York are the windswept moors, open, unfenced, treeless expanses of heather and grass. The town of **Haworth,** just west of Leeds, was the home of the famous Brontë family, and visitors can walk across the moors to the house on which *Wuthering Heights* was based.

The Lake District: This northwest area of England is composed of mountains, lakes, and dales, and is a marvelous place to hike and drive. This lovely, intensely green area is linked with William Wordsworth, whose Dove Cottage can be seen at **Grasmere,** and Beatrix Potter, who lived and worked in the area, and whose home can also be visited. The Lake District is 900 square miles of some of the most attractive and unspoiled countryside in Britain.

Scotland

A sparsely populated, spacious, and beautifully green landscape coupled with interesting, ancient cities makes Scotland a place every visitor should see. Reminders of Sir Walter Scott, Robert Burns, and Mary, Queen of Scots, are to be found throughout the country. Prestwick Airport for Scotland is about 32 miles from Glasgow. The bus fare into the city is £2.20 (half-price for children).

Edinburgh: One of the most beautiful and sophisticated cities in Britain, Edinburgh is the social and cultural center of Scotland. Its old city has winding streets, **Edinburgh Castle,** and the **Palace of Holyroodhouse,** the Queen's official residence in Scotland. The new town section of the city has the Georgian **Princes Street,** with shops on one side and **Princes Street Gardens** on the other. The **Edinburgh International Festival of Music and Drama,** world famous for its excellence, takes place every summer in late August and early September. Across the River Forth, in the county of Fife, is picturesque **St Andrews**—a university town and the mecca for golfers around the world. Other famous golf courses can be found at **Gleneagles, Turnberry, Troon,** and **Muirfield.**

Glasgow: The only complete medieval cathedral in Scotland is in Glasgow, Scotland's largest city. Located on the banks of the River Clyde, and essentially an industrial town, Glasgow has many fine parks. Nearby is the **Loch Lomond National Nature Reserve.**

The Highlands and Western Isles: The gateway to this remote and beautiful northern area of Scotland is the centrally located town of **Perth.** To the northwest is **Fort William,** overshadowed by Britain's highest mountain, **Ben Nevis,** and within easy driving distance of the famed **Loch Ness. Aberdeen,** one of Britain's most famous fishing ports, is now also the center of the offshore oil-drilling industry. From here you can drive to **Balmoral Castle,** which is not open to the public. However, royalty is always present at the **Braemar Highland Games** which takes place the first Saturday in September; during the winter months, enjoy a weekend's skiing at the winter resort areas of **Aviemore** and the **Cairngorms.** The "capital of the Highlands," **Inverness,** is—like the other Scottish cities mentioned here—an excellent place to shop for tartans, knitwear, tweeds, and native craft items.

The best known of the western islands is the **Isle of Skye.** The outer islands include the **Outer Hebrides,** the **Orkneys,** and the **Shetland Isles.** Further information for reaching these islands by air or sea is obtainable from the **British Tourist Authority,** London; New York, Chicago, Los Angeles, and Dallas in the US.

Wales

United with England for 700 years, the Welsh people have their own language and literature and have retained their own individuality and culture, made famous by Dylan Thomas. Wales offers the visitor superb scenery and facilities for the outdoor sportsman.

South Wales: This scenic area includes **Tintern Abbey** in Gwent and the narrow **Valley of Rhondda** that leads toward the hilly and green **Brecon Beacons. Caerphilly Castle** is located northwest of Cardiff, the capital city of Wales.

Central and North Wales: Central Wales, with the Cambrian mountains running north and south through it, is great country for the sportsman interested in fishing, sailing, and hiking. The university town of **Aberystwyth** is here. In North Wales, a hiker's paradise, is **Snowdon,** the highest mountain in England and Wales (3,560 feet). **Snowdon National Park** has magnificent views and beautiful areas for climbing and walking. The business and tourist center of **Caernarvon** is here, as is **Caernarvon Castle,** official seat of the Prince of Wales. To the northwest are the **Menai Straits, Anglesey,** once the sacred home of the Druids, and towering masses of rock in wild, barren countryside. Music lovers from around the world gather for the **International Eisteddfod** which takes place at **Llangollen,** Clwyd, the second week in July.

Northern Ireland

The beautiful countryside of Northern Ireland makes it a lovely place for a vacation; the unspoiled scenery of the countryside contrasts starkly with the current political unrest. In a quieter time, the visitor would do well to spend his days relaxing and walking or playing golf at one of the many well-known golf courses.

SOURCES OF FURTHER INFORMATION

Pan Am: 193 Piccadilly, London W1. Tel: (01) 734-7292; Lombard House, Great Charles Street, Queensway, Birmingham 3, Tel: (021) 236-9561; 10 King Street, Manchester 2, Tel: (061) 832-7626; 127 Buchanan Street, Glasgow, Tel: (041) 248-5744. **British Tourist Authority:** 680 Fifth Avenue, New York, NY 10019 Tel: (212) 581-4700; 612 South Flower Street, Los Angeles, CA 90017 Tel: (213) 623-8196; John Hancock Center Suite #3320, 875 North Michigan Ave, Chicago, IL 60611 Tel: (312) 787-0490; 64 St James's Street, London SW1 Tel: (01) 499-9325.

Greece

WHAT'S SPECIAL

Greece combines past greatness and present vitality with a wonderful climate. Here you will discover the history and culture of ancient civilizations and still enjoy all the comforts of the 20th century. Greece has one of the longest coastlines in Europe, beautiful and varied scenery—from the mountains of the north, the plains of Thessaly, and the rich valleys of the Peloponnese to the golden beaches of Attica—and enchanting islands, ideal for a relaxing holiday.

COUNTRY BRIEFING

Size: 50,944 square miles   **Population:** 9,500,000

Capital: Athens   **Capital Population:** Greater Athens 3,600,000

Climate: Mild Mediterranean climate; over 300 days of sunshine a year. February has the most rain. South of Athens and on the islands the weather is ideal 10 months of the year; elsewhere spring and fall are best.

Weather in Athens: Lat N37°58′; Alt 351 ft.

Temp (°F)	Jan	Feb	Mar	Apr	May	Jun	Jul	Aug	Sep	Oct	Nov	Dec
Av Low	42°	43°	46°	52°	60°	67°	72°	72°	66°	60°	52°	46°
Av High	54°	55°	60°	67°	77°	85°	90°	90°	83°	74°	64°	57°
Days no rain	24	22	26	27	28	28	30	30	28	27	24	24

Government: A republic.

Language: Modern Greek; English and French are widely understood and spoken.

Religion: 90% Greek Orthodox. Other denominations in Athens include Moslem, Protestant, Roman Catholic, and Jewish.

Currency: Drachma. 100 leptas = 1 drachma.

	5 Dr	10 Dr	20 Dr	50 Dr	100 Dr	500 Dr	1,000 Dr	1,500 Dr
US (dollars, cents)	.09	.18	.36	.89	1.79	8.95	17.89	26.84
UK (pounds, pence)	.04	.09	.17	.43	.86	4.28	8.55	12.83

Public Holidays:

New Year's Day, 1 Jan	Labor Day, 1 May
Epiphany, 6 Jan	Pentecost
Independence Day, 25 Mar	Feast of Virgin Mary, 15 Aug
Shrove Monday	National Day, 28 Oct
Good Friday	Christmas Day, 25 Dec
Easter Monday	Boxing Day, 26 Dec

HOW TO GET THERE

Flying time to Athen's Hellinikon Airport from New York is 10 hours; from Rome, ¾ hour; from Istanbul, 1¼ hours. Time in Greece: GMT+2. Daylight Saving Time observed.

REQUIREMENTS FOR ENTRY AND CUSTOMS REGULATIONS

A valid passport is required. Vaccination certificates required only when entering from an infected area. UK, Canadian, and US citizens may stay in the country up to three months without a visa, as may nationals of most British Commonwealth and most European countries. Thereafter a special permit is required—available from the Athens Aliens Bureau (9 Halkokondili Street—tel: 362 8301 or 362 2601) or from the nearest police station in smaller towns. Any amount of foreign currency and gold may be freely imported, but any sum in excess of US$500 should be declared on arrival if it is to be re-exported. Up to Dr1,500 in Greek currency may be imported or exported. Personal checks and travelers' checks can be freely re-exported, as can up to US$500 in banker's orders within 1 year of entry. Duty-free allowance: 200 cigarettes or 200 grams tobacco; 1 bottle liquor; 1 bottle wine; 60 grams perfume; gifts and new articles intended for personal use to the value of US$150, and a reasonable supply of food. Be prepared to show binoculars, cameras, record players, typewriters, etc.; although exempt from tax, they must be entered on your passport for re-exit purposes. Special license required for the exportation of antiquities. The importation of drugs and weapons, apart from licensed shotguns, is strictly forbidden.

AIRPORT INFORMATION

Hellinikon Airport is approximately 6 miles from Athens city center. Airport bus (yellow) to downtown Athens runs every 20 minutes; fare is Dr45, including luggage. Regular local buses (blue) run every 35 minutes to Athens (#184) and every hour to Piraeus (#185) but take no luggage—fare Dr15. Taxis are also available, approximate fare to city center Dr250. There is no departure tax for international flights. The airport has a hotel reservation counter and a duty-free shop.

ACCOMMODATIONS

Very wide range of high-standard accommodations. Apart from deluxe hotels, the other five hotel categories are regularly inspected and classified by the government. Athens hotels:

Rates are in US$ for a double/twin room with bath or shower

Acropole Palace, 51, 28th Octovriou (from $34)

Alfa, 17 Halkokondili (from $20)

Amalia, 10 Amalias Avenue (from $44)

Ambassadeurs, 67 Sokratous (from $30)

Astor, 16 Karageorgi Servias (from $30)

ATHENAEUM INTER·CONTINENTAL, Syngrou Avenue (luxury class, rates unavailable)

Athenee Palace, 1 Koloktroni Square (from $49)

Athens Hilton, 46 Vassilissis Sofias (from $105)

Attika Palace, 6 Karageorgi Servias (from $30)

Caravel, 2 Vassileos Alexandrou (from $68)

Elektra, 5 Ermou (from $30)

Esperia Palace, 22 Stadiou (from $30)

Grande Bretagne, Syntagma (Constitution) Square (from $90)

Holiday Inn, 50 Mihalakopoulou (from $58)

King George, Syntagma Square (from $78)

King Minos, 1 Pireos (from $30)

Kings' Palace, 4 Eleftheriou Venizelou (from $45)

Meridien, Syntagma (Constitution) Square (from $98)

Olympic Palace, 16 Filelinon (from $30)

Park, 10 Alexandras Avenue (from $59)

Royal Olympic, 28-34 Diakou (from $55)

St George Lycabettus, 2 Kleomenous (from $50)

The above hotels are all centrally located within 1 mile of Constitution Square.

USEFUL INFORMATION

Banks: International banking facilities available in Athens, in some other towns, and on major islands. Large amounts of foreign currency can be exchanged only at the Bank of Greece or the American Express Company in Athens. Banking hours in general are 8-2, Mon-Fri. Some banks also open evenings. The National Bank of Greece (2 Karageorgi Servias Street, Athens) is open 8-9, Mon-Fri; 8-8, Sat-Sun.

Mail: Stamps available from post offices, kiosks, and hotels. Mailboxes small, bright yellow.

Telephone Tips: Most street newsstand kiosks have telephones. The charge for a local call from coin phones is Dr2. Booths available elsewhere.

Long-distance calls from hotels, or at 15 Stadiou Street, open 8-12pm (dial 161 for overseas service from regular phones). Useful numbers in Athens:

Pan Am 323 5242

Airport Information (Olympic Airways) 981 1201

Airport Information (International flights, except Olympic) 979 9466 or 979 9467

Accommodation Offices 323 7193

Tourist Information Center 322-2545 or 322-1459

First Aid Center 166

Domestic Operator 151 or 152

International Operator 161 or 162

Emergency Police 100

Tourist Police 171

Fire 199

Auto Assistance 104

American Embassy 712 951

British Embassy 736 211

Canada and US are connected via the automatic exchange direct with Greece. (International prefix: 001.)

Newspapers. English-language newspapers and magazines available; the *Athens News* and *Athens Post* are in English. *The Athenian,* an English-language monthly, lists useful tourist information, including cultural events, restaurants, nightlife, addresses, and phone numbers.

Tipping: 10-15% included on hotel prices and restaurant checks, but waiters expect about 10% extra, and hotel staff Dr50. In cafés, bars, and restaurants, tip Dr5-10, depending on the class of the establishment. Taxi drivers—10%, but not obligatory. Luggage porters, Dr10 (per piece of luggage); hotel porters, Dr10-20 (depending on class of hotel); chambermaids, Dr200 per week; cloakroom attendants, Dr20; tour bus drivers, Dr20; hairdressers, 10-20%. In general tip Dr10 for small services.

Electricity: 220 volts 50 cycles AC is standard throughout Greece. Only in a very few districts is it still 110 DC.

Laundry: Laundry and dry-cleaning services available in Athens and major towns; 24-hour service in major hotels.

Hairdressing: Most deluxe and A-class hotels have salons (shampoo, cut, and set, about Dr1200; man's haircut from Dr310).

Photography: Photographic equipment is available but rather expensive; black and white 35mm film costs from Dr182 (36 prints), and color costs from Dr198 (24 prints) and Dr250 (36 prints). Prices are higher at kiosks than in shops. Black and white film developed within a week; color, about a week to 10 days, and longer in the tourist season.

Clubs: Kiwanis, Rotary (3 Kriezotou Street), Lions, American Club (tel: 801 2987).

Babysitting: In Athens can be arranged through hotels. Expect to pay about Dr200-250 an hour.

Rest Rooms: In hotels, restaurants, cafés; public lavatories in the main squares of major cities.

Health: English-speaking doctors and dentists. Further information obtainable from hotels and the **Medical Association,** 61 Akadimias Street, Athens (tel: 361 7141). Imported pharmaceuticals and toiletries available. Drinking water safe in Athens and resorts. Avoid well water. Bottled mineral water also obtainable. It is advisable to wash fruit before eating.

TRANSPORTATION

Public transportation is inexpensive. There is a comprehensive network of road, sea, and air services. Plenty of local buses; long-distance buses link major cities. Athens also has trolley buses and a subway service to suburban areas. Price per ride on trolley, bus, or subway is Dr10. Some buses and trolleys require exact change. Renting a car costs around US$20 per day, plus about US20¢ per kilometer; there is an 18% tax. A valid international driving license is required. Chauffeur-driven cars are also available. Taxis can be hailed on the street or ordered through hotels; metered taxis start with a flat charge of Dr15 and then go up at the rate of Dr12.50 per kilometer within the Athens-Piraeus area. Minimum fare: Dr50. Extra charges are Dr10 per piece of luggage, Dr20 for boarding between midnight and 5am, and Dr10 when boarding at any public transport terminal. Country-wide bus tours with English-speaking guides operate. Every important area of mainland Greece may be reached using the Greek railroad network. Food usually available, and there are sleeper cars on the Inter-Continental Express. The Greek State Railways Organization also runs luxury buses to connect areas not on the rail route. Car and passenger ferries from Piraeus serve the major islands, and from late March through October, 2- to 7-day Greek Island cruises operate. Yachts can also be chartered. Olympic Airways offers an extensive network of domestic flights to many islands and mainland airports.

FOOD AND RESTAURANTS

It is not difficult to find international food, but try the Greek cuisine; there is a variety of unusual and tasty dishes. Prices in restaurants and *tavernas*, except in those of the luxury class, are under strict control and are reasonable. In *tavernas* the atmosphere and food are distinctly Greek. Delicious and unusual appetizers include *taramasalata* (fish roe dip), *tsatziki* (cucumber, yoghurt, and garlic dip) and an eggplant dip. *Avgolemono* or egg and lemon soup is a specialty, and the egg and lemon combination often appears as a sauce with entrées. Lamb dishes are great favorites and there is excellent seafood, including *barbounia* (red mullet), *marida* (like white-bait), squid, and octopus. Among the most popular Greek dishes are *dolmades* (vine leaves stuffed with ground meat and rice—made into smaller *dolmadakia*, they are served as appetizers); *moussaka* (a casserole with alternate layers of eggplant, ground meat, and béchamel sauce); *pastichio* (another casserole, with ground meat and macaroni); and *keftedes* or Greek meatballs. These, too, are made into smaller *keftedakia* and served as appetizers. Desserts are sweet and sticky—*baklava* is made of flaky *phyllo* pastry, honey, and nuts, and *kadaife* is a sugary mixture of nutmeats in a shredded pastry. *Kourabiedes* are rich, almond-flavored cookies covered with powdered sugar.

Dinner in a large hotel or deluxe restaurant in Athens, like **Dionysos** opposite the Acropolis (Philopappos Hill—tel: 913 778), which serves both lunch and dinner, costs from US$20 per person, with wine. Try **Balthazar** (at Tsoha and Vournazou 27), **Athens Cellar** (Anagnostopoulou 1, Kolonaki), and **Gerofinikas** (Pirandou 10). Some medium-priced restau-

rants—average price of dinner per person US$10-15, including wine—
are **Corfu** (6 Kriezotou Street, Constitution [Syntagma] Square—tel: 361
3011); **Floka** (9 Eleftheriou Venizelou Street—tel: 323 4064); **Zonar's** (9
Eleftheriou Venizelou Street—tel: 322 6990); and **Stagecoach** (6 Loukianou Street—tel: 730 507), which serves American-style steaks. For French
cuisine try **L'Abreuvoir** (51 Xenokratous Street, Kolonaki—tel: 729 106).
In one of the inexpensive restaurants or *tavernas*, dinner for one costs
from US$7-10 (including wines). An excellent Plaka *taverna* with music
is **Xynou** (Angelou Yerondos 4), while the **O Platanos** (Diognous 4) is
inexpensive. **Ta Tria Adelphia** (Elpidos 7, Victoria Square) is a moderately
priced *taverna*. Also try the traditional meal of hors d'oeuvres washed
down with ouzo, beer, or wine. The most famous one in Athens is **Apotsos**
(Venizelou 10). Across the street is the smaller **Orfanides** (Venizelou 7).
Outside the city are **Psaropoulos** (Glyfada); **Blue Pines** at Kifissia, 8½
miles north of the city; the **Club House** at Vouliagmeni (15 miles away);
and the fish restaurants along the **Mikrolimano** yacht harbor in Piraeus.

Snack foods available everywhere at street stalls are *souvlaki* (roasted,
skewered chunks of meat) and *giro* (shredded lamb pressed into a circular
form from which slices are cut for a sandwich), *tiropetes* and *spanakopetes*
(triangles of phyllo pastry and cheese or spinach). *Feta,* a crumbly, white
goat cheese, is one of the ingredients of the typical Greek salad that
makes a good, light lunch for a day at the beach. And Greek yoghurt
(yiaourti) is delicious, especially at breakfast with fruit and honey.

DRINKING TIPS

Drinks are served at any time. *Ouzo,* the national aperitif, has a strong
aniseed flavor. It is very potent, and most people take it with water
and ice. A characteristic wine is *retsina,* with a strong taste of resin.
There are also many unresinated wines, and each region produces its
own special variety. Greek wines range in both price and quality, but
even inexpensive table wines are quite drinkable. There is good and
inexpensive brandy. Imported drinks tend to be expensive. Small cups
of strong Greek coffee are drunk, accompanied by a glass of water. The
sugar is already in it and usually quite a lot—so ask for it *metrio* (medium
sweet) or *sketo,* without sugar. Two popular cafés in Athens are **Floka**
and **Zonar's.** Also popular are the cafés around Kolonaki Square.

ENTERTAINMENT

Nightlife in Greece is lively, especially during summer, and there is something to suit every taste. The **Athens Festival,** a series of nightly plays,
concerts, opera, and ballet, is held from July to the end of September
at the ancient **Herod Atticus Theatre** just below the Acropolis. Tickets
from the Festival Office (4 Stadiou Street) or from the theater. **Sound
and Light** performances are given in Athens, Corfu, and Rhodes in English and other languages from April through October. In Athens alone,
there are many winter theaters and open-air summer theaters presenting
both classical and modern plays. Opera and concerts are presented at
the **Olympia Theater** in winter, and summer concerts at the **Lycabettus**

Theater and the **Herod Atticus Theater.** The famous **Dora Stratou Folk Dancers** give performances nightly during the summer season at the open-air theater on Philopappos Hill. There are numerous movie houses, outdoors in summer, which show American and European films with Greek subtitles, and there is a wide variety of nightclubs, discothèques, tavernas, and *bouzoukias* for local color, dinner, dancing, and Greek music. Many of these are to be found in the narrow winding streets of the picturesque Plaka district at the foot of the Acropolis. Lively nightspots include **Athinea** (6 Panepistimiou Street), the **Supper Club** at the Hilton Hotel, **Annabella** (at Agios Kosmas, a suburb near the airport), **On the Rocks** (Varkiza—30 miles outside Athens), and for *bouzouki* music, **Dilina** (Glyfada—south of Athens along the coast) and **Fantasia** at Glyfada during summer and at 50 Keffallinias Street in winter. For cabarets try **Copacabana** at Voula (along the coast beyond Glyfada) during summer and at 10 Othonos Street during winter.

Outside Athens, numerous annual events include the Fire-walking Ceremony at Langadas, near Salonika—21 May; ceremonies in Piraeus and other naval harbors to celebrate **Naval Week,** late June; the open-air **Epidaurus Festival** of ancient Greek drama that takes place weekends from July to mid-August; other open-air drama festivals in the ancient theaters of **Philippi** in Macedonia, and **Dodoni** in Epirus, during August. At Daphni, near Athens, there is a **Wine Festival** from July through September, with many different varieties of wine which can be sampled for a small admission charge, plus dancing, singing, floor shows, and *bouzouki* music. In Thessaloniki, the **Demetria Festival** of drama, opera, ballet, and music is held during October.

SPORTS

Spectator sports include soccer, basketball, and horse racing, which takes place twice weekly on the **Faliron Race Course;** auto racing is popular, and the most important event is the annual **Acropolis rally,** in the second half of May. The Greek seas are hunting grounds for amateur anglers and spear-fishing enthusiasts. Underwater activities take place at many of the islands in areas defined by the Archeological Society, and there is freshwater fishing in lakes, including **Loutraki** and **Ioaninon.** Information from the **Association of Underwater Activities and Fishing** (Agios Kosmas), Hellenikon (tel: 981 7166). Visitors may hunt hare, quail, and partridge throughout Greece; the **River Evros** area is especially popular. Information and hunting permits from the Department of Hunting and Fishing in the Ministry of Agriculture (2 Acharnon Street, Athens). Yacht races take place in and off **Faliron Bay,** and yacht owners, if accompanied by a member, are welcome at the **Hellenic Yacht Club** (Mikrolimano, Piraeus—tel: 417 9730). For details on yachting and canoeing, contact the **Greek Yacht Brokers' Association** (25 Loukianou Street). There are new golf courses on the islands of **Corfu** and **Rhodes** and at the **Glyfada Golf Course and Club** (tel: 894 6820) down the coast. There are horseback riding stables at the **Helenic Riding Club** (18 Paradissou Street, Maroussi—tel: 681 2508) and the **Athens Riding Club** (Gerakas, Agia Paraskevi—tel: 659 3803). Visitors are welcome at the **Athens Tennis Club** (2 Vassilissis Olgas Avenue—tel: 923 2872) and at the **Panhellinios Gymnastics Club** (26 Mavromateon Street—tel: 823 3720). Climbing, hiking, and mountaineering are popular on the mainland and in Crete, and during the winter months there is skiing at **Mt Vermio** in Macedonia, **Metsovo** in Epirus, and **Mt Pelion** in Thessaly. The ski center at **Mt Parnassus,** near Delphi, is the closest to Athens and has the most modern facilities. Further information is obtainable from the **Greek Skiing and Alpine Association** (7 Karageorgi Servias Street, Athens—tel: 323 4555). Target shooting is practiced at the **Kaisariani** shooting ranges outside Athens, and fencing is mainly practiced in Athens at the **Segas** building, 25 Panepistimiou Street, and at the **Panhellinios Gymnastics Club.** Various sporting events take place in the **Panathenaic Stadium,** built for the 1896 Olympic Games, and a vast **Sports Center** at Agios Kosmas on the Saronic Gulf comprises a whole complex of sportsgrounds, tennis courts, etc., plus a hostel with 46 twin-bedded rooms.

SHOPPING

Shopping hours vary according to the category of shop and day of the week, but in general, shops open at 8am and close 1:30-2:30pm, Mondays through Saturdays. Many shops are open evenings on Tuesday, Thursday, and Friday from 5:30-8:30pm. It is customary to bargain in the street market at **Monastiraki** in Athens, open every morning but particularly busy on Sundays. Greek handicraft articles are a good buy in any part of Greece and include woven fabrics and small fabric bags from **Arahova** (near Delphi); wood-carved articles from **Vitina** (near Tripolis) and **Metsovo;** island knitwear; textiles from **Mykonos;** handmade silver jewelry from **Epirus;** gold and silver ornaments from **Rhodes;** ceramics and alabaster from **Crete; Skyros** pottery; handwoven shirts and dresses; sandals; brass and copper; worry beads; embroidery; *flokati* (long pile rugs in vivid colors). Also of interest are sponges, honey, *ouzo,* and brandy. There is a permanent exhibition of Greek folk art and handicrafts at 9 Mitropoleos Street, Athens. The main shopping areas for all types of clothing, jewelry, and Greek handicrafts are along the main streets which lead off **Syntagma** (Constitution) **Square,** in **Monastiraki,** and around the old quarter of Athens—the **Plaka** district. There are many small, high-quality fashion boutiques, art galleries, and specialty shops for prints, antiques, handicrafts, and other items in the **Kolonaki** section of Athens, a short walking distance from the business section. Many major stores will pack and ship purchases.

WHAT TO SEE

In **Athens,** maps and information brochures are available from the National Tourist Organization office at 2 Amerikis Street or from the Tourist Information Office in the National Bank on Syntagma Square. Bus tours can be arranged through hotels or travel agencies. Admission to the **Acropolis** and all other ancient monuments and museums is free on Sundays. Museum hours vary according to the season. The most famous archeological site in the world is surely the hill of the **Acropolis,** dominated by the **Parthenon,** the sacred temple of Athena, and one of the most skillfully contrived pieces of architecture in existence. From here there is an excellent view of Athens, Piraeus, and the sea. On the hill around the Parthenon stands the **Erechtheion**—famous for its porch of graceful Caryatids (maidens); the imposing **Propylaea,** the entrance gate to the Acropolis; and the exquisite little temple of **Apteros Nike,** also called the Wingless Victory. On the southeastern slopes of the Acropolis is the **Theater of Dionysus,** built in the 5th century BC, where the plays of Aeschylus and Sophocles were first performed, and on the southwestern slope the theater of **Herod Atticus,** now the site of summer events in the **Athens Festival.** Just southeast of the Acropolis, note the beautiful **Monument of Lysicrates**—334 BC. A little farther, the soaring **Arch of Hadrian** still stands, and just behind it is the **Temple of the Olympian Zeus**—one of the greatest temples of the Hellenic world. Northwest of the Acropolis are the ruins of the **Agora,** the marketplace and civic center, and nearby, the **Temple of Hephaestus** or **Thesseion** is marvelously preserved. Directly north of the Acropolis, there are the remains of **Hadrian's Library,** the **Roman Forum,** and the **Tower of Winds,** built in the 1st century BC to house a hydraulic clock and sundial. Relics of the Roman era are also to be found among the present-day houses of the **Plaka** (old town) district, now filled with picturesque tavernas. Visit the **Stadium,** also ancient, built into a hillside, and restored for the celebration of the first modern Olympic Games in 1896. Three Byzantine churches in Athens are definitely worth a visit; beautiful 12th-century **Agios Eleftherios** on Mitropoleos Square, the 11th-century **Kapnikarea** with its tiled gables on Ermou Street, the 10th-century **Agii Theodori** on Agii Theodori Square. The funicular railway from Kolonaki Square climbs to the top of **Lycabettus Hill,** where stands the little church of **Agios Georgios** (St George). From here, almost 1,000 feet above the city center, there is a marvelous view over Athens, the **Saronic Gulf,** and the **Plain of Attica.** Among Athens's museums, the **National Archeological Museum** is the most important for its classical sculpture and gold treasures from Mycenae. **The Benaki Museum** (corner Vassilissis Sofias Avenue and Koumbari Street) has a wide-ranging collection of regional costumes and *objets d'art,* and one of the best collections of Byzantine icons in the world is housed in the **Byzantine Museum** (22 Vassilissis Sofias Avenue). In downtown, modern Athens, you can stroll through the **National Gardens** near Syntagma Square to see the colorfully costumed *Evzones* guarding the Presidential Residence beyond.

Excursions out of Athens: Visit the 11th-century monastery of **Daphni**—which contains superb mosaics—on the road to Eleusis, and the Byzantine monastery and gardens of **Kaisariani** on the slopes of **Mount Hymettus. Marathon,** where the Athenians defeated the Persians, is 28 miles northeast of Athens, and at the southern tip of Attica lies **Cape Sounion** with the spectacular white temple of **Poseidon** overlooking the sea. A longer excursion can be made by car, train, or bus in 1 day to the major sites of the **Peloponnese.**

Nauplion, the former capital, is a pleasant little port with an old Venetian fort. Epidaurus was the center of the cult of Asclepius, the god of healing; you will see the vast temple and the largest (14,000 seating capacity), best-preserved ancient theater in Greece, with marvelous acoustics. Corinth has the remains of a temple of Apollo and the fountain of Pierene springing from high up on Acro-Corinth, a huge crusader castle.

Mycenae is a most important archeological site and the fabled home of Agamemnon. The treasures unearthed there are now in the National Archeological Museum in Athens, but you can still climb up through the famous Lion Gate to the underground beehive tombs. In the southern Peloponnese is Diros, a beautiful bay in the Gulf of Messinia, with sea caves where remains of a prehistoric community have been found.

Delphi, 100 miles west of Athens, is superbly situated in the southern foothills of Mount Parnassus. It was the sanctuary of Apollo and the Nine Muses and home of the famous Pythian oracle. Visit the ancient theater, the stadium, the Temple of Pronaea Athena, and the Museum with the well-known bronze statue of the *Charioteer*. Hotels in Delphi are the Amalia, Apollonos Street; Vouzas, 1 Pavlou & Friderikis; Castalia, Vas. Pavlou & Friderikis; and King Iniohos, Osiou Louka Street; all US$31-32 double BB.

At Olympia, 200 miles west of Athens, the first Olympic Games were held in 776 BC; the sacred flame burns eternally in the Stadium. The Museum contains the famous *Hermes* of Praxiteles. Hotels include the Spap Hotel (from US$39 double BB), the Xenios Zeus Motel (from US$22 BB), and the Xenia (from US$32 BB).

Thessaloniki (Salonica): This is the second-largest city in Greece and a commercial seaport, once a thriving Byzantine metropolis. Landmarks include the Triumphal Arch of Emperor Galerius and several early basilicas. Hotels include the Capitol, 8 Monastiriou Street (from US$30 double BB); the Macedonia Palace, Kennedy Avenue (from US$58 double BB); the Elektra Palace, Aristotelous Square (from US$30 double BB); and the Olympic Hotel, 25 Egnatius Street (from US$19 double BB). All are in the town center, except for the Macedonia Palace, which is a mile away.

Mount Athos, on a narrow peninsula in the northern Aegean Sea and one of the great beauty spots of Greece, is a strict monastic community. Women are not allowed to visit it, but male visitors may stay overnight. An entry permit, obtainable from the Ministry of Foreign Affairs in Athens, or from the Ministry of Northern Greece in Thessaloniki, is required. Kavala, the principal town of eastern Macedonia, is one of the loveliest seaside towns in Greece.

The Islands: Capital of the Dodecanese, Rhodes is an island of superb natural beauty and is famous as a vacation center. Rich in archeological treasures, with ruins covering the Hellenic, Roman, and Byzantine periods, its main attraction is the walled medieval city of the Knights of St John. The 15th-century hospital is now an archeological museum containing the *Aphrodite of Rhodes*. Other points of interest include the ancient city of **Lindos** with the **Temple of Athena;** the **Monastery of Philerimos** and the excavated town of **Kamiros.** There are excellent sports facilities and duty-free shops. There are plenty of nightclubs and a casino in the luxury **Grand Hotel. Sound and Light** performances are held April-October, the **National Theater** produces folk plays in Greek, and folk dancing takes place twice weekly June-October. The annual **Wine Festival** takes place from July to early September in Rodini Park, and on the offshore island of **Halki,** there are religious festivities on 15 August. Hotels in Rhodes:

Belvedere, Canaris Beach (from US$36 double BB)
Cairo Palace, Makariou Street (from US$31 BB)
Golden Beach, Trianta (from US$36 double BB)
Grand Hotel, Vassileos Constantinou Street (from US$56 double BB)
Ibiscus, Kos Beach (from US$36 double BB)
Miramare Beach, Trianta (from US$73 double BB)
Park, Riga Fereou Street (from US$36 double BB)
Rodos Bay, Trianta (from US$28 double BB)
Thermae, Makariou Street (from US$22 double BB)

From Rhodes you can visit the small islands of the eastern Aegean. **Kos** is a most delightful and a fertile green island with golden beaches, good for fishing and small-game hunting. Birthplace of Hippocrates, "Father of Medicine," it has a temple to **Asclepius,** god of healing, and a museum. Stay at the **Atlantis Hotel** (from US$26 double), the **Continental Palace** (from US$26 double BB), the **Caravia** or the **Ramira Beach** (both from US$26 double BB). Nearby **Patmos** was where St John wrote down his *Revelation;* the 11th-century monastery has a rich library. **Lesbos** was the birthplace of the poet Sappho. It is the third-largest island of Greece, with enormous olive groves and a petrified forest.

Corfu (**Kerkira** in Greek) is the most beautiful of the Ionian Islands. Its spectacular scenery and sophisticated tourist amenities make it an international holiday center. The ornate **Achilleion Palace** is now an elaborate casino, with restaurant, nightclub, and snack bar. There are beautiful villas, romantic Venetian castles, and early 19th-century Georgian architecture dating from the British occupation. The 16th-century **Cathedral** is dedicated to St Spyridon, the island's patron saint. There are marvelous water sports facilities and an 18-hole golf course. Daily flights from Athens take 55 minutes. Hotels: **Corfu Palace** (from US$92 double BB), the **Cavalieri** (from US$40 BB), the **Astron, King Alkinoos,** and the **Olympic** (all from US$32 double BB).

Mykonos is the most popular tourist island in the Cyclades and attracts many artists and international celebrities. It is a maze of winding streets, sparkling whitewashed houses, domed churches, windmills, and sundrenched cliffs rising sheer from the sea. It is 5½ hours by boat from Piraeus. Hotels include the **Alkistis,** Agios Stefanos Beach (from US$37 double BB), **Ano Mera** (from US$26 double BB), **Leto** (from US$39 double BB), **Aphroditi** and **Despotika** (both from US$26 double BB). **Delos** is 5 miles across the sea from Mykonos. A small, arid island, it was important

151

as the legendary birthplace of Apollo and Artemis. Acres of ruins and statuary attract archeologists, and precious relics are preserved in the museum. On **Thira** (Santorini), climb up above its cliffs to the crater of the volcano whose mighty eruption buried Minoan civilization. Hotels in Santorini include the **Atlantis** (from US$26 double BB). **Milos,** where the *Venus de Milo* was found, and **Paros,** famous for its white marble, are also in the Cyclades group.

Crete: Largest of the Greek islands, it is ideal for winter sunshine with sandy beaches, high mountains, and warm, flower-scented air. The amazingly advanced Minoan civilization flourished here 5,000 years ago. **Knossos, Phaestos,** and **Gortyna** are the three most ancient cities, and splendid royal tombs and palaces have been unearthed. The murals in the **Palace of Minos** at Knossos are world-famous. The **Iraklion Museum** exhibits the rich finds from the excavations. Among the wide range of activities are mountaineering, hunting, water sports, and a lively nightlife, with many local tavernas, clubs, and discothèques. Festivities of **St John the Baptist** (bonfires and folk dances) take place on 24 June. Crete is 45 minutes by plane from Athens; boats from Piraeus and interisland boats. Hotels in Crete:

Atlantis, Merembelou and Yghias Streets, Iraklion (from US$42 double BB)

Xenia, Venizelou Street, Iraklion (from US$26 double BB)

Minos Beach, Agios Nikolaus (from US$83 double BB)

Doma, Hania (US$22-26 double BB)

Diktyna, Hania (US$15 double)

Xenia, Rethymnon (US$20 double)

Spetsai and **Hydra** are picturesque islands in the Saronic Gulf, easily accessible by boat from Piraeus.

In the North Aegean, off the eastern coast of central Greece, are the Sporades islands—**Skiathos, Skopelos, Alonnissos,** and **Skyros.** They are favored by many visitors because they are green and wooded, and, like the rest of the Greek islands, they possess an incomparable climate.

SOURCES OF FURTHER INFORMATION

Pan Am, 4 Othonos Street, Syntagma Square, Athens, and any Pan Am office around the world; **National Tourist Organization,** 2 Amerikis Street, Athens; **Greek National Tourist Organization,** Olympic Tower, 645 Fifth Avenue, New York, NY 10022 and Crocker-Citizens Building, 627 West Sixth Street, Los Angeles, CA 90017; **National Tourist Organization of Greece,** 195-197 Regent Street, London W1R 8DL.

Hungary

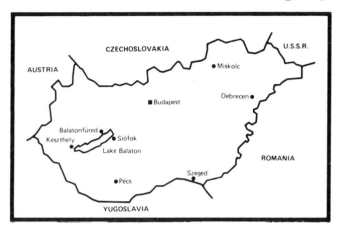

WHAT'S SPECIAL

In Hungary you can drive in a horse-drawn gig over the *Puszta,* the great Hungarian plains, go for a swim in Europe's largest warm-water lake, spend the night in a sumptuous palace where the Esterhazy aristocracy once lived, or dine on magnificent goulash, sipping Bull's Blood (a local red wine) to the strains of soulful gypsy violins. You can wander through the pleasant café-lined streets of the twin cities of Buda and Pest, go on a cruise down the River Danube, join in the festivities at a traditional village wedding, or just lie in the sun by Lake Balaton.

COUNTRY BRIEFING

Size: 35,919 square miles   **Population:** 10,700,000
Capital: Budapest   **Capital Population:** 2,050,000

  Climate: Winters in Hungary are rather harsh and cold, but the snow cover in the mountains lasts only 60-90 days. Summers are warm and pleasant, with temperatures in the upper 70s and low 80s, while the long fall is usually dry and sunny. Best time to go: May-September.

Weather in Budapest: Lat N47°31'; Alt 394 ft

Temp (°F)	Jan	Feb	Mar	Apr	May	Jun	Jul	Aug	Sep	Oct	Nov	Dec
Av Low	26°	28°	36°	44°	52°	57°	61°	59°	63°	45°	37°	31°
Av High	35°	40°	51°	62°	72°	78°	82°	81°	74°	61°	47°	38°
Days no rain	24	22	24	22	22	22	24	25	23	23	22	22

Government: A socialist people's republic.
Language: English is spoken in hotels.

Religion: Roman Catholic.
Currency: Forint. 100 fillers = 1 forint.

	1 ft	10 ft	20 ft	50 ft	100 ft	500 ft	1,000 ft	1,500 ft
US (dollars, cents)	.04	.37	.73	1.83	3.65	18.25	36.50	54.75
UK (pounds, pence)	.02	.18	.35	.87	1.74	18.71	17.41	26.12

Public Holidays:

New Year's Day, 1 Jan
Liberation Day, 4 Apr
Easter Monday
Labor Day, 1 May

Constitution Day, 20 Aug
The Great October Socialist
 Revolution Day, 7 Nov
Christmas Day, 25 Dec
Boxing Day, 26 Dec

HOW TO GET THERE

Flying time from New York is 8¼ hours; from Frankfurt, 1¼ hours, from Munich, 1 hour. Time in Hungary: GMT + 1.

REQUIREMENTS FOR ENTRY AND CUSTOMS REGULATIONS

Any Western visitor to Hungary needs a valid passport and an entry visa, which as a rule is obtainable at Hungarian consulates within 48 hours and is valid for a 30-day visit within 6 months of issue. Two passport-picture-size photographs must be presented with the visa application forms. The cost of a visa is US$6 or its equivalent in convertible currency, US$8.50 for a double-entry visa allowing you to leave and re-enter. Tourists arriving by car or plane may obtain their visas at border crossing stations or at Ferihegy Airport. No visas are issued at the frontier railway stations.

Extensions to the 30-day period are possible through the Aliens Registration Office KEOKH. Népköztársaság út 93, Budapest VI, or through the large Budapest hotels.

Duty-free allowances are 2 liters of wine, 1 liter of spirits, 250 cigarettes or 50 cigars or 250 grams tobacco per person over 16 years of age; gifts to the total value of ft5,000 on the first entry of each calendar year. Travelers' checks and cash can be exchanged at travel bureaus, at exchange offices on the border, in hotels, at stations, and at the Hungarian National Bank, the National Savings Bank, and their branch offices. Quite a few stores, restaurants, and hotels in Hungary accept Western credit cards. At a number of stores in Budapest, tourists may do their shopping with American Express, Carte Blanche, Diners Club, Visa, or Eurocard credit cards.

AIRPORT INFORMATION

The international airport for Budapest is Ferihegy, 10 miles from the city. There are buses every 20 minutes from 5:30am-10:30pm to Vörösmarty Terminal; there is no charge. Taxis can be scarce, and the fare to the heart of town is ft140-180 including tip. If you are renting a car during your stay, you can have it waiting for you at the airport. Ferihegy has a duty-free shop and hotel reservation counter.

ACCOMMODATIONS

There are over 260 hotels in Hungary, but even so there is a general shortage of hotel rooms during the summer months (June-September); reservations are highly recommended. Budapest and Balaton hotels offer off-season reductions from 16 November-1 April. There are also 60 first-class camping sites (details from the **Hungarian Camping and Caravanning Club**, 1088 Budapest VII, Múzeum utca 11—tel: 141 880), as well as a large number of motels and youth hostels. Delightful holiday cabins with a bathroom and kitchen equipped with a refrigerator can also be rented in Balaton resorts, but if you really want to get to know Hungarian people, there is no better way than by becoming a "paying guest" in someone's home. Details of accommodations in A/I, A/II, and B category hotels can be had from **Danubius** (1395 Budapest V, Martinelli tér 8—tel: 173 115), from **HungarHotels** (1364 Budapest V, Petöfi Sándor utca 16—tel: 183 018), from **Pannónia** (1443 Budapest V, Kígyó utca 4-6—tel: 183 910), and from **IBUSZ** (1364 Budapest V, Felszabadulas tér 5—tel: 186 866). Paying-guest rooms can be reserved through any IBUSZ bureau, through the **Cooptourist** and **Volantourist** travel agencies, and through the tourist offices. The **IBUSZ Hotel Service** office (Budapest Petöfi tér 3) is open 24 hours a day.

Rates are in US$ for a double/twin room with bath or shower including breakfast.

Aero, Ferde u. 1-3 (from $30 BB), near airport

Astoria, Kossuth Lajos u. 19 (from $49 BB)

Beke, Lenin körút 97 (from $46 BB)

Budapest, Szilágyi Erzsébet fasor 47 (from $52 BB), at foot of Buda Hills

DUNA INTER · CONTINENTAL, Apáczai Csere János út 4 (from $75)

Europa, Buda Hills (from $38 BB), about 33 miles from center but with fast access

Gellért, Gellért tér 1 (from $72 BB)

Hilton, Hess András tér 1-3 (from $68), in Buda Hills

Olympia, Eötvös u. 40 (from $37 BB), in Buda Hills

Palace, Rákóczi út 43 (from $33 BB)

Royal, Lenin körút 49 (from $55 BB)

Sport, Tassvezér út 711 (from $47 BB), on outskirts

Szabadság, Rákóczi út 90 (from $44 BB)

Thermal, Margaret Island (from $72 BB), on island in Danube

Hotels are centrally located unless otherwise indicated. It is advisable to secure and confirm reservations in advance.

USEFUL INFORMATION

Banks: Open from 8:30-3, Mon-Fri.

Mail: Stamps can be obtained at post offices and tobacconists.

Telephone Tips: Phones in public booths, hotels, and post offices. Local calls cost ft2. Useful numbers:

Pan Am 171 441

Airport Information 572 122

IBUSZ Hotel and Tour Information
184 848

Emergencies 04

Long Distance Operator
(Domestic Calls) 01

Long Distance
(International) 09

Time 08

Legation of Great Britain
182 880

US Legation 124 224

Newspapers: Some imported English-language newspapers and magazines are available in hotels. The local English-language publication on sale at newsstands is the *Daily News.*

Tipping: Although officially discouraged, it is quite customary. In restaurants, leave about 10-15%. Porters are tipped ft15, per piece of luggage; cab drivers, ft10-15; hotel porters, ft10-15, cloakroom attendants, ft2-4. Hairdressers and barbers, 20%.

Electricity: 220 volts 50 cycles AC, throughout the country.

Laundry: Dry-cleaning and laundry services in most hotels.

Hairdressing: Over 300 beauty salons in Budapest alone. Shampoo from ft80; man's haircut with shampoo from ft50.

Photography: Bring your own film because familiar brands will be found only in the larger hotels and will be expensive. Developing 3-4 days.

Babysitting: In Budapest the cooperative Tempo (Bajcsy Zsilinsky utca 54—tel: 127-051) will arrange.

Rest Rooms: In restaurants, cafés, and bars; some public facilities; women, *nök,* men *férfiak.*

Health: Many Hungarian doctors and dentists speak English. Ordinary drugs available. Tap water in Budapest and major towns safe.

TRANSPORTATION

Bus, subway, streetcar, and trolleybus services in Budapest. Taxis can be hailed in the street. If you want an English-speaking driver, call 222-222 or 666-666. Weekly rates for car rental from US$76. Deposit of about US$150 needed. Roads generally very good.

FOOD AND RESTAURANTS

Hungarian goulash *(Gulyás)* is world-famous, but there are many other inviting, lesser-known specialties. *Halászlé* is fish soup; try *Borjú-paprikás* (veal chops in paprika sauce); *Töltöttkáposzta* (layered cabbage); *Rántott Csirke* (chicken roasted in breadcrumbs); or the veal stew called *Borjú Pörkölt.* For dessert there is strudel or the rich pastries. The newly restored **Gundel** (Allatkerti ut 2), in the City Park, offers traditional Hungarian haute cuisine accompanied with fine music, and luscious pastries in the Pastry Shoppe. Recommended in Budapest are the two restaurants at the Duna Inter • Continental Hotel: **Bellevue** for international cuisine, **Csárda** for local specialties. Try **Margit Sziget** (Margitszigét) for international cooking; **Alabárdos** (Országház út 2) for paprika crayfish; **Mátyás**

Pince (Március tér 15) for perch. The celebrated **Hungaria** (Lenin körút 9), where the playwright Ferenc Molnar used to work, is not only a restaurant but one of the grand cafés of Europe. The specialty at **Fehér Galamb** (Szentháromság u. 9) is meat prepared over an open fireplace. For old Hungarian atmosphere try **Arany Szarvas** (Szarvas tér 1), which features game on its menu, **Kerék** (Bécsi út 103), and **Postakocsi** (Fötér 2). Music accompanies the meals at **Kis Royal** (Márvány u. 19) and **Régi Országház** (Országház út 17), both featuring gypsy music; **Pest-Buda** (Fortuna u. 3) has music from the early 19th-century Hungarian Biedermeyer period; **Százéves** (Pesti Barnabás u. 2) has zither music; **Kóborló** (Attila u. 27) has a pianist; and **Vasmacska** (Laktaanya u. 3) features brass music in a saloon-like atmosphere. Two scenic restaurants are **Halászbástya** (Szentháromság tér), with a view of the Danube and Pest from the Fisherman's Bastion, and **Hármashatárhegy**, built on one of the highest points of the Buda Hills. A traditional atmosphere can be found at **Borkatakomba** (Nagytétényi út 65), **Fortuna** (Hess András tér 4), **Kárpátia** (Károly u. 4-8). **Szeged** (Bartók Béla út 1), in the style of a fishermen's inn, with waiters in folk costumes, specializes in fish soup.

DRINKING TIPS

Hungary is the home of the sweet, golden *Tokay* dessert wine and *Bull's Blood* of Eger is the famous Hungarian red wine, but there are many others, and also apricot, plum, and cherry brandies. Whisky and soda will cost about US$3-6 (ft90-180).

ENTERTAINMENT

All theaters, opera houses, and concert halls are state-owned, and performers, directors, designers, and stage technicians are state employees. As a result tickets are at very low prices. There are two opera houses, the **State Opera House** and **Erkel Theater**, with 70-80 operas in their repertoire. There is also the **Municipal Operetta Theater**, or the open-air performances during the summer on **Margaret Island**, and the open-air stage at the **Zoo**. The **State Puppet Theater** (Népköztársaság út 69) is internationally known. There are 11 other theaters in Budapest, and also many orchestras and string and wind ensembles. Theater tickets are in great demand and it is best to try the tourist agencies or the box office although sometimes they can be obtained in advance from the **Budapest Tourist Board** (Roosevelt tér 5), or the **Central Booking Agency for Theaters** (Népköztársaság út 18). Foreign films are usually dubbed; films by Hungarian directors are internationally famous. There are nightclubs with dancing and floor shows at all major hotels. Also recommended are the **Moulin Rouge** (Nagymező út 17); **Maxim Variety Club** (Akácfa utca 3); **Eden Bar** (Széna tér 7); **Pipacs Bar** (Aranykéz út 5, overlooking the city from Gellért Hill); **Fortuna Bar** (Hess András tér 4); and the famous **Casanove Night Club** (Batthyányi tér 4).

SHOPPING

Stores in Budapest are open from 10-6 on weekdays, 10-3 on Saturdays—most are state-owned. Department stores are open longer on weekdays—

9-7 or 8. Best buys are Herendi and Zsolnay china and porcelain sets, which you'll find in the porcelain shop on Kigyó utca, and a variety of arts and crafts—embroidered slippers, woodwork, dolls, peasant blouses, table sets, and embroidered tablecloths. Classical records and foreign books are a particularly good buy, especially at the **Bookstore** on Váci útca. Large department stores are **Szabadság Aruház** in Kalvin tér, **Luxus Aruház** in Vörösmarty tér, and **Corvin Nagyfuház** in Blaha Lujza tér.

SPORTS

Soccer is the most popular sport. There are tennis courts and a mini-golf course at the **Vörös Csillag Hotel** and tennis courts at the **Sports Ground**, Üllöi út 129; swimming pools in Budapest; hiking and climbing in summer and skiing in winter in the **Buda Hills**; freshwater fishing (**Hungarian Anglers' Association,** Budapest V, Október 6 utca 20) and excellent hunting (contact **Mavad, I,** Uri u. 39); swimming, yachting, and water-skiing in summer and ice sailing in winter at **Lake Balaton.** Horseback riding is very popular in this equestrian country and there are guided riding tours, ranging up to 10 days, with accommodations in old castles and manors, and outdoor picnics along the way. The Riding School at **Tata** is the departure point for many of the programs.

WHAT TO SEE

First, go on one of the excellent tours organized by the **Budapest Tourist Office** (Roosevelt tér 5) to get oriented. This will take you to the **House of Parliament;** to **Hösök Tere** (Heroes' Square), with monuments to the heroes of Hungary; to the **People's Stadium;** and then across the Danube to **Margaret Island** to see the **National Sports Swimming Pool, Budapest's Lido,** and the largest open-air theater in the capital. Then again across the Danube to **Buda,** the other half of the city, which is full of important historical monuments: the **Royal Castle;** the **Hungarian National Gallery,** set within the walls of the old Buda castle; the 700-year-old **Matthias Church,** where the former kings of Hungary were crowned; the turreted **Fisherman's Bastion;** and the **Citadel** on Gellért Hill. Then there are the remains of what was once the Roman town of **Aquincum** in the northern part of the city, the **Aquincum Museum** (Szentendrei út 139), and the towers of **Magdalen** and **St Nicholas,** built in the 14th and 15th centuries. The **Art Gallery** (Hösök Tere) puts on excellent exhibitions by local and foreign artists, and next door, the **Museum of Fine Arts** (Dózsa György út 41) has paintings by Giotto, Titian, Raphael, Monet, and many others. The **Hungarian National Museum** (Muzeum körút 14-16) has fine historical collections and the Crown of St Stephen, recently returned to Hungary by the US. The **Folklore Center** (Fehérvári út 47) has evening programs of folk dancing and traditional Hungarian music. Take a night cruise on the Danube or the **Budapest-by-Night** tour.

Hungary has some 400 thermal springs, of which more than 120 are in Budapest itself. In Roman times, Aquincum was a spa and later, when the Turks occupied Hungary, Turkish baths were built over many of the springs. Today, the baths not only provide up-to-date medical treatment but also have a lighter side and play a major role in the city's social life. Among them are the **National Institute for Rheumatology and Physiotherapy** and the **Lukács Baths,** both with departments for the treatment of patients from abroad; the **Széchenyi Baths,** one of the largest in Europe, with a popular swimming pool; the **Császár Baths** and **Rudas Baths,** both with Turkish baths built in the 16th century. The **Géllert Hotel** has a medicinal bath, and both hotels on Margaret Island (**Thermal** and **Grand Hotel Margitsziget**) are spa hotels.

Outside Budapest, **Balatonfüred,** on the northern shore of Lake Balaton, **Hévíz,** with the modern Thermal Hotel, and **Balf,** where there are accommodations in an old castle, are a few of the health resorts with medicinal baths.

Lake Balaton, 65 miles from the capital, is Hungary's playground and the largest freshwater lake in Europe. In summer, the water has an average temperature of 77°F. A warning: if you are out on the lake and see a yellow flare followed by a red one, return immediately—it means there is a violent storm coming.

SOURCES OF FURTHER INFORMATION

Pan Am, Duna Inter · Continental, Apáczai Csere János út 4, or any Pan Am office around the world. **IBUSZ,** 1364 Budapest V, Felszabadulas tér 5; 630 Fifth Avenue, New York, NY 10020; **Danube Travel** (General Agents for IBUSZ in UK), 6 Conduit Street, London W1R 9TG.

Iceland

WHAT'S SPECIAL

Iceland has deep coastal fjords, vast icefields, scores of volcanoes, and dramatic hot springs, an important source of heat for the island. Its people are among the most literate in the world; it was back in the 12th century that they developed the art of storytelling—the sagas—and later, writing. Their language has remained unchanged for centuries.

COUNTRY BRIEFING

Size: 39,702 square miles   **Population:** 229,000
Capital: Reykjavik   **Capital Population:** 85,000
  Government: A republic
  Language: Icelandic (English taught in schools)
  Religion: Lutheran
  Climate: Mild. Best time to visit, June-September.
  Currency: Icelandic krona; 100 aurar = 1 krona; 6.57Kr = US$1.

HOW TO GET THERE

Flying time to Reykjavik's Keflavik Airport from New York is 6 hours; from Frankfurt, 3¾ hours; from London, 2¾ hours. Time in Iceland: GMT.

REQUIREMENTS FOR ENTRY AND CUSTOMS REGULATIONS

Current passport but no visa required except for Scandinavian nationals; visa not required of US, Canadian, or UK citizens, or of citizens of most other countries. You may take into the country up to Kr400 and take out Kr400 in denominations up to Kr50. You are allowed to take out the same amount of foreign currency as you brought in. Duty-free allowance: 200 cigarettes; 1 bottle liquor; 1 bottle wine.

AIRPORT INFORMATION
From Keflavik Airport there is a 45-minute bus ride into Reykjavik costing Kr22. Taxis are also available, costing Kr350. There is a Kr112 departure tax.

ACCOMMODATIONS
First-class hotel accommodations can be found in Reykjavik, Akureyri, Husavik, Stykkisholmur, and Höfn. Edda hotels—there are 13 of them— are run by the Iceland Tourist Bureau in school dormitories throughout the country during summer only; a double room with bath costs about US$40, breakfast US$7 per person, sleeping bag place US$12 per person. Hotels in Iceland:
Rates are in US$ for a double/twin room with bath or shower
  Borg, Austurvöllur Square, Reykjavik (from $42 winter, $74 summer), in center city
  Esja, Sudurlandsbraut 2, Reykjavik (from $45 winter, $84 summer), 1½ miles from center city
  Hekla, Raudarárstig 18, Reykjavik (from $32 winter, $60 summer), in center city
  Holt, Bergstadastraeti 37, Reykjavik (from $38 winter, $68 summer), in center city
  Höfn, Höfn (Hornafjordur) (from $35 winter, $59 summer)
  Husavik, Husavik (from $35 winter, $59 summer)
  Kea, Hafnarstraeti 89, Akureyri (from $37 winter, $66 summer), in center city
  Loftleidir, Reykjavik Airport (from $45 winter, $84 summer)
  Saga, Birkimelur, Reykjavik (from $45 winter, $74 summer), in new residential section, ½ mile from center city
  Stykkisholmur, Stykkisholmur (from $45 winter, $59 summer)
  Vardborg, Geislagötu 7, Akureyri (from $30 winter, $46 summer), in center city

USEFUL INFORMATION
Banks (only in principal cities) open 9:30-3:30, Mon-Fri. Mailboxes are often a slit in the wall with *Post* written above. A local telephone call costs 20Kr. Useful numbers: **Pan Am agent,** 21085; **Airport Information,** 26622 domestic flights, 22333 international flights; **Tourist Offices,** 25855 and 23025. **Tipping;** not customary. **Electricity:** 220 volts 50 cycles AC.

TRANSPORTATION
There is no railroad. The country relies on its bus network and internal airline, Icelandair, with scheduled flights and connections to all corners of country.

FOOD AND RESTAURANTS

Some national dishes are smoked mutton *(hangikjot);* singed and boiled sheep's head *(svid);* salted cod *(saltfiskur);* and *skyr,* similar to yoghurt. Established restaurants in the capital include the **Naust** (Vesturgarta 8—tel: 17759), for seafood; the **Saga Grill Room** (Hagatorg—tel: 28033, for international and local dishes; the **Loftleidir Hotel** (at Reykjavik Airport—tel: 22321), for smörgåsbord; the **Hotel Holt** (Bergstadastraeti 37—tel: 21011), for seafood and special lamb dishes. Many new restaurants have opened, offering variety, lower prices, and better quality and service to diners as a result of their competition. These include **Torfan** (Amtmannsstig 1—tel: 13303), for seafood; **Hlidarendi** (Noatun 2—tel: 11690), for seafood and steaks; **Versalir** (Hamraborg 4—tel: 45688), for international and local dishes; **Rán** (Skolavordustig 12—tel: 10848), for seafood and international dishes; **Laugass** (Laugaasvegur 1—tel: 31620), for pizza and local dishes; and **Braudbaer** (Thorsgotu 1—tel: 25090), for local dishes. Among fast-food chains to be found are **Kentucky Fried Chicken** and numerous hamburger places.

DRINKING TIPS

Liquor sold in state licensed shops and licensed restaurants.

ENTERTAINMENT

Hotels **Borg** and **Saga**, the **Klubbur**, **Leikhuskjallarinn**, **Sigtun**, and **Thorscafe** all have dancing. **Odal** and **Hollywood** are discothèques.

SHOPPING

Best buys are Icelandic sweaters, sheepskin and ponyskin rugs, ceramics, silverwork and filigree, and smoked salmon. Visit **Glit** ceramics on Hofdabakka for good bargains and to watch craftsmen at work on lava ceramics.

WHAT TO SEE

Reykjavik is a smokeless city because it is heated by natural hot springs; you can visit hot-spring reservoirs. See Reykjavik's **University** and **National Museum.**

Easily reached in one day's sightseeing from Reykjavik are the town of **Hveragerdi** where flowers and fruit are grown in greenhouses heated by hot springs; the magnificent **Gullfoss** waterfall; the **Great Geysir** area, with many hot springs and Strokkur, the most active geyser; and **Thingvellir**, where the oldest Parliament in the world (Althing) was founded in 930. The Iceland Tourist Board's "Golden Circle" excursion visits all four attractions in a 9-hour trip costing about US$30. A 2-hour flight will take you to see the active volcano, **Mount Hekla**, in southwest Iceland, and there are day trips by air to see the **Westman Islands**, scene of recent volcanic destruction. Recommended is Sverrir Thoroddsson Air Charter, Reykjavik Airport (tel: 28420).

SOURCES OF FURTHER INFORMATION

Pan Am agent, Polaris Ltd, Austurstrati 18, PO Box 1311, Reykjavik, and any Pan Am office around the world; **Icelandic National Tourist Office,** 75 Rockefeller Plaza, New York, NY 10019; **Iceland Tour Information Bureau,** 73 Grosvenor Street, London W1.

Ireland

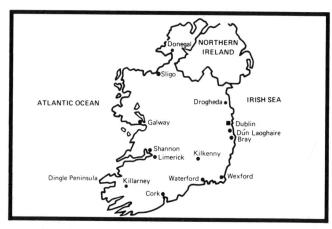

WHAT'S SPECIAL

William Makepeace Thackeray wrote in his *Irish Sketch-Book:* "It is clear that for a stranger the Irish ways are the pleasantest, for here he is at once made happy and at home." True when written and true today of a land in which the population is not half that of London, in which there are no crowds or weekend traffic jams (although there is pressure on accommodations in the summer). Progress is creeping up on Ireland— more cars on the road, modern buildings going up here and there— but it is still a place for a relaxing vacation.

COUNTRY BRIEFING

Size: 27,000 square miles   **Population:** 3,365,000
Capital: Dublin   **Capital Population:** 544,000
   Climate: Rainy, mild winters; warm summers, influenced by the Gulf Stream. The best time to visit is April to October.

Weather in Dublin: Lat N53°22′; Alt 155 ft

Temp (°F)	Jan	Feb	Mar	Apr	May	Jun	Jul	Aug	Sep	Oct	Nov	Dec
Av Low	35°	35°	36°	38°	42°	48°	51°	51°	47°	43°	38°	36°
Av High	47°	47°	51°	54°	59°	65°	67°	67°	63°	57°	51°	47°
Days no rain	18	17	21	19	20	19	18	18	18	19	18	18

Government: A Parliamentary democracy.
Language: English and Gaelic.
Religion: Roman Catholic.
Currency: The Irish pound, or punt (IR£), is divided into 100 pence.

Irish bills and coins have different value and are not interchangeable with UK currency. Most hotels will change currency.

Public Holidays:

New Year's Day, 1 Jan	Bank Holiday, 1st Mon June
St Patrick's Day, 17 Mar	Bank Holiday, 1st Mon Aug
Good Friday	Christmas Day, 25 Dec
Easter Monday	St Stephen's Day, 26 Dec

HOW TO GET THERE

Flying time to Shannon Airport or Dublin Airport (¼ hour flying time between the two) from New York is 6 hours; from Caracas, 10½ hours; from London, 1 hour. Time in Ireland: GMT+1. Daylight Saving Time observed.

REQUIREMENTS FOR ENTRY AND CUSTOMS REGULATIONS

Passport. Vaccination certificates required only if arriving from an infected area. No pornographic materials or books on the government's censorship list can be brought into the country. Visitors may not take out currency or travelers' checks in excess of £100. Duty-free allowance for visitors from Common Market countries: 300 cigarettes or 75 cigars or 400 grams tobacco; 1½ liters spirits and 3 liters wine; 75 grams perfume and ⅜ liter toilet water; other goods to the value of £120, with no one item exceeding £52. For visitors from other European countries: 200 cigarettes or 50 cigars or 250 grams tobacco; 1 liter spirits and 3 liters wine; 50 grams perfume and ¼ liter toilet water; other goods to the value of £27. For visitors from non-European countries: 400 cigarettes or 100 cigars or 500 grams tobacco; 1 liter spirits and 2 liters wine; 50 grams perfume and ¼ liter toilet water; other goods to the value of £27.

AIRPORT INFORMATION

Shannon Airport in the west of the country is 16 miles from the city of Limerick. Buses from the airport to city center run every 15 or 20 minutes and cost £1.45. Taxis are also available, fare about £5.50. The Tourist Information Desk in the Arrivals Terminal or the Tourist Information Office at 62 O'Connell Street, Limerick (tel: 47522) can help with accommodation reservations. Shannon's duty-free shop (for international flights only) is one of Europe's busiest.

Dublin Airport is 5 miles from the Central Bus Station *(Busaras)* downtown. Airport buses (every 15 minutes) meet each flight, and the fare is £1.20. Taxis are also available at about £5. The airport has a hotel reservation counter, duty-free shop, and a Tourist Information Office.

ACCOMMODATIONS

Irish cities have an ample supply of all classes of hotels from the very modern to the old established. But with its great rural attractions, Ireland also offers a wide variety of out-of-town accommodations. Some medieval castles offer accommodations, ranging from US$25 (room only, single) to US$70 per night. Thatched cottages in small villages are ideal for families, and many farmhouses accept visitors for about £65 a week, full board. Bed and breakfast houses charge about £5 single a night; hostels charge about £11 a night. Trailer sites and camping parks are available, and for a really leisurely touring vacation, modernized horse-drawn tinkers' wagons are for rent. Rates are slightly lower in winter but are high in Dublin during the Rugby International weekends and the Dublin Society Horse Show. The **Tourist Information Office** at 14 Upper O'Connell (tel: 747733) will help find accommodations, and the **Irish Hotel Central Reservation Service** in Dublin (tel: 781200) can also help. A 12½% to 15% service charge is added to hotel bills. Dublin hotels:

Rates are in US$ for a double/twin room with a bath or shower

Berkeley Court, Lansdowne Road, Ballsbridge (from $90), 1 mile from center

Blooms, Anglesea Street (from $44)

Burlington, Upper Leeson Street (from $60)

Clarence, 6-8 Wellington Quay (from $29)

Gresham, O'Connell Street (from $40)

International Airport (from $55), at airport

Jury's Dublin, Ballsbridge (from $86), 1 mile from center

Marine, Sutton (from $56), near airport

Royal Hibernian, Dawson Street (from $80)

Shelbourne, St Stephens Green (from $90)

Tara Tower, Merrion Road (from $36), 3½ miles from center

All hotels listed above are centrally located unless otherwise indicated.

USEFUL INFORMATION

Banks: Open 10-12:30 and 1:30-3 Mon-Fri, until 5pm Thurs. At Dublin airport open 7:30am-11:30pm daily in summer, 8:30am-9:30pm daily in winter. At Shannon open year round 7:30am-5:30pm Mon-Fri, and 7:30am-5pm Sat-Sun.

Mail: Some tobacconists sell stamps, and small post offices are often found in general stores. Mailboxes are green. The General Post Office, O'Connell Street, Dublin, is open Mon-Sat from 8am-11pm; on Sundays and public holidays it is open from 9am-11pm for stamps, telegrams, and registered letters.

Telephone Tips: Public telephone booths are on streets, in hotels, and in most restaurants and pubs. Coin operated. To use, lift receiver, insert two 5p coins (for local call), dial, and press button "A" to speak. If there is no answer, or you hear an engaged signal (short, rapid, high-pitched beeps), press button "B" for money to be returned. For operator-controlled phones, lift receiver and dial 10. In rural areas only, lift receiver and wait. Since phone service is often poor, it is sometimes necessary to use telex or telegrams for urgent messages. Useful numbers in Dublin:

Airport Information 370191	**Time** 1191
Tourist Office 747733	**Weather** 1199
Directories 190	**Emergency** 999

Tipping: In many restaurants and in hotels a 10%-15% service charge is added to bills and no additional tip is expected. Tipping is not customary in pubs and you never tip in cinemas or theaters. The usual tip for taxi drivers is 30p for a normal ride, at least 50p for anything greater. Tip porters 30p to 50p and cloakroom attendants 30p.

Electricity: 220 volts 50 cycles AC.

Laundry: Good dry-cleaning and laundry services; 24-hour and some 1-hour services in the cities. Major hotels have express service (to dry-clean a suit £3; to launder a shirt, about £1). Laundromats in main towns.

Hairdressing: Few hotels have salons, but there are good facilities in large department stores (shampoo and set, about £4, tip 30p-50p; man's haircut, £3).

Photography: Good supplies of equipment in all towns, with prices among the lowest in Europe. Black and white film takes 1-2 days to be developed, color 2-3 days.

Clubs: Rotary meetings are held at the Jury's Hotel, Ballsbridge, Monday lunchtime. Lions also meet at Jury's Hotel.

Rest Rooms: Public facilities in street. Women, *Mná;* men, *Fir.*

Health: Imported pharmaceuticals available and quite inexpensive. Drinking water excellent.

TRANSPORTATION

The city bus service is very efficient but complicated by the use of Gaelic on the destination indicators. Suburban trains serve a 15-mile radius of Dublin. Metered taxis can be hailed in the street; they are also readily available by phone or from a stand. Minimum charge is 80p. Rental cars are readily available; you must be over the age of 21 and have a valid driving license in your own country—the international license is not required. Driving is on the left, and although the country roads are often quite deserted, the cities are congested during the rush hours—8:30-9:30am and 5-6:30pm. Warning: Don't drive a car if you have consumed even as little as two pints of beer. Police crack down mercilessly on anyone they suspect by applying the roadside "Breathalyzer" test. If the crystals in the plastic bag turn green (even that second pint will do it for some people), the offender faces fines up to £500 or 6 months in jail (or both). The law applies to residents and visitors alike. The use of seat belts is compulsory for drivers and front seat passengers. (Children under 12 in the front seat may use some other suitable restraint.) Penalties for non-use are severe.

A reasonable train service serves major cities, with dining cars but no sleepers. "Rambler" tickets for unlimited travel by rail or by rail and bus are available from the CIE (**Coras Iompair Eireann** or National Transport Company) on Upper O'Connell Street, Dublin, or from any city railroad station. A 15-day "Rambler" ticket costs US$84 (rail) or US$102 (rail and bus). An 8-day ticket costs US$58 (rail) or US$72 (rail and bus). Aer Lingus flies to Shannon Airport (for Limerick), Cork, and Belfast. Ferries cross the River Shannon between Tarbert and Killimer and the Atlantic between Galway and the Aran Islands.

FOOD AND RESTAURANTS

Irish food is at its best when unpretentious, so that the high quality of the meat and the freshness of the vegetables can be appreciated. Dublin Bay prawns, oysters, trout and salmon, dairy-fed pork and bacon, free-range eggs, butter, and soda bread are all superb. *Colcannon* is a potato and cabbage dish, and *mixed coddle* is boiled bacon and sausages. Irish stew (meat, potato, and vegetables) is simple and always tasty. Steak tends to be well done unless requested otherwise. The average meal per person costs about £20 in an expensive restaurant, £12 in a medium-priced one, and £6 in an inexpensive one. The best hotel restaurants in Dublin are at the Royal Hibernian (tel: 772991), **Jury's** (Ballsbridge, tel: 767511), and the Shelbourne (tel: 766471). **Snaffles** (47 Lower Leeson Street—tel: 762227) has Irish country hotel cuisine, and the **Soup Bowl** (Molesworth Mews—tel: 767649) specializes in duckling. **Sutton Castle,** a little out of Dublin, in Sutton (tel: 324476), has good Irish and French food. Many pubs serve lunches or light snacks such as sandwiches, meat pies, and salads. The **Brown Thomas** department store (15 Grafton Street) serves open sandwiches, and **Bewley's Oriental Cafés** on Westmoreland and Grafton Streets serve inexpensive lunches and good coffee. Grafton Street also has several good American hamburger restaurants in the £3-6 range. **Captain America's** is in Grafton Court, while **McDonald's** is at the city center end of Grafton Street.

DRINKING TIPS

To the Irish, conversation is the greatest of all arts and distillation the finest of the sciences; they never tire of combining the two in a congenial pub. Most of the "spit-and-sawdust" atmosphere has disappeared. Irish women prefer to use the lounge bar of a pub, leaving the public bar as a male preserve. Imported beer, lager, wine, and liquor are for sale, but the most popular drink is Guinness, a dark beer (stout) with a thick creamy head. Whisky (different in taste from Scotch whisky) is another native brew, and the whisky liqueur, *Irish Mist,* is delicious. Irish coffee is served with whisky and cream. *Poteen* is a liquor sometimes sold in illegal drinking houses called *shebeens* in remote rural areas—it is extremely strong. Alcohol is not sold to anyone under 18, but everybody else can drink from 10:30am-11pm in winter, till 11:30pm in summer. Dublin, Waterford, Limerick, and Cork pubs close for "holy hour" between 2:30-3:30. A whisky and soda costs about £1.10 and a bottle of wine from £3.50.

Hotel bars are always popular, particularly on Sundays. Pubs in central Dublin often attract fashionable crowds. **Neary's** (Chatham Street) is a theater pub. **Davy Byrnes** (mentioned in *Ulysses*), once frequented by the leaders of the 1916 Rising, now has a literary clientele. The **Brazen Head** (Bridge Street), by the river, is Dublin's oldest pub. The **Lord**

Edward (Christchurch Place) is very cozy with its open fire, quite unlike the noisy, rambunctious **O'Donoghue's** in Merrion Row, off the southeast corner of St Stephen's Green—very crowded but good for traditional Irish music.

ENTERTAINMENT

The most popular form of entertainment in Dublin is probably the poetry and ballad sessions in pubs. The **Abbey Tavern** at Howth has a good seafood menu to accompany the entertainment, and during the season there are cabarets at Jury's, the Burlington, and the Shelbourne hotels. Discothèque restaurants are **Zhivago Club** (Baggot Street) and **Annabel's** (Leeson Street, behind the Burlington Hotel). Jazz is played at **The Baggot Inn** (Baggot Street) on Wednesdays. Dublin's most famous theaters are the **Abbey,** where Yeats plays are frequently performed, and the **Gate,** with an international repertoire. The **Dublin Theater Festival** is held in October and the **City of Dublin International Festival of Music** in June. There is little opera or ballet, and films tend to be censored, but one good house for noncommercial movies is the **Irish Film Theater,** Earlsfort Terrace, off the southwest corner of St Stephen's Green. Irish traditional folk dancing and singing can be seen at the *fleadh* (festivals), which are held throughout the year all over the country.

SHOPPING

Stores open 9-5:30, Mon-Sat. Best buys are linen, tweed (from Donegal), crystal (from Galway and Waterford, Cavan, Dublin, and Kilkenny), knitwear, particularly the fishermen's sweaters from the Aran Islands, pipes, walking sticks, Belleek china, and souvenirs of Connemara marble. Major department stores in the capital are **Brown Thomas, Switzer's,** and **Arnott's,** all on Grafton Street, and **Clery's** on O'Connell Street. The **Dublin Woollen Co.** (Metal Bridge Corner) specializes in tweeds. **Market Ireland** (75 Grafton Street) has glass, jewelry, tweed, knitwear, and Irish musical instruments and records. **Irish Heraldic Industries** (51 Middle Abbey Street) and **Historic Families** (8 Fleet Street) specialize in heraldry and family crests. Most antique shops are south of the river and include the **Fine Art Showrooms** (27 South Anne Street), the **Georgian Shop** (54 South William Street), **Edward Bulter** (14 Bachelors Walk), and **Louis Wine** (32 Grafton Street). There is a lighthearted weekday market called **Daisy Market** on East Arran Quay, also the **Iveagh Market,** which is on Francis Street.

SPORTS

Two games peculiar to Ireland are hurling and Gaelic football. The **All-Ireland finals** of these games are held in Croke Park, Dublin, in September. Rugby has an enthusiastic following, and during the **International** weekends (competitions held between England, Scotland, Wales, Ireland, and France), the capital is packed with fans. Ireland is famous for its bloodstock, and horse racing takes place almost daily throughout the country from March to September. The **Dublin Horse Show** is the most important event in the equestrian calendar. Held in August, over 2,000 horses, military and civilian, compete. An important event on the international sporting calendar is the four-day **International Indoor Horse Show** in November. Hunting and horseback riding are available to visitors everywhere. Ireland is ideal for all quiet outdoor activity. There is no overcrowding at beaches, golf courses, lakes, or streams. The fishing, both inland and offshore, is superb.

WHAT TO SEE

Dublin is a gracious city with lively, interesting people. The spirit of eccentric Dubliners like Wilde, Shaw, Swift, O'Casey, Behan, and Joyce still flourishes in many well-known and loved "characters." The buildings of *"Eblana,"* as Ptolemy called it in the 1st century, have been gradually replaced, leaving only the beautiful 18th-century houses and squares of the Georgian period as relics of a bygone age. **St Patrick's** and **Christchurch** cathedrals date back to the 11th and 12th centuries, but their facades are more modern. Swift lies buried in St Patrick's, and in Christchurch there is an old monument to Strongbow, the Norman earl who invaded Ireland in 1169. A good way to see Dublin is on foot, and the Tourist Office (14 Upper O'Connell Street) provides leaflets describing walking tours.

Through the center of Dublin flows the river **Liffey.** From its principal bridge, named after Daniel O'Connell, can be seen the delicate ironwork tracery of **Halfpenny Bridge** and the tulip domes of the **Guinness Brewery.** North of O'Connell Bridge stretches **O'Connell Street,** the main city thoroughfare, with its impressive **General Post Office,** stronghold of the 1916 Easter Rising. Also on the north bank is the **Custom House,** one of the finest buildings in Dublin. South of the Liffey is **College Green,** with the **Bank of Ireland,** formerly the Irish House of Parliament, and **Trinity College,** founded in 1591 by Elizabeth I. The **Old Library** houses beautiful illuminated Celtic gospels, of which the oldest is the 7th-century *Book of Durrow.* Trinity's most famous manuscript, the *Book of Kells* (8th century), is in the Library. Oscar Wilde was born at 21 Westland Row at the far end of the College. **Grafton Street,** the main shopping center, leads up to **St Stephen's Green,** and in the area between the Green and Trinity lies the best of Georgian Dublin. Here are **Leinster House,** seat of the Irish Government; **Mansion House,** home of the Lord Mayor; and the **National Gallery,** with French, Dutch, and Flemish collections and lovely paintings by Jack B. Yeats, brother of the poet. **Merrion Square,** adjoining Upper Merrion Street where the Duke of Wellington was born, is still one of the most fashionable parts of town. The **National Museum,** Kildare Street, contains outstanding examples of Celtic Art, including the famous **Tara brooch** (dating back to the early 700s AD), the **Ardagh Chalice,** and the superb stone-carved **Cross of Cong** (1123). **Dublin Castle,** at the top of Dame Street, was the symbol of British rule in Ireland from 1200 until 1921. The **State Apartments,** furnished with Donegal carpets, have painted ceilings and carved wood panels. A delightful little building is **Marsh's Library,** near St Patrick's Cathedral

(Kevin Street Upper). It was built in 1702, and its interior is virtually unchanged. **Phoenix Park** is one of the world's largest, with zoo, deer park, racecourse, and polo ground.

Dun Laoghaire (pronounced Dunleary), 7 miles down the coast, is the terminus of the mail-steamer from Britain. It has a fine harbor, the headquarters of several yacht clubs, and all facilities for swimming, tennis, golf, sailing, and dancing. The **Martello Tower** at Sandycove, at the southern end of town, figures in the opening chapter of *Ulysses* and appropriately houses the **James Joyce Museum** (open May to September). Stay at **Fitzpatrick's Castle Hotel,** about 3 miles south at Killiney (from US$54 double). Dun Laoghaire has two fine restaurants on the seafront: **Restaurant na Mara,** over the railroad station, and the **Mirabeau,** near the Tower, expensive but good. Seaside resorts within easy reach of Dublin are **Bray** (to the south), the most popular; **Howth, Portmarnock, Malahide, and Skerries** (to the north). Howth is a fishing village famous for the rhododendrons in the **Howth-Castle** grounds, and **Malahide Castle** houses a collection of Irish period furniture as well as part of the National Portrait Collection. The restaurant in **O'Shea's Hotel** in Bray and the **King Sitric Restaurant** in Howth are recommended. Twelve miles from Dublin a mile-long avenue of lime trees leads to **Castletown House,** Celbridge, Ireland's finest Georgian country house, with a famous Long Gallery hung with Venetian chandeliers. **Russborough,** near Blessington (about 16 miles from Dublin) is another lovely Georgian house and home of the Beit art collection. The beautifully landscaped grounds of **Powerscourt Estate** (12 miles from Dublin) include ornamental Japanese and Italian gardens, formal terraces, and deer herds. The River **Dargle** runs through Powerscourt woods and drops off a rock shelf to form a 398-foot-high waterfall.

Monasterboice, 35 miles north of Dublin, is an early Christian monastic community, with ruined medieval churches, a 9th-century round tower, and other remains. It is worth a trip to see the High Crosses. The **Cross of Muireadach** is 17 feet 8 inches high and has 50 sculptured panels. Four miles from Monasterboice are the beautiful ruins of the 12th-century Cistercian **Mellifont Abbey,** on the banks of the river Mattock. **Brugh na Boinne,** along the north bank of the River Boyne, is a pre-Christian cemetery, the legendary burial place of kings. It consists of a series of Neolithic burial mounds—the principal ones are at **Newgrange, Knowth,** and **Dowth**—dating back to 2,500 BC. The mound at Newgrange contains a remarkable passage-grave, one of the finest in Europe.

The monastic community of **Glendalough,** the "glen of the two lakes" (30 miles south of Dublin), should be visited for its lovely surrounding countryside as well as its interesting remains. In the southeast is the historic city of **Kilkenny** on the river Nore, with a prominent castle, a fine 13th-century cathedral, and many picturesque buildings. The showrooms of the **National Design Workshop** are in the town.

Near the coast is **Waterford,** famous for its glass in the 18th century. The modern factory where the classic shapes are decorated may be visited. Three good angling rivers flow into Waterford Harbor. The **Ardee**

Hotel (from US$40 double) and the **Tower Hotel** (from US$36 double) are in this area.

Wexford is a pretty old town with swans swimming in its fishing harbor. The **Opera Festival** at the end of October has built up an international reputation for rare Italian opera. Stay at the **Talbot Hotel** (from US$34 double), at **White's Hotel** (from US$42 double), or, 13 miles south in Rosslare, at the **Strand Hotel** (from US$34 double).

The West of Ireland: Shannon Airport has an excellent duty-free shop and a connecting bus to Colbert Station, Limerick. **Bunratty Castle,** with a fine 15th-century keep and period furniture and tapestries, lies between the airport and the city. Medieval banquets, with traditional Irish entertainment, are served all year round in the castle. Ballads and story-telling are just two of the attractions of the fascinating Folk Village adjoining the castle grounds. **Limerick,** at the mouth of the River Shannon, dates from the 9th century and has much of historic interest; it is also a busy, thriving city. The violence of its history can be read in the stones of its impressive castle and the remains of its siege-battered town walls. **St Mary's Cathedral** still contains the ancient tomb-slab of its founder Donald O'Brien, who died in 1194. Hotels and the main shopping center are in the vicinity of O'Connell Street. Stay at **Jury's Limerick,** Ennis Road (from US$66 double); **Hanratty's,** Glentworth Street (from US$32 double); or the **Cruises Royal,** 7 O'Connell Street (from US$32 double). **Dromoland Castle,** 15 miles from Limerick, now a luxury hotel (from US$99 double), was the birthplace of William Smith O'Brien, a leader of the Young Ireland Movement. Nearby is the **Clare Inn** (from US$58 double). Thirteen miles upstream is **Killaloe,** beautifully situated on the Shannon, where it swells into Lough Derg. This small town, an ideal center for fishing, boating, and river cruising, boasts a masterpiece of Romanesque art in the **Cathedral of St Flannan:** a doorway richly carved and decorated, said to have been the entrance to the tomb of Murtagh O'Brien, King of Munster (died 1120). Further up the Shannon near Athlone is **Clonmacnoise,** a celebrated early Christian center of learning, founded by St Kiernan in 548. Among the well-preserved ruins are two round towers, a cathedral, eight churches, and some of Ireland's famed sculptured High Crosses. Cabin cruisers can be hired at Killaloe (tel: 76251).

Galway is a quaint old town of narrow streets and houses built Spanish-fashion around courtyards. Columbus is said to have prayed here on his way to discover the New World. The Galway River is famous for salmon, and in season the fish can be seen gathering under the **Salmon Weir Bridge.** The **Oyster Festival** is held in September. **Seoda,** featuring traditional Irish music, song, dancing, and mime, is performed during July and August (excluding Race Week) in **An Taibhdhearc,** Galway's Irish-language theater. In Galway, stay at the **Great Southern Hotel,** Eyre Square (from US$54 double); the **Corrib Great Southern,** Dublin Road (from US$32 double); or the **Imperial,** Eyre Square (from US$28 double).

Steamer services connect with the barren **Aran Islands,** where the fishermen and small farming communities are predominantly Irish-speaking and there are some remarkable prehistoric forts. **Inisheer,** the smallest of the three islands, is entirely Gaelic-speaking and very primitive. West of Galway is **Connemara,** a beautiful wilderness of tiny lakes and mountain glens. The rivers teem with fish, and shaggy ponies trot among the white-washed stone cottages. Near **Clifden** is a stone commemorating Alcock and Brown's first flight across the Atlantic.

Westport, on lovely hill-enclosed Clew Bay, is a great center for big-game fishing (shark and porbeagle) and hill walking. **Croagh Patrick** (2,510 feet) is climbed by thousands of pilgrims on the last Sunday in July, many of them barefooted. Ireland's first **Zoo Park** is on the beautiful estate of **Westport House** overlooking Clew Bay. Stay at the **Great Western Hotel,** at Mulrany in County Mayo (from $66 double); at **Ashford Castle,** Cong, County Mayo (from US$82 double); at **Breaffy House Hotel,** Castlebar, County Mayo (from US$30 double); or at **Hotel Westport,** County Mayo (from US$32 double). Stay at the **Great Western Hotel,** at Mulrany in County Mayo (from US$66 double), or at the **Ashford Castle Hotel,** Cong, County Mayo (from US$82 double).

Donegal: The most northerly county of Ireland is also one of the wildest. It has a magnificent coastline dotted with fishing villages and is a strong-hold of cottage industries and the Gaelic language. In the hills of Donegal, women still weave the famous tweed. **Sligo,** a good place to buy tweed, is in the heart of Yeats country. All around are lakes for fishing, golf courses for sport, wooded glens for walking, and prehistoric remains for sightseeing. Stay in Sligo at the **Hotel Innisfree** (from US$25 double) or at the **Sligo Park** (from US$50 double).

Cork is very lively during its **Choral Festival** in April and the **Film Festival** in June. The best restaurants are the **Oyster Tavern** (Market Lane), **Arbutus Lodge** (in wooded suburb of Montenotte), and **Lovett's** at Greggs Cross. Hotels are **Jury's Cork,** Western Road (from US$79 double), with very good food; the **Imperial,** South Mall (from US$44 double), also with very good food; the **Metropole,** MacCurtain Street (from US$50 double); and the **Silver Springs Hotel,** Tivoli (from US$60 double), both of the latter with good food, too. Cork is attractively situated on the River Lee; downstream is **Cobh,** Ireland's principal port. The main excursions from Cork are to **Blarney Castle** and its stone and to **Cashel,** former capital of the Kings of Munster. The southwest of Ireland has a very mild climate. Tours from **Killarney** (by boat or by horse-drawn jaunting cars) are the best way to appreciate the lakes and mountains. Hotels in Killarney:

Aghadoe Heights, Tralee Road (from US$40 double)

Dunloe Castle, opposite the Gap of Dunloe and the River Laune (from US$64 double)

Gleaneagle, Muckross Road (from US$28 double)

Great Southern, (from US$54 double)

Killarney Ryan Motor Hotel, Cork Road (from US$24 double)

The **Dingle Peninsula:** This is the most westerly peninsula in Ireland, and indeed in Europe. Stay at the **Ostan Dun-an-Oir,** Ballyferriter (from US$44 double).

SOURCES OF FURTHER INFORMATION

Any **Pan Am** office round the world; **Tourist Information Office,** 14 Upper O'Connell Street, Dublin; **Irish Tourist Board,** 590 Fifth Avenue, New York, NY 10036, and in Chicago, San Francisco, Los Angeles, and Toronto; and 150 New Bond Street, London W1Y OAQ.

Italy

WHAT'S SPECIAL

Italy offers an infinite variety in its geography, climate, and people. In the north there are snow-capped mountain peaks, in the south the palms and orange groves of Sicily. In the summer the beaches of the Adriatic and Italian Riviera are among the most popular in Europe, and in the winter the Alps and the Dolomites are a snow-covered playground. Then there are the great cities of Rome, Florence, Venice, and Milan, rich in historic and artistic treasures.

COUNTRY BRIEFING

Size: 119,690 square miles   **Population:** 56,999,047
Capital: Rome   **Capital Population:** 2,911,671

Climate: The weather varies from very warm to freezing depending on place and time of year. April to November are usually sunny and warm—hot in midsummer. Rome is pleasant all year round, but there is a rainy season in winter.

Weather in Rome: N41°48′; Alt 377 ft

Temp (°F)	Jan	Feb	Mar	Apr	May	Jun	Jul	Aug	Sep	Oct	Nov	Dec
Av Low	39°	39°	42°	46°	55°	60°	64°	64°	61°	53°	46°	41°
Av High	54°	56°	62°	68°	74°	82°	88°	88°	83°	73°	63°	56°
Days no rain	23	17	26	24	25	28	29	28	24	22	22	22

Government: A democratic republic.
Language: Italian.

Religion: Roman Catholic.
Currency: Lire.

	L 100	L 500	L 1000	L 2500	L 5,000	L 7,500	L 10,000	L 50,000
US (dollars, cents)	.09	.44	.88	2.19	4.38	6.57	8.74	43.69
UK (pounds, pence)	.04	.21	.42	1.05	2.09	3.14	4.18	20.88

Public Holidays:

New Year's Day, 1 Jan
Easter Monday
Labor Day, 1 May
Anniversary of the Republic, 2 June

Assumption *(Ferragosto)*, 15 Aug
All Saints' Day, 1 Nov
Immaculate Conception, 8 Dec
Christmas Day, 25 Dec
St Stephen's Day, 26 Dec

HOW TO GET THERE

Flying time to Rome's Leonardo da Vinci Airport from New York is 8¼ hours; from Mexico City, 13¼ hours; from London, 3¼ hours; from Istanbul, 2½ hours. Time in Italy: GMT+1. Daylight Saving Time observed.

REQUIREMENTS FOR ENTRY AND CUSTOMS REGULATIONS

A valid passport; no visa for visits up to 3 months, but a smallpox and/or cholera vaccination if coming from an infected area. You may bring in any amount of non-Italian currency but only 200,000 lire (in note denominations of 50,000 lire or less) per person. Only 200,000 lire can be taken out; 50,000 and 100,000 lire notes may not be exported. Duty-free allowance: 400 cigarettes or 100 cigars or 1 pound tobacco; 1 bottle liquor, 2 bottles wine; 50 grams perfume; 2 still cameras with 10 rolls film, 1 movie camera with 10 reels film; portable radio (subject to a small license fee); personal effects such as clothing, jewelry, books, sporting and household equipment. If you wish to export works of art or antiquities, apply to the Export Department of the Italian Ministry of Public Education.

AIRPORT INFORMATION

Leonardo da Vinci Airport is 21 miles from Rome. There is a regular airport bus service to and from the terminal at Stazione Termini, Via Giolitti (L1,500). Taxis cost around L30,000 (establish fare in advance). There is an extra charge for luggage. Tip luggage porters L500 and up per bag plus a small additional tip. An airport departure tax of L4,200 (international departures only) is included in the price of the ticket. At departure, be sure to advise the bus or taxi driver whether you are traveling nationally or internationally.

ACCOMMODATIONS

Italian hotels *(alberghi)* are officially classified by the government as deluxe, 1st class, 2nd class, 3rd class, and 4th class, and prices are fixed by law. Some hotels choose to be classified as 2nd class for tax reasons, while providing really first-class accommodations. Check on the supplementary charges before taking a room in the hotel; you may not wish to have the extras. Many hotels include breakfast in the price quoted. Most *pensioni* in Italy are bright, clean, and friendly and generally a good bargain. Italy has about 60 youth hostels, and they cost about L5,000 and up per night, including taxes, sheets or sleeping bag, heating, hot water, and breakfast. Rome hotels:

Rates are in US$ for a double/twin room with bath or shower

Bernini-Bristol, Piazza Barberini 23 (from $115)
Carriage, Via delle Carrozze 36 (from $45)
Cavalieri Hilton, Via Cadlolo 101 (from $153)
D'Inghilterra, Via Bocca di Leone 14 (from $86)
Eden, Via Ludovisi 49 (from $101)
Excelsior, Via Vittorio Veneto 125 (from $155)
Flora, Via Vittorio Veneto 191 (from $93)
Le Grand, Via Vittorio Emanuele Orlando 3 (from $173)
Hassler-Villa Medici, Piazza Trinità dei Monti 6 (from $151)
Hotel Britannia, Via Napoli 64 (from $69)
Quirinale, Via Nazionale 7 (from $82)
Regina Carlton, Via Vittorio Veneto 72 (from $90)
Savoy, Via Ludovisi 15 (from $95)
Sitea, Via Vittorio Emanuele Orlando 90 (from $69)

With the exception of the Cavalieri Hilton, on a hill overlooking Rome about ½ hour from the center, all the above hotels are centrally located.

USEFUL INFORMATION

Helpful Hints: Women should always carry handbags securely under the arm that is away from the curb. Men should not carry passports or wallets exposed in back pockets. Never leave your car unlocked and never leave valuables in it, even for the shortest absence.

Banks: In Rome the Banca del Lavoro, near the Pan Am office, represents the major US banks. American Express is at Piazza di Spagna 38; Thomas Cook, Via Veneto 9-11. Banks open 8:30-1 Mon-Fri. Hotels cash travelers' checks, and you can change money at any Exchange Bureau *(cambio)*, railroad station, or airport (you will definitely get a better rate at the bank or *cambio*).

Mail: Stamps available from post offices, hotels, and tobacconists. Mailing from the Vatican post office (St Peter's Square) can save several days' delivery time overseas. Vatican stamps are available only at the Vatican post office.

Telephones: To use public phone booths, buy tokens *(gettoni)* from newsstands, tobacconists, or any café with a public phone (local calls L100). Long distance or international calls can be made from your hotel or, in Rome, from the post office at Piazza San Silvestro. Useful numbers in Rome:

Pan Am 4773
Italian State Tourist Office 49 711   **Directories** 12
Rome Tourist Office 46 18 51   **Time** 161
Overseas Operator 170   **Weather** 1911

Newspapers: Most English-language newspapers and magazines available. In Rome, the newsstands on Via Veneto, Via del Corso, and near St Peter's Square are the best supplied with foreign publications. Local English-language newspapers are the *International Daily News* and the *Daily American.*

Tipping: Taxi drivers, 15%; luggage porters, L500 and up per piece of luggage at railroad stations; hotel concierge, L800 per day plus an additional tip for any extra services; chambermaids, L500 per day or L2,000-2,500 per week. Waiters and bartenders, 5-10% of bill (where service is included—otherwise give 12-15%); cloakroom attendants, L300; hairdressers, shampoo girls, barbers, 10% divided among those providing services. Tip museum guides and movie ushers L300, more if theater or opera seats are very expensive. Tip church attendants L1,000 for showing you around, turning on lights, etc.

Electricity: Current is not uniform. Some places have 220 volts 50 cycles AC (e.g. Milan), but large areas have 110-127 volts 50 cycles AC. Rome and several other towns have both. Check before you plug in. Plug converters and small transformers are available almost everywhere.

Laundry: Most hotels have a quick and reliable laundry service. Dry-cleaning takes longer. (Cost of dry-cleaning a suit, from L6,000; laundering a shirt, from L2,200).

Hairdressing: Major hotels have their own salons. (Shampoo and set from L10,000-15,000; man's haircut with shampoo from L8,000-15,000. Tip 10%.)

Photography: Plenty of supplies in every large town. Black and white processing can generally be handled in 2-3 days, the same with color slides from Ektachrome; take Kodachrome home for development. Prices for film—L2,200 for black and white (20 exposures), L3,900 for Kodacolor (24), L11,000 for Kodachrome (36). Prices vary enormously, and if you are staying a while, it is cheaper to have film shipped to you.

Clubs: Kiwanis, Lions, Rotary, American Chamber of Commerce, American Club, and American Women's Association all meet in Rome.

Babysitting: Most hotels will arrange this. In Rome, Organization Unlimited (Via dei Leutari 29—tel: 654 45 21).

Rest Rooms: Signs to look for: women, *Signore;* men, *Signori.*

Health: Most hotels will be able to put you in touch with an English-speaking doctor. Rome has excellent hospitals. The **Salvator Mundi International** has American-trained staff. Tap water is safe in major towns, but bottled water is available everywhere. Wash all fruit.

TRANSPORTATION

There is fire and fury in Roman driving, and rush-hour traffic is intense, but there are plenty of taxis and bus service is good. To get a taxi, go to the nearest taxi stand. They can also be called by phone, but you pay extra depending on the distance traveled by the cab to pick you up. There is also an extra L1,000 night and holiday charge, and an extra charge per piece of luggage. Rome's efficient bus service costs L100 per ride. Get on at the rear door and drop a L100 coin or two L50 coins into the ticket machine. The fare is the same no matter how far you travel. The traditional way to see Rome is by horse-drawn carriage— for about L30,000 per hour and up; bargaining is possible. Much cheaper is the "Essential Rome" tour by special city bus. It leaves every day at 3:30pm from the large square in front of Stazione Termini, costs L3,000, and in 3 hours will help you get your bearings with the benefit of a guide. If you're headed for the beaches at Ostia or the ruins of Ostia Antica, the Metropolitana, Rome's subway, will save you time; otherwise, it is not yet a very extensive system. To see the city from the air, you can hire a small plane or a helicopter at the Urbe Airport (Via Salaria 825). Regular air services link all the main cities with Rome. Italian long-distance buses are first-class. Some have bars, hostesses, and interpreters. For information about the routes, prices, etc., contact CIT (Compagnia Italiana Turismo) at Stazione Termini or at Piazza Cola di Rienzo 33 (tel: 38 80 57). If you plan to travel by rail, see your travel agent or the Italian State Railroad representative before you leave home, as there are many worthwhile reductions and special facilities available to tourists. The Eurailpass is accepted in Italy.

FOOD AND RESTAURANTS

All you need to eat well in Rome is a good appetite. The *tavola calda* is the Italian equivalent of a lunch bar, and you eat quickly, standing at the counter or perched on a high stool. **Babington's Tearooms,** at the foot of the Spanish Steps, is more British than Italian in flavor, which means it is one of the best places to get a good homemade breakfast. Unlike many Italian eateries, it is open all day long for lunch, snacks, or tea. **La Capricciosa** (Largo dei Lombardi 8) has good food at reasonable prices, is known for pizzas as well, and is open till 2am. It is wise to phone ahead since restaurants have one closing day a week. Among restaurants whose cuisine tends to be international rather than Italian are **El Toulà** (Via della Lupa—tel: 68 17 96), **George's** (Via Marche 7— tel: 48 45 75), **Sans Souci** (Via Sicilia 20—tel: 46 04 91), and **Mahona** (Via A. Bertani 6/7—tel: 581 04 62), all expensive. The **Hostaria dell'Orso** (Via Monte Brianzo 93—tel: 656 42 50) is elegant and expensive, in a landmark building that was already a hostelry in the 14th century. **Cesarina** (Via Piemonte 109—tel: 46 08 28) is strictly Italian, with Bolognese cooking the specialty, as it is at **Dal Bolognese** (tel: 36 11 426), off Piazza del Popolo, with a sidewalk terrace for summer dining. Parliamentarians and journalists eat at **La Pentola** (Piazza Firenze 20—tel: 654 26 07) for its excellent Tuscan dishes; for a good Tuscan steak try **Il Buco** (Via S Ignazio 8—tel: 679 32 98), where the game is also good. At **Al Fogher** you can dine by candlelight in the atmosphere of a delightful country house; cuisine is of the Friuli region. **Le Cabanon** (Vicolo della Luce— tel: 68 81 07) is expensive, but you dine to music in elegant surroundings, while **I Due Ladroni** (24 Piazza Nicosia—tel: 656 10 13) is average to high priced and is a good place for a business dinner. **Ranieri** (Via Mario de' Fiori—tel: 679 15 92), near the Spanish Steps, is old-fashioned and quietly refined, with more than a century of experience. **Passetto** (Piazza Zanardelli 14—tel: 654 36 96) is consistently good, a favorite on many lists and just off Piazza Navona. **Da Pancrazio** (Piazza del Biscione 92—tel: 656 12 46) occupies the lower section of the ancient Theater of Pompeii and is full of columns, statues, and busts. **Piccolo Mondo** (Via Aurora 39—tel: 475 45 95) caters to the celebrity crowd; another restaurant popular with theater folk is **Al Moro** (Vicolo delle Bollette 13—tel: 678 34 95). **La Carbonara,** in Campo dei Fiori, is fashionable, and its excellent Roman cooking is inexpensive. **Dino e Pino** (Piazza Montevecchio 22—tel: 656 13 19) is a small chic tavern, with a warm intimate atmosphere, personalized service, and average prices; they turn out a broad sampling of Italian regional specialties. For fairly modest prices, try the **Trattoria Nazzareno** (Via Magenta 35/37—tel: 49 57 72), near the main Rome railway station. A favorite place for summer dining is across the Tiber in Trastevere, a quarter of the city whose residents, the *trasteverini,* consider themselves the only true Romans. Outdoor restaurants crowd the streets, among them **Sabatini,** a superb fish restaurant just a few steps behind Piazza Santa Maria in Trastevere. In the square itself are **Galeassi** and **Alfredo,** with tables around the central fountain. Restaurants with a difference are the **Ambasciata d'Abruzzo** (Via Tacchini 26—tel: 87 82 56), where the waiters are an entertainment in themselves, and **Da Meo Patacca** (Piazza dei Mercanti 30—tel: 581 61 98), in Trastevere, where they are even more so. With costumed waiters, strolling musicians, and premises decorated as Hollywood might have done it, the restaurant unselfconsciously caters to tourists and when you're in the mood, it's great fun. For a complete switch, enjoy French cuisine at **L'Eau Vive** (Via Monterone 85—tel: 654 10 95), where the waitresses and cooks are nuns. Among hotel restaurants, the **Massimo D'Azeglio** (Via Cavour 18—tel: 46 06 46) is outstanding, famous for its classic food and superb desserts. Lunch in Rome begins at 1 and goes on until 2:30 or 3; dinner begins at 8. Eating in Rome is not as economical as it once was: dinner for two in the majority of restaurants ranges from L15,000-L30,000; in an expensive one from L25,000 to L50,000. But there are many anonymous *trattorie,* often family operations, where dinner for two can be had for L15,000. Many restaurants close for holidays in August. If *pane e coperto* (bread and cover charge) appears on the menu, you pay that whether you eat anything else or not, and if you want to leave room for good things to follow, it is quite acceptable to order a *mezza porzione* (half portion) of pasta.

DRINKING TIPS

Italians drink vermouth as an apéritif and wine with the meal; they usually finish off with a cognac, a small glass of Sambuca (a licorice-flavored liqueur), or a hair-raising distilled wine called *grappa*. *Chianti* is probably the best-known Italian wine, but the quality varies, so look for the sign of the black cockerel on the label and settle for reliable makes, such as Frescobaldi, Melini, and Ricasoli. Other good red wines *(rossi)* are Barolo, Valpolicella, Bardolino, and a full-bodied wine from Sicily called Corvo. Connoisseurs say that Brunello di Montalcino is the best Italian red wine. Some of the best white wines are Orvieto, Frascati, and Soave; if you like a sweet, light sparkling wine, Asti Spumante is very refreshing. Martini and Cinzano are famous Italian apéritifs, but for a change try Punt e Mes, Campari, or Rosso Antico. Strega is an interesting liqueur. In general, better wine is in bottles, not in carafes. Rome is full of fascinating drinking places. Perhaps the best known is the **Café de Paris,** of *La Dolce Vita* fame, on the famous Via Veneto. A whisky there would cost from L4,000 and a half bottle of wine from L6,000. Via Veneto is also lined with the chairs, tables, and umbrellas of **Doney's** and **Harry's Bar.** The **Caffè Greco** (Via Condotti 86) was a favorite haunt of Mark Twain, Oscar Wilde, and Buffalo Bill. The **Baretto,** on the same street, is one of the places to be seen having your before-dinner drinks—if you can get in; there are only six seats. **Rosati,** in Piazza del Popolo, is another popular spot for the before-dinner apéritif or the after-dinner coffee. Across from Rosati's is **Canova Bar,** which also has good snacks and pastries. The **Bar Zodiaco** (Viale Parco Mellini 90) and the lovely **Monte Mario** near the Observatory are pleasant, and the **Bar Tre Scalini** has a delightful terrace in Piazza Navona, one of Rome's most beautiful squares. All three are also good for an ice cream or a *granita di caffè con panna* (a coffee-flavored ice with whipped cream). The Hassler-Villa Medici has an excellent bar with impressive decor.

ENTERTAINMENT

Romans love to see and be seen, and delight in watching the world go by, whether from a table at a corner café or a more swank lookout on the Via Veneto. But for something livelier, there are numerous alternatives. **Club 84** (Via Emilia 84), near the Veneto, has long been on the scene and remains one of Rome's best nightclubs—live music. **La Clef** (Via Marche 13), also near the Veneto, is a sophisticated bar with live piano and disco music as well. Flashy and very much in vogue is **Jackie O** (Via Boncompagni 11), a nightclub-disco with a plush restaurant down-stairs where you can wine and dine. **Scacco Matto** (Via Ferdinando di Savoia 6) has live music, turn-of-the-century opulence in its decor, and it, too, has a restaurant on the floor below. **Bella Blu** (Via Luciani 21) is an elegant and small restaurant-nightclub. A young crowd gathers at the **Scarabocchio,** a discothèque in Trastevere (Piazza Ponziani 8). A drink at any of these will cost about L10,000 and be warned that in Rome, the second drink usually costs no less than the first. Other possibilities: **La Taverna Ulpia** (Piazza del Foro Traiano), where the music is live but a bit softer, more romantic than elsewhere; the large **Much More** (Via Luciani 52), near the Veneto, with lots of lights and confusion; **La Biblioteca del Valle** (Largo del Teatro Valle 9) where the younger set can still manage an evening on L10,000. **The Piper Club** (Via Tagliamento 9) alternates dancing with cabaret. For a more intimate but still lively evening, there's **Tony's Piano Bar** at the Hotel Savoy; a whisky here would cost from L4,000.

The official season of opera interspersed with ballet runs from the end of November to May at the **Teatro dell'Opera.** In the summer you can go to the opera in the grandeur of one of ancient Rome's most magnificent buildings, the ruins of the **Baths of Caracalla.** Your hotel porter will help you to obtain tickets, and for a comprehensive guide of current productions, see the *International Daily News,* the *Daily American, Coming Events,* or *This Week in Rome.* Theater and opera performances usually begin at 9:15pm, and most Roman theaters close one day a week, so check beforehand. During the summer, concerts are held in some of the beautiful churches in Rome. The **Pasquino,** near Piazza Santa Maria in Trastevere, shows English-language films with the original soundtrack. There are many festivals on the Roman calendar, and you can obtain all the information you need from the Tourist Office (Via Parigi 11—tel: 46 18 51).

SHOPPING

Rome's most tempting shopping area is the network of streets between Piazza di Spagna and Via del Corso, with Via Condotti as its backbone, a street where the best, the most fashionable, and the most expensive can be found in almost every category. **Bulgari,** the renowned jeweler, is just one of the storefronts here. Via Sistina and its side streets at the top of the Spanish Steps, the Via Veneto area, plus the less expensive Via Nazionale, are other places. For shoes, sandals, and boots, the highest quality is at **Albanese** (Via Lazio 19) and **Ferragamo** (Via dei Condotti 66). For a huge selection at reasonable prices try **Charles al Corso** (Via del Corso 109). **Anticoli** (Piazza Mignanelli 22) and **Perroni** (92 Piazza di Spagna) are among the best glove shops in town. **Fendi** (Via Borgognona 36 A/B) is a good place for gifts—key chains, handbags, wallets, anything in leather. Most expensive is **Gucci,** in Rome at Via Condotti 21. **Laura Aponte** (Via Gesù e Maria 10) is known for knitwear and **La Mendola** (Piazza Trinità dei Monti 15) for creations in silks and cottons. Famed **Emilio Pucci** can be found at Via Campania 59 and **Valentino** at Via Gregoriana 24 for *alta moda,* at Via Bocca di Leone 15-18 for women's ready-to-wear. On Via Condotti are **Battistoni** and **Runci,** two of the best men's shops, or try **Enzo Ceci** (Via della Vite 52). **Roland's** (Piazza di Spagna) has both men's and women's clothing. Other temptations in Rome are gold and silver jewelry, and antiques. For the latter, go to **Via del Babuino,** or to **Via de' Coronari. Alinari** (Via del Babuino 98) has an extensive collection of old prints and reproductions of Italian works of art. **Rinascente,** the department store, has two locations (Piazza Colonna and Piazza Fiume) and is good for gifts. **Standa,** at many locations, is something of a five-and-dime, good for small items and things you forgot. In general, shops are open 9-1 Tues-Sat, then 4-8 in summer and 3:30-7:30 in winter. In summer, shops tend to close Saturday afternoon also. Many accept credit cards. For good buys in almost everything, particularly clothing, try the **Viale Libya** area. Rome has a Flea Market every Sunday morning at **Porta Portese,** and the food market at **Campo dei Fiori** is one of the most colorful in Rome.

SPORTS

The **Rome International Horse Show** is held every year in May. Many boxing, basketball, and tennis events are held in the spectacular **Palace of Sports** (built by architect Pier Luigi Nervi, the "wizard of reinforced concrete"). You can swim in the **Cavalieri Hilton** pool, or go horseback riding at the **Whip Club** (Via Trigoria—tel: 501 14 05); there are lessons for beginners at the **Farnesina Riding Club** (Via Monte Farnesina 18). The **Acqua Santa Golf Club** (Via Appia Nuova 716—tel: 78 34 07) has special facilities for nonmembers. Rome has two bowling alleys—the **Brunswick** (Via dell'Acqua Acetosa) and the **Roman** (Viale Regina Margherita). You can play tennis at the **Cavalieri Hilton** and at many tennis clubs. There are over twenty 18-hole golf courses throughout the country. Permits can be obtained for fishing and hunting.

WHAT TO SEE

Rome

No stay in Rome will be long enough to enable you to enjoy all its splendors, nor can we do more than point you in the right direction. There are excellent guided tours, and you should take volumes of literature to read.

You can start with the **Capitoline Hill.** Climb the stairs to the **Campidoglio,** the beautiful square built according to the design of Michelangelo, with the golden-bronze statue of Marcus Aurelius. To the left as you go up you can see the famous church of **Santa Maria d'Aracoeli,** and on the right is the cage of the live she-wolf, symbol of the wolf who suckled Romulus and Remus, founders of Rome. The **Capitoline Museum** houses fabulous mosaics and the celebrated sculpture of the *Satyr of the Capitol* by Praxiteles. Nearby is **Piazza Venezia,** dominated by the monument dedicated to Vittorio Emanuele II; and behind that are the **Roman Forum,** center of political life, the judiciary, and business in ancient Rome; the **Palatine Hill;** the **Imperial Forums;** **Trajan's Column;** the **Arch of Constantine;** and the **Colosseum.** In this huge arena, dating from 80 AD, Christians, gladiators, and beasts fought and died in front of crowds of up to 60,000, many under the reign of Nero, whose spectacular **Domus Aurea** (Golden House) is a 2-mile-long mass of underground ruin near the Colosseum.

Those Christians did not die in vain. Their monument is the **Vatican,** a self-contained state ruled by the Pope. Stand in the great square designed by Bernini and admire the magnificent dome of **St Peter's** designed by Michelangelo. Inside St Peter's—the world's largest church—is Michelangelo's *Pietà* and the baroque *St Peter's Pulpit* by Bernini. In front of this is the crypt where St Peter is buried. Adjoining St Peter's is the **Vatican Museum,** where you can visit the **Sistine Chapel** with Michelangelo's superb ceiling and his mural of the *Last Judgment.* See also the **Rafael Rooms** with superb frescoes, the great **Library**, the **Picture Gallery** of Italian Masters, and the wonderful collection of tapestries, sculptures, robes, maps, and other treasures.

On Sunday mornings (except in summer, when the Pope moves to his residence in Castel Gandolfo) crowds flock to St Peter's Square to await the Pope's appearance on the balcony of his study and his Papal blessing of those gathered below. If you wish to attend one of the weekly general audiences—held Wednesdays either at the new Pope Paul VI Hall just off St Peter's Square or in St Peter's Church, apply through the Prefetto della Casa Pontificia (Prefecture of the Pontifical Household). US visitors should apply to the Bishops' Office for United States Visitors to the Vatican, 30 Via dell' Umiltà, 00187 Rome (tel: 679-0658 and 679-2256). Apply well in advance: the Bishops' Office must submit its requests to the Prefecture by the Thursday preceding the Wednesday selected; they receive the tickets the following Tuesday at their office, from where you pick them up. If you don't have time to apply in advance, you can still drop by the Bishops' Office (near Trevi Fountain) on the morning of an audience—there may be uncollected tickets available. Pope Paul VI Hall seats over 6,000, with standing room for several thousand more.

Further places of great interest in Rome are along the **Via Appia Antica**, where you will find the **Catacombs**; the great fortress of **Castel Sant'Angelo** (near the Vatican), originally built as Hadrian's tomb; the basilicas of **Santa Maria Maggiore, St John in Lateran,** and **St Paul's Outside-the-Walls.** See the **Villa Borghese,** which houses a wonderful collection of paintings and sculpture; the archaeological collection at the **Museo Nazionale Romano** in Piazza della Republica; and the **Museo Nazionale di Villa Giulia,** which has one of the most important Etruscan collections in the world. You should also see the great **Baths of Caracalla;** the **Pantheon,** founded in 27 BC and one of the best-preserved temples in the city; and the church of **San Pietro in Vincoli** (St Peter in Chains), which houses Michelangelo's *Moses.* Wander through the quaint streets of **Trastevere,** and do not miss the mosaics on the facade of **Santa Maria in Trastevere,** possibly Rome's first church dedicated to the Virgin Mary. Do not miss the **Spanish Steps,** especially lovely at Easter when the stairs are banked with azaleas in bloom, and from **Piazza di Spagna,** make your way to **Piazza del Popolo** with its baroque churches and the **Egyptian Obelisk.** Another beautiful square is **Piazza Navona** with its three fountains, the center one designed by Bernini.

For a little light relief, throw two coins in the **Trevi Fountain** to ensure your return to Rome; take the children to the **Villa Borghese Zoo** and **Gardens** (open daily), or go to the Punch and Judy Show at the **Pincio** (weekends only—check times at your hotel or any tourist office).

Around Rome: It is only 30 minutes by Metro (L200) to **Ostia Antica**—ruins of what was a thriving seaport of 10,000 inhabitants in the 4th century BC. Rome's closest beach, **Lido di Roma,** is nearby. If you have not been dazzled already by the city's fountains, you can see other superb examples at **Tivoli,** in the gardens of the 16th-century **Villa d'Este,** which is near the great ruins of **Hadrian's Villa,** built by the Emperor in 135

AD. Tivoli is about 20 miles from Rome and is reachable by bus from Viale Castro Pretorio, or by train from Stazione Termini.

Siena: If you are anywhere near Siena on 2 July or 16 August, the *Corsa al Palio* is a must. Participants in this exciting horse race in the **Piazza del Campo** (the main square) dress up in 15th-century costume— and since each entry represents a section of the city, spirits among the spectators are high. Stay at the **Continental,** Via Banchi di Sopra 85 (from US$47 double), the **Moderno,** Via Baldassarre Peruzzi 19 (from US$36 double), the **Park Hotel Marzocchi,** Via di Marciano 16 (from US$95 double), or the **Villa Scacciapensieri,** Via di Scacciapensieri 24 (from US$90 double).

Assisi: This particularly attractive and enchanting rose pink city was the home of St Francis. His life is depicted in Giotto's frescoes in the 13th-century **St Francis' Basilica.**

Pisa: Another fascinating town of the Tuscany region, Pisa has its 12th-century cathedral and its **Leaning Tower,** one of the most photographed monuments in the world. Now about 14 feet off center, it is still slipping. Galileo was born here and used the tower in his gravity theory.

Florence: 180 miles north of Rome, Florence is one of the great cities of the world. Everywhere you turn in this incomparable town you will see exquisite masterpieces of architecture and art which recall the days when Florence, under the rule of the powerful Medici family, was the undisputed leader of the Renaissance world. In 1966 a sealed room was discovered beneath the base of the Medici chapels. Open to the public, the walls are covered with Michelangelo's charcoal sketches made while he was hiding from his enemies. You can visit magnificent places like the **Galleria degli Uffizi,** designed by Vasari in 1574, where you will see Botticelli's *Birth of Venus,* and the **Palazzo Pitti,** in the **Boboli Gardens,** which has a modern art gallery and a silver museum as well as works by Raphael, Titian, and Giorgione. Donatello's famous statue of **St George** is in the **Bargello Museum** (a prison in the 16th century). The second pair of bronze doors which Ghiberti designed for the Baptistry of the **Cathedral of Santa Maria del Fiore** were described by Michelangelo as "gates of Paradise," and the building itself, with its celebrated Giotto's **Campanile** (bell tower) is a glowing masterpiece of colored marble. Dante was baptized here. Every square and every ancient building is a work of art—the 13th-century church of **Santa Croce,** where Machiavelli and Michelangelo are buried; the Dominican monastery of **San Marco,** with its beautiful Fra Angelico frescoes; the **Accademia di Belle Arti,** where you can see Michelangelo's superb statue, *David.* A copy is in the **Piazza della Signoria,** which is a busy square in the city and one of the most beautiful open-air galleries in Europe.

Florence is also one of the top gourmet cities in Europe. Try a *bistecca alla Fiorentina,* a thick T-bone steak, generally grilled, or the *tortino di carciofi* (eggs with artichokes). Places to enjoy these masterpieces include **Buca Lapi** (Via del Trebbio 1R); **Il Coccodrillo** (Via della Scala 7); **The Open Gate** (Viale Michelangelo); **Ristorante Ponte Vecchio,** near the famous 14th-century bridge; **Sabatini** (Via Panzani 41) and **Otello**

(Via Orti Oricellari 36). **Sabatini** (Via de' Panzani 9), with an elegant atmosphere, is moderate to expensive. Popular *trattorie* are **Bordino** (Via Stracciatella 9); **Leo in Santa Croce** (Via Torta 7R); **Cammillo** (Borgo San Jacopo 57R); lunch at **La Loggia**, Piazzale Michelangelo, on a hill overlooking all of Florence; **Mamma Gina** (Borgo San Jacopo 37R) for typical Tuscany trattaria, and **Sostanza** (Via del Porcellana 25). Try **Antico Fattore** (Via Lambertesca 1) for good, fairly inexpensive Florentine cooking. If you want to eat American-style now and then, **Doney's** (Via Tornabuoni) has a good line of snacks as well as specialties such as *scampi alla Medici*. **Harry's Bar** is a favorite meeting place, and the **Jolly Club** is a lively discothèque.

Shopping in Florence: Gloves are a particularly good buy at **Manco** on Via Tornabuoni, and **Salvatore Ferragamo** on the same street is world famous for shoes. Florence is the place, too, for all high-quality leather, handbags, marble-inlay mosaics, lacquer trays, handsome tooled leather book wallets, wallets, purses, etc. For jewelry try the booths all along the **Ponte Vecchio**, the only bridge in Florence not blown up in World War II. **Eurostovile** (Via Nazionale 81-85) will mail their pottery, ceramics, and ornaments for you. Go to the **Officinia Farmaceuticha di Santa Maria Novella** (Via Scala 16) for personally blended perfumes; it's worth the trip just to watch the perfume masters at work. A good place to hunt for bargain souvenirs is the **Straw Market** around the corner from Piazza della Signoria. Hotels in Florence:

Rates are in US$ for a double/twin room with bath or shower
  Anglo-Americano, Via Garibaldi 9 (from $95)
  Augustus & dei Congressi, Vicolo dell'Oro 5 (from $70)
  Columbia-Parlamento, Piazza San Firenze 29 (from $32)
  Continental, Lungarno Acciaiuoli 2 (from $60)
  Excelsior Italia, Piazza Ognissanti 3 (from $190)
  Grand Hotel Minerva, Piazza Santa Maria Novella 16 (from $86)
  Jolly Carlton, Piazza V Veneto 4-A (from $85)
  Lungarno, Borgo San Jacopo 14 (from $80)
  Plaza e Lucchesi, Lungarno della Zecca Vecchia 38 (from $95)
  Ritz, Lungarno della Zecca Vecchia 24 (from $65)
  Savoy, Piazza della Republica 7 (from $130)
  Villa Medici, Via il Prato (from $145)

Fiesole: Just outside Florence, with the medieval **Monastery of St Francis** on the hill above. Superb views from the terraces. There is also an 11th-century cathedral and a Roman theater.

Naples: 140 miles south of Rome, dominated by **Vesuvius.** Do not miss a visit to the city's **Museo Nazionale,** which houses an interesting collection of antiquities found at the ruins of **Herculaneum** and **Pompeii.** Try some of the Neapolitan specialties, like the *pizza* (the best in Italy)— and of course ice cream, spaghetti, and seafood. The Neapolitan version of a fresh fish fry *(frittura di pesci)* is well worth sampling. Good restaurants to try are **Le Arcate** (Via Aniello Falcone 249—tel: 68 33 80) and **La Sacrestia** (Via Orazio 116—tel: 66 41 86). Fish is excellent along the **Santa Lucia** waterfront—try **La Bersagliera** (Banchina Santa Lucia—tel:

39 06 92). The **San Carlo Opera House** in Naples is one of the most important in the world; the season is usually from December to April. There are many good hotels in Naples; listed below are a few to choose from:

Excelsior, Via Partenope 48 (from US$161 double)

Jolly Ambassador's, Via Medina 70 (from US$68 double)

Mediterraneo, Via Nuova Ponte di Tappia 25 (from US$59 double)

Parker's Hotel, Corso Vittorio Emanuele 135 (from US$55 double)

Royal, Via Partenope 38 (from US$84 double)

Vesuvio, Via Partenope 45 (from US$83 double)

Pompeii: Only half an hour from Naples lie the ruins of the great city destroyed by an eruption of Vesuvius in 79 AD. Take the trip by cable car to the moon-like landscape of the crater of **Vesuvius.** Naples is a good center for visiting spots like **Positano,** a dream of a fishing village; **Amalfi,** at the end of one of the most hair-raising scenic drives in Europe; **Sorrento,** where the Roman Emperors had their summer palaces and which is now a booming beach resort; and of course **Capri,** the lovely little island famous for its **Blue Grotto** and for the late Gracie Fields, the British entertainer, from whose restaurant by the sea, **Canzone del Mare,** you can swim between courses. Recommended hotels in Capri are the **Club Hotel Villa Pina** (from US$50 double); **La Pergola Hotel** (from US$56 double); **Hotel Punta Tragara** (from US$180 double).

Venice: Built on 118 islands crisscrossed by 160 canals and linked by 400 footbridges. There are no roads, only canals; no traffic, only the water buses, water taxis, and gondolas. A labyrinth of alleys and stairs and little bridges link the main waterways. Have coffee at **Caffé Quadri, Caffé Avena,** or **Caffé Florian** (the oldest café in Venice) in the grandest square in Europe—**Piazza San Marco**—with its hordes of pigeons who feast from your hands. Make a special visit to the square in the evening. See the **Cathedral of St Mark** at one end of the square, and climb the 325-foot-high 14th-century **Bell Tower,** where bronze figures chime the bells, or the 15th-century **Clock Tower** for superb views over Venice. The **Palazzo Ducale,** where the Doges lived in princely style, has Tintoretto's masterpiece, *Paradise,* in the Grand Council Chamber. See also the **Rialto Bridge,** the **Accademia** and **Museo Civico Correr** art galleries, the **Ca' d'Oro,** the **School of San Giorgio degli Schiavoni** with famous Carpaccios, and the **School of San Rocco** with magnificent Tintoretto paintings. And see **Harry's Bar,** on the **Grand Canal** (entrance on Calle Vallaresso), made famous by Ernest Hemingway. When shopping in Venice, look for fine handmade lace, jewelry, leather goods, and above all, glass. You could go to the island of **Murano** and see the glass being made, to the island of **Burano** for lace, and to **Torcello** for its cathedral with beautiful mosaics. Luxury hotels in Venice include the **Danieli Royal Excelsior** (from US$196 double), right next door to the Doge's Palace; the **Cipriani** (from US$220 double), on Giudecca Island; the **Gritti Palace** (from US$219 double); and the **Bauer Grunwald** (from US$218 double). The garden terrace at the Bauer Grunwald is a delightful place for summer dining and dancing. The canal-side Terrace restaurant at the **Monaco**

& **Grand Canal Hotel** (from US$120 double) offers a magnificent view, good service, and excellent Italian dishes. For lunch, the **Tavernetta da Carlo e Renzo** has local atmosphere and excellent food. **La Taverna Felice, La Caravella, Al Giglio,** and **Da Raffaele** are good places for dinner; for seafood specialties, try **Do Forni, Al Graspo de Uva, Malamocco,** and **Antico Panada.** The **Taverna La Fenice** is conveniently located beside the famous theater of that name but is expensive, while the **Madonna,** in the Calle della Madonna, is more modestly priced. Places to visit from Venice include the **Lido,** just across the lagoon. It has a marvelous beach, with fine hotels like the **Excelsior Palace** (from US$197 double), and a casino.

Ravenna: Near the Adriatic coast, it has many fine buildings dating from the 5th and 6th centuries and is famous for its mosaics. Visit the **Basilica di San Vitale,** a remarkable building with mosaics covering the walls of the choir. There are also large mosaics in the church of **Sant' Appollinare Nuovo,** with a beautiful round bell tower. The burial place of Dante is in the **Basilica San Francesco,** a 5th-century building with a Romanesque bell tower. **Faenza,** 20 miles southwest of Ravenna, is famous for ceramics.

Vicenza, with its fine Palladian villas—and Palladio's last work, the **Teatro Olimpico**—is less than 40 miles from Venice. **Verona** has one of the best-preserved Roman amphitheaters in the world (where operas and concerts are held in the summer months in the arena, which comfortably seats 25,000 spectators), plus many wonderful medieval buildings, a fabulously wealthy **Museum of Art,** and a 15th-century house on Via Cappello where Juliet is supposed to have lived. She is alleged to be buried on the Campo della Fiera. **Padua** is certainly worth a visit. See Donatello's *Gattamelata,* outside the **Basilica del Santo** and Giotto's frescoes in the **Scrovegni Chapel.**

Italian Lakes: Lombardy and **Piedmont** have clear mountain air and the snow-capped peaks of the Alps. The most famous lakes are **Lake Maggiore,** which Italy shares with Switzerland, **Lake Como,** and **Lake Garda,** the largest of the Italian lakes, about 2 miles wide and 40 miles long. There is skiing and sailing, and in June one of the greatest car races in the world, the **Italian Grand Prix,** takes place at **Monza,** just outside Milan, which is the capital of Lombardy district. Take a boat at Como and sail down to **Bellagio,** a lovely resort town where the lake forks. There are two good 18-hole golf courses in the Lake Como region— **Villa d'Este** and **Menaggio Cadenabbia. Stresa** is the main summer resort on Lake Maggiore, opposite the lovely islands of **Isola Bella** and **Isola dei Pescatori.** The **Hotel Grand et des Iles Borromées** (from US$116 double) has first-class food, tennis courts, and a private beach. Other hotels are the **Bristol** (from US$51 double); **La Palma** (from US$40 double); and the **Regina Palace** (from US$55 double). **Brescia** is a good spot to start your tour of Lake Garda. Stay at the **Vittoria** (from US$55 double) and, on Lake Garda, at the **Regina Adelaide** and **Eurotel** hotels. Brescia has interesting Roman and Renaissance monuments.

Milan: Once the capital of the Kingdom of Italy, Milan is a thriving modern city and one of the best shopping centers in Italy. **Via Montenapoleone** and **Corso Vittorio Emanuele** are good places to start. The **Galleria Vittorio Emanuele II** is attractive—a glass-covered arcade where you can shop in smart stores and boutiques and stop for coffee or a meal at one of many excellent restaurants. But Milan is also a great art center, and the **Brera Gallery**, the **Poldi-Pezzoli Museum**, and the **Castello Sforzesco** house some of the most important art collections in Italy. Landmarks include the famous Gothic **Cathedral,** third-largest church in the world, and the **Church of Santa Maria delle Grazie,** where Leonardo da Vinci's painting of *The Last Supper* decorates the wall of the former Dominican refectory. **La Scala** (season usually from December to June) is one of the greatest opera houses in the world. Milan is one of the gourmet cities of Italy, and restaurants which back up this claim include **Marchesi** (Via Bonvesin de La Riva 9), the only restaurant in Milan with two Michelin stars; **Malatesta** (Via Bianca di Savoia 19), superb French and international cuisine from US$25 per person; **Giannino's** (Via Amatore Sciesa 8-10); **Boeucc** (Piazza Belgioioso 2); and **Savini's** (Galleria Vittorio Emanuele II). If you want good trattoria-style restaurants, go to **Bagutta** (Via Bagutta 14), **Da Bice** (Via Borgospesso 12), **Don Lisander** (Via Manzoni 12a), and the **Taverna del Gran Sasso** (Piazzale Principessa Clotilde 10). Milan hotels:

Rates are in US$ for a double/twin room with bath or shower

Anderson, Piazza Luigi di Savoia 20 (from $75)

Atlantic, Via Napo Torriani 24 (from $80)

Cavour, Via Fatebenefratelli 21 (from $87)

Duomo, Via San Raffaele 1 (from $94)

Excelsior Gallia, Piazza Duca d'Aosta 9 (from $121)

Grand Hotel Fieramilano, Viale Boezio 20, in a residential area next to Milan fairgrounds (from $100)

Grand Hotel et de Milan, Via Manzoni 29 (from $111)

Jolly President, Largo Augusto 10 (from $110)

Jolly Touring, Via Ugo Tarchetti 2 (from $90)

Lord Internazionale, Via Spadari 11 (from $52)

Marino alla Scala, Piazza della Scala 5 (from $75)

Mediolanum, Via Mauro Macchi 1 (from $53)

Milano Hilton, Via Galvani 12 (from $120)

Palace, Piazza della Repubblica 20 (from $173)

Plaza, Piazza Diaz 3 (from $95)

Principe e Savoia, Piazzale della Repubblica 17 (from $179)

Royal, Via Cardano 1 (from $67)

Select, Via Baracchini 12 (from $85)

Windsor, Via Galileo Galilei 2 (from $70)

The above hotels are all centrally located unless otherwise indicated.

Turin: About 80 miles from Milan along the *autostrada,* Turin is the elegant capital of Piedmont, with wide streets and beautiful squares— some of its devotees claim that **Piazza San Carlo** is second only to Piazza San Marco in Venice. Very much a businessman's city—home of Fiat,

Lancia, and Martini and Rossi Vermouth—Turin has fine hotels and first-class restaurants: try **Cambio** on Piazza Carignano, **Cucolo** on Via Roma, and the fascinating **San Giorgio,** once a medieval castle in the **Parco del Valentino** on the shore of the Po. Other good restaurants are **Urbani,** with excellent desserts; **Muletto,** with delicious Piemontese cooking; and **Da Benito,** known for its seafood. Charming but expensive is the **Villa Sassi,** located on the outskirts of the city in lovely gardens. Landmarks are the **Palazzo Madama,** once the home of Queen Maria Christina, now a museum of fine art with some exquisite porcelain and glass, and the **Castello del Valentino,** royal palace of the Savoy kings of Italy, in the Parco del Valentino. Turin's greatest treasure is the 15th-century **St John's Cathedral,** with its facade of white marble. In the cathedral's **Chapel of the Holy Shroud** is an urn containing what is believed to be the shroud in which Jesus' body was wrapped when taken from the cross and which still retains the marks of his head and body. Turin hotels:

Jolly Hotel Ambasciatori, Corso Vittorio Emanuele 104 (from US$92 double)

Jolly Hotel Principi di Piemonte, Via P Gobetti 15 (from US$80 double)

Majestic, Via Rattazzi 10 (from US$63 double)

Sitea, Via Carlo Alberto 35 (from US$69 double)

Turin Palace, Via Sacchi 8 (from US$65 double)

ITALIAN RIVIERA

The **Riviera dei Fiori** (Coast of Flowers) begins at **Ventimiglia** near the French border and sweeps right along the coast to **Savona.** Spring comes early, and that is when you will see fields and fields of carnations. You can swim happily from May to September. The liveliest resort on this holiday coast is **San Remo,** which has luxury hotels, fashionable beaches, a gambling casino, and a funicular railroad which can take you up to the snows of **Mount Bignone** in about 45 minutes. There is a golf course halfway up the mountain, and you can play golf all year round at **Garlenda,** about 10 miles from **Alassio,** just farther down the coast. Hotels in San Remo are the **Royal,** Corso Imperatrice 74 (from US$80 double), **Grand and Des Anglais,** Corso Imperatrice 34 (from US$50 double), and **Grand Londra,** Corso Matuzia 2 (from US$68 double).

Other fascinating places to visit include **Genoa,** birthplace of Columbus (they celebrate his birthday with carnivals on 12 October). Hotels in Genoa: **Columbia Excelsior,** Via Balbi 40 (from US$145 double); **Bristol Palace,** Via 20 Settembre 35 (from US$75 double); and **City Hotel,** Via San Sebastiano 6 (from US$42 double).

Rapallo has excellent swimming and an underwater fishing school; stay at the **Cuba & Milton,** S Michele di Pagana (from US$32 double), or the **Astoria,** Via Gramsci 4 (from US$43 double). Eat at the **U Giancu,** a large, family-run trattoria. See **Santa Margherita,** which boasts two of the best restaurants in the area, the **Trattoria dei Pescatori** and **All Ancora,** and the enchanting **Portofino,** once a little fishing village, now a millionaires' playground, with luxury yachts in the harbor alongside painted fishing boats. There are very good seafood restaurants including **Il Pitos-foro** (guitar serenades while you eat) and **Delfino,** famous for its traditional seaside *trenette al pesto* (pasta in a basil-garlic sauce).

Italian Mountains: This is another Italy of towering, snow-capped mountain peaks and icy rivers. In the spring, the high Alpine meadows are carpeted with flowers, and the slopes are green with a spike pattern of vineyards. Though the sun is hot in summer, there are still high places where you can ski—**Solda,** for example, has an international slalom competition in July. The **Dolomites** are an all-year-round playground, with the winter season at its peak over Christmas and New Year's, and from the end of January until the middle of February. The major resort is **Cortina d'Ampezzo.** Stay at **Cristallo Palace** (from US$87 double); **Miramonti Majestic** (from US$110 double); or the **De La Poste** (from US$99 double).

Cortina has one of the greatest bobsled runs in Europe, a fine ice stadium, ski jumps, ski trails, and a mountain railway to the top of **Mount Tofana,** a height of nearly 11,000 feet. This resort is on a par with St Moritz, and you can ski all day and dance all night if you are in the mood. All this fresh air will give you an appetite, and there are plenty of places to satisfy it—for example, with great helpings of local specialties like *Selchcarré mit kraut* (smoked pork with sauerkraut) and *knödel* (dumplings). There is a strong Austrian influence about the food in this part of Italy. **El Toulà** is one of the top restaurants in Cortina d'Ampezzo, and others to note include **Al Fogher** and the less elaborate but very good **Capannina. Da Peppe Sello** has rustic decor and reasonable prices. **El Camineto,** located 3 miles outside of Cortina at Rumerlo, offers good local specialties and a spectacular view of the valley and the Dolomites. Another major resort is **Courmayeur,** near the entrance of the Mont Blanc tunnel, with the highest mountain in Europe (15,781 feet). It is famous for the cable car ride over the glaciers to Chamonix, in France.

ITALIAN ISLANDS

Sicily has green valleys, flowers, fishing villages, lovely resorts, a great capital city, **Palermo,** and some of the best-preserved and most magnificent Greek temples in the world. Scenic **Taormina,** built on a hill high above the Straits of Messina, is a year-round resort. The sea below the town is crystal clear and the view of the still-active volcano, **Mount Etna,** stunning. **San Domenico Palace,** a converted 14th-century monastery, is Taormina's leading hotel (from US$120 double), but the **Jolly Diodoro** (from US$59 double), **Timeo** (from US$76 double), **Bristol Park** (from US$65 double), and **Villa Belvedere** (from US$39) are also good. Other places to visit include **Monreale,** with remarkable mosaics in the Norman cathedral; the ancient city of **Syracuse,** founded in the 8th century BC; the ruined temples at **Agrigento, Segesta,** and **Selinunte;** and the crater of Mount Etna. Palermo has an important opera house where the season usually begins in February. Puppet theaters are a great feature of Palermo. There are festivals in January (Twelfth Night) and at Easter, and Palermo has a month-long drama and ballet festival in July.

Sardinia: Until the Aga Khan discovered it and began the luxury **Costa Smeralda** development, Sardinia was largely unexploited. It is the second-largest island in the Mediterranean (9,300 square miles), with a landscape ranging from the petrified forest at **Laerru** to the red cliffs and pink sand beaches of **Arbatax.** Visit **Cagliari,** the capital of the island and a cosmopolitan port thousands of years ago. Costa Smeralda hotels include **Cala di Volpe,** Cala di Volpe (from US$146 double); **Cervo,** Porto Cervo (from US$194 double); and **Pitrizza,** Porto Cervo (from US$162 double). **Porto Rotondo** is one of the smartest spots on the Costa Smeralda, and **Santa Margherita di Pula,** another holiday complex, has a nightclub and lots of sporting facilities. You will probably eat in your hotel, but the **Trattoria Sacchi** at **Nuoro** is excellent. The island has good bus and train service to principal towns. Sardinia is a 1-hour flight from Rome.

SOURCES OF FURTHER INFORMATION

Pan Am, via Bissolati 46, Rome, and any Pan Am office around the world; **ENIT,** Ente Nazionale Italiano per il Turismo, Via Marghera 2, Rome, and at other major points of entry in Italy; **Italian Government Travel Office,** 630 Fifth Avenue, New York, NY 10020; and in Chicago, San Francisco, and Montreal; **Italian State Tourist Department,** 201 Regent Street, London W1.

Liechtenstein

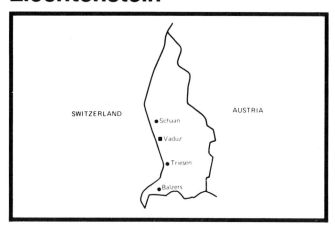

WHAT'S SPECIAL

One of the smallest nations in the world, Liechtenstein is a sovereign and independent state with a government elected by the people, without an army—but with its own police. Liechtenstein uses the Swiss franc as its currency, and its history may be traced back to the 12th century CE.

The high mountain peaks, the beautiful pastures, orchards, vineyards, and the sweep of the Rhine provide a thousand different views of this last feudal remnant of the Holy Roman Empire. The principality traces its origins to Hugo von Liechtenstein—younger son of Mannegold the Second, and the *minnesinger* (or bard), Ulrich von Liechtenstein, whose son was instrumental in forging an alliance with the Austrian Hapsburg empire. For the visitor there is skiing in winter, an array of good food and wine, and the delicate sounds of the 27-note *hackbrett*, a lyrelike instrument. And there are postage stamps.

COUNTRY BRIEFING

Size: 60.66 square miles   **Population:** 25,220
Capital: Vaduz   **Capital Population:** 4,614
   Climate: Mild, similar to Switzerland, snow in winter, pleasantly warm in summer.

Weather in Vaduz: Lat N47° 08'—Alt 1,761 ft.

Temp (°F)	Jan	Feb	Mar	Apr	May	Jun	Jul	Aug	Sep	Oct	Nov	Dec
Av Low	24°	25°	32°	39°	46°	52°	55°	55°	50°	41°	34°	26°
Av High	36°	39°	49°	58°	65°	72°	75°	73°	66°	56°	45°	36°
Days no rain	21	20	22	18	18	15	17	18	19	20	20	21

Government: A constitutional monarchy.

Languages: German is the official language, while English is widely spoken.

Religion: Roman Catholic.

Currency: Swiss franc. 100 centimes (or rappen) = 1 Swiss franc.

Public Holidays:

New Year's Day, 1 Jan	Corpus Christi
Epiphany, 6 Jan	Assumption Day, 15 Aug
Easter Monday	All Saints' Day, 1 Nov
Labor Day, 1 May	Immaculate Conception, 8 Dec
Ascension Day	Christmas Day, 25 Dec
Whit Monday	St Stephen's Day, 26 Dec

HOW TO GET THERE

Flying time to Zurich from New York is 8¼ hours; from Frankfurt ¾ hour; from Munich ¾ hour. Then from Zurich travel by road to Liechtenstein. Time in Liechtenstein: GMT+1.

REQUIREMENTS FOR ENTRY AND CUSTOMS REGULATIONS

A valid passport. No formalities or restrictions when entering from Switzerland. From elsewhere, entry regulations are as for Switzerland.

ACCOMMODATIONS

Hotels, mountain inns, bed and breakfast boarding houses, pensions, camping grounds at **Bendern** and **Triesen,** and a motel with a splendid view 2 miles from **Vaduz** on the Triesenberg Road. Liechtenstein hotels are:

Rates are in US$ for a double/twin room with bath or shower

Gasthaus Kulm, Triesenberg (from $33)
Hotel Adler, Vaduz (from $36)
Hotel Engel, Vaduz (from $32)
Hotel Gorfion, Malbrun (from $36)
Hotel Linde, Schaan (from $28)
Hotel Malbruner, Malbun (from $41)
Hotel Real, Vaduz (from $43)
Hotel Schlöessle, Vaduz (from $45)
Hotel Waldeck, Gamprin (from $26)
Landhaus Vaduzer-Hof, Vaduz (from $39)
Motel in Liechtenstein, Triesen (from $28)
Park Hotel Sonnenhof, Vaduz (from $66), overlooking the town
Tourotel, Gaflei (from $39)
Turna Hotel, Malbun (from $31)

USEFUL INFORMATION

Banks: Open 8-12, 1:30-4:30; Mon-Fri. Exchange office in City Hall is open 8:30-3 Sat, 10-3 Sunday. Currency and travelers' checks can also be changed at Quick Tourist Office, Vaduz. **Postage** stamps can be obtained at the post office or at postcard shops. Mailboxes are yellow with a red cross. Coin-operated **telephones**—insert coin, dial number; if there is no reply, the coin will be returned. Local call costs 40 centimes. Useful numbers: **National Tourist Office,** Vaduz 2 14 43, and branch office in Malbun 2 65 77; **Quick Tourist Office,** 2 33 33 and **Vaduz Tourist Office,** 6 62 88. On **tipping,** a service charge of 15% is generally included in restaurant bills. 10-15% is the general rule. **Electric current** is 220 volts 50 cycles AC. **Laundry, dry-cleaning, hairdressing,** and **photographic facilities** are all available. For **babysitters,** ask your hotel. **Health:** imported pharmaceuticals are available, and many doctors and dentists speak English.

TRANSPORTATION
There is a good bus service; phone for fixed-rate taxis.

FOOD AND RESTAURANTS
Food is much the same as in Switzerland and at about the same prices. Many hotels have good restaurants. In Vaduz try hotels Real (tel: 2 22 22); for gourmet food, expensive: Park Hotel Sonnenhof (tel: 2 11 92) also highly considered; Engel (tel: 2 10 57); Adler (tel: 2 21 31); Vaduzer-Hof (tel: 2 21 40), and **Landgasthof Mühle** (tel: 2 41 41). **Hotel Meierhof** (tel: 2 18 36) and **Mittagsspitze** (tel: 2 36 42) are in Triesen; **Hotel Dux** (tel: 2 17 27) and **Linden-Pic** at the Hotel Linde (tel: 2 17 04) are in Schaan; also in Schaan are the **Schaanerhof** (tel: 2 18 77) and the **Sylva** (tel: 2 39 42). Also try the **Landhaus** (tel: 3 21 31) in Nendeln and the **Waldhof** (tel: 3 11 38) in Schaanwald. The **Old Castle Inn** (tel: 2 10 65) is in the style of an English pub and offers international cuisine, and in the restaurant **Torkel** (tel: 2 44 10), surrounded by landmarks of Old Vaduz, the fine wines from the Prince's own vaults are served. Also worth noting is the **Löwen** at Schellenberg (tel: 3 11 62) where Liechtenstein specialties, as Sparback wild boar and *Liechtensteiner Tafelspitz* can be enjoyed in a 300-year-old setting.

DRINKING TIPS
Imported wines, liquor, and beers are available. The wines from the **Hofkellerei des Fürstens** are remarkably good as is the local **Vaduzer** rosé. There are no restrictions on the sale of drinks; drinks and coffee can be enjoyed in hotel bars and lounges.

ENTERTAINMENT
Movie houses in Vaduz, Schaan, and Balzers. Regular concerts and theatrical performances.

SHOPPING
Stores open 8-12 and 1:30-6:30 Mon-Fri; though some souvenir shops remain open during luncheon; Saturday till 4pm; Friday till 9pm in Schaan only. Among best buys are low-priced cameras, Swiss watches, cuckoo clocks, musical boxes, whistling wooden carved figures of men,

local pottery, scarves, and dirndl dresses for children. Swiss chocolate and rare Liechtenstein stamps make ideal gifts for under US$10.

SPORTS

In summer, hiking, trout fishing (permit required and obtainable from the Tourist Office in Vaduz), horseback riding, and miniature golf at **Vaduz;** swimming and tennis in Vaduz and **Schaan;** mountain climbing at **Triesenberg, Steg,** and **Malbun.** Excellent skiing from December to April. **The Liechtenstein Miniature Golf Sports Club,** Vaduz, **Liechtenstein Ski Association, Liechtenstein Tennis Club,** and **Liechtenstein Angling Club,** Vaduz, welcome visitors.

WHAT TO SEE

In **Vaduz** you will get a complete picture of the country's history and folklore in the **National Museum.** The **Picture Gallery** at the *Engländerbau* (English Building) on Vaduz's main street is open daily and houses magnificent paintings from the Prince's world-famous collection, including works by Rubens, Van Dyck, and Frans Hals. Don't miss the display of beautiful Liechtenstein stamps at the **Postal Museum.** Above the capital towers the **Castle**—home of Prince Franz Josef II (Head of State of the Principality of Liechtenstein). The village of **Balzers** is dominated by the medieval **Castle of Gutenberg;** for romantic ruins, see **Wildschloss** above Vaduz, a robber baron's hideout, and **Neu Schellenberg,** a historic fortress. In the same area is the picturesque church of **Bendern.** At **Triesen,** look for **St Mamerten chapel** with its remarkable frescoes. Conservation areas protect the country's rich plant and animal life. As a result, although Liechtenstein is host to a number of modern industries, the visitor is never aware of their intrusion in landscape. There are ceramics factories at **Schaan** and **Nendeln,** where gifts can be purchased. For a wonderful panoramic view of the Rhine Valley, take the road from Vaduz which twists and climbs past the castle to the little resort village of **Triesenberg** (2,890 feet). This is the start of the skiing region. See the **Regional Museum. Gaflei** is a starting point for long hikes along the ridge of the **Dreischwestern Massiv. Steg** (4,300 feet), impressively situated in a high Alpine valley with rushing mountain streams, is a peaceful summer resort. **Malbun** (5,250 feet) is the winter sports center with a chairlift and five ski lifts.

SOURCES OF FURTHER INFORMATION

Any **Pan Am** office around the world. **National Tourist Office,** Vaduz and Malbun; **Quick Tourist Office,** Vaduz; **Swiss National Tourist Office,** 608 Fifth Avenue, New York, NY 10020. **Swiss National Tourist Office,** Swiss Center, 1 New Coventry Street, London W1V 3HG.

Luxembourg

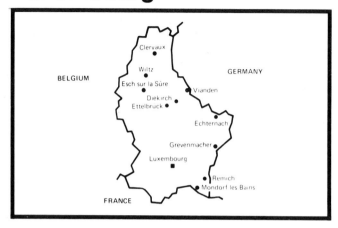

WHAT'S SPECIAL

On the one hand Luxembourg is a "pocket" state with fairytale castles and a strange language; on the other it is one of the wealthiest countries per capita in the world. While the smallest country in the Common Market, it is the seat of the European Court of Justice, the European Community (Common Market) Parliament, and other EC administrative offices.

COUNTRY BRIEFING

Luxembourg covers an area of 1,000 squares miles, and its **population** is 364,000. The **capital,** Luxembourg City, has a population of 80,000. **Climate** is temperate without extremes. July and August are the hottest months, with temperatures reaching the mid-70s; May and June are the sunniest months. It is an independent constitutional Grand Duchy. Letzeburgisch is the everyday language, but French is the official one, and German is universally spoken; many people also speak English. **Religion—** Roman Catholic. **Currency** is the Luxembourg franc (28.90F to US$1), which has the same value as the Belgian franc, though it is rarely accepted in Belgium. Belgian francs, however, are widely accepted in Luxembourg. **Public Holidays:** New Year's Day, 1 Jan; Easter Monday; May Day, 1 May; Ascension Day; Whit Monday; National Day, 23 June; Assumption Day, 15 Aug; All Saints Day, 1 Nov; All Souls Day, 2 Nov; Christmas Day, 25 Dec.

HOW TO GET THERE
Flying time to Luxembourg's Findel Airport from New York is 9 hours; from Frankfurt, ¾ hour; from Brussels, 1½ hours; from Paris 2 hours. Time in Luxembourg: GMT+1.

REQUIREMENTS FOR ENTRY AND CUSTOMS REGULATIONS
Passport or, if a Common Market citizen, identity card; no visa required or vaccination certificate, unless coming from an infected area. No currency regulations. Duty-free allowance for visitors from non-European countries: 400 cigarettes or 500 grams tobacco or 100 cigars; up to 4 bottles wine; 2 liters alcohol. Visitors from other Common Market countries: 300 cigarettes or 400 grams tobacco or 75 cigars. Up to 4 bottles wine, 1½ liters alcohol.

AIRPORT INFORMATION
Findel Airport is 4 miles from Luxembourg City. Taxis (300LF) and bus service (city bus 16LF, plus 16LF for baggage, Luxair bus 60LF) to city. Duty-free shop at airport, and hotel reservations counter at National Tourist Office in city terminal (tel: 48 79 99).

ACCOMMODATIONS
Different types of accommodations are abundant—a few luxury hotels in Luxembourg City and many more modest ones which are clean, simple, and good.
Rates are in US$ for a double/twin room with bath or shower
  Aerogolf Sheraton, rue des Trèves (from $60), near airport 4 miles from city center
  Alfa, 16 Place de la Gare (from $44), city center
  Cravat, 29 Boulevard Roosevelt (from $53), 1 mile from city center
  Eldorado, 7 Place de la Gare (from $47), city center
  Holiday Inn, Centre Européen, Kirchberg (from $47), near airport 3 miles from city center
  Kons, 24 Place de la Gare (from $59), city center
  Rix, 20 Boulevard Royal (from $44), 1 mile from city center
  Senator, 38 rue Jos. Junck (from $32), city center

USEFUL INFORMATION
Banks open 8:30-12, 1:30-4:30 or 5pm Mon-Fri. Banks open weekends at railway station and airport. Money can also be changed at border posts, hotels, and many stores. **Mail:** stamps from machines, in souvenir shops, and post offices. The main post office across from the train station has a 24-hour telegram and postal service. Mailboxes yellow. **Telephone** booths, coin-operated, in restaurants and cafés; local calls 3LF. Useful numbers: **Tourist Office** 48 79 99; **Local information** 017; **International information** 016; **Time** 19; **Weather** 18; **Emergency** 012. English-language newspapers available. **Tipping:** service charge in restaurants and hotels, so tips not expected though appreciated if you've received special treat-

ment; 10-20% to taxi drivers; porters 20LF per piece of luggage. **Electricity** is mostly 220 volts; some areas still use 110 volts. **Laundry:** express laundry and dry-cleaning services available in major hotels (dry-cleaning a suit, from 160LF; laundering a shirt from 60LF). Laundromats in most towns. **Hairdressing** salons in some hotels (shampoo and set from 320LF; a man's haircut from 180LF; tip 15-20%). **Photography:** black and white and color film available; 1-2 days to develop black and white, less than a week for color. **Clubs:** Lions, Rotary, Round Table, Kiwanis. For **babysitting**, contact the Tourist Office. **Rest Rooms** usually near town halls and in public squares and in cafés. Women, *Damen;* men, *Hommes, Messieurs* or *Herren.* **Health:** many doctors and dentists speak English; imported pharmaceuticals available.

TRANSPORTATION

Luxembourg City has a good bus service, and services link all other towns and tourist spots. Metered taxis available by phone or from stands (basic charge of 90LF, with additional charge of 17LF per kilometer; tip 10%; night fares 50% higher). Chauffeur-driven or U-drive cars available. The Eurailpass is accepted in Luxembourg.

FOOD AND RESTAURANTS

Food is rather French, but with a German and Belgian influence. Specialties include *quiche Ardennaise,* Ardennes ham, venison in season, and *écrevices* (crayfish) *à la Luxembourgeoise* during the summer. In Luxembourg City *coq au vin* is a specialty at the exclusive **Au Gourmet** (8 rue Chimay). Other expensive restaurants are the **Hostellerie Grünewald** (10 rue d'Echternach) and **Des Empereurs** (11 Avenue de la Porte Neuve). **Cordial** (1 Place de Paris) is less expensive. Also good are the French cuisine at **Saint Michel** (32 rue de l'Eau) and the delicious, freshly caught fish at the **Simmer Restaurant,** along the Moselle River at Ehnen.

DRINKING TIPS

Brewing is a traditional industry, and the people of Luxembourg are great beer drinkers. The well-known brands are *Henri Funck, Mousel, Diekirch,* and *Boefferding. Moselle* wines are also produced. Bars open from 6am to 1am. Nightclubs open until 3am. Women welcome.

ENTERTAINMENT

Nightlife is rather staid, but there are some nightclubs in the capital. Try **Chez Nous** and **Splendid** (both in rue Dicks) for cabarets; **Plaza** (Avenue de la Liberté); **Black Bess** (Avenue de la Liberté); and **Bugatti** (rue des Bains). **Jazz Club Melusina** (rue de la Tour Jacob) frequently features internationally known groups. Plays, operas, and ballet can be seen at the **Luxembourg Theater,** Rond Point Schumann, and during the summer, concerts are often held in public squares. Try to visit the open-air theater and music festival in **Wiltz** during July and August and also the modern theater in the **Casemates,** Luxembourg City, in July.

SHOPPING
Stores open 8am-12 and 2-6 Monday through Saturday. No bargaining.

SPORTS
Soccer is the main spectator sport. The **Luxembourg Golf Course,** near the Aerogolf Sheraton, four miles from the city, is open to visitors. There are also many opportunities for river and lake fishing (permit 200LF for fly fishing, 400LF for boat fishing).

WHAT TO SEE
Luxembourg City, founded in 963, was once one of the strongest fortresses in Europe; you can still walk through the **Casemates,** a 14-mile-long network of underground passages hewn out of solid rock. The city has 91 bridges, the newest being the **Grand Duchess Charlotte Bridge,** 178 feet high, which links it with the Kirchberg Plateau. A walk along the **Chemin de la Corniche,** a footpath around the city, provides good views of the bridges and the many valleys. A city sightseeing bus leaves the central station bus terminal daily at 9:30; the tour includes a visit to the US military cemetery at Hamm. During the summer there are guided tours (some in English) of the **Ducal Palace,** built 1580 and renovated in the 19th century. One of the oldest parts of the City is the **Marché aux Poissons** (fish market). Here are the **Museum of History and Art** and the **Natural History Museum,** while in Luxembourg Park is the **J P Pescatore Museum.** The 15th-century **Cathedral** has beautiful stained-glass windows. **La Place d'Armes** is surrounded by several cafés with seating outdoors during nice weather and live concert music. Children will enjoy a trip to **Bettembourg,** 7 miles to the south of Luxembourg City, where the **Parc Merveilleux** has a miniature zoo and farm, a fairy wood, a mini-train, and boats. Not far to the northeast is **Walferdange,** which also has a children's park. At **Rumelonge,** the **Mining Museum** is unique in Europe. Most outdoor attractions open only from Easter through the end of September. An interesting excursion outside the city could include a drive along the Moselle and its wine region with a stop to sample fried Moselle fish and wine, a visit to **Echternach,** then on to the impressive chateau from the Middle Ages at **Vianden,** and to **Cleraux** and **Wiltz.**

SOURCES OF FURTHER INFORMATION
Any **Pan Am** office around the world; **National Tourist Office,** PO Box 1001, Luxembourg City; **Luxembourg National Tourist Office,** 1 Dag Hammarskjold Plaza, New York, NY 10017; 36-37 Piccadilly, London W1V 9PA.

Malta

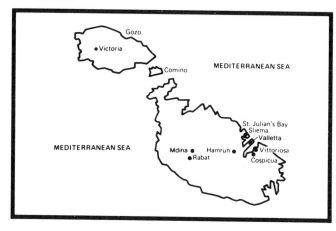

WHAT'S SPECIAL

Lying between Sicily and North Africa are Malta and her sister islands of Gozo and Comino. There are modern hotels, nightclubs, discothèques, an elegant casino, and a coastline with first-class facilities for swimming and all water sports. But Malta is also the historic island of the Knights of St John of Jerusalem, who from 1530 to 1798 built palaces and churches and defended their fortress against all invaders, including the Turks during the Great Siege of 1565. Valletta, the island's capital, designed by Francesco Laparelli, Michelangelo's assistant, is named after Jean de Valette, the heroic Grand Master who organized the island's defenses at the time of the Siege. At the beginning of the 19th century the British came, staying until the island was granted independence in 1964.

COUNTRY BRIEFING

Size: Malta, 95 square miles
Gozo, 26 square miles   **Population:** 347,000
Capital: Valletta   **Capital Population:** 15,300
  Climate: High summer can be very hot, but there is usually a light breeze. Winters are mild, and an equable climate can be enjoyed throughout the year.

Weather in Valletta: N35°54'; Alt 233 ft

Temp (°F)	Jan	Feb	Mar	Apr	May	Jun	Jul	Aug	Sep	Oct	Nov	Dec
Av Low	51°	51°	52°	56°	61°	67°	72°	73°	71°	66°	59°	54°
Av High	59°	59°	62°	66°	71°	79°	84°	85°	81°	76°	68°	62°
Days no rain	18	20	25	27	29	30	31	30	27	25	21	18

Government: An independent republic within the British Common-wealth, with a Parliament and President.

Language: Most people speak English, Maltese, and Italian.

Religion: Principally Roman Catholic. Anglican, Presbyterian, and Methodist churches in Valletta, also a synagogue.

Currency: Maltese pound; 100 cents = £M1.

	1¢	5¢	10¢	50¢	£M1	£M5	£M10	£M20
US (dollars, cents)	0.03	0.13	0.26	1.32	2.64	13.21	26.41	52.83
UK (pounds, pence)	.01	.06	.12	.63	1.26	6.30	12.60	25.20

Public Holidays:

New Year's Day, 1 Jan

Freedom Day, 31 March

Good Friday

St Joseph the Worker, 1 May

The Assumption, 15 Aug

Republic Day, 13 Dec

Christmas Day, 25 Dec

HOW TO GET THERE

Flying time to Malta, Luqa Airport from New York is 9 hours; from London 2½ hours; from Rome 1¼ hours. Time in Malta: GMT+1. Daylight Saving Time observed.

REQUIREMENTS FOR ENTRY AND CUSTOMS REGULATIONS

A valid passport for visits up to 3 months; North American, European, or Australian visitors need no vaccination or inoculation certificates. Any amount of foreign currency can be brought in but it should be declared at customs. You can take out what is left of the foreign currency declared on arrival. Maltese currency up to £M50 allowed in, but only up to £M25 per person can be exported. Duty-free allowance: 200 cigarettes or the equivalent in cigars or tobacco, 1 bottle spirits and 1 bottle wine, perfume not exceeding £M2 in value.

AIRPORT INFORMATION

Luqa Airport is 4 miles from Valletta. There is an airport bus service. Taxis are metered. Tip porters 10 cents per bag. Airport departure tax, £M2. Duty-free shop and exchange counter open 24 hours a day.

ACCOMMODATIONS

Most hotels charge for bed and breakfast, though full- and half-pension terms can be arranged. Your travel agent, or the **National Tourist Organization** (The Palace, Valletta), will give you a complete list of hotels. There is also an **Information Office** at 1 Freedom Square (formerly known as Kingsgate Arcade), Valletta. A list of agents dealing in furnished accommodations is also available. Prices for villas and apartments begin around £M100 a week. Most hotels add 10% service charge. Rates are usually lower November-March.

Rates are in US$ for a double/twin room with bath or shower

Castille, St Paul Street, Valletta (from $31 BB)

Cavalieri, Spinola Road, St. Julian's (from $46 BB), 5 miles from Valletta

Corinthia Palace, De Paule Avenue, San Anton, Attard (from $79 BB), 5 miles from Valletta

Cumberland, 111 St John Street, Valletta (from $24 BB), center of town

Delphina, Dragonara Road, St Julian's (from $31 BB), 5 miles from Valletta

Dolmen, Oawra, St Paul's Bay (from $46 BB), 8 miles from Valletta

Dragonara, St Julian's (from $96 BB), 5 miles from Valletta

Fortina, Tigne Sea Front, Sliema (from $46 BB), 4 miles from Valletta

Grand Hotel Excelsior, Floriana (from $59 BB), near town center

Grand Hotel Verdala, Inguanez Street, Rabat (from $78 BB), 5 miles from Valletta

Hyperion, Oawra, St Paul's Bay (from $34 BB), 8 miles from Valletta

Imperial, Rudolph Street, Sliema (from $34 BB), 4 miles from Valletta

Malta Hilton, St Julian's (from $119 BB), 5 miles from Valletta

Mellieha Bay, Ghadira, Mellieha (from $40 BB), 16 miles from Valletta

Osborne, 50 South Street, Valletta (from $34 BB), center of town

Phoenicia, Floriana, Valletta (from $88 BB), near town center

Preluna, Tower Road, Sliema (from $43 BB), 4 miles from Valletta

St Julian, Dragonara Road, Paceville, St Julian's (from $34 BB), 5 miles from Valletta

Villa Rosa, St George's Bay (from $55 MAP), 6 miles from Valletta

USEFUL INFORMATION

Helpful Hints: People are still sensitive here about dress that is too revealing—so no bikinis away from the beach. Do not wear abbreviated clothes when you go into churches.

Banks: Open 8:30-12:30 Mon-Fri, 5:00-7:00 Fri, and 8:30-12 noon Sat. Thomas Cook's, on Republic Street in Valletta, will change money and travelers' checks, as will most hotels.

Mail: The General Post Office in Valletta is open 8-6:30 Mon-Sat, until noon Sundays and public holidays. The post office at Luqa Airport is open daily, including Sundays and public holidays, from 7:30-7:30.

Telephone Tips: Cost of a local call from a public booth is 3 cents (all instructions written in English). Useful numbers:

National Tourist Organization Malta	**Time** 95
24444/28282	**Weather** 855011
Directories 90	**Emergencies** 99
	Overseas Operator 94

Newspapers: Malta has two English-language newspapers—*The Times* and *The Daily News.* UK newspapers arrive same day.

Tipping: Give waiters and bartenders 10% of the bill, same for taxi drivers. Tip hairdressers 10%, and give hotel porters and chambermaids 20 cents, cloakroom attendants 10 cents.

Electricity: 240 volts 50 cycles AC.

Laundry: Good fast service (24 hours). Dry-cleaning a suit, from £M1.50; laundering a shirt, from 30 cents.

Hairdressing: Many first-class hotels have their own hairdressing salons, and you pay accordingly. Shampoo and set, from £M5; man's haircut, from £M1.

Photography: Plenty of photographic supplies available; film costs from 50 cents for black and white, from £M1 for color. Processing black and white film, 24 hours; color about a week.

Clubs: Rotary Club, Lions Club, Kiwanis.

Babysitting: Only when hotels provide their own services.

Rest Rooms: Plentiful, with signs all in English.

Health: Standards of hygiene are high and tap water safe to drink. Imported pharmaceuticals easily available at reasonable prices. Most doctors and dentists speak English.

TRANSPORTATION

Green island buses link all the towns and villages with Valletta's terminal outside Freedom Gate; destination is displayed according to bus number. Taxis are metered but the meters are seldom used and the price for the trip should be arrived at before starting out. Car rental available from £M5 per day (not including gas). A chauffeur-driven car would cost about £M7.50 per day. Water taxis, which ply across the Grand Harbor, can be rented from the quays near the Customs House. A car ferry links Malta with Gozo several times daily. Driving is on the left; speed limits are 25 mph in towns, 40 mph outside.

FOOD AND RESTAURANTS

The Maltese are marvelous cooks and have a distinctive local cuisine, although many hotels have settled for an Anglo-Italian compromise and you may have to look around for local specialties. **Alexandra's** in South Street, Valletta, makes a good starting point for a gourmet's tour. Try *fenkata* (rabbit) or *bragioli* (beef roulades). If you want a steak or scampi, the **Whisper Knightclub and Farmhouse** in Mosta is the place to go. Also, the **Lantern** (Sappers Street, Valletta) is recommended for lunch and after the theater. *Timpani*, a luscious concoction of puff pastry, macaroni, meat, and eggs, is very Maltese, and they say the best place to eat it (order in advance) is in Gozo, at the **Royal Lady** in Mgarr. Fish is excellent in Malta, and restaurants like **Palazzo Pescatore** and **Gillieru's** in St Paul's Bay specialize in seafood.

DRINKING TIPS

Maltese wines are well worth sampling; names to make a note of are *Lachryma Vitis, Marsovin Reserve, Regatta,* and the government-produced *8th September.* Bars are open from 6am until the last customer leaves. A bottle of local wine could cost you as little as £M1 and rarely more than £M2 in a first-class restaurant. A whisky and soda would cost about 60 cents. *Cisk* lager (pronounced Chisk) and *Blue Label* and *Hop Leaf* are good home-brewed beers. The **Cafe Cordina** in Palace Square, Valletta, is the smart place for a drink, and **Magic Kiosk** in Sliema is a popular open-air café on the waterfront. In Gozo the local wine is reputed to be very strong.

ENTERTAINMENT

Throughout Malta there are about 30 fiestas occurring on Sundays between May and October. These are usually heralded by firework displays on the preceding Saturday. In Valletta the second weekend in May is "King Carnival" and the whole city is festive for three days. The festivities consist of a parade down Republic Street, music, fireworks, dances at Freedom Gate, and traditional fancy-dress balls in many hotels. The **Mnarja** (the weekend preceding June 29) is a great folk festival, with street races where horses and donkeys are ridden bareback. But there is a carnival atmosphere all the time at places like the **Buskett Roadhouse** and **Barrel & Basket** in Rabat; **Il Foresta** at Ta'Qali, and **Tigullio's** in St Julian's Bay. Also try the **Whisper Knightclub and Farmhouse, Palazzo Pescatore,** the **Sky Room** at the Preluna Hotel in Sliema, and the **Phoenicia Hotel.** Then there is the elegant **Dragonara Palace Casino,** at St Julian's Bay, where you can dine, dance, or try your luck at roulette, blackjack, chemin-de-fer, punto banco, or baccarat. Discos can be found in Sliema and St Julian's and on Gozo, but on the whole, nightlife in Malta is quiet. From October to May the 18th-century **Manoel Theater** has plays, concerts, opera, and ballet. Several movie houses show American and British films in English.

SHOPPING

Malta is famous for its heavy lace and handwoven cloth and the traditional lacemakers of Gozo are now turning out high-fashion garments which combine modern styles with ancient skills. Have a look in the **Malta Lace Store** in Rabat. Pottery, ceramics, glazed tiles, and wall plates make attractive low-priced souvenirs. Maltese jewelers, following a tradition that goes back hundreds of years, are still producing some of the most exquisite gold and silver filigree work in the world. **La Rosa Jewelers** on Zachary Street has a good selection. Other good buys are pipes; dolls dressed in traditional costume; model *dghajsas* (typical Maltese boats or water taxis); and wickerwork—the place to go is **Art Cane** at the **Crafts Village** at Ta'Qali or **Cane Alley** in Hamrun. From Hamrun come wrought-iron work, copperware, and brassware (especially dolphin door knockers). You can buy French perfumes in Malta for less than you would pay in Paris, at shops like **Rosina Depares** (Old Bakery Street, Valletta). Mdina glass is famous, and you can see the displays in the factory at the Ta'Qali Crafts Village, near the old town of Mdina. **Bernard's** in Valletta makes men's suits to order in British cloth. From the **Malta Crafts Center,** a permanent, government-run handicrafts exhibition opposite St John's Cathedral in Valletta, you will be directed to the right places to buy souvenirs. Most of the major stores will pack and ship purchases for you. Stores open 9-12:30 and 4-7 in summer, 4-7 in winter. **Republic Street,** the main shopping street in Valletta, is closed to traffic.

There is an open-air market in **St John's Square** Mon-Sat mornings from 7-12 and on Sunday at **St James Ditch.**

SPORTS

The warm clear water is ideal for all water sports—skin-diving, water-skiing, sailing, and fishing. Clubs which offer facilities include **Malta Sports Club,** Marsa; **Dragonara Water Sports Center,** St Julian's Bay; **Mellieha Boat and Ski Club; Union Club,** Sliema. The **Dragonara Water Sports Center** and **Bonett's,** in Sliema, offer both diving equipment and instructors for hire. Golf is played all year round on the 18-hole course at the **Marsa Sports Club,** Marsa (tel: 620842). Many major hotels have tennis courts. Sailing regattas, including the Middle Sea race from Malta to Sicily and back, are held frequently between April and November. Trotting and flat races are held every Sunday afternoon from October to May at the **Marsa Racecourse.**

WHAT TO SEE

In **Valletta** you could start in **Castille Square** and walk or drive round the **Bastions,** to give you some idea of the scale and splendor of the city. The Knights of St John built the walls 400 years ago. In the great **Cathedral of St John,** one of the grandest churches in Europe, the earliest Grand Masters of the Order are buried in the crypt. There is a museum attached. Close to the **Palace of the Grand Masters** is the **Armory,** with its collection of weapons used by the Knights. The **National Museum** on Republic Street has an important archaeological collection. Here you can purchase an inexpensive season ticket to cover all museum entrances for six months (special concessions for students from the Director of Museums). There are temples at **Tarxien, Hagar Qim,** and **Mnajdra,** which date back to the Copper Age. Other interesting archaeological sites include the **Ghar Dalam** cave near Birzebbuga, which contains fossils of Ice Age animals, and the mysterious underground temple of **Hal Saflieni Hypogeum,** which is one of the wonders of the ancient world and dates back nearly 5,000 years. About 7 miles from Valletta is **Mdina,** "the Silent City," ancient capital of Malta. The cathedral there is supposed to have been built on the spot where St Paul met the Roman governor Publius, who was the island's first convert to Christianity.

Rabat is a sprawling suburb of Mdina and a great center for some of the oldest crafts on the island—Malta weaving, pottery, glass. It is also where St Paul is believed to have lived in the **Grotto** for three months after his shipwreck. Visit the **Roman Villa** and **Museum of Roman Antiquities** and **St Paul's and St Agatha's Catacombs.** All these museums and places of interest are closed on public holidays. There is an admission fee, but you can buy inexpensive day tickets to cover entrance to all museums. Children would probably enjoy a visit to **Blue Grotto,** a delightful 10-minute sail on a sunny day. Try a half-hour sail in a glass-bottom boat to the submarine reel off **Dragonara Point.**

Gozo: From the Citadel in **Victoria** you can get a magnificent view of this fertile little island with its picturesque villages and majestic rugged cliffs. Visit the megalithic temples at **Ggantija** and the cave where Calypso is supposed to have entertained Ulysses for seven years (just above Ramla Bay). In Victoria you can stay at the **Duke of Edinburgh Hotel,** 114 Racecourse Street (from US$24 double BB), and in Marsalforn at the **Calypso Hotel** (from US$34 double BB).

Comino: This tiny island covers an area of one square mile; it has no cars. The **New Comino** and **Nautico Club** hotel offers all vacation amenities.

SOURCES OF FURTHER INFORMATION

Pan Am agent, Tumas Ltd, Regency House, 254 Kingsway, Valletta, and any Pan Am office round the world; **National Tourist Organization,** The Palace, Valletta; **Information Center,** 1 City Gate, Arcade, Valletta; **Malta Mission to the UN,** 249 East 35th Street, New York, NY 10016; **Malta Government Tourist Office,** 24 Haymarket, London SW1Y 4DJ.

Monaco

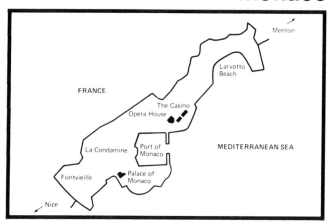

WHAT'S SPECIAL

Monaco lies at the foot of the southern Alps, on the shore of the Mediterranean near the French/Italian border. One of the tiniest countries in the world, it is full of aristocratic charm and dignity, a gathering place for the famous and wealthy who come to enjoy the elegant atmosphere of the exclusive beaches and luxurious hotels, to attend the fashionable galas, and to saunter in splendid surroundings by the gambling tables of the Casino de Monte Carlo. A tiny world of its own.

COUNTRY BRIEFING

Monaco, with a **population** of 25,000 (about 4,500 of whom are Monégasque), covers an area of 465 acres. Sheltered from the northern winds by the barrier of the Alps, its **climate** offers a mild winter and warm summer; there are about 180 days of sunshine during the year. Winter, 15 Dec-15 Mar, is the smart time to go. The official **language** is French, but a Monégasque dialect is spoken by the residents. Many people speak English and Italian. The Principality of Monaco is a hereditary and constitutional monarchy. The executive is under the authority of Prince Rainier. Roman Catholicism is the **religion. Public Holidays:** New Year's Day, 1 Jan; St Dévote, 27 Jan; Good Friday; Easter Monday; Labor Day, 1 May; Whit Monday; Assumption, 15 Aug; National Day, 19 Nov; Christmas, 25-26 Dec. **Currency** is as for France (5.1F = US$1).

HOW TO GET THERE

Flying time to Nice from New York is 8¼ hours; from London, 1¾ hours; from Rome, 1¼ hours. From Nice take a helicopter or road to Monaco. Time in Monaco: GMT+1.

REQUIREMENTS FOR ENTRY AND CUSTOMS REGULATIONS

No formalities are required if you want to cross the frontier between France and Monaco and there are no customs barriers between the two countries.

AIRPORT INFORMATION

The airport for Monaco is Nice-Côte d'Azur International Airport (France), 12 miles away. There are buses from the airport to Monaco, running from 9am-8pm; the fare is 25F. A taxi from the airport will cost about 120F. A helicopter leaves every ½ hour from Nice airport for the 6-minute flight to Monaco; fare is 150F per person.

ACCOMMODATIONS

Monaco has accommodations that are the last word in luxury, with swimming pools, restaurants, air conditioning, and sauna baths. Young people can stay at the **Centre Mediterranéan** at Cap d'Ail for about US$10-15 a day, including all meals and entertainment at the center's cinema, theater, and discothèque. If you would rather stay on a yacht, you can rent one complete with crew for US$200-3,000 per day, from **Agence Maritime** (1 bis Avenue du Président J. F. Kennedy). If you require assistance in finding accommodations, the **Direction du Tourisme et des Congrès** is at 2a Boulevard des Moulins. Monte Carlo hotels:
Rates are in US$ for a double/twin room with bath or shower
   Alexandra, 35 Boulevard Princesse Charlotte (from $30)
   Balmoral, 12 Avenue de la Costa (from $40)
   Beach Plaza, 10 Avenue Princesse Grace (from $50)
   De Paris, Place du Casino (from $100)
   Hermitage, Square Beaumarchais (from $80)
   Loew's, 12 Avenue des Spélugues (from $50)
   Métropole, Avenue de Grande-Bretagne (from $65)
   Miramar, 1 Avenue du Président J. F. Kennedy (from $35)
   Old Beach, Route du Beach (from $100, open summer only)
   All hotels listed above are centrally located.

USEFUL INFORMATION

Banks open 9-12 and 2-4 Monday to Friday; the exchange office of the Credit Foncier de Monaco (Casino agency) is open daily, including Sundays and holidays, from 10am to midnight. Banks have an exchange service open Saturday mornings. American Express is at Avenue de Monte Carlo (tel: 30 96 02) and at 35 Boulevard Princess Charlotte (tel: 30 96 52); First National City Bank at 2 Avenue des Spélugues (tel: 30 27 07); Barclays Bank at 31 Avenue de la Costa. **Postage** stamps can be bought at tobacconists as well as post offices and hotels. Although some rates are the same as for France, Monaco stamps must be used. A local call from a public **telephone** booth costs 50 centimes. Useful numbers: **Airport Information** (Nice), (93) 83 19 40; **Tourist Information** and **Accommodation Offices**, 30 87 01, 50 60 88, and in English, 50 07 51; **Operator and Directories**, 12; **Time**, 11; **Police**, 17; **Fire**, 18. **Electricity** is 220 volts 50 cycles AC. Most hotels have converters. **Laundry, dry-cleaning, photography, hairdressing,** and **tipping** are all as for France. **Clubs:** Kiwanis; Lions meets every second Thursday at Hotel Hermitage; Rotary on the first, third, and fourth Wednesday of each month at Hotel Métropole. For a private **babysitter,** call 50 63 71. **Health:** many doctors speak English, and imported pharmaceuticals and toiletries are available from pharmacies at reasonable prices. The nearest US consulate is in Marseille (France), (tel: 42 54 92 00).

TRANSPORTATION

Fares on the local buses are 3.30F, but you can buy a book of eight tickets for 13.30F. Taxis are also available; you can phone or go to the nearest stand. Taxis have meters and a minimum charge of 10F during the day, 13-15F at night. Cars can be easily rented, with or without chauffeur, in Monaco or Nice. There are bus services to Nice and Menton every 30 minutes; also buses to La Turbie, Roquebrune Village, and to Italy. French National Railways has trains to all neighboring towns.

FOOD AND RESTAURANTS

Do try the marvelous fish and wine stew called *stocafi,* and the local version of ratatouille called *tian.* **The Grill** on the top floor of the **Hôtel de Paris** is a luxurious restaurant with magnificent cuisine, a 150,000-bottle wine cellar, and a sublime panorama. Order the *soufflé de langouste* or *selle d'Agneau farcie aux rognons.* **Rampoldi** (3 Avenue des Spélugues); **Le Bec Rouge** (12 Avenue St Charles), and **Le P'tit Bec** (11 Avenue de Grande-Bretagne) are all very elegant, and the food is also excellent at **Les Ambassadeurs** (Galerie Charles III) and **La Calanque** (33 Avenue St. Charles). The view from the **Restaurant des Privés** (in the Casino) is quite something, but you should also go to **La Chaumière** (Boulevard du Jardin Exotique). For good value go to **Le Pinocchio** (30 Rue Comte Felix Gastaldi), a charming spot, and **Saint Nicolas** (6 Rue de l'Eglise), both situated near the Prince's palace. **Tip Top** is great for a late-night breakfast of scrambled eggs (11 Avenue des Spélugues), and **Le Drugstore** (Place du Casino) is open for snacks 24 hours a day.

DRINKING TIPS

As in France, sipping a glass of cool lager or a refreshing *Pastis* in one of the sidewalk or beach cafés is a favorite pastime. The **Café de Paris,** close to the Casino, has an orchestra and is one of the popular meeting spots. Another popular spot is **Britannia,** near Tip Top on Avenue des Spélugues.

ENTERTAINMENT

Throughout the winter, the famous **Orchestre National de l'Opéra de Monte Carlo** gives concerts in the **Salle Garnier** (in the Casino) and in the auditorium of the new **Congress Center** near Loew's Hotel, while during the summer the orchestra performs in the **Cour D'Honneur** of the Palace. Top international ballet companies perform in Monaco during the Christmas, New Year, and Easter holidays; the opera season is from February to March; theater plays are from December to May; and you can enjoy summer variety shows at the **Théâtre aux Etoiles.** English or American movies are shown at the **Gaumont Cinema,** and in summer you can see a different movie every night of the week in the open-air cinema near the Sport Club d'Eté.

In winter, galas are held in the **International Sporting Club,** while during the summer there are gala evenings every Friday and dinner dances with top international entertainers every night at the **Sport Club d'Eté.** If you prefer your entertainment to be more free and easy, go to **Maona, Jimmy's,** or **La Boccaccio,** all of them lively discos on Avenue Princesse Grace, or to **Le Tiffany's,** Avenue des Spélugues.

The **Casino de Monte Carlo** is famous throughout the world. Public gaming rooms are open from 10am. It will cost you 20F for the pleasure of strolling through the Salle des Amériques, which has craps, blackjack tables, and American roulette. Make your way to the other splendid gambling rooms, where the minimum stakes *(unité de mise)* are indicated at each table—about 10F. There is roulette, chemin de fer, baccarat, trenteet-quarante, anything you would care to try. But if you want to rub shoulders with the tycoons and play for the really high stakes, you will have to obtain a special card and pay considerably more to get into the *salons privés* (private salons, open 4pm). You must be 21 or over to be permitted into the Casino. Casual dress is permitted. **Loew's Hotel** has its own casino.

SPORTS

Boxing, fencing, and soccer are played and gymnastics performed. Pebbly **Monte Carlo beach** costs 25F for entry in midsummer, but the sandy **Larvotto Beach,** though less exclusive, is much more popular. There are marvelous heated sea-water pools where you can go swimming the year round (**Piscine des Terrasses,** Avenue d'Ostende, and **Loew's** swimming pool). Undersea exploration, regattas, cruises, and big-game fishing are organized in summer by the **Yacht Club de Monaco** (Quai Antoine 1er), which also has a sailing school. There is water-skiing off the beaches, and boats are for hire (**Navigator,** 12-14 Quai Antoine 1er). For tennis and squash, the **Monte Carlo Country Club** is open all year round—entrance fee 80F; July-September 120F. The **Golf Club** has an excellent 18-hole golf course, 3,000 feet above sea level on Mont Agel—green fee for the day, 70F; on Saturdays and Sundays, 100F—and there is miniature golf at the **Park Princesse Antoinette.** For winter sports, Monaco is only 2 hours away from the **French Alps.** In January and May, motor sports fans flock to Monte Carlo for the famous **Rally** and for the **Monaco Grand Prix.**

WHAT TO SEE

Monaco-Ville: The old city, with narrow climbing streets, has the Romanesque **Cathedrel of Monaco,** in whose crypt lie the tombs of the Princes of Monaco. Perched on the Rocher de Monaco is the storybook palace— **Palais du Prince, Princier,** whose outer walls act as a continuation of the perpendicular rock. Some parts of the palace date back to the 13th century. You must visit the **State Apartments,** surrounded by arcades decorated with frescoes; the magnificent **Salle du Trône** (throne room); and the vast state rooms where official receptions take place. Do go and listen to an evening concert in the **Cour d'Honneur** during the summer. The Palace is open to the public from July to September, 9-12:30 and 2-7pm; entrance fee for adults 20F, 6-14 years 10F, under 6 free. The **Art Gallery** in the Palace has some very interesting Napoleonic souvenirs, important archives, and the Prince's stamp collection. The Gallery is open daily (except Mondays) from 9:30-11:30 and from 2-7. In the Palace Square, the **Changing of the Guard** in their colorful uniforms takes place every day promptly at 11:55. The **Musée Océanographique** is open daily from 9-7 throughout the year. Founded in 1910 by the scientist Prince Albert I, its aquarium is one of the most beautiful and richest in Europe. There is also a fascinating department of applied oceanography, and you can see the cabin of the Prince's ship, with the scientific instruments he invented. Entrance fee—adults 20F, 6-15 years 10F, under 6 free. The **National Museum** of automatons and dolls is open from 10-12:15 and from 2:30 to 6:30. The automatons work only from 3:30 to 5:30. Entrance fee is 10F for adults, children 5-15 years 5F.

La Condamine is the name of the harbor district which links Monte Carlo with the Rocher de Monaco. Hanging on the side of the rock, with a wonderful view of the whole principality, the **Jardin Exotique** has a most extraordinary collection of cacti. From here you can go through the **Observatoire Grottoes,** with their caverns full of strange and brilliant stalactite and stalagmite formations, and then to the **Museum of Prehistoric Anthropology,** also founded by the enlightened Prince Albert I, which contains beautiful collections of Roman antiquities; combined entrance fee for adults, 12F.

Fontvieille is the industrial area whose appearance will soon be completely changed by the creation of a futuristic city built on land entirely reclaimed from the sea.

Monte Carlo is the sophisticated and elegant entertainment center of Monaco. The **Casino,** surrounded by beautiful gardens, is an enormous and ornate building, marbled and mirrored, with crystal chandeliers everywhere. There is also a concert room and a theater, the **Salle Garnier,** where Serge Diaghilev introduced the Ballets Russes de Monte Carlo during the season of 1911; it is still the setting for ballets, opera, drama, and concerts that brighten up the social season. Also visit **St Paul's Anglican Church** on the Avenue de Grande-Bretagne.

The events of the year include the **International Television Festival** in February, the pre-Lenten **Carnival,** the **Monte Carlo Open** at Easter, the **International Circus Festival** in December; the year's most fashionable occasion is the **Monégasque Red Cross Gala** in August.

SOURCES OF FURTHER INFORMATION

Any **Pan Am** office around the world; **Direction du Tourisme et des Congrès,** 2a Boulevard des Moulins, Monte Carlo (tel: 30 87 01); the **Monaco Government Tourist Office,** 20 East 49th Street, New York, NY 10017; and 34 Sackville Street, London W1X 1DB.

Netherlands

WHAT'S SPECIAL

Amsterdam is the heart of one of Europe's most extraordinary and individualistic countries. Approximately 30% of the present land area of these "Low Countries" has been reclaimed from the North Sea, and without the protecting dikes more than 50% of the land would be flooded. With the exception of the hilly southeastern panhandle, the *polders* of Holland stretch smooth, green, and flat as far as the eye can see, and canals and waterways weave through the countryside. Ancient windmills and modern pumps work constantly to literally bail the country out, and everywhere, of course, are the famous dikes that keep the North Sea in its place. The Dutch will impress the visitor with their forthright, industrious spirit and their unobtrusive but droll sense of humor. Holland's small size makes it a place the tourist can see much of in a short time; beauty, color, and novelty are found everywhere.

COUNTRY BRIEFING

Size: 15,892 square miles (and growing)

Capital: Amsterdam

Population: 14,000,000

Capital Population: 711,982

Climate: Winters are mild, summers are warm rather than hot. Late springtime sees Holland at its best.

Weather in Amsterdam: Lat N52°23'; Alt 5 ft

Temp (°F)	Jan	Feb	Mar	Apr	May	Jun	Jul	Aug	Sep	Oct	Nov	Dec
Av Low	34°	34°	37°	43°	50°	55°	59°	59°	56°	48°	41°	35°
Av High	40°	41°	46°	52°	60°	65°	69°	68°	64°	56°	47°	41°
Days no rain	12	13	18	16	19	18	17	17	15	13	11	12

Government: A constitutional monarchy of 11 provinces ruled by the Queen and a bicameral parliament. The seat of the government is at The Hague.

Language: The official language is Dutch, but almost everyone speaks some English.

Religion: 40% are Roman Catholic, 30% Protestant, 6% other religions, and 24% are uncommitted.

Currency: Guilder (or florin). 100 cents = 1 florin.

	25c	50c	f1	f10	f25	f50	f100	f200
US (dollars, cents)	.10	.20	.39	3.92	9.81	19.61	39.22	78.44
UK (pounds, pence)	.05	.10	.19	1.87	4.69	9.37	18.74	37.49

Public Holidays:

New Year's Day, 1 Jan	Ascension Day
Good Friday	Whit Monday
Easter Monday	Christmas Day, 25 Dec
Queen's Birthday, 30 Apr	Boxing Day, 26 Dec

HOW TO GET THERE

Flying time to Amsterdam's Schiphol Airport from New York is 7 hours; from London, 1 hour; from Frankfurt, 1 hour; from Brussels, ¾ hour. Time in the Netherlands: GMT+1.

REQUIREMENTS FOR ENTRY AND CUSTOMS

A valid passport is required of all visitors. No visa necessary for visits of up to 3 months, but you need a smallpox vaccination certificate if you are coming from an infected area. Europeans from Common Market countries may bring in 300 cigarettes or 75 cigars or 400 grams tobacco; 3 liters alcoholic beverage less than 22% or 1½ liter alcoholic beverage greater than 22%; 75 grams perfume; other goods to a total value of f500—provided all the above originate in Common Market countries. Other travelers are allowed 200 cigarettes or 50 cigars or 250 grams tobacco; 2 liters alcoholic beverage less than 22% or 1 liter greater than 22%; 50 grams perfume; other goods to a value of f90—unless the items imported originate in Common Market countries in which case the higher allowances apply. Customs authorities will seldom bother visitors if the value limit is not exceeded and items are clearly for personal use.

AIRPORT INFORMATION

Schiphol Airport is 13 feet below sea level. It is one of the most modern and efficient airports in Europe. There is a bus every 30 minutes from the airport to the downtown terminal on the Museumplein. The distance is 8 miles, and the bus fare for the 25-minute ride is f6. Taxis will take you for f40, depending upon the amount of luggage. In the airport concourse there is an Amsterdam Computer Reservation Service. There is no arrival or departure tax.

ACCOMMODATIONS

Amsterdam has accommodations of all types, from the luxurious to the barge hostels on the canals. Even in the inexpensive hotels you can be sure that all will be clean and civilized. During off-peak season (winter but not Christmas) you can expect reductions of up to US$3 on a double room and US$2 on a single; however, these figures are merely a rough indication of possible discounts. Bed and breakfast in a typical canal house will cost from about US$35, and pensions will charge about US$20 per person. Students and others with economy in mind should be able to find somewhere for US$10 or over a night without much trouble. Breakfast will not leave you wondering how you will last until lunchtime; the Dutch believe in starting the day with a hearty meal. For information about accommodations try the airport bureau upon arrival or the **VVV** (the local tourist office), tel: 26 64 44, or 22 10 16 after 5:30pm and on Sundays. They are good at finding accommodations off the beaten track; reservations cannot be made final over the phone, however.

Amsterdam hotels:

Rates are in US$ for a double/twin room with bath or shower

American, Leidsekade 97 (from $72)

Amstel, Prof Tulpplein 1 (from $100)

Amsterdam Hilton, Apollolaan 138 (from $84.20)

Amsterdam Marriott, Stadhouderskade 19-21 (from $85)

Amsterdam Sonesta, Kattengat 1 (from $85)

Apollo, Apollolaan 2 (from $75), on the waterfront

Arthur Frommer, Noorderstraat 46 (from $65)

Caransa, Rembrandtsplein 19 (from $59)

Carlton, Vijzelstraat 2-18 (from $70)

Doelen, Nieuwe Doelenstraat 24 (from $59)

Eurocrest, De Boelelaan 2 (from $64)

Grand Hotel Krasnapolsky, Dam Square 9 (from $97)

Novotel, Europa Boulevard 10 (from $80), near Rai Convention Center

OKURA INTER · CONTINENTAL, Ferdinand Bolstraat 175 (from $75), near Rai Convention Center

Pulitzer, Prinsengracht 315-331 (from $100)

Schiphol Airport Hilton, Schiphol International Airport (from $84.20), at airport

Victoria, Damrak 1-5 (from $72)

Except where noted, all the above hotels are centrally located.

USEFUL INFORMATION

Helpful Hints: A reasonable display of good manners will get you through most situations in Holland. Everyone shakes hands frequently, and gentlemen stand for ladies in crowded buses and streetcars. It is in order to strike up a conversation with your neighbor in a café. The

Dutch for "thank you" is *Dank U*. One point: the Dutch normally refer to themselves as *Nederlanders*.

Banks: Open 9-4 Mon-Fri. Also open Thursday night 5-7. Travelers' checks may be cashed at American Express, Thomas Cook & Son, stores, restaurants, and hotels, and at the "Grenswisselkantoor" (exchange bureau) in the Central Station, open every day 9am-11pm.

Mail: Stamps can be bought and letters mailed at all hotels and post offices. Some mailboxes (red and gray-colored, mounted on walls) also have stamp dispensers.

Telephone Tips: Public telephones in street booths, restaurants, and cafés. All fully automatic, coin operated; a local call costs 25 cents. To call long distance outside Europe you may have to go to a post office. Useful numbers in Amsterdam:

Pan Am 17 83 15

Schiphol Airport Arrivals/Departures 51 10 43 2

Tourist Information(VVV) 26 64 44

Taxis 77 77 77

Long Distance/Europe 0010

Theatre Information and Reservation Bureau 22 90 11

Long Distance/Outside Europe including USA 0016

Ambulance 55 55 55 5

Fire 21 21 21

Police 22 22 22

Newspapers: International editions of many leading English-language newspapers on sale in Amsterdam every day. All important international news and fashion magazines available.

Tipping: Tipping is not essential but is well appreciated. All cafés and restaurants include 15% service in the check. Tip also included in hairdresser and barber costs. Taxis, included in meter reading, but you may leave the small change. Rail and airport porters normally have a fixed rate per piece, but they also expect a 15% tip on top. If no fixed rate, about 50 cents to f1 per piece. Checkroom or washroom attendants or theater ushers, 25 cents; tour guides, about f1 for a half-day excursion. Hotel services are also included in the bill, but you may give 50 cents-f1 per bag to porters, 50 cents-f1 per night to chambermaids; 50 cents-f1 to the doorman for hailing you a cab.

Electricity: 220 volts 50 cycles AC.

Laundry: All major hotels have an express laundry and dry-cleaning service (dry-cleaning a suit from f12; laundering a shirt from f5). Coin-operated laundromats are big business.

Hairdressing: Facilities in all the main towns and in the big hotels (shampoo and set from f40; men's haircut from f25).

Photography: Photographic services are excellent and the standard of film processing good. Processing of color film takes about a week in Amsterdam and 2 weeks in the provinces. Black and white processing takes only 2-3 days in the city.

Clubs: Several international clubs meet in Amsterdam, including International Round Table (tel: 35 78 44); Kiwanis (tel: 24 22 20); Lions (tel: 03 40 4); and Rotary (tel: 23 24 05); American Women's Club meets the first Thursday every month in an Amsterdam hotel.

Babysitting: Student Babysitting Organization (Roeterstraat 34-36, Amsterdam—tel: 23 17 08).

Rest Rooms: Women, *Dames Toilet;* men, *Heren Toilet.*

Health: Most doctors and dentists speak English, and there is a Central Doctors' Service (tel: 64 21 11 or 79 18 21). If you want to buy pharmaceuticals, you will find them at the *apotheek,* toiletries at the *drogist.* There is one or the other on most main streets, but the products are comparatively expensive.

TRANSPORTATION

Services are excellent. In Amsterdam, public transport is by streetcar, bus, and taxi. The city streetcars cover just about the whole city, and you shouldn't have to wait more than 5-10 minutes for one. Most routes start at the Central Station. Apart from buying a ticket valid for one day's unlimited travel for f4.75, you can also obtain a 6-trip ticket for f2.85. Streetcar stops are marked *Tramhalte,* and tickets for buses and streetcars are on sale from kiosks, dispensers nearby, and at the VVV. Much the same applies to the bus service. Bus stops are all marked *Bushalte,* and the two services complement each other well. Amsterdam's taxi drivers all use meters. To get a taxi, call 77 77 77 or go to a taxi stand. At night you can hail cabs, but do not waste time on the ones with the "taxi" light out.

The traffic in Amsterdam is heavy between 8 and 9am and 5 and 6pm, so try to avoid these rush hours. Take special care near streetcars— they have absolute priority. Anything approaching from the right also has right of way. In the countryside you will find the roads well planned and clearly marked.

Outside Amsterdam you will find Holland has an enviable electric railroad system, with regular services to just about anywhere you might want to go. For the sake of comfort and at a minimal extra cost, it is well worth traveling first class. The Eurailpass is accepted in the Netherlands.

FOOD AND RESTAURANTS

The Dutch give a great deal of thought to eating. French *haute cuisine* is the aspiration of the leading restaurateurs, although well on a par with these are the many Indonesian restaurants—a reminder of the country's colonial experience. Breakfast resembles lunch—cheese, ham, or eggs, with a selection of breads: white, brown, black rye, rusks, and, often, gingerbread, accompanied by orange juice and coffee. A cup of coffee at midmorning is an institution that keeps body and soul together until *koffietafel*—a light lunch that tends to repeat the breakfast menu. *Borrel* time happens around 5pm, when everyone sits down for a drink and a chat. Dinner is served anywhere between 6 and 10. A cautionary note: many restaurant kitchens close at 10, so it is best to plan on eating early.

Among the wholly Dutch dishes to be found on restaurant menus, look for *Erwtensoep*—the world's thickest, most delicious pea soup; *Rode-*

kool met Bloedworst—a dish of red cabbage, black pudding, and sliced apples; *Boerenkool met Rookworst*—a tasty cook-up of kale, mashed potato, and smoked sausage. Seafood stands out for its excellence on many menus, and the Dutch are famous for herring preparations. In the Indonesian restaurants, try *Rijsttafel;* it means "rice table." Your meal may consist of up to 10 or 20 dishes. Generally speaking, the cost of eating out works out at about US$40 per person in a really high-class restaurant; US$12-15 in a family restaurant; and around US$10 in lunch bars. In addition, over 700 restaurants all over the country offer a fixed price tourist menu at about US$7.50 per person. At *Haringstallen* (herring stalls) you can buy pickled or salted herrings, with or without chopped onion, and, alternatively, there are the *Broodjeswinkels,* Holland's sandwich bars, with fillings from smoked eel to spiced raw ground beef. Cost, a couple of florins.

Amsterdam's **De Boerderij** is excellent. It is an old house off the downtown Leidseplein (tel: 23 69 29). French and traditional Dutch fare star on the menu, with game in season. For wining and dining in style, try the **Dikker en Thijs** (Prinsengracht 444—tel: 26 77 21) and the **Excelsior** (Nieuwe Doelenstraat 2—tel: 23 48 36); expect to pay about f90 per person. **Apollo Hotel** (Apollolaan 2—tel: 73 59 22) has a lovely terrace, and game is the specialty here from mid-October to mid-December. Easier on the budget is **Le Bon Mariage du Vin et Fromage** (Herengracht 338—tel: 23 10 40); as the name implies, it is a wine and cheese cellar. One of the most outstanding and popular restaurants in the city is the **'T Swarte Schaep** (Korte Leidsedwarsstraat 24—tel: 22 30 21)—a low-beamed rustic restaurant with mainstream French cuisine, open until midnight. To sample *Rijsttafel,* try the Indonesian **Manchurian** (Korte Leidsedwarsstraat 51); it, too, is open until midnight. Another fine Indonesian restaurant is the more expensive **Sama Sebo** near the Rijksmuseum (Pieter Cornelis Hooftstraat 27—tel: 72 81 46).

At the **Fong Lie** Chinese restaurant (PC Hooftstraat 80—tel: 71 64 04), the check for two should not be more than f80 (reserve in advance), and the same is true of **Lotus** (Binnenbantammerstraat 5—tel: 24 26 14). **De Oesterbar** (Leidseplein 10—tel: 26 34 63) is a first-class seafood restaurant open until midnight, costing about f45 per head. Very good traditional Dutch food may be had at **Dorrius** (Nieuwe Zijds Voorburgwal 336—tel: 23 56 75). A very good French restaurant in the Jordaan quarter is the **Café-Bistro Cartouche** (Anjeliersstraat 177—tel: 22 74 38).

DRINKING TIPS

The national drink of the Netherlands is *Jenever.* It is gin, but quite different from the average dry martini's backbone. It is oilier and sweeter than dry gin and is made with a variety of spices. Normally, it is drunk chilled and straight. Many of the Dutch liqueurs are as sought after as their French counterparts and not nearly so expensive. A Dutch specialty is *Advocaat*—a potent egg flip. The Dutch are also skilled brewers, and the internationally known *Amstel Bier* makes an excellent companion for *Rijsttafel.* All international brands of liquor are available, and drink

prices vary enormously. Beer costs from f1.50-4 a glass, whisky from f4-9; nightclub drinks are more expensive.

ENTERTAINMENT

There are many excellent movie houses in Amsterdam, showing American and British films with the original soundtracks. For programs buy a copy of *This Week in Amsterdam,* on sale at newsstands and at the local tourist office every Wednesday. The performance times vary, but there are usually four shows a day at 1:30, 3:30, 7:30, and 9:30pm.

Holland has many famous orchestras, opera companies, and ballet companies. Among the top names regularly performing are the **Concert Gebouw Orkest, De Nederlandse Operastichting,** and the **National Ballet.** Performances take place at the **Concert Gebouw** (Van Baerlestraat 98) and at the **Stadsschouwburg** (Leidseplein 26). The **VVV** always has programs of cultural events in Amsterdam and throughout Holland.

There are two nightspot areas in the city, one near the **Rembrandtsplein,** the other around the **Leidsedwarsstraat.** Generally speaking admission to nightclubs and discothèques is free, although a few charge up to f2.50 entrance. For nightclubs, try the **Blue Note** (Leidsedwarsstraat 71), which has dancing, bands, and cabaret acts that go on until the small hours. There is a pleasant feeling at the **Picadilly** on Thorbeckeplein. Another suggestion for entertainment is **Louis Seize** near Rembrandtsplein (Reguliersdwarsstraat). Other bars with music worth hearing are the somewhat arty **Pinky Club** (Leidseplein 8) and the bar located in the **Marriott Hotel** (Leidsebosje). To dance to lively music try the **King's Club** discothèque (Korte Leidsedwarsstraat 85), **Juliana** (under the Hilton Hotel), or **Atalaya** (Kleine Gartmanplantsoen near Leidseplein).

SHOPPING

Most stores in Holland are open weekdays 9-6; shops open Thursday night 7-9; most shops close at 4pm on Saturday. Department stores, larger shops, and supermarkets have a mandatory half-day closing once a week, usually Monday mornings. Good buys for visitors include diamonds, Delftware porcelain, traditional dolls, pewterware, liqueurs, and, of course, paintings and antiques. There is also a vast amount of Indonesian bric-à-brac for sale, including batik prints, masks, figurines, and weapons. Three good department stores in Amsterdam are **De Bijenkorf** (Damrak), **Metz & Co** (Leidestraat), and **Vroom & Dreesman** (Kalverstraat). You will also find some good bargains if you explore the antique shops along **Nieuwe Spiegelstraat** or the **Flea Market** near Waterlooplein. For Delftware try **Focke & Meltzer** (P C Hooftstraat 65). And for Indonesian curios go to **MLJ Lemaire** (Prinsengracht 841). If you are setting out for a day's unspecified shopping, start off at **Kalverstraat**—the street offers a good cross section of shops.

SPORTS

The inland areas of water provide good sailing and water-skiing. There are numerous golf clubs throughout the country, and the resorts and large towns have tennis courts. There are riding clubs. Skating is popular in winter.

WHAT TO SEE

Amsterdam: One of the joys of Amsterdam is that all the sights are within easy reach of the visitor, and the best way of finding your bearings is to take a few leisurely strolls through the downtown area. The layout of the city center (four concentric canals and three major squares) is ideally suited to this. Make your way to the Central Station and work outward from there. Another trip that is not to be missed is a cruise through the canals in the famous glass-topped boats. The tour lasts 1-1¾ hours; there is a multilingual commentary, and the fare is from f6 per person. There are innumerable art museums and galleries: don't miss the **Rijksmuseum** (the richest collection of Dutch paintings in the world), the **Vincent Van Gogh Museum,** and the world-famous **Stedelijk Museum** (modern art); all three are on the Museumplein. Also visit the newly restored **Historical Museum** housed in the former 17th-century municipal orphanage on the Kalverstraat. Take note that all of the Netherlands' museums are open 10-5 and on Sundays 1-5. Amsterdam is the diamond-cutting capital of the world. Take a guided tour of a diamond merchant's workshop: both **Asscher's** and **A van Moppes & Zoon** welcome visitors.

The house in which Anne Frank took refuge during the Nazi pogroms of World War II can be visited. In complete contrast, visit the bulb-flower exhibition at the lovely **Keukenhof Gardens** at Lisse; open from the end of March to mid-May, 8am to sundown. Not far from Amsterdam (an easy day trip) are the picturesque villages of **Spakenburg Hoorn** and **Enkhuizen.**

The Hague: To avoid confusion, understand that the Dutch call it *Den Haag,* and they write it *'s-Gravenhage.* This is the seat of the government (since 1247), the Diplomatic Corps, and the International Court of Justice. For splendid pageantry be there on the third Tuesday in September, when the Queen presides over the State Opening of Parliament. Around the beginning of June, The Hague prepares for the world-famous **Holland Festival of Music and Ballet.** The Hague is also home to the renowned **Mauritshuis Collection,** Plein 29, an assembly of Dutch Masters housed in a 17th-century mansion. There is also a collection of Piet Mondrian's work at the **Gemeente Museum,** Stadhouderslaan.

Four tips for dining out in The Hague: First, the **Royal Restaurant** (Lange Voorhout 44), undeniably expensive, but the French food is exquisite. Formality is the keynote here. **'t Gemeste Schaap** (Raamstraat 11) is moderately expensive, but the food is good and the traditional Dutch ambiance makes it well worth a visit. **Pancake House** (Maliestraat), near the Des Indes hotel, is inexpensive and good. And at Scheveningen, The Hague's seaside resort, is the **Bali Restaurant** (Badhuisweg 1) opposite the Kurhaus Hotel. The *Rijsttafel* at the Bali is reputed to be the finest in Holland. Scheveningen also boasts a casino, with blackjack and roulette.

Hotels in The Hague: **Promenade,** 1 van Stolkweg (from US$75 double);

Parkhotel De Zalm, 53 Molenstraat (from US$78 double); Des Indes, 56 Lange Voorhout (from US$90 double); the Bel Air, Kennedy Laan (from US$70 double); and the newly opened Kurhaus (from US$90 double); entrance to the adjoining casino is US$3.50.

One of Holland's most famous attractions, the miniature village of Madurodam, can be found not far from The Hague. In this extraordinary 1:25 scale model of a Dutch town, trains run, the bands play, and at night the city lights up just like a real one. If you have ever wondered how Gulliver really felt, do not miss Madurodam. It is open from the Thursday before Easter until the first Sunday in October. Admission is f5, f2.50 for children. All the proceeds from Madurodam go to charity.

Rotterdam owes its ultra-modernity to its utter devastation in the Second World War. The visible result of this "fresh start" is one of the most dynamic and efficient seaports in the world. Situated on the estuaries of the Maas (Meuse) and the Rhine, Rotterdam is one of the major European trade centers, and the world's largest port. There are frequent pleasure cruises through the heart of the dock area (from Willemsplein Landing Stage), and, for a panoramic view of the city, go to the top of the 605-foot Euromast. At street level you should not miss the Boymans-van-Beuningen Museum, which houses many of the works of Hieronymus Bosch, the medieval painter.

Hotels in Rotterdam: Atlanta, 4 Aert van Nesstraat (from US$65 double); Central, 12 Kruiskade (from US$65 double); Euromotel, 61 Vliegveldweg (from US$38 double); Park, 70 Westersingel (from US$74 double); Rijnhotel Rotterdam, 1 Schouwburgplein (from US$80 double); Rotterdam Hilton, 10 Weena (from US$90 double); Savoy, 81 Hoogstraat (from US$61 double); and Zuiderpark, 485 Dordtseweg (from US$49 double).

Delft: This is the home of Delftware pottery and is very picturesque. Most of the houses have been preserved in their original 17th-century condition. Visit the Porceleyne Fles, where you can see the real Delftware on display. It carries a mark featuring a triple signature depicting a vase topped with a straight line, the stylized letter "F," and the "Delft." Contrary to popular opinion, Delftware comes in many colors and designs. Do not be taken in by the name "Delft Blue" on sale in souvenir shops; it is good but not quite the same thing. If you are keen on antiques, try to visit during the annual Delft Antique Dealers' Fair. The dates vary but the VVV will tell you when the next one starts. For your stay, try the Central Hotel, 6-8 Wijnhaven (from US$37.50 double).

Giethoorn: If you can possibly fit in a trip to this roadless village some 24 miles north of Zwolle, then do so—it is another world. There are angular wooden footbridges linking the houses, but otherwise everything that moves does so by boat—including cattle on their way to pasture and the Sunday congregation on their way to church.

Haarlem: The colorful birthplace of Frans Hals (the Laughing Cavalier). There are many fine medieval gabled houses here, and a city hall (Stadhuis) begun in 1250. Haarlem is the world center of tulip growing. Stay at the Lion d'Or, 34 Kruisweg (from US$58 double).

Gouda: This town affords a chance to see the famous cheese market which takes place every Thursday morning between mid-May and September. There is also a magnificent **Carillon** built in 1561. Visit **St Jan's Church,** known for its stained-glass windows made in the 16th century by the brothers Jan and Dirk Crabeth. In December (the date varies, so check with the VVV), there is the **Gouda by Candlelight** festival that takes place in the market square. The high spot is a moving performance of choral singing. In Gouda stay at the **De Zalm,** Markt 34 (from US$37.50 double).

Zandvoort: To catch the full flavor of European Grand Prix Motor Racing, visit Zandvoort in early June for the **Dutch Grand Prix.** Hotels are: **Astoria-Zon en Duin,** 155-159 Dr. C. A. Gerkestraat (from US$40 double); **Bouwes,** 7 Badhuisplein (from US$63 double); **Bouwes Palace,** 2-4 Burg. van Fenemaplein (rates on request); and the **Hoogland,** 5 Westerparkstraat (from US$45 double). Zandvoort also has a casino.

Utrecht: Capital of the province of the same name, Utrecht is the fourth largest city of the Netherlands and also one of the oldest. The magnificent Gothic **Cathedral,** made from imported stone, provides an unrivaled view of the city; on a clear day you can see the steeples of Amsterdam. The biennial fairs, which started as the Royal Netherlands Industrial Fair in 1917, have made it an important international business center. Hotels are: **Holiday Inn,** 24 Jaarbeursplein (from US$65 double); **Smits,** 14 Vredenburg (from US$50 double); and the **Hes,** 2-4 Maliestraat (from US$50 double).

SOURCES OF FURTHER INFORMATION

Pan Am, Schiphol Airport Station Building, Amsterdam, and any Pan Am office around the world; **Tourist Information Office (VVV),** Stationsplein, Amsterdam; and Nassauplein 31, The Hague; **Netherlands National Tourist Office,** 576 Fifth Avenue, New York, NY 10036; 143 New Bond Street, London W1.

Norway

WHAT'S SPECIAL

Norway is as much sea as land, more mountain than plain, more forest than meadow, only 2.6% cultivated. Steep cliffs drop dramatically into clear blue waters. Fjords open on to islands and more islands. In the south are clusters of white-painted fishermen's houses; in the north, long treeless stretches where the Lapps bring their reindeer herds to graze. Even in Oslo the countryside is near.

COUNTRY BRIEFING

Size: 125,181 square miles   **Population:** 4,092,500
Capital: Oslo   **Capital Population:** 451,700

    Climate: Half of Norway is within the Arctic Circle, but the Gulf Stream tempers the climate to mild on the coast. The mountain air is cold and dry; summers are sunny. May-June is spring; July-August is most popular, but September is also good. Winter sports are available from January to April. Oslo has 19 hours of daylight at midsummer.

Weather in Oslo: Lat N59°56′; Alt up to 308 ft

Temp (°F)	Jan	Feb	Mar	Apr	May	Jun	Jul	Aug	Sep	Oct	Nov	Dec
Av Low	20°	20°	25°	34°	43°	51°	56°	53°	45°	37°	29°	24°
Av High	30°	32°	40°	50°	62°	69°	73°	69°	60°	49°	37°	31°
Days no rain	13	17	23	30	24	18	14	18	6	8	11	12

Government: A constitutional monarchy.
Language: Norwegian—English widely spoken.
Religion: 96% Lutheran.

Currency: Krone. 100 øre = 1 krone.

	25 øre	50 øre	1 Kr	10 Kr	50 Kr	100 Kr	200 Kr	300 Kr
US (dollars, cents)	.04	.09	.18	1.76	8.80	17.60	35.20	52.80
UK (pounds, pence)	.02	.04	.09	.84	4.21	8.41	16.82	25.23

Public Holidays:

New Year's Day, 1 Jan
Maundy Thursday
Good Friday
Easter Monday
Labor Day, 1 May

Constitution Day, 17 May
Ascension Day
Whit Monday
Christmas Day, 25 Dec
Boxing Day, 26 Dec

HOW TO GET THERE

Flying time to Oslo's Fornebu Airport from New York is 7¾ hours, from London, 2 hours, from Frankfurt, 2¼ hours. Time in Norway: GMT+1.

REQUIREMENTS FOR ENTRY AND CUSTOMS REGULATIONS

Valid passport; visa not required. Vaccination certificates only if coming from an infected area. There is no restriction on the amount of Norwegian currency imported; you may deport with up to Kr2,000 in Norwegian currency. Bills higher than Kr100 may not be brought in or taken at departure. There are restrictions on the import of firearms, livestock, meat, and live plants. Duty-free allowance: 200 cigarettes or 250 grams of other tobacco products and 200 cigarette papers; 2 liters wine and 2 liters beer or 1 liter wine and ¾ liter liquor. Antiques and similar objects may not be exported without permission. You may not bring in pets (dogs and cats); there are heavy fines if they are found in cars or aboard vessels.

AIRPORT INFORMATION

Fornebu Airport is 5 miles from Oslo. The airport bus fare into town is Kr12. Taxis—which may be in short supply at rush hours—cost Kr60. The airport has a duty-free shop for liquor and tobacco products and a hotel reservations counter.

ACCOMMODATIONS

The tourist trade and the number of good hotels are growing in Norway, but there is still a shortage of rooms during the summer in the cities. Accommodations designated Hotel, Town Hotel, Mountain Hotel, and Tourist Hotel are subject to strict government specifications. Inexpensive and reliable places to stay are the student hostels available to tourists in summer and the (strictly nonalcoholic) Mission hotels. Ask at local tourist offices for the names of private homes willing to put you up (minimum of three nights). The chain of Norwegian youth hostels is of a very high standard. Those fond of outdoor life will find the mountain huts adequate and extremely economical. For information write to **Den**

Norske Turistforening (Stortingsgaten 28, Oslo). Local tourist offices will help you to find accommodations for a small fee and a deposit. There is a bureau for personal application at the East Railway Station in Oslo, open 8:30am-11pm from mid-May to mid-September; closed the rest of the year. Oslo hotels:

Rates are in US$ for a double/twin room with bath or shower

Astoria, Akersgaten 21 (from $100 BB)

Bristol, Kristian IV's gaten 7 (from $105 BB)

Carlton, Parkveien 78 (from $80 BB)

Continental, Stortingsgaten 24/26 (from $106 BB)

Forbundshotellet, Holberg Place 1 (from $70 BB)

Grand, Karl Johansgate 31 (from $118 BB)

KNA Hotellet, Parkveien 68 (from $103 BB)

Nobel, Karl Johansgate 33 (from $90 BB)

Norum, Bygdøy Allé 53 (from $76), near Vigeland Sculpturepark

Panorama Sommerhotel, Sognsveien 218 (from $60 CP), near Sognsvann Lake

Scandinavia, Holbergs Gate 30 (from $113)

Stefanhotellet, Rosenkrantzgaten 1 (from $83 BB)

Viking, Biskop Gunnerusgaten 3 (from $107 BB)

All hotels listed are centrally located unless otherwise indicated.

USEFUL INFORMATION

Helpful Hints: Working hours are 8-3:30 or 4, Mon-Fri. Lunch is usually a snack in the office; the main meal at 5pm. Dress is informal in Oslo. If invited to someone's home for the evening, take flowers. A peculiar Oslo habit is giving the address of a building in a street around the corner from the entrance. For example: a hotel listed as being in Karl Johansgate will be found in Rosenkrantzgaten, and one supposedly in Rosenkrantzgaten will be in Grensen.

Banks: Hours vary, but practically all banks are open between 9 and 3. Oslo banking hours are 8:15-3:30, Mon-Fri (to 6 on Thurs); June through Aug 8:15-3:00 (to 5:00 on Thurs), closed Saturday and Sunday. Money can be changed at Fornebu Airport from 7am-10:30pm Mon-Sat and at Gardermoen Airport 7am-5pm Mon-Sat, Sundays from 8-6; also at the Railway Station from 8am-9pm weekdays, Saturday to 7pm, and Sunday to noon.

Mail: Stamps can be bought at newsstands. Mailboxes are red with a yellow posthorn symbol.

Telephone Tips: To make a call you need a 1Kr piece. Booths in streets, cafés, shops, stations, etc. Useful numbers in Oslo:

Pan Am 41 56 00	Oslo Travel Association 41 48 63
Airport Information 12 01 20 SAS, international and domestic flights; 53 29 40 Braathens SAFE, domestic flights	Directories and Operator 018 Police 11 00 11 Tourist Information—Bergen 31 66 00

Newspapers: Foreign English-language newspapers available in major cities and resort areas.

Tipping: A 15% service charge is generally added to hotel and restaurant bills. No other tip expected, but round off the bill. Taxi drivers—round off to the nearest krone. Baggage porters should get Kr3 per piece, minimum Kr5; cloakroom attendants, Kr3 per piece; hotel porters about Kr1 per person per night, with a minimum of Kr5; hairdressers—tip not really necessary.

Electricity: 220 volts 50 cycles AC. Hotels do not always have converters.

Laundry: Good but expensive express service in major hotels (to dry-clean a suit, from Kr70; laundering a shirt Kr10).

Hairdressing: Shampoo and set, from Kr75 in city center; men's haircut Kr50 with tip.

Photography: Processing takes about 2 days. Equipment easy to get and low-priced. A roll of 35mm film (36 exposures) costs from Kr33.25 for Kodacolor, from Kr25 for black and white, processing not included. Kodachrome, processing included, costs Kr55 for 20 exposures, Kr80 for 36 exposures.

Clubs: Rotary—Grand Hotel, Thurs, 12:15 (tel: 33 52 24 during office hours); Lions (tel: 55 97 90); Kiwanis, Continental Hotel, Thurs, 4:15pm; International Friendship League (tel: 14 29 07).

Babysitting: There are no official offices; try the hotel desk.

Rest Rooms: *Toalett;* Women, *Kvinner;* men, *menn.*

Health: Doctors and dentists usually speak English. Reciprocal agreement with British National Health Service for British citizens. Imported pharmaceuticals fairly expensive. For 24-hour dispensing service, tel: 41 24 82.

TRANSPORTATION

Oslo has buses, subways, and streetcars. Municipal buses are red or silver; private ones are yellow or blue, and the main terminal is by the Rådhus (the town hall). You may pay cash or buy a punchcard (11 rides, one free). The municipal subway terminal is at East Railway Station Square; a private subway called *Holmenkollbanen* has a terminal at the National Theater.

Taxis are in short supply during rush hours (8:30am, 3:30-4pm) and in bad weather. Reserve in advance where possible by phoning 38 03 86 from 9am-3pm and 6-11pm, minimum notice 1 hour; otherwise, call 348. To get a cab in the street go to a stand (green boxes) or hail one. Taxis are metered, with extra charges for more than two passengers, after 10pm, and for baggage. Car rentals available, but avoid the rush hour in Oslo. Parking in the city center is at meters only, free after 5pm. Ask the Tourist Information for a *Tourist Parking Map* to explain things. Roads outside Oslo are not good and frequently interrupted by fjords, where you will have to wait for the ferry. Only 200 miles a day should be attempted.

A good train service links all major towns. Sleeper cars and food are available. The Eurailpass is accepted in Norway. The Scandinavian Rail Pass allows 21 days or 1 month of unlimited travel in Denmark, Norway,

Sweden, and Finland. Buy it in Scandinavia or in some European countries—it is not sold outside Europe. SAS and two internal airlines run domestic services to many towns in Norway, and this is certainly the easiest way to reach the north (flying time to Tromsø is 1¾ hours from Oslo, for example). Good steamer services up and down the coast are the best way to see the fjords. Daily car ferry services between Oslo and Copenhagen, Frederikshavn, Aarhus, and Kiel (less frequent in winter). Car ferries also go from Oslo, Bergen, Stavanger, and Kristiansand to Newcastle-upon-Tyne and Harwich, England. There is year-round ferry service between Kristiansand and the Danish ports of Hirtshals and Hanstholm.

FOOD AND RESTAURANTS

Norwegians generally eat a good breakfast at 8, have a snack at about noon, and eat their main meal *(middag)* at 5pm—usually two courses. They may have another snack at 9pm. Restaurants are open from 9 or 10am until midnight. A Norwegian breakfast in Oslo costs about US$7, but that includes a cold assortment of fish, ham, and cheese served with thinly sliced bread, along with hot dishes such as eggs and cereal and, of course, coffee. A full dinner in a top restaurant will cost about US$25, but it is possible to eat well for less than that, and US$8 is enough for a sandwich or a hot dish in a cafeteria. Norwegian cuisine is rich in specialties (mostly seasonal, including elk and reindeer steaks). Meat comes served as *fenalar*, which is cured and baked leg of mutton; thin slices of *spekeskinke*, a cured ham eaten with scrambled eggs and chives; or *kjottkaker*—meatballs mixed to a secret recipe. But the real glory of Norsk cooking is the seafood. Fresh-caught shrimp or crabs are sold at night on the sidewalks. Fjord shrimp *(reker)* are eaten within hours of being caught, with a sprinkle of lemon. Herrings *(sild)* can be served in about 50 different ways as part of the cold table *(koldtbord)*. This heavily laden board is a normal way to serve lunch in many hotels: you take one dish at a time, returning for more, until you are satisfied. Other fish dishes are the famous poached cod *(kokt torsk);* salmon *(laks)* similarly cooked, or just smoked, or cured with dill *(gravlaks)*. Trout *(ørret)* is likely to come to you smoked, sautéd in sour cream *(stekt i rømme)*, or freshly poached *(kokt)*. Oslo has no lack of top-class restaurants. The traditional artists' restaurant is **Blom** in a little courtyard off Karl Johansgate—number 41 (tel: 33 09 56). The most beautiful room is claimed by the **Grand Hotel,** the Speilsalen (Mirror Room)—(tel: 33 48 70), where you can dance. One place where cooking is taken seriously is the **Hotel Continental** (tel: 41 90 60). Noted for its grills is the **Tre Kokker** (Drammensveien 30—tel:44 26 50), and for its enterprise, the **Bristol** (Kristian IV's gaten 7—tel: 41 58 40), which is a nightclub, an intimate place in the evening, and a reasonable lunch spot by day. The **Holberg** (tel: 11 30 00) at the Scandinavia Hotel is a pleasant place to eat, as is the **Scanorama Bar** on the 21st floor of the same hotel; at the latter, enjoy a sandwich lunch or evening drink while overlooking Oslo. The Maritime Museum is not a place you would expect to eat, but if you fancy fish, note the

number of its **Najaden Restaurant** (tel: 55 44 90), on the Bygdøy peninsula. The airport too has its own claim to gastronomic fame—the **Caravelle** (tel: 12 02 20). In a slightly less expensive bracket are two delightful old cafés: **Engebrets Café** (Bankplassen 1—tel: 42 12 62) and the **Grand Café** in the heart of town next to the Grand Hotel (Karl Johansgate 31—tel: 33 48 70). Popular with writers and actors is the **Theatrecafen** in the Hotel Continental (tel: 41 90 60). The **Astoria** (Akersgaten 21— tel: 33 67 00) is good for a quiet meal and dancing. Oslo also offers a whole series of places specializing in the view. At the top of the Viking Hotel is a top-class dinner and dance restaurant, the **Crystal Garden** (tel: 33 64 70) overlooking Oslo. Or take the half-hour train ride to Holmenkollen Hill. By the famous ski jump you can eat well at the **Holmenkollen Restaurant** (tel: 14 62 26) as you gaze at the sun going down over the fjord. To eat from the highest perch of all, stay on the train till the last stop, at **Frognerseteren.** The restaurant there (tel: 14 37 36) serves Norwegian specialties indoors or outdoors, and the view is magnificent. For a beautiful lakeside setting in an old private home, coupled with individual cooking, go 20 miles out to the **Villa Sandvigen** on the old E6 to the south (tel: 80 51 15). The **Tourist Office** issues a useful leaflet listing low-priced restaurants in Oslo. Two names are the **Kaffistova** chain (three in all, centrally situated) and the **Mollhausen** chain at several locations in downtown Oslo, including one in Karl Johansgate. You can eat well also on the *pølse* (hot dogs) sold from little kiosks.

DRINKING TIPS

Norway is not a good place for drinking though it produces one of Scandinavia's best aquavits—*Linie. Akevitt* is the national drink, best taken with some food, or you may find it unexpectedly strong. The government does its best to discourage drinking by high taxes, by rigid driving laws (three weeks in jail, no option), and by some idiosyncratic laws governing the sale of liquor (never before 3pm or after 11:45pm). No liquor at all is sold on Sunday, or to persons under 20. Package goods can be bought only from the bank-like **Vinmonoplet,** a government-run monopoly open in Oslo 10-4 weekdays, except Thurs 10-5; 8:30am-1pm Sat. In some towns, weekday closing is 4:30pm. One way to get around these restrictions is to drink Irish coffee on weekends and to go to a country hotel on a Saturday. Wine and beer, on the other hand, can be served in a restaurant on any day. Beer is sold in three strengths: *Export* (strong), *Pilsner* (lager), and *Brig* (very light). *Vorterøl* is nonalcoholic. *Bokkøl* is a dark beer. Whisky is very expensive—over US$4 a glass, but note that unless stated otherwise you will be served a double measure—5 centiliters instead of the usual 2½. A bottle of red wine will be over US$8. There are plenty of pub-like places to drink in, and in summer there are sidewalk cafés.

ENTERTAINMENT

American and English movies are often shown in Norway with their original soundtrack. But the glory of Oslo is its theater. The **National**

Theater is a temple of the classics, of course, where you will catch something of the original spirit of Ibsen. It has its own experimental group, the *Amfiscenen,* which performs upstairs. At Rosenkrantz 10 is the lively, young **Oslo Nye Theater.** There are two more which perform in the so-called New Norwegian Language, and the famous **Chat Noir,** a seasonal cabaret theater. There are few nightclubs: the **Bristol,** the **Telle** (Klingenberggaten 4), open weekdays, and the **Qvarten Slap-Inn** (Rådhusgaten 19). Several restaurants offer music and dancing, however, including **Bonanza Western Restaurant** (Grand Hotel), **Pigalle** (Grønlandsleiret 15), and **Ribo** (Universitetsgaten 26). You can watch folk dancing on Monday, Wednesday, and Friday evenings in summer at 9pm in the **Theater Hall** (Rosenkrantzgate 8), and in the restaurant in the **Folk Museum** (Bygdøy) at 8pm on weekdays. For jazz, try the students' club (Studentbyen, Sognsveien 85) on Sundays. Discothèques include **KROA; Chateau Neuf; Club 7; Hawk Club; Loftet** (Hotel Continental). The **Regnbuen Restaurant** (Klingenberggatten 5) has a good cabaret.

SHOPPING

Norwegian hand-knitted sweaters are as well known as the pewter, glass, and furs. But not so well known is that Swiss watches cost less than in Switzerland, owing to an export plan whereby goods can be sent tax free directly to the harbor or airport. **Michelet** (Prinsengate 21) will organize things for you. Another surprise may be the furniture, both hand-carved traditional and modern design. Go to **Impuls** (Rosenkrantzgate) for a modern display and an excellent collection of textiles—including some from Ceylon. **Forum** is nearby on the corner, a state-run store to display the best Norwegian crafts. An enormous store on several floors selling crafted wood, sealskin, slippers, embroidery, and toys is **Husfliden** (Møllergaten 4), and on the other side of the Cathedral you will find **Brukskunstentret Basarhallene,** which specializes in modern arts and crafts. Beautiful enamels on silver are a Norwegian specialty; these can be bought at **David-Andersen** (Karl Johansgate 20). For individual and quite reasonably priced hand-blown glass, go to **Glasmagasinet** (Stortovet 9), and for your Saga mink or blue fox fur, take a look at the stock at **Pels-Backer** (Kongensgate 31). Nearby is the **Steen & Strom** department store. For sweaters you will have a wide choice, but try **William Schmidt** (Karl Johansgate 41). Smaller knitted items—gloves and stockings—make useful presents.

SPORTS

Skiing is as natural as walking to most Norwegians, making it the most popular sport for 4 months of the year. Because it was invented here, it is the original kind, with long narrow skis you kick over the untrodden snow. Norwegian skiers get their excitement from speed-skating and ski jumping, although *slalom* is a Norwegian word too. In the summer they walk, climb, sail, swim, and play tennis. A unique event for golfers is the **Midnight Cup,** played at Trondheim in June. Southern Norway is good for riders, too; the sturdy, local horses can take you over miles of wild and free terrain. There are plenty of trout everywhere, and some of the best salmon fishing in the world is to be had in the north. A compulsory fishing license (Kr30) is obtainable from post offices. In the middle of August, Stavanger celebrates its **Sea Fishing Festival;** fees, including the boat, are Kr500, or Kr300 for juniors. Hunting (for elk or reindeer) takes place throughout Norway in the fall. Hunters should write for information to Norges Jegerforbund (Grønlandsleiret 39, Oslo 1). For winter sports enthusiasts, the best time of the year is the end of February to the beginning of March, when there are the **Speed Skating Championships,** the famous **Holmenkollen International Ski Event,** and the **World Cup Slalom** at Voss.

WHAT TO SEE

To explore **Oslo,** beginning from the center, walk from the Stortinget down Karl Johansgate to the **King's Palace.** On your left are the **Studenterlunden,** gathering place of all Oslo, and the **National Theater,** guarded by statues of Ibsen and Bjørnson. Opposite is the **University;** its **Aula** (center building) was painted by Munch. (There is also the **Munch Museum** in Oslo, Tøyengalen 53.) Behind the University are two very important collections: to the left, the **Historical Museum** with its gold and silver work dating from Viking times; to the right, the **National Gallery,** where the definitive collection of Norwegian art hangs, plus some important works by Matisse, Cézanne, Van Gogh, and others. You could now turn up St Olavsgate to the **Kunstindustrimuseet** (Museum of Applied Arts). The most remarkable objects here are the beautiful medieval tapestries—some of the earliest and best in Europe. Look particularly for the **Baldishol Tapestry,** dated 1180. Or you could walk through the recently built part of Oslo, toward the great red-brick **Rådhuset** (Town Hall) whose huge, square twin towers you have seen on all the photographs. Modern as it is, it is worth a visit for the wealth of decoration inside by Norwegian artists—carvings, tapestries, and huge murals. Now you are a mere step away from the ferry to **Bygdøy** (Pier C, mid-April through September; use the No 30 bus year round). Look back as you cross for a good view of the city; but leave yourself a good half day—preferably more—for the sights of Bygdøy. First is a ship that has been farther north and south than any other—the **Fram,** polar expedition ship of Nansen and Amundsen. In the museum next to it is the famous **Kon-Tiki,** balsa raft of another adventurous Norwegian, Thor Heyerdahl. On the same peninsula are the visible relics of the wild men who started it all: three **Viking Ships,** preserved on the fjords for 1,000 years. Walk over to the **Folkmuseum,** a park of 150 original ancient buildings gathered from all over Norway. Among them is a 12th-century stave church and Ibsen's own study. There are demonstrations of crafts here and folk dancing in the evenings. You can eat here too, or at the Maritime Museum overlooking the fjord.

Facing you across the water is Oslo's castle, the **Akershus Slott.** This Renaissance fortified palace was built by Christian IV on the burned-out remains of a medieval fortress. In the grounds is a museum of Norway's heroic Resistance movement, perhaps the most dedicated of the war. Still to be seen in the city is the **Cathedral**, built in 1695 but heavily restored in recent times. On the edge of town to the east near the Botanic Gardens is a gallery devoted to the works of **Edward Munch**—Norway's greatest painter, who has been an important influence on modern Western art. And to the west is a museum and park full of sculpture by **Vigeland**, variously described as "inspired," "obscene," "unforgettable." Nearby is Oslo's own **City Museum**. At the **Ekeberg Nature Park**, overlooking the fjord, there are ponies to ride, a camp site, and a restaurant. Finally, you should take the subway from the National Theater to **Holmenkollen** to see the famous ski jump that dominates the city. An elevator takes you up the tower for a panoramic view, and at the base is the **Ski Museum** with, among other things, a 2,500-year-old ski. Higher up the hill is a better view yet—the best in the north—from **Tryvannstarnet** observation tower: you can see over 11,600 square miles.

Farther out of town, about 7 miles, is the **Henie-Onstad Arts Center**. You can get there on the *Båtservice* (boat) from Pier C, or by bus No 32, 36, or 37. A modern building houses the impressive 20th-century collection of Sonja Henie and her shipowner husband; exhibitions and concerts are also held here. The top-class **Pirouette** restaurant looks out across the water. To the south of Oslo, about 2 hours away, you may want to visit the old whaling ports of **Sandefjord** and **Tønsberg**, Norway's oldest town, near where the Viking ships were found. Main attractions are the old houses, the fortress on the hill, and the **Vestfold Folk Museum**. Lunch at the **Grand** or the **Handverkeren**, and stay at the **Klubben Hotel**, near the harbor (from US$82 double BB).

Sandefjord has the **Whaling Museum** (open 12-5), with a replica of the huge blue whale, and an excellent hotel, the **Park**, about 200 yards from the Quay (from US$66 double BB). Across the fjord (ferry from Horten to Moss) is **Fredrikstad**. Craftsmen here make pottery, glass, and textiles—you can watch them at work and buy their wares from 9-3 weekdays, 9-12 Saturday. A good restaurant here too: the **Tamburen**.

To the north about 3 hours lies **Lillehammer**. If you can spare the time for a longer trip, a memorable way to get there is the 6-hour lake voyage by ancient steamer (over 100 years old) from **Eidsvoll**. Lillehammer is a fully developed tourist center, gateway to the central mountains. Its most important attraction is the **Sandvig Collection**, an open-air museum of peasant buildings, crafts, and way of life, collected before these things began to disappear. See especially the stave church and the workshop. Two of Norway's most famous writers lived in this area too: Sigrid Undset and Bjørnstjerne Bjørnson, whose home you can visit.

The south coast is Norway's Riviera. Here, still unspoiled, little fishing towns of white-painted houses huddle round the harbors. There are islands, beaches, long pine-clad valleys, and a good road (the E18) and railway to link them. **Kristiansand** is the largest town, from which you can take a bus or drive up into the picturesque **Setesdal** valley. Stay in Kristiansand at either the **Caledonien**, Vestre Strandgate 7 (from US$104 double BB), or the **Emst**, Rådhusgaten 2 (from US$74 double BB). **Kragerø** is picturesque and secluded; **Risør** is romantic; from **Arendal** (stay at the **Central,** from US$75 double BB) you can visit **Merdøy Island** with its relics of sailing days; from **Lillesand** you can take a ship through the skerries along the coast. **Telemark**—scene of the most famous acts of heroism of Norway's Resistance—is the inland region southwest of Oslo. In the village of Kviteseid you can stay at the **Vrådal Turist** (from US$45 double). Telemark is best seen from the deck of the gracious *Victoria,* which cruises 65 miles up the Bandak canal to **Dalen.** Every valley in this region has something to offer—sometimes unexpected, such as the ancient church at **Eidsberg** with its museum containing a 200-year-old washing machine. Around the southwest coast, **Stavanger,** headquarters of Norway's oil industry, is widely known for the wooden homes that are still a substantial part of the town's housing, and for the 12th-century **Cathedral.** Hotels in Stavanger are the **SAS Royal Atlantic** (from US$106 double BB), the **Mission Hotel Sankt Svithun** (from US$78 double BB), or the **KNA** (from US$73 double BB).

The fjord country, a vast area, is probably best seen from **Bergen.** University student hostels are available to visitors in the summer; details at the **Information Office** (Tovgalmenningen). The **Hotel Norge** has rooms from US$80 double. For eating, the **Bellevue** restaurant (Bellevuebakken 9) is popular. Fish, especially salmon, is a specialty in Bergen. This city is historically a rival to Oslo for dominance and well worth as much time as you can spare. See **Bryggen,** the old quarry with its ancient wooden houses, and the **Hanseatic Museum.** The **Fantoft Stave Church,** dating from 1150, a strangely Oriental-looking building, should not be missed. Nor should Grieg's house, **Troldhaugen,** a national memorial to the great composer at **Hop.** Recitals are held here during the **Bergen International Festival,** which takes place in the summer, May to June, for two weeks. **Mariakirken,** a 12th-century church and the oldest building in Bergen, and the 13th-century **Bergenhus Fortress** and **Håkonshallen** are other unique attractions. Take the **Fløyen** cable car for a magnificent view and the **Fana Folklore** excursion for some genuine folklore and music. Exploring the fjords is best done by boat. If you decide to drive, you need patience and the latest ferry timetable. You also need a good head for heights on many of these roads. For nondrivers there are excellent bus services timed to meet the ferries, plenty of comfortable hotels, even mountain huts for walkers.

Hardangerfjord is the most lush, with pretty painted villages and, in spring, miles of pink and white blossoms in fragrant orchards. Stay at the **Seljestad Motel** off Highway E76 (from US$92 double MAP); prices are reduced according to the length of stay. **Sognefjord** is the most awe-inspiring.

North of **Trondheim** distances are vast and the scenery rugged, so that drivers are advised not to count on doing more than 200 miles a day. The midnight sun is visible from 5 June to 9 July, inside the Arctic Circle at **Bodø;** at **Tromsø** from 21 May to 26 July; at **North Cap** from 14 May to 30 July. Other attractions of the Northland are the

Lapps—the migrant people who live by, and with, their great reindeer herds.

SOURCES OF INFORMATION

Pan Am, Akergaten 64, Oslo, and any Pan Am office around the world; **Oslo Tourist Information Office,** Rådhuset, Oslo 1; **Norway Travel Association,** H. Heyerdahlsgate 1, Oslo 1; **Norwegian National Tourist Office,** 75 Rockefeller Plaza, New York, NY 10019; **Norwegian National Tourist Office,** 20 Pall Mall, London SW1.

Poland

WHAT'S SPECIAL

Heroic deeds of patriotism, endless struggles across a flat land to build and preserve an independent heritage against invasions from both east and west—these are what spring to mind at the mention of Poland. But there is much more: great plains studded with sporting lakes, rivers, and dense forest, impressive mountains with good skiing, a lovely coastline. And then there are great cities, often rebuilt from the fragments of war, lovingly restored not just to be lived in and enjoyed, but as monuments of great culture and learning. For this is the land of Chopin and Copernicus, of art galleries and opera; a land that made a great musician a prime minister—Paderewski. Wander off the beaten track and you will find Europe's last remaining herd of bison, a medieval leaning tower to rival Pisa's, and a tennis court and chapel in one of the world's oldest salt mines. You will find Poland and its people very special and well worth a visit.

COUNTRY BRIEFING

Size: 121,000 square miles   **Population:** 35,700,000
Capital: Warsaw   **Capital Population:** 1,650,000
  Climate: Hot dry summers and cold winters.

Weather in Warsaw: Lat N52°13′; Alt 394 ft

Temp (°F)	Jan	Feb	Mar	Apr	May	Jun	Jul	Aug	Sep	Oct	Nov	Dec
Av Low	21°	23°	28°	38°	48°	53°	56°	55°	48°	41°	32°	35°
Av High	30°	32°	41°	54°	67°	72°	75°	73°	65°	54°	40°	32°
Days no rain	23	21	25	23	23	19	20	20	21	21	23	23

Government: Polish People's Republic.
Language: Polish. Some people speak English. Orbis guides and hotel staff speak French and German, as well as English.
Religion: Roman Catholic.
Currency: Złoty. 100 groszy = Złoty. Rate of exchange is official exchange rate for tourists.

	g	Zł	Zł	Zł	Zł	Zł	Zł	Zł
	50	1	5	10	50	100	500	1,000
US (dollars, cents)	.02	.03	.16	.32	1.60	3.20	16.00	32.00
UK (pounds, pence)	.01	.01	.08	.15	.76	1.53	7.63	15.26

Public Holidays:

New Year's Day, 1 Jan
Easter Monday
Labor Day, 1 May
Victory Day, 9 May
Corpus Christi

Polish National Day,
  22 July
All Saints Day, 1 Nov
Christmas Day, 25 Dec
Boxing Day, 26 Dec

HOW TO GET THERE

Flying time to Warsaw's Okecie Airport from New York is 9 hours; from Frankfurt, 1½ hours; from Caracas, 13½ hours. Time in Poland: GMT+1.

REQUIREMENTS FOR ENTRY AND CUSTOMS REGULATIONS

Passport and visa required. Apply to a Polish Consulate with passport, two photos, visa fee, and a copy of a travel voucher or exchange order furnished either by Orbis, the Polish Travel Office, or a travel agent representing Orbis. A travel voucher is issued when services such as hotel accommodations, meals, car rentals, etc., have been prepaid. When such services have not been prepaid, a set minimum of currency must be exchanged in advance for each day of the expected stay—US$15, or US$7 for people of Polish origin, students, or young people 16-24 years of age. An exchange order is issued for this amount by the travel agent, to be presented upon arrival in Poland in exchange for the equivalent in Polish currency. No Polish currency is allowed into or out of the country. There is no limit to the amount of foreign currency in cash or travelers' checks taken into Poland, but it must be declared and you cannot take out more than you brought in. Duty-free allowance: 250 cigarettes, 50 cigars, or ½ pound of tobacco; 2 liters wine or liquor.

AIRPORT INFORMATION

Okecie Airport is 7 miles from Warsaw. Bus service to city terminal costs Zł1.5. Taxi fare, Zł50-70. There are special unmarked taxis called Polonez cars with a fixed rate of Zł120 to any hotel in Warsaw (waiting time Zł170 per hour). Drivers wear a "Taxi" badge. Polish Airlines' bus links international and domestic airports, fare Zł5. Tip luggage porters Zł10 to Zł20 per bag. Airport has a duty-free shop, a hotel reservation counter, and a small Luna hotel.

ACCOMMODATIONS

Orbis, the Polish Travel Office, runs several deluxe hotels and many more which are first-class. It also provides more modest pension accommodations, which can be reserved by the week. The less expensive hotels are usually run by the local town councils and by the **Polish Tourist Association (PTTK)**, which has a network of tourist houses and hostels, mountain chalets, and water sport centers all over the country. There are also youth hostels and hostels for students which open in summer only. Campers will find a wide choice of sites, most of which are run by PTTK. About 25 to 30 small inns have been constructed in western and southern Poland; prices are about US$20-30 for a double room. Visitors are advised to reserve hotels (through Orbis) well in advance. Warsaw hotels:

Rates are in US$ for a double/twin room with bath or shower

Europejski-Orbis, Ulica Krakowskie Przedmiescie 13 (from $84 BB)

Forum-Orbis, Nowogrodzka 22-24 (from $84 BB)

Grand Orbis, Ulica Krucza 28 (from $64BB)

Novotel-Orbis, Ulica Pierwszego Sierpnia 1 (from $44 BB), 10 minutes from city center near Okecie Airport

Solec-Orbis, Ulica Zagorna 1 (from $64 BB)

Vera-Orbis, Kostrzewy 16 (from $64 BB)

VICTORIA-ORBIS (INTER · CONTINENTAL), Krolewska 11 (from $84 BB)

All hotels listed above are centrally located unless otherwise indicated.

USEFUL INFORMATION

Banks: Hours vary, opening 8 or 9am to 12 or 2pm, Mon-Sat. All Orbis hotels have a currency exchange desk. There are branches of the Polish National Bank in all towns and cities. Keep all exchange receipts. They are necessary to reconvert Polish money into foreign currency at departure. (You can reconvert only an amount in excess of the set daily minimum for expenses.)

Mail: Stamps can be obtained at hotels and newspaper kiosks *(Ruch)* as well as post offices, which are open from 8am-8pm Monday-Friday. Mailboxes are red (foreign and national) or green (local).

Telephone Tips: There are street booths, and you can also make calls from hotels, restaurants, and cafés. Coin-operated, local calls cost Zł1. Useful numbers in Warsaw:

Pan Am 26 02 57	**Operator** 900
Airport Information 46 96 45 and 46 96 70	**Directories** 913
	Police 997
Tourist Information (Orbis) 26 16 68 and 26 02 71	**Fire** 998
	Ambulance 999

Newspapers: Some English-language newspapers available.

Tipping: Restaurants usually include a 10% service charge; when it is not included, leave a 10% tip. Give taxi drivers 10% of fare; hotel porters Zł20; cloakroom attendants Zł5.

Electricity: 220 volts 50 cycles AC. Converters available at hotels.

Laundry: Express service in major hotels. Also laundry shops and dry-cleaning shops, but no laundromats. Dry-cleaning a suit, from Zł50; laundering a shirt, from Zł20.

Hairdressing: First-class hotels have salons (shampoo and set from Zł100, tip about Zł10, men's haircuts from Zł50-60).

Photography: Film and equipment on sale in Poland is mostly Polish and East German. Developing takes 3-7 days for black and white, and up to 10 days for color (Kodak can be developed in some private laboratories). It is illegal to take photographs of industrial, transport, or military installations, and no pictures may be taken from the air.

Babysitting: Hotels may oblige.

Rest Rooms: Charge Zł2. Women, *Dla Pán, Dla Kobiet,* or *Damska;* men, *Dla Panów, Dla Mezczyzn,* or *Méski.*

Health: Some doctors and dentists speak a little English. Drinking water safe; milk is pasteurized.

TRANSPORTATION

In Warsaw metered taxis are obtainable at stands or ordered by phone. The charge is Zł7 for the first kilometer and Zł4.50 per kilometer thereafter; double fare between 11pm and 5am. For a Radio Taxi, call 909. A pleasant way to see the city is by horse-drawn carriage—but fix the charge first. Warsaw has bus and streetcar services; tickets are bought at newspaper kiosks before boarding. Poland has a network of long-distance buses (PKS), and the railroad system is also quite extensive, providing connections with all main cities. Remember that it is 75% more expensive to travel by express train than on ordinary passenger services. Internal air services are run by Polish Airlines (LOT). Coastal and inland steamer services are a restful way of seeing the country in the summer.

Car rental or chauffeur-driven cars may be obtained through Orbis in cooperation with Avis, Hertz, and Europcar. Car rental stations are in Warsaw, Gdańsk, Katowice, Cracow, Lodz, Olsztyn, Poznań, Szczecin, and Wroclaw. Cars available are the Polish-made Fiat 125P, Fiat 132P, plus Mercedes and Ford Granada. International driver's license required. Rates for self-drive cars range from US$15.40 per day plus 16¢ per kilometer for Soviet and Polish made cars up to US$30 for larger Western cars. Tourists arriving in cars with foreign plates must pay for gas with fuel coupons purchased from Orbis for foreign currency. The Poles run a novel system for hitchhikers; for those over 17 the PTTK sells books of coupons entitling them to 2,000 kilometers of travel during the summer season. These coupons are handed over to the motorist who gives them lifts, and the motorist with the most coupons wins a prize.

FOOD AND RESTAURANTS

Polish food is generally hot, spicy, and filling. Goose, duck, and hare are popular and are usually served with sauerkraut. Knuckle of pork served with cabbage, peas, and *Zywiec* beer *(golonka i piwo Zywiec)* is a Poznań specialty, while *Bigos,* a hunter's stew of rabbit, pork, or beef, and cabbage, often cooked in wine, can be found anywhere. *Go-*

POLAND

labki, spiced meat wrapped in cabbage, is another popular dish, and you must not miss the excellent Polish ham *(szynka)* and the famous beet soup *(barszcz),* which is often accompanied by *ouchkas,* a kind of mushroom ravioli. Many of the best restaurants are to be found in Orbis hotels, and they usually have international as well as Polish menus. While there is a shortage of meat, sugar, candy, chocolate, and even vodka, Orbis hotels have sufficient supplies. Good places to try outside the hotels include **Kamienne Schodki** in the Old Town Market Square (Rynek Starego Miasta 26—tel: 31 08 22), specializing in roast duck, and **Rycerska** (Szeroki Dunaj 11), serving excellent veal and roast meat. Good Hungarian food, music at **Kuznia Krolewska** (Wilanów—15 kilometers out of town—tel: 41 59 01) and at **Budapest** (Marszalkowska—tel: 25 34 33), with music, dancing, and a wine-cellar atmosphere. **Baszta** (Pyry—20 kilometers out of town—tel: 43 06 96) has Russian specialties as well as good Polish food. The food and service are excellent at the Victoria Hotel's three restaurants—the **Canaletto,** serving Polish specialties, the **Boryna** (brasserie), and the **Hetmanska** (grill specialties). The Europejski Hotel has an excellent restaurant and a lunch bar with good food and quick service, though it is often crowded. The Forum Hotel has two restaurants, **Maryla** and **Soplica,** with onion soup believed to be better than it is in Paris. **Krokodyl** (Rynek Starego Miasta 19), a restaurant by day and a nightclub at night, serves Polish and continental dishes. It is advisable to make reservations for Saturdays or holidays, when restaurants become heavily booked. Tourists should not forget the shortage of meat in Poland. Some restaurants of lower categories have meatless days on Wednesday or Thursday.

DRINKING TIPS

Coffee houses *(Kawiarnia)* are an institution in Poland. People go there to read newspapers and to meet their friends. Among the most popular in Warsaw are the upstairs coffee houses at **Krokodyl** and **Kamienne Schodki** in the Old Town Market Square, and **Retro-Emocja,** Mokotowska 57, which serves Italian pizza and good coffee. Some privately owned small cafés in the Stare Miasto district occasionally serve hot dogs. Vodka *(Wodka)* and beer *(piwo)* are widely drunk. Vodka is taken straight as an aperitif, as a mealtime drink, and as a liqueur. There are no drinking restrictions for those over 18, and bars are open all day and often until 2am in Warsaw and other main cities. Women are welcome in all bars. In Warsaw it is fun to visit some of the wine cellars, especially **Fukier** in the Old Town Market Square, which is inexpensive. **U Michala** (Freta Street 9) is small and intimate and serves excellent wine with spices. There are at least 20 other small cafés in the Old Town area, some selling popcorn in summer.

ENTERTAINMENT

To many who live in the land of Chopin and Paderewski, music is a way of life. The Polish calendar is studded with music festivals large and small. One of the most enjoyable is the **Chopin Festival** at **Dszniki**

Spa every August. From June-September Chopin recitals are given on Sundays at his birthplace in **Zelazowa Wola** near Warsaw, and his music can also be heard frequently in the city at recitals in beautiful **Lazienki Park** and also at **Ostrogski Palace.** The **Warsaw Autumn International Contemporary Music Festival** is a big event, and the city also has the **International Jazz Jamboree** in October. Season tickets for the Warsaw Philharmonic Orchestra at the **National Philharmonic Hall** can be obtained. The **Congress Hall** in the towering **Palace of Science and Culture** is also an impressive setting for shows and concerts. Warsaw's **Grand Opera House,** rebuilt since the war, stages excellent performances, and several other towns (including **Poznań** and **Gdańsk**) are especially interesting and have many lively shows, including satire. Movie houses show some English and American movies with original soundtrack and Polish subtitles.

Visitors should try and see a festival combining Poland's wealth of folk dance, song, and costume. The biggest is the **Harvest Festival** in September, which is held every year in a different town. The **Cracow Youth Festival** takes place in May. **Sopot** has an international festival of song in August, and in October there is an international festival of amateur song and dance ensembles at **Zielona Góra,** which features many of Poland's famous regional groups.

Songs often dominate the nightclub scene in Warsaw. In some nightclubs there are floor shows and strip tease is performed. Principal nightclubs in Warsaw are the deluxe **Europejski** (known to locals as **Kamieniolomy**) in the Europejski Hotel; the **Krokodyl,** with waitresses in traditional dress; the **Adria** (Moniuski 8), deluxe nightclub and restaurant; the **Kongresowa,** in the Palace of Science and Culture complex; the **Black Cat** in the Victoria Hotel; **Marathon,** Foksal & Kopernika streets. There are also jazz clubs. Connoisseurs will enjoy the **Piwnica Wandy Warskiej** in the Old Town Market Square, young people the **Remont** (Warynskiego, corner of Polna), and **Stodola** (Batorego 10) discothèques, and professionals the **Akwarium** (Emilii Plater Street). For other tastes, there is classical music at the **Ambassador** restaurant opposite the American Embassy on Aleje Ujazdowskie Street.

SHOPPING

Stores (other than food stores) are open from 11-7 Mon-Sat, closed Sun. Polish craftwork is fascinating; wood carvings, boxes, and handwoven rugs come mostly from the Zakopane region. Other souvenirs include costume dolls, glass, amber jewelry, embroidery, paper cutouts, and models of firearms from the 16th and 17th centuries.

In Warsaw and other cities, **Cepelia** stores specialize in folk craft articles. **Orno** shops have a wide selection of silverwork and jewelry. **Desa** is the place to go for works of art and antiques as well as reproductions, though most antiques will need an export permit. Desa, Orno, and Cepelia stores accept hard currency or Polish currency, but **Pewex** stores are strictly hard currency shops, and souvenirs can be purchased despite a shortage of consumer goods, even of essentials, in other Polish stores.

Found mostly in hotels, Pewex stores sell a variety of handicraft items, gold and silver jewelry, other souvenirs, and cigarettes, wines, and liquor. Warsaw's largest department stores are **Wars** (across from the Palace of Culture), **Junior,** and **Sawa** (Marszalkowska Street). An unusual shopping expedition is to **Rutkowskiego Street** in Warsaw, where many small private shops selling gloves, hats, dress material, and jewelry are hidden away in courtyards or in upstairs rooms. Tourists may take out, duty-free, purchases up to the value of Zł1,000, and above that anything purchased for hard currency and for which they have the sales receipt. If items above the Zł1,000 limit were bought with zlotys, they will be taxed on departure. Crystal, especially, is heavily taxed if bought with Polish currency, and leather and fur goods bought with Polish currency are not allowed out at all.

SPORTS

Opportunities for sailing, canoeing, fishing, swimming, and water-skiing are excellent in the vast **Masurian Lake District,** which has 2,700 lakes, most of them linked by rivers or canals. A newly constructed hotel at Mragowo (from $26 double BB) has sailboats, a tennis club, and a sauna. Otherwise, hotels are scarce, but there are plenty of campsites. The dense forests in this region are good for hunting. Game includes stag, boar, wild duck, goose, hare, pheasant, and blackcock. Orbis will arrange hunting trips with accommodations in foresters' huts. Fishing is supervised by the **Polish Angling Association,** and to fish you must buy a 1-7- or 14-day license costing from US$7 (obtainable from Orbis). **Zakopane,** 2,720 feet above sea level on the slopes of the dramatic **Tatra** mountains, is the center for mountaineering and skiing holidays. Stay at the **Kasprowy-Orbis Hotel** (from US$64 double BB) on the slope of **Gubalowka Mountain.** The climbing season is from June-September, and there is superb skiing from December-April. The highest of Zakopane's three ski jumps is regarded as one of the most technically perfect in the world. Poland's Baltic coastline has many delightful sandy beaches for swimming, and **Sopot** is the major seaside resort. There is no golf in Poland, but some tennis clubs welcome visitors, and Orbis will arrange horseback riding holidays on selected stud farms. Horse racing is held (May-November) in **Warsaw, Sopot,** and **Wroclaw,** with Polish-bred Arabian horses participating; there's also steeplechase racing at these spots.

WHAT TO SEE

Warsaw, once a medieval fortified town, lies on the River Vistula amid the plains of central Poland. It became the country's capital only toward the end of the 16th century. The restored **Old Town** *(Stare Miasto)* now looks as it did then. Warsaw street scenes by painters of the Canaletto School were used as a guide during the restoration work after World War II, which left the city almost totally destroyed. These paintings can be seen in the **National Museum,** which also has works from Polish and other European schools and a rare collection of Nubian frescoes. Warsaw has about 30 museums and art galleries. Among the most interesting are the **Historical Museum of the City of Warsaw,** with scale models of the town from prehistoric to modern times; the **Museum of Martyrdom,** showing the persecution of the Poles by the Nazis; the **Chopin Museum** at Ostrogski Palace; and the **Poster Museum** at Wilanów.

Dominating the Warsaw skyline now is the 765-foot-high **Palace of Science and Culture,** which houses theaters, restaurants, scientific institutions, a swimming pool, and a vast Congress Hall. From the top you get a spectacular view of the whole of the city, including the modern residential quarter of the Muranów, which replaces the Jewish ghetto destroyed when Warsaw's Jews heroically rose up against the city's Nazi occupiers and fought to their death. Here is the impressive **Monument to the Heroes of the Ghetto.**

Castle Square with its 17th-century **King Sigismund Column** is the best starting place for a tour of Old Warsaw. The itinerary from there past the **Royal Castle,** which is still being rebuilt, and up **Krakowskie Przedmieście Street,** with its baroque churches and palaces and fine patrician houses, to **Nowy Swiat,** is known as the Royal Route. Where the two roads join is the **Church of the Holy Cross.** The heart of Frédéric Chopin is kept in an urn there, at his request, though his body is buried in France, where he died. Its winding alleyways, old houses, and medieval barbican (defensive towers) give the **Old Town** an unforgettable charm. The marketplace (Rynek Starego Miasta) is one of the finest in Europe, and the 14th-century **St John's Cathedral** has been rebuilt in the original Gothic style. The 17th- and 18th-century **New Town** *(Nowe Miasto)*, which has a fine marketplace, has also been restored. Visitors should find time to wander in gracious **Lazienki Park** and see the 18th-century lakeside palace. Try to visit, too, baroque **Wilanów Palace** on the south side of the city, which has many artistic and historic treasures.

Nieborów, a 17th-century palace in beautiful grounds, is about 50 miles south of Warsaw. **Zelazowa Wola,** Chopin's birthplace, is about 35 miles west, on the road to Poznań. Other towns of interest in the Warsaw area include **Warka,** a picturesque vine-growing town with a museum commemorating General Kazimierz Pulaski, who commanded troops in the American Revolutionary War; and **Løwicz,** center of a folklore region, with an interesting **Museum of Folk Art. Kampinos Forest,** outside Warsaw, is a national park where elks still roam.

Unlike Warsaw, **Cracow,** one of the most beautiful medieval towns in Europe, was undamaged in the war. It lies 200 miles to the south of Warsaw and was once the capital of Poland. The **Royal Castle** towers over the town on Wawel Hill and houses an art collection containing the famous *Arras Tapestries.* Nearby is the **Cathedral** where Polish kings are buried. **The Sigismund Chapel** is a fine example of Renaissance architecture. The arcaded **Cloth Hall** in the Market Square was built in the 14th century and rebuilt during the Renaissance. On the first floor is a collection of Polish paintings. A medieval bugle call is played every hour from the tallest of **St Mary's Church** towers. Inside is the famous 15th-century altarpiece carved by Wit Stwosz. The **Czartoryski Museum** has works by Leonardo da Vinci and Rembrandt, and the **Jagiellonian Univer-**

sity, founded by Casimir the Great in 1364 and now a museum, has magnificent Gothic buildings ranged around a courtyard. The museum houses a priceless collection of instruments used by Copernicus and other medieval astronomers. Hotels include the **Cracowia-Orbis,** with double rooms from US$75 BB; the **Holiday Inn,** with double rooms from US$75 BB; and the **Francuski Motel,** with double rooms from US$59 BB.

At **Wieliczka,** 8 miles from Cracow, you can visit the oldest salt mines in the world. They have been worked since the 10th century and are still being worked today. Deep underground are carved passages and grottoes and even a chapel and a tennis court. There is also a huge natural crystal grotto. Visit **Auschwitz** (Oswiecim), 40 miles from Cracow, the former Nazi concentration camp where millions of people from 26 nations perished in the years 1940-45. There is now a museum in the camp.

In 1973, Poland celebrated the 500th anniversary of the birth of its great astronomer, Copernicus. Follow the **Copernicus Trail,** which covers places where he lived and worked. Starting in Warsaw, the trail leads to **Olsztyn,** which is the gateway to the beautiful Masurian Lake District (see Sports), through **Frombork,** with its 14th-century cathedral buildings, and to **Gdańsk,** the historic Polish port. Try to see the animated cathedral organ in the suburb of **Oliwa.** In Gdańsk, stay at the **Monopol-Orbis** (from US$34 double BB); the **Novotel-Orbis,** the **Posejdon-Orbis,** or the new **Heweliusz-Orbis** (all from US$37double BB). Nearby are **Gdynia,** a modern port, and **Sopot,** Poland's big seaside resort. When in Sopot stay at **Grand-Orbis Hotel** situated on the beach (from US$47 double BB). There are many beautiful beaches along the Baltic shore, which is known as the "Amber Coast" because of the ancient trade in amber throughout this region. The Copernicus Trail continues through **Malbork,** whose 14th-century **Castle of the Order of Teutonic Knights** is said to be the best-preserved medieval structure in central Europe. The trail ends at **Torun,** Copernicus's birthplace, which has a medieval "leaning tower." Stay at the **Hotel Orbis-Kosmos** (US$25 double BB). Other places of tourist interest include **Poznań,** where the **International Trade Fair** is held (the **Merkury-Orbis,** Roosevelta 20, and the **Polonez-Orbis,** Stalin-gradzka 54-68, both US$74 double CP); **Wroclaw,** with Gothic town hall and modern pantomime groups has the **Panorama** (from US$34 double BB); and **Szczecin,** ancient capital of Western Pomerania, situated at the mouth of the Oder River. Stay at the **Arkona-Orbis** (from US$62 double BB) or the new **Reda-Orbis** (from US$69 double BB). The all-year health resort of **Kolobrzeg** is northeast of Szczecin, along the Baltic coast. Stay at the **Solny-Orbis** or at the **Skanpol** (both from US$55 double CP). Worth seeing are the **Tatra** mountain region and **Bialowieza** nature reserve near the Russian frontier, where Europe's only bison are protected in their wild state. Also visit **Czestochowa,** where there's the **Jasna Gora Monastery,** Polish Catholicism's most sacred shrine. The monastery possesses a picture of the Czestochowa Virgin Mary (Black Madonna), subject of a religious cult dating back to medieval times and regarded by Polish Catholics as the Queen of Poland. Stay at the **Patria-Orbis**

Hotel (Ochotnikow Wojenncyh 1, from US$64 double BB) or the newly constructed **PZM-Czestochowa** motel (from US$58 double). In eastern Poland you may visit the ancient town of **Lublin** with a beautiful 16th-century castle and the Old Town. Lublin's Catholic University (Katolicki Uniwersytet Lubleski), where Pope John Paul II taught ethics, is the only Catholic university in the country.

SOURCES OF FURTHER INFORMATION

Pan Am, Inter · Continental Victoria Hotel, Krolewska 11, Warsaw, and any Pan Am office around the world; **Orbis,** Krakowskie Przedmiescie 13, Warsaw; **Polish Embassy,** 2640 16th Street, Washington, DC 20009; **Polish National Tourist Office,** 500 Fifth Avenue, New York, NY 10036; 313 Regent Street, London W1.

Portugal

WHAT'S SPECIAL

After Roman occupation by Julius Caesar, Portugal, then known as Lusitania, was conquered by the Moors in 711. In 1147 the great stronghold of Lisbon was recaptured by Alfonso I and Christian Crusaders, and 100 years later Alfonso III completed the ousting of the Moors. Moorish influence can still be seen in the architecture of houses in the Algarve, in the narrow streets of Lisbon's Alfama quarter, in Arab dialect, in towns like Silves in the south, and, above all, in the *azulejos* (beautiful tiles, predominantly blue) which cover the walls of many buildings.

Under Prince Henry the Navigator in the 15th century, the Portuguese set out to navigate and explore the globe and became one of the greatest and wealthiest countries in the West. A sense of this past grandeur is still vividly preserved in Portugal's rich cultural heritage.

COUNTRY BRIEFING

Size: 35,387 square miles
Capital: Lisbon

Population: 9,904,000
Capital Population: 757,700

Climate: In the north the climate is an Atlantic one, while the south is more Mediterranean. The heat of the high summer is tempered by the influence of the Atlantic on the coastal areas. The southern Algarve coast has a year-round mild climate; Lisbon, hot in summer, can be wet and windy January through April.

Weather in Lisbon: Lat N38°43′; Alt 313 ft

Temp (°F)	Jan	Feb	Mar	Apr	May	Jun	Jul	Aug	Sep	Oct	Nov	Dec
Av Low	46°	47°	49°	52°	56°	60°	63°	64°	62°	57°	52°	47°
Av High	56°	58°	61°	64°	69°	75°	79°	80°	76°	69°	62°	57°
Days no rain	22	20	21	23	25	28	30	30	26	24	20	21

Government: A constitutional republic.

Language: Portuguese is the official language. In cities many people speak French or English as a second language.

Religion: 90% Roman Catholic.

Currency: The escudo. 100 centavos = 1 escudo. The written sign for the escudo is very similar to the dollar sign; the escudo sign comes between escudos and centavos.

	1 escu.	5 escu.	20 escu.	50 escu.	100 escu.	500 escu.	1000 escu.	1500 escu.
US (dollars, cents)	.02	.08	.33	.82	1.64	8.21	16.42	24.63
UK (pounds, pence)	.01	.04	.16	.39	.78	3.92	7.85	11.77

Public Holidays:

New Year's Day, 1 Jan
Shrove Tuesday, Feb
Good Friday
Liberty Day, 25 Apr
Labor Day, 1 May
National Day, 10 June
Feast of St Anthony (Lisbon only), 13 June
Feast of St John (Oporto only), 24 June

Assumption Day, 15 Aug
Proclamation of the Republic, 5 Oct
All Saints Day, 1 Nov
Independence Day, 1 Dec
Feast of the Immaculate Conception, 8 Dec
Christmas, 24-25 Dec

HOW TO GET THERE

Flying time to Lisbon's Portela de Sacavem Airport from New York is 6½ hours; from London, 1½ hours, from Madrid, 1 hour. Time in Portugal: GMT+1. Daylight Saving Time observed.

REQUIREMENTS FOR ENTRY AND CUSTOMS REGULATIONS

A valid passport required. Visas are not necessary for US, Canadian, British, or West European citizens. Other nationals should check with their Portuguese consulate. If coming from, or passing through, a place where cholera is present, a vaccination certificate against this must be produced. Portugal occasionally has outbreaks of cholera, so the tourist may be required to be vaccinated before leaving the country if this occurs. Currency in the form of travelers' checks, credit cards, and foreign or Portuguese banknotes can freely be taken into the country, but for personal expenses only and not for investment or land purchase. Up to 5,000 escudos in Portuguese currency per person may be brought into the country. Gold cannot be exported (except personal jewelry) other than through the Bank of Portugal. The duty-free entrance allowances are 2 quarts liquor, and up to 5,000 escudos worth of tobacco, perfume, and small souvenirs.

AIRPORT INFORMATION

Portela de Sacavem Airport is about 6 kilometers from Lisbon. Taxis are available at all times and cost about 100 escudos to the city center. City transport system buses go by the airport to the center every 15 minutes or so, but have very limited luggage space. No arrival or departure tax. Lisbon airport has a duty-free shop where wines, liquors, perfumes, and tobacco can be bought. There is a nursery for children and an information desk run by the tourist office.

ACCOMMODATIONS

An annual *Hotel Guide* published by the State Department of Tourism gives basic details of all hotels all over the country. Prices are, on the whole, reasonable for good standards of rooms and service. One of the best bargains is the chain of about 20 *pousadas* or small state-sponsored inns, with stay limited to no more than 3 days. Prices run from US$41 for a double room with bath in luxury category inns, to US$29 in plainer ones. These inns are often situated in scenic spots with tourist appeal and are sometimes converted buildings of historic interest such as castles or palaces. There are also many private *estalagems* (inns) around the country. Special tourist discounts are available for North Americans under the Silver Platter Program. Any Portuguese tourist office can provide details. There are plenty of camping grounds and trailer parks; details in a Tourism Department guide. Tourists between the ages of 14 and 30 years can get accommodations in youth hostels by applying to Tourism Estudantil, Rua Fernano Pedroso (near Praça de Londres), in Lisbon; it is advisable to have a youth hostel card when making reservations. Pensions in Lisbon are inexpensive and of good standard, and the State Tourism offices can advise on these. Lisbon hotels include:

Rates are in US$ for a double/twin room with bath or shower

Altis, Rua Castilho 11 (from $84)

Avenida Palace, Rua 1 de Dezembro 123 (from $66)

Borges, Rua Garrett 108 (from $27)

Diplomatico, Rua Castilho 74 (from $48)

Do Guincho, Praia do Guincho (from $70), 20 miles from Lisbon

Dom Carlos, Avenida Duque de Loulé 121 (from $38)

Eduardo VII, Avenida Fontes Pereira de Melo 5-C (from $38)

Embaixador, Avenida Duque Loulé 73 (from $46)

Estoril-Sol, Parque Palmela, Cascais (from $90), 18 miles from Lisbon

Excelsior, Rua Rodrigues Sampaio 172 (from $38)

Fénix, Praça Marquês de Pombal 8 (from $48)

Flórida, Rua Duque de Palmela 32 (from $48)

Lisboa Penta, Avenida dos Combatentes (from $51)

Lisboa Plaza, Travessa do Salitre 7 (from $50)

Lisboa Sheraton, Rua Latino Coelho 2 (from $88)

Lutécia, Avenida Frei Miguel Contreiras (from $50), 3 miles from city center

Palacio, Parque do Estoril (from US$95), 15 miles from Lisbon

Ritz, Rua Rodrigo da Fonseca 88-A (from $106)
Tivoli, Avenida da Liberdade 185 (from $66)
Tivoli Jardim, Rua Júlio César Machado 7-9 (from $60)
All hotels centrally located unless otherwise indicated. Many of the above hotels give special rates for longer stays.

USEFUL INFORMATION

Banks: 8:30-12 and 1-2:30, Mon-Fri; closed Sat. Major banks have affiliations with US banks. American Express has offices in Lisbon. There are banks outside the main cities, and you can change currency and travelers' checks in most banks and hotels throughout Portugal.

Mail: Mailboxes in Portugal are red, usually round, standing on the sidewalk.

Telephone Tips: Telephone booths are reasonably available. You need a 1-escudo, 2.50-escudo, or 50-centavo coin for area calls in Lisbon. You cannot make long-distance calls from most booths; these are made (apart from hotels, etc.) by asking for the number in a Central Post Office or telephone office and then paying when the call is over. Useful numbers in Lisbon:

Pan Am 362591	Emergencies 115
Tourist Office 575091	Weather 16
Airport Information 889181	Telegram 10
Time 15	Information Service 16
Directories 12	

Newspapers: Foreign newspapers are available in Lisbon and the major tourist resorts. A local English publication called *Anglo-Portuguese News* is published every two weeks.

Tipping: Customary and usually around 10-15%. Taxis 15%. Luggage porters 15 escudos per bag. Hotel porter 20 escudos. Cloakroom attendants 20 escudos. Restaurants 10-15%, if no service charge is added to the bill. Hairdressers 10-15%.

Electricity: Voltage is 210-220 volts 50 cycles AC. In certain parts of the country voltage is 110 AC. Some hotels in resorts have converters.

Laundry: Dry-cleaning and laundry services are good. For 24-hour service, an extra 25% may be charged. (From 240 escudos to dry-clean a suit, from 20 escudos to have a shirt laundered.)

Hairdressing: Portuguese hairdressers are usually very good. First-class hotels have their own salons (shampoo and set or man's haircut and shampoo both from 250 escudos; tip 15%).

Photography: Film is available, but expensive. Black and white film can be developed and printed in a day in Lisbon shops. It is best to save color film for development at home. Cost of black and white film is from 238 escudos; color from 900 escudos with processing included.

Clubs: There are a number of clubs for foreigners which welcome visitors to their meetings. Useful ones to note are the American Club of Lisbon, Rua Castilho 38, Lisbon; Royal British Club, Rua da Estrela 8, Lisbon; Ladies Club, Rua Nova da Trindade 1-2, Lisbon; Historical

Association, Rua Luis Fernandes 3, Lisbon; The British Club, Rua das Virtudes 11, Oporto; Stella Maris, Rua Fresca 78, Leça de Palmeira (Oporto). The Kiwanis club is also active in Portugal.

Babysitting: Services can be arranged through some of the hotels. During the day Becassine, Avenida Antonio Augusto Aguiar 84-2, Lisbon (tel: 41307), takes infants and children from 8am-8pm.

Rest Rooms: In restaurants, cafés, railway stations, airports, gas stations, usually free. For women, *Lavabos de Senhoras* ("S" on the door); for men, *Lavabos de Homens* ("H" on the door).

Health: Many doctors and dentists speak English. Imported pharmaceuticals available, but expensive. Local water safe for drinking, but bottled local mineral waters available.

TRANSPORTATION

There are adequate road links between Lisbon and the major towns and cities, although many of the secondary roads and some main roads are poorly maintained. Portugal has one of the highest road-accident rates in Europe. Hazards include unlit donkey carts at night and a general non-observance of the traffic code. Cost of a chauffeur-driven rented car would be from US$29-65 per day, plus mileage and the driver's meals; without chauffeur about US$11-48 plus mileage. Driving in Lisbon is fast and furious and is best avoided altogether, particularly in older quarters like **Alfama.** Although there is no jay-walking law, for safety's sake it is best to find a spot controlled by a policeman or a traffic light before crossing the street. The Metro is state-owned, and the set fare for any distance is 12.50 escudos. The green and black Lisbon taxis are among the least expensive in Europe. Fares are metered within the municipal area. For out-of-town destinations a kilometer rate is charged and the price will include the return trip even if you don't use the taxi. If you have over 66 pounds of baggage you may be charged an extra 50% on the fare. The Lisbon bus company, **Carris,** used to be English-owned and still has double-decker buses and old-fashioned streetcars; maximum fare 20 escudos. In addition, there are three special streetcars or *elevadores* which inch their way up particularly steep hills; in the "Baixa," the main downtown shopping and banking center, there is an elevator designed by Eiffel which carries passengers from Rua do Ouro up to the "Chiado" shopping district above. For sightseeing, **Cityrama** or **Claras** buses leave Marques do Pombal in Lisbon daily between 2 and 2:30pm.

From Lisbon to the nearby resorts of Estoril and Cascais there is a good electric train service taking about 35 minutes. The state railroad (CP) has trains connecting all the principal cities. There are overnight sleepers to Oporto and the Algarve from Lisbon, and fares are comparatively inexpensive. Unlimited-mileage tickets are available for train trips over 1,500 kilometers. These *Bilhetes Kilométricos* are available from railway stations. A long-distance bus service also links the main towns.

TAP runs internal flights to Faro in the Algarve and Oporto, each taking about 40 minutes, and also flies to Funchal, Madeira, and airports in the Azores.

FOOD AND RESTAURANTS

Portuguese food places a strong accent on fish and seafood. Fish is abundant in this maritime country, and Portuguese cooks are highly skilled in preparing it. Restaurants all have their own versions of the popular *caldeirada,* a stew made of different kinds of fish mixed with vegetables. The national dish is dried cod *(bacalhau).* Seafood is surprisingly expensive. It is usually sold by weight in restaurants.

Meat is not as traditional as fish and seafood but is available in a number of delicious ways. In Lisbon steaks cooked in earthenware dishes, often topped with a fried egg, are popular. Liver *(iscas)* sliced thinly and sautéed, served with salad and fresh green beans, is another popular dish. Pork, veal, and chicken are also popular, either made into thick stews in the north or, as pork is in the Algarve, cooked with wine, mussels, and onions *(cataplana).* Soups are a favorite meal opener, thick and nourishing. There is the *caldo verde* potato and cabbage soup, or tomato soup perhaps with an egg floated in it, Madeira style. Bread soups *(acorda)* are still made, with bread as a basis eked out with game or other meats and vegetables.

There are some good local cheeses: *azeitao,* from the hills south of Lisbon, and *serra,* another mountain cheese made from ewe's milk. Meal times in Portugal are breakfast from 8:30-10; lunch from 12-2:30; dinner from about 7:30 onward. In the city, lunch can often be eaten as what is called a *snack,* much more substantial than the word implies for us. Popular *snack* bars to try in Lisbon are the **Monumental** a few steps from the Ritz Hotel and the **Tivoli** at the Tivoli Jardim Hotel. Also good for a snack is the cafeteria in the basement of the Sheraton. An expensive restaurant costs from US$30 up with wine, a medium about US$20, and an inexpensive one about US$8. Among the more elegant restaurants in Lisbon are **Aviz** (Rua Serpa Pinto 12B—tel: 328391) and **Tavares** (Rua da Misericórdia 35—tel: 321112), which has an upstairs dining room with superb cooking and more reasonable prices than the downstairs room. **O Faia** (Rua da Barroca 56—tel: 369387) is one of the few places where you can listen to *fado* music and have good food too. To dine out with a view, try the Tivoli Hotel Terrace, or **Tagide** (Largo da Biblioteca Publica 18—tel: 320720), a popular luxury restaurant with a splendid view of the city and river. The Sheraton Hotel also has a rooftop restaurant with view. At **A Gondola** (Avenida de Berna 64—tel: 770426) you can dine out of doors on Italian or Portuguese cuisine. You enter **Portas do Sol** (Rua de S Tomé 86—tel: 861633) through an antique shop which spills over into the restaurant. Try their truffle omelette. Nine miles outside the city at Queluz the **Cozinha Velha,** the former royal kitchens of the Queluz Palace (tel: 950232), serves superb Portuguese cuisine. **Hotel Palacio dos Seteais** at Sintra (tel: 980681) is known for its decor and surroundings and is best at lunch or afternoon tea.

DRINKING TIPS

Portugal produces some fine table wines that are among Europe's best bargains. Most widely known are the red wines produced in the Dão region and known as a type by that name. These wines improve with age, so check the vintage date to make sure the wine is not less than 5 and preferably over 10 years old. Bucelas is a fine, dry white wine, once esteemed throughout Europe and still excellent even if less fashionable. Portugal's unique *vinhos verdes* (literally green wines) are young red or white wines with a slight sparkle and should be drunk well-chilled. The rosé wines, such as Mateus, that have gained fame outside the country are seldom drunk by the Portuguese themselves. For an after-dinner drink, there are the world-famous port wines from Oporto, or Madeira wine, or, for braver spirits, *Bagaço,* the fiery national schnapps-like drink. The domestic beers, like *Sagres,* are worth favoring over the more expensive imports. Women are welcome but seldom go alone to bars. A popular place for a drink or quiet, intimate dining is the resort town of Cascais, 20 minutes by train from Lisbon. Try **Os Doze** (Rua Frederico Arouca 71, Cascais—tel: 286 5334). In Lisbon, the **Port Wine Institute** bar (Rua São Pedro de Alcantara 45—tel: 323307) should not be missed. It features a cellar where you can sample some 200 ports.

ENTERTAINMENT

Lisbon is definitely a place for film buffs. Movie houses are numerous and cheap and they show films virtually uncut and with original soundtrack. There is a short—January through April—opera season at the beautiful 18th-century **San Carlos Theater**. The **National Theater Company** performs Portuguese and foreign classics at the recently refurbished **Dona Maria Theater** in Rossio Square. The **Gulbenkian Foundation** provides ballet, concerts, and recitals at its handsome center on Avenida de Berna. Vaudeville survives in the popular *revistas* in the Parque Mayer theater area, with emphasis on unsophisticated chorus lines and double-meaning word gags. The elegant **Casino** at Estoril has its own nightclub and movie house. In Lisbon night haunts to visit include **Ad Lib** (Rua Barata Salguiero, 28-7°—tel: 561717), **Carousel** (Ritz Hotel—tel: 681571), **Stone's** (Rua do Olival 1), and in Cascais where many of the liveliest and most fashionable discothèques are found, the **Van Go Go** (Travesa Alfarrobeira, 9—tel: 283377).

The *fado,* a swelling, romantic lament sung to the plaintive accompaniment of the Portuguese guitar, is a unique part of Lisbon nightlife. For the full flavor, hear it over dinner or late night drinks in *fado* houses in the city's old quarters. And try not to talk while the singers are performing; the Portuguese take their *fado* seriously. Fado houses to try: **Lisboa a Noite** (Rua das Gaveas 69), **Parreirinha d'Alfama** (Beco do Espirito Santo 1—tel: 868209), or **Picadeiro Casa de Fados** outside of Cascais. Regional folk dances are sometimes included in shows, especially at **O Faia** (Rua da Barroca 56), **Luso** (Travessa da Queimada 10-16), and **A Tipoia** (Rua do Norte 102).

SHOPPING

Stores are open from 9-1 and 3-7 Mon-Fri. Some shops open at 9:30am; some open Saturday morning, but every store is closed Saturday afternoon. Lisbon's main shopping area is in the **Baixa** quarter and in the **Chiado** district around the **Rua Garrett.** Good buys in Portugal include jewelry, leather, china, and cork (visit **Mr Cork,** Rua da Escola Politécnica 4-10). For filigree gold and silver jewelry, try the shops in the **Rua Aurea;** for shoes, handbags, and accessories, embroideries, and household linens, go to the department stores listed below, and for Madeiran products visit **Ann Leacock's** boutique in the arcade beneath the Ritz hotel. China and pottery of all kinds can be bought from the big stores or from **Vista Alegre,** Largo do Chiado 18. Antique hunters should see the shops in the **Rua de Sao Bento** and **Rua D. Pedro V.** Good stores to visit: **Fabrica Ceramica Viuva Lamego** (Largo Intendente P Manique 25) for traditional tiles and ceramics; **Casa das Ilhas Adjacentes** (Rua Sao Bento 392) and the **Casa Regional de Ilha Verde** (Rua Paiva de Andrada 4) for island crafts; **Grandela** (Rua Aurea), a major department store; **Galeão** (Rua Augusta 190/6) for handbags and hand luggage; **Drugstore Apolo 70** (Avenida Julio Dinis 10), a young drugstore-style shop with clothing and souvenirs; and **Casa Quintão** (Rua Ivens 30) for rugs. Shopping centers, with little shops where you can buy anything from a goldfish to a pair of shoes, have mushroomed all over Lisbon and are open from morning to midnight. Good ones include **Imaviz,** in the basement of the building adjoining the Sheraton Hotel, and the **Terminal,** in the Rossio train station in downtown Lisbon.

It isn't customary to bargain except in the markets, but some stores give discounts on travelers' checks, etc. Most major stores will pack and ship abroad. Markets in Lisbon yield some good buys, mainly of smaller household items. The best known is the **Feira de Ladra** ("Thieves' Fair") held in the Campo Santa Clara on Tuesdays and Saturdays. For food, try the **São Pedro** market along the narrow street in Alfama in the mornings. The main market is **Praça da Ribeira,** near Cais do Sodre, with fish, fruit, vegetable, and flower sections.

SPORTS
The sports passion for most Portuguese is soccer, and there are some fine teams. More fascinating to the visitor, however, might be Portuguese bullfighting, which in Lisbon can be seen at the **Campo Pequeno** bullring on some Thursday evenings and some Sunday afternoons from Easter to October. Unlike Spanish bullfighting, the bull is not killed. It is advisable to check a schedule, because bullfights are now held irregularly.

There are good sporting facilities for tourists in most parts of the country. Golf, tennis, water sports, fishing, and hunting facilities are the most common. Tennis is available at Lisbon, Estoril, and in the Algarve as well as at many of the first-class hotels. Golf has always been prized at Estoril, and now the Algarve has three championship golf courses: **Penina, Vila Moura,** and **Vale do Lobo.** There are other good golf courses around the country. Horseback riding is popular both around Cascais and in the Algarve, where there are English-run riding schools. Swimming in the sea is possible near Lisbon at Cascais and Estoril. The Algarve has the country's best sandy beaches, though the little fishing villages north of Lisbon in the **Nazaré** and **Ofir** areas have larger beaches with high sea breakers. The **Arrábida** area, south of Lisbon, is also good for swimming, though beaches are small. In spite of being a fishing-oriented country, Portugal has not developed fishing as a sport for visitors. The best is organized from the **Hotel Espadarte** at Sesimbra, south of Lisbon, though local fishermen will often take out visitors on request. Swordfishing is the big attraction at Sesimbra. There is also some freshwater fishing in the **Minho** and **Lima** rivers in the north and the **Serra da Estrela** lakes. Hunting takes place from 1 October, and game is shot around the Cascais area. Contact **Equipagem de Santo Humberto,** Rua Visconde de Seabra 2-4D, Lisbon. Other sports clubs welcoming visitors include **Tenis de Monsanto,** Lisbon, **Clube de Ténis Estoril, Clube de Golfe Estoril,** and the golf clubs in the Algarve; **Clube dos Amadores de Pesca de Portugal,** 175 Rua de Salitre, Lisbon (for fishing); **Clube de Equitacao de Cascais** (in Marinha woods, for riding); and **Clube Internacional de Ténis,** Rua Amoreiras 193, Lisbon.

WHAT TO SEE

Lisbon is a city of hills, and atop the highest the **Castelo de São Jorge** is the oldest monument in the city, dating back to the Visigoths. There are pleasant, tree-lined walks here and views over the city and Tagus River. Beneath it are the cobbled, labyrinthine streets of the **Alfama** district, the old quarter which, along with the Castle, survived the tremendous Lisbon earthquake of 1755. See the **Casa dos Bicos,** the house of pointed stones. Other traces of early Lisbon are the ruins of the 14th-century **Carmo Church,** which has an archaeological museum.

São Vicente is a huge church in Largo São Vicente, of interest as the Pantheon of the former Braganza kings and queens. São Roque is the most ornate and rich of Lisbon's churches (in Largo Trindade Coelho). Of chief importance is the **Chapel of St John the Baptist,** which was the most costly chapel of its time (early 18th century) to be built in Europe. Among Lisbon's museums, see the **National Museum of Art** (Rua das Janelas Verdes) with paintings by European masters and a collection of 15th- and 16th-century Portuguese primitives. The **Gulbenkian Foundation** (Avenida de Berna) houses the superb art collection of the late oil magnate Calouste Gulbenkian. The works range from ancient Egyptian to the French Impressionists. The Gulbenkian Center also has many special exhibits which are worth checking when visiting. In the **Ricardo Espirito Santo Foundation,** a museum of the decorative arts in the Alfama district, you can see reproductions of antique furniture. Museums are open 10am-5pm, closed Mondays and public holidays.

At **Belém,** a riverside suburb on the western outskirts of the city, the impressive **Jerónimos Monastery Church** marks the place where Portugal's great navigators began their voyages of discovery in the 15th and 16th centuries. The church is a perfect example of the ornate Gothic style called Manueline after the king (Manuel I) who reigned when Portugal was expanding the known frontiers of the world. The **tomb of Vasco da Gama** is inside. At the river's edge are the 16th-century **Tower of**

Belém, another fine example of Manueline style, and the modern **Monument to the Discoveries.** Nearby is the **Museum of Popular Art,** which houses an attractive collection of regional arts and crafts, and adjoining the Jerónimos Church is the **Naval Museum** with a collection of models, paintings, and artifacts illustrating Portuguese maritime history. A few blocks east of the church, adjoining the 18th-century **Belém Palace** that is the official residence of the president, is the **Coach Museum,** with a famed collection of 16th-, 17th-, and 18th-century coaches displayed in what was once the palace riding school.

Parks and gardens to enjoy are **Parque Eduardo VII** and, in it, the **Estufa Fria** (Cold Greenhouse) which uses wooden slats rather than glass to regulate light and temperature; the **Estrela Gardens;** and the **Zoo,** which has a reputation for rearing rare young animals in captivity.

Near Lisbon: The **Costa do Sol** is west of the city. **Estoril,** 15 miles from Lisbon and reached by electric train from Cais do Sodre station, is a sophisticated beach resort, the chosen home in exile of European royalty. Centerpiece of the resort is the **Parque do Estoril,** formal gardens leading from the railway station at the water's edge up to the **Casino,** where there are bars, restaurant, nightclub, and a cinema, in addition to the gaming rooms. **Cascais,** a few miles farther along the coast, is the last stop on the electric railway line. It remains an unspoiled fishing village despite the growing popularity of its beaches. Wednesday morning, when the open-air market is in full swing, is a good time to visit. At **Guincho,** beyond Cascais where the Costa do Sol rounds the headland to meet the open Atlantic, the sea is rough and dramatic with a dangerous undercurrent, but the beach is a vast stretch of golden sand. At its end is **Cabo do Rocha,** the westernmost point of Europe.

Away from the coast, 9 miles northwest of Lisbon, **Queluz** has the small but charming 18th-century rococo **Queluz Palace,** surrounded by formal gardens. Visiting dignitaries are housed here, and there is a restaurant in the palace kitchen. **Sintra,** 15 miles northwest of Lisbon, has the **National Palace,** begun in the 16th century and a former summer home of Portuguese kings—the azulejo tiles are among the finest in Portugal. The **Pena Palace,** also at Sintra, dates from the 19th century. It is set in the midst of the rare plants of its own palace grounds and those of the nearby **Monserrate Gardens.**

Setúbal, 25 miles southeast of Lisbon, is reached by road across the suspension bridge spanning the Tagus. It has, among many points of interest, the **Church of Jesus,** the ruins of **Cetobriga,** the **Castelo de São Filipe** (now a *pousadá*), the medieval fortress of **Palmela,** and the marketplaces. Near Setúbal lies the beautiful beach of **Portinho da Arrábida,** which can be reached by driving through the hills of the **Arrábida National Park.**

The Algarve: The Algarve coast in the south of Portugal, stretching 100 miles from the Spanish border to Cape St Vincent in the west, is Portugal's main vacation area. The coast is dotted with small resorts, hotels, and villas.

Among the places to visit (moving from east to west) is **Monte Gordo,** a resort with a good beach (further to the west, it becomes rocky and dramatic). Hotels in Monte Gordo are **Das Caravelas** (from US$43 double MAP) and **Vasco da Gama** (from US$85 double MAP). **Praia da Rocha** on the western stretch of the Algarve is one of the finest towns in the area to be developed into a resort. **Faro** is the area's capital and has some lovely old churches around its harbor. **Faro beach,** about 5 kilometers away, is a long sandy shoal with a sheltered lagoon behind it and is a good area for water-skiing. A good place to stay is the **Eva Hotel** (from US$34 double). **Albufeira** is the main resort on the coast, with many bars, boutiques, and hotels, including the **Balaia** (from US$73 double) and the **Boa Vista Hotel** (from US$30 double). Older towns now developing satellite resorts around them include **Lagoa,** a town that makes inexpensive pottery and wine; **Carvoeiro,** where foreigners buy fishermen's houses and where there are good restaurants; and **Lagos,** where Henry the Navigator built fortifications. The coast culminates in the rugged squared-off cliffs around **Cape Saint Vincent,** a superb viewpoint to watch shipping vessels pass by and see the old lighthouse. Inland, **Loulé** is a market town known for its typical tall chimneys, its old market, and the shops where locals make copperware. **Silves** is an ancient Moorish town of narrow streets climbing up to a massive restored castle which dominates the skyline. **Monchique** is a spa town high in the hills which back the coast and is worth visiting for the spectacular views. Among restaurants worth trying are **Aquario** and **Alfaghar** in Faro; **Jose Roque** on Faro beach, a simple fishermen's restaurant but excellent value; **Jul Bar, Alfredo's,** and **Boa Vista** at Albufeira (there are plenty of nightclubs here); **O Patio** and **O Bistro** and **Togi's** at Carvoeiro, **Sete Marés** at Portimão, and **Rouxinol** on the road to Monchique.

Northern Portugal: Moving north on the straight coastal roads from Lisbon, there is the charming area of fishing-village resorts of which **Nazaré** is the best known. You can stay at the **Dom Fuas Hotel** (from US$32 double). Visits can be made to the great monasteries of Portugal: **Mafra, Batalha,** and **Alcobaça.** Nearby is **Fátima,** Portugal's famous Christian shrine (105 miles northeast of Lisbon). Pilgrimages to the sanctuary are made on the 13th of each month, and the crowds are especially large from May to October.

The center of romantic Portugal, associated with her famous poet Camões, is **Coimbra,** the university town, with narrow streets climbing a steep hill. Here you can buy the famous blue pottery copied from 17th- and 18th-century designs and see the collection of jewelry and sculpture in the **Machado de Castro** museum. For children, there is the **Portugal dos Pequeninos,** a park of reproductions of famous Portuguese buildings big enough for children to enter. Accommodations can be found at the **Astoria Hotel** (from US$38 double) and the **Braganca Hotel** (from US$13 double). If you want the luxury of staying in a palace (open in summer only), there is the **Palacio Hotel** at Buçaco, set in a very lush and wooded area. In this district is **Viseu,** the capital of the Beira Alta, where the cathedral square, with its marvelous 16th-century churches and palace, is an excellent example of Portuguese architecture. In the palace are paintings by Vasco Fernandes. The **Grao Vasco Hotel** will put you up for US$48 minimum in a double room. **Oporto** is Portugal's second city and is said to have given its name to the country. The city is split by the river Douro, which makes a deep gorge here spanned by some impressive iron bridges. On the other side is **Vila Nova da Gaia,** where all the port houses are situated. These welcome visitors and are generous in their sampling facilities. Details of the visits can be obtained from the Port Wine Institute, Rua de Ferreira Borges. The Oporto people eat well and heartily. Recommended restaurants are at the **Hotel Infante Sagres, Escondidinho, Tres Irmaos,** and **Montenegro.** At **Leça** on the river mouth there are several good seafood restaurants, such as **Boa Nova, Garrafão,** and **Bem Arranjadinho.** In the **Foz do Douro** area are nightclubs and discothèques.

Outside Oporto, the mountains of the **Douro River** area rise rugged, harsh, and inhospitable, though they provide the grapes for the production of port. North beyond this, the country becomes lush and gentle around the rivers of the **Cavado Lima** and **Minho,** and along the coast there are small resorts like **Ofir, Esposende,** and then **Viana do Castelo,** which has the excellent **Santa Luzia Hotel,** perched on a hill overlooking the town (from US$40 double). Inland one can follow the Lima to **Barcelos,** where the characteristic brown and yellow pottery is produced. Near here is the ancient town of **Braga.**

Madeira: This beautiful Portuguese island is 600 miles southwest of the mainland and 1½ hours away by air. It has mild temperatures year round and is the home of the famous Madeira wines. Mountainous, and intensely cultivated and terraced, the island produces—besides the grapes—tropical fruits and a profusion of flowers, enough so that it is sometimes described as the floating garden of the Atlantic. **Funchal,** where a third of the population of approximately 300,000 lives, is a city of narrow, cobblestoned streets and the capital. Madeira is a quiet spot for a relaxed vacation of sightseeing, walking, swimming, fishing, and water sports. Though the island has only one beach, at **Prainha** near Canical, all major hotels have pools, many heated, and often built at the edge of the sea to allow a dip in either. Among the things to see and do, a most unusual excursion is the trip to the villages of **Monte** or **Terreiro da Luta** for the magnificent view over Funchal, then the return to the city via the *carro*—a 2-mile toboggan slide downhill over cobblestones worn smooth from the days when hill villages used to send their produce to market this way. This ride is made in a large basket on wooden runners with two men keeping pace alongside to control the trip by means of ropes.

In Funchal, visit the **Mercado dos Lavradores,** liveliest early in the day. The stalls of costumed flower vendors are at the entrance to the market, and the bustling fish market is nearby. See also the **Museum of Sacred Art** with a display of the island's church treasures; **Quinta** das Cruzes, an old villa housing a collection of 16th-century Portuguese furniture, with an orchid house attached; the **Municipal Museum** and **Aquarium;** the **Se Cathedral.** For a taste of Madeira, there are many wine "lodges" in the city, or stop at the showroom of the **Madeira Wine Association.** For a broad selection of local handicrafts including the island's famous embroidery, tapestries, and wickerwork, visit the **Casa do Turista.**

Outside of town, there are walking tours mapped by the Tourist Office, many following the old *levada* system of irrigation channels. Starting points are scattered throughout the island and the walks range from 1 to 10 miles in length. A half-day excursion not to be missed is the drive to **Porto Moniz,** a picturesque fishing village at the northwest corner of Madeira, with spectacular scenery along the way. In the center of the island, closer to Funchal, is the village of **Curral das Freiras,** nestled among high mountain peaks. **Porto Santo,** 25 miles north of Madeira, is a smaller, flatter island with a 4-mile sand beach along its south shore. In Madeira, stay at the **Casino Park Hotel,** Avenida do Infante (from US$70 double), the **Madeira Palacio,** Estrada Monumental (from US$70 double), the **Madeira Sheraton,** Largo Antonio Nobre (from US$88 double), or **Reid's,** Estrada Monumental (from US$148 double MAP). All except the Madeira Palacio are within easy walking distance of town. The island's **Casino** is next door to the Casino Park and if you wish to try your luck, remember to take your passport with you.

The Azores: These nine islands with a population of nearly 300,000 are 800 miles from the mainland, or 2 hours by air. **São Miguel** is the largest, and **Ponta Delgada** on São Miguel is the capital and largest city of this archipelago of farmers and fishermen. The Azores have been known since the 15th century and played a part in the great voyages of discovery to the New World. Several expeditions set off from here and Christopher Columbus dropped anchor on his return from his first voyage to America. The islands are volcanic in origin, full of hot springs, extinct craters, and crater lakes. According to legend, one of the latter— the **Caldeira das Sete Cidades** on São Miguel—is the watery grave of one of the seven lost cities of Atlantis. Coastlines in the Azores are indented with inlets and bays, there are sandy beaches, the climate is mild, the soil fertile, and the vegetation luxuriant. Hydrangeas especially are characteristic and in all colors they break through the carpet of green on every island. Besides São Miguel, the islands include **Terceira,** with **Angra do Heroismo,** the oldest town in the Azores (1534); **Santa Maria; Faial,** known for its yacht harbor; **Pico,** with the highest peak and the well-known *verdelho* wine; **São Jorge; Graciosa,** with its windmills; and remote **Flores** and **Corvo** islands. There are international airports on Santa Maria and Terceira, and on São Miguel there are connections with the mainland; other airports are served by inter-island flights only. Accommodations are in 4- and 3-star hotels on São Miguel, Terceira, and Faial; in smaller hotels and boarding houses on the other islands.

SOURCES OF FURTHER INFORMATION

Pan Am, Praça dos Restauradores 46, Lisbon, and any Pan Am office round the world; **Portuguese National Tourist Board,** Avenida Antonio Augusto Aguiar 86, Lisbon; **Portuguese National Tourist Office,** 548 Fifth Avenue, New York, NY 10036; New Bond Street House, 1/5 New Bond Street, London W1Y ODB.

Romania

WHAT'S SPECIAL

Romania's landscape resembles a natural citadel; the Carpathian Mountains at its center descend step-like toward its plains, which are crisscrossed with rivers. Romania has the tideless Black Sea with its magnificent beaches, the Danube Delta, lakes, and several rivers. The spring offers flowers and festivals; the summer, sun and sea; the autumn, harvest festivals; and the winter, snow and skiing in the mountains.

COUNTRY BRIEFING

Size: 91,699 square miles   **Population:** 22,300,000

Capital: Bucharest   **Capital Population:** 1,832,000

   Climate: Dry, hot, sunny summers; cold, dry winters (with heavy, periodic snowfalls in the mountains). Long, mild, and sunny autumns; spring is sunny too, but with more rainfall.

Weather in Bucharest: Lat N44°25; Alt 269 ft

Temp (°F)	Jan	Feb	Mar	Apr	May	Jun	Jul	Aug	Sep	Oct	Nov	Dec
Av Low	20°	24°	33°	41°	51°	58°	61°	60°	53°	44°	35°	26°
Av High	33°	38°	51°	63°	74°	81°	86°	86°	76°	65°	49°	37°
Days no rain	25	23	25	24	23	21	24	26	25	26	24	25

   Government: Socialist republic.

   Language: The Romanian language is Latin-based and is related to French, Italian, Spanish, and Portuguese. French widely spoken; English becoming more so.

Religion: Most believers are Romanian Orthodox; remainder are Roman Catholics, Lutherans, Jews, and Muslims.

Currency: Leu. 100 bani = 1 leu (plural lei).

Rate of exchange is official exchange rate for tourists.

	50 b	1 Leu	5 Lei	10 Lei	50 Lei	100 Lei	500 Lei	1,000 Lei
US (dollars, cents)	.03	.07	.33	.67	3.33	6.67	33.33	66.67
UK (pounds, pence)	.01	.03	.16	.32	1.58	3.18	15.90	31.80

Public Holidays:

New Year, 1-2 Jan   Liberation Day, 23 and 24

Labor Days, 1 and 2 May   Aug

HOW TO GET THERE

Flying time to Bucharest's Otopeni Airport from New York is 10 hours; from Frankfurt, 2½ hours; from Belgrade, 55 minutes. Time in Romania: GMT+2.

REQUIREMENTS FOR ENTRY AND CUSTOMS REGULATIONS

A tourist visa is obtainable at a Romanian Embassy abroad or at frontier points and Romanian airports. There is no visa fee for citizens of the US or other countries that have a waiver agreement with Romania; in other cases the visa fee is the equivalent of US$5.50. With a tourist visa, at least US$10 or the equivalent must be exchanged per person per day. Tourists entering Romania individually or in groups with prepaid arrangements for the duration of their stay and confirmations issued by travel agencies are exempt from this mandatory per diem exchange. It is also not imposed if the visitor possesses a business visa, an official invitation to visit Romania, is of Romanian origin, or is a long- or short-term resident of the country returning from a visit abroad. Children under 14 years of age are also exempt. It is advisable not to change large sums into local currency, as many purchases are made in dollars. Exchange receipts should be kept until leaving the country. No round-trip ticket or vaccination certificates are required (unless you are coming from an infected area). No Romanian currency may be imported or exported, and on departure local currency must be reconverted and the official receipt for the original transaction must be produced. You may bring in personal articles, including jewelry, two cameras with 24 rolls or cassettes of film, a small movie camera with two reels of film, pair of binoculars, portable radio, tape recorder, television set, a portable typewriter, and personal sports equipment. Duty-free allowance: 2 liters whisky, 5 liters wine, 300 cigarettes, presents valued up to 2,000 lei, medicines as necessary for the duration of the stay. Antiquities and art objects of great value can be taken out of the country only with the permission of the competent museum authorities.

AIRPORT INFORMATION

Otopeni Airport is 12 miles from the center of Bucharest. Bus fare from airport is 8 lei, but because the city terminal is not centrally located, it is advisable to take a taxi, fare about US$16-18. The airport has a children's nursery, duty-free shop, hotel reservation counter, tourist information desk, and currency exchange bureau.

ACCOMMODATIONS

A range from the luxurious **Inter · Continental Hotel** in Bucharest to country inns, villas, motels, student hostels, and camping sites. Except for top hotels in Bucharest, there is a general reduction of 25% between 15 October and 15 December, and again from early March to end of May in the mountains. Confirmation of reservations is essential. Hotels in Bucharest:

Rates are in US$ for a double/twin room with bath or shower

Astoria, 27 Boulevard Dinicu Golescu (from $46 CP)

Athénée Palace, 1-3 Strada Episcopiei (from $72 CP)

Cişmigiu, 18 Boulevard Gheorghiu-Dej (from $15 CP)

Continental, Calea Victoriei 56 (from $65 CP)

Dorobanţi, 1 Calea Dorobanţi (from $52 CP)

Hanul lui Manuc, 5 Strada 30 Decembrie (from $36 CP)

INTER · CONTINENTAL BUCHAREST, 4 Boulevard Nicolae Balcescu (from $94)

Lido, 5 Boulevard Magheru (from $60 CP)

Modern, 46 Boulevard Republicii (from $36 CP)

Negoiu, 16 Strada 13 Decembrie (from $29 CP)

Nord, 143 Calea Grivitei (from $52.50 CP)

Parc, 3 Boulevard Poligrafiei (from $36 CP), near exhibition grounds

Union, 11 Strada 13 Decembrie (from $36 CP)

All hotels centrally located unless otherwise indicated. Confirmation of reservations is essential.

USEFUL INFORMATION

Helpful Hints: Handshaking is a common form of greeting. Gallant Romanian men frequently kiss women's hands. Children welcome in all public places.

Banks: Money can be changed at the National Bank of Romania (25 Strada Lipscani), the Romanian Bank for Foreign Trade (3 Strada Eugen Carada), at Carpati tourist offices at frontier points and within the country, and at bank desks in the large hotels. Bank checks, letters of credit, and payment orders can be cashed only at offices of the National Bank or the Romanian Bank for Foreign Trade. Hotel and border exchange desks generally open from 7:30am-10pm.

Mail: Stamps at cigarette and newspaper kiosks, hotels. Mailboxes *(Posta)* are orange-yellow.

Telephone Tips: Phones in restaurants, cafés, candy stores, hotels, and in streets. Useful numbers in Bucharest:

Pan Am 13 63 60	**Carpati Head Office** 14 51 60
Airport Information 33 31 37	**Overseas Calls** 090
International Tourist Service	**Directories** 131
Agency 14 19 22	**Time** 058

Newspapers: US and UK newspapers are available; *Lumea* (The World), and *Romanian News* are local English-language publications.

Tipping: Not customary, but for special services something like a pack of cigarettes is appreciated. Tipping is also sometimes helpful in obtaining a hotel reservation.

Electricity: 220 volts 50 cycles AC.

Laundry: Dry-cleaning and laundry efficient in all main hotels (from 40 lei to dry-clean a suit; from 3.50 lei to launder a shirt).

Hairdressing: Salons in first-class hotels (shampoo and set, from 25 lei; man's haircut from 10 lei).

Photography: Black and white, color and movie film available in big towns and resorts. Roll of black and white, from 17 lei; color from 30-40 lei. Five to ten days to develop color; less for black and white.

Babysitting: Services can be arranged in first-class hotels. Some hotels, mainly at sea resorts, have play areas for children.

Rest Rooms: In hotels and places of entertainment and street conveniences. Women, *WC Femei;* men *WC Bărbați.*

Health: Your hotel will get you a doctor (or dentist) who can speak English. Toiletries and pharmaceuticals widely available and inexpensive, though some medicines are sold only on prescription. Drinking water safe.

TRANSPORTATION

Metered taxis can be hailed in the street or ordered in advance through hotel porters. Buses, trolley buses, and streetcars operate in cities, but tend to be very crowded. There are good rail links with the main towns. Unlimited travel tickets *(bilet in circuit)* can be purchased from railroad terminals. Tarom, the state airline, links major cities. Chauffeur-driven cars available at US$50 per day. Speed limit in built-up areas 60 kmh; in open country, 80-100 kmh.

FOOD AND RESTAURANTS

Spicy, aromatic dishes of pork, chicken, and smoked sausage accompanied by *mămăligă* (corn meal cooked firm) are typical of Romanian cuisine. Sample *sărmăluțe in foi de vița* (ground meat wrapped in vine leaves, sprinkled with borscht, and served with sour cream or yoghurt); *pui la ceaun* (chicken cooked slowly in a rich garlic sauce in a cast-iron pot). Try also grilled beluga and pike or carp on a spit. You can afford Romanian caviar. In the brasseries and cafés try savory sausage, paté *ghiveci călugăresc* (monk's hotchpotch—vegetables cooked in oil); *mămăligă* with cheese, cream, or eggs; *bulzul* (a ball of *mămăligă* stuffed with cheese and butter). Meals are usually rounded off with fresh fruit and cream, ice cream, or pastries (cheese pancakes, plum puddings, brioche, or sweetmeats like *baclava* and *sarailie*). Bucharest restaurants in the first-class hotels are good, or have a meal in one of the open-air restaurants in summer or fall. Open-air Romanian evenings are a specialty of the **Pădurea Baneasa** restaurant in the forest just outside the city (60 Ploiești Road), with folk singing and dancing. **Carul cu Bere** (Beer Wagon) at 3

Stavropoleos Street is worth a visit, also the **Crama cu Vin** (Wine Cellar) in its basement. At **La Doi Cocoşi** (The Two Roosters), 6 Străuleşti Street, specialties include chicken and home-baked bread. For music as you dine try **Berlin** (4 Strada Constantin Mille), with Romanian as well as German cuisine; **Bucur** (2 Strada Poenaru Bordea); **Doina** (4 Şoseaua Kiseleff), which is in a park and has an open garden dining area during warm weather. Many consider **Bucuresti** (26 Calea Victoriei) the best traditional Romanian restaurant in the city, and good Romanian food can also be found at **Cina** (1 Strada C.A. Rossetti) near the Athénée Palace Hotel. An interesting place to eat is **Hanul lui Manuc** (in the hotel of the same name), which is a complex of three different restaurants. A good seafood restaurant is **Pescăruş** (Parcul Herăstrău) in Bucharest on the lakefront. The price of a good meal with wine averages around 160 lei per person.

DRINKING TIPS

The national drink *Tuica* (plum brandy) is potent straight and is served as an aperitif. There are several excellent *vins du pays,* five kinds of brandy, and several liqueurs. Imported liquor is fairly expensive. No special liquor licensing laws.

ENTERTAINMENT

Romanians are proud of their opera, theater, ballet, and symphony orchestras. Every major city has its own concert hall, opera house, and theater. Bucharest has 58 movie houses and 25 theaters and concert halls. The most notable theater companies are those of the **LS Bulandra Theater,** the **National Theater,** and the **Jewish State Theater of Bucharest.** Symphony concerts are given in the beautiful **Athenaeum** concert hall. Movie houses are open from 10am. *Tăndarică* is a type of Romanian Punch and Judy show. To dance and see a floorshow, go to the Athénée Palace (1 Strada Episcopiei), the **Atlantic** (35-37 Strada Colonadelor), the **Melody** (4 Strada Pictor Verona), and the **Balada,** on the Inter • Continental Bucharest Hotel roof.

SHOPPING

Stores open 9-1 and 4-8 Mon-Sat; some open Sunday mornings from 8am-noon. In the capital a trip to the **Lipscani** street market should not be missed. Shop at **Comtourist** shops, where you get 20% discount on purchases made with foreign currency. In Bucharest they're located at 48 Strada Mendeleev, 5 and 7 Boulevard Magheru, 21 and 25 Strada Academici, 40 and 87 Calea Victoriei, 11 Calea Dorobanţi, 137 Calea Griviţei, 40-44 Strada 30 Decembrie, and 30 Boulevard Nicolae Bălcescu. Main department stores in Bucharest are **Unirea** (1 Piaţa Unirii), **Victoria** (17 Calea Victoriei), **Cocor** (33 Boulevard 1848), and **Bucur** (2 Şoscaua Colentina). In these, a 20% discount is given on purchases made in lei if you present the exchange receipt.

SPORTS

Romanians, with a fine Davis Cup record, are addicted to tennis. You can get a game in all the Black Sea resorts, municipal parks, and sports clubs. Prices are moderate and include showers. Black Sea resorts offer safe swimming and lots of beach games and aquatic sports. A chain of lakes at the northern end of Bucharest provide good beaches and water sports. Best areas for horseback riding enthusiasts are **Bucharest, Ploiesti, Poiana Braşov, Timişoara,** and **Mangalia.** Mountain climbers, and in winter, ski and bobsled buffs, make for the **Carpathians.** On the **Danube Delta** there is fishing and bird-watching.

WHAT TO SEE

Bucharest has been called "the Paris of the Balkans." It has beautiful gardens and parks and lakes, and just beyond are woods and forests. Things to see include the **Stavropoleos Church,** the neo-classical **Romanian Atheneum,** and **Mogoşoaia Palace,** now a museum of feudal art, about 12 miles away. The **Arts Museum** houses works of the 19th-century Grigorescu, Romania's foremost painter, with medieval, traditional, and modern works. There are also the **Minovici Museum,** the **Ethnography & Folk Art Museum,** the **Museum of Romanian History,** and the **Village Museum,** which has examples of village architecture from all over the country. See also the **Hanul lui Manuc,** a restaurant and hotel with verandas, galleries, and belvederes.

The Black Sea: **Constanta,** a popular resort in itself, is the stepping stone to the other resorts along the coast, and is a 4-hour drive or 25-minute flight from Bucharest. Eat seafood at the **Pescarul,** Dobrogea Pie and shish kebab at the **Dobrogea Wine Cellar,** and fishermen's patties washed down with the local Murfatlar wine at the **Furnica.** Stay at the **Continental Hotel,** 20 Boulevard Republicii, or the **Palace Hotel,** 5 Strada Remus Opreanu (both from US$26 double). Visit the **Archeological Museum,** the **Roman mosaic,** and the **Statue of Ovid,** the Latin poet who spent the last years of his life here in about 17 AD. About 40 miles to the north of Constanta lie the ruins of the ancient city of **Histria,** built in the 6th century BC by Greek colonists. At **Adamclisi,** about 40 miles in the opposite direction, is the **Tropaeum Trajani** erected by the triumphant Romans 1,800 years ago. From Constanta 1- and 2-day excursions are run by the National Tourist Office along the coast into the **Danube Delta** and **Central Moldavia.** See the painted monasteries of **Bucovina,** whose colors are undimmed after almost 500 years, and the natural wonder of the **Bicaz Gorge.** From **Mamaia,** 3 miles from Constanta, stretch some 38 miles of broad flat beach along which are strung resorts full of modern Miami-type hotels. Best-known are **Saturn, Neptun, Cap Aurora, Jupiter,** and **Venus.** Mamaia, on a tongue of land between the sea and **Lake Siutghiol,** is probably the most popular and lively of the resorts. Not far away is the quieter spa resort of **Eforie Nord,** where health enthusiasts can try their first mud bath, rinsing off in the warm therapeutic waters of **Lake Techirghiol.** Romanian spas and health resorts, mineral springs, and mud baths are world-renowned for their therapeutic value. Other popular year-round health resorts are **Mangalia,** also on the Black Sea, **Băile Felix** in Transylvania, and **Băile Herculane** in Banat.

Braşov, just over 100 miles from Bucharest, in the Transylvanian section of the Carpathians, is Romania's second city and a good tourist center. Stay at the **Carpaţi** (double from US$50), or there is the **Postăvarul Hotel,** 2 Politehnicii Street (from US$28 double).

Also in Transylvania is the well-preserved medieval town of **Sighişoara. Timişoara,** the town of gardens, is particularly attractive because of its picturesque parks, old quarters and baroque public buildings, and its many historical monuments. **Cluj-Napoca,** with a rich historical past, is one of Romania's largest industrial and cultural centers.

SOURCES OF FURTHER INFORMATION

Pan Am, Inter·Continental Hotel, Bucharest, and any Pan Am office around the world; **Carpati National Tourism Office,** 7 Boulevard Magheru, Bucharest; **Romanian National Tourist Office,** 573 Third Avenue, New York, NY 10016; 98-99 Jermyn Street, London SW1.

Spain

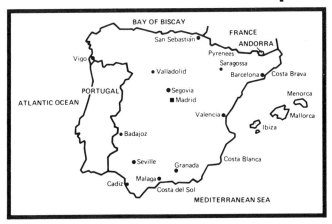

WHAT'S SPECIAL

There is an excitingly "different" feeling about Spain, with its sunny beaches, rich art galleries, grandiose churches, fiestas, and bullfights. Somehow the Pyrenees seem much more than just a physical separation between Spain and the rest of Europe. Two totally different religious cultures have gone into its making—the Roman Catholic, whose fervor launched the Inquisition, and the Muslim, legacy of 700 years of Moorish rule (711-1492). The Spanish temperament as a result is a mixture of flamboyance, passion, and sentiment. It is only when travelers sample Spain's wide variety of climate and scenery and see the tremendous contrast between ancient cities and thriving tourist hotels that they realize just how big this country is and how deep its feelings.

COUNTRY BRIEFING

Size: 197,897 square miles   **Population:** 38,719,648
Capital: Madrid   **Capital Population:** 3,368,466

Climate: Mediterranean. It can be rainy on the northern Atlantic and Cantabrian coasts. Madrid, with very hot summers and snow in the mountains in winter, is best visited in spring or fall.

Weather in Madrid: Lat N40°25'; Alt 2,188 ft

Temp (°F)	Jan	Feb	Mar	Apr	May	Jun	Jul	Aug	Sep	Oct	Nov	Dec
Av Low	33°	35°	40°	44°	50°	57°	62°	62°	56°	48°	40°	35°
Av High	47°	51°	57°	64°	71°	80°	87°	86°	77°	66°	54°	48°
Days no rain	22	19	20	21	22	24	28	29	24	23	20	22

Government: Constitutional monarchy.
Language: Spanish.
Religion: Predominantly Roman Catholic.
Currency: Peseta. 100 centimos = 1 peseta.

	5 ptas	25 ptas	50 ptas	100 ptas	500 ptas	1000 ptas	2000 ptas	3000 ptas
US (dollars, cents)	.05	.27	.55	1.10	5.48	10.96	21.92	32.88
UK (pounds, pence)	.02	.13	.26	.53	2.62	5.24	10.48	15.71

Public Holidays:

New Year's Day, 1 Jan
Epiphany, 6 Jan
St Joseph's Day, 19 Mar
Maundy Thursday
Good Friday
May Day, 1 May

Corpus Christi
St James's Day, 25 July
Assumption Day, 15 Aug
Columbus Day, 12 Oct
Immaculate Conception, 8 Dec
Christmas Day, 25 Dec

HOW TO GET THERE

Flying time to Madrid, Barajas Airport from New York is 6 hours; from London, 1 hour; from Frankfurt, 1½ hours; from Casablanca, 2½ hours. Time in Spain GMT+1.

REQUIREMENTS FOR ENTRY AND CUSTOMS REGULATIONS

Passport. Vaccination certificates for smallpox, cholera, and yellow fever necessary only if coming from an infected area. Up to 50,000ptas may be brought into the country and 3,000 taken out. Spain is very strict on drug control. Duty-free allowance: 200 cigarettes or 50 cigars or 250 grams tobacco; 1 bottle liquor and 1 bottle wine; small quantity of perfume for personal use; gifts—no duty-free allowance. There are duty-free shops in international airports for out-bound passengers.

AIRPORT INFORMATION

Barajas Airport is 9 miles outside Madrid, to which it is connected by a frequent airport bus, price 80ptas. Taxis with a meter are available to and from the airport for about 500ptas to most hotels. Barcelona airport is 7½ miles from the city center. No departure tax.

ACCOMMODATIONS

Spanish hotels are still among the best bargains in Europe, and you get what you pay for. First-class hotels have all modern conveniences. Less expensive hotels are not air-conditioned and can be oppressive in summer. To supply the need for accommodations in country areas, the government has set up luxurious *paradores* (often converted palaces), *albergues* (or wayside inns) intended for stops not exceeding 48 hours, and *refugios,* mountain cabins in remote and mountain areas. Pensions average US$20-30, and hostels are divided into three classes with prices beginning at US$10. Most hotels offer breakfast from 80-350ptas. Madrid hotels, centrally located unless otherwise indicated, include:

Rates are in US$ for a double/twin room with bath or shower
Agumar, Reina Cristina 9 (from $37)
Barajas, Barajas, Madrid 22 (from $71), at the airport
Castellana, Paseo de la Castellana 57 (from $53)
Colon, Doctor Esquerdo 117-119 (from $37), 20 minutes from downtown
Emperador, Avenida José Antonia 53 (from $47)
Eurobuilding, Padre Damián 23 (from $97), 20 minutes from downtown
Gran Hotel Velázquez, Velázquez 62 (from $35)
Luz Palacio, Paseo de la Castellana 67 (from $81)
Melia Castilla, Capitan Haya s/n (from $81), 20 minutes from downtown
Mindanao, San Francisco de Sales 15 (from $72), 20 minutes from downtown
Monte Real, Arroyo Fresno 17 (from $89), 25 minutes from downtown
Palace, Plaza Cortes 7 (from $83)
Plaza, Plaza de España 8 (from $61)
Principe Pio, Onésimo Redondo 16 (from $40)
Ritz, Paseo del Prado 5 (from $122)
San Antonio de la Florida, Paseo de la Florida 13 (from $109)
Sanvy, Calle Goya 3 (from $23)
Sideral, Casado del Alisal 14 (from $51)
Villa Magna, Paseo de la Castellana 22 (from $118)
Wellington, Velázquez 8 (from $74)

USEFUL INFORMATION

Helpful Hints: Siesta is from 1:30-4:30, when stores, offices, museums, and even churches are closed, in most of Spain. Always dress respectfully in churches. Wearing beach attire off the beach is discouraged, especially in northern Spain, but possible on the Costa Brava and Costa del Sol.

Banks: Open 9-2 Mon-Fri, 9-1 Sat in summer. There are banks in all towns, and currency and travelers' checks can be changed by travel agents, American Express, and hotels.

Mail: Stamps can be bought at tobacconists, known as *estancos,* and at post offices *(oficinas de correos).* Mailboxes are yellow cylinders. The main post office in Cibeles Plaza in Madrid stays open until midnight.

Telephone Tips: In restaurants, cafés, and booths in *telefónicas,* public telephone buildings. Telephones are coin and token operated. To use, insert 5ptas and dial. Tokens are obtained from cashier or coat attendant. Restaurants and hotels will get your number for you. Useful numbers in Madrid:

Directories 003	**Pan Am** 241 42 00
Foreign Telephone Information 051	**Airport Information** 231
Police 091	4436
Operator 0	**Ambulance** 252 3264

Newspapers: English-language newspapers and magazines are available, and a local publication is the *Iberian Daily Sun.*

Tipping: Restaurants—5-10% in addition to the 15% service charge; taxis—10-15%; porters—25ptas per bag; hotel porters—25ptas per bag; chambermaid—100ptas; cinema usher—10ptas; hairdressers and barbers, 10-15%.

Electricity: 110-120 volts 50 cycles AC. New buildings have 220 volts. Many hotels have converters.

Laundry: Plenty of dry-cleaners, but few laundries, although some laundromats are in the main cities. Hotels and "Express" dry-cleaners provide a 24-hour service (from 225ptas to dry-clean a suit; from 75ptas to launder a shirt).

Hairdressing: First-class hotels have salons. Cost is from 400ptas for shampoo and set; man's haircut from 250ptas.

Photography: Equipment available, but fairly expensive. One-day developing service possible, but usually it takes up to 4 days.

Babysitting: Services are usually arranged through the hotel or in Barcelona contact El Canguro (Amigo 18—tel: 227 4989). Babysitters must be accompanied home or given taxi money.

Health: Except in Madrid, use bottled water and peel all fruit. Few doctors or dentists speak English, but there is a British-American hospital at Calle Del Limite, University City, Madrid. Imported pharmaceuticals available but expensive.

TRANSPORTATION

Madrid has buses which are crowded, microbuses (only slightly more expensive and you can get off between stops), and a subway which costs only 15ptas per ride (25ptas on Sunday). Ticket books for the bus are available in central bus stations. Taxis have meters (the only extras are for luggage—10ptas per bag) and can be hailed in the street. At night they show a green light when free. Rental cars are readily available. Roads are adequate, driving is on the right, and horn blowing and U-turns are forbidden in major cities. Intercity bus services are limited, but in summer long-distance tourist buses operate to major towns. Trains serve all areas, but second-class travel is primitive and overcrowded. The Eurailpass is accepted in Spain. To avoid endless standing in line at stations, buy tickets at travel agencies. Iberia Airlines flies to Barcelona, Valencia, Malaga, Seville, and several other cities.

FOOD AND RESTAURANTS

Mealtimes are late, especially in Madrid. Lunch is between 1:30 and 4 and dinner 8:30-11:30. As compensation, drinks are often accompanied by *tapas,* delicious hors d'oeuvre-type tidbits: in Madrid ask for a *chato,* a glass of wine with *tapas.* Regional specialties such as the Valencian *paella,* saffron-flavored rice with chicken and shellfish, can usually be found throughout the city. *Gazpacho,* an iced soup made with tomatoes, oil, garlic, and lemon, is delicious in the heat of summer. *Zarzuela,* seafood with sauce, is one of the many excellent fish dishes, and *calamares,* deep-fried squid, is another. *Cocido* is a rich casserole of chicken, meat, sausage, and chickpeas. The average meal comprises four courses: soup, vegetables, fish or eggs, fish or meat, and a dessert. An expensive meal costs $22, medium-priced restaurants charge about $9, and inexpensive ones $5 (per person). *Tabernas* are small cafés serving primarily drink, but their food is excellent and can be as little as $3.00.

Restaurants in Madrid: Between 15 July and 1 September, many restaurants in Madrid are closed for holidays; first-class ones are closed in August, and a few remain closed through the first week in September. **Puerta de Moros** (Calle Don Pedro 10—tel: 265 3035) is a first-class international restaurant in a converted palace; its specialty is *pollo al barco* (baked chicken) and game. The **Jockey** (Amador de Los Ríos 6—tel: 419 1003) is an elegant and expensive establishment serving superb smoked salmon. The **Horcher** (Alfonso XII 6—tel: 222 0731) is renowned for its excellent German cuisine. **Lucio** (Cava Baja 35—tel: 265 3252) has a lively atmosphere and an elite clientele; reservations necessary. Some restaurants well above average are **Club 31** (Alcalá 58—tel: 231 0092) for international food; **Charlot** (Serrano 70—tel: 225 6577), Art Nouveau-decorated with excellent French and Spanish cuisine; **Las Lanzas** (Espalter 8 y 10—tel: 230 5079), specializing in Madrilenian cuisine; **Lhardy** (Carrera de San Jerónimo 8—tel: 221 3385), where you can order a meal from an 1839 menu; **Principe de Viana** (Dr. Fleming 7—tel: 259 1448), serving Basque food and free house wine; **Zalacain** (Alvarez de Raema 4 y 6—tel: 261 3011), also specializing in Basque and French cuisine and the elegant, expensive eating place of Spanish political leaders and leading businessmen; **El Bodegón** (Del Pinar 15—tel: 262 8844) with superb, classic Castilian cooking; the **Ritz Restaurant** (Paseo del Prado—tel: 221 2857) for French and Spanish dishes; and **La Trainera** (Lagasca 60—tel: 226 1181) for seafood only.

Less expensive are **Alcalde** (Jorge Juan 10—tel: 276 3359); **Bali-Hai** (Calle de la Flor Alta 8—tel: 231 2550), with Polynesian decor and drinks, Cuban band, and Chinese food; **Rugantino** (Velázquez 136—tel: 261 0222), tasty Spanish and Italian food; **Alduccio** (Concha Espina 8—tel: 250 0077); **Casa Paco** (Plaza Puerta Cerrada 11—tel: 266 3166) for excellent steaks, fish soup, and serrano ham; **El Schotis** (Cava Baja 11—tel: 265 3230), which should not be missed by steak lovers; **Jai-Alai** (Balbina Valverde 2—tel: 261 1116), a friendly Basque restaurant; **Mesón de San Javier** (Calle del Cende 3—tel: 248 0925); and **Viejo Valentin** (San Alberto 3—tel: 231 0035), both Madrilenian. Still less expensive are **Hosteria Piamontesa** (Costanilla de los Angeles 18—tel: 248 3414) for Spanish and Italian food and **Edelweiss** (Jovellanos 7—tel: 231 5114) for wonderful German food with a Spanish accent.

Less central establishments are the deluxe **Mayte Commodore** (Serrano 145—tel: 261 8606); **José Luis** (Rafael Salgarde 11—tel: 259 3129); the open-air **Los Porches** (Paseo Pintor Rosales 1—tel: 248 5197); the excellent Chinese **House of Ming** (Paseo de la Castellana 74); and the two moderately priced restaurants in the Parque de Atracciones—the **Basque Vasco** (tel: 463 8032) and the **Valenciano** (tel: 403 8031).

DRINKING TIPS

Many bars *(tascas)* open at 9am and close with the last customer. Imported alcohol is available but expensive. A whisky and soda costs 125-300ptas; a liter bottle of ordinary wine 70-325ptas. Soft drinks tend to cost more than Spanish liquor. A delicious accompaniment to meals (or by itself) is *Sangría*—a brimming jug of red wine, soda, and fruit. There is naturally a wide variety of famous sherries, and *coñac* is Spanish brandy, which runs from cheap and rough to first-class quality. Champagne *(Champán)* is sparkling wine, but less expensive than the French equivalent. Light beer *(cerveza)* is always sold ice-cold. *Horchata* is a popular nonalcoholic drink made from *chufa* nuts. In Madrid the **Plaza Mayor** and its immediate neighborhood is a popular rendezvous for before-dinner drinks. **Café Gijon** (Paseo de Calvo Sotelo 21) is an old established café. For a taste of the student nightlife in Madrid, visit the *Moncloa barrio* near the university.

ENTERTAINMENT

Guidepost is a useful publication covering most of the entertainments in the capital. Movies are generally dubbed, except in the **Salas Especiales,** where they are shown with original soundtrack. Performances usually begin at 7 and 10:30pm. The **British Institute** and the **Casa Americana** often run movies, plays, and concerts. Classic Spanish drama can be seen at **El Teatro Espanol** and **Teatro Maria Guerrero.** Concerts and opera are performed in the **Teatro Real.** *Zarzuela* is Spanish comic opera and is a combination of dancing, singing, and burlesque. In season it can be seen at the **Zarzuela Theater,** which at other times features operettas, top dance groups, and music. *Flamenco,* the best-known Spanish folk music and dance, is always included in nightclub floor shows, although it is often more rewarding at less commercialized spots such as the **Corral de la Moreria** (Moreria 17); **Las Brujas** (Norte 15); **El Duende** (Señores de Luzon 33); and the **Café de Chinitas** (Calle Torija 7). The **Pasapoga** nightclub (Avenida José Antonio 37) and the **Lido** (Alcalá 20) both have good cabarets. **El Biombo Chino** (Isabel la Católica 6) has flamenco twice nightly, and the **Molino Rojo** (Tribulete 16) specializes in international cabaret. In summer the open-air **Pavillón** (no floor show) and **Florida,** in Retiro Park, are popular.

The major religious festivals are as colorful in Madrid as everywhere in Spain. The capital's major events are the **Feria de San Isidro,** 2 weeks in May when top bullfighters perform in the two stadiums, and the **Verbena de la Paloma** (14 August), when the garlanded streets of the Paloma district are the scene of fireworks, music, and dancing until dawn.

SHOPPING

Hours are 9:30-1:30, 4:30-8, closed Sundays. Best buys include suede and leather goods, hand-made rugs, shoes, damascened steel and gold inlay from Toledo, wood carvings, ceramics (especially the attractive tiles), Majorcan glassware and artificial pearls (black and white), embroidered linen, lace, and antiques. Most stores will pack and ship purchases. Some shops offer 5% discount to US visitors. The **Calle Serrano** and **Avenida de José Antonio** are two of the main shopping streets in Madrid. **Galerias Preciados** (Plaza Callao, Plaza Arapiles, and Calle Goya), **El Corte Inglés** (Calle Preciados, Calle Goya, Paseo de la Castellana, and Calle Princesa), and **Sears** (Calle Serrano) are the major department stores. The **Mercado Nacional de Artesania** (Floridablanca 2), **Empresa Nacional de Artesania** (Velázquez 132), and **Obra Sindical de Artesania** (Paseo de San Jerónimo) are excellent handicraft centers. **Kreisler's** (Calle Serrano 19) sells a wide range of high-quality souvenirs, including mantillas, fans, and Toledo thimbles and scissors. **Casa Bique** (Castellana 60) combines a first-class boutique trade (leather and knitwear) with the more expensive craftware (handcarved furniture). **Forum** (Calle Hermosilla 20) specializes in wrought iron and **Linares** (Plaza de las Cortes) in antiques.

Spanish haute couture has an international reputation, and top fashion houses include **Eisa** (Balenciaga) (Avenida José Antonio 9); **Marbel** (Avenida de Nazaret 1); and **Flora Villareal** (Paseo Castellana 9). **Nieves** (Avenida José Antonio 55) is a linen shop specializing in beautiful handsewn lingerie, and **Rafhael Garcia** (Avenida José Antonio 40) has embroidered shawls. **Durán** (Serrano 30) is a jewelry shop with good antique pieces, and **Alexandre** (Calle Velázquez 39) has inexpensive costume jewelry. **Loewe** (Avenida José Antonio 8 and Calle Serrano 26) has the most famous chain of leather shops in Spain. The **Calle del Prado** is lined with antique shops and the **Calle Libreros** with second-hand bookstalls. Every Sunday morning a **Stamp Fair** is held under the arches of the Plaza Mayor. Shops and stores have fixed prices, but you can bargain Sunday mornings at the **Rastro**, Madrid's flea market in the Plaza de Cascorro and spreading down Ribera de Curtidores.

SPORTS

Bullfighting is, of course, the major sporting interest of young and old alike. Fights can be seen anywhere in Spain from Easter to October. In July each year in **Pamplona** full-bred bulls are run through the streets as a challenge to young bloods. *Pelota*, the original *jai alai*, the fastest ball game in the world, is played at *frontones* (pelota courts) in **Bilbao, Guernica,** and **San Sebastian.** Soccer has a large following. Golf and tennis are available in the major towns, and partridge and clay-pigeon shooting are popular pastimes. **La Mancha** is a good area for quail and partridge and the **Ebro Delta** for wild duck. Hunting—for deer, chamois, bear, wild boar—is from October to February in the mountain regions, and horses can be ridden there also. There is skiing in the **Pyrenees** and the **Sierra Nevada** in winter, and the Madrilenians ski in the sierra at **Navacerrada.** Freshwater fishing for trout, salmon, pike, and many others is possible in lakes, rivers, and reservoirs. There is deep-sea fishing in the **Bay of Biscay** (licenses needed for hunting and fishing). The **Golf Club,** Puerta de Hierro, Madrid, welcomes visitors.

WHAT TO SEE

Madrid: The **Prado** (open 10-5 in winter, 10-6 in summer, and 10-2 Sundays and holidays), one of the world's most famous museums, is in the center of Madrid on the Paseo del Prado, and has an incomparable collection of Goya, Velázquez, and El Greco, also masterpieces by Rubens, Titian, and Bosch. The **Royal Palace** (Palacio Real) has Flemish tapestries, porcelain, furniture, and 15th- to 18th-century armor. Part of the **Convent of the Descalzas Reales** is open to the public (daily 10:30-1:30, weekdays 4-6, except Thursday), where paintings by Titian and Rubens hang in rooms still furnished as in the 16th century. Goya painted the frescoes in the small chapel of San Antonio de la Florida where he is buried. The **Museo Taurino**, in the Plaza de Toros, is a bullfighting museum. Retiro Park affords lovely wooded and lakeside strolls among small temples, colonnades, and statuary. On summer evenings, open-air ballet and *zarzuela* are performed. Thirty-one miles from Madrid is **El Escorial**, the vast monastery-palace built by Philip II, whose chapels, patios, fountains, gardens, cloisters, and apartments are in a black and barren setting. Near El Escorial, **Valle de los Caídos** (Valley of the Fallen) is the burial place for the dead of Spain's Civil War and is dominated by a colossal cross.

Other excursions from Madrid are to the medieval walled city of **Avila**, home of Saint Teresa, and to **Segovia**, with its castle and Roman aqueduct. **La Granja**, a small Versailles, has world-famous tapestries, within reach of Segovia.

Toledo is a short drive from Madrid and stands over a gorge of the river Tagus. Best view of the walled city is from the **Alcantara Bridge**. See the Gothic cathedral, cloisters, and the **Church of Saint Tomé** with its paintings by El Greco, who lived here. His house is now a museum. Toledo is well known for inlaid gold metalwork.

Barcelona is the most prosperous and cosmopolitan city in Spain. Spanish is spoken, but the dominant language is Catalan, similar to French. A replica of Columbus's ship is in the harbor. Its most picturesque aspect is seen in the old **Barrio Gotico** (Gothic Quarter) around the 14th-century **Cathedral**. At noon on Sundays the traditional local dance, the *sardana*, is performed in front of the cathedral. Close by are the **Palacio de la Diputacíon**, seat of the ancient parliament of Catalonia, the **Avuntamiento**, and many other attractive old palaces and mansions. Barcelona's 19th-century architect, Gaudi, produced the large but still unfinished **Church of la Sagrada Familia**, the strange structural decorative designs of which characterize Gaudi's other major works, the two animal-shaped houses in the **Paseo de Gracia**, his playground at **Parque Guell**, and the **Guell Palace (Museum of Spanish Theater)**. A funicular rises to **Montjuich Park**, where the **Palacio Nacional** houses the **Museum of Catalan Art** with primitive paintings. Also in the park is the **Pueblo Español**, a reconstructed Spanish village. Folk art is made and sold at the Pueblo, and in summer there are folklore evenings. The **Museum of Modern Art** in the Parque de la Ciudadela has some of Salvador Dali's works, and Picasso is on show in the **Picasso Museum** on Calle Moncada. The **Plaza de**

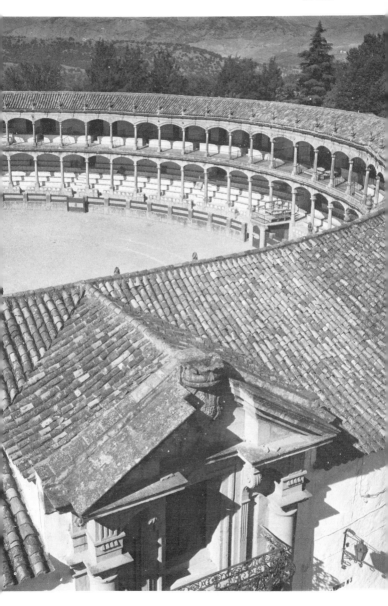

Cataluna is the city center. Best restaurants are the **Reno** (Calle Tuset—tel: 227 9308); **Atalaya** (Avenida Generalísimo 523—tel: 239 4661); the **Cosmos** (Plaza Teatro 34—tel: 302 3023); **Finisterre** (Avenida Generalísimo 469—tel: 230 9114); and **Orotowa** (Consejo de Ciento 335—tel: 302 3128). Less expensive are **Agut d'Avignon** (Trinidad 11—tel: 302 6034) and **Au Perigord** (Roberto Bassas 32—tel: 230 9102). Barcelona's major festival is **Nuestra Señora de la Merced,** celebrated 20-24 September. The main excursion is to the mountain monastery of **Montserrat,** founded in 880 AD. The two prides of Montserrat are the *Black Virgin,* reputedly carved by St Luke, and Escolania, a children's choir with a 700-year-old history. The **Museum** in the village contains works by El Greco, Caravaggio, and Correggio. Hotels in Barcelona, centrally located unless otherwise indicated:

Rates are in US$ for a double/twin room with bath or shower

Arenas, Capitan Arenas 20 (from $50), near university, 10 minutes from center

Astoria, Paris 203 (from $34), modern district, 15 minutes from center

Avenida Palace, Avenida José Antonio 605 and 607 (from $70)

Balmoral, Via Augusta 5 (from $49)

Colon, Avenida Catedral 7 (from $50)

Cristal, Diputación 257 (from $47)

Diplomatic, Via Layetana 122 (from $78)

Gran Hotel Cristina, Avenida del Generalísimo Franco 458 (from $41), modern district, 10 minutes from center

Majestic, Paseo de Gracia 70 (from $67)

Manila, Ramblas 111 (from $51)

Presidente, Avenida del Generalísimo Franco 570 (from $64), modern district, 10 minutes from center

Princesa Sofia, Plaza Pio XII (from $98)

Ritz, Avenida José Antonio 668 (from $72)

Roma, Mallorca 163 (from $31), modern district, 15 minutes from center

Sarria Gran Hotel, Avenida Sarria 48 (from $77), near university, 10 minutes from center

The **Costa Brava,** Spain's Riviera, lies between the Pyrenees and Barcelona. A superb coastline of cliffs and pine-backed sandy coves and bays, it is now one of the most crowded holiday areas in the world. There are hundreds of good hotels, plenty of water sports, and a lively nightlife.

Valencia: Famous for its *paella,* its oranges, and its lively *fiestas,* Valencia was liberated for a time from the Moors by the legendary El Cid in 1094; Moorish influence can still be seen in many of its fine white houses. The **Cathedral** was built in the 13th century, although the main facade is baroque. The magnificent purple agate chalice is claimed to be the Holy Grail, used at the Last Supper. Among the richly decorated rooms of the **Palacio de la Generalidad** is the Golden Room, with a beautiful ceiling. The 15th-century **Lonia** (Exchange), with its Orange Court, has a lovely vaulted Silk Room with spiral columns. An excellent collection of ceramics is housed in the **Dos Aguas Palace.** During the

Fallas de San José (12-19 March), a week of flower battles, fireworks, bullfights, and music culminates in the traditional burning of huge painted effigies. The **Summer Fair** *(Feria)* is the last week in July and is attended by bullfights and elaborate firework displays.

Alicante is the principal town of the superb resort coast known as the **Costa Blanca** and is dominated by a huge Moorish castle. A worthwhile excursion is to **Elche**, where a 3,000-year-old stone bust of a woman (now in the Museo Arqueologico) attests to its ancient origin. The town is famous for its date-palm forest, which supplies all Spain with fronds for Palm Sunday, and for its annual **Mystery Play** (14-15 August) performed to 13th-century music. Good accommodations and water sports.

Granada: The spectacular **Alhambra Palace** is a poignant epitaph to the triumph of the Catholic monarchs and the despair of the defeated Moors who still mourn its loss. With imposing towers and halls, rooms decorated with lacy carvings, colored tiles, and gold mosaics, courtyards with fountains and hidden gardens smelling of jasmine, it is unparalleled in Europe. The Alhambra is the concert stage of the **Guitar and Spanish Classic Music festivals** in June. In Granada's cathedral the victors lie beneath tombs in the Royal Mausoleum. Hotels are the **Alhambra Palace,** Peña Partida 2 (from US$47 double); **Luz Granada,** Calvo Sotelo 34 (from US$49 double), **Melia Granada,** Angel Ganivet 7 (from US$51 double), and the **Washington Irving,** Paseo del Generalife 2 (from US$27 double).

Cordoba: Most famous for its 8th-century **Mosque,** supported by hundreds of columns of marble, jasper, and onyx and illuminated by 4,000 bronze and copper lamps. It is so impressive that it dwarfs the cathedral built in one section of it. In the heart of the old Jewish quarter stands one of the only two synagogues in Spain. The museum in the Alcázar (Spanish for fortress or palace) has Roman mosaics.

Málaga: An attractive Andalusian city, popular as a winter resort because of its mild climate. Special winter festivities are held mid-January to mid-February, and the local fiesta is held the first week in August. The unfinished 16th-century **Cathedral** has beautifully carved choir stalls and paintings by Van Dyck and Andrea del Sarto. The 11th-century **Alcazaba** was one of the strongest fortresses built by the Moors.

Costa del Sol: Extends from Málaga to Estepona. **Torremolinos** is the most popular resort, thanks to its fine 5-mile beach. **Marbella,** more exclusive, with another lovely beach, is quieter. Hotels include:

Rates are in US$ for a double/twin room with bath or shower

Al Andalus, Avenida de Montemar, Torremolinos (from $42)

Andalucia Plaza, Nueva Andalucia, Marbella (from $45)

Atalaya Park Hotel & Golf Course, Carretera Cádiz-Málaga, km 175 Estepona-Marbella (from $58)

Golf el Paraíso, Carretera Cádiz, km 173, Estepona (from $49)

Holiday Inn, Carretera Cádiz, km 238 Guadalmar, Torremolinos (from $68)

Melia Don Pepe, Finca las Marinas, Marbella (from $108)

Seghers Club, Carretera Cádiz-Málaga, km 159 Estepona (from $9)

Algeciras is a ferry departure point for North Africa. The hotel **Reina Cristina** has excellent food. Double rooms from US$55.

Seville has the largest Gothic **Cathedral** in the world, with two famous Murillo paintings and Christopher Columbus's mausoleum. The bell-tower is a Moorish minaret topped by a large bronze statue so accurately balanced that it acts as a weather vane. The Alcázar is a classic example of *mudejar* or Arab-Christian architecture. The sights include the 15th-century palace called the **House of Pilate;** the **Hospital de la Caridad,** with paintings by Murillo and Zurbarán; the **Museum;** and the **Lonja,** which houses a collection of New World documents. The **Springtime Fair** follows Easter with bullfights and Andalusian dancing. Stay at the **Colon,** Canalejas 1 (from US$61 double); the **Maria Luisa Park,** Asuncion 79 (from US$61 double); and the **Luz Sevilla,** Martin Villa 2 (from US$60 double).

Burgos, home of the 11th-century hero El Cid and former capital of old Castilla, has a fine Gothic **Cathedral.**

Santiago de Compostela in the west was a famous place of pilgrimage in the Middle Ages. The **Feast of St James** (25 July) still attracts thousands of pilgrims for a week. The original Romanesque facade of the **Cathedral** is now the right-hand outside wall. Across the Plaza de España is the **Renaissance Rajoy Palace,** now the Town Hall. Also in the square are the old **Pilgrims Hostal** and the 15th-century **San Jerónimo College.**

San Sebastián is a fashionable Atlantic summer retreat only 12 miles from the French border, situated on a bay between two low mountain peaks. It is never excessively hot.

Leon features a cathedral with some of Spain's finest stained-glass windows.

SOURCES OF FURTHER INFORMATION

Pan Am, Edificio España, Plaza España, Madrid, or any Pan Am office around the world. **Secretariat of State for Tourism,** Calle Alcalá 44, Madrid 14; **Spanish National Tourist Office,** 665 Fifth Avenue, New York, NY 10017; **Spanish National Tourist Office,** 67 Jermyn Street, London SW1.

Sweden

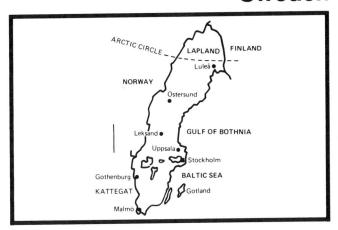

WHAT'S SPECIAL

Larger than California but smaller than Texas, Sweden is a land of lakes, forests, and islands, with a glorious summer and the space to enjoy it. It is one of the most prosperous countries in Europe and heavily industrialized, but for the tourist there are long open-air days by lovely lakes in the summer and skiing in the winter. There is space and freedom and a high standard of living. You'll enjoy a taste of it.

COUNTRY BRIEFING

Size: 173,665 square miles   **Population:** 8,300,000
Capital: Stockholm   **Capital Population:** 1,400,000

Climate: The best time for a summer holiday is May-September, when the weather is warm and sunny, never humid. Enjoy the midnight sun in Lapland in June and July, but also go there later, in September, for lovely fall colors and fewer mosquitoes. For winter sports, February and March are the best months, but you can ski in northern Lapland virtually all year round.

Weather in Stockholm: Lat N59°21'; Alt 146 ft

Temp (°F)	Jan	Feb	Mar	Apr	May	Jun	Jul	Aug	Sep	Oct	Nov	Dec
Av Low	23°	22°	26°	32°	41°	49°	55°	53°	46°	39°	31°	26°
Av High	31°	31°	37°	45°	57°	65°	70°	66°	58°	48°	38°	33°
Days no rain	23	21	24	24	23	23	22	21	22	22	21	22

Government: A constitutional monarchy.
Language: Swedish. English widely spoken.

Religion: Lutheran predominates.

Currency: Krona (pl. Kronor). 100 öre = 1 krona.

	25 öre	50 öre	1 Kr	5 Kr	50 Kr	100 Kr	200 Kr	300 Kr
US (dollars, cents)	.05	.10	.20	1.02	10.21	20.41	40.82	61.23
UK (pounds, pence)	.02	.05	.10	.49	4.88	9.75	19.51	29.26

Public Holidays:

New Year's Day, 1 Jan
Epiphany (Twelfth Night)
Good Friday
Easter Monday
Labor Day, 1 May
Ascension Day
Whit Monday

Midsummer's Day (Sat nearest 21/22 June)
All Saints Day (Sat nearest 2 Nov)
Christmas Day, 25 Dec
Boxing Day, 26 Dec

Special Events: Walpurgis Night, 30 Apr, festivities to celebrate arrival of Spring. St Lucia's Day, 13 Dec, "Queen of Light" processions. Nobel Prize Ceremony, 10 Dec.

HOW TO GET THERE

Flying time from New York 9 hours; from London 2½ hours; from Caracas 13½ hours; from Tokyo 16 hours. Time in Sweden: GMT+1.

REQUIREMENTS FOR ENTRY AND CUSTOMS REGULATIONS

Passport. Smallpox and cholera vaccinations if coming from an infected area. Customs: 6,000Kr is the limit that may be brought in or taken out in Swedish notes and coins. Foreign currency is unrestricted. Duty-free allowance (for residents outside Europe): 400 cigarettes or 100 cigars or 500 grams of tobacco; 2 liters of either wine or liquor and 2 liters of beer. (Cigarettes and tobacco allowances are half this for European residents.) Import restrictions on certain foodstuffs and live plants and on weapons, ammunition, and drugs. You are allowed to export antiquities (except for some special ones considered Swedish "national treasures") and an unlimited number of gifts.

AIRPORT INFORMATION

Arlanda International Airport is 27 miles from the center of Stockholm. An airport bus meets each incoming flight; the fare to the city center is 19Kr for adults, half for children aged 7-12, and free for children under 7. The taxi fare is about 175Kr. Duty-free shop at the airport. No arrival or departure tax.

ACCOMMODATIONS

Accommodations range from luxury hotels to log cabins, with alternatives in between. Summer hotels are modern, comfortable, and reasonably priced. There are several chains of modern, well-equipped, and well-furnished motels, average price 225Kr for a double room with shower. There are also "family rooms" with more beds at little more than the double-room price. Additionally, there are farm and manor-house holidays, mostly in southern Sweden, and youth hostels, chalets, and log cabins. Hotel checks, a voucher system available in two price categories (with or without private bath) and honored by more than 400 hotels, cut costs from May through September. For help in finding accommodations go to the **Turisbyrå** (tourist bureau), in any town; in Stockholm, the **Hotellcentralen** at the Central Railway Station is an official service booking hotel and boarding house rooms. In addition, several nationwide hotel chains can provide reservations. These include **SARA** (Stockholm tel: 34 97 30), **RESO** (tel: 23 75 00), and **ESSO** (tel: 24 55 50). Young people should contact the **Stockholm Student Reception Service** (Körsbärsvägen 1, tel: 15 50 90), which rents rooms at low cost to students. Hotels in Stockholm, inclusive of service charges:

Rates are in US$ for a double/twin room with bath or shower

Amaranten, Kungsholmsgatan 31 (from $95)

Anglais, Humlegårdsgatan 23 (from $110)

Aston, Mariatorget 3 (from $75)

Birger Jarl, Tulegatan 8 (from $76 CP; no bar or hard liquor sold in this church-run hotel)

Bromma, Brommaplan 1 (from $66 CP), 10-15 minutes by cab from city center

Carlton, Kungsgatan 57A (from $100)

Continental, Klara Vattugränd-Vasagatan (from $95 CP)

Diplomat, Strandvägen 7C (from $113)

Esso Motor, Uppsalävägen Ulriksdal, Järva Krog (from $48), 10-15 minutes by cab from city center

Esso Motor, KungensKurva (from $48), 10-15 minutes by cab from city center

Grand, S Blasieholmshamnen 8 (from $120)

Lady Hamilton, Stor Kyrkobrinken 5 (from $110 CP)

Lord Nelson, Västerlånggatan 22 (from $85 CP)

Malmen, Götgatan 49-51 (from $73 CP)

Mornington, Nybrogatan 53 (from $100)

Park, Karlavägen 43 (from $115)

Reisen, Skeppsbron 12-14 (from $110)

Sheraton, Tegelbacken 6 (from $130)

Strand, Nybrokajen 9 (from $90)

Sjöfartshotellet, Katarinavägen 26 (from $67)

Wellington, Storgatan 6 (from $110)

All hotels listed above are in central Stockholm unless otherwise indicated.

USEFUL INFORMATION

Arrive punctually for appointments, as the Swedes do. An invitation to a Swedish home in the evening may not include dinner, as families usually eat around 6pm. Take flowers or candy for your hosts, or a bottle of liquor you may have bought tax free.

Banks: Open 9:30-3 Mon-Fri; in large towns and the center of Stockholm, certain banks are open unti 6pm. Closed Sat. Bank at Arlanda Airport open 7 days a week, 7-9.

Mail: Stamps at post offices and newspaper kiosks.

Telephone Tips: Public telephone booths and phones in restaurants, cafés, and tobacconists' shops. Local calls cost 1Kr. Useful numbers (*note:* 08- is the prefix for Stockholm—omit if calling within Stockholm):

Pan Am 23 19 20

Tourist Information
(English) 22 18 40

Airport Information
(International flights) 780 3030
(Domestic flights) 780 2260

Telephone Services Operator (internal
Sweden) 000
(external Sweden) 0011

Directory Inquiries
90140 (for local numbers
from any city) 90160 (for
long-distance numbers
from any city)

Time 90510

Weather 23 95 00

Emergencies 90000

Telegrams (abroad and
domestic) 0021

Newspapers: English-language dailies available in larger towns, magazines at all kiosks. For business information about Sweden, read *Sweden Business Report,* an English fortnightly available from Affärsvärlden. A six-times-a-year magazine giving good general information about the country is *Sweden Now,* available at major newsstands.

Tipping: In hotels and restaurants, a service charge of 12½-15% is generally included in the bill, and there is no need to give a further tip (though in top-class restaurants waiters may expect a few kronor extra). Airport and hotel porters get 3Kr for one bag, 2Kr for each extra bag. Cloakroom attendants get 3Kr per item. Taxi drivers and hairdressers receive 10-15% of the bill.

Electricity: 220 volts 50 cycles AC.

Laundry: Services reliable but expensive (dry-cleaning a suit express, from 65Kr; laundering a shirt, from 20Kr).

Hairdressing: Plenty of salons (shampoo and set, from 60Kr; man's haircut, from 35Kr).

Photography: Film and equipment widely available. Black and white film (35mm, 36 exposures) costs 10Kr and Instamatic (20 exposures) 7.50Kr; color film (35mm), 65Kr including processing. Developing takes 2-4 days.

Clubs: Kiwanis, Lions, Rotary, RAC, Junior Chamber of Commerce. Ask the Tourist Board for details of meetings.

Babysitting: Hotels can arrange this; some department stores have supervised playrooms.

Rest Rooms: Not many public ones. Try hotels and department stores. Women, *Damer;* men, *Herrar.*

Health: Swedish medical care is of a very high standard, and most doctors and dentists speak English. Nonprescription drugs about same price as in the US. Water safe to drink.

TRANSPORTATION

In Stockholm there are buses and the subway *(tunnelbana)*. Standard fare of 4Kr on both for inner-city travel. Buy a 20-coupon *rabatthäfte* at any kiosk for 10 inner city trips for 25Kr. Tourist cards allowing 24 hours of unlimited inner-city travel are available for 20Kr; a tourist card allowing 3 days of unlimited inner-city travel costs 40Kr including free entry to Skansen Outdoor Museum, Gröna Lund Amusement Park, and Kaknäs Tower. If planning to stay longer than 3 days, a good travel bargain could be a 70-*kort* (70-card), costing 80Kr and good for unlimited travel for one month. (However, new cards are needed the first of each month.) Ferries are an important part of the transportation system: many people rely on them in the summer to travel to summer houses on the islands in the archipelago. Phone for a taxi or hail one in the street. They are metered and expensive. Special tourist limousines with English-speaking guides can be hired from Freys Hyrverk (tel: 67 03 60) at about 145Kr per hour. If taxis are hard to get, call Freys, which cost about 40% more than normal taxis but are available 24 hours a day. You can rent a car from about 80Kr a day including tax, plus a charge of about 1.05Kr per kilometer. Check whether rates include comprehensive insurance; by paying a little more you can get exemption from liability for all damage. Sweden drives on the right. Driving laws are very strict. Do not risk exceeding speed limits, and drinking two beers or two glasses of wine is enough to make you liable for prosecution. Watch where you park: any infringement could mean a 100-150Kr parking ticket or, worse, a towaway costing you 350Kr plus a 150Kr fine. All-night parking is prohibited on some streets.

Swedish railroads offer a fast, efficient, and comfortable service linking all main towns. The new Scandinavian Rail Pass is good for 21 days of unlimited travel in Sweden, plus Denmark, Norway, and Finland, and is also good for ferry crossings between Sweden and Denmark. The pass can be bought in Scandinavia and certain European cities, but not outside Europe. The Eurailpass is also accepted in Sweden. There is an extensive bus network. In the north, the Post Office carries passengers in mail coaches. Internal air services are operated by SAS and LIN, the domestic line. Car ferries link Sweden with Finland, Denmark, Germany, Holland, and the UK.

FOOD AND RESTAURANTS

Smörgåsbord, a cold table made up of many different dishes, takes so long to prepare that families have it only on special occasions and at Christmas. There are meat dishes such as *små köttbullar*, small savory meatballs usually accompanied with lingonberry (similar to cranberry) sauce. Fish and meat dishes are meant to be eaten separately. Delicacies you should not miss are *gravlax*—dill-cured salmon, smoked reindeer, smoked eel, and (in season) ptarmigan, fresh reindeer, and moose, served in various rich sauces. Traditional dishes you might be served in a Swedish home include *Janssons Frestelse* (Jansson's temptation), a dish of anchovies, potatoes, and onions, served with a drink of *snaps* before the main course; and *ärter med fläsk*—a filling pea soup with pork, traditionally served on Thursdays and followed by *plättar* (pancakes) with lingonberry jam. In the summertime you might be invited to a crayfish *(kräftor)* party, at which a glass of *snaps* accompanies each claw consumed. There are over 50 varieties of crispbread *(knäckebröd)* and many different kinds of yoghurt. As the cost of living in Stockholm is higher than in New York, top restaurants are expensive, and dinner will not cost less than 130Kr each—probably more. There are more moderate establishments where the check will be about 60-80Kr each. In a self-service restaurant or in department stores (**Domus, Epa, Tempo, Ahlens**) a meal will cost from about 20Kr, exclusive of drinks. Hot dogs with mashed potato are sold by street vendors or in snack bars (look for **Varm Korv**). Best lunches at low prices (about 18Kr) are in the pizzerias, which have excellent pizza, but also generally have a simple luncheon dish of some Swedish specialty as well. Stockholm and other large cities have a number of **McDonald's; Clock** is a similar Swedish-owned chain. Most restaurants in downtown areas serve special lunches between 11am and 2pm—usually a main course, salad, milk or beer, and coffee, for about 18Kr.

The **Operakällaren** (pronounced *shellaren*) has a reputation as one of the best 15 restaurants in Europe (Karl XIIs torg—tel: 11 11 25); it also has a bar and a lunch bar offering Swedish fare at lower though still expensive prices; good for lunch. Under the same management is the elegant **Riche** (Birger Jarlsgatan 4—tel: 10 70 22). **Teatergrillen** (Nybrogatan 3—tel: 10 70 44) and **Stallmästaregarden,** housed in a 17th-century inn near the Haga Park (tel: 24 39 10), are also in the luxury class. There are several excellent restaurants in the Old Town, notably **Aurora** (Munkbron 11—tel: 21 93 59, closed Sunday), a cellar in a beautiful 17th-century house; **Fem Små Hus** (Nygrand 10—tel: 10 87 75), furnished with antiques; **Cattelin** (Storkyrkobrinken 19—tel: 20 18 10), with Swedish and French fish specialties—crayfish soup is very good—and a lovely atmosphere, like a Left Bank bistro; and **Diana** (Brunnsgränd 2—tel: 10 73 10). **Gourmet,** a short walk from the city center (Tegnergatan 10—tel: 31 43 98) is considered by many to be the best restaurant in Stockholm; it is closed weekends June through August. All of these are in the moderate to expensive range, and you should reserve in advance. Remember that Swedish people dine very early and only the more expensive restaurants can be relied on for dinner after 8pm. Fish is the dish Swedes prepare best, and one newly opened place is **Erik's,** located on a beautifully converted coastal freighter, docked along Strandvagen, a five-minute stroll from the Royal Dramatic Theater. From an oyster bar on the upper deck level, diners have a beautiful view of the Stockholm waterfront (tel: 60 60 60). All kinds of fish dishes, particularly shellfish, are available in **Ostermalmshallen,** a 100-year-old market hall that has a restaurant among the retail vegetable, fish, and meat stalls; crowded at lunch. Another good fish restaurant is **Glada Laxen** (Regeringsgatan 23—tel: 21 21 90), highly popular for lunch; closes at 2:15 in summer, 6 in winter. **Källaren Bohemia** (Tunnelgatan 1—tel: 21 53 10) is an excellent, medium-priced restaurant featuring Czechoslovakian food. Other good, medium-priced restaurants include **Cassi** (Narvavägen 30—tel: 61 74 61) and **Prinsen** (Master Samuelsgatan 4—tel: 10 13 31), both very popular for lunch, but here, as elsewhere in Stockholm, if you go late (1:30pm onward) you will miss the crowds. A delightful and unusual luncheon restaurant is the **OGO Konditori** (Kungsgatan 27—tel: 23 22 20), which serves wonderful pastries. **La Brochette** (Storgatan 27—tel: 62 20 00), considered to be one of the best French restaurants in the city, is in the medium-priced class. The restaurant in the Sverigehuset (Hamngatan 27—tel: 21 56 51) is convenient for lunch, coffee, or a drink if you are shopping. A number of acceptable Chinese restaurants have opened in Stockholm in recent years.

DRINKING TIPS

Drinking is expensive, and the government tries to discourage drunkenness and alcoholism. *Akvavit,* or *snaps,* is very good served ice-cold with *smörgåsbord* or with any herring dish—it is generally not drunk on its own. With meals the Swedes drink wine or beer. The state liquor monopoly provides excellent wines at relatively low cost. A bottle of good wine will cost from 18Kr and up in the liquor stores and at least twice that in a restaurant. Beer costs from 8Kr. Whisky is expensive, 25-35Kr, according to where you drink it and what size you order. Restaurants do not serve liquor at all before noon (1pm Sundays); many are licensed only for wine and beer. The best places to have a drink are the bars attached to restaurants or in hotels. Pubs are now very popular, try **Engelen** (Kornhamnstorg 59B—tel: 10 07 22), **Stampen** (Gråmunkegränd 7—tel: 20 57 93), or **The Tudor Arms** (Grevgatan 31—tel: 60 27 12).

ENTERTAINMENT

The **Dramatic Theater** presents classic and modern plays from mid-August to June; the **Royal Opera and Ballet** perform during the same period. Opera buffs should not miss the **Drottningholm Court Theater,** the only 18th-century theater in Europe still in its original building and using original sets. Operas from the 18th century are performed there during the summer. You can go by bus, but the pleasantest way is by boat from **Klara Mälarstrand,** near the City Hall. The boats return after the performance, and some have a restaurant on board. Other theaters and concert halls are closed in summer, but there are open-air concert halls and folk dancing in **Skansen.**

There are not many real nightclubs, but you can dance in most of the big hotels and several good restaurants and discothèques. A few of the most popular are **Atlantic** (Teatergatan 3), **Bolaget** (Grev Turegatan 16), **Nya Bacchi** (Järntorgsgatan 5), **Maxim** (Drottninggatan 81), and **Berns** (Näckströmsgatan 8). **Shazam, Kolingen,** and **Hayati's** are places for the young at heart. More sedate are **King Creole, Hamburger Börs,** and the nightclub in the **Strand Hotel.**

SHOPPING

Stores in Stockholm open 9:30-6 weekdays, 9-2 Sat. Best buys: Swedish glass, handwoven textiles, wooden objects, women's and children's clothes, and furs. The three largest department stores are **NK** (Hamngatan), **Ahléns** (near Sergels Torg), and **PUB** (Hötorget). **Domus** is smaller, but budget priced. Specialized stores with the best Swedish glass are **Nordiska Kristallmagasinet** (Kungsgatan 9) and **Svenskt Glas** (Birger Jarlsgatan 8).

For handicrafts and textiles, try **Konsthantverkarna** (Mäster Samuelsgatan 2)—permanent exhibition and sale; **Handarbets Vänner** (Djurgårdsslätten 82-84, south of Skansen); **Libraria** (Västerlånggatan 48); **Svenskt Hemslöjd** (Sveavägen); and **Klockargardens Hemslöjd** (Vasagatan 42)—regional crafts. An excellent selection of Scandinavian silver jewelry is at **Gallerie 22** in the Sheraton Hotel.

Some of the best furniture and interior design shops are **Otto Dahlin** (Sveavägen 62), **Carl Malmsten** (Strandvägen 5B), **Nordiska Galleriet** (Nybrogatan 11), **Svenskt Tenn** (Strandvägen 5A), **Åhlbergs Möbelhus** (Sveavägen 5), and **Solna Möbler** (Sergelarkaden, in the square opposite Parliament House). Take a trip out to **IKEA**, which has an export service, for furniture and household accessories at very low prices.

Gustavsberg (Birger Jarlsgatan 2) is the place to go for ceramics. For modern printed textiles try **Gürs & Company** (Norrlandsgatan 14); **PUB** has some interesting designs. There are antique shops and art galleries all over the Old Town. For women's clothes the best areas are along Västerlånggatan in the Old Town, Norrmalmstorg and Biblioteksgatan (between **NK** and Stureplan), and around Hötorget. In this last area look for **Hennes** (budget priced—opposite **PUB**) and **Blommor & Bin** (Kungsgatan) for colorful and unusual things for adults and children. A newly opened indoor mall, **Gallerian**, stretching for several blocks and with main entrance on Hamngatan opposite the **NK** department store, has dozens of shops, an excellent fish restaurant, a pizzeria, and ice cream parlors. In the basement level is the **Stadsauktion** (City Auction), a combination flea market, antique shop, art gallery, and book sale that's been going on for over 300 years. Viewings are Wednesdays and Saturdays, and the auctions are held Mondays, Tuesdays, Thursdays, and Fridays; closed during the summer months.

SPORTS

From December-May everybody skis, and good facilities for both downhill and cross-country skiing exist. In summer the Swedes leave town for summer houses on islands or near one of their 100,000 lakes, for swimming, yachting, and fishing. A wide variety of fresh- and sea-water fish makes Sweden especially rewarding for fishermen. Ask the local Tourist Board about permits and special trips, or write to **Fritidsfiskarna,** Fack 104, 40 Stockholm or phone 67 07 40. A unique attraction is salmon fishing in the heart of downtown Stockholm, where Lake Mälaren flows out to the Baltic. There are over 200 golf courses—one beyond the Arctic Circle where you can play at midnight in summer. As for hiking in the north of Sweden and Lapland, only the experienced should try it alone: distances are vast, and it is easy to get lost. The **Swedish Touring Club** organizes tours. Sweden also offers good hunting, mainly in autumn and winter for moose, roe deer, hare, capercaillie, blackcock, and other small game birds. A permit and insurance are required and are obtainable from the County Council *(Länsstyrelse)* either of the region where you intend to shoot or of the region through whose custom post you will pass when entering Sweden. The Tourist Board can supply addresses.

WHAT TO SEE

Stockholm was founded on an island in the 13th century, and as it grew, it spread to 13 other adjacent islands. If you could do only three things in Stockholm, one should certainly be to explore **Gamla Stan** (the Old Town where the city began) set in the middle of Lake Mälaren. Another should be to take a trip by boat through the waterways separating the rest of the city islands. A third would be to go to **Skansen.** In Gamla Stan there is the **Royal Palace** with the King in residence, but you can wander through the State rooms. Try to be here for the changing of the guard at noon (1pm on Sundays) in summer. There is also the oldest church in Stockholm, **Storkyrkan,** home of the Reformation in Sweden and scene of coronations. On a tiny island just off Gamla Stan is the **Riddarholmenskyrka,** an old church where the kings and queens of Sweden were traditionally buried. Also see the **Stortorget,** the old main square of Gamla Stan. You will find just walking through the narrow, virtually traffic-free old lanes of this area rewarding and every lane will lead you eventually back to the water. Next, take a boat trip. Two tours—**Under Stockholm's Bridges** and the **Royal Canal Tour**—leave hourly during the summer from the pier near the Grand Hotel and take from one to two hours. Or take a longer trip into the **Skärgården,** Stockholm's archipelago of some 24,000 islands that dot the water as Lake Mälaren stretches eastward toward the Baltic. There are daily steamer sailings during the summer that link some of these islands. Finally, go to **Skansen,** Stockholm's open-air museum. Set on a hill over the water, it shows you centuries-old farmsteads, manors, and craftsmen's shops, with the craftsmen there in summer. There is music and folk-dancing (7:30pm; 2:30 and 4pm on Sundays), a restaurant, zoo, and children's park. Two of the other important sights are nearby: the royal warship **Wasa,** which keeled over and foundered in 1628 a few yards from launching and was raised again in 1961 after four years' work, and the **Nordiska Museet,** which has exhibits of daily life in Scandinavia as far back as the 16th century. Further on from Skansen is **Prins Eugen's Waldemarsudde,** a collection of paintings, many by the artist-prince himself, in a beautiful gallery, his bequest to the nation. To get a broader view of Stockholm, take a No 69 bus from Karlaplan (which you can reach by subway or bus) out to the **Kaknäs Tower,** a new, tall (508 feet) television tower. Two speedy elevators take you up for a panoramic view. You will want to visit the **Stadshuset,** the imposing red-brick city hall by the water and a remarkable piece of 20th-century architecture. See particularly the courtyard, the Golden Hall, and the Terrace. The **National Museum** has an outstanding collection of Impressionists and Rembrandts. Across a bridge from here is an island, **Skeppsholmen,** full of museums; most fun is the **Moderna Museet,** which has a large room set aside for children to work and play in. Nearby are the **Östasiatiska Museet** (Far Eastern Antiquities) and the **Architecture Museum.** Those who know and like the work of sculptor Carl Milles will want to go out to **Lidingö** (subway to Ropsten, bus to Torsvikstorg) to see his work and collection displayed in his old home by the water. In general, Stockholm museums are open from 10am-4pm, but times vary with the seasons.

Around Stockholm: Easiest of the excursions you can make from the city is to **Drottningholm**—either by water or road, or by subway to Brommaplan and from there by bus. (Travel time from downtown is about 30 minutes.) This is a royal palace in the country, a Swedish Versailles. It is notable chiefly for its theater, a perfectly preserved 18th-century court theater with everything intact. In the grounds is the **Chinese Pavilion.**

Uppsala is probably the most important place to go outside Stockholm. It was first a Viking religious center, then a Christian one, now the location of the oldest university in Scandinavia. Three miles outside the town are the three great burial mounds of **Old Uppsala.** The Gothic **Cathedral,** once the site of a gold-sheathed pagan temple, has the tombs of St Erik and King Gustav Vasa, the 16th-century founder of the Swedish state. Facing it is the library, **Carolina Rediviva,** with almost 20,000 manuscripts and the **Silver Bible,** a 5th-century manuscript, written in pure Gothic. Try to be in Uppsala for the student festivities on 30 April, **Walpurgis Night. Sigtuna,** the Swedish capital of nine centuries ago, has a main street credited as being the oldest street in the country. In the same area is **Skokloster Castle,** a 17th-century general's mansion that has been maintained reverently ever since. At the western end of Lake Mälaren, one of Sweden's most distinguished castles can be visited on an excursion by water (three hours from Stockholm, leaving at 10am): **Gripsholm,** beautifully maintained and furnished and hung with royal portraits, a 16th-century castle begun by King Gustav Vasa. In the opposite direction—an hour by steamer seawards—stands the ancient fortress town of **Vaxholm,** which used to guard the city from the sea.

Some of the best medieval artistic talent of Sweden was lavished on church wall painting. Reformation zeal plastered it over; now it can be seen again, but only in country churches. Some of the best is at **Sala,** an old silver-mining town, **Härkenberga,** and **Täby Kyrkby,** a Stockholm suburb that has the work of Albertus Pictor. Stay at the **Sala Stadshotell,** Bråstagatan 5 (from US$77 double).

Some distance away on the main road is **Örebro**—a thriving city with ultramodern architecture; but at its heart stands the **Castle,** a 13th-century building islanded in the river, where Bernadotte was made ruler of Sweden. A visit here is perhaps easiest on your way to Gothenburg or Oslo.

Dalarna: The center of Sweden is easy to visit and rewarding in folklore and local crafts. Dalarna means "The Valleys" and the province has preserved the more picturesque aspects of the old life better than most areas. About 6 hours by road or 4½ by rail from Stockholm, it centers on **Lake Siljan,** where the old boats still carry folk-costumed families to church on Sunday. Best time to go is for the Midsummer maypole dances (around 23 June) and early July for the church-boat races. Later in the month is the open-air miracle play at **Leksand,** where there is a museum full of the traditional Dalarna painting. In Leksand stay at the **Tre Kullor** (from US$40 double). Nearby are two picturesque lakeside resorts, **Tällberg** and **Rättvik**—the latter with a preserved and typical old farmstead, "Gammelgård" (open 12 June-15 August). In Tällberg stay at the **Green Hotel,** above Lake Siljan (from US$65 double). Hotels in Rättvik: the **Lerdalshöjden,** with double rooms from US$60, the **Persborg** (from US$40 double), and **OK Motorhotell** (from US$40 double). History credits **Mora** with being the cradle of Sweden's 16th-century War of Independence; it is now chiefly notable for the works of the great painter Anders Zorn. Stay at the **Mora Hotel,** where double rooms are from US$65 CP, or at the **Esso Motor Hotel** (from US$48 double). Do not miss the ancient copper mines at **Falun**—the oldest (700 years) business company in the world, Stora Kopparberg, was founded here—and the fascinating museum.

To the south, and on the way to Oslo, lies the province of **Värmland,** a picturesque but industrious part of Sweden known chiefly from the writings of Selma Lagerlöf.

Gothenburg and the Southwest: Gothenburg (Göteborg) is Sweden's second-largest city and by far its largest port. Life centers upon its maritime activity as gateway to the west. See the great fishing harbor, **Fiskhamnen,** the **Maritime Museum,** the **Aquarium,** and the outdoor **Maritime Museum** at Lilla Bommen, where the Göta Canal steamers leave for Stockholm. It also boasts Sweden's largest amusement park, a sort of Tivoli, called **Liseberg** (open end of April to mid-September), and the **Art Museum** has a collection well worth seeing, including fine Rembrandts. The **Concert Hall** next door attracts international musicians with its superb acoustics. Probably the best way to see the city is from its Dutch-designed canals: *Paddan* boats leave regularly from **Kungsportsbron** at the north end of The Avenue (fare 12Kr). There are other boat excursions along the coast and among the islands. Hotels are:

Rates are in US$ for a double/twin room with bath or shower

   Europa, Köpmansgatan 38 (from $74)

   Excelsior, Karl Gustavsgatan 9 (from $52)

   Opalen, Engelbrektsgatan 73 (from $93 CP)

   Park Avenue, Kungsportsavenyen 36-38 (from $107 CP)

   Rubinen, Kungsportsavenyen 24 (from $93)

   Scandinavia, Köpmansgaten 10 (from $60; special weekend rates $48 CP)

   Tre Kronor, Norra Kustbanegaten 15-17 (from $75 CP)

   Windsor, Kungsportsavenyen 6 (from $90)

Student hostels are available in summer, when some hotels actually reduce their rates. Ask for details of the **Göteborgstrip** money-saving plan at the Tourist Office (Parkgatan 2—tel: 13 60 28). The southwest is a favorite vacation area for Swedes. Very popular with the young is **Marst-**

rand, a day excursion from Gothenburg, a little old town on an island brooded over by a 17th-century fortress, where there is an international regatta early in July. Most fashionable resort is **Båstad**—125 miles south of Gothenburg—where you should visit the **Norrviken Gardens.** Further south is **Helsingborg,** stepping-off point for Denmark.

The South: **Skåne** is fertile country, dotted with the castles of its prosperous lords. There is strong Danish influence: for many, Copenhagen is a nearer capital than Stockholm. Largest city (third-largest in Sweden) is **Malmö,** which has an amusement park—**Folkets Park**—open in the evenings and a castle which contains an art gallery and museum. Restaurants: **Savoy, Tunneln,** and **Trölls Jins Kru** for regional specialties. The cultural capital of Scandinavia for centuries was **Lund,** only 10 miles inland from Malmö. The beautiful Romanesque **Cathedral** is a must: go at noon to see the medieval astronomical clock perform. Nearby is a superb **Museum** of old buildings, including a painted church, peasant houses, workshops, and a house filled with ceramics from all over the world. As you journey south from here, you will be able to see the well-preserved medieval city of **Ystad** with its Franciscan monastery, the 13th-century **St Mary's Church,** and **Per Hälsas Gård.** Stay at **Ystads Saltsjöbad** (from US$67 double). Other sights in this area are **Simrishamn,** an idyllic village; the church at **Maglehem;** Dag Hammarskjöld's farm at **Backäckra;** and the 15th-century fortress of **Glimmingehus.**

Småland is a rocky, forested region with hundreds of lakes, and small villages and towns. Småland is today known for its many small, family-owned factories and private entrepreneurs, but 100 years ago it was from this province that poverty-stricken farmers emigrated by the thousands to America, recreating their red-painted, high-roofed wooden barns. This is where the famous glass factories are: **Kosta, Boda,** and **Orrefors.** Tourists are welcomed by English-speaking guides who show them glass-blowers working now as they have for centuries, and it is a great opportunity to buy beautiful glass at bargain prices. See, too, the glass museum at **Växjö.** Even more interesting to many will be the exhibition devoted to the emigrants to America at **Utvandrarnas Hus** (Emigrants' House) here. The best way to see this region is to take the steamer up the **Göta Canal,** which passes through the lakes and forests of central Sweden from Gothenburg to Stockholm. On the way is huge **Lake Vättern:** visit the hotel restaurant **Gyllene Uttern** ("golden otter") on the Gothenburg-Stockholm road near Gränna—magnificently housed in an old castle, complete with tiny chapel.

On the east coast, at **Kalmar** is the bridge linking it with **Öland**—the longest in Europe. Here is the **Castle,** once called "the lock and key of Sweden" because of its strategic importance. It has a beautiful chapel and the best Renaissance room in Scandinavia. The **Cathedral** is 17th-century baroque. Across the water is the holiday island of **Öland,** remarkable for its flora (30 kinds of wild orchid), fauna (bird sanctuaries), and landscapes. Further out into the Baltic is the equally popular island of **Gotland.** This has everything to please the vacationer, including a sunny dry climate and an interesting history. Brilliant and powerful in the 12th century, **Visby** is now a tourist's dream: near-complete city walls and 17 medieval ruined churches covered with rambling roses. To get there take a direct flight (45 minutes) or ferry (5½ hours) from Stockholm. Stay at **Tofta Strandpensionat,** outside Visby, with double rooms from US$72, or in the city at the **Visby,** with double rooms from US$76.

Half of Sweden is to most Swedes simply The North, **Norrland.** This is a country of vast forests, rivers down which logs are transported, huge iron-ore mines, and barren moors where only the Lapps run with their reindeer herds. It is a wonderful area for fishermen and for skiers. And, of course, it has the perpetual daylight of the Arctic summer. The area near **Östersund**—the logging city—is very popular for winter sports, **Åre** in particular. Östersund has one of Sweden's best open-air museums— the **Jamtli.** Nearby is **Frösön** village on the island in Lake Storsjön with magnificent views, a medieval church, and Sweden's most northerly rune-stone. Capital of the far north is the ore-mining town of **Kiruna.** Stay at the **Ferrum Hotel** (from US$76 double CP). But perhaps the most interesting towns are **Lulea** on the coast, with its great collection of Lapp ethnographica in the **Norbotten Museum,** and **Gammelstad** nearby—an old wooden town the Lapps come to for festivals and wed-dings. Those wanting a holiday in deepest Lapland might try the **Laplan-dia Sportshotel,** Rikgränsen.

SOURCES OF FURTHER INFORMATION

Pan Am, Jakobstorg 1, Box 1614, Stockholm, and any Pan Am office around the world; **Tourist Center** at Sverigehuset, Hamngatan 27, Stock-holm; **Swedish National Tourist Office,** 75 Rockefeller Plaza, New York, NY 10019; **The Tourist Secretary,** The Royal Swedish Embassy, 23 North Row, London W1R 2DN.

Switzerland

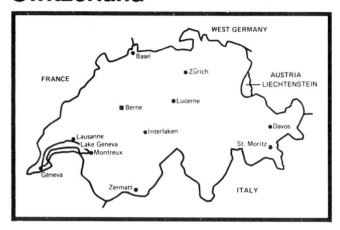

WHAT'S SPECIAL

Switzerland is one of the most remarkable countries in the world and has remained at peace with its neighbors since the Treaty of Paris in 1815. As a neutral state Switzerland has taken its duties seriously, and the sovereign cantons are still united to ensure "Freedom, Independence and Security against all attacks by enemy powers." While there is no standing army or airforce, all citizens are trained and detailed to a military unit from the age of 20 until they reach 50. The system is similar to that found in Sweden and Israel, and outside of annual training, the forces are "on leave" and carry out their civil occupations.

The ensuing peace has enabled the Swiss to build an effective year-round tourism industry that is second to none, for the country itself enjoys some of the finest mountain landscapes in the world. Its Alps are legendary, its sweeping mountain lakes spectacular, its villages attractive while its towns are thoughtfully planned.

It unites three languages and cultures—French, German, and Italian—reflected in the variety of food, architecture, and traditions you will find in different areas. More recent immigration has included Tibetans with group settlements in the Toss River Valley (canton Zürich), and there's an exotic Tibetan Institute at Rikon. If the Swiss are pioneers in the art of hotel and restaurant management, as bankers, they are known worldwide. Their railroads and their precision watches are feats of engineering skill, though the watch industry has experienced a recession in recent years. Politically neutral, Switzerland hosts the European Office of the United Nations and the headquarters of many other international organizations; the International Red Cross was founded here. It is a peaceful, stable country, whose industrious and tidy people enjoy great prosperity and live surrounded by outstanding natural beauty.

COUNTRY BRIEFING

Size: 15,941 square miles   **Population:** 6,329,000
Capital: Bern   **Capital Population:** 142,900

   Climate: Very cold in the mountain areas, with much snow. In the cities, the summer temperature seldom gets above the 80s, and humidity is low. The clear air and lack of wind make sunbathing in mountain areas possible even in winter. Daily weather reports covering the main holiday resorts are posted in all the important railroad stations and outside post offices in holiday resorts. For detailed information on the state of roads and Alpine passes, tel: 163 (from anywhere in Switzerland; no area code necessary) if you understand German, Italian, or French. For winter sports, the best time to go is between December and the end of April.

   Weather in Geneva   Lat N46°12′; Alt 1,329 ft

Temp (°F)	Jan	Feb	Mar	Apr	May	Jun	Jul	Aug	Sep	Oct	Nov	Dec
Av Low	29°	30°	35°	41°	48°	55°	58°	57°	52°	44°	37°	31°
Av High	39°	48°	51°	58°	66°	73°	77°	76°	69°	58°	47°	40°
Days no rain	21	19	21	19	19	19	22	21	20	20	19	21

   Government: Switzerland is a federal republic. Each of its 26 cantons (20 full cantons and 6 half cantons) sends representatives to legislative bodies corresponding to the US Senate and House of Representatives. Switzerland, founded in 1291, is the oldest existing democracy. Its modern form dates back to 1848.

   Language: The national languages of Switzerland are German (central, northern, and eastern regions), French (in the west), Italian (in the south), and in the Grisons area Romansh, spoken by 1% of the population. English is taught in schools and widely spoken.

   Religion: Predominant faiths are Roman Catholic and Reformed Protestant.

   Currency: Swiss francs. 100 centimes or rappen = 1 Swiss franc.

	10¢	50¢	SF 1	SF 10	SF 20	SF 50	SF 100	SF 200
US (dollars, cents)	.05	.25	.49	4.91	9.82	25.55	49.09	98.18
UK (pounds, pence)	.02	.12	.23	2.35	4.69	12.21	23.46	46.92

Public Holidays:

New Year's Day, 1 Jan	Whit Monday
Good Friday	Labor Day, 1 May
Easter Monday	Christmas Day, 25 Dec
Ascension Day	Boxing Day, 26 Dec

HOW TO GET THERE

Flying time to Zürich's Kloten Airport from New York is 8¼ hours; from London, 1¼ hours; from Frankfurt, ¾ hour. Flying time to Geneva's

Cointrin Airport from New York is 7¾ hours; from London or Frankfurt, 1 hour. Time in Switzerland: GMT+1.

REQUIREMENTS FOR ENTRY AND CUSTOMS REGULATIONS

A valid passport; no visa or vaccination certificates are needed unless coming from an infected area. Duty-free allowance for US residents: 400 cigarettes or 100 cigars or 500 grams of tobacco; 1 liter of over 25% alcohol spirits; 2 liters of under 25% alcohol spirits; ½ liter of perfume; children under 17 have half this allowance. There are no limits on Swiss products taken out of the country, except watches. You can have up to five sent to your home or ten delivered to your aircraft without an export license from the Swiss Horological Chamber, but remember your country's duty-free allowance.

AIRPORT INFORMATION

Zürich's Kloten Airport is 7 miles from the city center and is linked with its air terminal in the main station *(Hauptbahnhof)* by a 10-minute ride on a shuttle train that operates at 20-minute intervals; fare is SF5.20 1st class, SF3.40 2nd class. Many mainline trains also stop at the airport's underground station, providing direct connections with other parts of Switzerland. Taxis available at all times, from the airport to city center costing about SF35, and as in most major Swiss cities, the tip is included in the fare. Basel-Mulhouse Airport (actually on French soil, but you go through Swiss customs) is 4 miles from the town center; the bus fare is SF4.50 to the terminal at the main station. There are no airport arrival or departure taxes. At all airports there are duty-free shops and hotel reservation counters. Tip porters at least SF1 per piece of luggage.

Geneva's Cointrin Airport is 2½ miles from the Cornavin air terminal located in the main railroad station. Taxi fare to the terminal is about SF15, and the bus fare SF3.50. Airport buses depart every 15-20 minutes between 7am and 11pm and 40 minutes before flight time for flights earlier than 7.

A direct bus service links Cointrin with the Tourist Office terminal in Lausanne at 90-minute intervals, 7:45am-10:30pm from the airport, 5:45am-8:30pm from Lausanne; the trip takes 50 minutes and cost SF15, children SF7.50.

ACCOMMODATIONS

The Swiss have few rivals when it comes to high standards in hotels. To help you choose, the **Swiss Hotel Association** publishes a guide listing its 2,200 members. It includes pensions, spas, and climate resorts; lists of camping sites are available from tourist offices. A list of Youth Hostels for young people under 26 can be obtained from the **Swiss National Tourist Office**. Hotel reservations can be made at main stations from June to September, from morning-10pm. There are special off-peak season rates, but many hotels may close in their off season (e.g. winter sports hotels may close in summer). Investigate package stays and tours.

USEFUL INFORMATION

Banks: Open 8:30-4:30 Mon-Fri. American Express and Thomas Cook & Son have branches in all major Swiss cities. Citibank has branches in Geneva, Lugano, Lausanne, and Zürich; the Bank of America, Morgan Guaranty, Chase Manhattan, Chemical Bank, and Manufacturers Hanover are in Zürich. You can also change currency and travelers' checks at official exchange offices at railroad stations, airports, and in many hotels.

Mail: You can buy postage stamps at post offices and sometimes at postcard kiosks. Mailboxes are yellow and set in walls, with the Swiss flag emblem on them. There are also stamp and postcard machines.

Telephones: The telephone system is automatic, and all numbers within Switzerland can be reached by direct dialing. Besides the phone booths in the post and telegraph offices, you will find booths on the street with directions for use in several languages, giving details on call charges. Local calls cost 40 centimes. Useful numbers:

Pan Am	**Airport Information:**
(Geneva) 32 38 34	(Basel) 57 25 11
Tourist Office	(Geneva) 98 31 11
(Basel) 25 38 11	(Zürich) 812 71 71
(Bern) 21 12 12	**Police** 117
(Geneva) 28 72 33	**Time** 161
(Lausanne) 27 73 21	**Weather & Avalanche**
(Zürich) 211 40 00	**Bulletin** 162
Information in English	**Road Conditions** 163
Swiss numbers 111	**National Tourist Office**
International numbers 191	(Zürich) 202 37 37
	International Service 114

Newspapers: International daily newspapers available; local tourist-oriented English-language publications like the *Zürich Weekly Bulletin* and the *Basel Weekly Bulletin* are available in key cities.

Tipping: Because service is included in hotel or restaurant checks, it is not necessary to give more. Porters get SF1 for each bag they carry; taxi drivers expect 12-15%, except in cities, where service is included in fare; hairdressers, 15%. Cloakroom attendant should receive SF1 if the service charge is not posted.

Electricity: 220 volts 50 cycles AC in most places.

Laundry: Dry-cleaning and laundry services available in large cities and some resort hotels. The service is excellent, the work beautiful, but prices high (dry-cleaning a suit, from SF15; laundering a shirt from SF4). There are numerous discount, 3-hour cleaners in all major cities.

Hairdressing: Shampoo and set from SF20; man's haircut from SF12. Tip about 15%.

Photography: A good selection of equipment, black and white and color film all over the country. Black and white film costs about SF6 for a roll of 36; Kodacolor, SF4.50 for 24; Kodachrome SF10 for 20 including processing.

Clubs: Rotary, Lions, and Kiwanis clubs meet regularly in the larger cities. Rotary meets at the Carlton-Elite in Zürich and Kiwanis at the

Zunfthaus zur Waag. Local US consulates will give information about meetings of the Swiss Friends of the USA and the Swiss Society for Cultural Relations with America, as well as local American Clubs and other organizations.

Babysitting: Can usually be arranged through the advice of the local tourist office and at your hotel.

Rest Rooms: Rest rooms in hotels, restaurants, as well as in most stores are free of charge. In stations the charge is usually 20 centimes. Women, *Damen, dames, signore;* men, *Herren, messieurs, signori.*

Health: Many doctors and dentists speak English. Imported and world-renowned Swiss-made pharmaceuticals in chemists. (Visitors often confuse drugstores with the Swiss word *Droguerie* which is actually where one buys toiletries. *Pharmacie* is where you buy medicinal items.) There is a Swiss spa or sanitarium for almost every ailment and Switzerland is one of the great healing centers of the world.

TRANSPORTATION

Travel by train, bus, boat, or air in Switzerland and you will journey comfortably and arrive punctually. The railroad network is entirely electric, and all principal cities are served. The Eurailpass is accepted in Switzerland. You can also buy round-trip tickets for 10 days (but they can be extended) for 25% less than the price of two one-way tickets, and children under 6 can ride free. Up to 16 they pay half fare. The long-distance Swiss Postal Motor Service links mountain areas not reached by rail; you can reserve seats at any post office in Switzerland. Switzerland's larger lakes have a well-organized service of fast, comfortable steamers, most of which serve food. The most convenient way to pay for a Swiss trip is to buy a **Swiss Holiday Card** available from the Swiss National Tourist offices before departure. It entitles the holder to unlimited travel on the entire network of the Swiss Federal Railways, including most private and mountain railroads, the postal motor buses, and lake steamers. It also entitles the holder to purchase locally an unlimited number of transportation tickets at a reduction of up to 50% for excursions to mountain tops not included in the ticket. It is available at half price for children from 6-16, and you can buy 4-day, 8-day, 15-day, or 1-month passes.

In the cities there are buses, trolleys, and taxis. On all local routes tickets must be obtained at automatic vending machines before boarding the vehicle. The cost varies from city to city, but is generally in Geneva's range of 60 centimes for a very short ride to SF1 for a longer one. Taxis are readily available, and the best way to get one is at a stand or by phone. Taxis are metered. The overall speed limit in Switzerland outside urban areas is 100 kilometers (62 miles) per hour, except on expressways.

FOOD AND RESTAURANTS

Switzerland is divided gastronomically just as it is linguistically, and each region has its specialty. You will have *fondue* and *raclette* (melted cheese dishes) in the French section; all kinds of *Wurst* (sausages), roasts, wild game in season, and special hashed potatoes *(rösti)* in the German areas; *Bündnerfleisch* (beef hung up to dry in the mountain air and then served paper thin) in the Grisons. *Fondue bourguignonne* is popular everywhere; you spear a piece of meat and dip it in sizzling hot oil, then into one of a variety of piquant sauces. Italian specialties in the Ticino include *risotto* (rice, tomatoes, and mushrooms); *osso buco* (leg of veal); *zabaglione* (a dessert of egg yolks, marsala, and sugar); and spaghetti and ravioli. Cheese is an important food item; there is cream cheese *(Vacherin)* made in the Jura and Alpine pastures, and the famous Gruyère and Emmental; Bagnes and Conches, rather hard, used for *raclette;* cheese cakes *(Ramequins);* mountain cheese like Urner; or the cheese soup *(Käsesuppe)* made in central Switzerland. You can buy marvelous cakes and pastries, especially in Zürich and Lucerne.

Usual meal times are: breakfast 7-9:30, lunch 12-2, dinner 6-11. Tea, coffee, or chocolate with pastries from 4-5pm. In an expensive restaurant expect to pay US$35 (without wine, which comes high) per person for dinner; in a medium-priced restaurant, US$15, and in an inexpensive place US$8. The Zürich Tourist Office publishes a list of restaurants where visitors can dine for less than SF10 (US$5).

DRINKING TIPS

Switzerland is a major wine-importing country that also produces its own incredible range of fine wines. The Swiss enjoy it with meals, and as a favorite apéritif. Their own wines are excellent; drink them young from the local vineyards. The tastiest red wines come from Ticino, Lake Geneva, Neuchâtel, and the southern Valais (Dôle). The best whites include *Hermitage, Fendant,* and *Johannisberg* from the Valais (the highest vineyards in Europe); *St-Saphorin* and *Dézaley* from the Vaud. *Glühwein,* a hot spiced wine, is the inevitable après-ski drink. Grisons wines include *Maienfeld, Chur, Malans, Jenins,* and *Zizers.* Some fine Rhine-type wines are produced in the Schaffhausen region. Liqueurs are delicious and strong; *Marc, Kirsch* (originally cherry liqueur), *Pflümli, Williamine* are the best known. Most imported wines, liquors, and beers are available. The average price of a whisky and soda begins at SF8. A bottle of ordinary red wine would cost about SF8 in a shop, SF20 in a restaurant. By all means sample local "open" wines by the deciliter and save money. Restaurants tend not to have drinking bars.

ENTERTAINMENT

Music, opera, and theater are all first class in Switzerland, and the major towns hold important arts festivals, including the **Zürich June Festival,** **Montreux Jazz Festival** (end of June, early July), **Locarno Film Festival** (July), **Yehudi Menuhin Festival** at Gstaad (August), and the **International Festival of Music** in Lucerne (August-September). Throughout the summer you can listen to organ music weekly in **Bern Cathedral** and at **Grossmünster Cathedral** in Zürich. Concerts can be heard in the delightful setting of the **Hôtel de Ville courtyard,** Geneva. Serious playgoers should see performances (in German) at the **Zürich Schauspielhaus,** one of Europe's best (closed in summer).

English and American movies are usually shown with original soundtrack, with German and French subtitles. Performances are not continuous, and seats can be reserved in advance.

Many resorts have casinos with gaming rooms. *Boule,* a modified form of roulette, is the only game. Do not expect to see fortunes made and lost; the limit per bet is SF5. There is occasional horse racing in larger cities, and winter racing on snow tracks in Davos, Arosa, and St Moritz.

You are bound to come across some unique local festivity, from cow contests in the Valais to the Alps festival in the Bernese Oberland, where champions compete in flag swinging, alphorn blowing, and Alpine wrestling. In Zürich there is a big spring festival, the **"Sechseläuten"**—in the Engadine the "Chalanda Marz"—organized by the descendants of craft guilds with a costumed parade, numerous floats, and the burning of winter in effigy. Other celebrations include **Swiss National Day,** 1 August, celebrated all over the country with speeches and fireworks; the **Geneva Festival,** with its battle of flowers in mid-August; the **Wine Festival** at Neuchâtel in September; the **Onion Market,** Bern, November; the **Escalade Festival** at Geneva with torchlit processions through the streets in December; and the **Vogel Gryff Festival of Three Guilds** in Basel, a river festival with rafts and processions in January. Not to be missed are the **Wine Expositions** on lake steamers in Zürich and Geneva; this happens end of October-November and is a tippler's delight.

SHOPPING

Stores open in larger cities 9-6:30 weekdays, 9-4 Sat. Smaller stores may be open earlier, closed during lunch hour. English is frequently spoken.

What to buy? The world's finest selection of watches, although the saving is not as large as before Orient competition. Switzerland is famous for its precision-made products: movie cameras, optical instruments, stainless steel knives, and typewriters. Music boxes, wood carvings, cuckoo clocks, and Swiss chocolate make good presents. Most large towns have intriguing little antique shops and fine bookstores—art books are beautifully produced here. Ski clothes and equipment are naturally top quality. Folkcraft items may be bought at *Heimatwerk* shops located in the larger cities.

Good regional buys include embroidery and lace at **St Gallen;** wood carvings, pottery, and leather in the **Bernese Oberland;** wines from **Neuchâtel, Valais, Vaud;** cheese from **Valais, Emmental, Gruyère;** leather from **Spiez.**

SPORTS

The best season for winter sports is December to the end of April, and there are three main areas: **Valais, Grisons,** and the **Bernese Oberland.** Among popular resorts are **Zermatt, Davos, Klosters, Pontresina, Bad Scuol, Flims, Laax, Lenzerheide, St Moritz, Gstaad, Arosa, Verbier, Wen-**

gen, **Mürren,** and **Villars.** Ski and mountain-climbing schools are govern-ment-supervised, and their instructors officially qualified. Lessons are moderately priced, and skis and ski boots can be rented. Cross-country skiing is also very popular.

In summer there are swimming, boating and water-skiing, golf, horse-back riding, rifle shooting, and trap shooting. There is freshwater fishing on **Lake Geneva, Neuchâtel, Bienne,** and **Morat.** In Bern you can get a fishing license from the **Amthaus** (Hodlerstrasse 7).

Spectator sports include soccer, cross-country bike racing, traditional sports like wrestling, *Hornussen* (which, say the Swiss, is a combination of golf and baseball), and *boccia,* a kind of bowls, in the Ticino. Several sporting clubs welcome visitors, including the **Champel Tennis Club** (12 avenue Calas, Geneva) and the **Montreux Tennis Club.** There are 90 branches of the **Swiss Alpine Club.**

WHAT TO SEE

Bern: Switzerland's capital is one of Europe's best-preserved cities, with attractive arcaded streets and decorative fountains. The **Bear Pit,** near **Nydegg Bridge,** is the home of Bern's heraldic animals. **Bern Cathedral** is a handsome example of late Gothic style in Switzerland, with beautiful stained-glass windows and carved choir stall. The nearby clock tower has a famous 16th-century astronomical clock with figures that move four minutes before every hour. The **Art Museum** houses the largest collection of Paul Klee's work in the world. The **City Historical Museum** displays Charles the Bold's booty, and the **Swiss Postal Museum** has one of the world's largest stamp collections open to the public. In the **Botanical Gardens** you can see rare plants native to mountains from the Pyre-nees to the Himalayas. From Easter to the end of October, the old part of the city is illuminated from dusk to midnight, and you will get a good view from the **Rose Garden.** Notable restaurants to try in Bern are the **Casino** (Herrengasse 20—tel: 22 20 27), for moderate prices, music, and fish, specialties; the **Grill Room** at the Hotel Bellevue Palace has good international cuisine (tel: 22 45 81); the **Grill** at the Schweizerhof (tel: 22 45 01) serves excellent Swiss food. A favorite of artists is the **Café du Commerce** for inexpensive Spanish *paella* (Gerechtigkeitgasse 74). A local favorite is **du Théâtre** (Theaterplatz 7), known for its fine general cuisine. The **Klotzlikeller** (Gerechtigkeitgasse 62) is a lively wine cellar, and **Feller** (Marktgasse 31) is good for coffee and cakes.

Nightlife in Bern: There is the **Kursaal** (casino) for dancing and small-time gambling. **Mocambo** (Genfergasse 10) and **Chikito** (Neuengasse 28) are nightclubs with well-known bands for dancing, bars, and cabaret. You might also try the **Babalu** (Gurtengasse 3) or the **Cadillac** (Laupen-strasse 10) for relaxed dining and dancing.

In Bern, the old part of town has excellent antique shops and art galler-ies. Some specialty stores are **J Otto Scherer** (Kramgasse 26) for antique clocks; **Oberlander Heimatwerk** (Kramgasse 61) for handicrafts; and **A & W Muggli** (Hirchengraben 10) for Swiss typewriters. A good depart-ment store is **Loeb** (Spitalgasse 47). Bern hotels include:

Rates are in US$ for a double/twin room with bath or shower

Alfa, Laupenstrasse 15 (from $53)

Bären, Schauplatzgasse 4 (from $53)

Bristol, Schauplatzgasse 10 (from $53)

Hotel Bellevue Palace, Kochergasse 3-5 (from $74)

Kreuz, Zeughausgasse 41 (from $46)

Schweizerhof, Schweizerhoflaube 11 (from $74)

Silvanhof, Jubilaumsstrasse 97 (from $54), near US Embassy, 10 minutes from city center

All hotels listed are centrally located unless indicated otherwise.

Zürich: Zürich is Switzerland's largest city, but seems more like a resort than a commercial and financial center; it is beautifully situated among wooded hills around the shores of a lake. Its fine modern architecture contrasts with the quaint little alleys and squares of the Old Town, crammed with antique shops and elegant boutiques. There is an opera house, theater, and concert halls. Zürich's **Art Museum** (Heimplatz 1) has fine medieval and modern art, including a Giacometti collection. The **Heidi Weber House of LeCorbusier** (Bellerivestrasse 8) was the architect's last building. The **Museum Rietberg** (Gablerstrasse 15, closed Mon) has some of the finest Eastern antiquities in the world. In the **Schweizerisches Landesmuseum,** near the main station, you will see the art and history of old Switzerland, and the **Thomas Mann Archives** preserves documents, souvenirs, and manuscripts of the famous German writer (Schönberggasse 15, near the University; open Wed and Sat, 2-4). The **Wohnmuseum** (Bärengasse 20-22; open Mon, 12-5, Tue-Sun, 10-5) offers a delightful glimpse of Zürich living in the 17th and 18th centuries. The **Grossmünster** (Cathedral), reputedly founded by Charlemagne, is worth visiting.

You will get an excellent meal with regional specialties at **Veltliner Keller** in the Old Town (Schüsselgasse 8—tel: 221 32 28). For expensive French gourmet cuisine, make for the **Hotel Eden du Lac grill** (Utoquai 45). James Joyce, who wrote some of *Ulysses* in Zürich and is buried here, liked the **Kronenhalle** (Rämistrasse 4), where you can enjoy the ambience while admiring original paintings by Picasso, Braque, Matisse, and Bonnard. For memorable dining in atmospheric settings try the **Zunfthaus** (guild) restaurants. To eat well but inexpensively, try the **Zeughauskeller** (near Paradeplatz) and **Feldschlössen** (Bahnhofstrasse 81), and other **Mövenpick** eateries. For memorable summer dining, try the fish specialties at **Fischstube** or **Casino** in Zurichhorn Park. The **Petit Palais** (Baur au Lac Hotel) is a chic nightspot, and the **Mascotte** (Bellevueplatz) has dancing and good jazz. There's also entertainment at **Hazyland** plus a few good discothèques.

Zürich is a shopper's paradise: the fashionable shopping street is the **Bahnhofstrasse** (protected by the 1974 historic preservation law), leading south from the main railroad station and ends at Quai General Guisan. The largest department stores are **Jelmoli** (Seidengasse 1) and the nearby **Globus;** the oldest and most famous confectionery shop is **Confiserie Sprüngli** (Bahnhofstrasse 21) while the **Teuscher Confiserie** (Storchen-

gasse 9) makes exquisite chocolates. For leather goods go to **Leder-Locher & Cie** (Münsterhof 18); for souvenirs, handicrafts, and the most complete toy shop **Franz Carl Weber** (Bahnhofstrasse 62); on Thursday afternoons visit the Weber toy museum and for watches go to almost any store on Bahnhofstrasse. There are over 20 private art galleries, many in the Old Town. Zürich hotels:

Rates are in US$ for a double/twin room with bath or shower

Alexander, am Postgebäude (from $51)

Ascot, Lavaterstrasse 15 (from $64)

Atlantis, Döltschiweg 234 (from $82), near residential section

Guesthouse Atlantis, adjacent to main hotel, offers accommodations (from $50)

Baur au Lac, Talstrasse 1 (from $102), near the lake

Bellerive au Lac, Utoquai 47 (from $66), on the lake

Carlton Elite, Bahnhofstrasse 41 (from $82)

Chesa Rustica, Limmatquai 70 (from $56)

Continental, Stampfenbachstrasse 60 (from $71)

Dolder Grand, Kurhausstrasse 65 (from $97), in residential section

Eden au Lac, Utoquai 45 (from $92)

Engematthof, Engimattstrasse 14 (from $48)

Europe, Dufourstrasse 4 (from $61)

Florhof, Florhofsgasse 4 (from $51)

Florida, Seefeldstrasse 63 (from $41)

Holiday Inn, Mövenpick Zürich Airport (from $51), 15 minutes from center

Nova-Park, Badenerstrasse 420 (from $61)

Opera, Dufourstrasse 5 (from $53)

Savoy Hotel Baur En Ville, Poststrasse 12 (from $92)

St Gotthard, Bahnhofstrasse 87 (from $77)

Seehotel Meierhof, Zürich-Horgen (from $51)

Schweizerhof, Bahnhofplatz 7 (from $82)

Waldhaus Dolder, Kurhausstrasse (from $89)

Zum Storchen, Weinplatz 2 (from $82)

Zürich Airport Hilton, Zürich Airport (from $71), 15 minutes from center

All hotels listed are located in central Zürich unless otherwise indicated.

Geneva: Switzerland's most international city has 2,000 years of history behind it. Julius Caesar was the first to mention it, and Calvin preached reform and austerity here from **St Peters Church** in the 16th century; it was the birthplace of Jean-Jacques Rousseau and the Red Cross was founded here in 1864. Geneva is now headquarters of over 200 international organizations and the European seat of the United Nations; as a result it is a polyglot, cosmopolitan city with excellent restaurants, shops, and entertainment facilities. The **Petit Palais** (2 terrasse Saint-Victor) shows modern art from Renoir to Picasso. The **Art and History Museum** (11 rue Charles-Galland), the **Ariana Museum** (10 avenue de la Paix), for porcelain and pottery, and the **Voltaire** (25 rue des Délices) and **Jean-Jacques Rousseau** (Promenade des Bastions) museums are especially interesting. There is the annual **Fête de Genève** every August; other exhibitions include one for watches and jewelry in September, and the **Auto Show** in March.

Restaurants to try are **La Perle du Lac** (128 rue de Lausanne—tel: 31 35 04) in a lovely garden by the lake, with fish specialties and moderate prices; **Restaurant Le Duc** (Quai du Mt Blanc, 7—tel: 31 73 30), which has its fish flown in daily from France; **Le Gentilhomme** (Hotel Richemond—tel: 31 14 00); **Le Boeuf Rouge** (7 rue de Paquis—tel: 32 75 37), for French Lyonnaise cooking; or **Restaurant des Eaux Vives** (Place des Eaux Vives—tel: 36 46 40) and **Le Béarn** (4 quai de la Poste—tel: 21 00 28), expensive and famous—try *saucisson sous la cendre;* **L'Or du Rhône** (19 boulevard George Favon—tel: 28 55 91), for steaks and chicken grilled over an open fire; **Café du Dézaley** (63 boulevard du Pont d'Arve—tel: 29 55 91), moderately expensive, good Valais specialties; **Les Armures** (1 Puits-St Pierre—tel: 28 91 72) for Swiss cheese specialties. For lunch try **Restaurant L'Aioli** (Place du Port, 2—tel: 28 50 68). There is a good floor show and dancing at **La Tour.**

Where to shop in Geneva: for cameras, **Photo Mont-Blanc** (17 rue de Mont-Blanc); for candies, **Chocolâterie du Rhône** (2 rue du Rhône); a good department store—**Au Grand Passage** (13 rue du Marché); sports equipment, **Charles Sports** (23 quai des Bergues); souvenirs and wood carvings, **A l'Ours de Berne** (28 quai Général Guisan), and watches from **A Collet** (8 place du Molard), **Clarence** (3 rue du Marché), while **Patek Philippe's** shop is to be found at Quai General Guisan, 22—tel: 20 03 66. Hotels in Geneva include:

Rates are in US$ for a double/twin room with bath or shower
Angleterre, 17 Quai du Mont Blanc (from $77)
Arbalète, 3 Tour-Maitresse (from $87)
Beau Rivage, 13 Quai du Mont Blanc (from $94), on the lake
California, 1 Rue Gevray (from $56)
De Berne, 26 Rue de Berne (from $48)
De La Paix, 11 Quai du Mont Blanc (from $92), on the lake
Des Bergues, 33 Quai des Bergues (from $97)
Du Rhône, Quai Turrettini (from $87)
Hilton International, 19 Quai du Mont Blanc (from $99)
Noga Hotel d'Alleves, Passage Kleberg 13 (from $50)
Hotel Rotary, Rue du Cendrier 18-20 (from $77)
INTER · CONTINENTAL GENEVA, 7-9 Pt Saconnex (from $87), 10 minutes from city center near UN
Penta, near airport (from $66)
Président, 47 Quai Wilson (from $145)
La Réserve, 301 route de Lausanne (from $94), on lake, 10 minutes from city center
Le Richemond, Jardin Brunswick (from $94)
Suisse, 10 Place Cornavin (from $43)
Windsor, 31 Rue de Berne (from $46)
All of the hotels listed are centrally located unless otherwise indicated.

Basel was founded by the Romans in 44 BC. The chemical drug industry is located here. Its position on the Rhine at the junction of France, Germany, and Switzerland also makes it an important port.

Perhaps Basel is most famous for its *Faslnacht* (Shrove Tuesday) **Carnival,** which lasts several days. There are many museums and art galleries, including the **Art Museum** *(Kunstmuseum)* in St Albangraben, with one of the finest collections of modern art in Europe and a fine Holbein collection. Do not miss the 11th-century **Cathedral** *(Münster),* where Erasmus is buried, or the lovely square and medieval houses surrounding it. There is an excellent zoo.

The main shopping street is the **Freiestrasse.** Among good department stores, **Magazine zur Rheinbrücke** (Greifengasse 24) and **Globus** (Markplatz). For handicrafts, **Heimatwerk Basel** (Freiestrasse 45 and 81); sports equipment, **Kost-Sport** (Freiestrasse 51). Good restaurants include **Safranzunft** (Gerbergasse 11), an old Guildhall restaurant; **Chez Donati** (St Johannsvorstadt) for good, reasonably priced Italian food; the **Euler & Grand Hotel** (Centralbahnplatz 14) and **Bruderholz** (Bruderholzallee 42), with garden atmosphere, for excellent, though more expensive cuisine. Basel hotels:

Rates are in US$ for a double/twin room with bath or shower

Basel, Münzgasse 12 (from $61)

Basel Hilton, Aeschengraben 31 (from $77)

Drei Könige am Rhein, Blumenrain 8 (from $82)

Euler & Grand, Centralbahnplatz 14 (from $77)

International, Steinentorstrasse 25 (from $66)

Krafft am Rhein, Rheingasse 12 (from $43)

Schweizerhof, Centralbahnplatz 1 (from $64)

All of the hotels listed are located in central Basel.

Lucerne is a traditional vacation center and one of Switzerland's prettiest towns as well as a watch shopping center. It is famous for its carved stone lion and medieval wooden bridge with its painted roof. Worth seeing too are the **Collegiate Church,** the town ramparts, and the baroque interior of the **Jesuit Church.** There is an **Art Museum,** an unusual **Transport Museum,** including a planetarium, the recently opened **Hans Erni Haus** with more than 300 works by Switzerland's most famous living artist, and a museum of Swiss costume. The **Glacier Gardens** contain skulls and bones of prehistoric animals. There is an annual **Music Festival** in Lucerne held in August and September—reserve in advance. You will have splendid views of the town and lake from the heights of **Pilatus** or **Rigi,** reached by mountain railroad. **Vitznau** and **Weggis** are pretty lakeside resorts, and **Altdorf** is famous as the scene of William Tell's legendary arrow shot. Lake excursions to take include a ride across Lake Lucerne to **Bürgenstock,** a plush resort with spectacular views, and over to **Trieschen,** Wagner's home, now a museum. Some good restaurants: **Château Gütsch** (Kanonenstrasse); **Zum Wilden Mann** (in the hotel), with a medieval atmosphere; **Galliker** (Kasernenplatz), for medium-priced Swiss specialties; and the **Old Swiss House** by the Lion of Lucerne.

Lausanne on Lake Geneva is an education center of Switzerland. Its university dates from the 16th century. Many international conferences are held here at the **Palais des Congrès.** It was a favorite retreat of exiled royalty. From the elegant suburb of **Ouchy,** where Byron stayed, you can take a steamer trip to **St Sulpice** to see the best-preserved Romanesque church in Switzerland. Nearby is the lovely lakeside village of **Vevey** associated with Rousseau and Victor Hugo, home of the Swiss multinational Nestlé world headquarters, and the fabled **Hotel Trois Couronnes** (from US$61).

For dining out try **La Grappe d'Or** (3 Cheneau-de-Bourg); **Le Mandarin** (7 avenue du Theâtre)—Chinese; **Chez Godio** (2 Place Pepinet) and a typical Swiss cellar, **Carnotzet du Petit Chêne,** Alpha-Palmiers Hotel (34 Petit-Chêne) for cheese specialties. At **Crissier,** just outside Lausanne, **Girardet's** restaurant at 1 rue d'Yverdon has won recognition as one of Europe's best eating places.

Shopping in Lausanne: For cameras—**Schnell & Fils** (4 place St François); jewelry from **A l'Emeraude** (5 place St François); watches from **Bijoux Windsor** (34 avenue de la Gare); and sports equipment from **Sports-Ausoni** (5 place St François).

Lausanne hotels: **De la Paix,** 5 Avenue Benjamin-Constant, the **Royal Savoy,** 40 avenue d'Ouchy, and the **Victoria,** 46 avenue de la Gare, have double rooms from US$51. Also **Le Beau-Rivage** on Lake Geneva at Ouchy (from US$87), a patrician hotel. The **Chateau Ouchy** and **La Résidence,** both near the lake, offer double rooms from US$51.

Montreux has attracted visitors since the 18th century, when young British aristocrats on the "grand tour" visited Europe to complete their education. Its palms and pomegranates testify to its mild winter. **Chillon Castle,** immortalized by Byron and a few miles away on the lake, is one of the most romantic sights in Europe. You can take a 1-day trip to see **Mont Blanc.**

Try the **Taverne du Château de Chillon,** an open-air restaurant facing the lake, the **Bavaria** (café-type), or the **Vieux Montreux**—a typical cellar restaurant.

The Montreux casino has dancing, a restaurant, and a cabaret, and the **Hungaria** has a floor show and dancing. Lake trips can be taken on steamers where dancing is featured. Hotels in Montreux:

Eurotel, Grand-Rue 81 (from US$53)

Excelsior, Rue Bon Port 21 (from US$46)

Grand Hôtel Suisse & Majestic (from US$53)

Montreux Palace (from US$92)

National, Chemin du National 2 (from US$53)

All hotels listed are centrally located.

Interlaken is the chief town of the Bernese Oberland, situated between Lake Thun and Lake Brienz with a fantastic view of the **Jungfrau.** The name derives from the German for "between the lakes." Stroll along the Höleweg and admire the brilliant summer flowers and incredible scenery. Take the rack-railroad to the **Schynige Platte,** or the boat excursion to the **Griessback Falls.** There are beaches and a swimming pool, golf, riding, sailing, and water-skiing. Interlaken is a good base for rambling in the surrounding mountains, for excursions on the two lakes, and for trips high up into the Jungfrau area. Europe's highest railroad takes you to over 11,300 feet. There is a casino (summer only) where you can gamble, or just listen to music. Hotels in Interlaken:

Beau-Rivage, Höheweg 211 (from US$50)

Belvédère, Höheweg 95 (from US$39)

Bernerhof, Bahnhofstrasse 16 (from US$34)

Métropole, Höheweg (from US$49)

Victoria Jungfrau (from US$57)

All of the hotels listed are centrally located. Interlaken enjoys a low, middle, and high season, so rates fluctuate, slightly.

Nearby in this canton is **Gstaad,** one of the most popular holiday resorts of the Bernese Oberland. All winter sports are available here, and in summer there are golf and tennis tournaments. The **Gstaad Palace,** with its own swimming pool, tennis courts, and golf, has double rooms from US$112 low season to US$184 high season. The **Grand Hotel Alpina** and **Park-Hotel Reuteler** have double rooms from US$77-117. The **Grand Hotel Bellevue** has double rooms from US$66-102.

Zermatt, 5,302 feet up near the Matterhorn, is free of all traffic, and exhaust fumes are unknown. With the longest skiing season in Europe, it draws visitors from the world over. But it has also attracted summer visitors ever since 1865, when Edward Whymper made the first ascent of the Matterhorn. The view from the **Gornergrat,** at 10,289 feet, is unique, while the highest cable-car in Europe takes one to the breathtaking **Little Matterhorn** at 12,533 ft. There are many hotels, holiday apartments, and rooms to rent. A few notable ones are the **Grand Hotel Zermatterhof** and **Mont Cervin,** both from US$122; the **Nicoletta, Alex,** and **Monte Rosa,** from US$98; the **Hotel Walliserhof** (from US$86); and **Parnass** (from US$57); all near the station. Zermatt also has a middle and low season.

The Grisons: Many of the most popular ski resorts are in this area; St Moritz, Davos, Arosa, Flims, Laax, Pontresina, Savognin, Lenzerheide, Bad Scuol, and Klosters. It has some of the highest, most rugged mountains in Europe. But it is also worth visiting at other times of year, especially late spring. See the **Swiss National Park** for its wildlife and the **Engadine Valley** for its charming villages, such as **Guarda,** with its decorated peasant houses, Bad Scuol, **Zoaz** and **Tarasp,** dominated by a dramatic 11th-century castle.

Arosa: A smart, fully developed ski center, Arosa is 1 hour from **Chur,** the canton's pretty, medieval capital, by train or car. There are three natural ice rinks plus one artificial rink and an excellent ski school. The Casino *(kursaal)* is the focal point of Arosa's nightlife. Stay at the **Alexandra Palace Hotel** (US$87-148) or the **Park Hotel** (US$56-138).

Davos, one of the most sophisticated skiing resorts, has particularly pure air and bright sunshine. It was the setting for Thomas Mann's "Magic Mountain." It offers good food, lively entertainment, and ample sports facilities. Stay at the **Schweizerhof** for first-class accommodation (US$58-

113); **Seehof** (US$91-107); **Derby** (US$92-122); the less expensive **Bellavista Sport,** Davos-Platz (US$47-82); or the **Belvedere Grand Hotel** (US$98-143).

St Moritz is the world's most fashionable winter sports resort. International celebrities come here to enjoy its excellent skiing and social life. But it is beautiful, and less expensive, in summer. There are many first-class hotels, shops, and facilities for all kinds of sport. The **Palace Hotel,** superior de luxe (US$112-219), and the **Carlton** (US$87-143), are both in St Moritz-Dorf; the **Kulm** (US$82-132); and the **Hotel Belvedere** (US$51-71).

The Ticino, on the far side of the Gotthard, is Italian-speaking Switzerland, and everything changes; climate, language, architecture. From Alpine valleys the road runs down to Locarno, Brissago by Lake Maggiore, on to Lugano, and then down into the southern Mendrisiotto. It is a warm, relaxing, and beautiful region. **Locarno** on Lake Maggiore is pretty and is said to have more sunshine than anywhere else in Switzerland. Take a lake excursion to the **Isles** of **Brissago,** with their subtropical gardens. **Lugano** has a beautiful position in a bay by Lake Lugano. In the **Abbey Church of Santa Maria degli Angeli** there are magnificent frescoes by Luini, a pupil of Leonardo da Vinci. **La Villa Favorita** contains the magnificent private art collection of Baron von Thyssen-Bornemisza, open to the public in summer. Lugano's many hotels include the **International au Lac Hotel,** via Nassa 68 (from US$44); **Splendide Royal,** Riva a Caccia 7 (from US$82); and the **Arizona,** via Massagno 20 (from US$48). Cooking is, of course, mostly Italian with Ticinese specialties.

Northeastern Switzerland: The main town here is **St Gallen,** which lies between Lake Constance and Mount Säntis. It is an ancient city with a fine **Cathedral** and the **Abbey Library,** containing priceless books and manuscripts. St Gallen is the center of commercial and industrial life in the east and is famous for its fine cotton, lace, and embroidery.

SOURCES OF FURTHER INFORMATION

Pan Am, rue du Mont Blanc, 7, 3rd floor, Geneva, or any Pan Am office around the world; **Office du Tourisme,** rue Tour de l'ile 1, Geneva; **Offizielles Verkehrsbüro,** Main Station, Basel, and Blumenrain 2, Basel; **Swiss National Tourist Office,** Bellariastrasse 38, Zürich. Other offices at 608 Fifth Avenue, New York, NY 10020; 250 Stockton Street, San Francisco, CA 94108; 104 South Michigan Avenue, Chicago, IL 60603; and Suite 2015, Commerce Court West, Toronto, Ontario, Canada, The **Swiss Center,** 1 New Coventry Street, London W1.

USSR

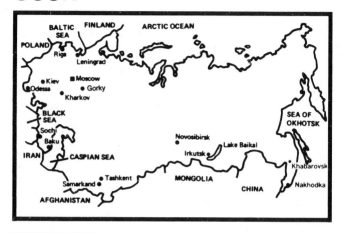

WHAT'S SPECIAL

From earliest times the migrations of Huns and Tartars and the civilizations of ancient Greece, Byzantium, and Islam have left their mark on the 8 million square miles of the USSR. But in little more than 65 years since the Bolshevik Revolution, the Soviet Union has risen from a feudal economy to become the world's second most powerful industrial state. Inside the Kremlin is the Supreme Soviet, the nation's Parliament. Throughout all of the 15 republics it represents, you would not expect to find the same traditions or attitudes to life. In fact, this sprawling nation that spans two continents has historically been a meeting ground of Muslim, Asian, and European cultures—a mosaic of over 150 nationalities. The diversity of her peoples, climate, and landscape is reflected in painting, music, dance, architecture, literature, and drama. Moscow is a microcosm of the Soviet Union, for there you can see Tartars, Ukrainians, Uzbeks, and Georgians working and studying together.

Tourism in the USSR is generally well organized. The network of low-priced transportation is opening up the country to tourists, and even the 7-day journey to Khabarovsk on the Trans-Siberian Express is a worthwhile experience. Foreigners are looked upon with lively curiosity and people will be eager to meet you.

COUNTRY BRIEFING

Size: 8,649,490 square miles   **Population:** 266,600,000
Capital: Moscow   **Capital Population:** 8,099,000

Climate: Ranges from extreme Arctic conditions in Siberia to subtropical along the Black Sea coast. From June through September, the USSR near Europe has weather similar to that in the northern US. Crimea and the Caucasus in the south have mild winters and hot summers. February is springtime in the Central Asian part of the Soviet Union; summers there are torrid; the fall is warm.

Weather in Moscow: Lat N55° 46′; Alt 505 ft

Temp (°F)	Jan	Feb	Mar	Apr	May	Jun	Jul	Aug	Sep	Oct	Nov	Dec
Av Low	9°	10°	17°	31°	44°	51°	55°	52°	43°	34°	23°	13°
Av High	21°	23°	32°	47°	65°	73°	76°	72°	61°	46°	31°	23°
Days no rain	20	19	23	21	22	20	19	19	21	20	20	22

Government: The highest legislative authority is the Supreme Soviet of the USSR. The Council of Ministers, the executive and administrative body, is appointed by the Presidium of the Supreme Soviet. Real power lies with the Communist Party, which oversees all other organs of government.

Language: Russian is the official language; the multinational population speaks more than 100 other languages in addition, however. English, especially among students, is sometimes spoken, and a few people speak German and French. Interpreter guides can be arranged through Intourist Hotel Bureaus.

Religion: Officially atheist. The largest denomination is the Russian Orthodox Church. There are a substantial number of Muslims, quite a few Protestants, a large Jewish population, not many Roman Catholics.

Currency: Rouble. 100 kopecks = 1 rouble. Rates of foreign exchange are established by the Soviet government at the beginning of every month.

	5 Kop	10 Kop	50 Kop	1 Roub	5 Roub	10 Roub	25 Roub	50 Roub
US (dollars, cents)	.07	.14	.68	1.36	6.80	13.60	34.00	68.00
UK (pounds, pence)	.03	.07	.32	.65	3.24	6.49	16.22	32.44

Public Holidays:

New Year's Day, 1 Jan

International Women's Day, 8 Mar

Labor Day, 1 & 2 May

Victory Day, 9 May

Constitution Day, 7 Oct

Revolution Day, 7 & 8 Nov

HOW TO GET THERE

Flying time from New York to Moscow, Sheremetyevo Airport is 11 hours; from Frankfurt, 3½ hours; from Mexico City, 15 hours; from Tokyo, 10½ hours. Time in Moscow, Leningrad, and Kiev: GMT + 3.

REQUIREMENTS FOR ENTRY AND CUSTOMS REGULATIONS

Passport and visa required; smallpox, yellow-fever and cholera certificates are needed if entering from an infected area. Whether traveling individually or in a group, arrangements including visa applications are handled by travel agencies appointed by and representing Intourist, the Soviet national tourism bureau. Visas are issued only after arrangments are made and the travel agent has received a confirmation number from Intourist, and they are valid only for the duration of the specific tour booked or the individual travel itinerary submitted as part of the visa application. Allow a minimum of two weeks for the visa to be issued, though it is best to apply well in advance up to a maximum of three months prior to the projected date of entry. Visitors whose visas are not in proper order may be detained in a special detection hotel. If you want to visit relatives outside the approved tourist areas, you must have a special visa and an officially approved invitation; start making arrangements several months in advance. You must register with the local police upon arrival and have this registration entered on your visa. The import or export of roubles is forbidden. There is no limit to the amount of foreign money taken into the USSR either in travelers' checks or bills, but the amount must be declared on the customs declaration form. This will be checked against your receipts for money exchanged during your stay and will enable you to convert unused roubles back into your own currency. Valuables must be declared, too. It is important for the visitor to retain his or her copy of the official declaration of the exact amount of foreign currency and valuables, since this copy will be checked on departure. Duty-free allowance: 200 cigarettes or 250 grams other tobacco products; 1 liter liquor and 2 liters wine; 1 still camera and 1 movie camera; gifts worth not more than 30 roubles; perfume for personal use. No works of art or antiquities (such as icons) may be taken out without the permission of the Ministry of Culture (see *Memo for a Foreign Tourist* published by Intourist for details). Items dated prior to 1945 count as antiques. No arms may be taken in or out with the exception of hunting rifles. Hunters must present an Intourist voucher stating that they are following an approved hunting itinerary and must register the serial number of all rifles on the customs declaration form. All rifles must be taken out of the country when the hunter leaves. Although you may of course bring a reasonable amount of reading matter for your own use, do not bring or distribute any printed matter that could be considered pornographic or detrimental to the Soviet Union's interest.

AIRPORT INFORMATION

The New International Terminal 2 was opened in Moscow's Sheremetyevo Airport in 1980. There is an Intourist Information Office in the terminal where a car can be hired to take you to the city center or your hotel, a distance of about 20 miles. The cost per person is 16 roubles for one, 8.50 roubles each for two, and 6 roubles each for three. Taxis are available until midnight, or have Intourist to call one. The taxi fare into Moscow is about 12 roubles. The airport has no duty-free shops.

ACCOMMODATIONS

All types and classes of accommodations, from deluxe hotels to motels and campsites, must be reserved prior to arrival and can be booked for you by Intourist-appointed travel agents. There are special rates for young children, students, and groups. A minimum of 6 weeks' notice is needed to obtain accommodations through Intourist, and though you can ask for a particular hotel, you may be put up elsewhere. Space is especially tight in summer and during trade fairs. Super deluxe suites of three to four rooms cost US$134 single or double, suites of one to two rooms, $95. First-class rooms cost US$66 double, $56 single. (Arrangements and rates for businessmen are slightly different; check with Intourist for details.) Tourist class is available only to visitors from Socialist countries. All hotels used to accommodate foreigners have an Intourist Service Bureau that can arrange sightseeing in addition to that included in the room rates, theater tickets, or restaurant reservations. Listed below are some recommended hotels though it is to be repeated that Intourist will not guarantee you the hotel of your choice. Tell friends your hotel room telephone number to enable them to telephone you, otherwise they will have difficulty in getting through. Hotels in Moscow:

Belgrad, 5 Smolenskaya Street
Berlin, 3 Zhdanov Street
Cosmos, 150 Mira Prospect
Intourist, 3-5 Gorky Street
Leningradskaya, 21-40
   Kalanchevskaya Street
Metropol, 1 Marx Prospect
Minsk, 22 Gorky Street

Mozhaiskaya, 165
   Mozhaiskoye Highway
National, 1-14 Marx Prospect
Peking, 5 Bolshaya Sadovaya
   Street
Rossiya, 6 Razin Street,
   opposite the Kremlin
Ukraina, 2/1 Kutuzovsky
   Prospect

USEFUL INFORMATION

Helpful Hints: Never drop litter in the streets—even a cigarette will offend the tidy citizens, and it is illegal. Do not sell clothes, American cigarettes, or other personal effects to individuals. Refer to the Soviet Union, not Russia. A hat is essential and overshoes very useful. Be sure to bring all your own toiletries and a bathplug, especially if traveling outside Moscow.

Banks: Open 9-1 Mon-Fri, 9-12 Sat. Exchange bureaus in hotels are open 8:30am-11:30pm daily. Airports and railroad stations also have exchange bureaus. American Express is at 21A Sadova Kudrinskaya. Large cities also have branches of state banks. Always keep receipts of currency exchanges (see Customs Regulations). Do not change money except at official places, as black-market transactions are very heavily penalized. Keep some of your own currency for hard-currency shops and "dollar bars," where you must pay in foreign currency.

Mail: There are post office facilities in the larger hotels.

Telephone Tips: You can call from all hotels, some bars and restaurants, and public booths. In the latter the telephones work with a 2-kopeck coin. Insert coin, listen for dial tone, then dial. If the number connects, coin will drop. If an operator replies in Russian, say "Po-Angliiski" and wait for someone who speaks English. Useful numbers in Moscow:

Pan Am 223-51-83	**Intourist Representative**
Operator and Directories 09	**at Sheremetyevo** 578-59-71
Intourist 203-60-62	**Overseas Calls** 8194
	US Embassy 252-24-51

Newspapers: Hotel lobbies sell Soviet-approved foreign books as well as newspapers and magazines in Russian and many foreign languages. The locally published English-language paper is the *Moscow News.*

Tipping: Frowned on officially, but the following rates will be cheerfully received: cloakroom attendants, 20 kopecks; hairdressers, 10-15% of check; taxi drivers, 10-15%; waiters, 10-15% unless service is included; porters at airports and railroad stations, 25-50 kopecks per bag. Guides and interpreters will be more grateful for small gifts of Western origin.

Electricity: Mostly 220 volts 50 cycles AC, some 127 volts; European-type plugs and wall outlets. Converters generally not available.

Laundry: Larger hotels have 24-hour dry-cleaning and laundry service.

Hairdressing: Nearly all hotels of any size have salons.

Photography: Color and black and white film available; Kodak not always obtainable and only Agfa can be processed. It is strictly forbidden to photograph anything which might have strategic importance; this may include ships, bridges, and railroads in some areas.

Babysitting: Can possibly be arranged through hotel service bureaus or Intourist.

Rest Rooms: In restaurants, hotels, bars, museums, parks, railroad stations; look for a male of female silhouette on the door. The name is pronounced like the French word, toilette—*twalet.*

Health: Free care for everybody including foreigners—there is a tourists' clinic at 2 Gruzinsky Proyezd. Soviet dentists not recommended.

TRANSPORTATION

Moscow's subway is the cleanest and most grandiose in Europe, with marble halls and chandeliers, and it covers the entire city; price 5 kopecks for any distance. Buses, trolleys, and trains run from 6am-1am; fares are a flat rate of 5 kopecks on buses and trains, 4 kopecks on trolleys. Streetcars run from 5:30am to 1:30am and cost 3 kopecks a ticket. There are self-service ticket machines at the entrance to all public transport vehicles, so keep correct change ready for these. Books of tickets can be bought from the driver. Taxis can be recognized by a checkered band on both sides of the car and a green light on the top right-hand corner of the windshield. If the light is on, the taxi is free—you can hail them in the street. You can also call a taxi from your hotel or get one at a taxi stand. Fixed-route *(marshrootnoye)* shared taxis circulate around central Moscow; you can board them at stops located near bus stops. The fare is 15 kopecks per person but you must know in Russian where you want to get off and tell the driver as you enter.

Car rental: A small car costs 9.10 roubles per day plus 1.50 roubles for insurance, with a charge of 10 kopecks per kilometer (gas extra). A station wagon is 9.40 roubles plus 1.50 roubles insurance per day, and

15 kopecks per kilometer. After the first 10 days the price is progressively reduced. Cars must be ordered seven days in advance. A car with driver can be hired for US$27 for the first hour and $8 per hour thereafter. A guide-interpreter charges US$21 for the first four hours and $4 for each extra hour. You must have an international driver's license, certificate of car registration, a **Motoring Tourist's Memo** (obtainable on arrival) with details of your itinerary, and, if bringing a car from abroad, a certificate of obligation to take the car out again. When driving across the country, never deviate from the prescribed routes, and check on distance to the nearest gas station; these are often widely spaced.

Aeroflot has flights connecting most cities. Railroad travel: "Soft class" (first class) is fairly comfortable, with deluxe accommodations available on express trains. Warning: large parts of the USSR are closed to foreigners.

FOOD AND RESTAURANTS

Moscow is a multinational city, but food tends to be standard everywhere. Try the *shashliks, kebabs,* and *pilafs* typical of Georgia, one of the Soviet Union's southern republics, as well as the heavier types of central European cooking. Russian specialties beside caviar are *blinis,* a type of pancake made with a variety of fillings and served with sour cream; *zakuski,* hors d'oeuvres often of cold meats, salmon, herring, or sturgeon; *borsch* and *shchi,* a kind of cabbage soup. Yoghurt is a national dish, and ice cream is excellent. The samovar for making tea is still part of the Russian way of life. Average meal times: breakfast 8:30-9:30, lunch 1-2:30, dinner 7:30-8. There are usually three courses at main meals, and breakfasts may include cold cuts of meat, eggs, and cheese, as well as coffee, tea, and bread. Service in restaurants is liable to be very slow. Meal prices average 10 roubles per person for lunch or dinner. All hotels have their own restaurants, many with loud, "conversation-stopping" dance bands. Menus show a wide variety of tantalizing dishes but only those with prices beside them are available. Order your entire meal at the same time while you have your waiter.

In Moscow the **Aragvi** (6 Gorky Street—tel: 229-37-62) specializes in Georgian food; try the chicken *tabaka.* The **Rossiya Hotel** restaurant is on the 21st floor and has a spectacular view of Red Square and the Kremlin. **Seventh Heaven,** a revolving restaurant, is 300 meters up on the Ostankino television tower. You could also try the **Uzbekistan** (29 Neglinnaya Street—tel: 294-60-53), noted for its Uzbek food, or the **Slavyansky Bazaar** (October 25th Street— tel: 228-48-45) for Russian specialties. Reservations are essential; ask your hotel service bureau to make them. A special Intourist "Degustatsiya" program in Moscow allows one to buy a voucher for certain restaurants; this provides reservations, a large set menu, and drinks. Cafés serve cookies, cakes, fruit juice, ice cream, coffee, and tea. Some of the most pleasant are in the parks of Culture and Rest. Street kiosks serve drinks, ice cream, and *pirozhki* (little pies). Outside the city, set in beautiful surroundings, are the **Russkaya Izba** (561-42-44), **Rus** (174-42-02), and **Arkhangelskoye** (562-03-28).

DRINKING TIPS

You can buy liquor in a variety of places: bars, restaurants, and stores. Beer can be bought at street kiosks; vodka with unusual flavors and Soviet wines, as well as other drinks, are available at restaurants. Crimean and Georgian wines, sweet or dry, are good. **Dollar Bars** are places where you can buy imported drinks, but only with foreign currency. A whisky and soda costs about $2.00. Dollar bars are at the Intourist, National, Rossiya, Metropol, Berlin, and Cosmos hotels in central Moscow. Not dollar bars, but very good are the **Moscow Hotel Bar** (7 Marx Prospect) and the **Arbat Restaurant Bar** (Kalinin Prospect). In the University district near Leninsky Prospect and the Faculty of Arts at Marx Prospect, you can visit some of the cafés popular with students.

ENTERTAINMENT

With the exception of nightclubs, there is every form of entertainment in Moscow. If you are looking for late-night entertainment, there are cabarets and floor shows. The best-known are those at the **Intourist Restaurant** (in the Intourist Hotel—tel: 203-40-80) and at the **Arbat Restaurant** (Kalinin Prospect—tel: 291-14-03). Other hotels have dining rooms with dance-type jazz. There are also two discothèques, **Metelitsa** (Kalinin Prospect) and **Sinaya Ptitsa** (Chekhov Street), which are very popular with Soviet youth. They are open from 7pm-11pm and you are advised to go early to be sure of getting in. The average closing time is 11pm, except at the dollar bars at the National and the Intourist, which are open until 1am.

Among Moscow's 30 theaters there are several which can be enjoyed with little or no knowledge of Russian. These are the **Bolshoi,** with its famous opera and ballet companies, the **Obraztsov Marionette Theater,** the **Theater Roman,** with vivid gypsy mime, at the Sovetskaya Hotel, the **Stanislavsky and Nemirovich-Danchenko Musical Theater,** and the **Operetta Theater.** The **Kremlin Theater,** inside the Kremlin, is designed for operatic and theater productions as well as wide-screen movies. The **Central Theater** for children has plays written especially for them. The **Moscow Arts Theater,** the **Maly,** and the **Mayakovsky** have such splendid productions of the classics and acting of such quality that the language becomes unimportant. The **Beryozka Dance Company,** the **USSR Folk Dance Company,** and the **Soviet Army Song & Dance Company** should be seen. The **Moscow State Circus** with its spectacular trained animals (especially bears) is unique. There also is a charming, smaller circus in Moscow with its own program.

Concerts: At **Tchaikovsky Hall** and the Large and Small Halls of the **Conservatory,** you can hear (among others) the **State Symphony Orchestra** and Russia's top soloists. Performances all start at 7pm and finish around 9:30-10pm. Seats are inexpensive but tickets fairly hard to get, so ask the Intourist Service Bureau to make reservations. Tickets for all entertainment should be reserved well in advance.

Festivals: For winter visitors to Moscow there is the **Russian Winter Festival** held from 25 December through 5 January. This is the high point of the Moscow theater season, with visiting companies of performers from all over the Soviet Union. It is the Soviet equivalent of the Christmas season, with troika rides, a New Year's tree, Grandfather Frost, and the Snow Maiden.

The **Moscow Stars Festival** in early May opens the spring season of concerts, opera, ballet, and theater. Festival tours are sold at special rates and include tickets to theaters and concerts.

There are some 120 movie theaters in Moscow. When US and European films are shown, they have dubbed soundtracks in Russian. The best-known movie houses are the **Rossiya**, the **Zaryadye**, and the huge **Octyabr**. The **Mir** shows movies-in-the-round, and at the **National Economic Exhibition** you can see the Soviet Circarama. Movie houses open at 9am, and the last show begins about 9pm. Price is about 50 kopecks, and seats must be reserved early in the day of the performance.

SHOPPING

Large department stores like GUM and TSUM open 8am-9pm Mon-Sat. Smaller stores are open 11am-8pm Mon-Sat (lunch from 2-3pm). All stores close Sundays. There are hard-currency **Beriozka** stores in the lobbies of large hotels and at 25A Luzhnetsky Proyezd. Stores for tourists often have information desks where foreign languages are spoken. Food shops in general are open from about 7am to 11pm. The best shopping streets are **Gorky Street** and **Kalinin Prospect**. **Detski Mir** (Children's World), 2 Marx Prospect, and **Dom Igrushky** (House of Toys), 8 Kutuzovsky Prospect, with their mammoth toy collections, are wonderlands for children—fun for adults too. There are good antique shops at **32 Arbat Street** and **46 Gorky Street**. Paintings and prints can be found at **46 Gorky Street**. Export of Russian art and cultural articles is strictly controlled; check with your Intourist representative before buying. You will hardly be able to avoid the traditional painted wooden dolls and carved toys at the Beriozka souvenir shops. The **Rossiya Hotel** and the Beriozka at 25A Luzhnetsky Proyezd have the largest selection. Less usual gifts are the hand-embroidered shirts and blouses at the **Russian Souvenir Shop** (9 Kutuzovsky Prospect). Russian perfumes are on sale at **4 Arbat Street, 12 Pushkin Street,** and **6 Gorky Street**. Books and phonograph records are extremely inexpensive in the USSR, and art books are a particularly good value; at **8, 16,** and **46 Gorky Street, 4 Arbat Street, 31 Kropotkinskaya Street** (foreign currency only), and **26 Kalinin Street** you will find good collections. **GUM** (3 Red Square), the largest department store in the Soviet Union, **TSUM** (2 Petrovka), and **Moskva** (56 Leninsky Prospect) are leading stores worth a visit. If you are feeling adventurous, buy a rug from Baluchistan (or Kazakhstan) at **9 Gorky Street**. Fur coats, caviar, Russian champagne, or exotic vodkas can all be bought at Beriozka shops. The two main markets where farmers sell produce from their private plots are **Tsentralny Rynok**, Central Market (15 Tsvetnoy Boulevard), and **Cheryomushkinski Rynok** (3 Lomonosovski Prospect). It is not customary to bargain.

SPORTS

Probably the most popular spectator sport in the Soviet Union is soccer, and there are stadiums that seat over 100,000—such as the **Lenin Stadium** in Moscow. Ice hockey is also popular. In Moscow, there is a swimming pool at **Kropotkinskaya Embankment** open year round except for 6 weeks Aug-mid Sep, 7am-8:30pm. Tickets must be bought prior to the session desired and sessions last from 45 minutes to one hour. Ice skating and cross country skiing take place in the city's parks in winter; cross country skis can be hired in the **Sokolniki** and **Izmailovo** parks. Horse racing, trotting and flat racing, is held on Fridays, Sundays, and Wednesdays. Chess players in the parks and certain cafés are usually happy to accept a challenge from visitors.

WHAT TO SEE

Facing **Red Square**, *Krasnaya Ploschad* (which also means beautiful square), is the **Kremlin**—the heart of Moscow and seat of the government. Behind its 15th-century walls are palaces, museums, and cathedrals. The Kremlin is open daily except Thursday, 10am-7pm; admission is free, but it is well worth joining an Intourist guided tour. A museum to visit is the **Armory Museum**, with its dazzling collection of precious jewels and splendid gold and silver, including Fabergé masterpieces, armor, weapons, and icons; open daily except Thursday, 9:30am-5pm. Within the walls you can also see the 15th-century **Cathedral of the Annunciation**, with precious icons; the **Cathedral of the Assumption**, with its gilt cupolas, where the tsars from the 15th century onwards were crowned; the 17th-century **Patriarch's Palace**; the **Church of the Twelve Apostles**; and the **Cathedral of the Archangel Michael**. In the main square the **King of Bells**, 22 feet high and the heaviest in the world (200 tons), is matched by the **King of Cannons**, 18 feet long and weighing 40 tons. Outside the Kremlin there is always a long line of people waiting to see Lenin's embalmed body in the **Mausoleum**; foreign visitors are ushered through to the head of the queue. At the south corner of the square is **St Basil's Cathedral**, with its brilliant onion-shaped domes, built by Ivan the Terrible.

The best collection of icons, Russian paintings, and sculpture is in the **Tretyakov Gallery** (10 Lavrushinsky Pereulok), near the Kremlin. The **Pushkin Museum of Fine Art** (12 Volkhonka Street) has a large collection of antique Oriental and European Renaissance art and sculpture. French painting is particularly well represented. The **Andrei Rublyov Museum** (10 Pryamikov Street) is devoted to the works of this great master of icon painting. The **Novodyevichi Monastery** near Luzhniki houses an art and history museum; the graves of many famous Russians are in the cemetery here. The houses of some of Russia's greatest writers and composers have been preserved as museums. Among them are the houses of **Pushkin, Tolstoy, Dostoevsky, Glinka, Gorky, Ostrovsky**, and **Chekhov**. Opening and closing times of museums vary enormously and almost all are closed at least one day a week. Before setting out, check with the hotel service bureau. **Gorky Park** and the **Moscow Zoo** (1 Bolshaya Gruzinskaya Street) should be seen. There are boat trips on the **Moskva River,** lasting about an hour and a half, which give a fascinating view of the city. In the **Arkhangelskoye Estate,** 10 miles from Moscow, is a beautiful late 18th-century palace. Just outside Moscow is the **Ostankino Palace,** a wooden mansion with precious works of art, and the **Botanical Gardens, Suzdal,** to the northeast, has many fine monasteries and churches. The **Zagorsk Monastery,** 50 miles north of Moscow, is one of the most famous in the USSR. At **Yasnaya Polyana,** Tolstoy's house and estate are preserved intact, while 20 miles south of Moscow, on the **Gorky Estate** where Lenin lived and worked, is a museum dedicated to him.

Leningrad: From 1713-1918 St Petersburg was the capital of Russia, and its magnificence is largely the result of Peter the Great's admiration for the art and architecture of Western Europe. Italian and French craftsmen and architects designed the palaces of the aristocracy. The **Fortress of Peter and Paul,** built as a bastion against attacks from Scandinavia, was the beginning of a great building program. The result is a beautiful combination of great townhouses, parks, gardens, and tree-lined avenues. The former Winter Palace is part of the **Hermitage Museum,** one of the finest collections of art and antiquities in the world. It undoubtedly has more masterpieces of Western painting than any other museum, from Raphael and da Vinci to Matisse and Picasso. There are some 600 bridges across the **Neva,** and the town is at its most romantic in the **White Nights** from the end of June through July, when it never gets really dark. You must see the **Cathedral of Our Lady of Kazan** and the **Cathedral of St Isaac of Kiev.** From the **Admiralty,** walk down Nevsky Prospect to the 18th-century **Stroganov Palace.** Visit the **Russian Museum,** with its collection of traditional Russian art from the 10th century onwards. Excursions to nearby places include the town of **Pushkin,** site of Catherine the Great's palace, and **Petrodvorets,** with landscaped gardens and fountains in an exquisite park—only 30 minutes away by hydrofoil. Hotels: The best hotels are the **Leningrad,** 5/2 Pirogovskaya Embankment; **Astoriya,** 39 Gertsen Street; **Evropeiskaya,** 1/7 Broadsky Street; **Sovetskaya,** 43 Lermontovski Prospect; **Rossiya,** 11 Chernyshevski Square; **Prebaltiskaya,** 14 Korablestroeley Street. All these hotels have restaurants, and there is very good Slav cuisine at the **Sadko,** next door to the Evropeiskaya Hotel; the **Olen** restaurant specializes in game dishes. The best shops are on **Nevsky Prospect;** the **DLT** department store is at 23 Zhelyabov Street.

The **Ukraine,** second-largest republic of the Soviet Union, has its own language, culture, and traditions. **Kiev,** its capital, is the third-largest city in the USSR. The town is built along the banks of the **Dnieper** and is full of green parks; its main street, **Kreshchatik,** is lined with chestnut trees. One of its most magnificent buildings is the gilded, multidomed **Cathedral of St Sophia.** Its interior is richly decorated with mosaics and frescoes. Southeast of the town is the 55-acre complex of the **Kievo-Pecherski State History and Culture Reservation,** with the cave dwellings of the first monks of the Pecherski Monastery, their catacombs, and 10th- and 11th-century churches. The **Taras Shevchenko** museum commemorates the Ukraine's great poet and has artifacts of ancient Kiev. At the **Shevchenko Opera House** you can see the opera and ballet companies; there are also the Ukrainian and Russian drama theaters and the **Musical Comedy Theater.** On the river banks there are some charming open-air restaurants; try **Okhotnik, Mlin, Natalka, Vetryak,** and **Khata Karasya** for Ukrainian cuisine. Other large cities in the Ukraine are **Kharkov, Lvov, Donetsk, Zaporozhye,** and **Odessa,** the Ukraine's largest Black Sea port. Hotels in Kiev: **Dnipro,** 1-2 Leninsky Komsomol Square; **Lybed,** Pobeda Square; **Moskva,** 4 Oktyabrosky Street; **Slavutich,** 1 Entuziastov Avenue; **Ukraina,** 5 Shevchenko Boulevard.

The Black Sea Coast is the playground of millions of Russians who come to relax in the former palaces of the aristocracy, now vacation homes for workers. **Yalta,** on the southern tip of the Crimean peninsula, has a year-round mild and sunny climate. There is a **Chekhov Museum** in the writer's former house. Other popular resorts are **Sochi, Sukhumi, Mishkov,** and **Batumi.**

Georgia: Farther east, running up from the shores of the Black Sea into the Caucasus Mountains, lies Georgia—which boasts more citizens over 120 years of age than all the rest of the world. **Tbilisi** (Tiflis), founded in the 5th century, is the capital as it was the capital of the former kingdom of Georgia. One of the oldest cities in the USSR, it was for centuries a stopping-off point along trading routes between Europe and the Far East. Marco Polo visited in the 13th century and described it then as a "fine city of great size" where silk and many other fabrics were woven. To see the terrain through which these early travelers passed, take the cablecar to the top of **Mt Mtatsminda,** from where you can view the city itself and the Caucasus Range beyond and try the Georgian food at the **Mtatsminda Restaurant.** Tbilisi has museums, parks, botanical gardens, a 6th-century basilica, a cathedral, fortress, and castle to visit. About a half-hour drive away is the ancient capital of **Mtskheta,** with the 11th-century **Svetitskhoveli Cathedral,** burial place of Georgian kings.

Central Asia and **Kazakhstan:** East of the Caspian Sea and touching Afghanistan and China is a land of huge mountains, lakes, and desert. **Tashkent,** fourth-largest city in the USSR and capital of Uzbekistan, has many masterpieces of Muslim architecture. Legendary **Samarkand** is a magnificent city of mosques, palaces, and gardens. The richly decorated mosque of **Shakhi-Zinda** is a unique complex of medieval tombs and mausoleums. **Bukhara,** too, has magnificent mosques and minarets whose interiors are amazingly cool in spite of the scorching sun outside. See the **Mausoleum of Ismail Somani.**

Siberia is the same size as the continental US and, until recently, something of an unexplored wilderness of forest and lake. The Trans-Siberian Railway takes you to the Siberian cities of **Novosibirsk, Irkutsk** (by **Lake Baikal**), and **Khabarovsk.** You can also fly to these cities to save time.

The Baltic Republics: Tallin, capital of Estonia, formerly a heavily fortified walled town, has medieval Gothic buildings, the massive **Toompea Castle,** and tall towers. **Riga,** the capital of Latvia, also has its old town, with gabled roofs and spires of ancient churches. The **Cathedral** is the principal landmark. **Vilnius,** the capital of Lithuania, has an interesting old center and is dominated by its historic **Castle of Guediminas.**

SOURCES OF FURTHER INFORMATION

Pan Am, Suite 239, Metropol Hotel, 1 Prospect Marx, Moscow, and any Pan Am office around the world; **Intourist,** 1 Gorky Street, Moscow; 630 Fifth Avenue, New York, NY 10020; 292 Regent Street, London, W1; **American Express Travel Service,** 21A Sadova Kudrinskaya, Moscow.

Yugoslavia

WHAT'S SPECIAL

Yugoslavia is a fusion of six republics bordering seven countries—all of which makes for a wide diversity in customs, cultures, language, and history. It may be a difficult country to govern, but it is a highly interesting one to visit. The Slovenian region has magnificent mountain scenery; Bosnia has an Oriental atmosphere and exotic ruins; Serbia, medieval monasteries and churches with beautiful frescoes; Croatia has the spectacular Istrian and Dalmation coasts, medieval seaports and lovely summer resorts, and hundreds of starkly beautiful islands and islets; Montenegro has dramatic mountains inland, lush sun-drenched sandy beaches, palm-fringed Boka Kotarska fjord, and old walled cities; Macedonia, the home of Alexander the Great, offers untouched folkways and magnificent Lake Ohrid.

COUNTRY BRIEFING

Size: 98,766 square miles **Population:** 22,400,000
Capital: Belgrade (Beograd) **Capital Population:** 1,400,000
 Climate: December-April for winter sports.

Weather in Belgrade: Lat N44°8′; Alt 453 ft

Temp (°F)	Jan	Feb	Mar	Apr	May	Jun	Jul	Aug	Sep	Oct	Nov	Dec
Av Low	27°	27°	35°	45°	53°	58°	61°	60°	55°	47°	39°	30°
Av High	37°	41°	53°	64°	74°	79°	84°	83°	76°	65°	52°	40°
Days no rain	23	22	24	21	22	21	25	24	24	23	23	22

Government: A socialist federal republic including Bosnia Herzegovina, Croatia, Macedonia, Montenegro, Serbia (with two autonomous provinces, Kosovo and Vojvodina), and Slovenia.

Language: There are three Slav languages, although English, German, and Italian are fairly widespread. There are two alphabets, Latin (generally in western Yugoslavia) and Cyrillic.

Religion: Orthodox, Roman Catholic, Muslim, Protestant.

Currency: Dinar. 100 paras = 1 dinar.

	1 D	5 D	10 D	50 D	100 D	200 D	500 D	1,000 D
US (dollars, cents)	.03	.16	.33	1.64	3.29	6.57	16.43	32.85
UK (pounds, pence)	.01	.08	.16	.78	1.57	3.13	7.48	15.67

Public Holidays:

New Year, 1-2 Jan

Labor Day, 1 May

Partisan Day, 4 July

Republic Days, 29-30 Nov

HOW TO GET THERE

Flying time to Belgrade's Surcin Airport from New York is 9 hours; from London, 2¾ hours; from Frankfurt, 1¾ hours. Time in Yugoslavia: GMT+1.

REQUIREMENTS FOR ENTRY AND CUSTOMS REGULATIONS

Visitors need a current passport, along with visas obtainable on entry; no limit to the amount of foreign currency that can be brought in. The limit of local currency is D1,500 in and D1,500 out per person (in denominations up to D100). Duty-free allowance: 200 cigarettes or 50 cigars or ½ pound tobacco; ¾ liter liquor, or 1 liter wine; reasonable amount of perfume for personal use; personal effects within reasonable amounts.

AIRPORT INFORMATION

Belgrade Airport is 7½ miles from the city center; taxi fare is D400. Bus fare into the city is D25 for the airport bus. Tip porters D20 per bag. Airport departure tax is D50 for Europe, D60 for intercontinental flights.

ACCOMMODATIONS

Luxury establishments are still fairly rare, but steadily growing in number. Rates are generally lower in the cooler months. Boarding houses and tourist settlements provide inexpensive accommodations. Belgrade hotels:

Rates are in US$ for a double/twin room with bath or shower

Balkan, Prizrenska 2 (from $27 CP)

BELGRADE INTER · CONTINENTAL, Vladimira Popovica 10, Novi Beograd (from $100 CP), 10 minutes from downtown

Excelsior, Kneza Milosa 5 (from $42 CP)

Jugoslavia, Partizanski Put 3 (from $66 CP), 10 minutes from downtown

Kasina, Terazije 25 (from $30 CP)

Majestic, Obilicev Venac 28 (from $39 CP)
Metropol, Boulevard Revolucije 69 (from $60 CP)
Moskva, Balkanska 1 (from $60 CP)
National, Bezanijska Kosa, Novi Beograd (from $31 CP), near airport
Palace, Topličin Venac 23 (from $28 CP)
Park, Njegoseva 2 (from $30 CP)
Slavija, Svetog Save 1 (from $33 CP)
Splendid Garni, Dragoslava Jovanovica 5 (from $27 CP)
Union, Kosovska 11 (from $27 CP)
All hotels listed above are in downtown Belgrade unless otherwise indicated.

USEFUL INFORMATION

Banks: Open 7am-7pm Mon-Fri, 7-1 Sat. Money can be changed at travel agents, hotels, and post offices. There is a Sunday-morning service counter open 9-12 at Knez Mihajlova 42, Belgrade. Most major credit cards are widely accepted.

Mail: Mailboxes are square and yellow. Bookstalls sell stamps.

Telephone Tips: Local calls cost D2. Useful numbers in Belgrade:

Pan Am Agent 441 484	Operator 900/901/902
Airport Information 675 992	Directories 988
Tourist Offices 635 622	Time 95
and 635 343	Police 92
Fire Station 93	Emergency 94

Newspapers: Most major English-language newspapers and magazines, as well as German, French, and Italian ones, are available in all larger cities and resorts. English versions of Yugoslav publications *Tourist News* and *Review* are available.

Tipping: 10% is a steady guide for general purposes.

Electricity: 220 volts 50 cycles AC.

Laundry: Good, inexpensive services available (from D150 to dry-clean a suit; from D30 to launder a shirt).

Hairdressing: Good hotels have salons (average cost of a shampoo and set from D140, 10% tip; man's haircut from D50, 10% tip).

Photography: Major cities and tourist resorts supply all film; black and white can be processed; best to take color home.

TRANSPORTATION

Taxis charge a fixed rate of D20, plus D12 per kilometer. Streetcars and buses in main centers have a set fare of D7-10.50, but coupons can be bought at tobacconists at a 40% discount. Low-cost rail and bus networks connect all major centers. There are a variety of excellent steamer services along the Adriatic coast, and daily and weekly cruises operate out of all major coastal centers. Ferryboats link the Yugoslav coast with Italian and Greek ports. Major highways along the Adriatic coast and down the center are good. JAT, the Yugoslav airline, Inex-Adria (Ljubljana), and Transadria (Zagreb) service all major cities and tourist resorts.

FOOD AND RESTAURANTS

Yugoslav food is based upon generous portions of meat with lots of onions, potatoes, and good coarse breads. *Čevapčiči*, barbecued veal, beef, or pork patties in long, sausage shapes, are tasty; *ražnjiči*, small pieces of barbecued veal on a skewer, are delicious with a piece of bread. Savory stews are rich, the egg-and-veal ragout *teleča corba*, or *djuveč*, a delicious mixture of eggplant, carrot, potato, rice, and meat with a grated cheese topping. *Punjene tikvice* (stuffed zucchini) and stuffed cabbage are tasty with tomato sauces. *Pohovani kačkavalj* is a delicious slice of fried matured cheese. Also try *bosanski lonac*, a spicy stew of cabbage, *zeljanica*, a spinach-egg-and-cheese pastry, as well as *gibanica*, a rich savory cottage cheese and egg pie, and corn pone with *kajmak*. The seafoods along the Dalmatian coast are excellent, and the oysters around the Limski Canal and Ston are exceptional. Yugoslav cheeses and sausages are strong and tasty. While in Belgrade visit the many restaurants with roving folk and gypsy groups in Skadarlija area, and sample the Serbian cuisine at **Dva Jelena** (Skadarska 32—tel: 334 885), which specializes in game and fish, and **Tri Šešira** (Skadarska 29—tel: 347 501) with its quaint authenticity. The restaurant at the Belgrade Inter·Continental has an exceptionally wide assortment of select national dishes. The writers' club, **Klub Knjizevnika** (Francuska 7—tel: 627 931), and **Zlatiborac** (Maglajska—tel: 441 546), both in town, and **Kumbara** (Beli Potok—tel: 321 654) and **Devetka** (Pionirski Grad—tel: 559 922), amid greenery on the outskirts of town, are great local favorites. **Dva Ribara** (Narodnog Fronta 21—tel: 328 807) serves excellent fish dishes. In the warm season, **Stadion** (Humska 1—tel: 648 179), **Graficar** (Vase Pelagica 31—tel: 651 467), **Milosev Konak** (Toplider 1—tel: 680 146), and **Seher** (Andre Nikolica 3—tel: 651 726) all have open-air grills and music. **Dom Lovaca** (Njegoseva 36—tel: 436 128) serves game; **Dušanov Grad** (Terazije 4—tel: 321 986), **Beogradjanka** (Masarikova—tel: 684 651), and **Dunavski Cvet** (Tadeusha Koscuskog 65—tel: 625 985) serve fine Yugoslav and international cuisine in contemporary settings, and **Romani Tar** (Terazije Square—tel: 333 280) is good for gypsy specialties and dancing. For Chinese food, try the **Peking** (Vuka Karadzic 2—tel: 628 371), with a set 16-course menu cooked by chefs from China. In summer you can dine aboard a Danube cruise boat; ask at your hotel. For less expensive meals, self-service centers can be found all over the city. Some of these are **Kasina, Luksur, Studentski Park,** and **Zagreb. Kalemegdan Castle** has a little outdoor restaurant overlooking the broad confluence of the Sava and Danube rivers.

DRINKING TIPS

Yugoslavia produces excellent wines at relatively low cost. A bottle ranges from about D100-180. White wines to try are *Ljutomer, Sylvanec, Traminec, Rebula,* and *Tokaj* from Slovenia, *Kutjevo, Belje* and *Marastina* from Croatia, *Zilavka* and *Blatina* from Mostar; good reds are *Barbera* and *Merlot* from Slovenia, and the strong and pungent *Dingac, Posip,* and *Grk* from Dalmatia. Try Yugoslavia's famous plum brandy *Sljivovica* (very potent). *Maraschino,* a liqueur, is tasty, and you will like Yugoslav beer. Drinking hours are not specifically regulated.

ENTERTAINMENT

While in Belgrade make sure you get a copy of *Belgradescope* from your hotel for a detailed and up-to-date account of nightlife. A highlight the year round, but especially in summer, is **Skadarlija,** a reconstructed turn-of-the-century street jammed with sidewalk cafés, hot-foot stands, and fine restaurants and featuring roving singers, poetry recitals, and art stalls. There are few nightclubs as such, but you will find that many restaurants have dancing and a good floor show, as do the bigger hotels. Nightclubs are attached to the hotels Belgrade Inter·Continental, Majestic, Yugoslavia, and Metropol, and other clubs are the **Lotos** and **Romani Tar.** There are casinos in Belgrade and other resort centers. Discothèques in Belgrade are the **Cepelin, Simonida, Kalemegdan, Adriatic,** and at the Hotel Balkan. Summer festivals throughout Yugoslavia provide music, drama, opera, ballet, and film. International theater and music festivals are held in Belgrade in the fall.

SHOPPING

Local handicrafts, popular with visitors, include costumed dolls, embroidered blouses, filigree jewelry, leather goods, carved wooden items, dyed wool rugs, and gold and silver work. Crystal is good and reasonably priced. There are numerous handicraft stores around Belgrade, such as **Amfora** (Terazije 6), several **Narodna Radinost** stores on Terazije and Knez Mihailova, where you will also find the **Galerija Sebastian** (an art, glassware, and ceramics shop) and a craft store called **Fontana,** and the Ulus artists' cooperative on Vasina Street. The **Beogradjanka** (Masarikova 5) and the **Belgrade** (Terazije 15-23) are department stores and a good source of just about everything.

SPORTS

The Adriatic coast is ideal for every kind of water sport. Log-rafting trips through the spectacular canyons and white water of the Drina and Tara rivers are very popular. Fishing along the coast and in the lakes and rivers of Yugoslavia is good, but usually a license is necessary; see the Yugoslav Tourist Information Office about this. Winter sports are excellent. International ski jumping contests are held in **Planica,** just south of the Austrian border, in late March; in the Slovene Alps, **Kranjska Gora, Pokljuka,** and **Pohorje** are three good resorts. So are **Bled** and **Bohinji** lake districts; in other parts of the country are **Jahorina, Kopaonik,** and **Zlatibor;** directly south in Macedonia, **Mavrovo** and **Popovo Sapka;** and nearby in Kosovo, **Brezovice.** Skiing here is considerably less expensive than in the better-known resorts of Europe.

WHAT TO SEE

Belgrade is at the confluence of the Danube and the Sava rivers. The great fortress of **Kalemegdan,** a great stone building in the form of a

terraced bastion, is a relic of the Turkish occupation. There are several imposing gateways, turrets, ramparts, and a "Roman" well (sunk by the Austrians). The **National Museum** in Belgrade has a rich collection of antiquities, and the **National Theater** just opposite stages the renowned annual opera season. Beautiful monastic frescoes can be seen in the **Fresco Art Gallery** and frescoes and icons of great beauty in the **Serbian Orthodox Church Museum.** If you cross the river to **Novi Beograd,** the new section of the city, you will find the **Sava Center**—a super-modern conference and concert center with late-night shopping, snack bars and restaurants, and the **Modern Art Museum,** which has examples of modern painting and sculpture. Other museums are the **Museum of Applied Arts,** the **Ethnographic Museum,** and the **Theatrical Arts Museum.** Don't miss a visit to Tito's tomb in the **House of Flowers** and the adjacent **25th May Museum** housing many of the gifts given to him during his lifetime. It is well worth taking a hydrofoil trip on the Danube. Also take a morning's walk through the open-air peasant markets.

Dubrovnik: This, the most famous of the Dalmatian coast, has not only managed to preserve its 16th-century atmosphere but has 250 days of sunshine, too. The ancient part of the town is encircled by high walls with huge guard towers. There are many outstanding buildings, including the **Church of Sveti Spas, St Saviour,** the **Sponza Palace,** and the **Rector's Palace.** During the summer festival in Dubrovnik, Shakespeare's plays are performed in the **Lovrijenac Fortress,** concerts are given in the Sponza Palace, and all the courtyards and squares are used for operas, plays, and music. Among restaurants are the **Dubravka Café, Rozari** for fine seafood, the cafés in *Prijeko ulica,* the **Jadran** at the old convent near the Onofrio fountain, and the **Ocean,** specializing in broiled meats. For something different, have lunch in the Benedictine abbey on the nearby isle of **Lokrum.** Hotels include: **Argentina** (from US$34 double), **Dubrovnik-Palace** (from US$66 double), **Dubrovnik-President** (from US$72 double CP), **Excelsior** (from US$36 double), **Grand Hotel Park** (from US$40 double), **Imperial** (from US$40 double), **Kompas** (from US$38 double), **Lero** (from US$29 double CP), **Libertas** (from US$76 double CP), **Plakir** (from US$60 double), and **Tirena** (from US$60 double). Nearby Dubrovnik, at Cavtat, is the new luxury **Croatia** (from US$77 double). Rates are for the high season, July through September, and, as in all coastal towns, are up to 50% lower in other months.

Split: North of Dubrovnik, Split was built around a 4th-century Roman palace of the Emperor Diocletian, which has been made the center of the annual **Split Summer Festival.** Of interest are the Venetian Gothic and Renaissance buildings, medieval churches, and towers. The **Mestrovic Gallery** contains the works of famous Yugoslav sculptors. For hotels, try the **Lav,** about 6 miles south of the center (from US$70 double), the **Marjan,** Obala Jna 8 (from US$41 double), the **Park,** Setaliste 1, Maja 15 (from US$38 double), and the **Split** (from US$34 double).

The Adriatic islands are worth a visit: **Korcula,** the birthplace of Marco Polo, is renowned for its wine and colorful traditional dancing. **Mlet** island is nearby with lush vegetation, two lakes, and beaches. **Hvar** is an Adriatic paradise with a uniquely mild all-year climate. A regularly scheduled car ferry departs Dubrovnik several mornings a week, stopping at Korcula, Hvar, Split, at Zadar on the Dalmatian coast, and at the island of Rab, arriving at Rijeka the next morning. The island of **Krk** (which can be reached from Rijeka) is the scene of the **Palace Haludovo Hotel** (from US$44 double), a luxury vacation enterprise whose wide-ranging facilities cater to the most extravagant needs. Also accessible from Rijeka are the islands of **Cres** and **Losinj.** Yugoslavia has countless other islands off its 1,550-kilometer coast, and dotting the length of the mainland are renowned seaside resorts equipped for everything from aqua-planing, mudbaths, and disco dancing. South of Split and Dubrovnik, there is **Hercegnovi,** one of Montenegro's oldest resorts, and in the fishing village of **Sveti Stefan** there is an exclusive new waterfront hotel named after the village (from US$104 double). In the north, there are the excellent amenities of **Portoroz** on the Slovenian coast, and **Porec** on the Croatian coast, both popular.

Opatija: In a glorious coast setting backed by green mountains, Opatija is a paradise of flowers, fruit, and trees. The attractive, modernized town was originally developed as a resort for wealthy Hungarian and Austrian nobility, and grand old hotels bear witness to this. An elegant old casino is a feature of the town, and the music festival, **October in Opatija,** is a favorite with visitors. There are some charming little restaurants in the town, and the **Café Jedro,** down in the port, is quiet and intimate. Opatija is convenient for an excursion to **Pula,** with its 1st-century Roman amphitheater, the magnificent **Plitvice Lakes** lying on 16 different levels all connected by waterfalls, and the caves of **Postojna** and **Rovinj,** a town dating from Roman times. During the winter months, skiing trips are arranged out of Opatija to **Platak** and during the summer to the Slovenian Alps.

Ljubljana: The capital of Slovenia, Ljubljana is surrounded by the peaks of the **Kamniske** and **Julijske Alps** and was built around a picturesque old fort. The old part of the town, dating from the 16th century, has been restored to its original baroque style. See the 17th-century **Franciscan Church** and the impressive **Ursuline Church,** with its magnificent facade. The **Tromostovje,** an ornamental bridge with three connecting spans, and a marble foundation in front of the town hall are the work of the Italian sculptor Robba. The **Slovenian Philharmonic Concert Hall,** dating from 1702, is where Beethoven conducted the first performance of his *Pastoral Symphony.* Ljubljana is convenient to nearby ski centers as well as the seaside resorts. Hotels include the **Slon** (from US$32 double), **Lev** (from US$33 double), **Union** (from US$39 double), and the **Holiday Inn** (from US$83 double).

Zagreb: The second-largest town in Yugoslavia, Zagreb is the capital of Croatia. It is dominated by the austere towers of the **Cathedral,** which is a formidable achievement in Gothic architecture. Another outstanding architectural monument is the **Church of St Marko,** which dates back to the 18th century. See also the old stone gates of the town. The city has twenty museums, eight art galleries, and an active theater and concert life. The **Zagreb International Fair,** held annually for hundreds of years, is one of the biggest in the world. Near Zagreb are many famous spas, such as **Krapinske, Stubiske,** and **Tuheljske.** Hotels in Zagreb are the **Beograd-Garni** (from US$29 double), the **Dubrovnik-Garni** (from US$32 double), the **Esplanade,** Mihanoviceva 1 (from US$55 double), the **International,** Miramarska (from US$30 double), the **Palace,** Strossmayerov Trg 10 (from US$39 double), and the **INTER·CONTINENTAL ZA-GREB,** Krsnjavoga 1 (from US$92 double).

Sarajevo is an interesting Oriental town with a large Turkish bazaar and many mosques, but it is notorious as the place of the assassination on 2 June 1914 of Archduke Ferdinand of Austria, which precipitated the First World War. The river Miljacka flows through the town, with 10 bridges of different styles crossing it. Hotels include the **Bristol** and the **Europa** (from US$36 double CP).

Skopje is the political and cultural center of Macedonia. This city has many monuments dating back to the 15th and 16th centuries, the **Church of St Saviour,** the baths of **Daut Pasha,** and the **Mustafa Pasha** mosque. The earthquake of 1963 destroyed much of Skopje, but help from architects from all over the world has made for its rapid regrowth. Among Skopje hotels are the **Continental** (from US$32 double), the **Grand** (from US$31 double CP), and the **Bellevue** (from US$28 double CP). One of the world's ecological wonders is virgin **Lake Ohrid** with its unique rose-colored trout and man-made pearls. It straddles the Yugoslav-Albanian border, one hour's flight from Belgrade.

SOURCES OF FURTHER INFORMATION

Pan Am, Hotel Slavija in Belgrade, and any Pan Am office around the world; **Tourist Information Center** (in the Underground passage), Terazije Square, Belgrade; **The Yugoslav State Tourist Office,** 630 Fifth Avenue, New York, NY 10020; **Yugoslav National Tourist Office,** 143 Regent Street, London WI.

Africa

EUROPE

ASIA

Casablanca

TUNISIA MEDITERRANEAN SEA

MOROCCO

WESTERN SAHARA

ALGERIA

LIBYA

EGYPT

Tropic of Cancer

MAURITANIA

MALI

NIGER

CHAD

Khartoum

SUDAN

SENEGAL

Dakar

GAMBIA

GUINEA

UPPER VOLTA

NIGERIA

ETHIOPIA

IVORY COAST

Abidjan Accra

Lagos

CENTRAL AFRICAN REP.

SOMALI REP.

Monrovia

GHANA

TOGO

Douala

UGANDA

KENYA

LIBERIA

BENIN

CAMEROON

SIERRA LEONE

Equator

Nairobi

GUINEA-BISSAU

EQUITORIAL GUINEA

Libreville

CONGO

ZAIRE

TANZANIA

GABON

Dar es Salaam

CABINDA

Kinshasa

ATLANTIC OCEAN

Luanda

MOZAMBIQUE

ANGOLA

ZAMBIA

MALAWI

SOUTH WEST AFRICA (NAMIBIA)

RHODESIA (ZIMBABWE)

MALAGASY REP.

Tropic of Capricorn

BOTSWANA

Johannesburg

SWAZILAND

REP. OF SOUTH AFRICA

LESOTHO

Cape Town

iNDIAN OCEAN

AFRICA CURRENCY CONVERSION

Country	United States $				United Kingdom £			
	5¢	10¢	50¢	$1	5p	10p	50p	£1
Algeria dinars • centimes	.21	.42	2.08	4.17	.44	.88	4.35	8.72
Benin francs	12.50	25.00	125.00	250.00	26.13	52.25	261.30	522.50
Cameroon francs	12.50	25.00	125.00	250.00	26.13	52.25	261.30	522.50
Egypt pounds • piastres	3.42	6.85	34.25	68.49	7.15	14.32	71.58	143.14
Ethiopia birr • cents	.10	.21	1.03	2.07	.21	.44	2.15	4.33
Ghana cedi • pesewas	.14	.27	1.37	2.75	.29	.56	2.86	5.75
Guinea sily • corilles	.90	1.81	9.03	18.05	1.88	3.78	18.87	37.72
Ivory Coast francs	12.50	25.00	125.00	250.00	26.13	52.25	261.30	522.50
Kenya shillings • cents	.38	.76	3.82	7.63	.79	1.59	7.98	15.95
Liberia dollars • cents	.05	.10	.50	1.00	.03	.05	.24	.48
Libya dinars • dirhams	.02	.04	.18	.36	.04	.08	.38	.75
Morocco dirhams • centimes	.24	.48	2.38	4.76	.50	1.00	4.97	9.95
Nigeria naira • kobo	.03	.05	.27	.53	.06	.10	.56	1.11
Senegal francs	12.44	24.88	124.38	248.76	26.00	52.00	259.95	519.91
Seychelles rupee	.33	.67	3.33	6.65	.69	1.40	6.96	13.90
South Africa rands • cents	.04	.08	.42	.84	.08	.17	.88	1.76
Tanzania shilling	.41	.82	4.10	8.20	.86	1.71	8.57	17.14
Tunisia dinar • millimes	21.74	43.48	217.39	434.78	45.43	90.87	454.35	908.69
Uganda shilling • cents	.39	.77	3.86	7.72	.82	1.61	8.07	16.13
Zaire zaire • mukata	.16	.31	1.55	3.10	.33	.65	3.24	6.48
Zambia kwacha • ngwee	.04	.08	.41	.83	.08	.17	.86	1.73

Algeria

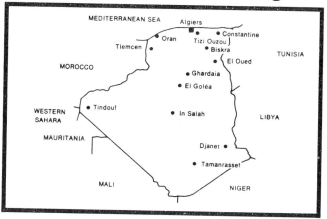

WHAT'S SPECIAL

For years the preserve of the French traveler, Algeria's attractions are now becoming known to the world, thanks to the country's fostering of its potential as a tourist destination. Once ruled by Berbers, then conquered by Phoenicians and Romans, Algeria fell to the Arabs in the 7th century and took up the religion of Muhammad. Today, its people and customs are as varied as its landscape. In the north, Mediterranean beaches are a summer playground. Farther inland, the cedar-covered mountains of the Atlas chain offer winter sport. To the south, there is the diversity of the Algerian Sahara; sand dunes near El Oued; the stony wasteland of the M'zab region, relieved only by the pastel-colored M'zabite towns that have inspired, it is said, the best of modern architects; the "lunar" landscape of the Hoggar. Here in the southern part of the country, there is no vegetation except for date-palm trees in oases, but there are oil and gas in great quantities.

COUNTRY BRIEFING

Size: 919,590 square miles   **Population:** 18,524,786
Capital: Algiers   **Capital Population:** 2,500,000

Climate: Coastal areas have a Mediterranean climate, with mild temperatures and a rainy season from October to May. Inland, in the Atlas mountains, there is more seasonal variation in temperature and snow in winter. The desert is dry, with extreme daily temperature variations (on the average, 100°F during the day and 40°F at night) and frequent cold winds. Autumn is the best time to travel in the Sahara.

Weather in Algiers: Lat N36°50'; Alt 194 ft

Temp (°F)	Jan	Feb	Mar	Apr	May	Jun	Jul	Aug	Sep	Oct	Nov	Dec
Av Low	48°	50°	51°	55°	59°	65°	69°	71°	68°	63°	55°	50°
Av High	59°	61°	65°	68°	73°	78°	84°	84°	80°	73°	67°	61°
Days no rain	20	19	22	25	26	28	30	30	26	24	19	19

Government: A popular democratic republic.

Language: Arabic is the official language; French is widely spoken. English is spoken in some hotels.

Religion: Islam is the state religion.

Currency: Dinar. 100 centimes = 1 dinar

				1	5	10	50	100	500
	10c	20c	50c	DA	DA	DA	DA	DA	DA
US (dollars, cents)	.02	.05	.12	.24	1.20	2.40	12.00	24.00	120.02
UK (pounds, pence)	.01	.02	.06	.11	.57	1.14	5.72	11.45	57.24

Public Holidays:

New Year's Day, 1 Jan

Labor Day, 1 May

Independence Day, 5 July

Anniversary of the
Revolution, 1 Nov

Mouloud, Id ul Fitr, Id ul Adha, and Ashura are Muslim holidays whose dates vary according to the lunar calendar.

HOW TO GET THERE

Flying time to Algiers' Houari Boumediène Airport from New York is 9 hours; from Frankfurt, 2 hours; from Rome, 2½ hours. Time in Algeria: GMT+1. Daylight Saving Time observed.

REQUIREMENTS FOR ENTRY AND CUSTOMS REGULATIONS

Passport. A visa is required of US and Canadian citizens, but not of some European, Middle Eastern, and African citizens. Visas cost $5.25 and can be obtained from Algerian embassies and consulates and allow a stay of up to 90 days. They can be renewed in Algeria for stays of up to 3 months at any local Wilaya (Town Hall) office. Smallpox vaccination certificates not required; yellow-fever and cholera vaccinations required if coming from an infected area. Duty-free allowance: 200 cigarettes or 50 cigars or 400 grams tobacco per adult; 1 liter alcoholic beverage per person. Gold coins cannot be imported or exported without an authorization from the Algerian Central Bank. Personal jewelry containing gold, pearls, or precious stones must be declared at customs upon entry. Import of foreign currency is unrestricted but the total amount must be declared at customs and a copy of the declaration kept by the visitor. It must be presented at departure to allow the re-export of any remaining foreign currency. No Algerian currency may be brought in or taken out.

AIRPORT INFORMATION

Houari Boumediène Airport is 13 miles from Algiers. Bus fare to the downtown terminal at 1 rue Colonel Ahmed Ben Abderrazak (near Hotel Aletti) is DA5 for the 30-minute ride. Taxi fare to the city center is about DA70. Tip luggage porter DA5. The airport has a duty-free shop, a bank (open 7am to 7pm), two car rental agencies, but no hotel reservation counter. No departure tax.

ACCOMMODATIONS

Algeria has been making considerable efforts recently to develop its tourist industry, and practically every beach resort, mountain resort, or oasis can boast of a new hotel or holiday village, run by the state or local government. Many of them, designed in harmony with the environment, are of architectural interest themselves. There is a hotel reservation service run by **ALTOUR** (an agency of the Algerian National Tourist Office) located in the city center at 5 Boulevard Ben Boulaid (tel: 65 15 50). Hotels in Algiers and in nearby beach resorts include:

Rates are in US$ for a double/twin room with bath or shower

Albert ler, 5 Avenue Pasteur (from $32)

Aletti, Rue Asselah Hocine (from $52.50)

Aurassi, Avenue Frantz Fanon (from $87.50)

Du Port, Sidi Ferruch (from $30), on seacoast 17 miles from Algiers

El Manar, Sidi Fredj (from $34), on seacoast 17 miles from Algiers

El Minzah, Staoueli (from $34), on seacoast 16 miles from Algiers

El Riadh, Sidi Fredj (from $32.50), on seacoast 17 miles from Algiers

Oasis, 2 Rue Kerrar Smain (from $21)

Unless otherwise indicated, above hotels centrally located in Algiers.

USEFUL INFORMATION

Helpful Hint: The Algerian weekend begins Thursday afternoon and runs through Friday.

Banks: Open 8:30-4 except Thurs. and Fri. Currency and travelers' checks can be changed at hotels but it is advisable to use the banks.

Mail: Stamps can be bought at post offices and at some hotels.

Telephone Tips: Local calls cost 50 centimes at post offices, DA1 in restaurants and cafés. Useful numbers in Algiers:

Air Algérie 76 43 50/51	Police 17
Airport Information 76 10 18/35	Fire 14
ALTOUR 64 15 50	Telephone Inquiries 19
Tourist Information Office 64 68 64/68	International Calls 16

Newspapers: There are no local English-language publications. Foreign newspapers are sometimes available in the city center.

Tipping: A service charge is generally included in restaurant and hotel bills.

Electricity: 110-115 volts 50 cycles AC in older parts of cities; 220 volts 50 cycles AC elsewhere.

Laundry: Reliable dry-cleaning and laundry services in main hotels; 24-hour service available in larger towns.

Hairdressing: Available in most first-class hotels.

Photography: Black and white and color films are available, but it is better to bring your own because you may not always find what you need.

Clubs: Lions and Rotary

Rest Rooms: Women's, *Dames;* men's, *Hommes.* Generally no charge.

Health: Few doctors or dentists speak English, but health care, should you need it, is free at hospitals and infirmaries. Pharmaceuticals are reasonably priced. Tap water outside the large cities is unsafe to drink; Saida, the Algerian bottled mineral water, is available everywhere, as is Mouzaia, a bottled, sparkling mineral water. You will need sunglasses, a wide-brimmed hat, moisturizing cream, and lip pomade in the southern regions, as well as woolen clothes for the night.

TRANSPORTATION

Taxis can be hailed in the street or called from a stand (tel: 62 33 33). There is good intercity bus service throughout the country. Information concerning timetables and prices is available by calling the National Travel and Transport Company (SNTV) offices in Algiers (tel: 63 10 79 or 60 93 23). A rail network connects Algiers with cities and towns along the coast and with certain inland points. Tickets can be bought at the National Railroad Transport Society (SNTF) passenger office at 3 rue Maitre Ali Boumendjel (tel: 63 32 34/36) or at the Main Station, rue d'Along (tel: 64 73 80). Air Algérie flies to Algeria's largest cities (for reservations, tel: 64 24 24 for national flights; 64 24 28 for international flights). Cars can be rented at the Algiers airport or in major cities through Altour and through private companies. Cost is approximately DA150 per day, plus 70 centimes per kilometer and compulsory insurance. Chauffeured cars cost approximately DA600 per day. Do not attempt to cross the Sahara from June to mid-September, when sandstorms are frequent and the heat intense. There are three major routes across the Sahara, hard-surfaced in the northern part, but changing to unsurfaced tracks in the south. Roads are classified according to the degree of risk they present. Class A roads are safe for all vehicles. Motorists whose itinerary will take them over any Class B roads must apply for a travel permit from authorities at the point of departure. The permit will be granted only if the car is in proper condition to make the trip and if it is stocked with the necessary spare parts and with emergency and first-aid equipment. En route, the driver must contact the police at each stage of the trip—they have the authority to cancel the next stage if road conditions warrant it. Private cars may travel alone on B1 roads, which are well-traveled and well-maintained tracks. On the seldom-used and little-maintained B2 tracks, cars must travel in convoys of two or more and night driving is prohibited. Class C roads may not be used—they are dangerous.

FOOD AND RESTAURANTS

International cuisine is served in hotels and many restaurants in Algiers, but you won't want to miss the local specialties: *chorba,* a spicy, long-simmered soup containing mutton, chick peas, tomatoes, and onions in various combinations; *couscous,* the Algerian staple made of semolina flour steamed over and then served with its stew of meat, vegetables, and spices; *melfouf,* skewered mutton with slices of onion, tomato, and green pepper; *mechoui,* barbecued lamb or mutton done on a spit; *bourek,* pastry stuffed with meat, fried egg, and onions; *lhamlahlou,* meat with prunes. Algerian pastries, often thick with honey and nuts, are typically North African. You'll find Algerian cooking at **El Djenina,** 10 Avenue Franklin Roosevelt (tel: 59 29 12); **El Baçour,** 1 rue Patrice Lumumba (tel: 63 50 92); **La Casbah,** 56 rue Khélifa Boukhalfa (tel: 66 11 14); and **El Koutoubia,** 54 rue Didouche Mourad (tel: 63 98 56). For fish dishes, go to the **Pêcherie,** or fish market, where you'll find many small restaurants, including **Sindbad,** Rampe de la Pêcherie (tel: 62 10 65). Restaurants in Algiers serving European food only are **Le Carthage** (tel: 60 28 63), **El Djenan,** the former Chez Catherine (tel: 78 48 17), and **Villa d'Este** (tel: 81 95 02), which is also noted for its fish. While first-class restaurants have elaborate menus, very few of the dishes offered are available. Dinner in a first-class restaurant will cost DA70-80, excluding wine; in a medium restaurant, DA35-50; in an inexpensive one, about DA15. A meal for one in a tourist restaurant will cost about DA50, excluding wine.

DRINKING TIPS

Coffee is the national drink. Mint tea, served in small glasses and drunk any time of the day, is also popular. Algerian wines are strong but good, especially the red ones, and they are expensive. The cheapest wine in a restaurant will cost about DA30 a bottle. Local wines to ask for are: (red) Cuvée du Président, Medea, Mascara, Coteaux de Tlemcen, Dahra; (white) Blanc de Blanc, Medea, Mascara, Coteaux de Tlemcen; (rosé) Alicante, Medea, Mascara, Coteaux de Tlemcen, Pelure d'Oignons. El Bordj is a pleasant aperitif. Because of Muslim traditions, there are no local liquors, and imported spirits are available only if you are willing to pay extremely high prices. A bottle of whisky, for example, costs about DA350. There are drinking spots everywhere in Algiers, but the most pleasant cafés are to be found in tourist centers such as Moretti, Sidi Fredj, Zeralda, and Tipasa, along the coast outside of Algiers. There are no licensing hours.

ENTERTAINMENT

The **Théâtre National Algérien** (Place Mohamed Touri) performs regularly in Algiers, and there are regional theaters in **Oran** and **Constantine.** Check to see if the play is in French or Arabic. During the summer, go to the outdoor theater at Sidi Fredj, 15 miles from Algiers, to hear singers from all over the world. Tickets cost about DA35. The **Algerian Cinemathèque** in downtown Algiers shows Arab and foreign film classics (26 rue Larbi Ben M'Hidi). Major hotels provide music for dancing. There are nightclubs or discothèques at the tourist centers of Moretti, Sidi Fredj, Zeralda, and Tipasa, and in Algiers. During the course of the year there are many local agrarian festivals that give visitors a chance to sample regional folklore. You'll see folk dancing and the *baroud* (mock battle)

in March or April at the **Spring Festival** in Biskra, and camel races at
the **Date Festival** in Touggourt in April. Among others are the **Orange
Festival** in Boufarik in April or May, the **Cherry Festival** in Miliana in
May, and the **Sheep Festival** in Djelfa in June. The **Mediterranean Cultural Festival** takes place in Timgad in April.

SHOPPING

Stores in Algiers are open 9-12 and 3-7, closed Fridays. Traditional handicraft skills, once passed from generation to generation but recently in
danger of extinction, are now being developed and promoted by the
National Society of Traditional Handicrafts. Among the most interesting
are carpets; woven wool and goat-hair blankets; baskets and wickerwork;
pottery and ceramics; gold and silver jewelry; copper, brass, and iron
work; gold- and silver-thread embroidery on velvet, silk, and leather;
carved wood objects; decorated leather belts, slippers, bags, and saddles.
You'll even find "affanes" from El Oued—wool and camel-hair slippers
meant for walking on sand. Important handicraft centers are **Bou Saada,**
regions of the **Kabylia, M'Zab,** and **Hoggar,** and **Tlemcen,** but even if
you never leave Algiers, you'll find a broad selection of handicraft items
on display and for sale at shops maintained by the National Society. Its
headquarters in Algiers are at 1 Boulevard Front de Mer in the Bab el
Oued section (tel: 62 77 26/29), and other shops are at 2 Boulevard
Mohamed Khemisti, 3 rue Ali Boumendgel, and 1 rue Didouche Mourad.
In Oran, the shop is at 3 place Emir Abdelkader. Prices are fixed in
these shops, and in general, bargaining is no longer a regular practice
in Algeria.

SPORTS

Seven hundred and fifty miles of Mediterranean coastline provide the
opportunity for swimming and numerous other water sports, including
sailing, water-skiing, wind-surfing, and fishing. Horseback riding—on fine
Arabian horses—is available at beach resorts, mountain resorts, or
(through hotels) at some oases. For information, write to the Federation
des Sports Equestres, 21 rue Didouche Mourad, Algiers. There are tennis
courts at newer hotels, and Algiers, Oran, and Constantine all have tennis
clubs. Algiers has an 18-hole golf course near the **Olympic Stadium** (Che-
raga Road). Hunting for quail, partridge, hare, and wild boar is popular
in Algeria. The Algerian National Tourist Office has a **Tourist Hunt Service**
which arranges hunts for groups of 4-12 tourists (tel: 64 68 64). The
Hotel Tamgout in Yakouren is a favorite of wild-boar hunters. There is
skiing from December to February or March in the Atlas Mountains at
Chrea, and from November to May at **Tikjda** and **Tala Guilef** in the
Kabyl Mountains. Tikjda is also the spot where Algerian mountain
climbers are trained. Mountain climbing in the **Hoggar** is possible from
October to March.

WHAT TO SEE

Algiers is an important seaport built on steep hills, and sightseeing can
be tiring. Along the waterfront, elevated boulevards above vaulted ware-

houses provide a close-up view of activity in the harbor. In the center of town, the tiered gardens and stairs of Boulevard Mohamed Khemisti rise to the **Esplanade de l'Afrique** for another view. Do not miss the **Kasbah**, the old district with narrow streets dating from the period when Algiers was ruled by Turkish Deys. It, too, climbs the hills, but you can begin your visit at the top by taking a taxi to the 16th-century **Citadel**. Among the sights in the Kasbah: the **Safir Mosque;** the **Sidi Abderrahmane Mosque** and nearby "medersa" or Islamic school; **Mustapha Pasha Palace;** the **Museum of Popular Arts and Traditions,** which houses masterpieces of Algerian handicrafts in a palace of the 16th century (called **Dar Khadoudja El Amia**); the **Ketchaoua Mosque;** and the 16th-century **Dar Aziza Bent El Bey,** formerly the Archbishop's Palace. At the foot of the Kasbah, see the 11th-century **El Kebir** or **Great Mosque,** the oldest in Algiers, and, nearby, the **El Djeddid Mosque** (Fishermen's Mosque). The **Bardo Museum of Prehistory and Ethnography** and the **Museum of Classical and Moslem Antiquities** are also worth a visit. Finally, take a drive to **Notre Dame d'Afrique,** where the view of the city and Algiers Bay is magnificent, especially in the evening.

The coastal road west of Algiers passes the popular beaches of **El Djemila, Moretti, Sidi Fredj,** and **Zeralda** before reaching **Tipasa,** a resort town with important Roman ruins in a beautiful setting. In a cedar forest about 40 miles southwest of Algiers, in the Atlas Mountains, is the winter resort of **Chrea.** Nearby are the **Chiffa Gorges** and the **Monkey's Stream** (Ruisseau des Singes), where you'll see monkeys all over the mountain.

Kabylia is east of Algiers, a region of unspoiled seacoast and picturesque mountain villages, noted for its figs and olives and for the independence of its people (who speak the Kabyl dialect rather than Arabic). The track along the sea from **Azzefoun** to **Cap Sigli** is especially scenic. Accommodations are available at the **Lala Khedjidja Hotel** (from US$29 double) and the **Beloua Hotel** (from US$28 double) in **Tizi Ouzou,** the main town of the region, about 60 miles from Algiers.

Constantine, capital of eastern Algeria, occupies a natural fortress position on top of a rocky plateau cut through by the canyons of the Rhumel River. Suspension footbridges connect one part of the city with another and allow vertiginous views downward. See the 19th-century **Palace of Ahmed Bey,** which once housed a harem of 300 women; the **National Museum,** with valuable Roman, Christian, and Muslim relics; the **Kasbah;** the 13th-century **Great Mosque** (Djemaa el Kebir); and other mosques of the later Turkish period. Between Kabylia and the Constantine region, there is a marvelous coastline drive from **Bejaia** to **Jijel. Djemila** (near Setif) is a major North African Roman site. In Constantine, stay at the **Cirta Hotel,** 1 Avenue Rahmani Cherif (from US$25.50 double).

South of Constantine, the **Aures Mountains** lie between **Batna** and **Biskra,** and the green countryside changes to a dry, pre-Saharan landscape. **Timgad,** at the foot of the Aures, was founded in the 1st century AD by the Roman Emperor Trajan. The ruins are the most complete example remaining of a provincial Roman city. The oasis of Biskra, Algeria's date capital, follows a broad *oued* (river) surrounded by thousands of date palms. **Hamman es Salihine** spa, known to the Romans as "Ad Piscinam," is just outside the city. A half day from Biskra are the valley of the **Oued el Abiod,** the oasis of **M'Chounèche,** and **Balcon de Rhoufi,** which has a splended view of an ancient village nestled in the palms. In Biskra, accommodations at **Les Zibans Hotel** are available from US$30 double.

Bou Saada is the closest place to Algiers (150 miles) to experience the atmosphere of a Saharan town. It has sand dunes and palms, camels, and white koubbas (mausoleums), and fine craftsmen. Accommodations are at **Le Caid Hotel** (from US$37.50 double). **El Oued,** farther southeast near the Tunisian border and in the sea of sand known as the **Souf,** is a winter resort. A colorful market takes place every morning; it is very crowded on Fridays. **Du Souf Hotel** has double rooms from US$34.

Not to be missed are the five cities of the **M'zab,** settled in the 11th century by a puritanical sect of Muslims who took refuge in this rocky wasteland to preserve their religion. Today the towns rise like multicolored pyramids in a Cubist painting, superb examples of Saharan architecture; and the lush M'zabite gardens seem a miracle in the desert. The best way to see the five towns—**Ghardaia, El Ateuf, Bou Noura, Melika,** and **Beni Isguen**—is with a guide available from the Algerian National Tourist Office in Ghardaia, the capital of the region. Visitors to Beni Isguen, the holiest of the cities (where non-M'zabites may not spend the night), should avoid wearing short skirts or shorts, should not smoke, and should not photograph anyone. In Ghardaia stay at **Les Rostemides** (from US$34 double).

El Goléa, 165 miles from Ghardaia, was once a stop on caravan routes across the desert, as was **In Salah,** 255 miles from El Goléa and the first typical town of the deep south. Below In Salah, the hard-surfaced road becomes a track leading to **Tamanrasset,** the last outpost of the Algerian Sahara and an administrative and market center for the nomads who populate this otherwise desolate region. From here you can hire a guide for a tour of the **Hoggar Mountains.** The tour, including the **Assekrem Plateau,** takes about 5 days by camel or 1 day by car. Another unforgettable landscape is the **Tassili N'Ajjer Mountains,** famous for prehistoric rock paintings and carvings. The trip to this rewarding open-air museum is by donkey from **Djanet,** an oasis town in the southeast corner of Algeria.

Oran, 270 miles west of Algiers, is the capital of western Algeria and the country's second-largest city. It is Spanish in character, a result of nearly 3 centuries of Spanish occupation (1509-1791). The 16th-century **Santa Cruz Fort** in the **Murdjadjo Hills** provides a view of the city, the harbor of **Mers-el-Kebir** to the north, and the **Sebkha** or Salt Lake of Oran to the south. See also the 18th-century **Mosque of the Pasha** and the **Demaeght Museum** with prehistoric exhibits. Inland, **Tlemcen** has a famous past as a center of Islamic art and culture; it has shrines that are still the object of veneration by pilgrims. Among the monuments from the 12th to 14th centuries are the **Great Mosque,** with its faïence-encrusted minaret; the **Sidi Bel Hassen Mosque,** now a museum; the

Agadir Minaret; the mausoleum, medersa, and mosque of **Sidi Bou Mediene** in the village of **El Eubad** just outside of Tlemcen; and the mosque at the **Mansourah ruins,** a beautiful example of Muslim art. Accommodations are available in Oran at the beachfront hotel, bungalows, and villas of **Les Andalouses** tourist center, 18 miles from Oran (from US$30 double).

SOURCES OF FURTHER INFORMATION

Any **Pan Am** office around the world; **Algerian National Tourist Office,** 25/27 Rue Khélifa Boukhalfa, Algiers; **Embassy of Algeria,** 2118 Kalorama Road NW, Washington DC 20008; 54 Holland Park, London W1.

Benin

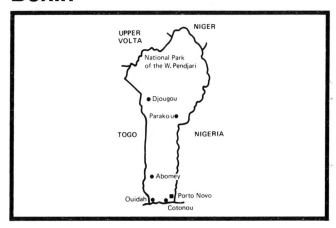

WHAT'S SPECIAL

Benin's national parks and game reserves are among Africa's finest,
and there are beautiful beaches and bamboo villages. Agriculture is the
mainstay of this country, formerly Dahomey; palm trees (for palm
oil and by-products), peanuts, coconut, cotton, coffee, and tobacco are
cultivated. There is swimming and hunting, plenty to see, and some
nightlife.

COUNTRY BRIEFING

Size: 44,696 square miles   **Population:** 3,370,000
Capital: Porto Novo   **Capital Population:** 104,000
    Principal town and port is Cotonou (population: 178,000).
    Climate: Equatorial in the south and tropical in the north. Best season
to visit is November-March, the dry season.

Weather in Cotonou: Lat N6°21'; Alt 23 ft

Temp (°F)	Jan	Feb	Mar	Apr	May	Jun	Jul	Aug	Sep	Oct	Nov	Dec
Av Low	74°	77°	79°	78°	76°	74°	74°	73°	74°	75°	76°	76°
Av High	80°	82°	83°	83°	81°	78°	78°	77°	78°	80°	82°	81°
Days no rain	29	26	26	23	20	17	24	28	24	22	24	30

Government: An independent republic.
    Language: French is the official language; English is spoken in most
hotels. The major languages are Fon, Yoruba, Bariba, Dendi, and Mina.
    Religion: Majority of the population animists; there are Roman Catho-
lic and Protestant churches and Muslim mosques.

Currency: CFA franc.

	CFA 5	CFA 50	CFA 100	CFA 500	CFA 1,000	CFA 5,000	CFA 10,000	CFA 15,000
US (dollars, cents)	.02	.20	.40	2.00	4.00	19.98	39.95	59.93
UK (pounds, pence)	.01	.10	.19	.95	1.91	9.53	19.06	28.59

Public Holidays: New Year's Day, 1 Jan; Easter; Labor Day, 1 May; Ascension Day; Whitsunday; Benin Armed Forces Day, 26 Oct; National Day, 30 Nov; Christmas Day, 25 Dec; Feed Yourself Day, 31 Dec. Dates of Ramadan and Tabaski, Muslim celebrations, change yearly.

HOW TO GET THERE

Flying time to Benin's Cotonou Airport from New York is 11¼ hours; from Paris, 7½ hours; from Lagos, ½ hour. Time in Benin: GMT+1.

REQUIREMENTS FOR ENTRY AND CUSTOMS REGULATIONS

Passport and visa, obtainable from consulates of Benin or France, and an onward ticket. Visas will not be granted to travelers with South African visas already in their passports. Smallpox, yellow fever, and cholera vaccination certificates required. Unlimited foreign currency can be brought in but must be declared on arrival. The export of articles of historical value is prohibited. Duty-free allowance: 50 cigarettes or 25 cigars or ¼ pound of tobacco. Reasonable amount of liquor and perfume for personal use. Authorization from Ministry of Interior is required for all weapons.

AIRPORT INFORMATION

From Cotonou Airport into the city is 3 miles, taxi fare US$3. No need to tip driver. Tip luggage porter CFA100. There is no departure tax.

ACCOMMODATIONS

Hotels in Benin are controlled by the government which has a tendency to consider creature comforts non-essential. As a result, accommodations do not begin to compare with facilities found in neighboring West African countries. The better hotels in Cotonou (inclusive of tax) are:
Rates are in US$ for a double/twin room with bath or shower
  Benin-Sheraton, PO Box 1901 (from $50), on beach
  De la Plage, PO Box 36 (from $26), in residential area
  Du Port, PO Box 884 (from $23), centrally located

USEFUL INFORMATION

Banks are open 8-11 and 2-4 Mon-Fri. **Pan Am agent** in Cotonou is at Air Afrique (tel: 313 444). **Tipping** is at your discretion. **Electricity** is 220 volts. First-class **laundry** service at major hotels. All **photographic film** available, but very expensive. Tap water is not drinkable. It is a good idea to take a quinine-base tablet for 10 days before your trip, during your stay, and for 15 days after your departure.

TRANSPORTATION

The railroad system is shared with Niger. An 8-hour train ride will take you to Parakou, central Benin, for CFA4,000 (first class). Travel is inexpensive but crowded. Bus services connect major towns, where taxis are reliable and reasonable, about CFA200 for any journey around town, CFA500 for ½ hour, and CFA1,000 for an hour. Rental car rates are high, beginning at US$20 per day, and gasoline is expensive also. Most roads are unpaved, except for those joining Benin with her neighbors. (If traveling by road, be aware that the border between Benin and Togo closes at 6pm sharp.) In Benin, as in several West African countries, it is best not to rent a car unless you also pay for a driver, since the driver is responsible in the event of an accident, and very likely responsible for supporting the injured African and his family for years to come.

FOOD AND RESTAURANTS

In the south, maize, manioc, yams, vegetables, and pork are the basis of the local cooking. In the north, dairy products and big-game meat are standard fare. French cuisine predominates in many hotels and restaurants. In Cotonou, dine at restaurants in the Benin-Sheraton, De la Plage, and Du Port hotels, or try **Les Trois Paillotes** for typical dishes and dinner dancing. French food is good at **Pam Pam**, and **Chez Pepita** specializes in seafood.

ENTERTAINMENT

There is dancing at most large hotels, such as the **Kings Club** at Hotel Du Port. The Benin-Sheraton has a nightclub and disco. Other clubs are **Canne a Sucre** and the **Lido.** Movie houses in Cotonou and Porto Novo show European and American movies.

SHOPPING

Benin is renowned for its handcrafted wares. In the former capital of Abomey and the village of Baname, various craftsmen still produce jewelry, elongated statuettes, tapestries, roco wood furniture, ebony masks, swords, and daggers. Samples of these wares can also be found in the large stores of central Cotonou and Porto Novo. For some enjoyable haggling, visit the delightful "lagoon market" at **Dan Topka** near Cotonou.

SPORTS

Hunting safaris should be arranged before arriving in Benin. The hunting season lasts from 1 December to 1 July; for all game a temporary license is issued, obtainable at Cotonou or Porga upon presentation of a gun license and two photographs or a passport. You can hunt all wildlife but must pay a tax for each animal or bird killed. At Cotonou there is a yacht and tennis club (**Club du Bénin**).

WHAT TO SEE

Cotonou's beaches are superb, but swimmers should beware of undertow. From Cotonou you can visit the fascinating lake village of **Ganvié**, whose 46,000 inhabitants live in bamboo huts on stilts above the water. A canoe ride around the village is possible but it's better to take the tour by motorized pirogue. Excursions can be arranged through the Tourist Office in Cotonou (tel: 312 687 or 313 271) or through hotels. Rates vary according to the number of people making the trip. **Porto Novo** was once the residential area of the wealthy families of Cotonou. **Ouidah**, 26 miles west of Cotonou, has the restored fort of the Portuguese explorers and the **Temple of the Serpents**, which houses fetish pythons.

The fortified township of **Abomey**, built in the mid-17th century and the original capital of Benin, is 90 miles northwest of Cotonou. The historical museum and the tombs of the former Kings of Abomey are of great interest to art lovers, as are the works of the many local craftsmen. In the north is the **National Park of the Pendjari.** There are good hotels at **Porga** and facilities for seeing the animals of Africa in a natural environment. Parks are open from November-March only.

SOURCES OF FURTHER INFORMATION

Pan Am, c/o Air Afrique, Avenue du Gouverneur Ballot, Cotonou, and any Pan Am office around the world; **Office du Tourisme du Benin** (Tourist Office), PO Box 89, Cotonou; **Benin Mission to the UN,** 4 East 73rd Street, New York, NY 10021; **Embassy of Benin,** 2737 Cathedral Avenue NW, Washington, DC 20008.

Cameroon

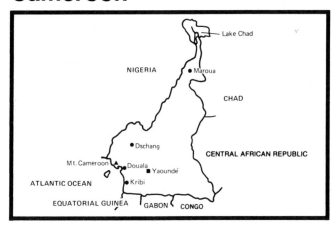

WHAT'S SPECIAL

Cameroon is known as Africa in miniature; it has all the features of the continent—rolling savannah country, broad rivers, equatorial forests, white-sanded Atlantic beaches, and all the animals, including elephants, giraffes, antelopes, and monkeys. The people, too, are a cross-section of Africa, an enormous variety of tribes and races living harmoniously.

COUNTRY BRIEFING

Size: 183,591 square miles   **Population:** 8,300,000
Capital: Yaoundé   **Capital Population:** 500,000
  Climate: Rainy season May through September. Best time to visit is October through April.

Weather in Douala: Lat N4°03'; Alt 26 ft

Temp (°F)	Jan	Feb	Mar	Apr	May	Jun	Jul	Aug	Sep	Oct	Nov	Dec
Av Low	73°	74°	73°	73°	73°	72°	71°	71°	72°	71°	73°	73°
Av High	86°	86°	86°	86°	86°	83°	80°	80°	81°	81°	84°	85°
Days no rain	27	22	19	18	15	11	7	7	9	11	20	25

Government: A united republic since 1972.
Language: French and English are both official languages.
Religion: Mainly Muslim in the north, Christian and animist in the south.

Currency: CFA franc.

	CFA 5	CFA 50	CFA 100	CFA 500	CFA 1,000	CFA 5,000	CFA 10,000	CFA 15,000
US (dollars, cents)	.02	.20	.40	2.00	4.00	19.98	39.95	59.93
UK (pounds, pence)	.01	.10	.19	.95	1.91	9.53	19.06	28.59

Public Holidays:

New Year's Day, 1 Jan
Youth Day, 11 Feb
Good Friday
Labor Day, 1 May
National Day, 20 May
Ascension Day

Djoulde Soumae, 12 Aug
Assumption Day, 15 Aug
Union Nationale Camerounaise Day, 1 Sept
Christmas Day, 25 Dec

The end of Ramadan, the Muslim fast period, is a holiday, and 70 days later is the Sheep Festival.

HOW TO GET THERE

Flying time to Douala Airport from New York is 11 hours; from Rome, 5½ hours; from Lagos, 1¼ hours. Time in Cameroon: GMT+1.

REQUIREMENTS FOR ENTRY AND CUSTOMS REGULATIONS

Passport, round-trip or onward ticket required; no visa required for stays up to 20 days. Smallpox and yellow-fever vaccinations required. Duty-free allowance: 400 cigarettes or ½ pound tobacco or 125 cigars; 2 bottles liquor, and perfume for personal use. No foreign currency restrictions; only CFA25,000 or 500 French francs may be taken out of the country without an exchange receipt, more with the receipt.

AIRPORT INFORMATION

Douala Airport is 8 miles from the city center. Taxis meet flights, and the fare is CFA2,000, though some drivers will ask for more. Some hotels provide a transfer service. There is no departure tax. Tip airport porters CFA100 per bag.

ACCOMMODATIONS

In Yaoundé, Douala, and other main cities there is a choice of international-type hotels. In tourist and safari areas, campsites provide accommodations based on *bukara*—the local village dwellings plus modern comforts and conveniences. The Waza National Park has a hotel. Hotels in Douala:

Rates are in US$ for a double/twin room with bath or shower
Akwa Palace, PO Box 4007 (from $50)
Hotel des Cocotiers, PO Box 310 (from $30)
Residence de Joss, PO Box 1218 (from $15)
Sawa Novotel Douala, PO Box 2345 (rates on request)
The above hotels are centrally located in Douala.

USEFUL INFORMATION

Banks are open 7:30-11:30 and 2:30-3:30 Mon-Fri, closed Sat. **Stamps** can be bought at post offices only. There are few **telephone** booths, but phones are available in restaurants and post offices. The *Cameroon Times* and *Cameroon Outlook* are published weekly in English. **Tipping** is customary, as is 10% service charge in restaurants. **Electricity** is variable between 110-220 volts. First-class hotels have **laundry** and **dry-cleaning** services, and some hotels have **hairdressing** salons. Black and white and color film available in major cities, but developing takes a long time. It is safe to drink tap water in the larger cities.

TRANSPORTATION

There are public transportation systems in Yaoundé and Douala. Taxis are available with fixed charges but no meters; the minimum fare is CFA300, CFA500-600 at night. Privately owned buses can be rented by groups. Cars rent for US$20 a day minimum, plus charges for mileage and gas. Drive on the right. Roads are poor, especially in the rainy season. A railroad network connects main cities; there are also long-distance buses. Quickest and most comfortable travel is by Cameroon Airlines (Cam-Air).

FOOD AND RESTAURANTS

The restaurants in principal hotels provide an international cuisine. The local fish is good, and so are the fruit and vegetables. There are restaurants in the cities, mostly French or Italian. In Yaoundé try **Le Dauphine**, **Trappola**, **Le Cintra**, and **Les Boucarous**. Douala has **Le Paris** (Avenue Ahmadou Ahidjo—tel: 42 12 89), **L'Auberge**, and **La Cascade**, all expensive restaurants serving French food. Also in Douala **Al Vesuvio** (Bonanjo) has Italian cuisine, and **Le Lyonnais** (near the Beauséjour Hotel) serves a good Spanish paella. For Chinese dishes try **Lotus** (Bonanjo) behind the Palais de Justice, **l'Astor** or **Le Dragon d'Or**. A meal in an expensive restaurant will cost US$13 and up per person and in an inexpensive one US$5-7.

DRINKING TIPS

Gold Harp, "*33,*" and other locally produced beers are fair. Other drinks are imported. A whisky and soda costs US$2.25, a bottle of red wine about US$6.50. No restrictions on drinking hours.

ENTERTAINMENT

There are movie houses in the towns, usually showing French movies or others with a soundtrack dubbed into French. In Douala **La Frégate**, **La Jungle, Cosmos,** and **Kings** are European-type nightclubs, and in Yaoundé there are the **Pacha Club, Balafon, Le Caveau,** and **Papagaho**.

SHOPPING

Shops open 9-12:30 and 4-7 Mon-Sat. Best buys include beadwork, ivory and copper articles, carved masks, pottery, wickerwork, tooled leatherware, and embroidered table linen. Lizard and snakeskin handbags and wallets are particularly attractive and reasonably priced (check your country's import custom laws for restricted items). In Douala, **Ali Baba, Galerie Africa,** and **Reine Sherman's** stock native art and handcrafts; supermarkets such as **Monoprix, Cie Soudanaise,** and **Supercam** have a wide range of goods. Markets are **New Bell** and **Deido,** in Douala.

SPORTS

Boxing and soccer are the country's favorite sports. Swimming, except on the beaches, can be dangerous. For safari hunting the best region lies between Garoua and N'Gaoundere. Hunters must pay a firearm tax and obtain a permit, either from the Secretariat Rural, S/c du Directeur des Eaux et Forêts in Yaoundé, or S/c du Chef de l'Inspection Nord des Chasses, BP 50, in Garoua. For hunting guides apply to Safaris Jacques Guin, BP 9, Maroua. Tourist offices in larger cities provide information.

WHAT TO SEE

Yaoundé is a fine, tree-lined, modern city. **Mount Febe** is only 10 minutes drive away, with accommodations at the **Independence Hotel,** PO Box 474, Yaoundé (from US$26 double); and **Sheraton-Mont Febe Palace,** PO Box 4178 (from US$26). Go to the **Nkolbisson Agricultural Center—** see the **Rock of Akok;** visit the **Nachtigall falls** in **Obala.**

Douala, the largest city and the commercial center, lies on the Wouri River, in the equatorial forest region. Look for the imitation Chinese Pagoda of **Manga Bell,** the **Centenary Temple,** and the **Cathedral** on Avenue Ahmadou Ahidjo.

Kribi, with white sandy beaches, is on the coast 125 miles south of Douala. North of Douala, **Dschang** is an agreeable mountain resort. In the far north, there are magnificent landscapes and first-class safari country at **Kapsiki, Rumsiki,** and **Logone. Maroua** is a convenient center for the **Waza Wild Life Reserve,** one of the most beautiful in Africa. There are national parks too at **Boubandjidah, Benoue,** and **Kalamaloue.** In the west lies **Mount Cameroon,** once called the Chariot of the Gods, and on its slopes the charming town of **Buea** rests, at 4,500 feet.

SOURCES OF FURTHER INFORMATION

Pan Am agent: **Cameroon Airlines,** Avenue De Gaulle, Douala, and any Pan Am office round the world; the **General Delegation for Tourism,** Yaoundé; **Cameroon Mission to the UN,** 22 East 73rd Street, New York, NY 10021; the **Cameroon Embassy,** 2349 Massachusetts Avenue NW, Washington, DC 20008; 84 Holland Park, London W11.

Egypt

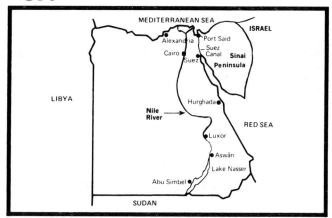

Note: All Sinai Territory is scheduled to be returned to Egypt in April 1982.

WHAT'S SPECIAL

The Arab Republic of Egypt, lying at the crossroads between the continents of Europe, Asia, and Africa, has two faces: the Egypt with 5,000 years of history and the new Egypt with modern hotels and every recreational facility.

COUNTRY BRIEFING

Size: 386,101 square miles   **Population:** 42,000,000
Capital: Cairo   **Capital Population:** 9,500,000

   Climate: Distinct winter and summer seasons, with a short spring and fall. Hot weather begins in May, and the average temperature is about 97°F in summer. As the rainfall is very low (25mm in Cairo) and the air very dry, the summer heat is bearable and there is a sharp drop in temperature after sundown. Winters are from December to March: it is usually warm, but the temperature does sometimes fall as low as 40°F in Cairo.

Weather in Cairo: Lat N29°52′; Alt 381 ft

Temp (°F)	Jan	Feb	Mar	Apr	May	Jun	Jul	Aug	Sep	Oct	Nov	Dec
Av Low	47°	48°	52°	51°	63°	68°	70°	71°	68°	65°	58°	50°
Av High	65°	69°	75°	83°	91°	95°	96°	95°	90°	86°	78°	68°
Days no rain	30	27	30	30	31	30	31	31	30	31	29	30

Government: A Presidential Republic with a cabinet and a People's Assembly.

Language: Arabic. English is widely understood in larger cities, and some French is spoken.

Religion: 90% of the population is Sunni Muslim, and Islam is the official state religion. There is a sizable Coptic Christian minority. Catholic and Protestant churches and synagogues in main cities.

Currency: Egyptian pound. 100 piastres = £E1. Rate of exchange is official exchange rate for tourists.

	PT 2	PT 5	PT 10	PT 50	£E 1	£E 5	£E 10	£E 20
US (dollars, cents)	.03	.07	.15	.73	1.45	7.25	14.50	29.00
UK (pounds, pence)	.01	.03	.07	.35	.69	3.46	6.92	13.83

Public Holidays:

Fixed holidays:

Revolution of Mar 8th, 8 Mar

Labor Day, 1 May

Evacuation Day, 18 June

National Day, 23 July

Proclamation of the Union, 1 Sept

Suez Day, 24 Oct

The following holidays depend on lunar calendar and vary from year to year. Birthday of the Prophet; Ramadan Bairam, for 4 days; Arafat Day; Kourban Bairam, for 4 days; Islamic New Year. NB: Government offices and banks and many shops are closed on the Muslim day of worship, Friday. Other shops and services as well as the Khan El Khalili Bazaar merchants close or close early on Sunday.

HOW TO GET THERE

Flying time to Cairo International Airport from New York is 11¼ hours; from Rome, 3 hours; from Istanbul, 2 hours. Time in Egypt: GMT+2. Daylight Saving Time observed.

REQUIREMENTS FOR ENTRY AND CUSTOMS REGULATIONS

Valid passport, return or onward ticket, and visa required. Israeli citizens are allowed entry in special cases and with the approval of the Egyptian government. Entry visas, valid up to one month, are obtainable from Egyptian Consulates or on arrival. Visitors not traveling with a prepaid tour and staying more than 72 hours must exchange the equivalent of £E100 upon arrival. Those staying less than 72 hours are exempt from this exchange requirement and will be granted a transit visa. Entry visas can be extended up to six months with proof of the transfer of adequate funds to cover expenses during the period of residence. No vaccination or inoculation certificates for smallpox or yellow fever unless coming from an infected area.

Duty-free allowance is officially 200 cigarettes or 50 cigars or ½ pound tobacco, and 2 bottles liquor, though reasonable amounts of liquor and cigarettes are usually allowed; jewelry, photographic equipment, typewriters, etc. should be declared at customs. Up to £E20 in Egyptian currency allowed in, none allowed out. There are no limits on the amount of foreign currency brought in but it must be declared on Form D which is kept and presented on departure, along with the receipts of all currency exchange transactions. Everyone entering Egypt must register with the Ministry of the Interior within 7 days. Most hotels provide this service for guests but if you must do it in person, go to the Mugamma Building on Tahrir Square with your passport.

AIRPORT INFORMATION

Cairo International Airport is 15 miles from the city center. Egypt Air runs a 24-hour bus service to the terminal on Opera Square (fare PT10 for adults and children). Also public bus service every 25 minutes. Both buses are usually jammed. Taxi fare to city £E4-5. Luggage porters are tipped PT25 per bag. Departure tax £E3. Duty-free shop at airport.

ACCOMMODATIONS

There is a wide choice of accommodations, but reservations must now be made at least 3 months in advance and tourists should have written confirmation. Rates are among the lowest in the world, even in one of Cairo's deluxe hotels. Comfortable accommodations are also to be found in Alexandria, Luxor, and Aswan, and in resorts along the Egyptian Riviera. Youth hostels in Cairo, Giza, Alexandria, Luxor, and Aswan are open to students with a valid international membership card; price is PT12-17 per bed. For information, contact the Egyptian Youth Hostels Association, 7 Abdel Hamid Said Street, Cairo. A service charge of 12% as well as 2% tax is included on hotel bills. For help in finding accommodations contact the **Ministry of Tourism:** Head office in Cairo, 5 Adly Street (tel: 923000); Pyramid Office, on Pyramid Road (tel: 850259); in Alexandria, at Saad Zaghlul Square (tel: 25985). Hotels in Cairo, centrally located unless otherwise indicated, include:

Rates are in US$ for double/twin room with bath or shower

Atlas, 2 Mohamed Rushdy Street, Opera Square (from $27)

Cairo International Airport, Cairo International Airport (from $29), at airport

Cleopatra, 2 Abdel Salam Aref Street (from $36)

Continental, 10 Opera Square (from $24)

El Nil, 4 Ragheb Street, Garden City (from $30)

Grand, 17 26th July Street (from $16)

Heliopolis Sheraton, Uruba Street, Heliopolis (from $60), at airport

Holiday Inn, Pyramid Road, Giza (from $51), 40 minutes from Cairo

Jolie Vie, Pyramid Road, Giza (from $58), 40 minutes from Cairo

Khan El Khalili, Ataba Square (from $20)

Mena House Oberoi, Al Ahram Street, Giza (from $60), 9 miles from Cairo

Meridien, Corniche El Nil (from $61)

Nile Hilton, Tahrir Square (from $65)

President Hotel, Zamalek Island (from $51), 10 minutes from Cairo

Shepheard's, Corniche El Nil Street, Garden City (from $51)

Sheraton, 2 Kubri El Gala Square, Giza (from $60), 9 miles from Cairo

Victoria, 66 El Goumhouria Street (from $18)
Windsor, 3 Alfi Street (from $18)

USEFUL INFORMATION

Banks: Open 8:30-12:30, Mon-Thurs and Sat; 10-12 Sun; closed Fri. Traveler's checks can be changed at hotels. American Express is at 15 Kasr El Nil Street and in the lobbies of the Hilton, Sheraton, and Meridien hotels; Thomas Cook & Son, 4 Champolion Street.

Mail: Stamps are on sale in most souvenir kiosks and shops as well as post offices. Central Post Office, Ataba Square, always open.

Telephone Tips: The Egyptian telephone system is notoriously bad. Blocks of numbers are often changed. Dialing slowly and deliberately will reduce the frequency of wrong numbers. Improvements have begun, however, and it is now possible to call from the extreme southern suburb or Maadi to the rest of Cairo. Local calls can be made from stores and kiosks or post offices for PT5, but a call from a hotel or restaurant phone will usually cost PT10. Useful numbers in Cairo:

Pan Am 747399	**Airport Information** 964255-9
Tourist Office (Head office) 923657	**Tourist Police** 912644
(Pyramid office) 850259	**Directories** 125
	Operator 10

Newspapers: The *Egyptian Gazette,* and its Saturday edition called *The Egyptian Mail,* are the local English-language newspapers. The *International Herald Tribune* and some English newspapers are available, along with *Time, Newsweek,* and *The Economist* and an unpredictable assortment of foreign magazines. Best to look in the bookshops of the major hotels.

Tipping: In restaurants a 10-12% service charge is usually included in the check, but you should still leave an extra 10% tip. Porters get PT10 per piece of luggage; taxi drivers 10% of fare. Tip the hotel porter PT20 or PT25 and the chambermaid PT20 or PT25. Tip higher in first-class hotels. The hotel keeps most of the service charge.

Electricity: In most of Egypt, 220 volts 50 cycles AC; in Alexandria, 110/120 volts 50 cycles AC; fluctuates in Heliopolis and elsewhere. Transformers available.

Laundry: Laundries in Cairo and Alexandria. Major hotels have dry-cleaning and 24-hour service (suit dry-cleaned from £E2-3; shirt laundered from PT30-40).

Hairdressing: Salons are available in major hotels (shampoo and set from E£10-20; man's haircut from E£2 up; tip 10%).

Photography: Equipment and film available in major cities; reasonably expensive. Color costs £E7 for slide film and E£5 for color print film; black and white is about E£2, while color prints cost PT35 each. Developing usually takes a week, but Kodachrome stills and color movie films of any kind cannot be processed locally. Because the quality of processing and printing, film is generally poor; it is best to wait until you return home. Military installations, public utility buildings, bridges, and the broadcasting station may not be photographed.

Clubs: Automobile Club, Cairo Yacht Club, Touring Club, Rotary Club.

Babysitting: Services available at first-class hotels.

Rest Rooms: In hotels and restaurants. Very few public conveniences. Women, *Hammam Sayyedat;* men, *Hammam Regal.*

Health: Some doctors and dentists speak English. Hotel doctors handle small problems, but foreigners seriously ill are generally advised to return home. If you become critically ill, the Maadi Military Hospital, located in a Cairo suburb, and the Anglo-American in Gezera (tel: 806163-5) are recommended. Bring any special medications with you. Water in Cairo and Alexandria generally is considered safe to drink, but milk should be boiled.

TRANSPORTATION

Bus services in major towns exist, but are generally packed to capacity; taxis are inexpensive. You can hail a taxi in the street or go to a stand. Charge is PT12 for the first kilometer, PT1 for each additional 300 meters; a short trip costs PT25-50. Tourists may have to wait hours downtown for taxis as they are in short supply. Best to rent one by the hour (£E2.50-3) and keep it with you. Chauffeured cars can be rented at an average rate of £E20-50 per day (including fuel).

Good railroad service connecting Cairo and Alexandria, Minia, Luxor, Fayyoum, and Aswan. The regular Cairo to Luxor-Aswan trips are very rough but on the two deluxe trains that make the trip daily the smooth ride is well worth the extra money. Air-conditioned buses available between Cairo-Alexandria and Cairo-Fayyoum. Egypt Air operates regular flights between major cities.

FOOD AND RESTAURANTS

The average meal in Egypt consists of several different dishes, all laid out together, which you sample at will. Most hotels serve European food, and there are many good restaurants in Cairo and Alexandria. In Cairo these include the **Aladin** (26 Sherif Street); **Kursaal** (17 Alfi Street); **Estoril** (12 Talaat Harb Street); **Indian Tea House** (23 Talaat Harb Street); and **Grillon** (8 Kasr El Nil). The **Seahorse** (Cornice El Nil) is noted for its delicious seafood, the **Liban** (20 Adly Street) for its Lebanese food, the **Felfella** (15 Hoda Shaarawi Street), for its Egyptian cuisine and atmosphere, and the **Arabesque** includes a bar and art gallery with the restaurant. The **Swiss Chalet Bar-b-Que** (3 Ahmed Nessim Street) is also good. The **Omar Khayyam Floating Palace** is in an exotic houseboat near the Gezira Sporting Club and **La Lanterne** has a garden for outdoor dining just off Pyramid Road. If you are in the suburb of Maadi, try the **Sweet Hotel Restaurant** on Road 13. Two self-service restaurants, **Cairo Tower** and **A l'Americaine**, are on 26 July Street and Talaat Harb Street. In Alexandria go to **Santa Lucia** (40 Saad Zaghlul Street); **Maxim** on Maamura Beach; or **Petrou** (5 El Missak Street).

A dinner for one in an expensive restaurant will cost about US$20; in a medium-priced restaurant, about US$5; and in an inexpensive restaurant about US$2. Food from street stalls is not recommended for the tourist passing through.

DRINKING TIPS

Local wines are quite passable, and the Egyptian Stella beer is good, but quality control is poor. Watch out for flat or green beer when you order. Imported liquors expensive (about US$5 for a whisky and soda; about US$20 for a bottle of red wine in a restaurant). Egyptian rosé or white wines are not bad at US$4.50.

ENTERTAINMENT

The best way to spend an evening in Cairo is to rent a felucca (native boat) and sail up the Nile. Most boats have charcoal broilers aboard if you want to take along some steak or shrimp. Another outstanding evening activity in and around Cairo is the *Son et Lumière* spectacle. You sit at the foot of the illuminated pyramids and sphinx and listen to the story of one of the world's greatest civilizations. Shows start at sunset, and you should check in the "Round and About" section of the *Egyptian Gazette* for information on performances in English. There are *Son et Lumière* shows at **Karnak** and **Luxor;** for information call 53260. Occasional ballets by visiting ensembles. The **Planetarium** at the Exhibition Grounds opens daily at 7pm except Wednesdays.

For good floor shows and dancing, the **Auberge des Pyramids** (352 Al Haram Street) and the **Sahara City** nightclub behind the pyramids are particularly recommended for visitors. **Aladdin** (Sheraton Hotel) has oriental and western floor shows, as well as an excellent dance floor, and you can spend a romantic evening on the **Omar Khayyam Floating Palace.** There are supper clubs with dancing in the roof gardens of several hotels, the most exclusive of which is the **Pyramid Roof** at the Nile Hilton. Also popular are the **Tamerina Stereo Club,** the **Arizona,** and the **Ramses Night Club,** all on Pyramid Road, Giza, and the **Cairo Airport Stereo.** If you want to gamble, go to the **Montaza Palace Night Club** in Alexandria; also the Sheraton Hotel, the Shepheard Hotel, and the Nile Hilton in Cairo, which have casinos. The Hilton has what it terms the most elegant discothèque in the Middle East or Europe (adults only).

SHOPPING

Cairo shopping hours, designed to relieve downtown congestion and save energy costs, are 9am-8pm daily except Friday and Sunday; on those days, only some stores are open. Stores open outside Cairo every day, 9-1 or 1:30 and 4 or 5pm to 8 or 9pm. Most department stores, including **Circural, Hanneau, Chemla,** and **Be'a El Masnu'aat** are on 26 July Street, Kasr El Nil Street, and Talaat Harb Street. Best buys in Egypt are lengths of printed cottons and linens; gold and silver jewelry; brass and copperware encrusted with different metals; wood carvings; and leather goods. Buy yourself a camel saddle ottoman. At the **Khan El Khalili Bazaar** in the center of the Old City, and the bigger bazaar on the **Mousky Road,** you are expected to bargain.

SPORTS

Soccer is very popular in Egypt, as are the frequent athletic contests held in Cairo's **Gezira Sporting Club.** Horse racing can be seen from mid-October to mid-May in Cairo and in Alexandria during July and September. There are several rowing and yachting clubs along the Nile. The **Gezira Club** (Gezira—tel: 802272) and the **National Sporting Club** (tel: 802114) have swimming, water skiing, golf, tennis, squash, riding, and racing facilities, as well as playgrounds for children. Golf is available at the **Mena Golf Club** (tel: 853779) in the Pyramids zone. **Maadi Sporting and Yacht Club** (tel: 35091) has sailing, water skiing, swimming, bowling, tennis, films, and social gatherings. Horseback riding around the pyramids and the surrounding desert areas in the early morning hours is an exhilarating experience, and the stables are generally good. Recommended are the **MC** and the **SA** stables, both located close to the sphinx at the pyramids. Roads are well marked. The cost is about US$4.50 an hour. Horses can be ridden even in remote desert areas. There is wild duck shooting at various locations. For information go to the **Egyptian Shooting and Hunting Club** in Doqqi (tel: 802171). Egypt has a beautiful unspoiled coastline along the Mediterranean. Beaches at **Agami** near Alexandria, long preferred by tourists, are becoming crowded. There is more space at **Sidi Abdel Rahman,** about 60 miles west of Agami. The Red Sea is now being opened to tourism as well and has some of the best diving in the world, with all kinds of colorful fish and corals to interest the amateur or the professional. There are glass-bottom boats as well. Two first-class resorts, about 520 km southeast of Cairo, are the **Sheraton Hurghada** and the **Club Mediterranée,** each with a swimming pool, extensive seawater sports, and other recreational facilities. The resort can be reached in 40 minutes by a daily flight, or in 7 hours by a bumpy bus ride at a reasonable price. Reservations must be made well in advance. For information on sporting facilities, go to the **Touring Club of Egypt** (10 Kasr El Nil Street—tel: 977243).

WHAT TO SEE

The three great **Pyramids of Giza** and the **Sphinx** are the main tourist attractions. You can ride by camel around the pyramids, or go by bus or taxi. An hour's drive from Cairo is the **Step Pyramid** of King Zoser, at Sakkara, the most ancient stone building in the world, dating back to 2,816 BC. Tickets to all Pharaonic and Islamic monuments are issued by the **Department of Antiquities** (Tahrir Square, Cairo). See the **Citadel of Saladin,** built in 1183. Perhaps the most beautiful of the many mosques in Cairo is **Al Azhar,** founded in the 10th century along with its university, one of the oldest in the world. Other mosques are the **Ibn Touloun** and the **Sultan Hassan.** You should also see the very old Coptic churches within the **Fortress of Babylon,** the ex-King's palaces, and the **Barrage,** north of Cairo. The **Egyptian Museum** (Tahrir Square) has Pharaonic treasures 5,000 years old. **Abdin Palace Museum** in El Goumhouria Square was the Royal Palace of former King Farouk and his predecessors. There are also the **Coptic** and **Islamic** art museums. For a superb view of the city, particularly at sunset, the **Cairo Tower** on Zamalek Island is a must; there is a small restaurant at the top of the tower.

Alexandria, 140 miles northwest of Cairo, is a seaside resort with perfect Mediterranean weather. Once one of the three main centers of the Christian world, it now houses the **Graeco-Roman Museum,** which contains more than 40,000 valuable relics dating as far back as the third century BC. Here also you will see **Pompey's Pillar** standing 25 meters high in the ruins of the **Serapium Temple,** the **Roman Amphitheater,** with its 12 marble terraces, the Catacombs of **Kom El Shuqqaffa,** and the **Al Montaza Palace,** the residence of the former royal family. Hotels in Alexandria: **Cecil,** 16 Saad Zaghlul Square (from US$22 double); **Palestine,** Montaza Palace (from US$28 double); **San Stefano,** Al Geish Avenue (from US$22 double).

Luxor, 316 miles by air south of Cairo, has a history dating back to the 27th century BC and rose to importance under the deity "Amun Ra." It is part of the ancient city of Thebes, capital of the mightiest empire of ancient times. The heart of the city, with the beautiful columned halls and galleries of the **Temples of Luxor** and **Karnak,** lies on the east bank of the Nile. A ferry takes you to the **City of the Dead** and the famous **Valley of the Kings,** where in November 1922 the tomb of the boy king Tut Ankh Amun was discovered, the **Valley of the Queens** at the extreme south of the Necropolis, and the **Funerary Temples** of the Kings. Hotels in Luxor: **Luxor,** Maabad El Karnak Street (from US$27 double); **Savoy,** Al Nil Street (from US$27 double); and **Winter Palace,** Al Nil Street (from US$86 double).

Aswân, site of one of the largest and highest dams in the world, lies farther up the Nile. Here you must visit the **Island of Elephantine,** where you will see the **Nilometer** and the **Necropolis of the Sacred Rams;** the **Aswân Museum,** where the mummy of one of the sacred rams is on display; the **Exotic Gardens;** and, just south of Aswân on an island reached either by sailing boat or motor launch, the magnificent **Temples of Philae.** Hotels in Aswân: **Amun,** Amun Island (from US$33 double); **Aswan Oberoi,** on Elephantine Island (from US$21 double); **Cataract,** Abtal Al Tahrir (from US$19 double); **Kalabsha,** Abtal Al Tahrir (from US$14 double); and **Cataract,** Abtal Al Tahrir (from US$40 double).

Once threatened by the waters of the Aswân High Dam and now superbly reassembled over the new **Lake Nasser,** the four colossal figures of **Ramses II,** the greatest Pharaoh of ancient Egypt, stand guard at the entrance to the **Great Temple of Abu Simbel,** 166 miles south of Aswân. Just north of the Great Temple lies the smaller temple carved out of the cliffs in honor of the Goddess of Love and Beauty and of Nefertiti, wife of Ramses II. Twice a week, hydrofoils skim visitors over the waters of the Nile to these unforgettable sights. Departure at 5am from El Sad Ali quay in Aswân—you'll be back by 5:30pm. Round-trip ticket, including breakfast, lunch, tea and entrance fee is £E26.50.

SOURCES OF FURTHER INFORMATION

Pan Am agent, Emeco Travel, 2 Talaat Harb Street, Cairo, and any Pan Am office around the world; **Egyptian Ministry of Tourism,** 5 Adly Street, Cairo; **Egyptian Government Tourist Office,** 630 Fifth Avenue, New York, NY 10020; 62a Piccadilly, London W1.

Ethiopia

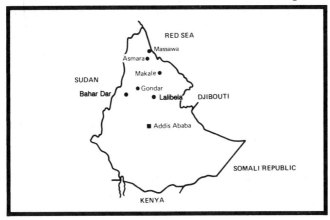

WHAT'S SPECIAL

Ethiopia is still a country for travelers rather than tourists, a place where unique scenery and customs compensate for the occasional lack of comfort. The people of this ancient land have long lived an agricultural and, until recently, largely feudal way of life often compared to that of 17th-century Europe. In 1974, the 58-year reign of Emperor Haile Selassie, the "Lion of Judah," came to an end, and Ethiopia now has a provisional military government. The country's physical features—mountains and desert eastern regions—imposed a history of isolation and though occupied by the Italians from 1936-1941, the country has remained proudly independent of outside influences. Its history and relics of early Christianity together with a wealth of craft skills provide the visitor with plenty to see. Note: Tourists are advised that due to the political situation in Ethiopia, not all areas of the country are currently open to visitors, though it is the government's intention to ease restrictions in the future. Before planning a trip, check with an Ethiopian embassy or consulate for the most recent regulations governing travel by foreigners beyond the capital city.

COUNTRY BRIEFING

Size: 471,776 square miles   **Population:** 30,500,000
Capital: Addis Ababa   **Capital Population:** 1,327,200
  Climate: On the high plateau the climate is comfortable year round and cool at night. In the Red Sea area, around Massawa, temperatures can be extremely high. The rainy season is from early June to the middle

or end of September. Best time to visit is from the end of September until June.

Weather in Addis Ababa: Lat N9°20'; Alt 8,038 ft

Temp (°F)	Jan	Feb	Mar	Apr	May	Jun	Jul	Aug	Sep	Oct	Nov	Dec
Av Low	43°	47°	49°	50°	50°	49°	50°	50°	49°	45°	43°	41°
Av High	75°	76°	77°	77°	77°	74°	69°	69°	72°	75°	73°	73°
Days no rain	29	23	23	20	21	10	3	3	9	28	28	29

Government: A provisional military government.

Language: Amharic; English is the second language.

Religion: About 40% Christian (Ethiopian Coptic); about 40% Muslim; the remainder animist.

Currency: Birr. 100 cents = birr 1.

	Birr 5¢	Birr 50¢	Birr 1	Birr 5	Birr 10	Birr 50	Birr 100	Birr 125
US (dollars, cents)	.02	.24	.48	2.42	4.83	24.15	48.31	60.39
UK (pounds, pence)	.01	.11	.23	1.15	2.30	11.52	23.04	28.81

Public Holidays:

Christmas, 7 Jan
Epiphany, 19 Jan
Adwa Day, 2 Mar
Good Friday

Labor Day, 1 May
New Year's Day, 12 Sept
Revolution Day, 13 Sept
Feast of the True Cross, 28 Sept

Christmas, Good Friday, and Easter are observed in accordance with a program issued by the Ethiopian Orthodox Church. Maloud, Id ul Fitr, and Id ul Adha are Muslim holidays celebrated according to the lunar calendar.

HOW TO GET THERE

Flying time to Addis Ababa International Airport from New York is 16 hours; from Rome, 5½ hours; from Nairobi, 1¾ hours. Time in Ethiopia: GMT+3.

REQUIREMENTS FOR ENTRY AND CUSTOMS REGULATIONS

Passport, round-trip ticket, and visa are necessary. Tourist visas must be obtained in advance from Ethiopian embassies or consulates; transit visas, valid up to 72 hours, are obtainable on arrival. Health certificates covering yellow fever and cholera are required. There are no restrictions on the amount of foreign currency brought into or taken out of the country provided it is declared on entry and the receipt presented at departure. No more than ETB 100 can be exported. Exporting of animal skins and some historic antiques is restricted without special licenses. Guns and ammunition require permits for import. Duty-free allowance: 100 cigarettes or ½ pound tobacco; 1 bottle liquor, reasonable amount of perfume; gifts to the value of US$3.

AIRPORT INFORMATION

Addis Ababa International Airport is at Bole, 4 miles from the city center. There is public bus (ETB5) service from 6am to 8pm from the center of Addis to the airport, and airline buses connect with flights, ETB2 (no charge for luggage). Taxis are available and cost ETB10-12 per person between the airport and hotels. There is an airport departure tax of ETB8. The airport has a hotel reservation desk, a duty-free shop, and the **ETTE Warehouse,** a vast supermarket of duty-free goods of all kinds. Visit this a few days before leaving, and goods bought can be delivered to your departure flight.

ACCOMMODATIONS
Addis has a small but good selection of first-class hotels and one deluxe hotel, the Hilton. Accommodations outside the cities are extremely limited, and reservations should be made well in advance through local travel agents. Less expensive but very simple accommodations are available. There are no off-season reduced rates. Hotels in Addis Ababa:
Rates are in US$ for a double/twin room with bath or shower
   Addis Ababa Hilton, PO Box 1164 (from $44)
   D'Afrique, PO Box 1120 (from $25)
   Ethiopia, PO Box 1131 (from $25)
   Ghion, PO Box 1643 (from $30)
   Harambee, PO Box 3340 (from $20)
   Ras, PO Box 1632 (from $20)
   Wabi Shebelle, PO Box 3154 (from $25)
   The above hotels are all centrally located.

USEFUL INFORMATION
   Banks: Open 9-12 Mon-Fri. Hotels will cash travelers' checks.
   Mail: Stamps only at post offices and hotels.
   Telephone Tips: Phones in cafés and stores. Useful numbers:

Pan Am (Addis) 445776	International Calls 98
Airport Information (Addis) 182222	Intercity 99
	Telegrams 94
Tourist Office (Addis) 447470	Time 902
Directories 97	Police 91

   Tipping: Customary. A service charge is usually added to bills in hotels and restaurants; for good service add a further 5%. Porters, ETB.50 per piece of luggage; no need to tip taxi drivers; hairdressers, ETB2; hall porter, ETB1 or more depending on size of hotel; chambermaid, ETB1. No need to tip museum guides. Village people photographed will expect ETB2.
   Electricity: 220 volts 60 cycles AC.
   Laundry: Hotels provide laundry services; in addition Addis has laundries and can provide 24-hour service (dry-cleaning a suit, ETB6 in town, ETB15 at hotel; laundering a shirt, from ETB1).
   Hairdressing: Major hotels have salons; Addis has other salons too (shampoo and set, ETB15-25; man's haircut, ETB10).
   Photography: Film available in Addis Ababa, but it is advisable

to take plenty with you, particularly up country. In the cities it takes 3-5 days to have film processed.

Clubs: Rotary, Lions, Skal.

Babysitting: Available only at major hotels.

Rest Rooms: In hotels, shops, and restaurants. Few public ones. English signs.

Health: Doctors and dentists speak English. Imported pharmaceuticals are available in cities. Toiletries are expensive. Anti-malarial pills should be taken if visiting lake or Blue Nile areas or the Rift Valley. Drink bottled water.

TRANSPORTATION

There are bus and taxi services within the big cities. In the small country towns, rough horse-drawn carts are the local taxi transport. Taxis are blue-and-white with "taxi" on the license plate. There are no fixed rates; bargain before you start. Luggage does not cost extra, but an extra charge is added per passenger. Rental cars are available, though there are few paved roads beyond the larger cities. Traffic away from city centers is light, but flocks of sheep, goats, cattle, children, carts, etc. are all hazards to watch for, particularly at night. Major tourist spots (when travel is not restricted) are linked with Addis by Ethiopian Airlines flights, mostly by DC3 planes.

FOOD AND RESTAURANTS

Ethiopian cuisine is virtually a one-dish food. *Injera* is a bread made from fermented grain and looks like thin foam rubber; it is made in large circles and served with *wat*, highly spiced curry-like lamb, goat, or perhaps cottage cheese. The food is usually served on trays on a round woven basket, around which diners sit on small stools. *Tej* is a fermented honey drink that goes with it. This type of food can be sampled very inexpensively by tourists in the little restaurants run by the **Ethiopian Women's Association** in most tourist cities. International menus are available at all hotels for visitors, and Italian dishes predominate, particularly in the north. Tea is weak, and coffee—the country's main export—is good. In Addis there are international restaurants, including French and Chinese. For Ethiopian food in Addis, try the **Addis Ababa Restaurant** (Weatherall Street); **Harrar Messaub** (Abebe Damtew Avenue); **Mintamir Yifat** (Asfa Wossen Avenue); **Maru Dembya National Restaurant** (Ras Desta Damtew Avenue). An inexpensive but delicious Chinese meal can be had at **China Restaurant** (Ras Desta Damtew Avenue) or the **Hong Kong** (off Churchill Road). Other good restaurants include **Kara Mara, Kokeb, Castelli,** and **Cottage.**

DRINKING TIPS

Ethiopian wines, beers, and brandy are excellent and not expensive. Imported drinks are available; most people drink Scotch in bars and nightclubs. *Talla* is a fermented barley and oats drink made by the local people. A Scotch and soda is ETB3-6; a bottle of local wine costs ETB10-

25, imported wine, ETB40-100. Unaccompanied women are welcome in bars in major cities and sightseeing areas; otherwise, it is best not to go alone.

ENTERTAINMENT
The National Theater has presentations in Addis; movie houses show American, English, Russian, and Chinese movies with original soundtrack and/or English subtitles. Nightlife in Addis centers in the Ghion, Hilton, Ras, and Wabi Shebele hotels, and in clubs like the Venus Night Club and Night Fever. Other small spots should be visited at the visitor's discretion.

SHOPPING
Stores are generally open 9-1 and 3-8 Mon-Sat. The massive market in Addis has a crafts section, and near the market, the small crafts shops and the Ethiopian Handicraft School are worth a visit. *Falasha* pottery is much less expensive in the village where it is made. Typical buys are silver crosses from Lalibela, fly whisks, woven baskets, small primitive paintings, amber, carved chairs and stools, woven items, pottery, necklaces, and clothes from Makale. You should bargain hard everywhere except in stores and you'll find it easier to do if you have a guide who speaks the language and has some idea of the value of the item you want.

SPORTS
Spectator sports are soccer, basketball, and gymnastics. There is tennis, horseback riding, swimming, fishing, and hunting. Sports clubs welcoming visitors are Guido Farm Makanissa for horseback riding and the Ethiopian Golf Club.

WHAT TO SEE
In Addis the National Palace can be visited on tours run by the Ethiopian Tourist Organization or by local operators. The Ethiopian Museum gives a good background to the arts and crafts of the country. Visit also Africa Hall, the Menelik II Mausoleum, Trinity Church, Parliament, the National Archaeological Museum, St George's Cathedral, the Handicraft School, and the Mercato market area. Day trips can be taken south to the lakes and to the Koka Dam, where there is the pleasant Koka Hotel (from US$30 double), formerly the Emperor's summer palace; or west of Addis to the scenic Blue Nile Gorge, about a 2½ hour drive away. Principal festivals to see are Epiphany and Maskal. The latter commemorates the finding of the True Cross and involves, in Addis, the lighting of a huge bonfire in a special square, with processions of soldiers carrying lighted brands.

From Addis, the main scenic itinerary is along the Historic Route to Bahar Dar to see island monasteries and the Tississat Blue Nile Falls; to Gondar to see the ancient castles of King Fasilidas and the Black Falasha or Jewish tribe living there; Lalibela for the wonderful red rock churches dating from the 12th century; **Axum** for the ancient ruins of the kings, the palace of the Queen of Sheba, and the crowns of the emperors.

SOURCES OF FURTHER INFORMATION

Pan Am agent, Admas Air, National Theater Building, Churchill Rd., PO Box 3331, Addis Ababa, and any Pan Am Office round the world; **Ethiopian Tourism and Hotels Commission,** PO Box 3183, Addis Ababa; **Wonderland Tourist,** PO Box 2895, Addis Ababa, Ethiopia; **Ethiopian Mission to the UN,** 866 UN Plaza, New York, NY 10017; **Embassy of the Provisional Military Government of Socialist Ethiopia,** 17 Princes Gate, London SW 7.

Ghana

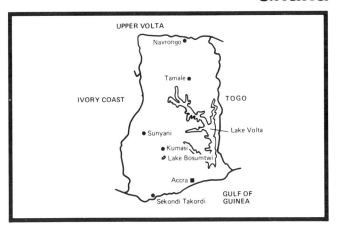

WHAT'S SPECIAL

Symbols and dancing are two distinctive features of the life of the Ghanaian. At state functions chiefs and their elders sit in a semicircle symbolizing the crescent moon; at *durbars* the royal umbrellas rising high in the air indicate the various shades of power of the chiefs in the royal procession. The most important events in the community are accompanied by special dances to show their meaning and significance. But side by side with all this tradition and symbolism there are modern hotels, delicious dishes and drinks, beautiful beaches, color scenery, and a warm welcome for the vacationer in what was formerly known as the Gold Coast.

COUNTRY BRIEFING

Size: 92,100 square miles   **Population:** 11,742,000
Capital: Accra   **Capital Population:** 564,000
   Climate: Seasons are marked by changes in rainfall rather than temperature. Best time to visit is from mid-June to mid-December and February.

Weather in Accra: Lat N5°33′; Alt 88 ft

Temp (°F)	Jan	Feb	Mar	Apr	May	Jun	Jul	Aug	Sep	Oct	Nov	Dec
Av Low	73°	75°	76°	76°	75°	74°	73°	71°	73°	74°	75°	75°
Av high	87°	88°	88°	88°	87°	84°	81°	80°	81°	85°	87°	88°
Days no rain	30	26	27	24	22	20	27	28	26	25	27	29

Government: A republic within the British Commonwealth.
Language: English. Many local dialects.
Religion: Christians, Muslims, and animists.
Currency: The Cedi. 100 pesewas = ₵

	10p	50p	₵1	₵5	₵10	₵25	₵50	₵100
US (dollars, cents)	.04	.18	.36	1.82	3.64	9.09	18.18	36.36
UK (pounds, pence)	.02	.09	.18	.87	1.74	4.34	8.67	17.34

Public Holidays:

New Year's Day
Independence Day, 6 Mar
Good Friday
Holy Saturday

Easter Monday
Republic Day, 1 July
Christmas, 25-26 Dec

HOW TO GET THERE

Flying time to Accra's Kotoka Airport from New York is 10½ hours; from London, 7½ hours; from Dakar, 3½ hours; from Monrovia, 1¾ hours. Time in Ghana: GMT.

REQUIREMENTS FOR ENTRY AND CUSTOMS REGULATIONS

Passport, visa, and onward ticket, plus cedi vouchers purchased from Ghana's embassies abroad before being granted a visa. These can be exchanged for cedis at banks in Ghana. Hotel bills are expected to be paid in cedi vouchers, travelers' checks, or foreign currency. Yellow-fever and cholera vaccination are required. Take antimalarial precautions. There are no restrictions on duty-free importation of liquor and tobacco for personal consumption. No limit on the amount of foreign currency brought in, but it must be declared. No more than ₵20 can be taken out.

AIRPORT INFORMATION

Kotoka International Airport is 7 miles from Accra; airport bus fare is ₵2, taxi fare ₵11. Tip porters ₵2 per bag. Departure tax is ₵5. The airport has a duty-free shop.

ACCOMMODATIONS

Hotel reservations can be made either directly or through an airline or travel agent. Assistance with inexpensive hostel or guest house accommodations is available through **Ghana Tourist Board,** PO Box 3106 (tel: 27114 or 28933). Hotels in Accra are:

Rates are in US$ for a double/twin room with bath or shower

Ambassador, Independence Avenue (from $40)
Avenida, Kojo Thompson Road (from $37)
Continental, Liberation Road, near airport (from $40)
Granada, airport residential area (from $68)
Penta, Osu residential area, near downtown (from $65)
President, Sobukwe Avenue (from $61)
Star, Switchback Road, near airport (from $40)

Unless otherwise indicated, the above hotels are all centrally located. Prices do not include 10% government tax and other charges.

USEFUL INFORMATION

Banks: Open 9-2 Mon-Thurs, 9-3 Fri. Major hotels also change money.

Telephone Tips: There are no coin-operated booth phones. Calls may be made from restaurants, cafés, and post offices. Useful numbers in Accra:

Pan Am 21151	Tourist Information 27114 or 28933
Airport Information 76111	Tourist Office 65461

Tipping: Although service charge is generally included in hotel and restaurant checks, modest tipping is expected for good service. A "dash," or tip in advance, is often expected for special services.

Electricity: 240 volts 50 cycles AC.

Photography: Film available in major towns, but very expensive.

TRANSPORTATION

Local airlines serve main centers and railways serve the three regional capitals of Accra, Kumasi, and Takoradi, but most traveling is done by road. Buses are operated by the Akuaba Tourist Travel Agency (PO Box 2059, Accra—tel: 28020) and the State Transport Corporation (PO Box 7384, Accra—tel: 21918). Mini "tro-tro" buses operate around the towns and between centers. Taxis have no meters; bargain over the price beforehand. To rent a car costs about anywhere from about US$18 an hour for a limousine to US$289 a day for a group tour bus.

FOOD AND RESTAURANTS

The local seafoods and tropical fruit are fresh and mouth-watering. Local dishes to try are palm nut soup, *banku* (made from corn meal), and *fufu* (pounded yam, cocoyam, and cassava in the form of a dough). Good liquor and beer are produced locally, and better establishments offer imported brands as well. Whisky in Ghana means Scotch. In Accra you can dine at the **Palm Court, Jade Gardens,** and **Mandarin** (Chinese); the **Tropicana, Commodore,** and **Club 400** (Middle Eastern); the **Terra Nova** (Spanish); and the **Moustache** and **Edwards** (continental). Almost all major hotels have restaurant facilities. For dinner and dancing try the Continental, Ambassador, and Star hotels, and for nightclubbing **Tip Toe, Club Papito, Pussycat, Black Caesar's, Stereo Spot, High Society Disco,** and **Keteke.**

SHOPPING

Among the best buys are traditional African wood and ivory carvings, African jewelry, native sandals, basketry, shirts, and colorful cloth. Department stores include the **Glamour, Rose Pillars, Farisco, Kingsway, GNTC,** and **UTC.** Souvenir buying can be done on High Street. Good small shops are available in the Ambassador and Continental hotels. The **Ghana Tourist Development Company** has a duty-free shop.

SPORTS

There are excellent opportunities for swimming and water sports along the coast, fishing in the rivers, and deep-sea fishing off the coast. Hunting is restricted, and you must have a permit. Information can be obtained from the Chief Game and Wildlife Officer (Department of Game and Wildlife, Box M239, Accra—tel: 63793). There are public tennis courts at the **Accra Sports Stadium** and the **Kaneshi Sports Complex,** and polo grounds adjacent to the Granada Hotel near the airport. Horse races are held Saturday afternoons, and soccer is played on Sunday afternoons.

WHAT TO SEE

In **Accra** see the **Arts Center, Glo Art Gallery, National Museum,** and the **University. The Castle** is the present seat of government. The tropical gardens in African Liberation Square and the **Botanical Garden** at Aburi are worth seeing. Beautiful beaches close by are **Labadi Pleasure Beach, Busua Pleasure Beach,** and **Paradise Beach,** Tema.

Kumasi, "the garden city of West Africa," dates from the 17th century and reminders of this time are the **Manhyia Palace** and the legendary sword of **Okomfo Anokye.** Visit the **Kumasi Fort** (the military museum). Stay at the **City Hotel** (from US$40 double). Kumasi is close to the great lake **Bosumtwi** and to the villages of **Bonwire,** noted for *kente* weaving, **Ntonso** for Adinkra cloth printing, and **Ehwia** for stool carving.

Ghana has 350 miles of tropical coastline, beautiful beaches, palm trees, and good fishing. The coast is dotted with fortresses. **Elmina Castle,** built in 1482 by the Portuguese, is the most famous. **The Mole Game Reserve** in northwest Ghana is an area of 1,800 square miles where you can go on safari to see wildlife in a natural environment. There is an excellent motel here, the **Mole Game Reserve Motel** (from US$20 double), with swimming pool. The great, man-made **Volta Lake** has a variety of tropical aquatic life. You can stay in Akosombo at the **Volta Hotel** (from US$17 double).

SOURCES OF FURTHER INFORMATION

Pan Am, Cocoa House, Liberty Avenue, PO Box 1119, Accra, and any Pan Am office around the world; **Ghana Tourist Board,** PO Box 3106, State House, Accra; **Ghana Tourist Office,** 19 East 47 Street, New York, NY 10017; **High Commission for Ghana,** 13 Belgrave Square, London SW1.

Guinea

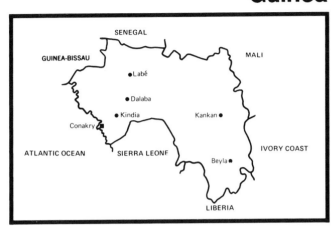

WHAT'S SPECIAL

Once administered by France, Guinea became Africa's second independent republic in 1958. The country offers hunting, fishing, and sea bathing, but tourism is not encouraged. Its mineral wealth (including about one-third of the world's reserves of high-grade bauxite, over two billion tons of high-grade iron ore, and significant diamond deposits), hydroelectric power potential, agriculture, and fishing make its economy potentially one of the strongest in Africa.

COUNTRY BRIEFING

Area, 94,925 square miles; **population** 5,665,000, of whom 575,000 live in Conakry, the **capital. Climate** is tropical; dry season (Nov-Mar) is sunny, warm, and humid; rainy season (May-Oct) is cooler and often very wet. Lightweight clothing is advised. The official **language** is French and the **religion** Muslim (animist, Roman Catholic, and other denominations also represented). The **currency** is the syli (100 corilles = 1 syli); 100 Guinean sylis = US$5.54.

HOW TO GET THERE

Flying time to G'Bessia Airport from New York is 8¾ hours; from London, 6½ hours; from Dakar, 1¼ hours. Time in Guinea: GMT.

REQUIREMENTS FOR ENTRY AND CUSTOMS REGULATIONS

You will need a passport, visa, and round-trip ticket. Smallpox, yellow-fever, and cholera vaccination certificates are required, and malaria precautions must be taken. Tetanus, typhoid, and typhus shots are recommended. All currency must be declared, and Guinean currency may not be taken in or out. Personal effects may be brought in duty-free but must be declared; guns and ammunition are forbidden. Duty-free allowance: travelers may bring into the country up to 1,000 cigarettes and 1 bottle whisky. Entry is impossible without a visa, and departure requires an exit visa.

AIRPORT INFORMATION

G'Bessia Airport is 9 miles from Conakry; taxis are the only means of transport, and the fare is about US$8. Departure tax is 100 sylis for points within Guinea, 150 sylis for other destinations. The duty-free shop in the airport accepts only foreign currency.

ACCOMMODATIONS

There is one good, brand new, and fully air-conditioned hotel—**Hotel de l'Unité** (tel: 43286 or 43921, telex: Hotelpi 31 39). Price of a single room is US$75 CP, or a double room US$80 CP. Other hotels are the **Hotel de l'Independence** (tel: 4349/92), **Caymayenne** (tel: 61139), and the **G'Bessia** (tel: 61145).

USEFUL INFORMATION

Banks are open 8am-1pm. **Mail** service is poor (mail is sometimes censored and can get "lost"); **phone service** is unreliable (sometimes unavailable), though long-distance calls can be made. English-language **newspapers** prohibited. **Tipping** is optional; **hairdressing** salons are limited and expensive. A government permit is needed to take **photographs.** Always boil or filter water; wash fruit and vegetables. Pharmaceuticals and toiletries scarce, so bring them with you. **Electricity** is European style: 220 volts, 50 cycles.

TRANSPORTATION

Buses and taxis are available but rather unreliable. There is irregular train service between Conakry and Kankan, 412 miles away. Most roads can be managed throughout the year, though some tend to be muddy during the rainy season. National airline is Air Guinée.

FOOD AND ENTERTAINMENT

Dining in Guinea is limited. Restaurants are not considered up to international standards, but a few of those in Conakry are **Le Petit Bateau** (for chicken and a nice view of sea and sky), **L'Aiglon, Rat Palmist, Paradis, Grillon, Oasis, Avenue Bar, L'Escale de Guinée,** and **Syli Bar** for local dishes. The average price of a meal in these restaurants is US$20 per person. Facilities for entertainment are limited; nightclubs include the **Jardin de Guinée, La Paillotte, La Minière, La Kaloum, Joliba, Palace Night Club, Tam-Tam,** and **Neuf Février,** most of which have dancing, and there is cabaret at the **Hotel G'Bessia** and **L'Osise.** Conakry also has several movie theaters, including the air-conditioned **Syli Cinema.**

The **National Orchestra of Guinea** is equipped with purely African instruments, and ballet galas at the **People's Palace** are exciting.

SHOPPING

There are shops and two big markets. Shops owned by the government are open from 7:30-3 Mondays, Thursdays, and Saturdays; Fridays from 7:30-1. Private shops are open from 8-6 and some are open at night. The locally dyed materials are very pretty; handicrafts tend to be expensive.

WHAT TO SEE

Conakry is laid out in a series of rectangular blocks. Visit the market square on the Route de Niger, the fish market, and the **Place de la République.** Also, if possible, try to see the Guinean sculptures and ethnographic displays in the **Musée National.** The islands of **Soro, Tamara,** and **Kassa** are beautiful. Boats leave from Port Conakry every Sunday during the dry season from November to March and cost 100 sylis. Travel in the interior is possible only with government authorization, which may be withheld in the event of political unrest. The most beautiful scenery is to be found in the mountains of the **Fouta Djallon,** with its stunning **Kinkon Falls.**

SOURCES OF FURTHER INFORMATION

Ministry of Information, Conakry, Guinea; **Embassy of Guinea,** 2112 Le Roy Place, Washington, DC 20008.

Ivory Coast

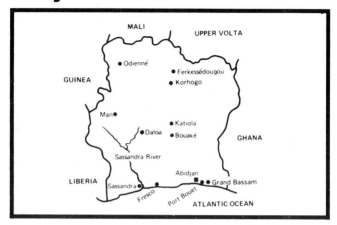

WHAT'S SPECIAL

With its comparatively stable political background, an expanding economy, and the natural advantage of a coastline possessing wide beaches and beautiful lagoons, the Ivory Coast has become a popular West African vacation spot. Visitors will find special tourist villages built for them inland. Ebrie lagoon close to Abidjan is a beautiful resort.

COUNTRY BRIEFING

The **area** is 129,687 square miles and the **population** 7,500,000, of whom 900,000 live in the **capital,** Abidjan. **Climate** ranges from the humid equatorial region of the south through a central tropical area to the cooler savannah of the north; best time to visit is November through April. The Ivory Coast is a **republic,** the **language** is French, the **religion** mainly animist, and the **currency** the CFA franc (CFA 250 = US$1).

Public Holidays:

New Year's Day, 1 Jan	National Day, 7 Aug
Easter Monday	Assumption Day, 15 Aug
Labor Day, 1 May	Tabaski, 28 Sept
Ascension Day	Independence Day, 7 Dec
Whit Monday	Christmas Day, 25 Dec

In addition, Islamic holy days are observed. Dates vary, since they are based on the lunar calendar.

HOW TO GET THERE

Flying time to Abidjan, Port Bouet Airport from New York is 10¾ hours; from Dakar, 3¼ hours; from Monrovia, 1¼ hours. Time in Ivory Coast: GMT.

REQUIREMENTS FOR ENTRY AND CUSTOMS REGULATIONS

Passport, visa, valid health certificate for smallpox and yellow fever, and round-trip or onward ticket plus a letter of financial responsibility are required. Visitors from some European and African countries can stay for up to 3 months without a visa. Certain works of art require an export permit from the National Museum, PO Box 1600, Abidjan. Duty-free allowance: 50 cigarettes or 25 cigars or ¼ pound tobacco; 1 bottle liquor.

AIRPORT INFORMATION

Port Bouet Airport is 10 miles from Abidjan. Taxi fare to Cocody, the residential area of Abidjan, is about CFA3,000; to the Plateau district, the city center, about CFA1,800. Tip taxi drivers 10%, luggage porters CFA100 per bag. No departure tax. There is a duty-free shop and a hotel reservations counter.

ACCOMMODATIONS

The Ivoire Inter·Continental Hotel, in the Cocody district of Abidjan, is almost a town in itself. In its two skyscrapers are contained three restaurants, a cinema, a nightclub, shops and a supermarket, a bowling alley, a swimming pool, and a congress hall seating 2,000. There is a separate casino, built in African straw-hut style, a heliport, a marina, and extensive gardens. Abidjan has several other good hotels, all with air-conditioning, and tourist centers such as Man and Daloa also have modern hotels, many of them government-sponsored. There are tourist villages along the coast at Assinie and Assouinde, 50 miles east of Abidjan, and camping facilities at Man and at Gouessesso, where you can sleep in the straw huts of a native village specially constructed for tourists with all the modern conveniences. Hotels in Abidjan:

Rates are in US$ for a double/twin room with bath or shower

   Akwaba, PO Box 7058, along the coast, 4 miles from Abidjan (from $67)

   Le Parc, Avenue Chardy, Plateau (from $70)

   FORUM GOLF, Boulevard Lagunaire, Riviera (from $56)

   IVOIRE INTER·CONTINENTAL, Boulevard de la Corniche, Cocody (from $93)

   Novotel, 10 Avenue de General De Gaulle, Plateau (rates on request)

   Relais de Cocody, PO Box 767, Cocody (from $26)

   Sebroko Abidjan, PO Box 8239, Baie du Banco (from $63)

   Tima, Boulevard de la Republique, Plateau (from $64)

The Plateau district is Abidjan's business center, about 10 minutes by taxi from the Cocody residential district and about 5 minutes from the native quarter of Treichville. The Riviera district, beyond Cocody, is 15 minutes from the city center. The Sebroko Abidjan is about 5 minutes' drive from the Plateau district.

USEFUL INFORMATION

Banks usually open 8am, but this varies. **Postage stamps** available at post offices and hotels; **phone booths** in post offices, hotels, cafés, restaurants. Useful numbers in Abidjan: **Pan Am,** 44-21-32; **Tourist Board,** 32-51-97. **Tip** waiters 5-10% above service charge. **Electricity** is 220 volts 50 cycles AC. **Laundry** prices high but service good. **Hairdressing** salons in first-class hotels. **Photographic** equipment available but because film is expensive, bring your own supply. **Health:** doctors and dentists speak English. Tap water safe in first class hotels in Abidjan; bottled water is recommended elsewhere; wash fruit and vegetables; take antimalarial drugs. It is advisable to carry antitetanus and snakebite serum on hunting expeditions.

TRANSPORTATION

Abidjan has a bus service, but taxis are fast, numerous, and inexpensive. Hail one or phone a stand. Abidjan is linked to other major cities by Air Ivoire, which runs daily services. There is also a train service running from Abidjan to the north, with sleeping and restaurant facilities. Boats can be rented to sail the lagoons round Abidjan. Car rentals start at about US$20 per day, plus mileage, gas, and 17.6% tax. (If you rent a car, hire a driver also. In many West African countries, the driver is responsible for any accident and can be held responsible for the future support of any injured party and his or her family.) Main roads are paved; beware of dirt roads where there has been heavy rain, as they often become impassable.

FOOD AND RESTAURANTS

The Ivory Coast national dish is *foutou*—yams or bananas with groundnut or palm-seed sauce. *Atiéké* is the Ivory Coast version of couscous. Try these and other African dishes at **Attoungban** or **Nanau Yamousso,** both in Abidjan's African quarter of Treichville, or at the **"421"** in Cocody. Hotels such as Ivoire Inter·Continental, Relais de Cocody, and Hotel le Parc have excellent international menus. Other cuisine includes Vietnamese at **Au Petit Lac** (tel: 22-65-76), **Baie d'Along** (tel: 35-77-79), **La Pagode** (tel: 35-62-71), **Mekong** (tel: 22-22-66), and **Chez Jacky** (tel: 32-11-86); Lebanese at **Horizon** (tel: 32-27-99); Moroccan at **Le Marrakech** (tel: 32-51-64) and **La Maison du Maroc** (tel: 22-69-60). There are many restaurants, among them **Chez Valentin** (tel: 32-47-16), **Le Coq d'Alsace** (tel: 22-26-17), **Au Vieux Strasbourg** (tel: 32-30-46), and **Acapulco** (tel: 32-10-88), with international menus—usually with the emphasis on French cooking. Two other popular restaurants are **Le Seu de Bois** and the **Santa Maria.**

DRINKING TIPS

There are two locally brewed beers, but typical Ivory Coast drinks are *bandji,* made from palm extract; *tchapalo,* a distilled millet wine; and *lemouroudji,* lemon juice with ginger. Imported wines, liquors, and beers are available, but expensive. A whisky and soda will cost from US$4.50-6.75. There are no restrictions on drinking hours and bars are open all day and until late at night. Women are welcome. Popular bars are the **Rendez-Vous** at Hotel Ivoire, the terrace of the Hotel le Parc, and **Pam-Pam.**

ENTERTAINMENT

Abidjan has many nightclubs offering both "Western" and African entertainment. The discothèque at the new **Novotel** is rapidly becoming the "in" spot, or try the **Ascot,** the **Pussy Cat,** and **Inn Club,** or any of the hotel nightclubs. For jazz go to the **Blue Note,** and for real African atmosphere visit **Le Sous-Marin,** anchored in the lagoon, or the **Boule Noire** in Treichville. Gamblers can try their luck at the Hotel Ivoire's **Elephant d'Or Casino.** There are a dozen movie houses to choose from, showing French movies or American and English ones with French soundtracks. Traditional African dances are most exciting. In Abidjan these are performed quite frequently, especially on national holidays and fête days, but it is even better to see them in their native settings at places such as Man, Gouessesso, and Korhogo.

SHOPPING

Stores open 8-12 and 3-7 Mon-Sat. Abidjan has several picturesque markets, where bargaining is necessary (but fun). The best are in the native quarters of **Treichville** and **Adjamé,** but there is also a curio market opposite the Hotel le Parc. Ivory objects are reasonably priced in the shop at the Ivoire Inter·Continental. Look also for silver, gold, or bronze jewelry, loincloths, wood carvings, chiefs' emblems and breastplates, pottery from Katiola, Korhogo tapestries, Ashanti dolls, and the picturesque African masks.

SPORTS

Abidjan's lagoon is a perfect spot for water sports like sailing and waterskiing, and it is also excellent for line-fishing. Beautiful beaches extend along the coast from Abidjan to Fresco, Sassandra, and beyond, but swimmers should beware of strong currents. Many hotels have swimming pools, some private, some public. Many species of fish are found off Abidjan, including tuna, sharks, barracuda, sailfish, scad, and bluefish. Deep-sea fishing can be arranged through hotels or at the **Yacht Club.** The hunting season (elephant, buffalo, hippopotamus, panther, and some game birds) is from December to June, notably in the Korhogo area in the north of the country. A license is necessary. Fees begin at CFA2,000 and vary with the species hunted. A "kill" tax is levied and also varies with the species. Visitors can play tennis at the **Abidjan Sports Club** or at the Ivoire Inter·Continental hotel (the latter also has ice skating). There is horse racing at **Club de l'Etrie** and **Club de l'Epron.**

WHAT TO SEE

Known as "the pearl of the lagoons," **Abidjan** is a mainly modern city with many skyscrapers, especially in the central plateau area. The **Museum** on Avenue Chardy has a large collection of African art. Beyond Adjamé on the northern outskirts is a **Zoo,** and further on is the **Banco National Park,** a vast tropical rain forest area with some rare and valuable trees. At **Bingerville,** 10 miles east of Abidjan, there is an interesting **Botanical Garden** with orchids, and also the **School of African Art,** with a display of masks. At **Grand-Bassam,** the former capital of the Ivory Coast, you can see some fine examples of French colonial architecture.

Along the coast amid the banana and pineapple plantations are picturesque fishing villages like **Port Bouët** and **Fresco,** and there are beautiful beaches at **Sassandra, Assinie,** and **Grand-Lahou.** The latter also has a game reserve noted for its elephants. There is a large wildlife park at **Bouna** in the northeast corner of the country, and photo-safaris can be arranged to these reserves. Four- to five-day tourist trips are also organized to the interior of the country, where you can visit African towns and villages and watch exciting tribal dances. At **Man** there is a liana bridge, its fragile-looking creepers swaying high above a waterfall, and in nearby villages you can see the famous masked stilt dance of the Yacouba and Dan tribes. Stay African-style—but in Western comfort—at the tourist village of **Gouessesso,** which boasts an artificial lake, a swimming pool, and tennis courts. In this area the Africans perform a ritual acrobatic dance. Around **Korhogo,** in the land of the Sénoufou and Malinké tribes, the mysterious panther-man, in animal mask and garb, leaps to the rhythm of age-old chants and drumbeats. Try to see the ironsmith's village of **Koni;** the 17th-century mosque of baked earth at **Kassoumbarga;** the weavers of **Waranie-ne;** the pottery-making village of **Katiola; Bouaké,** the country's second largest town; and **Yamoussoukro,** with its mosque and sacred crocodile lake.

SOURCES OF FURTHER INFORMATION

Pan Am, c/o Air Afrique, Hotel Ivoire Inter·Continental, Abidjan, and any Pan Am office round the world; **Ivory Coast Embassy,** 2424 Massachusetts Avenue NW, Washington, DC 20008; 2 Upper Belgrave Street, London SW1.

Kenya

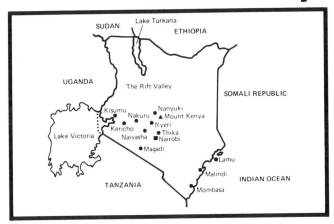

WHAT'S SPECIAL

Kenya is a young country politically, and yet it was here on the shores of Lake Rudolf that a 2-million-year-old skull of early man was found. The equator divides it into almost equal halves, yet due to the effects of altitude in its Highlands, its climate and vegetation vary from lush equatorial rainforests, through temperate zones and grasslands, to desert conditions. Its magnificent scenery and wildlife attract every kind of tourist, and Kenya has something to offer all of them. You can fish in the lakes of the cool inland plains, climb snow-covered mountains, see jungles and waterfalls, and go on safari for a sight of the world's most exotic and beautiful animals: the elephant, lion, leopard, buffalo, antelope, and black rhinoceros and, among birds, the flamingo. As a conservation measure, hunting has been banned by the government, and greater emphasis is now given to photographic safaris, which are superbly organized. Kenya's coastline is a beautiful contrast to the bush country, with white sandy beaches and the blue of the Indian Ocean.

You will meet beautiful people, famous for their crafts and music, living a simple age-old life and rightly proud both of their country's history and of its present stability and racial harmony.

COUNTRY BRIEFING

Size: 225,000 square miles
Capital: Nairobi

Population: 15,300,000
Capital Population: 835,000

Climate: Hot and humid on the coast, cool in the Highlands; it can be cold at night, especially June–August. There are two rainy seasons. December-March is the driest and hottest season.

Weather in Nairobi: Lat S1°16′; Alt 5,971 ft

Temp (°F)	Jan	Feb	Mar	Apr	May	Jun	Jul	Aug	Sep	Oct	Nov	Dec
Av Low	54°	55°	57°	58°	56°	53°	51°	52°	52°	55°	56°	55°
Av High	77°	79°	77°	75°	72°	70°	69°	70°	75°	76°	74°	74°
Days no rain	26	22	20	14	14	21	25	24	24	23	15	20

Government: Independent republic within British Commonwealth.

Language: Swahili is the official language, but English is widely spoken and written in both government and business circles.

Religion: The population is Christian, Hindu, and Muslim; some of the remoter tribes still practice animism.

Currency: Kenya shilling, 100 cents = 1KS.

	10¢	50¢	1 KS	5 KS	10 KS	50 KS	100 KS	500 KS
US (dollars, cents)	.01	.07	.13	.66	1.31	6.57	13.14	65.70
UK (pounds, pence)	—	.03	.06	.31	.62	3.13	6.27	31.34

Public Holidays:
New Year's Day, 1 Jan
Good Friday
Easter Monday
Labor Day, 1 May
Madaraka Day, 1 June

End of Ramadan (Id ul Fitr), variable
Kenyatta Day, 20 Oct
Jamhuri Day (Independence Day), 12 Dec
Christmas Day, 25 Dec
Boxing Day, 26 Dec

HOW TO GET THERE

Flying time to Nairobi, Jomo Kenyatta International Airport from New York is 16½ hours; from Rome, 8½ hours; from Caracas, 16 hours; from Bombay, 7 hours. Time in Kenya: GMT+3.

REQUIREMENTS FOR ENTRY AND CUSTOMS REGULATIONS

Passport. Citizens of the US and most other countries must have a visa obtainable from the Kenya Tourist Office, Kenyan embassies, or consulates for a fee of US$3.05. Citizens of Commonwealth countries (other than British citizens of Asian origin) and citizens of certain other countries do not require visas. A round-trip or onward ticket is also necessary. International certificate of inoculation against yellow fever and cholera required. Smallpox inoculation certificate needed if traveling from an infected area. No restrictions on foreign currency, but you may not import or export Kenyan currency. Nor may you take out more foreign currency than you brought in. Tourists should check current currency regulations upon arrival. There is an illegal market in Kenya, but it can get you into trouble. Cameras, film, and personal effects are admitted duty-free; a police permit is needed for firearms and ammunition. Duty-free allowance: 250 grams of tobacco (200 cigarettes or 50 cigars); 1 liter alcohol; ¼ liter perfume; radios, typewriters, and tape recorders must be declared and a returnable deposit paid. You may also have to pay a deposit on souvenirs brought in from other countries.

AIRPORT INFORMATION

Nairobi's new Jomo Kenyatta International Airport is 15 miles from the city center. Buses run to the Kenya Airways Terminal, Koinange Street, Nairobi; fare on the bus is 20KS, and the driver will drop you at your hotel for a slight tip. The taxi fare is 126KS. Departure tax of 80KS. Duty-free shop and hotel reservation counter.

ACCOMMODATIONS

Reasonably priced accommodations. Coast hotels offer reductions of 10% and more out of season. Inexpensive accommodations are available in guest houses, but are not always to be recommended. The national parks have comfortable game lodges and camping sites, most of which have bathrooms, showers, and good drinking water. The average charge for the latter is US$9.80 per person per night. For advice on accommodations write to the Senior Tourist Officer, **Ministry of Tourism,** P.O. Box 54666, Nairobi, or tel: 331030. Hotels in Nairobi, in the downtown area unless otherwise indicated, include:

Rates are in US$ for a double/twin room with bath or shower

Ambassadeur, Moi Avenue, PO Box 30399 (from $45.50 BB)

Excelsior, Kenyatta Avenue (from $45.50)

Fairview, Bishop's Road, PO Box 40842 (from $28.90), 1½ miles from city center

INTER · CONTINENTAL NAIROBI, City Hall Way, PO Box 30353 (from $80.20)

Mayfair, Waiyaki Way, PO Box 42680 (from $33.10 BB), 1½ miles from city center

Milimani, Milimani Road, PO Box 30715 (from $45 BB)

Nairobi Hilton, Mama Ngina Way and Moi Avenue, PO Box 30624 (from $76.50)

Nairobi Serena, Kenyatta Avenue, PO Box 46302 (from $77.50)

New Stanley, Kenyatta Avenue, PO Box 40075 (from $73.50)

Norfolk, Harry Thuku Road, PO Box 40064 (from $72.80)

Panafric, Kenyatta Avenue, PO Box 30486 (from $56.50), ½ mile from city center

Six Eighty, Kenyatta Avenue, PO Box 43436 (from $57.00)

USEFUL INFORMATION

Be discreet when taking photographs; you should always ask permission and give a tip to tribesmen who pose at tourist centers. Do not take pictures of the Arab women on the coast or in the Arab quarter of Mombasa. *Jambo* (hello) is the general greeting, but business people, accustomed to meeting foreigners, prefer to be addressed in English. Women should not walk alone in the streets at night, nor go into the older parts of town in very short skirts. Remember to pronounce the country's name with a short e—Kĕnya—as in the name Ken.

For clothes, nonsynthetic materials are more comfortable. Elaborate safari outfits are not necessary—cotton slacks or jeans and shirts are quite adequate. Comfortable shoes or lightweight boots are essential, and binoculars and a flashlight will come in handy. A lightweight raincoat is a wise precaution if you are going in the rainy season, and you will need a wrap or sweater for evenings in the Highlands. Dress is fairly informal in the evening, but a jacket and tie are *de rigueur* in some smart Nairobi bars and restaurants. An open-necked shirt and slacks are fine in others.

Banks: Open 9-1 Mon-Fri, 9-11 Sat. Some open 8:30-2:30 Mon-Fri and remain closed on Saturdays. Travelers' checks can be changed in hotels as well as banks.

Mail: Postage stamps can be bought in hotels and in post offices. Postal addresses are box numbers, as mail is collected from private mailboxes.

Telephone Tips: Phones in booths, and in cafés. International services good, but there may be some delays on trunk calls outside Nairobi. Useful numbers in Nairobi:

Pan Am 28379 and 822206
  or 822313 (airport)
Information 991
Nairobi City Council
  Telegrams 990

Operator 900
International Calls 0196
Emergencies 999

Newspapers: English-language as well as German, French, and other foreign newspapers and magazines obtainable at newsstands in Nairobi. Many local publications in English, including *The Daily Nation*, the *Standard, Weekly Review, Viva, Sunday Nation,* and *Nairobi Times,* and *The Sunday Standard*.

Tipping: In restaurants a service charge of 10% is often included in the check, in which case you are not expected to tip but may leave a little extra if you wish; if not included, tip 10-15%. Taxi drivers also expect about 10%, minimum 1KS; same for hairdressers. Porters receive 1KS per piece of luggage; give hotel porters 5KS for showing you to your room and give the chambermaid 20KS at the end of your stay. Tribesmen dressed up for photos naturally want a tip. Bargain; as a general rule pay about half what they ask.

Electricity: 220 volts 50 cycles AC.

Laundry: Fast laundry and dry-cleaning services through hotels (dry-cleaning a suit, from 20KS; laundering a shirt, from 18KS).

Hairdressing: First-class hotels have salons (shampoo and set from 120KS; a man's haircut from 80KS).

Photography: Film available in all major towns. Black and white 30KS (developing takes 24 hours); color 116KS (Kodachrome 11 cannot be processed locally). It is forbidden to photograph the President unless permission has been granted.

Clubs: Kiwanis, Lions, Rotary, and Round Table.

Babysitting: Hotels will arrange services.

Rest Rooms: Rely on hotels. Outside English-speaking areas, ask for *Choo ya wanawake* (women) or *Choo ya wanaume* (men).

Health: Doctors and dentists speak English and are very well qualified. Imported pharmaceuticals and toiletries expensive. Water safe to drink in Nairobi and in tourist hotels everywhere. Take antimalarial precautions (some programs entail taking pills for a week before arrival and for a week after departure, some require that pills be taken for several weeks after return). As Nairobi is over 5,000 feet, give yourself a day or so to adapt, and do not underestimate the sun's strength; it is deceptive in the Highlands and you can easily get a sunburn.

TRANSPORTATION

There is an inexpensive bus service in Nairobi, but it is not much used by tourists. To get a taxi it is best to phone one of the taxi companies; otherwise try a stand (there are ones by the New Stanley, Hilton, and Norfolk hotels). Taxis are often distinguished by a yellow stripe. Agree on the fare before setting off. Cars can be rented from 165-240KS per day, plus 5.70-7.05KS per kilometer. Chauffeur-driven cars cost from 730-865KS a day, plus about 5.70-7.05KS per kilometer. Buses and jeeps can be rented for safaris. You must be over 23 to hire self-drive cars, and foreign licenses are valid for 90 days. Check carefully what insurance coverage you are getting; you will have to pay extra for complete exemption for liability. Drive on the left. Out of town, natural hazards include potholes, animals (especially cattle), unwary cyclists, and treacherous mud on unsurfaced roads in rainy weather. Consult the **AA of Kenya** about road conditions. It is not advisable to drive on the Escarpment at night.

For long-distance travel, the train service is slow (Mombasa to Nairobi, 350 miles, takes 13 hours) but comfortable, in first class at least, and it is a relaxing way to see the country. You can reach Nakuru as well as Mombasa by rail, and there are sleeper and restaurant cars. Reserve in advance through Kenya Railways in Nairobi (tel: 212121). Alternatively there is a long-distance bus service linking major towns, not normally used by tourists. Kenya Airways and various charter companies (such as Sunbird) can fly you all over the country; all game parks have landing strips. There are regular flights to Mombasa, Kisumu, and Malindi from Nairobi. There is a ferry across Kilifi Creek at the coast and round the ports on Lake Victoria.

FOOD AND RESTAURANTS

Hotels serve international food, with the English tradition predominating. Good beef, raised in the Highlands, and seafood are specialties, and you will also come across fresh trout and unfamiliar game. Nearest to the national dish is *ugali*, a corn and bean dish. *Posho*, a corn-based porridge, is the staple dish of the lower class. Local curries are very good. Restaurants are reasonably priced in Kenya. The average price for dinner in a first-class restaurant is about US$32 for one, about US$17 in a medium one, and under US$15 in an inexpensive one.

Recommended restaurants in Nairobi include **Alan Bobbe's Bistro** (Caltex House, Koinange Street—tel: 21152) and the **Café de France** at the French Cultural Center (tel: 331435), both with French cuisine. Traditional Kenyan dishes are at the **African Heritage Café** (tel: 28145). Several hotels have good restaurants: the **Amboseli Grill** in the Hilton (tel: 334000), which holds dinner dances; and **Le Château** at the Inter • Continental Hotel (335550). There are several good Chinese restaurants, among them the **Hong Kong** (Koinange Street—tel: 28612), the **Mandarin** (Tom Mboya Street—tel: 20600), and the **Pagoda** (1st Floor, Shankardass House, Moi Avenue—tel: 27036). The **Red Bull** serves German cuisine (Silopark House—tel: 28045), and **Lavarini's** (Moi Avenue—tel: 20359) and **Marino's** (Mama Ngina Way—tel: 27150) both serve Italian and continental specialties. For delicious seafood there's the **Tamarind** (off Harambee Avenue—tel: 338959), and for charcoal-grilled meats, the **Carnivore** (on the Langata Road 4 miles outside Nairobi—tel: 501775). The Inter • Continental **Coffee Banda** is ideal for coffee or a light snack.

DRINKING TIPS

A social gathering place is the **Thorntree Café** in the New Stanley Hotel in Nairobi. Local beer is good, and imported liquor is available. A whisky and soda costs around US$2.30, and an ordinary bottle of wine from US$11.50. There are no prohibitions on the sale of liquor, and bars are normally open 11-2 and 5-11. There are many pleasant bars in hotels, such as the **Big Five** cocktail lounge in the Inter • Continental. Women should be escorted outside hotels and main tourist areas.

ENTERTAINMENT

The **National Theater,** the **Donovan Maule Theater Club,** and the **French Cultural Center** all perform plays, and there are several movie houses, including two drive-ins. There are various nightclubs in Nairobi, and the major hotels provide attractions; there is dancing at the Inter • Continental Hotel's **Le Château** supper club, at the Hilton and Panafric hotels, and at the **Bacchus Club** (Standard Street; daily membership US$3.50). Three casinos—at the **International, Paradise,** and **Safari Park** hotels— provide music and dancing as well as gaming. There is a strong and rich tradition of folk music in Kenya which you can hear at the **Music Festival** held in Nairobi at the beginning of July or at many other smaller festivals throughout the country. There is also the **Bomas of Kenya,** a government-sponsored traditional song and dance troupe, which gives daily performances in its auditorium on Forest Edge Road off Langata Road.

SHOPPING

You will find a wide range of wood carvings, such as Masai figures and spears, beadwork, Kisii stone carvings, sisal mats and baskets, and colorful tie-dye and batik fabrics, all at reasonable prices. In Nairobi, several good shops are in the Hilton Hotel area. **Afrique Sculptures** on Muindi Mbingu Street is good for carvings, and the main market, **Koinange Street,** is the place for basket work and wooden bowls—you can bargain as much as you like. General stores are on **Moi Avenue** and **Kenyatta Avenue**.

SPORTS

Almost every kind of sport is available. For golf there are seven courses in the Nairobi area, six of which are of 18-hole championship standard. You can go horseback riding almost everywhere; many hotels have stables or arrangements with riding schools, and polo is available. On the coast, the Indian Ocean offers every kind of water sport—surfing, scuba diving, sailing, water-skiing, and deep-sea fishing. In the interior you can sail or water-ski on the huge lakes or fish for trout in the mountain streams. The mountains are a challenge to climbers. Soccer, rugby, field hockey, athletics, tennis, and swimming are popular spectator sports. Autoracing enthusiasts will enjoy the annual Kenya **Safari Rally,** usually held in April. Nairobi is the center for safari trips.

WHAT TO SEE

Nairobi is a pleasant modern city and the best base for traveling in the country. The **Kenyatta Conference Center** is a cylindrical skyscraper rising from a mammoth hall shaped like an African hut and is situated in gardens. See the **National Museum,** outstanding for its displays of animals and flora arranged in natural settings, its prehistoric exhibits, and a range of African weapons and ceremonial headdresses. Next to the museum is the **Snake Park,** where you can see a wide range of snakes and reptiles. Both are at Museum Hill, about 1½ miles from the city center.

The **National Parks** have been created to protect Kenya's magnificent wildlife, and a visit to any of them will richly reward animal lovers and photographers. Special "photo-safaris" can be arranged. **Nairobi National Park,** the closest to the city—5 miles from the center—is the habitat of cheetahs, giraffes, lions, leopards, buffalo, rhinos, hippopotami, and there is an "animal orphanage" which children will love.

The **Great Rift Valley,** a deep trench in the earth's crust that is up to 80 miles wide and stretches from the Red Sea to Mozambique, is a dramatic spectacle. It can be seen from the top of the Ngong Hills on its eastern edge, 10 miles out of Nairobi. In clear weather you will also see as far as the snow-covered peaks of Mount Kenya and Mount Kilimanjaro in neighboring Tanzania.

The floor of the valley is the site of huge soda lakes that host hundreds of thousands of brilliantly colored flamingoes that feed on the algae. **Lake Magadi,** crusted with pink and white soda, is southwest of Nairobi, and northwest is **Lake Nakuru** and its national park, one of the most famous bird sanctuaries in the world. Also in this direction, the 35-square-mile **Menengai Crater.** In the Rift Valley there are two hotels at Naivasha: the **Lake Naivasha Hotel,** PO Box 15 (US$82 double AP); and the **Safariland Club,** PO Box 72 (US$56 double AP). Lake Naivasha can be reached comfortably in 1½ hours from Nairobi.

Thika, 25 miles from Nairobi, is the center of a large area of coffee plantations, and you should see the **Chania Falls.** At **Olorgesailie National Park,** southwest of the capital, hand axes dating back ½ million years are on exhibit.

Mount Kenya (17,058 feet and Africa's second highest peak) is just south of the equator, covered on its lower slopes by huge forests which are the home of many wild animals. Mount Kenya is also a national park, as popular with mountain climbers as it is with animal lovers. This is Central Kenya's Highlands area, extending west from Mount Kenya to include the Aberdare Mountains and **Aberdare National Park.** Here is the famous **Tree Tops Hotel,** PO Box 47557, Nairobi (US$96 per person MAP inclusive of transport from Nairobi), first of the Highlands' viewing lodges where guests can watch animals—elephant, buffalo, rhino, bongo, and giant forest hog—come to drink at the waterhole below. Other viewing lodges are **The Ark,** PO Box 49420, Nairobi (US$109 double MAP), in the Aberdares, and the **Mountain Lodge,** PO Box 30471, Nairobi (US$97.50 double AP), near Mount Kenya.

Amboseli National Park lies close to the Tanzania border, about 140 miles south of Nairobi. Zebra, elephant, wildebeest, and gazelles can be seen grazing on its savannahs. Places to stay here are the **Amboseli Serena Lodge** (US$72.90 double AP), also the **Amboseli New Lodge** (US$110.30 double AP), and the **Kilimanjaro Safari Lodge** (US$108 double AP).

Other national parks are the **Masai Mara Game Reserve** across the border from Tanzania's Serengeti National Park, habitat of grazing animals and the great cats, and the only place in Kenya to see the great wildebeest migration; **Meru National Park,** north of Mount Kenya, for lions, zebra, reticulated giraffe, kudu, and the white rhinoceros; **Samburu Game Reserve** in the dry northern region, with Grevy's zebra, reticulated giraffe, oryx, and impala among many other species; **Marsabit National Park,** farther north, home of some of Kenya's largest and oldest elephants.

Tsavo National Park is not only Kenya's largest—its 8,000 square miles make it one of the largest national parks in the world. It is divided into two sections, Tsavo East and Tsavo West, by the Nairobi-Mombasa Highway, and the two sections have separate entrance fees. As in the Highlands, Tsavo has lodges with waterhole views: **Kilaguni Lodge,** PO Box 30471, Nairobi (US$103 double AP), where herds of buffalo frequent the waterhole, and **Ngulia Lodge,** PO Box 30471, Nairobi (US$103 double AP), both in Tsavo West, and **Voi Safari Lodge,** PO Box 30471, Nairobi (US$85 double AP) in Tsavo East. Both sides of the park also have safari camps and self-service lodges.

Mombasa: The atmosphere here is quite different from Nairobi. Forty percent of the population is Muslim, and there are 49 mosques. **Mandhry Mosque** is the oldest, built in 1570, and is one of the many in the picturesque **Old Town,** whose narrow, winding streets and black-veiled women are reminiscent of Morocco and Tunisia. Go down to the **Old Harbor** to see the *dhow* boats, which arrive in December on the winds of the northeast monsoon from the Persian Gulf, as they have for 2,000 years. They bring in dates, salt, and carpets and take back sisal, limes, and ghee. Mombasa's most important historic monument is **Fort Jesus,** built by the Portuguese in 1593 and now a museum. For eating out here you will find a wide range of curry restaurants, of which the **Singh** (Mwembe Tyari Road) and the **Taj Hotel** are recommended. In the Old Town, try the **Rekonda Hotel,** Kobokono Street, for tasty Arab food. For seafood, try the **Tamarind** on the far side of the old Nyali Bridge. In the tiny shops of Arab craftsmen you will find attractive souvenirs such as old jewelry and coffee pots, and down in the tiny Old Kilindini Road there is the goldsmiths' community. Or buy a *kanga*—brightly colored cloth, often with sayings in Swahili printed on it, and worn sarong-style.

Hotels in Mombasa: **Serena Beach,** PO Box 90352 (US$113 double AP); **Mombasa Beach,** PO Box 90414 (US$97.50 double AP); **Nyali Beach,** PO Box 90581 (US$102.50 double AP), 3 miles; **Whispering Palms,** PO Kikambala, via Mombasa (US$67 double AP); **Whitesands,** PO Box 90173 (US$80 double AP), 8 miles.

Malindi, 75 miles north of Mombasa, was the Portuguese headquarters in East Africa until 1593, when it was moved down to Mombasa. Its most interesting monuments are two tombs, dating from the 15th century, one a tall pillar and the other low and paneled, and Vasco da Gama's pillar, with a cross of Lisbon limestone, brought here by the explorer himself. **Malindi Bay Beach** and **Silversands** are perfect for swimming and surfing. The **Malindi Marine Park** has excellent snorkeling. Hotels in Malindi include the **Sinbad Hotel,** PO Box 30 (US$78 double AP), and the **Indian Ocean Lodge** (US$170 double AP including wine at meals).

Lamu, further north again, is an old Arab town, built on an island without roads or cars, a holy place where hundreds of Muslim pilgrims come each year to celebrate the Prophet's birthday. The town is remarkable for its carved wooden doors and fine ebony and ivory carved chairs which were made here until recently and can still be bought. There is also fine silverwork. Hotels are **Petley's Inn,** PO Box 4 (US$65 double MAP), in town on the waterfront, and **Peponi Hotel,** PO Box 24 (US$64 double AP), in the nearby Arab village of Shela next to an 8-mile uninhabited beach.

SOURCES OF FURTHER INFORMATION

Pan Am, Hilton Hotel, PO Box 30544, Simba Street, Nairobi, and any Pan Am office round the world; **Kenya Tourist Development Corporation,** PO Box 42013, Nairobi; **Ministry of Tourism and Wildlife,** PO Box 30027, Nairobi; **Kenya Tourist Office,** 60 East 56th Street, New York, NY 10022; 9100 Wilshire Boulevard, Doheny Plaza, Suite 111-112, Beverly Hills, CA 90212; 13 Burlington Street, London W1X 1FF.

Liberia

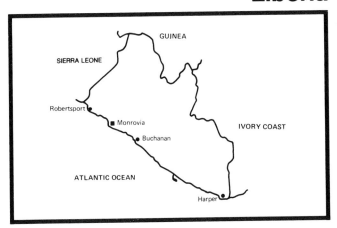

WHAT'S SPECIAL

Liberia was bought by the American Colonization Society from six tribal kings in 1821 to promote a "back to Africa" movement among freed American Negro slaves. The first settlers began to arrive the following year and in 1847 Liberia became an independent republic, its constitution modeled on the American pattern and its capital named after American President James Monroe. Firestone, Goodrich, and Uniroyal all have large rubber plantations here, and the country has received a considerable amount of US development assistance. A military coup in April 1980 toppled the slave-descendent government. The new government is generally pro American despite isolated cases of harrassment.

COUNTRY BRIEFING

The **area** is 43,000 square miles and the **population** 1,700,000, of whom about 229,000 live in the **capital**, Monrovia. The **climate** is tropical and very humid; best time to visit is November-March during the dry season. Liberia is an **independent republic;** the **language** is English and the **religions** Christianity and Islam. The **currency** is the Liberian dollar, at par with the US dollar. Since Liberia does not issue paper currency, US paper currency is used, supplemented by Liberian coins.

HOW TO GET THERE

Flying time to Monrovia, Roberts International Airport from New York is 8¾ hours; from Dakar, 2 hours; from Lagos, 2½ hours. Time in Liberia: GMT.

REQUIREMENTS FOR ENTRY AND CUSTOMS REGULATIONS

Passport, visa, round-trip or onward ticket; smallpox, yellow-fever, and cholera certificates. Duty-free allowance: 200 cigarettes or 1 pound tobacco; 1 quart wine or liquor. No currency restrictions.

AIRPORT INFORMATION

Roberts International Airport is 38 miles from Monrovia. Shared taxis (L$25) meet planes. If arriving late, it might be advisable to stay overnight at the Roberts Field Hotel—the journey to Monrovia is often difficult at night due to heavy rains and fog, and is dangerous as well because of the unsettled political situation. Departure tax is L$5. There is a duty-free shop.

ACCOMMODATIONS

The range is from the luxury-class Ducor Inter · Continental to inexpensive hotels and motels, but many lack amenities due to the political upheaval. Some are air-conditioned. No off-peak special rates. Hotels in Monrovia:

Rates are in US$ for a double/twin room with bath or shower
  Carlton, 285 Broad Street (from $24)
  DUCOR INTER · CONTINENTAL, Broad Street, Mamba Point (from $55)
  Holiday Inn, 100 Carey Street (from $40, not affiliated with international hotel chain)
  Travellers' Roost, Broad Street (from $18)
  All the above hotels are in the heart of Monrovia.

USEFUL INFORMATION

Banks open 8-12 Mon-Thurs, 8-2 Fri; closed Sat except for the International Trust Company, which is open 8-11. There are phones in hotels, restaurants, and cafés. Useful numbers: **Pan Am** 224624; **National Tourist Office,** 222148. Airmail editions of British and American **newspapers** and weekly newsmagazines are available, and Liberian newspapers are in English. **Tipping** is customary 10-15% in restaurants; porters, 50¢-$1; taxi drivers are not tipped. **Electricity:** 120 volts 60 cycles AC except at the Ducor Inter · Continental Hotel where current is 220 volts. Main hotels have express **laundry** services. **Hairdressing** salons are found in major hotels (shampoo and set from L$8; man's haircut from L$5 plus tip). There is a good selection of black and white and color **film** and equipment. **Clubs:** Kiwanis. **Health:** Doctors, dentists speak English. Imported pharmaceuticals and toiletries are available at reasonable prices. Wash fruit; drink boiled water. Anti-malarial medication is strongly recommended.

TRANSPORTATION

There is a bus service and plenty of taxis, which can be hailed on the street (fixed charges of 35 cents within Monrovia and 60 cents to suburbs).

Long-distance buses link Monrovia with other major cities. Air Liberia has connections to coastal and interior towns, and small airplanes can be chartered for journeys elsewhere. It is possible to travel along the coast by ship; inland, some villages are linked by canoe, others only by bush trail. Regular or chauffeur-driven cars can be rented, and there are good roads in and around Monrovia. In the interior many roads are dusty in the dry season and rough and slushy in the rains. Drive on the right.

FOOD AND RESTAURANTS

Main hotels have European, American, and sometimes Asian food, but it is interesting to try local dishes made with palm oil, rice, meat, and vegetables like cassava leaf and eggplant. Go to **Angie's** for outstanding Liberian specialties or to **Rosaline's Restaurant** (Carey Street), another good place for local food. The Ducor and Carlton hotels (both on Broad Street) have a range of international dishes; the dining room at the Holiday Inn is good, with a varied menu. **Julia's** on Gurley Street has excellent French cuisine, while Italian food is the specialty at the **Lark** on Warren Street. The **Mandarin** (Broad Street) has excellent Chinese cuisine, and **Salvatore** serves European delicacies. Go to the **Wimpey Coffee Shop** (Broad Street) for coffee and snacks.

ENTERTAINMENT

A curfew that lasted almost a year broke the habit of going out, and now there is no nightlife.

SHOPPING

Stores open 9-12 and 3-6 Mon-Fri, 9-12 Sat, with some open 2-6 Sat. African souvenirs include ivory and wood carvings, gold and silver jewelry and trinkets, usually inexpensive, and tie-dye materials. You can bargain in the market.

SPORTS

Liberians are enthusiastic soccer fans, and in the dry season matches are held in Monrovia's **Antoinette Tubman Stadium.** The Ducor Inter · Continental Hotel has tennis and swimming facilities. There are beaches near Monrovia, but sea swimming can be dangerous because of currents.

WHAT TO SEE

Liberia has a beautiful coastline, with sandy beaches, narrow lagoons, and rocky promontories. Inland there are plains, dense forest with trees reaching to 200 feet, and a mountainous area topped by **Mount Wutiri** (4,528 feet). Tourists with their own transportation should drive down the coast to **Buchanan,** where the **Louiza Hotel** has good accommodations, then up through **Nimba County** past tribal villages of mud huts and back to Monrovia through **Bong County. Monrovia's Cultural Center** is worth a visit. **Robertsport,** west of Monrovia, has the country's largest freshwater lake and a good hotel, the **Victoria.** The **Firestone Rubber Plantation** near Roberts International Airport offers tours. **Harper** has an interesting "dead island."

SOURCES OF FURTHER INFORMATION

Pan Am, 53 Broad Street, Monrovia, and any Pan Am office around the world; **Ministry of Information, Cultural Affairs and Tourism,** Capitol Hill, Monrovia; **Liberian Embassy,** 21 Princes Gate, London SW7; **Liberian Information Center,** 1050 17th Street NW, Washington, DC 20036.

Note: Because of the political situation in Libya, it has not been possible to provide complete information for this chapter.

Libya

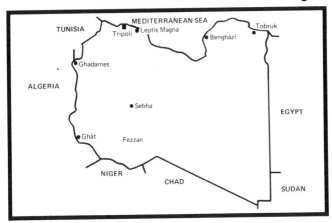

WHAT'S SPECIAL

Beyond the fertile coastal strips, the beaches, and the high-rise apartment buildings and modern hotels of Tripoli and Benghazi, Libya presents a different face: vast desert, ancient cities, and great ruins from Roman times, with little oasis towns further inland. First a Greek, then a Roman colony, Libya was under Turkish rule until 1911 and was an Italian colony until 1944. It gained independence in 1951 and in 1969 became a republic. In the 1960s oil was found.

COUNTRY BRIEFING

Libya covers an **area** of 679,358 square miles and has a **population** of 2,600,000. Tripoli (population 750,000) is the **capital**. The coastal fringe has a Mediterranean **climate**. Inland there are hot days and cold nights. **Language:** Arabic; some English and Italian spoken. **Religion:** Sunni Muslim. **Currency:** the Libyan dinar, divided into 1,000 dirhams (LBD .36 = US$1.00). **Public holidays** are 8 Mar; 28 Mar; 25 May; 11 June; 23 July; 1 Sep; 7 Oct. There are also movable religious holidays.

SOURCES OF FURTHER INFORMATION

Any **Pan Am** office around the world; **Libya Tourist Board,** Haiti Street, PO Box 891, Tripoli; **Embassy of the Libyan Arab Republic,** 5 St James's Square, London SW1.

Morocco

WHAT'S SPECIAL

Morocco, on the northwest coast of Africa, is closer to Europe than any other African nation and it is this geographical situation that suggests the fascinating blend of the old and the new to be found here. In the countryside, farmers with their camels continue tilling the soil much as they have done for centuries, undisturbed by the jet traffic overhead. The minarets of the mosques in older cities such as Fez and Marrakesh reflect the continuing vitality of local customs and a style of life absent in the sophisticated cities of Casablanca and Rabat, whose skylines are punctuated with modern skyscrapers. The contrast is continued in nature; the hilly Er Rif area, the fertile Mediterranean and Atlantic coastal sections, and the dramatic stretches of the snow-capped Atlas Mountains offset the bleak and dramatic wasteland of the Sahara beyond. Tourism is a thriving industry in Morocco, and the visitor will find fashionable resorts, good hotels and restaurants, and a lively nightlife.

COUNTRY BRIEFING

Size: 177,117 square miles
Capital: Rabat

Population: 20,368,000
Capital Population: 865,000

Climate: Sunshine 300 days a year. Mild to hot along the western coastline; very hot in summer in the south and toward Marrakesh. Evenings cool in mountain and desert areas. You can visit any time of the year, but specially recommended are: for seaside, May-September; Marrakesh and inland, January and February; winter sports, December-April.

Weather in Casablanca: Lat N33°35′; Alt 190 ft

Temp (°F)	Jan	Feb	Mar	Apr	May	Jun	Jul	Aug	Sep	Oct	Nov	Dec
Av Low	45°	46°	49°	52°	56°	61°	65°	66°	63°	58°	52°	47°
Av High	63°	64°	67°	69°	72°	76°	79°	81°	79°	76°	69°	65°
Days no rain	23	20	23	23	26	29	31	31	29	25	22	22

Government: A constitutional monarchy.

Language: Arabic. French is spoken widely; Spanish in the north only. English is poorly understood. Berber tongues are spoken in the mountains.

Religion: Islam.

Currency: Dirham. 100 centimes = 1 dirham.

	5F	10F	20F	50F	1D	10D	100D	200D
US (dollars, cents)	.01	.02	.04	.10	.21	2.10	21.01	42.02
UK (pounds, pence)	—	.01	.02	.05	.10	1.00	10.02	20.04

Public Holidays:

Throne Day, 3 Mar
Labor Day, 1 May
Youth Day, 9 July

Anniversary of the Green
March, 6 Nov
Independence Day, 18 Nov

There are five Muslim holidays whose dates vary according to the lunar calendar: Aid El-Seghir, Aid El-Kebir, Mouloud, the 1st of Moharram, and Achoura.

HOW TO GET THERE

Flying time to Casablanca's Nouasseur Airport from New York is 8 hours; from London, 2½ hours, from Madrid, 1½ hours. Time in Morocco: GMT.

REQUIREMENTS FOR ENTRY AND CUSTOMS REGULATIONS

Passport. Nationals of most countries need no visa for a stay up to three months. Cholera certificate necessary if arriving from an infected area. Import of foreign currency is unrestricted but the amount must be declared at customs. Keep all exchange receipts in order to reconvert, on departure, up to 50% of the amount originally exchanged for Moroccan currency. Dirhams may not be imported or exported. Duty-free allowance: 200 cigarettes (1 carton) or 50 cigars or 1 pound of tobacco; 1 bottle liquor or 3 bottles wine.

AIRPORT INFORMATION

Nouasseur Airport in Casablanca is 20 miles from the city's center. Buses run every hour, fare 5 dirhams; taxis are easily obtainable, fare 60 dirhams. Tip luggage porter 1 dirham per piece. Rabat Airport is 6 miles from the city, but few international flights land there.

ACCOMMODATIONS

There are luxury to budget-priced hotels, youth hostels, and pensions. Peak season is 15 October-15 June in the south and 15 May-15 September in the north, when rates are higher and advance bookings advisable. Hotels in Rabat, centrally located unless otherwise indicated:

Rates are in US$ for a double/twin room with bath or shower

Balima, Avenue Mohammed V (from $17)

Hotel Chellah, Rue d'Ifni (from $27)

Hotel De La Tour Hassan, 26 Avenue Abderrahman Annegai (from $47)

Rabat Hilton, Aviation-Souissi (from $53), 2 miles from city center

USEFUL INFORMATION

Banks: Open Mon-Fri from 8:15-11:30 and 2:15-4. (Hours are shorter during the summer and during Ramadan, the month-long period of fasting that culminates in the Aid El-Seghir holiday.) Currency may also be changed at hotels and travel agencies and at airport and port exchange bureaus.

Mail: Stamps from post offices or hotel porter.

Telephone Tips: Cost of a local call is 0.60 dirham from a phone booth, 1 dirham in restaurants and cafés. Useful numbers:

Pan Am agent 246047 (Rabat)	**Tourist Offices** 21252 (Rabat)
271122 (Casablanca)	270469/222267 (Casablanca)
Police 19	30258/30314 (Marrakesh)
Fire 15	38239 (Tangier)
Operator 10	**Airport Information**
Local International Operator 12	21252 (Rabat)
Telephone Inquiries 16	339040 (Casablanca)

Newspapers: No local English-language publications, but American and English newspapers are obtainable.

Tipping: Service charge of 10-15% is generally included in the restaurant and hotel bill.

Electricity: 110-120 volts 50 cycles AC.

Laundry: Good in major cities and reliable hotels; 24-hour service available (from 15 dirhams to dry-clean a suit, from 4 dirhams to launder a shirt).

Hairdressing: Some major hotels have salons (shampoo and set from 50 dirhams, tip 2 dirhams; man's haircut from 50 dirhams, tip 10%).

Photography: Black and white and color film are available in major cities, along with a selection of equipment.

Clubs: Check at local tourist office.

Babysitting: See hotel reception.

Rest Rooms: Women, *Dames;* men, *Hommes.*

Health: Some doctors and dentists speak English. Imported pharmaceuticals available (mainly French and rather expensive). Drink tap or bottled water and avoid food from street stalls.

TRANSPORTATION

There are buses and plenty of taxis available in major cities. Taxis have meters, and Grand Tourisme (limousines) charge a fixed rate. Royal Air Maroc, Royal Air Inter, trains, and bus services link major cities. Rental cars are available in Casablanca, Rabat, Tangier, Marrakesh, Agadir, Fez, and Oujda. Road travel is generally good. Gas is expensive. Car ferries

link Tangier and Ceuta with Algeciras and Malaga in Spain and with other points in Europe. The crossing between Algeciras and Tangier takes 2½ hours, between Algeciras and Ceuta 1 hour.

FOOD AND RESTAURANTS

Couscous, a flavorful blend of spiced semolina and meat sauce cooked over broth, is the national dish and should certainly be tried by the visitor. There are many other tasty local dishes, and the Moroccans are justifiably proud of their culinary art. However, if you prefer more familiar foods, international cuisine is readily available in the principal towns and cities, and there are many good French restaurants. The appetites of those who are partial to seafood will also be satisfied in Morocco, especially in the string of restaurants along the coast near Casablanca. In Rabat try the **Diffa Room** (tel: 21401) at the Tour de la Hassan Hotel for national dishes; for good seafood dishes try **Le Provençal** in the town of Temara, 12 miles from Rabat. For Moroccan food at its best try the **Al Mounia** restaurant (95 Avenue Prince Moulay Abdallah, Casablanca—tel: 222669) and **La Maison Arabe** (5 Rue Derb Ferran, Marrakesh—tel: 22605), where you also see folk-dancing performances (make table reservations in advance). Also in Marrakesh are **Ksar el Hamra** (28 Rue Goundafi—tel: 23297) and **Dar es Salam** (Derb Riad Jadid—tel: 23520) for national specialties. For French specialties go to **La Tour d'Argent** (40 Avenue Es-Slaoui, Fez—tel: 24871), and **Relais de Père Louis** (1 Rue de Dimack, Rabat—tel: 22315).

DRINKING TIPS

Mint tea is the national drink, and the making of it is considered to be an art acquired at a very early age. Moroccan wine is generally of good quality and inexpensive to buy, as is the local beer. Other liquor is available—best drinking places are the numerous outdoor cafés and the hotel bars; the average price of a whisky is US$3.50, a bottle of ordinary red wine US$4.

ENTERTAINMENT

In Rabat, performances in various languages take place at the **Mohammed V** theater. In Casablanca, for nightlife, try the Americanized **Basin Street, La Réserve, La Notte,** or **Calypso** discothèques. There is gambling at the **Casino** in Mohammedia (15 miles from Casablanca), also in Tangier and Marrakesh. American, European, and Arabic movies are shown with French dubbing.

SHOPPING

French imports are widely available in all major cities, but traditional Moroccan crafts make excellent souvenirs. These include colorful caftans, copperware, fine tooled leather goods, and silver and gold jewelry. The best places to shop in the older cities such as Fez, Marrakesh, and Meknès are the *souks,* or markets, but in the larger and more modern cities there are many stores which sell the same range of goods. Visit **Coopartim,** which has a branch in Rabat on the corner of Rue Aljabarti and Rue Renard, and in Casablanca on the Avenue des FAR. Prices are fixed in the stores, but bargaining is a regular practice in souks.

SPORTS

You can enjoy tennis, water sports at all resorts, and deep-sea fishing around Tangier. Golf is very popular—good at Casablanca, Mohammedia, Tangier, and Marrakesh; exceptional at Rabat at the **Dar es Salam Royal Golf Club** (45 holes), 7 miles southeast of the city (tel: 20202). Try the hunting, chiefly wild boar and wild fowl, in the **Arbaoua Hunting Reserve for Tourists.** Climbing in the **Atlas Mountains** is popular, and in winter there is skiing at **Oukaimeden** and **Ifrane.** Horseback riding is possible at riding clubs, which issue temporary subscription cards, and at some hotels with stables. Excursions on horseback from village to village in the Atlas Mountains can be arranged.

WHAT TO SEE

Casablanca is the industrial and commercial center of Morocco. It is a modern city of tall white buildings, many retaining the ornate style of the country's traditional form of architecture. The centrally located **United Nations Square** is a good place to begin any tour. Nearby is the park which commemorates the foundation of the Arab League and the Roman Catholic **Sacré Coeur Cathedral,** built in this century. There is also the modern **Notre Dame de Lourdes,** noted for its stained-glass windows and walls. For a different prospect visit the **Great Mosque** in the Old Medina, the original Arab residential and commercial quarter, and the **Royal Palace,** one of several in Morocco. Along the coast north of Casablanca there are many excellent beaches, especially at **Mohammedia,** 15 miles away. Hotels in Casablanca, centrally located unless indicated, include:

Rates are in US$ for a double/twin room with bath or shower
  Casablanca, Place Mohammed V (from $51)
  El Mansour, 27 Avenue des FAR (from $64)
  Marhaba, 63 Avenue des FAR (from $27)
  Noailles, 22 Boulevard de 11 Janvier (from $14)
  Transatlantique, 79 Rue Colbert (from $22)

Rabat: Though another modern city and the capital since 1912, Rabat—along with Fez, Marrakesh, and Meknès—is one of Morocco's four "imperial cities," capitals of former powerful Moroccan dynasties whose architectural achievements remain in the mosques, palaces, and *medersas,* or koranic schools, admired today. Rabat has ancient walls, splendid old gateways, and delightful public gardens. Visit the **Royal Palace** on a Friday morning when the King is in residence and the Royal Guard is on parade. Also go to the **Oudayas Kasbah,** or fortress, where there is a good view over the sea and the estuary of the Bou-Regreg River. The **Handicrafts Museum** is in a small 18th-century palace in the Kasbah Gardens. The **Tower of Hassan,** built in the 12th century as part of a mosque that was never completed, now includes the **Mausoleum of King Mohammed V,** first ruler of modern, independent Morocco. Outside the walls of Rabat is the fortified Roman village of **Chellah. Salé,** on the opposite side of the gulf known as the Bou-Regreg, was once notorious as a base for Mediterranean pirates.

Tangier, known as the "Crossroads of the World," was an international city between World War I and 1956, and it remains cosmopolitan. (Inland, in contrast, medieval **Tetouan** and **Chaouen** were closed to Europeans until 1920.) Tangier is renowned for its almost perfect climate and for the **Sultan's Palace** in the Kasbah. The palace apartments, now a museum, contain Moroccan arts and crafts from all regions. From the Kasbah, the steep and narrow streets of the old city, or Medina, lead toward the **Grand Socco,** the main marketplace; the **Petit Socco,** a small square with cafés and old hotels; and the **Mendoubia Gardens.** Hotels in Tangier include the **Intercontinental,** Boulevard de Paris (from US$62 double); the **Rif,** Avenue d'Espagne (from US$53 double); the **El Minzah,** 85 Rue de la Liberté (from US$62 double); and **Les Almohades,** Avenue des FAR (from US$62 double).

Fez is the oldest city in the land, founded by Moulay Idriss I of the Idrisside dynasty in the 8th century, and capital to succeeding dynasties as well. Visit the tombs of the Merinides Princes, the dynasty under whose rule in the 14th-century the city reached its greatest splendor. The **Medina** in Fez is a dense, labyrinthine collection of alleyways, souks, and monuments, one of the most interesting in Morocco and best visited with a guide. (Check with your hotel or go to the Syndicat d'Initiative). In the Medina, see the **Bou Inania Medersa,** a magnificent example of 14th-century Moroccan architecture. The **Karaouyine Mosque,** begun in the 9th century, is the largest mosque in North Africa; only Muslims are permitted entry. Nearby is the mosaic-tiled **Nejjarine Square** and its fountain. Hotels in Fez:

De Fez, Avenue des FAR (from US$57 double)
Les Merinides, Route Fez-Nord (from US$27 double)
Palais Jamai, Bab Guissa (from US$62 double)
Zalagh, Rue Mohammed Diouri (from US$22 double)

Meknès, 37 miles from Fez, became an imperial city in the 17th century when Moulay Ismael of the Alaouite dynasty made it his capital. In the Medina, see the gates of **Bab Mansour** and the **Jamai Palace,** now the **Museum of Moroccan Arts.** The **Mausoleum of Moulay Ismail** is open to non-Muslims. About 17 miles from Meknès is **Moulay Idriss,** a holy city, with the **Mausoleum of Moulay Idriss I,** founder of Fez. Entry to the sanctuary is limited to Muslims, but the town itself is interesting, especially in mid-August, when it is the site of an important **moussem,** a pilgrimage that culminates in colorful festivities. At **Volubilis,** a few miles away, there are extensive Roman ruins; finds from the excavations here are in the Antiquities Museum in Rabat. The **Transatlantique Hotel** in Meknès (Rue El Meriniyine) has double rooms for US$40.

Marrakesh, the oasis city, is famed for its perfect twilight and red-ochre color; it is the gateway to the Sahara. Founded by the Almoravids in the 11th century, it was one of Islam's greatest cities. Most exotic of sights is the **Jemaa El Fna Square:** acrobats, jugglers, water sellers, snake charmers, and others are the cast of characters in a show that began long before tourists with their cameras arrived. Now a tip is expected if you shoot—one dirham per subject. The **Café de France,** on the square, is a place to sit down and enjoy the spectacle. Among the gems of Marrakesh, see the **Koutoubia Mosque,** nearby, the **Saadian Tombs,** the **Medersa Ben Youssef** and its exquisite courtyard, and the **Menara Gardens.** The **Bahia Palace** has five gardens, and the ruins of the **El Badii Palace** are the site of the annual **National Folklore Festival** held in early June. Visit the wonderful souks and, finally, go sightseeing in a horse-drawn carriage around the old city gates and beyond.

From Marrakesh, arrange a tour over the **Atlas Mountains** to the south, the route of the Kasbahs, or castle fortresses. Visit the pastoral mountain peoples of the south, with their colorful costumes and unique folklore, and see **Ouarzazate** and the **Valley of the Draa** and **Goulimine.** In Marrakesh stay at the **Mamounia,** Avenue Bab Djedid (from US$111 double); the **Palais El Badia,** Avenue de la Ménara (from US$58 double); the **Es Saadi,** Avenue El Qadissia (from US$98 double MAP); or at **Les Almoravides,** Arset Djebel Lakhdar (from US$22 double).

Agadir, on the Atlantic coast 325 miles from Casablanca, has long beaches with fine sand and a climate that allows year-round swimming. Nearly destroyed by an earthquake in 1960, it is a rapidly growing resort city and the starting point for excursions to southern Morocco. Visit **Essaouira** to the north, one of the many places which still has traces of early Portuguese influence. Hotels in Agadir:

Les Almohades, Quartier des Dunes (from US$62 double)
Atlas, Boulevard Mohammed V (from US$27 double)
Marhaba, Avenue Mohammed V (from US$27 double)
Royal, Boulevard Mohammed V (from US$17 double)
Sahara, Boulevard Mohammed V (from US$52 double)

SOURCES OF FURTHER INFORMATION

Pan Am agent, Royal Air Maroc, 44 Avenue de l'Armée Royale, Casablanca, and Avenue Mohammed V, Rabat; and any Pan Am office around the world; **Office National du Tourisme,** Avenue d'Alger 22, Rabat; **Moroccan National Tourist Office,** 521 Fifth Avenue, Suite 2800, New York, NY 10017, and 174 Regent Street, London W1.

Nigeria

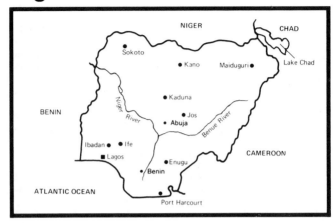

WHAT'S SPECIAL

Nigeria is both the most populous country in Africa and, it is thought, potentially one of the richest. It is one of the world's major producers of oil, turning out some two million barrels of crude a day. The country is a fascinating mixture of people, culture, and tradition—from the Hausa and Fulani in the north to the Yoruba and Edo in the west and the Ibo in the east. It is this diversity of race and culture that may well prove Nigeria's great strength in the future. From the archaeological point of view the country is fascinating. Recent discoveries at Nok in the central plateau have revealed a culture some 4,000 years old, with evidence of the superb pottery, bronze, hardware, and other crafts that continue to form a distinctive aspect of Nigeria today.

COUNTRY BRIEFING

Size: 356,669 square miles　　　**Population:** 80,000,000
Capital: Lagos　　　　　　　　 **Capital Population:** 4 to 5 million
　Climate: There are two seasons—dry and rainy. Around Lagos the dry season is from November-April. This is the best time to visit; although it is hot, there is a cool but dry "harmattan" spell between December and February.

Weather in Lagos: Lat N6°27'; Alt 10 ft

Temp (°F)	Jan	Feb	Mar	Apr	May	Jun	Jul	Aug	Sep	Oct	Nov	Dec
Av Low	74°	77°	78°	77°	76°	74°	74°	73°	74°	74°	75°	75°
Av High	88°	89°	89°	89°	87°	85°	83°	82°	83°	85°	88°	88°
Days no rain	29	25	24	20	15	10	15	21	16	15	23	29

Government: A federal republic of 19 states.

Language: English. Hausa, Ibo, and Yoruba are the major ethnic languages.

Religion: Muslim, Christian, and animist.

Currency: Naira. 100 kobo = 1 naira.

	10k	50k	N1	N5	N10	N50	N100	N500
US (dollars, cents)	.19	.94	1.87	9.37	18.74	93.69	187.37	936.85
UK (pounds, pence)	.09	.45	.89	4.47	8.94	44.69	89.34	446.88

Public Holidays:

New Year's Day, 1 Jan	National Day, 1 Oct
Good Friday	Christmas Day, 25 Dec
Easter Monday	

Islamic holidays of Id-el-Fitr, Id-el-Kabir, and Id-el-Maulud are also observed. They are based on the lunar calendar.

HOW TO GET THERE

Flying time to Lagos, Murtala Mohammed International Airport from New York is 11¼ hours; from Dakar, 4½ hours; from Monrovia, 2½ hours; from Nairobi, 4¼ hours. Time in Nigeria GMT+1.

REQUIREMENTS FOR ENTRY AND CUSTOMS REGULATIONS

Passport, visa or entry permit, and an onward ticket. Vaccination certificate for yellow fever is required. No Nigerian currency may be taken into or out of the country, though departing Nigerian citizens may have up to N50 in their possession and may return with it. Duty-free allowance: 200 cigarettes or 50 cigars or ½ pound tobacco; 1 liter liquor; 1 liter wine; ½ pint perfume.

AIRPORT INFORMATION

The new Murtala Mohammed International Airport Ikeja is 14 miles (60 minutes) from the city center and most hotels. Although taxis are metered, the fare must be arrived at by bargaining and should cost N15-20. Car hire services are available at all airports but are not cheaper. Tip porters N1 for all baggage. There is an airport departure tax of N5. Other international airports are Kano in the north, 5 miles (30 minutes) from Kano City, and the new Port Harcourt in the south, 12 miles (5 minutes) from city center.

ACCOMMODATIONS

There are first-class hotels and government rest houses which are clean and inexpensive. A service charge of 10% is paid on room, food, and beverages. All hotels require a full-stay deposit in advance. Hotels in Lagos:

Rates are in US$ for a double/twin room with bath or shower

Airport, Ikeja (from $65), 2 miles from airport

Bristol, 8 Martins Street (from $65)

Eko Hotel, Victoria Island, facing "bar beach" (from $90)

Federal Palace, Victoria Island (from $90)
Ikoyi, Kingsway Road (from $65)
Mainland, 2-4 Denton Street (from $70)
Except for the Airport Hotel, all the above hotels are centrally located.

USEFUL INFORMATION

Banks: Open 8-3 Mon, 8-1 in Lagos and 8-1:30 elsewhere Tues-Fri. All banks cash travelers' checks and offer better rates than hotels.

Mail: Mailboxes are available in all hotels as well as at post offices.

Telephone Tips: Public coin-box phones are not common in Nigeria, though they can be found. In general, check at the post office. There are 7 international telephone and telex booths variously located. Many hotels accept international call bookings. Direct dialing to almost anywhere in the world is now available. Cost of a local call is 25k. Useful numbers in Lagos:

Pan Am 661731/41 **Tourist Office** 638080

Airport Information 935800

Newspapers: Over 70 daily and weekly papers are published in English. Imported papers are available one day after issue.

Tipping: A 10% service charge in hotels and restaurants is common.

Electricity: 220 volts 50 cycles AC.

Laundry: Facilities available in all hotels: there are dry-cleaning shops and laundromats in Lagos.

Photography: Black and white film costs just under N3-4, color about N8-10. It takes a week to develop black and white; color can be processed locally.

Clubs: Rotary, Island, Kiwanis.

Health: All doctors speak English, and facilities are reasonable. Drink only bottled water and take antimalarial precautions.

TRANSPORTATION

Nigeria Airways connects all major centers; 2,200 miles of railroad link Lagos, Port Harcourt, Kano, Ibadan, Kaduna, Jos, and Enugu. For comfort, travel first class. In the high-water season, vessels take passengers and cargo to Jebba on the Niger and Yola on the Benue. Within cities, buses are always crowded. Taxis are fairly easy to find, and although fitted with meters, bargaining is customary.

FOOD AND RESTAURANTS

Nigerians like their food hot, and it is generally well-spiced with red and green peppers. Local dishes feature cassava, corn, vegetables, and tropical fruits. Along the coast the seafood is excellent, and it includes barracuda, red snapper, and prawns. One of Lagos' fine restaurants is the **Summit** at the Eko Hotel, and there are other good restaurants at the Ikoyi, Mainland, and Federal Palace hotels. The **Mandarin,** Airport Road, serves Chinese food and there are fine Chinese restaurants at the Ikoyi and Federal Palace as well. Other places to try in Lagos are **Club**

Bagatelle (208 Broad Street); **Bacchus Club** (57 Awolowo Road); **Cathay, Quo Vadis,** and **Tabriz.** The nightclub at the Eko Hotel's **Peacock** has an excellent range of cocktails, live band and disco music. The **Beachcomber** in Maryland and the **African Shrine** close by in Ikeja have all-night entertainment. **Phoenicia Restaurant-Nightclub,** Martins Street, offers a range of continental and Middle Eastern dishes and the **Nefertiti Restaurant-Nightclub** on Ikorodu Road is Egyptian in flavor, with weekend floor shows.

DRINKING TIPS

Locally produced beer and liquor are of a high standard. Imported drinks are expensive, a whisky and soda costing N3-5 and a bottle of red wine N20-25. Bars and local "pubs" called "beer parlors" are open in cities most of the day and late into the night.

SHOPPING

The range of goods is smaller now than before due to import restrictions, but craftwork abounds and is superb—brass pots and kettles; leather goods; calabash gourds; carvings or figures in ivory, ebony, clay, and bronze; handwoven fabrics in bright colors; unusual masks; earthenware pots; basketry; and camelhair blankets. In Lagos, shop at **Kingsway Stores, Leventis Stores, Bhojson,** and **Chelleram's** (all on Marina), or at the **Union Trading Company** on Broad Street. A great many of the arts and crafts can be seen outside almost all hotels. Price bargaining is customary. Colorful, exotically embroidered local wear is available at many street corner stalls as well as boutiques. **Chique Afrique, Shade's,** and **Craft Village** are three excellent boutiques at the **Falomo Shopping Center** near the Ikoyi Hotel.

SPORTS

Sailing, motor boating, fishing, and swimming in Lagos and along the coast. Swimming at Lagos' main beach, "bar beach," is dangerous; try **Tarkwa Bay** instead. Soccer, boxing, and athletics are popular and there are facilities for these all year round in major cities. There is hunting in the northern states; a license is necessary. Major annual sporting events include the **All Nigeria Lawn Tennis Open** (October) and the **International Ogbe Hard Court** in Benin City (November).

WHAT TO SEE

Lagos is a modern city built on a series of islands connected to each other and the mainland by bridges and overpasses. The **Museum of Nigerian Antiquities** has a fine collection of Nigerian art. The **National Theater** is a most modern and fascinating structure. **Tarqua Bay,** near Lagos, is a popular beach.

Ibadan, meaning "between the forest and the savannah," is the headquarters of the Yoruba tribe. About 90 miles northeast of Lagos, it is famous for its beautiful **University** and its medical school. Hotels in Ibadan are the **Premier,** Mokola Hill (from US$88 double), and the **Greensprings,** Ife Road (from US$65 double).

The museums at **Ife** (55 miles east of Ibadan) and **Benin** (150 miles east of Lagos) show the origins of bronze casting, and the Ife Museum has a very fine collection of bronze heads. The famous **Olumo Rock** in **Abeokuta,** 50 miles from Lagos, is a historic attraction.

Jos, the mining center, has a museum housing a series of terra cotta objects discovered at Nok and one of the largest zoos in Africa. The **Yankari Game Reserve,** Bauchi State, is 135 miles from Jos. Its great variety of game, facilities, including accommodations at the famed Wikki Warm Springs, restaurants, and cultural presentations are well worth the distance. Excursions and conducted tours can be arranged.

Kano, 600 miles northeast of Lagos, still heralds the arrival of its visitors with silver trumpets. A 500-year-old city founded by the Muslims, it was once the center of an active caravan trade with the Mediterranean. It has exotic markets and beautiful leatherwork. Stay in the city at the **Central Hotel,** Bompai Road (from US$70) or in the Bompai area at the **Daula Hotel** (from US$70).

A new federal capital city, 450 miles from Lagos, is being built at **Abuja,** an idyllic plateau just north of the confluence of the Niger and Benue rivers.

SOURCES OF FURTHER INFORMATION

Pan Am, 21-25 Broad Street, Lagos, and any Pan Am office around the world; **Nigerian Tourist Association,** 47 Marina, Lagos; **Consulate of Nigeria,** 575 Lexington Avenue, New York, NY 10022; **Nigerian High Commission,** 9 Northumberland Avenue, London WC2.

Senegal

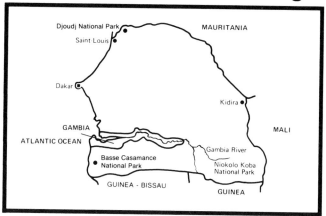

WHAT'S SPECIAL

Senegal's wonderful beaches, tropical vegetation near the coast, colorful markets, and warm weather make it a country of outdoor interests. The Western and French influence can be seen in Dakar, with its wide avenues and handsome buildings, but in the hinterland, traditional African village life continues. The economy is based on the cultivation of peanuts, which account for half of the country's agricultural production and for the livelihood of a great percentage of its population. Senegal is a friendly country that makes visitors welcome.

COUNTRY BRIEFING

Size: 76,124 square miles   **Population:** 5,000,000
Capital: Dakar   **Capital Population:** 800,000
    Climate: June-September, brings hot, dry weather. From October through May it is warm and dry, with cool nights—the best time.

Weather in Dakar: Lat N14°42'; Alt 131 ft

Temp (°F)	Jan	Feb	Mar	Apr	May	Jun	Jul	Aug	Sep	Oct	Nov	Dec
Av Low	64°	63°	64°	65°	68°	73°	76°	76°	76°	76°	73°	67°
Av High	79°	80°	80°	81°	84°	88°	88°	87°	89°	89°	86°	81°
Days no rain	31	28	31	30	31	28	24	18	19	28	29	31

Government: An independent republic.
    Language: French is the official language, Wolof, Serer, Diola, Toucouleur, Peul, and Malinke the six national ones; there are over 20 local Senegalese languages.

Religion: Muslim 90%; Christian 5%; remainder animist and other beliefs.

Currency: The CFA franc.

	CFA 50	CFA 100	CFA 500	CFA 1,000	CFA 5,000	CFA 10,000	CFA 15,000
US (dollars, cents)	.20	.40	2.01	4.03	20.13	40.26	60.39
UK (pounds, pence)	.10	.19	.96	1.92	9.60	19.20	28.81

Public Holidays:

New Year's Day, 1 Jan
Maouled
Easter Monday
Independence Day, 4 Apr
Labor Day, 1 May
Ascension Day

Whit Monday
Day of Association, 14 July
Korité
Assumption Day, 15 Aug
Tabaski
All Saints Day, 1 Nov
Christmas Day, 25 Dec

HOW TO GET THERE

Flying time to Dakar's Yoff Airport from New York is 7 hours; from London, 4¾ hours; from Monrovia, 1 hour and 50 minutes. Time in Senegal: GMT.

REQUIREMENTS FOR ENTRY AND CUSTOMS REGULATIONS

Passport, and visa obtainable from the Dakar Immigration Service (Ministry of the Interior) or from Senegal's US and European Consulates. Any group of four or more tourists with valid passports may obtain visas upon arrival at Yoff Airport; no forms or photographs necessary. Yellow fever vaccination required and antimalarial precautions advised during the rainy season June-September. Currency must be declared on arrival; there is no restriction on the amount of foreign currency allowed into or out of Senegal, except that no more may be taken out than was brought in. Antiquities considered to be part of Senegal's heritage may not be exported without a certificate from the Ministry of Culture. Duty-free allowance: 200 cigarettes or 50 cigars or 9 ounces tobacco; reasonable amounts of liquor; perfume for personal use.

AIRPORT INFORMATION

Yoff International Airport is 9 miles from the center of Dakar. Bus services operate; a taxi costs CFA1,500 to the center. There is a duty-free shop, bank, post office, rental car information counter, hotel reservations counter, and nursery. Tip porter CFA100 per bag.

ACCOMMODATIONS

There are many very pleasant hotels, some right by the beaches. Information about hotel accommodations can be obtained from the hotel reservation counter at the airport. Hotels in Dakar:
Rates are in US$ for a double/twin room with bath or shower
Croix du Sud, 20 Avenue Albert Sarraut (from $45)
De la Paix, 38 Rue de Thiers (from $30)

Indépendence, Place de l'Indépendence (from $60)
Lagon II, Route de la Corniche Est (from $60)
Massata Samb, Route de la Plage de N'Gor (from $50), on oceanfront,
10 miles from center city
Méridien (N'Gor, Diarama, and N'Gor Village) Hotels, Route de N'Gor
(from $60), on oceanfront, 10 miles from center city
Nina, 43 Rue du Dr Theze (from $50)
Pacha, 42 Avenue Lamine Gueye (from $60)
Teranga, Place de l'Indépendence (from $70)
The above hotels are centrally located unless otherwise indicated.

USEFUL INFORMATION

Banks: Open 8-11:30 and 2:30-4:30 Mon-Fri. Many smaller towns
do not have banks, so it is best to change travelers' checks in Dakar.

Mail: Stamps only at the post office. A few mailboxes on streets, or
mail letters at the post office.

Telephone Tips: Phones generally in restaurants and cafés. A local
call costs CFA40. Useful numbers in Dakar:

Pan Am 22 57 86   Airport Information 21 74 31
Senegal Tourist Office
   21 98 13 & 21 66 29

Newspapers: Foreign newspapers available.

Tipping: Usually 10%; CFA100 standard for special services.

Electricity: 110 and 220 volts 50 cycles AC.

Laundry: Fair service but expensive; 24-hour service in hotels (dry-
cleaning a suit, from CFA1, 500; laundering a shirt, from CFA300).

Hairdressing: Average cost of shampoo and set, from CFA2,000; a
man's haircut, from CFA1,200.

Photography: Film is expensive; it is best to bring your own. Black
and white takes 2 days to be developed, color 10 days.

Rest Rooms: Women—*Dames;* men—*Hommes.*

Health: Some doctors and dentists speak English. Pharmaceuticals
are expensive. Consult your doctor about an antimalarial program prior
to departure for Senegal. In general, pills are begun about two weeks
before entering a malaria zone and are taken during the visit and for
several weeks after leaving.

TRANSPORTATION

Bus tickets in Dakar cost CFA75 per fare stage. Taxis have meters and
cost CFA20 per kilometer (double from midnight to 5:30am), plus pick-
up charge of CFA70. On long trips, decide on price before leaving. There
are two main railroads—Dakar to Saint-Louis (160 miles) and Dakar to
Kidira (400 miles). Car rentals available. A passenger launch operates
between Dakar and Gorée Island.

FOOD AND RESTAURANTS

Fish, the basis of Senegalese cuisine, is always served with a spicy sauce.
The national dish is *tiébou dieune*—fish, sea snails, vegetables, rice, and

pimento. Also try *mafé* (chicken with peanut sauce); *yassa* (chicken marinated in lemon, pimento, and broiled onions); *fou fou* (fish or meat served with *gombo* sauce, *pasta,* or local couscous). Try **Le Cauri** (Rue Bourgi—tel: 22 55 59) and **Guet Ndar** (Pointe des Almadies, 10 miles from downtown) for delicious Senegalese specialties. For French cuisine, go to **Le Ramatou** (Route de N'Gor—tel: 20 03 40) and **Restaurant Le Lagon** (Route de la Petite Corniche—tel: 21 53 22). **Le Virage** (Route de N'Gor—tel: 20 06 57) has unusual fish dishes. The restaurants of the **Croix du Sud** and **N'Gor** hotels serve beautifully prepared foods, as do **Chez Raphael** (4 Rue Parent—tel: 21 27 19), **Le Rond Point** (Place de l'Indépendence—tel: 22 10 29), and **La Mandrague** (Plage de N'Gor—tel: 20 02 23). Vietnamese food is served at **La Baie d'Along** (Avenue Bourguiba—tel: 21 16 69) and **Kim Son** (Route de N'Gor—tel: 20 06 05). Dinner with wine can range from US$5 up to US$25.

ENTERTAINMENT

The **Théâtre National Daniel Sorano** is a splendid modern theater. Folklore dances are performed on Saturday nights and Sundays by local groups in the villages, at the request of travel agents. Senegalese folklore also includes wrestling matches and performances of games called *faux lion.* For enjoyable nightclubs try **L'Aristo** (55 Rue Bourgi) or **Le Mandingo** at the Hotel Teranga. Outside the city, there is **Le Timmis** at the Méridien (N'Gor) Hotel. Dakar's **Casino du Cap Vert** is also on the Route de N'Gor. Other places to try include **La Wahoo** at the N'Gor Village, **Le Sahel** at Place Sahm-Priba, **Le Jandeer** at Soumbedioune Artisan Village, and **L'Aldo** at the Indépendence Hotel.

SHOPPING

Stores open 8:30-12 and 3-6:30 Mon-Fri. One of the most worthwhile spots for shopping in Dakar is the artisan village of **Soumbedioune**—weavers, jewelers, sculptors, leather workers, and shoemakers sell their fabrics, jewelry, art, and musical instruments at reasonable prices. You can bargain in the markets. For wonderful African dress materials, pottery, masks, and carvings there are many good shopping streets around the Place de l'Indépendence, Avenue Roume, Avenue William Ponty, Avenue Albert-Sarrault, the **Kermel Market** in Place Kermel, the **Sandaga Market,** Avenue Lamine Guèye, and the **Tilene Market,** Avenue Blaise Diagne, in the Medina quarter.

SPORTS

Outdoor sports abound, and many clubs welcome visitors—tennis (**Sporting Club**—tel: 21 36 73); golf (**Golf Club de Cambérène**—tel: 22 40 69); sailing (**Cercle de la Voile de Dakar**—tel: 21 07 20); water-skiing (**Ski Nautique au Lagon**—tel: 21 53 22); horseback riding (**Cercle de l'Etrier**—tel: 21 52 63). Hunting allowed from December to May, and you must have a license. Air Afrique organizes expeditions to the **Maka Diama Hunting Reserve,** 20 miles from Saint-Louis; cost is CFA21,000 for one day, or CFA12,000 for a half day. There are many fine beaches, but be careful of the current—swim only when others are around. You can go on fishing expeditions, craft and crew supplied, for a full day for CFA40,000 for four persons, half day at CFA32,000 (**Centre de Pêche Sportive de Dakar**—tel: 21 28 58).

WHAT TO SEE

Apart from the markets, a comprehensive range of African crafts can be seen at the **IFAN Museum** (Fundamental Institute of Black Africa), Place Tascher, opens 8-12 and 2:30-7, closed Mondays and public holidays. The **Musée Dynamique**, Corniche de Fann, has modern art exhibitions. See the basalt cliffs at **Cape Manuel** and the colorful park and zoo at **Hann.**

Bus tours go to **Cape Almadies,** the westernmost point in Africa, with its old fort, oyster beds, and lobster reserves. Take a ferry to the island of **Gorée,** lying 1½ miles offshore from Dakar, where you can see the **House of Slaves** from which the Africans were put on ships to go to the Americas. The **Historical and Oceanographic Museums** are also interesting.

The town of **Saint Louis,** 160 miles from Dakar, was formerly the capital of Senegal and Mauritania. From the fishing quarter each morning you can see 400 to 500 fishing boats cross the bar to fish off shore. Later visit the fisherman's cemetery, where the tombs are surrounded by fishing nets; the **IFAN Museum** and the picturesque market are worth seeing. Some 30 miles north of Saint-Louis, **Djoudj National Park** is a bird sanctuary where there are crested cranes, flamingoes, storks, and pelicans in abundance.

Niokolo-Koba National Park, 2,315 square miles of Senegal's southeast corner, has lions, elephants, hippos, water buffalo, and the Derby eland, the largest antelope in the world. **Basse Casamance National Park,** in the south below the Gambia River, is a forest park, but there are birds and animals, especially monkeys, there, too.

Also of interest are the plantations of **Sangalkam** and the fishing village of **Cayar.** Try to visit the latter at 4pm when the boats return. **Joal,** about 60 miles south of Dakar, is 15th-century Portuguese port with many old houses.

SOURCES OF FURTHER INFORMATION

Pan Am, 2 Place de l'Indépendence, Dakar; and any Pan Am office around the world; **Direction de la Promotion Touristique,** PO Box 4049, Dakar; the **Senegal Government Tourist Bureau,** Pan Am Building, 200 Park Avenue, New York, NY 10017; **Embassy of the Senegal Republic,** 11 Phillimore Gardens, London W8.

Seychelles

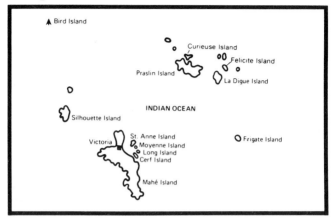

WHAT'S SPECIAL

The 92 Seychelles Islands, having survived relatively undisturbed for the past 600 million years, have recently become one of the most fashionable places to visit. These islands lie in the western Indian Ocean, 575 miles northeast of Madagascar and 1,000 miles due east of Mombasa, Kenya. Hotels have been built on the major islands, particularly on Mahé, and a tourist's life there becomes more comfortable every day. The islands are particularly noted for their wide variety of flora and fauna.

COUNTRY BRIEFING

The area of the archipelago is about 171 square miles, and the **population** 62,000. The **capital** is Victoria, on the island of Mahé. The **climate** is pleasant, with only slight variations from 75-90°. June-August is coolest; March-May is the northwest monsoon season and May-October the southeast; the humidity is always high and at times can be uncomfortable. The Seychelles were a crown colony within the British Commonwealth and became independent in 1976. The **language** is English (but French and Creole are widely spoken), the **religion** basically Roman Catholic, and the **currency** the rupee (Rs6.65 = US$1). **Public holidays** are: New Year's, 1 and 2 Jan; Good Friday; Easter Monday; Labor Day, 1 May; Corpus Christi Day; Independence Day, 29 June; Assumption Day, 15 August; All Saints Day, 1 Nov; Immaculate Conception, 8 Dec; Christmas, 25 Dec.

HOW TO GET THERE

Flying time to Seychelles' Mahé Airport from New York is 19½ hours; from Rome, 11½ hours; from Nairobi, 3 hours. Time in Seychelles: GMT+4.

REQUIREMENTS FOR ENTRY AND CUSTOMS REGULATIONS

Passport and current certificate of inoculation against cholera and yellow-fever necessary if traveling from an infected area. A visa is not required. All visitors receive a Visitors Pass on arrival valid for a 1-month stay and renewable. A round-trip ticket is usually necessary, and a visitor who does not have one may be asked to deposit an amount equivalent to the price of a return ticket with the Principal Immigration Officer. No restrictions on bringing in or taking out foreign currencies, nor are there any currency controls. It is forbidden to import firearms or spear-fishing guns. Personal effects may have to be declared, and radios, particularly, are sometimes liable for duty. Radios for personal use must be declared to avoid duty and then re-exported at the end of the visit. Duty-free allowance: 200 cigarettes or 50 cigars or ½ pound tobacco; 1 liter liquor and 1 liter wine; 125 cc perfume, ¼ liter toilet water.

AIRPORT INFORMATION

Seychelles International Airport is at Pointe la Rue, about 7 miles south of Victoria on the east coast of Mahé. Buses offer inexpensive transportation to all parts of Mahé, which is some 17 miles long and 5 miles wide. One can travel into Victoria by taxi, bus, or camion (basically a truck with wooden seats). Taxi fare is Rs10 for the first mile and Rs5 for each additional mile. Coach transfer services run by tour operators cost about Rs50-70 per person between the airport and hotels. Although efforts will be made to find accommodations should you arrive without hotel bookings, it is likely you will be put on the next outgoing flight if nothing can easily be found. There is a duty-free shop with adequate stock. There is a departure tax of Rs100.

ACCOMMODATIONS

There are large and small resort hotels, guesthouses, and holiday apartments. The Tourism Division (PO Box 56, Victoria, Mahé) can supply a list of accommodations but there is no accommodation service—you must reserve a room well in advance and confirm your reservation with a deposit. A service charge of 10% is added to hotel bills. Hotels on Mahé:
Rates are in US$ for a double/twin room with bath or shower

Barbarons Beach, Barbarons (from $100)
Beau Vallon Bay, Beau Vallon (from $88)
Coral Strand, Beau Vallon (from $76)
Fisherman's Cove, Bel Ombre (from $110)
Mahé Beach, Port Glaud (from $80)
Northolme, Glacis (from $85)

Reef, Anse aux Pins (from $85)
Residence Danzilles, on sea (from $53)

USEFUL INFORMATION

There is a Standard Bank and a Barclays Bank in Victoria, as well as Barclays Bank branches in La Misere on Mahé and in Grand Anse on Praslin. Banks are usually open from 8:30-1 Mon-Fri; some are open later in the day and on Saturday mornings. The Central **Post Office** in Victoria is open 8-12 and 1-4 Mon-Fri, and 8-12 Saturday. Generally no **phone booths,** but there are phones in hotels. **Tipping:** porters Rs1 per bag; waiters 10%; hairdressers Rs2-3; taxi drivers optional unless they have served as sightseeing guides. **Electricity** is 240 volts AC. **Laundry** and dry-cleaning services in large new hotels and in Victoria—with some degree of risk. **Film** and photographic equipment available; Kodak film can be processed in Mahé, but others are sent to Nairobi. **Babysitting** services at all hotels. No public **rest rooms. Doctors** and **dentists** speak English.

TRANSPORTATION

On **Mahé** there are buses to the rural districts, and taxis. Cars can also be rented from Rs200 per day or Rs1,200 per week with unlimited mileage. A taxi can be hired for about Rs60 per hour; the rate is negotiable. There are roads covering about 100 miles of Mahé. Travel to **Praslin** and **La Digue** is by ferry, which leaves Victoria at 8am every Mon, Wed, and Fri and returns in the evening; first-class round trip is Rs135. An air-conditioned boat, *La Belle Coralline,* does the same trip for Rs200 at 7:45am Tuesdays and Thursdays. Local tour operators run regular excursions to these and other islands. There is air service from Mahé to Praslin, Bird, and Denis islands.

FOOD AND RESTAURANTS

The large new hotels on Mahé aim for a European or international standard. Local fruits and vegetables are good, and the islanders excel at Creole cooking and curries. The best of the "local" restaurants are unlisted, but the tourist office at the airport or in Victoria will assist you. Most hotels try to include one local dish in the menu, and the weekly Creole buffet dinner at the **Mahé Beach** is excellent. The **Corsaire Restaurant** (Bel Ombre Point) and the **Fisherman's Cove** both have interesting food. **Julian's Bar** at Anse à la Mouche is one restaurant serving Creole food exclusively. **La Marmite,** Victoria, also specializes in local Creole dishes. **Penelope's** at Beau Vallon serves French and Creole food. You might also like to visit the **Bougainville Hotel** and the **Mandarin** restaurants. Because much of the food on the island is imported, prices of European menus tend to be high.

DRINKING TIPS

The Seychelles have a brewery, where they produce *Seybrew,* a lager that costs about Rs7 a bottle in most hotels. The locals also drink what they call a "toddy," which tastes rather like ginger ale and is sometimes mixed with Guinness (stout). Imported beers are expensive. British gin and whisky cost about Rs12 per drink in hotels.

ENTERTAINMENT

Entertainment on the islands is scarce and not very elaborate. Movies are shown nightly in the **Olian Cinema** in Victoria. There is no theater or concert hall, but most of the larger hotels have bars and nightclubs offering dancing, folk dancing, barbecues, and shows. Worth a visit are the **Takamaka** discothèque at the Coral Strand Hotel, and the **Tonic** at Glacis. For other events, it is best to check *The Nation*.

SHOPPING

Facilities are limited. The **Home Industries** shop in Victoria is part of a government cooperative selling handicrafts, and there is a market outside the building on most days. There are many handicrafts made from coconuts, raffia, land coral, and tortoiseshell (which cannot be brought into the US since tortoise is an endangered species) as well as woven articles. The **Oceana Crafts** boutique turns out tie-dye and block prints, sarongs, and T-shirts. Otherwise shopping is done in the local supermarkets. Locally grown and prepared spices such as pepper, nutmeg, and vanilla are usually souvenirs.

SPORTS

Soccer is the national game, and there are matches each week at the **People's Stadium** in Victoria. There are badminton and squash clubs, a cricket club, and an athletic association. The **Reef Hotel** has a nine-hole golf course, open to all. The **Béolière Club** on the west coast has minigolf. There is swimming, boating, water-skiing, snorkeling, and surfing. It is best to check with the tourist authority about swimming and skindiving in some of the deserted bays around the Victoria coast (or see the warning signs), as the currents can be very strong. The **Marine Charter Association** arranges big-game fishing. There is a **Yacht Club** in Victoria. There are now very good opportunities for scuba-diving; all tour operators rent equipment; lessons are given by the **Seychelles Underwater Center** and by **Tecnosub**. Major hotels have tennis courts.

WHAT TO SEE

Mahé, the largest and most populated of the islands, has many features to recommend it. Most of the island is surrounded by coral reefs, and the warm, sparkling blue water is safe for swimming. A car is almost a necessity for exploring, as the coastal roads weave through some of the most exciting coastal scenery in the world. Particularly noteworthy is the drive over the hills to **Grand Anse** and the coastal trip south from Victoria, the only town. Also near Victoria is **Beau Vallon,** one of the best beaches. Victoria has a museum, **Botanical Gardens,** with an orchid garden, and **State House,** a large colonial edifice with sweeping green lawns and expansive verandas.

SEYCHELLES

The Seychelles are the home of numerous rare birds; big game fish are plentiful in deeper waters, and the coral reefs and submerged plateau offer some of the world's most colorful underwater scenery.

Praslin, the second largest of the islands, can be reached by either boat or plane. Although the island is only 21 miles from Mahé, the boat journey takes about 2½ hours, so it may be advisable to consider staying on Praslin a few days. In the center of Praslin is the **Vallée de Mai,** where you can see the coco-de-mer palm, which produces fruit weighing up to 40 pounds. Hotels in Praslin are **Château des Feuilles,** Pointe Cabris (from US$120 double MAP), **Paradise Hotel,** Côte d'Or (from US$80 double MAP), **Indian Ocean Fishing Club,** Grand Anse Beach (from US$40 double), and **The Flying Dutchman,** Grand Anse (from US$55 double).

La Digue, the next island out, with a population of about 2,000, is about ¾ hour by boat from Praslin. You will see coconut palms, ox carts, pigs, and chickens. Hotels in La Digue: **Gregoires,** Anse Réunion (from US$87 double MAP); **Cabane des Anges,** Anse Réunion (from US$65 double MAP).

Bird Island, 7½ hours from Mahé by boat or 30 minutes by air, is a small, palm-studded island surrounded by white sand and clear water. It is the site of a rookery for thousands of sooty, noddy, and fairy terns, has an excellent open-air restaurant and small overnight bungalows. One-day flying excursions from Mahé are possible and some hotels have a reciprocal agreement so that one night on Bird Island can be substituted for a night on Mahé.

SOURCES OF FURTHER INFORMATION

Any **Pan Am** office around the world; **Tourism Division,** PO Box 56, Victoria, Mahé; **Permanent Mission of the Republic of Seychelles to the United Nations,** 820 Second Avenue, Suite 203, New York, NY 10017.

South Africa

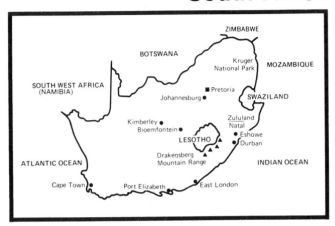

WHAT'S SPECIAL

South Africa is a land of year-round sunshine and good beaches, unbeatable fresh food (particularly the fruit), game reserves, and buildings ranging from contemporary through Edwardian baroque to Flemish Renaissance. The theaters and movie houses have local and imported plays and movies—occasionally censored—and there is much activity in ballet and concerts.

COUNTRY BRIEFING

Size: 471,445 square miles   **Population:** 21,794,000
Capital: **Capital Population:**

   Pretoria   (administrative)   543,950 (Pretoria)
   Cape Town (legislative)   691,296 (Cape Town)

   Climate: No extremes. It is generally sunny and temperate, and the number of hours of sunshine is among the highest in the world. Winters are generally mild, although there is snow on the mountain ranges in the Cape Town and Natal areas during the winter months. May-August is about the best time to travel, and June-September the best time to see Kruger National Park. December-February is the best time to enjoy a Mediterranean summer in Cape Town.

Weather in Cape Town: Lat S33°54′; Alt 56 ft

Temp (°F)	Jan	Feb	Mar	Apr	May	Jun	Jul	Aug	Sep	Oct	Nov	Dec
Av Low	60°	60°	58°	53°	49°	41°	45°	46°	49°	52°	55°	58°
Av High	78°	79°	77°	72°	67°	65°	63°	64°	65°	70°	73°	76°
Days no rain	28	26	28	24	17	19	18	18	23	26	27	28

Government: A republic.

Languages: Two official languages—Afrikaans and English.

Religion: Dutch Reformed Church, Church of England, Roman Catholic, and other Protestant denominations.

Currency: Rand. 100 cents = R1.

	1¢	10¢	20¢	50¢	R1	R10	R20	R40
US (dollars, cents)	.01	.12	.24	.59	1.19	11.85	23.70	47.40
UK (pounds, pence)	—	.06	.11	.28	.57	5.66	11.33	22.65

Public Holidays:

New Year's Day, 1 Jan

Good Friday

Easter Monday

Ascension Day

Republic Day, 31 May

Settler's Day, 1st Monday in Sep

Kruger Day, 10 Oct

Day of the Vow, 16 Dec

Christmas Day, 25 Dec

Family Day, 26 Dec

HOW TO GET THERE

Flying time to Johannesburg's Jan Smuts Airport from New York is 16 hours; from Rio, 8 hours; from Rome, 10¼ hours. Time in South Africa: GMT+2.

REQUIREMENTS FOR ENTRY AND CUSTOMS REGULATIONS

Passport and round-trip ticket necessary. Visitors who do not have a round-trip ticket may be required to make a cash deposit up to R1,000, refunded upon departure. Visas are necessary for citizens of the United States and of most other countries. Yellow-fever and cholera vaccinations are required if coming from an infected area. Foreign currency should be declared on entering; the amount of currency taken out is restricted to the amount taken in. The amount of South African currency taken into or out of South Africa is restricted to R200. It is best to reconvert all local currency before leaving. Permits are necessary for firearms brought into the country and are issued at the point of entry. Duty-free allowance: 400 cigarettes, or 50 cigars or 250 grams tobacco; 1 liter liquor, 1 liter wine, 300 milliliters perfume, and other articles up to the value of R80. Used cameras, radios, binoculars, tape recorders, typewriters, camping and sporting equipment also duty free. Some magazines and books are banned in South Africa.

AIRPORT INFORMATION

Jan Smuts International Airport, the major airport, is 10 miles from the center of Johannesburg. There is a bus from the airport to the downtown terminal which operates daily from 6am to 11pm, or whenever there is an incoming or outgoing international flight. The bus fare is R1.80 for adults, 90 cents for children, and there is no extra charge for luggage. Taxis are available at all times; the fare from the airport to the town center is about R15. SAA has connecting flights between Jan Smuts International Airport and the internal airports in all main cities and towns. No arrival or departure tax. Duty-free shop and hotel reservation counter. Porters are tipped 20 cents per piece of luggage.

ACCOMMODATIONS

Special accommodations available include the excellent caravan and camping parks and the rest camps in the Drakensberg mountains and in the various game reserves (including Kruger National Park). For inexpensive accommodations, there are one-star hotels in most towns and youth hostels. A list of the latter is available from the **South African Youth Hostels Association,** National Secretary, PO Box 4402, Cape Town 8000, or from any **South African Tourist Corporation (Satour)** office. Very few student accommodations. Information about hotels may be obtained from the Visitors' or Publicity Bureaus in the different city centers. There is also a hotel guide available from Satour listing all hotels, motels, game park rest camps, caravan and camping sites, beach cottages, holiday flats, and bungalows. Hotel rates are lower out-of-season (Feb-Mar, May, Aug-Sep). See regional centers for hotel accommodations.

USEFUL INFORMATION

Banks: Open 9-3:30 Mon-Fri (Wed 9-1); Sat 9-11.

Mail: Stamps available only from post offices.

Telephone Tips: Phone booths are in hotels, restaurants, and cafés. Useful numbers:

Pan Am	**Operator Service**
Cape Town 43-7992	Johannesburg 0020
Johannesburg 21-9391	Pretoria 0020
Pretoria 27059	**Directory Enquiries**
Airport Information 975-0183	Pretoria 1025
National Tourist Bureau	**Time,** Johannesburg 1023
Johannesburg 21-5241	Pretoria 1025
Pretoria 48-6531	Cape Town 1025
Johannesburg Hospital	**Johannesburg Ambulance**
643-0111	35-4141
Capetown Hospital 47-3311	**Capetown Ambulance**
	51-5151

Newspapers: English-language newspapers available. Local English-language publications are *The Star, The Rand Daily Mail, The Citizen,* and the *Sunday Times* in Johannesburg; the *Cape Times* and *Cape Argus* (Cape Town), *The Friend* (Bloemfontein), and *The Natal Mercury* and *The Natal Daily News* (Durban).

Tipping: 10% is more than adequate. Usually there is a 10% service charge included on checks. Tip a bit extra if service has been exceptionally good. Porter (per piece of luggage) 50 cents; taxi drivers 10%; hotel porter 50 cents; chambermaid at your discretion; cloakroom attendants 20 cents; gas pump attendants 20 cents.

Electricity: 220-230 volts 50 cycles AC (Pretoria 250 volts).

Laundry: Dry-cleaning services available throughout the country in all but the smallest towns, and laundromats are becoming popular. Hotels have good express services (dry-cleaning a suit, from R2.80, laundering a shirt from 60 cents).

Hairdressing: Salons are good, particularly at major hotels. Tipping not necessary (shampoo and set from R6.75; man's haircut from R5).

Photography: Good equipment, black and white and color film available in major cities. Black and white film, 35mm, 36 exposures, R10; color film, 35mm, 36 exposures, R20, inclusive of processing. Color film takes 3 days; black and white 2-5 days.

Clubs: Rotary, Lions, Jaycees, Round Table.

Babysitting: Arranged through hotels. Also by university students; contact the universities in Cape Town, Johannesburg, Pretoria, Durban, and Pietermaritzburg.

Rest Rooms: In town centers, restaurants, hotels, and railroad stations. Women, *Dames;* Men, *Here.*

Health: Doctors and dentists speak English. Imported pharmaceuticals available, not necessarily expensive. Water safe to drink in towns, but not from inland rivers. Many rivers and lakes are not suitable for bathing, as they may be contaminated with bilharzia. Precautions against malaria are advisable in the Kruger National Park and Hluhluwe Game Reserve.

TRANSPORTATION

Buses and taxis are the only services available within the cities. Taxis do not cruise; phone or go to a stand. Rates vary from city to city but are usually 70 cents initially, going up in units of 60 cents per kilometer and R5 per hour waiting time. It is possible to rent a car from US$13 per day, plus a charge ranging from approximately US13 cents per kilometer. A chauffeur-driven car will cost about US$58 per day. Drive on the left; maximum speed in open spaces is 90 km per hour. An international driver's license is necessary, but US visitors may use their state licenses if in South Africa on a temporary basis. Gas stations open from 6am-6pm Mon-Fri, 6am-noon Sat, closed Sun. Petrol permits allow visitors to obtain gas at any time from emergency filling stations; they can be obtained at any magistrate's office—in Johannesburg at 1023 Magistrate's Court, Main and West Streets. The railroad service is excellent. All major towns are served by rail links. South African Railways operate bus tours all over the country. Internal airlines are SAA, Magnum, Air Services, Border Air, United Air, and Namaqualand Air Services. SAA flies from Johannesburg to Cape Town, Durban, Port Elizabeth, East London, Bloemfontein, Kimberley, and Maseru.

FOOD AND RESTAURANTS

Eating is usually good. Except for a few specialties, there is a choice of good, plain food, or the fairly standard international fare available almost everywhere. The cuisine in restaurants is basically European, employing local meat, vegetables, and seafood. To some extent this is indicative of the country's Dutch and English origins, although some of the dishes are influenced by Asian cooking. The range of seafood is fairly extensive—such as lobster tails, Cape salmon, and oysters. It is worth sampling the venison—either kudu, springbok, or blesbok—and you might try *bobotie* (curried ground meat), *biltong* (dried meat), or *sosaties* (kebab). *Putu,* cornmeal, is served with meat and sometimes cooked on a *braaivleis* (a popular South African tradition equivalent to a barbecue). In addition, many good and inexpensive wines are produced in the Cape province. Standard eating hours in larger restaurants or hotels are 7-9am, 12-2, and 7-9. A meal in an expensive restaurant will cost from US$25 per person; in a medium-priced one from US$15, and in an inexpensive one from US$8. Look for inexpensive eating places in **Hillbrow,** Johannesburg, **Seapoint,** Cape Town, and **Sunnyside,** Pretoria. For recommended restaurants see listing under various cities.

DRINKING TIPS

Van der Hum is a tangerine-flavored and brandy-based liqueur; beer is also popular, and Castle and Lion are two good lagers. *Hansa* beer is a specialty imported from South West Africa, where it was first brewed by German settlers. South African sherries and brandies are well known, and the wines are good as well. A bottle of good wine, *Delheim* or *Nederburg,* will cost about R2.50 per bottle; the average price of a whisky and soda will be about 50 cents. Sale of liquor is restricted on Sundays and religious public holidays. Bars are open at different times, varying from province to province, but generally 10am-11:30pm. Women are not normally allowed in bars, but there are a number of hotels with bars which admit women. Liquor stores close from 1pm Saturday until 9am Monday, and it is necessary to make weekend purchases before the shops close.

ENTERTAINMENT

You can choose from theater, ballet, movies, symphony concerts, and occasionally, opera. As South Africans go out on weekends, particularly Saturdays, it is wise to reserve in advance for Friday or Saturday night activities. Nearly everything is closed on Sunday, including movie theaters. Better-known theaters in the country are **Nico Malan Opera House** (Foreshore, Cape Town); **Civic Center** (Braamfontein, Johannesburg); **H B Thom Theater** (University of Stellenbosch, Cape Town), and **The Baxter** (Rondebosch, Cape Town). There are annually two seasons of both opera and ballet. One of the most exciting theatrical ventures is the **Maynardville Open Air Theater** in Cape Town, which has a season in January-February. **The Symphony Concert** seasons vary from city to city, and there are concerts at 1pm on Thursdays at the **Johannesburg City Hall.** There are a number of nightclubs; try **Ciro's Nightclub** (45 Kruis Street, Johannesburg); **Top of the Carlton** (Carlton Hotel, Johannesburg); **La Bohème** (Volkskas Building, Pretoria); **Blaises Bistro** (22nd Floor, Sanlam Building, Cape Town); **Vineyard** (Newlands—7 miles from Cape Town); **Lanzerac** (Stellenbosch, 36 miles from Cape Town). Many nightclubs in South Africa do not have liquor licenses, and patrons must "bring your own." Nightclubs cannot serve liquor after midnight on Saturday.

SHOPPING

Stores open 8:30-5 Mon-Fri; 8:30-12:45 Sat. Native art work (Bantu wood carvings, pottery, and beadwork), gold and silver jewelry, dolls, leather or skin goods, or clay figures are good buys. **Cape Town** is a good place to buy antiques and objects of historical interest. Some of the more interesting shopping areas include the **Fruit and Flower** and **Flea Markets** on the Parade in Cape Town, and **Adderley Street,** also in Cape Town. Stores are **Greaterman's,** Pritchard Street, Johannesburg, and **Stuttaford's,** Adderley Street, Cape Town; **John Orr's,** Eloff Street, Johannesburg; **Garlick's,** Carlton Center, Johannesburg, Adderley Street, Cape Town, and in Church Street, Pretoria; **Ivy's Curios** in Johannesburg, Durban, and Cape Town; **Lilliput's Toy Shop** in Johannesburg and Pretoria (Polley's Arcade); **Goodman's Gallery** and **Everard Read Gallery,** Johannesburg; **Jack Lemkus Sports** in Pretoria and Cape Town; **Binnehuis** in Cape Town and Stellenbosch.

SPORTS

The most popular spectator sports are soccer, rugby, cricket, and horse racing, although baseball is gaining in popularity. All sports are racially segregated. There is also auto racing, tennis, golf, horseback riding, swimming, and freshwater and deep-sea fishing, limited hunting, hiking, and mountain climbing. Useful addresses in Cape Town for sports activities: **Western Province Golf Union,** Scotts Building, Cape Town (tel: 41-0381); **Atlantic Underwater Club,** Bay Road, Cape Town (tel: 49-7147); **Royal Cape Yacht Club,** Duncan Road, Duncan Docks (tel: 21-1354); and **The Mountain Club of South Africa,** 97 Hatfield Street, Cape Town (tel: 45-3412).

WHAT TO SEE

Pretoria: South Africa's administrative capital, Pretoria is 36 miles from Johannesburg and is the country's fourth-largest city. Pretoria is quiet; it has more than 300 miles of streets lined with jacaranda trees, which bloom in October and give the whole city a purplish appearance. It is one of South Africa's oldest cities, and, in places like **Paul Kruger's House** (Church Street West), it is possible to trace many links with the old Transvaal Republic. The current center of administrative facilities is in the **Union Buildings,** which overlook the city from Meinjieskop. Also see the **Voortrekker Monument,** dedicated to the pioneers of the north, the **Pretoria Art Museum** (Park Street, Arcadia), with its fine collection of African works, and the **Melrose House** (Jacob Maré Street, opposite Burgers Park), where the Boer War peace treaty was signed in 1902. The **Visitors' Information Bureau** is in the Munitoria Building, corner Vermeulen and Van der Walt Streets (tel: 41-2461) and is open on weekdays and Saturday mornings. Two excellent restaurants to try are **Restaurant Elite** (Fran Du Toit Building, Paul Kruger Street), expensive, and **La Provence** (Schoeman Street), medium. Hotels in Pretoria: **Boulevard,** 186 Struben Street (from US$47 double BB), **Burgerspark,** Minnaar and Van der Walt Streets (from US$32 double), **Continental,** 152 Visagie

Street (from US$43 double BB), and **New Union,** 572 Church Street (from US$52 double BB).

Johannesburg has evolved in less than a century from a small mining camp into a large and thriving city. Its gold fields have produced a bit more than a thousand million ounces of gold, or one-third of the gold mined worldwide since the Middle Ages. This, plus the golden-colored piles of sand or "mine dumps" left after the extraction of the metal from rock, give the city its nickname—the Golden City. Half-day tours of the surface workings of a mine are possible on Wednesday or Friday mornings at a charge of R4. Apply at least two weeks in advance to the Public Relations Adviser, Chamber of Mines of South Africa, PO Box 809, Johannesburg 2000. Tours of the historic **Simmer and Jack Gold Mine** take place at 8:30am weekdays and include both the underground and surface workings; charge R10. Reserve 1 day in advance by contacting Simmer and Jack Gold Mine, PO Box 192, Germiston 1400 (tel: 51-8571). At the **Hall of South African Achievement,** on the eighth floor of the Johannesburg Stock Exchange, Diagonal Street (tel: 833-6580), there is an exhibition of the mining and industrial wealth of the country. The **Mining Museum,** depicting gold mining at the turn of the century, is at Crown Mines near the Johannesburg city center. A shaft system is in operation. There is a restaurant and African tribal dancing is staged every Sunday (tel: 35-8711). Other museums include the **Africana Museum** (in the Public Library building), the **Geological Museum** (also in the Public Library), the **Railway Museum** (in the railroad station grounds under the Johann Rissik Bridge), and the **Planetarium. The Art Gallery,** designed by Sir Edwin Lutyens, has one of the best collections of paintings in South Africa, among them works by Pissarro, Bonnard, Sisley, and a number of English Pre-Raphaelite painters. The **Jan Smuts House** at University of the Witwatersrand, Braamfontein, is a memorial to Field Marshal Jan Christiaan Smuts. The 882-foot **J. G. Strijdom Post Office Tower** (the tallest building in Africa) and the 772-foot **Brixton Tower** on Brixton Ridge provide panoramic views of the city. The **Transvaal Snake Park,** at Halfway House, has about 1,000 snakes from all over the world. The **Zoological Gardens** are in **Hermann Eckstein Park** along with a restaurant, a swimming pool, and boating on the zoo lake. **The Wilds,** a reserve for South African flora, has been called the most attractive park in Johannesburg. Some restaurants here include **Bougainvilia,** Rosebank (expensive); **Three Ships,** Carlton Hotel (French, expensive); **Three Vikings,** 61 Marshall Street (Danish, expensive); **Pot Luck,** Melle and Smit Streets (expensive); **Colony,** Hyde Park Hotel (medium); and the **East African Pavilion,** 256 Bree Street (Indian, inexpensive). Hotels in Johannesburg:

Rates are in US$ for a double/twin room with bath or shower

    Carlton, Main Street (from $87)

    Casa Mia, 37 Soper Road, Berea (from $43 BB)

    Crest, 7 Abel Road, Berea (from $35 BB)

    Dawson's, 117 President Street (from $35 BB)

    Holiday Inn, Jan Smuts International Airport (from $40)

Landdrost, 88 Plein Street (from $78)

Milpark Holiday Inn, Owl Street and Empire Road (from $54)

Moulin Rouge, Claim Street, Hillbrow (from $51 BB)

President, Eloff and Plein Streets (from $58)

Quirinale, 27 Kotze Street, Hillbrow (from $41 BB)

Rand International, 290 Bree Street (from $64)

Skyline, 27 Pretoria Street, Hillbrow (from $34 BB)

Southern Sun's Airport Hotel, Jan Smuts International Airport (from $57)

Sunnyside Park, 2 York Road, Parktown (from $50)

Towers, Kerk Street (from $65)

Victoria, 25 Plein Street (from $32)

With the exception of hotels at Jan Smuts International Airport, the above are all located in central Johannesburg.

South Africa's most modern and spectacular hotel/resort is **Sun City,** 167 kilometers from Johannesburg in Bophutha Tswana. Gambling is not permitted publicly in South Africa, except for horse racing, but there are no restrictions in Bophutha Tswana. Sun City has a casino, Las Vegas-type entertainment, and all resort facilities. Double rooms are from US$68.

Kimberley is synonymous with diamonds, first discovered there in 1871. A visit to the **De Beers Recovery Plant** where the diamond washing process takes place can be arranged through the De Beers Head Office at 36 Stockdale Street. It is possible to see the "Big Hole"—360 feet deep and nearly a mile in circumference—where 14,500,000 carats of diamonds have been found. Nearby is the **Kimberley Open Mine Museum,** open daily 8-6. The **William Humphreys Art Gallery** includes a collection of antiques (open weekdays 10-1 and 2:30-5:30; Saturdays 10-1; Sundays 2:30-5:30). Hotels in Kimberley: **Kimberley Grand,** 120 Old Dutoitspan Road (from US$43 double BB); and the **Savoy,** De Beers Road (from US$52 double BB).

Cape Town: The Cape Province is the largest in South Africa, and Cape Town dates back to 1652. Of interest are its valleys, beaches, high mountains, harbors, the naval base, fishing villages, and vineyards. The **Castle of Good Hope** dates back to 1666 and is the oldest building in South Africa. The **State Rooms** have a lovely collection of furniture and art objects, and the **Military Museum** is also in the building, which was the residence of early Cape governors. There are tours of the premises at 10, 11, and 12am, and at 2, 3, and 4pm. Among buildings in the Cape Dutch style are **Koopmans De Wet House** (1701), 35 Strand Street; **The Old Town House** (1755), with a great collection of 17th-century Dutch and Flemish masters which includes Frans Hals' *Portrait of a Woman;* **Rust en Vreugd** (1777) on Buitenhant Street; **The Groote Kerk** (clock tower dates from 1703) on Adderley Street; and the **Old Supreme Court. Government Avenue,** which looks onto the **Houses of Parliament,** the **Public Library,** the **Municipal Botanical Gardens,** the **National Gallery,** and the **South African Museum,** is planted with oak trees dating from the 17th century. It is also possible to visit the **Houses of Parliament** (July-December, Mon-Fri, 9:30-noon and 2-3) on application to the chief messenger. The **South African Museum** has Bushmen exhibits. The **Kirstenbosch Botanical Gardens** are also worth visiting. Good restaurants include **Ascot Grill**, Arthur's Seat Hotel; **Cafe Royal**, Church Street; **Constantia Nek**, Constantia, 10 miles from town; **Harbour Cafe**, within the harbor area; **Ons Huis**, Bloubergstrand; **Kronendal**, Hout Bay; **Lanzerac**, Stellenbosch; **Nelson's Eye**, 9 Hof Street, Gardens; **La Perla**, Beach Road, Seapoint; and **De Chavonnes**, in the President Hotel at Sea Point. Among Cape Peninsula sights is **Table Mountain**, with a 4,000-feet cable car journey up to the observation deck, depending on the weather; it is best to call the Visitors' Bureau (43-4811) to see if the cars are running. The **Marine Drive** takes in the entire coastline from Cape Town to Cape Point along both sides and includes the **Cape of Good Hope Nature Reserve**, which covers the whole of the southern tip of the peninsula. The **Zoopark**, in Tygerberg (20 miles north of the city), is Cape Town's new zoo. Hotels in Cape Town:

Rates are in US$ for a double/twin room with bath or shower

    Arthur's Seat, Arthur's Road, Sea Point (from $52 BB)

    Capetonian, Pier Place (from $59)

    Claridges, 47 Main Road, Green Point (from $50 BB)

    De Waal, Mill Street (from $62)

    Eastern Boulevard Holiday Inn, Coronation and Melbourne Roads, (from $56)

    Elizabeth, Beach Road, Sea Point (from $50 BB)

    Heerengracht, St George's Street (from $83)

    Mount Nelson, Orange Street (from $72)

    Newlands, Main Road, Newlands (from $62)

    President, Beach Road, Sea Point (from $98)

    Town House, Corporation Street (from $42)

Sea Point, Green Point, and Newlands are each 5-10 minutes by taxi from downtown Cape Town.

    Durban, on the east coast, is a year-round sun-soaked resort and provides some of the best South Africa has to offer in the pleasure department. The north and south beaches, with the **Marine Parade** (where most of the great hotels are located), provide good surfing, and there are cafés, amusement parks, theaters, and swimming pools. The **Centenary Aquarium** is on the beach at the foot of West Street and has more than 1,000 fish fed twice a day by a scuba diver. The **Snake Park** houses venomous species from all over the world and is one of the largest producers of snake-bite serum in southern Africa. On the first Saturday in July is the **Durban July Handicap**, a great social highspot. Also notable is the **Shembe Festival** taking place before the full moon near the end of July, usually over a weekend near the 25th. The **Visitors' Information Bureau** in Durban is at the Church House, Church Street (tel: 32-6421). A few hours' drive from Durban is the beautiful **Royal Natal National Park**. In addition to flora and fauna there is excellent swimming, riding, and superb scenery. Restaurants in Durban include those in the Edward, Maharani, and Elangeni hotels (luxury).

Hotels in Durban:

Rates are in US$ for a double/twin room with bath or shower
   Beverly Hills, Umhlanga Rocks (from $97 BB)
   Blue Waters, Snell Parade (from $45)
   Edward, Marine Parade (from $58)
   Elangeni, Snell Parade (from $65 BB)
   Four Seasons, Gillespie Street (from $38 BB)
   Holiday Inn, North Beach (from $53)
   Maharani, Marine Parade (from $86)
   Oyster Box, Umhlanga Rocks (from $62 BB)
   Royal, city center (from $72)

Kruger National Park is one of the largest game reserves in the world and stretches from the Crocodile River in the south some 200 miles to the Limpopo River in the north; it is about 40 miles wide, covering an area of about 7,500 square miles. Best time to visit is during the winter and spring months (June to October), when grass is low and it's easier to spot the animals. Elephants, giraffes, zebras, lions, leopards, cheetahs, wildebeests, and especially impala are common and there are at least 450 species of birds.

The **Drakensberg** mountain range stretches 600 miles and is called the "spine" of South Africa. The mountains are at their most spectacular between Natal and Lesotho, and it is in this area that one finds most of the mountain resorts. In winter the mountains are often covered with snow. There is the **Drakensberg Garden Hotel,** PO Underberg, Natal, (from US$38 double).

Zululand is a territory of 10,500 square miles incorporated into Natal in 1897. Abundant wildlife—of the savannah, forest, or wetland—is found in the area's five main game parks. **Hluhluwe Game Reserve** is best known for its rhino, and **Ndumu Game Reserve** for its birds, including the rare suni. Other parks are **Umfolozi Game Reserve, Mkuzi Game Reserve,** and **St Lucia Reserve and Park. Ulundi** is the capital of the territory. At **Hluhluwe** there is the **Holiday Inn,** PO Box 92 (from US$47 double) and the **Zululand Safari Lodge,** PO Box 116 (from US$85 double BB).

Bloemfontein, the capital city of the Orange Free State, was settled by Dutch pioneer farmers and eventually became a center for trading. It has good hotels and a variety of sporting facilities. There is the **Bloemfontein Hotel,** East Burger Street (from US$60 double) and the **President Hotel,** 1 Union Avenue (from US$59 double BB).

SOURCES OF FURTHER INFORMATION

Pan Am, Airways Wing New Station Building, Cape Town; Shell House, Smith and Aliway streets, Durban; Merino Building, Bosman and Pretorius streets, Pretoria; and any Pan Am office around the world; **Johannesburg Publicity Association,** Shop 153, Upper Shopping Level, Carlton

Center, Commissioner Street, and Cape Town Center, Railroad Station Building; **Cape Town Visitors' Bureau,** Lower Adderley Street, and **Durban Visitors' Bureau,** Church House, Church Street; **South African Tourist Corporation,** Arcadia Center, 130 Beatrix Street, Arcadia 1108 Pretoria; 610 Fifth Avenue, New York, NY 10020; Suite 721, 9465 Wilshire Boulevard, Beverly Hills, CA 90212; Suite 1001, 20 Eglinton Avenue West, Toronto, Ontario M4R 1K8; 13 Regent Street, London, SW1Y 4LR.

Tanzania

WHAT'S SPECIAL

Tanzania has Africa's highest mountain, Kilimanjaro, its deepest and longest freshwater lake, Tanganyika, and Selous Game Reserve, the largest in the world, with the largest number of elephants in Africa. At Olduvai Gorge, near the Ngorongoro Crater, relics of early toolmakers who lived 1¾ million years ago have been found. There are also 500 miles of unpolluted white beaches, historic towns such as Zanzibar and Kilwa, and the chance to do some big-game hunting and fishing. The tourist will find much to enjoy in Tanzania and its clove-producing islands.

COUNTRY BRIEFING

Size: 362,844 square miles   **Population:** 17,500,000
Capital: Dar es Salaam   **Capital Population:** 830,200

Weather in Dar es Salaam: Lat S6°50'; Alt 47 ft

Temp (°F)	Jan	Feb	Mar	Apr	May	Jun	Jul	Aug	Sep	Oct	Nov	Dec
Av Low	77°	77°	75°	73°	71°	68°	66°	66°	67°	69°	72°	75°
Av High	87°	88°	88°	86°	85°	84°	83°	83°	83°	85°	86°	87°
Days no rain	23	22	19	11	16	24	25	24	23	24	21	20

Government: An independent republic within the British Commonwealth.

Language: Swahili. English also spoken.

Religion: Muslim and Christian, with animism practiced by some tribes.

Currency: Tanzania shilling. 100 cents = 1 Tanzania shilling.

	10¢	50¢	1 sh	5 sh	10 sh	50 sh	100 sh	500 sh
US (dollars, cents)	.01	.06	.12	.61	1.22	6.11	12.21	61.06
UK (pounds, pence)	—	.03	.06	.29	.58	2.91	5.82	29.12

Public Holidays:

Zanzibar Revolution Day, 12 Jan
Chama Cha Mapinduzi
    Anniversary, 5 Feb
Good Friday
Easter Monday
Union Day, 26 Apr

Workers' Day, 1 May
Saba Saba Day, 7 July
Independence and Republic
    Day, 9 Dec
Christmas Day, 25 Dec

Maulid Day, Idd-El-Fitr, and Idd-El-Hajj are Muslim holidays whose dates vary years according to the lunar calendar.

HOW TO GET THERE

Flying time to Dar es Salaam International Airport from New York is 18 hours; from London, 11½ hours; from Caracas, 16½ hours; from Tokyo, 19½ hours. Time in Tanzania: GMT+3.

REQUIREMENTS FOR ENTRY AND CUSTOMS REGULATIONS

Passport and round-trip ticket are required. Visas are required of all except Commonwealth citizens and citizens of countries which have a full visa abolition agreement with Tanzania. Vaccination certificates for yellow fever and cholera are required if coming from an infected area. The border with Kenya is closed and entry directly from Kenya via air is not allowed either. Import and export of Tanzanian currency forbidden. US dollars must be declared on arrival and exchanged only through authorized foreign exchange dealers. Import of firearms and ammunition requires special police permits; pornographic literature, gold, diamonds, South African products, and opium cannot be imported. Unaccompanied baggage (items costing US$15 or over) being sent abroad requires Bank of Tanzania approval. Duty-free allowance: 200 cigarettes or 50 cigars or 250 grams of tobacco; 1 liter of wine or spirits; ¼ liter perfume; one camera; one radio; one tape recorder.

AIRPORT INFORMATION

Dar es Salaam International Airport is 8 miles from the city center. Taxi fare is about T120-150sh. There is no airport arrival tax, but departure tax is T40sh. The airport has a duty-free shop and hotel reservations counter.

The Kilimanjaro International Airport is 25 miles from Arusha and Moshi and is the closest to the northern game circuit. All international airport facilities are available.

ACCOMMODATIONS

There is a variety of hotels, including some owned by the government, in the cities. Elsewhere there are luxury tent camps on permanent sites, temporary safari camps and wild-life lodges. Some hotels offer off-season rates in April, May, and June. Hotels in Dar es Salaam:

Rates are in US$ for a double/twin room with bath or shower

Africana, Kunduchi (from $49 BB), 12 miles

Agip Motel, City Drive (from $55 AP)

Bahari Beach, Kichangani (from $63 BB), 17 miles

Kilimanjaro, Azania Front (from $63 BB)

Kunduchi Beach, Kunduchi (from $63 BB), 15 miles

New Africa, Maktaba Street (from $55 BB)

Oyster Bay, Toure Drive (from $50 BB), 4 miles

Twiga, Independence Avenue (from $48 BB)

Hotels are centrally located unless otherwise indicated.

USEFUL INFORMATION

Banks: Open 8:30-12:30 Mon-Fri; 8:30-11:30 Sat.

Mail: Stamps at post offices, in hotels, and at tobacco stands.

Telephone Tips: Some restaurants and cafés have phones, and there are booths in major towns. Useful numbers in Dar es Salaam:

Pan Am 21747/23526	Directories 991
Airport Office 42368	Operator 00
Tourist Offices: Dar es Salaam	Time 993
20373/28181 Arusha 3300	Emergencies 999
Reservations 23491	

Newspapers: The *Tanzanian Daily News* and *Sunday News* are English-language newspapers. European and American periodicals, paperbacks, and other books are on sale in some shops.

Tipping: Service charge of 5% in hotels and restaurants. Otherwise tipping is officially discouraged and not necessary, though you may tip if you wish to do so.

Electricity: 240 volts 50/60 cycles AC.

Laundry: In major towns 24-hour laundry and dry-cleaning services operate, but the standard is not adequate for better fabrics. Dry-cleaning a suit, from T30sh; laundering a shirt, from T25sh.

Hairdressing: Some first-class hotels have salons (shampoo and set, from T120sh; man's haircut, T60sh).

Photography: Equipment and film are not readily available. Bring an adequate supply. Regulations prohibit photographing certain buildings, such as international airports and army installations.

Babysitting: Hotels can usually arrange.

Rest Rooms: In public buildings, restaurants, and hotels.

Health: Many doctors and dentists speak English, but medical services are not good. Even basic imported pharmaceuticals and toiletries are practically unavailable. In large hotels water is safe, but elsewhere keep to bottled drinks. It is essential to take an antimalarial prophylactic, as Tanzania is malaria-free only above 6,500 feet. Swimming or paddling in still or slow-moving water must be avoided, as the tropical disease bilharzias is common. Hookworm is also prevalent, but the risk can be minimized by wearing shoes or sandals out of doors. Shortages of the common medicinal drugs occur frequently, so bring a reserve supply. Medical facilities for routine treatment are barely adequate.

TRANSPORTATION
The bus service in Dar es Salaam is inexpensive. Taxis can be found at stands or called by phone, they have no meters, but fixed rates are usually charged—negotiate first. Night fares can be up to 20% extra, subject to negotiation. Slow trains with sleepers and restaurant cars go from Dar es Salaam via intermediate towns to Mwanza, Kigoma, Mpanda, Tanga, and Arusha. Travel by Uhuru Railway Line is also possible between Dar es Salaam and Mbeya, en route to Lusaka, Zambia. Long-distance bus services are operated by Tanzania Railways Corporation, Kamata, and others. There are steamer services from Dar es Salaam to Zanzibar and other ferry services to the ports, offshore islands, etc. Air Tanzania runs flights from Dar es Salaam to Mwanza, Tabora, Dodoma, Kilimanjaro, Bukoba, Kigoma, Tanga, Lindi, Mtwara, and the islands of Pemba, Zanzibar, and Mafia. Self-drive cars and buses with driver can be rented. Cars start at US$110 a day; kombis (modern 12-seater bus) are US$122 a day. A 40-seater bus can be rented at US$50 per day plus $1.35 per kilometer, and a 25-seater bus at US$37 a day plus US$1.15 per kilometer. An extensive and improved road network links Dar es Salaam with Morogoro, Moshi, Arusha, Tanga (all within a day's drive), and other centers. Drive on the left. Visitors should keep to well-lit and well-populated streets when walking at night.

FOOD AND RESTAURANTS
National dishes like *mishikaki* (charcoal-broiled meat), *ndizi na nyama* (bananas and beef), and *wali na nyama* (beef curry) can be found in most Tanzanian restaurants; another Tanzanian specialty worth a try is *nyama ya mbuzi* (goat meat). Breakfast is usually served from 6:30-9:30, lunch from 12-2, and dinner from 7-11, with local variations. The average hotel and restaurant meal is four courses, but light snacks like kebabs, Bagia meat balls, hamburgers, and hot dogs can be bought elsewhere. Dinner in an expensive restaurant costs about US$10-15 for one; in a medium-priced one US$7.50, and in an inexpensive one US$4-5. Dar es Salaam offers a good gastronomic choice, from the excellent international cuisine of the **Motel Agip** (City Drive—tel: 23511) to the succulent seafoods of the **Oyster Bay Hotel** (Toure Drive—tel: 68631) and the **Palm Beach Hotel** (Upanga Road—tel: 28891). The best eating is at the **Bahari Beach** (Kichangani—tel: 47101) and the **Bushtrekker** (Ohio Street—tel: 25091).

DRINKING TIPS
Local beers, wines, and liquors are plentiful, and there are also imported ones available in major hotels. Locally brewed beers include Chibuku,

Crown, Safari, Snow Cap, and Kilimanjaro. *Konyagi* (local gin) is recommended, and *Dodoma Red* and *Dodoma Rosé* are local wines. The price of a local whisky and soda is about T30sh; a bottle of local wine about T90sh.

ENTERTAINMENT

Professional theater, classical music, opera, and ballet do not exist, but Dar es Salaam has popular bands and an amateur theater group. A popular nightspot is the **Simba Room** at the Kilimanjaro Hotel. **Savanah Club** (Morogoro Road—tel: 53326) is a typical African nightclub. Discothèques include those at the **Africana, Bahari Beach,** and **Kunduchi Beach** hotels.

SHOPPING

Stores are open from 8:30-12 and 2-6 Mon-Sat. Best buys include Makonde and other ebony wood carvings, clay carvings, primitive paintings, gemstones, shells, and skins. Regional specialties include suede from the Moshi tannery, Zanzibar chests, Masai masks, shields, spears, and meerschaum pipes from Arusha. Gifts for under US$20 include wood and clay carvings, masks, shields, and spears, meerschaum pipes, and baskets. Bargain in markets and stores where prices are not marked. Worth a visit are the **National Arts Center Tanzania, Tausi Handicraft Shop, Zanzibar Antiques,** and **Afro Fashions,** all on Independence Avenue, Dar es Salaam, and the **Silver Curio Shop** and **Tourist Pride Curio Shop** on Maktaba Street. The **Kariakoo Market** has inexpensive handicrafts. Shops in **Bagamoyo Road** specialize in Makonde and other ebony wood carvings, and those on **Independence Avenue** specialize in curio items.

SPORTS

Soccer is a popular spectator sport. In Dar es Salaam there is golf and tennis, horseback riding, and sailing all the year round. Outside the capital there is swimming along the coast, sailing at **Tanga,** deep-sea fishing at **Mafia** and **Tanga,** freshwater fishing at **Kilimanjaro** and the lake areas, and hunting and mountaineering at **Mount Kilimanjaro.**

WHAT TO SEE

Dar es Salaam is Arabic for "the haven of peace," and the city takes its name from its land-locked harbor fringed with palms. Nowadays it is a bustling commercial port and the political and administrative center of Tanzania. The official residence of the President is near the harbor entrance. Modern office buildings stand among older wood-beamed German buildings; Arab mosques and twisting narrow streets of Arab origins can be seen. The **National Museum,** in Shaban Roberts Street, contains the skull of the "nutcracker man," the *Australopithecus boisei,* 1,750,000 years old. It also has a fine collection of African—especially Makonde—Arab, Persian, and Chinese art and crafts. In the **Village Museum,** there is a traditional African village.

Arusha, the administrative center of Northern Tanzania, is an old trading post. Its modern shops and lively bazaar are overlooked by **Mount**

Meru. Arusha National Park is only 45 minutes' drive from the city. Hotels in Arusha include the **New Arusha** ($34 double) and the **Mount Meru** (US$63 double BB). The **Hotel Seventy Seven** (US$55 double BB) and the **New Safari Hotel** (US$32 double BB) are in **Moshi**, 20 miles away.

Lake Manyara National Park, 65 miles southwest of Arusha, covers over 123 square miles. Go there to see its 350 species of birds, buffalo, elephant herds, and tree-climbing lions. Stay at the **Lake Manyara Hotel**, on a cliff overlooking the lake (US$63 double BB).

Mount Kilimanjaro, 19,340 feet high, is majestic and snow-capped but not inaccessible. It can be climbed in 5 days, sleeping at mountain huts, as long as you have good boots, warm clothes, sunglasses, and stamina. Hotels in the foothills: **Kibo**, Private Bag, PO Box 102, Marangu and the **Marangu**, PO Box 40, Moshi ($36.70 double AP).

Ngorongoro Crater, 112 miles from Arusha, is nearly 10 miles across and 2,000 feet deep, and herds of zebra and wildebeeste, lions, elephants, buffaloes, and rhinos wander freely around it. Stay at **Ngorongoro Wild Life Lodge**, PO Box 9500 (US$63 double BB).

Selous Game Reserve covers over 15,500 square miles southwest of Morogoro. It is the largest game reserve in the world.

Serengeti National Park, 225 miles from Kilimanjaro International Airport, and over 5,000 square miles in area, has a spectacular concentration of migratory game. Stay at the **Seronera Wildlife Lodge** or **Lobo Wildlife Lodge**, both US$63 double BB.

Zanzibar, off the Tanzanian coast and 15 minutes flight from Dar es Salaam International Airport, is known as "the island of cloves." Zanzibar was an early Arab and Persian trading area which came under Portuguese control in the 16th and 17th centuries and under Arab domination later. Arab rule reached its zenith under Sultan Seyyid Said (1804-56). The town of Zanzibar is famous for its **Stone Town** of ornate Arab houses, its Arab fort, and the former Sultan's palace. Deserted beaches and coves can be reached by taxi. Consult your hotel for the best ones to go to. Hotels include the **Africa House**, PO Box 317 (US$10.10 single BB), the **Zanzibar**, PO Box 392 (US$8-9 single BB), and the **Ya Bwawani**, PO Box 6701 (US$34.50 double BB).

SOURCES OF FURTHER INFORMATION
Pan Am, Kilimanjaro Hotel, PO Box 1428, Dar es Salaam, and any Pan Am office around the world; **Tanzania Tourist Corporation**, PO Box 2485, Dar es Salaam; 201 East 42nd Street, New York, NY 10017; **Tanzania Tourist Representative**, 43 Hertford Street, London W1Y 7TF.

Tunisia

WHAT'S SPECIAL

Tunisia is situated between Algeria and Libya and has 750 miles of coastline on the Mediterranean. It is in many ways an oasis. Its acceptance of the Western world contrasts with the attitude of its nationalistic neighbors, Algeria and Libya; its modern hotels, from Tunis to Hammamet and on down the coast to Sousse, Sfax, and Djerba, offer reasonable accommodations; it retains the old French colonial influence, but loses none of its authentic Arab flavor. You can spend vacation time in Tunisia in almost any way imaginable—on the wide sandy beaches, drinking smooth, inexpensive local wine, and then, when the sun goes down, wandering back through the orange groves to the hotel and dancing outside under the stars. If you are robust and an eager sightseer, you can trek down into the Sahara and *really* "get away from it all."

COUNTRY BRIEFING

Size: 63,378 square miles   **Population:** 6,500,000
Capital: Tunis   **Capital Population:** 1,100,000

Climate: Sunny all year round, though it rains frequently in winter. Very hot in desert regions, but fresh light breezes on coast. Best months: April to October.

Weather in Tunis: Lat N36°47′; Alt 217 ft

Temp (°F)	Jan	Feb	Mar	Apr	May	Jun	Jul	Aug	Sep	Oct	Nov	Dec
Av Low	43°	44°	47°	51°	56°	63°	68°	69°	66°	59°	51°	44°
Av High	58°	61°	65°	70°	76°	84°	90°	91°	87°	77°	68°	60°
Days no rain	18	16	20	21	25	25	20	28	23	22	19	17

Government: A republic.

Languages: Arabic; French is the working language. English is spoken in main hotels and tourist shops.

Religion: Islam. A few Christian churches in Tunis, and synagogues throughout the country.

Currency: Dinar. 1,000 millimes = 1 dinar.

	10 mill	50 mill	100 mill	500 mill	1D	5D	10D	25D
US (dollars, cents)	.02	.11	.23	1.15	2.29	11.45	22.90	57.26
UK (pounds, pence)	.01	.05	.11	.55	1.09	5.46	10.92	27.31

Public Holidays:

New Year's Day, 1 Jan
Mouled
Anniversary of Revolution, 18 Jan
Independence Day, 20 Mar
Labor Day, 1 May
Victory Day, 1 June
Youth Day, 2 June
Aid el Feter, 22 July

Republic Day, 25 July
President Bourguiba's
  birthday, 3 Aug
Women's Day, 13 Aug
Commonwealth Day, 3 Sept
Aid el Kebir
Evacuation Day, 15 Oct
Muslim New Year
Christmas, 25 Dec

HOW TO GET THERE

Flying time to Tunis' Carthage Airport from New York is 9 hours; from Frankfurt, 4 hours; from Rome, 1 hour; from Casablanca, 3¼ hours. Time in Tunisia: GMT+1.

REQUIREMENTS FOR ENTRY AND CUSTOMS REGULATIONS

Passport. No visa required if staying less than 4 months. Tourists must have a round-trip or onward ticket and sufficient foreign currency for their stay. Vaccination certificates not required unless coming from an epidemic area. Duty-free allowances: 200 cigarettes or 50 cigars or 14 ounces tobacco; a reasonable number of small gifts, including food and drink, not exceeding US$25 in value. It is forbidden to import or export Tunisian dinars, but you may take in any amount of foreign currency. Important: remember to keep all exchange receipts, since you cannot reconvert to foreign currency more than 30% of the amount previously exchanged into dinars.

AIRPORT INFORMATION

Tunis-Carthage International Airport is 4 miles from the city center. Fare into town by airport bus is 175 mill. A taxi will cost about D2 by day, D3 at night. There is a duty-free shop, hotel reservation counter, a bank open when there are flights, and car rental desks. There are three other international airports in Tunisia: the Monastir-Skanes, the Djerba Melita, and Tozeur.

ACCOMMODATIONS

A wide range exists, from deluxe hotels to youth hostels and *marhalas* (inexpensive accommodation organized by the Tunisian Touring Club).

Rates in tourist hotels are 10-25% lower out of season (Nov-Mar) except during the Christmas week. A 7.5% government tax and a 15% service charge are usually added to bills. Students can stay in youth hostels costing US$3 a night. *Marhalas* cost about US$2 per night. Hotels in Tunis, centrally located unless otherwise indicated, include:

Rates are in US$ for a double/twin room with bath or shower, service and tax included

Abou Nawas, Sidi Bou Saïd (from $38), resort area, 35 minutes from Main Square

Africa, 50 Avenue Habib Bourguiba (from $72)

Baie des Singes, Gammarth (from $41), resort area, 35 minutes from Main Square

Hilton, Notre Dame-Le Belvédère (from $67), hilltop, 20 minutes from Main Square

Hotel du Lac, 2 Rue Mont Calmé (from $42)

International Tunisia, 49 Avenue Habib Bourguiba (from $67)

Majestic, 36 Avenue de Paris (from $32)

Megara, Gammarth (from $29), resort area, 35 minutes from Main Square

Reine Didon, Carthage (from $29), resort area, 30 minutes from Main Square

USEFUL INFORMATION

Banks: Open 8-11 Mon-Fri in summer; 8-11, 2-4 in winter. There are not many banks outside the principal cities, but foreign currency and travelers' checks can be exchanged at most hotels and the larger shops. Remember to keep exchange receipts.

Mail: Stamps can be bought at tobacco shops as well as at post offices.

Telephone Tips: Telephones in post offices, cafés, and restaurants. Local calls cost 50 mill. In a café buy a *jeton* from cashier. Useful numbers (Tunis):

Airport Information 289.000	Police service (for foreigners)
Tourist Information Office	243.000
259.133	

Newspapers: Some English-language newspapers available.

Tipping: Restaurants: 10% (except when already added to bill); airport/railway porters: 200 mill each piece of luggage; taxis 10%; hairdressers/barbers 200 mill; hotel porters 200 mill; chambermaids D1 at end of stay.

Electricity: 110-115 volts 50 cycles AC in older parts of city; 220 volts 50 cycles AC in the country and in most hotels.

Laundry: Dry-cleaning and laundry service in most hotels is reliable and speedy (dry-cleaning a suit, from D2.3; laundering a shirt, from 350 mill).

Hairdressers: Good salons in most first-class hotels (shampoo and set, from D3.5; man's haircut from D2.5).

Photography: Both black and white and color film are available in

the main cities, but it is safer to take it with you. It takes about 2 days to develop black and white or color.

Clubs: Kiwanis, Lions, Rotary.

Babysitting: Most hotels will help.

Rest Rooms: There is no charge, and they are marked *Dames* for women and *Hommes* or *Messieurs* for men.

Health: Not many doctors or dentists speak English, so arm yourself with a French dictionary. Pharmaceutical goods (mainly French) are available. It is advisable to drink mineral water outside the large towns. It is inadvisable to eat oysters, mussels, or any other shellfish.

TRANSPORTATION

There are plenty of taxis, which can be hailed in the street or called by phone (tel: 241.812 or 241.313). There is bus service, and a train which leaves the Avenue Bourguiba every 15 minutes for Carthage, Sidi Bou Saïd, and other places along the coast. There is good train service between Tunis and Gabes. The roads are good, and long-distance taxis known as *louages* have reasonable rates which are fixed from point to point and are usually posted. Car rentals cost from about US$18 to US$52 per day plus 12-30¢ per kilometer depending on the type of car, in addition to the cost of gas at about 250 mill per liter. A deposit of the approximate amount of the total rental is required except for those holding an accepted credit card. An international driver's license is preferred though not necessary, but you must be over 21 years of age and you must have had a valid driver's license for at least one year.

FOOD AND RESTAURANTS

Try the many traditional *patisserie* (pastry) and Tunisian dishes (such as *couscous*) at **Le Chateau** (26 Rue Sidi Bou Krissane, Medina—tel: 264.687), **Le Malouf** (108 Rue de Yougoslavie—tel: 243.180), or **Le M'Rabet** (Souk Et Trouk, Medina—tel: 263.681); folk music and dancing in all three restaurants. For top international cuisine go to the **Hungaria** (11 Rue Ali Bach Hamba—tel: 245.4690), **The Pub** (1 Rue Attaturk—tel: 243.436), **Le Palais** (8 Avenue de Carthage—tel: 256.326), and **Chez Slah** (15 bis, Rue Pierre de Coubertin—tel: 258.588). All hotels serve European food to nonresidents. Medium-priced restaurants include **Chez Nous** (5 Rue de Marseille—tel: 243.043), **Le Strasbourg** (100 Rue de Yougoslavie—tel: 241.139), **L'Orient** (4 Rue Ali Bach Hamba—tel: 242.058), **Le Paradiso** (Italian) (33 Rue Lt. M.A.Taj—tel: 256.198), **Asia House** (Avenue Charles Nicole, El Menzah—tel: 289.995). Inexpensive restaurants are **Le Bagdad** (31 Avenue Bourguiba—tel: 259.068), **Le Capitole** (60 Avenue Bourguiba—tel: 246.601), **Le Carthage** (10 Rue Ali Bach Hamba—tel: 255.164), and **Le Carcassonais** (8 Avenue de Carthage—tel: 256.768).

On the Byrsa Hill in Carthage the **Reine Didon** (tel: 275.344) offers good food and a view over ancient Carthage and the Bay of Tunis. In Sidi Bou Saïd, a reasonable restaurant with a view is the **Dar Zarrouk** (tel: 270.703). Good fish restaurants on the coast at La Marsa and Gammarth are **Le Golf, Le Pecheur,** and **Les Dunes.**

Bars serve deliciously elaborate snacks called *kemia:* tiny fried fish, olives, pickles. Tunisian snacks are appetizing and not expensive (but you should be cautious when buying from street vendors). A *cassecroûte* is a sandwich with tunafish, tomato, pickles, olive oil, and red peppers. Enjoy dates filled with almond paste, the orange-blossom or rose-flavored pastries, and sugar syrup-soaked snacks.

DRINKING TIPS

There are no licensing hours. Wines are good, but relatively strong—local ones to ask for are (red) Chateau Feriana, Magon, Sisi Saad, (rosé) Chateau Mornag, Coteaux de Carthage, Sidi Rais, and (white) Domaine Karim, Muscat de Kelibia. A pleasant apéritif is a *muscat* or a *kina* from the Thibar estates. *Celtia* (rather like lager) and *Stella* are two good local beers. Local liquor is *Boukha*, made from figs; it tastes like vodka and is drunk straight, if you can stand it, on the rocks, or with Coca-Cola. *Thibarine*, a local liqueur, is very good. There are imported spirits at expensive prices.

Delightful drinking spots in Tunis: **Café de Paris** (62 Avenue Bourguiba), very central and luxurious; **Café Africa** (50 Avenue Bourguiba); and **Café de Tunis**—smaller, more typically Tunisian. At Sidi Bou Saïd, **Café des Nattes** is an historic café in a beautiful setting.

ENTERTAINMENT

The most exciting place to see a play is at the Roman amphitheater at **Dougga** (in June) or at the International Festivals at **Carthage** or **Hammamet** (July/August), where the theater is by the sea. Check to see if the play is in French or Arabic. There are plays at the **Tunis Municipal Theater** and symphony concerts in Tunis in winter. Some US movies are shown, usually dubbed. Most hotels have their own nightclub or discothèque where you can dance or watch belly-dancers. Other nightclubs in Tunis: **Monseigneur** (2 Rue de Marseille), with a floor show; the **Crazy Horse,** Le Colisée; the **Baba Club,** 3 Rue Vésoul; the **Tunis Club,** corner Avenues Bourguiba and Paris; **La Potinière,** Rue de Hollande; or **Les Dunes** at Gammarth.

SHOPPING

Stores are open from 8:30-7 (closed at 12 for 2-3 hours) and 8-8 (closed 12-4) in summer; in some towns they close on Fridays. Local handicrafts are excellent, and you will find the best of these at fixed prices at the **ONA** (Office National de l'Artisanat), corner of Avenue Bourguiba and Avenue Carthage in Tunis; also in Sidi Bou Saïd, Bizerta, Monastir, Gabès, and Djerba. A 10% discount is given for payment in foreign currency, and shipping can be arranged to all parts of the world. Look for rugs, carpets, blankets, caftans, leatherware, ceramics, jewelry, and exquisite silver and copper inlay. You must not miss shopping in the *souks*—miles of covered alleys. You will find plenty of good-value gifts for less than US$10, and haggling is part of the fun. The most interesting *souks* in Tunis are the **Souk el Attarine** for perfume; **Serrajine** for embroidered leatherwork; **Souk el Berka,** for gold jewelry; **Souk du Cuivre,** for Tunisian cooking pots and pans; and the streets near the **Great Mosque** for rugs and carpets.

SPORTS

The country has 750 miles of coastline, so there is plenty of swimming and sailing and some water-skiing, wind-surfing, and skin-diving. Most hotels by the sea have their own tennis courts and facilities for horseback riding. You can even ride camels. Horse racing takes place in Tunis every Sunday from October to June. There is a pleasant **Golf and Country Club** at the **Soukra** (tel: 238.025), a tennis club in Tunis at 20 Rue Alain La Savary, Cité Jardin (tel: 280.425), and a horseback riding club at the Soukra (tel: 236.054). All three clubs welcome visitors. A new golf course recently opened at the **Port El Kantaoui Project** near Sousse. Wild boar and buffalo hunting, mountain climbing, and deep-sea fishing are other sports. There is a **Club Mediterranée** at Korba, Skanes, and Djerba.

WHAT TO SEE

Tunis has wide boulevards, smart shops, good restaurants—as well as the *souks.* Get your bearings about the ancient world at the **Bardo Museum,** then set foot in the remains of **Carthage,** in the northern suburbs. Visit the **Great Mosque** in the Medina and the zoo in **Belvedere Park.** Nearby **Sidi Bou Saïd** (the St Tropez of Tunisia) has cobbled streets and a charming café on the hill. Go and see the huge flocks of flamingoes in the **Lake of Tunis** and the **Lake of Rades.**

Hammamet: This is a modern resort with wide-horizoned beaches of platinum sand and graceful modern hotels among groves of oranges and lemons. There is plenty of entertainment, with excellent nightclubs and drama and ballet festivals. Hotels in Hammamet: **Les Colombes** (from US$25 double); **Omar Khayam** (from US$25 double); **Phenicia** (from US$35 double); **Sheraton** (from US$37 double); **Sinbad** (from US$37 double); **Yasmina** (from US$25 double). In **Nabeul,** 15 miles from Hammamet, accommodations are available at **Les Narcisses, Les Pyramides,** and the **Lido** (all from US$22 double).

Sousse is 87 miles along the coast from Tunis and is the jumping-off point for **Kairouan,** the holy city of minarets and mosques. Near Sousse are **Skanes** and the fortified medieval town of **Monastir.** About 40 miles from Sousse is the immense **Colosseum of El Djem** dominating the flat sands. Hotels in Sousse are: **El Hana** (from US$33 double); **Hannibal Palace** (from US$55 double); **Scheherazade** (from US$21 double); **Sousse Palace** (from US$25 double); and **Tour Khalef** (from US$21 double).

Djerba is identified as the island of the lotus eaters which Ulysses found so beguiling. Ancient Muslim and Jewish quarters are here. Visit the **Synagogue of La Ghriba** at Hara Srira, a famous place of pilgrimage. See the ancient pottery center at **Guellala,** watch the weavers at **Sedoui-**

kech, or spend the day on a boat with the sponge fishermen. Hotels on Djerba Island are **Dar Djerba** (from US$25 double); **Djerba Menzel** (from US$22 double); **Les Sirènes** (from US$20 double); **Medina** (from US$17 double); and **Ulysses Palace** (from US$21 double).

Another ancient city to try and see is **Dougga**—the largest Roman ruins in Tunisia; **Utica**, with Roman villas and Punic sarcophagi, is also worth a visit, as are **Sbeitla** and **El Djem**.

The **Sahara Desert** is an awe-inspiring world of rippling sand dunes, mirages, camels, and palm-fringed oases—just as you might expect. Try to visit the dazzling white **Chott El Djerid** salt desert where you are sure to see a mirage. Nearby **Tozeur** is a good base from which to see the herds of dromedaries. The **Oasis Hotel** (from US$21 double) has a swimming pool. The nearby twin oasis of Nefta, 15 miles away, has the **Sahara Palace Hotel** (from US$56 double).

Sfax, in the east, is a large industrial city, but there are ancient fortifications, elegant 17th-century houses, and a medina to see, plus the peaceful **Kerkennah Islands**, complete with some interesting Roman ruins and the centuries-old traditions of their people.

Bizerte, northwest of Tunis, has a well-preserved medina with its mosques. Its winding streets end at the **Old Port** where there are cafés, small docks, and a unique atmosphere. Farther west along the coast is **Tabarka**, famous for its coral.

SOURCES OF FURTHER INFORMATION

Any **Pan Am office** around the world; **Office National du Tourisme Tunisien**, 1 Avenue Mohamed V, Tunis, also at Tunis/Carthage airport; **Tunisian National Tourist Office**, 630 Fifth Avenue, Room 863, New York, NY 10020.

Note: Because of the political situation in Uganda, it has not been possible to provide complete information for this chapter.

Uganda

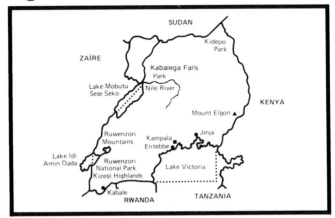

WHAT'S SPECIAL

Many seasoned travelers consider Uganda to be the most beautiful country in Africa. One-sixth of its surface is water and the rest ranges from high mountains through dense jungle to rolling grasslands and dry scrublands in the northeast. Along the western border, the Ruwenzori Mountains, fabled "Mountains of the Moon," straddle the equator yet are clothed in snow—they are the legendary home of Rider Haggard's "She." Uganda's three game parks and numerous reserves have been among the best in Africa: Kabalega Falls National Park with the celebrated falls (formerly Murchison Falls) plunging 150 feet on the Nile and a population of one of the world's rarest animals, the white rhino; Kidepo Valley National Park; and Ruwenzori National Park. The source of the Nile is at Jinga on the shores of Lake Victoria, the second largest lake in the world.

Uganda's tourist industry has declined in the last decade since the military coup by General Idi Amin in 1971, and despite his downfall in 1979, conditions in the country remain unsettled. Potential visitors should check with the US Embassy in Nairobi to determine regulations governing foreigners as well as the advisability of making such a trip.

COUNTRY BRIEFING

The **area** is 93,981 square miles and the **population** 13,000,000, of whom 332,000 live in the **capital**, Kampala. The **climate** is sunny all year round. The seasons are not precise, but there are usually two dry periods a year—from December to February and in June and July. **English** is spoken and the **religions** are Christian and Muslim. **Currency** is the Ugandan shilling; 100 cents = 1 shilling. **Public Holidays:** New Year's Day, 1 Jan; Second Republic Day, 25 Jan; Easter; Labor Day; 1 May; Independence Day, 9 Oct; Christmas Day, 25 Dec; Boxing Day, 26 Dec, and certain **Muslim** holidays.

SOURCES OF FURTHER INFORMATION

Uganda Tourist Board, PO Box 4241, Kampala; **Ministry of Tourism, Game and Wildlife,** PO Box 1764, Kampala; **Uganda Mission to the UN,** 801 Second Avenue, New York, NY 10017; **Embassy of Uganda,** 5909 16th Street NW, Washington, DC 20011; **High Commission for Uganda,** Uganda House, Trafalgar Square, London WC2.

Zaïre

WHAT'S SPECIAL

Zaïre has all the best elements of Africa: game reserves, tremendous rivers and lakes affording fishing, magnificent mountains with bamboo forests, native villages, and a mixture of tribes, including some 80,000 Pygmies.

COUNTRY BRIEFING

Area is 905,063 square miles, with a **population** of 27,750,000, of whom 2,500,000 are in the **capital**, Kinshasa. **Climate** tropical; two rainy seasons. Best time to visit, June-Sept. Official **language** is French, with four main African dialects spoken. **Religions** are Roman Catholic, Protestant, Eastern Orthodox, Kimbanguiste, Muslim, and animist. **Currency** is the zaïre; 100 mukata = 1 zaïre, 3.1 zaïre = US$1. **Public Holidays:** 1 Jan, 4 Jan, 1 May, 20 May, 24 June, 30 June, 14 Oct, 27 Oct, 17 Nov, 24 Nov, 25 Dec.

HOW TO GET THERE

Flying time from New York, 18 hours; from Rome, 6½ hours; from Caracas, 13½ hours; from Tokyo, 16 hours. Time in Kinshasa: GMT+1.

REQUIREMENTS FOR ENTRY AND CUSTOMS REGULATIONS

Passport, visa; yellow fever and typhoid inoculation certificates; smallpox and cholera inoculation certificates when traveling from an infected area; round-trip or onward ticket and proof of adequate funds to cover stay in Zaïre. Visas are obtainable from the Zaïre Mission to the UN or from Zaïre embassies around the world. It is illegal to import or export the zaïre. All foreign currency or other means of payment imported into Zaïre must be declared on a currency declaration form at the time of entry. Any subsequent exchange of currency must be recorded on the form, and the form presented at time of departure. Travelers over 16 years of age may bring in duty free up to 1 kilo of tobacco and tobacco products; 1 bottle liquor; also personal effects such as electric razors, irons, regular cameras, movie cameras, and tape recorders, but no more than one of each.

AIRPORT INFORMATION
N'Djili Airport is 18 miles from Kinshasa. Taxis are available (60-100 zaïre). Duty-free shop and hotel reservations counter.

ACCOMMODATIONS
There are good central hotels, although accommodations are sparse in the rest of the country. Hotels in Kinshasa:
Rates are in US$ for a double/twin room with bath or shower
> INTER · CONTINENTAL KINSHASA, Avenue des Batetela, Gombe residential quarter, outside main business and diplomatic area (from $123)
>
> Memling, 5 Avenue République du Tchad (from $100)
>
> Okapi, Zone de N'Galiema, Binza quarter, about 6 miles from center (from $65)
>
> Unless otherwise noted, the above hotels are in the center of Kinshasa.

USEFUL INFORMATION
Banks open 8-11:30am Mon-Fri. Useful **phone numbers** are: **Pan Am,** 23371; **Tourist Office,** 22417/25828/25629. **Tip** 10% in restaurants. **Electricity** is 220 volts 50 cycles AC. Hotels have good express **laundry** services. Drink only bottled or boiled water. There are a number of restrictions on picture-taking in Zaïre. Tourists are advised to check with the National Tourist Office for details prior to using their cameras.

TRANSPORTATION
City buses are overcrowded and unreliable. There are group taxis carrying up to four passengers, and the one who has the most distant destination gets off last; bargain before entering the cab. Taxis may also be hired by the hour at the cost of 120 zaïres; for trips outside Kinshasa, the charge is 80 zaïres per hour plus 2.50 zaïres per kilometer. SOTRAZ (tel: 22.226), near the Kingabwa, supplies taxis and there is a car rental bureau at the Inter · Continental. Roads are not good, and car rentals cost about US$100 per day. Long-distance travel is by train, special bus, and air, although river boats are available. On Lakes Tanganyika and Kivu there is a range of boats available for travel, including rapid motor boats.

FOOD AND RESTAURANTS

Hotels and restaurants serve Belgian and international cuisine. **Restaurant de La N'sélé** specializes in local dishes such as *moambé*, chicken cooked in palm oil and served with rice and spinach. Other good restaurants include **La Devinière**, in a villa with a view of Mt N'Galiema from the terrace, **L'Etrier, Stirwen, Chez Nicola, Pergola, Plein Vent, Kin's Inn, La Raquette, Grill, Mediterranée,** the **Restaurant du Zoo, Méditerranée,** and the **Guest House** at Ndolo. Service may sometimes be slow, and food is comparatively expensive in Zaïre.

DRINKING TIPS

Primus, Skol, and *Regla* brands of beer are produced in Kinshasa, and in the major towns of Shaba province, *Simba* and *Tembo* are made. The national wine is *Vin de Palme.* Imported liquor is expensive.

ENTERTAINMENT

There are attractions offered by hotels. Recent movies are shown nightly at 8:30pm at four theaters. Among the nightclubs are **L'Etoile** at the Inter · Continental Hotel, **Safari** at the Hotel Okapi, **Les Anges Noirs, Le Maxims, Olympic, Las Vegas,** and **VIP.** The **Playboy Casino** is a restaurant and disco with a car that passes the Inter · Continental and Memling hotels to transport guests.

SHOPPING

Shops open 8-noon and 3-6. Best buys are hand-carved African masks, semiprecious jewelry, ivory and ebony work. The best spot to purchase African artifacts is the open-air **Zandoya Bikeko** souvenir market near the Memling Hotel. Be prepared to bargain for anything you buy. Usually you can get an item for half the asked price. Some knowledge of French is essential to conclude negotiations. Kinshasa shops sell imported goods from Europe, but prices are high.

SPORTS

Tennis is extremely popular and can be played in Kinshasa at the **Funa Sports Center** or at the Inter · Continental Hotel, where squash courts and a swimming pool are also available. The local population is fond of football which is played in the **Stade du 20 Mai.** There are occasional international boxing matches. Fishing can be enjoyed on the rivers, but hunting has been suspended for an indefinite period.

WHAT TO SEE

In **Kinshasa** visit the **Académie des Beaux Arts** with its African art sales room and ethnological museum, the **Presidential Gardens** and **Zoo** at Mt N'Galiema, and **St Ann's Cathedral.** Just outside of town is the **Presidential Domain of La N'Sélé,** a model farm, recreation center, and residential complex with pagodas and pools for swimming and fishing. Follow the **Zaïre River** by road to see the rapids or **Pool, Zongo Falls,** the **Botanical Gardens** at Kisantu (75 miles from Kinshasa), tribal fishermen, and their villages. Also south of the capital is the forest of **Mayumbe** with primitive tombs. In the eastern part of the country is the scenically beautiful area around **Lake Kivu**, including the snow-capped **Ruwenzori Range. Epula**, where the rare animal okapi is tracked and captured for national parks, is located further north. **Virunga National Park**, a good place to see hippos and gorillas, **Garamba National Park**, the habitat of buffaloes and the white rhino, and **Maiko National Park**, also important for gorillas, is the northeast region; **Upemba National Park** in the southeastern part of the country. **Salonga, Kundelungus**, and **Kahuzi-Biega** are other national parks. It is also possible to climb the two active volcanic peaks of **Nyamulagira** and **Nyragongo**.

SOURCES OF FURTHER INFORMATION

Pan Am, 7 Boulevard du 30 Juin, PO Box 791, Kinshasa, and any other Pan Am office around the world; **Commissariat General au Tourisme,** PB 9502, Kinshasa; **Republic of Zaïre Mission to the UN,** 866 2nd Avenue, New York, NY 10017; **Embassy of the Republic of Zaïre,** 1800 New Hampshire Avenue NW, Washington, DC 20009; 26 Chesham Place, London SW1.

Zambia

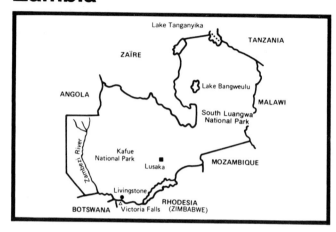

WHAT'S SPECIAL

Zambia has been haunting the imagination of travelers since Livingstone discovered the "smoke that thunders"—Victoria Falls—in 1885. Rich in wildlife, Zambia has one of the most important game reserves in Africa, as well as Lake Tanganyika, which is like an inland sea. Fishermen's tales of Goliath tiger fish and Nile perch of more than 100 pounds are true. The country is rich in folk art, tribal customs, and dancing. There are elegant modern cities, luxurious hotels, and an efficient transport system.

COUNTRY BRIEFING

Size: 290,587 square miles **Population:** 6,000,000
Capital: Lusaka **Capital Population:** 600,000

Climate: Although Zambia is in the tropics, most of the country lies on plateaus from 2,000 to 7,000 feet high, where the night-time temperature can drop to near freezing in the cool season, May-July. Rainy season, November-April.

Weather in Lusaka: Lat S15°25′; Alt 4,191 ft

Temp (°F)	Jan	Feb	Mar	Apr	May	Jun	Jul	Aug	Sep	Oct	Nov	Dec
Av Low	63°	63°	62°	59°	54°	50°	49°	53°	59°	64°	64°	63°
Av High	78°	79°	78°	79°	77°	73°	73°	77°	84°	88°	84°	80°
Days no rain	10	11	16	27	30	30	31	31	30	28	19	14

Government: An independent republic within the British Commonwealth.

Language: English is the official language.

Religion: Predominantly Christian; other denominations represented.

Currency: Kwacha. 100 ngwee = K1

	1n	5n	10n	50n	K1	K5	K10	K50
US (dollars, cents)	.01	.06	.12	.61	1.21	6.07	12.13	60.66
UK (pounds, pence)	—	.03	.06	.29	.58	2.90	5.79	28.93

Public Holidays:

New Year's Day, 1 Jan
Youth Day, 14 Mar
Good Friday
Easter Monday
Labor Day, 1st Mon in May
African Freedom Day, 25 May
Christmas Day, 25 Dec

Heroes Day, 1st Mon in July
Unity Day, 1st Tues in July
Farmer's Day, 3 Aug
Independence Anniversary, 24 Oct

HOW TO GET THERE

Flying time to Lusaka Airport from New York is 18½ hours; from Lagos, 7½ hours; from Nairobi, 2½ hours. Time in Zambia: GMT+2.

REQUIREMENTS FOR ENTRY AND CUSTOMS REGULATIONS

Passport, visa, obtainable from nearest Zambian diplomatic mission or nearest UK government representative; tourists may also obtain visas at the point of entry. Visa fee is K2.75. Round-trip ticket; fever and cholera certificates are required if arriving from an infected area, which includes a forced landing in an area in which yellow fever is endemic. Visas not required for British Commonwealth citizens unless arriving from Rhodesia, or for those under 16 years of age. No Zambian currency may be brought into the country, only K10 allowed out; foreign currency must be declared and cannot be exported in excess of the amount imported. Keep the currency declaration form for presentation at departure. Duty-free allowance: 200 grams cigarettes or 250 grams cigars or tobacco; 1 bottle liquor; 1 bottle wine; a camera and reasonable quantities of film.

AIRPORT INFORMATION

The International Airport is 16 miles from the center of Lusaka. Taxis are available, fare about K10. Zambia Tours & Lodges transports passengers between the airport and hotels. There is a duty-free shop and hotel reservations desk. Tipping porters is not required. Departure tax is K4 for local flights and K8 for international flights.

ACCOMMODATIONS

Apart from private hotels, there are government rest houses in tourist areas and government lodges in the national parks, including the Safari Villages in Kafue and South Luangwa National Parks. Rates are subject to a 10% sales tax, and major hotels add a 10% service charge. Hotels in Lusaka:

Rates are in US$ for a double/twin room with bath or shower

INTER · CONTINENTAL LUSAKA, PO Box 32201, Haile Selassie Avenue, 2 miles from city center (from $45 BB)

Pamodzi, PO Box 34450, Church Road (from $43 BB)

Lusaka, PO Box 30044 (from $21 BB)

Ridgeway, PO Box 30666, ½ mile from center (from $32 BB)

USEFUL INFORMATION

Banks: Open 8:15-12:45 weekdays except Thurs, when they close at noon, and Sat, when they close at 11am. Major hotels offer banking services from 8:15am to 10pm daily. It is advisable to keep all exchange receipts.

Mail: Stamps obtainable at post offices and hotels.

Telephone Tips: Coin-operated booth phones. Useful numbers in Lusaka:

Airport Information 75801	Emergencies 999
Directories & Operator 0	Tourist Information 72891/5

Newspapers: English-language newspapers available. Local English-language dailies: *Daily Mail* and *Times of Zambia*.

Tipping: A 10% service charge is usually included in restaurant and hotel bills; when baggage handling is not included in transfer charges, tip 40 ngwee per bag. Officially tipping is not allowed.

Electricity: 220 volts 50 cycles AC.

Laundry: Very efficient. Most hotels have reliable 24-hour service (dry-cleaning a suit from K2.75; laundering a shirt, from 90 ngwee).

Hairdressing: Most first-class hotels have salons (shampoo and set from K10).

Photography: Equipment available, but best to bring your own because prices are high and shortages common. Film cannot be purchased without prepaid processing. There are many places you cannot photograph including bridges, railways, airports, power stations, hospitals, government buildings (particularly State House, the President's residence), Parliament Building, Mulumgushi Hall, the Bank of Zambia, court buildings, post offices, and military and police installations.

Clubs: Rotary, Lions, Jaycees.

Rest Rooms: All hotels and restaurants. Signs in English.

Health: English-speaking doctors and dentists, modern efficient treatment. Imported pharmaceuticals available but expensive. Water safe to drink in large towns; elsewhere, boil. Take insecticide spray to the Kafue and South Luangwa National Parks for protection against the tsetse fly. Antimalarial prophylactics should be used outside the major cities, and are available without prescription.

TRANSPORTATION

Good network of internal flights and train services link most of the large cities on the Copperbelt, Zambia's industrialized province. Express and local service is also available on the TANZAM Railway between New Kapiri Mposhi, Zambia, and Dar es Salaam, Tanzania. There is train service between Lusaka and Victoria Falls. United Bus Company of Zambia (UBZ) provides bus service to Copperbelt cities and to the Tanzanian border. Cars can be rented in Lusaka or Livingstone, from about US$20 per day plus mileage; international driving license and refundable deposit required. Drive on the left. Drivers can be hired for an additional K8 per day from 7:30am to 5pm, with 8 ngwees for each additional hour.

FOOD AND RESTAURANTS

Mainstay of the local menu is *Mealie-Meal,* a kind of corn mash mixed with boiling water and eaten with fish and meat. There is international cuisine in large hotels like the **Inter · Continentals** at **Lusaka** and **Livingstone** (the Musi · O · Tunya Inter · Continental). In Lusaka, the **Woodpecker Inn** (Independence Avenue) is a high-class restaurant with continental food, including such specialties as imported oysters. The **Kudu Inn** (Longacres) serves continental and local food. For good Chinese food, there is the **Shanghai Restaurant** (Kulima Tower, Katunjila Road).

DRINKING TIPS

Chibuku is the national drink, based on ground soybeans. If your spirit fails you, imported liquor is available. Local bottled beer includes Mosi and Mchinga. Bars are always open; women welcomed when accompanied by a man.

ENTERTAINMENT

One of the top nightspots in Lusaka is the **Makumbi Room** at the Inter · Continental Hotel—music, dancing, floor show. On Friday nights traditional Zambian music and dancing alternates with a wide variety of Western-style music and dancing. There are casinos at the Inter · Continental and the Ridgeway. The **Woodpecker Inn** and **Studio 22** on the 22nd floor of Findeco House, Cairo Road, are popular nightclubs.

SHOPPING

Stores and supermarkets usually open 8-1 and 2-5; closed Saturday and Wednesday afternoons and all day Sunday. The larger supermarkets remain open until 6pm. Some souvenir sellers on streets are in business all the time. Lusaka has markets on **Cairo Road** and **Cha Cha Cha Road,** and the Livingstone market is on **Musi-O-Tunya Road.** Bargain only with street vendors. African carvings, beadwork, pottery, gemstones, and copperware are the most popular tourist items.

SPORTS

Lusaka has the **Lusaka Golf Club** and tennis facilities; badminton and squash are popular in main resorts. There is fishing in **Kasaba Bay.** The **Zambian National Fishing Competition,** held one week in March, is an outstanding event. Fishermen come from all over the world to try their hand against local people for the challenging tiger fish and Nile perch.

Private companies can arrange organized walking safaris in the national parks. Soccer is the national sport. Lusaka and Copperbelt cities have horse racing.

WHAT TO SEE

Zambia is, above all, the **Victoria Falls,** one of the natural wonders of the world. The awe-inspiring sound and sight of the avalanche of roaring water is unforgettable. From the **Knife Edge** footbridge, you can view the falls head on (take a raincoat and umbrella unless you want to be drenched by spray), or get other angles of the "smoke that thunders" from such vividly named vantage points as the **Boiling Pot.** If you are around on the night of a full moon you should go to the **Eastern Cataract** between 8:30-9:30pm, when the shining silver smoke is caught in a lunar rainbow and the sight is out of this world. At the Falls there is the **MUSI-O-TUNYA INTER · CONTINENTAL,** PO Box 151, Livingstone (from US$45 double BB). Dr. Livingstone's notebook, where he recorded his first impressions of the Falls, is in the nearby **National Museum,** which is well worth a visit. Take a sundowner cruise on the **Zambezi River,** where the hippos wallow and the crocodiles lie like logs. Do not miss the **Maramba Cultural Center,** really a village, where the ancient arts and crafts of Africa are kept alive and you can see blacksmiths, wood carvers, and mask makers at work. The reedskirted Makishi and traditional dancers from other regions perform here. There are daily flights to Livingstone, with special one-day round-trip excursion rates for tourists, and the **Zambia Tours & Lodges, Ltd,** runs all-inclusive weekend tours from Lusaka.

South Luangwa National Park is another must. Known as the "Crowded Valley" for the variety and quality of its game, it is considered by experts to be one of Africa's best-stocked sanctuaries. In its 3,500 square miles are some 100,000 elephants and other animals of the forest, wetland, and savannah—giraffes, leopards, monkeys, kudu, and wildebeest. It is a particularly good place to see hippopotamuses and the only place in Africa to see the Thornicroft giraffe. Open year round, the park is best seen during the dry season, June through October. Accommodations are at the **Mfuwe, Chichele,** and **Luamfwa Lodges,** open year-round and with swimming pools. The **Chibembe Safari Camp,** also with swimming pool, is open during the dry season only. Rates are about US$110–150 per person for a 3 day/2 night stay including all meals and two animal-viewing drives per day. The park is served by Zambia Airways' scheduled flights from Lusaka to Mfuwe Airport.

Kafue National Park covers 8,650 square miles and here, too, the animal and bird life is spectacular. You will see elephants, lions, lechwe (the little antelope all but exterminated by poachers and now roaming the vast Busanga Plains), and countless other species, as well as over 600 varieties of bird life. **Ngoma Lodge,** with swimming pool, and **Musungwa Safari Lodge** provide accommodations at rates comparable to those in South Luangwa. Zambia Airways runs scheduled flights from Lusaka and Livingstone to Ngoma in the dry season.

Walking safaris are an unusual feature of Zambia's national parks. Nowhere else do you wander on foot, come face-to-face with hippos and crocodiles, and catch such close-up pictures of the animals (an armed guard goes with you). Walking safari packages are available from the **Zambia Tours & Lodges, Ltd,** and **Wilderness Trails,** or from private companies. Sample rates: from US$385–500 per person for 6 days/5 nights including all meals and transport (airfare from Lusaka additional). Other novel adventures possible in Kafue are night drives to view nocturnal animals and boat trips on the Kafue River to see the aquatic ones and those along the shore.

If you want a sailing, fishing, sunbathing vacation, there are beach resorts at **Kasaba** and **Nkamba Bays** on Zambia's inland sea—**Lake Tanganyika,** 500 miles long and about 75 miles wide.

SOURCES OF FURTHER INFORMATION

Any **Pan Am** office around the world; **Zambia National Tourist Board,** PO Box 30017, Lusaka, Zambia; 150 East 58th Street, New York, NY 10022; Zimco House, 129/139 Finsbury Pavement, London EC2 INA.

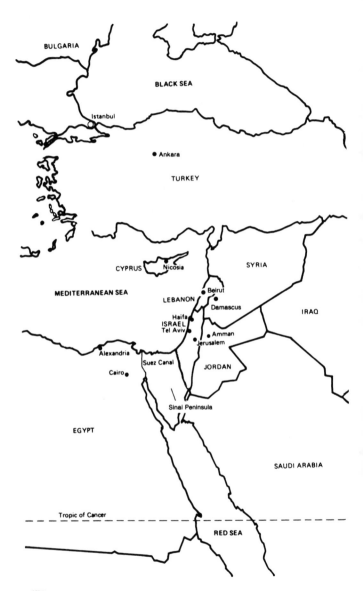

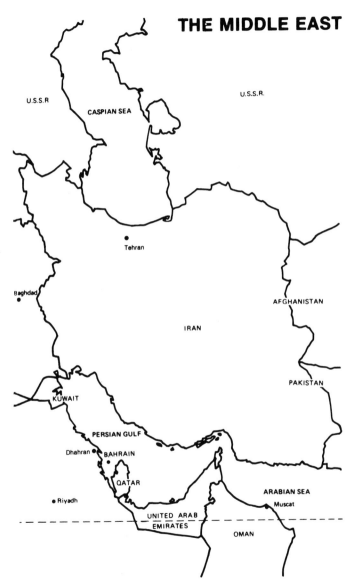

THE MIDDLE EAST

U.S.S.R

U.S.S.R.

CASPIAN SEA

Tehran

Baghdad

AFGHANISTAN

IRAN

PAKISTAN

KUWAIT

PERSIAN GULF

Dhahran BAHRAIN

QATAR

Riyadh

ARABIAN SEA

Muscat

UNITED ARAB
EMIRATES

OMAN

MIDDLE EAST
CURRENCY CONVERSION

Country	United States $				United Kingdom £			
	5¢	10¢	50¢	$1	5p	10p	50p	£1
Bahrain dinar • fils	.02	.04	.19	.38	.04	.08	.40	.79
Iraq dinars • fils	.02	.04	.18	.36	.04	.08	.38	.75
Israel shekels	.47	.93	4.67	9.34	.98	1.94	9.76	19.52
Jordan dinars • fils	16.13	32.26	161.29	322.58	33.17	67.42	337.10	674.19
Kuwait dinars • fils	.02	.03	.14	.27	.04	.06	.29	.56
Lebanon pounds • piasters	.21	.42	2.10	4.20	.44	.88	4.39	8.78
Saudi Arabia riyals • halalas	.17	.34	1.69	3.38	.36	.71	3.53	7.06
Syria pounds • piasters	.20	.39	1.97	3.94	.42	.82	4.12	8.23
Turkey liras • kurus	4.85	9.71	48.54	97.08	10.14	20.29	101.45	202.90

Bahrain

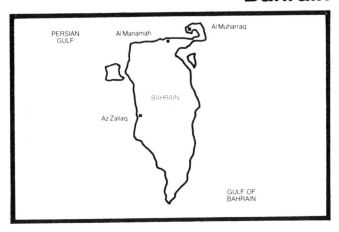

WHAT'S SPECIAL

This tiny island-emirate, forming an archipelago in the Persian Gulf between the Qatar Peninsula and the mainland of Saudi Arabia, is one of the most important banking services and financial centers in the Arab world. The discovery of oil in 1932, well before other exploration in the area, made it the first of the Arabian Gulf countries to provide its people with welfare services and schools. Its wealth, formerly derived from a thriving pearl industry, comes from a combination of trade and commerce, ship building, and oil.

COUNTRY BRIEFING

The land area of the 33 islands is approximately 258 square miles; **population** is 341,384, of whom about 150,000 live in the **capital** Manama on the principal island of Bahrain (30 miles long, 10 miles wide). Muharraq, the second-largest island, is connected to Bahrain by a causeway. **Climate:** October through May are generally pleasant, fair months, with occasional light rains, and the summer months of June through September are very hot and humid. **Government:** a monarchy; **language:** Arabic, with English widely spoken; **religion:** Muslim; **currency:** the Bahrain Dinar (1,000 fils = BD1; BD1 = $2.66).

Public Holidays: New Year's Day, 1 Jan; Bahrain National Day, 16 Dec; in addition Muslim holidays are observed.

HOW TO GET THERE

Fly to Dhahran, Saudi Arabia, and by connecting flight to Bahrain, Muharraq International Airport. Flying time from New York to Dhahran, about

12¾ hours; Dhahran to Bahrain, about 15 minutes. Time in Bahrain: GMT+3.

REQUIREMENTS FOR ENTRY AND CUSTOMS REGULATIONS

Passport. With the exception of citizens of the UK, Saudi Arabia, Kuwait, Qatar, Oman, and the UAE, visitors need a visa, obtainable from Bahrain embassies abroad. Transit visas valid for 72 hours can usually be obtained at the airport immigration office by passengers holding return or onward tickets. Passengers are advised to check with Bahrain Embassies abroad. Certificates of vaccination against smallpox and yellow fever required if entering from an infected area. Duty-free allowance: 200 cigarettes, 50 cigars, ½ pound tobacco, 1 bottle spirits, 8 ounces perfume.

AIRPORT INFORMATION

Muharraq International Airport is about 4 miles from the center of Manama. Taxis are available; rates are fixed at about BD3. Duty-free shop at airport. Tip porters not less than 100 fils.

ACCOMMODATIONS

It is advisable to book rooms early and to ask for confirmation by cable. Hotels in Manama:
Rates are in US$ for double/single rooms with bath or shower
  Aradous Hotel, Wali Al Ahd Road (S$47/D$80)
  Bahrain Hilton, north end of Old Palace Road (S$103/D$128)
  Delmon Hotel, Government Road (S$79/D$106)
  Gulf Hotel, Gudaibiya (S$84/D$100)
  Holiday Inn, off King Faisal Road (S/D from $93)
  Ramada Hotel, Gudaibiya on Old Palace Road (S$91/D$115)
  REGENCY INTER·CONTINENTAL HOTEL, center city (S$92/D$114)
These rates are subject to a 10-15% service charge. All hotels listed are centrally located.

USEFUL INFORMATION

Banks are open 8-11am, closed Fridays. English-language newspapers are the *Gulf Daily News* and the weekly *Gulf Mirror*. **Electricity** is 220 volts 50 cycles AC. **Tipping** is generally expected. **Laundry** and **dry-cleaning** services are available. There are **hairdressing** salons (wash and set up to US$8, man's haircut from about $3). **Photographic** equipment and films are available. **Health:** Tap water is generally safe for drinking, but Saliue and Brackish bottled water is available. **Toiletries** are available but expensive, **pharmaceuticals** frequently unavailable without a prescription. Available hospitals are the **American Mission Hospital** (tel: 253447), **Bahrain International Hospital** (tel: 251666), and **Salmaniya Hospital** (tel: 252761).

TRANSPORTATION

A bus system connects the various towns and villages of Bahrain and Muharraq; cost ranges between 25-50 fils. Taxis, operating on a fixed fee, are readily available and cars may be rented. An international driver's license is necessary.

FOOD AND RESTAURANTS

International dishes are widely served in most restaurants, accompanied by traditional Bahraini dishes and Middle Eastern foods. Some interesting restaurants in Manama are: the **Mandarin,** on Sheikh Daij Road (tel: 259775), has authentic Chinese food in elaborate surroundings; **Upstairs Downstairs,** off Juffair Road, specializes in English and American foods for downstair lunches and dinners and has an evening bistro upstairs; **Talk of the Town,** in the Ali Matrook Building on Zubara Road, serves Middle Eastern food with a background of music. For those who want a snack there is **Kentucky Fried Chicken,** on Osam bin Zaid Road, and the **Wimpy Coffee Bar,** on Al Khalifa Road. Food in the luxury hotel restaurants is largely continental in style. A full-course meal costs about BD10 per person.

DRINKING TIPS

There are few restrictions on the sale of alcohol and it is available in most hotels and restaurants. Imported whisky, beers, and wines are all obtainable.

ENTERTAINMENT

Many of the larger hotels have nightclubs or discos.

SHOPPING

Stores are open from 8am-12:30pm and 3:30-6:30pm; closed Fridays. Best buys include Persian carpets, Bahraini pearls, and gold jewelry. Local handicrafts can be found in most of the shops in Bahrain. Facilities range from modern department stores to the tiny shops in the winding streets of the Manama and Muharraq areas.

SPORTS

There are pools at the Aradous, Delmon, Ramada, Hilton, and Gulf hotels. Thoroughbred Arabian horses race at the new race track stadium where traditional camel races are also held.

WHAT TO SEE

Visit the **Portuguese Fort,** which is situated on the northern coast of Bahrain and can be reached by turning off the Manama-Budaiya Road. The **Burial Mounds,** scattered across the northern and western slopes of the island, are of great interest, and archaeological finds are housed in the **Bahrain National Museum** in **Muharraq,** former capital of Bahrain with many old buildings. Also worth seeing is construction of the traditional *dhow* fishing boats, mostly on Muharraq, and pottery-making at **Aali,** west of Isa Town on Bahrain. **Bahrain Explored** offers a variety of interesting group and individual tours of the island and its sights (tel: 742211).

SOURCES OF FURTHER INFORMATION

Pan Am, World Travel Services, Unitag House, Government Road, Bahrain, and any Pan Am office around the world; **Ministry of Information,** Department of Tourism, Bahrain; **Bahrain Embassy,** 2600 Virginia Avenue NW, Washington, DC 20037; **Bahrain Consulate,** 747 Third Avenue, New York, NY 10017.

Note: Because of the political situation in Iran, it has not been possible to provide complete information for this chapter.

Iran

WHAT'S SPECIAL

Iran (ancient Persia) is one of the oldest empires in the world, having celebrated its 2,500th anniversary in 1971. Less than 200 years ago, its present capital was little more than a village; today Tehran is a cosmopolitan city with broad avenues, modern buildings, and deluxe hotels. Some Iranian women still use the veil to great effect—even when wearing skirts.

COUNTRY BRIEFING

Size: 628,000 square miles   **Population:** 36,000,000
Capital: Tehran   **Capital Population:** 4,600,000

Climate: There are four distinct seasons, with summers very hot and dry and winters cold with intermittent snow. Best times to go are spring (March-May) and fall (mid-September to mid-November).

Weather in Tehran: Lat N35°41'; Alt 3,700 ft

Temp (°F)	Jan	Feb	Mar	Apr	May	Jun	Jul	Aug	Sep	Oct	Nov	Dec
Av Low	20°	24°	39°	49°	58°	66°	72°	71°	64°	53°	43°	27°
Av High	45°	50°	59°	71°	82°	93°	99°	97°	90°	76°	63°	51°
Days no rain	27	24	26	27	29	29	30	31	30	30	27	27

SOURCES OF FURTHER INFORMATION

Ministry of Information and Tourism, 174 Elizabeth Boulevard, Tehran; Iran Information and Tourism Center, Newton House, Suite 12, 118-119 Piccadilly, London W1.

Note: Because of the political situation in Iraq, it has not been possible to provide complete information for this chapter.

Iraq

WHAT'S SPECIAL

Iraq was once called Mesopotamia, meaning "land between the rivers." It is linked to the past through its long and fascinating history—the fertile crescent between the Tigris and the Euphrates is here—but it is firmly rooted in the present through its prospering oil industry, now helping to harness the power of these ancient rivers. In claiming to be the cradle of civilization, Iraq can point to the monuments, relics, and remnants of the Sumerian, Akkadian, Babylonian, and Assyrian civilizations, dating back to the fourth millennium BC. The Hanging Gardens of Babylon were here, as were the cities of Ur of the Chaldees and Nineveh.

COUNTRY BRIEFING

The **area** of Iraq is 167,568 square miles (37% desert land); **population** is 12,171,295, of whom over 3 million live in the **capital,** Baghdad. Climate: July and August are uncomfortably hot months; best times to visit are September-January and April-June. **Government:** Iraq is a republic. **Language** is Arabic and English is widely spoken; **religion,** Muslim; **currency,** the dinar (1,000 fils = 1 dinar; 1 dinar = US$2.76).

SOURCES OF FURTHER INFORMATION

Any **Pan Am** office around the world: **US Interests Section,** Belgian Embassy, Opposite Foreign Ministry Club, Masbah, Baghdad; **British Embassy,** Sharia Salah Uddin, Karkh, Baghdad; **Iraq Mission to the UN,** 14 East 79th Street, New York, NY 10021; **Iraqi Interests Section,** Embassy of India, 1801 P Street NW, Washington, DC 20036; **Iraqi Tourist Office,** 4 Regent Street, London W1.

Israel

WHAT'S SPECIAL

Israel, one of the youngest nations of the modern world, is also one of the world's oldest with a history dating back almost 6,000 years. Until 14 May, 1948, when the people of Israel proclaimed themselves an independent republic, the Jews had undergone the Diaspora, originally forced upon them by the Babylonians more than 2,500 years ago, and reinforced successively by the Greeks (creators of the original holocaust in 171 BC under Antiochus IV) and Romans, who completed the task with the destruction of the Temple Jerusalem in 70 AD under Titus Vespasian.

First called the Holy Land in the Bible, the area is still popularly known by that name, with Muslims, Jews, and Christians claiming sites that authenticate the history of their religions. The new nation has suffered terrorist violence and war from its inception, and the peace with Egypt is welcomed as providing plentiful opportunities for mutual endeavors that will raise the standard of living for all who live in the region.

Much of this formerly desert land, once owned by absentee landlords, has been made to bloom again. The extensive irrigation projects developed by the Israelis to transform the Negev has produced technology that is now being made available to other desert areas of the world.

COUNTRY BRIEFING

Size: 7,980 square miles   **Population:** 3,916,800

Capital: Jerusalem   **Capital Population:** 388,000

   Climate: Mediterranean, warm sunshine from April to October. Winter mild, with sunny days between periods of rain, November to March.

Weather in Jerusalem: Lat N31° 41'; Alt 2,485 ft

Temp (°F)	Jan	Feb	Mar	Apr	May	Jun	Jul	Aug	Sep	Oct	Nov	Dec
Av Low	41°	42°	46°	50°	57°	60°	63°	64°	62°	59°	53°	45°
Av High	55°	56°	65°	73°	81°	85°	87°	87°	85°	81°	70°	59°
Days no rain	22	17	28	27	30	30	31	31	30	30	26	24

Government: A republic, with a president as head of state.

Language: Hebrew. Signs also in English, which is widely spoken. *Shalom* (peace) used for hello and goodbye.

Religion: Of the population, approximately 3.28 million are Jewish, 494,000 Muslims, 92,000 Christians, and 50,000 Druzes and other religions.

Currency: Israeli Shekel. 100 agorots = 1 Israeli Shekel.

	1S	5S	10S	50S	100S	250S	500S	1000S
US	.11	.54	1.07	5.35	10.70	26.75	53.50	107.00
UK	.05	.26	.51	2.55	5.10	12.76	25.52	51.04

Public Holidays:

Jewish & Official Holidays (all movable feasts):
Purim
Pesach (Passover)
Shavuot
Independence Day

Rosh Hashana (New Year)
Yom Kippur (Day of Atonement)
Sukkoth (Tabernacles)
Chanukka (Feast of Lights)

HOW TO GET THERE

Flying time to Tel Aviv, Ben Gurion Airport from New York is 10½ hours; from Rome, 3 hours; from Istanbul, 1¾ hours. Time in Israel: GMT+2.

REQUIREMENTS FOR ENTRY AND CUSTOMS REGULATIONS

Passport, visa and round-trip ticket, but visa is not usually required for citizens of the Commonwealth, Great Britain, the US, Mexico, and many Western European countries. A smallpox vaccination certificate is required for entry from infected areas. An unlimited amount of foreign currency in cash or travelers' checks may be imported. Similarly, an unlimited amount of Israeli pounds. On departure, Israeli currency up to IS1,000 may be exported, while Israeli pounds up to a maximum value of US$3,000 may be reconverted. There is a stringent security check on all passengers and their baggage leaving from foreign airports and arriving in Israeli airports. Duty-free allowance: 250 cigarettes or 250 grams tobacco (for each person over 17); ¾ liter liquor; ¾ liter wine (for each person over 17); ¼ liter of perfume; and gifts up to US$100 value.

AIRPORT INFORMATION

Ben Gurion, 12 miles from Tel Aviv, is the International airport (tel: 972888). A 24-hour bus service, connecting with flights from the airport, goes to the Arlasoroff Street Railway Station Air Terminal. Bus fare is approximately $1, taxi fare $11, to Tel Aviv. Porters should be tipped the equivalent of 50¢ per piece of luggage. Duty-free shop and tourist information. There is an airport departure tax of US$10 or the equivalent in shekels.

ACCOMMODATIONS

Hotels of all grades available at all main centers and along the Mediterranean coast. There are other pleasant forms of accommodations. The **Israeli Government Tourist Office** has branches in Jerusalem, Tel Aviv, Haifa, Ben Gurion Airport, and elsewhere, but there is a great demand for accommodations, so reserve early. Youth hostels provide for basic needs, charging about US$3-5 for bed and breakfast depending on age, membership, etc. Recreation villages charge US$15-20 a day, including food and sporting facilities. There are 17 well-equipped camping sites. Christian hospices provide simple accommodations for pilgrims; kibbutz guest houses are also good and inexpensive (US$17-22 per person). Hotel rates in Israel are subject to a 15% service charge. Hotels in Jerusalem, centrally located unless otherwise indicated, include:

Rates are in US$ for a double/twin room with bath or shower

Ambassador Hotel, Sheikh Jarrah (from $34 CP)

American Colony, Nablus Road (from $27 CP)

Ariel Hotel, Hevron Road (from $52 CP)

Diplomat, Talpioth (from $55), residential area

Hilton, Givat Ram (from $60)

Holyland, Bayit Vegan (from $25.50 CP), 10 minutes from city center

INTER · CONTINENTAL JERUSALEM, PO Box 19585 (from $41.75)

Jerusalem Plaza, 47 King George Street (from $68 CP)

Jerusalem Tower, 23 Hillel Street (from $34 CP)

King David, King David Street (from $69 CP)

Kings, 60 King George Street (from $44)

King Solomon Sheraton, 32 King David Street (from $75)

Moriah, Keren Hayessod (from $53 CP)

Mount Scopus, Sheik Jarrach (from $31 CP), overlooking center

National Palace, Az Zahara Street (from $36 CP)

Palace, Mount of Olives Road (from $26 CP), 10 minutes from city center

Panorama, Hill of Gethsemane (from $35 CP)

President Hotel, Achad Ha'am (from $43 CP)

Hotel Ram, Jaffa Road (from $37 CP)

Ramada Shalom, Bayit Vegan (from $47 CP), 10 minutes from city center

Ritz, 8 Ibn Khaldoun Street (from $34 CP)

Tirat Bat Sheva, 42 King George Street (from $40)

USEFUL INFORMATION

Helpful Hints: Shabbat (Saturday, the Jewish Sabbath) begins at sunset on Friday and ends at sunset on Saturday and is a public and religious holiday. Banks, shops, offices are closed, public transport is limited to taxis, and streets with synagogues are closed to traffic. Some places of entertainment are also closed, and so are some cafés and restaurants. The dining rooms of hotels are open, but guests are sometimes asked not to smoke.

Banks: Open 8:30-12:30, Sun-Thurs (in larger branches also 4-5pm). Fridays and days before Jewish holidays, 8:30-12; closed Wednesday afternoon and Saturday. Travelers' checks can also be cashed at the large hotels and some travel agencies. Diners Club, American Express, and Carte Blanche credit cards are accepted in certain stores and hotels. Master Charge and Visa also accepted.

Mail: Main post offices open 7am-8pm; sub-post offices have a 3-hour lunch break and close at 6. Stamps and airmail letters can be bought at stationery stores and bookshops which carry the post office symbol (a white deer on a blue background).

Telephone Tips: Not many telephone booths, but public phones in cafés and drugstores. Useful numbers:

Pan Am agent (Tel Aviv)
   247272
Airport Information
   03 614656
Tourist Offices & Information:
   Beersheba 057 36001
   Bethlehem 02 942591
   Eilat 059 2268
   Haifa 04 666521
   Jerusalem 02 2412812
   (New City)
   Jerusalem 02 282295/6
   (Old City, Jaffa Gate)

Tourist offices (cont)
   Nazareth 065 70555
   Tel Aviv 03 223266/7
   Tiberias 067 20992
Directories 14
Fire 102
Police 100
International Calls 18
Cables 171
Accident 101

Note that area codes, 02/Jerusalem, 03/Tel Aviv, 04/Haifa are not used when dialing within a particular city.

Newspapers: *The Jerusalem Post* is published locally in English. Foreign periodicals are for sale.

Tipping: Not universal, but restaurants generally include 10% service charge. Taxi drivers and *sherut* taxi drivers not tipped. Hotel porters, 50¢ for each piece of luggage; chambermaids about 40¢ per day. In nightclubs a 25% tip is usual.

Electricity: 220 volts 50 cycles AC

Laundry: Major hotels have an express service. Laundry and drycleaning establishments in all towns and cities.

Hairdressing: Deluxe hotels and main towns have salons.

Photography: Black and white and color films on sale. Black and white developing takes about a week, color can take two weeks or more. In Tel Aviv, color film can be developed within 24 hours at Photo Farage on Dizengoff Street. No pictures may be taken of military installations and equipment or of restricted zones near the border.

יין פנה שמאלה
NO LEFT TURN

Clubs: Kiwanis, Rotary, Jaycees, Lions, Soroptomists, Automobile & Touring Club, B'nai Brith, Moadon Haoleh (for English-speaking immigrants), all meet in the main cities. American Canadian Club is in Hayakon Street, Tel Aviv.

Babysitting: Available in Jerusalem through the Student Employment Service of Hebrew University (tel: 02/585111). In Tel Aviv, through Students' Union of Tel Aviv University (tel: 03/420111), from 9-2. In Haifa, through Tourist Information Office (tel: 66521) or the Student Union of Haifa (tel: 04/240111, extension 247 or 776). Reserve one or two days in advance.

Rest Rooms: In hotels, restaurants, etc; women, *Sherutim Lenashim;* men, *Sherutim Legvarim.*

Health: Good English-speaking doctors available. Local offices of the Israel Medical Association will help find one (Beit Ha-Rofeh, Tel Aviv— tel: 256983). By calling your embassy, tourists will be directed to a listed physician, round the clock. The same service is offered by all embassies. Newspapers list emergency physicians and pharmacies on night duty in the main cities. Israeli Red Shield (Magen David Adom—the equivalent of the Red Cross) is at your service (tel: 101). Imported pharmaceuticals expensive. Drinking water pure.

TRANSPORTATION

Organized tours by plane, bus, or limousine cover the country. Most popular and least expensive form of public transport is the bus. Egged Inter-Urban Co-operative provides 15- or 30-day Run-About tickets for bus travel. Train service comfortable, reliable, and inexpensive. Limitations on travel imposed by *Shabat* will affect public transport on Friday nights and Saturday. Private metered taxis are expensive, with a 25% night surcharge. *Sherut* follow fixed routes between cities and charge 10-30% more than bus fare at fixed rates. Rental cars are available. Traffic drives on the right; speed limits are 50km per hour in built-up areas, 90 on highways. Only a few gas stations are open on Saturdays.

The local airline, Arkia, connects with Jerusalem, Tel Aviv, Haifa, Eilat, Rosh Pina, and Sharm-el-Sheikh. Many tourists fly to Eilat on the Red Sea and return by car or bus (ARKIA, 88 Ha'hashmonaim Street, Tel Aviv, tel: 03 266161 for all details).

FOOD AND RESTAURANTS

Israelis observe many of the strict Jewish dietary laws, and these set a pattern for restaurant meals, though not all restaurants serve "kosher" food. The rules forbid pork and shellfish in any form; also, meat and milk cannot be mixed, so that rules out butter, cream, and cheese with meat meals, though they may be eaten at other times. The spicy, oily specialties of the Middle East and the Mediterranean are supplemented by Italian pasta and German baking. There are French, Polish, North

African, Italian, and Oriental restaurants. Local fruit and vegetables are excellent. Good quick meals include *peeta* (the Oriental pancake bread) with a wide variety of fillings; *falafel*, *peeta* stuffed with chickpea balls, are served from kiosks everywhere. *Taheena* and *humus* are versions of the same theme.

Restaurants in Tel Aviv are plentiful. **Casba** (32 Irmiyahou Street—tel: 442617) serves European and Oriental food of an exceptionally high standard. The decor and the service are also excellent. **Zion Exclusive** (28 Pedium Street, Yemenite Quarter—tel: 57323) is famous for its Oriental and Yemeni cuisine; **La Barchetta** (326 Dizengoff Street—tel: 448405) for seafood; **Ron** (86 Retzif Herbert Samuel—tel: 53530) for Italian and French cuisine; and **Dan** (147 Ben Yehuda Street—tel: 220988) represents one of the successful attempts in Tel Aviv to revive East European Jewish cooking. For a Balkan meal, visit **Balkan Corner** (Sderot Rokakh—tel: 417440) or **Harel** (95 Ha'hashmonaim Street), which serves both Balkan and European dishes. **Assa** (49 Bograshov Street—tel: 287382) specializes in Bulgarian food only. Try **Casa Mia** (72 Frishman Street) or **Gondola** (57 Pinsker Street—tel: 283788) for a taste of Italy; **Triana** (12 Carlebach Street—tel: 264949) for a taste of Greece, and **Toutoune** (Simtat Mazal Dagim—tel: 820693) for French food. **The Café de Paris** (17 Trumpledor St, tel: 285803), **Versailles** (37 Geula Street—tel: 55552), and **La Couronne** (Pinsker Street) are also famous for French food. For Chinese fare, try **Mandy's Singing Bamboo,** 317 Hayarkon St (tel: 443400) or kosher Chinese at the Marina Hotel (Namir Square—tel: 282244), and for Indian food the **Tandoo,** 193 Dizengoff St (tel: 232386). Dairy and vegetarian food at the **Taste of Honey** (12 Frishman Street) and health food at **Banana** (334 Dizengoff Street). For American food go to **Mandy's Drug Store** (206 Dizengoff Street—tel: 234304) or **Sunny Boy** (196 Dizengoff Street—tel: 232919) for Southern fried chicken.

DRINKING TIPS

Israel produces several good table wines, and those made by Carmel Mizrachi and Friedman are all worth trying. There are locally made brandies and liqueurs—try Sabra. The average price of a bottle of local red wine is about US$2-3. Imported drinks are available; a whisky and soda costs upward of US$1. No restrictions on the sale of drinks; women welcome everywhere. Soft drinks, made from juices of locally grown fruit, are excellent. In Jerusalem try the **Atara** (Ben Yehuda Street) and **Navah** (Jaffa Street).

ENTERTAINMENT

There are several well-established theater companies performing classical, contemporary, and local plays, sometimes in English. There are 270 movie theaters. The **Israel Philharmonic Orchestra** gives 180 concerts a year throughout the country and because it is one of the finest orchestras anywhere in the world tickets are hard to come by. Plan to book seats well in advance of your visit. Its permanent home is the **Mann Auditorium** in Tel Aviv. There is a Chamber Ensemble, a National Opera Group, and several dance companies, both modern and classic. The **Israel Festival of Music and Drama,** in late summer, and the **Ein Gev Music Festival,** held at Passover at Lake Kinneret, draw wide audiences. The "Inbal" **Yemenite Folkloric Dancing Troup** is also worth seeing. There are many hotels and cafés with cabarets or other entertainment. There are also numerous discothèques; in Tel Aviv the most active nightlife is found in Old Jaffa, on Hayarkon Street near the old Tel Aviv port, and in the new cafés and restaurants around city hall. Go to **Aladin** (tel: 826766), **Omar Khayam** (tel: 825865) or **The Cave** (tel: 829018 in the Old City of Jaffa) for an Israeli folklore evening, to **Mandy's Piano Bar** (317 Hayarkon Street—tel: 443400), or the **Magic Carpet Club** in the Hotel Pal (closed Fridays). The **Ohalim,** in the Tel Aviv Hilton, is open on Friday night and Saturday afternoon. There is a floor show at **Zorba's** (Yafet Street 15—tel: 821243) in Jaffa. Other Israeli cities are quieter, but in Jerusalem there is Israeli singing and dancing at the **Taverna** (Nuzha Street) or the **Khan Piano Bar** (tel: 02 68283). In Haifa, there is dancing at **Club 120** (120 Yefe Nof Street) and at the **Shulamit Hotel.**

SHOPPING

Stores open 8:30-1 and 4-7, Sun-Thurs; 8:30-1 Fri; closed all day Sat. Look for articles made in attractive olive wood and pressed-flower pictures. Handmade articles by Arab and other craftsmen are colorful and original—they are less expensive outside the big towns. The leatherwork and camelskin bags are good buys. Brass and copperware, silver filigree jewelry, rugs, and embroidery are all vivid and characteristic merchandise. In the fascinating markets in the Old City of Jerusalem, at Jaffa, and at Mount Carmel, you can try your skill at bargaining. Fashion wear for men and women, knitted goods, and beachwear are all well made and not expensive. Furs and jewelry are good too. Goods purchased in major stores and in hotel duty-free shops are 30% less expensive when paid for in foreign currency; they are collected at the airport on departure.

Shalom Stores (Shalom Tower, 9 E'had Ha'am) in Tel Aviv is Israel's leading department store. **Maskit** (El Al Building, 32 Ben Yehuda Street, Tel Aviv, and 12 Rav Kook Street, Jerusalem) sells handicrafts and clothes; try **Iwanir** (Dizengoff Street 129) for knitwear, and shops on Dizengoff Street for leather goods. First class leatherwear is available from **Beged Or** shops at 102 Ben Yehuda Street in old Jaffa and on Dizengoff Street in Tel Aviv, as well as in the shopping arcades of the larger hotels. In Tel Aviv buy handicrafts and souvenirs from the **Arts & Crafts Gallery** (119 Rothschild Boulevard); leather and suede from **Snia** (133 Dizengoff Street). In Jerusalem, rugs, embroidery, and handicrafts are to be found at **I.M. Barakat Souvenirs** (11 David Street) and **Saa'di Barakat** (46-48

David Street); leather coats are to be found at **Danaya** (23 Hillel Street) and **Rosenblum** (Kikar Tzorfat), while for furs, try **Ben Basa** (26 Strauss St), **Jerusalem Furs Ltd** (5 Shattner Center) or **Scharf's** (11 Rivka St); **Beged Or** and **D'or** stores offer extremely good value in leatherware. In Haifa shop for women's clothing at **Apart** (2 Balfour Street) and **Ilka** (57 Herzl Street). Look for Bedouin work in Beersheba, at **Chen-Chen** (Egged Central Bus Station), **Opaz** (53 Herzl St) or the souvenir shop at the **Zohar Hotel,** olive wood in Bethlehem and Nazareth. Consult the useful little *Tourist Shopping Guide* that the Ministry of Tourism publishes, and look for the *Recommended for Tourists* sign that the Ministry grants shopkeepers. Tel Aviv's newest shopping complex, **Kikar Namir** (Atarim Square), overlooks the Mediterranean and is only a short walk from most Tel Aviv hotels. It has numerous restaurants, drugstores, and cafés and is the only shopping center open from 10am to midnight, including Fridays and Saturdays.

SPORTS
Swimming and water sports are very popular. There are splendid beaches on the Mediterranean coast, at **Eilat,** the Red Sea resort, and on **Lake Tiberias.** There is an 18-hole golf course at **Caesarea;** many of the big hotels have tennis courts, and there are facilities for horseback riding in Ashkelon, Caesarea, Natanya, **Gordon's Riding & Sport Club,** Tel Aviv, and at **Vered Hogalil** dude ranch in Galilee.

WHAT TO SEE
Jerusalem: Go to the **Old City,** with its eight-gated walls, to see the rooftops, archways, and alleys of former days. See the **Western Wall,** the last vestige of **Solomon Temple,** most sacred spot on earth to the Jews. Follow the **Via Dolorosa** with the 14 stations of the Cross—share the reverence of Christians at the **Church of the Holy Sepulchre** and the shrines in the **Garden of Gethsemane** (outside the walls of Jerusalem). The **Dome of the Rock**—called the **Mosque of Omar**—is the place, tradition says, where Abraham prepared to sacrifice Isaac, and from where, Muslims believe, Muhammad ascended to Heaven. Go as well to the City's museums—above all to the **Biblical and Archeological Museum,** housed in the Israel Museum, with the Shrine of the Book where visitors can see the Dead Sea Scrolls, ancient Biblical writings. Visit also the **Rockefeller Museum** and the **Bezalel Art Museum.** Explore the **Mea Shearim,** quarters of the ultra-orthodox Jews, and go to the **Knesset** (Israel's Parliament House), to see the floors and tapestries by Chagall, to the **Hebrew University,** and to **Hadassah Medical Center.** The **Biblical Zoo,** with every animal mentioned in the Bible, is worth a visit. Go outside the city to **Mount Herzl** and the tomb of Theodore Herzl, founder of modern Zionism, and to **Mount Zion** itself, to see the Tomb of King David and the Chamber of the Last Supper.

Tel Aviv is the place where the new state of Israel was proclaimed in 1948. This city, only 65 years old, bright and modern, is the largest in Israel, with a million inhabitants. Watch the bustling scene in **Dizengoff Square**—go to the shops and nightclubs. The **Tel Aviv Municipal Museum**, the **Haganah Museum**, and the **Haaretz Museum** all throw important light on the past. The new **Diaspora Museum** which traces the varied histories of these people following their forced dispersion by the Romans from their homeland is well worth the visit. There is also a zoo and a planetarium. When you are exhausted from a day's sightseeing refresh yourself with a drink at one of the numerous cafés in the Ben Yehuda and Dizengoff Street area. Hotels in Tel Aviv, centrally located unless otherwise indicated, include:

Rates are in US$ for a double/twin room with bath or shower

Ami, 4 Am Israel Chai (from $28 CP)
Astor, 105 Hayarkon Street (from $30.40 CP)
Avia, Savyon (from $45)
Basel, 156 Hayarkon Street (from $40)
City, 9 Mapu Street (from $32)
Commodore, Dizengoff Square (from $26 CP)
Concorde, 1 Trumpeldor St (from $35)
Dan, 99 Hayarkon Street (from $61 CP)
Diplomat Hotel, Hayarkon St (from $55)
Hyatt, (from $50)
Moriah Tel Aviv, 250 Hayarkon St (from $53 CP)
Ora, 35 Ben Yehuda Street (from $23 CP), near beach
Park, 75 Hayarkon Street (from $33.50)
Plaza, 127 Hayarkon Street (from $58)
Ramada Continental, 121 Hayarkon Street (from $56)
Ramat Aviv Garden, RAG, Haifa Rd (from $28)
Shalom, 216 Hayarkon Street (from $27.50 CP)
Sheraton, 123 Hayarkon Street (from $52)
Sinai, 11 Trumpeldor Street (from $35)
Tel Aviv Hilton, Independence Park (from $60)

Alongside Tel Aviv is **Jaffa,** 4,000 years old. Visit the **Artists' Quarter** overlooking the old harbor. See **St Peter's Monastery,** on the foundation of a 13th-century crusader's citadel. Look for bargains in the flea market by the clock tower.

Haifa: The third city and the "Gateway to Israel." Visit the **Bahai Gardens** and the **Bahai Temple;** the Museums of Japanese Art, Folklore, and Ancient and Modern Art; and the **Marine Museum.** Nearby is **Mount Carmel,** with its ancient foundation, the **Carmelite Monastery,** and **Elijah's Cave.** Restaurants to visit are **Pagoda** (1 Bat Galim Avenue) for a Chinese meal; **Balfour Cellar** (3 Balfour Street) for kosher meat and dairy food; the **Rondo Grill** in the Dan Carmel Hotel; **Bankers Tavern** (2 Habankim Street) for a varied menu; and **Misada Atlas** (Bat Galim Avenue) if you are a lover of seafood. Hotels in Haifa: **Ben Yehuda,** 179 Sea Road (from US$17 CP); **Dan Carmel,** 85 Shderoth Manassi (from

US$64 CP); **Nof,** 101 Hanassi Avenue (from US$40 CP); **Shulamit,** 15 Yirgat Sefer Street (from US$33 CP); and **Zion,** 5 Baerwald Street (from US$33 CP).

Acre was a crusader strongpoint, stronghold of Richard the Lion-Hearted. See the **Crypt of St John** and the **Mosque of Jazzar Pasha.** Accommodations at **Hotel Palm Beach** (from US$34 CP).

Northern Israel is the land of the **Sea of Galilee** *(Tiberias),* of **Capernaum,** of the **Mount of Beatitudes,** of **Mount Tabor** (said to be the Mount of the Transfiguration), of **Cana** and **Nazareth.** Accommodations in Tiberias (on the Sea of Galilee) include: **Galei Kinnereth** (from US$35 CP), **Tiberias Plaza** (from US$38 CP), and **Galilee Ginton** (from US$29 CP). In Nazareth, scene of Christ's childhood, see the **Church of the Annunciation,** with the ancient village well—Our Lady's Well—where Mary went to draw water with the other village women. Accommodations in Nazareth include the **Grand New Hotel** (from US$27.50 CP) and **Nazareth Hotel** (from US$28 CP). **Caesarea** was the chief port in Roman times and should be seen for its Roman and Crusader ruins; you can stay at the **Dan Caesaria** (from US$55 CP).

Bethlehem lies south of Jerusalem. Go there to visit the **Church of the Nativity,** with its grotto and silver star. See the **Shepherds' Fields** and **Rachel's Tomb.**

The **Negev** and the **Dead Sea:** Visit the ancient city of **Beersheba**—from there a scenic highway will take you to **Sodom** and the **Dead Sea,** the lowest point on earth (1,250 feet below sea level), dating back 100 million years. Swimming in the extraordinary, buoyant salt water is a rare experience. The scene is dominated by the flat-topped rock of nearby **Masada,** magnificent palace of Herod the Great and scene of the heroic resistance by Jewish nationalists to Roman forces 1,700 years ago. There is an easy cable car approach—or you can climb the ancient Snake Path. Hotels in Beersheba are the **Arava** (from US$16.50 CP); **Beersheba Desert Inn** (from US$31.25 CP); and the **Zohar** (from US$20 CP). On the Dead Sea in the small town of **En Boqeq** is the luxurious **Moriah Dead Sea** (from US$55 CP).

To the south lie **King Solomon's copper mines,** and beyond, the thriving Red Sea port and resort area of **Eilat.** Admire the way the surrounding Negev desert is being brought under cultivation. Hotels in Eilat: **Laromme Eilat,** Coral Beach (from US$55 CP); **Neptune,** PO Box 259 (from US$45 CP); **Queen of Sheba,** PO Box 196 (from US$43.50 CP); and **Red Rock,** PO Box 306 (from US$55 CP); **Caesar** (from US$45 CP); **Moriah Eilat** (from US$45 CP); and **Shulamit Gardens** (from US$46 CP).

Jericho: To the north of the Dead Sea is another ancient city—see **Elisha's Fountain** and **Herod's Winter Palace.** Seven miles away lies **Qumran,** famous for the discovery of the Dead Sea Scrolls.

SOURCES OF FURTHER INFORMATION

Pan Am agent, Andol Aviation Ltd., (G.S.A.), 9 Frishman Street, Tel Aviv, and any other Pan Am office around the world; the **Ministry of Tourism**

of the Israeli Government, 7 Mendele Street, Tel Aviv; 24 King George Avenue, Jerusalem; 350 Fifth Avenue, NY NY 10001; 795 Peachtree Street NE, Atlanta, GA 30308; 6380 Wilshire Boulevard, Beverly Hills, CA 90048; 437 Boylston Street, Boston, MA 02166; 5 South Wabash Avenue, Chicago, IL 60603; 59 St James's Street, London SW1.

Jordan

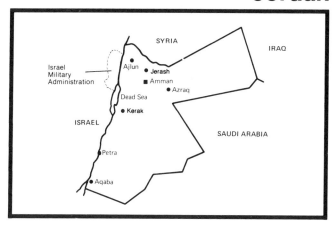

WHAT'S SPECIAL

The valley of the River Jordan is one of the most fertile areas in the world, and archaeologists have found proof that prosperous settlements existed there 4,000 years before the birth of Christ. In the desert lands beyond, fabulous cities like Petra were hidden under the sands for centuries until 19th- and 20th-century explorers and archaeologists discovered them again. It is a fascinating country.

COUNTRY BRIEFING

Size: 35,570 square miles   **Population:** 2,053,000
Capital: Amman   **Capital Population:** 1,188,000

Climate: Mostly warm, dry, and sunny, but the mountain areas have snow in winter and there is tropical heat in the desert.

Weather in Amman: Lat N31°57′; Alt 2,548 ft

Temp (°F)	Jan	Feb	Mar	Apr	May	Jun	Jul	Aug	Sep	Oct	Nov	Dec
Av Low	39°	40°	43°	49°	57°	61°	65°	65°	62°	57°	50°	42°
Av High	54°	56°	60°	73°	83°	87°	89°	90°	88°	81°	70°	59°
Days no rain	23	20	27	27	31	30	31	31	30	30	26	26

Government: Constitutional monarchy.

Language: Arabic. English widely spoken, some French.

Religion: Muslim; Christian minority.

Currency: Jordanian dinar. 1,000 fils = 1 Jordanian dinar.

	10fls	50fls	100fls	500fls	JD1	JD5	JD10	JD20
US (dollars, cents)	.03	.16	.31	1.55	3.10	15.50	31.01	62.02
UK (pounds, pence)	.01	.08	.15	.74	1.48	7.39	14.79	29.58

Public Holidays:

Arbor Day, 15 Jan

Arab League, 22 Mar

Independence Day, 25 May

King Hussein's Accession, 11 Aug

King Hussein's Birthday, 14 Nov

There are five additional Muslim holidays.

HOW TO GET THERE

Flying time to Amman International Airport from New York is 11½ hours; from Rome, 3¾ hours; from Cairo, 1¾ hours. Time in Jordan: GMT+2.

REQUIREMENTS FOR ENTRY AND CUSTOMS REGULATIONS

Passport and visa required, smallpox vaccination certificate only if coming from an infected area. Persons of the Jewish faith can enter Jordan, though they can expect their visa requests to be considerably delayed as their status is carefully checked in Amman. Israeli passports, however, will not be accepted. There is no restriction on the amount of foreign currency or travelers' checks which can be taken into Jordan. Duty-free allowance: 200 cigarettes or ½ pound tobacco or 25 cigars; 1 liter each of liquor and wine (opened bottles).

AIRPORT INFORMATION

Amman International Airport is 3 miles from the city. There is no bus service; taxis cost about JD1-2. Departure tax: JD2. There is a duty-free shop, a car rental counter, and a tourist information counter.

ACCOMMODATIONS

Amman has the luxury-class Jordan Inter • Continental and several other first-class hotels. The government has built a number of rest houses at tourist spots and sites of historical and archaeological interest, such as Petra. The rest houses provide meals, and their charges are reasonable, about JD6 double per night, excluding meals. In Amman there is a youth hostel, at the YMCA in Jebel Amman (tel: 41588). There are no off-season reductions, and there is no central source of assistance for finding accommodations, but the Ministry of Tourism and Antiquities will advise (tel: 42311). Hotels in Amman:

Rates are in US$ for a double/twin room with bath or shower

Al Cazar, Al Hashimi Street (from $19)

Ambassador, Shmesani (from $37)

Cameo, Jebel Amman (from $25)

City, H E Muhammad Street (from $25)

Commodore, Shmesani (from $31)

Granada, Jebel Amman (from $25)

Grand Palace, Amman University Street (from $31), about 4 miles from city center

Holiday Inn, Jebel Amman (from $67)

JORDAN INTER • CONTINENTAL, Jebel Amman (from $67)

Jordan Tower, Shmesani (from $25)
Merryland, Abdali (from $25)
Middle East, Shmesani (from $37)
Philadelphia, Al Hashimi Street (from $37)
San Rock (from $47), about 3½ miles from city center
Sheraton (from $75), about 4 miles from city center
Unless otherwise indicated, the above hotels are centrally located.

USEFUL INFORMATION

Banks: Open 8:30-1 Sat-Thurs.

Mail: Stamps at post offices or hotels.

Telephone Tips: There are a few street booths, found at main intersections, but they are usually not in working order. Phones are usually available in hotels, restaurants, cafés, and shops. Useful numbers in Amman:

Pan Am 41959	**Operator** and **Directories** 12
Airport Information 51401-9	**External Calls** 10 & 17
Tourism Authority 42312	**Emergencies** 19

Newspapers: English and American newspapers are available. The *Jordan Times* is published daily.

Tipping: Expected in restaurants (10%); porters, 100-200 fils; chambermaids, 150-200 fils; cloakroom attendants, 50-100 fils; taxi drivers, 10%, but not compulsory.

Electricity: 220 volts 50 cycles AC.

Laundry: Services slow but sure. Prices reasonable.

Hairdressing: Main hotels have salons (shampoo and set from JD2.5, tip 200 fils; man's haircut from 600 fils, tip 100 fils).

Photography: Good selection of equipment and film in major cities and tourist sites, but many camera shops seem to carry color only. Black and white and color prints can be developed in 1-2 days. You are not allowed to take pictures of military installations, including bridges. Be careful about everything you photograph; a good rule is "ask before you snap."

Clubs: Kiwanis, Rotary, and Lions.

Babysitting: No services.

Rest Rooms: Available in hotels, restaurants, shops. Usually called *Toilette*.

Health: Many doctors and dentists speak English. Hospital facilities in Amman are good. Imported pharmaceuticals and toiletries are reasonably priced. Milk should be boiled; fruit and vegetables should be well washed. Water is safe except in small villages and at wayside stands.

TRANSPORTATION

Amman has buses, and there are long-distance services linking main towns. Most tourists prefer the taxi services. In Amman taxis are plentiful and can be hailed in the street or ordered by phone. Charges are fixed and usually metered, but if the cab does not have a meter, it is a good idea to agree on the charge beforehand. Shared taxis operate between all major towns and cities, and rates are reasonable. Rental cars are available. Main roads are asphalt and fairly good; driving is on the right, and Jordanians claim they have no traffic jams. A train service links Amman with Damascus, in Syria, but is not recommended for fast journeys. ALIA, the Royal Jordanian Airline, flies between Amman and Aqaba, taking 25 minutes.

FOOD AND RESTAURANTS

Typical Arab foods include *kebabs* (meat roasted on skewers), *mensaf* (rice with lamb and yoghurt sauce), and *musakhan* (chicken in olive oil and onion sauce roasted in Arabian bread). These and other local specialties can be tried in Amman at the **Jerusalem Restaurant** on King Hussein Street (tel: 30168), the **Jordan Restaurant** on Prince Muhammad Street (tel: 38333), **Le César** (tel: 24431) in Jebel Webdeh, the **Orient** restaurant on Basman Street (tel: 36039), and the **New Orient** (tel: 41879) and **Diplomat** (tel: 25592) restaurants in Jebel Amman. The Jordan Inter · Continental Hotel (tel: 41361) and the **Royal Automobile Club** on Wadi Esseir Road (tel: 44261) both serve international food as well as Arab dishes. Try also the **Elite**, in Jebel Webdeh (tel: 22103), and **La Terrasse** in Shmesani (tel: 62831). Chinese food is the specialty at **Taiwan Tourismo** (Third Circle, Jebel Amman—tel: 41093), the **Chinese Restaurant** (Jebel Amman—tel: 38968), and **Mandarin Chinese Restaurant**, opposite the Holiday Inn (tel: 61922). For Turkish dishes go to **Istanbul** in Jebel Amman (tel: 28212). Also try the **Hussein Sports City Restaurant** (tel: 39334) and the **Paradise** (tel: 63311) both in Shmesani, and the **Mandaloun** near the Orthodox Club (tel: 43564). Snack foods include *shawarma* (sliced broiled lamb) and a large variety of desserts and cakes. These are usually taken with Turkish-style coffee.

DRINKING TIPS

The sale of liquor is unrestricted, and imported wines, liquors, and beers are available. A whisky and soda costs about JD1, and a bottle of *vin ordinaire* in a hotel or restaurant about JD2. *Arak* is the local apéritif. Bars open from noon to about 11pm, and women are welcome in hotel and restaurant bars. Remember that many Muslims do not drink alcohol.

ENTERTAINMENT

There are no theaters in Jordan, but numerous movie houses show British and American movies with original soundtrack. There are occasional concerts by visiting musicians. Tourists should try to see the folklore presentation given at the **Roman Amphitheater** in Amman and also visit the **Hussein Youth City** in Amman, which sometimes has interesting programs at the **Palace of Culture.** Several hotels have music and dancing, and there are a few nightclubs in Amman—**Le César** (tel: 24431) in Jebel Webdeh, the **Venus Club** (tel: 37236) in Jebel Amman, and the **Caravan** in the Jordan Inter · Continental. There are several discos, including some in the major hotels; those within the city limits stay open until 1am, outside until later.

SHOPPING

Stores open at 8 or 9 and remain open until 7. Some close for lunch from 1:30 to 3 or 3:30. Muslims close on Friday and Christians on Sunday. Prices are fixed in the shops, but you are expected to bargain in the markets *(souks)*. Best buys include rugs from Madaba, Hebron glassware, mother-of-pearl boxes and pins from Amman, carvings and boxes in olive wood, delicate bronze and silverwork, Palestine pottery, Oriental jewelry, and intricate cross-stitch embroidery. The art gallery in the lobby of the Jordan Inter · Continental sells oil paintings and watercolors as well as antiques. For handicraft items, try the **Jordan Crafts Center** near Second Circle, Jebel Amman. Also try **Jerusalem Exhibitions**, the **Bethlehem Store,** and the **Jordan Gifts Store,** all in Jebel Amman. **Jordan Souvenirs** on Prince Muhammad Street near the General Post Office specializes in old caftans. Most of Amman's gold and silver shops are located in the jewelry souk (market) in the center of the city in the King Feisal Street area. Some important ones are **Shafik al Halteh, Shamieh, Mashi, Khoury, George S. Nour,** and **Kopti Jewelry. Jabasini,** Jebel Amman, sells Western-style jewelry.

SPORTS

Horse racing and sometimes camel racing can be seen at the **Marka** racecourse, just outside Amman, during the summer. In the middle of the racetrack is a nine-hole golf course belonging to the **Amman Golf Club.** Golfers are advised to take old clubs, as the fairways are not grassed and the greens are sand. Soccer is a popular spectator sport. Facilities for this and other sports such as basketball, tennis, squash, and athletics are at the **Hussein Sports City** on the outskirts of Amman (membership required). There are several swimming pools in the capital, including a large one at the Inter · Continental Hotel. **Aqaba** is excellent for swimming, skin-diving, and water-skiing, and there is also deep-sea fishing there. Amman has an archery range at the **Royal Automobile Club,** and there is horseback riding in Amman at reasonable charges.

WHAT TO SEE

Amman is spread over seven steep-sided hills *(jebels)* and is today a handsome modern city with gleaming white limestone buildings. Little remains of its historic past except the ruins of the **Temple of Hercules** on Citadel Hill, near Jebel Hussein, and the fine **Roman Theater** opposite the Citadel, built into the curve of a hill by the Emperor Trajan in the 2nd century AD. It has excellent acoustics and seats 6,000 people for outdoor festivals and concerts. There are two museums devoted to ethnography within the amphitheater complex. On the Citadel, opposite the amphitheater, the **Jordan Archeological Museum** has a rare collection of Nabataean pottery, relics of the Crusades, and ancient artifacts from the area.

Jerash, 30 miles north of Amman, is one of the most beautifully preserved Greco-Roman cities in the world. Since the 1920s excavations have disclosed the magnificent colonnades, temples, and streets of this city—which was lost to the Western world from the time of the Crusades. You can now see the great **Triumphal Arch** erected in 129 AD to welcome the Emperor Hadrian, the **Temple of Artemis** with its impressive stairway and magnificent columns, the **Street of Columns** which leads out of the colonnaded **Forum,** the ornamental **Nymphaeum** fountain built in 190 AD, the **West Baths,** and the **Theater.** There is also a **Cathedral** built by 4th-century Christians and a **Museum** with interesting archaeological finds. From Amman to Jerash is a 45-minute drive, and you can stay in the rest house, complete with restaurant.

Castles and fortresses built in the 7th and 8th centuries, many now in ruins, are an impressive sight standing stark against the sand in the desert that lies to the north and east of Amman. They were built as fortresses, hunting lodges, pleasure palaces, and watch-posts by the Omayyad Caliphs. **Ajlun,** 41 miles north of Amman, is the site of a magnificent fortress built by one of Saladin's generals in 1184. The **Roman Fortress** at Azraq was used as headquarters by Lawrence of Arabia, and he described it as "magically haunted." The oasis of Azraq and over 1,000 square miles of desert have been turned into a **National Park** to preserve the wildlife, which includes a few herds of gazelles and ibex. Most impressive of the castles to the south of Amman is one from the Crusaders period located at **Kerak,** about 80 miles south along the King's Highway. The town of Kerak is within the massive fortified walls of the castle, built in the 12th century on a towering height overlooking the Dead Sea Valley. Visitors may enter the castle free of charge after registering with the Antiquities Inspector. Accommodations and meals are available at the government rest house.

Umm Qais, about 60 miles north of Amman, is on the site of ancient Gadara—scene of the Biblical tale of the Gadarene swine. Within yards of Jordan's northern border, Umm Qais commands a breathtaking view of the Sea of Galilee in Israel, and contains the ruins from the Roman, Hellenistic, Byzantine, and early Islamic periods—some of them restored by recent archaeological work.

Petra, the "rose-red city, half as old as time," can be visited on a fairly arduous day trip from Amman, but there is so much to see and it is so fascinating that it is much better to stay at the **Petra Rest House** just outside the entrance to the ruins. From nearby **Wadi Musa** you can hire a docile horse and multilingual guide, and after a short ride up the narrow gorge of the **Siq** you are confronted with one of the world's most beautiful and dramatic sights. Through a cleft in the dark rocks you suddenly glimpse, outlined in sunshine, the noble facade of **El Khaznah,** the **Treasury of Petra,** carved with delicate precision into the sandstone face of the mountain.

Wadi Rum, the vast desert valley where Lawrence of Arabia camped, lies between Petra and the Red Sea. Travelers on the **Desert Highway,** which runs for 209 miles from Amman to Aqaba, pass this eerie valley with its towering cliffs of weird and fantastic shapes. Land Rover tours to Wadi Rum, which include a stop for Arab coffee at the **Desert Camel Corps fort,** can be arranged from Aqaba. There are also planned caravan tours taking visitors into the desert for overnight camping; and daylight treks by camel, returning to the Desert Highway at **Quweira.** A thrilling view of Wadi Rum is possible from **Ras-en-Naqb,** where there is a rest house.

Aqaba, Jordan's only seaport, lies on the Red Sea backed by a rugged range of mountains. Though it dates from Biblical times, Aqaba is now an attractive modern winter resort with sandy beaches, excellent water sports, and good hotels, including the **Al Cazar,** PO Box 392 (from US$31 double), the **Aqaba,** PO Box 43 (from US$31 double), the **Coral Beach,** PO Box 71 (from US$31 double), the **Holiday Inn** of Aqaba, Kings Boulevard (from US$50 double), and the **Miramar** (from US$31 double). Aqaba has two museums: the **Gulf of Aqaba Museum** and the **Red Sea Museum.**

SOURCES OF FURTHER INFORMATION

Pan Am agents, United Travel Agency, Zahran, Amman, or any Pan Am office round the world; **Jordan Ministry of Tourism and Antiquities,** PO Box 224, Amman; **Jordan Information Bureau,** Suite 1004, 1701 K Street NW, Washington, DC; **Jordan Consulate,** 866 UN Plaza, New York, NY 10017, and 177 Regent Street, London W1.

Kuwait

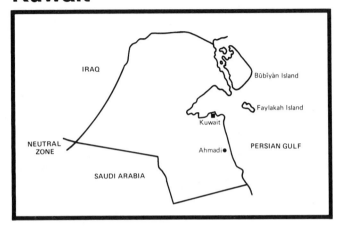

WHAT'S SPECIAL

Thanks to the discovery of oil in the 1930s, Kuwait is believed to be the richest country in the Middle East, with a per capita income that has now climbed to about $16,500 a year. The city of Kuwait is the showplace of a country whose oil riches benefit its people in housing, hospitals, schools, a generous pension system, and a fund for economic aid to developing countries. Modern cities have now mushroomed on a desert landscape once occupied only by oases and oil rigs.

COUNTRY BRIEFING

The **area** is 7,780 square miles and the **population** 1,350,000, of whom 750,000 live in the **capital,** Kuwait. Summer **temperatures** can reach 120°F, with no rain at all; winters are cool with most of the rainfall between January and March. The north wind (shimal) sometimes blows up severe sand storms. **Government:** Kuwait is an independent and sovereign Arab state, ruled by an emir with a unicameral national assembly; official **language** is Arabic, with English the second language. **Religion** is Muslim. **Currency** is the Kuwait dinar (1,000 fils = 1KD; 0.275KD = US$1). **Public holidays** include Kuwait National Day (25 Feb) and the Muslim Maloud, Leilat al Meiraj, Id ul Fitr, Id ul Adha, and New Year, all based on the lunar calendar. It is preferable to avoid a visit during the month of Ramadan because most of the city is closed.

HOW TO GET THERE

Flying time to Kuwait International Airport from New York is 13 hours; from London, 6 hours; from Bahrain 1 hour. Time in Kuwait: GMT+3.

REQUIREMENTS FOR ENTRY AND CUSTOMS REGULATIONS

Passport, visa, and round-trip ticket necessary. Smallpox vaccination certificate required; cholera and yellow-fever vaccination certificates if coming from an infected area. No currency regulations, but it is forbidden to bring any alcohol into Kuwait, and pornographic magazines are confiscated. Duty-free allowance: 100 cigarettes or 50 cigars, although they are less expensive in Kuwait.

AIRPORT INFORMATION

The Kuwait International Airport is 10 miles from the center of Kuwait. A taxi ride into town costs about KD2. Tip porters about 150 fils per bag.

ACCOMMODATIONS

Because of increased travel by Western businessmen, it is advisable to book rooms early and ask for confirmation by cable or letter. Hotels in the city of Kuwait:

Rates are in US$ for a double/twin room with bath or shower

Bristol, Fahad al-Salem Street (from $72)

Carlton, Fahad al-Salem Street (from $100)

Golden Beach, Gulf Street (from $105)

Kuwait Hilton, Benail al-Ghar (from $135)

Kuwait Marriott Marina, Safat (from $118)

Kuwait Sheraton, Fahad al-Salem Street (from $155)

Messilah Beach Hotel, Salmiyah, about 2 miles from the city (from $100)

Phoenicia, Fahad al-Salem Street (from $72)

Sahara, Al Sour Street (from $80)

Rates are exclusive of a 15% service charge. Unless otherwise indicated, the above hotels are centrally located.

USEFUL INFORMATION

Banks open 8:30-noon daily except Friday. English-language **newspapers** available; local English-language publications are the *Arab Times* and *Kuwait Times.* **Tipping** is customary and generally 10% unless a service charge has been added. Taxi drivers are not normally tipped, but long-distance drivers should be given 10%; hotel porter and chambermaid, 150 fils; cloakroom attendants, 100 fils. **Electricity** is 240 volts 50 cycles AC. Numerous **laundry** and dry-cleaning services. **Photographic** equipment available, also black and white and color film. Drinking water safe; imported pharmaceuticals expensive.

TRANSPORTATION

Buses, taxis, and rented cars available. Bus fare in the city of Kuwait is a flat 50 fils; taxi fare is from 500-750 fils within the city (if using a taxi for the day, agree on the price beforehand). Car rental counters at Sheraton and Hilton Hotels.

FOOD AND RESTAURANTS

Dishes tend to be strongly spiced and accompanied by the traditional flat bread. Tasty specialties are *sayyadiya*, fish and rice, and *harees*, a mixture of rice, yoghurt, and meat. Some interesting restaurants in the capital are **Abou-Nawas, Haroun al-Rashid,** the **KAC Tower** and **Kuwait Towers** restaurants, all with Arabic food; **Caesar's** (behind the Kuwait Sheraton), **Mandarin,** and **Silver Star,** with Chinese food; and **Khyber,** with Pakistani and Middle Eastern food. Food served in hotels is both Continental and Middle Eastern. A three-course meal costs about KD4-8 per person, including service charge. There are nightclubs at the large hotels.

SHOPPING

Stores are open 9-12 and 4:30-9, closed Fridays. Best buys include Persian carpets, brassware, copperware, and handbags imported from Egypt, Syria, and Lebanon. Try the department stores and boutiques on Fahed al-Salim Street. Older, more traditional handicrafts have become scarce, but some are to be found at the old **souk** off Palestine Street.

WHAT TO SEE

Sights in the old city of **Kuwait** include the old city gates and portions of the old city walls. The **Kuwait Museum** has good exhibits of Bronze Age, Babylonian (c. 1,500 BC), and Hellenic (c. 300 BC) remnants. The observatory in the modern **Kuwait Towers** building affords a view over all of the city. **Failaka Island,** 20 miles off the coast, has an **Ethnographical Museum** and archaeological excavations of a Bronze Age settlement and of a fortress town in existence at the time of Alexander the Great. The **Exhibition Center** of the Kuwait Oil Company is in **Ahmadi,** about 25 miles south of Kuwait City.

SOURCES OF FURTHER INFORMATION

Any **Pan Am** office around the world; **Kuwait Ministry of Guidance and Information,** Kuwait Airport; **Kuwaiti Embassy,** 2940 Tilden St NW, Washington, DC 20008, and 40 Devonshire St, London W1.

Note: Because of the political situation in Lebanon, it has not been possible to provide complete information for this chapter.

Lebanon

WHAT'S SPECIAL
The flow of foreign visitors to this beautiful country was virtually stopped by the political unrest of recent years. Now that normalcy is gradually returning, the Lebanese government is encouraging the travelers' return. Visitors will still find Beirut a modern capital with entertainment and comforts of an international standard. To the north and south of Beirut are 134 miles of coastline with many sandy beaches and, only an hour away, there are snowy mountains for skiing in the sun.

COUNTRY BRIEFING
Size: 4,015 square miles   **Population:** 3,200,000
Capital: Beirut   **Capital Population:** 1,000,000
   Climate: Though there are four distinct seasons, it is almost always cool in the mountains and usually quite warm near the sea. April through December is the best time to visit.
   Weather in Beirut: Lat N35°28′; Alt 111 ft

Temp (°F)	Jan	Feb	Mar	Apr	May	Jun	Jul	Aug	Sep	Oct	Nov	Dec
Av Low	51°	51°	54°	58°	64°	69°	73°	74°	73°	69°	61°	55°
Av High	62°	63°	66°	72°	78°	83°	87°	89°	86°	81°	73°	65°
Days no rain	16	16	22	25	29	30	31	31	29	27	22	19

Government: A republic.
   Language: Arabic. French is spoken extensively and about 35% of the population speaks English.
   Religion: Roughly 50% of the population is Muslim, 50% Christian.
   Currency: Lebanese pound. 100 piasters = L£1

SOURCES OF FURTHER INFORMATION

Any **Pan Am** office around the world; **Ministry of Tourism** Rue Banque du Liban, Beirut; **National Council of Tourism,** P.O. Box 5344, Hamra Street, Beirut; (tel: 340940); **Lebanon Tourist and Information Office,** 405 Park Avenue, New York, NY 10022; **Lebanon Tourist Information Office,** 90 Piccadilly, London W1.

Saudi Arabia

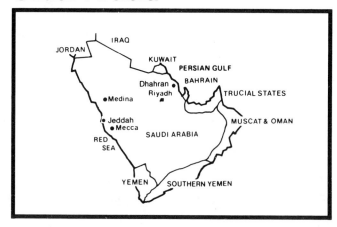

WHAT'S SPECIAL

Saudi Arabia is the cradle of Islam. The Prophet Muhammad preached the new religion 1,400 years ago, vanquished Mecca and Medina, and spread the faith throughout Arabia, to be carried later by his successors as far as China in the East and Spain in the West. Mecca, with the shrine of the Holy Kaaba, and Medina, site of the Prophet's tomb, are the two most venerated cities in Islam, the goal of more than 2,000,000 *hajjis* or pilgrims yearly who come from all over the world to fulfill their duty as prescribed by the Koran.

Modern Saudi Arabia has another side. It is the world's largest exporter of oil and also has the world's largest known reserves of oil. Due to a crash modernization program, it has rapidly become a magnet for businessmen associated with oil production, petrochemicals, minerals, and the requirements of building an infrastructure for urban and industrial expansion. Widely open to business, the country is closed to tourism. The foreign work force of two million is double the number of employed Saudis. The rigid rules of the Koran are the law of the land, and they are strictly enforced. Alcoholic liquors are prohibited, women still wear veils in public and they seldom work, drive, wear short skirts, or even ride alone in a taxi, and nightlife and any public entertainment are nonexistent.

COUNTRY BRIEFING

Size: 864,640

Capital: Riyadh

Population: 10,600,000

Capital Population: 1,000,000

Climate: Saudi Arabia is a tropical country with an immense variety of desert terrains and cloudless, sunny skies. Jeddah, the seaport on the Red Sea and the natural gateway to Mecca and Medina, is noted for hot and humid weather from late March through November; the winters are rather pleasant. Taif, in the mountains near Jeddah, is noted for its cool breezes during the summer months. Riyadh, perched on the Nejd Plateau, has torrid dry summers and icy dry winters. Dhahran, in the oil producing and exporting area, enjoys a moderate winter climate and a hot and humid summer from April to November.

Weather in Riyadh: Lat N24° 39'

Av Temp	Jan	Feb	Mar	Apr	May	Jun	Jul	Aug	Sep	Oct	Nov	Dec
Riyadh (°F)	31°	32°	47°	72°	78°	99°	115°	122°	119°	95°	91°	42°

Government: Monarchy.
Language: Arabic, English widely spoken in cities.
Religion: Islam. No public non-Muslim religious services.
Currency: Saudi riyals. 100 halalas = 1 riyal; US$1 = 3.38 riyals.

Public Holidays

There are four Muslim holidays: Maloud; Eid al-Fitr (Breaking of the Fast) lasts for a week at the end of Ramadan, the Muslim month of fasting; Eid al-Adha (The Sacrifice) lasts for ten days and coincides with the Pilgrimage to Mecca; Muslim New Year. Dates vary according to the lunar calendar. In addition, National Day is celebrated 13 September. Businesses are closed on Fridays (the weekly holiday), and open on Sundays.

HOW TO GET THERE

Flying time to Dhahran airport from New York is 12 hours; from Istanbul, 4¾ hours; from Bahrain, 25 minutes. Time in Saudi Arabia: GMT+3.

REQUIREMENTS FOR ENTRY AND CUSTOMS REGULATIONS

Passport, visa, and smallpox and cholera vaccinations are required. Persons of Jewish faith or those holding an Israeli visa will be refused entry. No restriction on currency or other imports, except alcoholic beverages, narcotics, pork products, and pornography, which are strictly forbidden.

AIRPORT INFORMATION

Dhahran and Riyadh Airports are all about 10 minutes from town. The new Jeddah International Airport, opened 1981, is one of the world's largest and most modern. Taxis from Dhahran and Riyadh to the city center are about US$7.50, from Jeddah US$6.

ACCOMMODATIONS

A large number of hotels have opened recently; more are being built or planned. There is an abundance of hotel space in the Eastern Province. However, occasional shortages still occur in Riyadh and Jeddah, especially

487

during the pilgrimage season. It is helpful to have a contact in the country who can make and reconfirm reservations.

Room rates are set by the government according to the class of the hotel. All the following hotels are classified as First Class or Luxury, and the rates given are for single rooms, including a 15% service charge.

Riyadh:

Al Khozama, city center, tel: 465 4650, telex: 200100 KHOZAM SJ (from US$90)

Attala, city center, tel: 478 9764, telex: 201665 RASIDE SJ (from US$95)

INTER · CONTINENTAL, city center, tel: 465 5111, telex: 201076 RUHIHC SJ (from US$112)

Khurais Marriott, 6¼ miles north of airport on Dhahran Highway, tel: 464-2133, telex: 200133 KHUMAR SJ (from US$100)

Saudia, Nassiriya Street, tel: 35051, telex: 201069 SAUDIN SJ (from US$75)

Jeddah:

Al Attas, city center, tel: 20400, telex: 48071 AMSK SJ (from US$80)

Kaki, Airport Road, tel: 48071, telex: 401379 AMSK SJ (from US$80)

Kandara Palace, Airport Road, tel: 6425700, telex: 401095 SJ (from US$95), 5 minutes from airport

Meridien, city center, tel: 45011, telex: 401327 HOMER SJ (from US$122)

Sands, Hamra District, tel: 57995, telex: 401534 STRACO SJ (from US$125)

Sheraton, Airport Road, tel: 47077, telex: 401512 SHERAT SJ (from US$122)

Eastern Province (Dhahran/Dammam/Al Khobar):

Al Gosaibi, Al Khobar, tel: 864 2466, telex: 670008 GOSHOTEL SJ (from US$98)

Carlton, Al Khobar, tel: 864 5214, telex: 670064 CARLTON SJ (from US$95)

Dammam, Dammam, tel: 832 9000, telex: 601108 DHOTEL SJ (from US$75)

Dammam Oberoi, Dammam, tel: 8345555, telex: 602071/2 OBHTEL SJ (from US$62)

Dhahran International, Dhahran, tel: 864 8555, telex: 601272 DIAH SJ (from US$120)

Marriott, Dhahran, tel: 864 8222, telex: 601226 DHAMAR SJ (from US$98)

Ramada, Al Khobar, tel: 864 5720, telex: 601227 RAMADA SJ (from US$82)

Mecca:

INTER · CONTINENTAL, (Muslim guests only), 4 miles from city center, tel: 31580, telex: 440006 QCAIHC SJ (from US$135)

Taif:

INTER · CONTINENTAL, tel: 732833, telex: 450055 MADARA SJ (from US$106)

Sheraton, tel: 41400, telex: 451092 SHERHD SJ (from US$102)

USEFUL INFORMATION

Banks: Open 8-12 every day except Friday. Citibank and the Saudi British Bank (formerly the British Bank of the Middle East) have offices in Jeddah and Riyadh and offer a full range of banking services.

Mail: Stamps at post offices. Hotels can handle mail.

Telephones: Available at hotels and restaurants.

USEFUL NUMBERS IN SAUDI ARABIA

Pan Am in Al Khobar (Dhahran/Dammam): 864 2977
Pan Am in Riyadh: 25 8659
Pan Am in Jeddah: 6675330
Saudia in Al Khobar: 864 2000
Saudia in Rivadh: 33333
Saudia in Jeddah: 33333
American Embassy in Jeddah: 670080
American Consulate in Dhahran: 43200
American Embassy Liaison Office in Riyadh: 477 2528
British Embassy in Jeddah: 604430
American Express in Jeddah: 31151

AREA CODE PREFIXES:

Riyadh 01,   Jeddah 021,   Taif 023,
Dhahran/Dammam/Al Khobar 03,   Mecca 022

Newspapers: English and American newspapers are available. There are two English-language dailies, the *Arab News* and the *Saudi Gazette,* and one English-language weekly business magazine, *Saudi Business.*

Tipping: A 10-15% tip is expected in restaurants and hotels, and is usually added to the bill. A small additional tip, up to about half of the service charge, is generally left for restaurant waiters. No tips to taxi drivers.

Electricity: Voltage is 110 and 120; process of standardization to 60 cycles AC is near completion.

Laundry: Services are available at hotels and dry-cleaning shops.

Hairdressing: Available at hotels. Prices reasonable.

Photography: An array of equipment of all kinds is available at duty-free shops.

Babysitting: Only at the Riyadh Inter · Continental Hotel.

Rest Rooms: Available at hotels and restaurants.

Health: Many English-speaking doctors and dentists.

TRANSPORTATION

In the three main cities, taxis and private cars are now commonly used, creating serious traffic jams at rush hours. Taxis are unmetered, and although the government posts rates, the prices are somewhat flexible. Taxi fare is about 15 riyals for an average ride, 20 riyals for a longer trip. Once a price is agreed on, no tipping is necessary. A comfortable, subsidized public bus system has begun service in Riyadh and Jeddah, with some intercity connections. Saudia, the national airline, maintains a cheap, dependable network of frequent flights by modern jet to some 30 cities within this vast country. Book early, since flights fill up quickly.

FOOD AND RESTAURANTS

The national dish in Saudi Arabia is the *kabsah,* made of either seafood or meat and rice. Arabs took this dish with them to Spain centuries ago, where it is now famous as Valencian *paella.* If you are invited to a gala meal, you might be served stuffed mutton garnished with almonds and eggs, and though you will be supplied with knives and forks it is often more diplomatic to eat with only your right hand. Other fine Western and Middle Eastern foods are served in hotels and restaurants. New restaurants are springing up fast, so check the English-language papers for the ads. Nonalcoholic beverages such as cider and grape juice are usually served with meals.

In Jeddah, restaurants offering Arabic selections include **Topkapi, Kaymak Glace, Al Hamra Casino, Alfleila Waleila, Morocco,** and **Nation's Beach. Shalimar** and **Spinzer** serve Pakistani food ; **Shangri-La** and **China Rose,** Chinese food; **Il Castello,** Italian food; or **Rebeia International,** Indonesian food. Go to the **Al Attas Oasis Hotel** cafeteria, an "American-style restaurant," for hamburgers, steaks, and salads, or to the **American Steak House** or the restaurants at the **Meridien, Sheraton,** and **Kaki** hotels. In Riyadh, try the **Japanese Steak House, Roma Restaurant** (serving Swiss and Italian dishes), and the **Oasis Restaurant** at the Inter · Continental Hotel. Recommended in the Dhahran, Dammam, and Al Khobar area are the Syrian menu at **Bassam Oasis,** and restaurants in the **Marriott, Ramada, Carlton,** and **Al Gosaibi** hotels.

SHOPPING

Stores are open 9-1pm and 5-10pm, and closed on Fridays. Best buys are electronic equipment, cameras, rugs, carved wood, gold jewelry, and brass and copperware imported from Iran, India, and Pakistan. Prices tend to be high, and in stores they are fixed. Prices in the souks, or markets, are flexible, and the gold souk in Jeddah is a good place to buy gifts. In souks, try to get 5-10% off, even on cameras and stereo equipment.

WHAT TO SEE

The most important attractions in Saudi Arabia are the Holy Shrines of Mecca and Medina, restricted to visitors of the Muslim faith. Other attractions are the impressive oil industry installations in the eastern zone, including Ras Tanura refinery and port on the Arabian Gulf, where crude oil is loaded daily into waiting tankers. The Red Sea is a magnificent natural underwater museum, where coral and volcanic formations of all shapes blend with a myriad of incredibly colorful fish and other aquatic animals and plants. All you need to see it are an inexpensive diving mask, snorkel, and swim fins or some other protection for the feet, such as canvas shoes. (The bottom is rocky, the coral sharp, and there are spiny, poisonous stonefish—so called because they look like stones—on the coral.) Scuba-diving has become very popular, although oxygen equipment is not necessary to see the colorful undersea life against the coral reef. Diving equipment is readily available in Jeddah. A few *dhows* cross daily between Al Khobar and **Bahrain,** leaving in the morning and arriving at **Manama** 3 to 4 hours later.

SOURCES OF FURTHER INFORMATION

Pan Am, PO Box 6, Dhahran International Airport, Dhahran, the Pan Am reservations and ticket office in Al Khobar just off King Abdul Aziz Street near Abdullah Fouad Center, and any Pan Am office around the world; **Saudi Arabia Consulate,** 866 UN Plaza, New York, NY 10017; **Saudi Arabia Embassy,** 30 Belgrave Square, London SWI.

Note: Because of the political situation in Syria, it has not been possible to provide complete information for this chapter.

Syria

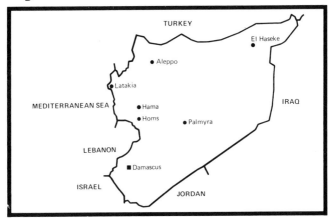

WHAT'S SPECIAL

Syria, ancient battleground of Phoenicians, Greeks, Persians and Romans, looks toward the Mediterranean in one direction, the Euphrates in another. History is everywhere; in the sites of Biblical fame, the temples of the Greco-Roman period, the ruins of Byzantine towns, the Turkish mosques, the Crusader castles of the Middle Ages. Geographically it is a mixed land: scorched deserts, coastal greenery, snow-capped mountains, and the warm Mediterranean Sea are the setting for a character and culture that are predominantly Arabic. Despite the gradual intrusion of 20th-century civilization, traditions die hard beyond the cities. Mechanization has barely touched the more remote areas, nomadic tribes wander on the steppes, and craftsmen follow ancient methods. Damascus, though modernized by comparison, can claim to be the oldest continuously inhabited city in the world.

COUNTRY BRIEFING

Size: 71,498 square miles   **Population:** 8,500,000
Capital: Damascus   **Capital Population:** 2,000,000
   Climate: Varies from relatively hot Mediterranean-type summers and warm, often rainy, winters on the coast to hot summers and cold winters inland. In the desert temperatures fluctuate.
   Weather in Damascus: Lat N33°30′; Alt 2,363 ft

Temp (°F)	Jan	Feb	Mar	Apr	May	Jun	Jul	Aug	Sep	Oct	Nov	Dec
Av Low	36°	39°	42°	49°	55°	61°	64°	64°	60°	54°	47°	40°
Av High	53°	57°	65°	75°	84°	91°	96°	99°	91°	81°	67°	56°
Days no rain	24	22	29	27	30	30	31	31	28	29	25	26

Government: A republic.

Language: Arabic. Some English and French spoken in tourist areas.

Religion: About 85% Muslim. Christian minorities include Greek Orthodox, Roman Catholic, Protestant and Syriac.

Currency: Syrian pound. 100 piasters = 1 Syrian pound.

SOURCES OF FURTHER INFORMATION

National Tourist Organization, 29 Ayar Street, Damascus; **Arab Information Center,** 747 Third Avenue, New York, NY 10017; **Syrian Arab Republic Embassy,** 2215 Wyoming Avenue NW, Washington, DC 20008; 5 Eaton Terrace, London SW1.

Turkey

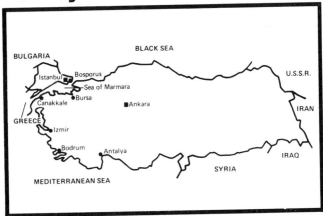

WHAT'S SPECIAL

Europe and Asia meet in Turkey, with the Bosporus Strait as the dividing line. On her borders are Greece, Bulgaria, the USSR, Iran, Iraq, and Syria. It is a country on which 12 different civilizations have left their mark, and it is rich in antiquities. There are ruins dating back to the Greeks, Romans, Selcuk and Ottoman Turks, Assyrians, Persians, and Hittites.

COUNTRY BRIEFING

Size: 296,000 square miles
Capital: Ankara
Population: 45,217,556
Capital Population: 2,500,000

Climate: Varies widely. The Anatolian Plain is hot in summer and freezing in winter, the Black Sea coast is mild and damp, and the Mediterranean coast is warm and sunny with an average annual temperature of 75°F. The best time of the year to visit is from April to October.

Weather in Istanbul: Lat N40°58'; Alt 96 ft

Temp (°F)	Jan	Feb	Mar	Apr	May	Jun	Jul	Aug	Sep	Oct	Nov	Dec
Av Low	36°	37°	39°	45°	53°	60°	65°	66°	61°	54°	48°	41°
Av High	45°	47°	52°	61°	68°	77°	81°	81°	75°	67°	59°	51°
Days no rain	19	18	22	24	26	26	28	28	25	22	29	16

Government: Republic
Language: Turkish. Some English, German, and French spoken.
Religion: 98% Muslim.

Currency: Turkey lira. 100 kurus = TL1

	50K	TL 1	TL 50	TL 100	TL 200	TL 500	TL 1000	TL 2000
US (dollars, cents)	—	.01	.52	1.03	2.06	5.16	10.32	20.64
UK (pounds, pence)	—	—	.25	.49	.98	2.46	4.92	9.85

Public Holidays:

New Year's Day, 1 Jan   Constitution Day, 27 May
Children's Day, 23 Apr   Victory Day, 30 Aug
Spring Day, 1 May   Republic Day, 29 Oct
Youth Day, 19 May

Two Turkish religious (Islamic) holidays are kept: the end of Ramadan and Kurban Bayram, the dates of which vary annually.

HOW TO GET THERE

Flying time to Istanbul, Yesilköy Airport from New York is 10 hours; from Frankfurt, 2¾ hours; from Rome, 2¼ hours. Time in Turkey: GMT+3.

REQUIREMENTS FOR ENTRY AND CUSTOMS REGULATIONS

US, British, and European (not Greek) citizens need a current passport but no visa. Currency regulations allow only TL1,000 to be taken into the country. Duty-free allowance: 200 cigarettes or 20 cigars; 2 quarts liquor (opened). No smallpox vaccination certificate needed unless coming from an infected area.

AIRPORT INFORMATION

Yesilköy Airport, Istanbul, is 30 minutes from the city center. The bus fare is about TL50, and a taxi will cost about TL900. There is a Tourist Information Office at the airport. Esenboğa Airport is a 40-minute ride from the center of Ankara. The bus ride is TL50, the taxi fare about TL1,200. Ciğli Airport is 45 minutes from downtown Izmir. There are duty-free shops at Istanbul, Ankara, and Ismir airports for the purchase of liquor and cigarettes by arriving or departing passengers.

ACCOMMODATIONS

There is a good range of hotels in the main cities, from luxury class to pensions. There are some very good campsites (by gas stations) on the main routes. Hotels, exclusive of 15% service charge, are:

Rates are in US$ for a double/twin room with bath or shower

Bebek, Bebek, on the Bosporus (from $23)
Büyük Tarabya, Tarabya, on the Bosporus (from $50)
Carlton, Yeniköy, on the Bosporus (from $41)
Cinar, Yesilköy, on the shores of the Marmara Sea, near airport (from $53)
Divan, Cumhuriyet Caddesi, Harbiye (from $48)
Dilson, Siraselviler Caddesi, Taksim (from $22)

ETAP Istanbul, Mesrutiyet Caddesi, Tepebasi (from $30)
ETAP Marmara, Taksim Square (from $60)
Harem, Selimiye, on the Asian side of the Bosporus (from $19)
Istanbul Hilton, Cumhuriyet Caddesi, Harbiye (from $93)
Istanbul Sheraton, Taksim Park (from $73)
Kalyon, Marmara Sea Coast Road, in the old city (from $30)
Keban, Siraseliler Caddesi, Taksim (from $22)
Macka, Emlak Caddesi (from $42)
Olcay, Aksaray, in the old city (from $20)
Opera, Inonu Caddesi, Ayazpasa (from $18)
Pera Palas, Mesrutiyet Caddesi, Tepebasi (from $42)
Plaza, Aslan Yatagi 19, Siraseliler (from $25)

Unless designated as in the old city, on the Bosporus, or on the Asian side, the above hotels are all centrally located in the new city.

USEFUL INFORMATION

Dress is conservative. Bathing suits are for the beach only. Women should enter a mosque wearing a headscarf; neither sex should wear shorts.

Banks: Open 9-5 Mon-Fri, closed Sat. There are authorized money changers; money can be changed also at airports and some hotels.

Mail: Mailboxes are yellow and marked PTT. Stamps can be bought at a few tobacco shops, as well as at the post office.

Telephone Tips: Cost of a local call is TL10. Useful numbers (Istanbul):

Pan Am 47 45 30
Airport 73 29 20
Tourist Information Bureau 40 68
    64, 49 57 76, 40 63 00
Long Distance (Turkish) 03
Long Distance (International)
    28 23 03 or 28 48 20

Directory Enquiries 01
Useful numbers (Ankara):
    Pan Am 13 88 91
    Airport 24 12 70
    Tourist Office 17 30 12

Newspapers: Foreign papers readily available in Ankara and Istanbul. Local English-language publication is the *Daily News.*

Tipping: 10-15% service charge in hotels and restaurants. In a bar or nightclub, a 10% tax is added. Tip porters TL25 for each piece of baggage, and chambermaids according to length of stay.

Electricity: 220 volts, 50 cycles throughout Turkey, except in some sections of Istanbul where 110 volts 50 cycles is used.

Laundry: Only good hotels have a fast, reliable laundry service (dry-cleaning a suit, from TL100; laundering a shirt, from TL35).

Hairdressers: Some hotels have salons—cost of a shampoo and set from TL250; man's haircut from TL100; tip TL15.

Photography: Istanbul, Ankara, and Izmir have a good selection of equipment. Black and white film, TL200-300; color TL700-1,750.

Rest Rooms: Women, *Bayanlar-Kadin;* men, *Baylar* or *Erkekler.*

Health: There are American, German, French, and Italian hospitals. Many doctors speak English.

TRANSPORTATION

The Bosporus Bridge links the European and Asiatic shores of Istanbul and charges a toll of TL100. Ferries also cross the Bosporus at many points; cost is TL10 per person and TL100 per car. Taxis (black and yellow checkerboard markings on the side) cost about TL250 for rides around the new section of the city and TL400 for a trip from the new to the old section. As taxis don't use meters, always bargain and determine fare first. The Turks also use a collective taxi they call a *dolmus*. These look the same as other taxis but have a yellow stripe instead of a checkerboard. They move only when full and travel on a fixed route with a set fare, usually about TL25. Buses around the cities are very crowded, but there is a good bus service linking major towns. Trains, although inexpensive, are slow and crowded. Turkish Airlines (THY) maintains a network of regularly scheduled flights between all major cities in Turkey. Renting a car will cost you about US$22-24 per day plus about 26¢ per mile. Major roads in Turkey are good.

FOOD AND RESTAURANTS

The national dish of Turkey is the *sis* (pronounced "shish") *kebab*, seasoned pieces of lamb or beef on a skewer with tomatoes and onion, eaten alone or with green salad and rice. Other specialties are *dolmas*, green peppers, cabbage, or eggplant stuffed with spicy rice and served cold in olive oil or stuffed with rice and meat and served hot; *börek*, a flaky pastry with a cheese or meat filling; *imam bayildi*, eggplant stuffed with ground beef, tomatoes, and onions. Yoghurt is a favorite and is served with the main course as a relish, or as a base for desserts. Turkish sweets are as tasty as some of their names suggest—*dilber dudagi* (beauty's lip) and *kadin gobegi* (lady's navel). Istanbul has plenty of good restaurants. The **Kalyon** (Marmara Sea Coast Road—tel: 26 62 50). The nearby inexpensive restaurants, including **Canli Balik**, that surround picturesque **Kumkapi Square** specialize in seafood. **Konyali** (Topkapi Palace—tel: 26 27 27) has great views of the Bosporus while you dine. **Pandeli's** (tel: 22 55 34) in the old Spice Bazaar (Misircarsisi) offers excellent Turkish dishes and views of the Galata Bridge in a cool, ceramic-tiled interior. For an inexpensive lunch inside the Covered Bazaar, try **Havuzlu**, while just outside the bazaar is **Vitamin**; arrive before 12 noon or after 1pm for each of these restaurants. The Hilton has a range of restaurants, including the **Terrace Coffee Shop** for snacks and the **Roof Rotisserie** (tel: 46 70 50). A delightful restaurant on the Istikâl Caddesi is the **Four Seasons** (tel: 45 89 41). Good restaurants to look out for while along the Bosporus are **Abdullah** (Emirgan—tel: 63 64 06), with both Turkish and international cuisine; **Facyo** (tel: 62 08 98), **Filiz** (tel: 62 01 41), **Kiyi** (tel: 62 00 02), **Palet I** (tel: 62 01 18), and **Palet II** (tel: 62 00 20), all at Tarabya and all good for fish; and **Sureya** (Bebek—tel: 63 55 76). Small, inexpensive seaside restaurants at **Rumeli Kavak**, on the European side of the Bosporus at the entrance to the Black Sea, specialize in fried mussels. A restaurant which has become a password among the young is the **Lale** (or Pudding Shop), Sultan Ahmet Square, with a very lively atmosphere where you can meet people easily. There are little *sis kebab* restaurants along the street near the Pudding Shop. More expensive but on the Square itself, is the **Delfino** (tel: 22 61 63), specializing in seafood.

DRINKING TIPS

Local wines are of good quality. Good reds to try are *Kavaklidere, Villa Doluca,* or *Buzbag;* among the white, sample *Villa Doluca* and *Riesling.* Turkish liqueurs are popular: *Rose,* made from rose petals, *Kahve,* from coffee, and *Portakal,* from oranges, bananas, raspberries, mint, cherries, and strawberries. *Raki,* with an anisette base, is good, as is the Turkish vodka. Also try Turkish beer. Turkish coffee can be ordered either sweet or with little or no sugar; the tea, or *cay,* is pungent but refreshing.

ENTERTAINMENT

Istanbul has its own symphony orchestra, opera company, and ballet company. The theater is very active, but plays are in Turkish. The **Istanbul Cultural Festival** is held yearly in July in such picturesque settings as **Rumeli Hisar Castle.** International in scope, the festival celebrates music, dancing, drama, and the visual arts throughout the city. Tickets to the various concerts and events can be obtained at the Ataturk Cultural Center (Opera House), in Taksim Square. **Sound and light** shows in Sultan Ahmet Square on summer evenings, with the Blue Mosque sensationally lit up, are given in English, French, German, and Turkish on different nights. Check the Tourism and Information office for rates and schedule. For Turkish belly dancing, go to any floor show, the best being at **Bebek Belediye Casino** or **Kervansaray** (Cumhuriyet Caddesi 30).

For something a little more sophisticated, **Cloud 9** on the Hilton roof stages a floor show in elegant surroundings, the **Parisienne** (Cumhuriyet Caddesi 8) has a strip show, and the **Galata Tower** (Sishane—tel: 447 395) frequently stages Western floor shows in addition to Turkish folk dance.

SHOPPING

The **Covered Bazaar,** a medieval supermarket with 4,000 little shops, is the mecca for all shoppers in Istanbul. Insist on a good price, and you will come away with some real bargains. Leather and suede suits and coats, ready-made or tailored for you, are an excellent buy, and the popular sheepskin coats, in all lengths, embroidered and in various colors, are tempting. Rugs and carpets can be sent home for you in a surprisingly small bundle. Bursa silks and embroidered wraps are appealing, as are the jewelry—pendants, bracelets, and rings in gold, silver, and antique silver. The Turkish puzzle ring is world famous. Wander around the maze of little streets behind the bazaar and you will find everything, including the street of traders beating copper and selling rows of copper pots, pans, kettles, and lamps. Most shops are open from 9am-7pm except Sundays. On Sundays in the old city a huge flea market is set up in **Bayezit Square** next to the University. **Istiklâl Caddesi** is a good street for slightly smarter shops. The best department store is **Vakko,** good for fabrics. **Beymen** is good for men's clothing. **Nisantas** and **Sisli** are also good shopping districts, full of boutiques.

SPORTS

There are yachting, sailing, scuba-diving, and other water sports on the various coastlines of Turkey. Fishing (without a license) is best on the Black Sea and Marmara. Local tourist bureaus will supply information about where you may fish. Hunting for wolf, lynx, and wild boar is good, but a license from local authorities is required (the Directorate of the nearest town). Winter sports: skiing, sledding, and skating are popular, especially at **Mt Uludağ.** Istanbul has yacht, tennis, golf, and riding clubs, and car rallies sponsored by the **Istanbul Touring Club** are becoming popular.

WHAT TO SEE

Istanbul's skyline is shaped by over 400 mosques. The biggest and best are grouped in the old city. The **Blue Mosque,** built by Sultan Ahmet in the 17th century, is the only mosque in the world with six minarets. Sound and light shows are held here on summer evenings. **St Sophia,** an amazing architectural feat, was completed in the 6th century and served first as a Christian church, then as a mosque, and now as a museum. Nearby is **St Irene,** one of Byzantium's earliest churches, built over the pagan temple of Aphrodite. There are concerts and recitals in the church during the Cultural Festival in July. Between St Sophia and the Blue Mosque is the ancient **Hippodrome,** built in 203, an ancient racecourse overlooking the Sea of Marmara. Close by, the **Museum of Mosaics** shelters a part of the floor of the **Constantine Palace,** built of beautiful mosaics. On the promontory formed by the Bosporus and the Golden Horn is the rambling, famous **Topkapi Palace** of the Ottoman Turkish sultans. Here is the world's finest collection of Chinese porcelain. The library holds priceless Arabic and Greek manuscripts; there are the magnificent gold- and silver-threaded robes of the sultans, and the jewels in the treasury, including an 88-carat diamond, huge emeralds, and peacock blood rubies, defy all description. Close to Topkapi are the **Museum of Archaeology** and **Museum of Oriental Antiquities.** Descend into Yerebatan Sarayi, the **Sunken Palace Cistern,** ancient vaults upheld by 336 columns. The **Süleymaniye Mosque** must be seen, also the **Kaariye Museum,** which has some of the greatest Christian mosaics of the Byzantine period. Close to the Edirne Gate are the remnants of the **Palace of Constantine Porphyrogenitus,** an impressive early structure. In the new city, right on the Bosporus, is the white marble baroque palace of **Dolmabahce,** built in the mid-1800s. Do not miss the **Flower Market** off Istikâl Caddesi near Galatasary Square.

    Ankara: You can fly to Ankara, capital of Turkey, from Istanbul in 45 minutes or take an overnight trip by train. Begin your tour with **Ataturk's Mausoleum** in Kabir Caddesi, a tribute to the leader of the War of Independence and father of the Turkish Republic. Other things to see are the **Roman Baths** dating from the 3rd century BC; the **Column of Julian,**

55 feet high, a relic of the 4th century; the **Temple of Augustus;** the **Haci Bayram Mosque;** the world-famous **Hittite Museum** on the **Citadel,** a walled ancient fortress; the government buildings and the **Presidential Palace** at Cankaya.

Restaurants in Ankara to try are the **Kristal Restoran,** formerly the Washington (Bayindir Sokak 28—tel: 12 19 52), for Turkish and international dishes, the **Kazan** (Ahmetagao-glu Caddesi 28/1 Cankaya—tel: 27 04 62), with mainly Turkish specialties and a panoramic view of Ankara, the **Reve** (Turanameksiz Sok, Gaziosmanpasa—tel: 27 16 92), and the **Kent Hotel Restaurant** (Mithatpasa Caddesi 4, Sihhiye—tel: 17 72 68). Top nightclubs are the **Gar Casino** (Demiryolu Gari—tel: 11 51 90) and the clubs in the hotels **Büyük Ankara, Dedeman,** and **Kent.**

Hotels in Ankara:

Rates are in US$ for a double/twin room with bath or shower

    Bulvar Palas, Atatürk Bulvari 141 (from $28)

    Büyük Ankara, Atatürk Bulvari 191 (from $61)

    Dedeman, Büklüm Sokak 1 (from $42)

    Kent, Mithatpasa Caddesi 6 (from $42)

    Marmara, Atatürk Ciftligi, in the environs overlooking Atatürk Farm (from $60)

    Mola, Atatürk Bulvari 80 (from $40)

    Stad, Mudafaai Hukuk Meydani, Ulus (from $36)

    Tunali, Tunalihilmi Caddesi 19, Kavaklidere (from $35)

Bursa: At the foot of Mount Olympus, this ancient town was built around a fortified castle. The **Green Mosque** is especially impressive with its cluster of 20 domes. Best Bursa hotel is the **Celik Palas** (from US$36 double). For winter sports, especially skiing, popular **Mt Uludağ** is only 21 miles southwest of Bursa. Uludağ's hotels range from the deluxe **Panorama** (from US$26 double) to the rustic **Fahri** (from US$55 AP).

Canakkale: It is via this town that you make your way to the ancient ruins of the legendary city of Troy, 30 miles south.

Cappadocia: Southeast of Ankara is the strange region that includes the Göreme Valley, with a landscape of eroded pinnacles and canyons, in which are built some 300 Byzantine-decorated chapels.

Izmir: Biggest port on the Aegean coast, see the ancient Greek **Agora,** dating back to the 2nd century BC. **Kadifekale,** the "velvet fortress" on top of Mt Pagos, dates from Alexander the Great. Izmir's large International Trade Fair takes place from 20 August to 20 September. Best hotel is the **Büyük Efes** (from US$33 double). Izmir is only a 2-hour drive from the first **Seven Churches of Christendom** that are mentioned in *Revelation* 1-111. At **Ephesus,** where St Paul was imprisoned, visit the house the Virgin Mary lived in; the **Temple of Artemis,** one of the seven wonders of the ancient world; the ruins of the **Basilica of St John;** and the great **Ephesus Theater,** which can hold 25,000.

At **Sardis** are the ancient ruins of the capital of Lydia, once ruled by the wealthy King Croesus. Today archaeologists have restored a magnificent Roman gymnasium and a Jewish synagogue of Roman times.

Bodrum, a resort village south of Izmir, was the birthplace of Herodotus, the father of history (484 BC), and has the remains of the **Mausoleum,** another of the seven wonders of the ancient world, and a superb **Crusader Castle; Didyma** has one of the largest classical temples ever built, that of Apollo. **Aphrodisias** is the city of the goddess; **Pamukkale** has hot springs, and nearby are the ruins of the ancient city of **Hierapolis.**

Turkish Riviera: Antalya, set against the Bey Mountains, is a beautiful resort. There are good beaches at **Konyaalti** and **Lara.** To the west of Antalya is **Termessos,** an ancient pre-Greek city almost a mile high in the mountains; **Finike,** with its tombs carved from rock; **Demre,** burial place of St Nicholas (Santa Claus); and the ruins of **Xanthos,** near **Kinik.** East of Antalya are the ruins of three Greek cities: **Perge,** where Paul won his first apostles; **Side,** with its amphitheater; and **Aspendos,** with the finest Roman theater extant. It is still used for drama festivals.

Alanya is an ancient citadel. **Silifke** is crowned by a fortress built first by ancient Armenians and then by Crusaders. **Tarsus** is the birthplace of St Paul.

SOURCES OF FURTHER INFORMATION

Pan Am, Hilton Hotel Arcade, Istanbul, and 175/3 Atatürk Bulvari in Ankara; the **Turkish Government Tourism and Information Office,** 821 United Nations Plaza, New York, NY 10017, and 49 Conduit Street, London W1.

THE PACIFIC AND ASIA

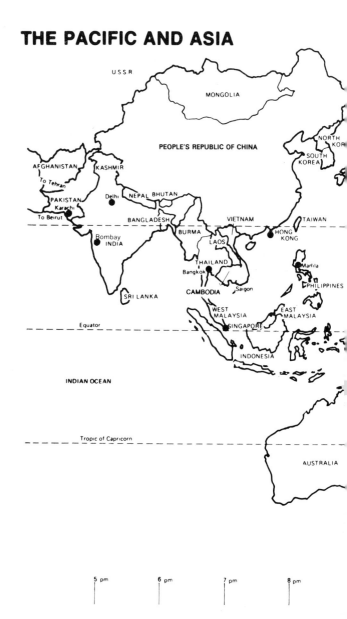

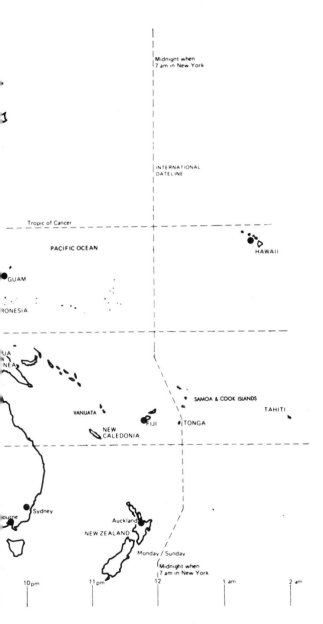

Midnight when
7 am in New York

INTERNATIONAL
DATELINE

Tropic of Cancer

PACIFIC OCEAN

HAWAII

GUAM

RONESIA

UA
N
NEA

VANUATA

FIJI

SAMOA & COOK ISLANDS

TAHITI

TONGA

NEW
CALEDONIA

ourne Sydney

Auckland
NEW ZEALAND

Monday / Sunday

Midnight when
7 am in New York

10 pm   11 pm   12   1 am   2 am

503

PACIFIC AND ASIA
CURRENCY CONVERSION

Country	United States $				United Kingdom £			
	5¢	10¢	50¢	$1	5p	10p	50p	£1
Australia dollars • cents	.06	.11	.57	1.14	.13	.23	1.19	2.39
Bangladesh takas • paisas	.85	1.69	8.43	16.85	1.78	3.54	17.67	35.32
Burma kyats • pyas	.35	.70	3.50	7.00	.73	1.47	7.34	14.68
Fiji dollars • cents	.04	.08	.40	.80	.08	.17	.84	1.68
Guam dollars • cents	.05	.10	.50	1.00	.10	.21	1.05	2.10
Hawaii dollars • cents	.05	.10	.50	1.00	.10	.21	1.05	2.09
Hong Kong dollars • cents	.28	.56	2.78	5.56	.59	1.17	5.83	11.66
India rupees • paise	.42	.83	4.17	8.33	.88	1.74	8.74	17.46
Indonesia rupiah • sen	31.45	62.89	314.47	628.93	65.93	131.84	659.27	1318.51
Japan yen • sen	11.06	22.12	110.62	221.24	23.19	46.37	231.91	463.82
Malaysia dollars • cents	.12	.23	1.17	2.34	.25	.48	2.45	4.91
Micronesia dollars • cents	.05	.10	.50	1.00	.10	.21	1.05	2.09
Nepal rupees • paisas	.60	1.20	6.00	11.99	1.26	2.52	12.58	25.14
New Caledonia francs • centimes	4.55	9.09	45.45	90.90	9.54	19.06	95.28	190.57
New Zealand dollars • cents	.06	.11	.57	1.14	.13	.23	1.19	2.39
Pakistan rupees • paisas	.50	.99	4.95	9.90	1.05	2.08	10.38	20.75
Papua New Guinea kina • toeas	.03	.07	.33	.65	.06	.15	.69	1.36
People's Republic of China renminbi • chiao	.09	.17	.87	1.73	.19	.36	1.82	3.63
Philippines pesos • centavos	.39	.78	3.91	7.81	.82	1.64	8.20	16.37

PACIFIC AND ASIA
CURRENCY CONVERSION

Country	United States $				United Kingdom £			
	5¢	10¢	50¢	$1	5p	10p	50p	£1
Samoa & Cook Islands tala • sene	.04	.08	.47	.94	.08	.17	.99	1.97
Singapore dollars • cents	.11	.22	1.09	2.17	.23	.46	2.29	4.55
South Korea won	33.33	66.67	333.33	666.67	69.87	139.77	698.81	1397.63
Sri Lanka rupees • cents	.89	1.79	8.93	17.86	1.87	3.75	18.72	37.44
Tahiti francs • centimes	4.55	9.09	45.45	90.91	9.54	19.06	95.28	190.59
Taiwan dollars • cents	1.82	3.65	18.25	36.50	3.82	7.65	38.26	76.52
Thailand bahts • satangs	1.05	2.10	10.50	21.01	2.20	4.40	22.01	44.05
Tonga pa'anga • seniti	.05	.09	.44	.88	.10	.19	.92	1.84
Vanuata francs • centimes	.28	.55	2.77	5.54	.59	1.15	5.81	11.61

Note: Because of the political situation in Afghanistan, it has not been possible to provide complete information for this chapter.

Afghanistan

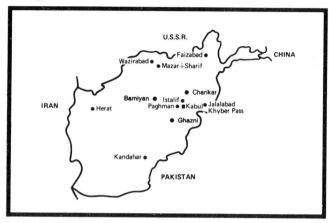

WHAT'S SPECIAL

Wedged among so many different countries, Afghanistan has often found itself the pawn in international differences. It has known the armies of famous warriors such as Alexander the Great, Genghis Khan, Tamerlane, the missionary soldiers of Islam, and the British in the Afghan wars. Today you can drive through Afghanistan on American highways and fly in to a Russian-built air terminal. Yet it remains one of the few countries in the world today where the tourist can see camel trains wending their way to the cities and where the villages of clay blend into the stone and the sand.

The capital, Kabul, is at an altitude of 6,000 feet; its ancient city walls can still be seen on the spurs of the two high hills that dominate the city. Beyond Kabul, major attractions are the drive along the ancient silk route through the Kabul Gorge into the Khyber Pass to the historic town of Jalalabad; the pair of enormous Buddhas carved into the cliff face at Bamiyan 1,500 years ago and the fresco-decorated Bamiyan caves; the holy city of Mazar-i-Sharif and the nearby ruins of Balkh, the "Mother of Cities," 4,000 years old; Kandahar, first capital of modern Afghanistan, where the sacred mantle of the prophet Muhammad is enshrined in the splendid mosque. Finally, there is Herat, conquered by Alexander the Great in the 4th century BC, levelled by Genghis Khan in the 13th century and again by Tamerlane in the 14th century, but reborn to flourish once more in a 15th-century "Golden Age."

COUNTRY BRIEFING

Size: 250,000 square miles   **Population:** 20,500,000
Capital: Kabul   **Capital Population:** 749,000
   Climate: Dry, hot summers and cold winters, especially in the north.
Spring and fall are milder.

Weather in Kabul: Lat N34°30′; Alt 5,955 ft

Temp (°F)	Jan	Feb	Mar	Apr	May	Jun	Jul	Aug	Sep	Oct	Nov	Dec
Av Low	18°	22°	34°	43°	51°	56°	61°	59°	51°	42°	33°	27°
Av High	36°	40°	53°	66°	78°	87°	92°	91°	85°	73°	62°	47°
Days no rain	29	25	24	24	29	29	31	31	30	30	28	30

Government: A republic.
Language: Pashtu and Dari (Persian).
Religion: Muslim.
Currency: Afghani. 100 puls = 1 afghani.

SOURCES OF FURTHER INFORMATION

Afghan Tourist Organization, Ministry of Information and Culture Building, Kabul; **Afghan Consulate,** 122 West 30th Street, New York, NY 10001; **Afghan Embassy,** 2341 Wyoming Avenue, NW, Washington DC 20008; **Afghan Embassy,** 31 Princes Gate, London SW7.

Australia

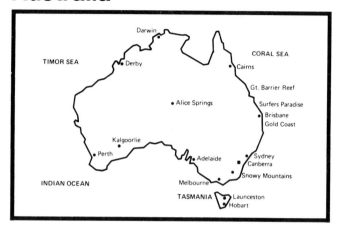

WHAT'S SPECIAL

Australia is in the unique position of being able to provide the visitor with a great range of experiences, from the still continuing domestic life of aboriginal tribes in the heart of this untamed country to the sophisticated cultural opportunities available in the Sydney Opera House. The character of the country is even now in the making and the continent itself, as big as the United States, still offers unlimited scope for both growth and expansion without the necessity of obliterating the past. For the land is old—so old that it has more unique features, flora, and fauna than any other country in the world. There's a lifetime of exploring possible here, and any one vacation could encompass a number of different aspects of this unique country. The marvelous Great Barrier Reef alone would fill one vacation, the "Outback" another. In July you can ski in the Snowy Mountains only 200 miles south of Sydney, while on Christmas Day, after church services, you can swim off the beaches near all the major cities. With even more time to spare you could walk among the stones of Tasmania, fossick for gems, ride the surf, race with an emu, or round up sheep and cattle with a jackaroo. Some things are essential—and very rewarding. It is important to visit at least part of the interior and not cling to the coastal cities. And you should meet the animals—strange marsupials; flightless, laughing, and mimicking birds; cuddly koalas; mammals that lay eggs; and the brilliantly colored parakeets and cockatoos. There is something in Australia for everyone.

COUNTRY BRIEFING

Size: 2,968,000 square miles   **Population:** 14,615,900
National Capital: Canberra   **Capital Population:** 220,900

   Climate: Tropical to temperate, but enormously varied. In the center, fiercely hot (up to 140°F); perhaps no rain for years. The northeast has over 100 inches of rain a year, and the Tasmanian mountains are normally snow-covered. Summer, November to April, is hot and humid in the north, pleasant in Victoria. Winter, June to August, can be cold in Melbourne and is ideal in Alice Springs, Darwin, and Brisbane.

Weather in Sydney: Lat S33°52′; Alt 138 ft

Temp (°F)	Jan	Feb	Mar	Apr	May	Jun	Jul	Aug	Sep	Oct	Nov	Dec
Av Low	65°	65°	63°	58°	52°	48°	46°	48°	51°	56°	69°	77°
Av High	78°	78°	76°	71°	66°	61°	60°	63°	67°	71°	74°	77°
Days no rain	17	15	17	16	18	18	19	20	18	19	18	18

   Government: Member of the British Commonwealth, with Dominion status. State and Federal parliaments are elected by popular vote.

   Language: English, with many Italian and Greek-speaking immigrants and other groups of Europeans all over the continent. Also small immigrant groups from Asia and Latin America.

   Religion: Predominantly Protestant.

   Currency: Australian dollar. 100 cents = 1 Australian dollar.

	5¢	20¢	50¢	A$1	A$5	A$10	A$20	A$50
US	.04	.18	.44	.88	4.39	8.78	17.56	43.90
UK	.02	.09	.21	.42	2.10	4.20	8.39	20.98

Public Holidays:

New Year's Day, 1 Jan	Anzac Day, 25 Apr
Australia Day, 1 Feb	Queen's Birthday, 3rd Mon June
Good Friday	Christmas Day, 25 Dec
Easter Monday	Boxing Day, 26 Dec

HOW TO GET THERE

Flying time to Sydney's Kingsford Smith Airport from Los Angeles is 13½ hours; from Honolulu, 9¼ hours; from Auckland, 2¾ hours. Flying time from Sydney to Melbourne's Tullamarine Airport is 1¼ hours. Time in Sydney: GMT + 10.

REQUIREMENTS FOR ENTRY AND CUSTOMS REGULATIONS

Passport, visa, and round-trip ticket required. Vaccination certificates required only if coming from infected zones. No limit on importing currency. Visitors staying in Australia less than six months may export currency only up to the value declared on entry. Duty-free allowance: 200 cigarettes or 250 grams of tobacco or cigars; 1 liter liquor; personal effects; dutiable goods up to the value A$200.

AIRPORT INFORMATION

(See under New South Wales and Victoria.)

ACCOMMODATIONS

Large cities have a wide range from luxury to inexpensive; motels are spreading all over the country. But don't expect to explore everywhere in luxury. Australians are not fussy and don't expect you to be. There are hostels in most towns for traveling workers (Australian workers move around a lot), and the climate and country in the coastal areas and southeastern Australia are ideal for campers. See individual regions for details.

USEFUL INFORMATION

Helpful Hints: In general, the one thing Australians hate is "putting on airs." Friendliness will get you everywhere. Dress is extremely informal at home and in resorts, slightly more formal in the cities.

Banks: Some downtown banks open 10-6 Mon-Fri, but services after 3pm are restricted to savings accounts. A very useful institution is the Bank of New South Wales. It has branches almost everywhere and also acts as a travel agent and adviser.

Mail: Stamps can be bought at some newspaper dealers and stores as well as at post offices. Mailboxes are red.

Telephone Tips: All coin-operated, with operating details posted in telephone booths.

Tipping: 10% in hotels and restaurants and at the barber or beautician. Hotel porters 20 cents per bag. Airport and railway porters have fixed rates. Taxi drivers receive odd change. In general, tipping is rather light, especially in rural areas.

Electricity: 240 volts AC—occasionally DC in the country.

Laundry: As good and easy to find as anywhere in the world.

Hairdressing: There are good salons in the cities and some hotels. Women's shampoo and set from A$15; men's haircuts from A$5.

Photography: Film and equipment easy to buy. Processing in 48 hours in the cities.

Health: Dentists, doctors, and hospitals are excellent. Water and milk can be drunk everywhere without fear. The only dangers to health are sharks, snakes, and heat. To avoid these heed local advice. Don't swim at unguarded beaches, and don't think you can explore the vast, largely uninhabited desert interior by yourself.

TRANSPORTATION

The vast distances make air by far the most convenient method of travel. There is a comprehensive, reasonably priced network of domestic lines run by Ansett and TAA. Other means of getting about include road, rail, and sea. Train journeys are an interesting, if slow, way to see the country: Sydney to Perth, for example, takes 3 nights, and in the Nullarbor Plain there's a 300-mile stretch of dead straight track. Cars can be rented easily but many roads in the outback country are unpaved tracks with little to see for hundreds of miles. The **Ansett Pioneer Express** bus service has "Aussie Pass" plans for travelers to visit most areas of interest in the continent at a cost of A$199 for 15 days, A$350 for 30 days, or A$440 for 2 months.

FOOD AND RESTAURANTS

Australians are great meat-eaters. Big steaks and legs of lamb are cheap and good. Seafood, too, is plentiful and includes varieties you won't have met elsewhere—such as the fighting barramundi, the mud crabs of Queensland, and the rock oysters of Sydney. And the fruit is juicy and abundant. There are few Australian national dishes, however—apart, perhaps, from kangaroo-tail soup; traditional cooking is simple. For sophisticated cuisine you will rely on the skills of the "New Australians"—recent immigrants from Italy, France, and Asia. Even so, your most memorable meal may be a steak barbecued on the back of a shovel over a *mulga* fire, washed down with billy tea. Mealtimes are early—12 onwards for lunch, 6-9 for dinner. But then shop hours and working hours are also early. Those on a budget should take full advantage of the fashion for smorgasbord and pizza, the traditional counter lunch at a hotel coffee shop, and buffet lunches in hotel bars.

DRINKING TIPS

Most bars—often called hotels or pubs—are open from 6am-10pm, and the beer is excellent. Australians are fierce in defense of their favorite brand, whether Swan Lager, Victoria Bitter, or Foster's. You drink it in 15-ounce glasses known as *schooners* or in 10-ounce glasses called *midis,* and it's stronger than US or British beer, although a lighter variety has been introduced. Local wine is very good; no need to pay for expensive imports. Average cost of a Scotch is $1.25, of wine about A$2.50 a liter. The **Marble Bar** in the Sydney Hilton, rescued from the old Adams Hotel, is a national monument.

SHOPPING

The bargains come from the soil, opals and gems of great rarity and beauty can be bought from jewelers in all big cities. A discount of about 20%, equivalent to a reduction in the sales tax, is available to tourists who can produce their passport and airline tickets. All Australian opals and gems qualify for the rebate. Sheepskin hats and coats are good buys. Many people take home a cuddly toy koala or a boomerang.

SPORTS

You've come to the right place. Australians are enthusiastic sportsmen, living for strenuous activity in the great outdoors. There are water sports in abundance, of course—some of the world's best swimming, surfing, skin-diving, and big-game fishing, and no lack of facilities since all the state capitals are coastal. Most towns have a racetrack—some have several. Tennis is a passion; there are lovingly kept greens for golf and bowls. You can ride, sail, and watch four kinds of football and cricket.

NEW SOUTH WALES

CAPITAL

Sydney, population 3,193,000. The oldest colony (1788), New South Wales is now the most populous state on the continent, yet with only a tenth of its area. In many ways New South Wales leads Australia, though other states might deny it. To visitors Sydney seems lively and forward-looking, its nightlife, theater, music, and industry, active and well advanced.

AIRPORT INFORMATION

Sydney's Kingsford Smith Airport is 6 miles from the city center. The airport bus into town costs A$1.60; a taxi, A$5. Departure tax is A$10 for overseas destinations.

ACCOMMODATIONS

A full range of hotels, luxury and modest, new and old. There are also a number of modern motels, suburban guesthouses, and YMCA, YWCA, and youth hostels. Hotels in Sydney, centrally located, include:

Rates are in US$ for a double/twin room with bath or shower

Boulevard, 90 William Street (from $94)

Carlton Rex, 56 Castlereagh Street (from $65)

Gazebo, 2 Elizabeth Bay Road, Kings Cross (from $69)

Hyatt Kingsgate, Kings Cross Road, Kings Cross (from $101)

Manhattan, Greenknowe Avenue, Potts Point (from $51 BB)

Menzies, 14 Carrington Street (from $90)

New Chevron, 81 Macleay Street, Potts Point (from $62)

New Crest, corner Victoria St & Darlinghurst Road, Kings Cross (from $59)

Sebel Town House, 23 Elizabeth Bay Road, Kings Cross (from $87)

Sydney Hilton, 259 Pitt Street (from $96)

Top of the Town, 110 Darlinghurst Rd, Kings Cross (from $57)

Wentworth, 61 Phillip Street (from $96)

TRANSPORTATION

A very useful subway line connects all the main shopping areas and the main-line train services. Buses are fairly plentiful and inexpensive, and the drivers most amiable. The many ferries are a delightful way to see the great harbor, or just to relax a moment from the hustle of the city. They leave every few minutes from Circular Quay and also make daily harbor cruises.

FOOD AND RESTAURANTS

The restaurant scene in Sydney is still young; even 10 years ago native Australians were not notably food-conscious. But tourists and recent immigrants have changed that with a vengeance. Now you will find dozens of places vying for patronage—and in the Kings Cross area they do so with youthful panache.

For the sake of the view, go to the **Summit** atop Australia Square Tower (tel: 279777) and be gently revolved. Either **Flanagan's Afloat Restaurant** (Rose Bay—tel: 371 7955) or the **Caprice** (Sunderland Avenue, Rose Bay—tel: 371 6799) will give you a romantic evening overlooking the water with seafood to match. The **French Restaurant** (379a Bourke

Street Darlinghurst—tel: 313605) serenades you with wandering musicians; French specialties, too, from **Le Provençal** (143 King Street—tel: 232 6670). Probably the top French restaurant is **Le Trianon** (29 Challis Avenue, Potts Point—tel: 358 1353), luxuriously decorated in Louis XIV style, and expensive. For a more intimate but equally elegant meal try **La Causerie** (100 Driver Avenue, Moore Park—tel: 358 6993). Other top restaurants are the **Garden Court** in the Wentworth Hotel (Phillip Street—tel: 230 0700) and **Chelsea** (119 Macleay Street—tel: 358 4333). The informal **Market Place,** at the Sydney Hilton on Pitt Street specializes in prime steaks and rack of lamb while the hotel's **San Francisco Grill** offers haute cuisine. Seafood is, of course, the great treat in Sydney—especially the local rock oysters. Eat them on the shell, fried in batter, or wrapped in a big juicy steak (called a carpetbagger). **Flanagan's** (92 Pitt Street—tel: 233 5433, and 4 Castlereagh Street—tel: 232 6868) will always have the day's catch on the menu; so will **Prunier's Chiswick Gardens** (65 Ocean Street, Woollahra—tel: 321619) and the **Doyle's Restaurant** (11 Marine Parade, Watson's Bay—tel: 337 2007, and 594 New South Head Road, Rose Bay—tel: 364187). For an exotic touch, you should go to one of the New Australian restaurants, such as **Beppi's** (Yurong & Stanley Streets—tel: 357 4558), where the food is authentic regional Italian, or the **Spanish Room** (Menzies Hotel, 14 Carrington Street—tel: 20232), where there's music too. Two Chinese restaurants are recommended: **Dixon** (51 Dixon Street—tel: 211 1062) and **Jade Terrace** (109 Foveaux Street, Surry Hills—tel: 212 2020). Two interesting moderately priced places are the **Argyle Tavern** (18 Argyle Street, Circular Quay—tel: 271613), where they roast lamb and whole suckling pig in a 137-year-old convict-built store, and the Indonesian restaurant **Slamat Makan** (362 Victoria Street, Darlinghurst—tel: 317905). Dine expensively or modestly at **Mother's Cellar** and for budget food, go to one of the branches of **Cahills.** The **International Restaurant,** at Kingsgate Shopping Center, is not only inexpensive but open all night.

ENTERTAINMENT

The **Sydney Opera House,** one of the world's architectural wonders, has four halls where top-quality drama, ballet, opera, and concerts are performed. You can eat before curtain time in the elegant **Bennelong Restaurant** or self-service **Harbour Restaurant.** Theaters are of top international quality here—lively and experimental, too. Of the dozen-and-a-half shows likely to be on, check at least the ones at the **Independent,** the **Ensemble,** and lunchtime at the **AMP.** The **Australian National Ballet** at the **Elizabeth** is well worth catching. The **Town Hall** features first-class music by international artists. For nightlife take a quick cab to **Kings Cross** and it's all around you—food plus music, and floor show plus food. Some names are **Polaris, Jason's Hofbrauhaus, Tabou.** There's a disco at the Hyatt Kingsgate, and classy places can be found in the big hotels, such as **Juliana's** (Sydney Hilton). **Hunter's Lodge** at Double Bay is well spoken of, as is **The Coachmen** (763 Bourke Street, Redfern) and **Fisherman's Lodge** at Watson's Bay. At **Les Girls** you can eat to an all-male revue.

It may be worth an excursion to Neutral Bay to the **Music Hall** for old-time food, drink, and melodrama.

SHOPPING

Two places where you can buy genuine aboriginal work and art at the right price are the **Bush Church Aid Society** (135 Bathurst Street) and the **Aboriginal Arts and Crafts Proprietary Ltd** (38 Harrington Street). All the profits go back to the people who make the goods. For opals and gemstones try **Opal Skymine** (6th Level, Australia Square), where there is a replica of a mine and an audio-visual presentation of the mining of opals; **Australian Opal Galleries** (28 Gilmore Road); and the **Opal Center** (4th floor, ASL House). Remember to take your passport and return ticket to qualify for the 20% discount to tourists. **Cornelius Furs** (Corner Castlereagh and King Streets) has the largest selection of furs in the southern hemisphere. For other shopping, try **Centrepoint**, 200 specialty shops in one building in the center of Sydney, or any of the shops or arcades around **Elizabeth, Pitt, Castlereagh,** and **George Streets.** And farther out, there are shopping centers such as fashionable **Double Bay.** On Friday and Saturday mornings, go to **Paddy's Market** in the Haymarket and see what young Australian artists are doing. Several of the best galleries are in the picturesque Paddington area—such as **Bonython, Berry Stern,** and **Realms.** Other picture galleries are the **Strawberry Hill** and **Prouds.** There are a number of duty-free shops, besides the one at the airport, in downtown Sydney.

SPORTS

Try swimming and surfing from any of over two dozen magnificent beaches (**Manly, Bondi, Palm Beach, Coogee,** and **Cronulla** for example). This can be as exciting to watch as to take part in—also true of sailing in the harbor and around the Heads (the approaches to the Pacific Ocean). For information call the **Royal Sydney Yacht Club** (tel: 927171). Freshwater fishermen will find some of the best trout fishing in the world up in the Snowy Mountains at **Lake Eucumbene.** Golfers have no lack of excellent courses, but may need an introduction to use them.

Depending on the season, there will be sporting events somewhere every week: tennis at **Rushcutters Bay,** rugby football in winter, cricket in summer, horse-racing and show jumping around Easter. And for skiers, the **Snowy Mountains** are at their best in September.

WHAT TO SEE

To get a good view of the city, first climb to a vantage point such as the **Harbor Bridge,** the observation floor of the AMP building, or the 48th floor "Skywalk" observation deck of Australia Square (admission A$2). Then take a ferry ride from Circular Quay—preferably to **Taronga Zoo Park**—or a ferry cruise of Sydney Harbor. These will give you a good idea of Sydney's superb waterfront situation. For an inkling of its history, walk around the **Old Rocks** area near the bridge. Old buildings to see are **Cadman's Cottage,** the **Customs House,** the **Conservatorium** of Music, the **Technical College,** and two Georgian buildings by the convict architect, Greenway—the **Law Courts** and **St James's Church** (all within walking distance of the center). Then drop in at the **Australian Museum** on College Street for an even broader view of the continent's natural history. You must see the fabulous **Opera House,** its concrete spires flying like sails on the waters of the harbor. During the day you can stroll the granite boardwalk around the Opera House and take a conducted tour of the interior. Get acquainted with Victorian Sydney in the **Paddington** district where row houses have iron lace balconies. **Vaucluse House** is a lovely 19th-century mansion surrounded by gardens. If interested in modern art, go to the **Art Gallery of New South Wales,** in the Domain. Try at all costs to catch a **Surf Carnival** (weekends in summer).

At **Koala Park,** 15 miles northwest of Sydney, a keeper will coax the furry animals down from the treetops so you can pet them and get close-up photographs. **Ku-ring-gai Chase National Park,** a bit farther away, has aboriginal rock paintings that may be 8,000 years old as well as wild-flowers and a koala sanctuary. You could take a meandering water trip on the pastoral **Berowra Waters** and **Hawkesbury River,** some 30 miles north of Sydney, or go to Gosford, 45 miles north along the Central Coast to see **Old Sydney Town,** a recreation of the original settlement at Sydney as it was in 1810. You can also see how poisonous snakes are handled at the **Gosford Reptile Park.** A day or two could be spent in the **Blue Mountains**—40 miles west of Sydney. Here are the famous **Jenolan Caves, Katoomba,** and rugged terrain of scrub forest or "bush" with trails for bushwalking. The 9-mile **Federal Pass Walk** takes you by **Leura Falls** and **Katoomba Falls.** Or take a **Jolly Swagman** tour which flies you to a sheep station inland and shows you the facts of Australian life—ending with a barbecue in the outback.

There are two times of the year that are special in Sydney: the Christmas and New Year holidays, which call for carols by candlelight, carnivals and merrymaking by night on the beaches, closely followed by the **Festival of Sydney,** a month-long program of entertainment and amusement with a gala concert to herald the New Year; and the **Royal Easter Show** with a grand gathering of cattle, horses and horsemen, sheepdogs, and axemen.

SOURCES OF FURTHER INFORMATION
Pan Am: 14 Martin Place, Sydney—tel: 233 1111; **New South Wales Government Travel Center,** 16 Spring Street, Sydney—tel: 231 4444; **Tourist Information Service**—tel: 949 5111.

VICTORIA

CAPITAL
Melbourne, population 2,739,700. Of all cities in Australia, Melbourne has the most old-world charm. It is generally considered more conservative and European in personality than Sydney. With its grand old Parliamentary buildings and the numerous church steeples piercing the skyline,

Melbourne is a refined city. It is also considered to be the commercial and financial center of Australia, and most of the country's leading companies have headquarters here.

AIRPORT INFORMATION

Melbourne International Airport is at Tullamarine, 15 miles from the city center. A taxi into the city costs about A$11.00, an Airways Coach A$2.50.

ACCOMMODATIONS

There is a wide range of good hotels. If you plan to visit Melbourne in March, when the *Moomba* is staged, or early November when the Melbourne Cup is being run, it is advisable to reserve ahead. Hotels in Melbourne, centrally located unless otherwise indicated:

Rates are in US$ for a double/twin room with bath or shower

Australia, 266 Collins Street (from $58)

Chateau Commodore, 131 Lonsdale Street (from $70)

Commodore Motel, 4 Queens Road (from $38), 1 mile from downtown

Melbourne Hilton, 129 Wellington Parade East (from $92), ½ mile from downtown

Noah's Melbourne, corner Exhibition and Little Bourke Streets (from $72)

Southern Cross, 131 Exhibition Street (from $65)

Victoria, 215 Little Collins Street (from $39)

Windsor, 103-115 Spring Street (from $54)

FOOD AND RESTAURANTS

Melbourne boasts almost as many and varied restaurants as Sydney, with cuisine of every imaginable country. **Mayfair Restaurant** (Southern Cross Hotel—tel: 630221); **Maxim's** (Toorak Road, South Yarra—tel: 265500); **Vlados Charcoal Grill** (61 Bridge Street, Richmond—tel: 425833); **Bims** (East Melbourne—tel: 413426); **Lazar Restaurant** (240 King Street, Melbourne—tel: 602 1822); **Pamplemousse** (20th Floor, National Mutual Centre, 447 Collins Street, Melbourne—tel: 627167), for superb views of the city; and **Le Château** (48 Queens Road, Melbourne—tel: 515211)— these are the most elegant restaurants. For fun, try **Peanuts Restaurant** (389 Lonsdale Street, Melbourne—tel: 671410). Look for **Pancake Parlors,** a national chain well represented in Melbourne; they are inexpensive, good, and open 7 days a week. One hour's drive from the city into the near hills brings you to several excellent dining places such as **The Baron of Beef** (Sherbrooke Forest—tel: 7501220) for fine beef and jolly entertainment; the **Cuckoo** (Mt Dandenong Tourist Road, Olinda—tel: 751 1003) for an excellent smorgasbord.

ENTERTAINMENT

Larger movie houses which show first-run films are in the city center. The **Melbourne Symphony Orchestra** presents a concert season from August to September at the Town Hall, and in summer concerts are regularly staged at the **Sidney Myer Music Bowl.** Opera and ballet are performed at the **Palais Theater** and **Her Majesty's Theater,** musical entertainment at **Tikki and John's,** Exhibition Street (call for advance reservations: 663 1756).

There are nightclubs attached to the leading hotels. Other clubs are the **Troika,** out of town at 17 Beach Road, Hampton (tel: 982176), with its gypsy music, dancing, and floor shows; **Smacka's Place** (55 Chetwynd Street, North Melbourne—tel: 328 1788), a jazz spot; the **Taboo** (16 Esplanade, St Kilda—tel: 941359); and the **Distillery** (519 St Kilda Road).

SHOPPING

Most of the city's shops are centered on **Collins, Bourke,** and **Swanston Streets. Myers** department store is the largest and sells just about everything. This area is riddled with arcades of small shops selling everything you could desire. **George's** of Collins Street is a more exclusive store. Australian opals can be purchased from one of a number of shops in the **Southern Cross Hotel** complex, or at **Altmann & Cherny** on Collins Street. Also on Collins is **Aboriginal Artifacts and Handicrafts,** where genuine handcrafted articles can be bought. There are duty-free stores on Queen Street and Exhibition Street.

SPORTS

Melbourne is "Australian Rules" football crazy, and throughout the winter (May-Sept) Saturday matches are crowded and exciting. "Aussie Rules" is a hard, fast game with long kicks and quick hand passes and high thrilling catches called "marks." It started in the 1850s, based on Gaelic football. The Melbournians are also very fond of racing, and **Flemington Race Course** is the scene of many big events, especially of the famed Melbourne Cup held on the first Tuesday in November. Facilities for golf, tennis, bowling, and swimming are all excellent. There are some good beaches south of the city and many pools in the city itself.

WHAT TO SEE

From Flinders Street Station move south down the tree-lined boulevard, St Kilda Road, where you will see the **National Gallery,** a superb building that houses a beautifully displayed, extensive collection of Australian and European paintings and artifacts. In the Great Hall, admire the stained glass roof created by Robert French. Across the road, you can walk into the glorious green of the **Botanical Gardens;** the **Shrine of Remembrance,** Melbourne's war memorial, and **Como Mansion** are close by.

If you head east up Collins Street out of the city, you will come to the grand-looking Government buildings and the **Treasury Gardens.** Just the other side of these are the **Fitzroy Gardens;** here you will find **Captain Cook's Cottage,** specially shipped out from Yorkshire. You'll also find the **Fairy Tree,** an imaginatively carved tree. Nearby, to the rear of the Melbourne Hilton, are several blocks of beautifully restored Regency and Victorian houses. Koalas, kangaroos, and other native Australian animals can be visited at the **Royal Park Zoo.** Drive out through the suburbs and up into the **Dandenongs.** These hills abound with rich green undergrowth and beautiful places to walk and picnic. For a glorious view of the city drive up to **Mount Dandenong** and have a meal at the restaurant as you admire the view. There are innumerable little villages through the hills, such as **Fern Tree Gully, Olinda, Sassafras, Belgrave,** and **Monbulk,** all set in lovely forest and mountain to make a charming day's tour. There are a number of day tours you can take from Melbourne throughout the state of Victoria, which is generally green and, except for its characteristic gum or eucalyptus trees, the most English part of the Australian mainland. The **Rippon Lea** gardens and mansion occupy 13 acres in Elsternick. Go up to **Ballarat** and **Bendigo,** both the center of the gold rush days of the 1850s and now two charming old provincial towns. Bendigo is popular for its rough-hewn pottery and Australian antiques. For a close look at the unique Australian wildlife—kangaroos, wombats, koalas, and others—drive 39 miles from Melbourne to the great **Sir Colin Mackenzie Wildlife Sanctuary** at Healesville. South of Melbourne you can take long drives along the coast, down to lovely **Mount Eliza** and **Arthur's Seat.** At Arthur's Seat, there is a chairlift to the peak and you have a view over **Port Phillip Bay.** The restaurant at the Seat serves good meals. There are numerous attractive seaside resorts on the other side of Melbourne—**Torquay, Anglesea,** and **Lorne.** Off the coast is **Cowes** (Phillip Island), with a seal colony, muttonbirds, and, an exciting reminder that Antarctica is not that far off, lots of fairy penguins. If you are in Melbourne during the winter, organize a skiing trip up to the **Australian Alps** in southeastern New South Wales and eastern Victoria. The popular centers near Melbourne are **Mount Buller** and **Falls Creek.**

SOURCES OF FURTHER INFORMATION
Pan Am: 233 Collins Street, Melbourne—tel: 654 4788; **Victorian Government Travel Center,** 230 Collins Street, Melbourne—tel: 630202.

CANBERRA

Population 220,900. The age-old rivalry between Melbourne and Sydney made it entirely appropriate to establish a capital elsewhere, and the site of Canberra was chosen in the early 1900s. It is one of the world's few fully planned cities, designed and landscaped by an American architect, Walter Burley Griffin, who trained under Frank Lloyd Wright and won an international competition for the city plan. Canberra—its name is from an aborigine word meaning "meeting place"—is the seat of the federal government and the center of diplomatic life in Australia.

ACCOMMODATIONS
There are government guesthouses that can be used by visitors and are less expensive than hotels, a YMCA/YWCA, and a youth hostel. Hotels in Canberra, centrally located:
Rates are in US$ for a double/twin room with bath or shower
   Canberra City TraveLodge, Northbourne Avenue (from $75)

Canberra International Motor Inn, Northbourne Avenue (from $68)
Canberra-Rex, Northbourne Avenue, Braddon (from $58)
Kythera Motel, 98 Northbourne Avenue, Braddon (from $35)
Noah's Lakeside International, London Circuit (from $88)
Parkroyal Motor Inn, 102 Northbourne Avenue, Braddon (from $79)
Spero's Motel, 82 Northbourne Avenue, Braddon (from $35)
Wellington, corner National Circuit and Canberra Avenue (from $45),
   1½ miles from downtown

EATING AND ENTERTAINMENT

Most restaurants are attached to the major hotels: **Noah's** (12 Rudd
Street—tel: 488011) at the Towne House Motel specializes in steaks; the
Parkroyal Motor Inn (tel: 491411) has excellent food in gracious surroundings; the **Carousel** (tel: 731808), on top of Red Hill, has beautiful views
of the city. The **Bacchus Tavern** (tel: 487939); **Charlie's** (7 Bunda Street—
tel: 488338); **Pizzeria** (tel: 489131); and the **Lobby Restaurant** (tel: 731563)
are all recommended. There are a number of movie houses and drive-
in theaters in Canberra, but there is very little other nightlife.

SPORTS

The streams around Canberra offer the best trout fishing in Australia.
One can also enjoy sailing on **Lake Burley Griffin,** horse-riding trails
around the lake, golf, tennis, swimming in the Canberra swimming pool,
and skiing in the **Alps** in southeastern New South Wales and eastern
Victoria.

WHAT TO SEE

Lake Burley Griffin cuts a wide swath between northern and southern
sections of the city and all around Canberra is bordered by parkland.
To get a lovely view of the city you can take a ferry trip along the
lake for A$3.50 (or A$9 with a smorgasbord lunch). Canberra's principal
shopping center is planned around a beautifully designed city square
with statues and a fountain, called the **Civic Center.** The city's outstanding
attractions are **Parliament House,** impressive and white, set in beautiful
gardens, the **Australian War Memorial,** and the **Museum.** At the **Royal
Australian Mint** you can see coins being minted. At **Mount Stromlo Observatory,** one of the largest observatories in the southern hemisphere, a
74-inch telescope is open to the public. If you phone 881111, extension
30, you can arrange a viewing at night. Tours of the **Australian National
University** are conducted daily. The copper-covered shell of the **Australian Academy of Science** forms one of Canberra's landmarks. The Parthe-
non-shaped **National Library** is a magnificent building. The **Government
Nursery** at Yarralumla covers 70 acres and is one of the largest civic
nurseries in the world. The **Tidbinbilla Tracking Station and Nature Reserve** is 20 miles from the city and is open to the public. A more ambitious
excursion is to **Kosciusko National Park** with the great **Snowy Mountains
Hydro-Electric Scheme** and **Mt Kosciusko,** Australia's highest peak. You
could ski here in August (several resort hotels) or follow trails in January,

and at any time marvel at one of the world's greatest feats of civil engineering. Whole rivers have been turned back through mountains to irrigate the parched interior and provide electric power.

SOURCES OF FURTHER INFORMATION
Pan Am, 28-36 Ainslie Avenue, Canberra—tel: 489184; **ACT Government Tourist Bureau,** corner London Circuit and West Row, Canberra—tel: 497555.

SOUTH AUSTRALIA

CAPITAL
Adelaide, population 933,300. Apart from the sheep and cattle country near Adelaide, most of this state is barren, a fiercely hot land of ancient desert and dry salt lakes. Adelaide itself is a gracious city, inlaid with gardens and churches. Until recently, it had the reputation of being quiet and strait-laced; now it is awakening to the possibilities of tourism and has a livelier pace. Every 2 years (even numbered) in March a 3-week-long **Adelaide Festival of Arts** is held—celebrating the performing arts of all Australia. And it helps that this is the wine capital of Australia. Its climate is dry, bright, and warm most of the year.

ACCOMMODATIONS
If you are coming for the Festival, make reservations 6 months in advance. Hotels in Adelaide, centrally located unless otherwise indicated:
Rates are in US$ for a double/twin room with bath or shower
  Adelaide TraveLodge, 223 South Terrace (from $47), ½ mile from downtown
  Gateway Inn, 147 North Terrace (from $75)
  Grosvenor, 125 North Terrace (from $64)
  Meridien Lodge, 21 Melbourne Street North (from $56), 1 mile from downtown
  Oberoi, 62 Brougham Place North (from $75), 1 mile from downtown
  Parkroyal, 226 South Terrace (from $75), ½ mile from downtown
  Royal Coach, 24 Dequetteville Terrace, Kent Town (from $74), 1 mile from downtown
  South Terrace TraveLodge, 208 South Terrace (from $65), ½ mile from downtown
  Town House, Hindley and Morphett Streets (from $70)

FOOD AND RESTAURANTS
Some of South Australia's "New Australians" have been here long enough to establish vineyards and to make Adelaide's food scene more exciting than most. Some good restaurants to try are **Benjamin's Lake Restaurant** (Memorial Drive, overlooking Torrens Lake); **Arkaba Steak Cellar** (22 Gilbert Place, off King William Street); **Alpine Restaurant** (South Terrace); **Little Amsterdam** (5 Gays Arcade, off Twin Street, a quarter-mile from

the city center); **Swains Seafood Restaurant** (207 Glen Osmond Road, Frewville); **Decca's Place** (93 Melbourne Street, North Adelaide); the **Magic Flute** (109 Melbourne Street, North Adelaide); the **Festival Theater Restaurant** at the Adelaide Festival Center; and the very elegant **Henry Ayers Restaurant** (288 North Terrace) in an old restored home. For lunches, snacks, and inexpensive food, try the pubs.

SPORTS

People fish this coast for white shark and tuna—**Yorke Peninsula** and **Kangaroo Island** are two key spots. At the mouth of the **Murray River** there is excellent wildfowling country. Otherwise, the full range of Australian sports, including some good beaches and municipal golf courses, is found in the city itself.

WHAT TO SEE

Start with the beautifully laid out city itself, its gardens and lawns by the lake, the Victorian suburban homes of North Adelaide with their lacy ironwork, and Melbourne Street for its boutiques, wine cellars, and vine-covered walks. Visit the **Adelaide Festival Center,** on King William's Road, and the **Botanic Gardens** with a collection of unusual water lilies. Easily reached are the **Mount Lofty** ranges, 5 miles east, from which you can see over the whole area, and **Cleland Conservation Park,** a reserve for kangaroos, koalas, wombats, wallabies, and other native Australian animals. There is enthralling scenery at other parks and reserves including **Belair Recreation Park**—where there's also the old **Government House,** now a museum—and **Para Wirra Recreation Park, Morialta Falls,** and **Torrens Gorge.** South Australia is where the opals are mined. A trip to the digs at **Coober Pedy** is recommended only for those who believe in beginners' luck and can stand temperatures up to 110°, but there is no lack of reputable dealers in Adelaide who will sell stones hot from the field. A 6-day trip can be made into really rugged outback country in the **Flinders Ranges.** Accommodations are available at **Wilpena Pound** and **Arkaroola.** In contrast, you could take a 5-day trip on an old paddle-steamer down the **Murray River** (A$255-300 per person), a lazy, sunny way to see some of Australia's richest pioneer country. But the four-star visit is to the **Barossa Valley,** where German immigrants so hopefully planted their first vineyards in 1847. Now they are thriving "wineries" producing wines, sherries, and ports to compare with the European originals. The **Barossa Valley Vintage Festival** is held every 2 years, alternating with the Adelaide Festival of Arts, but if you miss it, the state tourist bureau can tell you which of many wineries are open to tasters.

SOURCES OF FURTHER INFORMATION

Pan Am, Aston House, 13 Leigh Street, Adelaide—tel: 512821; **South Australia Government Tourist Bureau,** 18 King William Street, Adelaide—tel: 513281.

WESTERN AUSTRALIA

CAPITAL

Perth, population 883,600. This is the largest state, the most sparsely populated, the state with the greatest potential. It's rather like a brand new California. Things are moving in Western Australia: to the south, new agricultural techniques are reclaiming the desert; to the north, unimaginably huge deposits of minerals are being mined. Perth is a beautiful city, but for the most part this land is notable for the vastness of its scale and its lovely ruggedness. The Perth area has an ideal climate and plenty of beaches nearby to enjoy it. The heat elsewhere in the state can be overwhelming.

AIRPORT INFORMATION

From Perth Airport there is a 4-mile ride into the city. Taxis cost approximately A$6 and buses 45¢. Cars can be rented at the airport.

FOOD, RESTAURANTS, AND ENTERTAINMENT

Perth has a dozen live theaters and several good theater restaurants. Nightlife ranges from theater to movies, nightclubs, taverns, wine bars, and restaurants. Most hotels, taverns, and wine bars are open until midnight, nightclubs until 3am.

Among Perth's better-known restaurants, **Hilite 33** (44 St George's Terrace—tel: 325 4884) offers classic French cuisine and is Perth's only revolving restaurant. **Miss Maud's Swedish Restaurant** (97 Murray Street—tel: 325 3900) features ethnic cuisine and decor; **Ruby's** (37 Pier Street—tel: 325 7474) offers real Victorian elegance and excellent cuisine; **Rooms With A View** (18 The Esplanade—tel: 325 2000) has a delightful outlook on the Swan River and a dance band along with fine food. There are several good seafood restaurants, such as **Mischa's Seafood Restaurant** (137 James Street—tel: 328 7449) and the **Oyster Bar** (88 James Street—tel: 381 7449). **Dirty Dick's Elizabethan Rooms** (194 Cambridge Street, Wembley—tel: 381 3853) offer bawdy, rollicking fun, abundant food, serving wenches, minstrels, and a jester. A large number of restaurants are clustered around James Street; Williams Street is known for its inexpensive but good eating places. Many of Perth's restaurants are fully licensed to sell liquor, but it is a good idea to check with the restaurant beforehand. Some excellent restaurants are not licensed but have a tavern or hotel nearby where liquor may be purchased.

ACCOMMODATIONS

Hotels located in central Perth:
Rates are in US$ for a double/twin room with bath or shower
  Gateway Inn, 10 Irwin Street (from $60)
  Highways Town House, 778 Hay Street (from $54)
  Park Towers, 517 Hay Street (from $56)
  Parmelia Hilton, Mill Street (from $75)
  Sheraton Perth, 207 Adelaide Terrace (from $63)

Transit Inn, 37 Pier Street (from $58)
TraveLodge, 54 Terrace Road (from $49)

WHAT TO SEE

Perth is blessed with a major park inside the city itself. The foresight of a former governor established **King's Park,** 1,000 acres of virgin bush on a gentle range from which you can see over the river by which Perth stands. There are many other gardens: **Queen's Gardens** are a must for children.

The city has a short history, visible in its 19th-century buildings, most of them in St George's Terrace. The **Stirling House Museum** will give you some idea of what it was like in pioneer times. Farther out, **Rottnest Island** makes an interesting trip for its unique marsupial, the quokka, and a pleasant place to pass a sunny day. You can also drive out to the **Darling Ranges** for unspoiled scenery and spring flowers, or to see one of the daily performances of the famed Andalusian Dancing Horses at the El Caballo Blanco stud farm.

Farther afield, there is a 5-day tour to the lush, giant karri tree forests in the Manjimup and Pemberton area and on to the rugged coastline around Albany. The tour costs A$264. To the north, similar tours are available to Geraldton and the surrounding coastal and inland areas, costing A$250. These are areas where more than two-thirds of the world's wildflowers can be seen, with over half of them native to Western Australia. There are also local airline tours available, including fishing safaris from Carnarvon or a 10-day Perth-to-Darwin tour. Fly for a 2-day tour to historic Kalgoorlie and the Goldfields areas for A$189, or take an 8-day coach trip for A$360.

SOURCES OF FUTHER INFORMATION

Pan Am, 178 St George's Terrace, Perth—tel: 321 2719; **Western Australian Government Travel Center,** 772 Hay Street, Perth—tel: 321 2471.

NORTHERN TERRITORY

CAPITAL

Darwin, population 54,603. There is one road in the territory: they call it "the track." It runs south from Darwin to Alice Springs, passing through Tennant Creek on the way. And at the Alice it ends. At the center of Australia, there are rivers, too, which run (maybe) twice a year—when a 4-foot wall of water pours hundreds of miles out into the desert.

ACCOMMODATIONS

Hotels in the Northern Territory, located in city centers:
Rates are in US$ for a double/twin room with bath or shower
  Capricornia, 44 East Point Road, Fannie Bay, Darwin (from $37)
  Darwin, Herbert Street, Darwin (from $49)
  Don, 12 Cavenagh Street, Darwin (from $57)
  Koala Welcome Inn, Daly Street, Darwin (from $56)

Telford International, Dashwood Crescent, Darwin (from $56)
TraveLodge, 122 The Esplanade, Darwin (from $75)
Elkira Court, 134 Bath Street, Alice Springs (from $33)
Oasis Motel, Gap Road, Alice Springs (from $41)
Territory Motel, Leichardt Terrace, Alice Springs (from $49)

WHAT TO SEE

Darwin is in the tropics, a center for exploring the lush, wild country around it, which abounds in exotic animals: buffalo, crocodiles, wallabies, beautiful birds, and the curious termite colonies that punctuate the plains. Tours can be organized to wildlife parks or, more adventurously, by boat and four-wheel-drive vehicles into open country with aborigine guides. Aborgine settlements can also be visited either on **Bathurst Island** or **Melville Island.** *Pukamumi* poles, curved and painted by aborigines, are a prominent feature of Darwin itself. Accommodation in Darwin and its environs is adequate, but not luxurious. If you want to hunt buffalo, crocodile, or other wildlife, note that this is a strictly enforced conservation area, and you will do best to arrange to stay in one of the properly organized safari camps.

Alice Springs is in the center—the parched heart—of this continent; only a remarkable town could survive. "The Alice" has a population of only 14,000, but it fairly hums with life. By day it is a busy little town, filled in winter with tourists exploring the heartland. By night there are many bars in full swing—even nightclubs—and the sound of aborigine *corroborree* rites from the dry bed of the **Todd River.** Accommodations and facilities are increasing annually. It is virtually the only base from which you can explore the remarkable and beautiful natural features of this area. **Ayers Rock,** 275 miles southwest of Alice Springs, is the most famous. This is a gigantic red monolith rising from the desert—awesomely beautiful and long sacred to the aborigines, who have left their paintings on the walls of its caves. It changes color and aspect magically at sunset and sunrise, and it is possible to get 30 different pictures in as many minutes. Nearby is **Mount Olga,** a more modest sister to the Rock, which anywhere else would be a tourist attraction in itself. A trip here is most valuable if it includes an overnight stay. Nearer to Alice Springs are brilliantly colored **Stanley Chasm, Glen Helen,** and **Ormiston Gorges**—spectacular chasms. Remarkable in a different way is **Palm Valley,** where a living fossil grows—the *Livistona mariae* palm, found nowhere else in the world. A trip to this desert is usually combined with a visit to sacred aborigine sites and the **Hermannsburg Mission,** an aboriginal mission 175 miles southwest of Alice Springs, run by the Lutheran Church. Such excursions are usually made by four-wheel-drive vehicles, since there are no roads. An illuminating experience is to travel with the mail pilot on his run here to visit the largest cattle range in the world—over 1,000,000 acres. In Alice Springs itself are several interesting visits: **the Pitchi-Ritchi Museum and Bird Sanctuary,** the old telegraph station and its schoolhouse by the Springs, the flying doctor service, and the **School of the Air.**

SOURCES OF FURTHER INFORMATION

Pan Am, Mitchell Street, Darwin—tel: 818666; **Northern Territory Government Tourist Bureau,** 27 Smith Street, Darwin—tel: 816611; 51 Todd Street, Alice Springs—tel: 521299. Information on camping and national park attractions from **The Territory Parks and Wildlife Commission,** Gap Road, Alice Springs—tel: 522788.

QUEENSLAND

CAPITAL

Brisbane, population 1,015,200. Over half of Queensland is in the tropics—some of it still unsettled. Called the Sunshine State, it certainly can be among the warmest places in Australia. Apart from some beautiful country ranging from jungle to mountain, downs and desert, it has two famous tourist attractions: the coral gardens and islands of the Great Barrier Reef, and the Gold Coast.

ACCOMMODATIONS

Not as varied as in New South Wales. Hotels in Brisbane, centrally located unless otherwise indicated:
Rates are in US$ for a double/twin room with bath or shower
   Carlton, 103 Queen Street (from $35)
   Crest International, King George Square (from $77)
   Gateway Inn, 85 North Quay (from $70)
   Gazebo Terrace, 345 Wickham Terrace (from $57)
   Lennons Plaza, 66 Queen Street (from $66)
   Parkroyal Motor Inn, corner Alice and Albert Streets (from $76)
   TraveLodge, 355 Main Street, Kangaroo Point (from $62), 1 mile from
      downtown
   Zebra Motel, 103 George Street (from $62)

EATING AND ENTERTAINMENT

While the culinary standards are not as high as in other Australian cities, there are some good restaurants and good tropical seafood—barramundi, red emperor, coral cod, and the local specialty, mud crabs—and wonderful tropical fruit. The dinner hour is early and short, with many restaurants closed by 9pm. Some restaurants to try are **Captain Cook's Cabin** (243 George Street—tel: 217334) for seafood and **Baxter's** (166 Braun Street, Deagon), about 9 miles from the city, which has been serving seafood for well over a century. For European food, try **Allegro** (Central Station Plaza, Edward Street—tel: 229 5550) and enjoy chamber music while dining. At the **Living Room** (at the Gardens end of Edward Street—tel: 221 2805) you wine and dine while watching live theater. The **Wine Cellar** (327 Queen Street, opposite Piccadilly Arcade—tel: 219436) has the largest stocks of wine in Brisbane.

SPORTS

Fishing, tennis, golf, sailing, surfing, skin-diving; but don't just dive in. Many Queensland resorts have surf patrols, and swimming at supervised beaches is strongly recommended.

WHAT TO SEE

Inland, the **Lamington National Park** is a beautiful area of unspoiled mountain country about 70 miles south of Brisbane. Some flora and fauna here are unknown in the rest of the world—the lyre bird, for example, that takes the voice it last heard; or the 3,000-year-old Antarctic beeches (nut bearing trees). You can stay in reasonable comfort at the **Green Mountain Guest House** or **Binna Bura Lodge.** An easy outing is to the **Lone Pine Koala Sanctuary,** the largest in Australia, to mingle with those lovable living teddy bears. Take the river launch for a leisurely cruise.

The **Gold Coast,** south of Brisbane, is a living stretch of sandy beaches and curling surf for those who love the sun, sand, sea, and their fellow creatures. The strip abounds in hotels, restaurants, and entertainments, among which are the boomerang factory at **Mudgeeraba** where you can watch the flight-testing; the **Currumbin** bird sanctuary, where at a signal flocks of lorikeets flutter in to perch on your head and arms; **Sea World,** which has daily shows with performing dolphins and other marine life; **Fleay's Fauna Reserve** at Burleigh Heads; and the **Auto Museum** at Kirra. At **Surfers Paradise,** there are water-skiing shows, speedboat rides, floor shows, and bowling lanes. North of Brisbane is the **Sunshine Coast** where the beaches are as good though much quieter than those to the south. Varying from 20 miles to 150 miles off the coast is the **Great Barrier Reef,** largest coral reef in the world—1,200 miles long—and in many ways a perfect vacation area, especially in winter. There are quiet green islands, brilliant coral, tropical fish, thousands of coves and beaches, transport and accommodations in plenty. Dedicated skin-divers should not miss it, neither should collectors of exotic sea shells. The islands of the **Whitsunday** group—**Brampton, Hayman, Lindeman,** and **South Molle**— are reached from Mackay and are very beautiful. Others to the north and south have their advantages—in particular **Green Island,** with its underwater observatory, and **Dunk Island,** both reached from Cairns. The most economical way to see the reef is by taking one of the package tours offered by several Australian companies at about A$300-400 for a 4-5 day cruise.

SOURCES OF FURTHER INFORMATION

Pan Am, 307 Queens Street, Brisbane—tel: 221 7477; 350 Flinders Street, Townsville—tel: 715197; **Queensland Government Tourist Bureau,** Adelaide and Edward Sts, Brisbane—tel: 312211.

TASMANIA

CAPITAL

Hobart, population 168,480. Tasmania, 140 miles south of the mainland, is the "apple isle," the smallest of the Australian states and the most verdant. It is a beautiful little island, with its rugged mountains, irregular coastline, orchard-line valleys, lonely alpine lakes, and colorful past.

ACCOMMODATIONS

Hotels in Tasmania, located in city centers unless otherwise indicated:
Rates are in US$ for a double/twin room with bath or shower

Four Seasons Downtowner Motor Hotel, 96 Bathurst Street, Hobart (from $58)

Four Seasons Town House, 167 Macquarie Street, Hobart (from $47)

Innkeepers Lenna Motor Inn, 20 Runnymede St, Hobart (from $70)

Wrest Point Hotel-Casino, Sandy Bay Road, Hobart (from $55), 1½ miles from center

Abel Tasman Motor Inn, 303 Hobart Road, Launceston (from $33), 2 miles from center

Colonial Motor Inn, 31 Elizabeth Street, Launceston (from $56)

Launceston Hotel, 107 Brisbane Street, Launceston 7250 (from $41)

Penny Royal Watermill Motel, 145 Paterson St, Launceston (from $41)

EATING AND ENTERTAINMENT

The seafoods in Tasmania are the island's specialty, notably the scallops and lobster. In Hobart the best restaurants are attached to the hotels. The **Wrest Point Casino** (tel: 250112) is situated overlooking the beautiful Derwent River, only 5 minutes from the city. It offers gambling and nightly entertainment. The **Chart Room** at the TraveLodge (tel: 342911) is also very good. The **Ball and Chain** restaurant is in an old restored warehouse on the waterfront (87 Salamanca Place—tel: 232222). A small place to try is the **Copper Kettle** (111 Main Road, in Moonah—tel: 282372). The **Old Hobart Bar** (Elizabeth Street) is an intriguingly decorated pub serving a good lunch. Halfway between Hobart and Launceston, at the historic village of Ross, the **Hotel Ross** serves home-cooked meals by the open fireplace. There are numerous movie houses and a few small theaters in Hobart. Nightlife is pretty much limited to hotel dancing, although the Wrest Point and **Carlyle** hotels do have a good floor show.

SHOPPING

Hobart's two main department stores, **Fitzgeralds** and **Myers,** have everything. For souvenirs, try **Rembrandts, Wards,** or **Ashtons.**

SPORTS

With its innumerable small bays and inlets, Hobart is a very popular yachting center. The annual **Sydney** to **Hobart Yacht Race,** departing Sydney on Boxing Day, is one of the major events of the year for yachtsmen the world over. Tasmania is also a popular place for hikers. The rugged mountains that cover large sections of the country are ideal for bushwalking and climbing. Fishing is excellent.

WHAT TO SEE

Hobart is a picturesque little town nestling under **Mount Wellington,** which rises to 4,166 feet above sea level. The 14-mile ride to the peak gives you a majestic view of the city. Renovated **National Trust Houses** are worth visiting. There are some 90 of them, many on Macquarie and Davey streets. A good starting place for a walking tour is the gift shop and information center at 25 Kingsway Place (tel: 348289), a cottage built by a local flour miller in 1875. **Constitution Dock** and **Salamanca Place,** where warehouses dating back to whaling days are being restored, are part of the historic waterfront area. From Hobart you can go on a cruise up the Derwent River to **New Norfolk** and the salmon hatcheries. A day trip out to the **Huon Valley,** the principal orchard district, is rewarding—especially if you return via the **D'Entrecasteaux Channel** with its lovely seascapes. Sixty miles from Hobart is **Port Arthur,** a penal colony used for about 40 years in the mid-19th century. The dreaded **Eaglehawk Neck,** where guard dogs once used to turn back escapees, and the crumbling ruins of the old guardhouse stand in memory of the convict days.

Launceston to the north is the second largest city in Tasmania, an area of parks and gardens set among rolling hills. **Cataract Gorge,** only 10 minutes from the city center, was chiseled out by the South Esk River. Nearby are the **Cataract Cliff Grounds and Park. Entally National House** is furnished with prized antiques from colonial days. The spring wildflowers at **Cradle Mountain-Lake St Clair National Park** are glorious and attract hundreds of people every year. Tasmania's east coast, with its beautiful beaches and good fishing areas, has many popular holiday resorts; **St Helens** is a good example. The west coast is rugged and densely forested. You can see much of this area by taking the Lyall Highway into **Queenstown,** and from nearby Strahan, a boat trip up the River Gordon. From Queenstown the fine new Murchison Highway completely encircles the island.

SOURCES OF FURTHER INFORMATION

Tasmanian Government Tourist Bureau, 80 Elizabeth Street, Hobart— tel: 346911. **Pan Am,** 31 Murray Street, Hobart—tel: 348212, and Pan Am offices in Sydney and Melbourne, and any Pan Am office around the world; **State Tourist Bureau** in each Australian capital city; **Australian Tourist Commission,** 3550 Wilshire Boulevard, Los Angeles, CA 90010; 1270 Avenue of the Americas, New York, NY 10020; Qantas House, 49 Old Bond Street, London WIX 4PL; Australische Fremdenverkehrszentrale, Neue Mainzerstrasse 22, Frankfurt am Main 6, West Germany; Air New Zealand House, 1 Queen Street, Auckland 1, New Zealand; CPO Box 16, Tokyo 100-91, Japan.

Bangladesh

WHAT'S SPECIAL

Bangladesh is a country of great, though not spectacular, natural beauty, with many rivers and a variety of vegetation. While it is not an obvious choice for a vacation, its attractions should not go unnoticed.

COUNTRY BRIEFING

The **area** is 55,126 square miles and the **population** 90,000,000, of whom about 1,680,000 live in the **capital,** Dacca. The **climate** is tropical. October-March are the best months to visit. Bangladesh has been **independent** since 1971; the **language** is Bangla; and 80% of the people are **Muslim.** The **currency** is the taka; 100 paisas = 1 taka. 16.85 takas = US$1. **Public Holidays** are National Mourning Day, 21 Feb; Independence Day, 26 Mar; Good Friday; National Revolution Day, 7 Nov; National Day, 16 Dec; Christmas, 25 Dec. Buddhist and Muslim religious holidays dates vary yearly according to the lunar calendar.

HOW TO GET THERE

Flying time to Dacca, Tejgaon Airport from Frankfurt is 11 hours; from Delhi, 2¼ hours; from Bangkok, 2¼ hours. Time in Bangladesh: GMT+5 hours 30 minutes.

REQUIREMENTS FOR ENTRY AND CUSTOMS REGULATIONS

Passport; visas are necessary for US and UK citizens but generally not required for citizens of British Commonwealth countries. Smallpox and cholera vaccination certificates required; yellow-fever certificates for those coming from an infected area. Only 20 takas may be taken into the country, with unlimited foreign currency; no more than 20 takas may be taken out and no more foreign currency than was brought in. Duty-free allowance: 200 cigarettes or 50 cigars or ½ lb tobacco; 2 bottles liquor; ½ pint perfume. Firearms may be imported, with permission.

AIRPORT INFORMATION
The major airport is Tejgaon (Dacca International), which is 6 miles from Dacca. There are taxis and buses to the town center, bus fare is 1 taka. Taxis are always available, and the fare is 150 takas. Airport departure tax is 50 takas.

ACCOMMODATIONS
Hotels and rest houses are available. Hotels in Dacca:

> **INTER · CONTINENTAL DACCA,** Minto Road (from US$67 double)
> **Purbani International,** 1 Dilkusha (from US$45 double)

USEFUL INFORMATION
Banks are open 9:30-1:00pm, Mon-Thurs; 9-11, Fri and Sat. It is unlawful to transact business in foreign exchange except through authorized dealers. There are some English-language publications, including the *Bangladesh Observer* and the *Bangladesh Times*. Useful **telephone** numbers: **Pan Am** 25 59 11; **Tourist Information Center** (at airport) 31 42 09, (at Inter · Continental), 28-05 79; **Bangladesh Tours and Travels (BIT),** 25 42 93/25 22 18; **Automobile Association of Bangladesh,** 40 22 41. **Tipping** is customary in hotels. Tip 5-10% on restaurant bills and 10% of bill to drivers of rented cars. Railway and airport porters expect up to 1 taka per piece of luggage. **Electricity** is 220 volts AC. Major hotels have a **laundry** service (dry-cleaning a suit, from 60 takas; laundering a shirt, from 15 takas). There are **hairdressing** salons in first-class hotels. Film and **photographic** equipment are available in limited quantities and are expensive. Drink boiled or bottled water, be careful when eating local food.

TRANSPORTATION
Buses and taxis available in the city. A car can be rented for about 40 takas per hour, plus 5.5 takas per mile. Rickshaws start at 2 takas and a 1½-mile ride will cost about 5 takas. Bargaining over transport fees has become almost a sport in Dacca, so negotiate the price before taking the ride. Some taxi drivers attempt to charge 150 takas no matter how short the journey. The roads are, at best, reasonable, but not all are surfaced. There are about 1,800 miles of railroad—but trains can be slow and uncomfortable. There is also a long-distance bus service linking major towns and districts. Boat travel is widespread, with special coaches for tourists in the boats. Contact Bangladesh Parjatan Corporation, Motijheel, Dacca (tel: 25 27 65) for booking. The internal airline is Bangladesh Biman (Air Bangladesh).

FOOD AND RESTAURANTS

There is a choice of local or Western-style food in hotels and large restaurants of the major cities, or a variety of curries and rice dishes available throughout the country. A meal in an expensive restaurant will cost about US$6. The buffet at the Inter • Continental, for example, is 100 takas. It is advisable to avoid foods that have been frozen, such as imported beef or seafood. A ½ pint of beer will cost 45 takas, and an imported bottle of scotch 700 takas. Restaurants include **Colon Ruchita** (tel: 25 44 46), **Sakura** (tel: 28 09 46), and **Mary Anderson-Floating Garden** (tel: 71 288).

SHOPPING

Stores generally open 9am-6pm (Mon-Fri), 9am-2pm(Sat), closed Sundays. Pink pearl, wood carvings, brassware, cottons, muslins, and silk are all available throughout the country at reasonable prices.

WHAT TO SEE

Dacca has hundreds of mosques, the most noted of which are the **Star Mosque** and the **Baitul-Mukarram Mosque. Chittagong,** on the river **Karnaphuli,** is the major port in this part of the country, situated on the Bay of Bengal. The town of **Cox's Bazar,** 94 miles south of Chittagong, has one of the longest natural beaches in the world.

SOURCES OF FURTHER INFORMATION

Pan Am agents, Bangladesh Biman Building, Motijheel, Dacca, and any Pan Am office around the world; **Bangladesh Parjatan Corporation** (National Tourist Organization of Bangladesh), Islam Chambers, 125-A Motijheel, Dacca 2; **Permanent Mission of Bangladesh to the United Nations,** 821 UN Plaza, New York, NY 10017; **Bangladesh Embassy,** 3431 Massachusetts Avenue NW, Washington, DC 20007; **Bangladesh High Commission,** 28 Queen's Gate, London SW7.

Burma

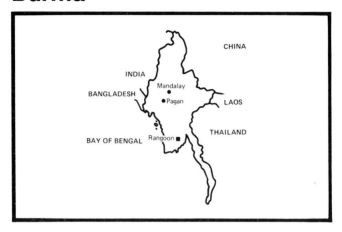

WHAT'S SPECIAL

Throughout the 1960s Burma and the Burmese people went their own way. Foreign visitors were barred; a diplomatic "do not disturb" sign hung over the country, and the government concentrated on radical programs of internal reform. Today the government is beginning to extend a cautious welcome to visitors (the people themselves have always been overjoyed to meet strangers), and the very fact that Burma is emerging from a period of isolation makes it a most unusual Southeast Asian country. This temporary isolation has enabled the Burmese to side-step the more tasteless aspects of modernization. Naturally, this "unspoiled" aspect of Burma means there are fewer deluxe tourist facilities than you will find in other parts of Asia. Nevertheless, for a glimpse of a deeply religious, fiercely independent people, living in a green and fertile "un-Westernized" country, you would do no better than to take advantage of the gap in the doorway to Burma. Among the people and places of South East Asia, Burma is unique.

COUNTRY BRIEFING

Area 261,789 square miles with **population** of 34,938,000 of whom over 3,000,000 live in the **capital,** Rangoon. **Climate:** Burma is monsoon country; during the dry summer months of March, April, and May, temperatures may reach 110°F. In early June the monsoon begins, bringing torrential downpours most afternoons. In November the rain stops and temperatures drop. Winter lasts until February, and this is the best time to visit. **Government:** Burma is a socialist republic ruled by a state council.

The **language** is Burmese, and about 10% of the people speak English. Ninety percent of the population are of the Buddhist **religion. Currency** is the kyat; 100 pyas = **K**s1; **K**s7 = US$1.

Public Holidays: National Mourning Day, 21 Feb; Independence Day 26 Mar; Good Friday; National Revolution Day 7 Nov; National Day, 16 Dec; Christmas, 25 Dec. In addition there are several Moslem and Buddhist holidays with variable dates, including Burmese New Year or the Water Festival (four days in April); the Full Moon of Kason or celebration of the birth and enlightenment of the Buddha (April or May); the beginning of Buddhist Lent (July); the end of Buddhist Lent or the Festival of Lights (October); and the Tazaungdaing Festival (November).

HOW TO GET THERE

Flying time to Rangoon, Mingaladon Airport from Frankfurt is 14 hours; from Hong Kong is 3½ hours; from Bangkok, 1 hour. Time in Burma: GMT+6 hours 30 minutes.

REQUIREMENTS FOR ENTRY AND CUSTOMS REGULATIONS

Entry regulations are strict. A valid passport and visa (obtainable from any Burmese Embassy or Consulate or British Consulate) are essential. Only two types of visa are issued to tourists: 24-hour transit visas and 7-day tourist visas. On arrival you must show an outbound ticket with a confirmed reservation within the period of the visa's validity. Children over 7 must hold visas separate from those of their parents. Note: visas must be obtained before departure for Burma; they will not be issued on arrival and cannot, furthermore, be extended once you arrive. Cholera certificate necessary; yellow-fever vaccination required for passengers arriving from infected areas; smallpox certificate not required. No restrictions on foreign currency, but import and export of Burmese currency is strictly prohibited. Duty-free allowance: 200 cigarettes or 50 cigars or ½ pound tobacco; 1 quart liquor; 1 pint perfume or eau de cologne; no gift allowance.

AIRPORT INFORMATION

Rangoon's Mingaladon Airport is 12 miles from the city center. There are government-owned pickups which charge **K**s25. The same trip by taxi costs about **K**s30, after bargaining. Burma Airways Corporation runs a free pick-up service between the airport and the BAC office in town, close to the Strand Hotel. Bus fare is 1 kyat, but the buses are usually very crowded with little room for luggage. Mingaladon has a duty-free shop.

ACCOMMODATIONS

Burma's hotels are modest by international standards. The three principal ones in Rangoon are: the **Strand** on the waterfront near the business center of the city; the **President (Thamada)**, also in the center; and the **Inya Lake,** overlooking the lake of the same name en route to the airport. Rates are subject to 10% service charge. Hotels in Rangoon:

Inya Lake, Kaba Aye Pagoda Road (from US$30 double)
President, 5 Signal Pagoda Road (from US$17 double)
Strand, 92 Strand Road (from US$20 double)

USEFUL INFORMATION

Banks open 10-2 Mon-Fri, 10-12 Sat. Phones in street booths, restaurants, and hotels. Useful numbers: Pan Am agents, 14555; Airport Information, 40567; Tourist Information, 77966/75328. Tipping is not widespread; in restaurants up to Ks2 if 10% service charge is not already included; porters, 1 kyat per bag; taxis, about 10%; hairdressers and roomboys, Ks2. Electricity is 220 volts, 50 cycles AC. Laundry and dry-cleaning services available in all big hotels (one day's laundry can be done for about Ks15). Health: there are English-speaking doctors and dentists. Imported pharmaceuticals are expensive and imported goods difficult to find. All water should be boiled and filtered and vegetables washed in mild disinfectant. Precautions should be taken against typhoid, dysentery, and malaria.

TRANSPORTATION

For travel in and around Rangoon, visitors are advised to rent a car with driver. Rates vary, but expect to pay about US$28 per day. Alternative means of transport include taxis (price subject to bargaining). Bus travel is strictly for the adventurous. Up-country, Burma Airways Corporation Fokker Friendships operate regular services on all the major towns, as do the National Railways and the Inland Waterways Transport Service.

FOOD AND RESTAURANTS

The local Burmese food is hot, spicy, and invariably served with rice. Chinese restaurants abound, and in most hotels you will find Western dishes on the menu. To avoid upset stomachs choose bland dishes. There are good restaurants at the Strand, Inya Lake, President, and Orient hotels. Other places to try in Rangoon are the Hai Yuan (University Avenue—tel: 31457), on the way to the Inya Lake Hotel; the Nam Sin (120 Prome Road—tel: 60407), about 8 miles from town; the Nanthida Café (Lewis Street Jetty); and the Karaweik, which is a floating restaurant on Kandawgyi Lake.

DRINKING TIPS

Bars all close at 10:30pm. An imported whisky and soda will cost from KS20, and both imported and local wines are available. Local beer (KS8 a bottle) compares favorably with the Indian brews. Try the Mandalay beer brewed in Mandalay.

ENTERTAINMENT

National music, drama, and dance can all be sampled at the National Academy or at the Fine Arts Theater, Jubilee Hall in Rangoon. Nightlife is very limited. There are movie houses, some showing American and English films with original soundtrack.

SHOPPING

Burmese jade, sapphires, pearls, and rubies are excellent buys, as are traditional handicraft items such as weapons and wood and ivory carvings. When buying gems, official receipts should be obtained in order to avoid problems in clearing customs on leaving the country. The **Diplomatic Shop**, near the main tourist bureau in Rangoon, and the duty-free shop at the airport both offer a selection of gems and the necessary receipts. Be careful if bargaining elsewhere, as the gems may be substandard or the receipts offered not recognized by customs officials.

WHAT TO SEE

For security reasons trips to certain areas up-country must have government approval. Your hotel will tell you the procedure, or check with Tourist Burma, the official hotel and tourist corporation.

Rangoon: Near the heart of Rangoon and standing on a small hill is one of the world's most revered Buddhist shrines, 2,500-year-old **Shwedagon Pagoda.** The *stupa* (or spire) of the temple soars 326 feet into the air and is capped with thousands of foot-square gold plates and thousands of diamonds and other precious and semi-precious stones. It is a breathtaking sight, attracting Buddhist pilgrims from all over the world. (Do not forget to remove your shoes in all Buddhist temples and pagodas). Along the covered stairways on the east side of the Pagoda you will find the **Shwedagon Pagoda Bazaar,** where the atmosphere is as colorful as the trinkets on sale; you should bargain and feel satisfied if you knock 30% off the starting price. If you possibly can, time your visit to coincide with the **Festival of Kason,** held during the full moon nearest to the end of April. People from all over the country flock to the Shwedagon Pagoda to pay homage to the **Banyan Tree** commemorating the Buddha's enlightenment, and the colorful, festive occasion is a chance to witness the traditional music and dancing that are a part of the celebration. Other sights worth seeing in Rangoon include the **Sule Pagoda,** nearly as old as the Shwedagon Pagoda; the modern **Kaba Aye** or World Peace Pagoda, and the nearby **Great Sacred Cave;** and the **National Museum.** If you can, catch a bout of traditional Burmese boxing, usually arranged on festive occasions.

Mandalay, about 365 miles north of Rangoon, is the physical and spiritual center of Burma and the home of the last two Burmese kings. Do not miss the **Kuthodaw Pagoda** with its 729 miniature pagodas, each housing a text of the Buddhist canon, the *Tripitaka,* or the village workshops where gold is beaten into leaf to adorn religious statuettes and shrines. A day trip by air from Rangoon should suffice, or stay at the **Mandalay Hotel** (from US$15 double).

Pagan boasts 16 square miles of ruined pagodas—the ruins of over 5,000 pagodas that graced the landscape during the height of the Pagan dynasty from the 11th to the 13th centuries. During that period, it is said, so many trees were cut to fire bricks for the pagodas that even the climate of the area changed. It is a place of breathtaking beauty and a place to ponder upon the might of Kublai Khan, who sacked the city in 1287. Further destruction came with an earthquake in 1975 and the government is now in the process of renovating the 30 most significant temples. Accommodations in Pagan are at the **Thiripitsaya Hotel** (from US$22 double).

Inle Lake: Located near the town of **Taunggyi,** Inle Lake is famous for its fascinating floating islands, stilt houses, and skillful fishermen (they row their boats standing with one leg wrapped around the oar!). Look for the islanders rowing to pray during the **Phaung-Dau-Oo-Pagoda Festival** in October; it is a moving and colorful sight. Try also to visit the nearby **Pindaya Caves.** You can stay in Taunggyi itself, at the **Strand Hotel** (from US$15 double).

Pegu is the nearest town to the **Imperial War Cemetery,** where 27,000 Allied servicemen from the Second World War are buried. Pegu is the site of the immense **Shwemawdaw Pagoda,** with its more than 50-foot-long image of the *Reclining Buddha.* It is a day trip from the city no visitor should miss.

SOURCES OF FURTHER INFORMATION

Pan Am agents: Burma Airways Corporation, 104 Strand Road, Rangoon, and any Pan Am office around the world; **Tourist Burma,** 77/91 Sule Pagoda Road, Rangoon; **Consulate General of Burma,** 10 East 77th Street, New York, NY 10021; **Burmese Embassy,** 19a Charles Street, London, WI.

Fiji Islands

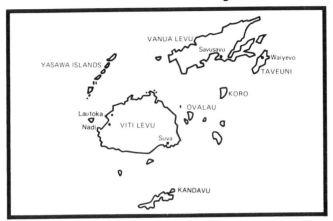

WHAT'S SPECIAL

Everybody has a dream desert island. Fiji can make that dream come true, three hundred times over. Lying like a handful of pearls in the Southwest Pacific, the 300 islands that make up Fiji have it all—and more: fantastic water sports—including spear and big-game fishing; great food—tropical feasts, Chinese, Indian, and European; rich entertainment—traditional and Western-style singing and dancing; and, above all, the sort of warm hospitality you'd expect from a people whose neighbors are thousands of ocean miles away.

Captain Cook was one of the first visitors, followed by Captain Bligh of the *Bounty*. Duty didn't permit them to stay, but many others since have stayed and settled—principally Indians and Chinese, who, with the Fijians themselves and some Europeans, form a truly harmonious and hospitable community.

COUNTRY BRIEFING

Size: 7,055 square miles
Capital: Suva

Population: 623,000
Capital Population: 80,000

Weather in Suva: Lat N3°07′; Alt 127 ft

Temp (°F)	Jan	Feb	Mar	Apr	May	Jun	Jul	Aug	Sep	Oct	Nov	Dec
Av Low	74°	74°	74°	73°	71°	69°	68°	68°	69°	70°	71°	73°
Av High	86°	86°	86°	84°	82°	80°	79°	79°	80°	81°	83°	85°
Days no rain	8	7	7	8	11	13	14	14	12	13	11	10

Government: Independent member of British Commonwealth.
Language: English, Fijian, and Indian dialects.
Religion: Various Christian denominations, Hinduism, Islam.
Currency: Fiji dollar, 100 cents = 1 Fiji dollar.

	5¢	10¢	50¢	F$1	F$5	F$10	F$20	F$50
US	.07	.13	.63	1.25	6.25	12.50	25.00	62.50
UK	.03	.06	.30	.60	2.98	5.96	11.93	29.81

Public Holidays: Where holidays are movable, they are given as approximate dates.

New Year's Day, 1 Jan
Muhammad's Birthday
Good Friday
Holy Saturday
Easter Monday
Queen's Birthday, June
Bank Holiday, 1st Mon in Aug

Fiji Day, 1st Mon in Oct
Diwali (Hindu), late Oct
Prince of Wales's Birthday, 14 Nov
Christmas Day, 25 Dec
Boxing Day, 26 Dec

HOW TO GET THERE

Flying time to Nadi Airport from Los Angeles is 10 hours; from Honolulu, 5 hours; from Sydney, 3¾ hours. Time in Fiji: GMT+12.

REQUIREMENTS FOR ENTRY AND CUSTOMS REGULATIONS

Passport and round-trip ticket are sufficient for a stay of 1 month, and permission to extend is easily obtainable. Visas are not required for US, UK, or Commonwealth citizens, or for cruise passengers whose liner is calling in port. Other nationals may be issued a permit valid up to 4 months. Smallpox, cholera, and yellow-fever certificates required if entering from an infected area. Duty-free allowance: 200 cigarettes, or ½ pound of cigars or tobacco; 1 quart liquor; 4 ounces of perfume for personal use; gifts to the value of $20.

AIRPORT INFORMATION

Nadi is the international airport. It is about 5 miles from the town (a taxi costs F$4). Coral Coast Express bus operates between Nadi and Suva (135 miles), stopping at principal hotels en route; F$15 one way. Air Pacific operates shuttle services (40 minutes) between Nadi and Nausori Airport near Suva; single fare F$26. Fiji Air operates twice-daily air/taxi service between Nadi and Nausori, stopping at airfields en route for access to coast resorts. Buses from Nausori to Suva (12 miles) cost F$1. Taxi fare is F$10. A departure tax of F$5 is levied at Nadi and Nausori airports on all international departures. There are duty-free shops at Nadi and Nausori airports.

ACCOMMODATIONS

Fiji hotels have a wide variety of style and character. Of special note are the resort hotels on Viti Levu's south coast, near Nadi airport and on outer islands. There are luxury hotels and medium-priced ones. Most provide pools, sight-seeing facilities, and constant entertainment for all guests. *Bures* or native cottages, with straw roofs but with air conditioning and modern plumbing, are also provided by these hotels and are very pleasant vacation homes. Hotels from luxury to budget class exist in Suva and elsewhere. There is a very good group of island resort hotels, as Fiji has more than 70 hotels. A selection grouped by area:

Rates are in US$ for a double/twin room with bath or shower

NADI

Fiji Gateway (from $30), opposite airport
Mocambo (from $33), near airport
Regent of Fiji (from $80), 20 minutes from airport on beach
Tanoa (from $37), near airport
TraveLodge (from $71), near airport
Westgate (from $33), 2½ miles from airport

CORAL COAST (Viti Levu Island)

The Fijian (from $95), on Yanuca Island
Hyatt Regency Fiji (from $61), at Korolevu, 65 miles from Suva
Korolevu Beach Hotel (from $34), 65 miles from Suva
Man Friday Resort (from $43), 55 miles from Suva
Naviti Resort (from $49), 58 miles from Nadi
Pacific Harbour Resort (from $75), at Deuba, 35 miles from Suva

SUVA

Courtesy Inn (from $46), centrally located in Suva
Grand Pacific Hotel (from $41), on Suva Harbor
Tradewinds Hotel (from $39), on Suva Bay
TraveLodge (from $71), waterfront location

OUTER ISLANDS

Castaway Island Resort (from $51), 15 miles off Lautoka
Castaway Taveuni (from $39), on Taveuni
Mana Island Resort (from $56), 21 miles from Lautoka
Namale Plantation Resort (from $39), on Vanua Levu
Plantation Island (from $55), 20 miles off Lautoka
Savusavu TraveLodge (from $37), on Vanua Levu
Toberua Island Resort (from $72), on Toberua
Treasure Island Resort (from $55), 10 miles off Lautoka

USEFUL INFORMATION

Banks: The Australia and New Zealand Bank, the Bank of Baroda, the Bank of New South Wales, the Bank of New Zealand, Barclays, and National Bank of Fiji have branches in Suva and other main centers. Hours: 10-3 Mon-Thur, 10-4 Fri. Hotels and stores will change currency and travelers' checks.

Mail: Stamps can be bought only at post offices, and letters can be mailed in mailboxes and in some hotels.

Telephone Tips: There are public coin-operated phone booths—automatic services in all main centers. A local call costs F5 cents. Useful numbers:

Pan Am Nadi 72100; Suva 22641

Fiji Visitors Bureau Nadi 72433; Suva 22867

Overseas Calls 012

Directory Inquiries 010

Operators 018

Emergencies 000

Newspapers: The *Fiji Times* and *Fiji Sun* are published daily in English; there are also two tourist newspapers available, as well as international English-language newspapers and periodicals. Radio Fiji broadcasts international news from Radio Australia, BBC, and Voice of America.

Tipping: Tipping exists, but is not inevitably expected—it is given only for real personal service. Luggage porters at the airports should be given F20 cents a bag.

Electricity: 240 volts 50 cycles AC throughout the country. Some hotels have 110 volts for shavers.

Laundry: Laundry and dry-cleaning services are good and inexpensive. There is a 24-hour service in the main hotels and the towns. The cost of dry-cleaning a suit is about F$2.50, laundering a shirt from F$1.

Hairdressers: The first-class hotels have hairdressing salons: shampoo and set, from F$7; man's haircut average F$3. Men do not tip, women only if they wish.

Photography: Photographic equipment can be bought in the duty-free shops; film is available in the main townships. Color film (negatives) and black and white take 24 hours to process.

Clubs: Branches of the Rotary Club, Lions, Jaycees, Apex, Quota, Soroptomists, Royal Suva Yacht Club, PPSEAWA, Fiji Arts Club, and Alcoholics Anonymous. The Visitors Bureau will give details.

Babysitting: Provided in hotels.

Rest Rooms: Free public lavatories are provided in department stores and hotels.

Health: British, Australian, New Zealand, and some American pharmaceuticals readily available at about US prices. Doctors, dentists, and hospitals readily available.

TRANSPORTATION

Transportation is good, in all its various forms. There is a local bus service round the island from Suva, stopping at most villages and townships and the main hotels.

Local airlines: Fly Air Pacific from Nadi and Nausori (Suva) throughout Fiji. Fiji Air links Nausori and Nadi with all smaller airfields, such as Lakeba, Bureta, Deuba, Korolevu, Natadola, and Malololailai.

Trading cutters depart frequently to outer islands.

There is a daily bus service between Suva and Lautoka. Taxis are available, readily in Suva and Nadi, scarcer elsewhere; they can be phoned or picked up at many stands. Taxis are metered in the main centers and cost an initial F20 cents plus 40 cents per mile. Fare should be negotiated with the driver before journeys of more than 15 miles. Drive on the left.

FOOD AND RESTAURANTS

Fijian food is delicious and different. Go to a *Magiti* (feast) and you'll picnic under the southern stars on pig, taro, and fish, succulently baked in a traditional earth oven, backed up by *kokoda* (raw fish marinated in coconut cream) and heaps of exotic fresh fruits. Other regular local delicacies include prawns, baked dalo, *rourou*, and many more. There is also a great tradition of Chinese and, of course, Indian food. If you tire of all that variety, there is plenty of good European cuisine available. Restaurants in Suva to try are **Scotts**, Suva TraveLodge, **Biddy's Steak House**, Le Normandie, and Grand Pacific and Tradewinds hotels for waterfront dining, **New Peking, Bamboo Terrace, Nanking Inn, Courtesy Inn**, and **Wan Q.**

DRINKING TIPS

Yaqona, made from the ground root of the pepper plant, is the national drink and is nonalcoholic. It is drunk ceremonially at weddings, funerals, and all important occasions as well as socially in the villages and in *kava* saloons in the towns. The locally brewed beer is good. Bars are open from 11-2 and 4-9. Young people under 18 are not permitted entrance; women alone should patronize hotel bars only. The hotel bars and lounges are usually more attractive and sell liquor and varied drinks. Prices are very reasonable. A whisky and soda costs about F$1.

ENTERTAINMENT

The larger hotels and resort hotels have dance bands and floor shows (mainly Fijian cultural singing and dancing). Nightclubs flourish at the **Golden Dragon, Lucky Eddie's,** and **Rockefellers,** all in Suva; **Fijiana** in Nadi; **Raymond's** in Lautoka. These nightspots are not elegant, but lively, and drinks are reasonably priced; cover charge of about F$2.50. **Viseisei Village,** 8 miles from Nadi Airport, has a program of folk singing and dancing every Friday evening. The **Cultural Center and Marketplace of Fiji** stages spectacular live cultural shows most afternoons at Pacific Harbour, 35 miles from Suva.

SPORTS

Water sports are first-class. Resort hotels have pools, beaches, and facilities for all sports. The beaches of many of the islands are fabulous. You can go scuba-diving, skin-diving, and snorkeling in the reef. Deep-sea fishing is organized from launches belonging to the hotels. Harpoon guns are not allowed into Fiji. There is river fishing in the larger islands. There are golf courses at Suva, Nausori, Nadi, Lautoka, Ba, Vatukoula, Fijian Hotel, and a magnificent 18-hole championship course (designed by Robert Trent Jones) at **Pacific Harbour.** Tennis, horseback riding, bowls, and squash are available. Excellent public tennis courts are available in Suva. There is a **Newk's Tennis Ranch** at the Regent of Fiji (Nadi), and fine courts and a resident pro at Pacific Harbour Resort.

SHOPPING

Superb stores in the main towns sell a first-class range of goods—watches, radios, photographic equipment, typewriters, electric razors, binoculars, sporting goods (including fishing tackle), jewelry, and perfume in every variety—all at duty-free prices. In Suva three large department stores in the main shopping center stock just about everything—they are **Burns Philp, Morris Hedstrom,** and **Narseys.**

Local best buys are all kinds of handicrafts and curios, silver and tortoise-shell jewelry, Indian silk saris, wooden carvings, coral—even grass skirts and recordings of Fijian music. The **Fiji Museum Shop,** the **Government Handicraft Centre** in the Development Bank, and **Polynesian Handicrafts,** on Queen's Road, all in Suva, sell handicrafts reasonably. Shopping hours are Mon-Fri 8-4:30, Sat 8-12; occasionally stores are open Sunday afternoon when liners are in port.

WHAT TO SEE

Viti Levu: **Suva,** the capital, is a South Sea port straight from the pages of a Somerset Maugham novel. Fast cruising liners lie alongside shabby trading schooners busy unloading copra and bananas from their holds; the streets are a bustling mixture of Fijians, Chinese, Indians, and Europeans. You can take water-bus tours up the Rewa River to **Nakamakama** village, where good food and entertainment greet you. Unique Fijian firewalking is staged regularly at a number of hotels in Suva, on the Coral Coast, and at Nadi. Indian religious firewalking is held in temples during winter months (March-October).

The port of **Lautoka** is 15 miles north of Nadi. It is the center of the sugarcane industry and the jumping-off point for some interisland cruises. From Nadi, there are half-day trips to the splendid **Nausori Highlands.** All round the island of Viti Levu there are things to look at—little South Sea villages, palm-backed beaches, and coral reefs.

Northeast of Suva and not far by ferry or plane is **Levuka,** on the island of Ovalau, the site of Fiji's former capital. **Kandavu,** an island south of Suva, is the place to hear sea island maidens lure the turtles to shore with their sweet singing.

Vanua Levu: This is the second largest of the Fijian Islands, 45 minutes flight from Suva. It has fine vacation attractions, water sports, particularly good hotels in **Savusavu** and at **Labasa,** and sugarcane and copra plantations to visit.

Southeast of Vanua Levu is the lovely island of **Taveuni** with its range of volcanic cones and lush tropical plantations and fruits; in the **Yasawa** group—west of both Viti Levu and Vanua Levu—there are more volcanic islands, with a wondrous collection of beaches strewn with rare shells.

SOURCES OF FURTHER INFORMATION

Pan Am agents: Pan Air Ltd, 189 Victoria Parade, Suva, and Nadi Airport, Nadi; and any Pan Am office around the world; the **Fiji Visitors Bureau,** PO Box 92, Suva; **Pacific Area Travel Association,** 228 Grant Avenue, San Francisco, CA 94108.

Guam

Area 212 square miles					**Population** 109,900							
Capital Agana					**Sales Tax** None							

Weather

	Jan	Feb	Mar	Apr	May	Jun	Jul	Aug	Sep	Oct	Nov	Dec
Av Temp (°C)	25	25	25	26	26	27	27	26	26	26	26	26
Days of Rain	12	10	7	10	6	10	12	12	13	13	8	5

Time Zone No named zone. When it is 12 noon Monday in New York City it is 3am Tuesday in Guam.

The largest of the volcanic Mariana Islands in the Western Pacific between the Philippines and Hawaii, Guam combines the beauty of the tropics with the modern conveniences of the Western world. It has a healthy and pleasant climate, beautiful sunsets, fragrant flowers, white beaches, and a crystal-clear sea. Guam's strange formations of rock and coral are the result of the immense volcanic unheavals that formed the Marianas and the surrounding Pacific deeps. Man-made history ranges from early cave drawings and the mysterious latte stones which signposted the Malaysian migration across the Pacific, to Magellan's arrival in 1521, and more recent reminders of Spanish occupation, and later of World War II.

The island is now an unincorporated territory of the United States and is populated by 60% indigenous Chamorros and 20% mainland Americans, with a heavy sprinkling of Hawaiians, Filipinos, Chinese, Japanese, Koreans, and Micronesians. Its people are US citizens and, although they do not vote in national elections, they are represented in Congress. Since 1970 the island has elected its own governor and there is an elected, one-house legislature. The US Department of the Interior supervises the government of the island.

All Guamanians are fluent in English, although "Chamorro" is widely spoken. The predominant religion is Roman Catholic; however, Protestant denominations are represented. Several major American banks have offices on the island; US currency is used. There is a daily air mail service and overseas phone calls can be made through the overseas operator. Electrical outlets are 120 volts, 60 cycles AC.

WHAT TO SEE

Guam Museum in **Agana** gives a digest of over 5,000 years of history; also visit the **Micronesian Area Research Center** in the **University of Guam Library.** See the Spanish buildings, forts and bridges around the charming Chamorro villages of **Merizo, Umatac** and **Inarajan;** the mysterious coral columns called *latte.* Take a coral-watching trip in a glass-bottom boat. Visit the **Plaza de Espana** in Agana or Lovers' Point at **Puntan dos Amantes,** which also boasts one of the world's finest sunsets nightly. Several companies offer bus tours of the island for six hours, $30 per person with lunch, or four-hour tours of the central area, $22, including lunch. Private cars with guides are available through major hotels at $100 per half day. **Lanchon Antigo** or "Old Village" is a living museum in Inarajan Village—oldest community in Guam. It provides an authentic re-creation of Chamorro village life with demonstrations of traditional craft working, food preparation and the performing arts.

HOW TO GET THERE

Flying time to Guam International Airport from San Francisco is 12 hours; from Honolulu, 7 hours; from Manila, 3½ hours. The airport is 2 miles from Agana, the main village; resort hotels at Tumon Bay are less than 15 minutes from the airport. Taxi fare into Agana is about $5. In addition, hotel buses meet planes, cost about $3.80 to hotel row; hotel call phones are available in the airport customs area. Rental cars are handy everywhere.

ACCOMMODATIONS

A wide range of modern hotels are available overlooking picturesque Tumon Bay. Among the higher prices are the **Hilton** (646-1841), **Okura** (646-6811), and **Reef** (646-6881), averaging from about $57 twin. A new resort is the **Pacific Islands Club** (646-7865, S/D$75), part of a beach complex. Medium priced hotels include the **Dai-Ichi, Fujita Guam Tumon Beach, Guam Horizon, Terraza Tumon Villa, Joinus:** average, $34 twin. Economy priced hotels in the Agana area include the **Magellan,** about $25 twin. Hotel room tax: 10%; most hotels have an additional 10% service charge.

RESTAURANTS

Restaurants reflect the cultural heritage of the island; there is American, Japanese, Spanish, Filipino, Mexican, Chinese, and Chamorro as well as

continental cuisine. Chamorro dishes are primarily made of coconuts, rice and taro with roast pig, barbecued spare ribs, and chicken all spiced with **finadeni** sauce. True Chamorro food is almost impossible to get except at the Public Market stands in downtown Agana, and at the frequent village or private fiestas, but restaurants for other foods abound. Elegant American and continental dining can be had at the **Galleon Grill** in the Hilton, the **Flamboyan** at the Okura, **La Fuente** at the Kakuei, the **Salzburg Chalet, Don Pedro's Castle;** all are in the Tumon resort hotel area. Japanese food excels at the **Kuramaya** at the Dai-Ichi, **Genji** at the Hilton, the **Top of the Reef.** The **Sakura, Yakitori II, Furosata,** and others are slightly less expensive. Go to **Nina's Papagayo** or **Joe and Flo's** for Mexican food; to the **Toh Kah Lin** in the Okura, **China House** at the Dai-Ichi, plus a half dozen others around town for Chinese food; **Chuck's** or **Suehiro's** for steaks, both in the Tumon area. And the **Hale Kai** on San Vitores Road for fresh seafood. There are **McDonald's, Colonel Sanders, Shakey's,** and other pizza and hamburger havens, too.

SHOPPING

The superb duty-free shops are full of low-priced luxury items. Look for Oriental goods; gems, art objects, jewelry, silks, brocades, batiks, pearls.

Other good buys include photographic and stereo equipment, European and Japanese china and crystal, perfume and Swiss watches. Wood carvings and needlework from the Philippines can be purchased as well as shell products, ceramics and wood carvings.

Americans can purchase up to $600 (instead of $300) of non-US-made goods and be exempt from duty on returning home.

SPORTS

First-class water sports of every conceivable kind are available; scuba-diving is outstanding. Equipment may be rented from the **Coral Reef Marine Center** or the **Marianas Divers** in Agana. Guam's offshore waters are a fisherman's paradise; trawling for marlin, tuna, dolphin, barracuda, bonito, and sailfish can be done in chartered boats from **Coral Reef Marine Center, Agana,** or **Merizo Boaters Association, Merizo.** There are several 18-hole golf courses; **Country Club of the Pacific** and the **Windwards Hills Golf Course** have clubhouses and swimming pools. Horseback riding is available at **Talofofo Bay;** bowling, tennis, greyhound racing, and cock-fighting are also offered.

FURTHER GUAM INFORMATION

Guam Chamber of Commerce, PO Box 283, Guam 96910. **Guam Visitors' Bureau,** PO Box 3520, Agana, 96910; tel: 646-5278/9.

Hawaii

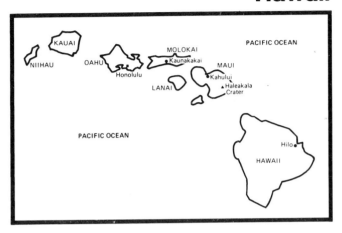

WHAT'S SPECIAL

Thrown up by a volcanic cataclysm from the ocean bed a million years ago, Hawaii still has infrequent, though spectacular, volcanic eruptions that can be safely viewed by the lucky tourist who happens to arrive at the island of Hawaii at the right time. But even without the volcanoes, the variety of this island group is fascinating. There are unusual birds and animals, scenic wonders and moods to choose—from the brash excitement of Honolulu on Oahu to the quiet beauty of an old whaling town on Maui. There's a fascinating history to discover, from the arrival of the Polynesian outriggers when Charlemagne was still writing the map of France, to the visit of Captain Cook, who named these the Sandwich Islands, after the Earl of Sandwich; the story of the missionaries from New England, and the one of the King and Queen who died of measles on a visit to London in 1824; the ingenuity of Mr. Dole in establishing the pineapple on a big scale, the sadness of Pearl Harbor, and, finally, the happy assumption of statehood in 1959. It's quite an extraordinary history book. And quite an extraordinary collection of peoples and races—Polynesian, Asian, European, and American.

COUNTRY BRIEFING

Size: 6,425 square miles
Capital: Honolulu

Population: 965,000
Capital Population: 365,114

   Climate: Little variation in temperature: warm in winter, not too hot in summer. It's the ideal vacation spot all year round.

Weather in Honolulu: Lat N21°19′; Alt 38 ft

Temp (°F)	Jan	Feb	Mar	Apr	May	Jun	Jul	Aug	Sep	Oct	Nov	Dec
Av Low	66°	66°	67°	68°	70°	72°	73°	74°	73°	72°	70°	68°
Av High	79°	79°	80°	81°	82°	84°	85°	86°	86°	85°	82°	80°
Days no rain	21	18	22	21	24	24	23	24	23	21	20	20

Government: US state.

Language: English is the official language. Hawaiian and Japanese are heard often, and pidgin, a kind of shorthand English, is heard everywhere.

Religion: Polynesian beliefs have been superseded by Christianity, although many people practice Buddhism and Shintoism.

Currency: US dollar.

Public Holidays:

US public holidays are observed. State holidays are:

Chinese New Year, 25 Jan (1982)

Prince Kuhio Day, 26 Mar

Lei Day, 1 May

Kamehameha Day, 11 June

Admission Day, 3rd Fri in Aug

Aloha Week, Sep or Oct

HOW TO GET THERE

Flying time to Honolulu International Airport from New York is 11½ hours; from San Francisco, 5¼ hours; from Guatemala City, 9½ hours; from Tokyo, 6½ hours. Time in Hawaii: GMT−10.

REQUIREMENTS FOR ENTRY AND CUSTOMS REGULATIONS

Valid passport and visa are required for non USA and Canadian travelers. Visas may be obtained from an American consul office.

AIRPORT INFORMATION

The bus fare from Honolulu International Airport to Waikiki beach is $4 per person. There is also a municipal bus that travels between the airport and Waikiki, fair 50¢, no baggage allowed. Taxis cost about $15 per person and the Gray Lines Airporter Service costs $3.50 per person, $6.00 round trip. The airport has a hotel reservation counter.

ACCOMMODATIONS

Some of the world's most luxurious hotels are to be found in Hawaii. Many are located along the beaches, which are open to the public and offer a wide range of recreational facilities. Others boast a truly authentic Polynesian atmosphere enhanced by twilight serenades. Although prices can be very high in such a popular vacation resort as Hawaii, there are off-the-beach hotels which need cost no more than $20. National Park areas on Maui have cabins ($8 per person per night) and inexpensive camping facilities. Hotels in Honolulu:

Rates are in US$ for a double/twin room with bath or shower

Ala Moana Americana, 410 Atkinson Drive (from $42)

Cinerama Reef Towers, 227 Lewers Street (from $28)

Colony East, 2895 Kalakaua Avenue (from $65-70)

Coral Reef, 2299 Kuhio Avenue (from $33)

Coral Seas, 250 Lewers Street (from $20)
Edmunds Hotel Apartments, 2411 Ala Wai Boulevard (from $16)
Hale Pua Nui Hotel Apartment, 228 Beach Walk (from $29-33)
Hawaiian Regent, 2552 Kalakaua Avenue (from $49)
Hilton Hawaiian Village, 2005 Kalia Road (from $52)
Holiday Isle, 270 Lewers Street (from $32)
Hyatt Regency Waikiki, 2424 Kalakaua Avenue (from $65)
Ilikai, 1777 Ala Moana Boulevard (from $60)
Imperial Hawaii, 205 Lewers Street (from $31)
Moana, 2365 Kalakaua Avenue (from $41)
New Otani Kaimana, 2863 Kalakaua Avenue (from $39)
Park Shore, Kalakaua & Kapahulu Avenue (from $35)
Princess Kaiulani, 120 Kaiulani Avenue (from $34)
Royal Hawaiian, 2259 Kalakaua Avenue (from $65)
Sheraton-Waikiki, 2255 Kalakaua Avenue (from $60)
Waikikian, 1811 Ala Moana, Honolulu (from $44)
Waikiki Circle, 2464 Kalakaua Avenue (from $23-30)
Waikiki Pacific Isle, 1850 Ala Moana Boulevard (from $55)
Waikiki Prince, 2431 Prince Edward Street (from $22)
Waikiki Surf-Side, 2452 Kalakaua Avenue (from $29)
Waikiki Terrace Apartment Hotel, 339 Royal Hawaiian Avenue (from $17)
White Sands Garden Hotel, 431 Nohonani Street (from $26)

USEFUL INFORMATION

Banks: Open 8:30-3 Mon-Thurs, 8:30-6 Fri.

Mail: Stamps can be bought in some drugstores, some supermarkets.

Telephone Tips: Public street phones are coin-operated. Cost of local call 15¢. You can also find telephones in restaurants and cafés. Useful numbers in Honolulu:

Pan Am 955-9111   **Hawaii Visitors' Bureau** 923-1811

Newspapers: Local newspapers are the *Honolulu Advertiser* and *Honolulu Star Bulletin,* both in English. Mainland publications available.

Tipping: Taxis 10-15%; porters 25-50¢ per bag or whatever seems appropriate; restaurants 10-15%; service charge is not usually included in the bill.

Electricity: 110 volts 60 cycles AC.

Laundry: Hotels have excellent 24-hour and express services. Dry-cleaning a suit, from $5 to $7; laundering a shirt, from $1.15 to $1.75.

Hairdressing: Cost of a shampoo and set from $12, plus 10-15% tip; a man's haircut, from $5. Tip also 10-15%.

Photography: All films and equipment available. Camera shops have one-day processing services.

Clubs: Rotary (tel: 922-5526), every Tuesday noon at Royal Hawaiian Hotel; Elks, Monday, 7:30pm (2933 Kalakaua Avenue—tel: 923-5722).

Rest Rooms: The local names are *Wahine* for women, and *Kane* for men.

Health: Excellent facilities available. Water and milk safe.

TRANSPORTATION

Honolulu's Mass Transit Lines buses are known as **TheBus** and go almost everywhere on Oahu. The fare is 50¢ for adults, including free transfers, and is free to senior citizens with a pass. Guided bus **Circle Island Tour** around the island (about 100 miles) costs $14.80 per person and is very comfortable, but you can do it on your own aboard TheBus from Waikiki: Take Bus #5 or Bus #8 to the Ala Moana Shopping Center; transfer to a Wahiawa/Kaneohe Bus for a 4-hour circle trip via Pearl City, Wahiawa, Waialua, Haleiwa, Kahuku, the Polynesian Cultural Center, Kahaluu, and Kaneohe. When you've circled back to the end of the line at Ala Moana you'll need another 50¢ for the return to Waikiki. (TheBus also circles in the opposite direction.) Waikiki-Ala Moana buses run every 10 minutes from 6:15am to 8pm and then every 30 minutes to midnight. Bus schedules are available. Wahiawa/Kaneohe buses run from Ala Moana at hourly intervals from 7:05am to 9:15pm weekdays, from 7:30am Saturdays, and from 8:30am to 8:15pm Sundays. The weekly visitors' guide *Where* (free at most hotel desks) details all the possible minicost excursions. Taxis are best called by phone; they are metered at $2 for the first mile and $1 each additional mile. Limousines with chauffeur cost $18 up per hour (minimum, 2 hours). Those who'd like to drive themselves will find driving conditions in Honolulu similar to those in any other US city and the selection of rental cars available also similar.

Inter-Island Tours: Hawaiian and Aloha Airlines run dozens of inexpensive flights between nine island airports, and there are several air-taxi charter and helicopter services.

FOOD AND RESTAURANTS

Traditional Hawaiian food conjures up all the romance of a tropical island. The **Luau** is a classic feast at which a pig is steamed for hours in an underground oven. The accompaniment to this and most other local dishes is *poi*, a taro root paste. *Lomi lomi* salmon is salmon marinated in onion and tomato; chicken *luau* is chicken cooked with taro tops and coconut cream. The **Royal Hawaiian, Outrigger, Sheraton-Waikiki,** and **Hawaiian Village** hotels have regularly scheduled *luaus.* Local seafood is, of course, excellent, particularly crabs, squid, tuna, lobster, and *mahimahi,* a delicately flavored island fish. Fresh fruit in season—papaya, mango, pineapple, passion fruit, and guava—is out of this world. Most restaurants serve American food, with the exception of the popular Japanese, Chinese, and Korean establishments. Top cuisine in Waikiki is found in **Michel's** in the Colony Surf Hotel and **Canlis' Restaurant** (2100 Kalakaua Avenue), the **Maile Room** at the Kahala Hilton, and the **Monarch Room** at the Royal Hawaiian Hotel. **The Third Floor** restaurant in the Hawaiian Regent Hotel is one of the places to go for elegant dining, or try **Bagwells** in the Hyatt Regency Waikiki. The **Tahitian Lanai** in the Waikikian Hotel features Hawaiian food cooked with European fastidiousness, and the **Willows** (901 Hausten Street—a little outside Waikiki) has superb Hawaiian food two nights during the week. The **Pagoda Float-**

ing Restaurant at the Pagoda Hotel has its own carp pool. Prices range from $17 per person and up, in expensive restaurants, to $8 per person in less expensive places. Chop suey houses outside Waikiki are far cheaper. *Saimin* is a Japanese noodle soup served at stalls and inexpensive restaurants.

DRINKING TIPS

Juices made from local fruits are always delicious. Try guava nectar and passion fruit juice. Poolside bars serve pleasant refreshments, and Japanese *sake* houses in Honolulu offer rice wine and beer.

ENTERTAINMENT

Entertainment is plentiful and various; probably your first move should be to consult *Where* or the *Waikiki Beach Press* to see what and where the action is. Most of the best entertainment is at major hotels, with lavish floor shows and visiting artists. The **Monarch Room** at the Royal Hawaiian and the **Maile Room** at the Kahala Hilton are two of the top places. For a more Polynesian flavor try the **Canoe House** at the Ilikai, the **Tapa Room** at the Hilton Hawaiian Village, and the **Hala Terrace** at the Kahala Hilton. Dancing, dining, and floor shows are also to be found at **Duke Kahanamoku's** cabaret restaurant, in the International Market Place. Most nightclubs have hula dancers, and a few spots feature Tahitian and Samoan entertainment. Traditional and modern hula can be seen free at the **Kodak Hula Show,** Tuesday through Friday at 10am at the Waikiki Shell. If you're interested in the very traditional entertainment, the outdoor theater at the **Polynesian Cultural Center** in **Laie** (on Oahu's north coast) stages genuine Polynesian dancing and singing. Plays, ballet, and concerts are performed in the halls of the Honolulu **International Center.** The **Honolulu Symphony** is Hawaii's major orchestra, and the **Royal Hawaiian Band** presents concerts of Hawaiian music. Top international entertainers appear at the open-air **Waikiki Shell.** Polynesian water ballet is performed weekly at the **Sheraton-Waikiki Hotel.** Stage plays are produced by the **Honolulu Community Theater,** the **University of Hawaii** (in the John F. Kennedy Theater), and the **Hawaii Performing Arts Theater** in Manoa Valley.

SHOPPING

Look for perfume, native jams and jellies, hand-blocked linens, silk, shell and black-and-pink coral jewelry, and attractive loose-flowing women's *muumuus.* Hawaii is also a good place for Chinese and Japanese curios and other Asian goods. The **International Market Place** (2330 Kalakaua Avenue) is a shopping area specializing in arts and crafts from the Pacific islands. **Ala Moana Shopping Center** (1450 Ala Moana Boulevard) is one of the largest in the world, with 155 stores supplying just about everything. **Sears Roebuck** department store in the center specializes in locally made goods. **Fort St Mall, Kahala Mall,** and **Ward Warehouse** are other popular shopping areas. **Liberty House** and **Carol and Mary Ltd** are excellent stores with several branches in Waikiki and Honolulu. **Blair**

Ltd (404 Ward Ave) has attractive wood carvings, both domestic and decorative. For first-rate Japanese goods try **Iida** or **Shirokiya** at Ala Moana Shopping Center.

SPORTS

Surfing is a year-round favorite. Golf is also very popular. There are 35 courses throughout the state—**Makaha Valley** boasts two exceptional 18-hole courses. You can cruise in outrigger canoes and catamarans, and there are a number of yacht clubs that sponsor weekly sculling regattas. Instructors and equipment can be rented for scuba- and skin-diving. Surfing is the all-time favorite. There are fully equipped charter boats for marlin fishing, or you can learn to cast nets the native way. Bird and game hunting is excellent in the mountain regions of **Oahu, Molokai, Maui, Lanai,** and **Kauai,** and some areas allow game hunting with bow and arrow. For pre-hunt practice, archery targets are available in **Kapiolani Park,** Honolulu. Tennis courts can be found in Kapiolani Park and at **Ala Moana Park.** For those who like to hike and quietly admire the spectacular scenery, there are mountain trails on all the islands and numerous campsites where you can put up for the night. Popular spectator sports include boxing, wrestling, baseball, football, and polo.

WHAT TO SEE

Oahu: Between the Pacific and the Koolau mountains stretches all 15 miles of Honolulu. The luxury hotels of **Waikiki** and the smart downtown **Fort St Mall** shopping and business center are only a part of this varied cosmopolitan city. **Chinatown,** between Nuuanu Avenue and River Street, is a colorful mixture of food markets, tattoo parlors and dives, and genuine Chinese restaurants, laundries, and curio shops. In contrast, the surrounding hills are very elegant residential suburbs. **Diamond Head,** with its famous crater, is at the eastern end of Waikiki. In the center of town, in a park oasis, is **Iolani Palace,** the only royal palace on American soil. The building is an exuberant Victorian structure built by the merry monarch, King Kalakaua, who used to play billiards and poker in the basement. The gilded thrones (replicas) are covered with Chinese brocade. Hawaii's first church, **Kawaiahao Church,** built of coral blocks, was the royal chapel. Sunday services are in English and Hawaiian. A fascinating memorial to the men and women responsible for bringing Christianity to the islands is the **Mission Houses** (across from City Hall), built in New England style and kept as a museum with original domestic and personal mementos. **Bishop Museum,** on Kalihi Street, has a wonderful collection of Hawaiian art, culture, and religious relics and also houses a planetarium. The **Academy of Arts** embraces both Oriental and Western art and has some rare masterpieces. Limousines (4-7 passengers) can be rented for tours of Honolulu from $22 per hour. Tours are arranged to pineapple canneries, woodworking shops, sugar mills, and perfume factories.

Pearl Harbor is just north of Honolulu, and the US Navy runs a free cruise to see the sunken hulls of the battleships *Arizona* and *Utah.* **Nu-**

uanu-Pali cliff, which towers over the Honolulu-Windward Oahu road, has a look-out point cut into its steep sides from which the views are stupendous. At **Makapuu Point** (30 minutes from Honolulu) is the **Sea Life Park,** where you can descend three fathoms beneath the waves to observe a living reef with its fish and plant life. There are porpoise and whale performances and a reconstructed native fishing village. The **Polynesian Cultural Center** at Laie is another living museum, with reconstructed primitive villages. **Byodo-In Temple** in the Valley of the Temples Memorial Park is a replica of the 900-year-old National Treasure of Japan in Kyoto;

Hawaii: The largest of the islands is famous for the spectacular fiery rumblings of its active volcanoes and the beauty of its countless varieties of orchids—Hawaii has the world's largest orchid-growing industry. Set amid these colorful floral fields is **Hilo,** second-largest city in the islands. Hotels include: **Hilo Lagoon** (from $32 double); **Naniloa Surf** (from $49 double). **Volcano House** (from $31 double), high up on **Kilauea** crater, is the best center for exploring the unearthly region of **Hawaii Volcanoes National Park.** A trail leads through a romantic forest and out into the cracked lava of **Halemaumau,** the crater within a crater, looking like the end of the world. Other park routes lead to spooky **Devastation Trail** and the **Chain of Craters Road** (check with Park HQ before hiking). West of Kilauea is **Mauna Loa,** the world's largest volcanic mountain, with a forest of rare trees and birds on its slopes. Black sand beaches at **Kaimu,** near Kalapana, and at **Puna Lu'u,** near Ka'u, one north and the other just south of the park's shoreline, get their color from pulverized lava. **Akaka Falls,** 15 miles north of Hilo, is a lovely waterfall set in magnificent tropical gardens.

The **Kona** coast is a good deep-sea fishing area, and hunting for wild goats is another sporting activity here. Hotels are the **Kona Surf, Keauhou Beach, Kona Hilton,** and **Hotel King Kamehameha,** averaging $46-55 double.

Maui—the Valley Isle—is formed by two linked volcanoes. Villages, horse trails, and a well-paved highway wind up the side of **Haleakala,** the widest volcano in the world, which gives stunning cloud effects at sunrise and sunset. The barren cinder cones of the volcano (the floor is 19 miles across) can be explored on foot or horseback. The **House of the Sun Observatory** is 10,000 feet up on the edge of the crater. Between **Haleakala National Park** and the sea is a vast natural jungle, much of it still unexplored. In the **Kipahulu Valley** of plunging waterfalls and rare birds are the **Seven Pools,** where the legendary mother of Maui used to wash her tapacloth clothes. In **Wailuku** is the fascinating museum of **Hale Hoikeike,** better known as the Old Bailey home, a stone structure built 1834-1850, with beautiful silver and wooden objects of Hawaiiana. The road from Wailuku to Hana is noted for its spectacular scenery.

Former capital of the Hawaiian Kingdom, **Lahaina** was the scene in the 19th century of violent conflicts between missionaries and whalers. It boasts the biggest banyan tree in the islands. **Kaanapali,** a top resort, has an elegant hotel complex built around the excellent Kaanapali golf course. At **Kahakuloa Hawaiian Village,** the fishermen and small farmers have preserved their more primitive way of life. Hotels in Maui:

Rates are in US$ for a double/twin room with bath or shower

INTER · CONTINENTAL MAUI, Wailea Beach (from $75)

Kaanapali Beach, Lahaina (from $53)

Maui Beach, 170 Kaahumanu Avenue, Kahului Bay (from $38)

Napili Kai Beach Club, Lahaina (from $90)

Napili Village Hotel, Lahaina (from $40)

Royal Lahaina, Lahaina (from $58)

Sheraton-Maui, Kaanapali Beach (from $65)

Kauai—the Garden Isle—was the movie location for *South Pacific.* Sweet-scented flowers bloom all year amid lush tropical greenery. Pineapple and sugar are important industries, and rice is grown and harvested by hand. Outside Wailua is **Heiau Holo-Holo-Ku,** one of the most ancient of Hawaiian religious sanctuaries, with fierce statues and a stone altar for human sacrifice. Beyond the temple enclosure are the royal birthstones on which royal infants were born. The **Wailua,** or sacred river, can be explored by motor launch. **Fern Grotto** is a romantically lovely cave where ferns trail from the rocks. **Waimea Canyon** is a stunning miniature of the Grand Canyon—in glorious technicolor. Two of the best beaches on the island are **Hanalei** and **Poipu Beach.** Hotels are the **Coco Palms,** PO Box 631 (from $54 double); **Kauai Surf,** PO Box 1729, Lihue, Kauai (from $55 double); **Poipu Beach,** Koloa, Kauai (from $46 double); **Sheraton Kauai,** PO Box 303, Poipu Beach (from $67 double); **Kauai Beach Boy,** Waipouli Beach, Kapaa, Kauai (from $44 double); **Islander Inn-Kauai,** PO Box 68, Kapaa, Kauai (from $43 double).

Molokai: The wild-deer hunting and game-fishing prospects of the Friendly Isle may be explored from **Molokai Shores** (from $38 double), **Sheraton Molokai** (from $55 double), and the **Pau Hana Inn** (from $15 double). Horses can be hired from **Pau-o-Haku Ranch.**

Lanai: Wholly owned by the Dole Pineapple Company and with a population of only 2,000, this island is an ideal spot for a quiet vacation. The **Lanai Lodge** in Lanai City has 11 rooms (from $35 double). There is a 9-hole golf course where anyone can play, no fee charged. Swimming is at **Manele Beach** and **Shipwreck Beach,** both accessible by 4-wheel vehicle which can be rented at Lanai City. Hiking, hunting, and fishing are also possible on Lanai.

SOURCES OF FURTHER INFORMATION

Pan Am, 2342 Kalakaua Avenue and 1021 Bishop Street in Honolulu, and any Pan Am office around the world; **Hawaii Visitors' Bureau,** 2270 Kalakaua Avenue, Waikiki; Room 1407, 441 Lexington Avenue, New York, NY 10017; Room 203, 3440 Wilshire Boulevard, Los Angeles, CA 90010; Suite 1530, Marshall Field Annex, 25 East Washington Street, Chicago, IL 60602; Room 615, 209 Post Street, San Francisco, CA 94108.

Hong Kong

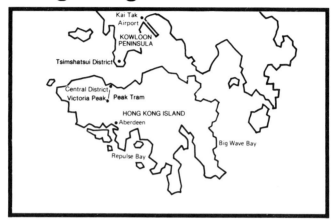

WHAT'S SPECIAL

The Hong Kong of today is modern offices and apartment blocks and factories resting amidst the few remaining evidences of an older China of walled villages and ancient temples. Yet, for all its striving toward a Western modernity, Hong Kong remains intrinsically a Chinese city-state, ruled by a British colonial administration. It is bustling with world commerce, with hundreds of international banks, stock companies, and trading organizations; the numerous stores are stocked with low-priced wares from every corner of the globe. Across the border from the still semirural but rapidly growing New Territories lies the Peoples' Republic of China and a very different pattern of life.

The first Europeans to sail into the area were Portuguese navigators whose voyages paved the way for the foundation of Macao, Portugal's 16th-century beachhead on the Cantonese coast. By the late 1600s the lure of a flourishing trade with the Orient had also attracted the British, whose East India Company kept up a lively commerce throughout the 18th century in the area, based in Canton. But with the introduction of opium into the bartering scene, Sino-British relations degenerated rapidly. The famous "opium wars" that followed were settled by the 1842 Treaty of Nanking, which ceded Hong Kong to the British. Kowloon was added to the Crown possessions in 1860, and the New Territories and adjacent islands were leased from China in 1898.

COUNTRY BRIEFING

Size: Hong Kong, Kowloon, and the New Territories have a combined area of 404.8 square miles.

Population: 5,147,900

Capital: Hong Kong has no capital as such, though the Central District (formerly known as Victoria) is the downtown commercial area.

Climate: Mild, with heat and humidity rising as spring wears on, and a rainy spell in summer. Winters are chilly enough for an overcoat. Best season—autumn.

Weather in Hong Kong: Lat N22°; Alt 109 ft

Temp (°F)	Jan	Feb	Mar	Apr	May	Jun	Jul	Aug	Sep	Oct	Nov	Dec
Av Low	56°	55°	60°	67°	74°	78°	78°	78°	77°	73°	65°	59°
Av High	64°	63°	67°	75°	82°	85°	87°	87°	85°	81°	74°	68°
Days no rain	27	23	24	22	18	12	14	16	18	25	28	28

Government: British Crown Colony.

Language: Chinese (mostly Cantonese dialect) and English.

Religion: Buddhism, Taoism, and ancestor worship. About 10% are Christians.

Currency: Dollar. 100 cents = HK$1.

	5¢	10¢	50¢	HK $1	HK $10	HK $50	HK $100	HK $200
US (dollars, cents)	.01	.02	.09	.18	1.84	9.19	18.37	36.74
UK (pounds, pence)	—	.01	.04	.09	.88	4.39	8.78	17.56

Public Holidays: Chinese holiday dates vary from year to year according to the cycles of the moon, and these are given as approximate dates. The combined Chinese, Christian, and British Public Holidays are as follows:

New Year's Day, 1 Jan
Chinese New Year (3 days), 25-27 Jan
Ching Ming Festival, 5 Apr
Good Friday, 9-10 Apr
Easter Monday, 12 Apr
Queen's Birthday, 21 Apr
Tuen Ng (Dragon Boat) Festival, 25 June

First weekday in July
First Monday in Aug
Liberation Day, last Mon in Aug
Chung Yeung Festival, 25 Oct
Christmas Day, 25 Dec
Boxing Day, 27 Dec

HOW TO GET THERE

Flying time to Kai Tak Airport, Hong Kong from San Francisco is 14 hours; from Frankfurt, 14 hours; from Delhi, 5¼ hours; from Tokyo, 4¼ hours. Time in Hong Kong: GMT+8.

REQUIREMENTS FOR ENTRY AND CUSTOMS REGULATIONS

Most visitors staying less than 30 days require only a valid passport and an onward or round-trip ticket; visas must be obtained for longer stays. A smallpox vaccination certificate is not required. There are no restrictions on currency. Duty-free allowance: 200 cigarettes or 50 cigars; 1

quart liquor. Drugs, guns, and ammunition are prohibited. No restrictions on goods taken out of the country.

AIRPORT INFORMATION

Kai Tak Airport is in Kowloon, across the harbor from the city center. Airport bus to Hong Kong Island costs HK$2.50. Taxis are available, with fares to downtown Kowloon averaging about HK$15, and HK$25-35 via new tunnel to Hong Kong Island, a 20-minute ride.

There is an airport departure tax of HK$20. The airport has a duty-free shop, but all of Hong Kong is duty free. Kai Tak Airport also has a hotel reservations counter.

ACCOMMODATIONS

Hong Kong boasts some of the most luxurious hotels in the Far East. There are moderately priced hotels on both sides of the harbor and a number of inexpensive guest houses, mostly in Kowloon. For young people there is the International Youth Hostel at 90 Hung To Road, Kowloon, and for budget-minded travelers of all ages two YMCAs in Kowloon and one on Hong Kong Island.

Rates are in US$ for a double/twin room with bath or shower

Ambassador, Nathan/Middle Road, Kowloon (from $43)

Astor, 11 Carnarvon Road, Kowloon (from $76)

Empress, 17-19 Chatham Road, Kowloon (from $43)

Excelsior, Gloucester Road, Hong Kong Island (from $72)

FURAMA INTER · CONTINENTAL, 1 Connaught Road, Hong Kong Island (from $88)

Grand, 14 Carnarvon Road, Kowloon (from $39)

Hilton, 2 Queen's Road, Hong Kong Island (from $67)

Holiday Inn, 50 Nathan Road, Kowloon (from $57)

Holiday Inn Harbour View, Salisbury Road, Kowloon (from $72)

Hong Kong, 3 Canton Road, Kowloon (from $57)

Hyatt Regency Hong Kong, 67 Nathan Road, Kowloon (from $54)

International, 33 Cameron Road, Kowloon (from $46)

Lee Gardens (Forum Hotel), Hysan Avenue, Causeway Bay, Hong Kong Island (from $70)

Mandarin, Connaught Road, Hong Kong Island (from $88)

Merlin, 2 Hankow Road, Kowloon (from $46)

Miramar, 134 Nathan Road, Kowloon (from $66)

Nathan, 378 Nathan Road, Kowloon (from $40)

New World, 22 Salisbury Road, Kowloon (from $74)

Park, 61-65 Chatham Road, Kowloon (from $48)

Peninsula, Salisbury Road, Kowloon (from $88)

Plaza, 310 Gloucester Road, Hong Kong Island (from $66)

Regent, Salisbury Road, Kowloon (from $111)

Royal Garden, Ching Yee Road, Kowloon (from $85)

Sheraton-Hong Kong, 20 Nathan Road, Kowloon (from $75)

The above hotels are all centrally located unless otherwise indicated.

USEFUL INFORMATION

Banks: Open 9-4 Mon-Fri, 9-12 Sat. Money can also be changed in the larger hotels, in shops catering to the tourist trade, and at official money changers. Banks include Citibank, Chase Manhattan, Bank of America, and an American Express Office.

Mail: Stamps are normally bought at the post office, but in the larger hotels you can buy them from the information desk. On the outlying islands and in the New Territories, some food stores are authorized to sell stamps and collect mail. Mailboxes are cylindrical, 4 feet high, and painted bright red.

Telephone Tips: Public phones are usually painted red or pink. A local call costs HK50¢. Calls from private phones within Hong Kong are free. Kowloon numbers are prefixed by 3-, Hong Kong Island numbers are prefixed by 5-, and New Territories and outlying islands by 0-. Useful numbers:

Pan Am 5-231111	**Information** 108
Tourist Office 5-244191	**Emergencies** 999
Airport Information 3-829220	

Newspapers: There are five locally published English-language newspapers in Hong Kong: *The South China Morning Post, The Hong Kong Standard, The Star,* the *International Herald Tribune,* and the *Asian Wall St. Journal.* Foreign English-language newspapers are available at lobby newsstands in the better hotels.

Tipping: Tipping is customary. When a 10% service charge is included in any bill, an extra 5% may be left; otherwise 10-15%. Here are some general outlines: taxi drivers, 10% of charge, minimum HK30¢; porters, HK$1 per piece of luggage; restaurants, 10-15% of bill; cloakroom attendants, HK$1 per item; hairdressers, 15%.

Electricity: 200-220 volts 50 cycles AC. Hotels have converters.

Laundry: Most large hotels have dry-cleaning and laundry services and will do express jobs if these are required. There are many dry-cleaners, laundries with delivery service, and laundromats.

Hairdressers: Most hotels all have hairdressing salons. The average cost of a shampoo and set is HK$45-65.

Photography: All major brands of photographic equipment are available. Both color and black and white film can normally be developed locally (except Kodachrome, which must be sent overseas); most photo processing is finished within 24 hours.

Clubs: Rotary, Lions, and Kiwanis. Other civic and social associations include the Toastmasters, Soroptimists, Skal Club, American Club, Foreign Correspondents Club, Australian Club, YMCA, and YWCA.

Babysitting: Services can be arranged through hotels.

Rest Rooms: Facilities are commonly found in hotels, bars, and all transportation terminals. A HK$1 tip to the attendant is usual.

Health: Most, if not all, doctors and dentists speak English. Imported pharmaceuticals and toiletries are available and not expensive. Travelers are advised not to drink water from tap except in better hotels.

TRANSPORTATION

There are bus, minibus, and ferry services; the Peak Tram travels from the center of the city to the top of the Peak (a suburb high above the city) for HK$2. A few rickshaws still operate for the delight of tourists, but you should agree on the price first. Taxis are plentiful. You can hail one on the street or get one at a taxi stand; they can also be summoned by phone. They have meters, and in Hong Kong the charge is HK$4 for the first mile and HK50¢ for each additional mile. When traveling through the Cross Harbour Tunnel in either direction between Hong Kong Island and Kowloon, the taxi fare will be HK$10 additional to cover tunnel fees. This is not registered on the meter. The Kowloon railroad covers the 22-mile stretch to the Chinese border, with eight stations along the way. The MTR subway system connects Hong Kong Island with Kowloon via an under-harbor tunnel, then makes a wide arc through northeast Kowloon; fares from HK$1.20-3.70, depending on length of journey. The Star Ferry links Hong Kong and Kowloon; *wallah wallahs*, or motor boats, also make the crossings. The outlying islands are served by the Hong Kong and Yuamati Ferry Co. Rent-a-cars are from HK$15 hourly, HK$100 daily, and HK$550 weekly. Chauffeur-driven cars cost from HK$20 hourly. You drive on the left.

FOOD AND RESTAURANTS

Cantonese cuisine sets the keynote in Hong Kong, but you will find the entire range of Chinese cooking represented in the colony's numerous restaurants and eating places. Shark's fin soup, sweet and sour pork, Peking duck, bird's nest soup, chicken and almonds, *fou yong hai* (egg and crab), toffee apples, and literally dozens of other delicacies are all there, waiting to be sampled in their original glory. For a light lunchtime treat, try *dim sum,* a typically Cantonese array of pork, chicken, shrimp, and vegetable tidbits carried around on large trays by girls who call out the names of the dishes.

When it comes to eating out the choice is enormous, from the floating restaurants of Aberdeen (some of them multistoried) to the luxurious, Western-style **Mandarin Grill** and **Pierrot** in the Mandarin Hotel (tel: 5-220111), the Hilton's **Eagle Nest** (tel: 5-233111), or **Hugo's** at the Hyatt Regency (tel: 3-662321). Eminently notable is the **Peak Tower Restaurant** (Upper Peak Tram Station, Hong Kong—tel: 5-97260), with magnificent views and food to match. For Cantonese fare, try the **Tai Tung** (271 Des Voeux Road Central—tel: 5-497772), which has an ample *dim sum* menu at noon. For Peking dishes it's the **Peking Restaurant** (144 Gloucester Road, Hong Kong—tel: 5-754212), and don't miss the duck. The **Luk Yu Tea House** (24 Stanley St., Hong Kong—tel: 5-232973) is so steeped in local color that the menus are all in Chinese, so bring along a Chinese-speaking friend. The **Fung Lum Restaurant** (20-22 Leighton Road, Happy Valley, Hong Kong—tel: 5-777669) is another excellent spot for Cantonese cooking. For all-round Chinese menus try the **Chung Chuk Lau** at 30 Leighton Road, Happy Valley, Hong Kong (tel: 5-7902086). For French cuisine there is **Marseille** (5a Hart Avenue, Kowloon—tel:

3-672905) and **La Renaissance** (73 Hennessy Road, Wanchai, Hong Kong—tel: 5-285511).

DRINKING TIPS

All the usual drinks are available, though alcohol is not usually drunk with Chinese meals; it is the tea that comes into its own here, in a rich and inexhaustible variety. There is, however, Chinese rice wine, called *shiu hing*. For beer, try San Miguel, the most popular, and also try a Tsingtao from China, a good light brew. There are several good English-style pubs, including the **Jockey** in Union House and the **Bull and Bear** in Hutchison House, both in the Central district. There are no restrictions on the serving or selling hours.

ENTERTAINMENT

There are performances by the **Hong Kong Philharmonic** and recitals by visiting artists in the concert halls at the **City Hall** and the **Hong Kong Arts Centre**; Chinese opera can be heard at **Laichikok**—an amusement park in Kowloon—or the **Mandarin Theater Restaurant**. Films are big entertainment here; Hong Kong makes more films than Hollywood. A local movie house is well worth a visit. Many films are dubbed in English or have English subtitles.

Heading our list of night spots in Kowloon is the **Miramar Theater Restaurant** at the Hotel Miramar (tel: 3-681111), which provides a floor show featuring Chinese opera against lavish, Peking-inspired sets. There is also **Bar City**, a collection of six entertainment spots in the New World Center ranging from modern disco through jazz and country-and-western to a traditional British pub and a Korean *boite*. Also in Kowloon are the **Kingsland Night Club** in the Maramar Hotel (tel: 5-681111) and the **Oceania Restaurant & Nightclub** (Ocean Terminal, Kowloon—tel: 3-670181). In Hong Kong, night owls will find their way to the **Macambo** (King's Theater Building, Hong Kong—tel: 5-222296), **The Den** disco at the Hilton, the **Captain's Bar** at the Mandarin, or **The Bottoms Up Club** (14 Hankow Rd., Kowloon—tel: 3-675696).

SHOPPING

Shops are open 9-6 (or later in some districts) Mon-Sat, and often Sunday too. Among the best buys are silks, ivories, jade, jewelry, and fine tailor-made suits and shirts (remember to allow time for the fittings). There are also imported cameras, watches, and stereo equipment. The shopper will do well to obtain a copy of the Hong Kong Tourist Association's comprehensive *Stop & Shop*. Bargaining is customary, except at large department stores, where prices are fixed. In Kowloon, try the **Shui Hing** department store on Nathan Road and the **Ocean Terminal** and **Ocean Centre** shopping complex next to Star Ferry Pier or **Lane Crawford** in the Central District. The **Merchandise Emporium** in Kowloon is loaded with bargains, as is the **Chinese Arts & Crafts (HK) Ltd** (Star House, Salisbury Road, Kowloon), which has a Hong Kong branch at Shell House, Queen's Road Central. For a food market full of local color and exotic products, try the smaller markets in the Central, Wanchai, and Causeway Bay districts.

SPORTS

You can enjoy golf (at the **Royal Hong Kong Country Club** or **Fanling Golf Course** in the New Territories), tennis (at park courts), and riding (in the **New Territories**); swimming, surfing, and water-skiing are available at the many beaches, especially at **Repulse Bay**. Those who would rather watch—and bet—will find the horses running twice weekly Oct-June at the **Happy Valley Racecourse** and the splendid **Shatin Race Track** in the New Territories.

WHAT TO SEE

Hong Kong: A train ride to the top of the **Peak** is a must. It will give you a superb view of the city, harbor, and outlying islands. The Peak district—an exclusive suburb dotted with mansions—is itself worth a visit. The heart of the downtown section is the Central District, with its banks, shops, and office buildings. To the east, along the waterfront, is the colorful **Wanchai** area of Suzie Wong fame. **Tiger Balm Gardens,** a public park built by the promoter of a patent medicine of the same name, has bizarre Chinese sculptures and, in its **Haw Par Mansion,** a remarkable collection of jade. For tickets to the latter, apply at the Hong Kong Standard (635 King's Road, North Point). On the opposite side of the island is **Aberdeen,** known for its houseboats and floating restaurants. Not far away are the beaches of **Deep Water Bay** and **Repulse Bay.** For guided tours, call the Tourist Office at 5-244191. To recapture these earlier times it is necessary to visit the remaining Tanka (boat people) whose lives are spent upon the water. Their years pass aboard their fishing junks, where they are born, mature, and die. Here still are small temples where the pious maintain their personal dedication to the many deities of the Chinese tradition, and where prayers are daily offered to Kuan Yin, Buddhist Lady of Mercy and Tin Hau, the goddess of those who live and work upon the sea.

Kowloon and the New Territories: This is the leading industrial zone of the colony and, paradoxically, the doorway to the rural peace of the New Territories. The center of Kowloon itself (the name means "Nine Dragons") rivals Hong Kong across the harbor with its shops, neon signs, and heavy traffic. Especially bustling is the Tsimshatsui district, site of the **Ocean Terminal,** a modern complex of 100 shops built beside a 1,200-foot pier, and the new adjoining **Ocean Centre** complex.

The New Territories, though adjacent to Kowloon, are administered separately. The Kowloon-Canton railway cuts across them, and a ride to the Chinese border is an excellent way of getting acquainted. Along the way is **Shatin,** home of the **Temple of the Ten Thousand Buddhas.** A popular spot to view China is **Lok Ma Chau,** not far from Fanling and overlooking the farmlands of China.

Macao: This city has the distinction of being the oldest European settlement in the Far East—and bears it proudly. Situated on a short peninsula stretching out from the Chinese mainland, Macao has an area of just under seven square miles and is linked to Hong Kong by jetfoil, hydrofoil (75 minutes), and ferry (2½-3 hours). The jetfoils cost HK$45 per person weekdays, HK$50 weekends; hydrofoils HK$30 weekdays, HK$40 weekends; ferries HK$20 for a seat or HK$100 for a first class cabin for two. The Hong Kong government departure tax is HK$8 per person. The province also includes two small islands, mostly forested. While the Peoples' Republic of China claims sovereignty over Macao, it remains an Overseas Portuguese Province, administered by a Lisbon-appointed governor, and sending a delegate to the Portuguese National Assembly. Here the visitor can enjoy a striking glimpse of 16th- and 18th-century splendor, Portuguese style. Its baroque churches, splendid old mansions, and cobbled streets are charming reminders that Macao is, in effect, a bit of southern Europe at the doorstep of mainland China. Among the landmarks are the significant **Governor's Palace;** the facade of the **Church of St Paul,** built in the 16th century; the steepled **Cathedral; St Dominic's, St Augustine's, St Lawrence's,** and **St Joseph's.** They and the older shuttered, arcaded houses around them could be transplanted without difficulty to northern Portugal or northwestern Spain. But Macao does not lack modern hotels. The **Lisboa** (Avenue Dr Oliveira Salazar) has 400 rooms, swimming pool, sauna, and eight restaurants, including a theater restaurant and nightclub (from US$37 double). The **Estoril** (Avenue Sidonio Pais), another leading establishment, has a casino, Olympic-size swimming pool, supper club, bars, and special facilities for children, including a fully equipped playground and wading pool (from US$28 double). Another recommended hotel is the **Matsuya,** Calcada de San Francisco (from US$24 double). The smaller but newer **Sintra** (from US$30) is close to the heart of the city. Nightclubs and casinos can be found in the city (the gambling is especially lively), and there is a choice of restaurants with excellent Oriental and Portuguese cuisine. A passport (but no visa) is needed for most Western tourists. Those needing visas may obtain them at the Consulate-General in Hong Kong (14th floor of the Central Building in Pedder Street). Entry tax HK$25. The **Government Information and Tourism Office** near Government House is helpful in arranging tours to outlying **Coloane** and **Taipa** islands where there are pleasant small inns and beaches. The new **Macao Trotting Club** on Taipa meets twice a week: one evening midweek and at 2pm Sundays. Comfortable coach service runs from the Lisboa Hotel to the harness raceway two hours before starting time. Entry tickets are sold on the coaches.

SOURCES OF FURTHER INFORMATION

Pan Am: 103 Alexandra House, Chater Road, Hong Kong, or any Pan Am office round the world; **Hong Kong Tourist Association,** 35th Floor, Connaught Centre, Hong Kong; Hong Kong Bank Building, 160 Sansome Street, Suite 1102, San Francisco, CA 94104; 548 Fifth Avenue, New York, NY 10036; 333 N Michigan Ave, Chicago, IL 60601 (also offices in Los Angeles, Seattle, and Washington, DC); and 14/16 Cockspur Street, London SW1.

India

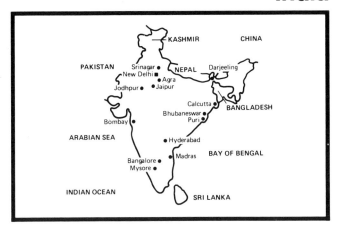

WHAT'S SPECIAL

India has many problems but is undergoing a slow, often frustrating revolution in its social and economic life. It is the cradle of two of the world's greatest religions and a land of beautiful temples and mosques, rock carvings, mausoleums and holy cities, dance dramas, and colorful religious festivals. Its world-famous Taj Mahal is in itself reason enough to visit India. Young people from all over the world come to India for peace and meditation, but it is also a land in which you can have an adventurous and exciting vacation.

COUNTRY BRIEFING

Size: 1,262,813 square miles   **Population:** 690,000,000
Capital: New Delhi   **Capital Population:** 4,800,000

Climate: Winters, from November-March, are dry with bright, sunny days; pleasantly cool in the south, bracing in New Delhi, but rather severe in the mountain regions of the north. Summers, April-June, are also generally dry but increasingly hot. There are frequent dust storms in the plains, though in the southern region it is usually humid, with cool afternoon breezes from the sea. In Calcutta, summer months are warm and humid. June-October are the months of the southwest monsoon, when India, with the exception of the southeast area, receives 85% of its rainfall. The southeast receives most of its rain from mid-October through the end of December. Best time to visit: winter months.

Weather in New Delhi: Lat N28°35′; Alt 714 ft

Temp (°F)	Jan	Feb	Mar	Apr	May	Jun	Jul	Aug	Sep	Oct	Nov	Dec
Av Low	44°	49°	58°	68°	79°	83°	81°	79°	75°	65°	52°	46°
Av High	70°	75°	87°	97°	105°	105°	96°	93°	93°	93°	84°	73°
Days no rain	29	26	30	29	29	26	23	23	26	30	30	30

Government: A federal republic; British Commonwealth nation.
Language: Hindi and English.
Religion: Hindu, 84%; Muslim and other faiths represented.
Currency: Rupee. 100 paise = 1 rupee.

	Paise 50	Re 1	Rs 2	Rs 5	Rs 10	Rs 50	Rs 100	Rs 500
US (dollars, cents)	.06	.12	.24	.60	1.20	5.98	11.96	59.80
UK (pounds, pence)	.03	.06	.11	.29	.57	2.86	5.72	28.58

Public Holidays

Republic Day, 26 Jan
Good Friday
Independence Day, 15 Aug

Mahatma Gandhi's Birthday, 2 Oct
Christmas Day, 25 Dec

In addition, there are other public holidays whose dates fall on Hindu, Muslim, Buddhist, or Sikh festival days and vary from year to year: Pongal/Sankranti, Jan; Holi, Feb/Mar; Buddha Purnima, May/June; Id, variable; Janmastami, Aug/Sep; Ganesh, Aug/Sep; Dussehra, Sep/Oct; Bakrid, Oct; Diwali, Oct/Nov; Muharram, variable; Guru Nanak Jayanti, Nov.

HOW TO GET THERE

Flying time to Palam Airport, New Delhi from New York is 16¾ hours; from London 10 hours; from Caracas 20¾ hours; from Tokyo 10 hours. Time in India: GMT+5 hours 30 minutes.

REQUIREMENTS FOR ENTRY AND CUSTOMS REGULATIONS

Passport and a landing permit (issued on arrival, valid for 30 days), or Tourist, Entry, or Transit Visa, issued by Indian Missions abroad (not needed by citizens of UK). A Tourist Visa is valid for 3 months and Transit Visas for 15 days. If arriving from an infected area (Africa and South America are considered as such), you need a yellow-fever vaccination certificate. Inoculations against smallpox, typhoid, tetanus, hepatitis, and poliomyelitis are strongly recommended. A valid certificate of vaccination against cholera is compulsory. Special permits required to visit restricted or protected areas of Darjeeling, Sikkim, Assam, Arunachal Pradesh, Meghalaya, Manipur, Nagaland, Tripura, Andaman, and Nicobar islands, and the Laccadive, Minicoy, and Amindivi islands.

Duty-free allowance: 200 cigarettes, or 50 cigars or ½ pound tobacco, 1 quart wine, one-fifth pint liquor; ½ pint toilet water and reasonable amount of perfume; one still camera with 5 rolls film (or 2 still cameras with 25 rolls film each if entered on a Tourist Baggage Re-export Form—TBRE); one 8mm or 16mm movie camera with 10 reels film (or an additional 20 reels with TBRE); personal effects including one watch (plus one extra with TBRE), personal jewelry; 3 sporting firearms with a total of 200 cartridges and an additional 400 cartridges on payment of duty (you must have an Arms Possession License); travel souvenirs not exceeding Rs500; you will have to agree in writing to re-export "high-value articles." Entering with more than $1,000 requires the filling out of a customs declaration form. Foreign currency should be changed at banks and other authorized agencies and receipts kept in order to convert remaining rupees back into foreign currency when leaving. No Indian currency (except rupee travelers' checks) can be brought in or taken out. The import of dangerous drugs (including hashish), live plants, gold coins, gold and silver bullion, and silver coins not in use is prohibited. On leaving India you must take with you what you brought in, especially what has been declared on your passport, including all "high-value articles" and souvenirs brought in from other countries. You may take out souvenirs bought in India without limit, precious stones and jewelry to the value of Rs10,000. If you want to export any antiquities, you should consult the Government Tourist Office for advice. Export of protected-animal skins and furs is strictly prohibited. Export of ivory is also banned, but a few trinkets, such as a bracelet and earrings will be allowed.

AIRPORT INFORMATION
The international airport for New Delhi is Palam, 8 miles from the city center, and a regular bus service is available. EATS also provides regular coach service to the city center to major hotels (fare is Rs8 per person). A taxi to Connaught Circus will cost about Rs25. Government tourist (ITDC) cars and coaches can also be hired. There is no arrival tax, but departure tax is Rs100. Porterage handled by an agency for 1 rupee per piece of luggage. Duty-free shop and tourist center at the airport.

ACCOMMODATIONS
There are modern "Western-style" hotels in all large cities and tourist centers, as well as the more austere "Indian-style" establishments. The better hotels have air-conditioned rooms and private baths, but you should reserve well in advance to avoid disappointment. Most of the Indian state governments run travelers' lodges and tourist cottages. Rates run from Rs60 to Rs100 for a double room with bath. Air conditioning, a necessity in summer, can bring the rate up to around Rs150. There are also houseboats on the banks of the river Jhelum and on the Dal and Nagin Lakes in Kashmir. Some hotels add a 7 to 10% service charge to room rates. An additional 10% "hotel receipts tax" may go into effect this year. If you need help in finding accommodations, there is a 24-hour Government Tourist Office desk at the airport (tel: 392745 in the international section and 393481, extension 286, on the domestic side) and at 88 Janpath (tel: 320005 and 320008). Hotels in New Delhi (with air conditioning included in price):

Rates are in US$ for a double/twin room with bath or shower

Akbar, Chanakyapuri (from $44), 5 miles from center city

Ambassador, Sujan Singh Park (from $37), 3.5 miles from center city

Ashoka, Chanakyapuri (from $53), 4 miles from center city

Broadway, Asaf Ali Road (from $23), 1.5 miles from center city

Claridges, 12 Aurangzeb Road (from $47), 3 miles from center city

Hans, 15 Barakhamba Road (from $41)

Imperial, Janpath (from $45)

Janpath, Janpath (from $33)

Kanishka, Lajpat (from $41), 1 mile from center city

Lodhi, Lala Laipat Rai Marg (from $27), 4 miles from center city

Maidens Oberoi, Alipur Road (from $31), 6 miles from center city

Maurya Sheraton, Sarder Patel Road (from $68), 4 miles from center city

New Delhi YMCA Tourist Hotel, Jai Singh Road (from $23)

Nirula's, Connaught Circus (from $29)

OBEROI INTER·CONTINENTAL, Dr Zakir Hussain Road (from $70), 3.5 miles from center city

President, 4/23 Asaf Ali Road (from $20), 1.5 miles from center city

Qutab, New Mehrauli Road (from $32), 9 miles from center city

Rajdoot, Mathura Road (from $38), 5.5 miles from center city

Ranjit, Maharajah Ranjit Singh Road (from $24), 1 mile from center city

Taj Mahal, 1 Man Singh Road (from $61), 3 miles from center city

Vikram, Ring Road (from $35), 7 miles from center city

Unless otherwise indicated, all the above hotels are centrally located.

USEFUL INFORMATION

Banks: Open 10-2 Mon-Fri, 10-12 Sat. The State Bank's tourist counter is open 5-7pm every evening except Sunday in G Block, Connaught Place, New Delhi, while the airport branch is open 24 hours. Many hotels also run 24-hour currency exchange facilities. Changing money through unauthorized channels is illegal, and furthermore you might find yourself with a handful of counterfeit Indian currency.

Mail: Stamps available from post offices (open 10-5) and some hotels. The airport post office and the main Parliament Street post office downtown are open 24 hours and the Eastern Court Post Office in Janpath, New Delhi, until 8pm. International telegrams can be sent through Eastern Court. For important letters, be sure to ask for a certificate of mailing or send registered (post office facility open 10-3, and at Parliament Street until 9pm). Be sure to have envelopes with high denomination stamps cancelled in your presence, or use aerograms.

Telephone Tips: Phones in some street booths, restaurants, cafés, hotels, and post offices, but these are generally very busy. Useful numbers:

Pan Am, New Delhi 322273
  Bombay 244020
  Calcutta 443251
Tourist Office, New Delhi 320005 or
  320008
  Bombay 293144
  Calcutta 441402
  Madras 86240 or 86249
Operator 199
Directories 197

International Calls 186
Time 174
Special Information 176
Police 100
  Calcutta 443521
  Madras 87964
Fire 101
Ambulance 102

Newspapers: English-language newspapers and magazines available in all major towns. Local publications in English are the *Statesman*, the *Times of India*, the *Indian Express*, the *Hindustan Times*, the *Economic Times*, and *Amrita Bazar Patrika* (Calcutta-based newspaper).

Tipping: Use your discretion. Apart from the customary 10% tip in a restaurant (less in those which have a 10% service charge), do not flash money around. One rupee and some loose change is a safe and generous tip for anyone. Taxi drivers are not usually tipped.

Electricity: 220 volts 50 cycles AC in most places.

Laundry: Dry-cleaning and laundry services usually reliable. Hotels generally give good service (dry-cleaning a suit, from Rs30, laundering a shirt, from Rs8).

Hairdressing: Salons in major hotels and in main shopping centers (shampoo and set, from Rs25; man's haircut, from Rs10).

Photography: Equipment available in major cities only and the selection of standard films is limited. It is best to bring film with you. Black and white film can be processed in 1-2 days, but there are only two laboratories processing color film in New Delhi and Bombay, and it could take over a week. Check with Mahatta & Co, 59M Block, Connaught Circus, New Delhi (tel: 3530008).

Clubs: Rotary, Lions, Roundtablers, Gymkhana Club, Kiwanis, India International Center, National Sports Club of India, and Press Club of India.

Rest Rooms: Use hotels and restaurants.

Health: All doctors and dentists speak English. Most pharmaceuticals are produced locally and are in good supply; imported pharmaceuticals and toiletries are expensive. Before leaving for India, it's best to ask your doctor about gamma globulin and antimalarial drugs.

TRANSPORTATION

Buses in the oldest areas of New Delhi are usually crowded and slow. Taxis are plentiful at all hours; you can hail one in the street or go to a taxi stand. They have a meter, but make sure that it is set and working; fares start at Rs2, then about Rs1.40 per kilometer, plus about Rs2 surcharge per trip. There is a 15 paise to Rs1 charge for suitcases, depending on weight, and a 25% increase in fares after 11pm. Scooter taxis (Rs1, then about Rs.80 per kilometer, plus about Rs1 surcharge) are available for the adventurous, as is the tonga—horse and cart. Four-wheel Victoria carriages are available at the Victoria railway terminus in Bombay, but though they can be used on back roads all day, they can be used on main roads only in the evening. No cars for rent in New Delhi or most other cities, but you can rent a chauffeur-driven car for Rs150-200 for an 8-hour day. Go to India Tourism Development Corp (L Block, Nirula Hotel Building, Connaught Circus), Mercury Travels (Jeevan Tara Building, Parliament Street, New Delhi 1), the Orient Express Co (70 Janpath), or SITA Travels (F-12 Connaught Place); or try negotiating an economy rate at any taxi stand (as little as Rs120).

The Indian railroad system is the second largest in the world and covers all cities. The Reservations Office is at State Entry Road (tel: 344877). Indrail passes (unlimited travel tickets) are available for seven days ($80 air conditioned, $15 second class) to 90 days ($300 air conditioned, $75 second class), and can be purchased from the Railway Tourist Guide, Baroda House, Copernicus Road, at India Gate, New Delhi. Payment must be made in convertible foreign currency. Children 5-12 pay half-fare. Long-distance bus services connect all major cities, but can be un-comfortable. Indian Airlines Corporation (IAC) operates daily scheduled services between New Delhi and Calcutta, Bombay, Madras, Hyderabad, and many other cities and a 14-day "Discover India" special for $375. Details from the IAC Office at Kanchanjunga Building, Barakhamba Road (tel: 40071).

FOOD AND RESTAURANTS

Curry of course—meat, chicken, vegetable, fish, coconut, peas, and cottage cheese—the variety is infinite and the quality unforgettable. Madras curry is particularly hot. Try the Bombay specialty, *Bhelpuri,* puffed rice, flour, potatoes, and onions drenched in chutney, or the very popular *biriyanis,* prepared with chicken or meat and whole spices covered in rice and garnished with grapes, cashew nuts, and eggs. Other specialties include *pork vindaloos* and sausages, or the superb *tandoori* dishes: chicken or meat cooked slowly in special *tandoor* earthenware ovens. Or *dahl,* which looks like thick pea and bean soup. Delicious too are the *chapathis,* flour-and-water dough rolled thin and cooked like pancakes; *idlis,* fluffy steamed rice-cakes and *masala-dosais,* pancakes stuffed with vegetables (both South Indian dishes); and *paan* dessert, consisting of betel leaf with lime paste stuffed with grated betel nut, aniseed, and cardamom. Very sweet Indian desserts include *gulab jamun, burfi, jalebi* (more tasty when served hot), and *Ras Malai* (a Bengal milk dessert).

International cuisine is available in major hotels, but sample the North Indian food at the **Moti Mahal,** near the Delhi Gate in Old Delhi—Punjabi and *tandoori* dishes to the strains of folk music. The **Woodlands Restaurant,** in the Lodhi Hotel, offers eight dishes of South Indian vegetarian food, coffee, and desserts for a very reasonable price. The **Panch Mahal** at the Akbar Hotel, New Delhi's first 5-star vegetarian restaurant, offers completely orthodox dishes, without the onions and garlic the Marwaris

people from Rajasthan state refuse to eat. Everything comes on a platter; spiced vegetables, lentils, rice, puffed fried *chapathis*, festive Indian bread, chutneys, and pickles. Indian musicians and dancers entertain. Recommended too are the **Moghul Room** at the Oberoi Inter · Continental; the **Tandoor,** in the Hotel President; the **Peacock** at the Ashoka Hotel; the **Mayur** at the Maurya Sheraton; the **Sheesh Mahal's** buffet at the Akbar; the **Orbit's** buffet at the Janpath; the **Ashiana** at the Ambassador Hotel; the **Embassy** in Connaught Place; and **Gaylord** in Connaught Circus. The **Nirula** in Connaught Place is self-service with stand-up counters for those in a hurry. If you prefer Chinese food, go to the **Mandarin Room** of the Janpath Hotel, the **Café Chinois** at the Oberoi Inter · Continental, or **Chungwa** in Defence Colony. **Fujiya,** at Malcha Marg, serves good Chinese and Japanese cooking, while the Maurya's **Bali Hi** is noted for its Indonesian fare (try their coconut soup). French cuisine is featured at the **Supper Club** of the Ashok Hotel, which has nightly dinner-dances and entertainment, and at the **Auberge** in the Hotel Maidens in Old Delhi. A meal in an expensive restaurant will cost upwards of US$8; in a medium-priced one, from US$2-3.50; in an inexpensive one, less than US$1.70. For Indian snacks, which are very good, try any of the café restaurants on Connaught Circus, but avoid street stalls. Drink bottled mineral water only even in the best hotels and restaurants, and never eat salads.

DRINKING TIPS

Prohibition of drinking is in force in the states of Gujarat, Tamil Nadu, and Bihar. New Delhi, Bombay, and Calcutta are not in these areas, though Madras is in the state of Tamil Nadu—but other states have many "dry days" when no liquor is sold. An All-India Liquor Permit, available from Government Tourist Offices, allows you to buy, transport, and consume liquor in dry states or on dry days elsewhere (except in Gujarat), but you may not buy anyone a drink who is not a holder of a liquor permit. You may therefore find that most of your drinking is confined to hotel bars and permit rooms licensed by the government. A whisky and soda (imported Scotch) costs anywhere up to Rs50. Local whisky is not always palatable to visitors. Imported wines are very expensive, costing from 250 to Rs.400 a bottle. Local beers are fine, about Rs18 a bottle. *Feni* is a very potent drink made from the juice of cashews. Indian tea is excellent, but do try a *Lassi*—sour milk shake.

ENTERTAINMENT

The dance is one of the most cultivated art forms in the country and an integral part of Indian life, having both spiritual and social significance. There are four major schools of dancing in India: the classical **Bharata Natyam** of South India, the **Kathakali** of Kerala, the **Kathak** of North India, and the **Manipuri** of Eastern India. In New Delhi, there are dance performances at the **Fine Arts Theater** (Rafi Marg), the **Bharatiya Kala Kendra** (Kamani Hall, Copernicus Marg), **Triveni Kala Sangam** (Tansen Marg), the **Roof Top** of the Oberoi Inter · Continental, the **Ashok's Con-**

vention Hall, and theaters in the Mandi House Circle area. There are concerts and Indian operas in various concert halls. Every evening there is a Sound and Light spectacle at the Red Fort—except during monsoons. A small selection of English and American films are shown with original soundtrack in some movie houses.

Try the nightclubs and restaurants in the best hotels in New Delhi, such as the Supper Club at the Ashoka Hotel, the Bali Hi at the Maurya Sheraton, the Café Chinois at the Oberoi Inter · Continental, and the Sensation at the Oberoi Maidens.

SHOPPING

Stores in New Delhi are open from 9:30-7, some on Sunday. Larger stores, especially those in the main shopping areas, close for lunch from 1:30-2:30. Smaller shops, such as those in Old Delhi, may be open all day. Some of the best shops are around Connaught Circus, where you will find handcrafts, brassware, stone and wood carvings, exquisite jewelry, blue pottery, delightful papier maché puppets, terracotta and clay toys, delicate *Phulkari* (flower craft), oriental furniture, Kashmir shawls, and wall hangings. The government emporia have fixed prices in all major cities and tend to be less expensive than private and hotel shops. Most are permitted to accept payment in foreign exchange. Don't be fooled by signs in general shopping areas claiming a shop is "Government Approved." In New Delhi, all government emporia are on Baba Kharak Singh Marg, near Connaught Circus. The Kashmir Government Emporium, on Connaught Circus, is the best place to go, with a wide variety of goods. Also excellent are the Central Cottage Industries Emporium on Janpath and Khadi Gramodyog Bhavan, in the Regal Buildings, 1 Connaught Square. The Handloom House, in Connaught Place, has garments for men and women; satins, silks of all kinds, filigree, brocades—Rs100 and upwards for most ready-made saris. For kaftans, kurtas, and "pantsuits" made from handwoven silks and cottons you might also try the Maharani of India and the Sona Boutique in the Ashok Hotel, or the Kamal Silk Emporium on Asaf Ali Road. For precious stones and jewelry go to Monohar Lall Bujjan Mall in the Janpath Hotel or the Ambassador Jewellers in the Claridges Hotel. Beautiful ivory chess sets and other articles are at the Ivory Mart, and the Indian Art Palace, in E and F Blocks of Connaught Place. The Ivory Palace in Old Delhi is worth a visit to see how things are made.

Visit the Chandni Chowk, the pungent, colorful, and infinitely fascinating bazaar of Old Delhi—but go in a scooter taxi to avoid bicycles, street urchins, and beggars. Try bargaining at 10% of the quoted price in order to end up paying 50%.

SPORTS

Soccer, hockey, polo, cricket, wrestling, swimming, and trekking (in Kashmir, Himachal Pradesh, and Uttar Pradesh) are very popular. There is horse racing in major cities. The Delhi Golf Club has an excellent course open to visitors, and there are two horseback riding clubs. There are swimming pools at the **Chelmsford Club** (Raisina Road), **National Sports Club** (Mathura Road), and **Gymkhana Club** (Safdarjung Road), with facilities for tennis and badminton—temporary membership available. Permits should be obtained for fishing and shooting. For full details of the finest shooting and fishing areas, plus instructions for obtaining permits, write: Government of India Tourist Office, 88 Janpath, New Delhi 110001.

WHAT TO SEE

The North

New Delhi's most magnificent monuments are **Jama Masjid,** a remarkable mosque in red stone and white marble, and the **Red Fort,** completed in 1647. Inside its walls are relics of the **Imperial Palace** of Shah Jahan, builder of the Taj Mahal, the **Dewan-I-Am,** the Hall of Public Audience, the **Diwan-I-Khas** or Hall of Private Audience, the **Rang Mahal,** or Pleasure Palace, once reserved for the royal ladies, the **Pearl Mosque** or Moti Masjid, the **Royal Baths** of beautifully carved and inlaid marble, and the **Sawan** and **Bhadaun** pavilions where royalty witnessed cultural performances. A museum of paintings and relics is housed in the **Shish Mahal,** the Palace of Mirrors.

From the Red Fort to the Fatehpuri Mosque runs the wide and sprawling **Chandni Chowk,** once reputed to be the richest street in the world. In New Delhi itself, see the former **Viceregal Lodge,** the **Central Secretariat,** and the circular colonnaded edifice of the **Rajya Sabha** and the **Lok Sabha,** the two Houses of Parliament. Also visit the **Jantar Mantar,** the observatory built by the astronomer Maharajah Jai Singh II in 1710; the impressive **India Gate,** memorial to the dead of two World Wars, built when the British raj was at its height of pomp and glory; the **National Museum,** which has relics of the 5,000 BC Indus Valley Civilization as well as Brahminical, Jain, and Buddhist sculptures, and old manuscripts such as the *Bhagavad Gita;* the **Raj Ghat,** marking the spot where Mahatma Gandhi's mortal remains were cremated in 1948; the **Gandhi Smarak Sangrahalaya,** containing many personal belongings of Gandhi, and the **Nehru Museum** at Teen Murti·Marg, a similar memorial, called **Shantivana,** to the great national leader Jawaharlal Nehru; and the **Buddha Jayanti Park,** a garden commemorating the 2,500th anniversary of the birth of Lord Buddha. Children will love the **Doll's Museum** and the **Children's Library** on Bahadur Shah Zafar Marg, and the **Delhi Zoo,** where they will see Vijay and Sohrab, a pair of white tigers, and many other exciting animals.

Engulfed in modern New Delhi are the remains of at least seven royal cities; there are hundreds of outstanding historical monuments, dating back 1,000 years. Most ancient is the tank and *ghat* of **Suraj Kund** (Sun Pool) built in the 11th century just south of New Delhi. The **Qutb Minar,** a 243-foot Tower of Victory 7 miles south of New Delhi, was started by Sultan Qutb-ud-Din around 1200 AD. In the village of **Mehrauli** is the octagonal tomb in memory of Adham Khan, who was hurled to his death over the parapet of the palace on the orders of Akbar in the 16th century. About 8 miles east of Qutb is the massive fort and mausoleum of **Tughlakābād.** The **Ashoka Pillar,** standing in the Firozshah Kotla, was already 1,500 years old when it was brought to the city by Firoz Shah, last of the Tughlaq dynasty. In the Purana Qila stands the red octagonal building called the **Sher Mandal.** The tomb of Emperor Humayun, an architectural forerunner of the Taj Mahal, is in the middle of the spacious walled garden.

Agra, the city of the Taj Mahal, lies 125 miles south of New Delhi, connected to the capital by the special "Taj Express" which leaves New Delhi at 7am and can bring you back by 10pm. Regular express trains from New Delhi, Madras, Bombay, and Calcutta also stop at Agra. There are also flights to Agra from New Delhi, Calcutta, Varanasi, and other cities; air-conditioned buses for day tours are also available (check with government tourist offices). If you are coming from New Delhi by road the first monument of Agra is the tomb of **Akbar the Great** at Sikandra. The central mausoleum is a four-storied affair, of which the top story is in marble and the bottom three in red stone. The extraordinarily beautiful **Taj Mahal,** one of the wonders of the world and a masterpiece in marble, was built in 12 years by an army of 20,000. Dominating the city of Agra is the massive **Red Fort,** the creation of successive emperors. Twenty-two miles southwest of Agra is the deserted city of **Fatehpur Sikri,** once the imperial capital and now a collection of abandoned but well-preserved mosques, mansions, and palaces. **Bharatpur Bird Sanctuary,** where cranes come from as far away as Siberia, is 55 km from Agra Airport. Stay at **Bharatpur Forest Lodge** (from US$19 double). In Agra, hotels are **Clark's Shiraz,** 54 Taj Road (from US$41 double), 8 miles from the airport and 1 mile from Taj Mahal; **Grand,** 137 Station Road (from US$12 double), 7 miles from the airport and 2.5 miles from Taj; **Holiday Inn,** Taj Ganj (from US$41 double), 9 miles from the airport and 1 mile from Taj; **Laurie's,** Mahatma Gandhi Road (from US$15 double), 3 miles from the airport and 6 miles from Taj; **Mayur Tourist Complex,** Fatehabad Road (from US$14 double), 9 miles from airport and 1 mile from Taj; **Moghul Sheraton,** Taj Ganj (from US$63 double), 8.5 miles from airport and 1 mile from Taj; **Mumtaj-Ashok,** 181/2 Fatehabad Road (from US$27 double), 9 miles from airport and 1 mile from Taj; **Hotel Saurabh,** Jasoria Enclave, Fatehabad Road (from US$23 double).

On the banks of the sacred river Ganges, halfway between New Delhi and Calcutta, stands **Varanasi** (Benares), Hinduism's greatest city, where for thousands of years pilgrims have cleansed themselves of their sins by taking a dip in the holy waters. Local craftsmen are world-famous for their silks and brocades. **Clark's Hotel,** Mall Road, has double rooms for US$34; **Diamond Hotel,** Bhelupur, for US$15; and **Varanasi Ashok,** Mall Road, for US$25.

The walled "pink city" of **Jaipur,** the capital of the state of Rajasthan, is encircled by rugged hills crowned with medieval fortresses. Among the famous buildings are the **Hawa Mahal** (Palace of the Winds), the **City Palace,** housing a collection of weapons, rugs, manuscripts and paintings, and the **Amber Palace,** dominating the city. Hotels in Jaipur are the **Clark's Amer** (from US$50 double), 2 miles from the airport and 8 miles from the city; **Jaipur Ashok,** Jai Singh Circle, Bani Park (from US$28 double); **Rajasthan State,** Mirza Ismail Road (from US$15 double), 12 miles from the airport and 1 mile from the city; **Rambagh Palace,** Bhawani Singh Marg (from US$44 double), 7 miles from the airport and 2 miles from the city; **Welcome Hotel,** Mansingh Sansar Chandra Road (from US$50), 7 miles from the airport and in city center area.

Udaipur is on Lake Pichola. Here you will see the **Maharajah's Palace,** with its peacock mosaics, and the **Jag Niwas** and **Jag Mandir** palaces, built on islands in the lake. The **Lake Palace Hotel,** 15 miles from the airport (from US$35 double), is a completely refurbished 18th-century oriental white palace set in the middle of Lake Pichola; or stay at the **Lake End Hotel,** Alkapuri, Fateh Sagar (from US$35 double); or **Lakshmi Vilas Palace** (from US$21 double).

Chandigarh, designed by a team of architects led by Le Corbusier, is the joint capital of the states of Punjab and Haryana and rises out of the jungle at the foot of the Shiwalik range about 150 miles from New Delhi. The **High Court Building** is one of Le Corbusier's masterpieces. The hotel here is the **Oberoi Mount View** (from US$38 double), 7 miles from the airport and 2 miles from the city center.

The **Valley of Kashmir** is one of the most beautiful regions in the world—a land of rivers, misty lakes, and flower meadows. **Srinagar,** the capital, with a population of 485,000 is 1½ hours flying time from New Delhi. Lying on the shore of the lovely Lake Dal, the two halves of the city are joined by nine bridges over the Jhelum River. You can stay on a houseboat with all facilities and servants, from Rs200 for a deluxe double berth and full board or Rs80 for "C" category comfort, or at first-class hotels such as the **Oberoi Palace,** former home of the Maharajah of Kashmir (from US$64 double), 12 miles from the airport and 3 miles from the city center; the **Hotel Broadway** (from US$44 double), or **Nedou's** (from US$15 double), both on Maulana Azad Road in the center of the city or **Shahanshah,** Boulevard Srinagar (from US$64). The beautiful formal gardens include **Shalimar,** "the abode of love," and **Nishat,** the "garden of pleasure." In the **Kashmir Government Emporium** and the **Central Market** you will find the wonderful woven rugs for which Kashmir is famous. If you visit carpet warehouses, beware of prices; bargain down to 50%.

The East

Calcutta, long the capital of British India and one of the largest cities in the world, is still the commercial center of modern India. Its population is over 9,500,000, and it is one of the world's problem cities—no slums are as appalling as Calcutta's **Bustees.** And yet Calcutta is a dynamic port handling 40% of India's exports. **Dum Dum Airport** is 12 miles from the city center (taxi to heart of town, from Rs40-50). Hotels in Calcutta:

Rates are in US$ for a double/twin room with bath or shower

Airport Ashok Hotel, 1 mile from airport (from $38)

Fairlawn, 13A Sudder Street (from $29)

Great Eastern, 1-3 Old Court House Street (from $35)

Hindusthan International, 235/1 Acharya Jagadish Chandar Bose Road (from $57)

New Kennilworth, 1 Russel Street (from $14)

Oberoi Grand, 15 J Nehru Road (from $66)

Park, 17 Park Street (from $40)

Rutt Deen, 21B Loudon Street (from $35)

Unless otherwise indicated, all the above hotels are centrally located.

Begin a tour of the city at the **Chowringhee Maidan,** the huge open square dotted with reservoirs and monuments, in the center of Calcutta. Climb the 218 steps of the **Ochterlony Monument** for a superb view. On the eastern side of the Maidan is the **Chowringhee Road,** the entertainment and cultural heart of the city. See the great white marble **Victoria Memorial,** off Cathedral Road, a treasure-house of British colonial relics; **St John's Church,** where many British notables are buried; and **Dalhousie Square,** with imposing buildings and the Government Office overlooking the enormous Red Tank. **Chitpore** is the main center for souvenir hunters, where you will find the **Nakhoda Mosque,** the largest in the city, capable of accommodating 10,000 worshipers. In Budree Das Temple Street the **Jain Temple,** glittering with precious stones, stands in formal gardens. Other interesting places are **Fort William,** built in 1773; the **India Museum,** the biggest in the country; the **Marble Palace,** with paintings by Western old masters; the **Asutosh Museum** in the Centenary Building at Calcutta University; and the **Arts and Prints Museum** (31 Park Mansions, Park Street). Visit the **Zoo** and the **Belur, Dakshineswar,** and **Kalighat** temples. **Handloom House,** Lindsay Street, and **Cottage Industries,** Jawaharlal Nehru Road, sell beautiful handmade saris and other handicraft items.

Amber Restaurant (Waterloo Street, a few blocks from the Great Eastern Hotel) serves superb Indian food. **Skyroom, Trinca's,** and **Mocambo,** all on Park Street, have good Indian and Western dishes. **Blue Fox,** also on Park Street, is a restaurant with a small band and a dance floor; **Maxim's** (Great Eastern Hotel) specializes in *moghul* and *tandoori* dishes; while **Nanking** (2 Blackburn Lane) and **Waldorf** (Park Street) serve good Chinese food. There is no prohibition in Calcutta. There are many movie houses in the Chowringhee Road area.

By rail from Calcutta you can go on an excursion to peaceful **Santiniketan,** 93 miles away, home of the international university founded by the poet Rabindranath Tagore. There is a tourist lodge (from US$8 double) for overnight stays. If you want to visit **Darjeeling,** the Himalayan outlook of West Bengal, you need a special permit. Permits may be obtained at the Bagdogra airport, or the Foreigners Regional Registration offices in Bombay, New Delhi, Calcutta, or Madras. Permit is valid for 7 days. Fly to **Bagdogra,** then take the miniature train through dense green jungle, terraced tea gardens, and pine-scented forests up into the mountains. Stop at **Central Hotel**, Robertson Road, Darjeeling (from US$17 double), **Oberoi Mount Everest**, 29 Gandhi Road (from US$50 double), or **Windamere**, Observatory Hill, The Mall (from US$15 double). From Darjeeling, take a predawn trip to **Tiger Hill** to see the sun rise over **Mount Everest**. Farther east, in the state of Assam, is the **Kaziranga Wild Life Sanctuary**, famous as the habitat of the one-horned rhino. Permits (valid for 7 days) to visit Kaziranga and other tourist spots in this restricted region are obtainable at the Gauhati airport if arriving by air; otherwise, you must apply in advance at the Trade Advisor to the Government of Assam in Calcutta or at Indian missions abroad. **Patna**, about 300 miles northwest of Calcutta, and accessible by rail or by plane, is the focal point for excursions to the ruins of **Bodh Gaya**, sacred to Buddhists, and the ruins of India's ancient university of **Nalanda**. For overnight stays, there are resthouses at Rajgir (from US$8) and **Hotel Pataliputra Ashok**, Beerchand Patel Path (from US$14 double), **Hotel Republic**, Lawlys Building, Exhibition Road (from US$12), **Welcome Group-Maurya**, South Gandhi Maidan (from US$38 double), and **Satkar International**, Frazer Road (from US$23). **Bhubaneswar** in the state of Orissa, south of Calcutta, is the cathedral city of India; about 500 ancient temples still stand. Every stone is carved, sculptured, ornamented. Places to stay are **Hotel Prachi**, Janpath, Bhubaneswar (from US$18 double), and **Kalinga Ashok**, Gautam Nagar (from US$18 double). To the west are the Jain and Buddhist rock caves of **Udaygiri** and **Khandagiri**, dating back to the 2nd century BC. To the southeast, at **Dhawalagiri**, you will find the even earlier stone edict of **Ashoka**. At **Puri** in June/July every year the **Car Festival** is held, when the image of Lord Jagannath is carried on a gigantic car in the spectacular procession. There are resthouses (within US$13 double) for overnight stays. **Konarak** is famous for its magnificent Sun Temple, or Black Pagoda, standing on 24 enormous wheels and pulled by seven magnificent horses. Nearby are tourist lodges from US$13 double.

The West

Bombay, the "Gateway to India," is the country's most cosmopolitan city, both in appearance and outlook. Stretching like a huge hand into the Arabian Sea, a finger and thumb enclosing the Back Bay, this is India's second-largest city, with a population of about 7 million. Bombay's airport, also known as Santa Cruz, is 9 miles from the city center (taxi to city center about Rs50). In the city there are taxis, bus and streetcar services, and a railroad commuter service operating from Churchgate and Victoria terminals. Hotels in Bombay:

Rates are in US$ for a double/twin room with bath or shower

    Airport Plaza, 70C Nehru Road, Vile Parle East, Santa Cruz Airport (from $40)

    Ambassador, Churchgate Extension (from $48)

    Bombay International, 29 Marine Drive (from $45)

    Centaur, Santa Cruz Airport (from $57)

Fariyas, 25 Off Arthur Bunder Road (from $39)

Heritage, Victoria Road, Byculla (from $25), 2 miles from center city

Holiday Inn, Juhu Beach (from $54), 9 miles from center city

Horizon, Juhu Beach (from $50), 9 miles from center city

Nataraj, 135 Netaji Subash Road (from $17 double), 1.5 miles from center city

Oberoi Towers, Nirmal, Nariman Point (from $72 double)

President, 90 Cuffe Parade, Colaba (from $50 double), 1 mile from center city

Ritz, 5 Jamshedji Tata Road (from $23), 1 mile from center city

Sea Rock, Lands End, Bandra (from $50)

Sun-n-Sand, Juhu Beach (from $38 double), 9 miles from center city

TAJ MAHAL INTER · CONTINENTAL, Apollo Bunder (from $63 double)

West End, 45 Marine Lines (from $25)

Unless otherwise indicated, the above hotels are centrally located.

Make your way to the **Gateway of India,** an imposing pavilion commemorating the visit of King George V and Queen Mary in 1911. On the island of **Elephanta** you can see some of India's finest temples, with amazing sculptured figures of gods and goddesses. Other places of interest are the **Prince of Wales Museum,** near the Gateway, and the **Marine Drive,** ending at Chowpatty Beach. The **Babulnath Temple** overlooks the beach. Around the bay, Walkeshwar Road climbs to **Malabar Point,** where the **Raj Bhavan** (Governor's house) is situated near the 11th-century temple of the Sand Lord. Overlooking the sea are the **Hanging Gardens,** where the view is magnificent, and the **Kamala Nehru Park.** The **Jain Temple** stands on top of a ridge on Malabar Hill, while the famous **Mahalakshmi Temple** is perched on the water's edge. Also visit the **Jehangir Art Gallery,** the **Raja Bai Tower** of Bombay University Library (permission required), and, of course, one of Bombay's exhilarating shopping centers: **Colaba Causeway, Crawford Market, Mohata Market,** or **Jhaveri Bazaar,** the goldsmith and jewelry center.

Regional foods include *Sri-Khand* (sweet yoghurt), *Bhajias* (onions, potatoes, and edible leaves), the famous *Bombay Duck* (dried fish), and *Bombay Halwa* (a variety of sweets). Some recommended restaurants with dancing and floor shows are the **Apollo Room** (Taj Mahal Hotel); **Four Seasons** (Nataraj Hotel); the **Other Room** (Ambassador); **Little Hut** (Ritz); and **Talk of the Town** (Veer Nariman Road). Bombay also has a selection of Chinese restaurants including the **Golden Dragon** at the Taj Mahal Inter · Continental (tel: 243366) and the **Outrigger** at the Oberoi Towers (tel: 234343), where the average price for a meal for two will be Rs120-125. Others that top the list for quality and popularity are the **Nanking,** near the Gateway; the **Oriental** at the Centaur Hotel; and the **Gazebo,** Hill Road, Bandra—all in the Rs45-90 range for two meals.

Fascinating excursions out of Bombay are to **Kanheri National Park,** 28 miles away; the **Lakes of Bombay; Ambarnath,** with its beautiful 11th-century **Chalukyan Temple;** and **Karnala Wild Life Sanctuary** on the road to Goa. In the neighboring state of Gujarat to the north is **Sasangir,** famous for the only surviving Asiatic lions which now number 250. There is the **Sasangir Forest Lodge** (from US$19 double).

Goa, 250 miles south of Bombay, is one of the most colorfully exciting spots in the East. This tiny former Portuguese territory is bordered by 65 miles of palm-fringed sandy beaches and has regions of incredible beauty, towns with quaint Latin squares, Hindu temples, and marvelous cathedrals. The **Basilica of Bom Jesus,** with the tomb of St Francis Xavier, is a place of pilgrimage. On the bank of the Mandovi River lies **Panjim,** a pleasant base for your visit to Goa. You can stay at the **Hotel Mandovi,** PO Box 164 (from US$25 double). Or there is the **Fidalgo,** Swami Vivekanand Road, Panji (from US$31 double), **Fort Aguada Beach Resort,** Sinquerim (from US$50 double), **Lapaz,** Vasco da Gama (from US$19 double), and **Zuari,** Vasco da Gama (from US$15 double).

Madhya Pradesh in Central India is the second-largest state in the country. Its capital **Bhopal** lies on the shores of two enchanting lakes. You can stay at **Ramsons International,** Hamidia Road (from US$31 double). In the Chattarpur District see the magnificent temples of **Khajuraho,** profusely sculptured and decorated. The **Khajuraho Ashok** (from US$25 double) is 5 km from Khajuraho airport. No trip to India is complete without seeing the astonishing sculptures at **Ajanta** and **Ellora,** both in Maharashtra (easy to reach from Bombay or Aurangabad), with their rock-hewn temple caves dating back to the 2nd and 3rd centuries AD.

The South

Madras (population over 3 million) lies on the east coast of India. See the old moated **Fort St George,** the **Madras High Court Buildings,** the **Cathedral of San Thome,** and the Hindu temples of **Kapaleswarar** and **Parthasarathy.** The **National Art Gallery** on Pantheon Road has a fine display of South Indian bronzes. The **Marina** is one of the longest beaches in the world. About 35 miles from Madras are the ruins and beautiful sea bathing resort of **Mahabalipuram,** a showplace of 7th to 10th century BC Pallava dynasty architecture. There are cave temples and the famous "rathas," shrines cut from rock. The magnificent temple town of **Kanchipuram** is further inland, about 45 miles from Madras. The temples of Kailasanatha and Vaikunta Perumal are 1,200 years old—and Kanchipuram silks are world famous. Hotels in and near Madras:

Rates are in US$ for a double/twin room with bath or shower

  Chola Sheraton, 5 Cathedral Road (from $50), 2 miles from center city

  Connemara, Binny's Road (from $29), 1 mile from center city

  Dasaprakash, 50 Poonamallee High Road (from $14), 2 miles from center city

  Fisherman's Cove, Covelong Beach (from $35), 20 miles south of Madras

  Maris, 9 Cathedral Road (from $11), adjacent to Chola

  Savera, 23A Edward Elliots Road (from $29), 2 miles from center city

Sudarsan International, 12A Monteith Road (from $38), 1 mile from center city

Taj Coromandel, 5 Nungambakkam High Road (from $44), 2 miles from center city

Temple Bay, Ashok Beach Resort, Mahabalipuram (from $19), 35 miles from Madras

V.G.P. Golden Beach Resort, Injambakkam (from $16), near Mahabalipuram, 35 miles from Madras.

Hyderabad is the capital of the state of Andhra Pradesh; its notable buildings include the **Char Minar** with four minarets 180 feet high, the **Mecca Masjid** mosque, and the **Falukama Palace,** home of the Nizam. The **Salar Jung Museum** has some very beautiful jade. **Warangal,** 8 miles away, is famous for its carpets and cottons. In **Hanamakonda** there is a thousand-pillared temple with the black basalt figure of Nandi, the Sacred Bull of Siva. Hotels in Hyderabad:

Rates are in US$ for a double/twin room with bath or shower

Annapurna, Manpally Station Road (from $17)

Ashoka, Lakdi Ka Pul (from $14)

Asrani, 1-7-179 Mahatma Gandhi Road, Secunderabad, the twin city to Hyderabad (from $18)

Ritz, Hill Fort Palace (from $32)

Welcome Group Banjara, 13 Banjara Hills, (from $54)

Karnataka (Mysore) is a hilly and wooded state. See the huge **Gol Gumbuz** mausoleum in Bijapur, the 11th-century temple of **Chenna Kesava** at Belur, the wonderful carvings on the temples of **Halebid,** and the **Hoysala Temple** at Somnathpur. At Shravanabelagola is the 1,000-year-old giant **Jain statue of Lord Bahubalik,** visible over a distance of 26 km. For the Belur and Halebid temples and the Jain statue stay at nearby Hassan (**Hassan Ashok,** Bangalore-Mangalore Road, 185 km from Bangalore airport and 1 km from Hassan railway station, from US$18 double). For the Somnathpur Temple stay at Mysore at the **Krishnarajasagar** (from US$27 double) or **Lalitha Maham Palace,** the palace of the Maharajah (from US$24 double). Hotels in Bangalore:

Rates are in US$ for a double/twin room with bath or shower

Ashok, Kumara Krupa, High Grounds (from $35)

Bangalore International, 2A/2B Crescent Road, High Grounds (from $15)

Barton Court, Mahatma Gandhi Road (from $25)

East-West, Residency Road (from $32)

Harsha, 11 Venkataswamy Naidu Road, Shivajinagar (from $18)

West-End, Race Course Road, High Grounds (from $25)

On the western coast lies the state of **Kerala,** most famous perhaps for the **Kathakali** dance dramas. **Trivandrum,** an attractive little city near India's southernmost point, is known for its ivory work. You can stay at the **Belair,** 7 km from Kovalam Beach (from US$29). **Kovalam,** 6 miles from Trivandrum, has one of the world's most magnificent beaches. Stay at **Kovalam Beach Resort Hotel** (from US$35), or in palm tree-sheltered cottages on the beach at **Kovalam Grove Beach Cottages** (from US$29). There are boats for hire. The setting is paradise, but be prepared for slow service and a restricted menu at the **Kovalam Hotel** and the cottages.

Quilon has been a port since Phoenician times; from here you can explore the extensive backwaters of the state. Seventy miles to the east is the **Periyar Wildlife Sanctuary. Kanya Kumari** (Cape Comorin) is the southernmost tip of India. **Cochin** is the chief port of Kerala, has a scenic background of green fields, lakes, and lagoons, and is called the "Queen of the Arabian Sea." It has a 400-year-old synagogue belonging to a small and almost extinct Jewish community. Hotels in Cochin are the **Casino,** Willingdon Island (from US$11 double), **Malabar Hotel,** Willingdon Island (from US$22 double), and the **Sea Lord Hotel,** Shanmugham Road, Erna-kulam, near Cochin (from US$19 double).

SOURCES OF FURTHER INFORMATION

Pan Am, Chandralok Building, 36 Janpath, New Delhi; Taj Mahal Inter · Continental Hotel, Bombay, and any other Pan Am office around the world. **Government of India Tourist Offices:** 88 Janpath, New Delhi 1; 123 N Karve Road, Churchgate, Bombay 20; 4 Shakespeare Savani, Calcutta 16; 35 Mount Road, Madras 2, and other principal cities. Also at 30 Rockefeller Plaza, New York, NY 10020; Suite 204, 3550 Wilshire Boulevard, Los Angeles, CA 90010; Suite 1016, Royal Trust Tower, Toronto Dominion Center, Toronto, Ontario; 21 New Bond Street, London W1.

Indonesia

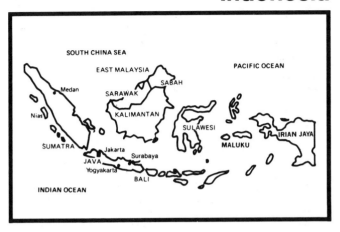

WHAT'S SPECIAL

Indonesia, the fabled East Indies land of more than 13,000 islands, is a country of infinite variety and intrigue. For those seeking something very different, it is a country well worth visiting.

Java, with some 90 million people, is the most heavily populated of the islands. It is graced with rice paddies and majestic volcanoes, and its history stretches back to "Java man," one of the oldest examples of *homo sapiens*. The "Outer Islands" are potentially some of the wealthiest regions of the world. There is densely forested Sumatra; Sulawesi, a mixture of modern and primitive cultures; Stone-age Irian Jaya; Kalimantan, or Indonesian Borneo, island of jungles, elephants, monkeys, and strange reptiles; and the myriad of fascinating smaller islands—Bali, island of the gods; Komodo, island of dragons and home of the world's largest lizards, which grow up to 10 feet in length; Nias, where the people still obey traditional laws based on a megalithic culture; Ambon, part of colorful Maluku (formerly called the Moluccas), glorious coral island with beautiful tropical beaches; and the famous Krakotoa, the volcanic island which erupted in 1883.

COUNTRY BRIEFING

Size: 735,268 square miles   **Population:** 148,085,000
Capital: Jakarta   **Capital Population:** 8,000,000

Climate: Tropical. Monsoons bring a wet season from November to March and a dry season from June to October. The best time to visit is the dry season, partly because it is more pleasant at this time and partly because this is the season of the festivities.

Weather in Jakarta: Lat S6°10'; Alt 26 ft

Temp (°F)	Jan	Feb	Mar	Apr	May	Jun	Jul	Aug	Sep	Oct	Nov	Dec
Av Low	74°	74°	74°	75°	75°	74°	73°	73°	74°	74°	74°	74°
Av High	84°	84°	86°	87°	87°	87°	87°	87°	88°	87°	86°	85°
Days no rain	13	11	16	19	22	23	26	27	25	23	18	17

Government: Indonesia is a republic with a president at its head.

Language: Indonesian is the official language, English the second. More than 300 languages and dialects are found throughout the archipelago.

Religion: Mostly Muslim; Bali is mainly Hindu.

Currency: Rupiah. 100 sen = 1 rupiah.

	R 25	R 50	R 100	R 500	R 1,000	R 5,000	R 10,000	R 20,000
US (dollars, cents)	.04	.08	.16	.79	1.59	7.95	15.89	31.78
UK (pounds, pence)	.02	.04	.08	.38	.76	3.80	7.59	15.19

Public Holidays:

Festivals abound in Indonesia; some of the holidays are listed below:

New Year's Day, 1 Jan

Good Friday

Maulid Nabi Muhammad (birth of Muhammad), date variable

Ascension Day

Waicak Day (celebrating birth of Buddha), date variable

Galunggan in Bali (a New Year feast lasting 10 days), 9 June

Sekaten (Hindu festival), date variable

Independence Day, 17 Aug

Idul Fitri (Muslim festival), date variable

Idul Adha (Muslim festival), date variable

Christmas Day, 25 Dec

HOW TO GET THERE

Flying time to Jakarta, Halim Perdanakusuma Airport from San Francisco is 18¼ hours; from Hong Kong, 4½ hours; from Singapore, 1 hour. Jakarta: GMT+7.

REQUIREMENTS FOR ENTRY AND CUSTOMS REGULATIONS

A valid passport endorsed with a tourist visa for 30 days and a round-trip ticket are required. A smallpox vaccination certificate is no longer required but cholera and yellow-fever certificates are necessary for those who have been in an infected area. It is recommended that antimalarial precautions be taken. No more than 2,500 Indonesian rupiahs (US$4) may be brought into the country or exported. No controls on foreign currency but no more may be taken out than was brought in. Electrical equipment and cameras may be noted on your passport by customs. Weapons, pornography, and narcotics are forbidden. Duty-free allow-

ance: 200 cigarettes or 50 cigars, and 2 pounds tobacco; 2 bottles liquor; a reasonable amount of perfume and gifts.

AIRPORT INFORMATION
Halim Perdanakusuma Airport is 7 miles from the center of Jakarta. The taxi fare from the airport is about 2700R. Departure tax is 2,000R for international flights, 1,000 for domestic flights. The airport for Bali is Ngurah Rai, near Denpasar. There are duty-free shops at both airports.

ACCOMMODATIONS
Apart from a few hotels of international standing in Jakarta, Bali, Surabaya, and Yogyakarta, the tourist will find it difficult to find acceptable accommodations. The best hotels to stay at are those built over the last five years or so. Less expensive accommodation is readily available but should be used with caution. Any travel agent or the **Jakarta Visitors' Information Center** (Jakarta Theater Building—tel: 364 093) will suggest suitable hotels. Rates shown below are exclusive of a 21% tax and service charge. Hotels in Jakarta, centrally located unless otherwise indicated:

Rates are in US$ for a double/twin room with bath or shower

Aryaduta Hyatt, Jalan Prapatan 44-46 (from $42)

BOROBUDUR INTER·CONTINENTAL, Jalan Lapangang Banteng Selatan (from $61)

Indonesia Sheraton, Jalan Thamrin (from $40)

Jakarta Hilton, Jalan Gatot Subroto, Senayan (from $63), 10 minutes from city center by taxi

Jakarta Mandarin, Jalan Thamrin (from $63)

Sahid Jaya, Jalan Sudirman (from $52), 5 minutes from city center by taxi

Sari Pacific, Jalan Thamrin (from $58)

USEFUL INFORMATION
Helpful Hints: Ensure that all your documentation for traveling in Indonesia is up to date and that all reservations for travel and accommodation are made in advance. Be very careful about food, and never drink tap water.

Banks: Open 8-12 Mon-Fri, 8-11am Sat. You can change your money in the larger hotels and at authorized money changers. All major towns have banks, and Jakarta has a number of international banks.

Mail: Stamps can be purchased at post offices, hotels, and some shops. Mailboxes are round and are painted red and yellow.

Telephone Tips: Hotels are the best places to use phones, although there are some public booths, coin operated. Useful numbers in Jakarta:

Pan Am, 371711   Directorate-General of
Tourism 348480

Newspapers: Some foreign newspapers are available; local English-language newspapers include the *Indonesian Observer* and *The Indonesia Times.*

Tipping: Tipping is not customary, although it is becoming increasingly common in the popular tourist hotels. Hotels usually charge 10% service, and some restaurants also add 10% to their bills. Even so, give the hotel chambermaid 100R a day, and tip your waiter about 150R. Tip for taxi drivers should be about 10% of metered fare; for porters, about 150R per piece of baggage.

Electricity: 220 volts 50 cycles AC in most hotels.

Laundry: The better hotels have efficient service.

Hairdressers: The most reliable are found at better hotels.

Photography: Film available in most cities.

Rest Rooms: Use rest rooms only at hotels and better restaurants. Women's, *Perempuan;* men's, *Laki Laki* or *Pria.*

Health: In Jakarta, best in case of illness is the Metropolitan Medical Center, located in Hotel Wisata International directly behind the Indonesia Sheraton. The Jakarta Visitors' Information Center can direct you to other English-speaking doctors and dentists. Pharmaceuticals can be purchased in any "apotik," particularly the state-owned Kimia Farma.

TRANSPORTATION

Surface transportation is not always easy. It is easier and quicker to fly, and Garuda Airlines can take you to most centers. There is train service in Java, but train and bus services tend to be uncomfortable, crowded, and unreliable. Air-conditioned buses may be hired for group travel at reasonable cost. Taxis are available in Jakarta but limited in other cities. If there is a meter, ask that it be used. If not, you'll have to bargain. Ask your hotel clerk for proper rates. The most reputable taxi in Jakarta is Bluebird (tel: 341 286), with door-to-door service. There are thousands of *becak* pedicabs around the cities. If you want to rent a car and driver it's easier to do so through the hotel, although you may have to bargain for the price. There are no self-drive cars available.

FOOD AND RESTAURANTS

Western cuisine is served in hotels. Eating Indonesian is a very spicy and tasty experience, and one of its most enchanting forms is the traditional *rijsttafel.* This features a bowl of steamed rice accompanied by numerous dishes of spiced meats, fish, vegetables, and sauces. *Sate,* consisting of slices of barbecued beef, lamb, pork, or chicken with a spicy sauce, is a delicate favorite. Try *soto,* the local soup, or *gadogado,* a mixture of vegetables cooked in a spicy peanut sauce; in Bali, the specialty is *babi guling,* delicious roasted pig. Tea and coffee are, of course, a real specialty of the islands.

There is a wide variety of places to eat in the main cities, but elsewhere the hotels usually offer the best cuisine. While in Jakarta try **Pemuda Restoran** across from the antique stalls on Jalan Surabaya for delicious fried shrimp, squid, and chicken (open evenings only), or the **Satay House Senayan** (Jalan Paku Buwono—tel: 715 821 or Jalan Kebon Sirih—tel: 346 237) for authentic Indonesian dishes in a pleasant setting. The **Oasis** (Jalan Raden Saleh 47—tel: 347 819) is the city's premier restaurant, with Western food served in an old colonial home. **Le Bistro** (Jalan Wahid

Hasyim 75—tel: 347 475) has French food and a cozy atmosphere. Also popular is the very contemporary **Bodega,** while the **Jaya Pub** (counter lunch style) appeals to the younger set. An outdoor Mexican restaurant, **The Green Pub,** is well advertised.

DRINKING TIPS

Liquor laws are not restrictive, and all imported liquors are available in tourist hotels. The three local beers (sold for about 1,000R per glass in major hotels) *Bintang, Anker,* and *San Miguel* are popular with visitors and cheaper than the imports. Some interesting rice and palm wines can be found in the outer provinces and in small stalls. They should be tried with caution because of the alcohol content.

ENTERTAINMENT

Indonesia is particularly noted for the charm of its dancers, puppets, and traditional drama and most Jakarta hotels will have monthly schedules of events. Traditional dances are held in a Balinese setting at the **Hilton Indonesian Bazaar** (Jalan Pintu Gelora V, tel: 583 051) nightly except Monday. Havanese dance drama is performed at the **Bharata Theater** (Jalan Kalileo 51, Pasar Senen) nightly except Monday. **Taman Ismael Marzuki or TIM** (Jalan Cikini Raya) is Jakarta's cultural center. Traditional and modern Indonesian dance, drama, and art can be seen here nightly.

There is horseracing at Jakarta's **Pulo Mas Racecourse** every Sunday. The **Ancol Dreamland Seaside Park** provides water sports, nightclubs, and a jai alai arena. The **Nirwana** at the Hotel Indonesia Sheraton is a popular nightclub, and the **Pit Stop** (Hotel Sari Pacific) and the **Oriental Club** (Jakarta Hilton) are lively discothèques. There is a casino on the top floor of the **Jakarta Theater.**

In **Bali** there is a dance for every occasion. While there you should witness the *Ketjak* (monkey dance) performed by over 200 people and held in the village of **Kuta Beach** weekly, as well as in outlying villages. While in **Yogyakarta,** go out to the temple at **Prambanan,** between the months of May and October, during the full moon, for the enchanting **Ramayana Ballet** staged on the site of the ancient temple. Movies are popular, though the censor tends to have a heavy hand.

SHOPPING

Indonesia is one of the best shopping countries of the Orient. The quality of crafts is very high. The handicrafts of Bali are the most famous—wood carvings, figurines in bone mounted on wood, intricately designed palm leaf fans. The specialities of Java are leather shadow puppets, dolls, Indonesian daggers (the delicately fashioned *kris* worked in silver), beautiful batiks, silverware, and crocodile and snakeskin leather goods. The best streets for shopping in Jakarta are **Palatehan I, Majapahit, Agus Salim, Jalan Surabaya,** and **Kebon Sirih Timur Dalam.** Recommended stores are the third floor of **Sarinah Department Store, Banuwati** (Java Boutique), **Pigura Arts & Gifts,** and **Wisma Nasional.** All the crafts of the islands can be found in Jakarta, though prices are generally lower in Bali or Yogyakarta. Be prepared to bargain (except at Sarinah), offering no more than a quarter of the initial price asked and settling, usually, at no more than half.

SPORTS

Indonesia has clubs offering the usual sports of golf, tennis, swimming, fishing, and various spectator sports. On the island of **Madura,** bull races are held on the first Sunday of September at **Bangkalan** and on the first Sunday of October at **Pamekasan.** Each team in the race has two bulls, colorfully decorated with bells and ornaments, and they pull sleds manned by jockeys. It is exciting, funny, and colorful. On **Bali,** there is a cockfighting arena in Denpasar which stages fights every Saturday and Sunday.

WHAT TO SEE

Java: Jakarta is not a particularly interesting city. However, visitors should visit the **National Museum,** which has a very fine collection of porcelain. The **Jakarta City Museum** houses relics of the Dutch colonial era. **Sunda Kelapa,** the sailing port, is near the City Museum and is worth a visit, as is **Mini-Indonesia,** a project which has houses and cultural artifacts from all the regions of Indonesia.

From Jakarta make the 40-mile trip to **Bogor** and be rewarded with the beautiful **Botanic Gardens.** This 275-acre showplace houses over 10,000 different species of tropical plants and is superbly landscaped. Near Bogor is the **Puncak** mountain region, the vacation playground of many Jakarta residents; the region abounds in hotels, pools, gardens, and golf courses. Also near Bogor is **Bandung,** a bustling city near the smoldering volcano, **Tangkuban Prahu.** Visitors can actually enter the mouth of the crater.

In central Java is the cultural center of Indonesia, **Yogyakarta.** Here you can find the finest batik in the country and beautiful leather goods and silverware. The best place to go shopping for these is the main street of **Malioboro.** Nearby is the **Sultan's Palace** with exquisitely embellished pavilions. Hotels to stay at are the **Sheraton Ambarrukmo-Palace** (from US$35 double) and the **Mutiara** (from US$28.30 double). Twenty miles northwest of Yogyakarta is majestic **Borobudur,** the largest Buddhist temple in the world.

East Java is less tourist-oriented than the west, a land of brooding cone-shaped volcanoes and tropical jungle. **Surabaya** is the provincial center, but one should also visit the **Penataran Temple** at Blitar, the 12th-century **Singosari Temple** near **Malang,** the **Majapahit** complex at **Mojokerto,** and the ruins of the first Muslim settlement from the 13th century. A delightful experience is to attend the **Candra Wilwatikta** amphitheater in **Pandaan,** 34 miles from Surabaya, which stages traditional dances in a glorious mountain setting. Performances take place from May to October on weekends when the moon is full. In Surabaya, stay at the **Hyatt Bumi** (from US$46 double).

Kalimantan, Sulawesi, and Irian Jaya have an abundance of exotic flora and fauna, and tours can be arranged through Jakarta travel agents, though the trip is likely to be rugged. Conditions are primitive and transport is difficult, while accommodation in these remote centers is generally in the form of rest houses. But for the traveler who wants to see birds of paradise in abundance, for instance, Irian Jaya is well worth a visit.

Sumatra is the home of wild animals such as the elephant, the rhinoceros, the famous Sumatran tiger, and the gibbon. Medan, the largest city in Sumatra, has Indonesia's largest mosque and the palace of the Sultan of Deli. Bukittinggi, 57 miles from Padang and located in one of the most beautiful parts of the whole of Indonesia, has a fine museum and zoological gardens.

Bali: Bali is one of the most hauntingly beautiful tourist spots in the world today. Its ancient and colorful traditions, temples, and ceremonies still resist the onslaught of the 20th century. So if you have time for only one stop in Indonesia, Bali should be that stop. It is a legend in itself. Denpasar is the center of Bali, but most hotels and restaurants are located in the tourist-oriented beach resorts at Sanur and Kuta. Hotels on Bali include the BALI BEACH INTER·CONTINENTAL, Sanur (from US$52 double); Bali Hyatt, Sanur (from US$51 double); La Taverna Bungalow, Sanur (from US$33 double); Bali Oberoi, near Kuta (from US$65 double); and the Legian Beach, near Kuta (from US$22 double). The beach at Kuta is especially lovely.

A visit to the Bali Museum will give you an idea of the quality and range of Balinese arts and crafts. It is worth visiting the museum before you purchase your souvenirs. Good places to shop are the Bali Art Foundation, C. V. Sura, or Pandy's, on Sanur Beach. In west Bali, places of interest are the monkey forest of Sangeh or the romantic temples of Tanah Lot, set on a cliff and overlooking the sea. In eastern Bali is the most holy of all temples—Pura Besakih, the mother temple, on the side of the sacred volcano, Mount Agung. In central Bali there's an elephant cave, the Peliatan palace of fine arts, holy temples, and, near some springs, a whole complex of temples and an old monastery.

SOURCES OF FURTHER INFORMATION

Pan Am, Hotel Borobodur Inter·Continental, Jalan Lapangang Banteng Selatan, Jakarta, and any Pan Am office around the world; Jakarta Tourist Information Center, Jakarta Theater Building, Jalan Thamrin, Jakarta; Directorate-General of Tourism, Jalan Kramat Raya 81, Jakarta; the Indonesian Consulate, 5 East 68th Street, New York, NY 10021; Indonesian Embassy, 38 Grosvenor Square, London W1.

Japan

WHAT'S SPECIAL

Japan is stunning and special. It has the power and influence of a continent, yet is a string of "offshore" islands. It can display the most neon-lit, skyscrapered, and expressway-lined face, yet find its inspiration in the quiet beauty of a small, formal rock garden. It can run its trains at lightning speed, yet spend hours on a small conversational courtesy. Perhaps you could call the Japanese "the professionals" in their own tradition. A picture, a play, a garden, a meal, even a judo match, all aim at graceful perfection, symmetry, or formal movement. But they will tackle an alien tradition with equal professionalism. In handling a camera, playing golf, running a symphony orchestra, or sorting out a traffic jam, they will rival anyone. Tokyo is the biggest, the most challenging, and perhaps the most expensive city in the world, yet it has an aboriginal village only an hour away.

COUNTRY BRIEFING

Size: 145,766 square miles   **Population:** 117,360,000
Capital: Tokyo   **Capital Population:** 11,608,000

   Climate: Since most of Japan lies in the North Temperate Zone, its climate may be likened to that of London, Paris, Seattle, or Portland. Spring and fall—the first blossom-scented, the second sunny and mild—are the ideal tourist seasons.

Weather in Tokyo: Lat N35°41'; Alt 19 ft

Temp (°F)	Jan	Feb	Mar	Apr	May	Jun	Jul	Aug	Sep	Oct	Nov	Dec
Av Low	29°	31°	36°	46°	54°	63°	70°	72°	66°	55°	43°	33°
Av High	47°	48°	54°	63°	71°	76°	83°	86°	79°	69°	60°	52°
Days no rain	26	24	21	20	21	18	21	22	18	20	23	26

Government: Japan's Emperor presides symbolically over a constitutional government.

Language: Japanese. English is spoken by many people in the tourist industry, but a phrasebook is an excellent investment (*Say it in Japanese* and the *Berlitz Translator* are among the best available in most book stores.) It is best to have a hotel clerk or someone write out names and addresses in Japanese characters.

Religion: Buddhism and Shintoism are the major faiths. There are also churches of all Christian denominations.

Currency: Yen. 110 sen = 1 yen.

	Y 10	Y 50	Y 100	Y 500	Y 1000	Y 5000	Y 10000	Y 20000
US (dollars, cents)	0.05	0.23	0.45	2.26	4.52	22.59	45.17	90.34
UK (pounds, pence)	0.02	0.11	0.22	1.08	2.16	10.80	21.59	43.17

Note: Care should be taken to distinguish between 10,000 and 5,000 yen bills, which look the same.

Public Holidays:

New Year, 1 Jan	Public Holiday, 4 May
Adult's Day, 15 Jan	Children's Day, 5 May
National Foundation Day, 11 Feb	Respect for the Aged Day, 15 Sept
Vernal Equinox Day, 20 or 21 Mar	Autumnal Equinox Day, 23 or 24 Sept
Emperor's Birthday, 29 Apr	Sports Day, 10 Oct
Constitution Memorial Day, 3 May	Culture Day, 3 Nov
	Labor Thanksgiving Day, 23 Nov

Holidays falling on a Sunday are celebrated the following Monday.

HOW TO GET THERE

Flying time to Narita Airport from New York is 13¾ hours; from Los Angeles, 11 hours; from London, 19½ hours; from Hong Kong, 3½ hours. Time in Japan: GMT+9.

REQUIREMENTS FOR ENTRY AND CUSTOMS REGULATIONS

US citizens entering Japan must have a valid passport and visa. Other nationals should inquire whether a visa is necessary. For stays of more than 61 days, apply for an Alien Registration Certificate. Round-trip tickets are required only for transit stays of 72 hours or less. Neither a smallpox vaccination certificate nor a cholera certificate is required. There are no restrictions as to how many yen a visitor may bring into the country; up to Y3 million in Japanese currency may be taken out. Leftover currency may be reconverted up to Y5 million without an official Record of Purchase, a document issued by the bank where the original exchange took place. One may not take out of the country any works of art officially designated as "national treasures." Duty-free allowance: 400 cigarettes or 100 cigars or 500 grams (1.1 pound) of tobacco; 3 bottles of liquor; 2 ounces of perfume. If you have friends in Japan, bear in mind that Scotch and cognac are extremely expensive, and take advantage of the allowance to bring some very welcome gifts.

AIRPORT INFORMATION

Narita is 41 miles from the city center. There is an airport limousine bus service to the Tokyo City Air Terminal (TCAT—tel: 665-7156) at Hakozaki (Nihonbashi) in central Tokyo with fare of Y2,300 for adults and Y1,150 for children and handicapped, luggage included. Buses leave every 5-15 minutes from 6am-8:40pm. Average time required between the airport and city is approximately 90 minutes. Taxis are plentiful but not recommended for the ride to downtown because they cost approximately Y12,000 (US$53). For those making connections to domestic flights at Haneda Airport, there is a limousine bus service available from 8am-6:20pm, frequency every 30 minutes. Fare is Y2,500 and the trip takes 1 hour 40 minutes. Japan's other principal international airport is Osaka. Airport limousine buses leave every 10 minutes from the Arrival Building for the 30-minute trip to downtown Osaka (fare: Y250), and every 20-30 minutes for the 60-minute trip to major hotels in Kyoto (fare: Y520). Taxis are available to downtown Osaka at about Y1,000 and to Kyoto at about Y2,500. Narita Airport has a duty-free shop, hotel reservation counter, and a tourist information center. If you're leaving Japan from Narita, save Y1,500 for the airport tax.

ACCOMMODATIONS

Nowhere does the traditional Japan meet the modern world so smoothly as in the hotel scene. Tokyo, Osaka, Kobe, Kyoto, and all large cities have modern Western-style hotels alongside the smaller, colorful Japanese inns which can be found all over the country. Of these, about 5,000 have become members of the **Japanese Ryokan Association**—a select network of immaculate hostelries where the kimono life is more than a figure of speech; and maid furnishes guests with this most beautiful and functional garment when they take possession of their room. *Ryokans* will also introduce foreigners to the relaxing delights of *ofuro*, or the Japanese bath. The average charge of JRA-member *ryokans* ranges from Y6,000 (US$28) and up (without bath) per person to Y8,000 (US$37) and up (with bath) per person. A 10% tax and 10-20% service charge (in lieu of tip) are normally added to the bill.

For the budget-minded, Japan offers a hotel system that welcomes visitors regardless of age or sex. More than 300 hostels—called *Kokumin Shukusha* or People's Lodges—are run by the government and charge from Y3,900 for a bed in dormitory-style accommodation, with breakfast and dinner included. For more information apply to the **Japan National Tourist Organization** offices, or call in Tokyo 437-5361. Another organization, the **International Youth Hostel Federation,** 1 2-chrome, Ichigaya, offers lodging to members of Youth Hostel Associations abroad. Charges here are about Y1,050 for a bed or Y2,100 with two meals.

Hotels in Tokyo:

Rates are in US$ for a double/twin room with bath or shower

Akasaka Tokyu, 2143 Nagata-cho, Chiyoda-ku (from $75)

Century Hyatt Tokyo, 2-7-2 Nishi Shinjuku, Shinjuku-ku (from $66)

Ginza Nikko, 8421 Ginza, Chuo-ku (from $59)

Ginza Tokyu, 9-5-15 Ginza, Chuo-ku (from $71)

Imperial, 1-1-1 Uchisaiwai-cho, Chiyoda-ku (from $97)

KEIO PLAZA INTER · CONTINENTAL, 2-2-1 Nishi Shinjuku, Shinjuku-ku, in the new Metropolitan Center complex (from $71)

Marunouchi, 1-6-3 Marunouchi, Chiyoda-ku (from $73)

Miyako, 1-1-50 Shiroganedai, Minato-ku (from $66)

New Japan, 2-13-8 Nagata-cho, Chiyoda-ku (from $80)

New Otani, 4 Kioi-cho, Chiyoda-ku (from $87)

Okura, 3 Aoi-cho, Akasaka, Minato-ku (from $97)

Pacific, 3-13-3 Takanawa, Minato-ku (from $75)

Palace, 1-1-1 Marunouchi, Chiyoda-ku (from $68)

Tokyo Hilton, 2-10-3 Nagata-cho, Chiyoda-ku (from $91)

Tokyo Prince, 3-3-1 Shiba Park, Minato-ku (from $71)

Unless otherwise indicated, the above hotels are centrally located.

Whether you choose hotel, hostel, or Japanese inn, reservations are strongly recommended.

USEFUL INFORMATION

Helpful Hints. To say that courtesy reigns supreme among the Japanese is to put it mildly. As you settle in, a few Japanese expressions out of a phrasebook will help; even more helpful will be a positive, cheerful attitude before the bland and self-effacing manner in which your questions may be answered. Remember that when he or she seems to be beating about the bush, your interlocutor is not being devious—this is simply being polite.

Banks: Open 9-3 Mon-Fri, 9-12 Sat. Money can also be changed in hotels, department stores, and duty-free shops, most of which will cash travelers' checks as well. Among the American banks with branches in Tokyo and Osaka are Chase Manhattan, Citibank NA, and Bank of America.

Mail: Sources of postage stamps other than post offices are stationery shops and cigarette kiosks, or any place that displays a red, double-crowned "T" on a white background. There are also special blue mailboxes that provide express service *(sokutatsu).*

Telephone Tips: Public telephones (red, pink, blue, and yellow) are found virtually everywhere in Japan. The automatic dial system is used in most cities. Insert a Y10 coin, wait for the tone, then dial. Local calls cost Y10 for the first 3 minutes; keep adding Y10 coins if you want to continue the call. The smaller red telephones are used only for local calls within the city; the larger red phones, and the pink, blue, and

yellow ones are convenient for long distance calls as well as local calls because they can take up to six to ten Y10 coins. (Yellow phones take up to nine Y100 coins, so they are very helpful for an expensive long distance call.) Excess coins will be returned. Blue phones can be used for dialing the operator, information, or any emergency number. Ask your hotel operator to place overseas calls. There is a 25% discount for Sunday calls to the US and Canada. Useful numbers in Tokyo:

Pan Am 240-8888

Police 110

Tourist Information Center 502-1461

Telegrams (overseas) 270-5111 (domestic) 115

Operator 0051

Information 104

Fire and Ambulance 119

Newspapers: Foreign newspapers, including many in English, are available in Tokyo. The city has four English-language dailies of its own: the *Asahi Evening News*, the *Japan Times*, the *Mainichi Daily News*, and the *Daily Yomiuri*.

Tipping: It is not the custom to tip in Japan, and, with few exceptions, a tip is given only for extras or out-of-the-way services. Exceptions include porters at airports and train stations, who are given Y200 per piece of luggage. These are charges, rather than tips. Rental-car drivers usually receive up to Y1000 per day. Taxi drivers are tipped only if they have rendered some special service—certainly if they have given a hand with the luggage. Restaurants and hotels add a 10-20% service charge to their bills, and their staff, including porters and hairdressers, require no tipping.

Electricity: 100 volts 50 cycles AC in the east, including Tokyo; 100 volts 60 cycles AC in the west including Osaka and Kyoto. In major hotels, you may find two outlets—one for 110 volts and one for 220 volts, or a converter may be available.

Laundry: Express-service laundry and dry-cleaning facilities available at major hotels. Shirts are almost always starched unless you specify otherwise—the phrase is *nori irranai*.

Photography: Equipment and film can be found in all Japanese cities. Color film can be developed in 3-4 days, black and white in 24 hours.

Clubs: In Tokyo there are branches of the Rotary Club (tel: 201-3888); Lions International (tel: 494-2931); Kiwanis (tel: 242-0637); YWCA (tel: 293-5421); YMCA (tel: 292-7421); American Club (tel: 583-8381).

Babysitting: Two agencies in Tokyo are the Tokyo Domestic Service Center (tel: 584-4769) and the Shibuya Employment Agency (tel: 463-9141). There is also a baby hotel in New Otani Hotel (tel: 265-1111); charge is Y15,000 per night.

Rest Rooms: Facilities can be found in department stores, restaurants, coffee shops, bars, etc., though the tourist should be warned that some are used for both sexes. *Toire* (or *O-te-arai*) is the general word.

Health: Many doctors and dentists speak English. There are imported pharmaceuticals in drugstores as well as excellent Japanese products. The water is safe and you can eat all the fresh fruit and vegetables you want.

TRANSPORTATION

Tokyo has a bus and subway service, though the uninitiated would do well to abstain during the unbelievably crowded rush hours. Both are, however, a quick and inexpensive way of getting about. You pay cash on public conveyances, with a minimum fare of Y80 or Y100 on the subway (there are private and municipal lines), Y110 on the bus. Books of tickets can be bought from the **Japan Travel Bureau** (1-1 Marunouchi, Chiyoda-ku, Tokyo).

Traffic is dense and drives on the left. Taxis are readily available—hail one in the street. No tipping unless, as said before, the driver has rendered some extra service.

Japan's railroads are among the finest in the world, with such showcase trains as the "bullet" super-express from Tokyo to Osaka and on to Hakata, which clips along at 130 miles an hour. The Japanese National Railway system (JNR) covers the entire country. JNR has a special rail pass allowing unlimited travel on all railroads (including the "bullet"). There are 2 kinds: 1st Class and Ordinary Class. The price of 1st Class for 7 days, Y30,000; 14 days, Y48,000; 21 days, Y66,000: for the Ordinary Class 7 days, Y21,000; 14 days, Y33,000; 21 days, Y44,000 (pass does not include sleeping cars). Children under 11 are ½ price. These passes can be purchased outside of Japan through your travel agent. JNR also runs its own ferry services linking Honshu to various other islands. There are three local airlines: Japan Airlines (JAL), All Nippon Airways (ANA), and Toa Domestic Airlines (TDA). There are also luxury cruises around the islands, the most popular being the Osaka-Beppu route through the Inland Sea, stopping at Kobe and several other ports. The 14-hour trip is sponsored by the Kansai Steamship Co Ltd. Car rental agencies are to be found in most large cities. Note that international drivers' licenses are valid in Japan. If you do not have an international license, then you must obtain a Japanese license at the Samezu Traffic Police Office, between Tokyo and Haneda Airport.

FOOD AND RESTAURANTS

Japanese food—an endless combination of simple ingredients served in dishes of all colors and shapes—is a delight for the eye as well as the palate. Preparation time is usually short, the flavor deriving from the deft use of vinegar, soy sauce, horseradish sauce, and other quick-acting condiments. Many dishes are, in fact, put together right at the table. The result is food that (though it can be "hot" in the best tradition—watch out for the green horseradish sauce) is light, greaseless, and wholesome.

The dish usually associated with Japan is, paradoxically, a relative newcomer to the country's cuisine. It is *sukiyaki*, which came into favor approximately a century ago when the Buddhist strictures against meat eating were relaxed. With a base of beef (cut into thin strips), it is a light, delicious meat-and-vegetable stew cooked in stock and flavored with soy sauce. Another favorite is *tempura*—prawns, fish, or vegetables deep-fried to golden perfection and served with a variety of dips. Rice is the Japanese staple par excellence and fish the traditional protein food. They combine in *sushi*, perhaps the most typically Japanese dish of all, which takes the form of rice patties topped by pieces of raw pickled fish. *Sashimi*, the raw-fish specialty that tops them all, consists of delicate fish fillets treated in soy or green horseradish sauce and garnished with vegetables.

Snack foods abound; chief among them is *soba*, a hearty, soup-like noodle dish sold in shops called *soba-ya*. Its variations are endless, all cooked in meat or fish broth and with bits of pork, beef, fish, egg, or vegetables swimming alongside the buckwheat pasta.

Prices vary considerably, reaching the top brackets in the *ryoriya* class, where the decor, ambiance, and service match the food. Dinner for one in a luxury establishment (Japanese and foreign) will cost around Y40,000 (US$200), in a medium-priced restaurant around Y10,000 (US$50), and in an inexpensive place about Y2400 (US$12), all prices without drinks. Foreign cuisine is to be found in abundance, especially in the Roppongi district, where French, Czech, and Greek restaurants do a lively business. For those wishing to go native in style, however, here is a brief and far from exhaustive list of the better *sukiyaki* and steak houses in Tokyo: **Akasaka Misono** (2-14-31 Akasaka, Minato-ku—tel: 583-3389); **Zakuro** (TBS Building, 5-3-3 Akasaka—tel: 582-6841); **Suehiro** (6-11-2 Ginza—tel: 571-9271); **Mansei** (6 Araki-cho, Shinjuku-ku—tel: 351-4789); **Mon Cher Ton Ton** (3-12-2 Roppongi, Minato-ku—tel: 402-1055). A good shop is **Otsuna**, also in the Roppongi section.

For *yakitori* (grilled, skewered chicken) try **Tatsumi** (2-7-8 Akasaka—tel: 585-0024). There are *tempura* places all over town; a medium-priced one is **Ten-ichi** (6-6-5 Ginza—tel: 571-1949). To vary the fare, try a Chinese restaurant, **China House** (2-24-3 Nishi-shimbashi—tel: 431-7371). For good French cooking try **Maxim's de Paris** (Sony Building, 5-3-1 Ginza, Chuo-ku—tel: 572-3621), one of Tokyo's most expensive restaurants.

DRINKING TIPS

Sake is the only typically Japanese drink. It is served hot as an aperitif, or it can take the place of white wine. But note that two small bottles—called *choshi*—are more than enough to complement a meal and lift your spirits to a prudent cruising altitude. Imported wines and soda will cost Y900 (US$4.25) and up. Ordinary domestic wine (some Japanese brands are quite palatable) cost Y800 (US$4.25) to Y2,000 (US$9-10) a bottle. A French wine, on the other hand, may cost as much as Y25,000 (US$118).

Drinks may be served up to about midnight, and there are bars and drinking places to suit all tastes. The **Starlight Lounge** at the Okura Hotel is one of many elegant hotel bars in Tokyo—with a superb view of the city into the bargain. Down on the Ginza is **Gin-Pari** (tel: 571-0085), in the Chuo Shintaku Building, livened with French chansonniers. At **L'Ambre** in Shinjuku (1-15-13 Kabuki-cho, Shinjuku-ku—tel: 200-1971) is a Nocturne Club with Chopin, Beethoven, and Mozart records playing

in the background. **Tact** (6-9 Ginza—tel: 571-3939) has bands of various kinds from rock music to Hawaiian. For a jukebox-and-hostesses evening, try the **New Yorker** at Shinbashi (tel: 580-0098), and for simple Japanese-style ambiance, go to **Wakamatsu** (Ginza Coa Building, 5-8 Ginza, Chuo-ku—tel: 571-1672).

ENTERTAINMENT

In a city the size of Tokyo, entertainment comes in a multitude of packages. Visitors will have to budget their time well and wisely—the scene is lively in the extreme. The performing arts will, of course, call for the most careful planning, with a check of the daily papers as to what's playing and when (curtain time can be anywhere between 4 and 6pm), plus, in the case of *Kabuki* and the *Noh* drama, a bit of boning-up on the background of these exquisite theatrical experiences. *Kabuki* is to Japan what Shakespeare's works are to Britain, Schiller's to Germany, or Lope de Vega's to Spain—the nation's cherished classical theater, preserved in all its purity for the delight of succeeding generations. Sing-song recitative, dancing, beautiful costumes, stylized makeup, and elaborate sets make it a unique spectacle as staged in several Tokyo theaters, chief among them the **National Theater** and the **Kabukiza.**

The *Noh* plays, seven centuries old and even more stylized, are opera-like pieces in which the actors often wear masks. Three drums and a flute provide the music for the simple allegorical tales, which are spun on a plainly decorated stage. *Noh* may be seen in a number of Tokyo theaters, including the **National Theater;** for programs check the daily papers, and for tickets apply at the box office or department store ticket bureaus. *Bunraku* or puppet plays complete the Japanese theatrical treats. Like the *Kabuki* and *Noh* dramas, they are performed at the ultramodern **National Theater** (4-1 Hayabusa-cho, Chiyoda-ku—tel: 265-7411).

Those who have been exposed to the growing stream of Japanese conductors and instrumentalists who perform in the West will not be surprised at the scope and quality of the concert-going in Tokyo and Osaka. There are no less than 8 symphony orchestras in the capital itself, among them the **Tokyo Metropolitan Symphony** and the **Yomuri Nippon Symphony,** which perform at the **Metropolitan Festival Hall.** Opera and ballet companies appear regularly at the **Metropolitan Festival Hall** and the **Hibiya Hall.** Films, another artistic export of the country, can be seen with both Japanese and English soundtracks.

The nightlife is just as lively as that of New York or Paris and can be extremely expensive. Duly warned, therefore, a nightclub-cum-cabaret set-up to try is the **Golden Gessekai** (3-10-4 Akasaka—tel: 584-1151). The **Copacabana** (3-6-4 Akasaka—tel: 585-5811) offers music and a floor show, with cover charge of Y4000. At the **Crown** (5-6-13 Ginza—tel: 572-5511), you'll find the same amenities and similar prices. The well known **Passatempo** is at the Roppongi Crossing, and **Club Morena,** which has a restaurant, is also in that lively district. **J & R** is a lively discothèque in the building of its name (5-4-9 Ginza—tel: 572-7381). **Mugen** is another swing-ing disco where you can dance until midnight (3-8-17 Akasaka—tel: 584-4481). The hours are late in nightspots in the **Ginza, Shinjuku** (which has the longest nights), **Roppongi,** and **Akasaka** sections.

SHOPPING

The wide choice of Japanese goods abroad will suggest, to some extent, the stocks that lie in store back home in Tokyo. Nor are Japanese goods limited to assembly-line products; folk crafts, paintings, and sculpture are there too for the imaginative shopper and memento-hunter. In gen-eral terms, the best buys will be cameras and hi-fi equipment (and the best discount area for these is around the **Akihabra Station** on the Keihin-tohoku Line), clocks, watches, lacquerware, porcelain, ivory, pearls (Y3,500 up), *cloisonné* objects and jewelry, kimonos of all types, and contemporary paintings and sculptures (there are 300 art galleries in Tokyo). Gifts for under US$12 might take the form of a lacquered candy bowl (Y2,000 up), a *cloisonné* brooch for Y2,000, fans from Y1,500 up, and paper goods ranging from paper wallets (Y1,000) to lanterns (Y2,500). Department store hours are 10-6; closed on different days; smaller shops may open at 9.

There are many large stores such as **Ise tan** (13-14 Shinjuku), open 10-6 and closed Wednesdays. Quality clothing and accessories are to be found in this large store, which even has a children's playground on the roof. Its fine arts department on the seventh floor of the main building has beautiful woodblock prints, and the basement boasts an enormous food section. There are fashions for all ages and sizes (they carry larger-than-Japanese wear for Western men). **Nippondo Tokei** (5-7-5 Ginza) has watches galore. **Ando Cloisonné Co Ltd** (5-6-2 Ginza) has beautiful samples of this artistic craft in brooches, vases, cigarette lighters, etc., ranging in price form Y2,000 to as much as a million yen. **Mitsukoshi** (1-7-4 Nihonbashi-Muromachi) is one of Tokyo's largest department stores and its most conservative one, highly favored by the Japanese, closed Monday. **Takashimaya** (2-4-1 Nihonbashi), closed Wednesday, is as large as Mitsukoshi. **Matsuya** (3-6-1 Ginza, Chuo-ku), open 10-6, closed Thursdays, has an excellent housewares department and folk art section. **Hayashi** is the best-known kimono center. It has three branches, one at the Hilton and two in the International Arcade (4-2 Yuraku-Chuo, Chiyoda-ku).

SPORTS

There are abundant golf courses (over 650), tennis, and swimming, though you may need an introduction to the many private clubs. Mountaineering, as might be expected in a country with such rugged topography, ranks high in the Japanese sporting world. Skiing is practiced with enthusiasm in Northern Honshu—**Akakura** and **Shiga Heights** have excellent facili-ties, as have the slopes around **Mount Madarao** near Nagano—and espe-cially in **Hokkaido,** center of all snow sports and site of the 1972 Winter

Olympic Games. **Tenguyama Ski Resort** near Otaru is one of the region's 16 skiing grounds, most of which have lifts and T-tows. For hunting enthusiasts, there are various national hunting grounds set aside by the Government, and rivers offer good fishing throughout the year. In Tokyo, you can watch judo at the **Kodokan Judo Hall** (1-16-30 Kasuga, Bunkyoku—tel: 811-7151). Instruction is also available. Karate training is given at the **Kokusai Karatedo Renmei** (3-3-9 Nishi-Ikeburuko, Toshima-ku—tel: 984-7421) and at the **Nippon Karate Kyokai** (1-6-1 Ebisu-Nishi, Shibuya-ku—tel: 462-1415).

The great spectator sport of *sumo* takes place during a series of 15-day tournaments six times a year. You can see *sumo* three times a year in Tokyo at **Kuramae Kokigikan** in January, May, and September. This traditional Japanese wrestling between giants in loincloths is not to be missed by addicts of the manly art of self-defense in *all* its exotic manifestations. The **KK** is at 2-1-9 Kuramae, Taitoku (tel: 851-2201).

WHAT TO SEE

Tokyo: This is the world's largest city and perhaps the fastest-paced. There are blocks of office buildings as far as the eye can see, expressways, traffic jams, rush-hour mobs in subways and buses. But this modern face, if striking, is only half the picture. Underlying Tokyo's asphalt jungle exterior are layers of history and unchanging tradition. At the heart of the city is the **Emperor's Palace,** set in 250 acres of landscaped grounds and surrounded by a labyrinthine moat. It stands on the site of a 15th-century castle, as remote and serene as any fortress out of Japan's feudal past. Nearby is the **Diet Building,** home of the nation's Parliament; to the east, across **Hibiya Park**—ablaze with chrysanthemums in November—stretches the bustling **Ginza** district, lined with restaurants and smart shops.

From the **Tokyo Tower** you will get a superb view of the city, whose **Meiji Shrine** and **Ueno Park** are musts on the excursion list. The first is a pilgrimage center which, though built in the purest Shinto style, dates only from 1920, having been erected in memory of the Emperor Meiji, grandfather of the present sovereign. In the **Iris Garden,** considered the finest in Tokyo, there are 1,000 varieties of the flower in late May. The **Meiji Shrine Outer Gardens** are close by. Also known as the **Olympic Park,** they are the site of the enormous **National Stadium,** two baseball parks, the **Memorial Picture Gallery.** More than a playground, **Ueno Park** is a vast cultural and artistic complex. Sharing its acreage with temples and shrines are the **Art Academy, Metropolitan Festival Hall, Tokyo National Museum, Fine Art Gallery, Tokyo University of Arts, National Science Museum,** the **Museum of Western Art,** and the city's zoo.

Honshu: Tokyo is located on Honshu, the largest of four islands that make up Japan and considered its mainland. It has an area a little larger than that of Great Britain and contains 34 of the country's 47 prefectures. Mountains abound in the central zone, from the peaks of **Nikko National Park** to the scenic **Fuji** district. Stretching across this region are the major cities of Osaka, Yokohama, and Nagoya, and other places rich in history, art, and architecture.

Nikko: There is an old Japanese adage that runs: "Never say *kekko* (splendid) until you have seen Nikko." It could not be more true. In this Alpine region 93 miles north of Tokyo is found some of the finest religious architecture of the Japanese people. Chief among these treasures is the 18th-century **Toshogu Shrine,** vermilion-lacquered and decorated with intricate carving. Sharing Toshogu's idyllic setting in the Nikko National Park are the **Rinnoji Temple,** the **Futaarasan Shrine,** the elaborate **Daiyuin Mausoleum,** a five-story pagoda, and other monuments to Buddhist piety. A drive to **Lake Chuzenji** along the twisting Irohazaka Highway will reveal spectacular panoramas of this mountain, whose **Kegon Waterfall** and **Dragon's Head Cascade** should not be missed.

Yokohama: As Japan's leading port, Yokohama (population 2.8 million) is the gateway to the nation. It has many attractions of its own, among them the **Sojiji Temple and Monastery,** one of the largest Buddhist centers in Japan. The city's **Sankeien Gardens** are also worth a visit; laid out in the classic Japanese style, they enclose a graceful pagoda, the **Rinshunkaku Hall**—a fine example of domestic architecture of the feudal era—and the **Choshukaku Pavilion,** a ceremonial teahouse also dating from the 17th century. No visit to the Yokohama area would be complete without a trip to the **Kamakura,** if only for a look at its famed *Daibutsu* or Great Buddha. This magnificent 13th-century statue, 39 feet high and 96 feet in circumference, portrays the great master in prayerful repose. Hotels in Yokohama: **Hotel Empire,** 700 Matano-cho, Totsuka-ku (from US$57 double); the **Yokohama Prince,** 3-13-1 Isogo, Isogo-ku (from US$57 double); and the **Hotel New Grand,** 10, Yamashita-cho, Naka-ku (from US$54 double).

Izu-Hakone-Fuji: Another great national park stretches southeast of Yokohama to embrace the regions of Izu, Hakone, and Fuji. **Izu** is a rugged peninsula with a great many hot springs and numerous spas. **Hakone,** another great resort area, is the site of the largest open-air museum of modern sculpture in the world. There is a motor boat and catamaran service across the lake, known as **Lake Ashi** to the Japanese. But perhaps the most famous lakes of the region are Fuji's five, ranged in a perfect semicircle around the Sacred Mountain, **Mt Fuji.** The majestic, 12,388-foot peak is shrouded in snow most of the year. To have seen it is, in a very real sense, to have seen Japan's loftiest symbol. Hotels in the Fuji Lakes area: **Fuji View Hotel,** 511 Katsuyama-Mura, Minamitsuru-gun (from US$61 double); the **Mt Fuji Hotel,** 1360-83 Lake Yamanaka (from US$71 double); and the **New Yamanaka Hotel,** 352-1 Lake Yamanaka (from US$71 double, with an extra charge from 28 Apr-5 May, 20 July-31 Aug, 30 Dec-5 Jan).

Kanazawa: If Fuji is a must for the visitor whose time in Japan is short, Kanazawa in northwestern Honshu offers a rewarding side trip for those who can travel farther for a close look at some beautiful relics of the nation's feudal past. The town, which grew around its own beautiful castle, has streets lined with ancient samurai dwellings, a *Noh* theater, and small shops selling the dolls and ceramics for which the district is famous. Its **Kenrokuen Park,** adjacent to the castle, is considered one of the three most beautifully landscaped gardens in all Japan.

Nagoya-Ise: Modern, industrial, and busy, Nagoya lies between Tokyo and Osaka and with those cities is part of Japan's commercial core. Over it rises its stately 17th-century castle, reconstructed after the war and open to the public. From Nagoya excursions go out to the Shinto shrines of **Ise Jingu,** built in the simplest ancient Japanese style, and traditionally razed every 20 years to be replaced by new ones (the last reconstruction took place in 1973). The Ise area is also known for an unusual industry; it was at Toba Harbor that Kokichi Mikimoto first grew cultured pearls. In **Mikimoto Island** the visitor can see the oyster beds and watch women divers retrieving gems from the depths of the sea. Hotels in Nagoya: **International Hotel New Nagoya,** 3-23-3 Nishiki, Naka-ku (from US$47 double); **Nagoya Castle Hotel,** 1-15 Hinokuchi-cho, Nishi-ku (from US$57 double); and the **Nagoya Miyako,** 2 Nishiyangi-cho, Nakamura-ku (from US$52 double).

Nara: Designated the first permanent capital of Japan in the year 710, Nara, 15 miles from Osaka, has the lion's share of the nation's most ancient and venerable architecture. Among its features are the **Kofukuji Temple,** founded in the 7th century, the charming **Kasuga Shrine** with its 3,000 lanterns, a five-story pagoda that is the second highest in the country, a **National Museum** with an excellent collection of ancient swords, and the **Todaiji Temple,** which houses the country's largest Buddha, cast in the 8th century and towering 53 feet high. **Nara Park** is a deer sanctuary where the animals, unbelievably tame, roam freely among the cedars, wisteria, and oaks of an enchanting forest. In Nara, stay at the **Nara Hotel,** 1096 Takabatake-cho, Nara City (from US$49.50 double).

Osaka: With a population of 3 million, Osaka is, after Tokyo, the leading metropolis of Japan. It is a trading city par excellence, built on the bay of its name and crisscrossed by canals. Its theaters, nightclubs, and department stores—which cluster around the **Umeda** district—can compare with those of the nation's capital. Among its tourist attractions are **Osaka Castle,** built in the 16th century by the warrior Hideyoshi Toyotomi, the **Temmangu Shrine,** established in the 10th century, and the **Shitennoji Temple** (or *Teenoji* for short), whose foundation dates back to the 6th century. Osaka is known for its many *Kabuki* and *Noh* theaters and was the birthplace of the classic puppet plays or *Bunraku.* In summer the city is the setting for Japan's leading music festival. Hotels in Osaka: *Rates are in US$ for a double/twin room with bath or shower*

    Hanshin, 2-3-30 Umeda, Kita-ku (from $50)

    New Hankyu, 38 Kobuka-cho, Kita-ku (from $44)

    Osaka Grand, 2-22 Nakanoshima, Kita-ku (from $52)

    Osaka Royal, 2-1 Tamae-cho, Kita-ku (from $80)

    Osaka Tokyu, 7-20, Chaya-machi Kita-ku (from $58)

    Plaza, 2-2-49 Oyodo Minami, Oyodo-cho, Oyodo-ku (from $71)

    Toyo, 3-16-19 Toyosaki Nishi-dori, Oyodo-ku (from $61)

    Kyoto: In the course of its 10 centuries as the capital (794-1868), Kyoto gathered unto itself such treasures of art, architecture, and landscaping that it has become synonymous with the very spirit of Japan. Its streets are a succession of mansions, temples, and shrines, presided over by the Emperor's ancient palace (still used on ceremonial occasions). Among its 1,500 Buddhist temples is the **Nishi Honganji**, a small city in itself complete with libraries, exquisitely decorated pavilions, two *Noh* stages, and gardens with mirror-like ponds. **Nijo Castle**, another former residence of the Imperial Family, is a moated 17th-century structure. For a model of a Japanese rock garden—a veritable masterpiece of raked sand and stone—see the one outside the **Ryoanji Temple**, or the one by the **Nanzenji Temple**. Hotels in Kyoto: **Fujita**, Nishizume, Nijo-Ohashi, Nakagyo-ku (from US$66 double); **International**, 284 Nijo-Aburanokoji, Nakagyo-ku (from US$66); **Kyoto**, Oike, Kawara-machi, Nakagyo-ku (from US$64); and the **Miyako**, Sanjo Keage, Higashiyama-ku (from US$57).

Kobe: This is a beautifully sheltered port on the scenic Inland Sea. Its rotating **Port Tower** will give the best view of the city, the harbor, and the beautiful backdrop of the **Rokko Mountain Range**. Kobe's **Ikuta Shrine**, another bright vermilion gem, is under the tutelage of the goddess Wakahirume-no-Mikoto, patroness of the city. On the outskirts is the beach of **Suma**, with a large sports complex and an excellent aquarium. Hotels in Kobe: the **Kobe International**, 8-1-6 Goko-dori, Fukiai-ku (from US$59 double); the **Oriental**, 25 Kyomachi, Ikuta-ku (from US$57 double); and the **New Port**, 7 Hamabe-dori, Fukiai-ku (from US$52 double).

Kurashiki: This quiet town off the obvious tourist track is a miniature industrial city and an art center of note. At the **Ohara Art Gallery** you can see works of El Greco, Corot, Rodin, Gauguin, and Picasso. The **Kurashiki Folkcraft Museum** shows some 3,500 samples of Japanese craftsmanship, including rugs, textiles, pottery, and bamboo ware. There is an archaeological museum, and a historical museum specializing in 12th-century objects, from musical instruments to household utensils.

Hiroshima: The city that passed into modern history as the first target of the atom bomb has been completely rebuilt, from its ancient castle to its tranquil **Shukukeien Garden**. Its most famous landmarks are the memorials to the holocaust of 1945: the **Atomic Bomb Memorial Dome**, the **Peace Memorial Park** and **Peace Memorial Hall**, and the **Cenotaph for the Victims**.

Inland Sea: This is the long, narrow body of water between Honshu and Shikoku. A cruise among its pine-covered islands—there are nearly 600 of them—is one of the most beautiful trips-within-a-trip of any visit to the Far East.

In the spring the **Island of Shikoku**, south of Honshu, attracts thousands of Buddhist pilgrims in their traditional white garments to its 88 Buddhist temples, all of them founded by, or associated with, the 8th-century priest Kukai.

Takamatsu: Gateway to Shikoku, the city of Takamatsu offers the tourist in its exquisite **Ritsurin Park** a fine example of the Japanese art of harmonizing forest, fountains, and boulders. Until the reaccession of Okinawa, the island of **Kyushu** was the southernmost Japanese territory. It is considered the birthplace of the country's civilization, having served in the 7th century BC as base of operations for the Emperor Jimmu, founder of the Yamato Court in Nara. Given its proximity to the Asiatic mainland, Kyushu has always figured prominently in Japanese history as the hub for trade with Korea and China.

Nagasaki: During the centuries of Japan's isolation, Nagasaki remained the nation's only contact with the outside world, and even before the bamboo curtain descended about the country, the city was open to Chinese influence. Both its **Kodaiji** and **Sofukuji Temples** are known as "Chinese Temples"; the first served Chinese residents of the city, while the second (also founded in the 17th century) reflects the Chinese architecture of the Ming Dynasty. A victim of the atomic age like Hiroshima, Nagasaki has its own **Peace Park,** laid out on the exact spot where the explosion occurred on 9 August 1945.

Northern Honshu and **Hokkaido** are Japan's Far North and the nation's great outdoors. The northeastern portion of Honshu Island—or Tohoku district—is a land of lakes, mountains, and spas. Across the Tsugaru Strait lies Hokkaido, famous for its snow country and the winter sport facilities which made it the site of the '72 Olympics' skiing, skating, and tobogganing events.

Aomori: The gate to Hokkaido is set among apple orchards. Lumber is its principal industry and the charming *Kokeshi* dolls, carved in wood, one of its traditional crafts. The **Lake Towada** region, a national park, lies directly south. The S-shaped crater lake with its wooden shores and pine-covered islands is stocked with trout and favored by fishermen in the summer months.

Sapporo: A neat city of over 1 million and the center for the 1972 Winter Olympics, it has a university, botanical gardens, and the **Ainu Museum** among its chief tourist attractions. The latter is of special interest for the light it sheds on the fast-diminishing *Ainu,* a people of Japan's Far North said to have no racial affinity with the rest of the Japanese. Though as an ethnic group they are now largely integrated, there are still Ainu villages in Hokkaido where this unusual remnant of the country's prehistoric past maintains its customs and primitive way of life. Their ancient snow country is today marked out with ski lifts, skating rinks, and other amenities for lovers of winter sports.

On 15 May 1972, the **Ryukyu Islands** reverted to Japan after more than 20 years under US administration. **Okinawa** is the largest, and in regaining it, Japan has added a subtropical paradise to its already varied geography; sunbaked beaches and lush vegetation are the features of the archipelago, whose people sprang from a mixture of South Sea Island and Oriental blood. Among the features of **Naha,** the capital, is the reconstructed **Shuri Castle,** which has been turned into **Ryukyu University;** its Gate of Courtesy, or *Shurei-no-mon,* dates from the 16th century. A complete restoration has also been accomplished in the **Sogenji Temple,** burial place of Okinawa's kings. The island's beaches are perfect for swimming and deep-sea diving, and its **Underwater Observatory** will delight young and old.

SOURCES OF FURTHER INFORMATION

Pan Am: Kokusai Bldg, No. 1-1, Marunouchi 3-Chome, Chiyoda-ku, Tokyo; 4-1-4 Honmachi, Higashi-ku, Osaka, and any Pan Am office around the world; the **Japan National Tourist Organization,** 2-10-1 Yuraku-cho, Chiyoda-ku, Tokyo; 45 Rockefeller Plaza, New York, NY 10020; 333 North Michigan Avenue, Chicago, IL 60601; Commerce Street, Dallas, TX 75201; 1737 Post Street, San Francisco, CA 94115; 624 South Grand Avenue, Los Angeles, CA 90017; 2270 Kalakaua Avenue, Honolulu, HI 96815; 165 University Avenue, Toronto M5H 3B8 Ontario, Canada.

Malaysia

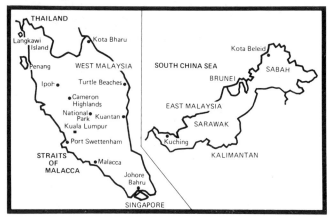

WHAT'S SPECIAL

Geographically Malaysia is two places—the peninsula of Malaysia and the northwestern area of Borneo made up of the states of Sabah and Sarawak. In human terms, however, it is a whole collection of fascinating places—deep impenetrable jungle and rubber plantations, marvelous sandy and secluded beaches, and rugged mountains topped with cool hill stations that seem to have been shipped from England complete with pubs, cottages, pines, and misty golf courses. There are great dredges mining the land of tin; fine bustling cities of mosques, temples, and modern buildings; hot, steamy ports where you can relive the world of Conrad, with rusty steamers plying for rubber, tin, timber, and pepper; and the villages of the Sea Dayaks, with houses on long stilts. There are Malays and Chinese, Indians, Kadazans, Muruts, Ibans, Bidayuhs, and Europeans, all with independent traditions yet bustling together to make this one of the richest and most colorful countries in Southeast Asia.

COUNTRY BRIEFING

Size: 127,316 square miles   **Population:** 13,435,588
Capital: Kuala Lumpur   **Capital Population:** 937,875
    Climate: Although near the equator, Malaysia does not suffer extremes of heat. Days are sunny and humid, the nights reasonably cool. Monsoon weather affects most of the country during the winter; Sarawak and Sabah can be very wet between November and January. The best time to visit is March to October.

Weather in Kuala Lumpur: Lat N3°07′; Alt 127 ft

Temp (°F)	Jan	Feb	Mar	Apr	May	Jun	Jul	Aug	Sep	Oct	Nov	Dec
Av Low	72°	72°	73°	74°	74°	73°	72°	73°	73°	73°	73°	72°
Av High	90°	92°	92°	91°	91°	91°	90°	90°	90°	89°	89°	89°
Days no rain	17	14	14	10	15	17	19	17	13	11	10	13

Government: An independent elective constitutional monarchy.

Language: Bahasa Malaysia (Malay) is the national and official language, with English widely used in commerce and industry. Many dialects of Chinese are spoken.

Religion: Most Malays are Muslim and most Chinese are Buddhists.

Currency: Malaysian ringgit. 100 sen (sign: ¢) = 1 Malaysian Ringgit (sign:$)

	10¢	50¢	M $1	M $5	M $10	M $50	M $100	M $500
US (dollars, cents)	.04	.21	.43	2.14	4.28	21.42	42.84	214.20
UK (pounds, pence)	.02	.10	.21	1.02	2.05	10.24	20.47	102.37

Public Holidays: Chinese, Hindu, and Muslim holidays vary from year to year according to the phases of the moon. Chinese and Hindu dates always occur within the same general period each year, while the Muslim dates each year occur 10 days earlier than the year before.

Mouloud, Jan 8-9
Chinese New Year, Jan 25
Labor Day, May 1
Wesak Day, May
Birthday of Yang di- Pertuan,
  June
Hari Raya Puasa,
  Aug 12-13
National Day, Aug 31
Deepavali, Oct
Hari Raya Haji, Oct 20
Christmas, Dec 25

HOW TO GET THERE

Flying time to Kuala Lumpur's Subang Airport from San Francisco is 18 hours; from Bangkok, 1¾ hours; from Singapore ¾ hour. Time in Kuala Lumpur: GMT+7 hours 30 minutes.

REQUIREMENTS FOR ENTRY AND CUSTOMS REGULATIONS

Passport; cholera and yellow-fever certificates if coming from an infected area. Import of Malaysian currency must not exceed M$10,000, and export must not exceed M$5,000. Passengers entering with currency over US$60 or its equivalent should declare this on arrival, to avoid difficulty on departure. Permits needed for plants and firearms. Duty-free allowance: 200 cigarettes or 50 cigars or ½ pound of tobacco; 1 quart each of liquor, malt beverages, and wine.

AIRPORT INFORMATION

Subang International Airport is 14 miles from Kuala Lumpur. Airport buses, running half-hourly between 7am and 11pm, cost M50¢ (M25¢ for children). The taxi fare to town is M$12. Subang has a duty-free shop and a hotel reservation counter. Airport departure tax is M$7.

ACCOMMODATIONS

In Kuala Lumpur and the larger cities, good hotels with air-conditioned rooms are always in demand and should be reserved well in advance. Government rest houses, found in most towns, are simple but clean and comfortable, and cost around M$17 for a room. Some hotels offer 10-20% reductions in off-peak season. The Malaysian Tourist Development Corporation, at Wisma MPI, Kuala Lumpur, or Subang Airport, Kuala Lumpur, will provide assistance. Hotels in Kuala Lumpur and on Penang Island:

Rates are in US$ for a double/twin room with bath or shower

Casuarina Beach Hotel, Batu Ferringgi Beach, on northern tip of Penang, about 10 miles from downtown Georgetown (from $36)

Century, 32-34 Jalan Klang, Kuala Lumpur (from $23)

Eastern & Oriental, 10/12 Farquhar Street, Georgetown, Penang (from $35.50)

Equatorial, Jalan Sultan Ismail, Kuala Lumpur (from $51)

Federal, 35 Jalan Bukit Bintang, Kuala Lumpur (from $50)

Holiday Inn, Jalan Pinang, Kuala Lumpur (from $47.80)

Jaya Puri, 2 Jalan Barat, Petaling Jaya, 5 miles from Kuala Lumpur (from $45.45)

Kuala Lumpur Hilton, Jalan Sultan Ismail, Kuala Lumpur (from $63.35)

Malaya, 162 Jalan Cecil, Kuala Lumpur (from $63)

Mandarin, 202-A Macalister Road, Georgetown, Penang (from $17)

Merlin, Jalan Sultan Ismail, Kuala Lumpur (from $43)

Merlin, 25-A Farquhar Street, Georgetown, Penang (from $34.30)

Palm Beach, 105-A Batu Ferringgi, about 10 miles from downtown Georgetown, Penang (from $26)

Rasa Sayang, Batu Ferringgi, about 10 miles from downtown Georgetown, Penang (from $49.55)

Regent of Kuala Lumpur, Jalan Imbi, Kuala Lumpur (from $56.50)

The above hotels are all centrally located unless otherwise indicated.

USEFUL INFORMATION

Banks: Open 10-3 Mon-Fri, 9:30-11:30 Sat. Banks in the smaller towns and hotels, and money changers handle travelers' checks and currency.

Mail: Stamps from post offices and hotel porters. Mailboxes are red.

Telephone Tips: Telephones are available in restaurants and cafés and in public booths. To use—insert M10¢, dial, press button, and speak. Useful numbers in Kuala Lumpur:

Pan Am 425044	Operator 102
Tourist Office 423033	Time 0
Tourist Information 80778	Emergency 0
Kuala Lumpur Tourist Association 423033	

Newspapers: English-language publications available, several published locally—*The New Straits Times, Malay Mail, Star,* and *Straits Echo.*

Tipping: Not mandatory. Taxi drivers—not necessary, but 10% is welcome; luggage porters, M$1; hotel porters, M50¢ per case; restaurants, 10% of bill, nothing extra if the service charge is included; hairdressers, M$2; tourist guides, M$1.

Electricity: 220 volts 50 cycles AC. Hotels have converters.

Laundry: Services are quick and efficient. Main hotels provide good express and 24-hour cleaning services. Dry-cleaning a suit, average cost from M$3; laundering a shirt, from M$1.

Hairdressers: Major hotels have hairdressing salons. A shampoo and set costs from M$15, tip M$1; a man's haircut from M$7.

Photography: Black and white and color film are generally available. Color film takes about 3 days to be developed, black and white usually 24 hours.

Clubs: Kiwanis. Rotary meets every Wednesday, 12:45 at the Merlin Hotel, Kuala Lumpur. Jaycees meet the first Sunday of every month at the Station Hotel. Lions meet the third Thursday of the month at the Merlin Hotel (8pm). Apex meetings are the first and third Wednesday of the month at Hotel Majestic (7:30pm).

Rest Rooms: In hotels, restaurants, stations, and stores. Local names are: women, *Perempuan;* men, *Laki Laki.*

Health: Most doctors and dentists speak English. Imported pharmaceuticals and toiletries are available and fairly cheap.

TRANSPORTATION

In the city the bus service is good. Bicycle rickshaws, called *trishaws,* are for rent but are rarely used by foreigners. Taxis can be hailed; if you call one by phone, the charge includes the distance from the stand to the pick-up point. In Kuala Lumpur and Penang taxis have meters, and the fare is M60¢ for the first mile and M20¢ for each additional half-mile. An extra M10¢ is charged for each passenger after the first two, M10¢ for each suitcase.

The railway connects Kuala Lumpur with Penang, Butterworth, Singapore, and Thailand. The service is efficient and comfortable, providing air-conditioned carriages (first class) and buffet cars. There are night expresses with sleeping compartments. Ekspres Raayat is an air-conditioned railway service between Penang and Singapore which cuts 4 hours from the normal service. Daily ferry services, operating every 20 minutes, connect the island of Penang with Butterworth. The Straits Steamship Company operates to ports in Sarawak and Sabah. Main towns in Malaysia are connected with frequent flights by Malaysian Airline System.

It is possible to rent self-drive and chauffeur-driven cars. Traffic drives on the left. In West Malaysia roads are excellent. On the east coast, travel can be difficult during the monsoon months, October to January. In East Malaysia the road network is limited; many are suitable only for jeeps. In Sabah many roads are seasonally limited.

FOOD AND RESTAURANTS

Each ethnic group of this potpourri of races contributes a distinctive brand of cuisine to the country. A favorite Malay delicacy is *satay,* meat barbecued on bamboo skewers and dipped in sweet chili and peanut sauce. *Rendang* is beef braised with ginger, and *panggang golek* is spicy roast duck. Bird's nest soup (a specialty of Borneo) and shark's fin soup are two of many famous Chinese dishes. *Meehoon* is a kind of spaghetti, and *rojak* an assortment of salad vegetables. *Tiffin*, a heritage of British colonial life, is served on Sundays in the **Majestic** and **Federal** hotels. Breakfast served 7–9, lunch 12:30–2:30, dinner from 7:30–9:30. Snack food is very popular, and street stalls abound everywhere. *Satay*, savory noodles, fried rice, even fish and chips, are all available; Chinese food stalls are particularly good and very hygienic. Steamed dumplings filled with pork, salted eggs, beans, or chestnuts are a Chinese delicacy traditionally eaten at the **Dragon Boat Festival** in June.

Malay food is at its best eaten in a Malay home, but three good substitutes in Kuala Lumpur are the **Bintang Restaurant** (44 Jalan Sultan Ismail—tel: 425151); **Majid Satay House** (Jalan Ipoh); and the **Yazmin Restaurant** (Ampang Shopping Centre). Good Chinese restaurants are the **Hakka** (Chin Woo Auditorium); **Kum Leng** (119 Jalan Pudu); and **Akasaka** (72 Jalan Hicks). Good Cantonese food is served in the **Imperial Room** at the Malaysia Hotel (tel: 427862) and the **Dragon Room** at the Merlin Hotel (tel: 480033). Both these hotels also have first-rate European restaurants. For French cuisine, try **Regent Court** in the Kuala Lumpur Regent. The **Coq d'Or** (121 Jalan Ampang—tel: 83522) serves excellent European and Chinese food. The best Indian restaurants are the **Akbar** (Medan Tuanku—tel: 920366) and the **Bilal** (33 Jalan Ampang—tel: 80804). The **Campbell Road** is a fine area for good, inexpensive Malaysian food. The average price of a meal in a first-class establishment is M$35 for one including drinks; in a medium-priced one M$9–12.

DRINKING TIPS

Imported beer, wines, liquor, and soft drinks are available, but the local equivalents should be tried; Tiger, Anchor, and Gold Harp beers are well known to generations of sailors, and freshly brewed coconut beer, usually sold out of town at local bars, is very good. Coconut water *(ayer kelapa)* can be drunk as an aperitif, and Sabah's local spirit is served at any time. Sugarcane water, a cool drink served with crushed ice, is a refreshing soft drink. Alcohol can be bought at any time during the day, but not after midnight. Whisky and soda costs about M$3.30 in a bar. The **Scots Bar** in the Hotel Merlin, **The Bar** in the Federal Hotel, the **Lobby Bar** in the Equatorial Hotel, and the **Aviary Bar** in the Hilton, along with the **Alcazar Cocktail Lounge** in the Ming Building and the **Brass Rail** on Medan Tuanku, are favorite drinking spots in Kuala Lumpur.

ENTERTAINMENT

Air-conditioned movie theaters have frequent afternoon and evening performances of Malay, Chinese, and English films (original soundtracks). Concerts and local variety shows are performed at the **Stadium Negara**. Malay drama called *makyong* (all female) and *menora* (all male) is a mixture of dance and story, dance being typical Malaysian entertainment. The most common dance is the *ronggeng,* originally a courtship dance; no physical contact takes place, and the dancers invent songs in praise of their partners. In the amusement park (every main town has one), the *ronggeng* can be danced with Malay or Indonesian hostesses. These parks also feature Chinese opera and dance, and cabarets with Western music and *taxi* dancers. *Wayang kulit* is the Malaysian form of shadow plays—puppet figures acting out stories from the great Hindu epics.

Nightlife in Kuala Lumpur is mostly limited to hotel entertainment places such as the **Dragon Court,** the **Tomorrow** discothèque, and the **Harlequin** at Hotel Merlin (tel: 480033); the **Continental Room** and **Latin Quarter** at the Federal Hotel (tel: 27701); the **Regent Club** discothèque at the Regent Hotel (tel: 425588); **Tin Mines** discothèque and **Paddock** supper club at the Hilton (tel: 422122); and the **Century High Ball** at the Century Hotel (tel: 22481). **The Hut** in Petaling Jaya (5 miles out of town) is a restaurant offering shows with folk and classical dances, shadow plays, and Malay music.

SHOPPING

Stores open from 9-6 and close on Sundays; some close at noon Saturday, but in Chinese quarters many stay open all week. Best buys are handmade silverware and beautiful hand-loomed silver- and gold-embroidered material called *kain songket* (Malaysian brocade). For a humbler purse, the pewterware (made from Malaysian tin) and the batik are very good. **Jalan Mountbatten** and **Jalan Tuanku Rahman** are the main shopping streets of Kuala Lumpur, and the **Ampang Shopping Complex** on Jalan Ampang is one of the best. **Jalan Campbell** also has a shopping complex. There is a government-run **Malaysian Handicrafts Center** on Jalan Mountbatten, and another at the **Bukit Nanas Tourist Complex.** The **Selangor Pewter Works** has a shop on Jalan Tuanku Rahman. **Weld Supermarket,** Jalan Weld, is good for handicrafts. The **MARA** building on Jalan Tuanku Rahman has various shops selling sarongs, batiks, and evening-dress lengths of fabric. There is no bargaining in stores; elsewhere it is expected. The **Malay Bazaar** comes into its own on Saturday night, when the "Sunday" market or *Kampong Bahru,* flourishes.

SPORTS

Rugby, soccer, cricket, tennis, and badminton are all popular. There is horse racing all year round, rotating between Kuala Lumpur, Ipoh, Penang, and Singapore. There are swimming pools in the larger towns and golf courses at **Kuala Lumpur,** the Genting Highlands, Fraser's Hill, Cameron Highlands, and Langkawi Island. Good sea angling is to be had in and around the lagoons and islands, and freshwater fishing is available in the **National Park.** *Bersilat,* the Malay art of self-defense, was introduced at court in the 15th century. Demonstrations, with rhythmic beatings of gongs and drums, are given at ceremonies and festivals. The **Royal Selangor Golf Club** and **Royal Selangor Flying Club** welcome visitors; apply to the secretary.

WHAT TO SEE

Kuala Lumpur: Three rivers flow into this spacious city of tree-lined streets and contemporary buildings. Founded in 1859 by a group of tin miners, Kuala Lumpur's most picturesque face is seen in the older streets of thatched *kampongs* on stilts. Modern interpretations of national and religious architecture give the city a skyline of domes and minarets. Best examples are the Moorish-style **Railroad Station,** and the beautiful **National Mosque.** Situated in the Lake Gardens are **Parliament House** and the **National Museum,** with a good collection of local antiquities and flora and fauna (open daily 9:30-6, closed Fridays between noon and 2:30pm). The **National Art Gallery** in the Tuanku Abdul Rahman Hall, Jalan Ampang, displays work by Malaysian artists. Eight miles north of Kuala Lumpur are the **Batu Caves,** vast natural caverns that, during the festival of Thaipusam, are the goal of Hindu penitents who, with spikes, climb the hundreds of steps to the cave shrine. Tin dredgings can be seen along the road to the Batu Caves, and the tin mines of **Ampang Village** (5 miles) are well worth a visit. Malaysia's second major industry is rubber, and a rubber plantation lies along the road to the **National Zoo** (about 8 miles); early in the morning women can be seen tapping the trees for rubber. The hill resort of **Genting Highlands** is 30 miles north of Kuala Lumpur at an altitude of 5,600 feet. The resort has Malaysia's one and only casino, an 18-hole golf course, swimming pools, waterfalls, cave temples, amusement parks, a flower nursery, and indoor gymnasium, and facilities for bowling and horseback riding. Accommodations in the four hotels range from economy chalets (US$20 double) to luxury penthouses (US$150 double).

Penang: Ringed with sandy beaches, the island rises in densely wooded slopes to a central range of hills (funicular to Penang Hill). Accommodations on Penang Hill, where the temperature is a pleasant 65°F, are to be had at the **Penang Hill Hotel** and at government vacation cottages. On the hill of **Ayer Itam** is a Buddhist temple with a seven-tiered pagoda housing 1,000 Buddhas. Among many architectural reminders of the British are **Fort Cornwallis, St George's Church** in Farquhar Street, Georgetown, the double-spired **Cathedral of the Assumption,** and most of the civic buildings. The **Snake Temple** lives up to its name, and live poisonous snakes entwine about the carvings and writhe in the courtyard. The dome of the **Waterfall Temple** is covered with gold, and the statue of the goddess Mariamman is decked with real diamonds and emeralds. Penang, a free port, is a shopper's paradise—cheap luxury goods, antiques, and curios. The **Dawood** and **Hammediyah** restaurants serve good Malay food.

Malacca: About halfway between Kuala Lumpur and Singapore, this is the oldest city in Malaysia. Founded as a Malay Kingdom, it was for centuries the center for gold, ivory, tin, spices, and silks. It fell under a succession of so-called "protective" influences: first the Chinese, then, in the 16th century, the Portuguese, followed by the Dutch in 1641 and the British in 1824. You can visit the oldest Chinese temple in Malaysia—the **Cheng Hoon Teng**—and behind this is **Bukit China Hill**, one of the oldest and largest Chinese burial grounds outside China. There are early Portuguese churches—one once held the remains of Saint Francis Xavier. The **Porta de Santiago** is the gateway of the original Portuguese port. There are also the **Tranquerah Mosque** and the comprehensive **Malacca Museum.** You can find accommodations at the **Travel Inn** or **Palace Hotel.** The east coast of West Malaysia affords hundreds of miles of unspoiled, golden beaches dotted with small villages. Offshore islands are a miniature tropical paradise, many with romantic legends attached to them.

Langkawi Island: North of Penang and within sight of Thailand, this island has black-sand beaches, blue lagoons, colored cliffs, and jungles rich in wild orchids. At **Pantai Dato Syed Omar** beach, the **Langkawi Country Club Hotel** has a golf course and all facilities for water sports (from US$20 double). The tiny **Emerald Island** just off Pangkor is a skindiver's and coral hunter's dream.

The Cameron Highlands: Numerous paths wind through the dense trees and cascading waterfalls of the Highlands, about 140 miles north of Kuala Lumpur. The hills, covered with wildflowers, are alive with beautiful butterflies. This cool hill resort, at an altitude of 6,500 feet, offers a golf course, tennis, badminton, and swimming. Arrangements can be made to visit tea plantations. Two good hotels to stay at are **Fosters Smokehouse** (from US$32 double) and the **Merlin Hotel** (from US$30 double). **Fraser's Hill** is another famous resort; similar in nature to the Cameron Highlands, it is a two-hour drive from Kuala Lumpur. Fraser's Hill Development Corporation has details of the hotel and government-operated guest houses. (Write the General Manager, c/o Fraser's Hill Development Corporation, Pahang, Malaysia.) Note: There is one-way traffic control on the mountain road, so check descent and ascent times.

National Park: **Taman Negara** in West Malaysia covers 1,677 square miles of river and jungle and can be reached only by plane or riverboat. In this virgin paradise, observation blinds overlook salt licks where tiger, panther, elephant, deer, and other wild life come to feed. Angling is good on the many little-used rivers of the park with their endless pools and rapids. The headquarters at **Kuala Tahan** has a rest house, cabins, and a supplies shop. Camping equipment, with mosquito nets, is available.

Sabah: Kota Kinabalu (Jesselton) is the modern capital of Sabah, an ideal center for exploring the homeland of its little-known native peoples. A good hotel there is the **Hyatt Kinabalu International** (from US$47 double). The satellite town of **Tanjong Aru** extends, literally, into the sea, with a "floating village" *(kampong ayer)* built on stilts in the still water. *Tamu besar* is market day, and this colorful Sunday scene of farmers bringing in their produce accompanied by wives in local costume can be seen at **Tuaran,** 21 miles away. The colorful horse-riding tribe, the *Bajau,* attend the *tamus,* and their home is **Sorob.** The *Kadazans* are Sabah's racial group, and the best place to see these people in their black garments and tinkling chain decorations is in **Papar** and its surrounding villages. *Muruts,* who still use blow-pipe guns, live mainly in the district of **Tenom.**

Kuching: The capital of Sarawak, one-time land of the headhunters, was the home of a Briton who established his own dynasty, that of the White Rajah. The **Palace** *(Astana)* was built by Sir Charles Brooke, the second rajah. The small town has many Chinese temples, Muslim mosques, and a picturesque bazaar. The famous museum has a superb collection illustrating the lives, history, and arts of the people of Sarawak. The primitive *Dayaks* (Ibans) inhabit "long-houses," the entire village living under the same palm-leaf roof. Conducted tours are made to their tribal villages. June 1 is **Dayak Festival Day,** when the end of the harvesting of paddy rice is celebrated. A cockerel is killed and offerings made to the gods; war dances, cockfights, and blow-pipe demonstrations follow. The **Niah Caves** north of Sarawak show signs of occupation by Paleolithic and Neolithic Man; a 40,000-year-old skull was found here (cast in Kuching museum).

SOURCES OF FURTHER INFORMATION

Pan Am, Equatorial Hotel, Jalan Sultan Ismail, Kuala Lumpur, and any Pan Am office around the world; **Tourist Development Corporation,** Wisma MPI and Subang International Airport, Kuala Lumpur; **Kuala Lumpur Tourist Association,** Central Railway Station Building, Jalan Sultan Hishamuddin, Kuala Lumpur; **Malaysian Tourist Information Centre,** Transamerica Pyramid Building, 600 Montgomery Street, San Francisco, CA 94111 and 17 Curzon Street, Mayfair, London W1.

Micronesia

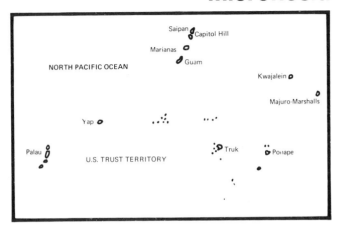

Area 700 square miles					**Population** 135,660							
Capital —					**Sales Tax** None							
Weather	Jan	Feb	Mar	Apr	May	Jun	Jul	Aug	Sep	Oct	Nov	Dec
Av Temp (°C)	25	28	28	28	30	30	30	30	28	28	28	25
Days Rain	8	9	12	16	9	23	22	22	19	17	14	12

Time Zone No named zone. When it is 12 noon Monday in New York City, it is 3am Tuesday in Guam.

Micronesia is many separate places: 2,141 variations on the tropical theme, with the usual liberal lacings of sand, sea, surf. The name itself means literally, "tiny islands"; there are in fact seven districts—Yap, Truk, Ponape, Kosrae, Palau, the Marshalls, and the Marianas. The whole territory is equal in size to the continental United States, while its actual land mass is about half the size of Rhode Island. Culturally and ethnically Micronesia has a checkered past. The original natives came from Southeast Asia, but from the 18th century onwards the islands have been occupied in turn by the Spanish, Germans, Japanese, and Americans; all left their marks. The Mariana Islands are on their way to attaining Commonwealth status with the US, while the other six districts currently are deliberating their future political status. The US trusteeship which provides the binding link of these distant territories comes to an end in the near future. Already residents of the islands of Koror, Babelthuap, Peleliu, Angaur, Kayangel, Sonsorol, Tobi and Pulo Anna have voted to join together as the Republic of Belau. (Belau appears at left on the map as Palau, and the new Republic will have an area of 190.6 sq. miles with a population of 14,800.)

Meanwhile, in the northwest Trust Territory, Saipan and residents of adjacent isles have already proclaimed the Commonwealth of the Northern Marianas. Area, 184.5 sq. miles with a population of 15,790. The bulk of the population lives on Saipan, the remaining 3,000 divided between Agrihan, Alamagan, Pagan, Rota and Tinian.

The islands of the central Trust Territory, including Ponape, Truk, Kosrae, Yap and the numerous atolls around, will be part of the Federated States of Micronesia. Kolonia on Panape is to become the seat of the new federal government. Land area is some 280 sq. miles with a population of around 65,000.

At the eastern edge of the Trust Territory are the Marshall Islands (and atolls), who have voted for independence. Majuro will become the seat of government for the 29,670 islanders. Total area of this new territory is about 70 sq. miles. All new mini-nations are expected to maintain alliances with the US in matters of foreign affairs and defense, which will result in the continuation of funding for government/economic and related activities.

The islands are, by and large, unspoiled and undeveloped, and visiting many of them is likely to be an adventure in the truest sense of the word. There *are* facilities for tourists—currently a great number of comfortable new hotels are opening on most of the islands—but life is still primitive. However, the sea is blue and inviting, the beaches are white and empty, and the lush backdrop of island scenery is as widely varied as the tropical climate.

Tropical Climate—rainy season in southern districts mid-May to late November, but the rain is rarely heavy.

Government—US Trust Territory with appointed Resident Commissioner for the Marianas and High Commissioner for the other six districts.

Language—English, Japanese, Micronesian dialects.

Religion—About 50% Catholic.

Currency—US dollar.

Public Holidays are the same as USA.

REQUIREMENTS FOR ENTRY AND CUSTOMS REGULATIONS

Passport, United States visa, and round-trip ticket are required for periods of 30 days or less. US citizens, visiting for the same amount of time, only need proof of identity for entry. Smallpox and cholera inoculations are required only if entering from an infected area. Tetanus, typhoid, and paratyphoid injections are strongly recommended. Change currency other than US dollars before arrival, as facilities are limited.

AIRPORT INFORMATION

Continental/Air Micronesia has regular services from Guam to Saipan, the Majuro-Marshall Islands, Ponape, Truk, Palau, Rota, and Yap. Airports have no hotel reservations counters. Hotel representatives meet flights in all districts and provide transportation. Taxis are generally available.

ACCOMMODATIONS

Accommodations are extremely varied—from good to practical—and are within minutes of airports. Due to the scarcity of rooms in some districts, single guests may be asked to share twin-bedded rooms with other single guests. (See district sections for specific hotels.)

USEFUL INFORMATION

Banks are open Mon-Fri. Currency can be changed only at a bank, although hotels and some shops take travelers' checks. Each district has a branch of a major bank (e.g. Bank of America or Bank of Hawaii), whose opening hours vary.

Only post offices sell stamps, and letters can be mailed only at district post offices or through hotel facilities. P.O. Hours: Mon-Fri. 7:30am-4:30pm; Sat. 9am-noon.

Phone systems are found in hotels, restaurants, and other public facilities. Saipan has the only pay phones (25¢ local calls). To operate the interisland service, dial direct. Radio-telephone communications are in operation for other districts.

English-language newspapers and magazines are available. The former include the *Guam Pacific Daily News, Marianas Variety,* and *Micronesian Independent.*

Tipping is not required, but it is much appreciated.

Electricity—110 volts 60 cycles AC in areas that have electricity.

Laundry service is adequate in most hotels, but dry-cleaning is available only in the Marianas.

Very few hairdressers, except at hotels on Saipan; shampoo and set from US$10, man's haircut from US$3.

Photographic equipment is available in hotels and shopping areas. Processing, however, is not available.

Rotary Club in Saipan only. Kiwanis in Commonwealth of the Northern Marianas.

Babysitting facilities can be found in hotels.

Rest rooms can be found in hotels, restaurants, and stores. No charge.

Doctors and dentists speak English. Imported pharmaceuticals are available in government clinics in each district.

TRANSPORTATION

There are no buses on the islands other than tourist services and taxis are the best and most reliable form of transportation. Alternatively, one can rent a car; prices are from US$15-20 a day, and chauffeur-driven cars cost more. Roads can be rough. The internal airlines are Air Micronesia and Air Pacific International, both of which link up most of the islands. Government field trip ships travel to outer islands; a boat with outboard motor can be hired for US$40 and up per day, guide/operator included.

FOOD AND RESTAURANTS

Fish, of course, is available in vast quantities—clams, eels, *langusta,* octopus—plus coconut crabs, mangrove clams, fruit bats, and yams. Try *kela-*

guin (a chewy mixture of diced chicken and shredded coconut) in the Marianas and breadfruit in Truk. The Japanese *sashimi* (slices of raw fish dipped in a peppery sauce) make a tasty snack with beer throughout the islands. The **Chamorro Village** is a new restaurant offering local food specialties and entertainment. Prices are reasonable. The food served in hotels is basically American, and adventurous eating will depend on your willingness to look for something more exciting. If you let people know that you want more than ordinary tourist food, you may be quite agreeably surprised. Hotel staff members can usually arrange for you to eat "out" somewhere—if you're in luck, it may be at the wedding feast of a member of their own family, where the eating is likely to be notably different. Otherwise, look for small native restaurants near the various town centers.

DRINKING TIPS

When on Ponape, drink *sakau*, which is obtained from the root of the sakau plant. Otherwise, imported wines, liquor and beers are available. Alcoholic-beverage drinking permits, varying in cost from US$1-3, are required in the Marshalls, Ponape, and Yap districts. The best bars are in hotels, most of which have food and are near the ocean. Truk recently became "dry" but that legislation may be repealed.

ENTERTAINMENT

Amateur theater groups, old films, local bands in nightclubs, and some native dance performances brighten the island evenings. Nightclubs with music include the following: Saipan—major hotels, **Oleai Room, Marianas Inn, Big K, Puppy Club, Tapa Bar;** Palau—**Peleliu Club, Factory Club;** Ponape—**Nan Madol Hotel;** the Marshalls—**Kitco Downtown Club;** Truk—**Christopher Inn, Maramar Hotel;** Yap—**Rai View Inn, O'Keefe's Community Club.**

SHOPPING

Handicraft shops can be found on all the islands, and Ponape black pepper and wood carvings are two of the best buys at handicraft cooperatives and stores. **Majuro** has *kili* bags woven by former Bikini islanders, stick charts, seashells, and coconut-fiber flowers. **Palau** and **Ponape** are known for their carvers, who make wooden story-boards depicting island legends, model outrigger canoes, carved wooden houses and tortoiseshell jewelry. The **Yapese** make miniature stone money, lavalavas, and grass skirts. On **Saipan** buy lacquered turtles, stuffed coconut crabs, and all kinds of seashell goods. On **Truk** look for love sticks and war clubs. The **Marianas** offer wishing dolls, coconut masks, and wood carvings.

SPORTS

Scuba-diving, snorkeling, deep-sea fishing, and swimming are enjoyed in all districts. There is outstanding scuba-diving among the coral reefs and drop-offs of Palau and the 60 or so sunken Japanese warships in the Truk Lagoon. Tennis and hiking are available in all districts, golf in Saipan only. Hunting and yachting are limited.

WHAT TO SEE

Yap: On Yap, life in the small, thriving District Center of **Colonia** provides an interesting mixture of loincloths and jukeboxes, grass skirts and motorcycles. In the villages see the huge slabs of stone money, some of them 14 feet across, lying about near roadsides and houses. Visit the **Yap Museum** in Colonia, or see the stone money bank in Rull. Hotels are the **Rai View Inn, Colonia** (tel: 485, from US$22 double), and the **ESA Hotel** (from US$25 double).

Northern Marianas: Saipan is the center of the Marianas, background for some of the fiercest battles of World War II. The best beaches of the Marianas are on Saipan, most of them decorated with rusty remnants of the war. Hotels here are **Hafadai Beach Hotel** (S$23/D$26) at the beach; **Mariana Hotel** (S/D$25) on the hillside overlooking the village of Garapan; **Royal Taga Hotel,** on the beach at Susupe (from US$30 double). There is also the new **SAIPAN BEACH INTER · CONTINENTAL INN,** Micro Beach (from US$45 double), and **Saipan Grand** (from US$50 double).

Tinian: Fleming Hotel (S$15/D$25).

Palau: Two hundred islands make up the district of Palau, the central town of which is **Koror.** Take a boat through the **Rock Islands** and see the atoll of **Kayangel.** Hotels are **Palau Continental,** Koror (from US$53 double); the **New Koror Hotel,** Koror (from US$20 double); the **Barsakesau Hotel,** Koror (US$30 double).

Truk: One of the world's largest lagoons, this circle of coral has the largest population of all the six districts. More war mementoes are here, scattered about the island. See the **Japanese Lighthouse** and the **Truk Trading Company,** called "a general store to end all general stores—part tropical outpost, part American frontier." Hotels are the **Bayview,** Moen (from US$14 double), the **Christopher Inn** (from US$20 double), in Moen near the airport. There is also **Truk Continental Hotel,** Moen (S$53-58/D$58-65).

Ponape: Perhaps the most beautiful and most "typical" of all South Sea islands, Ponape has few beaches but numerous freshwater streams, waterfalls, and lagoons where you can picnic and swim.

Kolonia is the district center of Ponape—a wonderful shanty of a town. Forty minutes away from Kolonia by boat is **Nan Madol**—ruined walls, pathways, canals, and the temple of **Nan Dowas.** Hotels in Kolonia: **Cliff Rainbow Hotel** (S$15-22/D$18-25) just 15 minutes from the airport, near Kapinga Village; **South Park Hotel** (S$25-40/D$28-45) overlooking Sokehs Bay; **Hotel Nan Madol,** also at Sokehs (S$16-19/D$24-26); **Hotel Pohnpei** (US$20 double); and **The Village** (S$35-45/D$40-50).

Majuro-Marshalls: Thirty-four island groups, 870 reefs, and the sea available in more than a dozen shades of blue—those are the attractions of the Majuro-Marshalls. The sea predominates here and provides all the entertainment you'll want. Hotels are the **Eastern Gateway Hotel,**

Majuro (US$30 a/c, US$21 non-a/c double), and the **Hotel Majuro,** Majuro (from US$18 double).

SOURCES OF FURTHER INFORMATION

Pan Am: Skinner Plaza, Agana, Guam, and any Pan Am office around the world; **Micronesia Regional Tourism Council,** PO Box 682, Agona, Guam 96910 (tel: 646-1250); **Northern Marianas Visitors Bureau,** PO Box 861, Saipan, Marianas Islands 96950; **Pacific Area Travel Association,** 228 Grant Avenue, San Francisco, CA 94108.

Nepal

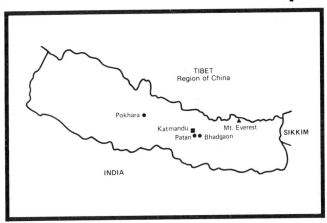

WHAT'S SPECIAL

The Himalayas have for centuries served as a barrier between Nepal and the outside world. This isolation has developed an exotic and individualistic culture in a spectacular setting, which has had a profound effect on the character and outlook of the people of Nepal. Not only will you marvel at the hand of nature, but the artistic achievement of the Nepalese will delight you.

COUNTRY BRIEFING

Size: 54,362 square miles   **Population:** 14,608,000
Capital: Katmandu   **Capital Population:** 600,000

Climate: From tropical to Arctic, depending on the altitude. Monsoons from early June to late August. Best season to visit is the fall, September to November.

Weather in Katmandu: Lat N27°42'; Alt 4,388 ft

Temp (°F)	Jan	Feb	Mar	Apr	May	Jun	Jul	Aug	Sep	Oct	Nov	Dec
Av Low	23°	30°	36°	42°	51°	61°	65°	66°	58°	48°	36°	26°
Av High	72°	75°	78°	84°	90°	95°	88°	86°	88°	83°	78°	73°
Days no rain	30	23	29	24	21	15	10	11	18	27	29	31

Government: A kingdom.
Language: Nepali. English taught in some schools.
Religion: 85% Hindu and 12% Buddhist.

NEPAL

Currency: Rupee. 100 paisas = 1 rupee.

	Re 1	Rs 2	Rs 5	Rs 10	Rs 50	Rs 100	Rs 250	Rs 500
US (dollars, cents)	.08	.17	.42	.83	4.17	8.33	20.83	41.67
UK (pounds, pence)	.04	.08	.20	.40	1.99	3.97	9.94	19.88

Public Holidays:

Prithbi Jayanti, Jan
Basant Panchami, Feb
Democracy Day, 18 Feb
Shivaratri (Night of Lord Shiva), Mar
Bisket Festival, Apr
Buddha Jayanti, May
Numerous other local holidays

Teej Women's Festival, Aug
Cow Festival (Gaijatra), Aug
Rain God Festival (Indrajatra), Sep
Dasain (Durga Puja), Oct
Festival of Lights, Nov
King Birendra's Birthday, Dec

HOW TO GET THERE

Flying time to Katmandu's Tribhuvan Airport from New York is 18 hours; from Frankfurt, 8¾ hours; from Hong Kong, 5 hours; from Delhi, 1¼ hours. Time in Nepal: GMT+5 hours 40 minutes.

REQUIREMENTS FOR ENTRY AND CUSTOMS REGULATIONS

Passport; visa for 30 days, available from nearest Royal Nepalese Embassy, or for 7 days, obtainable on arrival—both can be extended by applying to the Central Immigration Office, Ram Shah Path (Putali Sadak), Katmandu. A fee of US$11.50 is charged, and three photographs are required. Cholera, smallpox, and typhoid vaccinations are required; yellow-fever if coming from an infected area. A permit is generally required to visit places outside the Katmandu Valley, although some of these are already covered by your entry visa; see the Central Immigration Office in Katmandu. For entry you need proof of having over US$250 and a round-trip ticket. You are not permitted to take Indian currency in or out, and you can deal only in Nepalese currency while in the country. No other currency restrictions. Duty-free allowance: 200 cigarettes, 20 cigars; 2 bottles of liquor, 1 bottle of beer or 12 cans; one camera with 12 plates or 6 rolls of film, one movie camera with 2 reels of film; one portable record player with 10 records, one portable musical instrument, one transistor radio, one pair of binoculars, and one tape recorder with six tapes; perfume for personal use. The import of firearms and ammunition requires a license which must be obtained in advance from the Ministry of Foreign Affairs, the Home Ministry, or the Panchayat, His Majesty's Government of Nepal, Katmandu. Antiques must be certified at the National Archives Building, Ram Shah Path, Katmandu, before they can be exported.

AIRPORT INFORMATION

Tribhuvan Airport is 3½ miles from Katmandu. Royal Nepal Airlines bus service to city center, Rs5; the taxi fare into town is Rs25. An embarkation tax of Rs100 is levied on departure. Duty-free shop. Tip porters Re1 per bag.

ACCOMMODATIONS
Reserve well in advance, as the popularity of Nepal is increasing. Luxury-class hotels are well equipped with all facilities; other hotels are not so well equipped. Lodges and youth hostels are even less expensive than the hotels. Hotels in Katmandu, exclusive of a 10% government tax, include:

Rates are in US$ for a double/twin room with bath or shower
  Blue Star, Tripureshwar (from $26.90), 1 mile from center city
  Crystal, Juddha Road (from $31.50)
  De l'Annapurna, Durbar Marg (from $53.80), ½ mile from center
  Malla, Leknath Road (from $48.16), ½ mile from center
  Manaslu, Lazimpat (from $12.50 BB), 1 mile from center
  Mount Makalu, Juddha Road (from $12.50 BB)
  Narayani, Pfulchowk (from $32.50), 2 miles from center
  Panorama, Khichapokhari (from $9)
  Paras, Juddha Road (from $7)
  Shangrila, Lazimpat (from $39.20), ½ mile from center
  Shanker, Lazimpat (from $43.70), 1 mile from center
  Siddhartha, Kanti Path (from $31.50), ½ mile from center
  Soaltee-Oberoi, Tahachal (from $60.48), 2 miles from center
  Woodlands, Durbar Marg (from $34.75), ½ mile from center
  Yak and Yeti, Lal Durbar (from $58.24), ½ mile from center
  Yellow Pagoda, Kanti Path (from $33.25), ½ mile from center
  Unless otherwise indicated, the above hotels are centrally located.

USEFUL INFORMATION
Banks open 10am-2pm Sun-Thurs, 10am-noon Fri; closed Sat. Hotels may carry on banking transactions from 8am-8pm every day except Saturday. **Phones** in restaurants, cafés, and telephone exchange offices. Useful numbers in Katmandu: **Pan Am agent,** 15824; **Tourist Information,** 15818; **Emergencies,** 11999; **Inquiries,** 00. **Electricity** supply is 220 volts 50 cycles AC. **Laundry** and dry-cleaning services in and around Katmandu; extra charge for 24-hour service. **Hairdressing** salons in first-class hotels (shampoo and set from Rs35; man's haircut from Rs10). **Photographic** supplies available in Katmandu. Two days to develop black and white; color not processed locally. Nepalese word for **rest room** is *Shauchalaya*. Cleanest ones are in hotels and restaurants. **Health:** doctors speak English. Drink only bottled water.

TRANSPORTATION
Outside Katmandu Valley the only paved roads are the highways leading to Tibet, the highway down to India, and a road to Pokhara. Therefore transport is easiest by air. Royal Nepal Airlines flies to 35 domestic destinations. Airport tax on domestic flights is Rs15. In Katmandu, metered

taxis are readily available at Rs2 per kilometer, and rickshaws for Rs2 per kilometer. There are many tours by bus (around the Katmandu Valley) and by airplane. For views of Mount Everest and other peaks you can take one of three different morning flights (at 8:30am, 8:35am, and on certain days at 8:40am) in a 44-seater Avro for US$50. The flight takes about an hour. Tours of Katmandu in a Rhino bus will cost about Rs30. There are also scheduled bus services between Katmandu and Pokhara, Katmandu and Birgunj (Indian border), Pokhara and Bhairahawa/Sunauli (Indian border), Katmandu and Janakpur/Biratnagar, Katmandu and Trisuli, and Katmandu and Barabise/Kodari (Chinese border).

FOOD AND RESTAURANTS

Nepalese curries are based on chicken or pork, include vegetables, and are served with tasty Nepalese rice. Nepal produces a wide variety of cheeses, and the local desserts are very sweet. For Western cuisine, the major hotels usually have the most extensive menus. Restaurants in Katmandu with Western cuisine are the **Park** at Ranipokhari and the **Yak & Yeti** (Lal Durbar), set in an old palace. For traditional Nepalese and Indian dishes try the **Nook** (Kanti Path), **Mascara** (Kanti Path), **Ming Ming** (Durbar Marg), **Paradise** (Dharma Path), **Amra Pali** (Pyukha, New Road), **Indira** (New Road), **Tung Fong** (Kanti Path), and the **Eden** (Ombahal).

DRINKING TIPS

Local drinks include a mild beer called *jand* and some liquors under the name of *Rakshi*. Imported liquor is relatively expensive (a whisky and soda would cost up to Rs25). Coffee and tea are the most popular local drinks.

ENTERTAINMENT

There are no nightclubs in Katmandu. The **Casino Nepal** at the Soaltee Hotel and the band at **Hotel de l'Annapurna** provide nightly entertainment. There are four movie houses, which occasionally show English films.

SHOPPING

Buy only after hard bargaining. Things to look for are hand-wrought cigarette and jewel boxes decorated with semiprecious stones; brooches, bracelets, and necklaces; Buddhist prayer wheels in silver and copper; religious figures; wood and ivory carvings; Hindu dancing masks; delicately fine rice paper; homespun cottons and woolens; and Nepalese and Tibetan carpets. In Nepal an antique is considered an object over 100 years old and are not usually permitted to leave the country. So if buying an item which is not an antique but could cause doubt, be sure to obtain a certificate from the **National Archives Building**, Ram Shah Path, Katmandu, stating that the object is not over 100 years old. Best places to buy are at the **Cottage Industries** and the **Handicraft Emporium**, the **Patan Industrial Estate** (for metal and wood craft), the **Balaju Indus-**

trial District, the New Road and Ason areas, and the Mangal Bazaar in Patan City.

SPORTS

Raft trips are the latest method of exploring the untouched areas of Nepal, with the added excitement of shooting white water rapids. Among other agencies, contact **Himalayan River Exploration**, Durbar Marg, PO 170 Katmandu, (tel: 12808), TelexNP216; or **Himalayan Travels and Tours**, Durbar Marg, PO Box 324, Katmandu. However, trekking is the only way to reach the remote mountain villages and to experience the grandeur of the Himalayas at first hand. Hitherto prohibited areas such as **Jomosom** (including Muktinath) and **Manang** are now open to trekkers. You must have a permit from the Central Immigration Office, Ram Shah Path (Putali Sadak) Katmandu; tel: 12336, and trekking arrangements can be made through any travel agent in Katmandu. The season lasts from mid-September to May. Fishing for trout and salmon is popular; for salmon try the **Pokhara Valley** and for trout the **Mardi Khola**.

WHAT TO SEE

Katmandu is a medieval city set 4,500 feet above sea level in the terraced foothills of the Himalayas, guarded by the white tops of **Jugal Himal, Ganesh Himal, Himal Chuli, Gauri Shankar,** and **Lang Tang** peaks. Visit **Hanuman Dhoka**, the traditional seat of royalty, with its multi-roofed temples and palaces all intricately carved; the **Temple of the Living Goddess**, with profusely carved wooden balconies and latticed windows; and the temple of **Kastha Mandap**, said to be built from the timber of a single tree. Buddhist stupas (shrines) like **Swayambhunath** and **Bouddha** (or **Baudhnath**) are massive and artistic.

Near to Katmandu is **Nagarkot**, a mountain resort with a sweeping view of the eastern region of the Himalayas, including Mount Everest. **Patan**, 3 miles south of Katmandu, is a city abounding in Buddhist monuments and Hindu temples.

Bhadgaon, 9 miles east of Katmandu, is the home of Nepalese medieval art. It is a goldmine of stone sculptures, wood carvings, temples, and palaces. **Durbar Square** is full of pagodas and statues. The **Golden Gate** is a masterpiece in sculpture and embellishments. The **Picture Gallery** in Bhadgaon contains many valuable and beautiful works of Tantra art. **Namche Bazar** is the gateway to the Everest region; 180 miles from Katmandu, it gives you a panoramic view of **Sagarmatha** (Everest), **Lhotse, Nhuptse,** and **Ama Dablam.** This region is the home of the Sherpas. **Pokhara Valley,** a 45-minute flight from Katmandu, is one of the most picturesque spots in Nepal. The beautiful lakes of the valley, fed by the glaciers of the **Annapurna Range,** make this region ideal for trekking. Hotels in Pokhara are **Dragon** (from US$20.20 double), **Fishtail Lodge** (from US$26.90 double), and **New Crystal** (from US$30.80 double).

Tiger Tops is a modern "treetop" hotel in the heart of a 1,000-square-mile wildlife sanctuary (Meghauli, Royal Chitwan National Park), with double rooms from US$114 per person and $2 tax. Bookings are accepted for a minimum of two and a maximum of four nights at the lodge. Group rates are available at US$99.75 per person. There are tented camps approximately 14 miles from the main lodge at US$61.75 per person, plus $1 tax and a park fee (payable only once) of $4.20. For confirmed bookings at the lodge, a 50% deposit is required 60 days prior to arrival in Nepal. Round trip airfare Katmandu to Tiger Tops is US$61 and airport taxes are extra. Tiger Tops operates from 15 September to 20 June. Tiger Tops also opened **Tharu** village camp at nearby Nawalpur. Guests can sample Tharu rice wine and cuisine, visit Tharu villages, and participate in village dancing. Tharu camp is open October through May. The **Elephant Camp** at Chitwan National Park costs US$127.50 per person for two nights, US$195 double. Three nights per person is US$171.50. Group rates available at US$121.50 per person for two nights, US$159.50 per person for three. A 50% deposit is required 30 days in advance. The Elephant Camp is open from 15 September to 15 May. Animal photography and elephant-back excursions are featured, and the transfer from airport to the camp can be made either by elephant or jeep. Another unique hotel is the **Hotel Everest View,** Songboche (Khumjung), located opposite Mount Everest and reached by charter flight. Double rooms are available from US$199.50 per person AP and a deposit of $100 is required in advance. A two-night stay is possible at a reduced rate per person AP for the two nights. Rates include all arrangements at the hotel, round trip airfare from Katmandu, and the trekking permit fee. Hotel Everest View operates from 1 October through 31 May.

SOURCES OF FURTHER INFORMATION

Pan Am's agent: Tiger Tops (Private) Ltd, PO Box 242, Durbar Marg, Katmandu and any Pan Am office around the world; **Tourist Information Center,** Ganga Path, Basàntpur, Katmandu; **Department of Tourism,** Katmandu, tel: 11293 or 14519; **Permanent Mission to the UN,** 711 Third Avenue, New York, NY 10017; **Royal Nepalese Embassy,** 12a Kensington Palace Gardens, London W8.

New Caledonia

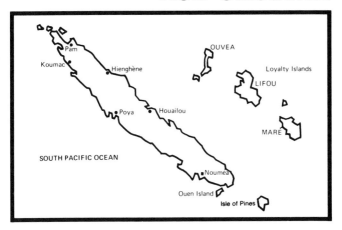

WHAT'S SPECIAL

It was Captain Cook, that avid Pacific tourist, who named this South Sea island New Caledonia when he landed on it in 1774. But in fact its resemblance to its rugged Scottish namesake is in name only. Encircled by a coral reef, the second largest in the world, and fanned by warm trade winds that give the air a special luminosity, this sunny island is also known as *L'Ile de Lumière*, or Island of Light. New Caledonia has an ideal climate, long white beaches, fascinating marine life, unusual birds (such as the flightless cagou, which barks), giant fern forests, purple bougainvillea, and some of the biggest nickel mines in the world.

COUNTRY BRIEFING

With its dependencies—the Isle of Pines, the Loyalty, Chesterfield, and Ouen Island—New Caledonia covers an area of 7,335 square miles. Total **population** is 136,000. Of these 61,000 live in the **capital,** Nouméa. New Caledonia is a French overseas territory, with representation in the French parliament. French is the official **language. Currency** is the French Pacific franc (CFP); CFP90.9 to US$1. **Public Holidays** are 1 Jan; Good Friday; Easter Monday; 1 May; Ascension Day; Whit Monday; 14 July; Assumption Day; 24 Sep; 2 Nov; 11 Nov; 25 Dec.

HOW TO GET THERE

Flying time to Nouméa's Tontouta Airport from Los Angeles is 14¾ hours, from Honolulu, 8¼ hours; from Tokyo 10½ hours. Fly to Nadi (Fiji), Sydney, or Auckland, then by connecting flight to Nouméa's Tontouta Airport. Nadi is the closest point, and flying time from Nadi to Tontouta is just under 2 hours. Time in New Caledonia: GMT+11.

REQUIREMENTS FOR ENTRY AND CUSTOMS REGULATIONS

Valid passport and onward ticket, but no visa required for stay of up to 30 days for nationals of most countries, including USA. Citizens of France and EEC countries may stay longer without visas. Smallpox vaccination required if arriving within 14 days from an infected area. Yellow fever and cholera vaccinations required if arriving within five days from an infected area. Duty-free allowances: 1000 cigarettes or 250 cigars, or 2Kg. of tobacco for passengers originating from North America, Europe, Africa; 200 cigarettes, or 50 cigars or 400 grams of tobacco for those originating in Oceania. One liter of spirits allowed all arrivals. Amateur photographers are allowed to enter with two still cameras (providing they take different size pictures), and one movie camera. Cameras must be declared on arrival.

AIRPORT INFORMATION

New Caledonia's international airport is Tontouta Airport, 35 miles from Nouméa. Transportation to town is airport bus (fare CFP600), and by taxi (fare CFP3000 per car). The airport has a duty-free shop.

ACCOMMODATIONS

In Nouméa the **Government Tourist Board** (Rue de Sébastopol) gives help with finding accommodations. There are special rates in off-peak seasons. New Caledonia has over 30 hotels, most of them in the capital city. One of the best and most informal resorts is on Ouvea Island. Hotels in New Caledonia:

Rates are in US$ for a double/twin room with bath or shower

Isle de France, Anse Vata, 3 miles from center of Nouméa, near beach (from $45)

Lagon, Anse Vata, near beach (from $39)

Motel Anse Vata, Val Plaisance, near beach (from $29)

Nouméa, Baie des Citrons, 2 miles from center of Nouméa, near beach (from $31)

Nouvata Hotel and bungalows, Anse Vata, Nouméa (from $41)

Paradise Park Motel, Nouméa (from US$33)

Relais de Fayaque, Ouvea Island (from US$87 AP)

Sébastopol, Rue de Sébastopol, downtown Nouméa (from $25)

Turtle Club, Ouen Island (from $77AP)

USEFUL INFORMATION

Banks open 7-11am and 1:30-3:30pm, Mon-Fri; 7:30-11am, Sat. **Telephones** are token operated: a local call costs CFP12. Useful numbers in Nouméa: **Tourist Office** 726-32; **Tourist Information** 726-16; **Operator** 10; **Directories** 12. No English-language **newspapers** available, but some English-language magazines are on sale. No **tipping** or cover charges.

Electricity: 220 volts 50 cycles AC. Reliable, expensive 24-hour **laundry** and dry-cleaning services in hotels. **Hairdressing** services are available in Nouméa; shampoo and set from CFP1500, man's haircut from CFP700. Black and white and color **film** available, processing of either in 24 hours. Rotary, Lions, and Kiwanis **clubs** hold meetings in Nouméa. Inquire at your local hotel for **babysitters. Health:** imported pharmaceuticals available but expensive. Tap water is safe to drink.

TRANSPORTATION

Nouméa's public transportation is supplied by inexpensive blue minibuses known locally as "baby cars." There are also long-distance bus services linking the capital to towns on the island. Air Calédonie flies to the east coast and to the neighboring islands from Magenta Airport, 4 miles from Nouméa (taxi CFP400). Reservations must be made in advance by passengers wishing to transfer from Tontouta Airport for the domestic flights. There are plenty of taxis obtainable from taxi stands in Nouméa. They have meters and are very expensive; extra charge for night fares. You can rent chauffeur-driven cars (extra charge for an English-speaking driver) or a self-drive car, available to drivers over 25 in possession of an ordinary driver's license. Rental cars cost about CFP1500 a day, plus mileage and insurance.

FOOD AND RESTAURANTS

New Caledonia boasts a large number of fine restaurants and informal eating places, most offering superb French cuisine and many featuring French regional dishes on their daily menus. Most food is imported from France, including excellent cheeses and wines, but some restaurants make imaginative use of local delicacies such as crayfish, mangrove oysters, and tropical fruits. Nouméa Tourist office publishes an excellent, regularly updated restaurant guide that lists each establishment in price brackets, from haute cuisine to snacks. In Nouméa try **Brasserie St Hubert** (middle price, bar and sidewalk café); **La Rotonde** (expensive); **Chez Nicholas** (middle price, family-style cooking); **Maffia** (expensive); **Flamboyant** for French dishes. The **Esquinade** is especially good for its seafood, and the **Creperie Bretonne** for its crepes. **El Cordobes** and **O'Churasco** serve Spanish food. There are plenty of pizzerias: **Le Rustic**, and of course Chinese and Vietnamese food as well; try **Asia** (Vietnamese), **Mandarin**, and **Grande Muraille. Ramayana** on Rue de Sébastopol specializes in Indonesian cooking. Most restaurants offer a daily entree from about CFP800 (including a carafe of wine). Cost of a more lavish meal a la carte, with wine, is about CFP1800.

DRINKING TIPS

Bars are open all day from about 8am to 10pm or midnight. Good quality French wines are expensive, but carafe wine is much cheaper and quite acceptable, along with beer. A whisky can cost about CFP400 a shot; champagne by the bottle is CFP5000. Women usually are welcome to drink in hotels or sidewalk cafés.

ENTERTAINMENT

Three movie houses and two drive-ins show French films. Nouméa's nightclubs, known as *boîtes de nuit,* stage continental or Polynesian floor shows, the most dramatic being the Wallisian sabre dance. A major attraction is a "Pilou-Pilou," a program of Melanesian war dances accompanied by an earth-oven feast. Nouméa has a number of nightclubs in the center of town and along the hotel areas of Baie des Citrons and Anse Vata. They include **Commodore, Casanova, Tivoli, Biarritz, Bounty, Don Camillo.** All are very lively and operate often as discos. There is a good gambling casino at the **Casino Royale,** where stakes can run high at baccarat, roulette, craps, and black jack. Dress is semi-formal at the casino.

SHOPPING

Hours are 7:15-11am and 2-5:30 or 6pm. Some small shops are open on Sundays. There are modern, French-style stores in the Rue de l'Alma, where smart French clothes and luxury goods are inexpensive. Two of the largest department stores are **Ballande,** in the Rue de l'Alma, and **Maison Barrau,** 22 rue Anatole-France, both in Nouméa. Good island souvenirs are curios made of local shells, coral, and mother-of-pearl; native wood carvings; and handicrafts made of bark, ceramics, and beads. A made-to-measure silk dress can be run up for a customer in 2-3 days. A number of shops are licensed to sell luxury goods duty-free. Savings of up to 30% are possible. The Tourist Office's "Duty-Free Shopping" leaflet has details.

SPORTS

A truly New Caledonian sport takes place at **Anse Vata** on Saturday afternoons and Sunday mornings when determined-looking Melanesian ladies dressed in colorful smocks, known as "Mother Hubbards," play an unusual form of cricket. Also on Saturday afternoons, and all day on Sunday, the local men play a game with steel balls, called *pétanque,* in the square opposite the old town hall. Popular sports are sailing, water-skiing, deep-sea fishing, skin-diving, and lagoon swimming. Excellent tennis courts (municipally owned) are available at Anse Vata, and there is a first-class **Squash Center** near town. There is also horse racing, with a season from early August to late September. For golfers there is one 9-hole course in Nouméa.

WHAT TO SEE

Good examples of Melanesian folk art are on show at the **Museum** and **Art Gallery** in Nouméa. Contrast the modern architecture of the **South Pacific Commission Building** with the old church of **La Conception** and **St Joseph's Cathedral.** Well worth a visit is the noted **Aquarium** for tropical marine life, or you can see underwater creatures in their natural habitat on a cruise through the lagoon in a glass-bottomed launch. Trips in these crafts are run frequently to **Amidée Island,** on which the world's third-highest lighthouse stands. Native animals are scarce; there are no snakes, but you will see some unusual birds and a vivid array of flowering plants and trees. More than 2,300 different species have been recorded; 77% of these are unique to New Caledonia. They are best seen on the east coast, where there is also a much more Melanesian atmosphere rather than on the west coast. On a trip to the east coast the tourist can meet the friendly Melanesian people in their picturesque villages and see their thatched huts.

SOURCES OF FURTHER INFORMATION

Any **Pan Am** office around the world, and the **Government Tourist Office, Immeuble Le Central, Nouméa.**

New Zealand

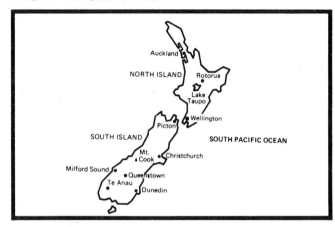

WHAT'S SPECIAL

New Zealand is made up of two islands that have some of the most magnificent and dramatic natural features in the world: the Alpine peaks of Mount Cook and its neighbors (all over 10,000 feet), and the towering walls of majestic fjords, on South Island; and a thermal region displaying bursting geysers, bubbling mud pools, and boiling lakes on North Island.

New Zealand has been discovered and rediscovered, first by the Maoris—who called the land Aotearoa (long white cloud)—and who settled in North Island, with their own language, music, and culture. Then in 1642 the white men—the *pakehas* to the Maoris—arrived. Tasman, their leader, called the land New Zealand after his own province in Holland. But he did not settle, nor did Captain Cook who came briefly more than 100 years later. Not until 1840 did the British arrive to stay, and they drew up the Treaty of Waitangi to share rights with the Maoris. New Zealand has kept close ties with Britain—the institutions and way of life are British, and everywhere there is an agreeable and informal friendliness that makes the visitor welcome.

COUNTRY BRIEFING

Size: 103,736 square miles **Population:** 3,107,000
Capital: Wellington **Capital Population:** 350,000
(Auckland is the largest city, with population 801,200.)

Climate: New Zealand has a cool temperate climate, without extremes of heat or cold, or distinct wet and dry seasons.

634

Weather in Auckland: Lat S36°47'; Alt 85 ft

Temp (°F)	Jan	Feb	Mar	Apr	May	Jun	Jul	Aug	Sep	Oct	Nov	Dec
Av Low	60°	60°	59°	56°	51°	48°	46°	46°	49°	52°	54°	57°
Av High	73°	73°	71°	67°	62°	58°	56°	58°	60°	63°	60°	70°
Days of rain	21	18	20	16	12	11	10	11	13	15	15	19

Government: An independent member of the British Common-wealth, New Zealand has a unicameral parliamentary system, with Queen Elizabeth II represented by a Governor General.

Language: English is the official language, universally spoken, although Maoris also speak their own language.

Religion: Chiefly Protestant (65-70%), and Roman Catholic (15-18%).

Currency: Dollar. 100 cents = 1 New Zealand dollar. At the current rate of exchange, the New Zealand dollar is virtually equivalent to the US dollar.

	¢ 0.05	¢ 0.10	¢ 0.50	NZ$ 1	NZ$ 5	NZ$ 10	NZ$ 20	NZ$ 100
US (dollars, cents)	.04	.09	.44	.88	4.40	8.80	17.60	88.00
UK (pounds, pence)	.02	.04	.21	.42	2.10	4.21	8.41	42.06

Public Holidays:

New Year's Day, 1 Jan
New Zealand Day, 6 Feb
Good Friday
Easter Monday
Anzac Day, 25 Apr
Queen's Birthday, first Mon in June

Labor Day, fourth Mon in Oct
Christmas Day, 25 Dec
Boxing Day, 26 Dec
Anniversary Day: each
  province has its own
Auckland, 29 Jan
Wellington, 21 Jan

HOW TO GET THERE

Flying time to Auckland International Airport from Los Angeles is 11 hours, from Honolulu 8 hours, from Sydney 2½ hours. Time in New Zealand: GMT+12. Daylight Savings Time is observed.

REQUIREMENTS FOR ENTRY AND CUSTOMS REGULATIONS

Passport, except for residents of Australia who are British subjects. Visa not required of British subjects or British Commonwealth citizens, but non-Europeans must have temporary entry endorsements on their passports. US citizens do not need visas for a stay of 30 days or less. Most other nationals do, unless they hold a forward booking for within 20 days. Currency: no restrictions, except that import of NZ currency is prohibited. Maori artifacts may not be exported. Pistols and revolvers may not be imported, and a license must be obtained for other firearms. Narcotics are prohibited. Duty-free allowance: 200 cigarettes or 50 cigars or ½ pound of tobacco; one-fifth US gallon of liquor and one-fifth of wine.

AIRPORT INFORMATION

International Airport, Auckland, is 13 miles from the city. Airport buses connect with all aircraft arrivals. Fare is NZ$3.50. Taxis are available at all times—fare NZ$20 for two people. There is an airport departure tax of NZ$2. The airport has a duty-free shop, hotel reservations counter, and car rental counters.

ACCOMMODATIONS

There is no official grading of hotels, but there are good ones in the principal cities and tourist areas and standard hotels elsewhere. Inexpensive accommodations at guesthouses and motels are generally available. Motels often cost about half the price of hotels, and most of them have complete cooking facilities and inevitably a pint of milk in the refrigerator. Some sheep stations and farms take paying guests, providing an unusual way of seeing huge farming areas. Reductions of various kinds are often made in off-peak seasons. The **New Zealand Government Tourist Bureau** will give helpful advice and information. Trailer camps, or camp sites, are very popular. As they are to be found in places of great natural beauty, they are often very pleasant. **The New Zealand Automobile Association** will give details. The **Tourist Hotel Corporation** (THC) runs a chain of hotels in national parks and resort areas. Hotels in New Zealand:

Rates are in US$ for double/twin room with bath or shower

Abel Tasman Hotel, Willis and Dixon Streets, Wellington (from $60)

Airport Inn, Massey Road at Mangere, 2 miles from International Airport, Auckland (from $48)

Auckland TraveLodge, 96-100 Quay Street, Auckland (from $72)

Burma Lodge, Burma Road, Johnsonville, Wellington (from $46)

Clarendon, 78 Worcester Street, Christchurch (from $42)

Chateau Commodore, Corner Deans Avenue and Kilmarnock Street, Christchurch (from $59)

INTER · CONTINENTAL AUCKLAND, Corner Waterloo Quadrant and Princes Street, Auckland (from $77.50)

James Cook, The Terrace, Wellington (from $70)

Noah's Hotel, Worcester Street and Oxford Terrace, Christchurch (from $75)

Royal International, Victoria Street West, Auckland (from $50)

Russleys, Roydvale Street, 2 miles from airport, Christchurch (from $46)

St George, Corner Willis and Boulcott Streets, Wellington (from $45)

Shaw Savill Lodge, Kemp Street, Kilbirnie, Wellington, about a mile from the airport (from $49)

South Pacific, Corner Queen and Custom Streets, Auckland (from $70)

United Service, Cathedral Square, Christchurch (from $34)

White Heron Lodge, 138 St Stephen's Avenue, Parnell, Auckland (from $60)

Unless otherwise noted, the above hotels are centrally located.

USEFUL INFORMATION

Banks: Open 10-4, Mon-Fri. Banking facilities at International Airport. There are banks throughout the country, and travelers' checks can be changed at large city hotels and in some shops.

Mail: Red mailboxes are attached to street lamp posts.

Telephone Tips: There are telephone booths and public phones available in many restaurants; they are coin-operated. A local call is NZ6¢. Useful numbers in Auckland:

Pan Am reservations 34-164
New Zealand Government Tourist
    Board 798-180
Directories 102
Emergencies 111

Airport Information 56-324
Accommodations Offices
    Hotels 794-660
    Motels 799-444

Newspapers: Local and national newspapers are in English; they include the *New Zealand Herald, Evening Post, The Press,* and the *Otago Daily Times.*

Tipping: Tipping is still not general, though with the growth of tourism it is becoming more widespread. Usually 10% in restaurants and to hotel lounge waiters (barmen are not tipped). Porters and hall porters get NZ10¢ or NZ20¢ for each piece of baggage handled. Taxi drivers receive this if they help with baggage, otherwise they are not tipped.

Electricity: 230 volts 50 cycles AC.

Laundry: There are good laundry and dry-cleaning facilities in the cities, many with 24-hour services, and there are laundromats in the principal cities. The major hotels also have good services, and some hotels provide guest laundry and pressing rooms. Average cost to dry-clean a suit, from NZ$4; to launder a shirt, from NZ$1.50.

Hairdressing: There are good hairdressing salons in the towns, but only a few in the hotels. Shampoo and set costs from NZ$10, men's haircut, from NZ$3.50. Tipping is not usual.

Photography: Black and white and color film are available everywhere. There are reliable developing services—24 hours for black and white, up to a week for color. Black and white film costs about NZ$3.58, color NZ$4.40.

Clubs: Rotary, Lions, Jaycees, Zonta, Kimonia, Overseas League, Royal Commonwealth Society, Travel Club, English Speaking Union of Kiwanis—all have branches in the principal cities. Local Public Relations offices will give details of meetings.

Babysitting: Available in large towns. Information can be found at hotels, or in the local telephone directory.

Rest Rooms: There are public facilities in streets, as well as in restaurants, some shops and some gas stations.

Health: A high standard of medical, hospital, and dental services is nationwide. Imported pharmaceuticals and toiletries are available. Water is good. Tourists injured while in New Zealand are eligible for compensation of medical and hospital costs arising from the accident regardless of fault. The scheme covers a reasonable period of recovery but allows no recourse to damage suits.

TRANSPORTATION

The total length of New Zealand is 1,000 miles, and there are 57,300 miles of roads, 3,220 miles of railroads, and 7,750 miles of regular internal air routes. There is a local bus service in cities and scheduled bus services throughout the country linking with good rail services, providing a reliable and efficient transportation network. Inter-Island Steamers connect North and South Islands, sailing from Wellington to Picton; advance bookings recommended. Air New Zealand links the principal cities of both islands and there are buses provided for passengers to and from airports and city terminals at NZ$1 to 3. Mount Cook Airlines offers scheduled services from North Island to South Island's scenic highlights and unscheduled "Flightseeing" excursions at resort areas.

Taxis are readily available and can be found at stands or called for by phone. They have meters, and rates per mile are approximately NZ40¢. Rental cars are available from NZ$25 a day, and many visitors tour in rented campers. Roads are good, except in remote areas. Traffic drives on the left.

FOOD AND RESTAURANTS

New Zealanders prefer plain and wholesome food, though continental cooking is gaining ground. Often food consists of first-class ingredients simply cooked, and, as so much meat and dairy produce comes from New Zealand farms, it is fresh and excellent. The lamb is outstanding and eaten in large quantities, but beef and pork are also very good. New Zealand is one of the world's largest dairy producers, so eggs, cheese, butter, cream, and ice cream are splendid. The waters around New Zealand provide some exotic specialties, including crayfish (rock lobster), whitebait, *paua* (abalone), scallops, and oysters fresh from the sea. Some restaurants serve wild game specialties such as venison and hare. The Maoris eat mutton-bird, the young of the sooty shearwater seagull. Visitors may try it, but it is an acquired taste. Scones and *piklets* (pancakes) appear at teatime, and *pavlova*, a rich meringue dessert, is one of the local specialties.

New Zealand only recently moved into the luxury restaurant trade, so standards of international cuisine vary, and few restaurants of quality exist outside the main cities. The restaurants of the principal hotels are usually good and reliable. Some places to try in Auckland are **Antoine's**, for French food and a restored colonial atmosphere (tel: 798-756), the **Bell House** in Pakuranga for continental dishes (tel: 564-015), and the **Ponsonby Fire Station** (tel: 769-499). Bars often provide simple cold food cheaply.

DRINKING TIPS

New Zealanders are beer drinkers, and the local beer is good and inexpensive. Wines are produced locally and are served with meals in hotels and restaurants. Pleasant white and red table wines cost from NZ$6 a bottle. Imported wines are usually available. Most hotel bars are open from 11am-10pm. Bottles can be bought at bars, or at package stores, up to 10pm except Sunday. Only those over 20 are allowed in bars. New Zealand's pubs are used for leisurely social drinking and there are some other delightful drinking spots. In the many vineyards of the Henderson area of Auckland visitors may sample the best of New Zealand wines free of charge.

ENTERTAINMENT

The standard of musical and theatrical life in New Zealand is improving. The **New Zealand Symphony Orchestra** tours the country giving concerts. All the large cities have professional theater groups. There are several Maori music concerts, and touring artists from Australia, the UK, and America visit frequently. The major cities have a few nightclubs and many pubs offer live entertainment. Movie houses show current British and American films. The pastoral and agricultural life of the country is reflected in the big national and regional agricultural shows, the country's biggest get-togethers and entertainment, with sheep-shearing and tree-falling contests. Auckland has its **Easter Show** in April or May, its **Royal Agricultural and Pastoral Show** in November.

SHOPPING

Stores are open 9-5 Mon-Thurs; 9-9pm Friday; 9-12 Saturday, closed Sunday. Jewelry made from the iridescent *paua* shell set in silver is charming and Maori handicrafts are attractive—they are expert wood carvers and also make ornaments out of greenstone, which looks like jade. These can be found mainly on the North Island. Sheepskin rugs are good and so are all kinds of knitted garments including handmade wool sweaters. In Auckland the shopping district is **Queen Street** and the neighborhood close to the principal hotels. Good shops include **The Disabled Servicemen's Shop** (58 Queen Street) and **Smith & Caughey Ltd** (246 Queen Street). **Christchurch** is promising territory for collectors of English antiques.

SPORTS

The national sport—and passion—is rugby, and matches can be seen in the main cities. But New Zealand also offers splendid tennis, soccer, and cricket. Clubs welcome visitors as temporary members—the National Tourist Board will give details. Golf is played on glorious courses on both islands—there are 325 registered clubs which make visitors welcome. It is usual to take a letter of introduction from one's home club secretary. The beaches offer swimming, surfing, and skin-diving from October to April, and there is yachting in many harbors. The **Regatta** held in Auckland on Anniversary Day is one of the biggest in the world. Deep-sea fishing off 300 miles of North Island beaches will take the sportsman less than an hour to spectacular fighting fish—marlin, shark, tuna—from January to April. Freshwater fishing in lakes and fast-running rivers is exciting and rewarding. The game-bird shooting season opens the first Saturday in May. Firearms must be registered. Hunting—for deer and chamois—is not as easy as it used to be because the animals have been driven to inaccessible areas where the terrain is rough and a guide, becoming harder to find, is essential. The **Hunting & Fishing Officer,** Tourist & Publicity Department, PO Box 527, Rotorua, will give details.

Hiking and tramping (long-distance mountain walking) through some of the world's most exciting scenery is very popular—contact the **New Zealand Federation of Mountaineering Clubs** (PO Box 1604, Wellington). For mountain climbing, contact the **New Zealand Alpine Club** (PO Box 2211, Christchurch).

Skiing: June through September are the most reliable months for downhill skiing on some of the world's best snow playgrounds, stretching for miles over glaciers and down mountainsides. Contact the **New Zealand Ski Association** (PO Box 2213, Wellington). **Mount Ruapehu** on North Island is reached from Chateau Tongariro. **Mount Cook** and the Alpine range are on South Island. Equipment can normally be rented at areas and through hotels. There is a well-stocked shop at the Tourist Hotel Corporation's **Hermitage Hotel,** Mount Cook. Horse-racing meetings are held at **Auckland** and **Wellington. Christchurch** and **Dunedin** feature flat racing and the popular harness racing.

WHAT TO SEE

North Island—the most populated island: Wellington and Auckland lie about 350 miles apart on North Island, and the three routes linking them cover the island's chief attractions.

Auckland, the city in which visitors first arrive, is placed astride two seas, **Waitemata Harbor** and **Manukau Harbor,** which provide contrasting glorious views. The town is built on sloping hills, surrounded by forests. A scenic drive above the city to take in the setting is a must, while a waterfront drive displays the seaside location. **Mount Eden,** behind the town, was once a Maori fort; here, and from nearby **One Tree Hill,** there is a magnificent view. The **War Memorial Museum** in 200 acres of gardens houses one of the best Maori collections in the world. The **Zoological Park** has specimens of the unique kiwi. Several airlines arrange "Flightseeing" trips over the city and its surroundings, with glimpses of South Island across the Strait. The **Bay of Islands,** 140 miles north of Auckland, is wonderful for water sports and fishing. Close by is **Treaty House,** where the Treaty of Waitangi was signed. For hotels in this area try **THC Waitangi** (Waitangi, Bay of Islands), double room from US$62; or the **Duke of Marlborough** (The Strand, Russell, Bay of Islands), double room from US$35.

Wellington, the capital since 1865, is another superbly situated city surrounded by steep hills. There are cable cars running up to fine views, city bus trips, and aerial tours. The **Dominion Museum** and **Art Gallery** hold displays of Maori and South Sea Island art and life. The **Botanical Gardens** (over 63 acres) have beautiful flower displays, especially over Christmas, which, of course, falls in high summer. The **Ngauranga Gorge** gives access to West Coast swimming resorts. **Petone,** 8 miles away, has a memorial to the first settlers—a replica of the bow of their ship and a stained-glass window. Wellington restaurants—located mostly in the downtown area—are **Beefeater Arms** (tel: 738-195), the **Coachman** (tel: 848-200), **Bacchus** (tel: 846-592) for a variety of dishes from a continental menu, and **Plimmer House** (tel: 721-872) for beef and seafood.

The **Central Route,** from Auckland to Wellington via Rotorua, passes through the pleasant town of **Hamilton** on the Waikato River, then reaches the extraordinary **Rotorua,** center of the thermal area. Here the most spectacular phenomena in the world can be seen—geysers, boiling mud, hot pools, hot springs, spouts of gushing steam. The peculiarities of the area—like Lake Rotorua, where the waters are icy but the sandy shores too warm for bare feet to walk on—must have sounded for years like incredible travelers' tales. Rotorua is also the center of Maori life and culture, with a model village, displays of carving, and concerts of Maori music and singing. Bus trips make these fabulous sights easily accessible from Rotorua, and there are a great many to choose from, organized by the Tourist Board.

The **East Coast Route** skirts the Bay of Plenty, with **Tauranga,** a paradise for deep-sea fishermen, and the golden sands for swimming and surfing at **Ohope Beach.** Try the **Sunseeker** motel (23 West End, Ohope Beach).

The **West Coast Route** passes, about 130 miles from Auckland, the tiny village of **Waitomo,** honeycombed with caves with limestone stalagmites and stalactites twisted in amazing, distorted shapes. (You might stay at the **Waitomo Hotel,** which is inexpensive.) The high spot of a visit to the caves is a boat trip to **Glow Worm Grotto,** lit by an unearthly blue-green radiance given off by tens of thousands of insect larvae covering the roof and walls. Southward the road reaches **Egmont National Park,** circling an extinct volcano—**Mount Egmont**—as harmonious and symmetrical against the sky as Japan's Fujiyama. **New Plymouth,** the major town in the district, stages a nine-day **Festival of Pines** every February, combining art, music, and sport. The **Westown Motor Hotel** (Maratahu Street, New Plymouth) has double rooms from US$36. **Wanganui,** 50 miles on, has a unique service for visitors—dial 8888 and a voluntary guide will show you around—and you can stay at the **Vacation Hotel,** 379 Victoria Avenue (from US$38 double).

South Island—characterized by fjords and inlets: **Christchurch,** the capital of South Island, has been called "the most English town outside England." But today its heart is an ultra-modern **Town Hall** and cultural center. Through the town flows a river called the Avon, crossed by 37 stone bridges, bordering the **Botanic Gardens.** The **Canterbury Museum** has comprehensive Maori and Antarctic collections and a charming replica of the 1860 Christchurch Street. The **McDougall Art Gallery** is nearby.

In the Southern Alps 116 miles from Christchurch is **Mount Cook,** a year-round resort named after New Zealand's tallest peak, which so impressed the Maoris with its 12,350-foot height that they call it *Aorangi,* the Cloud-Piercer. Most thrilling experience for many visitors is a spectacular flight in a ski-equipped airplane that rides low over the mountains and then glides to a stop on a snowfield covering the **Tasman, Fox,** or

Franz Josef glaciers. Intermediate and expert skiers are ferried to the Tasman Glacier by plane for a 10-mile run during the spring-to-fall ski season. Alpine Guides for skiing and mountaineering are headquartered in a rental shop at the deluxe **THC Hermitage Hotel,** Mount Cook (from US$62 double).

Queenstown, on **Lake Wakatipu,** was once a gold-mining center and is now a large and lively resort city with many shops. Excursions include a launch trip across the lake to **Walter Peak** sheep station, skiing and chair lift rides at **Coronet Peak,** a gondola ride to **Bob's Peak,** jet-boating on the **Shotover River,** and exploring old gold-mining settlements en route to **Skippers Canyon.** In Queenstown, stay at the **TraveLodge,** Beach Street (from US$65 double). **Fjordland National Park** covers 3 million acres of South Island—wild, rugged country and a coastline cut by 13 fjords. Peaks rise thousands of feet straight out of the sea, cascades crash down sheer slopes, dark pine forests loom in the distance—all combining to create a magnificent world. Much of this—perhaps New Zealand's grandest scenic treasury—can be reached by road, motor launch, or air. Remote **Te Anau,** at the southern end of majestic **Lake Te Anau,** is the gateway to Fjordland National Park. The **THC Te Anau Hotel,** in a lakeside garden setting facing snow-capped mountains, has double rooms from US$50. Across the lake from Te Anau is a glowworm cave and it's now possible to drive to the underground hydro-electric station at **Lake Manapouri** and on to **Doubtful Sound.** From Te Anau to **Milford Sound** there are two scenic routes: for the athletic, the 33-mile **Milford Track,** a 5-day walk; for the less energetic, a bus or car trip past exotic flora, waterfalls, a mirror lake, then through the **Homer Tunnel,** an engineering feat. Milford Sound is the most startling and magnificent of the fjords, dramatic in its rugged grandeur. At its head is the **THC Milford** which takes 80 guests and is a center for exploration (from US$58 double). A 2-hour motor launch trip visits the 540-foot **Bowen Falls, Stirling Falls, Mitre Peak, Mount Pembroke,** and enters the Tasman Sea. And the launches are welcomed by grampuses—large creatures like porpoises, which surface and follow the boats.

North of Fjordland Park, the coast of South Island reveals dramatically contrasting scenes, with subtropical forests and great glaciers—the twin glaciers Franz Josef and Fox flow through land where orchids and the crimson rata flowers grow. (An inexpensive hotel here is the **Fox Glacier.**)

Some 82 miles north of Christchurch is **Hanmer Springs,** a center for skiing, riding, fishing, golf, and year-round swimming—there are thermal springs.

SOURCES OF FURTHER INFORMATION

Pan Am: 3 Shortland Street, Auckland, and any Pan Am office around the world; **New Zealand Government Tourist Bureau:** 80-84 Wakefield Street, Wellington; 99 Queen Street, Auckland; 630 Fifth Avenue, Suite 530, New York, NY 10020; New Zealand House, Haymarket, London SW1.

Pakistan

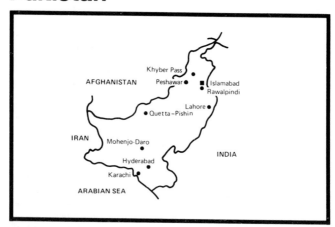

WHAT'S SPECIAL

Founded in 1947, Pakistan is one of the world's younger nations. Situated at the eastern end of the great Khyber Pass, it lies astride the ancient land route to the Indian subcontinent and the East. The influences of migration, invading armies, trade, and travel have left a country with a rich culture and a fascinating history of struggle and strife. Having achieved independence with the division of a predominantly Hindu India, this Muslim nation later lost its eastern wing when Bangladesh was established in 1971.

COUNTRY BRIEFING

Size: 310,403 square miles   **Population:** 82,000,000
Capital: Islamabad   **Capital Population:** 250,000
   Climate: Relatively dry; warm winter days, chilly nights; summer, April-June, is much hotter. Heavy rains June, July, and August. Coastal Karachi is tempered with sea breezes. Best time to visit is September-March.

Weather in Karachi: Lat N24°48′; Alt 13 ft

Temp (°F)	Jan	Feb	Mar	Apr	May	Jun	Jul	Aug	Sep	Oct	Nov	Dec
Av Low	55°	58°	67°	73°	79°	82°	81°	79°	77°	72°	64°	57°
Av High	77°	79°	85°	90°	92°	92°	91°	88°	88°	91°	87°	80°
Days no rain	30	24	25	30	31	25	20	25	27	31	30	30

Government: An Islamic republic.
Language: Urdu; many other dialects and English spoken.

Religion: 98% Muslim.
Currency: Rupee. 100 paisas = 1 rupee.

	50ps	Re1	Rs5	Rs10	Rs50	Rs100	Rs500	Rs750
US (dollars, cents)	.05	.10	.51	1.01	5.07	10.13	50.65	75.98
UK (pounds, pence)	.02	.05	.24	.48	2.42	4.84	24.21	36.31

Public Holidays: There are weekly holidays on Fridays and many Muslim holidays based on the lunar calendar, including 10th Muharram, Birthday of the Holy Prophet, Last Friday of Ramzan, Eidul Fitra (2 days), and Eidul Azha (2 days). Fixed holidays are:

Pakistan Day, 23 Mar
May Day, 1 May
Bank Holiday, 1 Jul
Independence Day, 14 Aug
Defence Day, 6 Sep
Anniversary of the Death of Quaid-i-Azam, 11 Sep
Birthday of Quaid-i-Azam & Christmas, 25 Dec
Bank Holiday, 31 Dec

HOW TO GET THERE

Flying time to Karachi Civil Airport from New York is 15¼ hours; from Tokyo, 10¼ hours; from Hong Kong 5½ hours. Time in Pakistan: GMT+5.

REQUIREMENTS FOR ENTRY AND CUSTOMS REGULATIONS

Passport; a tourist visa is required only for tourists who plan to stay longer than 30 days. Smallpox, cholera, and yellow-fever vaccinations only required if coming from an infected area. No limit on foreign currency imported; only Rs20 can be taken out, and only Rs80 can be brought in. Duty-free allowance: 200 cigarettes or 50 cigars; ½ pint perfume; up to US$50 worth of gifts; no liquor allowed.

AIRPORT INFORMATION

The taxi fare into town from Karachi Airport is Rs35 for the 10-mile trip. Airport to city buses stop at the Beach Luxury and the Inter·Continental hotels and cost Rs10 per person. Tip porter Re1 per bag. Departure tax is Rs100. Duty-free shop and hotel reservations counter at airport.

ACCOMMODATIONS

Apart from hotels, there are hostels, rest houses, and Dak bungalows. Prices below do not include 15% excise duty on services and $1-3 per day bed tax. Hotels in Karachi:
Rates are in US$ for a double/twin room with bath or shower
Beach Luxury, New Queen's Road (from $50), 10 minutes from center city on harbor
Columbus, Clifton Road (from $32)
Gulf, Dawood Pota Road, Saddar (from $20)
Holiday Inn, Abdullah Haroon Road (from $70), near American Consulate
Hostellerie De France, Main Drigh Road (from $55), near Karachi Airport
INTER·CONTINENTAL KARACHI, Club Road (from $103)
The Inn (from $35), near Karachi Airport

Jabees, Abdullah Haroon Road (from $38)
Mehran, Shahrah-e-Faisal (from $55)
Metropole, Club Road (from $35)
Midway House, Stargate Road (from $45), near Karachi Airport
National City, Saddar Road (from $15)
North Western, 26 Beaumont Road (from $12), near Karachi Airport
All hotels centrally located unless otherwise indicated.

USEFUL INFORMATION

Helpful Hints: Remove shoes when entering a mosque; women should cover their heads. Do not take photographs of women.

Banks: Open 9-1 Saturdays-Wednesdays, 9-11am Thursdays. Closed Fridays. Hotels also change currency; do not use street money-changers.

Telephone Tips: Useful numbers in Karachi:

Pan Am 510121/4	**American Consulate General** 515081
Airport Information 415931	**Directories** 17
Tourist Office 514477/516397	**Emergencies** 222222

Newspapers: Numerous daily English-language papers, such as the Karachi *Morning News, Dawn,* and *Business Recorder* in the morning, and the *Daily News, Leader,* and *Star* in the afternoon; the *Pakistan Times* from Lahore and Islamabad, and *The Muslim* from Islamabad; and the *Khyber Mail* from Peshawar.

Tipping: Service charge added in all restaurants and hotels. When tipping for other services, use your discretion.

Electricity: 220/240 volts 50 cycles AC.

Laundry: Most establishments offer a 24-hour service (dry-cleaning a suit, from Rs16; laundering a shirt, from Rs4).

Hairdressing: First-class hotels have salons (shampoo and set from Rs15, a man's haircut from Rs10; tip 10%).

Photography: Film readily available in major centers. Black and white costs Rs15 a roll, and color Rs50 and up. One-day processing available for black and white, 2 days needed for color; not all makes processed locally.

Clubs: Sind Club, Boats Club, Karachi Gymkana, Karachi Race Club, Karachi Golf Club, Karachi Club.

Health: All medical practitioners speak English. Drink only bottled water; boil milk. Wash fruit and vegetables. Take antimalarial precautions. Salt tablets are advisable.

TRANSPORTATION

The railroad network is extensive, but when traveling go first class or in an air-conditioned coach for comfort; ideally, rent a "Tourist Car," which can be attached to any train. Costs are low, and you need to reserve ahead. Metered taxis cost from Rs2 per mile.

FOOD AND RESTAURANTS

Flaming red *tandoori* chicken is a most renowned Pakistani dish; eaten with a flat wheaten *nans;* other delicious chicken dishes are a specialty, too—chicken *peshaware,* chicken *mussallam,* chicken *tikka,* and chicken curries. The other basic meat is lamb. For good Pakistani food, the **Chandni Lounge** at the Hotel Inter·Continental (tel: 515021) is elegant; **Farooq** (tel: 511031) is also excellent. **Bundu Khan** (tel: 71659), **Shezan** (tel: 78984), **Cafe Grand** (tel: 512400), **Casbah** (tel: 551031), **Shezan Kohsar** (tel: 428628), **Three Aces** (tel: 516226), the **Seherzade** at the Holiday Inn (tel: 512309), the **Golden Horse Shoe** (tel: 432939), the **Bali** (tel: 430260) for Indonesian food, and **Alpha** (tel: 514177) are all good.

DRINKING TIPS

Beer and most liquors are produced locally; they are less expensive than imported ones, and their standard is reasonable. Liquor is prohibited for local Muslims, but foreign visitors may drink in bars in almost every major city.

ENTERTAINMENT

There are folk and English music shows at the **Inter·Continental.**

SHOPPING

Pakistan has glorious bazaars, with gold and silver jewelry, glass bracelets, hand-embroidered shawls, tapestry-style vests and caps, silk, and brocades. In Karachi try the **Cottage Industries** sales and display center, and wander around the old bazaars; you might visit **Bohri Bazaar,** the **Saddar Cooperative Market,** the little shops along **Bunder Road, Tariq Road** in the PECH (Pakistan Employees' Council Housing) Society area, and **Kahkashan Market** in Clifton, Karachi's beach, about 4 miles south of the city.

WHAT TO SEE

Karachi, on the Arabian Sea, is the largest and most populous city (nearly 3½ million people) in Pakistan. See the **Mausoleum** of the father of the nation, Quaid-i-Azam; the **Defence Housing Society Mosque; Frere Hall** in the Jinnah Gardens; the **National Museum** in Burns Garden; and **Clifton Beach** and **Hawks Bay.**

Close to Karachi are the hot sulphuric springs at **Manghopir** and the ancient town of **Thatta. Makli Hill** is unusual, with 6 square miles of richly decorated tombs. The **Chakundi Tombs** are 14 miles from Karachi. About 60 miles north is the **Shahjehan Mosque** in the Thatta District, built in 1647. The archaeological site of **Moenjodaro,** dating back to the 2d and 4th centuries BC, is approximately 412 miles north of Karachi.

Lahore, "the City of Gardens," is the educational and cultural center of the country and has priceless Mogul monuments. Best known are the **Shalimar Gardens;** the **Tomb of Emperor Jehangir,** a majestic four-towered mausoleum; **Lahore Fort;** and the world's largest mosque, **Badshahi.** Other Mogul treasures are **Wazir Khan's Mosque** and the tombs of **Anarkali** and **Noor Jehan. Lahore Museum** has Mogul exhibits. **The Mall** is the main shopping center. Places to dine are the **Shezan** (tel: 52654), **Cathy Chines** (tel: 58392), **Omar Khayam** (tel: 80077), **Nemat Kadah**

(tel: 62657), **Lords** (tel: 312235), and **Fletti** (tel: 53861). Hotels in Lahore:
Rates are in US$ for a double/twin room with bath or shower

Ambassador, 7 Davis Road (from $25)

Faletti's, Suhrawardy Road (from $40)

Indus, 56 Shahrah-e-Quaid-i-Azam (from $20)

INTER·CONTINENTAL LAHORE, Shahrah-e-Quaid-i-Azam (from $53)

International, The Upper Mall (from $32)

Lahore Hilton, 87 Shahrah-e-Quaid-i-Azam (from $53)

Orient, 74 McLeod Road (from $10)

Zonobis, Main Market, Gulberg II (from $12)

Hotels are centrally located unless otherwise indicated.

Peshawar has the best bazaars in Pakistan. The most fabled are the **Quissa Khawani Bazaar,** also known as the street of the storytellers, and the heart of the city, and the nearby **Bazaar Baterbazan** and **Mochilara.** Also visit the **Mahabat Khan Mosque,** the ancient **Bola Hissar Fort,** and the **Peshawar Museum.** The nearby **Khyber Pass** is a vital key to the defense of India and Pakistan. Close to Peshawar is the **Landi Kotal,** where the Pathans have an amazing bazaar. Hotels in Peshawar: the **KHYBER INTER·CONTINENTAL,** Khyber Road (from US$50 double) and **Dean's Hotel,** Islamia Road (from US$28 double).

Rawalpindi-Islamabad: These cities form the focal point for trips to the lovely summer resorts of the **Murree Hills,** the **Kaghan Valley,** and the lofty **Gilgit Peaks.** For a panoramic view of the twin cities, go up to the **Shakar Parian Hills.** There are also numerous archaeological sites nearby, some dating back to the 6th century BC. The best sites are **Taxila, Gir, Kalawan, Jaulain, Manikyala, Tarbela Dam,** and **Mangla Dam.** Hotels in Rawalpindi are **Flashman's,** 23 The Mall (from US$35 double CP); **INTER·CONTINENTAL RAWALPINDI,** The Mall (from US$56 double), and **Hotel Shalimar,** The Mall (from US$27). Islamabad has the **Holiday Inn,** Agha Khan Road (from US$60 double) and the **Islamabad Hotel** (from US$30). Places to dine are the **Alhamra** (tel: 63524), **Silver Grill** (tel: 64719), the **Maharajah** (tel: 66370), and **Shezan** (tel: 62774).

SOURCES OF FURTHER INFORMATION

Pan Am, Metropole Hotel, Abdullah Haroon Rd., Karachi, and any Pan Am office around the world. **Tourist Information Offices:** Shafi Chambers, Hotel Inter·Continental, Club Road, Karachi; 5 Transport House, Egerton Road, Lahore; Club Annexe, The Mall, Rawalpindi; 8-C Super Market, Shalimar 6, Islamabad; Dean's Hotel, Islamia Road, Peshawar. **Embassy of Pakistan,** 2315 Massachusetts Avenue NW, Washington, DC 20008; **The Consulate General of Pakistan,** 12 East 65th Street, New York, NY 10021; **Pakistan Embassy,** 35 Lowndes Square, London SW1.

Papua New Guinea

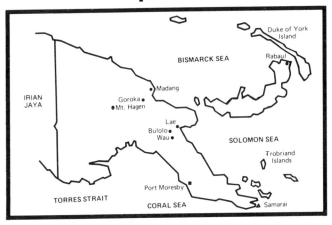

WHAT'S SPECIAL

Papua New Guinea comprises the eastern half of the island of New Guinea and a multitude of island groups lying off the coast. It is a unique country—not in terms of industrial, military, mineral, or agricultural strength or even its dramatic natural beauty, but rather for its people and their way of life. For here is one of the last places on earth where human beings virtually untouched by civilization are finally being thrust into the modern world. There are tribes in the highlands who, until a few years ago, thought they were the only people on earth. There existed, until recently, a "cargo cult" among some tribesmen, who believed that airplanes carried gifts from the gods and who built miniature airfields as welcoming shrines.

Now this country of stark mountains, deep ravines, rich forests, hidden rivers, and untouched people is being carefully opened up to progress and tourism. With its scores of lovely offshore islands, some comfortable modern towns and ports, and efficient transportation links, Papua New Guinea presents a dazzling prospect for the anthropologist and tourist alike.

COUNTRY BRIEFING

Size: 178,260 square miles   **Population:** 3,100,000
Capital: Port Moresby   **Capital Population:** 113,500
   Climate: Papua New Guinea is hot all the year round. The driest season is from May to December. The highlands can get rather cool at night.

Weather in Port Moresby: Lat S9°29'; Alt 126 ft

Temp (°F)	Jan	Feb	Mar	Apr	May	Jun	Jul	Aug	Sep	Oct	Nov	Dec
Av Low	76°	76°	76°	75°	75°	74°	73°	73°	74°	75°	76°	76°
Av High	89°	87°	88°	87°	86°	84°	83°	82°	84°	86°	88°	90°
Days no rain	23	21	22	25	29	27	29	29	28	29	27	25

Government: Papua New Guinea is a parliamentary state which gained its independence from Australia in September 1975. It is a member of the British Commonwealth of Nations.

Language: There are over 700 local languages. English is the language of government and commerce and is closer to an official language than any other; "pidgin English" and, to a lesser extent, Motu are the main oral languages of communication.

Religion: Traditional religious beliefs form an integral part of the native cultures. Christianity is represented in most cities and towns.

Currency: Kina (pronounced "keener"). 100 toea (pronounced "toyer") = K1.

	5t	20t	50t	K1	K5	K10	K20	K50
US (dollars, cents)	.08	.31	.77	1.53	7.65	15.30	30.60	76.50
UK (pounds, pence)	.04	.15	.37	.73	3.65	7.30	14.60	36.49

Public Holidays:

New Year's Day, 1 Jan
Good Friday
Holy Saturday
Easter Monday

Queen's Birthday, June
War Remembrance Day, 15 Aug
Independence Day, 16 Sep
Christmas Day, 25 Dec
Boxing Day, 26 Dec

In addition, each of the 19 provinces has its own special holiday celebrated only in that province.

HOW TO GET THERE

Flying time to Jackson Airport, Port Moresby from Sydney is 3¾ hours, Manila 5 hours, and Hong Kong 6½ hours. Time in Papua New Guinea: GMT+10.

REQUIREMENTS FOR ENTRY AND CUSTOMS REGULATIONS

Passport; round-trip or onward ticket. Citizens of many countries, including the US, Canada, UK, Australia, New Zealand, several surrounding Pacific and Asian nations, and most European nations need no prior visa for a stay up to 30 days, provided they are bona fide tourists and arriving by air at Port Moresby only, where they will be issued a Tourist Visa on arrival. Visas are required of others and are obtainable through PNG consular offices or, in countries where none exists, through the Australian High Commission or Consulate. Cholera and yellow-fever certificates required if arriving from an infected area. Anti-malarial precautions advised. Unlimited amounts of foreign currency may be taken in, but you must not leave with more than you imported. It is forbidden to import certain types of weapons, and animals are subject to import restrictions. Genuine relics and ancient artifacts cannot be taken out of the country without official permission. Duty-free allowance: 200 cigarettes or 250 grams of cigars or tobacco; 1 liter liquor; perfume for personal use; and gifts up to a total value of K200 per adult. Persons under 18 years of age are allowed K100 worth of duty-free goods but not liquor or cigarettes.

AIRPORT INFORMATION

Jacksons Airport, Port Moresby, is 7 miles from the city center. The taxi fare into town is about K6.50 to Waigani, about K6-9 to hotels. Some of the hotels have buses that meet the planes upon arrival. The airport has a hotel reservation counter and duty-free shop. Most other airports in Papua New Guinea are very small and have no such facilities. Departure tax for international flights is K10.

ACCOMMODATIONS

Lodgings are simple but good in Papua New Guinea, ranging from hotels and motels to guesthouses. For inexpensive accommodation try the YMCA or YWCA. No tax or service charge is added to hotel bills. Hotels in Papua New Guinea (Port Moresby, Lae, and Madang):
Rates are in US$ for a double/twin room with bath or shower
  Cecil, PO Box 12, Lae (from $28)
  Davara, Ela Beach Road, Port Moresby (from $43)
  Gateway, Jackson Airport, Port Moresby (from $52)
  Huon Gulf, PO Box 612, Lae (from $49)
  Islander, Waigani Drive, Port Moresby (from $56)
  Madang, PO Box 111, Madang (from $50)
  Melanesian, PO Box 756, Lae (from $60)
  Outrigger, Vanama Crescent, Port Moresby (from $32)
  Port Moresby TraveLodge, PO Box 3661, Port Moresby (from $68)
  Smuggler's Inn, PO Box 303, Madang (from $52)

USEFUL INFORMATION

Helpful Hints: Get hold of a "pidgin English" phrase book. It's very useful, e.g. *Apinun*—Good afternoon; *Wonem naem bilong yu*—What's your name?; *Paus bilong me stap we?*—Where is my suitcase?; *Bringim kaikai*—Bring me some food. The expressions "please" and "thank you," once unknown, are becoming more common as English becomes the standard language of commerce.

Banks: Mon-Thurs 9-3 and Fri 9-5. The exchange counter at Jacksons Airport is open for the arrival and departure of all international flights. Money can be changed at banks (in larger towns only), larger hotels, and some trading stores.

Mail: Stamps can be purchased at post offices, hotels, and some stores. Mailboxes are red.

Telephone Tips: Public telephones can be found at post offices and in restaurants; there are phone booths. These phones are operated by a 10-toea coin. Useful numbers in Port Moresby:

Airport 255844
Office of Tourism 272161/5
Air Niugini 259000

Trunk Inquiries 012
Overseas Calls & Inquiries 016
Police 255555

Newspapers: Foreign newspapers are available in major centers. Local English-language newspapers are the *Post Courier*, the *Times of Papua New Guinea*, and the *New Guinea News*.

Tipping: Not customary.

Electricity: 240 volts AC throughout the country. Large hotels have converters.

Laundry: Facilities available in major towns. For 24-hour service, hotels would be most reliable. Dry-cleaned suit, from about K4.50; laundered shirt, from about K2.

Hairdressing: Very few hairdressers in hotels; some in major towns. Cost for a shampoo and set, from about K6; for a man's haircut, from about K3.50.

Photography: The selection of photographic equipment is limited. Black and white film takes a couple of days to be developed, color about two weeks.

Clubs: Regular meetings of clubs such as Rotary, Apex, and other service clubs held in Port Moresby. Visiting members are welcome.

Health: Visitors should take anti-malarial tablets before, during, and up to a month after their stay. Hospital, medical, and dental facilities are fairly widespread, and all doctors and dentists speak English. European toiletries are readily available.

TRANSPORTATION

Port Moresby and Lae have limited bus services. Taxis are usually available. No train services. Air Niugini, the country's national airline, flies F28 jets and F27 turbo-props to over 15 domestic airports. Other outlying posts are connected by a network of smaller aircraft. Cars can be rented for about K14-20 per day plus mileage charges. Avis, Hertz, and Budget Rent-a-Car are represented.

FOOD AND RESTAURANTS

For the visitor to Papua New Guinea, the most exciting way to try the local foods is to attend a native feast. At these gala events roast pork is the specialty, accompanied by sweet potatoes, rice dishes, tropical fruits, and an array of other vegetable dishes. In Port Moresby, all the hotels have restaurants, many serving international cuisine. The new Trave-Lodge has a good restaurant, and so does the Islander and the Davara. For good Chinese food, go to the **Moonlight** (tel: 25 3168) or the **Mandarin** (tel: 25 3634) or the **Green Jade** (tel: 25 4013). For Indonesian food, go to **Akabar** (tel: 25 2347). Facilities in Lae and other main centers are good but naturally on a smaller scale.

DRINKING TIPS

South Pacific and San Miguel are popular locally produced beers. Imported wines, liquors, and beers are also available. A bottle of imported wine in a hotel or restaurant costs about K8, a whiskey in a bar or hotel about K1.50.

ENTERTAINMENT

Clubs and hotels form the basis of nightlife in Papua New Guinea. A lively band and a few drinks can make for a pleasant evening. The major towns have movie theaters that show current English and American films with original soundtracks. A number of local repertory groups regularly stage productions of light modern drama. You may be lucky enough to come across a spontaneous *singsing*, a coming together of villagers to sing and dance through the night in celebration of a wedding, the killing of a pig, planting or harvesting, or almost any other event. There are annual regional festivals of traditional culture that include *singsing* groups; the **Port Moresby Show** in June, for instance, and the **Morobe Show** (Lae) in October. The **Nabarosa Festival,** which takes place for a week in June, features local theater and dance, *singsings,* and craft and art displays (Madang). For an ideal opportunity to see the local people entertaining themselves in the grand manner, plan your visit to coincide with the **Eastern Highlands Show,** held in Goroka in even-numbered years. Thousands of tribespeople arrive from all over the Highlands to sing, dance, and parade in full regalia—vivid body paints, headdresses, beads, feathers, shells, and the famous mud masks.

SHOPPING

Stores open 8-4:30 five days a week and Saturday mornings. Among the bargains to take home are wood carvings, exotic masks, basketware, Madang pottery, elaborately decorated shells, painted shields, and necklaces made from shells and seeds. Hotels have artifact shops and in outlying districts the craftsmen themselves bring their wares to the hotel grounds each day. In Port Moresby, the government-run **Village Arts Center** on Rigo Road near the airport has a huge selection of artifacts from all over the mainland and the islands (open 8-5 Mon-Sat, 9-4 Sun). The **Girl Guides Handicraft Shop** (near Koki Market) has other items suitable as gifts or souvenirs. Other stores are **Burns Philp** on Musgrave Street, **Steamships Trading Company,** Champion Parade, plus innumerable Chinese stores.

SPORTS

Golf, tennis, and squash are all readily available. Sporting clubs are numerous, and the **Port Moresby Golf Club** is among the many that welcome visitors. Sports that are a feature of Papua New Guinea are fishing, hunting, and trekking. You can journey on the **Fly** and **Sepik Rivers,** rough it a little in the jungles and do some crocodile hunting, or go deep-sea fishing from **Wanigela** or off **Rabaul.** You can walk the **Kokoda Trail** and try to break the current record of 30 hours, 5 minutes. Undertaken at a more leisurely pace, it may take three days or more. There is good fishing also in the **Trobriand Islands.**

WHAT TO SEE

Port Moresby, capital of Papua New Guinea and seat of government, is a rambling city spread out along seven miles of tropical beaches. For a panoramic view of the town drive up to **Tuaguba Hill** or **Paga Point.** The spectacular new **National Museum and Art Gallery** at Waigani houses a selected range of traditional artifacts as well as current exhibits and is a good introduction to the country's many cultures. Also at Waigani, on the grounds of the University of Papua New Guinea, are the **National Botanic Gardens** with an outstanding orchid collection. Wander through the **Koki Market,** about 3 miles from the center, and enjoy the color, bustle, smells, and excitement of market day under the palm trees. Or visit the little village of **Hanuabada,** a tropical suburb on stilts. For natural beauty take a drive out to **Rouna Falls** and **Laloki Gorge,** or relax on the lovely **Ela Beach,** about a 5-minute walk from the center. The **Bomana War Cemetery** is worth a visit for its beautiful design and gardens.

Lae is a city of tree-lined avenues and gracious palm trees by the brilliant blue of the Huon Gulf. Pay a visit to the **Botanical Gardens** right in the center of town, with hundreds of species of plants and more of New Guinea's beautiful orchids. For a good meal **Melanesian Hotel** has a first-class restaurant.

To see an idyllic village set among palm trees, take a boat trip to the island of **Awasa Bosama,** or for good fishing take the boat out to **Samarai Island,** off the southeastern tip of the mainland. The **Trobriand Islands** are also renowned for their beauty. For the grandeur of mountain scenery, a drive up the **Markham Valley** is exciting, and a trip to **Bulolo** and **Wau** is well worth the effort. **Rabaul,** on the island of New Britain, nestles among the peaks of four volcanoes, the **Mother,** the **North and South Daughters,** and **Rabalankaia. Matupit** (still semi-active), a fifth volcano, is near the airport. Take a cruise around Rabaul's beautiful **Simpson Harbour,** the crater of an exploded volcano, and see the **Beehives,** cone-shaped islands of volcanic origin at the mouth of the harbor. Other features of volcanic interest are the hot springs and the **Vulcanological Observatory,** well worth a visit. While in Rabaul visit the "special" market (every Saturday), where the Chinese shops on **Kamerere Street** and **Casuarina Avenue** have a wide range of bargains, or go out to **The Duke of York Islands** and take advantage of the fishing in these waters. Hotels in Rabaul: **Hamamas Hotel,** PO Box 212, Mango Avenue (from US$43), **TraveLodge,** Mango Avenue (from US$65 double); **Kaivuna,** Mango Avenue and Namanula Street (from US$58 double). For dining out, the **TraveLodge Restaurant** offers good European cuisine.

The Highlands area of Papua New Guinea is the most densely populated in the country and one of the last to be penetrated by the outside world. **Goroka,** a picturesque mountain town set in a valley 5,000 feet above sea level, is the nerve center of the Eastern Highlands Province. Rent a car and explore the beauty of the towering **Bismarck Ranges** which loom over the town and provide a dramatic backdrop. At Goroka, tours can be arranged to visit the **Asaro Valley,** home of the world-famous Asaro Mudmen. According to legend, these tribesmen in some distant past had been driven into a river by their enemies. Emerging covered with mud, they frightened their attackers into retreat and have since then daubed themselves in mud and worn fearsome masks, also of mud. But their costume is only one of an incredible variety of face and body decoration you will see if you can make your visit to Goroka at the time of the **Eastern Highlands Show,** held in even-numbered years. It is a spectacularly colorful event, especially for camera enthusiasts, with thousands of natives parading and dancing. For your stay in Goroka, first-class accommodations are available at the **Bird of Paradise Hotel** (from US$45 double) and the **Lantern Lodge** (from US$35 double).

Mount Hagen is the keystone of the primitive Western Highlands Province, an area first reached by Western explorers in the 1930s. It is the center of the coffee and cattle regions and the gate to some of the most remote and spectacular areas, where villages are lost in the lush and rugged terrain. A side trip is to the **Bird of Paradise Sanctuary** at Baiyer River, 30 miles north of Mount Hagen, to see the exotic birds that are Papua New Guinea's national symbol. Accommodations in Mount Hagen are at the **Airport Hotel,** the **Highlander Hotel,** or the **Hagen Park Motel** (from US$43 double). The **Sepik River** region north of Mount Hagen is best seen from the river itself, a mile wide at its mouth and 700 miles in length. There are houseboat cruises of varying duration that will take you through dense jungle and swamp, past villages on stilts in the water or dry-land villages dominated by the richly decorated "haus tambaran" or spirit house. Accommodations in the area are in the towns of **Wewak, Maprik,** and **Angoram,** and are good though they should be reserved well in advance. Or stay at the **Karawari Lodge,** built in "haus tambaran" style on a tributary of the Sepik River at **Amboin.** Double rooms at US$84 per day AP include sightseeing tours along the river.

SOURCES OF FURTHER INFORMATION

Any **Pan Am** office around the world; **Papua New Guinea Office of Tourism,** PO Box 5644, Boroko; **Papua New Guinea Mission to the UN,** 801 Second Avenue, New York, NY 10017; **Papua New Guinea Embassy,** 1140 19th Street NW, Room 503, Washington, DC 20036. **Papua New Guinea Consulate-General,** 225 Clarence Street, Sydney, NSW, Australia.

People's Republic of China

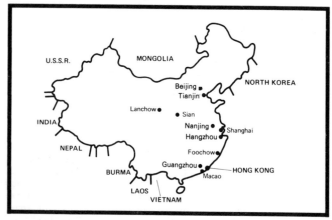

WHAT'S SPECIAL

No guide to the Pacific, or the world for that matter, can be complete without a mention of China. Like daylight through curtains, it persistently makes its presence felt in half the countries you visit, through its people, its trade, its traditions and customs. China is larger than continental Europe and contains over a quarter of the world's people. Its processes of civilization have matched those of Europe and the Middle East. Often China has led the West, in technical as well as cultural progress. Gunpowder and printing were known here centuries before they were developed in Europe. By 200 BC China possessed a national road network, standardized coinage, weights and measures, and script. By 200 AD a civil service and nationwide examinations had been developed, and the codification of laws had begun. Through all these and following ages the arts and sciences flourished astoundingly, leaving struggling Europe far behind. Agriculture and trade were very advanced by Western standards—there was a credit-exchange system in operation before the 9th century, and fairly sophisticated taxation. By the time Marco Polo and various missionaries arrived, the West still had a lot to learn.

A succession of wars—foreign invasions both military and trading, the Revolution in 1911 that turned China into a republic, the Sino-Japanese War from 1937-1945—culminated in the struggles that led to the establishment of the People's Republic of China in 1949. During all this time, and particularly since, increasing periods of introspection and isolation have left China something of a country apart, a country of mystery. Now this giant of life and history is opening up again to visitors and to trade, and more people are going there, not just statesmen and business-men. China is in the process of refurbishing more than 120 tourist destina-tions around the country and adding a network of new hotels and resorts with an eye to attracting 1 million tourists.

COUNTRY BRIEFING

China covers an area of about 3,691,501 square miles with a **population** of well over 900 million. The **capital** is **Beijing** (Peking), with a population of over 8 million. Because it is such a huge country, its **climate** is fairly wide-ranging, from some of the wildest deserts to the highest mountains on earth. In general, winters are cold and dry in Beijing, and summers are hot. Best time to visit is during spring or fall. In the south, the climate is subtropical, year round. China is a people's republic, and of the many regional variations of Chinese spoken, Mandarin and Cantonese dialects predominate. The official language is the Beijing dialect of Mandarin. However, all written languages are mutually intelligible because the writ-ing is ideogentic rather than purely phonetic. The **Pinyin** romanization system has been inaugurated which renders place names and personal names different from what many visitors are used to seeing. Peking, for example, is now Beijing, Canton is Guangzhou, Tientsin is Tianjin. Shanghai remains Shanghai. Mao Tse-tung is now Mao Zedong, Chou En-lai is Zhou Enlai. China is spelled Zhounghua. Your guide can help you understand the new place names. The **currency** is the renminbi (yuan); 10 chiao = 1 renminbi; 1.73RMB = US$1. **Public Holidays:** Chi-nese Lunar New Year, or Spring Festival, Jan or Feb; Labor Day, 1 May; Army Day, 1 Aug; National Day, 1 Oct. Time in China: GMT+8.

REQUIREMENTS FOR ENTRY AND CUSTOMS REGULATIONS

Passport, visa, and round trip ticket are required. Immunization against yellow fever and cholera are required only if arriving from an infected area. Importation of foreign currencies is allowed, but must be declared on arrival. The exchange into local currency can be made through the Bank of China or through facilities at visitors' hotels. Antiques over 150 years old and art treasures may not be exported except with special permits. One still camera and a small 8mm movie camera per family are permitted on entry. No 16mm movie cameras are permitted. Duty free allowance: reasonable amount of tobacco for personal use.

ACCOMMODATIONS

Chinese tourist hotels are comfortable and most are air conditioned. The average cost of the room varies from as little as US$12 per night in some of the smaller tourist centers to as much as US$150 or more for a suite in an exclusive Beijing Hotel. These prices, however, are academic as normally all reservations are made through China Travel Service and they designate which hotel you will stay at upon your arrival in each city and impose a service charge on packages, which generally include airport meeting and transfer by an interpreter, hotel, meals, guides, local air and rail transportation. Independent travel is not encouraged, although requests can be made to China Travel Service (Luxing-she) Changan Avenue, Beijing—tel: 667-850, or to CTS branches in Hong Kong, Tokyo, and Paris. A number of new hotels are in construction or in the planning stage but most will not be available until 1983-84. In Beijing, the **Beijing Hotel**, the **Minzu**, and **Xin Qiao** are being expanded with new wings and the main buildings are undergoing extensive refurbishing. A new airport hotel has been opened as has also the new suburban **Fragrant Hills Hotel** with 300 rooms. Hotel space is currently at a premium, especially during national holidays, and in Guangzhou, during the semi-annual Trade Fairs (15 Oct-15 Nov, and 15 Apr-15 May). Hotels in Guangzhou (Canton) include the enlarged and completely refurbished **Hotel Dong Fang**, the **Liu Hua, Bai Yun,** and **Beijing.** Most hotel prices have been brought into line with international levels for foreign tourists—averaging US$25-80 per day, but may be adjusted from time to time. In traveling elsewhere in China, accommodations are normally arranged by CTS in comfortable hotels or first-class guest houses. As all travel arrangements are handled by CTS, there is usually little or no choice in the accommodations. Service is generally good, and hotel food is excellent. Visitors are advised to carry a minimum of luggage and to wear easy-to-clean clothing. Tourists are almost always taken in groups with individual travel discouraged, though requests for sightseeing within each city will be entertained.

USEFUL INFORMATION

Currency and travelers' checks can be exchanged by banks or at special facilities installed in some hotels. MasterCard, Visa and Diner's Club are accepted at the Shanghai Arts and Crafts Trade Fair. MasterCard and Visa are now being accepted at the Shanghai Friendship store, and at the Beijing Friendship store. With an American Express card, you can cash a personal check up to $1,000 at the Bank of China in Shanghai, and this service is expected to expand to other larger cities. Credit facilities can be arranged in advance for telegraph and telephone calls overseas. Money can also be transferred into China by cable. As for **tipping**—don't. **Laundry:** 24-hour service is usually available at hotels. **Photography:** Chinese color and black and white film is available, and Kodak film is now available in some larger cities such as Beijing and Shanghai, but is expensive. Travelers are advised to bring enough film for their entire trip. You are free to take as many pictures as you like, except of military installations and inside certain museums, monasteries and temples. As the Chinese are shy, be sure to ask them before you take their pictures. Hotels have outgoing telex facilities but not incoming. International telephone calls are often easier to complete than calls inside China. Cable service is reliable. Mail service is very good. Airmail letter to US costs 70 **fen** (Chinese cents). **Hair styling** is available but technique and styles are not up-to-date. Shampoo and set costs 1-2RMB, a permanent 2RMB. **Health:** Use bottled or boiled water, which is supplied in every hotel room daily, and bring a supply of basic medicines. Local medical services are readily available to visitors.

TRANSPORTATION

Taxis cannot be hailed. They can be ordered at hotels, the International Club, or cab stands, and have a fixed rate. Non-tourists can hire chauffeured sedans for about US$25 per day in major cities. The airline within China is the **CAAC** and fares are relatively low. Typical air fares: Beijing-Shanghai US$110, Shanghai-Guangzhou US$140. First class is generally not available on flights within China. Railroads are used as the major cross-country means of transport, and rates for foreign visitors are higher than for residents but modest by international standards.

FOOD AND RESTAURANTS

Chinese food is some of the healthiest in the world and represents the first of what is known to Europeans as *haute cuisine:* it is also unique. Each region of China has its own distinctive form of cooking based upon local produce and the various ways in which it may be best enjoyed. Most of these culinary varieties can be enjoyed in the capital. Chinese food, using rice as its staple, is well represented in restaurants all over the world, and typical dishes such as steamed rolls and the delicious clear soups will be familiar to most travelers. Fish, especially shellfish, and pork are the most common additions to rice, frequently accompanied by sauce—sweet and sour, mild or spicy. One of the most pleasant restaurants in the capital is the **Ting Li Guan** at the Summer Palace. The famous Peking Duck is served at the **Quan Ju De** and the two **Bian Yi Fang's.** The good news for tourists is that Peking Duck style restaurants are being expanded so that more may enjoy this incredible art. The **International Club** has Western and Szechuanese food—very spicy. **Tang Chun Yuan** specializes in Kiangsu dishes. The best French cooking is at the **Peace Café** in the Dong Feng market. All hotels have restaurants serving European as well as Chinese food. An average meal costs about 7 to 12 yuan (about US$4.25). A full table for 12 runs about 130RMB or US$85 for a magnificent 10-course Chinese dinner in Beijing. Meal prices are being raised to accommodate the demands of tourists and these should be regarded as minimum figures. Smaller parties usually are seated with other diners at large, round tables. Visitors will find themselves seated in special sections reserved for overseas guests. While this certainly assures better service and often avoids waiting for a table, there are complaints that this tends to isolate the visitor from contact with Chinese people. International brands of wines and hard liquors are now available in the major hotels and Friendship stores, as is Coca-Cola.

ENTERTAINMENT

Movie houses predominantly show Chinese films, with no accompanying subtitles. Theaters stage modern and traditional works, including Beijing and Cantonese operas and even occasional Western ballets such as *Swan Lake.* Acrobatic shows are popular entertainment and worth seeing. Major cities have regular concerts. The most exciting time to be in the capital is on **National Day,** when the streets and square are packed with singing crowds, many in national costume, and bands playing spirited national music. At the **Summer Palace,** the **Working People's Palace of Culture,** and the city parks, there are almost continuous performances of opera, acrobatics, ballet, music, puppet shows, folk singing, and dancing. The **Beijing Hotel Café** is perhaps the busiest night spot in Beijing. Open until 11:30pm you can have drinks, cold snacks and even ice cream sundaes.

SPORTS

Sport is greatly encouraged in China, and the facilities are made available to visitors. Soccer, basketball, volleyball, ping-pong, gymnastics, and Chinese boxing and fencing are all popular spectator sports.

SHOPPING

The best buys in Beijing are porcelain, jade, rubbings of Tang dynasty works of art, silk, and small antiques. Nothing older than 150 years can be exported. Hand made silk rugs are good buys. Scrolls are quite inexpensive and make attractive gifts. **Wangfuching Road** is a good street for the shopping tourist, and antique shops in **Liu Li Chang** are worth exploring. While the stores are being renovated, the Liu Li Chang shops have been moved temporarily to the Temple of Heaven area. **Pai Huo Ta Lou** is Beijing's biggest department store. Never bargain in shops, stores, or markets as prices are set. **Friendship Stores** are open 7 days a week and are geared to foreign visitors. In the **Beijing Friendship Store,** all items from food (including hamburgers) to cloths and luggage are available. The **Shanghai Number 1** department store is a must for all visitors. A very busy store where the Chinese do their shopping, the use of a little language can get a tourist most any item.

WHAT TO SEE

Beijing (Peking): Among the modern buildings and party slogans are the wonderful historic monuments for which Beijing is famous. In the center of the capital is the golden-roofed **Forbidden City** with the many Imperial Palaces, including the **Palace Museum,** and just to the west lies a string of beautiful lakes surrounded by terraces and marble balustrades. In front of the Palace Museum is **Tien An Men** square, with the balcony from which Chinese leaders preside over parades. Just outside Beijing is the **Summer Palace,** with lovely pagodas, pavilions, temples, and courtyards, and other attractive hills decked with lakes, pavilions, and terraces. At the Summer Palace is the beautiful marble boat, built by the Dowager Empress. The 4,000-mile-long **Great Wall of China,** begun 2,500 years ago, is a must and can be climbed at Badaling outside of Beijing. The **Ming Tombs,** about 30 miles from Beijing, are approached by a road lined with statues of men and animals. In the underground mausoleum here there are carved marble thrones. Ten miles from Beijing is the beautiful 12th-century **Luouchiao** (Marco Polo bridge), made of white marble with carved, animal-topped balustrades. Although CTS makes arrangements, the following information about hotels in Beijing may be helpful. In the capital there are presently the four major hotels listed earlier that are used for tourism.

The **Beijing Hotel** is the most modern and is next door to the former French Beijing Hotel, now used exclusively by Chinese visitors to the capital. There's a full range of services, including a bank, post office, telegraph bureau, restaurants—the main dining room has an occidental and Chinese menu and caters to guests and nonresidents alike—souvenir and food store, plus a hairdressing salon and barbershop. There are private banqueting rooms and a Japanese restaurant on the second floor. This 16-story hotel has some 1,800 beds, and the rates are from RMB50-150, depending on room standard.

The **Minzu**—or Nationalities—**Hotel** is about eight minutes from downtown Beijing, just off West Chang An Avenue. There are two restaurants, one serving Chinese food, the other Western. There are three stores, post office, bank, and bookstore. There's also a women's hairdressing salon and barbershop. Rates, depending on standard of room, range from RMB15-50.

The **Xin Qiao Hotel** is located in the former "legation" quarter of the city, just a few minutes walk from the railroad station. There's a main restaurant serving Chinese food on the ground floor, while the Western menu is to be found on the sixth floor restaurant. Shops, post office and cable office, bank, and hairdressing salons. Rates from RMB15-45.

The **Youyi Binguan**, or Friendship Hotel, is about 20 minutes from downtown, and located in the northwest of the city. There are a number of accommodation buildings set around the main six-storied building in spacious grounds. Usual amenities, including the one open air swimming pool (open June-September) attached to a hotel here at present. Rates are from RMB15-30.

Destinations other than Beijing are opening rapidly. Package tours ranging from 1 day in Guangzhou to 20 days that include several cities are available from travel agents all over the world. Some special tours also include a Yangtze River cruise, Tibet, and Outer Mongolia. Passengers from the United States can fly directly into China through Beijing or Shanghai, or via Hong Kong and Guangzhou in the south.

Shanghai: Perhaps the world's most populous city, Shanghai numbers today more than 16 million people within its metropolitan area, and is one of the three municipalities—with Beijing and Tianjin—to be directly under central government control. Shanghai (which means *up from the sea*) is known to the Chinese as "Hu" from the word "hudu," a name given to the lesser known river—the Suzhou—around which the original settlement was made many thousand years ago, and which flows into the Huang Po (Yellow River) which is navigable year-round to vessels of up to 10,000 tons and has led the city to become China's major port. (The dock area runs more than 30 miles along the banks of the river which is about 200 yards wide and 30 feet deep at this point.)

Shanghai is best known for its Bund, a riverside boulevard with attractive gardens and flanked by European buildings that once housed merchant banks and trading concessions of former times. Today the offices are used by Chinese officials, though the city remains rather more cosmopolitan than many other Chinese cities, with its well-kept parks, theaters, and historic buildings and sights. Hotels include the former Palace Hotel—now the **Heping** (Peace) **Hotel** located on the Bund (Zhongsan Road, by the river); **Jinjiang Hotel,** similarly old fashioned, used mostly for visiting foreign delegations and notable for the fact that a telex service is available on the premises; **Shanghai Mansions,** in the heart of downtown, also has telex services; **Hengshan Hotel,** near the Gymnasium Center; the **Overseas Chinese Hotel** and **Guoji** (or International) **Hotel,** on Nanjing Road and formerly known as the Park Hotel.

Guangzhou (Canton): Gateway city of south China, just 80 miles from Hong Kong by rail, Guangzhou is uniquely different from north China. Located on a bend of the Pearl River, Guangzhou was brought to the 20th century during the 1920s when a modernization program was put into being. Further modernization came following the rise to power of the present government in 1949. Guangzhou has been a center of foreign trade for more than 2,000 years, and civic records show visits by Roman traders as early as the Han dynasty (200 BC-220 AD), while the first modern Europeans to visit were the Portuguese in 1514. The **Guangzhou Fair,** held semiannually (15 Oct-15 Nov and 15 Apr-15 May), is credited for almost 30% of China's foreign trade. Hotels include the **Dong Fang** (RMB25-50), and the **Bai Yun** (or White Cloud) hotels (from RMB35-90), fully air conditioned with more than 2,000 rooms. There are 12 hotels which cater to distinguished Chinese guests from abroad, including the **Kwangchuan,** the **Liu Hua**—located adjacent to the Trade Fair site— and **Renmin Mansion,** overlooking the Pearl River. Visits to well-kept Taoist temples and to Changshan University, named after the birthplace of Dr. Sun Yat-sen, the father of modern China, are recommended. Guangzhou is jammed during the month-long Trade Fairs when thousands of foreign businessmen flock to the city.

Hangzhou (Hangchow): One of China's traditional beauty spots, Hangzhou has long been a resort retreat for the nation's leaders, including the late Mao Tse-tung. Extensive lakes dot the city's suburbs, complete with delightful arch bridges, choice restaurants and inspiring vistas.

Suzhou, an ancient city on the old Imperial canal, claims it has the most beautiful gardens in all China. Designed in the Ming dynasty, they are beautifully kept to this day. The extensive network of canals are still the city's major thoroughfares. Suzhou has been named the sister city of Venice because of its famous **Grand Canal,** one of the oldest waterways in the world. Suzhou rose to prominence in 518 BC and has preserved its traditional appearance, with temples, pagodas, ponds, and waterways. It is also a shopper's paradise, noted for its jade carving, woodworking, laquerware, and silk. The city is known for its fine cuisine.

Guilin (Kwelin), a delightful resort city in the hills, was founded by Qin Shi Huang Di in 214 BC and is one of the most picturesque places in all of China. Guilin is famous for its mysterious mountains and excellent weather, and is being developed as a resort area both for foreign visitors and for Chinese citizens. The local fisherfolk still use trained cormorants to catch fish for them. Located in the subtropical region of China, the vegetation is lush. River trips, on launches pulled and poled over rapids and shallows, reveal incredibly beautiful crags, valleys, and bamboo groves, and village life along the embankment. The city itself is small and charming, ideal for a walking tour.

Other tourism centers include **Nanjing** (formerly Nanking), the "southern capital" of earlier times, today seat of government for the province of Jiang Su and located on the Chang River (better known as the Yangtze). The Yangtze River bridge, one of the longest bridges in China, is located here and connects Beijing with the lower Yangtze River Valley. It is also one of the Chinese's proudest accomplishments, completed after the Soviets removed their help. Much of the old city remains, including the city walls, built under the Ming dynasty in the 14th century, and people have been living here, say the archaeologists, since as early as 4,000 BC. Visitors normally stay at the **Nanjing Hotel,** one of the nicest in the entire province. The city is in a beautiful setting and is the site of the **Sun Yat-sen Mausoleum** and the **Ming Tomb.**

The city of **Loyang** has a quaint old section with narrow streets and some very interesting **Han Dynasty** graves containing early paintings. **Chufoo,** close to **Tsinan,** capital of Shantung province, was the birthplace of **Confucius.** It has a lovely temple and grounds, and the philosopher's grave a wood partly surrounded by early walls. **Xian**—Famous for the over 6,000 terra cotta life size statues of warriors and horses discovered in tact at the entrance of the Qin Shi-huang di Tomb, dating back to 210 BC. Excavations were begun at this site in 1974, when a group of farmers stumbled on some of the statues while digging a ditch for irrigation. A museum has now been built over the tomb, and some of the statues have been moved to exhibits in cities such as Beijing and Shanghai. Excavations are ongoing, and the most recent discovery was a bronze chariot used by the emperor.

SOURCES OF FURTHER INFORMATION

Pan Am offices, International Club, Jianguomen Wai, Beijing; **Jing An Guesthouse,** 370 Huashan Road, Shanghai; **China Travel Service** (Luxingshe), Ch'ang An Avenue, Beijing; **China Travel Service,** 77 Queen's Road Central, Hong Kong; **Chinese Embassy,** 100 Bronson Avenue, Ottawa, Canada; **China Touring Center,** 200 West 57th Street, New York, NY 10019; **Chinese Chargé d'Affaires,** 31 Portland Place, London W1.

Philippines

WHAT'S SPECIAL

Once a part of the Sri-Vishayan and Madjapit Empires of Indonesia, the Philippines was discovered for the Western world by Magellan in 1521 and became a colony of Spain. Filipinos proclaimed their independence from Spain in 1898 and set up a short-lived republic. That same year, because of the Spanish-American War, control passed to the United States, and the Philippines did not regain independence until 1946. The nation's history can be traced in its architecture, as well as its richly varied cultures.

The Philippines has much to offer. Islands have always held a special fascination for mankind and when you realize that the Philippines is made up of more than 7,100 islands, only a third of which are inhabited or even named, you can begin to understand the unique charm and attraction of the country for even the most seasoned travelers. It has some of the finest beaches in the world. Go north, and you can see whole mountain ranges carved into gigantic stairways—indelible monuments to the tribes who cultivated rice on the terraces thousands of years ago. Go south to the islands of Sulu, where you'll hear the chants of Muslim sea-gypsies, who live by gathering pearls from the sea bed. If you're adventurous, you can choose among exploring underwater caves, scaling a live volcano, shooting the rapids in a dugout canoe, or hunting wild boar through virgin forest. If you're a naturalist you'll want to see some of the world's smallest fish, hunt the most beautiful sea shells, and revel in the richest display of flowering plants and ferns in the Orient. And if you're fascinated by ancient customs and traditions, you'll find yourself with a full schedule. Whatever your interest, you'll be enchanted by the friendliness of a people whose own rich racial heritage has endowed them with a special gift of making each visitor, of whatever nation, feel thoroughly at home.

COUNTRY BRIEFING

Size: Eleven main islands account for about 96% of the total land area of 115,880 square miles. The archipelago stretches about 1,000 miles from north to south and is about 688 miles wide.

Population: Approximately 49 million.

Capital: Manila, the capital, includes Quezon City, three suburban cities, and 13 towns, and has about 8.5 million people.

Climate: Tropical, with two pronounced seasons: rainy, with risk of typhoons, June to October; dry from November to May. April and May are very hot, so the best time to visit is between November and March.

Weather in Manila: Lat 14°35'; Alt 47 ft

Temp (°F)	Jan	Feb	Mar	Apr	May	Jun	Jul	Aug	Sep	Oct	Nov	Dec
Av Low	69°	69°	71°	73°	75°	75°	75°	75°	75°	74°	72°	70°
Av High	86°	88°	91°	93°	93°	91°	88°	87°	88°	88°	89°	86°
Days no rain	25	25	27	26	19	13	7	8	8	12	16	20

Government: A republic. The transition to a parliamentary system of government was implemented in 1978 with the election of a National Assembly. In 1979 martial law was put into effect. The system was modified in April 1981 through a constitutional amendment providing for general elections. Martial law has been lifted throughout the Philippines, except for two regions in Mindanao.

Language: Pilipino is the national language. English and Spanish are widely spoken. English is used as a medium of instruction in schools. It is interesting to note that the Philippines is the third-largest English-speaking nation in the world. Many dialects still in existence.

Religion: About 85% of the population is Roman Catholic.

Currency: Pesos. 100 centavos = 1 peso.

	0.50	P1	P2	P5	P10	P50	P100	P500
US (dollars, cents)	.07	.13	.26	.64	1.28	6.42	12.83	64.15
UK (pounds, pence)	.03	.06	.12	.31	.61	3.07	6.13	30.66

Public Holidays:

New Year's Day, 1 Jan
Maundy Thursday
Good Friday
Araw ng Kagitingan, 6 May
Labor Day, 1 May
Philippine Independence Day, 12 June

Philippine-American Friendship Day, 4 July
All Saint's Day, 1 Nov
National Heroes Day, 30 Nov
Christmas Day, 25 Dec
Rizal Day, 30 Dec

HOW TO GET THERE

Flying time to Manila International Airport from San Francisco 14½ hours; from Honolulu 10 hours; from Guam 3 hours. Time in the Philippines: GMT+8.

REQUIREMENTS FOR ENTRY AND CUSTOMS REGULATIONS

Passport—a visa is not necessary for citizens of most Western countries for a stay of 21 days or less, provided you have a round-trip ticket. For an extension of your stay, to a total of 59 days, apply to the Commissioner of Immigration in the Philippines or to any diplomatic or consular office abroad. Vaccination certificates are required for smallpox; cholera and yellow-fever certificates also required if arriving from infected areas. You may be asked to take out a bond (redeemable on departure) if bringing in items like radios, typewriters, or tape recorders. The importation of narcotics and coffee is prohibited, and firearms are held by customs on arrival until the owner obtains an import permit from the Philippines police. Tourists do not have to fill out a customs declaration form upon arrival in the country. Their baggage is generally exempt from inspection, but they are asked to verbally declare any dutiable items. Items which may be brought in duty-free: wearing apparel, jewelry, toilet articles, a camera, and a reasonable amount of film and similar personal articles. Tobacco: 200 cigarettes, 50 cigars, or 3 pounds of pipe tobacco. Liquor: 1 quart of alcoholic beverages. Two kilos of packaged tea. Currency: tourists may bring in any amount of foreign currency without being required to fill in currency declaration forms though the amount of currency taken out should not exceed the amount brought in.

AIRPORT INFORMATION

Manila International Airport is about 6 miles from the city center. There is a regular public bus service to the center, and taxis are always available. Departing passengers must pay a departure tax of P25. The airport has a duty-free shop and hotel reservation counter.

ACCOMMODATIONS

The Ministry of Tourism can arrange accommodations and will supply a list of approved hotels and hostels. Most hotels add a 10% service charge; government hotel tax is 10%. In Baguio City there is a 25% reduction in rates in the off-peak season. Inexpensive lodging available in hostels (P50-100 nightly) and in YMCA/YWCA dormitories (single P77, double P100 nightly). Hotels in Manila include:

Rates are in US$ for a double/twin room with bath or shower

   Century Park Sheraton, Vito Cruz corner Adriatico (from $60)

   Holiday Inn Manila, 1700 Roxas Boulevard, Pasay City (from $53)

   Hyatt Regency Manila, 2702 Roxas Boulevard, Pasay City (from $66), near center city

   INTER·CONTINENTAL MANILA, Ayala Avenue (from $64), 6 miles from center city

   Manila, Rizal Park (from $75)

Manila Garden, Makati Commercial Center (from $60), 6 miles from center city
Manila Hilton, United Nations Avenue (from $70)
Manila Mandarin, Paseo de Roxas-Makati Avenue (from $72), 6 miles from center city
Manila Peninsula, Ayala Avenue-Makati Avenue (from $75), 6 miles from center city
Midtown Ramada, Pedro Gil, Ermita (from $55)
Philippine Plaza, 1146 Roxas Boulevard, Cultural Center (from $70)
Philippine Village, Manila Airport, Pasay City (from $50), 6 miles from center city
Regent of Manila, Roxas Blvd, Passy (from $52)
Silahia International, 1990 Roxas Blvd, Manila (from $55)
Tradewinds, South Superhighway, Makati (from $34), 6 miles from center city
Regent of Manila, Roxas Blvd., Passy (from $52)
Unless otherwise indicated, all the above hotels are centrally located. Hotel tax: 10%

USEFUL INFORMATION

Helpful Hints: One word of greeting you'll almost certainly hear: *Mabuhay,* a useful multipurpose word which can mean either "welcome" or, as a toast, "long life to you," and even "goodbye!" Social life—and dress—is lively and informal; Filipino women wear long evening dress only on the most strictly formal occasions. For men, the cool and comfortable *barong tagalog* or "manila shirt," woven from pineapple or banana fiber and worn outside the trousers, is worn on even very formal occasions. It can be very warm and humid, so bring cool, lightweight, and crease-resistant clothes.

Banks: Open 9-4 Mon-Fri. A 24-hour banking service is operated at Manila International Airport. In the provinces there are banks in all major towns, but they do not always exchange travelers' checks.

Mail: In addition to post offices, some shops will supply stamps. Letters take 5-10 days to reach both the United States and Europe.

Telephone Tips: Telephones are found in public booths, restaurants, cafés, and shops. For a local call, lift the receiver, deposit three 10-centavo coins, and wait for the dial tone; then dial the number you require. When the call is answered the money will drop automatically and make the connection. Useful numbers in Manila:

Pan Am 47-19-81	**Operator & Directories** 04
Tourist Information 59-06-25	**Long-Distance Operator** 09
Airport Information 80-62-05	**Overseas** 08
	Police 59-90-11

Newspapers: Leading daily newspapers are published in English. American magazines can easily be obtained in Manila.

Tipping: Many hotels and restaurants include a 10% service charge in your check—nothing extra is expected. If not included, add 10%. Taxi drivers 10% (optional); hairdressers P1 (optional); porters P1 per bag. In rural areas helpfulness often springs from genuine hospitality, and a tip may cause offense.

Electricity: 220 volts 60 cycles AC. Some hotels have 110-volt converters.

Laundry: Most hotels provide reliable 24-hour service. Rates are moderate—from P18 for dry-cleaning a suit; from P6.25 for laundering a shirt.

Hairdressing: Manila has many good hairdressers and barber shops, and first-class hotels may also have salons. Average cost for a shampoo and set from P10, for a man's haircut from P15.

Photography: Film and photographic equipment can be bought in major towns but is expensive. Black and white film can be processed in 24 hours; color can take from 48 hours to a week, depending on the film.

Clubs: Clubs in Manila include the Army & Navy Club, Elks Club, Manila Overseas Press Club, Manila Yacht Club, International Yacht and Tourist Club, Manila Boat Club, Manila Golf Club, Makati Sports Club, Wack Wack Golf and Country Club, Manila Polo Club, Club Filipino, Philippine Columbian Association, and Kiwanis Club of Manila. Rotary International meets every Thursday at the Manila Hilton, the Ermita Lions Club on the first and third Tuesdays of the month at the Army & Navy Club.

Babysitting: Services can usually be arranged through your hotel.

Rest Rooms: Women should look for the door marked *Babae;* men the one marked *Lalake.*

Health: Excellent medical and dental care available from American- and European-trained doctors and dentists. Cosmetic surgery is inexpensive and very good. Contact lenses are a fraction of their cost in Europe, the US. Tap water in Manila is safe to drink, and there is plenty of pasteurized milk. Play it safe by drinking boiled or bottled water and by avoiding raw vegetables when traveling in the provinces.

TRANSPORTATION

There are buses and taxis in all the big towns and also, in Manila, the so-called *jeepneys*—brightly painted jeeps converted to carry up to 10 passengers. The fare on jeepneys and buses, payable on boarding, is 60 centavos (P4.00 for air-conditioned Metro Manila buses) for any distance on a given route within city limits. The majority of taxis carry meters. Look for them at taxi stands outside hotels, or hail one in the streets. In Manila you can also ride by colorful horse-drawn *calesa*—rates for these depend on distance and time. There are car rental agencies for self-drive and chauffeur-driven cars. Traffic in the Philippines keeps to the right.

Many excursions by air-conditioned buses are run from Manila to places of interest on the main island, Luzon. The Ministry of Tourism can give details. Public bus lines cover much of the Philippines and are particularly extensive on Luzon because of its numerous concrete and asphalt highways. Two railroads operate: the Philippine National Railways on Luzon,

and the Philippine Railway Company on the island of Panay. The PNR extends from Manila north to Angeles, Cabanatuan, and San Fernando (La Union), and south to Quezon, San Pablo, Lucena, Naga, and Legazpi, for the volcano of Mount Mayon. You can reach the mountain resort of Baguio on the Northern line, via Damortis. Air-conditioned cars are available on day express trains, and there are first-class night express trains. Philippine Airlines operates on internal routes, and regular daily flights link Manila with all major centers, including Baguio. For travel between islands, steamship service is provided by several shipping lines at very reasonable rates. **Caution:** in spite of government measures, some of the extremely remote rural areas of the Philippines are still troubled with bandits; before you venture off the beaten track, check with the Ministry of Tourism.

FOOD AND RESTAURANTS

The cuisine of the Philippines is exceptionally varied and should appeal to all tastes. Favorite with the islanders is undoubtedly pork, whether served as *lechón,* a whole barbecued suckling pig, or as one of the many varieties of garlic, chicken, and pork casserole known as *adobo.* Other national dishes include *sinigang* (savory stewed fish with vegetables) and *lumpia* (vegetable roll). Rice is the staple food and is served with practically every dish. For dessert, Philippine fruits—mangoes, bananas, pineapples, papayas—are all excellent. Between-meal snacks—known as *meriendas*—are very popular; a favorite is hot chocolate and cakes. Mealtimes are generally the same as in Western countries. Prices for restaurant meals range from as little as P10. Western-style restaurants tend to be more expensive.

Restaurants in Manila which specialize in native foods are the **Zamboanga Restaurant** (8739 Makati Avenue, Makati, Rizal—tel: 89-49-32); **Las Conchas** (626 Makati Avenue, Makati—tel: 88-04-44); **Salambao** (Redemptorist Road, Parañaque, Rizal—tel: 83-92-92); and **The Bungalow** (1000 J Llanes Escoda Street—tel: 59-35-90). **Turo Turo sa Nayon** (Manila International Airport Avenue—tel: 83-19-84) not only serves specialties from the various regions of the country but also lets you see replicas of the various types of buildings and handicrafts typical of all the islands. Spanish food is at **El Comedor** in Malate, at **Jardin de Alba** in the Greenhills Shopping Center and at **Casa Marcos** on Roxas Boulevard, while the **Swiss Inn** (1394 General Luna Street, Paco—tel: 59-70-60) serves high-quality European food. French dishes are at **Au Bon Vivant** in the Ermita (near United Nations Avenue), Italian ones at **Cucina Italiana** in Malate and at the **Italian Village** in Makati and in Quezon City. **Max's Fried Chicken** (Roxas Boulevard, Baclaran, Pasay City—tel: 83-26-01) is memorable for just that— steaks are also served. If it's steak you want, Tomas Morato Avenue, Quezon City, is known as Manila's "Steak Street," site of **Alfredo's Steak House** (tel: 97-60-26). For Chinese food, **Kowloon House** (1533 A Mabini Street, Ermita—tel: 59-48-48), **Aberdeen Court** (7842 Makati Avenue, Makati, Rizal—tel: 89-93-72), and the **Mandarin Room** at the Hyatt Regency (tel: 80-26-11) are recommended. Try a

Polynesian menu at the **Luau** (155 Roxas Boulevard, Parañque, Rizal—tel: 83-40-60). Some of the best gastronomic treats are still in store at a variety of fine restaurants in the hotels, including **Hugo's Grill** at the Hyatt Regency, the **Rotisserie Grill** at the Manila Hilton, and restaurants at the Inter • Continental. Other popular spots are **Kamayan** on Pasay Road, Makati and Quezon Avenue (near Circle) in Quezon City, and **Barrio Fiesta**—in Ermita, Manila; West Avenue, and one on De Los Santos Avenue, Quezon City.

DRINKING TIPS

Favorites of the native population are *tuba,* a potent beverage fermented from the sap of palm trees, and *lambanog,* an even more potent coconut wine. There's also the excellent San Miguel beer. Minimum legal age for drinkers is 21. Hotel bars—the best bet for a leisurely drink—are open from 8am until about midnight, other bars much later. For the best martinis in town try the bar at the **Hilton,** while the **Inter • Continental** is tops for "Bloody Marys."

ENTERTAINMENT

At the **Philippine Cultural Center,** the **Folk Arts Theater,** the **Meralco Theater,** the **Philamlife Auditorium,** the **Rajah Sulayman Theater** in Fort Santiago, Intramuros, and the **Thomas Jefferson Cultural Center** in Quezon City, you can attend performances of contemporary theater, opera, music, and ballet, often with visiting European and American artists. Try to hear the distinctive native music or see a Filipino dance troupe—the **Bayanihan** and the **Filipinescas,** in particular, have won wide acclaim. The Bayanihan Troupe performs nightly at the Folk Arts Theater, and other troupes. Troupes sometimes appear in the better restaurants in the evening—see local papers for dates, times, and locations. Frequent festivals, fiestas, and religious pageants are part of the way of life—you can get a full list from the Ministry of Tourism. Some of the most spectacular are the **Procession of the Black Nazarene,** 9 January, in Quiapo, Manila; the **Ati-Atihan** carnival (third weekend in January) in Kalibo, Aklan province; the **Holy Week Morion** festival in the island province of Marinduque, when participants in colorful masks re-enact stories from the Bible; and the **Santacruzan,** a month-long gala street pageant celebrated in most towns in May.

Luncheon fashion shows present designs of local and international couturiers. Beautiful models are often featured in various restaurants such as **La Concha** at the Hyatt Regency and the **Top of the Hilton.** For nighttime entertainment in Manila you can choose from numerous nightclubs or supper clubs, offering various permutations of sophisticated food, floor shows, dancing, and hostesses. Among the most popular are **Where Else** at the Inter • Continental, **1571** at the Manila Hilton, the **Circuit** at the Hyatt Regency, **El Camarote** at the Holiday Inn, **Lost Horizon** at the Philippine Plaza, **Tipanan** at the Manila Peninsula, **Carousel Bar** at the Manila Mandarin, **Cellar Bar** at the Century Park Sheraton, and **Jungle Bar** at the Manila Hotel. Also worth trying are **Another**

World in Makati's Greenbelt Park, the **Gaslight Club** (Plaza Restaurant, Makati Commercial Center), and the **Sky Room** (Jai-Alai Building, Taft Avenue), where watching or betting on the games at the adjoining *fronton* makes an exciting alternative to dancing. **Bayside Club** and **Rino's** are on Roxas Boulevard, Manila's nightclub row fronting Manila Bay and often referred to as the Philippines' Las Vegas.

SHOPPING

Manila is a great undiscovered fashion center; some top French, Italian, and US designers have franchise arrangements, meaning you can pick up their creations for less than you'd pay back home. The **Makati** department store, for example, has a complete line of Dior models for less than Parisian prices. Tailors, too, rival the ones in Hong Kong and are no more expensive. Many local products are delightfully unusual and surprisingly inexpensive. Best buys are the hand-woven native textiles— *pina* (pineapple fiber) and *jusi* (raw silk), and articles and clothing made from these, often with colorful embroidery; *buntal* (Panama) hats; *abaca* (Manila hemp) bags and rugs from the Bicol provinces; exotic wood carvings from the northern mountain tribes; musical instruments from the Eastern Visayas; gold and silver filigree jewelry, brassware, and shellcraft from Mindanao; and black coral and mother-of-pearl from Sulu.

Principal shopping districts in Manila are **Ermita, Escolta, Rizal Avenue, Carriedo, Harrison Plaza** and **Quezon Boulevard.** In the suburbs are **Santa Mesa** and **Cubao** in Quezon City; the **Greenhills Shopping Center** in San Juan, Rizal; and the **Makati Commercial Center** in Makati, Rizal. A **Mabini Street** has many shops selling local handicrafts, and the **Divisioria Market** is a happy hunting ground for native fabrics. The main department stores are **Rustan's, Shoe Mart, Anson,** and the **Quad** at the Makati Commercial Center, **Berg's** (421 Escolta, Manila), **Good Earth Emporium** (Roces-Reyes Building, Rizal Avenue, Santa Cruz, Manila), and **Farmers Market, Rustan, Shoe Mart, Ali Wall I** and **II,** and **C.O.D.** in Cubao, Quezon City. Shops and stores are generally open 9-5, or later, sometimes with a break for lunch from 12 to 2. Souvenir shops and some stores are open Sunday mornings. Except in department stores, it is still customary to bargain for a reduction on the asking price. Major stores will pack and ship large purchases for you, but there is no tax-free export scheme for visitors in the Philippines.

SPORTS

Spectator sports like baseball, basketball, volleyball, tennis, and boxing are very popular in the Philippines, and there are regular events at the **Rizal Memorial Stadium** and at the famous 30,000-seat **Araneta Coliseum.** *Jai-alai,* a fast, exciting game of Basque origin, is played nightly, except Sundays, at the **Jai-Alai Building** on Taft Avenue. *Sipa,* a unique ball game that involves expert footwork, can be seen weekend afternoons at a park near the **San Lazaro Fire Station,** Manila. Cockfighting is a favorite weekend and holiday sport at cockpits in the suburbs and in all Philippine towns—it is also the most popular form of gambling among

Filipinos, though there is betting too at the daily *jai-alai* games and at horse racing on Saturdays and Sundays at the San Lazaro and Santa Ana race tracks.

If you want to get into the action yourself, you will find excellent facilities for year-round swimming and tennis everywhere; outstanding golf courses in Manila, Baguio, and Cebu City; yachting in Manila Bay; deep-sea fishing around Hundred Islands and in the Sulu Sea, except in the typhoon season (June to October); surfing on Quezon Beach and in Camarines Norte in December; horseback riding in Manila; mountaineering, freshwater fishing, and hunting in many locations. The Ministry of Tourism can give further information and put you in touch with sports clubs that welcome visitors.

WHAT TO SEE

Manila: For a glimpse of what the original Spanish walled city known as *Intramuros* was like before World War II reduced it to ruins, see the remains of Fort Santiago, a dungeon built by the Spanish and used as a prison by the Japanese during the war, and the surviving Church of San Augustin, the oldest stone church in the Philippines. Of the churches destroyed, only the Metropolitan Cathedral has been rebuilt, the sixth time since 1581. Also of historic interest are the 17th-century University of Santo Tomas, with its handicrafts museum, the Malacanang Palace, formerly the country home of the Spanish Governor-General and now the official residence of the President of the Philippines, and the Quiapo Church housing the shrine of the Black Nazarene which draws thousands of devotees every Friday. For a complete contrast, visit the modern suburb of Makati, a town planner's dream, with fine shops, restaurants, skyscrapers, San Andrés Church, and stunning residential areas. Makati also houses the Ayala Museum with its set of dioramas portraying episodes from Philippine history and is the site of the American Military Cemetery and Memorial. The National Museum, at Rizal Park, has fascinating relics of native art forms, and interesting contemporary art of all kinds can be seen at the Cultural Center of the Philippines, at the Luz Gallery in Makati, and at the Ateneo Art Gallery in Quezon City, as well as other museums and galleries. Opening hours are generally 9-5 weekdays only. Rizal Park, with its monument to the Philippine national hero, Dr José Rizal, is a favorite resort of Manilan families on Sunday afternoons, and on any day it is a good spot for enjoying the famous sunset over Manila Bay. Children can let off steam in the park's colorful gardens; they will also appreciate outings to Manila Zoo, the Aquarium, and the Nayong Pilipino (Philippine cultural Village), where the traditions and handicrafts of each area of the Philippines are beautifully presented and demonstrated. The Philippine Marine Life and Shells Museum is here also.

A hydrofoil trip to the island fortress of Corregidor, in Manila Bay, takes 50 minutes. See the historic World War II landing beaches, Milelong Barracks, and the Malinta Tunnel, wartime headquarters of General MacArthur and scene of the army's historic last stand.

Southern Luzon: Only half-an-hour's drive south of Manila is the church of **Las Pinas,** Rizal, famous for its remarkable bamboo organ, which is 150 years old and has withstood earthquakes, typhoons, war, and termites. Farther south, through countryside dotted with attractive stilt-house villages, rice fields, and tropical orchards, is **Tagaytay Ridge** and a spectacular view of **Lake Taal** and its unique volcano-in-a-lake-in-a-volcano.

At **Pagsanjan,** two hours' drive from Manila, on the eastern side of Laguna province, visitors can transfer to dugout canoes manned by expert native boatsmen for an unforgettable trip up river through steep, rocky gorges and lush jungle-type vegetation, to the roaring **Pagsanjan Falls.** The trip downstream is made doubly exciting by the thrilling experience of "shooting the rapids." Right on the southern tip of **Luzon Island,** in the province of Albay, the skyline is dominated by the perfect cone of **Mayon Volcano** (almost 8,000 feet), the most active of the Philippine volcanoes. This region is famous also for its beaches, hot springs, and boiling-mud lakes, and for *abaca* handicrafts. **Legazpi,** the main center, is 1½ hours from Manila by air, 12 hours by rail.

Northern Luzon: Baguio is about 150 miles north of Manila (less than an hour by plane) and is the summer capital of the Philippines. A cool climate, spectacular scenery, and beautiful parks and gardens make it one of the country's top resorts. From Baguio you can take a bus or car for a day's trip to the amazing **Banaue Rice Terraces,** sometimes called the "eighth wonder of the world." Carved out of the mountainside by the Ifugao tribes thousands of years ago, without the aid of metal tools, the terraces, if put end-to-end, would span halfway round the world. Ifugao tribesmen can still be seen here, clad only in loincloths and carrying spears. A little to the west of Baguio, down the coast, are the lowland beach resorts of **Bauang, San Fernando,** and **Poro Point.** Nearby are the delightful **Hundred Islands,** the Pacific's largest marine reserve. The islands are ideal for swimming, skin-diving, fishing, or just lazing on the beautiful white sandy beaches.

The Visayan Islands: If you have time, the southern islands of the archipelago will be well worth a visit. The oldest Spanish settlement and, after Manila, the largest city in the Philippines is **Cebu,** where you can still see the cross planted by Magellan during his voyage of discovery in 1521. Nearby in the beautiful **San Augustin Church** is the oldest Christian relic in the country, an image of the Holy Child. Cebu is 350 miles from Manila, about 1 hour by jet, or 2 days by boat. The island next to Cebu is **Bohol,** whose **Chocolate Hills**—mounds of earth sprawled over many miles of plains like huge chocolate drops—are still an unexplained mystery.

Still farther south is the island of **Mindanao,** home of some of the most colorful communities and exotic flowers and fruit in the Philippines. There are direct flights from Manila to **Zamboanga,** a busy port at the western tip of the island, known as the **"Gateway to Moroland"**—land of the Filipino Muslims. Apart from its mosque, and the *moro vintas*— the brightly striped broad-sailed craft of its fishermen—Zamboanga is noted for beautiful hanging gardens and parks, notably **Pasonanca Park,** rare fruits, a profusion of orchids, black coral, mother-of-pearl, silver jewelry, exquisite pearls, and Moorish brassware. Beyond Zamboanga are the islands of **Sulu,** whose people are also Muslim and live in villages built out on stilts over the sea. There, too, you will find a fascinating race of sea gypsies, whose main means of livelihood—fishing and pearl diving—have not changed for hundreds of years. Daily flights from Zamboanga take half an hour to **Jolo,** capital of the Sulu islands and the religious center.

SOURCES OF FURTHER INFORMATION

Pan Am, Delgado Building, Bonifacio Drive and 25th Street, Port Area, Manila, or any Pan Am office around the world; the **Ministry of Tourism,** Agrifina Circle, Manila; **Philippine Tourist Office,** 556 Fifth Avenue, New York, NY 10036; 447 Sutter Street, 6th Floor, San Francisco, CA 94108; Suite 919-920, 9th Level, Tower Building, Australia Square, Sydney 2000.

Samoa & Cook Islands

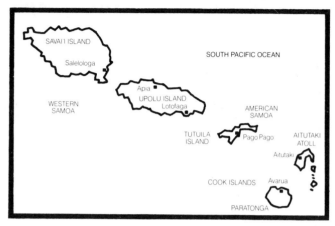

WHAT'S SPECIAL

Samoa is two countries, Western Samoa and American Samoa, united by a single description—lush green mountainous Pacific islands halfway between Hawaii and Australia. It's inspiring, too. Robert Louis Stevenson, Margaret Mead, and Somerset Maugham, with his legendary Sadie Thompson, found in its easy and peaceful ways much refreshment.

Despite the arrival of missionaries in the early 1800s and then the big jets 150 years later, Samoa is still one of the few places left whose culture and tradition have survived untouched, though in harmony with the modern world. Far away from the white sands, blue sea, and bustle of legendary Pago Pago, capital of American Samoa and gateway to both Samoas, the small villages in the sweep of the perfumed forests live on in timeless and almost tribal tradition. It is a tradition and a mood you will find very embracing. The two Samoas are ethnically identical though dissimilar sociologically and in their level of development. Though independent, Western Samoa is less developed but more picturesque than American Samoa. Perhaps the most crucial problem facing the two nations is the struggle to hold on to the extended family groupings—or *aigas*—while enriching the people through a move away from the traditional agricultural economy towards tourism.

COUNTRY BRIEFING

Area: 1,173 square miles   **Population** 155,000

Capital: Pago Pago, American Samoa; Apia, Western Samoa

   Climate: Tropical. The rainy season is December through April, and most visitors prefer to visit between May and November.

Weather in Samoa: Lat S13°48′; Alt 7 ft

Temp (°F)	Jan	Feb	Mar	Apr	May	Jun	Jul	Aug	Sep	Oct	Nov	Dec
Av Low	75°	75°	74°	75°	74°	74°	73°	73°	73°	74°	74°	74°
Av High	86°	86°	86°	86°	86°	85°	85°	84°	85°	85°	86°	86°
Days no rain	7	5	12	16	18	17	20	20	19	13	15	9

Government: American Samoa is administered by the US Department of the Interior which selects a governor. Western Samoa is a completely independent nation.

Language: The official language is Samoan, although English is spoken by about 85% of the population.

Religion: Christian Congregational Church; Roman Catholic; Mormon; Seventh Day Adventists; Methodist Church.

Currency: American Samoa's currency is the US dollar. Currency unit in Western Samoa is the tala; 100 sene = 1 tala. 85 sene = US$1. (or WS$1 = US$1.17)

Public Holidays: Same as US in American Samoa, with the addition of Flag Day, 17 April; White Sunday, 2nd Sunday in October; and the Swarm of the Palolo in late October or early November. Public holidays in Western Samoa are as follows:

New Year, Jan 1 and 2
Good Friday
Easter Sunday
Easter Monday
Anzac Day, 25 Apr
Whit Monday

Independence Celebration, June 1 and 2
Children's White Sunday, Oct 12 1980
Christmas Day, 25 Dec
Boxing Day, 26 Dec
New Year's Eve, Dec 31

Sunday is the regular weekly holiday and is strictly observed.

HOW TO GET THERE

Flying time to Tafuna International Airport from Los Angeles 10½ hours; from Honolulu 5½ hours; from Auckland 5 hours. Frequent daily shuttle service between Pago Pago and Apia. Time in the Samoas: GMT−11.

REQUIREMENTS FOR ENTRY AND CUSTOMS REGULATIONS

For entry into American Samoa, US citizens require proof of citizenship and round-trip ticket. Other nationals require passport, round-trip ticket, and a visa for stays of more than 30 days. For Western Samoa, requirements are valid passport, hotel reservations, return or onward ticket; no visa required for stays of less than 30 days. Visas are obtainable from Immigration Division, Prime Minister's Dept, Apia or any New Zealand diplomatic post or British consulate. Two passport size photos required. Smallpox vaccination certificates or yellow fever and cholera shots are not required for either territory by passengers from the United States, provided they do not arrive via an infected area. Duty-free allowance: 200 cigarettes or 50 cigars (or 1½ pounds of tobacco in Western Samoa); 2 fifths of liquor (1 fifth for Western Samoa). US citizens may leave with $600 worth of duty-free merchandise.

AIRPORT INFORMATION

Tafuna International Airport is 7 miles from town. Limousine fare into town is about US$3—luggage is charged by the piece. Taxis will do the trip for about US$5. No airport tax. Airport has a duty-free shop. Airport for Western Samoa is Faleolo, 23 miles from Apia. Transfers to downtown hotels cost approximately $2 by bus, $10 by taxi. Departure tax in Western Samoa about US$3.

ACCOMMODATIONS

Mostly up-to-date hotels, some with pools. There is an accommodation bureau at the **Office of Tourism**, PO Box 1147, Pago Pago American Samoa, 96799, tel: 633-5187. In Western Samoa, visitor information is available from the **Visitors' Bureau Department of Economic Development**, PO Box 862, Apia, tel: 731-630. Hotels in Samoa:

Rates are in US$ for a double/twin room with bath or shower

Aggie Grey's Hotel, PO Box 67, Apia, Western Samoa (from S$29/ D$61)

Motel Pago Pago (Herb and Sia's), PO Box 430, Pago Pago, American Samoa 96799 (S$13.75-14.50/D$17-19)

Pago Pago Rainmaker, PO Box 996, Pago Pago Bay, American Samoa (S$30-65/D$36-60)

Samoan Hideaway, PO Box 1195, Apia, Western Samoa; located at Mulivai Beach, 16 miles from Apia (S$19/D$24)

Tiafau Hotel, PO Box 34, Apia, Western Samoa (S$34/D$40)

Tusitala Hotel, PO Box 101, Apia, Western Samoa (S$50/D$57)

USEFUL INFORMATION

Helpful Hints: When visiting a Samoan home or *fale* that has no chairs, it is traditional etiquette to sit in a cross-legged position while addressing your hosts. One should not eat while walking through a village. If you are offered a cup of *kava* in a *kava* ceremony, it is customary to first tip a bit out of the cup onto the ground before drinking. If there is any *kava* left in the cup when you have finished, this should also be poured on the ground.

Banks: In American Samoa open 9-4 Mon-Fri; outside windows open till 4:30 Fri. In Western Samoa, 9:30-3 Mon-Fri, closed Sat and Sun. No banks outside the principal cities. Hotels and a few shops will change currency.

Telephone Tips: Local calls cost US10¢ at pay phones. Useful numbers in Pago Pago:

Airport Information 688-9145	Taxis 633-5445/633-5645/
Tourist Offices 633-5187	633-5545
Directory Inquiries and Operator 0	Time 633-4949
Weather 688-9130	Police 633-4441
Hospital 633-1222	Fire 633-5858

Newspapers: English-language newspapers are available in addition to the *Samoan News* and *News Bulletin,* in American Samoa, and the *Samoa Times Observer, Samoa Weekly* and *Savali* in Western Samoa.

Tipping: There is no tipping in Samoa.

Electricity: In American Samoa 110 volts (occasionally 230) 60 cycles AC. Hotels do have converters. In Western Samoa, 240 volts 50 cycles AC.

Photography: There is a good selection of photographic equipment available throughout the country. Processing takes about a week.

Clubs: The Rotary Club meets at the Pago Pago Rainmaker Hotel, American Samoa.

Rest Rooms: Public facilities are available in restaurants, hotels, bars, and around public places. There is no charge. Women, *Tamai'ta'i;* men, *Tane* (in Samoan).

Health: Most doctors and dentists speak English, and inexpensive pharmaceuticals are available at drugstores.

TRANSPORTATION

Buses or taxis. Polynesian Airlines and South Pacific Island Airways provide daily services between American and Western Samoa. Taxis are readily available for short journeys or sightseeing trips and can be identified by the "T" on their license plates. It is possible to rent a car from $25 per day in American Samoa, and for about $20 per day in Western Samoa.

FOOD AND RESTAURANTS

National dishes in Samoa include *palusami* (coconut juice, banana, and taro leaves), roast pic, taro, breadfruit, bananas, fish, and *poi* (mashed ripe bananas and coconut milk). Meal times are similar to US and European hours. **The Rainmaker Restaurant** in Pago Pago (in the Pago Pago Rainmaker—tel: 633-4241) serves international cuisine and is noted for its *fia fia,* traditional Samoan entertainment. **The Golden Dragon** (Pago Pago Village—tel: 633-4551) serves Chinese food exclusively. **Soli's Restaurant** in Pago Pago (tel: 633-4197) serves good food and is a lively nightspot. Other choices include **Mike Bird's Restaurant** and **Herb and Sia's Motel** restaurant. Western Samoa: **Aggie Grey's Hotel,** famous throughout the world for Polynesian cuisine and its weekly (usually Thursday) staging of *fia fia;* **Hotel Tusitala** for European food; and the **Tiafau Hotel.** Other possibilities include **Pintais** and **Leng Wai's** for Chinese fare, the **Faleburger, Morris Hedstrom's Café, O.F. Nelson's,** and **Ondres.**

DRINKING TIPS

In American Samoa bars are open from 8-5 daily and 8-12noon on Saturday. All bars are closed on Sunday but liquor is available at hotels to guests. Local drinks are *kava,* which comes from the root of the ava tree and is used as a ceremonial drink, and coconut milk. Other liquor, wines, and beers are imported and cost about US75¢ for a whisky and soda, US$1.70 plus for a bottle of ordinary wine. Bars worth visiting are the **Bamboo Room** in Pago Pago, the **Pago Bar,** which caters very much to the locals, the **Tumua Palace, Soli's, Evelani's, Seaside Garden, Tepatasi Terrace** and the **Tikki Club.** In Apia there are the **La Tanoa, Surfside, Aggie's Bar, Hotel Tusitala, Tiafau Hotel, Moon Glow, Mt Vaea,** and **Polyeurasian** nightclubs.

SHOPPING
There is an excellent assortment of local crafts—handwoven *tapa* cloth, *lava-lavas* and *puletasi* (traditional men's and women's costumes), shells, *laufala* mats, and carvings. US citizens may take home US$600 worth of goods duty free. Western Samoa has fine handwoven fabrics, baskets, bags, superb teak bowls, and shell and coconut jewelry, most of which can be bought from the shops in Apia. The best handicrafts are in the well-stocked **Government Handicrafts Corporation** store, next to the tourist office in downtown Apia, or from families selling their craftwares in the "New Market." Many of the small shops and general stores lining Apia's Beach Road also sell handicrafts.

SPORTS
Golf, tennis, swimming, surfing, scuba, skin-diving, spear fishing, yachting, climbing, horseracing, or fishing (including deep-sea fishing) are available year round. The beaches are magnificent—long and sandy and clean—and there are swimming pools on **Upolu,** Western Samoa.

WHAT TO SEE
Samoa is its own best attraction, and **Blunt's Point, Breaker's Point, Virgin Falls,** and **Solo Hill**—all within a short distance of Pago Pago—provide a visitor with a wide selection of Samoan scenery. From Solo Hill you can swing across Pago Pago Bay and up 1,600 feet to the top of **Mount Alava** on the Aerial Tramway. Other sights include **Assu Village** on "Massacre Bay," and the **Legislative Assembly Building, The Library of American Samoa, Matafno Mountain** (2,141 ft), **Museum of American Samoa** in the Old Post Office building, **Rainmaker Mountain,** the **Sadie Thompson Hotel** (actually Max Hallek Store No. 3, where Somerset Maugham is believed to have stayed when he visited Pago Pago in 1916 and supposedly wrote his famous short story "Rain"). The tuna canneries across Pago Pago Bay from Fago Toga and **Vaitogi Village** (home of the shark and turtle legend, whereby villagers have been known to call in these sea creatures by chanting) also are of interest.

On **Upolu,** Western Samoa, see the "scenic route," a 40-mile coastal stretch that takes in the **Falefa Falls,** the **Mafa Pass,** and the **Fuipisia Falls.** The atmosphere of Upolu is perhaps more quintessentially Polynesian than that of any of the other islands. It was on Upolu, at **Vailima,** that Robert Louis Stevenson made his home, and today you can see the restored house where he lived (now the official residence of the head of state), the **Road of Loving Hearts** and his grave on **Mount Vaea.** Other sights include **Parliament,** the **Courthouse,** the tombs of the **Samoan Kings,** some of the cocoa and copra plantations, the waterfalls

681

and freshwater pools. A day trip by launch to **Savai-Island**—the "cradle of Polynesia"—includes the *kava* ceremony, chants, and dances. In October or early November, Samoans celebrate the **Swarm of the Palolo.** At this time the *palolo,* or coral worms, swarm in the reef waters to lay their eggs, and the Samoans, who call the palolo the "caviar of the South Pacific," wade out with nets and cheesecloths to gather the eggs. The atmosphere is festival-like, and everyone is invited to go Samoan and join in the fun.

Cook Islands

An independent nation only since 1965, the 15 Cook Islands spread their 93 square miles of land area over 850,000 square miles of the Pacific Ocean, flanked to the west by Tonga and Samoa and to the east by French Polynesia. Formerly a New Zealand dependency, the islands are now self-governed, although outside affairs are still handled by New Zealand. Population of the Cook Islands is 18,128. The island of **Rarotonga** is the largest and most developed of the Cooks and is capital of the group.

Rarotonga has excellent tourist accommodations and a newly expanded International Airport close to Avarua, where approximately half of Rarotonga's 9,811 people live. Flying time to the Cook Islands from Western Samoa is about 4 hours. Most of the islands were discovered by Captain Cook (hence their name), although **Aitutaki,** 140 miles north and the only other island offering tourist facilities, was discovered by Captain Bligh shortly before the mutiny on the *Bounty.*

The climate of all the Cook Islands is pleasantly warm and mostly sunny year round. December to March is warmest and wettest and known as hurricane season, although such storms are a rarity. On Rarotonga, where the weather is perennially ideal, annual rainfall totals 80 inches.

There is a growing number of restaurants in Rarotonga. The **Arorangi Lodge** (from $20) 4 miles from town, stages three cabarets a week, including an excellent island-style buffet dinner. Bicycles and Honda scooters are available to rent at low rates. Luxury goods are duty-free in all shops. Accommodations on Rarotonga are also available at the **Raratonga Hotel** (S$39/D$44, suite $65), and **Lagoon Lodges** (S$20/D$25) at the beach. On the island of Aitutaki at **Rapae Motel** (S$18.10/D$21.30). For reservations contact the Cook Island Tourist Authority.

REQUIREMENTS FOR ENTRY AND CUSTOMS REGULATIONS

Bona fide visitors do not require an entry permit provided they possess a valid passport, have onward passage, and do not intend staying more than 31 days. A valid smallpox certificate is required of all visitors except citizens of Australia, Canada, New Zealand, the Pacific islands, and the United States, who are exempted provided they have not traveled outside those countries during the 14 days prior to entering the Cook Islands. Baggage is fumigated on arrival and delivered to the hotel about two hours after guests check in.

Visitors may bring 200 cigarettes, one-fifth of wine and one-fifth of spirits, two still cameras with 10 rolls of film, one pair binoculars, one portable radio, one record player (and 10 records), one typewriter, one portable musical instrument, all without duty. The importation of firearms, cartridges, and fireworks is expressly prohibited.

For more detailed information, write **Cook Island Tourist Authority,** PO Box 14, Rarotonga, Cook Islands.

SOURCES OF FURTHER INFORMATION

Any **Pan Am** office around the world; **Office of Tourism,** Government of American Samoa, PO Box 1147, Pago Pago, American Samoa 96799; **Office of Territories,** US Department of Interior, Washington DC Visitors' Bureau; **Department of Economic Development,** PO Box 862, Apia, Western Samoa; **Cook Island Tourist Authority,** PO Box 14, Rarotonga, Cook Islands.

Singapore

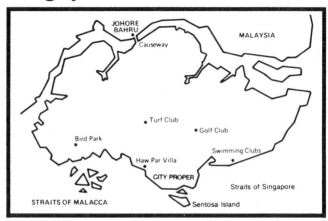

WHAT'S SPECIAL

Many places have been called "crossroads" or "gateways," but Singapore is one of the very few that can readily claim such titles. Its position helps; more ships and airlines pass by or stop here than almost anywhere else in the world. But above all it is the people. Ever since Sir Stamford Raffles established the East India Company here in 1819, this tip of Asia has drawn people of all races like a magnet. It has been called "instant Asia," and certainly the exciting yet harmonious mixture of Chinese, Malays, Indians, Pakistanis, Sinhalese, and many others is unique.

COUNTRY BRIEFING

Size: 226.4 square miles   **Population:** 2,400,000

Climate: Equatorial, with little variation of temperature throughout the year.

Weather in Singapore: Lat N1°20′; Alt 33 ft

Temp (°F)	Jan	Feb	Mar	Apr	May	Jun	Jul	Aug	Sep	Oct	Nov	Dec
Av Low	73°	74°	74°	75°	76°	76°	76°	76°	75°	75°	75°	74°
Av High	86°	87°	88°	88°	88°	88°	87°	87°	87°	87°	87°	86°
Days no rain	14	16	17	15	16	17	18	17	16	15	12	12

Government: An independent republic.

Language: Official languages are Malay, Chinese (Mandarin), Tamil, and English. Most Singaporeans speak English.

Religion: Christianity, Islam, Taoism, Buddhism, and Hinduism.

Currency: Singapore dollar. 100 cents = 1 Singapore dollar.

	10¢	20¢	50¢	S $1	S $5	S $10	S $50	S $100
US (dollars, cents)	.05	.09	.23	.46	2.31	4.64	23.19	46.37
UK (pounds, pence)	.02	.04	.11	.21	1.07	2.16	10.79	21.56

Public Holidays:

New Year's Day, 1 Jan

Chinese New Year, 25 Jan

Good Friday, 9 Apr

Vesak Day, May

National Day, 9 Aug

Hari Raya Haji, Aug

Christmas, 25 Dec

Also numerous festivals throughout the year.

NOTE: When a holiday falls on a Sunday, the following day becomes a public holiday.

HOW TO GET THERE

Flying time to Singapore Changi Airport in Singapore from San Francisco is 17¼ hours; from Tokyo, 7¾ hours; from Hong Kong, 3½ hours. Time in Singapore: GMT+7 hours 30 minutes.

REQUIREMENTS FOR ENTRY AND CUSTOMS REGULATIONS

A valid passport, and, if arriving from an infected area, yellow-fever and cholera vaccination certificates. Visas are not required for tourists, except for nationals of South Africa, Rhodesia, Taiwan, and the Communist bloc countries. Tourists are permitted to remain for 14 days but may apply for an extension at the Immigration Department. Currency regulations: there is no restriction on US currency and no limit on travelers' checks and their equivalent. Duty-free allowance: 200 cigarettes or 50 cigars or 8 ounces of smoking tobacco, 1 quart each of malt beverage, wine, and liquor. Firearms are not permitted, and magazines considered pornographic will be confiscated.

AIRPORT INFORMATION

Singapore Changi Airport is 12 miles from the city center. The airport arrival hall has an excellent accommodations bureau, car rental counters, and a duty-free shop. An air-conditioned, airport-to-hotel bus service (SABS) costs S$4 per person.Taxis about S$15 to city center. Airport departure tax is S$10 for international flights and S$4 for flights to Malaysia and Brunei.

ACCOMMODATIONS

Singapore has a dazzling array of modern hotels. International groups such as Hilton, Holiday Inn, Hyatt, Forum, and Western International are all well represented. In addition there is a wide selection of inexpensive accommodations, including the YMCA and YWCA. There is a 3% government tax on hotel bills. Hotels in Singapore:

Rates are in US$ for a double/twin room with bath or shower

  Century Park Sheraton, Nassim Hill (from $73)

Cockpit, Oxley Rise/Penang Road (from $50)
Equatorial, 429 Bukit Timah Road (from $62)
Goodwood Park, 22 Scotts Road (from $78)
Holiday Inn, 25 Scotts Road (from $62)
Hyatt, 10/12 Scotts Road (from $73)
Ladyhill, 1 Ladyhill Road (from $53)
Malaysia, Cuscaden Road (from $53)
Mandarin, Orchard Road (from $78)
Marco Polo, Tanglin Circus (from $75)
Ming Court, Tanglin Road (from $62)
Oberoi Imperial, 1 Jalan Rumbia (from $65)
Phoenix, Somerset Road (from $45)
Raffles, 1/3 Beach Road (from $52)
Shangri-La, 22 Orange Grove Road (from $90)
Singapore Hilton, 581 Orchard Road (from $74.40)
SINGAPURA FORUM, 585 Orchard Road (from $60)
York, 21 Mount Elizabeth (from $62)

All the above hotels are centrally located or a 5- to 15-minute taxi ride from the city center.

USEFUL INFORMATION

Banks: Most well-known banks have branches, open from 10-3 Mon-Fri and 9:30-11:30am Sat. There are also licensed money changers, but banks generally give the best rate.

Mail: Stamps can be bought only from a post office or hotel porter; if the hotel has no mail collection, use one of the bright yellow mailboxes on street corners.

Telephone Tips: There are public telephones in booths, restaurants, cafés, and shops, all operated by S10¢ pieces, inserted once the number has been answered; S10¢ a local call. Useful numbers:

Pan Am 2200711	International 104
Airport Information 800888	Emergencies 999
Information 103	Operator 100
Time 1711	

Newspapers: European newspapers are available, and the local *Straits Times* provides international news in English.

Tipping: Most hotels and restaurants add 10% service charge to the bill and tipping is officially discouraged. Taxi drivers are not tipped.

Electricity: The most common voltage is 230-250 volts AC, but the better hotels have outlets suitable for 110 volts 60 cycles AC. Check before using an appliance.

Laundry: Every hotel has a laundry service. Major hotels have excellent express facilities, and you can count on 24-hour service everywhere. Dry-cleaned suit—average cost from S$10; laundered shirt—average cost from S$4; lady's dress—about S$8.50.

Hairdressers: Most first-class hotels have hairdressing salons, where the average cost of a shampoo and set is from S$21; average cost of a man's haircut, about S$11.

Photography: There is a very wide range of film and developing services. Processing by Kodak labs takes 2 days for Ektachrome (slides) and Kodacolor (prints), but Kodachrome (slides) takes 2 weeks since processing is done in Australia; black and white in 24 hours. Film costs about S$5.50 for black and white; Ektachrome (36 exposures) costs S$10 with processing not included, Kodacolor S$6.50, processing included. Professional film facilities are also available.

Clubs: Rotary (five branches), Kiwanis, Lions, Skal, Apex, Toastmasters, and Junior Chamber of Commerce.

Babysitting: Some hotels have their own facilities, or the staff will arrange for a responsible sitter to come in.

Rest Rooms: Public facilities are not always the best, but it is easy to slip into a hotel, where standards are higher.

Health: Most doctors and dentists speak English, and there is a wide range of imported pharmaceuticals at standard prices. Singapore tap water is safe to drink.

TRANSPORTATION

There is a good supply of taxis and buses. A few trishaws (tricycle rickshaws) still remain but do not use fixed rates. The bus service is good between rush hours and inexpensive. There is a shuttle bus service (CBD 1 & 2) operating on two routes with stops close to major hotels and shopping centers. Service runs at 10-minute intervals from 9am-5pm weekdays, 9am-12:30pm and 3:30pm-8pm Saturdays, no service Sundays. Exact fare (S30¢) is required. Bus tours of Singapore and Johore last 3 hours and cost about S$16 and S$12 respectively. Chauffeur-driven limousines can be rented from $11-42 an hour (minimum 3 hours); self-drive cars require an international license and a returnable deposit—they cost from S$35-168 for 24 hours. Drive on the left. There are launches that tour the harbor and offshore islands, and junks (S$20 per person per hour) can be hired at Clifford Pier. The central business district is a restricted zone for private vehicles and taxis Monday through Saturday from 7:30 to 10:15. Entry during this period requires a daily license (S$4) or a monthly license (S$80).

FOOD AND RESTAURANTS

Dining out in Singapore is a problem—there is such a variety of superb cuisine, it is difficult to know where to start! There is Chinese food in the great tradition, or rather nine great traditions, including Cantonese, Peking, Hakka, and Szechuan. Shark's fin soup, drunken chicken, bird's nest soup, 100-year eggs, *tim sum* (an Oriental *smorgasbord*), and chili crab—they are all at their best here. Then there's superb *satay*, the great Malaysian kebab-style dish, Korean steaks, marvelous curries from India and Pakistan, Siamese *laksa*, Indonesian *rijsttafel*, as well as first-class Western haute cuisine. There are so many restaurants a choice is difficult, but for starters **The Golden Phoenix** (Equatorial Hotel—tel: 2560431); **Peking Mayflower Restaurant** (third floor, International Building, 360 Orchard Road—tel: 7373928); **The Cathay** (Cathay Building—

tel: 328121); and **The Great Shanghai** (Mayfair Hotel—tel: 328240) exemplify Chinese food. **Capitol Chinese Restaurant,** Szechuan cuisine features spicy dishes, and **Tai Seng** has exceptional food rarely tasted outside mainland China. The open-air food stall referred to locally as the **Satay Club,** on Queen Elizabeth Walk, is a great introduction to *satay,* and other Malay and Indonesian restaurants are the **Indonesia Cafe** (Apollo Hotel—tel: 432081) and **Aziza's** (36 Emerald Hill Road—tel: 2351130). **Rang Mahal** in the Oberoi Imperial Hotel (tel: 7371666), **Omar Khayyam** (55 Hill Street—tel: 361505), and the **Shalimar** (Tanglin Shopping Center—tel: 7370853) serve Indian food; while many of the hotels provide superb Western and Japanese food. Steaks, flown in from Australia and New Zealand, are the specialty at **Fosters Steak House** (Amber Mansions, Orchard Road—tel: 322939), not to mention Black Angus beef at the **Gordon Grill** (Goodwood Park Hotel, 22 Scotts Road—tel: 7377411). You can even get pizzas, tacos, borscht, escargots, and haggis. Perhaps the best advice is to obtain a free copy of the *Singapore Weekly Guide* from your hotel or at the Tourist Promotion Board, Tanglin Road.

DRINKING TIPS

Liquor, wines, and European drinks are available. The hotel bars serve drinks at all hours, and it is perfectly appropriate for an unaccompanied woman to order a drink. The local drinks are first-class beer (Tiger, Anchor), coconut water, and fruit juices, and one of the more diverting aspects of the meeting between East and West is the *Singapore sling—* gin, cherry brandy, and Benedictine, topped with a twist of lime. The perfect setting to try one is the **Palm Court** at the Raffles Hotel on Beach Road. A modest whisky costs an average S\$5 and a bottle of nonvintage wine S\$26.

ENTERTAINMENT

The variety of entertainment is rich, like the food. Many of the more expensive restaurants have floor shows featuring Western and traditional Asian dancing. Movie theaters are numerous—English and American films are shown with the original soundtrack, but it is often more fun to see Chinese and Indian films. It's worth taking in a Chinese dinner show. Try the **Neptune Theatre Restaurant** (Collyer Quay—tel: 913922) or the **Tropicana** (9 Scotts Road—tel: 7376433) for something more Western. Or if you want just drinks and dancing, most big hotels have discothèques, such as the **Lost Horizon** at the Shangri-La (tel: 7373644); the **Kasbah** at the Mandarin (tel: 7374411); the **Regency Lounge** at the Hyatt (tel: 7375511); and the **Black Velvet Club** at the Century Park Sheraton (tel: 7379677).

SHOPPING

Whether it's pewterware, batik, crocodile goods, watches, radios, antiques, jade, jade figurines, stones, fabrics, or cameras, Singapore has it—and more. Prices are highly competitive, so it's wise to do some comparison shopping. Few shops have fixed prices, so don't hesitate to bargain—discounts range from 10-30% off. Excellent values can be found in any one of the 11 Chinese Emporiums (fixed prices) scattered throughout the city. Look for Chinese silk, clothing, embroidered tablecloths, etc., at **Yuyi** (Orchard Building, opposite the Orchard Theatre) and at the **Chinese Emporium** (International Building, Orchard Road). Also highly recommended are **C.K. Tang** (310 Orchard Road), a department store with reasonable, fixed prices and a wide selection of goods, **Isetan Emporium** (Havelock/Outram roads), and **Klasse Department Store** (Lucky Plaza Shopping Center). A place not to be missed and synonymous with Singapore is **Change Alley in Raffles Place**—a maze of small shops and stalls where haggling is a must, even with money-changers. A short walk from Raffles Place leads to **North** or **South Bridge Road** or to **High Street**, the best area for colorful Indian fabrics and gold and jade jewelry. Two of the last areas where the flavor of "old" Singapore still lingers are **Thieves Market**, stretching along Rochor Canal, where an assortment of antiques, real and fake, can be found, and **Arab Street** for an excellent selection of batik, Indian silks, and semiprecious stones. There are many copies of antiques and dealers will say they are authentic. Be careful. Antiques that are 130 years old are not subject to duty. Be sure you have the proper authentication attesting to the age of each article, so that US Customs will not charge duty. For those who like to do their shopping under one roof, there are several large air-conditioned shopping centers—**Shaw Center, Lucky Plaza, Plaza Singapura, Orchard Towers, Far East Shopping Center,** and **Tanglin Shopping Center. Collyer Quay,** on the waterfront, has interesting shops.

Store hours vary but are generally from 9am to 5pm. For a change of pace, an outing to a **Pasar Malam** (night market) is recommended.

SPORTS

Horse racing, soccer, hockey, badminton, football, basketball, polo, and cricket are available as spectator sports. Three golf courses are open to visitors, **Singapore Island Country Club, Sentosa Golf Club** and **Seletar Golf Club.** There is golf, tennis, fishing, swimming, skin- and scuba-diving, water-skiing, yachting, and sailing for the energetic. A visit to newly developed **Sentosa Island** by cable car or ferry boat for a swim in the lagoon and boating is a welcome break from the bustle of Singapore. Swimming pools are a feature of the bigger hotels.

WHAT TO SEE

If you ever get around to taking time out from eating, shopping, and the nightlife, you will find a lot to see and do. Singapore is a place redolent of history, her own past and the past of myriad cultures. An excellent way to capture a feeling of place is to see **The Singapore Experience,** a 45-minute audio-visual presentation at the Cultural Theater, Grange Road (admission: S$5). The **Instant Asia Show,** performed daily from 9:45am at Grange Road, behind the Singapore Handicraft Center, offers an overall display of Malay and Chinese dancing, Malay fighting techniques, and snake-charming. Impressive examples of Oriental statuary can be seen at **Haw Par Villa,** better known as the Tiger Balm Garden, overlooking the sea at Pasir Panjang (admission free). This must be seen to be believed—acres of sculptured hillside and grottoes depicting the Chinese vision of the soul's pilgrimage. Also visit the **Jurong Bird Park,** teeming with exotic species; it is the site of the world's highest artificial waterfall. Then there are the **Mandai Orchid Gardens** on Mandai Road, a bewildering burst of color and perfume; also on Mandai Road are the **Zoological Gardens,** a beautifully landscaped zoo with more than 1,000 animals living in a natural environment. In Central Park off Clemenceau Avenue, the **Van Cleef Aquarium** gives close-ups of the tropical fish that surround Singapore, including turtles, octopus, king crabs, and monitor lizards. You ought to visit one of the temples: **Chettiar's Temple** on Tank Road, **Sri Mariamman Temple** on South Bridge Road, the **Sultan Mosque** on North Bridge Road, the **Thian Hock Keng Temple** on Telok Ayer Street. And while not an absolute must, the **National Museum** on Stamford Road, houses the Jade Collection as well as gives an insight into the history and ethnology of southeast Asia.

SOURCES OF FURTHER INFORMATION

Pan Am, G-3, Hong Leong Building, Singapore 0104, and any Pan Am office around the world; **Tourist Promotion Board,** Tudor Court, Tanglin Road, Singapore 19, tel: 2821111; **Singapore Tourist Promotion Board,** 251 Post Street, San Francisco, CA 94108; 342 Madison Avenue, New York, NY 10173; 33 Heddon Street, London W1R 7LB.

South Korea

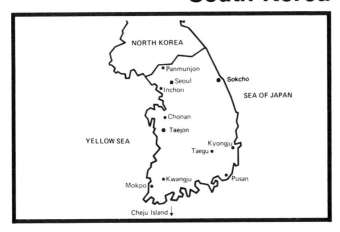

WHAT'S SPECIAL

Until the Korean War erupted on the international scene in 1950, Korea was virtually unknown to the West. The war brought misery and destruction, but in 5,000 years of history (in constant fear of an invasion from north or south) a deep-rooted resilience and a strong sense of national identity have survived in Korea. This characteristic spirit of unity is partly due to the 15th-century invention of a phonetic Korean alphabet. Korea now has one of the highest literacy rates in the world, and its people all write and speak one language. Many Koreans still carry a hand-carved seal bearing their names, but as more and more papers require one's signature, this is not as universal as it was twenty years ago. Despite its proximity to China and Japan, the country has developed its own unique culture. Age-old domestic traditions and social customs still flourish amidst increasing industrialization.

In the past, poet-scholars of Korea escaped to solitary country pavilions to sip wine, gaze at the moon, and cleanse their souls before returning to the outside world. Outside its cities, the great natural beauty and rural peace of this country, once called the Land of the Morning Calm, can still lend itself to such tranquil delights.

COUNTRY BRIEFING

Size: 38,452 square miles   **Population:** 37,440,000
Capital: Seoul   **Capital Population:** 8,360,000
    Climate: Korea is in the northern temperate zone, and 50% of its rainfall occurs from June to August. Spring and autumn are the most

pleasant times for a visit, as July and August are very hot and January and February rather cold.

Weather in Seoul: Lat N37°34'; Alt 285 ft

Temp (°F)	Jan	Feb	Mar	Apr	May	Jun	Jul	Aug	Sep	Oct	Nov	Dec
Av Low	15°	20°	29°	41°	51°	61°	70°	71°	59°	45°	32°	20°
Av High	32°	37°	47°	62°	72°	80°	84°	87°	78°	67°	51°	37°
Days no rain	23	22	24	22	21	20	15	18	21	24	21	22

Government: Republic under a president.

Language: Korean. Many people speak a few words of English.

Religion: Buddhism (8 million), Christianity (4.5 million).

Currency: South Korean won. 100 chon = 1 won

	won 10	won 20	won 50	won 100	won 500	won 1,000	won 10,000	won 20,000
US (dollars, cents)	.01	.03	.07	.15	.73	1.47	14.66	29.32
UK (pounds, pence)	—	.01	.03	.07	.35	.70	7.01	14.01

Public Holidays:

New Year, 1, 2, & 3 Jan

Independence Movement Day, 1 Mar

Buddha's Birthday, early/mid May

Memorial Day, 6 June

Constitution Day, 17 July

Liberation Day, 15 Aug

Moon Festival, late Sep/early Oct

Armed Forces Day, 1 Oct

National Foundation Day, 3 Oct

Hangul (Korean Phonetic Alphabet) Day, 9 Oct

Christmas Day, 25 Dec

HOW TO GET THERE

Flying time to Seoul Airport from San Francisco is 11¾ hours; from Singapore, 6½ hours; from Hong Kong, 3 hours; from Tokyo, 1¾ hours. Time in South Korea: GMT+9.

REQUIREMENTS FOR ENTRY AND CUSTOMS REGULATIONS

Passport; visa required except for stays of less than 72 hours. Currency and baggage declaration is required upon arrival. Jewels, gold, and narcotics are illegal imports. Duty-free allowance: 200 cigarettes or 50 cigars or ½ pound of tobacco; 2 bottles of liquor; personal effects regarded as essential for travel.

AIRPORT INFORMATION

Kimpo Airport is 10 miles from Seoul. A fairly frequent airport bus service (500 won) connects with the downtown City Hall Plaza terminal, and major hotels operate an airport pick-up service. The taxi fare to Seoul is 2,800 won. If you take a yellow "call taxi," the fare is about three times higher. The airport has a duty-free shop and hotel reservation counter. Departure tax, 2,000 won.

ACCOMMODATIONS

Korean-style hotels have heated floors and, as in private homes, cushions rather than chairs or beds. There are plenty of good Western-style hotels, with barber shops, beauty salons, and all modern conveniences. Hotels in Seoul:

Rates are in US$ for a double/twin room with bath or shower

Ambassador, 186-54, 2-ka, Chang Chung-dong (from $50)

Chosun, 87 Sokong-dong, Chung-ku (from $65)

Hyatt Regency, 747-7, Hannam-dong, Yongsan-ku (from $50)

King Sejong, 61-3, 2-ka, Chungmu-ro, Chung-ku (from $50)

Koreana, 1-61, Taepyong-ro, Chung-ku (from $42)

Lotte, 1 Sokong-dong, Chung-ku (from $52)

Pacific, 31-1, 2-ka, Nansan-dong, Chung-ku (from $38)

President, 188-3, 1-ka, Ulji-ro, Chung-ku (from $39)

Seoulin, 149 Surin-dong, Chongro-ku (from $35)

Seoul Plaza, 23, 2-ka, Taepyong-ro, Chung-ku (from $58)

Seoul Royal, 6, 1-ka, Myung-dong, Chung-ku (from $47)

Seoul Tokyu, 8 Yang-dong, Chung-ku (from $47)

Sheraton-Walker Hill, San 21, Kuangjang-dong, Sungdong-ku (from $46), about 10 miles from Seoul

Shilla, 202, 2-ka, Jangchung-dong, Chung-ku (from $47)

Tower, 5-2, Changchung-dong, Chung-ku (from $31)

Yoido, 1-496, Yoido-dong, Yongdungpo-ku (from $32)

Seoul Garden, 169-1, Dohwa-dong, Mapo-ku (from $32)

All hotels centrally located unless otherwise indicated.

USEFUL INFORMATION

Helpful Hints: Remove shoes before entering a private house or Korean-style restaurant. Koreans tend to avoid the use of first names. Foreigners are exempt from the midnight-to-4am curfew, but it puts a damper on much of the nightlife.

Banks: Open 9:30-5:30 Mon-Fri, 9:30-1:30 Sat. There are a few banks outside the principal cities, and currency can be changed at tourist hotels.

Mail: Stamps can be purchased and letters mailed in hotels. Mailboxes are red.

Telephone Tips: To use public phones in cafés, stores, and restaurants, insert a 10-won coin and dial. Some useful numbers: **Pan Am** 777-7701/03; **Korean Tourist Bureau** 72-1191/6; **Seoul Tourist Information Center** 75-6481/9.

Newspapers: English-language newspapers are available, and two local publications in English are *Korea Times* and *Korea Herald.*

Tipping: Not usual. 10% is usually added in hotels and restaurants. Taxi drivers, 10% if you wish; hairdressers, 10-15%; porters, 500-750 won; chambermaid and cloakroom attendant, 500-700 won.

Electricity: 110 volts 60 cycles AC.

Laundry: Same-day service is customary and very inexpensive. Major hotels have good express service. A shirt can be laundered for about 1,000 won; a suit dry-cleaned for about 4,500 won.

Hairdressing: First-class hotels have both ladies' and gentlemen's salons. A shampoo and set costs from 4,000 won (500 won tip), and a gentleman going to a barber for a haircut also gets a shave and a manicure all for 7,000 won (700-1,000 won tip).

Clubs: Rotary, Lions, Kiwanis.

Babysitting: Services do exist; ask at hotel.

Rest Rooms: Public facilities are free, but not very pleasant. The women's room is *Buin Yong,* the men's *Sinsa Yong.*

Health: Doctors and dentists in the Seoul Medical Center, the Severance Hospital, and other general hospitals speak English. Imported pharmaceutical goods and cosmetics are available at drugstores in downtown areas, including the Sokong Underground Arcade.

TRANSPORTATION

A subway in the inner-ring area of Seoul has been in operation since 1975. Other means of public transport include the city bus (difficult for foreigners to use). Mount Namsan, rising in the center of Seoul, has a cable car. Taxis can be found at cab stands but are not easy to catch during rush hours; most hotels operate their own transportation services.

There are five limited-access superhighways totaling 747 miles that put all of Korea within a one-day driving range. More than 1,390 miles of national roads are paved. Cross-country buses are inexpensive and often more direct than train services, which also connect main towns and major points of tourist interest. Korean Air Lines (KAL) flies to Pusan, Cheju, Taegu, Chinju, Sokcho, and Kwangju. A car ferry links Pusan and Mokpo with the southern islands of Japan and with Korea's southernmost island of Cheju.

FOOD AND RESTAURANTS

Though unfamiliar in the Western hemisphere, Korean food is very tasty. A simple Korean meal consists of soup, rice, a bowl of fish or meat, and *kimchi*—delicious hot pickled vegetables. *Pulgogi* is charcoal-broiled, marinated beef, usually prepared at your table, as is *sinsolo,* a superb casserole of meat, fish, eggs, vegetables, and genko nuts. *Kalbi* is beef spareribs. Spit-roasted chicken is served at special chicken restaurants. An expensive restaurant meal will be about 12,000 won and a medium-priced one about 6,000 won. Rice dishes cost less—"home rice," a kind of omelette with rice, costs 2,000 won at lunch bars. Generally avoid uncooked food (especially seafood), except peeled fruit.

A traditional Korean meal has anything from 17 courses upwards. The best place to try one is **Korea House** (80-2, 2-ka, Choong-ku—tel: 267-2375). Other good Korean restaurants in Seoul are **Jangwon** (235, Chungjin-dong, Chongro-ku—tel: 72-1807), **Hanil Kuan** (50-1, 2-ka, Myong-dong, Choong-ku—tel: 776-3388), **Pine Hill** (88-5, 2-ka, Juh-dong, Chung-ku—tel: 266-4404). Western restaurants include **Banjul** (12-16, Kwanchul-dong—tel: 73-1800), **Bear House** (39-1, 1-ka, Pil-dong, Choong-ku—tel: 266-4404), **La Cantina** (1-50, Ulji-ro, Chung-ku—tel: 777-2579), and **Cosmopolitan** (1-3, 1-ka, Myung-dong—tel: 776-0677). Japanese food is good at **Mijori** (14-5 Pukchang-dong—tel: 778-1131) and **Daebun** (66-4, 2-ka, Chungmu-ro—tel: 776-9917). Good Chinese restaurants are

Dongbo-sung (50-8, 2-ka, Namsan-dong, Chung-ku—tel: 28-2727), **Hee-Lai-Dung** (Namsan Foreigners' Apt.—tel: 792-6633), and **Arisan** (258-6, Etaewon, Yongsan-ku—tel: 793-7396). The city center is the best area for inexpensive eating places.

DRINKING TIPS

Imported liquor can be bought at Foreigners' Commissaries. Imported wine, liquor, and beers are available in tourist hotels. Korean wine is very good and locally-blended whisky is a favorite with foreigners. A bottle of local red wine costs 2,500-2,800 won; a bottle of locally-blended whisky, 14,000-16,000 won. A whisky and soda costs about 1,500-2,000 won. *Sul* (the spirit) is strong; *makoli* (the wine) is mild. Both are made from rice. Korean beer is very good and costs half as much in a bar as in a hotel. *Tabangs* are relaxing tea rooms, popular for after-lunch and after-dinner drinks, especially *ginseng* (noted for its medicinal qualities). There are no drinking restrictions for adults (over 20), but bars are closed in the morning.

ENTERTAINMENT

Movies are usually dubbed, and performances begin about 11am. Short runs of Western plays and operas are occasionally produced in Seoul. Korean traditional music divides into solemn, highly stylized court music and dance (at the **National Classical Music Institute**) and lively folk music, with its predominant sound of metal gongs, drums, and oboe. Traditional mask plays, part pantomine, part ballet, are very popular. **Korea House** (267-2375) presents programs of traditional Korean music and dance nightly at 8pm. Admission: 3,500 won.

Major hotels in Seoul have cabarets with bands and floor shows. **Tomorrow** is a nightclub at the **Chosun Hotel** (87 Sokong-dong, Chung-ku). Taxi drivers are mines of information on this score. The **Sheraton-Walker Hill Resort** has a casino as well as a nightclub with a lavish floor show, and there is another casino at the **Olympos Hotel** in Inchon, west of Seoul. Women are welcome, but Korean women do not always accompany their husbands. Expensive but elaborate *kisaeng* houses, resembling those of the Japanese geisha, provide traditional meals and entertainment. Recommended *kisaengs* are: **Chong-un Gak** (53-1 Chongun-dong), **Daeha** (56 Ikson-dong), and **Korean Mansion** (Sheraton-Walker Hill Resort).

SHOPPING

Amethyst and smoky topaz are the best of the beautiful gems mined in Korea. Silk and tweed (from Cheju Island) are of good quality and can be tailored for you. Cheaper buys are the fine inlaid lacquerware, brassware, embroidery, costume dolls, and grass rugs. Modern Koryo and Silla pottery are good reproductions of the high period of Korean ceramics. Major department stores are **Lotte, Mitopa, Shinsege, Cosmos,** and **Miz.** The main shopping streets are **Sokong-dong, Chongno,** and **Myong-dong. Lotte,** first avenue in Sokong-dong, is the most attractive shopping center and good for souvenirs. Good jewelry and handicraft shops are found in the **Sokong Underground Arcade** in front of the Chosun Hotel. Sprawling open-air and covered markets are at both the **East** and **South Gates. Pagoda Park Arcade** and the **Namdaemoon-ro** are antique and curio areas. You can bargain almost anywhere except in department stores and some downtown shopping areas.

SPORTS

Spectator sports include soccer, baseball, basketball, and boxing. Mass calisthenics are a dramatic interlude in the annual fall **National Athletic Meet.** Korean-style wrestling (*ssirum*) and bull-baiting (*so-ssa-um*)—and, in the country, dog fighting—are also popular. Skiing and winter sports are centered in the mountainous northeast of Korea; the main resort here is **Mount Sorak.** There are golf courses at the **Hanyang, New Korea, Seoul,** and **Kwan Ack Country Clubs,** Seoul.

WHAT TO SEE

Seoul: The **Great South Gate** and the less grandiose **East Gate** are two of the original boundaries of the city. Other reminders of a more regal age among Seoul's modern skyscrapers and expressways can be seen at the palace compounds with their distinctive Korean architecture. **Duksoo Palace** houses the **National Art Gallery. Changdok Palace** contains relics of royal residents, and many of the rooms have period furnishings; the **Secret Garden** attached to the palace is a delightful wooded park dotted with ponds, springs, and pleasure pavilions. **Kyongbok Palace,** behind the Japanese-built Capitol Building, has a lofty throne room and a beautiful banqueting hall. The **National Museum** inside the palace grounds displays a fine collection of items ranging from examples of semibarbaric culture to the sophistication of high court life. The smaller **Korean Folklore Museum** is also on the palace grounds. **Seoul Tourist Information Center,** behind City Hall, organizes free city tours. The **Han River,** cutting through the mountains that almost completely encircle the city, is an idyllic setting for a summer evening's boat ride.

Kyongju (about four hours from Seoul), the former Silla capital, has sights even more venerable. The **Pulguk-sa Temple** was completed in 742 AD. The museum contains objects excavated from the **Royal Tombs,** whose bulk can be seen looming over the rice fields in the distance. Nearby is the mountain-top grotto of **Sokkulam,** from which granite Buddhas gaze serenely out to the horizon at East Sea. A huge tourist complex was recently opened around **Bomun Lake** in Kyongju and further expansion is under way. The complex includes fine hotels, recreation facilities, and a golf course. Stay at the **Kyongju-Chosun Hotel,** 410, Sinpyong-dong, Kyongju City (from US$62 double) or **Kyongju-Tokyu Hotel,** 412, Sinpyong-dong, Kyongju City (from US$48 double). **Cheju Island,** 60 miles out to sea from the port of Pusan, has a mild climate all year and no curfew. The mountainous little island has scenic beauties and quaint customs. It is famous for its women divers, who gather pearls and abalone from the sea bed. Hotels to consider in this region are the

KAL, Cheju City, Cheju Island (from US$48 double), the **Cheju Tourist,** 1315, 1 Dong 2 Do Cheju, Cheju Island (from US$42 double), and **Sogwipo,** Cheju Island (from US$38 double).

SOURCES OF FURTHER INFORMATION
Pan Am, IPO-1644, Seoul, tel: 241451, and any Pan Am office around the world; **Korea National Tourism Corporation,** 460 Park Avenue, New York, NY 10022; **Korean Embassy,** 36 Cadogan Square, London SW1.

Sri Lanka

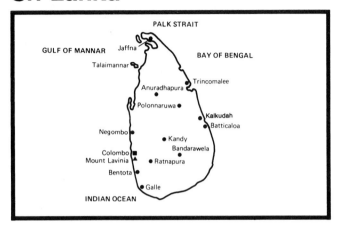

WHAT'S SPECIAL

An independent country since 1948, Ceylon in 1972 assumed its ancient name Sri Lanka—"resplendent land." The island has always been called Lanka, this having been the ancient island of the great Hindu legend, the Ramayana. Later, the Arabs called it Serendib, a word Horace Walpole took and rearranged and turned into Serendipity, or what Webster calls the "art of making happy discoveries by accident." Populated originally by the Sinhalese, it saw the birth of Buddhism when, in 247 BC, the first Buddhist monk arrived, and it was in those early centuries that many of its great cities were built.

The more than 14 million people in the country today include the Sinhalese, Tamils (descendants of early South Indian settlers), Moors (descendants of Arabs), Burghers (of Dutch and Portuguese origin), Eurasians, Malays, Europeans, and Veddhas, the latter being descendants of Sri Lanka aborigines. The cities are fascinating, and the country is covered by tropical forest, mountains, and flat sandy plains. The sun shines for months on end, and there are over 1,000 miles of beaches.

COUNTRY BRIEFING

Size: 25,332 square miles   **Population:** 14,500,000
Capital: Colombo   **Capital Population:** 600,000
   Climate: December-March is the best time to visit, though travel is possible throughout the year.

Weather in Colombo: Lat N6°55'; Alt 55 ft

Temp (°F)	Jan	Feb	Mar	Apr	May	Jun	Jul	Aug	Sep	Oct	Nov	Dec
Av Temp	81°	82°	82°	83°	82°	81°	81°	80°	81°	80°	79°	79°
Days no rain	21	24	20	14	10	10	13	17	13	9	11	19

Government: An independent democratic socialist republic within the British Commonwealth.

Language: Sinhala, Tamil, and English spoken.

Religion: Buddhism is the religion of the majority; Hinduism, practiced mainly by the Tamils, is the second largest affiliation; Islam and Christianity are also practiced.

Currency: Rupee. 100 cents = 1 rupee.

	50¢	Rs 1	Rs 2	Rs 5	Rs 10	Rs 50	Rs 100	Rs 500
US (dollars, cents)	.03	.06	.11	.28	.56	2.78	5.57	27.83
UK (pounds, pence)	.01	.03	.05	.13	.27	1.33	2.66	13.27

Public Holidays:

On full-moon days, all places of entertainment are closed, and no liquor is sold. Other holidays are:

Hadji Festival Day, Dec/Jan

Thai Pongal (Hindu Festival in honor of Sun God), 14 Jan

Independence Day, 4 Feb

Maha Sivarathri Day, Feb/Mar

Prophet Muhammad's Birthday, Feb/Mar

Sinhala and Tamil New Year, 13-14 Apr

Good Friday

May Day, 1 May

Wesak Poya Day, May

National Heroes Day, 22 May

Deepavali Ramzan, Oct/Nov/Dec

Christmas Day, 25 Dec

HOW TO GET THERE

Flying time to Colombo, Katunayake International Airport, from Frankfurt is 12½ hours; from Hong Kong, 5¾ hours; from Bangkok, 3¼ hours; from Singapore, 3½ hours. Time in Sri Lanka: GMT+5 hours 30 minutes.

REQUIREMENTS FOR ENTRY AND CUSTOMS REGULATIONS

Valid passport, smallpox, yellow-fever, and cholera certificates if coming from an infected area; onward ticket and sufficient funds. No currency from Sri Lanka, Pakistan, Indian, nor even Sri Lanka's own rupee can be imported. No restrictions on other currencies, but they should be declared. Goods can be exported freely, except tea (up to 6 pounds duty-free; 6-15 pounds expect a duty of Rs6 per pound). For gems of any value there must be proof that sufficient foreign currency was imported to cover their cost. The export of animals, alive or dead, or their skin, feathers, etc, is illegal. No antiques may be taken out of the country. Duty-free allowance: 200 cigarettes or 50 cigars or 375 grams tobacco; 2 regular-size bottles of wine and 1½ liters spirits; reasonable amount of toilet water or perfume for personal use. No guns of any type are permitted.

AIRPORT INFORMATION

Major airport is Colombo International Airport, Katunayake, 21 miles from Colombo. Buses and taxis are available to and from the city center. Some airlines provide transportation to and from Colombo. Taxis charge Rs200 per car (3 or 4 passengers) for transport from airport to Colombo. No arrival tax, but departure tax is Rs100.

ACCOMMODATIONS

Special types of accommodations include rest houses, bungalows in the national parks, and government cottages, all of which are inexpensive. Provincial guest houses and paying-guest accommodations are also not costly, rates being from Rs65 per person for bed and breakfast. Some hotels on the southwest coast reduce their rates in the off season, May-Oct. For help in finding accommodations in Colombo try the **Travel Information Center,** Ceylon Tourist Board, 25 Galle Face Center Road, Colombo (tel: 32178), or **Travel Bureau,** Ceylon Hotel Corporation, Hotel Ceylon Inter · Continental (tel: 23501/23504). In Kandy try the **Travel Information Office,** United States Library, Dalada Veediya (tel: 08 2661). Hotels in Colombo, exclusive of a 10% tax and, normally, a 10% service charge:

Rates are in $ for a double/twin room with bath or shower

    Brighton, 57 Ramakrishna Road, 5 miles from center (from $40); tel: 35211

    Ceylinco, 69 Janadhipathi Mawatha (from $33); tel: 20431

    Ceylon Inns, 501/1A Galle Road, 6 miles from center (from $27); tel: 83336

    CEYLON INTER · CONTINENTAL, 48 Janadhipathi Mawatha (from $64); tel: 21221

    Duro, 429 Galle Road (from $25); tel: 85338

    Galle Face, 2 Galle Road (from $45); tel: 28211

    Havelock Tourinn, 20 Dickman's Road, 5 miles from center (from $49); tel: 85251

    Holiday Inn, Galle Face (from $60); tel: 22001

    Janaki, 43 Fife Road, 3 miles from center (from $23); tel: 81524

    Lanka Oberoi, 77-83 Steuart Place (from $70); tel: 20001

    Mount Lavinia, 104 Hotel Road, 7 miles from center (from $35); tel: 071-5221

    Pegasus Reef, Santha Maria Mawatha, Hendala, 7 miles from center (from $60); tel: 070-205

    Ranmuthu, 112 Galle Road (from $39); tel: 33986

    Renuka, 328 Galle Road, 1 mile from center (from $47); tel: 26901

    Sapphire, 371 Galle Road, 6 miles from center (from $40); tel: 83306

    Sea View, 15 Sea View Avenue, 1 mile from center (from $15); tel: 26516

    Taprobane, 2 York Street (from $36); tel: 20391

    Tilly's Beach Hotel, 20 De Soysa Avenue, Mt Lavinia, 7 miles from center (from $33); tel: 071-3531

Unless otherwise indicated, all the above hotels are centrally located.

USEFUL INFORMATION

Banks: Open 9-1 Mon, 9-1:30 Tues-Fri.

Mail: Stamps at post offices, bookshops, and general stores.

Telephone Tips: Phones in cafés, restaurants, hotels, stores, and at all post offices; booths throughout the cities. Useful numbers in Colombo:

Pan Am agent 23177	Directories 138
Flight Information 27564	Accommodations Office
Tourist Offices 81801	23501/23504
Tourist Information 32178	Tourist Police 26941/21111

Newspapers: English-language newspapers available.

Clubs: Rotary, Lions, Jaycees, Apex. Women's clubs—The Inner Wheel and Zonta.

Tipping: Customary; 10% normally, although service is sometimes included. Porter, Rs2 per piece of luggage; hotel porter, chambermaid, cloakroom attendants all get about Rs2.

Electricity: 230-240 volts 50 cycles AC.

Laundry: Good laundry and dry-cleaning services, and laundromats are available throughout the country. In major hotels, a 24-hour service is usually available (dry-cleaning a suit, Rs5-12; laundering a shirt, Rs3-4).

Hairdressing: First-class hotels have salons (shampoo and set, Rs25-75; a man's haircut Rs30).

Photography: It is advisable to bring your own film. Black and white processing takes 1-2 days; color 2-4 days; Ektachrome or Kodacolor 3-7 days. Black and white film costs from Rs20; color Rs90-130. Permits are necessary to photograph certain archaeological sites, including those of Polonnaruwa, Sigiriya, Anuradhapura, and Mihintale. Apply to the Commissioner of Archaeology, Sir Marcus Fernando Mawatha, Colombo (tel: 94727), or (for Polonnaruwa, Sigiriya, and Anuradhapura) to the archaeological office at the site. There is no charge.

Rest Rooms: Signs, in English or symbol, prominently displayed in all modern hotels, railway stations, and other public places.

Health: Good medical care is available. All doctors and dentists speak English. Imported pharmaceuticals available. Drink only boiled, filtered or bottled water.

TRANSPORTATION

The Sri Lanka Transport Board buses provide transport within the cities; there is good train service between cities. Taxis also available. Cars can be rented through travel agents; rates from Rs280 per day, no extra charge for an English-speaking driver. Drive on the left. Roads good but narrow. Good long-distance express bus service links major towns and cities. Seats can be booked in advance on these buses for a reservation fee of Rs1. Inquiries at Central Bus Stand, Pettah (Colombo tel: 28081). The national airline, Air Lanka, connects the capital with provincial cities, and the Sri Lanka Air Force operates air charters by helicopter or small aircraft. Contact Heli-tours, Air Force Headquarters, Sir Chittampalam Gardiner Mawatha, Colombo 2 (tel: 31584 or 33184). Upali Travels (22

Janadhipathi Mawatha, Colombo 1—tel: 20465) operates a domestic air service to Jaffna, Trincomalee, and Anuradhapura daily, and has helicopters capable of landing at most tourist hotel grounds or attraction sites. Boats go from Jaffna to the surrounding islands and from Trincomalee to Seruvavilla or Mutur.

FOOD AND RESTAURANTS

Western food is readily available. Local specialities include rice and curry, a staple of the Sri Lankan diet. As the curries are hot, tourists should ask for "white curries" until their palates are ready for hotter dishes. The **Akasa Kade** (roof-top restaurant) in the Ceylinco Hotel serves excellent Ceylonese food, and the **Catseye Supper Club** at the Ceylon Inter · Continental has Ceylonese specialities along with international cuisine. Other restaurants serving Sri Lankan, Oriental, and Western food are **Ran Malu** at the Lanka Oberoi Hotel, **Palmyrah Restaurant** in Hotel Renuka (Colombo 3), **Emerald Tea and Coffee Shop** at Hotel Ceylon, Inter · Continental (Fort), **Alhambara** at Holiday Inn (Colombo 3). For Moghul food, try **Sea Spray Restaurant** in the Galle Face Hotel, **Omar Khayam** on Police Park Terrace (Colombo 5), and **Chez Amano**, Steuart Place (Colombo 3). Other tasty dishes are *lamprai* (rice boiled in stock with dry curries and then baked in banana leaf), *hoppers* (a cross between a muffin and a griddlecake with a wafer crisp edge), and *string hoppers* (steamed circlets of rice flour), some of which you can sample at the **Harbour Room** (Hotel Taprobane, York Street, Fort—tel: 20391) or at the **Green Cabin Café** (453 Galle Road, Colombo). The **Blue Leopard** (Hotel Taprobane), **Flame Room** (Havelock Tourinn), **London Grill** (Lanka Oberoi), **Renuka Restaurant** (Renuka Hotel), **The Fab** (474 Galle Road, Colombo 3), and **Supper Club** (Hotel Lanka Oberoi) all serve Western food. The **Windmill** (41 Galle Road) serves excellent light snacks. Also, for snacks, try the **Emerald Tea and Coffee Bar** at the Hotel Inter · Continental; the **Pagoda Tea Rooms** (Chattam Street, Fort), the **Coffee Shop** at the Lanka Oberoi Hotel, **Gardenia Tea and Coffee Shop** (Holiday Inn, Colombo 3), **Fountain Cafe** (Union Place, Colombo 2), **Perera and Sons** (Galle Road, Colombo 3), or **Bamboo Bar** at the Hotel Taprobane. Or try one of the numerous street stalls (called *boutiques*) where a variety of food is always available. The fruit includes pineapples, papaw, avocados and mangoes, rambuttans, oranges, grapefruit, beli, guava, sweet jak, cherry moir, pears, sour sap, watermelon, passion fruit, sapedilla, pomegranate, custard apples, jambus, mangosteens, and more than a dozen varieties of bananas. Sample the woodapple and durian (a great delicacy but with a noxious smell), or better still try *thambili*, the juice of the king coconut drunk straight from the shell. Go to the **Greenlands Hotel** (8 Shrubbery Gardens, Bambalapitiya, Colombo—tel: 81986), where vegetarian cooking is the order of the day. The **Ceyfish Restaurant** (1 Mohamed Marcan Markar Mawatha, Colombo) and **La Langousterie,** on the beach at Mount Lavinia, specialize in sea food; **Chopsticks** (91/1 Havelock Road, Colombo 5), **Park View Lodge** (70 Park Street, Colombo 2), **Nanking Hotel** (Chatham Street, Fort), and **Chinese Lotus Hotel** (Isabel Court, 265 Galle Road, Colombo 3), in Chinese cuisine; at the **Hotel Nippon** (123 Kumaran Rutnam Road, Slave Island, Colombo) there are Japanese, Chinese, and Western dishes.

DRINKING TIPS

The national drink, coconut toddy (the fermented sap of the coconut palm), is taken as a long drink and is distilled into *Arrack*, when it becomes as smooth and as strong as vodka—drunk straight or mixed. Sri Lanka also produces its own beer, gin, brandy and whisky. Imported beers, wines and liquors are available. The sale of liquor is restricted in sacred areas. Normal hours are 8am-1pm. *Arrack* bars are always open, except on full-moon days which are observed as public holidays in keeping with traditional religious custom.

ENTERTAINMENT

The **Symphony Orchestra of Sri Lanka,** Gilbert and Sullivan, and variety entertainment are available. Sinhala and Western plays and Sinhala translations of Western plays are staged frequently. Popular theaters are the **Lionel Wendt** (Guilford Crescent, Colombo 7), **Lumbini Theater** (Havelock Town, Colombo 5), **Tower Hall** (Maradana, Colombo 10—tel: 31878), **Nawarangahala (Theater Royal)** in Colombo, and the **John de Silva Memorial Hall** (Ananda Coomaraswamy Mawatha, Colombo 7). There are a number of movie houses, many of which show British and American movies. Most nightclubs in Colombo are in the major hotels; the **Blue Leopard** at Hotel Taprobane, **Supper Club** at Hotel Lanka Oberoi, the **Flame Room** in Havelock Tourinn (Dickman's Road, Colombo 5), the **Little Hut** at the Mount Lavinia Hotel, and the **Sunset Night Club** at Browns Beach Hotel, Negombo, have small groups providing music for dancing. In addition, there are programs of traditional dance, song, and drama from time to time in Colombo and in the provinces.

SHOPPING

Stores open 9-6, Mon-Fri. Best buys are gems, tea, batiks, and handicrafts. Ceylonese craftsmen work in silver, brass, tortoiseshell, horn, bone, ivory, wood, and terracotta. Buy some of their goods in **Laksala,** a government-sponsored emporium on York Street, Colombo, and at **Lakpahana,** 21 Race Course Avenue, Colombo. Also visit the **Sri Lanka Industrial Shop,** managed by the Ceylon Ceramics Corporation, at Katunayake International Airport. Sri Lanka has always been the treasury of the world in terms of gems—sapphires, rubies, amethysts, and other precious and semiprecious stones. The **State Gem Corporation** operates showrooms at 24 York Street, Colombo, at the **Hotel Ceylon Inter · Continental,** and at the airport. The corporation will also examine, at no charge, gems bought anywhere in the country and will certify whether they are genuine. Sri Lanka tea is considered among the best in the world and is freely available in stores. The **Ceylon Tea Board** has a sales counter at its main office, 574 Galle Road, Colombo 3, and another sales point at the airport. Near the business center is the **Pettah,** one of the most interesting shopping centers, with a variety of goods from antiques to bric-à-brac. In Kandy try the **Arts Association,** and in provincial towns the handicraft shops. Kandy is a particularly good place to buy silver, brass, and lacquerware. It is customary to bargain in markets.

SPORTS

Spectator sports include cricket, rugby, soccer, hockey, tennis, volleyball, netball, and basketball. You can go horseback riding on the Horton Plains, swimming on coastal beaches, surfing on the west coast near Colombo, yachting in Colombo and on the east coast, and deep-sea fishing on the south coast. For water-skiing, see Sun Stream Boat Service at the **National Holiday Resort,** Bentota (38 miles from Colombo on the west coast). Many major cities have golf courses; the **Royal Colombo Golf Club,** Model Farm Road, Colombo (tel: 95431) has an 18-hole course and facilities for temporary membership, as has the **Nuwara Eliya Golf Club** at Nuwara Eliya, 112 miles from Colombo (tel: Nuwara Eliya 0522.335). For tennis there are the **Ceylon Lawn Tennis Association,** 45 Edinburgh Crescent, Colombo (tel: 91425), and **Gymkhana Club,** 31 Maitland Crescent, Colombo (tel: 91025), **Women's International Club,** 16 Guilford Crescent, Colombo 7 (tel: 95072).

WHAT TO SEE

Colombo is gracious and is dotted with small parks and gardens, temples, museums, and many Victorian houses and administrative buildings. The streets are always crowded with ox carts, buses, pedestrians, market stalls, barefoot children, women in bright saris, and Englishmen in tweed jackets. See the **National Museum,** a collection of bronze and stone sculptures and many other items from ancient Sri Lanka. Visit the **Zoological Gardens** at Dehiwela (7 miles from Colombo)—one of the best in the world—with its beautiful landscaping, walk-in aviary, and elephant circus each evening at 5:15pm; the **Aquarium,** the only one of its kind in Asia, displays 500 varieties of aquatic life. Or see the **Raja Maha Vihare** temple at Kelaniya, especially in January, when a procession commemorates the visit of Buddha in pre-Christian times.

Seventy-two miles from Colombo is **Kandy,** one of the most beautiful cities in Sri Lanka. The **Sacred Tooth Relic** of the Buddha, brought to the country over 1,500 years ago, is housed here in the **Dalada Maligawa**—Temple of the Tooth—and is venerated by millions of Sri Lankan Buddhists. See the artificial lake in the center of town and just outside the town, the **Royal Botanical Gardens** at Peradeniya, 150 acres of tropical plants and a wonderful orchid collection. Not to be missed, if possible, is the **Përahera,** an ancient traditional festival continuing for 10 nights in July, or August, with processions of elephants, drummers, and dancers. Cradled in the bowl of five surrounding hills, Kandy is also the gateway to the mountains (over 6,000 feet high) and to several resorts, including **Muwara Eliya** (103 miles from Colombo). The center of the region is a beautiful landscaped town, with a park, golf course, and a lake. The countryside offers trout fishing, panoramic views, and a delightful spring-like climate. Hotels in the area are **Chalet Guest House,** 32 Gregory's Road (from US$23 double); tel: 08-4353; **Queens,** Dalada Vidiya (from US$22 double); tel: 08-2121; and **Suisse,** 30 Sangaraja Mawata (from US$22). **Hunas Falls Hotel,** Hunasgeria Group, Elkaduwa (from US$39 double) is located 17 miles out of Kandy, in the heart of a tea garden over 3,000 feet above sea level, and the **Grand Hotel Nuwara Eliya** (from US$22); tel: 0522-216. Rates do not include 10% tax.

During July and August see the popular **Kataragama Festival** at Kataragama (175 miles from Colombo), the jungle shrine dedicated to the Hindu god Skanda. Highlight of the festival is the fire-walking ceremony, where fervent devotees do an expiatory walk on a wide pit of red-hot coals.

The ancient cities and their many temples are also "musts." **Anuradhapura,** site of the holy Bo-Tree, is more than 2,000 years old. Here 119 kings ruled, while for 1,500 years Anuradhapura was the capital of the island, in addition to being Buddhism's capital city. Palaces, ruined temples, gardens, and fantastic reservoirs make up the whole of this ancient city. **Mihintale** and **Polonnaruwa** are also noteworthy ancient settlements, but perhaps the most interesting after Anuradhapura is **Sigiriya,** built by the parricide King Kassapa, who had the city literally carved from the top of a huge rock. Well worth seeing are the frescoes, still intact, of seductive dancing girls, painted onto the walls of the gallery in the 5th century AD.

Also see some of the resort areas which circle the island. **Negombo, Mount Lavinia, Bentota, Hikkaduwa, Galle, Hambantota, Kalkudah, Trincomalee,** and **Jaffna** are just a few.

SOURCES OF FURTHER INFORMATION

Pan Am agents: Shaw Wallace & Hedges Ltd, 353 Kollupitiya Road, PO Box 84, Colombo 3, or any Pan Am office around the world; **Travel Information Center,** 25 Galle Face Center Road, Colombo 3, Sri Lanka (tel: 32178, 31951, 36161). **Tourist Board,** Suite 308, 609 Fifth Avenue, New York, NY 10017; **Marketing Services (Travel and Tourism) Ltd,** 52 High Holborn, London WC1.

Tahiti

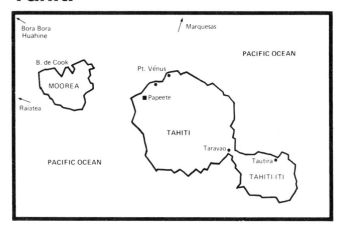

WHAT'S SPECIAL

Tahiti lies 2,400 miles south of Honolulu. Part of the Society Islands which are in turn part of French Polynesia (along with four other island groups—the Marquesas, Australs, Tuamotus, and Gambiers), the very name Tahiti has become synonymous with blue lagoons and beautiful beaches, with the sound of drums, with Gauguin, coconut palms, happy natives, and tribal music. And while it can hardly be said that Tahiti has been immune to progress, neither can it be maintained that the island has been spoiled. The present is treated with the same easy-going affection as the past here, and the legendary beauty of the island is undiminished.

Total escape is relatively easy. Large sections of Papeete, much of the island of Tahiti itself, and certainly many of the other Society Islands (Moorea, Bora-Bora, Huahine, Raiatea, and Tahaa) offer the expected retreats: complete peace, quiet, and palm trees. And Tahiti has its unique mixture of peoples—the French government officials, the Chinese shopkeepers, the European and American settlers, and the Tahitians themselves.

COUNTRY BRIEFING

Size: 386 square miles (Tahiti) 1,544 square miles (French Polynesia)

Capital: Papeete

Population: 140,000 (Tahiti) 138,000 (French Polynesia)

Capital Population: 30,000

Climate: Tropical, divided into two seasons. December-February is warm and moist with a good deal of rain; March-April can be wet, but May-November is cool and dry.

Weather in Papeete: Lat S17°32'; Alt 302 ft

Temp (°F)	Jan	Feb	Mar	Apr	May	Jun	Jul	Aug	Sep	Oct	Nov	Dec
Av Low	72°	72°	72°	72°	70°	69°	68°	68°	69°	70°	71°	72°
Av High	80°	89°	89°	89°	87°	86°	86°	86°	86°	87°	88°	88°
Days no rain	15	12	14	20	21	22	26	25	24	22	17	17

Government: Tahiti is part of French Polynesia, a French Overseas Territory with a French High Commissioner in residence and a locally-elected Territorial Assembly.

Language: Tahitian and French are the local languages. English is understood in Papeete.

Religion: About 55% Protestant, 30% Roman Catholic, some Seventh-Day Adventists and Latter-Day Saints, and a number of Buddhists and Confucianists.

Currency: French Pacific franc. 100 centimes = 1 CFP.

	CFP 5	CFP 10	CFP 20	CFP 50	CFP 100	CFP 500	CFP 1,000	CFP 5,000
US (dollars, cents)	.06	.11	.22	.55	1.10	5.50	11.00	55.00
UK (pounds, pence)	.03	.05	.10	.26	.52	2.62	5.25	26.24

Public Holidays:

New Year, 1/2/3 Jan
Chinese New Year, Jan/Feb
Good Friday
Easter Monday
Labor Day, 1 May

Ascension Day
Whit Monday
Bastille Day, 14 July
All Saints Day, 1 Nov
Christmas Day, 25 Dec

HOW TO GET THERE

Flying time to Faaa International Airport, Papeete from Los Angeles is 8 hours; from Honolulu, 5¾ hours; from Auckland, 4¾ hours. Time in Tahiti: GMT—10.

REQUIREMENTS FOR ENTRY AND CUSTOMS REGULATIONS

Passport and round-trip ticket necessary. A visa is not required unless staying more than 30 days. Yellow-fever and cholera vaccination certificates required if coming from an infected area. The luggage of all passengers coming from Fiji and Pago Pago will be kept for fumigation, which takes about two hours. Duty-free allowance: 400 cigarettes or 50 cigars or 500 grams of tobacco; one opened bottle of liquor (anisette alcoholic beverages prohibited); one still camera, and one movie camera with 10 rolls of unexposed film each.

AIRPORT INFORMATION

Faaa International Airport is 3½ miles from Papeete's town center. "Le Truck," an unscheduled bus service, stops in front of the airport and makes stops in Papeete, at hotels, and outlying districts; fare is CFP60-70, but it takes only light luggage. Taxis are available—a journey into Papeete costs US$2.50. The airport has a duty-free shop and hotel reservation counter operated by the **Tahiti Tourist Board.**

ACCOMMODATIONS

Hotels in Tahiti range from island-style, thatched-roof bungalows (called *fares*) to more conventional high-rise hotel or motel buildings. For those staying a long time, housekeeping cottages at moderate rates are available. In outlying districts, it is possible to rent rooms from the inhabitants, with or without meals, and usually with a communal bathroom. There is no service charge on hotel bills, but there is a 4% hotel tax. Hotels in Tahiti:

Rates are in US$ for a double/twin room with bath or shower
   Aimeo, Cook's Bay, Moorea (PO Box 627, Papeete) (from $115 MAP)
   Bali-Hai Moorea, Moorea (PO Box 415, Papeete) (from $85)
   Bali Hai Huahine, Fare, Huahine (from $110)
   Bali Hai Raiatea, Raiatea (PO Box 43, Uturoa) (from $85)
   Beachcomber, Papeete (PO Box 6014, Faaa) (from $77)
   Bora-Bora, Nunue, Bora-Bora (PO Box 1015, Papeete) (from $175)
   Kia Ora Moorea, Moorea (PO Box 706, Papeete) (from $175)
   Kia Ora Village, Rangiroa (PO Box 706, Papeete) (from $155)
   Maeva Beach, Papeete (PO Box 6008, Faaa) (from $75)
   Marara, Bora-Bora (PO Box 6255, Papeete) (from $110)
   Moorea Lagoon, Moorea (PO Box 1660, Papeete) (from $60)
   Royal Papeete, downtown Papeete (PO Box 919, Papeete) (from $34)
   Royal Tahitien, Papeete (PO Box 5001, Pirae) (from $150)
   Tahara'a, Papeete (PO Box 1015, Papeete) (from $85)
   Tahiti, Papeete (PO Box 416, Papeete) (from $32)

USEFUL INFORMATION

Helpful Hints: Tahiti is known for its informality, and women will find dresses and slacks acceptable in town. A long-sleeved shirt will come in handy on that occasional cool day. A raincoat is a must. Tipping is against the local traditions of hospitality. *Iaora* is the all-purpose local greeting, and *mauruururoa* means "thank you very much."

Banks: Open 7:45-3:30 Mon-Fri. One can also change money at the exchange counter at the airport.

Mail: The Papeete post office, located on Quai Bir-Hakeim, is the center of international communications and is open 7:30-11:30, 1:30-4:30 Mon-Fri.

Newspapers: The *Tahiti Bulletin* is the English-language publication, distributed free five days a week.

Tipping: Absolutely no tipping is expected, and no service charge is included in checks.

Electricity: 110 or 220 volts 60 cycles AC. Check before plugging in.

Laundry: 24-hour service in major hotels. Laundromats in Papeete.

Hairdressing: Good salons in major hotels.

Photography: Equipment, black and white film, and color film available in major cities only. Processing takes 48 hours for color, 24 hours for black and white.

Clubs: Lions meet on the second Tuesday of every month in the Maeva Beach Hotel, Papeete. Rotary meets every Monday evening for cocktails and dinner at the Maeva Beach.

Health: Many doctors and dentists speak English. Water is safe to drink, though many French bottled waters are available.

TRANSPORTATION

Transport consists of bus, *le Truck*, and taxi service. Taxis have fixed rates: initial cost CFP75, plus CFP50 per kilometer within Papeete and to the adjoining cities of Arue, Pirae, Faaa, and Punauia; CFP100 per kilometer to all other destinations. There is a minimum fare of CFP200. Prices are double in the evening (after 11pm), except for runs from hotel to airport and airport to hotel. There are a number of car rental establishments, where cars are available by the day or week. Cars can be rented for about CFP1800-2400 a day depending on type of car and minimum daily mileage. Road traffic on the island keeps to the right. There are no trains. Travel between the islands is by either plane or boat. The round-trip boat fare between Papeete and Moorea is CFP1,000-1,500 on a comfortable cruiser; round-trip air fare is CFP2,440. The internal airlines are Air Polynesia and Air Tahiti. They fly to Moorea, Raiatea, Bora-Bora, Maupiti, and Huahine in the Society Islands, and to all the other island groups.

FOOD AND RESTAURANTS

The variety of peoples living in Tahiti have done the island a service where cooking is concerned, for here their influence means you can eat "authentic" French, Chinese, or Tahitian food in addition to the standard international fare provided by the tourist hotels. Some of the Tahitian dishes available in most restaurants are *poisson cru* (marinated fish), *fafa* (young spinach-like taro leaves), and *poi* (a dessert of banana, pineapple, or papaya crushed into a fine paste—not to be confused with Hawaiian *poi*). A Tahitian specialty is the *tamaaraa* or native feast, when chicken or pork is cooked over red-hot stones and eaten sitting on the ground under the palm trees. Mealtimes are 6-8, 11-1, dinner 6-9. Prices vary from about CFP450 per person in some of the back-street or waterfront restaurants to about CFP1,600 per person in the most expensive restaurants. In a waterfront café you can have *gigot* or *escargots*, while down the road you can have a shrimp and octopus curry. The **Vaima** café on Quai Bir-Hakeim is a favorite spot for inexpensive meals. Good places for French food are the **Gauguin** in the Maeva Beach Hotel, **Michel et Eliane** (Vaima Center), both expensive. More moderate are **La Petite Auberge** (Rue General de Gaulle and Rue des Remparts) or the mountainside **Le Belvedere** (Route de Fare Rau Ape, Pirae—tel: 27344) and **La Chaumiere. Acajou,** near Vaima Center, has a famous chef and is also moderate. **Prince Hinoi** serves French and Chinese food (Avenue Prince Hinoi—tel: 28085), and **Waikiki**, Chinese (Rue des Remparts—tel: 29527). Less expensive Oriental cuisine may be enjoyed at **Dragon D'or**, and **Soupe Chinoise**. Elsewhere on the island try the restaurant in the Gauguin Museum, **Restaurant de Musée Gauguin**.

DRINKING TIPS

Be sure to try the good local beers, *Hinano* and *Manuia*. There are no restrictions on women in bars. Some popular spots in Papeete are the **Vaima** sidewalk café on the Quai Bir-Hakeim, **Manaya** on Avenue Bruat, and **Pitate**, Avenue Bruat.

ENTERTAINMENT

Many of the hotels have dancing and Tahitian music. There are also discothèques: **La Cave** with Tahitian ambiance (Royal Papeete Hotel—tel: 20129), **La Fayette**, again Tahitian (in Arue, 5 miles from Papeete—tel: 27024), **Whiskey-A-Gogo** (Quai Gallieni—tel: 29578); **Café de Paris** (Maeva Beach Hotel—tel: 28042); **Piano Bar** (Rue des Ecoles); and **Zizou Bar**, near the Kon Tiki Hotel. A *tamaaraa* can be arranged by a local tour representative. Numerous festivals are also endlessly diverting.

SHOPPING

Good buys are French products including perfume, bathing suits, silver, crystal, lingerie, and fabrics. Also interesting are Tahitian artifacts (especially carved *tikis*, or idols), materials, jewelry in mother-of-pearl and shell, Polynesian fashions (bikinis, skirts, ball gowns) in hand-blocked fabrics, woven hats, basketry and wood carvings. Shops usually open about 7:30am and close at 5pm (11am on Saturdays). The municipal market in Papeete is a good place for shopping; the best time to go is Sunday morning.

SPORTS

Tahiti has a first-rate golf course at **Atimaono Valley**, 25 miles from Papeete; green fee of CFP850 per day. Tours on horseback by the hour, day, or weekend can be arranged through the **Centre de Tourisme Equestre de Tahiti** and the **Club Equestre de Tahiti**. Horse racing takes place one Sunday a month at the **Hippodrome** at Pirae. Spectator sports include soccer and racing. Clubs that welcome visitors are: **Féderation Générale des Sociétés Sportives, Central Sport, Club Athlétique de Pirae**, and the **Yacht Club**. In Papeete there are good tennis courts and a diving and deep-sea fishing center.

WHAT TO SEE

Tahiti is really two separate mountain peaks, linked by an isthmus gently sloping down to the sea in a series of green ridges. The larger portion of the island is **Tahiti-Nui**, the small portion **Tahiti-Iti**. **Papeete** is the government seat of French Polynesia and as the largest city, has a fair amount to offer. One of the more off-beat attractions is the tomb of the last king of Tahiti, Pomare V, at Arue. There are also a number of museums: the **Papeete Museum,** the **Gauguin Museum** at Papeari (with memorabilia, a few originals, and many reproductions), and the **Museum of the Discovery** at Point Venus, a waxworks commemoration of the first European visitors to Tahiti. **Point Venus** is the spot where Captain Cook first dropped anchor at Tahiti in 1769. Papeari also has a beautiful **Botanical Garden,** and when you tire of looking at the gardens on land, you can take a two-hour glass-bottomed boat tour from the harbor in Papeete and visit the sea coral gardens. Not far from Papeete is the valley of **Fautaua,** scene of Pierre Loti's idyll *Rarahu,* and one of the island's noted beauty spots; there is a statue dedicated to Loti.

From Tahara'a Hotel's hill on Tahiti, the island of **Moorea** is visible about 12 miles away. The island is noted for its beautiful scenery and its simple, unaffected quality of life. Except for a small coastal strip, the 51 square miles of the island are composed almost entirely of rugged mountains, with hundreds of lofty blue peaks, and covered with blue and scarlet creepers. There is a 70-minute crossing by boat or a 10-minute flight.

Bora-Bora, with about 2,200 people, is 160 miles northwest of Tahiti and consists of a central island almost completely surrounded by a coral reef and smaller reef islands called *motus,* one of which serves as the airport. Two mountain peaks dominate the central island. The lagoon and the harbor of Bora-Bora is a large and magnificent stretch of water, and tours in glass-bottomed boats are available. The central village is **Vaitape.**

One hundred and forty miles from Papeete is **Raiatea,** the ancient center of Polynesian civilization. On Raiatea you can see fire-walking ceremonies, ancient pagan temples, and numerous archeological sites. The island, along with the neighboring island of **Tahaa,** has a population of 9,890 people, and the main settlement, **Uturoa,** is the second-largest city in French Polynesia. The only tourist hotel is the **Bali Hai,** Uturoa, Raiatea, which will arrange sporting excursions or visits to Tahaa.

On **Huahiné** there are a number of archeological sites and some old prayer houses and temples. The central village is **Fare,** with 600 people, which has a harbor, Farenui-Atea. The island's major hotel is the **Bali Hai Huahine.**

Nine hundred miles northeast of Tahiti are the eleven **Marquesas Islands;** six of them are inhabited, and **Nuku Hiya** is the administrative center. The 19th-century French painter Gauguin died and was buried on **Hiva Oa,** another island in the group. Melville wrote *Typee* here, and you can see in these islands a life-style that has gone on almost unchanged since their time.

SOURCES OF FURTHER INFORMATION

Pan Am, Vaima Center, Boulevard Pomare, Papeete—tel: 29640, and any Pan Am office around the world; **Tahiti Tourist Development Board,** Fare Manihini, Papeete; Suite 1704, 700 Flower Street, Los Angeles, CA 90017.

Taiwan

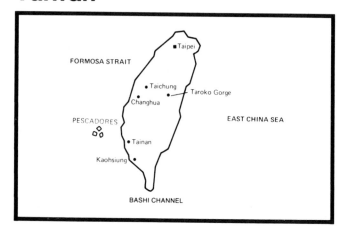

WHAT'S SPECIAL

Although the number of tourists to the island is markedly increasing, Taiwan does not wear its tourist attractions on its sleeve. The cities by and large may seem quiet after a visit to Japan or Hong Kong. The life-style is something you must experience in order to appreciate the subtle and not-so-subtle permutations of bustling street life in the older quarters. The National Palace Museum, whose art treasures from the whole range of Chinese dynasties appeal even to visitors who are not normally museum-goers, will provide at least a glimpse of ancient China. The Chinese name of Taiwan, meaning "terraced bay," is an apt description of the island's cultivated area, for outside the cities the terraces or rice paddies endlessly multiplied over an undulating landscape create some of the most distinctive scenery to be seen anywhere. Elsewhere much of the island proves the truth of the Portuguese name *Ilha Formosa,* or "beautiful isle."

COUNTRY BRIEFING

Size: 13,885 square miles   **Population:** 17,800,000
Capital: Taipei   **Capital Population:** 2,200,000

Climate: Subtropical, with moderate temperatures in the north, where there is a definite winter season (January-February), and slightly warmer temperatures in the south. Rain is heavy around Keelung and Taipei; the typhoon season is June-October.

Weather in Taipei: Lat N25°02′; Alt 30 ft

Temp (°F)	Jan	Feb	Mar	Apr	May	Jun	Jul	Aug	Sep	Oct	Nov	Dec
Av Low	54°	53°	57°	63°	69°	73°	76°	75°	73°	67°	62°	57°
Av High	66°	65°	71°	77°	83°	89°	92°	91°	88°	81°	75°	69°
Days no rain	22	15	19	16	19	17	21	19	20	22	23	23

Government: A republic founded in 1912.

Language: Mandarin is the official language. The Taiwanese dialect of Chinese is also widely spoken. English is understood in establishments catering to foreign tourists.

Religion: Buddhism and Taoism are the predominant faiths, but there are also Muslims and Christians. A number of churches offer English-language services, and a Jewish Community Center has been established.

Currency: New Taiwan dollar. 100 cents = 1 new Taiwan dollar

	50¢	NT$ 1	NT$ 10	NT$ 50	NT$ 100	NT$ 500	NT$ 1000	NT$ 2000
US (dollars, cents)	.01	.03	.27	1.37	2.74	13.71	27.42	54.84
UK (pounds, pence)	—	.01	.13	.65	1.31	6.55	13.10	26.21

Public Holidays:

Founding of the Republic of China, 1 Jan

Chinese New Year, Jan/Feb

Youth Day, 29 Mar

Tomb-sweeping Day and Death of Chiang Kai-shek, 5 Apr

Birthday of Confucius (Teachers' Day), 28 Sep

Double Tenth National Day, 10 Oct

Taiwan Retrocession Day, 25 Oct

Chiang Kai-shek's Birthday, 31 Oct

Dr Sun Yat-Sen's Birthday, 12 Nov

Constitution Day, 25 Dec

HOW TO GET THERE

Flying time to Taipei, Chiang Kai-shek International Airport from San Francisco is 13 hours; from Honolulu, 9½ hours; from Tokyo, 3 hours; from Hong Kong, 1½ hours. Time in Taiwan: GMT + 8.

REQUIREMENTS FOR ENTRY AND CUSTOMS REGULATIONS

Passports and visas are required. (In the United States, in the absence of diplomatic relations, Taiwan's visa-issuing organization is the Coordination Council for North American Affairs, with offices in many major cities.) Smallpox vaccination certificate not requried; a cholera certificate is necessary if arriving from an infected area. No more than NT$8,000 in cash may be brought in or taken out. Unlimited foreign currency may be imported and, if declared on arrival, taken out. Weapons, narcotics, and pro-Communist publications are prohibited. Unauthorized (pirated) reproductions of books or records are not supposed to leave the country, although customs officials generally do not object to small quantities that are clearly intended for personal use. Duty-free allowance: 400 cigarettes, 50 cigars, and 1 pound tobacco; 2 bottles of alcoholic beverages; a reasonable amount of personal belongings.

AIRPORT INFORMATION

Chiang Kai-shek International Airport is 25 miles southwest of Taipei, connected to the city by the North-South Highway. Taxi fare to the city center is about NT$800, and buses charging NT$50 per person leave every ten minutes. In addition, most major hotels provide inexpensive transportation for guests. There is no airport arrival tax, but the departure tax is NT$150. The airport has a duty-free shop and hotel reservation counter. Airport porters are tipped NT$20 per bag.

ACCOMMODATIONS

For inexpensive accommodations, try the local YMCA (19 Hsu Chang Street), the Federation of Overseas Chinese Associations (28 Tsinan Road, Section 2), or the International House (18 Hsinyi Road, Section 3). For help in finding accommodations check with the **Airport Service Center,** tel: (033) 834631, or the **Taiwan Visitors Association,** tel: 5943261. Hotels tend to be heavily booked in October, a holiday period during which thousands of Overseas Chinese return to Taiwan. Hotels in Taipei:

Rates are in US$ for a double/twin room with bath or shower

Ambassador, 63 Chung Shan North Road, Section 2 (from $60.55) = NT$2180

Central, 122 Chung Shan North Road, Section 2 (from $48.60) = NT$1750

Century Plaza, 132 Omei Street (from $33.30) = NT$1200

Grand, 1 Chung Shan North Road, Section 4 (from $62.50) = NT$2250, 15 minutes by taxi from city center

Imperial, 600 Lin Shen North Road (from $55.55) = NT$2000

Lai Lai Shangri-la Hotel, 12 Chunghsiao East Road, Section 1 (from $58.05) = NT$2090

Mandarin, 166 Tun Hwa North Road (from $50) = NT$1800

President, 9 Teh Hwei Street (from $57.50) = NT$2070

The Ritz, 155 Minchuan East Road (from $66.67) = NT$2400

San Polo, 172 Chung Hsiao East Road, Section 4 (from $50) = NT$1800

Taipei Hilton, 38 Chung Hsiao West Road, Section 1 (from $63.88) = NT$2300

Taipei Regency, 116 Jen Ai Road, Section 4 (from $50) = NT$1800

Taipei Sesame, 225 Hsin Yi Road, Section 4 (from $50) = NT$1800

All hotels are centrally located unless otherwise indicated. Service Tax: 10%

USEFUL INFORMATION

Helpful Hints: One useful expression is *Hsieh hsieh ni,* which means "thank you."

Banks: Open 9–3:30 Mon-Fri, 9–12 Sat. Otherwise money can be changed at tourist hotels and designated gift shops. There are major banks in cities outside the capital.

Telephone Tips: Telephones can be found in hotels, cafés, and restaurants, and there are also booths and wall phones on the streets. Pay phones take the NT$1.00 coin and each call is usually restricted to three minutes. Useful numbers in Taipei:

Pan Am 7652332
Tourist Bureau 7218541
Taiwan Visitors Association 5943261
Airport Service Center (033) 834631

Time (in Chinese only) 117
Water (in Chinese only)
166
**English-language
Information Operator**
3116796

Newspapers: Foreign English-language publications are available. Local ones include two daily newspapers, the *China Post* and *China News;* numerous business weeklies; and two monthly tourist magazines, *This Month in Taiwan* and *China Travel & Trade.*

Tipping: Rare and optional in Taiwan. The tourist board advises tipping only those who wait on you personally. Where applicable, one tips 10%, and there is often a 10% service charge on the bill. Hotel porter is usually tipped NT$10 per piece of luggage.

Electricity: 110 volts 60 cycles AC.

Laundry: 24-hour service available at hotels.

Hairdressing: First-class hotels have salons and barber shops—shampoo and set averages NT$250 and a man's haircut NT$150 (15% tip optional).

Photography: Good selection of photographic equipment, black and white film, and color film available in major cities.

Clubs: Lions International, Rotary, Kiwanis, and American Chamber of Commerce all meet in Taipei.

Rest Rooms: You will find them in hotels, railway stations, gas stations, airports, and restaurants.

Health: Do not drink tap water except in hotels with their own water supply. Many doctors and dentists speak English. A moderate range of imported pharmaceutical goods.

TRANSPORTATION

There are railway, bus, and domestic air services and cars with driver-guides. Tickets for city buses are sold at special booths. Taxis are easily found—hail one in the street—and their rates are among the lowest in the world. Often the meters haven't yet been adjusted to reflect the latest oil price increase, but the driver will have a chart showing the new rates. Few taxi drivers understand English, so it is advisable for visitors to have their destination written down in Chinese. There is a very good internal train service, on which hostesses will provide hot towels, newspapers, and tea. Trains and airplanes connect all the major cities; buses link major cities, towns, and villages.

FOOD AND RESTAURANTS

One of the joys of being in Taiwan is the chance to sample some of the world's best Chinese cuisine. There is great variety in the cooking from different regions of China—not only the Cantonese style most familiar to Americans, but also Szechuanese, Northern (Peking), Shanghainese, Hunanese, and others. The Chinese take food seriously, and Taipei alone boasts more than a thousand decent restaurants. Reservations are not necessary, but do dine early. Most restaurants close their doors at 9, and by 7:30 they may be out of some of the best dishes. A Chinese meal tastes better and is more fun eaten with chopsticks, but if you simply can't manage, ask for a knife and fork.

For something very different, try the Mongolian barbecue at the **Great Wall** (1 Linsen South Road) or **Genghis Khan** (176 Nanking East Road, Section 3). You fill a bowl with your own choice of raw vegetables, meats (beef, pork, chicken, lamb, venison), and sauces and spices, then hand it to a chef to cook in front of you on a huge grill.

One of the most popular types of cooking is that of Szechuan province, which tends to be quite spicy. Order chicken with peppers, shredded beef, and dry-cooked string beans, with pancakes to wrap them up in. Try the **China Restaurant** (26 Minsheng East Road) or the **Rong Shing** (45 Chilin Road). For fine Peking duck (with trimmings, a meal in itself), go to the **Peiping Chih Mei Lou** (162 Chunghua Road).

For Hunan cuisine (the honeyed ham is a must), visit the **Hua Hsin** (20 Pateh Road, Section 3, top floor) or **Charming Garden** (16 Nanking East Road, Section 1, 3rd floor). Other restaurants worth trying are the **Good Fortune** (261 Nanking East Road, Section 3) for Shanghainese style, **Fung Lum** (72 Lin Sen North Road) for Cantonese, and the **Ching Yeh** (1 Alley 105, Chungshan North Road, Section1), where you order from pictures on the menu, for typical Taiwanese fare. If you want to revert to a more familiar diet, there are excellent grill rooms in the **Grand**, **Taipei Hilton**, and **Taipei Regency** hotels. Or try the **Ploughman Pub** (9 Lane 25, Shuang Cheng Street), **Europa Haus** (21 Chang An East Road, Section 1), or the **President Steak House** (1–30 Shuang Cheng Street).

DRINKING TIPS

Leading foreign brands of liquor are available in Taiwan. The local beer, a government monopoly, is quite good. The Shaohsing rice wine goes well with a meal. Get the aged wine and ask for it to be warmed. Those who like their liquor fiery should appreciate the *Kaoliang*, made from sorghum, or the slightly more flavorful *Chu Yeh Ching*.

Some of the best drinking spots are the cocktail lounges and piano bars in the hotels, such as those in the **Hilton**, **President**, **Ambassador**, and **Taiwan Hotel** (28 Changchun Road). Most other bars in town (usually known as "clubs") tend to be for men only.

ENTERTAINMENT

You can find movies, concerts, and Chinese opera in Taipei. There are many movie theaters, showing both foreign films with the original soundtrack as well as Chinese movies. If possible, the opera should not be missed. **Peiping Opera** is the ancient form of Chinese theater, combining dialogue, ornate costume, and stylized movements in addition to music and singing. See it in Taipei at **Armed Forces Cultural Activities Center,** 69 Chung Hua Road. One astounding supper show is in the **Hoover Theater Restaurant,** 21–21 Fu Shun Street, where you can have a Cantonese meal while dancers swing from the ceiling. Other "theater restaurants" include the **Golden Dragon,** 50 Hua Yen Street, and the **First,** 41 Chung Hua Road, top floor. Nightclubs offering dancing and entertainment are found in six hotels—the **Ambassador, Central, Imperial, Majestic** (2 Min Chuan East Road), **President,** and **Taipei Hilton.**

SHOPPING

Stores are usually open every day from 9am (10:30 for some department stores) to 10pm. Good items are furniture, wood carving, Chinese carpets, jade and coral jewelry, pottery pieces, embroidery, semiprecious stones, lacquerware, and ceramics. The shops and stores designated by the "one price" insignia have fairly reasonable prices. You can bargain almost anywhere, and small shopkeepers will sometimes reduce their prices by as much as one-third. The major shopping areas in Taipei are **Chung Hua Market Buildings** (Haggle Alley) along Chung Hua Road, the **Shihlin** district, and the shops along **Chung Shan North Road.** Try the **Taiwan Handicraft Promotion Center,** 5 Chuang Shan South Road, for good handmade items at fair prices. One of the better department stores is the **Far Eastern,** with a main store at 32 Paoching Road and a branch at 68 Jen Ai Road, Section 4.

SPORTS

Spectator sports include basketball and Little League baseball. Swimming is good, either in the ocean or the pools at the first-class hotels. There is skin-diving off the shore rocks and along the coral reefs of southern Taiwan. Roller skating is popular in Taipei, as well as ice skating at the **Ice Palace** (Chung Shan North Road, Section 4, Taipei—tel: 8812287). Golf is becoming very popular, the best-known club being the **Taiwan Gold and Country Club,** 30 minutes from central Taipei. There is skiing on one of the mountains during the first two months of the year. Currently there is no hunting, as there is a large-scale movement to preserve wildlife, but there is good fishing in the island lakes and rivers.

WHAT TO SEE

Taipei is not pretty, but it has plenty of character. As a change from guided tours, get out your walking shoes and a good map and try the atmosphere in the streets. The people are friendly and helpful. You may find that some of the lesser-known, older sections like **Wan-hua,** with its snake stalls and food stands, are more to your liking than, say, the **Presidential Building.** Stroll around the area near the **Lungshan Temple** in Wan-hua after dark, when the colorful "night markets" open. One place you shouldn't miss is the **National Palace Museum,** which contains the world's largest and richest collection of Chinese art. The ancient porcelain and bronze pieces, carved jade and ivory, paintings, and calligraphy were once the property of the Imperial Court. Also of interest is the **Taiwan Provincial Museum** in Taipei with objects more directly related to Taiwan's history—collections of aboriginal pottery, wood carving, textiles, and weapons.

Taipei also has a number of temples, and one of the best of these is the brightly ornate **Lungshan,** more than 200 years old. The **Martyrs Shrine,** open daily 9–5, is also worth seeing. Taipei's **Zoo** is in Chung Shan North Road, Section 3, and also includes an amusement park for children.

Alternatively, visit the **Botanical Gardens,** within which you can find the **National Museum of History,** the **National Taiwan Arts Hall,** the **Central Library,** and the **New National Taiwan Science Hall.** Other major parks are **New Park** in the middle of the city, where local Taiwanese do their early morning fitness exercises, and **Yang Ming Park** atop suburban Grass Mountain.

An interesting day's excursion is a motor trip around Taiwan's northern coast, through the picturesque old town of **Tamsui,** past terraced fields and sandy beaches, and including stops at **Yehliu** and **Keelung.** Yehliu is a fishing port noted for the weird rock formations caused by the wind and the sea. Here you can see girls in coolie hats selling sea shells, and there is an abundance of seafood to eat or take away with you. Little or no English is spoken in Yehliu's restaurants, so get prices written down in advance. Keelung, a city nestled between hills, is Taiwan's major northern port, and there is a spectacular view of the harbor from a Buddhist shrine on one of the hilltops. Central Taiwan has a group of mountains called **Ali Shan.** From here you can see the "Sea of Clouds" sunset and sunrise over the 13,114-foot **Yushan** or **Jade Mountain,** formerly known as Mount Morrison. You ascend the mountain by a small, two-car, narrow-gauge forestry train, which takes 3 hours 40 minutes to pull you up through some of the most primitive and exciting scenery the mountain has to offer.

Taroko Gorge is one of the most famous sites of the island, a harrowing stretch of highway through 38 tunnels in mountains rich in marble. There is a bridge in the gorge called **The Bridge of Motherly Devotion,** which has marble railings and lions of marble guarding the entrance and exit.

Sun Moon Lake is another of the better-known sights of the island. In reality two lakes, one shaped like the sun and the other like a quarter moon, they are 2,500 feet above sea level and are surrounded on all sides by gentle green mountains. The **Shrine of Hsuan Chuang,** a monk who traveled to India in the 8th century to obtain Buddhist scriptures, stands on the shore.

Tainan is worth a visit. It is the oldest city on the island and still has much evidence of its long and varied past in the many old buildings still standing.

SOURCES OF FURTHER INFORMATION

Pan Am, represented by Taiwan Trading Corp, 35 Kuang Fu South Road, Taipei, and any Pan Am office around the world; **Tourism Bureau,** PO

Box 1490, Taipei; **Taiwan Visitors' Association,** 5th floor, 111 Min Chuan East Road, Taipei; **Republic of China Tourism Bureau,** 210 Post Street, San Francisco, CA 94108; 3660 Wilshire Boulevard (Suite 1060), Los Angeles, CA 90010; and 1 World Trade Center (Suite 86155), New York, NY 10048.

Thailand

WHAT'S SPECIAL

Say "Thailand" and a lot of good things come to mind. Say its ancient name, "The Kingdom of Siam," and a host of romantic and exotic images come rushing, for this country—the only one in Southeast Asia never to be colonized—is full of excitement and color. There are splendid temples, ancient cities, religious artifacts, classical dancing, elephants, deep jungle, the best rice in the world, and a capital laced with watery thoroughfares.

COUNTRY BRIEFING

Size: 198,250 square miles
Population: 48,000,000
Capital: Bangkok
Capital Population: 5,000,000

Climate: Hot and humid. The hottest months are March to May, the coolest November to February. The monsoon season lasts from June to October, but it does not rain continuously throughout the day. In Bangkok there is usually a heavy shower in the late afternoon. Best time to visit—November to April.

Weather in Bangkok: Lat N13°45'; Alt 7 ft

Temp (°F)	Jan	Feb	Mar	Apr	May	Jun	Jul	Aug	Sep	Oct	Nov	Dec
Av Low	68°	72°	75°	77°	77°	76°	76°	76°	76°	75°	72°	68°
Av High	89°	91°	93°	95°	93°	91°	90°	90°	89°	88°	87°	87°
Days no rain	30	27	28	27	22	20	18	18	15	17	25	30

Government: Thailand is a constitutional monarchy.

Language: Thai. Some Chinese languages also widely spoken. English spoken in areas catering to foreign visitors.

Religion: Buddhism—about 93% of the population.
Currency: Baht. 100 satangs = 1 baht.

	1 baht	5 baht	10 baht	20 baht	50 baht	100 baht	500 baht	1000 baht
US (dollars, cents)	.05	.24	.48	.95	2.38	4.76	23.81	47.62
UK (pounds, pence)	.02	.12	.23	.45	1.14	2.27	11.38	22.76

Public Holidays:

New Year's Day, 1 Jan
Magha Puja (Buddhist Festival), Feb*
Chakri Day, 6 Apr
Songkran (Thai New Year), 13 Apr
Coronation Day, 5 May
Visakha Puja (Buddhist Festival), May*

First Day of Buddhist Lent, July*
Queen's Birthday, 12 Aug
Chulalongkorn Day, 23 Oct
King's Birthday, 5 Dec
Constitution Day, 10 Dec
New Year's Eve, 31 Dec

*Exact date is based on lunar year.

HOW TO GET THERE

Flying time to Don Muang Airport, Bangkok, from Los Angeles is 22 hours; from Tokyo, 9 hours; from Hong Kong, 2½ hours; from London, 15½ hours. Time in Thailand: GMT+7.

REQUIREMENTS FOR ENTRY AND CUSTOMS REGULATIONS

Passport; visa necessary only for a stay longer than 15 days. Tourists must have an onward ticket. Vaccination certificates for cholera, and yellow fever are required only if coming from an infected area. No narcotics, pornography, or firearms (without special permission) may be brought into Thailand. Antiques or archaeologically valuable objects require a permit before they can be exported. Export of Buddha images is prohibited. Duty-free allowance: 200 cigarettes or cigars or 250 grams tobacco; 1 liter liquor; no duty-free allowance for gifts.

AIRPORT INFORMATION

Don Muang Airport is 18 miles outside Bangkok. A limousine service runs to hotels, carrying four passengers at 50 baht each. Hired individually, the price is 200 baht. Taxis are always available—the cost into town is approximately 150 baht. The airport has a hotel reservation counter. Beware of unofficial tours. Airport departure tax is 50 baht.

ACCOMMODATIONS

Modern hotels in Thailand have been built with an eye to the international businessman and traveler. Most of them have swimming pools, beauty parlors, shopping arcades, travel agents, and conference halls among their amenities. There are 60 hotels of all classes in Bangkok which cater to foreign visitors, and prices start from about US$10 per night. Far cheaper local-style hotels exist, where a room can be had for as little as 80 baht per night, but these do not always offer the facilities a foreign traveler might expect. The **Tourism Authority of Thailand**

(TAT) at Rajdamnern Avenue (tel: 2821143), with an office at Don Muang Airport, will advise but does not find accommodation. Hotels in Bangkok:

Rates are in US$ for a double/twin room with bath or shower

Amarin, 526 Ploenchit Road (from $51.38)

Ambassador, Soi 11 Sukhumvit Road (from $79.52)

Asia, 296 Phyathai Road (from $52.60)

Dusit Thani, Silom and Rama IV Roads (from $81.69)

Erawan, Rajprasong Intersection (from $73.40)

First, 2 Petburi Road (from $55.77)

Indra Regent, Rajaprarop Road (from $67.29)

Mandarin, 662 Rama IV Road (from $68.50)

Manhattan, Soi 15 Sukhumvit Road (from $55.08)

Manohra, 412 Suriwong Road (from $50.70)

Montien, 54 Suriwong Road (from $81.97)

Narai, 222 Silom Road (from $57.50)

Oriental, 48 Oriental Avenue (from $104.00)

Peninsula, 295/3 Suriwong Road (from $20.28)

President, 135/26 Gaysorn Road (from $74.63)

Rajah, 18 Soi 4 Sukhumvit Road (from $55.08)

Sheraton Bangkok, 80 Suriwong Road (from $79.82)

SIAM INTER · CONTINENTAL, Rama I Road (from $89.95)

Victory, 322 Silom Road (from $27.60)

Windsor, Soi 20 Sukhumvit Road (from $50.60)

Bangkok has no defined "center," as understood in Western cities, and the hotels listed above are located throughout the city. Taxis are plentiful, and tourist attractions are easily accessible.

USEFUL INFORMATION

Helpful Hints: Remove shoes before entering a home or temple. In the event of a misfortune in Bangkok, it is essential to immediately contact the Tourist Police (Tourist Assistance Center, Tourism Authority of Thailand Head Office, Rajdamnern Nok Avenue, Bangkok, Tel: 2810372, 2815051). Tourist Police officers speak English or other foreign languages and are familiar with the problems of visitors from abroad.

Banks: Open 8:30-3:30, Mon-Fri. Foreign currency can also be exchanged by authorized money changers who display the appropriate sign.

Mail: Stamps are bought at post offices and from some stationery shops. Mailboxes are red.

Telephone Tips: Telephones can be used in hotels, cafés, and restaurants. Public phone booths are coin operated. To use, insert a 1-baht coin, dial, push button, and speak. Cafés and restaurants sometimes charge 3 baht per call. Useful numbers in Bangkok:

Pan Am 2522121	**TAT** 2821143
Information 13	**Tourist Police** 2810372
	2815051

Newspapers: Foreign newspapers and magazines are available at the major hotels. Daily English-language newspapers published locally are

The Bangkok Post, The Nation (mornings), and *Bangkok World* (afternoons). A useful tourist publication is *Where,* a weekly newspaper available free from hotels and travel agents.

Tipping: Still optional, but customary in places frequented mainly by foreigners; some restaurants add a 10 percent service charge to the check. As a general rule, leave the loose change from the bill, but never leave only 1 baht—better to leave nothing. It is not necessary to tip taxi drivers. Luggage porters have a fixed charge of 2 baht per bag at the airport, 1 baht at the railway station. Hotel porters should be tipped 5 baht, and also hairdressers if you wish to tip.

Electricity: 220 volts 50 cycles AC. Some hotels have transformers for 110 volts.

Laundry: First-class hotels have good 24-hour laundry service. Dry-cleaners usually take 3-4 days; if urgent, some places offer 24-hour service.

Hairdressing: Many first-class hotels have hairdressing salons and barber shops. The average cost of a shampoo and set is from 50 baht; of a man's haircut, from 40 baht. Tipping optional, but 5 baht usual.

Photography: Black and white and color film are readily available in major cities; it takes 24 hours to have black and white film developed and 2 days for color. Kodachrome slides have to be sent overseas.

Rest Rooms: No public facilities, but ask in any hotel or restaurant for the *hong nam,* or "water room." The women's room is *Sukha Ying* and the men's *Sukha Chai.*

Health: Many doctors and dentists are British- or US-trained and speak excellent English. Many pharmaceuticals are imported, and you will probably find most of your favorite brands. Medical supplies are cheap but toiletries fairly expensive. Tap water is chemically treated; nevertheless, many people prefer to boil it for drinking purposes.

TRANSPORTATION

Traffic conditions in Bangkok are chaotic, and city driving is an unpleasant mixture of noise, exhaust fumes, and monumental traffic jams. Driving is on the left, but beware of motorcycles—which frequently decide otherwise. Buses are crowded, but so cheap that you can travel right across the city for a few baht. Taxis are everywhere and can be hailed in the street. Taxi drivers never use their meters, and it is essential to bargain beforehand. The minimum fare is 20 baht, and there are no extras, but—the price goes up if it is rush hour or raining heavily, or if the taxi is hired outside an expensive hotel or nightclub. The rickety three-wheeled taxis are slightly cheaper.

Whenever possible, forgo the chaos of city traffic in favor of water transportation. Water taxis are not the quickest form of getting around, as they are liable to double back to pick up another passenger hailing from the shore, but at 5 cents per mile this is one of the most pleasant ways of viewing the city. The State Railway of Thailand is the most efficient in Southeast Asia. Express and rapid trains have sleeping berths and air conditioning. At every station, vendors throng around the carriages selling local food and drinks. The long-distance bus service is very comfortable, air conditioned, and available for all major provincial cities daily; get tickets from travel agents. Thai Airways is the domestic airline, flying to Chiang Mai, Songkhla, and other cities.

FOOD AND RESTAURANTS

The invitation to a meal in Thailand is, literally translated, "come and eat rice." Rice is heaped onto your plate, and four or five dishes, plus several different sauce dishes, are placed in the center of the table. Food is "curried," but this can mean highly spiced as well as mouth-searingly hot. The first course is usually a clear soup, to which is added anything from shrimp balls to pineapple. Desserts are usually coconut concoctions, followed by tropical fruit. As some food is eaten with the fingers, damp cloths are provided. Interesting national dishes are *pla too* (fried, salted mackerel), *mee krob* (sweet crisp noodles with shrimp and banana flower stamens), and *tom yam* (spicy soup). In hotels and restaurants breakfast is from 7-10:30, lunch 11-2, and dinner 5-midnight. Street vendors are everywhere, cooking on-the-spot savories over charcoal grills and selling fruit and sweet treats. Noodle shops sell a wide variety of noodle dishes. For a Thai meal suitably mellowed for Western palates, try **The Piman** (46 Soi 49 Sukhumvit Road—tel: 3918107) and the **Maneeya Lotus Room** (518/4 Ploenchit Road—tel: 2510382); these restaurants have authentic Sukhothai period decor and Thai dancing every evening. **Chit Pochana** (62 Soi 20 Sukhumvit Road—tel: 3916401) offers the most extensive Thai food menu in town, with reasonable prices and a semi-outdoor setting. **Nick's Number One Hungarian Inn** (1 Sathorn Road—tel: 2862258) is the oldest European restaurant in Bangkok and serves lobster, oysters, venison, and beef stroganoff in an old rustic Thai castle. **The Two Vikings** (2 Soi 35 Sukhumvit Road—tel: 3911470) has French cuisine with good bouillabaisse and eel. Another good French restaurant is the **Normandie Grill** (Oriental Hotel—tel: 2349920). Also French is **Le Vendôme** (153/1 Soi Mahadlek Luang), near the Erawan Hotel, with gorgeous decor and specializing in frogs' legs and crêpes suzette. In addition to Thai food, and the wide variety of Chinese and European cuisines, Bangkok has Indian, Japanese, Korean, Muslim, and Vietnamese restaurants; the major hotels regularly feature "national weeks" with menus of various nations.

DRINKING TIPS

Locally made beers are Amarit, Singha, and Kloster. For *Mekhong*, the local rice whisky, go to local-style food shops and restaurants; it is cheap and not stocked in places catering to tourists. Virtually all famous brands of liquor are imported and available in hotels and bars, but beware of imitations; what is in the bottle is not always what is on the label. There is drinking to suit all tastes and pockets. From the refinement of the **Bamboo Bar** (Oriental Hotel) and the **Pool Bar** (Erawan Hotel) through the razzle-dazzle of the **Patpong Road** bars to the open-air noodle stalls, the visitor can watch a fascinating cross section of life while enjoying a drink.

ENTERTAINMENT

Bangkok has its fair share of movie theaters, showing English-language movies as well as Thai, Japanese, Chinese, and Indian films. Films are shown with their original soundtrack, but up-country they are dubbed on the spot by a man and woman acting all the parts. Occasionally, performances of Western opera, music, and ballet are staged in Bangkok. Thai classical dancing is a highly sophisticated art form: each dance tells a story—usually from a Sanskrit myth—and every graceful movement has its own significance. There are short programs of classical dancing at several of the Thai restaurants in Bangkok.

NIGHTLIFE

Bangkok has a full array of nightclubs. Some of the large hotels have nightclubs with floor shows and bands, such as the **Tiara** (Dusit Thani Hotel); but most hotel clubs draw young and energetic dancers. Among them are the **Casablanca** (Montien Hotel), and the **Cavern** (Sheraton Hotel). Thai nightclubs include **Lolita, Rofeno,** and **Sida** (all on Rajdamnern Avenue), which offer hostesses and dancing. The **Café de Paris** nightclub (Suriwong Road) offers floor shows, hostesses, and dancing.

SHOPPING

Major stores open at 9, close around 7pm; shops open at 8:30am, often closing at 10pm; small shops do as they please. Before going shopping, be sure to get a copy of the *Official Shopping Guide* issued by the Tourism Authority of Thailand and available free in most hotel lobbies. It contains much valuable advice and lists shops recommended by TAT. The best buys are Thai silk and cotton, celadon ceramics (a modern revival of an ancient technique, distinguished by a jade green color), niello ware (silver incised with lacquer), lacquerwork, wood carvings, and bronze work. Ideal gifts for less than US$10 are temple rubbings on rice paper and Thai dolls representing classical dancers and tribespeople in traditional costume. **Narai Phan** (75/2 Larn Luang Road) is the government-run handicraft center offering a large collection of crafts at reasonable prices. **Jim Thompson's Thai Silk Co** (9 Suriwong Road) has a very large selection of silk. For antique experts, Bangkok may prove interesting, but inexperienced buyers should beware. **Monogram Shop** (Erawan Hotel Arcade) and **Peng Seng** (corner Suriwong Road and Rama IV Road) are among the leading antique dealers. For antique bargain hunting, the **Thieves Market** in the Nakhon Kasem section of town is popular. Gems and jewelry are another fascinating field for bargain hunting, but again, there are risks. **Associated Lapidaries Ltd** (5th floor, 1 Patpong Road) issues a guarantee certificate with every purchase of jewelry or gemstones. **Pat Jewelry** is in the Dusit Thani Hotel and **Pat Gem** in the Siam Inter • Continental. **Yaowarat Road** in Chinatown has many gold shops, but care is necessary because the gold is not always of the purity claimed. The standard of Thai silverware, on the other hand, is government controlled. Some major stores have fixed prices, but almost every smaller shop will bargain—start at 50 percent of the marked price and try not to go much higher.

SPORTS

Thai spectator sports are in a class of their own. There is serious Thai boxing at **Rajdamnern Stadium** and **Lumpini Stadium.** Contestants use hands, feet, elbows, and knees, and native music accompanies each bout. Kite flying (February until April at the **Pramane Ground**) is practiced with elaborate "male" and "female" kites. *Takraw* is one of the oldest of Thai games. A hollow wicker ball is kept in motion by players using every part of their body except their hands. In country districts cockfighting and stick-insect fighting are popular. Individual sports facilities include golf, tennis, swimming (pools in big hotels), and yachting (at **Hua Hin** and **Pattaya**). In Bangkok, full horse-racing programs are offered weekends at **The Royal Bangkok Sports Club** and at the **Royal Turf Club of Thailand.**

WHAT TO SEE

Bangkok: There are some 300 temples in Bangkok, and the most impressive are the **Temple of the Emerald Buddha** (Wat Phra Keo) in the grounds of the Grand Palace (the Buddha is of translucent green jasper, and its vestments are changed three times each year by the king at a solemn ceremony); the **Temple of the Reclining Buddha** (Wat Po), always popular with stone-rubbers; the **Temple of the Golden Buddha** (Wat Traimit), housing a 10-foot-high statue of solid gold; and the **Temple of the Dawn** (Wat Arun), whose five towers rest on a series of terraces supported by statues of demons and angels. **The Marble Temple** (Wat Benjamabopit), housing a famous collection of Buddhas, is a beautiful example of Thai architecture.

Religious, regal, cultural, and ethnographic exhibits representative of all the great periods of Thai history are on display at the **National Museum** (9-12 and 1-4, closed Monday, Friday, and holidays). More intimate museums are the **Jim Thompson House** (9:30-3:30, closed weekends), and the **Suan Pakkard Palace** (9-12, closed Sunday), with their privately collected art objects and antiques. Also visit the **Sunday Market,** all day Saturday and Sunday at the Pramane Ground, where hundreds of stalls sell everything from antiques to exotic foods and wild animals. The **Ancient City,** 21 miles from Bangkok in Samut Prakarn, is very popular, as is the **Rose Garden,** in Nakon Pathom, 35 miles from Bangkok. With its authentic and unspoiled floating market, **Damnern Saduak,** 65 miles west of Bangkok, offers a view of waterborne life at its best (the original floating market in Bangkok is now less than satisfactory). Wooden houses rise out of the water on stilts, and the canals are filled with a multitude of small boats selling foodstuffs and other colorful wares.

Surin: Book in advance with TAT to attend the annual elephant roundup in November. See exciting demonstrations of elephants fighting and racing, of wild elephants being captured, and of folk dances of the region.

Chiangmai: One-and-a-half hours by air from Bangkok, Chiangmai is the second-largest city in the country and the northern capital. Built in the hill country, it presents quite a contrast to Bangkok. **Wat Phra Sing** is the largest temple in the city, and the sanctuary is a beautiful example of Thai style (built 1345). **Wat Chedi Luang** has another lovely sanctuary. The gardens of **Pu Ping Palace,** summer residence of the Royal Family, are open to the public on weekends. Visits can be arranged to the hill tribes and to see elephants at work in the jungles of the north. There are plenty of good accommodations, and the major Chiangmai hotels popular with international travelers have reservation offices in Bangkok.

Pattaya Beach: A tropical seaside resort, ideal for skin-diving, water-skiing, and sailing. Numerous air-conditioned buses make the trip daily from Bangkok, and there are a dozen resort hotels to choose from.

Ayutthaya: The ruins of the palaces and temples of this former capital of Thailand (founded 1350) cover 50 square miles. In the **Chao Sam Phraya National Museum** are bronze images of Buddha dating back 500-1,000 years.

Lopburi: This ancient city, once the capital of Siam and founded in the 5th century, is about 3 hours north of Bangkok by train. The **Phra Narai Rachaniwet Palace** is now the local museum housing ancient art objects and artifacts. The **Sacred Three-Spired Pagoda** (Prang, Sam Yod), a 3rd-century Buddhist sanctuary, is now the symbol of the province.

Kanchanaburi: In the rugged hill country some 75 miles from Bangkok are Neolithic burial sites and a sadder, more modern memorial—the cemeteries of the British, Dutch, Indian, Australian, and New Zealand soldiers who lost their lives building the notorious Death Railway in World War II. Related to this is the nearby bridge around which the plot of the fictional war movie, *The Bridge on the River Kwai,* was woven.

Phuket: An island on the Andaman Coast, Phuket is Thailand's most recently developed oceanside resort. Long a leading center of tin mining and rubber plantations, Phuket offers delightful unspoiled beaches and delicious seafood. It is easily reached by Thai Airways flights from Bangkok or Penang (Malaysia). There are four resort hotels.

SOURCES OF FURTHER INFORMATION

Pan Am, Siam Center, 965 Rama I Road, Bangkok, and any Pan Am office around the world; **Tourism Authority of Thailand,** Rajdamnern Nok Avenue, Bangkok; **TAT** New York office, 5 World Trade Center, Suite 2449, New York, NY 10048; **TAT** Los Angeles office, 510 West 6th Street, Suite 1212, Los Angeles CA 90014; **TAT** London office, 9 Stafford Street, London W1X 3FE.

Tonga

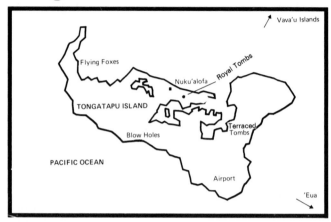

WHAT'S SPECIAL

Tonga is the last remaining Polynesian kingdom, a small, independent world of islands 1,100 miles northeast of Auckland that has somehow managed to retain its dignity while enjoying its contact with the modern world. It is a warm, coral-encircled dreamland where nobody goes hungry, because breadfruit, mangoes, sugarcane, and sweet potatoes grow at the edge of the villages, and fish abound in the sea. The natural courtesy and friendliness of the people make it difficult for anyone to feel a stranger. When Captain Cook landed here in 1773, he christened these islands the Friendly Isles, a name that has stuck, and of which Tongans are extremely proud. Today Tonga is a unique mixture of extraordinary natural beauty and cheerful modernity.

COUNTRY BRIEFING

Tonga is 269 square miles with a **population** of 92,000. Nuku'alofa is the **capital; population** 30,000. **Climate** is temperate—rainy season December to March. Average temperature is 75°F; May to November cooler. Tonga is an independent kingdom and a member of the British Commonwealth. Tongan is the official **language,** but English is widely spoken. **Currency** is the pa'anga (T\$), divided into 100 seniti. .88 seniti = US\$1. **Public holidays** are 1 January; Good Friday; Easter Monday; Anzac Day, 25 April; 4 May; 4 June; 4 July; 4 November; 4 December; 25 and 26 December.

HOW TO GET THERE

Flying time to Fau'amotu Airport, Tongatapu from New York is 18¾ hours; from Los Angeles, 13¾ hours; from Honolulu, 10½ hours; from Auckland, 2 hours. Time in Tonga: GMT+13.

REQUIREMENTS FOR ENTRY AND CUSTOMS REGULATIONS

Valid passport, round-trip ticket, proof of adequate funds for visit. A smallpox vaccination certificate is required if you have been in an infected area within 14 days previous to arrival; proof of yellow-fever inoculation, within 6 days. No currency restrictions.

AIRPORT INFORMATION

Airport for Nuku'alofa, the capital, is Fau'amotu, 13 miles from the city and linked to the city center by regular bus service. Fare, about T$1. A taxi to Nuku'alofa is about T$8. Duty-free shop.

ACCOMMODATIONS

In addition to hotels, there are guest houses and accommodations in private homes. Central accommodations service is provided by **Tonga Visitors' Bureau** (tel: 21733). Hotels in Tonga:

Rates are in US$ for a double/twin room with bath or shower

Beach House, Nuku'alofa (from $23 AP, sharing bathrooms—no private facilities available)

Captain Cook Vacation Apartments, Nuku'alofa (from $24)

Friendly Islander, Nuku'alofa (from $28)

Good Samaritan Inn, 12 miles from Nuku'alofa (from $17)

International Dateline Hotel, Nuku'alofa (from $34)

Moana Hotel, Nuku'alofa (from $10.50)

Pangaimotu Island, 2 km by boat from Nuku'alofa (from $37 AP)

Port of Refuge Hotel, Vava'u (from $27)

Stowaway Village, Vava'u (from $11)

Way-Inn Motel, Nuku'alofa (from $17)

USEFUL INFORMATION

Currency can be changed at the Bank of Tonga, in hotels, and in some larger stores. **Telephone** service is very limited—try the post office. Tipping is not encouraged. **Electricity** is 220 volts AC. Photographic **film** available, but no color processing. Doctors and pharmaceuticals are available, and you can drink the water in Nuku'alofa and hotels.

TRANSPORTATION

There is a regular bus service from the main town on each island to the outlying parts. Conventional taxis and colorful three-wheeled runabouts called *ve'etolu* are plentiful and cheap. Rental cars cost from T$160 per week including insurance and mileage. Local licenses are issued for T$2. Strict speed limit of 30 mph on all roads and 20 mph in Nuku'alofa and major villages. Ferry services connect all the Tongan island groups.

The Tonga Visitors' Bureau will give you information on these. Scheduled light aircraft services operate to the islands of Vava'u, Ha'apai, and 'Eua.

FOOD AND RESTAURANTS

The distinctive Tonga way of cooking is to use an underground oven, or *'umu*. One favorite and succulent dish is *lu-pulu*—beef marinated in coconut cream and baked in taro leaves. Another is coconut cream and sugar-caramel sauce poured over taro or dumplings. Staples of the Tongan diet are roast suckling pig, crayfish, crab, lobsters, and Tongan desserts are watermelon or other fresh fruit. Outdoor eating is common, but there are a few restaurants in Nuku'alofa, including **Fakalato,** the **Tong-Hua Chinese Restaurant, Basilica Restaurant,** under spectacular new cathedral of **St. Anthony of Padua, Latai Room,** and the **International Dateline Hotel** dining room, especially good on "Island Night." Not to be missed is the **Good Samaritan Inn,** well worth the 12-mile drive for French cooking, fresh seafood, and an informal atmosphere overlooking the beach.

DRINKING TIPS

Try *kava,* a Polynesian brew made from the root of the pepper plant, and *otai,* a wonderful fresh-fruit punch. Imported wines, liquor, and beers are on sale at reasonable prices. Hotel bars serve drinks from 10am-11pm. Popular drinking spots in Nuku'alofa are the **Yacht Club** (Vuna Road), the **Tonga Club** (Tupoulahi Road), the **International Dateline Hotel, Moana Hotel,** and **Joe's Hotel;** on Vava'u, the **Port of Refuge Hotel** and the **Vava'u Club.**

ENTERTAINMENT

The **International Dateline Hotel** and the **Port of Refuge Hotel** have cabarets featuring Tongan and Polynesian dancing as well as Western dancing. Nuku'alofa has four movie theaters. The most exciting Tongan entertainment of all is a feast, where 15 people may sit down to four suckling pigs, 15 crayfish, 20 chickens, and any amount of vegetables. Attend an evening feast at **Oholei Beach,** near Nuku'alofa, for a spectacular setting and entertainment.

SHOPPING

Look for woven mats, shell and bamboo curtains, stuffed animal toys, shell jewelry, slippers, grass skirts, woven hats, tapa cloth, wooden carvings, and many other native goods. Best handicrafts are at the **Langa Fonua Centre** in central Nuku'alofa, and at the open air market near the International Dateline Hotel. Some luxury Western goods can be purchased duty-free at airport and International Dateline Hotel shops.

SPORTS

There is good sailing and protected swimming. Modern, well-equipped yachts can be chartered at the Port of Refuge Hotel on **Vava'u Island,** and day cruises for fishing and skin-diving are available from **Pangaimotu**

Island (off Nuku'alofa). The best swimming beaches are **Ha'atafu, Mono-tapu, Hufangalupe, Pangaimotu Island,** and **Oholei.** The **Tonga Golf Club** (9 holes) welcomes visitors. Rugby is the main spectator sport.

WHAT TO SEE

In **Nuku'alofa** see the white-frame **Royal Palace,** spired and turreted with Victorian flourish, the new cathedral of **St Anthony of Padua,** opened in 1980 and constructed with the finest Tongan materials; also the **Royal Chapel** and the **Royal Tombs.** Perhaps Tonga's greatest beauties are the natural ones. Along a stretch of the southern coast of Tongatapu known as the **Blow Holes,** great geysers of water spout with an eerie whistling sound—Tongans call it *Mapu'a Vaea,* the Chief's Whistle. In the **Grove of the Bats** at Kolovai, the strange flying "foxes"—fruit-eating bats with fox-like heads—festoon the trees. Eastward from Nuku'alofa are Captain Cook's landing place, **Mu'a** village, and the wonderful terraced tombs of *Lapaha Langis*—huge terraced monuments of coral to the ancient king, dating from about 1200 AD. Then on to the **Ha'amonga Trilithon,** a massive arch made from three slabs of coral, probably used—like Great Britain's Stonehenge—as a seasonal clock. On **'Eua,** the great **Matalanga's Maui** and the **Lakafa'anga** cliffs rise sheer from a clear blue sea, and inland the great rain forests shelter the rare green-turquoise parrot and the white owl. The harbor of **Port of Refuge,** on the Vava'u islands, must be one of the most beautiful in the world.

SOURCES OF FURTHER INFORMATION

Any **Pan Am** office around the world; **Tonga Visitors' Bureau,** Box 37, Nuku'alofa, Tonga; **Pacific Area Travel Association,** 228 Grant Ave, San Francisco, CA 94108.

Vanuata

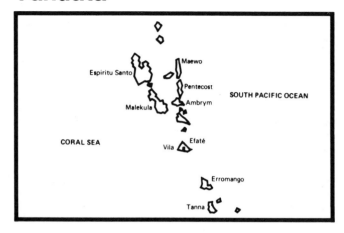

WHAT'S SPECIAL

Here is the lush, tropical South Pacific of James Michener's best seller: a chain of green islands 1,500 miles from Sydney and 600 miles from Fiji. With a wealth of sandy beaches and mountains covered in luxurious foliage, this is truly a virgin land brightened by a touch of European civilization. There are twelve main islands, and two towns—Vila and Santo (also known as Luganville)—rise on Efaté and Espíritu Santo respectively. The archipelago was first sighted in 1609 by the Portuguese Fernández de Queiros, who called it *Tierra Australia del Espiritu Santo* in the belief that he had discovered an immense Southern continent. It was Captain Cook in the 18th century who changed the name to New Hebrides in honor of that other more rugged island group off the coast of Scotland. In 1980 the country became the independent Republic of Vanuata. The primitive way of life and the beauty of the native crafts, added to the natural splendors of the 80-odd islands, make this one of the more exotic corners of the vast blue Pacific.

COUNTRY BRIEFING

Area, 5,700 square miles, with a **population** of 112,000. Of these, 16,000 live in Vila, the **capital.** The **climate** varies from tropical in the north to subtropical in the south; warm, humid season (with rainy spells) from November to April. Vanuata was a unique Anglo-French condominium (New Hebrides) for more than 70 years. The two colonial powers granted self-government in 1978, and independence in July 1980. **Languages** are French and English, various Melanesian dialects, and pidgin English;

although the new government is English-speaking. Vanuata is the only tax-haven country in the South Pacific. A new currency was introduced this year, the Vatu. Australian dollars are still acceptable as legal tender, but will gradually go out of use. US$1=5.54 New Hebrides francs. **Public holidays:** 1 Jan; Good Friday; Easter Monday; 1 May; 20 May; 15 Aug; 5 Oct; 30 Nov; Christmas and Boxing Day.

HOW TO GET THERE

Flying time to Bauer Field, Port Vile from Los Angeles is 13½ hours; from Honolulu 8 hours; from Sydney 4 hours; from Tokyo 9½ hours. Time in Vanuata: GMT+11.

REQUIREMENTS FOR ENTRY AND CUSTOMS REGULATIONS

Passport, visa (obtained from French or British Consulate; no visa required for French or British nationals or travel groups of not less than 15 persons who have obtained prior approval from the Chief Immigration Officer of Port Vila), and round-trip ticket required for a stay of up to 90 days. Smallpox vaccination certificate required only if arriving from an infected area. A "reasonable amount" of tobacco and liquor may be brought in; no firearms are allowed. No currency restrictions. The new government is expected to make changes in immigration laws and visa requirements. It is advisable to check requirements before traveling.

AIRPORT INFORMATION

Bauer Field Airport, 3 miles from Vila, has a hotel reservations counter and bus service to the downtown hotels (fare 300V). Taxis to Vila available up to 10pm. There is a departure tax of 400V.

ACCOMMODATIONS

Both the **Inter · Continental Island Inn** and **Hotel le Lagon** offer a variety of water sports and recreation facilities. Le Lagon also has a nine-hole golf course. Hotels in Vanuata:

Rates are in US$ for a double/twin room with bath or shower
  INTER · CONTINENTAL ISLAND INN, Vila (from US$43)
  Hotel Le Lagon, Vila (from US$57)
  Hideaway Island Resort, Mele Island, Vila (from US$22 with breakfast)
  Hotel Rossi, Vila (from US$20)
  Hotel Olympic, Vila (from US$26)
  Santo, Santo (from US$40)
  Relais Bougainville, Santo (from US$33)
  Tanna Bungalows, Tanna Island (from US$16)

USEFUL INFORMATION

There are eight **banks, mail** service, and a few public **phones. Tourist Information** is 2813. **Tipping** is considered offensive. **Electricity** is 220-240 volts AC. Hotels have **laundry** and dry-cleaning services and **hairdressing** salons. There is **photographic** equipment, and color processing. You can find **babysitters,** but not public **rest rooms. Health:** many doctors and dentists speak English; pharmaceuticals are available. Bottled water is recommended. Wash fruit and vegetables thoroughly. There is malaria on some of the outer islands. Take a supply of antimalaria pills to remain immune.

TRANSPORTATION

There are few buses, but taxis are readily available; fixed fares controlled by law, no need to bargain. Rental cars cost about 2500V a day, plus mileage and insurance. Roads are narrow, and outside of Vila there is very little traffic. Air Melanesiae flies from Vila to the principal islands, and various motor cruises are available for tours to the islands.

FOOD AND RESTAURANTS

Chinese, Vietnamese and French cuisines alternate with typical South Pacific dishes such as marinated fish, coconut crab, freshwater prawns, and lobsters. A Vanuata specialty is flying fox simmered in red wine. In Vila the main restaurants are at the **Hotel le Lagon, Hotel Rossi,** and the **Inter · Continental Island Inn** (featuring good French cuisine). Among restaurants with an enviable reputation, look for **L'Houstalet,** and **Pandanus** (French and South Pacific dishes); **La Hotte** and **Ma Barker's** (steaks); **Kwang Tung** (Chinese), **Ichise** (Japanese), **Le Buluana** (Melanesian). For pizza and snacks, try **La Pizza** or the **Solaise Motel.** The **Hideaway** serves smorgasbord and barbecues. In Santo there are restaurants in the **Hotel Santo,** and in the **Relais Bougainville.** The average price of a meal in an expensive restaurant will be between US$20-25, and in an inexpensive one about US$10-12.

DRINKING TIPS

The native drink, *kava,* a brew made from the root of the pepper plant, can be had in Melanesian villages; otherwise there are imported wines, liquor, and beer. The sale of liquor (by the bottle) is forbidden from 11am Saturday to Monday morning. Bars and lounges close at 11pm or midnight. Sidewalk cafés make delightful drinking places.

ENTERTAINMENT

French and English films are shown twice weekly. The nightclubs in Vila are **Le Privé, Solwata Club,** and **Le Tennis Disco.**

SHOPPING

Cameras, radios, French perfume, watches, and jewelry are all good buys at tax-free prices. Look for shell baskets, primitive masks, wood carvings, and hand-painted Tahitian material. The finest art can be found at the gallery/home of artist **Michoutouchkine,** near Hotel le Lagon. In stores it is not customary to bargain, but one does in markets, Chinese shops, and at shell sales on the beaches. Major stores include **Hebrida, Fung Kuei** (for appliances), and **Lo Lam,** all in Vila; **Burns Philp** in Vila and Santo. Shops open weekdays 7:30-11:30 and 2-5 or 7; Saturdays, mornings only.

SPORTS

There is year-round golf and tennis at **Vila** and **Santo,** and there is a squash court at the **BESA** (ex-servicemen's Club). Swimming and skin-diving in all the islands. Game-fishing from the **Hotel Rossi** in Vila.

WHAT TO SEE

Vila is a pleasant town on a peninsula between the harbor and a lagoon. Climb the hills behind the town for panoramic views. Visit the **Cultural Center's Museum** to see its displays of native carvings and ceremonial dress. Vila also has a small, talented, and highly creative artists' colony. Take in the Friday waterside market. Just outside the capital, **Mélé, Pango,** and **Erakor** have magnificent beaches; **North Efaté** has idyllic shores with tranquil pools sheltered by reefs. There are Melanesian leaf-villages all over the islands and old colonial-style buildings as well. Fly to **Tanna** (one hour by plane) and climb to the top of **Yasur,** its active volcano. At **Pentecost Island,** once a year around yam planting time in May, you may be lucky enough to see the land-divers hurling themselves off wooden towers with vines attached to their ankles. **Espiritu Santo Island** is very picturesque but quiet. Air Melanesiae operates daily services from Vila (flight time about one hour).

SOURCES OF FURTHER INFORMATION

Any **Pan Am** office around the world; **Tourist Information Bureau,** Box 209, Vila, Vanuata.

NORTH AMERICA

NEWFOUNDLAND

QUEBEC

ONTARIO

NEW
BRUNSWICK

PRINCE EDWARD I.

NOVA SCOTIA

TA

Montreal

ISCONSIN

Ottawa

Toronto

MICHIGAN

NEW YORK

MAINE
NEW HAMPSHIRE
VERMONT
MASSACHUSETTS
RHODE ISLAND
CONNECTICUT
NEW JERSEY

ILLINOIS

OHIO

INDIANA

PENNSYLVANIA
DELAWARE
WASHINGTON DC
VIRGINIA
WEST VIRGINIA
MARYLAND

JRI

KENTUCKY

TENNESSEE

NORTH
CAROLINA

SAS

ALABAMA

SOUTH
CAROLINA

ATLANTIC OCEAN

GEORGIA

MISSISSIPPI

FLORIDA

SIANA

F OF MEXICO

Canada

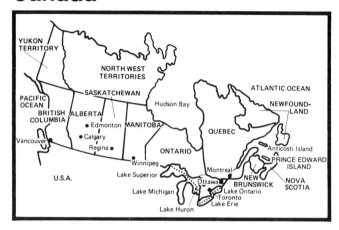

WHAT'S SPECIAL

Canada occupies the northern part of the North American continent, extending from the 49th Parallel to deep within the Arctic Circle. It is the second-largest country in the world, and its vast area embraces a variety of landscapes and life-styles. It is a country of rapidly developing urban complexes, but it also supports isolated fishing and trapping communities as well as seal-hunting Eskimos and Indians. It has two official languages and several different cultures. In Quebec City over 90% of the population is French-speaking, while in parts of British Columbia British traditions are still upheld, and Nova Scotians proudly wear Scottish Highland tartans. Canada is an exciting country to explore, because so much of it still remains virgin territory. Compared with its size Canada's population is tiny, and only 5% of the land is cultivated. Once away from the towns, modern man comes face to face with wild, untamed nature.

COUNTRY BRIEFING

Size: 3,852,000 square miles   **Population:** 23,809,800
Capital: Ottawa   **Capital Population:** 738,600

    Climate: Great extremes of temperature in the central and eastern areas mean brief, hot summers and snowbound winters. In the north it can be extremely cold, while the south Pacific coast of British Columbia is invariably mild. Best time to visit is May-October, or November-March for winter sports.

Government: An independent, federally governed nation within the framework of the British Commonwealth.

Language: English and French are both official languages.

Religion: Roman Catholic and Protestant are the largest religious groups.

Currency: The Canadian dollar. Can$1.20 = US$1. US currency is usually accepted in Canada, but you will want to convert to Canadian dollars if you are planning more than a brief visit. It is best to change at a bank to be sure of receiving the prevailing rate of exchange.

Public Holidays:

New Year's Day, 1 Jan	Labor Day, 1st Mon in Sep
Good Friday	Thanksgiving, 2nd Mon in
Easter Monday	Oct
Victoria Day, 24 May	Remembrance Day, 11 Nov
Dominion Day, 1 July	Christmas Day, 25 Dec
	Boxing Day, 26 Dec

There are also many local and provincial holidays.

HOW TO GET THERE
Flying time to Montreal from New York is 1¼ hours; from London, 8½ hours; flying time to Toronto from New York is 1¼ hours; from Los Angeles 4½ hours; flying time to Vancouver from New York is 6¼ hours; from Los Angeles, 2½ hours. Time in Ottawa, Toronto, and Montreal: GMT−5. Canada has seven time zones. Daylight Saving Time observed.

REQUIREMENTS FOR ENTRY AND CUSTOMS REGULATIONS
Passports, except for US citizens, who need proof of citizenship such as a birth or baptism certificate (a driver's license is not sufficient). Plants, except when accompanied by a US Department of Agriculture phytosanitary certificate, and meat products may not be imported. Dogs must have a rabies certificate signed by a veterinarian and showing vaccination within the previous three years. US and international driver's licenses are valid. Sporting guns need no entry permit but hunters should write in advance to the appropriate provincial or territorial capital for a nonresident license. Duty-free allowance: 200 cigarettes and 50 cigars and 2 pounds tobacco; 40 ounces of liquor or wine or 24 pints of beer or ale; gifts, except liquor and tobacco, worth up to $15 per recipient.

AIRPORT INFORMATION
Airport taxes are 8% of the ticket cost up to a maximum of $15 when going to the US; international flight passengers pay Can$10 per ticket. Major international airports have duty-free shops and hotel reservation counters. Porters receive 50 cents per bag, and taxis are available at most times. Airport buses meet flights, and there are regular bus services during peak hours. The fare is US$4.50 from Toronto International Air-

port into Toronto, or US$1.75-2.25 to the Islington, Yorkdale, or York Mills subway stations. Fare from Montreal International Airport (Dorval) into Montreal is $4; from Montreal's new Mirabel International Airport into the city, $7. Connecting time from Dorval to Mirabel is 2 hours 15 minutes for domestic connections and 2 hours 30 minutes for transborder flights. Mirabel handles all overseas flights.

ACCOMMODATIONS

Tourist and Convention Bureaus and Provincial Travel Bureaus are very helpful. If all else fails in Toronto, try the **Toronto Tourist and Convention Information Center** (Eaton Centre—tel: 979 3133). Some hotels give off-season reductions, mainly in mountain and seaside resorts. Alternative accommodations include Tourist Homes (where bed and breakfast is about $12 single and $16 double), pensions, guest ranches and farms, drive-in resorts, fly-in fishing and hunting camps, youth hostels, and trailer parks. Canada is one of the best countries in the world for camping, and the facilities are excellent. There are thousands of beautifully situated campgrounds, and a very high standard of individual privacy is maintained. For recommended hotels, see individual city listings.

USEFUL INFORMATION

Canadians are naturally friendly and hospitable. They are proud of their lovely scenery and delight in showing it off to visitors. You will always be welcome.

Banks: Open in major cities 10-3 Mon-Thurs, 10-6 Fri; closed Sat and Sun though branches may be open in some major shopping centers on Sat from 10-3. In remote areas banking facilities are often unavailable.

Mail: Stamps from post offices and from stamp machines. Mailboxes are free-standing, painted red.

Telephone Tips: Restaurant, café, and public phones are coin operated. To use, insert 10¢ or 20¢, depending on city, and dial. Useful numbers in Canada:

Pan Am (Toronto) 368 2941	**Operator** 0
(Montreal) 861 0521	**Directories** 411
(Vancouver) 684 2121	

Newspapers: In Quebec province, Montreal's *The Gazette* is the main English-language publication. *What's On in Ottawa, Montreal,* and *Quebec* are useful entertainment guides. A good business daily is Toronto's *The Globe and Mail,* available in most major cities across the country on a same-day basis, supplementing the dailies in individual cities.

Tipping: Service charge is not normally included in restaurant or hotel bills, and tipping is therefore essential. In restaurants, 12-15%; porters, 70 cents per bag; taxi drivers, 15-20%, 70 cents minimum; hairdressers, 15-20%; hotel porters, 70 cents per bag; chambermaids, $3-$4 per week; cloakroom attendent, 50 cents.

Electricity: 110 volts 60 cycles AC.

Laundry: Dry-cleaning and laundry services are good, fast, and inexpensive. Hotels and most laundries have 24-hour and express service (dry-cleaning a suit, from $5; laundering a shirt, from $1). Laundromats in all cities.

Hairdressing: First-class hotels have salons (shampoo and set from $10; man's haircut from $8).

Photography: The range of photographic equipment and services is unlimited. Black and white film can be processed in 24 hours, color in 2-3 days. Prepaid processing facilities are available.

Clubs: Rotary, Lions, Kiwanis, Optimist, Gyro, Richelieu.

Babysitting: Some hotels have services. For agencies consult the Yellow Pages phone directory.

Health: Excellent facilities available. Pharmaceuticals tend to be expensive.

TRANSPORTATION

Pedestrians should note that in the western provinces and Ontario, police are very strict with jaywalkers and those who cross against the lights. Traffic drives on the right everywhere, but road regulations vary slightly with each province. A potential trouble spot is that right turns on a red light are prohibited in Quebec unless there is a specific sign to the contrary. Quebec is the only province with this prohibition and police enforce the law strictly. Urban bus services are efficient and useful. Long-distance buses are air-conditioned and have rest rooms. Hitchhiking is not encouraged. Montreal and Toronto have subways and suburban train services. There are plenty of metered cabs in city centers which can be called or hailed. Car rental begins at about $23 per day. Some plans allow 100 km free per day and 18¢ to 20¢ per each additional km. Chauffeur-driven cars are available at a variety of prices. Highways are fast and good. The Trans-Canada Highway, the longest paved highway in the world, runs for nearly 5,000 miles from St. John's, Newfoundland, to Victoria, British Columbia. The Highway has "day parks" every 50 miles for picnic and rest stops and frequent "overnight parks" for campers. The Alaska Highway runs from Dawson Creek, British Columbia, to Fairbanks, and an all-weather highway goes from Grimshaw, Alberta, to Yellowknife on the north shore of the remote Great Slave Lake. Canadian National Railways (CNR) and Canadian Pacific Railways (CPR) passenger services, amalgamated and found in the phone book under Via Rail, are good; there is no finer way of appreciating the magnitude and variety of this unique country than by taking a cross-country rail trip from Montreal or Toronto to Vancouver (three nights), or flying to Edmonton or Calgary and taking the train through the Rockies. A Canrail pass gives unlimited rail travel for 22 days (Can.$345) or 30 days (Can.$395). It can be bought only in Canada at any Via Rail ticket office. Canadian air carriers serve all major cities and fly to remote areas.

FOOD AND RESTAURANTS

Fish is excellent everywhere, from the cod and lobster of the Atlantic to the salmon and shellfish of the Pacific seaboard and the unique Arctic char. The many inland lakes yield ample supplies of freshwater fish (good trout), and smoked Winnipeg goldeye is a local specialty of Manitoba province. Canadian ham, beef, and game are first-rate. National dishes include apple pie, buckwheat cakes, blueberry desserts, pumpkin pie, and maple sugar pie. Fish and brews (fish stew) is a specialty of the Maritimes, and cod tongues are a local delicacy found in Newfoundland, where one also finds seal steak and bakeapple (a berry) pie. Quebeçois dishes include pea soup, *tourtière* (meat pie), *cipaille* (game pie). International cooking is found in restaurants in the big cities, and Italian and Chinese cuisine is excellent, particularly on the west coast.

DRINKING TIPS

Liquor is served in beer parlors, beverage rooms, cocktail rooms (with or without meals), licensed restaurants and dining rooms (with meals), and at some sidewalk cafés. English-style pubs are popular, particularly in British Columbia, Toronto, and Montreal. Liquor, sold in province-run stores, can be bought in most places from 10-6 Mon-Sat. Minimum drinking age varies from 18 to 21. Bars are usually open 10am-midnight or 11am-2am. Canadian rye whisky is a favorite, and Canadian beers are stronger than most. Newfoundland *Screech* is a potent local rum.

SHOPPING

Hours 9:30-6 Mon-Wed and Sat, 9:30-9 Thurs and Fri. Best buys are coldweather clothes such as imported British woolens, leather (especially deerskin), and furs. Do not, however, buy the fur of animals on the endangered species list—anyone caught wearing these furs is subject to a fine as well as seizure of the garment. Other good buys are the many types of folk art, including beautiful Eskimo soapstone carvings (from $60, when available), west coast Haida Indian totem poles, masks and moccasins, wood carvings from St-Jean-Port-Joli (Quebec), and Nova Scotian weaving and pottery. British Columbian jade is worth hunting around for. **Eaton's, Simpsons-Sears,** and **The Bay Company** are old established department-store chains operating throughout the country. Major stores pack and ship purchases or deliver direct to airports and ports, with savings on tax when applicable.

SPORTS

Popular spectator sports are football, baseball, basketball, ice hockey (a national sport), rodeos, lacrosse, and Highland games. Other sports include superb fishing—salmon, trout, pike, bass, grayling, cod, and others—in coastal waters and the many inland lakes and rivers; hunting particularly in the forests of the north; skiing and mountain climbing in the Laurentians, Rockies, and Selkirks; canoeing in the forested wilderness of the northern Saskatchewan (maps of canoe routes are available from **Tourist Development Branch,** Power Building, Regina); snowmobiling, curling, yachting, water-skiing, horseback riding, tennis, and golf.

WHAT TO SEE ONTARIO

The soft rolling countryside of southern Ontario is distinguished by wide-spreading maple trees which turn to beautiful shades of red in the fall. In **Ottawa,** the capital, the imposing bulk of the **Parliament Buildings** rises from a hill dominating the city. There are free daily guided tours of the lavish interiors. (No parking on Parliament Hill, but there are numerous commercial parking lots within easy walking distance.) The **Peace Tower,** with a 53-bell carillon, is renovated. The guard is ceremonially changed in front of the **Parliament Buildings** at 10am June-September. **Laurier House** (335 Laurier Avenue), former residence of two Prime Ministers, was built in 1878 and retains its period furnishings. Interesting museums include the **National Gallery,** with an outstanding selection of European and Canadian art; the **Canadian War Museum,** with historical displays ranging from the Franco-Indian to the Second World War; the **National Aeronautical Collection** at Rockcliffe airport; the new **Currency Museum** (245 Sparks Street) in **Bank of Canada Building** has 100,000 items on history and development of world money; and **Bytown Museum,** housed in old office premises at the Rideau Canal, which has displays relating to the history of Ottawa. The canal links Ottawa with Kingston, and regular scenic boat cruises (May through October) leave the canal docks by the National Arts Center. The capital's main shopping area is **Sparks Street Mall,** a pedestrian area with sidewalk cafés, flowers, boutiques. Two places to go for local handicrafts are **Canada's Four Corners** (193 Sparks Street) and the **Snow Goose** (40 Elgin Street). **Byward Market** in one of the old parts of town (one block north of Rideau Street) is a lively scene when farmers gather to sell their produce on Tuesday, Thursday, and Saturday. There are two new and excellent wine bars in the Market area: **Vines** at 33 William Street, and **Daphne & Victor's** at 14 William Street. The winter carnival is held at the end of January, and the city is a riot of color in May during the tulip festival. Good restaurants in Ottawa include the **Chateau Laurier** (Major's Hill Park); **Al's Steak House & Tavern** (329A Elgin Street); **Stewart's Green Valley Restaurant** (Prince of Wales Drive); and the Chinese **Ta Tung Tavern and Restaurant** (1353 Cyrville Road). Noted for French cuisine are **Henry Berger** (69 Laurier Street) and **La Ferme Columbia** (St Joseph Blvd), both in Hull; **Mama Theresa's** (281 Kent St) Italian; **Old Fish Market** (54 York Street) for seafood; **Guadalaharry's** (18 York Street) Mexican food; **Japanese Village** (Laurier Street). Hotels in Ottawa with minimum daily rates for 2 persons/double room in US funds include: **Bytown Hotel,** 127 Metcalfe Street ($27); **Chateau Laurier Hotel,** Major's Hill Park ($46); **Deltas Inn of the Provinces,** 361 Queen Street ($58); **Four Seasons Hotel,** 150 Albert Street ($68); **Holiday Inn/Ottawa Centre,** 100 Kent Street ($47); **Holiday Inn/Market Square,** 350 Dalhousie ($39); **Lord Elgin Hotel,** 100 Elgin Street ($30); **Park Lane Hotel,** 111 Cooper Street ($35); **Skyline Hotel,** 101 Lyon Street ($55); **Talisman Motor Hotel,** 1376 Carling Ave (not downtown) ($46); **Auberge de la Chaudiere,** Hull, Quebec.

In the hills 8 miles out of Ottawa is **Gatineau Park** (25,000 acres), with a small pioneer museum. Lovely **Gatineau Valley** is a popular winter ski center. **Gracefield,** 60 miles north, is a lovely region of lakes and rivers and a good center for trout and bass fishing as well as moose, deer, and bear hunting in autumn.

Toronto, central to Canada's urban corridor along **Great Lakes** and **St Lawrence Seaway,** is now the largest metropolitan area in population and occupies 450 square miles near the west end of Lake Ontario. Architecture ranges from futuristic shell-shaped City Hall complex by Finnish architect Vilje Revell, and the 1815-foot CN Tower, world's tallest free-standing structure, to **Casa Loma,** a romanticized castle built in 1911. Historic buildings include grand **St Lawrence Hall,** adjacent to old market area; **Mackenzie House,** home of Toronto's first mayor and leader of 1837 Rebellion, still with its era furnishings; **Colborne Lodge** in 1836 style with English carriages in coach house; **Old Fort York,** a military post established in 1793, has colorful guard changes in summer; and **Todmorden Mills Museum Park,** where historic structures are open May through November. Within 18 miles of Toronto City Hall are **Black Creek Pioneer Village,** an early 19th-century farming community authentically recreated; **Metro Zoo,** one of the world's most modern, with a miniature train and covering 710 acres; **Canada's Wonderland,** new 320-acre family entertainment park at Maple with its own artificial mountain; **Ontario Science Centre** in suburban Don Mills, designed for visitors, young and old, to participate in demonstrations. Downtown, **Art Gallery of Ontario** has world's finest collection of Henry Moore sculpture; **Royal Ontario Museum** is being renovated; **McLaughlin Planetarium** next door offers audiovisual voyages to Jupiter and Saturn. On the waterfront, within 5 minutes drive of city center are **Harbourfront** with exhibits, antique market, varying entertainment and seafood dining. **Canadian National Exhibition** (late August-early September), annual exposition; **Ontario Place,** with ultra-modern structures, including domed **Cinesphere** theatre rising from water, and family dining. **Toronto Islands,** a 5-minute ferry ride, provides boating, cycling, picnicking, and a children's animal park (farm animals for city kids). Toronto has more than 50 companies providing live theatre year-round, including civic-owned **O'Keefe Centre,** with all entertainment bookings and home of **National Ballet Company; Royal Alex** for legitimate theatre and a large range of smaller dinner theatres. The 1815-foot **CN Tower** provides great panoramic view from observation levels and revolving restaurant that is located one third of a mile in the sky. Good restaurants include **Fenton's,** 2 Gloucester St, **Lhardy's,** 634 Church St, **Fernando's,** 36 Arthur Ave., and **Anesty's,** 16 Church St. At the major hotels are **Cafe de L'Auberge,** Inn-on-the-Park, in Don Mills; **Poseidon** (seafood), Harbour Castle/Hilton; Royal York Hotel's **Acadian Room;** Sheraton Centre's **Winter Palace; Truffles** in Four Seasons/Yorkville; Windsor Arms' **Courtyard Cafe,** 22 Thomas St, and the **Katsura** in the Prince Hotel. **Ed's Warehouse,** beside the Royal Alex, is for roast beef; the **Old Fish Market,** St Lawrence Market, and the **Mermaid** at 724 Bay Street are known for seafood. Multicultural Toronto has scores of restaurants to meet global tastes, among them: **Simpsons-on-the-Strand** at First Canadian Place and **Hind Quarter,** 23 St Thomas St (British); **Napoleon,** 79 Grenville St, **Gaston's,** 595 Markham St, **LeProvencal,** 23 St Thomas (French); **Noodles,** 60 Bloor W, **La Bussola,** 3434 Bathurst St, **LaScala,** 1121 Bay St (Italian); **Lee Gardens,** 358 Spadina Ave, **Pink Pearl,** 142 Dundas St W, **Sai Woo,** 130 Dundas St W (Oriental); **Jerusalem,** 955 Eglinton Ave W, **Taj Mahal,** 1158 Yonge St (Middle East and Indian). Hotels in Toronto are:

> Rates are in US$ for a double/twin room with bath or shower
> **Chelsea Inn,** 33 Gerrard St W (from $41)
> **Four Seasons/Yorkville,** 21 Avenue Rd (from $80)
> **Harbour Castle Hilton,** 1 Harbour Sq (from $70)
> **Hotel Toronto,** 145 Richmond St W (from $69)
> **Inn-on-the-Park,** Don Mills (from $56)
> **King Edward,** 37 King St E (from $84)
> **Westbury Hotel,** 475 Yonge St (from $54)
> **Park Plaza,** 4 Avenue Rd (from $58)
> **Prince Hotel,** 900 York Mills, Don Mills (from $58)
> **Royal York Hotel,** 100 Front St W ($61)
> **Sheraton Centre,** 123 Queen St W (from $67)
> **Sutton Place,** 955 Bay St (from $67)

Metro Toronto has six **Holiday Inns,** from 200-750 rooms, (from $38-50 double). In the near vicinity of Toronto International Airport are **Constellation Hotel,** 900 Dixon Rd (from $49 double) and **Skyline Hotel,** 655 Dixon Rd (from $49 double).

Stratford, 95 miles west of Toronto, is the home of the **Stratford Festival,** featuring Canada's famed theatre company in Shakespearian and other drama at Festival Theatre, June-October.

Niagara-on-Lake, about one hour by hydrofoil vessel from Toronto across Lake Ontario, or a 10-mile historic drive from Niagara Falls. Niagara-on-Lake was the capital of Upper Canada (Ontario) in the 1790's. The main street of the town has been restored to early 19th century authenticity. Shaw Festival, May through early September, presents work of George Bernard Shaw in Festival Theatre, plus wide-ranging program of dance, music, cabaret, musical comedy, and jazz.

Niagara Falls: The best views of the beauty and wonder of this great natural spectacle are from the Canadian side. Separated from the American Falls by Goat Island, the lovely curving sweep of the **Horseshoe Falls** drops 186 feet from a ledge 2,600 feet wide. At night the cascades are brilliantly illuminated. There is an observation platform at the base of the falls, and behind the curtain of falling water is the **Cave of the Winds.** Frequent boat trips in summer ride the torrent up the gorge almost to the foot of the thundering downpour. Downriver trips from **Whirlpool Rapids** travel the **Great Gorge** at its narrowest. For thrilling panoramic views visit the 775-foot-high **Skylon Tower** (with a revolving restaurant) and **Rainbow Bridge,** which spans the gorge downstream, or take a helicopter ride. Niagara's other attractions include an **Antique Auto Museum,** a **Wax Museum** of the famous and infamous, **Niagara**

Falls Museum, and **Table Rock House,** next to Horseshoe Falls, with a collection of replicas of the British Crown jewels.

QUEBEC

Quebec, the largest province in Canada, is a lovely place, with dense forests in the north (and many isolated fly-in hunting and fishing camps) and farmlands and smallholdings in the south.

Montreal, Canada's largest city and the second-largest French-speaking city in the world, has a lively cosmopolitan atmosphere and the best restaurants in Canada. Situated on an island in the St Lawrence river midway between the Great Lakes and the Atlantic, Montreal is a major port despite its distance of nearly 1,000 miles from the sea. Most central points of interest are accessible by subway. A focus of community life is majestic **Mount Royal,** a rural oasis in the center of the great metropolis. In summer concerts are staged, and in winter it is overrun by sports enthusiasts. **Château de Ramezay** on Notre Dame Street, a fine example of a French mansion, was the headquarters of the invading American army in 1775 and now houses an interesting Canadian historical museum. Also off Notre Dame Street is the **Place d'Armes,** a gracious square overlooked by **Notre Dame de Montréal,** the second-largest church in North America, which has beautiful stained-glass windows. Behind the Place d'Armes métro (subway) is **Chinatown,** and the nearby **Boulevard St Laurent** is monopolized by traders of all nationalities. **St Patrick's Church** is known for its Gothic-style architecture and fine interior décor, and **Marie-Reine-du-Monde** is a small-scale replica of St Peter's in Rome. Nearer the river are the cobbled streets and restored buildings of **Old Montreal. Place Jacques Cartier** is the center of this interesting area, with historical reminders among the modern boutiques. The famous sailors' church of **Notre Dame de Bon Secours** (1771) is near **Bon Secours Market,** dating from 1843. On the other side of Mount Royal is **St Joseph's Oratory,** a large pilgrims' church capable of holding 10,000 people. **Montreal Fine Arts Museum** has a good collection of Old Masters and Moderns and outstanding antique glass. More glass can be seen in the **Montreal Stock Exchange Tower,** at Place Victoria, where a fine chandelier of over 3,000 pieces of hand-blown glass hangs three stories down. Also worth visiting are **Manoir Lachine,** a fur-trading post built in 1671, the **Dow Planetarium,** and **Lafontaine Park,** with lagoons, gardens, and a lovely fountain, an open-air theater, and the fairytale **"Garden of Wonders." Man and His World,** the popular survivor from Expo '67, is one of the many attractions of Montreal's islands, which also have swimming and boating facilities. On **St Helen's Island** interesting military remains include a **Museum,** in a former barracks, the **Blockhouse** (now a museum), and the old powder magazine, converted into **La Poudrière,** a trilingual theater. The striking **Place Des Arts,** St Catherine Street West, houses one of Canada's most striking concert hall-theater complexes. A dramatic architectural addition to the city is the 65,000-seat saucer-shaped **Olympic Stadium** at Boulevard Pie IX and Sherbrooke Street, in the East End.

Montreal has over 4,000 international restaurants, and there is a good selection on **Mountain Street** between St Catherine and Sherbrooke Streets; **Café Martin** (2175 Mountain Street) and **Auberge St Tropez** (1208 Crescent Street) are both French. The temperature-controlled underground streets beneath Place Ville Marie and Place Bonaventure hold several others. **La Popina** (IBM Building, Place Ville Marie) and the luxurious **La Renaissance** (Place Westmount) are good. Excellent hotel dining rooms are **Bluenose** (seafood) in the Queen Elizabeth, **Pierre de Coubertin** in the Four Seasons, **Le Caf' Conc'** in the Chateau Champlain, and **Le Castillon** in the Bonaventure. Old Montreal boasts fine French cuisine; try **Le St Amable** (188 St Amable Street, Place Jacques Cartier), with local French-Canadian specialties as well, or **Les Filles du Roy** (415 Bonsecours). The most lavish restaurant is **Chez Bardet** (591 Henri Bourassa, Boulevard East).

Canada's largest city is always lively, and particularly so on **St Jean Baptiste Day** (24 June), **St Patrick's Day** (17 Mar), **Labor Day**, when the streets are filled with parades and pageants, and during the **Winter Season**. In August the **Festival of the Arts** and the **International Film Festival** take place. The Winter Season is at its gayest at resorts in the **Laurentian Mountains**, which extend from 25 to 150 miles north of the city. Ste-Agathe-des-Monts holds an international dog-sled derby during the season. The resort hotels are open all year, and the area is ideal for peaceful climbing. Hotels in Montreal:

Rates are in US$ for a double/twin room with bath or shower

   Bonaventure, 1 Place Bonaventure (from $78)
   Chateau Champlain, 1050 Lagauchetiere West (from $80)
   Holiday Inn-Downtown, 420 Sherbrooke Street West (from $54)
   Holiday Inn-Place Dupuis, 1415 St. Hubert (from $54)
   Hyatt-Regency, 777 University Street (from $67)
   Meridien, Complexe Desjardins (from $70)
   Quatre Saisons, 1050 Sherbrooke Street West (from $95)
   Queen Elizabeth, 900 Dorchester Boulevard West (from $85)
   RITZ-CARLTON INTER·CONTINENTAL, 1228 Sherbrooke Street West (from $71)
   Sheraton-Mount Royal, 1445 Peel Street (from $42.50)

All the above hotels are in downtown Montreal.

Quebec, Canada's oldest city, is built on a promontory rising steeply on the left bank of the **St Lawrence River**. Narrow streets wind up from the waterfront **Lower Town** to penetrate the encircling walls of **Upper Town**. The pastel-colored roofs of the old Lower Town houses, the predominance of French signs, the bohemian **Latin Quarter**, and the quaint horse-drawn carriages *(calèches)* invest Quebec with a unique Old World charm. Prominent among the new warehouses and commercial buildings of Lower Town is the church of **Notre Dame des Victoires**, built in 1688. The wall between the "towns" has been converted into **Dufferin Terrace**, a wide promenade 1,400 feet long and magnificently situated overlooking the river. Behind is the graceful bulk of **Château Frontenac**, an old Canadian Pacific Railway hotel. The **Ursuline Convent**, one of the oldest girls' schools on the continent, was founded in 1639, and the **Catholic Seminary** in 1663. On the flat plateau above the town are the **Plains of Abraham,** where Wolfe defeated Montcalm in 1759, taking Quebec for the British. The battlefield itself is now a park, popular with skiers and skaters in winter. The **Parliament Buildings,** standing in landscaped grounds, are in 17th-century French Renaissance style. There are guided tours of the attractive inner chambers. Also on the Plains are an interesting **Provincial Museum** and the **Bois de Coulonge.** The highest part of Quebec is **Cap Diamant,** crowned by the **Citadel,** summer residence of Canada's Governor-General. Quebec's **Winter Carnival** is the most festive in Canada. It takes place in the first two weeks of February, with a dizzy round of parades, costume balls, skating festivals, and curling competitions.

Good French restaurants in the city include **La Traite du Roy,** a 17th-century building with a discothèque in the basement, **Chez Guido,** with French and Italian food, **Le Croquembroche** (nouvelle cuisine) in the Hilton International, and the **Continental.** Hotels in Quebec:

Rates are in US$ for a double/twin room with bath or shower

Auberge des Gouverneurs, 3030 Sir Wilfred Laurier Boulevard, about 5 miles from downtown (from $54.50)

Auberge des Gouverneurs (Centre Ville), 690 St. Cyrille Boulevard (from $61.50)

Château Bonne Entente, 3400 Ste-Foy Road, about 5 miles from downtown (from $43)

Château Frontenac, 1 Rue des Carrières (from $65)

Holiday Inn-Ste-Foy, 3225 Hochelaga, about 5 miles from downtown (from $48)

Holiday Inn-Downtown, 395 Rue de la Couronne (from $59)

Le Concorde, 1225 Place Montcalm (from $55)

Quebec Hilton, 3 Place Québec (from $75)

Unless otherwise indicated, the above hotels are centrally located.

The **Gaspé Peninsula** is a beautiful region of little fishing villages, rocky cliffs, roadside shrines, and rugged hills. The peninsula ends with the **Perce Rock,** nearly 300 feet out of the water, through which the sea has bored an archway. The **Parc de la Gaspésie** attracts climbers to its 4,000-foot-high mountains, and there are government camps and cabins for trout and salmon fishers. The best is at **Le Gîte du Mont Albert.**

EASTERN PROVINCES

NEWFOUNDLAND

The most easterly part of North America, Newfoundland includes the Island of Newfoundland and the mainland area of Labrador, separated by the Strait of Belle Isle. Nova Scotia can be reached from the Island by air or, via the Cabot Strait, by ferry and car. The island of **Newfoundland** is full of lakes and bogs, rivers, falls, and rapids. Off the coast are the famous banks and shallows, rich in cod. Fishing, lumbering, and paper manufacturing are the chief commercial enterprises; most of the inhabitants live in scattered fishing villages along the coast. The main attractions for the tourist are fishing, hunting in the mountains, and incredibly beautiful scenery. A good view of the capital city, **St John's,** and the surrounding area can be had from **Signal Hill,** a point rich in the province's history. The **Trans-Canada Highway** starts at St John's and continues all the way to Vancouver, British Columbia. **L'Anse aux Meadows** in northern Newfoundland has a fascinating excavated Viking long-house.

Labrador, a large, triangle-shaped area is bounded by an Atlantic eastern coast with dramatic fjords. The cold Labrador current and the difficult terrain have left the area largely undeveloped, but the area contains tremendous deposits of minerals and a great potential for hydroelectric power, as seen in the complex at **Churchill Falls.**

NOVA SCOTIA

Almost an island, the seaside province of Nova Scotia is joined to the rest of Canada by the **Chignecto** isthmus. Its location on the Atlantic moderates winter and summer climates, and the coast has less severe temperatures than do the inland areas. Traditionally a fishing, farming, and mining province, Nova Scotia has become more industrialized in the past thirty years. However, modern fishing trawlers—replacing the wooden schooners of the past—still bring their catches to **Lunenburg** to be processed in one of the world's largest and most modern fish plants. Charming fishing villages such as **Peggy's Cove, Terence Cove,** and **Prospect** still remain, and remnants of the past are also found in the many historic sites and parks in the province, from grist mills and palisaded forts to the magnificent **Fortress of Louisbourg,** once the French stronghold in North America. Every area of the province has something different to offer in scenic variety; the tranquil farmlands of the Annapolis Valley, the rustic coves along the coast, and the stunning majesty and beauty of the **Cabot Trail,** a favorite tourist route skirting the spectacular mountainous coastline of the **Highlands National Park** on Cape Breton Island. The capital, **Halifax,** is the economic and cultural center for Atlantic Canada and offers first-class accommodations, restaurants, entertainment, and shopping. Here you will see the star-shaped **Citadel,** the city's best-known landmark; today it contains a military and historical museum.

PRINCE EDWARD ISLAND

Prince Edward Island is Canada's smallest province, 140 miles long and 11 miles wide at the broadest point, and one of its most charming areas. The warm sea (in the 70s in summer) laps against beautiful sandy beaches, and the red soil is tilled by people speaking a quaint dialect. Picturesque farms, fishing villages, country fairs, antique shows, and church lobster suppers all contribute to the unusual character of the island. Historic **Charlottetown,** where the article of Canadian Confederation was signed, has a good annual summer festival. The **National Park,** a 20-mile stretch of sandy beaches and dunes along the North Shore, has a fine golf course and is popular with campers and deep-sea fishermen. **Anne of Green Gables'** house in the Park is a lovely period building and should not be missed.

NEW BRUNSWICK

New Brunswick is a province of beautiful salmon rivers and small farms. Rivers flow from the richly forested regions of the north, which also produce millions of saw logs and cords of pulpwood annually. **Fredericton,** the provincial capital, is small, green, and clean. An educational and cultural center, the town boasts the **Beaverbrook Art Gallery,** one of the best in Canada, with a 10-foot-high painting by the surrealist Salvador Dali, and the **York Sunbury Museum.** The **Legislative Buildings** house many important paintings and a complete set of Audubon's bird pictures. Important manuscripts are on show at the **Harriet Irving Library** on the university campus.

At **Moncton** the Petitcodiac River clashes with the water from the **Bay of Fundy** at high tide, and it thunders into the town in an impressive tidal bore. This is particularly dramatic in April and September. Just outside the city is **Magnetic Hill,** where an optical illusion creates the mistaken impression of an uphill slope, when in fact you are going downhill. Nearby is **Shediac,** site of an annual mid-summer lobster festival. The **Reversing Falls Rapids** at St John is an interesting sight, best seen from the Tourist Bureau observation lounge at tide change. St John's **Provincial Museum** has some fine collections of Indian, French, and British colonial relics and shipbuilding displays. **Grand Manan Island** is the center of the fishing industry, providing much of the seafood for which the province is renowned. **Fundy National Park** is on the Bay, northeast of St John and south of Moncton. **Kouchibouguac National Park** has been developed on the east coast, and a string of provincial parks dot the province.

WESTERN PROVINCES

MANITOBA

Manitoba's landscape is two-thirds fertile prairie, the rest rocky, sometimes rolling, and densely forested. It has thousands of lakes, which provide sport (excellent fishing for pike, trout, and bass) and recreation for the visitor. In winter there is the additional thrill of ice-fishing. The hunting includes deer, black bear, elk, moose, caribou, and the rare snow goose. The national parks in the region have accommodations to suit every pocket: luxury hotels, motels, resort lodges, trailer and camping sites.

Winnipeg, the capital, is an attractive city with a lively interest in the arts. It is home to the **Royal Winnipeg Ballet** and the **Manitoba Theater Center.** Interesting reminders of its past history are **Upper Fort Garry** gateway, a relic of the Hudson Bay Company, located on Main Street opposite the CNR Station; the **Countess of Dufferin,** the first woodburning locomotive in the west; **Ross House,** the first post office in the west (on Higgins Avenue opposite the CPR Station); and **Seven Oaks House,** built in 1851, the oldest still habitable home in Manitoba (Rupertsland Avenue). Visit the huge **Grain Exchange** (9:30-1:30) and **Indian Handicrafts of Manitoba** (470 Portage Avnue). Traveling on the **Dash,**

a special bus that runs about every 5 minutes, you can go anywhere in the downtown core area for 10¢.

In Winnipeg, good food can be found at **La Vieille Gare** in the old Canadian National Railway Station (French); the **Old Swiss Inn,** with continental offerings (207 Edmonton Street); the **Rib Room** at the Charterhouse Hotel, for onion soup and roast beef; the **Selkirk Room** in the North Star Inn; **Oliver's Old Bailey** (185 Lombard Avenue), **Rae and Jerry's** (1405 Portage Avenue), and **Hy's Steak Loft** (216 Kennedy Street) for steaks and seafood. At the **Winnipeg Inn Hotel,** the **Velvet Glove** dining room has an 18th-century atmosphere, and the **Stage Door** dining room has cabaret. The **Factor's Table** in the **Fort Garry Hotel** is a replica of the original fort banqueting hall. Hotels in Winnipeg:

Rates are in US$ for a double/twin room with bath or shower.

Canada House, 340 Assiniboine Avenue (from $25)

Charterhouse, 330 York Avenue (from $45)

City Centre Motor Inn, 230 Carlton Street (from $26)

Delta's Marlborough Inn, 331 Smith Street (from $50)

Fort Garry, 222 Broadway Avenue (from $48)

Gordon Downtowner, 330 Kennedy Street (from $23)

Holiday Inn, 350 St Mary's Avenue (from $57)

International Inn, 1808 Wellington at Berry, adjacent to airport, about 4 miles west of city (from $43.50)

Delta's Marlborough Inn, 331 Smith Street (from $50)

North Star Inn, 288 Portage Avenue (from $62)

Sheraton-Carlton, 220 Carlton Street (from $39)

Winnipeg Inn, 2 Lombard Place (from $66)

Unless otherwise indicated, the above hotels are centrally located.

Lower Fort Garry, 19 miles north, is the only surviving stone fur-trading fort. It stands in a **National Historic Park** alongside a Red River settler's house, blacksmith's shop, and other period buildings. **Fort La Reine** museum and **Pioneer Village** are fascinating reminders of a bygone era. Summer rail excursions leave Winnipeg for **Churchill,** a Hudson Bay Trading Post since 1689. Indian and Eskimo communities live in this area, and **Churchill Eskimo Museum** has wonderful artifacts and carvings. **Fort Prince of Wales,** whose ruined walls are 14 feet thick, can be visited from Churchill by boat or dog-sled. Exciting festivals are the **Flin Flon Trout Festival** (late June), with street dancing, fishing contests, and a canoe derby, and the **Manitoba Trappers Festival,** held at **The Pas** in February.

SASKATCHEWAN

The terrain of Saskatchewan is diversified. In the north, the rugged granite of the Canadian Shield is dotted with lakes and clothed with evergreen forest. **Prince Albert,** home town of Canada's late statesman and ex-Prime Minister John Diefenbaker, is the major trading center and gateway to this area, which provides excellent hunting and fishing. The southern portion of the province is level prairie, its broad fields of wheat and other crops interspersed with large cattle ranches. In the extreme southwest are the **Cypress Hills,** rising to almost 5,000 feet. They possess their own unique fauna and flora. It was to this area that Sitting Bull fled after the battle of the Little Big Horn to escape United States retribution.

Saskatoon has the **Western Development Museum** showing life in the area at the turn of the century, the **Mendel Art Gallery** and **Civic Conservatory** (Canadian and European artwork including a gallery of Eskimo carvings), the **Memorial Art Gallery** with exhibits by Canadian artists, the **Ukrainian Museum of Canada,** and the legislative buildings. Hotels in Saskatoon:

Rates are in US$ for double/twin room with bath or shower

Bessborough Hotel, 601 Spadina Crescent (from $43)

Best Western Imperial 400 Motel, 610 Idylwyld North (from $27), northwest area

Confederation Inn Motor Hotel, 22nd Street and Circle Drive (from $25)

Holiday Inn, 90 22nd Street East (from $45)

King George Motor Hotel, 157 2nd Avenue North (from $29)

Park Town Motor Hotel, 924 Spadina Crescent East (from $38)

Sheraton Cavalier, 612 Spadina Crescent (from $35)

TraveLodge, 106 Circle Drive West (from $35)

Unless otherwise indicated, all the above hotels are centrally located.

Regina, with a population of 151,191, is the capital of Saskatchewan and a major commercial center for the rich wheat land and ranching country around it—land that is also rich in oil, gas, and potash. It is often called the "Home of the Mounties" because it was headquarters of the forerunners of Canada's Royal Canadian Mounted Police. Nightlife and entertainment are quite cosmopolitan in Regina. Among the larger downtown restaurants are the **Chinese Palace,** 4355 Albert Street; **L'Habitant** (French-Canadian cuisine), 1717 Victoria Avenue; **Dionysus Greek Dining Room,** 2727 Parliament Avenue; **Ranch Room,** Victoria and Scarth, and **Golf's Steak Houses Ltd** at Hamilton and Victoria; the **Copper Kettle,** 1953 Scarth Street; **Waldo's,** 3970 Albert Street; and **Miekas Kitchen,** 1810 Smith Street. Hotels in Regina:

Rates are in US$ for double/twin room with bath or shower

Holiday Inn, 777 Albert Street (from $36)

Imperial 400 Motel, 4255 Albert Street (from $26)

Landmark Inn, 4150 Albert Street (from $40)

Regina Inn, 1975 Broad Street (from $43)

Saskatchewan, Victoria Avenue and Scarth Street (from $46)

Sheraton Centre, 1818 Victoria Avenue (from $47)

Vagabond Motor Inn, 4177 Albert Street (from $27)

All the above hotels are centrally located.

ALBERTA

The **Canadian Rockies,** with their unparalleled beauty, provide opportunities for skiing, climbing, and fishing. **Banff** and **Jasper National Parks** are in the heart of the mountains, covering a region where the mountain peaks rise to 12,000 feet and ski trails range from championship runs to gentle nursery slopes. The 3,240-foot double chairlift is one of the steepest in the world. The town of **Banff,** with its beautiful and perfect location, is within easy reach of many ski trails. **Banff School of Fine Arts** organizes cultural events during the summer, and in late July there is an **Indian Festival** with tribal dancing and celebrations. The most famous ski resorts near Banff are **Mont Norquay, Sunshine Village,** and **Lake Louise.** From Banff you can visit **Lake Louise** and **Moraine Lake,** ride the gondola to the top of **Sulphur Mountain,** or enjoy a game of golf in the grounds of the **Banff Springs Hotel.** Between Banff and Jasper, the **Icefield Highway,** 142 miles long, passes **Athabasca Glacier. Jasper National Park** is 4,200 square miles of ice caps, mineral hot springs, and lakes. **Jasper** itself, an alpine village, has a string of lovely small lakes with sandy beaches.

Calgary, with a population of nearly 500,000, is the fastest growing city in Canada. Set in the foothills of the majestic Canadian Rockies and in the heart of cattle and oil country, it is packed during the **Calgary Exhibition and Stampede,** 10 days of rodeo held in early July and highlighted by the Stampede Parade. **Glenhbow Museum** has excellent historical and North American Indian displays, but the city is best known for its **Zoo** and **Dinosaur Park.** Alberta supplies three-quarters of the world's museums with dinosaur remains, and the Park has some staggering full-sized models of these enormous prehistoric creatures. **Heritage Park** brings the early West to life again and is staffed by oldtimers in period dress. Good restaurants in Calgary include many places for steaks, among them, **Blackbeard's** (235 10th Avenue SW), which has seafood as well; **The Moose Factory** (1213 1st Street SW) for crabs legs and steaks; **Pardon My Garden** (435 4th Avenue SW), for steaks, crepes, and seafood in delightful surroundings; **Heartland,** in the Sandman Inn, for provincial cooking; **Caesar's** (512 4th Avenue SW), where charcoal-broiled steak is the specialty; **Owl's Nest,** in the Calgary Inn, for steaks and ambiance; **Scotch and Sirloin** (820 10th Street SW), for seafood and beef. **Arestes** (2nd Avenue and 4th Street SE), with authentic Greek food, the **Japanese Village** (302 4th Avenue SW), and the **Silver Dragon** (106 3rd Avenue SE), serving superb Chinese cuisine, are among the city's many ethnic restaurants. The revolving restaurant at the top of **Calgary Tower** has a varied menu and a unique view. Hotels in Calgary:

Rates are in US$ for a double/twin room with bath or shower
   Airliner Inn, 4804 4th Street NE (from $35), near airport
   Chateau Airport, 2001 Airport Road NE (from $65), adjacent to airport
   Holiday Inn-Downtown, 708 8th Avenue (from $45)
   International, 220 4th Avenue SW (from $76)
   Palliser, 9th Avenue at 1st Street SW (from $65)
   Port O'Call, 1935 McKnight Boulevard NE (from $48)
   Sheraton Summit Inn, 202 4th Avenue SW (from $56)
   Unless otherwise indicated, the above hotels are all centrally located.
   Edmonton, the capital of Alberta, is divided by the deep Saskatchewan River valley. It is a booming city, rich in oil, and is considered by many

to be a model of modern urban design. There are a large number of parks, zoos, historic buildings, and recreational areas within the city limits. The best restaurants in Edmonton include the **Northcote Dining Lounge** (10020 100th Street), known for its seafood and its old steamboat décor, **Oliver's,** (10130 117th Street), for general fare, **Walden's** (10245 104th Street), with haute cuisine, **La Ronde** (101st at Bellamy Hill), and the **Mayfield Seafood Buffet** (16615 109 Avenue). **The Seven Seas** (10525 Jasper Avenue) specializes in Oriental cuisine. Hotels in Edmonton: *Rates are in US$ for a double/twin room with bath or shower*

    Cheateau Lacombe, 101st Street at Bellamy Hill (from $70)

    Edmonton Inn, Kingsway Avenue at 119th Street, adjacent to the industrial airport, about 2 miles from downtown (from $55)

    Edmonton Plaza, 101st Avenue and 100th Street (from $80)

    Four Seasons, 101st Street and 102A Avenue (from $90)

    Holiday Inn, 107th Street and 100th Avenue (from $47)

    Macdonald, 100th Street at Jasper Avenue (from $55)

    Sheraton-Caravan Hotel, 10010 104th Street (from $38)

    Unless otherwise indicated, all the above hotels are centrally located.

BRITISH COLUMBIA

Canada's most western province has high mountains, dense forests (the famous Douglas firs), and fast-flowing rivers. The **Fraser River** is the biggest salmon breeding ground in the world. The coastal area is remarkable not only for its mild climate but also for its many examples of Indian totem art.

    Vancouver, Canada's third-largest city, is superbly situated on the long, fjord-like **Burrard Inlet** (Vancouver Harbor), with a backdrop of forested slopes rising to the snow-capped peaks of the Coast Range. The city offers a wide variety of recreational facilities within easy reach—long sandy beaches near town, yachting from **Fisherman's Cove,** salmon fishing at **Horseshoe Bay,** steelhead trout in **Capilano River,** duck and geese shooting on the **Fraser Delta.** A lofty suspension bridge swings perilously across the width of the beautiful **Capilano Canyon,** and, from the top of Capilano Road, the **Skyride** cablecar rises up **Grouse Mountain** to **Grouse Nest Restaurant,** with a wonderful view. **Stanley Park,** a large (1,000 acres) natural forest area of fir and cedar, juts into the sea, forming one arm of the harbor entrance. Spanning the harbor is the beautiful **Lions Gate** suspension bridge. The park has an open-air theater, a zoo, an aquarium with performing whales, canoeing, bowling, and cricket. Vancouver is a friendly cosmopolitan city, and in summer young street musicians add a delightfully bright touch to the scene. The **University of British Columbia** has a museum of anthropology, a **Fine Arts Gallery,** and an interesting **Totem Park.** The old **Gastown** is the center of antique shops, boutiques, art galleries. Old **Hastings Mill Store** on Alam Road is an excellent pioneer museum. Vancouver's **Chinatown** is the second largest in North America, with Oriental curio shops, nightspots, and some superb restaurants. Good places to eat in Vancouver include the **William Tell** (722 Richard Street) for Swiss and Continental cuisine, **Le Napoleon**

(869 Hamilton Street) and **Le Pavillon** in the Four Seasons Hotel for French food. **Umberto's** (1380 Hornby Street) for Italian food, the **Cannery** (2205 Commissioner Street) and **La Cantina** (1376 Hornby Street) for seafood, and the **Carriage Room** at the Hotel Devonshire (849 West Georgia Street), known for steak and seafood. **Muckamuck** (1724 Davie Street) serves authentic American Indian food. The **Harbour House** on top of Harbour Centre at 555 West Hastings Street and the **Panorama Roof** at the Hotel Vancouver both have excellent meals with a view. Top festivals are the **Pacific National Exhibition, Oktoberfest,** and the **Squamish Loggers Sports Festival.** Hotels in Vancouver:

Rates are in US$ for a double/twin room with bath or shower

   Abbotsford, 921 West Pender Street (from $27.39)

   Bayshore Inn, West Georgia and Cardero Streets (from $41.50)

   Doric Howe Motor Hotel, 1060 Howe Street (from $31.54)

   Four Seasons, 791 West Georgia Street (from $96)

   Grosvenor, 840 Hose Street (from $34.03)

   Holiday Inn, 1133 West Hastings Street (from $40.67)

   Hyatt Regency, 655 Burrard Street (from $84)

The above hotels are all centrally located. Rates shown are exclusive of a 5% hotel tax.

Victoria, the capital of British Columbia on Vancouver Island, was named after the British Queen and has a mild winter climate, many fine parks and gardens, and a rather colonial atmosphere. It lies in a beautiful natural setting, surrounded by hills and overlooking the snow-clad Olympic mountains across the Juan de Fuca strait. Not to be missed when visiting the island are the beautiful and exotic **Butchart Gardens.** There are frequent ferries to the mainland (1¾ hours on the ferry itself, plus 20 miles on each end to the central cities) and to Seattle and Port Angeles, Washington. Victoria is close to beaches, woods, and lakes, and there are good facilities for yachting, golf, fishing, and hunting (grouse and deer). Ever-present reminders of the past are the Victorian **Parliament Buildings** and the stately **Canadian Pacific Empress Hotel** (721 Government Street, from $39.84 double). Other hotels in Victoria include the **Imperial Inn,** 1961 Douglas at Discovery Street (from $28.22 double), the **Courtyard Inn,** 850 Blanchard St (from $56), and **Century Inn,** 603 Pandora Avenue (from $29).

NORTHWEST TERRITORIES

An untamed, undeveloped, and seemingly endless landscape, the Northwest Territories comprise one-third of Canada's area and have a very small population. The land is rich in minerals but has few tourists; this is an advantage for the hardy vacationer who really wants to "get away from it all."

YUKON TERRITORY

The Yukon Territory is famed for its gold and its majestic isolation from modern development. Its huge mountains, beautiful lakes, and cold winter climate make it a breathtaking but rugged area for the outdoorsman who wants peace and quiet.

SOURCES OF FURTHER INFORMATION

Pan Am, 80 Bloor Street West, Suite 400, Toronto, and Pan Am general agents, Zizanis Travel Corp., 3 Place Ville Marie, Montreal; Pacific Western Airlines Ltd., 1018 West Georgia St, Vancouver; and any Pan Am office around the world; **Canadian Government Office of Tourism,** 235 Queen Street, East Tower, Ottawa; **Convention and Tourist Bureau of Metropolitan Toronto,** Eaton Centre, 220 Yonge Street, Toronto; **Montreal Municipal Tourism Bureau,** 155 Notre Dame West, Montreal; **Convention and Visitors Bureau of Greater Montreal,** Floor F, Place Bonaventure, Montreal; **Tourism British Columbia,** 1117 Wharf Street, Victoria; 800 Robson Street, Robson Square, Vancouver; **Canadian Government Office of Tourism,** 1251 Avenue of the Americas, New York, NY 10020, and Canada House, Trafalgar Square, London W1.

USA

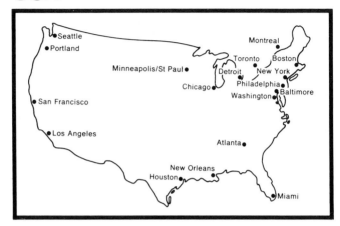

WHAT'S SPECIAL

The United States of America is an immense country—in size, wealth, energy, and skill. Physically, it straddles an entire continent. Its land is only partially devoted to producing its wealth and food; the bulk of it remains sparsely populated. It is possible to drive for hours and see no towns or settlements. The United States is still a young country and has been a "melting pot" of people from every corner of the world. The resultant mixture of races, cultures, religions, and ideologies has created the peculiarly American character, and the visitor will find warm hospitality everywhere. The country is incredibly rich in natural resources, not the least of which is the variety and drama of its landscape; some of the most spectacular scenery in the world can be found in its mountains, gorges, deserts, and fertile plains. United States cities offer exciting diversity in location and culture, too. Whichever areas you visit, you'll find much in your surroundings to interest and excite you. It is of course impossible to summarize or even list all the attractions and exciting places to visit in the United States; the visitor should realize that for every city, sight, and sound mentioned in this guide, there are a thousand others waiting in the world's most intriguing and diverse country.

COUNTRY BRIEFING

Size: 3,536,855 square miles, including Alaska and Hawaii. The United States is the world's fourth-largest country, after the USSR, Canada, and China.

Population: 222,020,000
Capital: Washington, District of Columbia.
Capital Population: 661,500
Climate: From the frozen Arctic tundra in Alaska to the tropical beaches of Florida, the United States has almost every climatic condition on earth.
Government: A republic consisting of 50 states and a federal district.
Language: English; many other languages spoken in ethnic areas.
Religion: Protestant, Roman Catholic, Jewish; Mormon (70% of the state of Utah); and many other smaller sects.
Currency: Dollars and cents (100 cents = 1 dollar). There are coins worth 1¢ (penny), 5¢ (nickel), 10¢ (dime), 25¢ (quarter), and 50¢ (half-dollar), and a rare 1-dollar piece. Paper money comes with face values of $1, $2 (rare), $5, $10, $20, $50, and $100.

Public Holidays:

New Year's Day, 1 Jan
George Washington's Birthday, third Mon in Feb
Memorial Day, last Mon in May
Independence Day, 4 July
Labor Day, first Mon in Sep

Columbus Day, second Mon in Oct
Veteran's Day, 11 Nov
Thanksgiving Day, fourth Thurs in Nov
Christmas Day, 25 Dec

HOW TO GET THERE

There are many money-saving travel plans for visitors to the USA. Your local agent will gladly give you detailed information. Decide on a gateway city: Chicago, Detroit, Houston, Los Angeles, Miami, New York, San Francisco, Seattle, or Washington. Many connecting routes within the states. Flying time to New York is 7½ hours from London, 9 hours from Rome, and 12½ hours from Tokyo. Flying time to Los Angeles is 11 hours from London, 12 hours from Paris, 9¼ hours from Tokyo, and 13 hours from Sydney. There are connecting flights to every area of the country. Time in Washington, DC, and in New York City: GMT−5.

REQUIREMENTS FOR ENTRY AND CUSTOMS REGULATIONS

All visitors to the United States, with the exception of Canadians entering from the Western hemisphere, must have a valid passport and a valid visa. Visas can only be obtained from an American consular office abroad. (No entry to passport holders from the countries of Cuba, Iraq, Korea Democratic Peoples Republic, Vietnam Socialist Republic). Visas for tourists and businessmen may be issued for a single entry or for multiple entries over a four-year period. In a few cases, they may be issued for multiple entries over an indefinite period. A smallpox vaccination certificate is required only of those who have been in an infected country within the previous 14 days. Duty-free allowance: 200 cigarettes or 50 cigars or 3 pounds tobacco or proportionate amounts of each; $100 worth of gifts (if staying longer than 72 hours and if this exemption has not already been claimed within the preceding six months). Remember that laws regarding liquor vary from state to state and that only those quantities permitted by the state in which you arrive can be released. No narcotics, meats, fruits or vegetables (without permit), plants, or furs or skins of endangered animals, such as leopard or crocodile, may be imported. If you bring in more than $5,000 in money or negotiable materials, you must file a report with Customs.

ACCOMMODATIONS

Accommodations in the United States run the gamut of visitors' requirements. Throughout the country there are luxury hotels offering every conceivable facility. Frequently such hotels feature lobbies containing shops, newsstands, hairdressers, jewelers, saunas, travel agents, car rental desks, and airline offices. These days the top US hotels set the pace for the rest of the world. So, if you are prepared to pay the money, you can take your choice. There are, however, many hotels in the US that offer clean, comfortable accommodations, excellent service, and a bill that will not reduce you to poverty. Note that most American hotel rates are quoted for rooms only; breakfast is usually extra, but US accommodations always include bath or shower, often television and air conditioning. The economy-minded will be able to get away with paying a lot less. Throughout the US there are many tourist homes (the equivalent of English guesthouses and European pensions) which offer rooms in private houses that are invariably clean and comfortable. Individual State Tourist Authorities will have lists of tourist homes available in the area. All across the nation you will find motor hotels and motels. Other accommodations for travelers include thousands of camping sites and trailer (caravan) parks and many youth hostels. In many cities the YMCA and YWCA offer excellent, inexpensive accommodations. For reasons of space we have not been able to include hotel recommendations for every important town in the US (except for New York). For a complete guide to the USA, purchase a copy of Pan Am's *USA Guide* from any Pan Am office.

USEFUL INFORMATION

Banking: Banks are plentiful throughout the USA. Hours vary, but most banks are open 9-3 Mon-Fri. Throughout the US there are very few banks which can exchange foreign currency (though there are facilities at the airports), so it is important to get dollar travelers' checks before you leave. You may find life simpler if you carry one of the internationally accepted credit cards such as American Express, MasterCard, or Visa.

Telephone Tips: Excellent, reasonably priced services; coin-operated phones available in street booths, restaurants, and stores.

Newspapers: US newspapers are local rather than national, although leading newspapers such as *The New York Times* and *The Wall Street Journal* will be available the same day in other major cities. Late editions of some foreign newspapers are also available at newsstands in major cities, but they are expensive.

Tipping: At US airports, tip porters about 50¢ for each piece of luggage they carry. In restaurants, the general rule is to leave a 15%-20% tip. It is not customary to tip restaurant head waiters unless you have received some exceptional service; in that case a $10 tip is sufficient. Checking your hat and coat calls for a tip of 50¢, depending on the type of place; hotel porters, 50¢; bellboys, 50¢ minimum, 25¢ per bag extra; 20% for meals served in your room; 20% in nightclubs. It is often worth getting a roll of half-dollar coins for use as tips. Taxis, 25¢ for fares up to 70¢; 50¢ for fares up to $1.50; and 20% for fares in excess of that. In a barber shop tip up to $1.50 for a haircut and 50¢ for a shave. Tip 50¢ for a shoeshine or having your clothes brushed.

Electricity: 110-115 volts 60 cycles AC. Power points take a 2-prong plug.

Laundry: Services are excellent, prices reasonable. Major hotels all offer a same-day or 24-hour laundry and dry-cleaning service. Individual coin-operated laundry and dry-cleaning services can be found in most shopping areas. Figure about $3.50 for a suit.

Hairdressing: Generally good; prices vary. Hotels have facilities, and there are good privately owned hairdressing shops everywhere.

Photography: The range of photographic equipment and services available in the US is unlimited. If you are shooting 35mm color film with prepaid processing, expect to receive your finished slides through the mail within 10 to 14 days of dispatch. In the cities black and white film processing takes a day or so, less if you take it direct to a film-processing laboratory. Most major cities now offer 24-hr (or less) color processing.

Clubs: Rotary, Lions, Jaycees, Kiwanis, American Women's, and Masonic. Most towns and cities have a chapter of these organizations, and they are delighted to welcome visitors. Cities and towns usually display signs indicating when and where meetings are held.

Rest Rooms: At gas stations, restaurants, and department stores.

Health: Excellent facilities, but generally expensive. If you already subscribe to medical insurance, you will find a small extra premium will cover you for travel.

TRANSPORTATION

If you arrive at New York's Kennedy Airport after a 7½-hour transatlantic flight, remember you are still only halfway to Los Angeles. The United States is truly vast. The most popular method of getting from city to city is by air; no US city is more than a half a day from the next. Every city is served by many airlines, domestic air fares are less expensive than their European equivalents, and there are numerous discounted fares for travel at off-peak hours. If you have time to spare, you will see even more of the country if you travel by car, bus, or train. Although distances are immense, cars are designed for long-distance cruising; the highways are built for it, gasoline is rather expensive, but services on the roads are superb. If you are thinking of renting a car, contact Hertz, Budget, National or Avis or ask the local **Pan Am** office to recommend a rental company. Rates vary, but expect to pay from around $200 per week for a compact (i.e. medium sized by world standards) car; air conditioning, well worth it in summer, costs a little extra. Special foreign-visitor discounts on standard rentals are offered by many rent-a-car companies. Gas works out at around $1.50 per gallon or more, depending on where you buy it. It is well worth contacting Amtrak (the US rail service) to see whether there is a scenic route going your way. From the north-east there are still services to the mid-West and West Coast via Chicago and New Orleans. Indeed, if you have four days to spare, one of the most interesting ways of making the cross-country journey is via The Crescent, which travels south from New York City via the Carolinas and Georgia to New Orleans, where there is an overnight stop, (from $900 double, including sleeping accommodation. You can use the train as your hotel in New Orleans). The train then continues its journey via Houston, San Antonio (Texas), through El Paso to Phoenix and so to Los Angeles where it arrives on the fourth day. There is also a train from Seattle to Los Angeles which makes its way down the western seaboard and is equipped with dome viewing cars. America's Greyhound or Continental Trailways bus services, with routes covering the entire nation, are one of the most economical ways of traveling overland. Tickets can be bought before you leave home or after arrival in the US. There is some difference in the plans offered by the two companies, but in general you can get 7 days of unlimited travel for $175, 15 days for $225, 30 days for $325. Purchase your ticket from a Pan Am travel agent, from Greyhound International Tourist Service Centers, or from Continental Trailways offices.

FOOD AND RESTAURANTS

Walk into a New York coffee shop or snack bar and order a hamburger. First, it will appear in a matter of moments; second, the chances are it will be twice as big as anything you have ever seen on a bun; and third, it will probably come with tempting fresh salads, sauces, or pickles on the side. It may cost twice as much as its European imitations, but it will be more than twice as good and twice as large. And that's typical of American cooking. Americans think big and they eat big. A typical breakfast menu will offer fruit juices, coffee, and "two eggs any style," with bacon, ham, sausages, chops, or griddle cakes and maple syrup. Toast and jelly or jam follows, with as much coffee as you can drink. At many places, breakfasts are discounted for early risers, and can be enjoyed for as little as $1.25. It is impossible to generalize about lunch and dinner menus. Salads, seafood, chicken, and of course, steaks, all rub shoulders on the average menu. Do not order a porterhouse steak unless you are really hungry. With steaks you will appreciate American baked potatoes—slit and with butter, sour cream, chopped bacon, or chives added. Favorite American snacks include hot dogs, clams, cheeseburgers, and Southern fried chicken. Almost anywhere you choose to eat in America, you will be impressed by the cleanliness of the restaurants and snack bars and with the overall attention to service. You will receive either a glass or pitcher of iced water while you are studying the menu. Out in the heartland you can always rely on the famous franchised restaurant chains like Howard Johnson's, where the standards of cooking and ingredients are dependably even. Another American exclusive is the drive-in restaurant. Just pull up in the parking lot, and a waiter or waitress clips a table onto your car windowsill and serves light meals and snacks. The cosmopolitan origins of the American people provide an enormous number of European, Mexican, Japanese, and Chinese restaurants. Certain parts of the US offer some noteworthy cuisine: New England lobsters, Appalachian hog jowl, spicy Southern creole dishes, and Southwestern chili con carne, to name but a few.

DRINKING TIPS

As a result of the inconsistent repeal of prohibition throughout the US, there are curious anomalies in liquor laws which you will discover as you travel from state to state and even from county to county. Generally, the licensing laws are far more lenient than elsewhere—for example, in Britain. And most visitors will find themselves able to drink anywhere at any time. Liquor and beer are favorite American drinks, the former mixed into a variety of exotic and uniquely American cocktails, the latter invariably served chilled and similar in taste to European lagers. The consumption of wine is on the increase, and some of the finer California wines are the equal of European vintages. But to catch the true flavor of American drinking, sample some typical cocktails, such as Sidecars, Manhattans, Whisky Sours, Screwdrivers, or Bloody Marys. Americans generally confine their drinking to their own homes or to cocktail bars located in hotels and restaurants. If you want to buy your own liquor, you can do so at a liquor store, sometimes called a "state store" or "package store." In many states you have to be 21 to purchase alcoholic drinks.

TIME ZONES

The continental United States has four main time zones: Eastern, Central, Mountain, and Pacific Standard time. When it is noon in an East Coast city, it is 11am in a Central Time Zone city, 10am Mountain Time, and 9am Pacific Time. Daylight saving time is observed in almost every state in an effort to conserve energy.

SHOPPING

Stores generally open 9-5 and do not close for lunch. Major department stores in cities have certain evenings when they remain open until 9pm. The "shopping malls" throughout the country offer a complete range of stores catering to all shopping needs. There is a wide range of products and gadgets in almost every US town, often at bargain prices. Good buys include household appliances (check to see if they're compatible with your electricity supply), cottons (sheets, towels, clothing), and musical equipment (tape recorders, records). Good souvenirs include Indian beadwork and leather goods, patchwork quilts, maple sugar products, and traditional silverware.

SPORTS

America's favorite spectator sport is baseball; almost as popular is football, a field game that blends dazzling action and ball passing. Ice hockey is also a prime attraction throughout the US, as is basketball, and soccer is fast gaining in popularity. Tennis and skiing are other favorite pastimes.

THE NORTHEAST AND NEW ENGLAND
NEW YORK

New York, the Empire State, reaches up to Buffalo and Niagara Falls along the Canadian border. The capital is Albany, linked to the vast metropolis of New York City by the huge Hudson River.

New York City

AIRPORT INFORMATION

John F. Kennedy International Airport is 16 miles southeast of midtown Manhattan; airport bus fare $4, taxi fare about $17, minibus fare $8 when arranged through your hotel, limousine about $30; La Guardia Airport is 9 miles east; airport bus fare $3, taxi fare about $14, hotel minibus fare $6, limousine about $25; travel time about 30 minutes. Newark Airport is 13 miles west; taxi fare about $25 plus tolls, hotel minibus fare $7.50, limousine about $40; travel time about one hour.

ACCOMMODATIONS

Although the city is well supplied with hotels, rooms are often scarce. Always arrange through your Travel Agent or Pan Am, or write or wire for a reservation and have it confirmed by the hotel, if possible. Prices given are minimum, and do not include the 8% tax. The following is only a representative list of hotels in New York City:
Rates are in US$ for a double/twin room with bath or shower

Times Square Area:

Abbey Victoria, 7th Avenue at 51st Street—10019 (from $44)
Howard Johnson's Motor Lodge, 851 8th Avenue at 51st Street—10019 (from $48)
Algonquin, 59 W 44th—10036 (from $67)
Ramada Inn, 790 8th Avenue—10019 (from $62)

Pennsylvania Station Area:

Statler Hilton, 7th Avenue and 33rd Street—10001 (from $74)

Hotels on West Side:

Barbizon Plaza, 106 Central Park South—10019 (from $75)
Loews Warwick, 65 West 54th Street—10019 (from $83)
Marriott's Essex House, 160 Central Park South—10019 (from $110)
New York Hilton, 1335 Avenue of the Americas—10019 (from $87)
New York Sheraton, 7th Avenue and 56th Street—10019 (from $84)

Sheraton Center, 811 7th Avenue at 52nd Street—10019 (from $89)

Wellington, 7th Avenue at 55th Street—10019 (from $32)

Hotels on East Side:

Barclay, 111 East 48th Street—10017 (from $106)

Berkshire Place, 21 East 52nd Street—10022 (from $115)

Doral Inn, Lexington Avenue at 49th Street—10022 (from $82)

George Washington, 23rd Street at Lexington Avenue—10010 (from $40)

Gotham, 5th Avenue at 55th Street—10019 (from $75)

Helmsley Palace, 455 Madison Avenue 10022 (from $140)

Lexington, Lexington Avenue and 48th Street—10017 (from $76.50)

Drake, 440 Park Avenue at 56th Street—10022 (from $110)

Pickwick Arms, 230 East 51st Street—10022 (from $36)

Plaza, 5th Avenue at 59th Street—10019 (from $100)

Regency, Park Avenue at 61st Street—10021 (from $105)

Roosevelt, 45 East 45th Street at Madison Avenue—10017 (from $71)

St Regis-Sheraton, 2 East 55th Street at Fifth Avenue—10022 (from $118)

Tudor, 304 East 42nd Street—10017 (from $55)

United Nations Plaza, 1 UN Plaza at 44th Street—10017 (from $125)

Waldorf-Astoria, 301 Park Avenue at East 50th Street—10022 (from $90)

Westbury, Madison Avenue at 69th Street—10021 (from $130)

EATING AND DRINKING

New York is one of the great restaurant cities of the world. If you are going to one of the more important and expensive places, make a telephone reservation. In the following list, "reasonable" means $12 or less per person for dinner without drinks or tips; "moderate" means $25; "expensive" means $50 or more. Very expensive restaurants average more than $75 per person. This list is only a brief sample.

Restaurants serving American specialties, moderately priced, include Ye Olde Dutch Tavern, Paul Revere's Tavern, Red Coach Grill, and Fraunces Tavern, open since 1719 (closed weekends). Among reasonable restaurants: the Coach House, Ye Waverly Inn, Once Upon a Stove, Landmark Tavern, the Steak and Brew restaurants, Downey's, and Weinerwald.

A few of the truly inexpensive "fast food" bars, with many locations each, are Chock Full O'Nuts, Nedick's, Prexy's, Zum Zum (German specialties), McDonald's, Burger King, Kentucky Fried Chicken, Arthur Treacher's Fish & Chips.

Meals with a view, expensive: Windows on the World on the 107th floor of the World Trade Center, and the Rainbow Room. Seafood, moderate to expensive: Gloucester House, Fin 'N Claw. For good steaks, moderate to expensive: The Cattleman, Adam's Rib. Broadway and theatrical atmosphere moderate to expensive: Sardi's, Stage Delicatessen, Backstage. Elaborate décor and menu, moderate-expensive: **Tavern on the Green** in Central Park; very expensive: **Four Seasons, La Caravelle, "21" Club.**

Restaurants by international menus: In Chinatown, reasonable: **Wah Kee, King Wu.** French, moderate: **Café Brittany, Café de France, Café Argenteuil.** Expensive: **La Côte Basque, Le Périgord, Brussels.** Very expensive: **La Caravelle, La Grenouille, Lutèce.** German, moderate: **Luchow's.** Reasonable: **Kleine Konditorei.** Italian, expensive: **Barbetta, La Fortuna.** Moderate: **Alfredo of New York, Gino's, Mamma Leone, San Marino, Piccolo Mondo.** Reasonable: **Eduardo's, Rocco's.** Japanese, moderate: **Benihana** (three locations). Reasonable: **Suehiro.** Jewish: **Lou C. Siegel, Ratner's, Katz's.** Middle Eastern: **Ararat.** Russian, moderate to expensive: **Russian Tea Room.** Latin American and Mexican, moderate: **The Castilian, El Faro, Xochitl.**

ENTERTAINMENT

Nightlife: New York probably has more places to go at night than any other city in the world—and there are all kinds of prices at all kinds of places, including the very sophisticated music spots and bars. Many of the leading hotels have one or more rooms with music, dancing, and entertainment. There are many other attractive places whose descriptions can be found in current copies of the *New Yorker* and *Cue-New York* magazines as well as newspapers. And remember—it is usually a good idea to make reservations.

Smart and expensive: The **Half Note Club** and **Eddie Condon's** feature top name jazz stars, while **Jimmy Ryan's** has Dixieland. The **Rainbow Grill** offers dining, disco-dancing and a floor show with a view of the New York skyline; **Riverboat** offers dining and dancing, but with a post-Civil War Mississippi décor.

Discothèques (some also serve food): New ones open and close frequently, so check locally at the time of your visit. Among the best: **Regine's, Sally's Disco, Le Cocu, Copacabana, Hippopotamus, Shepheard's, Xenon, New York New York, The Mudd Club** and **Thursday's.**

Less expensive, but fun: **Village Gate, Village Vanguard, Boomer's,** and **The Cookery.** These and many other places in Greenwich Village offer both well-known and new talent, all young and lively. Entrance fees range from $2.50 upwards depending on talent, and there is frequently a cover charge of $2 upwards, which may (or may not) include a drink. Some serve liquor, others coffee and soft drinks.

Some popular restaurant-bars, each with a large and interesting clientele, especially late in the evening, include **Elaine's, P.J. Clarke's, Michael's Pub, The Ginger Man** near Lincoln Center, **The Rendezvous,** the **Oak Room** (at the Plaza), **Four Seasons Bar, Chumley's, McSorley's,** and the **John Barleycorn. Charlie Brown's** in the Pan Am building is a popular drinking spot for the business crowd. Many others are found along First, Second, and Third Avenues.

Also recommended (all serve food and drinks): **Charley O's,** at Rockefeller Center; **Brasserie,** a popular medium-priced restaurant; the lobby of the **Algonquin Hotel,** intimate, popular for decades with writers and publishers, especially good after the theater.

Theaters: Seats for Broadway performances may be difficult to get. Theater ticket brokers sell tickets at list prices plus 10% of the total price but the discount ticket sales office at Duffey Square offers tickets for many shows at slightly more than half-price. The seats tend to be toward the sides of theaters, however. The off-Broadway and off-off-Broadway theater movements have grown tremendously and offer easy-to-get seats at generally low prices. They often have Sunday performances too.

Music: The world-renowned **New York Philharmonic** performs in **Avery Fisher Hall** at Lincoln Center. The great **Metropolitan Opera Company** in Lincoln Center presents a full program from September until spring and during the summer gives a series of free performances in New York City's parks. Tickets are increasingly difficult to get, however, and good seats are expensive. Unlike other nations, the US government provides no cultural subsidies. Other free outdoor summer musical events are those at the **72nd Street Bandshell,** Central Park Mall, and the **Damrosch Park Bandshell,** Lincoln Center, and the **Summergarden** series at the **Museum of Modern Art.** The **New York City Ballet** and the **New York City Opera** perform at Lincoln Center's **New York State Theater,** **American Ballet Theater** at the **Metropolitan Opera House.** New York City **Center** presents other important dance and musical events, and the stage of **Carnegie Hall** is home to orchestras, chamber ensembles, and solo artists from around the world.

SHOPPING

The principal retail shopping district extends from 34th to 59th Streets in Manhattan. The big department stores, **Macy's** and **Gimbel's,** are on the lower west side of this district, and **Bloomingdale's** is on the upper east side. In between run Fifth and Madison Avenues, the shopper's and window shopper's heaven. Along Fifth can be found **B. Altman, Lord & Taylor, Bonwit Teller,** and **Saks Fifth Avenue.** Discount department stores include **Mays, Alexander's,** and **Ohrbach's. Bergdorf Goodman** specializes in women's apparel.

FAO Schwartz is famous for toys, and **Hammacher-Schlemmer** is unique for housewares and unusual gadgets. The largest selections of cameras and photographic equipment are at **Willoughby's Camera Stores.** For records and related equipment, **Sam Goody's, The Record Hunter, G. Schirmer Music,** and **Liberty Music Shops** are among the outstanding stores. Among the larger bookshops are **Brentano's, Scribner's, Barnes & Noble, B. Dalton,** and **Doubleday. Rizzoli** and **French and European Publications** are international bookstores. For business and professional books, there is the **McGraw-Hill Book Store.** Among the best stores for jewelry, watches, silver, fine china, and glassware are **Tiffany, Cartier,** and **Georg Jensen.**

WHAT TO SEE

Museums: See the **American Museum of Natural History,** 79th Street and Central Park West (enormous collections of plant and animal life from earliest times to present); **The Cloisters,** Fort Tryon Park (priceless European medieval art in an exquisite setting on the Hudson); the **Frick Collection,** 70th Street and Fifth Avenue (outstanding art treasures in a beautiful building and chamber music concerts in fall); the **Library-Museum of the Performing Arts,** Lincoln Center, Broadway; the **Metropolitan Museum of Art,** 82nd Street and Fifth Avenue (one of the great art museums of the world); the **Museum of American Folk Art,** 49 West 53rd Street (changing displays of folk art from various periods and all areas of the country); the **Guggenheim Museum,** designed by Frank Lloyd Wright, 88th Street and Fifth Avenue (modern art); the **Whitney Museum,** 945 Madison Avenue (contemporary American art); the **Museum of Contemporary Crafts,** 29 West 53rd Street (changing exhibits of crafts and design); the **Museum of Modern Art,** 11 West 53rd Street (one of the best collections in the world). At the **South Street Seaport** on the East River you can board some of the magnificent old ships, now restored, that made New York's harbor the world's busiest.

Some other suggested sights are the **Bronx Zoo** and **Botanical Gardens;** the **Cathedral of St John the Divine; Central Park,** with its many activities (a zoo, a skating rink, Bethesda Fountain, a major meeting ground for young New Yorkers on warm weekends, facilities for plays and concerts), the **City Hall** district and the **Foley Square** courthouse area; **Fort Tryon Park; Chinatown; Columbia University;** the view from the top of the **Empire State Building;** the view from the observatory and roof of the **World Trade Center; Grant's Tomb; Greenwich Village;** the **Hayden Planetarium; Lincoln Center** guided tours; **Ford Foundation Building; Riverside Church; Rockefeller Center; Radio City Music Hall; St Patrick's Cathedral; Statue of Liberty** and **New York Harbor; Times Square** district; **United Nations; Wall Street** district and the **Stock Exchange,** open to the public weekdays 10-3:30; **Washington Square** and **Washington Arch.** "The New York Experience," located beneath the McGraw-Hill building, offers a multimedia history of New York City.

There are **Circle Line** cruises around Manhattan Island many times a day for $7.50 (children under 12, $3.75). From Memorial Day until Labor Day, the **Hudson River Day Line** has one-day trips to Bear Mountain, West Point Military Academy, and Poughkeepsie. For only 25¢ you can take the interesting ferry ride from lower Manhattan to **Staten Island.**

WHERE TO GO NEARBY

North of the city are the **Catskill** and **Adirondack** mountains, filled with hundreds of resorts, inns, hotels—popular both winter and summer. Swimming along the north and south shores of Long Island—from nearby **Jones Beach** to the exclusive private beaches farther out on the island— is a great summer sport for New Yorkers. Bathing along the nearby Jersey shore is also recommended. The **Pocono Mountains** bordering

Pennsylvania are popular for winter sports. The **Finger Lakes** are beautiful. Other interesting trips include the **Cornell University Campus, Ithaca,** with its gorges and waterfalls, and **Lower Enfield State Park.**

SOURCES OF FURTHER INFORMATION

Pan Am in New York City: Pan Am Building, 45th Street and Vanderbilt Avenue; 100 East 42nd Street; Fifth Avenue and 48th Street; 1 East 59th Street; World Trade Center. The reservations telephone number is 973-4000. **New York Convention and Visitors Bureau,** 2 Columbus Circle, New York, NY, answers questions for tourists and visitors and supplies maps and folders. The **New York State Travel Bureau,** 99 Washington Street, Albany, NY 12245, can provide information on areas outside New York City.

MAINE

By far the largest of the New England states, Maine has a rocky coastline, beautiful forests, lakes, and mountains; it is heavily snowbound in winter and a blaze of red and gold in the autumn. The principal cities are all on or near the coast and include **Portland, Lewiston, Bangor,** and **Augusta.** The whole state is very much a recreation area.

NEW HAMPSHIRE AND VERMONT

These two states share a similar terrain and a low population. Consisting mostly of forest, mountains, and green, rolling countryside, they are basically agricultural and produce much of the nation's maple sugar. There are many popular winter ski resorts throughout the area; principal cities are **Manchester** and **Burlington,** respectively.

MASSACHUSETTS

This historic state offers much to the visitor, from the glories of Cape Cod and the charm of Boston to the Berkshires further west. It is one of the most industrialized and densely populated states, but it also has substantial agricultural and dairy lands.

Boston

AIRPORT INFORMATION

Boston is served by regular transatlantic services from Europe (flying time about 7 hours) and by regular scheduled airline services from other US cities. Logan International Airport is 2 miles east of the business district via tunnels under Boston Harbor. Limousine and taxi fares average $2.50 to $6, depending on destination; subway or bus, 50¢. A new "share-of-cab" service to 138 surrounding cities and towns, with a maximum of four passengers per cab, costs each passenger an average of 50% less than the usual fare. Passengers are informed over airport loudspeakers of the destination of cabs that are leaving.

WHAT TO SEE

Boston is a must for any student of America's past, and many European visitors prefer it to any other US city. Most tourists enjoy wandering along the new Freedom Trail, a clearly marked walking tour covering about 1½ miles through the winding, narrow streets of old Boston. The trail passes 15 points of interest, including the **Boston Common,** which was a cow pasture where George Washington's soldiers drilled; **Park Street Church** and **King's Chapel;** the **Granary Burying Ground; Old South Meeting House; Old State House,** overlooking the site of the Boston Massacre; **Faneuil Hall,** often called the "Cradle of Liberty" because it was the site of Revolutionary meetings before the birth of the nation; **Paul Revere House,** home of the patriot immortalized in poetry and legend for warning of the arrival of the "Red Coats" by lantern from the **Old North Church;** and **Copp's Burying Ground.** Also worth visiting are the Federal mansions on **Beacon Hill,** now mostly private clubs, and **Louisburg Square,** for its early American architecture; the **Boston Athenaeum; Bunker Hill Monument,** scene of the decisive first major battle of the Revolution, and the **Boston Navy Yard,** where "Old Ironsides," the **USS Constitution,** is on view daily 10-4. The **Christian Science Mother Church** is impressive; across the street in the Christian Science Publishing Society building is the famous **Mapparium,** a huge hollow replica of the world. Also visit the fabulous **New England Aquarium. Harvard University,** founded in 1636 in nearby Cambridge, is an outstanding university; **Radcliffe College** for women is affiliated with it.

See the **Boston Museum of Fine Arts** (Roman, Greek, Oriental, and Near East art objects); the **Isabella Stewart Gardner Museum** (classic art, furniture); the **Children's Museum** (natural history exhibits); the **Children's Art Center** (contemporary art, children's programs); the **Museum of Sciences.** A wide range of city excursions is available and a two-hour tour costs around $7.

EATING AND ENTERTAINMENT

Local specialties include baked beans and brown bread, codfish balls, lobster and clam dishes, Indian pudding, and New England Boiled Dinner. Among the many fine restaurants are **Modern Gourmet** (rated by Bocuse as the best French restaurant in the US), the **Chart House, Jimmy's Harborside,** the **Locke-Ober** (where the late President John F. Kennedy dined while a Harvard student), the **Union Oyster House,** and the numerous Chinese restaurants in the **Hudson** and **Tyler Streets** district.

The **Boston Symphony Orchestra** performs during the winter season. The **Boston "Pops"** series is held during May and June. Boston is a good theater town, and many Broadway productions are presented at the **Shubert, Wilbur,** and **Colonial** theaters. There are also two "Off-Broadway" theaters and many summer playhouses near Boston. Experimental theater is offered by companies such as **The Theater Company** of Boston and the **Loeb Drama Center** and the **New Theater** in Cambridge.

WHERE TO GO NEARBY

Cape Cod, Martha's Vineyard, and **Nantucket** are fine vacation areas with old New England atmosphere. **Plymouth Rock** is only 37 miles south of Boston, just off State Highway 3. Nine miles north of Boston is the Saugus Ironworks, where Josephs Jenks founded America's iron and steel industry in 1646. **Cape Ann** is a delightful resort area only about 30 miles northeast of Boston. If you take the shore route you will pass through **Salem.** See the **House of Seven Gables, Peabody Museum, Essex Institute** museum, and the fishing town of **Gloucester,** which, with **Rockport** on Cape Ann, is continually painted by artists in summer. At **Old Sturbridge,** an hour's drive southwest of Boston, is a reconstructed early American village. In Western Massachusetts are the rolling hills of the Berkshires, offering music in a perfect setting—particularly the **Tanglewood** festival in Lenox and the **Jacob's Pillow** dance recitals near Lee. The best ski areas in the northeast are in Maine, New Hampshire, Massachusetts, and Vermont. They are only 2-4 hours from Boston.

SOURCES OF FURTHER INFORMATION

Pan Am: 150 Federal Street (tel: 482-6910); **Greater Boston Chamber of Commerce,** 125 High Street, 02110; **Information Center,** Boston Common; **Division of Tourism, Massachusetts Department of Commerce and Development,** 100 Cambridge Street, 02202.

RHODE ISLAND AND CONNECTICUT

Rhode Island, the smallest state and one of the most densely populated, has a rolling, hilly landscape cut by short, swift streams with numerous falls; **Newport** has summer mansions built during the 1890s by many of America's wealthiest families, and **Providence** is the capital. Connecticut, its neighbor to the west, is famous for its rural loveliness yet is highly industrialized; **Hartford** is its capital, and **Yale University** is in **New Haven.**

NEW JERSEY

New Jersey is filled with New York City commuter towns along the banks of the Hudson River, but it has many natural beauties as well. Its northern area lies within the Appalachian Highlands; to the south are a landscape of lowland plains and a string of popular beaches from **Atlantic City** to **Cape May** (see also under "Philadelphia—Where to Go Nearby"). **Princeton University** is famous; the capital of New Jersey is **Trenton.**

PENNSYLVANIA

This state is a progression of mountains and rolling hills, with narrow valleys and vast areas of wooded wilderness. It is called the "Keystone State" because of its position between the northern and southern colonies of early America. The Pennsylvania Dutch country is fascinating.

Philadelphia
AIRPORT INFORMATION

The international airport is 7½ miles southwest of the city. Limousine fare is $4.50; travel time 30 minutes.

WHAT TO SEE

Philadelphia, the fourth-largest city in the US, is in southeastern Pennsylvania on the Delaware and Schuylkill Rivers. It was founded in 1682

by William Penn. The Declaration of Independence and the Constitution of the United States were adopted and signed in Philadelphia. Known as the "City of Brotherly Love," today it is a handsome center of culture, education, science, and religion, as well as business and industry. Sights include **Independence National Historical Park; Fairmount Park; Philadelphia Zoo; Botanic Gardens; Bartram's Garden;** the **Franklin Institute** and **Fels Planetarium,** in the same building; the **Academy of Natural Sciences; Independence Hall** and the **Liberty Bell; Congress Hall,** which housed Congress from 1790-1800; **Betsy Ross House; Christ Church,** founded in 1695, where Washington, Franklin, Morris, and others worshiped; the **US Mint;** the **Old Custom House; Carpenter's Hall; Elfreth's Alley,** the nation's oldest residential street; colonial and Federal mansions in Fairmount Park, open to the public; **Friend's Meeting House; City Hall,** with its observation tower; **Edgar Allan Poe House; USS Olympia,** Commodore Dewey's flagship during the Spanish-American war; and **Old Fort Mifflin,** a well-preserved 18th-century bastion on the banks of the Delaware. Museums include the **Maritime Museum,** the **University Museum, Philadelphia Museum of Art,** the **Atwater Kent Museum** (folk art), the **Academy of Fine Arts** (American art), the **Museum of Art** (Western Art, 14th through 19th centuries), the **Philadelphia Art Alliance** (paintings and sculptures), the **Barnes Foundation** (works by Degas, Seurat and Picasso), the **Rodin Museum** (sculpture), and the **American Wax Museum.**

EATING AND ENTERTAINMENT

Philadelphia is one of the better places for gastronomes in the US with a wide variety of restaurants. Top rated are **Le Bec-Fin** and **La Panetiere, La Truffe** and **La Banane Noise,** all French restaurants. In addition, the city has local specialties which should be sampled; pepper pot (a spicy soup), scrapple (similar to ground sausage-meat), Lancaster smoked hams, and ice creams, softer and more custardy than ordinary ice cream.

The **Philadelphia Orchestra,** one of the best in the US, performs regularly at the **Academy of Music.** In summer there are outdoor concerts at **Robin Hood Dell** in Fairmount Park. The **Spectrum** and **Civic Center** present a varied repertoire of music, including big-name groups, country music stars, folk singers, and jazz. Excellent opportunities for theatergoers include the nearby **Bucks County Playhouse,** one of the nation's finest summer stock theaters.

WHERE TO GO NEARBY

Cherry Hill, 5 miles east of Philadelphia, has swimming, golf, summer theater, and points of historic interest. The **Pocono Mountains** are about 80-95 miles to the north; there are almost 200 vacation resorts in the vicinity of **Stroudsburg.** Other leading resorts are **Atlantic City,** New Jersey, 60 miles southeast; **Ocean City,** New Jersey, 68 miles southeast; **Wildwood,** 90 miles southeast; and **Cape May,** 95 miles southeast. About 35 miles north is **New Hope** in Bucks County, an artists' and writers' colony. The **Pennsylvania Dutch** country is about 40 miles west. **Valley**

Forge, 21 miles northeast of Philadelphia, is where Washington set up headquarters after the battle of Germantown; there is a beautiful park area with museum, historic buildings, and observation tower. **Washington's Crossing State Park,** 30 miles northeast, is the spot where Washington crossed the Delaware River; it has old buildings, grist mills, and historic land markers. **Ralph Stover State Park,** about 38 miles north, has picnic facilities.

SOURCES OF FURTHER INFORMATION

In Philadelphia, **Pan Am** is at 1617 John F. Kennedy Boulevard, (tel: 569-1330); the **Philadelphia Tourist Center** is at 1525 John F. Kennedy Boulevard (tel: 561-1200).

DELAWARE AND THE DISTRICT OF COLUMBIA

A tiny state, Delaware is called "the Diamond State" because of its size and its fertile soil; there is water everywhere, and the state, with **Dover** as its capital, is worth exploring. The District of Columbia is not a "state" in the strictest sense; the inhabitants can vote for their local government and in Presidential elections, but they do not have a voting representative in Congress. Located between Maryland and Virginia, the District is coterminous with the capital of the United States, Washington.

Washington, DC

AIRPORT INFORMATION

National Airport is 4 miles southwest of the city. Bus fare 75¢, subway fare 55¢, taxi fare about $7 for one passenger and 60¢ each additional passenger; travel time 25 minutes. Baltimore-Washington Airport is 22 miles north of the city. Limousine fare is $6; taxi $28-32 depending on destination. Pan Am services from Europe land at Dulles International Airport, 28 miles from downtown Washington. Limousine fare is $4.50 and taxi about $25 depending on destination. Limousine transfer service between Dulles and National Airport costs $4.25.

WHAT TO SEE

When the Founding Fathers were putting together the United States of America, they decided that the new nation's capital should not be located in any one colony but in a district of its own. President George Washington personally selected the site, a 60-square-mile area sandwiched between Virginia and Maryland, which was purchased from private owners. Washington has become a vital world center; it is an impressive national capital, characterized by its broad, tree-lined streets and imposing monuments.

See the Capitol district, including the **Capitol** itself (galleries open to the public when Congress is in session 9-4:30), the **Senate** and **House Office Buildings,** the **Supreme Court Building,** the **Library of Congress.** The **Smithsonian Institution** has been called the US government's "attic," because it's filled with a vast miscellany of objects; children have a wonderful time here. The Declaration of Independence, the Constitution, and the Bill of Rights are displayed in the **National Archives** on Constitution Avenue; open 9am-10pm weekdays and holidays, Sundays 1-10pm. The **Folger Library** has a fine collection of Elizabethan manuscripts and books and a complete collection for the study of Anglo-American civilization. All government departments and offices maintain their own specialized libraries. **Octagon House** is where President and Mrs. Madison lived after the British burned the original Executive Mansion in 1814. See the **Natural History Building**, the **Washington Monument**, and the **White House.** Along the Potomac are such attractions as the **Lincoln Memorial,** beautiful **Potomac Park** and the **Jefferson Memorial.** Visit **Arlington Cemetery** (Tomb of the Unknown Soldier, Kennedy graves), **Christ Church,** and **Washington Masonic Memorial.** Visit also **Mount Vernon,** George Washington's home. A visit to the **Bureau of Printing and Engraving** will show how money and stamps are made.

Museums: The **National Gallery of Art,** one of the outstanding museum buildings of the country, houses a fine collection; others include the **National Collection of Fine Arts** and **National Portrait Gallery,** opened in the massively handsome Old Patent Office Building in 1968; the **Museum of African Art** in the old Frederick Douglass home; the **Phillips Gallery,** painting from El Greco and Goya to the present day; the **Smithsonian Group** (including **Arts and Industries, Museum of Natural History, Smithsonian Building, Freer Gallery, Renwick Gallery**); the **Dumbarton Oaks Museum,** art collection; the **Corcoran Gallery of Art,** painting and sculpture; and the **Hirshhorn Museum and Sculpture Garden.**

Regular theater productions are given at the **National Theater** and the **Arena Stage,** national repertory productions in **Ford's Theater.** There is a **Shakespeare Festival** at the **Sylvan Theater** in summer. The **National Symphony Orchestra** gives regular concerts during the winter season. The new **Kennedy Center** incorporates an opera house, concert hall, movie theater, and the **Eisenhower Theater** for drama.

SOURCES OF FURTHER INFORMATION
Pan Am: 1660 K Street NW (tel: 833-1000). **Convention & Visitors Association,** 1129 20th Street NW, 20036; **International Visitors' Information Service,** 801 19th Street NW, 20006. (tel: 872-8747)

THE SOUTH

The style of life in the Southern and border states is still very different from that in the North more than 100 years after the bitter struggle of the Civil War (1861-65). The climate is warmer and the vegetation more lush, but the contrast goes further; the old traditions, the agriculture of cotton, tobacco, and citrus fruit, the generally slower pace of things—despite the lively and fast-growing cities of Atlanta, Miami, and New Orleans—make for a relaxing and easy atmosphere.

MARYLAND, VIRGINIA, NORTH AND SOUTH CAROLINA
These states were all originally settled in the 17th century, mostly from England, and the influence of that culture is still identifiable. The shared

coastline is an endless expanse of marsh and sand dunes broken by ports and resort towns; it offers fishing and water sports. Inland to the west there are the gorgeous and impressive **Blue Ridge** and **Great Smoky Mountains** of the Appalachian chain, with excellent hunting, hiking, and fishing. The capital cities of these states are, respectively, **Annapolis, Richmond, Raleigh,** and **Columbia.**

GEORGIA AND FLORIDA

The flat coastline of marsh and sand continues into Georgia and Florida; inland, Georgia is an area of pine and hardwood forests and of cypress in the famed **Okefenokee Swamp,** a wildlife refuge. Georgia was the last of the colonies to be settled; its capital is the culturally lively **Atlanta.** Florida has attracted millions to settle, retire, or vacation in its subtropical climate and on its beautiful beaches. Coupled with the establishment of the **Cape Kennedy** space complex, the many resorts and retirement villages sometimes overshadow Florida's great agricultural resources and the fascinating flora and fauna of the **Everglades. Disney World,** near Orlando, is a major vacation destination.

Miami

AIRPORT INFORMATION

Pan Am flights both international and domestic arrive at Miami International Airport, 7 miles northwest of midtown Miami and 12 miles from Miami Beach. Limousine fare into Miami or Miami beach is $3.50. Taxi fares are $8 into Miami, $12-18 to Miami Beach.

WHAT TO SEE

When the Florida boom flared up in the early 1920s, it seemed that everyone in America wanted to own property in Miami. **Miami Beach** is on a slim thread of land nearly 4 miles east of Miami between Biscayne Bay and the Atlantic Ocean. **Collins Avenue,** named after the man who first saw development possibilities in this former mangrove swamp, extends the full length of the beach for about 8 miles. From Bal Harbour southward, Collins Avenue is lined with huge oceanfront hotels and high-rise condominium apartment houses, each trying to be more opulent and stunning than the next. Miami Beach exists to give vacationers and conventioneers the time of their lives.

See the **Lowe Art Gallery** on the University of Miami campus at Coral Gables; the **Bass Museum of Art** in Miami Beach; **Spanish Monastery Cloisters,** North Miami Beach (an 800-year-old building transported from Spain); **Vizcaya** (Italian Renaissance palazzo with antique furnishings and gardens). The new **Omni** development in downtown Miami is a three-block-long complex of shops, restaurants, movie theaters, and a hotel.

Visit the elegant Bal Harbour shops north of Miami Beach and see the views from the causeways to Miami Beach and the yacht marinas, including the huge **Miamarina** off Biscayne Bay at 5th Street. See the art galleries and craft shops in Coconut Grove, the "Miracle Mile" of shops, **Venetian Pool,** and **Hialeah Race Track,** with its flamingoes. The

Museum of Science has exhibits spanning Florida's history from the peninsula's formation to space exploration far in the future. The **Seaquarium** on Rickenbacker Causeway has a performing killer whale, lion fish, porpoises, and seals.

EATING AND ENTERTAINMENT

The better eating places in Miami Beach are fairly expensive, especially in winter, and you cannot get in without a reservation unless you dine very early or after 8:30. The most famous entertainers and dance orchestras in America appear during the winter at Miami Beach hotel nightclubs; check local papers to see which stars are appearing and where. Ballet, opera, and other cultural performances are given in the **Dade County** and **Miami Beach Auditoriums, Gusman Hall,** and **Coconut Grove Playhouse.** There are occasional free concerts in **Bayfront Park Bandshell** in downtown Miami, usually on Friday night.

WHERE TO GO NEARBY

If you have a car, visit the oceanfront towns of **Hollywood** and **Fort Lauderdale** and those from **Delray Beach** to **Palm Beach. Lion Country Safari,** about 17 miles inland from West Palm Beach, is an exciting preserve of African animals. Nearer Miami and served by **Gray Line** tour buses are the popular **Parrot Jungle, Serpentarium, Monkey Jungle,** and **Coral Castle. Everglades National Park** is about 40 miles southwest of Miami. There is at least one racetrack open throughout the year in Greater Miami, and you can watch dog racing and jai-alai. **Fairchild Tropical Garden,** one of the world's finest collections of exotic trees and plants, is about 12 miles south of downtown Miami.

SOURCES OF FURTHER INFORMATION

Pan Am: 110 S.E. 3rd Ave, Miami FL 33131 and 147 Alhambra Circle in Coral Gables (tel: 637-6444); **Miami-Metro Department of Publicity & Tourism,** 499 Biscayne Boulevard, Miami 33132.

WEST VIRGINIA, KENTUCKY, TENNESSEE, AND ALABAMA

Separated from the coastal states by mountains, these states were opened up to settlement later, as the boundaries of the United States moved westward. The abiding characteristic is one of beautiful, rolling hills and forest, with much rich agriculture, principally tobacco, cotton, and corn. This is the land of "moonshine" (as well as excellent legally produced bourbon and rye), of "country music," hunting, and horses, particularly in beautiful, white-fenced Kentucky. **Charleston, Louisville, Nashville,** and **Birmingham** are some of the important cities in these states.

ARKANSAS, LOUISIANA, AND MISSISSIPPI

It was quite natural that the Mississippi River would open up the center of this huge continent. The Spanish traveled the area in 1540, closely followed by the French, who settled here and whose influence is still apparent, particularly in the Delta area of Louisiana where French is the second language. The terrain is generally flat except for the fine vacation highlands of the **Arkansas Ozarks**. The most important cities are **Little Rock, New Orleans,** and **Jackson.**

New Orleans

AIRPORT INFORMATION

Pan Am serves New Orleans International Airport, Moisant Field, which is 11 miles northwest of the city. Limousine fare is $4 and taxi fare about $11; travel time is about 20 minutes.

WHAT TO SEE

New Orleans is in southeastern Louisiana, on the Mississippi River. Famous for its Creole cuisine and fine restaurants, its Old French Quarter, its nightclubs, and its "Dixieland jazz," the city's character is a mixture of sophistication, honky-tonk, and Southern hospitality.

Undoubtedly the greatest attraction for tourists is the **French Quarter,** which still retains much of its original appearance of 250 years ago. Streets are narrow, and buildings have exquisite wrought-iron balconies and railings. There are patios and courtyards and many historic spots. **Bourbon Street** is best at night. **Royal Street** has some delightful shops filled with antiques, and it opens onto lovely courtyards. The **Louisiana Wildlife Museum** at 400 Royal Street houses an unusual collection of birds. See the **Cabildo,** erected in 1795, scene of the signing of the Louisiana Purchase; **Pontalba Apartments,** reputedly the first apartment houses in the US; **Absinthe House,** now a public bar; **Jackson Square,** with **St Louis Cathedral,** the oldest cathedral in the United States; the **Presbytère,** next door, and the many other well-preserved homes of historic New Orleans. Visit the **French Market,** recently renovated, and the adjacent coffee and *beignet* shops for the real flavor of the old city. Interesting, too, are the unusual old cemeteries called **Cities of the Dead,** with the highly decorated tombs of settlers. The new $163 million **Louisiana Superdome** is right in the downtown area, minutes from the French Quarter. Guided tours daily.

Museums include the **New Orleans Museum of Art;** the **Institute of Middle American Research** at Tulane University (Mayan collections); the **State Museum,** in the Cabildo; the **New Orleans Jazz Museum,** 833 Conti Street.

Principal parks: **City Park,** in the northern part of the city, has three public golf courses, many amusements and recreational facilities, and the famous **Duelling Oaks,** where affairs of honor were once settled. **Audubon Park,** in the southwestern part, has a zoo and aquarium.

EATING AND ENTERTAINMENT

New Orleans is one of the most famous cities in the country for food and restaurants; only New York and San Francisco compare with it. Its seafood, particularly shrimp, oysters, crawfish, and crab, is renowned, and local fish such as pompano, trout, and redfish are exceptional. Famous dishes include Oysters Rockefeller (baked with a spinach-herb mixture), *gumbos* (soups thickened with okra), and *café brûlot* (black coffee with spices and liquor). The **French Quarter** has many fine restaurants, of which **Antoine's** and **Brennan's** are probably the most famous. Also worthy of note are the **Embers Gallatoire,** crabmeat specialties, **LeRuth's** on the west bank of the river, the **Caribbean Room** at the Hotel Pontchartrain and the **Rib Room** at the Royal Orleans hotel. There are also pleasant coffee houses serving delicious pastries. In the French Quarter the nightclubs offer informal entertainment, much of it rough and ready and very lively after midnight. Many feature authentic Dixieland jazz. Walk down Bourbon Street—it is famous for its "honky-tonks." Among the many to visit are the **Al Hirt Club** (501 Bourbon), the **809 Club** (500 Bourbon), and **Your Father's Mustache** (426 Bourbon). **Pat O'Briens** (718 St Peter's Street) is also worth a visit for its "hurricane" drinks.

Music activities include concerts by the **New Orleans Philharmonic Symphony Orchestra** and performances by the **New Orleans Opera House Association.** Other musical events are the **Summer Pops** concert series, the **New Orleans Jazz Club** concerts, and musicals and operas put on by the New Orleans Recreation Department. The **Community Concert Association** presents a variety of musicians and dance companies. Some of America's most authentic Dixieland, played by oldtime jazzmen, is available at **Preservation Hall,** in the heart of the French Quarter. The **Beverly Dinner Playhouse,** a supperclub, puts on Broadway plays. The **New Orleans Theater for the Performing Arts** stages plays and musical productions. The **Free Southern Theatre** (1240 Dryades) is the oldest black arts institution in the South.

WHERE TO GO NEARBY

Fort Pike, 30 miles east, and **Fort Macomb,** 20 miles east of town, are old forts that have been restored. **Fontainebleau State Park,** on Lake Pontchartrain, 25 miles north, has water-sport facilities; beautiful **Lakeshore Drive** winds around the lake. **Chalmette National Historical Park,** about 6 miles south of the city, was where General Andrew Jackson defeated the British in 1815. There is a museum on the second floor of the restored **René Beauregard House** overlooking the battlefield. If you want to see the Bayou country, a 5-hour cruise on the *MV Mark Twain* will take you there. Delightful **Longue Vue Gardens** are just a few minutes' drive out of the central business district. For a taste of Louisiana's grand past, visit **Magnolia Lane Plantation** (open Wed-Sun, 1-5pm) or **Rosedown Plantation** in St Francisville, about 110 miles from the city. There are also 7-day cruises on the Mississippi River with stops at historic cities including **Nashville,** Tennessee and **Vicksburg,** Mississippi. Advance reservations may be made through your agent or the Delta Queen Steamboat Company. From 60 to 90 miles east of New Orleans are the Mississippi resorts on the Gulf of Mexico, including **Biloxi, Pass Christian, Gulfport,** and **Long Beach.** Swimming is best in hotel and motel pools.

SOURCES OF FURTHER INFORMATION

Pan Am: 3801 Canal St., New Orleans 70132 (tel: 529-5192); **Greater New Orleans Tourist & Convention Commission,** 334 Royal Street, New Orleans 70130.

THE MIDWEST AND NORTH CENTRAL STATES

Until the second half of the 19th century the Midwest, in terms of population and location in the Union, was very much "The West." The French, the British, and then the Americans all played a role in exploring, settling, and pushing back the frontiers. Central Europeans, Germans, and Slavs flocked to the Midwest in the latter part of the 19th century, and their influence and traditions are evident in the big cities.

OHIO, ILLINOIS, INDIANA, MICHIGAN, IOWA

These states are the industrial and agricultural heartland of America. The Great Lakes and the Ohio and Mississippi river systems are the key to the cities' development and settlement. Life is busy, efficient, and mostly prosperous, with plenty of recreation. There are cornfields and cattle ranches, auto plants, and some of the richest suburbs in the world. Major cities are **Cleveland, Chicago, Indianapolis, Detroit,** and **Des Moines.**

Chicago

AIRPORT INFORMATION

O'Hare International, Chicago's major airport is the country's busiest and is 23 miles northwest of the city. Airport bus fare $2.75; taxi, about $12; city bus or subway, 75¢. Average travel time about 45 minutes.

WHAT TO SEE

Chicago is a gigantic industrial and economic center. Fond of large-scale fairs and shows, proud of its tall buildings, it is typically American in its delight in anything big—commercial buildings, parks, zoos, conventions. The central business and shopping area is called **"The Loop"** because city-bound elevated trains make a complete circle there before heading back. This district contains most of the department stores and office buildings.

Principal sights are the **Adler Planetarium;** the **Art Institute of Chicago; Chicago Academy of Sciences; Chicago Historical Society;** the **Field Museum of Natural History;** the **Museum of Science and Industry;** the **Oriental Institute;** the **Museum of Contemporary Art.** See the 50-foot-high sculpture by Pablo Picasso outside the **Civic Center** and the huge bronze sculpture by Henry Moore at the **University of Chicago.** Chicago was the home of Frank Lloyd Wright and boasts 60 of his works. For a small fee, the public can view the Chicago panorama from two of its skyscrapers (John Hancock Center and the **Sears Tower**—the world's tallest building at 1,454 feet). Other points of interest are the **Buckingham Fountain, Chinatown, Marina City's** twin circular apartment towers on the riverside, the graceful French Renaissance **Wrigley Building,** the blue glass **Lake Point Tower** (70 stories), and the **Merchandise Mart.**

Chicago is justly proud of its 576 public parks. Outstanding are **Grant** and **Jackson Parks, Lincoln Park,** which features a children's zoo, and **Brookfield Zoo,** 14 miles west of downtown Chicago, where animals are shown in natural settings. **Illinois Beach State Park,** about 50 miles north, offers swimming, picnic facilities, stables, hiking trails, and a lodge.

EATING AND ENTERTAINMENT

There are good restaurants in major hotels and many cosmopolitan eateries. **Rush Street** contains one nightclub after another. There is a rich program of concerts, recitals, opera, ballet, and theatrical attractions at the **Civic Opera House,** several theaters, and the renovated and beautiful Louis Sullivan **Auditorium Theater.** There are many fine shops along **North Michigan Avenue,** Chicago's "Magnificent Mile," including **Water Tower Place,** with two department stores and 63 shops, seven restaurants, two movie houses, a theater, and a hotel. Especially outstanding in the Loop is famed **Marshall Field,** a marvelous department store, which has conducted tours Monday to Friday (reservations required).

SOURCES OF FURTHER INFORMATION

Pan Am: 18 South Michigan Avenue, 60603 (tel: 332-4900) and at O'Hare International Airport. **Chicago Convention & Tourism Bureau,** 332 South Michigan Avenue, 60604 (tel: 922-3530).

Detroit

AIRPORT INFORMATION

Detroit Metropolitan Airport, served by Pan Am, is 23 miles southwest of Detroit. Greyhound fare is $3.25, taxi fare about $16, travel time 40 minutes.

WHAT TO SEE

Detroit lies north of the river that shares its name and separates the city from Windsor, Ontario. Downtown Detroit is busy during the day, but nearly deserted after business hours. Although a fairly old city, it has few traditions and considerably more interest in the future than in the past. Much of the population is directly concerned with automobile manufacturing. Cadillac, Ford, and Lincoln Mercury auto production plants offer weekday tours. The **Detroit Institute of Art** displays works by a variety of masters and is open Tuesday through Sunday. The **Henry Ford Museum** and **Greenfield Village,** located about 15 minutes from downtown, display early automobiles, pre-industrial handicrafts, and reconstructions of important historical buildings. History buffs will enjoy the **Fort Wayne Military Museum,** a well-preserved pre-Civil War fort with original barracks and powder magazine.

In an area from 30 to 60 miles northwest of Detroit is a series of recreational parks. The most important are the several **Dodge Brothers'**

State Parks, **Kensington Park,** and **Island Lake** and **Proud Lake** areas. Canada is a 5-minute drive via the auto tunnel or Ambassador Bridge to Ontario.

EATING AND ENTERTAINMENT

Detroit has some fine international restaurants, and there are many lively night spots in the city and nearby suburbs. The **Fisher Theater** in the city's **New Center** area offers pre-Broadway productions and top road-company hits. The University of Detroit's **Performing Arts Center** offers concerts December through May and produces dramas and comedies in the University Theater July-August. The Detroit **Symphony Orchestra** gives a series of concerts during the winter.

SOURCES OF FURTHER INFORMATION

Pan Am: 1231 Washington Boulevard (tel: 354-0500) and at the International Airline Building, Metropolitan Airport; **Michigan Tourist Council,** 300 South Capital Avenue, Lansing MI 48926; **Convention Bureau,** 1400 Book Building, for general tourist information, maps, and booklets about the city; **City of Detroit, Department of Public Information,** City-County Building, Detroit 48226 (tel: 224-3755).

WISCONSIN, MINNESOTA, NORTH AND SOUTH DAKOTA

These states, heavily glaciated long ago, are filled with lakes (Minnesota has over 10,000), hills, lovely rural countryside dotted with dairy farms, and some spectacular gorges and canyons. They are all great vacation spots and marvelous places for the sportsman; **Mount Rushmore** is also an attraction in South Dakota. Principal cities, respectively, are **Milwaukee, Minneapolis, Fargo,** and **Sioux Falls.**

NEBRASKA, KANSAS, AND MISSOURI

Developed mainly in the latter half of the 19th century, these flat states of prairie and forest provide the country with much of its cereal crop. The winters can be cold, the summers hot and dusty. Major cities are **Omaha, Wichita,** and **St Louis.**

THE MOUNTAIN STATES

West of the great plains are the **Rockies** and behind them deserts, then more mountains. They formed a spectacular barrier to settler and explorer, railroad and road engineer.

COLORADO, IDAHO, MONTANA, WYOMING, UTAH, AND NEVADA

Of these states, Colorado, Wyoming, and Montana form possibly the most spectacular mountain vacationland on earth. Winter sports are dramatic, hunting and fishing equally so. **Yellowstone**—the world's first National Park—is an extraordinary combination of mountain, forest, lake, and bubbling geysers, with bear and moose still dominating their habitat. Through all this great wilderness thousands of settlers struggled on the way west. The best known are the Mormons, who eventually settled by the Great Salt Lake and established what is now Utah. The extraordinary cathedral-like red rock formations of **Bryce Canyon,** the great "spires" of **Zion,** and other immense natural sculptures provide an almost mystical experience for the traveler. Major cities include **Denver, Boise, Billings, Cheyenne,** and **Salt Lake City. Nevada,** apart from a few lush areas, is vast, waterless, unyielding desert and mountain, with little to offer except minerals. Yet here are two of the world's greatest centers of gambling and entertainment—the neon-lit fantasyland cities of **Las Vegas** and **Reno.**

THE SOUTHWEST

The superlatives used in describing the scenery of the Mountain States extend also to the Southwest, particularly Arizona and New Mexico. Some of the most ancient Indian settlements have been discovered in this area, and now these states contain nearly all the Indians in the United States. Much early Spanish exploration of the continent was in this area.

ARIZONA AND NEW MEXICO

These two states have amazing landscapes characterized by mountains, great deserts, deep canyons, and endless plains; the climate is quite warm and extremely dry. The scenery is spectacular, most of all in the **Grand Canyon** of Arizona, one of the natural wonders of the world. **Phoenix** and **Albuquerque** are the major cities.

OKLAHOMA AND TEXAS

Oklahoma and Texas are immensely rich in oil and are both characterized by great plains and prairies and big, blue skies. Texas, large enough to be a country in its own right, is one of the wealthiest states because of its oil and its cattle grazing; its size also means that it has four distinct climates and a variety of landscapes. Both states have excellent recreation areas; major cities are **Oklahoma City, Houston,** and **Dallas.**

Houston

AIRPORT INFORMATION

Houston Intercontinental Airport, served by Pan Am, is 17 miles north of the city. Bus fare $5 to hotels; taxi fare, about $27; travel time, 30 minutes.

WHAT TO SEE

Houston is 50 miles northwest of the Gulf of Mexico. The original settlement, founded in 1836, was the first capital of the Republic of Texas, and named in honor of General Sam Houston—first president of the Republic. The discovery of oil at Spindletop nudged Houston into the Petrochemical age, and the building of the **Lyndon B. Johnson Space Center** launched the city into the space age. At JSC, the US trains its astronauts and plans future forays into the universe.

Houston is one of the fastest-growing cities in the US. However, the social tempo is Southwestern—relaxed and friendly. City population 1,554,992; metropolitan area 2,886,962.

Sam Houston Park is a restoration area of early homes and buildings. In contrast is the skyline of today with the **Pennzoil Towers,** designed by Phillip Johnson; **Jesse Jones Hall for the Performing Arts;** the famed **Texas Medical Center,** and the **Astrodome,** an air-conditioned, covered sports arena.

ACCOMMODATIONS

The following is only a representative list of hotels in Houston: Rates are in US$ for an air-conditioned room with bath or shower

Downtown:

Hyatt Regency (654-1234, S$67-70/D$75-85)
Lamar (658-8511, S$48-62/D$58-72)
Sheraton Houston (651-9041, S$57-72/D$72-87)

Medical Center/Midtown Area:

Shamrock Hilton (668-9211, S$54-80/D$70-96)
Warwick (526-1991, S$65-100/D$80-115)

Galleria/Greenway Area:

Inter · Continental Houston (931-1400, opening in 1982)
Inn on the Park-Houston (871-8181, S$75-95/D$95-115)

NASA-Clear Lake Area:

Days Inn-Webster (332-4581, S$24.88/D$28.88)
Holiday Inn NASA (333-2500, S$58-76/D$72-90)
Host International Hotel (443-2310, S$58-62/D$66-70)

RESTAURANTS

Among outstanding Houston restaurants in the downtown area are: **Brennans** and **Hubers** for Louisiana Creole cooking; for French cuisine there is **Le Restaurant de France,** in the Hotel Meridien, and **Maxim's. Massa's** is an old Houston favorite; and for barbecue there's **Otto's,** serving a mild east Texas type of fare. In the Medical Center/Midtown area: **Che,** in the Plaza Hotel, serves continental cuisine. **Alfred's Village** specializes in kosher entrees, sandwiches, and pastries. For seafood try **Kaphan's, Guido's,** or **Pier 21. Red Lion Inn** serves delicious English prime rib. For barbecue, try the **Cellar Door.**

Dallas

AIRPORT INFORMATION

Dallas/Fort Worth Airport is 17 miles from each city. Bus fare $4 to hotels; taxi fare, $18; travel time, 40 minutes.

WHAT TO SEE

The city, founded in 1841, has become an important commercial and banking center. See the Dallas **Museum of Fine Arts; Owens Art Center,**

housing the **Bob Hope Theater;** the **Meadows Museum** of Spanish painting, the 20th-century sculpture court, and the **Pollack Art Galleries.** The
fall **Festival of Art** includes many fine art shows. See also the **Hall of
State, State Fair Grounds, John Neely Bryan's Cabin** on the County Courthouse lawn, the **Convention Center,** homes and scenery along **Turtle
Creek** and around **White Rock Lake,** famed **Neiman-Marcus** department
store, **Southern Methodist University** campus with its Georgian architecture, **Six Flags Over Texas** amusement park on the Dallas-Fort Worth
turnpike, the **Health and Science Museum,** and **Planetarium.**

EATING AND ENTERTAINMENT

Most of the major hotels serve all kinds of drinks and usually have dancing
and quite lavish entertainment. The **Dallas Summer Musicals** are a 12-
week summer season with Broadway stars and shows. The **Dallas Symphony** offers a home season. There are performances by the **Dallas Civic
Opera** and also by the visiting New York Metropolitan Opera Company.
There is a free **Shakespearean Festival** (with Broadway actors) at the
State Fair Bandshell for two weeks in July. The **State Fair of Texas** runs
for 17 days in mid-October. **Dallas Theater Center** is the only public
theater designed by Frank Lloyd Wright.

WHERE TO GO NEARBY

Lake Texoma, 100 miles from the city; **Bonham State Park,** about 105
miles; **Daingerfield State Park,** 138 miles; **Tyler State Park,** 99 miles;
and **Possum Kingdom State Park,** 85 miles.

SOURCES OF FURTHER INFORMATION

Pan Am: 340 North Belt East, Suite 227, Houston (tel: 447-0088); **Houston
Chamber of Commerce,** Chamber of Commerce Building, Houston, TX
77002 (tel: 651-1313); **Dallas Chamber of Commerce,** 1507 Pacific Ave,
Dallas 75201 (tel: 651-1020).

THE PACIFIC COAST

In many ways the Pacific Coast states make up the newest, most modern
part of the United States. Yet this area is also one of the oldest parts of
the country; some of the earliest Spanish settlements in the New World
were here. Then, in the mid-19th century, the promise of gold and fertile
land drew thousands of hopeful immigrants.

WASHINGTON, OREGON, AND CALIFORNIA

These states have mild climates and some of the most spectacular coastline scenery anywhere; inland the fertile soils produce much of the country's produce, timber, and minerals. Majestic mountains bisect the states,
and all three are ideal for the hiker and sportsman. California is the
most populous state in the union, and its residents claim to have the
best of the world's weather. Important cities are, respectively, **Seattle,
Portland,** and **Los Angeles** and **San Francisco.**

Los Angeles

AIRPORT INFORMATION

Los Angeles International Airport, served by Pan Am, is 16 miles from the central business district. Airport bus fare to downtown or Hollywood is $3.50.

WHAT TO SEE

Los Angeles, in southwestern California, sprawls over a vast area, extending 35 miles inland from the Pacific Ocean toward the mountains and the desert, the whole connected by an equally vast system of freeways. It is too varied a city to describe easily, and its population is too mixed for quick classification. Its residents came from all over the United States seeking the sun. To see the old Spanish landmarks, visit **Olvera Street,** with its shops, restaurants, and curiosities; it is most interesting in the evening. **The Old Mission Church,** on North Main Street at Sunset Boulevard, is the oldest in the city.

In central Los Angeles, visit **Chinatown's** shops and bazaars and dine in a Chinese restaurant. See **Little Tokyo,** recently restored as an authentic Japanese community. A few blocks north is **El Pueblo de Los Angeles State Historical Park. Arco Plaza** is downtown's "City Beneath the City"—with ten restaurants and 50 retail shops. The **Civic Center** is beautifully illuminated at night, bounded by the Hollywood Freeway, Grand Avenue, First Street and San Pedro Street. The art galleries on **La Cienega Boulevard** are especially interesting on open-house Monday nights, when Angelenos promenade to view the latest paintings and sculptures. Los Angeles movie and television studios are all interesting. Visit **Universal Studios** on daily 2-hour tours operated aboard candy-striped Glamor-Trams, or take the **Burbank Studios Tour** of Columbia Pictures and Warner Brothers' facilities. Both **CBS** and **NBC** have studio tours, and **Gray Line** has tours past the homes of the stars. The **Farmer's Market** is best visited in the middle of the day; enjoy an outdoor lunch there. See the ports of Los Angeles and Long Beach. **Disneyland,** southeast of Los Angeles in nearby Anaheim, is accessible by car from Los Angeles airport and by Gray Line Tours. Visit **Mann's Chinese Theater** to examine the footprints, handprints, and hoofprints of the stars.

Los Angeles **County Museum of Art,** on Wilshire Boulevard, consists of three pavilions holding up to $25 million worth of art treasures. Its outdoor décor is embellished with fine sculptures and mobiles. **Huntington Art Gallery** has paintings and sculpture; the California **Museum of Science and Industry** includes a space display and the **Shirley Temple Doll Collection.** The **County Museum of Natural History,** Southwest Museum, has Indian handicrafts and relics (closed mid-August to mid-September).

Parks and zoos include **Forest Lawn Memorial Park** in Hollywood Hills, with statues and historical memorials; **Marineland,** 25 miles south at Palos Verdes; and **Griffith Park,** on Mt Hollywood, with a zoo, observatory, planetarium, satellite exhibit, and travel museum.

EATING AND ENTERTAINMENT

There are hundreds of excellent eating places throughout the city and many nightclubs offering expensive dining, dancing, and entertainment.

Principal music groups are the Los Angeles **Philharmonic Orchestra,** the **Light Opera Association,** and the **Hollywood Bowl Association,** which sponsors the famous Symphony Under the Stars in July and August.

The **Music Center,** in the vicinity of the Civic Center, has been hailed as a "perfect" complex of buildings for musical and theatrical productions. Broadway presentations can be seen at the **Dorothy Chandler Pavilion,** the **Mark Taper Forum,** and the **Ahmanson Theater** in the Music Center, or the **Huntington Hartford Theater** in Hollywood.

WHERE TO GO NEARBY

If you enjoy the beach, **Santa Monica,** 15 miles west, and **Malibu Beach,** about 25 miles west, are ideal. **Long Beach,** with 8 miles of wide sandy beaches, now has the *Queen Mary* as a maritime museum and convention center. **Magic Mountain,** about 30 miles north of Los Angeles in Valencia, is a 200-acre amusement center. It boasts a wild collection of thrill rides, including the "Revolution," the world's largest steel rollercoaster with a 360-degree vertical loop. **Santa Barbara,** 92 miles northwest, is a famous resort with a good selection of accommodations. **Lake Arrowhead,** 83 miles east, is another good spot for a vacation. **Palm Springs,** about 125 miles southeast, is a famous winter resort in the desert, but extremely hot during the summer months. To the south of Los Angeles are such small communities as **Newport Beach, Balboa** and **Laguna Beach. La Jolla,** near San Diego, is one of the most beautiful small towns on the coast. **Huntington, Doheny,** and **San Clemente** beaches are all state park areas offering surf bathing and picnicking. **Palomar Mountain State Park,** about 100 miles southeast, has mountain scenery and camping; the **Palomar Observatory** is nearby. **Mount San Jacinto State Park,** 120 miles southeast, is a forest wilderness. **Joshua Tree National Monument,** approximately 160 miles east, has large numbers of Joshua trees, interesting roads, and wild animals. You can also drive through **Lion Country Safari,** a 500-acre preserve 60 miles south of Los Angeles where over 800 imported animals roam free.

SOURCES OF FURTHER INFORMATION

Pan Am: 514 West 6th St., Los Angeles 90017 (tel: 670-7301); **Southern California Visitors' Council,** 705 West Seventh Street, Los Angeles 90017; **Los Angeles Convention and Visitors' Bureau,** 505 South Flower Street, Los Angeles 90071.

San Francisco

AIRPORT INFORMATION

San Francisco International Airport, served by Pan Am, is 16 miles southeast of the city; limousine fare $1.75, taxi fare about $16.

WHAT TO SEE

San Francisco is in the central zone of California, on a peninsula bounded by the Pacific Ocean to the west, the **Golden Gate Bridge** to the north, and San Francisco Bay to the east. Built on hills between the mountains and the sea, San Francisco is a remarkably picturesque and sophisticated town noted for its well-dressed people. It is also a financial and business area of prime importance. Many of its streets have painfully steep gradients, and the weather is often on the damp side, but the loyalty of San Franciscans remains steadfast—and most visitors understand why.

Wandering about San Francisco can be fascinating. A 50¢ fare takes visitors anywhere on bus, cable car, or trolley, and transferring from one to another is possible. Call **Muni Railway** (tel: 673-6864) for directions and schedules. Because the city is compact, it is easy to walk between major points of interest. **Chinatown,** the largest Chinese community outside Asia, is next to the shopping district; the financial district and **Nob Hill** are near both; **North Beach** is just above Fisherman's Wharf, with seafood restaurants, markets, and shops. **Jackson Square,** a handsome collection of pre-Earthquake buildings refurbished as decorator shops, is a delightful five-square-block walk for the architecture enthusiast. Other points of interest include the **Civic Center,** with municipal, state, and federal buildings, the **Public Library,** the **Opera House,** and the **San Francisco Museum of Art,** in the Veteran's Memorial Building; the **M. H. de Young Museum** (the city's largest, housing an extensive collection of European and American art and, in the west wing, the Asian Art Museum, with the Brundage collection); the **California Palace of the Legion of Honor;** the **Maritime Museum;** the **Maritime State Historical Park;** the **World Trade Center;** the **Japan Center;** Telegraph Hill; **Ghirardelli Square;** the **Cannery;** the **Cable Car Barn;** the **Golden Gate Bridge,** connecting San Francisco with Marin County and the Redwood Highway; **Lincoln** and **Golden Gate** parks; the **Cow Palace; Mission Dolores;** the **Presidio,** a US Military reservation; **San Francisco-Oakland Bay Bridge; Stern Memorial Grove;** the **Fountain** on San Francisco's Embarcadero Plaza; the **Exploratorium** at the Palace of Fine Arts; and the new **Bay Area Rapid Transit System** (BART) with sleek, silent, computer-run trains. Take a tour of Alcatraz (leaves from Fisherman's Wharf).

EATING AND ENTERTAINMENT

A gourmet's paradise of seafood restaurants is located on the docks of **Fisherman's Wharf,** port of San Francisco's fishing fleet. **Ghirardelli Square** nearby is a pleasant plaza of restaurants and shops built within the framework of a 19th-century chocolate factory overlooking the bay. Try the local shrimp, Dungeness crabs, California rex sole, abalone, and clams; *cioppino,* a great local favorite, is a cross between soup and a stew, made with several kinds of seafood.

The city has a rich musical life. The San Francisco **Symphony Orchestra** gives concerts from early December to late May. The San Francisco **Opera Company's** fall season lasts 11 weeks beginning in mid-September, with the spring season beginning in February. The **San Francisco Ballet** performs in December and in the spring. The **Midsummer Music Festival** is held at Sigmund Stern Grove for 11 Sunday afternoons beginning in mid-June and extending into August. **Pop Concerts** are held at the Civic Auditorium during July and August. San Francisco is an active theatrical city, with regular professional productions given at the **Curran, Marines' Memorial,** and **Little Fox Theaters. Geary Theater** is the home of the American Conservatory Theater. The universities in the area also have frequent productions.

SHOPPING

Gump's, a famed city landmark, has unusual antiques and art objects. Among other stores are **I. Magnin, Macy's Emporium,** and **Abercrombie and Fitch.** Most stores remain open Monday evenings until 9. Shop in Chinatown; at the **Japan Center;** on Ghirardelli Square, with shops and restaurants; on **Union Square,** heart of the downtown shopping district, where the large department stores and apparel shops are located, and on **Union Street,** for antiques and boutique items; in the **Cannery,** formerly a fruit-packing plant, now housing specialty shops and restaurants; and at **Cost Plus Imports,** on Taylor Street, which carries exotic imports. **Upper Grant Avenue** in North Beach has specialty shops for leather and other handcrafted gift and apparel items. Exquisite home furnishing shops can be found in **Jackson Square.** Good regional buys are needlework, leathercrafts, objects d'art, and Oriental goods.

WHERE TO GO NEARBY

Suggestions for one-day trips include **Mount Tamalpais,** about 20 miles north of the city, or **Point Reyes National Seashore,** about 40 miles north. To the northeast of Mount Tamalpais are **Sonoma** and **Napa Valleys,** with vineyards and wineries. A guide for the wineries, both north and south, is available at the **Convention and Visitors' Bureau.** Much farther north is the redwood region, with the popular **Russian River** and **Clear Lake** resort areas; northeast of this district is **Mount Shasta** and its surrounding lake and streams. Going south from San Francisco along the coast, visit beautiful **Santa Cruz, Monterey Bay,** and **Carmel. San Luis Obispo** is about halfway to Los Angeles. California's many National Parks include **Redwood, Sequoia,** and **Kings Canyon,** with giant trees, and **Lassen Volcanic National Park,** with the only active volcano in the continental US; these should not be missed by any visitor, although they are some distance from San Francisco. San Francisco is a good starting point for an extended trip to beautiful **Yosemite National Park,** to the east, or to **Muir Woods National Monument,** just 17 miles north, comparatively small but magnificent with giant coast redwood trees. There are also 10 state parks within a radius of 150 miles of San Francisco, all with camping facilities. Several are situated along the coast, some in the famous redwood groves.

SOURCES OF FURTHER INFORMATION

Pan Am: 222 Stockton Street, San Francisco 94108 (tel: 397-5200), **Convention and Visitors' Bureau,** Fox Plaza, Market at Hayes Street, San

Francisco 94102; **Visitors' Information Center,** 476 Post Street, San Francisco 94102.

ALASKA

Alaska joined the Union as the 49th and largest state; it is more than twice the size of Texas. Alaska's game makes it a sportsman's paradise, and a profitable industry has developed from it. June through August are the best months to fish for huge trout, pike, and salmon. Hunting safaris bag Dall sheep, moose, deer, caribou, walrus, grizzly bears, and black bears from early August to mid-December.

Fairbanks is Alaska's most lively city. As the "Gateway to the Arctic," it is a popular departure point for excursions to the far north. It is also one of the best centers for Eskimo artifacts of all kinds.

Fort Yukon, just above the Arctic Circle, is a large Athabascan Indian fishing village and trading post. **Nome** still has a lot of Gold Rush atmosphere; you can pan for gold here, even on a short visit, and watch King Island Eskimos make beautiful ivory carvings. The Trans-Alaska oil pipeline runs 789 miles from Prudhoe Bay on the Arctic Ocean to Valdez on the Gulf of Alaska.

HAWAII

Hawaii, the 50th state to join the Union, is the perfect vacation destination, offering an ideal climate, sandy beaches, tropical flowers, hula dancers, and a great welcome. Hawaii is covered extensively in the **Pacific Section** of this Guide.

CENTRAL AND SOUTH AMERICA

CENTRAL AND SOUTH AMERICA
CURRENCY CONVERSION

Country	United States $				United Kingdom £			
	5¢	10¢	50¢	$1	5p	10p	50p	£1
Argentina peso • centavos	159.57	319.14	1595.74	3191.49	334.52	669.06	3345.37	6690.75
Belize dollars • cents	.10	.20	1.00	2.00	.21	.42	2.10	4.19
Bolivia pesos • centavos	1.23	2.45	12.25	24.51	2.58	5.14	25.68	51.38
Brazil cruzeiros • centavos	4.13	8.26	41.32	82.64	8.66	17.32	86.62	173.25
Chile peso • centavos	1.95	3.91	19.53	39.06	4.09	8.20	40.94	81.89
Columbia pesos • centavos	2.66	5.32	26.60	53.19	5.58	11.15	55.77	111.51
Costa Rica colons • centimos	.43	.86	4.29	8.58	.90	1.80	8.99	17.99
Ecuador sucres • centavos	1.51	3.01	15.06	30.12	3.17	6.31	31.57	63.14
El Salvador colons • centavos	.13	.25	1.25	2.50	.27	.52	2.62	5.24
French Guiana francs • centimes	.13	.26	1.28	2.56	.27	.55	2.68	5.37
Guatamala quetzals • centavos	.05	.10	.50	1.00	.10	.21	1.05	2.10
Guyana dollars • cents	.13	.25	1.27	2.55	.27	.52	2.66	5.35
Honduras lempira • centavos	.10	.20	1.00	2.00	.21	.42	2.10	4.19
Mexico pesos • centavos	1.19	2.38	11.90	23.81	2.49	4.99	24.95	49.91
Panama balboa • centesimos	.05	.10	.50	1.00	.10	.21	1.05	2.10
Paraguay guaranis • centimos	6.33	12.66	63.29	126.58	13.27	26.54	132.69	265.37
Peru sols • centavos	20.41	40.82	204.08	408.16	42.79	85.58	427.84	855.68
Suriname guilders • cents	.09	.18	.89	1.79	.19	.38	1.87	3.75
Uruguay pesos • centesimos	.53	1.06	5.32	10.64	1.11	2.22	11.15	22.31
Venezuela bolivars • centimos	.22	.43	2.15	4.31	.46	.90	4.51	9.04

Argentina

WHAT'S SPECIAL

A country as large as this is more like a continent. Region by region, it is as varied and different as the whole of North America with waterfalls that plunge hundreds of feet, soaring Andean peaks, a vast and fertile prairie land known as the "pampas," a top-notch ski resort, right down to frozen Antarctica.

The essence of Argentina is the richness of its land and the proud and independent gaucho who once roamed it. This is really cattle country with herds that total nearly 100 million grazers, but in the capital of Buenos Aires, the people are as sophisticated and cosmopolitan as those in Paris, London, or Rome. Life in Buenos Aires is lived in high style and fine restaurants and night spots abound. The Argentine people are a mixture of European immigrants and Indian stock, and all have one thing in common—a love of sport. Try your hand with them at hunting, fishing, sailing, skiing, mountain climbing, and horseback riding, or see a still-growing glacier, explore the jungle, swim from sandy beaches, or simply sit in the sun.

COUNTRY BRIEFING

Size: 1,072,749 square miles   **Population:** 27,800,000
Capital: Buenos Aires   **Capital Population:** 6,000,000
   Climate: There are vast changes from north to south, but in Buenos Aires it is temperate. There is no rainy season, so you can visit Argentina all the year round; but the best months are October-April.

Weather in Buenos Aires: Lat S34°35'; Alt 89 ft

Temp (°F)	Jan	Feb	Mar	Apr	May	Jun	Jul	Aug	Sep	Oct	Nov	Dec
Av Low	63°	63°	60°	53°	47°	41°	42°	43°	46°	50°	56°	61°
Av High	83°	83°	79°	72°	64°	57°	57°	60°	64°	69°	76°	82°
Days no rain	24	22	24	22	24	23	23	22	22	22	21	23

Government: A Federal republic, but under a military junta since 1976.

Language: Spanish is the main language, but English, French, Italian, and German are spoken.

Religion: Predominantly Roman Catholic, churches of all denominations. There are several English-speaking churches in Buenos Aires.

Currency: Peso.

	1,000 pesos	2,000 pesos	3,000 pesos	5,000 pesos	7,500 pesos	10,000 pesos	20,000 pesos	50,000 pesos
US (dollars, cents)	.31	.63	.94	1.57	2.36	3.13	6.27	15.67
UK (pounds, pence)	.15	.30	.45	.75	1.13	1.50	3.00	7.49

Public Holidays:

New Year's Day, 1 Jan
Holy Thursday
Good Friday
Labor Day, 1 May
National Anniversary of the Cabildo
   Abierto 1810, 25 May
Flag Day, 20 June
Corpus Christi, June

Independence Day, 9 July
Anniversary of San Martin's
   Death, 17 Aug
Columbus Day (Dia de la Raza),
   12 Oct
Immaculate Conception, 8 Dec
Christmas Day, 25 Dec

HOW TO GET THERE

Flying time to Buenos Aires, Ezeiza Airport from New York is 10¼ hours; from Miami, 8 hours; from Rio de Janeiro 3 hours. Time in Argentina: GMT−3.

REQUIREMENTS FOR ENTRY AND CUSTOMS REGULATIONS

Passport (should be carried at all times in Argentina). Visas are not required for citizens of the US, Canada, Latin American countries (except Cuba), Japan, and most European countries. Nationals of other countries should check with the nearest Argentinian consular office. Vaccinations against smallpox, cholera, and yellow fever required only when coming from infected areas. Cash and travelers' checks can be changed at the International Airport of Ezeiza (around the clock service), at any bank (open Mon-Fri 10am-4pm; not open weekends) or Casas de Cambio (exchange shops which are open Mon-Fri 10am-3pm and Sat 9am-12). The Casa de Cambio gives the best exchange rate. It is sometimes difficult to change currency in some of the smaller towns. Some hotels provide an exchange service. You can currently change as much money as you want. Currency may be changed back to dollars at banking and exchange institutions provided you have receipts showing that the original currency exchange was made at a bank or authorized exchange agency. No duties are charged on clothing, personal effects, etc. Cameras, typewriters, radios, etc., duty free if they have been used and only one of each is carried. Also duty free are 2 liters of alcohol, 400 cigarettes, 50 cigars, and about 11 lbs of foodstuff; perfume for personal use only; gifts up to a value of US$500. These allowances do not apply to tourists arriving from neighboring countries. Animals with a certified bill of health are allowed into the country.

AIRPORT INFORMATION

Ezeiza International Airport, Buenos Aires, is 26 miles from the city center. Buses meet every arrival and go to Plaza Once, a short cab ride from the city center; fare is US$14—no charge for children. Taxis and limousines called *remises* are also available; fare at press time is about US$45. Ordinary taxis can take passengers to the airport, but are not allowed to pick them up there.

The local bus service is slow and may not accept luggage. There is no arrival tax. At Ezeiza and other airports, departure tax for international flights is 15,000 pesos (about US$3) and 2,000 pesos for domestic flights. The duty-free shop is open 24 hours a day.

ACCOMMODATIONS

There is no central hotel reservation service and no off-season rate. Many hotels charge 24% service and 16% tax on top of the price of accommodations. If you are staying for a long visit, you can rent an efficiency apartment. The best way to do this is through advertisements in a local newspaper. Hotels in Buenos Aires:

Rates are in US$ for a double/twin room with bath or shower

Buenos Aires Bauen, Callao 350 (from $112)

Buenos Aires Sheraton, San Martin 1225 (from $120)

City, Bolivar 160 (from $55)

Claridge, Tucumán 535 (from $150)

Crillón, Sante Fé 796 (from $60)

Elevage Hotel, Maipu 960 (from $189)

Gran Hotel Buenos Aires, Marcelo T. de Alvear 767 (from $72)

Gran Hotel Internacional de Ezeiza, Ezeiza International Airport, 26 miles from city center (from $70)

Italia Romanelli, Reconquista 647 (from $45)

Libertador, Cordoba Maipu 1054 (from $90)

Plaza, Florida 1005 (from $126)

Presidente, Cerrito 850 (from $52BB)

Regidor, Tucumán 451 (from $90)

San Antonio, Paraguay 372 (from $23)

Sussex, Tucumán 572 (from $37)

Unless otherwise indicated, all of the above hotels are in the center of Buenos Aires.

USEFUL INFORMATION

Banks: Open Mon-Fri, 10-4; most closed weekends. Very few banks outside the big cities. Currency and travelers' checks can be changed at banks and authorized agencies (travel agent or money exchange).

Mail: Letters can be mailed at hotels or post offices. Post offices open 8-8 Mon-Fri, 8-2 Sat. International telegrams can be sent 24 hours a day from the central Post Office (Sarimento and Leandro N. Alem) or by calling 33-9251.

Telephone Tips: Phones are found in shops, cafés, bars, and Calle Florida. Tokens (fichas) needed to operate the phones can be bought from nearby shops or kiosks (listed on phone). Useful numbers in Buenos Aires:

Pan Am 45-0111	Police 101
Airport Information 620-0011	Fire 38-2222
Tourist Information 32-2232	Urgent medical attention 34-4001
Directories 110	
Time 113	Canadian Embassy 32-9081/88
US Embassy 774-7611	
UK Consulate 80-7071/9	Australian Embassy 32-6841/2574
Weather 31-0144	

Newspapers: English-language newspapers and magazines are available in Buenos Aires. The local newspaper in English is the *Buenos Aires Herald.*

Tipping: A service charge of about 22% is usually included in the bill or check, but something extra is expected—about 15% of a bill up to 30,000 pesos, otherwise 10%. Tip taxi drivers 10% of fare; porters, 10,000 pesos for 1 to 3 pieces of baggage, 20,000 pesos for over 3 pieces; hotel porter, 5,000 pesos; chambermaid, 7,500 pesos; washroom attendant, 3,000 pesos; hairdressers about 20-25% of the bill. It is customary to tip movie and theater ushers about 5,000 pesos. A tour guide is tipped about 5,000 pesos per person.

Electricity: 220 volts 60 cycles AC.

Laundry: Dry-cleaning and laundry services are good (dry-cleaning a suit, 40,000 pesos; laundering a shirt, 10,000 pesos).

Hairdressing: First-class hotels have salons (shampoo and set from 60,000 pesos; man's haircut from 50,000 pesos).

Photography: Color and black and white film available. Color slide film costs US$11 for a 36-exposure roll, and black and white costs US$6 for a 36-exposure roll. It takes 1-3 weeks to have color films developed.

Clubs: Rotary International; Lions; Kiwanis; Jaycees.

Babysitting: Hotels will usually oblige.

Rest Rooms: No public facilities in streets, but in bars, cafés, stores, restaurants, and movie theaters. *Bano de Damas* for women; men, *Bano de Caballeros.*

Health: Excellent British hospital in Buenos Aires (Perdriel 74). Some doctors and dentists speak English. Pharmaceuticals are relatively inexpensive. Drinking water safe in large cities. Bottled mineral water is available.

TRANSPORTATION

Buenos Aires has a good, inexpensive public transport system. Buses are cheap but usually crowded and operate 24 hours a day. Five subway lines serve downtown and a part of the metropolitan area until midnight—inexpensive. Trains serve Greater Buenos Aires with good, regular service. Some 26,000 taxis can be hailed or picked up at taxi "stops." Fares are the price shown on the meter unless traveling outside the city limits. Some cab drivers charge a small amount for each piece of luggage, but many don't.

Traffic is hectic. You can rent small European-type cars. An excellent railroad service links main cities and key resorts. There are four mainline stations in Buenos Aires. The three domestic airline services are Aerolineas Argentinas, all major cities; Austral Lineas Aéreas, major cities in the south; and LADE (Lineas Aéreas del Estado), smaller cities of the south.

FOOD AND RESTAURANTS

Argentina is beef country, and you will find the famous pampa-bred steaks on every menu. For an Argentine, the main meal would have five courses: hors d'oeuvres, soup, fish or meat, salad, dessert. For the visitor, three courses would usually be enough. International cuisine is readily available in major cities, but here are some of the local dishes: *parrillada,* a full course of mixed barbecued meats; *empanadas,* a sort of meat pie that you eat with your fingers, made of meat with raisins, hard-boiled eggs, and olives; *bife de lomo,* an excellent cut of meat and similar to filet mignon, well worth a try; *bife a caballo,* steak topped with fried eggs; *chorizo,* a spiced sausage; *churrasco,* a thick broiled beef steak; *tira de asado,* barbecued ribs; *puchero,* a stew; *puchero de gallina,* chicken sausages, chickpeas, potatoes, squash, and bacon all cooked together; *arroz con pollo,* a delicious heap of rice, chicken, eggs, vegetables, and local sauce. For a dessert try *dulce de leche,* a sweet caramel custard, or *panqueques,* a very inexpensive crepe suzette.

Meal times are standard, though dinner is usually served rather late, about 9-10pm. Prices are average to high; dinner for one at an expensive restaurant costs 100-150,000 pesos; at a medium-priced restaurant, 50-100,000 pesos; at an inexpensive restaurant, 20-50,000 pesos. Hotel restaurants with good international cuisine are at the **Claridge** (tel: 32-4001) and the **Plaza** (tel: 31-5011). For a choice of both local and international cuisine: **El Aljibe** (very expensive) in the Sheraton Hotel; **El Repecho de San Telmo** (Carlos Calvo 242—tel: 34-4473) in the old Spanish-colonial style—but book in advance. Other excellent typical restaurants are **La Cabana** (Entre Rios 436) and **Meson Espanol** (Av. Caseros 1750)—folk music provided at the latter. Also worth noting is **La Estancia** (Lavalle 941) where typical *asados* are served by waiters in gaucho dress. For French cuisine—but still at the expensive end of the price scale—try **Au Bec Fin** (Arenales 1223—tel: 44-7025); **La Casserolla** (Carlos Calvo 2000—tel: 23-3048). You can eat economically at **El Palacio de la Papa Frita** (Lavalle 735), open 24 hours; **Los Inmortales** (Lavalle 746 and several other locations) for Creole dishes, *empanadas,* and *asado;* **El Ceibal** (Avenida Cabildo 1421, and several other locations) for Creole food; **El Colonial** (Marcelo T. de Alvear 1202) for local cuisine. Visitors should beware of the 23% *laudo* (tax) which can turn an inexpensive meal into an expensive one. Some restaurants add the tax on, while others include it in the menu prices.

DRINKING TIPS
Argentina produces many excellent wines, a fact that is not well known outside South America because, until recently, little has been exported. Wine experts recommend the Cabernet Sauvignon; in general, the reds are considered to be superior to the whites. Restaurants serve their own house wine together with a bottle of sparkling mineral water. Also available are local beers, liqueurs, and champagnes. Imported wine and Scotch are expensive. A dry martini is called a *clarito.* Women are welcome in all bars.

ENTERTAINMENT
There are 125 movie houses in Buenos Aires, mostly centered on Lavalle and Corrientes avenues. Foreign films have Spanish subtitles. Performance times are generally at 1, 4, 6, 8, and 10pm, with late-night showings at midnight on Saturdays. The **Teatro Colón** houses the **National Symphony Orchestra** and its own opera and ballet companies. Most seasons start on 25 May with a gala performance attended by the President and government ministers. Internationally famous conductors, singers, and dancers make guest appearances throughout the season.

Serious music, often derived from early folk music, is played everywhere. And Argentina is the home of the tango. The legitimate theaters are closed for summer, and performances are in Spanish. There are also equivalents of off-Broadway experimental theaters.

Buenos Aires comes to life at night with discothèques, nightclubs, and folk entertainment. It all begins at 11pm. Take off for the **Mau-Mau** (Arroyo 866), the best discothèque in town, or the **Afrika** (Avenida Alvear 1885) for good beat bands. The **Michelangelo** has three different shows— tango, folk, and beat—held in three caves. To see the top tango artists go to the **Tango Norte.** For folk try **Poncho Negro, El Rancho de Ocho-A, La Casa de Herran, Figueroa Reyes, Bwana,** or **El Palo Borracho,** all with typical Argentine music and dances. Nightclubs with stage shows are **Karim** (C. Pellegrini 1143), **Karina** (Corrientes 636), and **King Club** (Cordoba 937). There are conducted night-spot tours.

SHOPPING
Stores are open 9-7:30 (some close for lunch) Mon-Fri, 9-1 Sat; closed Sun. The shops nearly all specialize in one particular kind of merchandise, or are sophisticated boutiques. An exception is the department store **Harrods** (Calle Florida). Best buys are leather goods and furs, alligator bags, and handmade shoes to match, although these items are no longer as cheap as they once were. Nutria is a good fur buy, and so are vicuña

and guanaco fur made up as ponchos, and jackets of antelope suede. Souvenir treasures might include a silver bowl, used for drinking yerba tea, which is the national drink, and the silver *bombilla* or drinking tube that goes with it; rugs and carpets, guitars, and, just for fun, a pair of *bombachas*, the baggy trousers worn by gauchos.

Calle Florida is a fashionable pedestrians-only shopping area where people watching is just as popular as window shopping. For leather goods, **Michel's** (Florida 787) has a good selection of excellent quality; **Le Faune** (Florida 791) features fine women's handbags and belts; the **El Trebel** shops, also on Calle Florida, have high fashion leather items. Wood carving is a highly developed art form in Argentina, and figurines and sculptures can be found at **La Estancia** (Florida 681); also good for handcrafts are **Guayruruo** (Charcas 515) and **The Casa Coya** (Sarmiento 999). Many other fine shops are along **Avenida Santa Fé.** Furs are in **Suipacha Street,** rugs and carpets in **Viamonte Street.** Bargaining possibilities and discounts can vary from store to store. For small gifts (about US$15-20) look for onyx carvings; alligator wallets, belts, and gloves; ponchos and woolen goods. There is a flea market in Buenos Aires at the **Plaza Dorrego** in San Telmo, open Sundays only from 8am-5pm and closed in January. Buenos Aires is also a center for the gems and silver in South America. **H Stern** and **Ricciardi** in the Plaza have Brazilian precious stones and jewelry.

SPORTS

National sports, apart from game hunting and trout and salmon fishing, are soccer *(futbol)*, boxing, horse racing, polo, and *pato*—a kind of basketball played on horseback. You can ride, play golf or tennis, swim, or surf. Guest cards to the clubs can be arranged (contact the Pan Am office). There is horse racing at the **Hipodromo de Palermo** and at the grass-turfed **Jockey Club** in **San Isidro,** and polo is played at **Hurlingham, Palermo,** and **Los Tortugas Country Club.** Horse shows are an important social event. Soccer games generate enormous enthusiasm, with 18 major stadiums in Buenos Aires alone. Games are usually on Sundays, with tickets ranging from US$5-50, generally available the day of the game.

WHAT TO SEE

In Buenos Aires, a good way to sight-see is to take a conducted tour. Buenos Aires Tur (Lavalle 1444) offers good tours with English-speaking guides on modern, double-decker buses. For those who prefer to sight-see independently, guides sometimes advertise in the "Herald." You should see the **Plaza de Mayo,** an important site in the tradition and history of Argentina. On one side is the **Casa Rosada** (the pink government house), on a second is the **Cabildo,** the old city hall with museum where the independence movement was planned, and on a third side is the **Cathedral,** where the remains of General Jose de San Martin, Argentina's liberator, rests. Buenos Aires was first founded at the Boca, the old waterfront district where Italian and seafood restaurants abound. Sometimes referred to as Little Italy, it is colorful and lively. Rent a horse-drawn carriage for a ride around **Palermo Park,** which has everything from rose gardens to a planetarium and a racecourse. Near the park are the **Botanical Gardens** and the **Zoo.** The **National Museum of Fine Arts,** one of the country's largest museums, houses a collection of paintings and sculptures by world masters as well as the major works of Argentine artists. Other museums worth visiting are the **National History Museum,** which shows Argentine history in objects, documents, and furniture (Defensa 1600, tel: 26-4588) and the **Argentine Museum of Natural Science** (Angel Gallardo 490, tel: 812-5243). You can take a boat trip to **El Tigre.** The delta is a huge network of streams and canals, creating hundreds of small islands, many of which are built up with luxury villas and unusual buildings rising from the water. Don't miss the chance to visit a cattle ranch *(estancia)*—many are within two hours of Buenos Aires by car or tour bus. Check with any tourism agency. Make sure that you see some Argentine handcraft fairs. You will see work done in leather, onyx, etc. These are to be found in various parks around the city. On Saturday or Sunday, between 10am and 6pm, try **Plaza de Vte. Lopez** (Calle Vincente Lopez between Junin and J.E. Uriburu), **Plaza Italia** (on the "D" subway line), or **Parque Lezama** (Calle Brazil between Defensa and Balcarce). The **Feria San Pedro Telmo** is an antique fair held in Plaza Dorrego on Sundays between 10am and 5pm.

There are various ways to see Argentina. Tours to all key resorts can be arranged through any of the many tourist agencies in the city center. You will find the **National Tourist Information Centre** (Santa Fe 883, tel: 32-2232) very helpful. English is spoken there. For those who have more time to spend, there are two plans made available to tourists by the government. The first is the **"Visit Argentina Tarriff"** which lasts 30 days and allows the traveler to see the whole country by plane. This tarriff is not available during January, February, July, or December. Minors are given discounts. The only conditions stipulated are no point may be visited twice, the ticket is not refundable, and only one airline may be used (either Aerolineas Argentinas or Austral). It is possible to trade off unused sections of your ticket for others if you change your itinerary. The second plan available is the **Argenpass,** a rail plan that permits travel anywhere in Argentina. Minors are charged at 50% of the full fare, and additional charges are made for first-class travel and the use of sleeping compartments. The pass is not transferable and is valid for one person for a duration of 20 days, two months, or three months. For slightly more, one can purchase the **"Amerail Pass"** which permits travel in Uruguay, Argentina, Brazil, Chile, Bolivia, and Paraguay. For railroad information contact C.I.F.A. office in Galeria Pacifica, Florida 753.

NORTH ARGENTINA

These are the strongly traditional provinces of the country. In the west, in the provinces of **Jujuy, Salta,** and **Tucumán,** is the beautiful, wild mountain country that was once the home of the early Inca civilization.

Many years later, in the fight for independence, it was the place where a small group of gaucho soldiers held back the invading Spanish army. On June 16, in **Salta**, a gaucho parade marches around the Guemes statue (set up to commemorate the battle). Locals play folk music with their *pincullos, charangos,* and *guitarras.* A Mardi Gras is held on Shrove Tuesday. A one-way plane ticket to Salta costs US$85. Accommodations include **Moteles Huacio,** Cas. Correo 154 (from US$18), **Salta Hotel,** Calle Buenos Aires (from US$18), and **Victoria Plaza Hotel,** Zuviria 16 (from US$15). Argentina's national independence was proclaimed in Tucumán, in a house that has been preserved in the city. A vivid, 50-minute description of the times of Argentine independence has been achieved through electronic means in a "Light and Sound Spectacle" in Tucumán. It relates, through the use of lights and music, the preparation of the 1816 Congress, the battles against the Spanish army and its eventual defeat in the **Battle of Tucumán,** and the signing of the Independence Act. Tickets are available at 24 de September St. every day. There are also many colonial buildings left over from the Spanish era to be seen in the streets. The province of **Jujuy** is noted for its spectacular scenery. **Hamahuaca** is noted for its natural beauty and its historic Indian past. At **Pucara de Tilcara** there is an ancient Indian fortress with relics of fighting days gone by. This is also the big game-hunting region.

In the northeast, 1,300 miles from Buenos Aires and deep into the jungle on the Brazilian border, is **Iguazú Falls.** The journey is 5½ hours by plane (or 6 days by boat). The falls are one of the most important sights in South America, greater than either Niagara or Victoria. Twelve miles from the point where the Iguazú River joins the Paraná is an amphitheater in the jungle measuring nearly 10,000 feet by 221 feet. It is here the river starts its race over the huge rocks to create a cascade of 275 falls. The spray rises 100 feet and bursts into rainbows filled with multicolored birds. A few miles downstream, in the middle of the jungle but in a space of 25 acres, stand the ruins of **San Ignacio,** a Jesuit mission set up to teach Catholicism to the natives. There are the remains of the old church, the priests' college, and the homes built for the Indians. The **Hotel Internacional Iguazú** is built right on the water's edge (from US$33 Sun-Wed, US$41.50 Thurs-Sat; from US$66 for a room with a view of the falls). Other hotels are available in Puerto Iguazú, 14 miles from the falls. The hotels **Esturion** and **El Libertador** are recommended. A bus service takes passengers to and from the falls regularly. A one-way plane ticket from Buenos Aires to Puerto Iguazú costs US$85. Planes are sometimes booked two to three weeks ahead. Four- and five-day tours are run by tourist agencies in Buenos Aires. Tours in all price ranges are available.

The Littoral Region (Corrientes, Entre Rios, and Santa Fé): This region is linked by the Paraná River, which runs along the three provinces. It is the land of the *dorado,* a fierce fighting fish. They usually weigh 25 to 35 pounds, but there have been catches of up to 55 pounds. The **International Dorado Fishing Tournament** is held annually in August at **Paso de la Patria** in the province of **Corrientes,** which is also the land of Indian myths. The people there speak the Guarani language as well as Spanish.

Entre Rios: This is a province of great beauty. The provincial capital **Paraná** is on the river, a city with a great cultural life. To the west of Entre Rios is the province of **Santa Fé.** The large, modern, and busy port of **Rosario** is on the right bank of the Paraná River and is the center of a thriving commercial and industrial region. The city has wide boulevards and magnificent theaters. It is also the place where General Manuel Belgrano hoisted the national flag for the first time, and there is a monument to commemorate the event. Hotels in the city of Corrientes are **Gran Hotel Corrientes,** Carlos Pellegrini—tel: 1058 (from US$33), and the **Hotel Provincial de Turismo,** Avenida Costanera y Entre Rios (from US$43).

Córdoba: The name both of a city and a province. The city was founded almost four centuries ago and has colonial architecture; towers, bell-towers, and churches of great beauty surround the extraordinary and majestic **Cathedral.** The **University** was founded in 1613, and the **Historical and Colonial Museum** is in the former Viceroy's House. Córdoba City is one hour by air from Buenos Aires and costs US$85. Hotels are **Crillón,** Rivadavia 85 (from US$70 double); and **Sussex,** Buenos Aires 59 (from US$55 double). The "Sierras," a lake-studded hilly region surrounding the city of Córdoba, is a popular vacation area, with boating, swimming, horseback riding, and hiking.

The **Cuyo Provinces** (San Luis, San Juan, Mendoza): Cuyo is a picturesque region at the foot of the Andes mountains in west Argentina. It extends from the plains of San Luis to the peaks of San Juan and Mendoza. As the visitor climbs up to a height of 21,000 feet, the scenery changes to the snow-covered peaks of the **Aconcagua.** There, high up in the Andes, is the monument to Christ the Redeemer, and nearby the famous **Puente del Inca** (Inca Bridge), a natural stone arch 150 feet long and 90 feet high. There are ski runs and skating rinks, making this a popular place for winter sports, and there is an annual **Snow Festival.** In Mendoza a winter sports center is **Las Cuevas.**

The fertile lands below the Andes make this the wine-growing region of Argentina. The world-famous **Vintage Festival** is held in March in **Mendoza,** a beautifully laid-out modern city. There are a number of wine-tasting tours of the local vineyards, and Argentine red wines have won numerous international prizes. Hotels are the **Plaza,** Chile 1124 (from US$55 double) and the **Balbi,** Las Heras 328/40 (from US$38 double).

SOUTHERN ARGENTINA

Mar del Plata (The Atlantic Beaches), 250 miles east of Buenos Aires on the Atlantic coast. This is the leading beach resort and the Riviera of Argentina. It has the largest casino in the world, apartments for rent, and some 1,500 hotels. The visitor can rent a cabana at **Bristol Beach, St James,** or the private **Playa Grande.** This is a great area for fishing, and the seafood is excellent. You can ride or make the trip to the *estancia,* the horse-breeding ranches at **Chapadmalal** and **Ojo de Agua.** Further south there is the beach resort of **Necochéa,** and inland is **Tandil,** in the cool of the hills. **Mar del Plata** is known as "The Happy City," and has the largest casino in the world. The season is late December through March. A convenient way to travel is the four-hour train ride aboard the **Marplatense,** which runs between Buenos Aires and Mar del Plata. Among hotels there are the **Benedetti,** Avenida Colón 2198 (from US$60); **Chateau Frontenac,** Alvear 2010 with an oceanfront location (from US$75); and **Gran Hotel Provincial,** Blvd Maritimo 2300, also beachfront (from US$85).

The Southern Lakes (Neuquén, Rio Negro, Chubut, Santa Cruz): Fly to **San Carlos de Bariloche,** the center for winter sports in this lake and mountain area. It is in the **Nahuel Huapi National Park,** an area that is divided into distinct regions. **Lake Nahuel Huapi** covers an area of 300 square miles and is at an altitude of 2,000 feet, surrounded by mountains rising to 12,000 feet. During the winter season (July to October) there is good skiing. The international competitions during the **Ski Festival** are followed by the **Snow Festival.** On lake Nahuel Huapi there is densely forested **Victoria Island.** One popular place on the lake is the area of flowers and plants of every kind that fills the peninsula of **Llao-Llao.**

Bariloche: Famous as a region for magnificent trout and salmon fishing. The best time to visit is from mid-November to mid-April. There is a special fishing area at **Lake Traful,** 4 hours from Bariloche. Fishing licenses are available in town at the Provincial Tourist Office, Centro Civico, Mitre 213, 2nd floor, or at the National Park Office, Santa Fe 690 in Buenos Aires. From Bariloche, it is possible to go sailing, walking, mountaineering (guides are available at tour agencies), skiing, fishing, and swimming. Hotels in Bariloche include **Bariloche Ski Hotel,** San Martin 352 (from US$56); **El Casco** (from US$85); **Tres Reyes** (from US$60); and **Tunquelen** (from US$90).

Take a boat trip to **Puerto Blest** at the end of a 10-mile fjord. You will pass **Cascada Blanca,** a huge waterfall fed by the great glaciers. From Puerto Blest you can go to **Puerto Alegre** on the Chilean border and continue into Chile, or return to Bariloche and Buenos Aires.

Hunting enthusiasts will find Bariloche a great location, and the season—for stag, Indian black buck, deer, boar, and geese, dove, and duck—runs from March to July. Hunting and fishing permits are readily obtainable.

Tierra del Fuego (Antarctica): The capital of the territory of Tierra del Fuego is **Ushuaia,** the most southern city in the world. The scenery is made up of lakes and forests of *lenga,* a tree with deep red leaves characteristic of this area. All roads lead to glaciers and snow-covered peaks. The largest lake, the **Fagnano,** stretches across the island from east to west for 60 miles. Trout and salmon can be fished from nearly all the lakes and streams, and in summer, wild geese, ducks, beavers, and a wide variety of bird life can be seen. Excursions can be arranged from Ushuaia. Don't miss "centolla," the delicious king crab that is fished from the Beagle Channel. Hotels are the **Canal del Beagle** (from US$35) and **Antartida** (from US$25 double).

SOURCES OF FURTHER INFORMATION

Pan Am, Avenida Roque Saenz Pena 832 6th floor, Buenos Aires, and any Pan Am office around the world; the **National Tourist Board**, Santa Fé 883, Buenos Aires; the **Argentina Consulate General**, 12 West 56th Street, New York, NY 10019; the **Argentine-American Chamber of Commerce**, 11 Broadway, New York, NY 10004; the **Argentine Information Office**, 150 SE 2nd Avenue, Miami, FL; the **Argentine Consulate**, 53 Hans Place, London SW1.

Belize

WHAT'S SPECIAL

Lying to the east of Guatemala on the low coastal plainlands that border the Caribbean Sea, Belize changed its name from British Honduras in 1973, to reflect increasing self rule—originally granted in 1964. The coastline and the islands, with secret harbors, coves, and bays, provided a haven to British privateers in the 16th and 17th centuries, who could forage on shore, and repair their ships from the immense stands of trees while waiting to attack Spanish treasure ships. Not surprisingly, settlements sprang up, British woodcutters (from Jamaica) harvested timber on a year-round basis, and by 1638 a permanent community had been established. Despite ineffective Spanish opposition, the British settlements endured, and by 1780 a British administrator had been appointed. Spain complained again, but a naval victory by a British squadron against a Spanish fleet in 1798 established British jurisdiction against future claims. From the beautiful coastal strip with its excellent beaches to the sharply rising Mountain Pine Ridge and the Maya mountains in the west, the country is relatively new to tourism. The mosaic of islands off the barrier reef, one of the largest in the world, provides marvelous opportunities for scuba-diving and game fishing, while inland there is hunting and history. The Cays are increasingly popular with visitors, and a good insect repellant makes sandflies almost no problem. One of the oldest civilizations in the world, the Mayan, is only now being discovered, with its sophisticated system of mathematics, astrology, and religion. There are ruins at Altun Ha, some 30 miles northwest of Belize City, and at Xunantunich, some 80 miles southwest.

Belize is famed for its orchids and wildlife. Some 450 varieties of birds make this an ornithologist's paradise. The limestone formations give rise to fascinating cave systems, often with evidence of primitive use. Hunting, mainly for jaguar, is a favorite sport. For the past 300 years, forestry has been the major economic activity and government today is looking for partners from abroad to develop not only those oil deposits, but farming, agriculture, and tourism.

COUNTRY BRIEFING

Size: 8,867 square miles **Population:** 152,000
Capital: Belmopan **Capital Population:** 7,000
  Climate: The climate is subtropical but with a brisk wind prevailing from the Caribbean, which is especially invigorating from October to March. October is one of the most pleasant months in which to visit.

Weather in Belize City: Lat N17°31'; Alt 17 ft

Temp (°F)	Jan	Feb	Mar	Apr	May	Jun	Jul	Aug	Sep	Oct	Nov	Dec
Av Low	67°	69°	71°	74°	75°	75°	75°	75°	74°	72°	68°	68°
Av High	81°	82°	84°	86°	87°	87°	87°	88°	87°	86°	83°	81°
Days no rain	18	22	27	25	24	17	16	17	15	15	18	18

Government: Belize is a British Crown Colony, but it is a self-governing state. Great Britain remains responsible for defense.
  Language: English, Spanish also widely spoken.
  Religion: Roman Catholic, Anglican, and Methodist predominate.
  Currency: Belize dollar. 100 cents = B$1. The Belize currency is linked to the US dollar at the rate of BZE$2 equals US$1.

	BZE 10¢	BZE 50¢	BZE $1	BZE $15	BZE $50	BZE $100	BZE $300	BZE $1000
US (dollars, cents)	.05	.25	.50	7.50	25.00	50.00	150.00	500.00
UK (pounds, pence)	.02	.12	.24	3.58	11.93	23.85	71.55	238.50

Public Holidays:

New Year's Day, 1 Jan	Commonwealth Day, 24 May
Baron Bliss Day, 9 Mar	National Day, 10 Sep
Good Friday	Pan American Day, 14 Oct
Holy Saturday	Garifuna Day, 19 Nov
Easter Monday	Christmas Day, 25 Dec
Labour Day, 1 May	Boxing Day, 26 Dec

If any of these days falls on a Sunday, the holiday is observed the following day. Early closing days: Wednesday and Saturday.

HOW TO GET THERE

Flying time to Belize International Airport from New York is 4¾ hours; from Miami, 2¼ hours; from Guatemala City, ¾ hour. Time in Belize: GMT−6.

REQUIREMENTS FOR ENTRY AND CUSTOMS REGULATIONS

Passport is the only proof of citizenship required for US citizens whose journey originated in the US or British citizens whose journey originated in a British possession, provided stay does not exceed 6 months. Visa required by nationals of some countries. Visitors' permits are obtainable at all points of entry to the country, without prior application. All tourists should have sufficient funds for their stay and a round-trip or onward ticket to another country. Immunization requirements should be checked before departure for Belize. Normally, none is required. Typhoid, tetanus, and polio vaccinations, though not necessary, are recommended. No limit on foreign currency brought in, but report what you have on entry. No fruit, firearms, or ammunition may be taken in. Duty-free allowance: 200 cigarettes or ½ pound tobacco; 1 quart liquor; one bottle perfume. There are restrictions on exporting Mayan antiques.

AIRPORT INFORMATION

Belize International Airport is about 10 miles northwest of Belize City, the major city, and about 60 miles from Belmopan, a planned city that is the seat of the national government. No entry tax, but departure tax of about B$8 if you stay more than 48 hours. Each airline has its own bus service to the center. Taxis are readily available at a cost of about B$16. There is a duty-free shop at the airport.

ACCOMMODATIONS

The **Belize City Tourist Board** (12 Regent Street—tel: 3013) provides assistance. Hotels in Belize City and in other districts:
Rates are in US$ for a double/twin room with bath or shower

Bellevue, 5 Southern Foreshore, Belize City (from $120)
Bliss Hotel, 1 Water Lane, Belize City (from $50)
Crossroads Hotel, Belize City (from $21)
El Centro Hotel, Belize City (from $65)
Fort George, 2 Marine Parade, Belize City (from $184)
Handyside Hotel, 11 Handyside Street (from $28.50)
Keller Caribbean Sports, 10 miles north of Belize City (from $20)
Mopan Travelodge, 15 Western Road, Tropical Park (from $28)
Palms Hotel, Western Highway (from $20)
Rio Haul Hotel, Northern Road (from $28)

At Ambergris Caye:

Ambergris Lodge, San Pedro, beachfront (from $70 AP)
Casa Solana Resort (from $70)
Coral Beach Hotel, San Pedro (from $24)
El Pescador, San Pedro (from $170 AP)
Paradise House Hotel, San Pedro (from $30)
Sea Breeze Hotel, Middle Street, San Pedro (from $30)

At Caye Chapel Island:

Caye Club Aquarius (from $75 AP)

At Cay Caulker:

Vega's Guest House (from $10)
Edit's (from $12)

At Corozal:

Don Quixote, Consejo Shores (from $100 AP)
Tony's Motel, South End (from $37)

At Mountain Pine Ridge:

Blancaneaux Lodge (from $80 AP)

At Placencia:

Rum Point Inn (from $120 AP)

At Stann Creek:

Pelican Beach Motel (from $40)

At Turneffe Island:

Turneffe Island Lodge (7 days, from $500 AP)

USEFUL INFORMATION

Banks: Open 8am-1pm Mon-Fri, 8am-11am Sat. Money can also be changed in hotels. Banks in Belize City: **Atlantic Bank** (6 Albert Street) open 1pm-3pm except Wed, Sat, and Sun; **Bank of Nova Scotia** (Albert and Orange Streets); **Barclays** (Albert Street); **Royal Bank of Canada** (60 Market Square); branches in San Ignacio, Belmopan, Dangriga, Orange Walk Town, Independence, San Pedro, Ambergris Caye, Punta Gorda, and Corozal Town.

Mail: Stamps from the post office or hotels; mail can be sent only from the post office. Money orders available in principal post offices of major cities.

Telephone Tips: Phones mainly in hotels and bars. Street booths are uncommon. Telegraph and radiotelephone service available. Useful numbers in Belize City:

Tourist Office 3013
Tourist Information 2999

Operator, Directories, Fire
110 & 112
Police 2222

Newspapers: English-language newspapers are the *Beacon* (weekly), *Belize Times* (Wed) and *Belize Sunday Times,* the *Reporter* (weekly), *Belize Newsletter* (weekly, published by Government Information Service), *New Belize Government Information Service* (quarterly), *British Honduras Chamber of Commerce Trade Directory* (annual).

Tipping: Customary but optional; the usual is to tip 10% for hotels and restaurants; the service charge is not included in the bill. Porters, B$2.

Electricity: 110-220 volts 60 cycles AC.

Laundry: Hotels offer a good express service. There is dry-cleaning service in Belize City (dry-cleaning a suit, from B$4, laundering a shirt, from B$1).

Hairdressing: Major hotels have salons, and there are inexpensive ones in the towns (shampoo and set, from B$7; man's haircut, from B$2-3.75).

Photography: A good selection of equipment and of black and white and color film in all major towns. For developing, color film has to be flown to Miami and back.

Clubs: Rotary, Kiwanis, and Lions.

Babysitting: Hotel staff will usually oblige.

Rest Rooms: Always marked in English; found in restaurants, hotels, and bars.

Health: Medical standards are high and specialists available. The main general hospital is in Belize City. Pharmaceuticals available, but supplies can be erratic. Boil all drinking water.

TRANSPORTATION

Out-of-town bus service available. Bus service in Belize City; taxis with a fixed rate of B$1 per person. A small addition is made for night journeys. There are nearly 1,000 miles of main and connecting roads. Car rental is available, and details should be obtained from the Belize City Tourist Office. There are no railroad services. A good long-distance bus service links most of the major towns, such as San Ignacio, Orange Walk Town, Corozal Town, Dangriga, and Punta Gorda. Maya Airlines operates internal flights linking Dangriga, Punta Gorda, Corozal Town, San Pedro, Ambergris Caye, and Sarteneja.

FOOD AND RESTAURANTS

Try the national dishes, composed of rice, beans, and lobsters cooked in a variety of ways. Also conch and *tamales*—cornmeal with meat or fish wrapped in the *waha* leaf. These are all available in the main restaurants. Similar to American and European traditions, an average meal consists of three courses: appetizer, the main course of meat or fish, and the dessert and coffee. International cuisine is readily available in Belize City and the first-class hotels. A service charge is not generally added to the bill, and tipping is usually on the order of 10%. Breakfast in Belize City hotels is usually quite early, between 7:30 and 8, lunch is from 12, and dinner from 7. In Belize City both the **Bellevue** and **Fort George Hotel** have good restaurants. Other popular eating places are **Best in the Town** (King Street); **Caribbean** (Regent Street); **China Inn** (Euphrates Avenue); **Tureto's** (Dean Street); **Golden Dragon** (Queen Street); **The Great Fisherman** (near the bridge, has good seafood); **Mom's Kitchen** (Albert Street); **Democratic Bar** (Daly Street); **Katie's Restaurant** (Barracks Street); **Blue Bird** and **Colonial Bread Shop** (Albert Street); **El Centro Hotel and Restaurant** (Bishop Street).

DRINKING TIPS

The national drink is rum. One local drink, known as "A and P," is an interesting combination of anise and peppermint. Imported wines, liquor, and beers are available. A bottle of Scotch costs in the region of B$15, and drinks can be sold in bars from 6am-9pm and in clubs from 9am-midnight. Restaurant bars are open 24 hours a day. Rum punch and *Rum Popo* are drunk as cocktails. The former is made with fruit juices and the latter with egg and nutmeg. It is not usual for women to be seen in street bars, though they are not unwelcome. For a leisurely thirst-quencher, try the numerous saloons and cafés. Visitors tend to congregate in the **Fort George Hotel.**

ENTERTAINMENT

There are four movie houses, the **Majestic, Palace, Belrio,** and **Eden,** showing English-language films. Nightlife is definitely Caribbean style. Recommended spots are the **Palms Motel** on the Western Highway just outside Belize City, the **Cross Roads Hotel, Shangrila, Haven, The Melting Pot, Castaways 2002,** and the **Belize Club.** The **Continental Hotel** also offers evening entertainment.

SHOPPING

Stores open from 8am-12noon and 1pm-4pm daily except Wed 8am-12noon. When you leave Belize, you must take back home some black coral novelty (**National Craft Centre,** 147 Cemetery Road has good selection), the famed wood carvings, straw hats, and other handicrafts, such as slippers made from Spanish toweling. Tortoiseshell is used to make many items, but it is illegal to bring anything made of this material into the US because of the endangered species laws. Also selling high-quality souvenirs is the **Cottage Industries** shop (26 Albert Street, Belize City). Well-stocked department stores are to be found along **Albert Street** and **Queen Street.** For high-quality sculpture see the **George Gabb Art Studio** on Albert Street. Also go to Belize City's market in the center of town, by the sea, where the prices are lower. It is not the custom to bargain.

SPORTS

Most sports can be enjoyed; tennis is played at **Tropical Park, St Mary's School,** and the **Belize Club**—guests welcome. There is horseback riding out in the Mountain Pine Forest, fishing nearby, and excellent swimming in the cold-water streams and pools. The hunting is very good—the place to go is the village of **Santeneja,** though most of the hotels will be able to arrange this for you. The island of **Turneffe** provides good facilities for its deep-water yachting and great fishing, while skin-diving and scuba-diving are popular off **Ambergris Caye.**

WHAT TO SEE

Sightseeing musts are the Mayan ruins, of which more are being discovered year by year. The tremendous wealth of history within the country is only just showing itself. Major sites include those at **Altun Ha,** 30 miles northwest of Belize City, where the world's largest jade head was discovered only a few years ago (it weighed more than six pounds); **Xunantunich,** 80 miles southwest of Belize City; and **St Herman's Cave** on Humming Bird Highway on the way to **Stann Creek Valley.** Tours of particular interest to the visitor include those of **Mountain Pine Ridge,** with its beautiful scenery, varied wildlife, greenery, and orchids. The **Belize City Museum** has a fine display of Mayan relics. Other places to visit are the **Anglican Cathedral,** the oldest cathedral in Central America (1857), in Belize City; **Corozal Bay,** which is ideal for fishing and swimming and is near the Mayan center of **Lubaantun; San Ignacio,** on the banks of the Macal River and 72 miles due west of Belize City, near the Mayan centers of **Cahal Pech** (Place of the Ticks), **Xunantunich,** and **Cerros.**

The beach resorts of Belize are increasingly sought by the experienced traveler for their unspoiled beauty and for the fact that the people one meets are adventurous too. Most popular with the younger crowd is **Cay Caulker,** reached by the ferry *Mermaid* from Belize City, a voyage of about four hours. The waters aren't too good close to the shore, but out at the reefs they're fine.

Ambergris Caye is now the destination of choice of many visitors to Belize, and there are a number of resort hotels. There are numerous other smaller cays, such as **St George's** and **Half Moon,** both beautiful, while **Goff's Cay** is tiny but has excellent swimming. **Cay Gable** has an excellent beach, and sandflies.

The **Placencia** resort area is growing—miles of unspoiled beach, while **Turneffe Island** offers very comprehensive island vacations. **Belmopan,** the capital, is a planned city created in 1970. Its only activity is government.

SOURCES OF FURTHER INFORMATION

Any **Pan Am** office around the world; **Tourist Board,** 12 Regent Street, Belize City; **Government Information Service,** Belmopan; **Belize Chamber of Commerce,** 43 Handyside Street, Belize City; **Caribbean Tourism Association,** 20 East 46th Street, New York, NY 10017; **West Indian Committee,** 18 Grosvenor Street, London W1.

Bolivia

WHAT'S SPECIAL

One thousand years ago Bolivia was still part of the fabled Inca Empire. Today, although its economy is based on tin, other minerals, and natural gas—it is self-sufficient for energy—it is still one of the poorest nations of the continent. There is significant production of iron ore and nonferrous metals (Bolivia is an important producer of tin), and mining remains the most important element of the nation's economy.

Bolivia became independent of Spain in 1825 when General Antonio Jose de Sucre defeated Spanish forces at Ayacucho, and the following year a constitution was adopted for the republic. Despite the independence movement, the social structure of the nation underwent little significant change. A series of unsuccessful wars brought about the cession of much of its land mass to larger neighbors.

Finally, in 1952 there was yet another revolution (there had been some 12 constitutions, 60 popular revolts, and a government every two years since independence) which was different. Universal suffrage was established, the tin mines were nationalized, and Indian serfdom was abolished. A compromise form of nationalistic capitalism has evolved since that time and while tourism is not a major concern, there are plenty of acceptable places to be found in most cities, though you may have to rough it elsewhere. Bolivia has the world's highest capital city, the highest golf course and ski run, and the highest navigable lake.

COUNTRY BRIEFING

Size: 424,162 square miles **Population:** 5,570,109
Governmental Capital: La Paz **Pop:** 791,358
Constitutional Capital: Sucre **Pop:** 78,944

*La Paz is the administrative capital, while Sucre is the legal and judicial capital.

Climate: There is a great range of climate depending on the altitude. Winters are generally dry and sunny. It is dry and sunny in the Altiplano, subtropical in the Yungas, tropical around Oriente. Best time to travel is May through November.

Weather in La Paz: Lat S16°30′; Alt 12,001 ft

Temp (°F)	Jan	Feb	Mar	Apr	May	Jun	Jul	Aug	Sep	Oct	Nov	Dec
Av Low	43°	43°	42°	40°	37°	34°	33°	35°	38°	40°	42°	42°
Av High	63°	63°	64°	65°	64°	62°	62°	63°	66°	71°	78°	65°
Days no rain	10	10	15	21	26	28	29	27	21	22	19	13

Government: Independent and sovereign republic of nine departments.

Language: Spanish. Quechua and Aymará also spoken. English spoken in hotels.

Religion: Predominantly Roman Catholic, some Protestant churches.

Currency: Peso boliviano. 100 centavos = 1 peso boliviano.

	PB 50c	PB 1	PB 5	PB 10	PB 50	PB 100	PB 200	PB 500
US (dollars, cents)	.02	.04	.20	.41	2.04	4.08	8.16	20.40
UK (pounds, pence)	.01	.02	.10	.20	.97	1.95	3.89	9.73

Public Holidays:

New Year's Day, 1 Jan
Carnival (Feb-Mar), two days
Holy Week, one day
Labor Day, 1 May
Corpus Christi, May

Independence Day, 6 Aug
Columbus Day, 12 Oct
All Souls Day, 2 Nov
Christmas Day, 25 Dec

HOW TO GET THERE

Flying time to La Paz's El Alto Airport from New York is 9¼ hours; from Caracas, 6 hours; from Buenos Aires, 3 hours. Time in Bolivia: GMT −4.

REQUIREMENTS FOR ENTRY AND CUSTOMS REGULATIONS

Valid passport, smallpox vaccination, cholera vaccination if coming from an infected area, and 90-day "tourist card" (renewable) are required for entry (tourist card can be obtained from Bolivian Consulates and airlines). There are no currency restrictions in operation; it is best to reconvert all money before leaving the country. When entering, declare all personal items (such as cameras or typewriters) to avoid any difficulties on departure. Duty-free allowance: 200 cigarettes or 50 cigars or 450 grams of tobacco; 2 quarts liquor; enough perfume for personal use. No restrictions on what you take out.

AIRPORT INFORMATION

The airport is El Alto, 15 miles from La Paz. Taxis are also available at all times, and the fare to the city center is about PB80 per person. There is a departure tax: PB25 for domestic flights and PB250 for international flights. The only facilities are a hotel reservation counter. Airport porters are tipped PB10.

ACCOMMODATIONS

For help in finding accommodations contact Instituto Boliviano de Turismo (tel: 367441/367442). Hotels in La Paz:

Rates are US$ for a double/twin room with bath or shower

  Copacabana, Avenida 16 de Julio 1802 (from $35)
  Crillón, Plaza Isabel la Católica (from $39)
  El Dorado, Avda. Villazon (from $30)
  Emperador, Plaza del Estadio (from $28)
  Gloria, Potosi esq. J. Sanginez (from $32)
  La Paz, Avenida Camacho 1277 (from $30)
  Libertador, Calle Obispo Cardenas 142 (from $33)
  Plaza, Avenida 16 de Julio (from $67)
  Sheraton, Avenida Arce (from $58)
  Sucre La Paz-Sheraton, Avenida 16 de Julio 1787 (from $32)
  All the above hotels are centrally located.

USEFUL INFORMATION

Banks: Open 9-12 and 2-4:30, Mon-Fri. Money can otherwise be changed at exchange offices.

Mail: Stamps available only at post offices.

Telephone Tips: Coin-operated telephone booths in restaurants and cafés. Useful numbers in La Paz:

Pan Am agent 41863	Directories 104
Airport Information 812492	Fire 119
Tourist Office 367463-4	Police 110
Tourist Information 367442	Ambulance 118
	Time 117

Newspapers: English-language newspapers can be bought. There is no local English-language publication.

Tipping: Customary; 10% in restaurants, 23% in hotels (included in bill). Otherwise: porter, PB10; cloakroom attendant, PB12; hairdressers, PB10; hotel porter, PB10; chambermaid, PB12; museum guides, PB20.

Electricity: 110-220 volts 50 cycles AC in La Paz. In Potosí only, it is 110 volts; in the rest of the country, 220 volts.

Laundry: Dry-cleaning and laundry services readily available, fast and good. A 24-hour service in all major towns and most hotels (dry-cleaning a suit costs PB45; laundering a shirt PB18).

Hairdressing: First-class hotels have good salons (shampoo and set PB50, tip PB5; man's haircut PB40, tip PB5).

Photography: Reasonable selection of equipment; black and white and color film available in major cities, but expensive. Film can be processed in a couple of days, but some must be sent out of the country. It is advisable to take film with you.

Clubs: Rotary International and Junior Chamber International. Rotary meets at Club de la Paz, Automobile Club at Calacoto plus a YMCA and German Club.

Babysitting: Services can be arranged through a few hotels.

Rest Rooms: In hotels and restaurants. Women, *Damas;* men, *Caballeros.* Often advisable to use only hotel facilities.

Health: Doctors and dentists speak English. Imported pharmaceuticals are available but expensive.

TRANSPORTATION

Good bus and taxi services available. Payment for both is by cash. The small "micros" offer good minibus service from PB3-6.50 and go through all city zones. In a taxi you often rent only a seat—someone else who is going your way may join you. Taxis have fixed rates—PB5 per person for short trips. In La Paz there are *Trufis,* cabs with colored flags that denote their route. Extra charges: PB4 for luggage; PB3 per person; and an extra PB2.50 at night. You can rent a car through Hertz, Bernardo Trigo 429 (tel: 325591). Average rate for rental cars is around PB100; for a chauffeur-driven car it is about PB60 per hour. Drive on the right. Some roads outside the city are poor. The train system is quite comprehensive and has sleeping cars and food service. The trains are slow (e.g., 2 days from Sucre to La Paz), but they do go through spectacular scenery. The new *ferrobus* is more efficient, with reclining seats and meals served on board. The internal airlines are Lloyd Aéro Boliviano and Transportes Aéreos Militares, which link most principal cities. There are hydrofoil cruises on Lake Titicaca from Crillon Tours (Avenida Camacho and Ayacucho).

FOOD AND RESTAURANTS

Bolivia, and more specifically La Paz, is not the place to go expecting the best in international cooking. The first-class hotels do have good food and sometimes international cuisine, but you can probably eat as well elsewhere, if not even better and more interestingly. Mealtimes are similar to US or European hours. Prices range from about PB150 for a meal in an expensive restaurant to PB40 in an inexpensive one. It is not a good idea to try green salads or uncooked vegetables, and bottled water is preferable to tap water.

Some of the best national dishes can be bought cheaply from stalls on street corners. *Empanada salteña,* a combination of meat, chicken, olives, raisins, potatoes, pepper, and hot sauce squeezed inside a cylinder of dough about the size of a hot dog is one of the most popular dishes and is available from most roadside stalls. Watch out for the word *picante* as a descriptive word—it means that the food is highly spiced with chili peppers. If you go for highly spiced foods, however, do try the *picante de pollo,* a chicken ("Southern fried") with rice, fried potatoes, hot peppers, and *chuno* or dried potato. Or have a *lomo montado,* which is a fried tenderloin with eggs, rice, and banana; or again, the *parrillada,* a kind of Bolivian mixed grill. There are a growing number of good restaurants, including **Don Roberto, Los Faros** (seafood a specialty), **Balneario Los Lobos, Las Vegas, Zlato, La Tablada, Verona, Esperanza, La Creperie** (French cuisine), **Maxim's, La Pergola, Monaco, La Florida, De Francesco, Ding Dong, Las Tablitas, Gargantua, Scaramusch, Caprice V, La Torre de Cristal,** among others. For national specialties try **Yotala, Naira, El Herraja, Las Tablitas** and **El Hilacata.**

DRINKING TIPS

Local whisky is good, as are wine and beer. Imported wines and liquor are available, but there is now a law prohibiting the importation of whisky; it does get smuggled in, and when available should cost about PB35. A bottle of ordinary red wine is about PB30. Drinks are sold either all day or from 2pm to midnight, and the sale of liquor is unrestricted to those over the age of 21. Women should be accompanied in bars. Hotels and coffee shops are good places for leisurely drinking, or look for places called *confiterias* which are all over La Paz. Some of the more popular *confiterias* are **Charlie's, Lonsdale, Briggite, Club del Jazz, Mac's Place, Saint George Pub, Scaramouche, Giorgissimo, Skorpio,** and the **Sky Room** at the Hotel Libertador.

ENTERTAINMENT

There is a resident symphony orchestra and a resident ballet company. For folk music and dance try **Las Penas Andinas, Naira, Las Naranjas** (at the Hotel Gloria), **De las Americas** (Hotel City-El Prado) and the **Internacional.** La Paz has a musical theater, where these and local dramatic companies perform. La Paz also has many movie houses where foreign films are shown, usually subtitled, but they are likely to be as much as four years old. The best known nightclubs are **El Hipopotamo, El Fogon, Discoteque, Candilejas, Michel Angelo, Senorial, Yes, La Casa Blanca.**

SHOPPING

Stores are open 9-12 and 2-6 Mon-Fri, 9-12 Sat. Best buys are vicuña, ponchos, alpaca sweaters, gold and silver jewelry, wood carvings, handwoven fabrics, pottery, native dolls, and rugs. The main shopping street is **Calle Comercio.** In the markets in **Comacho, Lanza,** and **Sopocachi,** the distinctive women vendors are noted for their bowler hats, intelligence, and aggressiveness. They will expect you to bargain. Some stores are **Artesanias Bolivianos** (Avenida Sánchez Lima 2320) for jewelry and rugs, **Flora** (Avenida Sagárnaga) for sweaters, **Fotrama** (Avenida 16 de Julio 1764) for handicrafts and rugs, **Calle Santa Cruz** also good for handicrafts, **Anticuario** (Calle Mercado) for antiques.

SPORTS

Spectator sports are soccer, football, tennis, and volleyball. The hunting in eastern Bolivia is probably about the best in the world today. To do it really properly you can go on a safari complete with bow and arrow and an Indian who plays the drums. The trout fishing at **Lake Titicaca** is also gaining world renown. Skiing is tremendous at 17,000 feet, but make certain you are acclimatized first. Tennis clubs in La Paz and Sucre both welcome foreign visitors. Otherwise, horseback riding, yachting (Lake Titicaca, all year), mountaineering (**Club Andino** at Chacaltaya), and golf are all available. Try the **Mallasilla Golf Course** on the outskirts of La Paz—the highest golf course in the world; you should add 30 or 40 yards to your drive!

WHAT TO SEE

The main thoroughfare through La Paz is the **Prado** or 16th of July Street. Here, near the Plaza Murillo, are the **Cathedral,** the **Presidential Palace,** and the **Congreso Nacional,** the seat of the legislature. Further along, at **Plaza Venezuela,** is the 16th-century **San Francisco Church** and monastery. See also the **National Museum of Art,** the open-air museum, and the collection of Tiahuanaco arts, as well as **Museum Casa de Murillo** (Calle Jaén) and **Casa de la Cultura** (Avenida Mariscal Santa Cruz y Calle Potosi). In January each year there is the Indian fair, the *Alacitas.*

The ruins of **Tiahuanaco,** 42 miles from La Paz on the plain of Kalasasaya, are from one of the earliest civilizations of America. Their precise date is unknown, although estimates range from 10,000 BC to 1,000 BC. See the **Temple of Kalasasaya** and the **Gates of the Sun and the Moon,** fantastic remnants of the sophisticated civilization that disappeared.

Not far from Tiahuanaco is **Lake Titicaca** (highest navigable lake in the world), half of which is in Peru. Here Indian reedboats share the waters with modern yachts and motor boats, and two of the lake's 36 islands are called the Islands of the Sun and the Moon, paying obvious homage to the ruins of Tiahuanaco. The fishing and hunting here are good, the lake having more than four varieties of edible fish, and the surrounding land is stocked with gull, duck, geese, widgeon, woodcock, grebe, plover, ibis, and gallinule. It was here that the former Aztec empire enjoyed a floating capital, and the Indians at Puno (the Uros) are thought to be the direct descendants of these earlier lords, living in their floating islands.

On the shores of the lake is **Copacabana,** a city that existed at the time of the Inca civilization and was used as a place of recreation by the royal family. The climate here is pleasant and temperate, the waters are warm enough for swimming, and the 17th-century city itself is one of the most pleasant old cities in Bolivia. See the **Statue of the Virgin** (which is said to possess miraculous powers), the Franciscan Fathers' **Monastery,** and the 17th-century sanctuary with its numerous paintings and jewels. The celebration of the **Festival of the Virgin of Copacabana** is on August 5th. It's possible to make just a day visit, though there are some small hotels if you want to stay over.

Another city of interest is **Sucre,** officially the constitutional capital of Bolivia and called the "white city" because of the white towers of its many churches. It is still the legal capital of the nation. Pleasantly quiet and isolated, there are many gracious buildings here of both the Spanish colonial and republican periods, in addition to which Sucre has the second-oldest (17th century) university in Latin America. Hotels are: **Hotel Municipal** (Avenida Venezuela); **Hotel Paris** (Calle Calvo 116); and **Hotel Londres** (Avenida Venezuela), all about US$20 double.

Cochabamba, an agricultural center, is a popular resort as well as Bolivia's third-largest city. The marketplace and shopping centers here are comparable to those in La Paz. Hotels are: **Gran Hotel Cochabamba** (Plaza U Anze); **Gran Hotel Ambassador** (Calle Espana 5696); **Hotel Capitol** (Calle Colombia, Esquina 25 de Mayo); and **Colón Hotel** (Plaza Colón 179), all from about US$40 double.

Potosí is yet another of the old Spanish colonial towns, full of winding streets and old mansions with colonial coats of arms. It was one of the first great cities of the Americas early in the 17th century, due in large part to the silver mines, which kept the Spanish treasury solvent. The **Central Hotel,** Calle Bustillo 1230 (from US$12 double) offers only modest accommodations, with no private baths; **Hotel Cuarto Centenario,** Avenida Villazón (from US$16), is the most comfortable.

Santa Cruz, the second largest city, is Bolivia's fastest-growing, a center of agriculture, industry, and of the natural gas boom. Its tropical climate contrasts with that of the Andean cities. It is forward-looking, with modern hotels—including the **Holiday Inn** (from US$45 double). Other important hotels are: **Cortez, La Siesta, Santa Cruz,** and **Bolivia.** The city also has an active nightlife. **Oruro,** 3 hours by bus from La Paz, is famous for the Diablada ceremony performed at **Carnival** (end of February or early March) by brilliantly costumed and masked dancers. The carnival goes on for 8 days of round-the-clock dancing.

SOURCES OF FURTHER INFORMATION

Pan Am's agent: Aircom Ltd. (G.S.A.), Edificio Alameda, Oficina No. 2, La Paz; or and Pan Am office around the world; **Instituto Boliviano de Turismo,** Plaza Venezuela-Edificio Hermann, La Paz; **Consulate General of Bolivia,** 10 Rockefeller Plaza, New York, NY 10020; **South American Travel Organization,** 100 Biscayne Boulevard, Miami, FL 33132; **Embassy of Bolivia,** 106 Eaton Square, London SW1.

Brazil

WHAT'S SPECIAL

Occupying nearly half of South America, Brazil is the fifth largest country in the world and is bigger than the continental United States. Everything is on a scale to match the sprawling Amazon jungles with broad-leafed trees and enormous shrubs, great pine forests in the Rio Grande, parched deserts in the northeast, the Iguaçu Falls, higher and larger than Niagara, no fewer than 4,603 miles of Atlantic coastline; and the tall, white buildings of Rio de Janeiro reaching up between bare, purple mountains.

And then there are the people. The "Cariocas" are as racially mixed as any in the world, friendly, hospitable, and uninhibited. They work hard—play hard as well on the beautiful beaches. Service in restaurants (even small inexpensive places) and hotels is especially friendly and good, delighting the experienced traveler. Their Carnival is the gayest in the world. Precious stones, sugar, soybeans, coffee, and iron ore all come out of Brazil, and there are still huge areas of the country that have scarcely been explored. Some historians have suggested that Sir Thomas More was inspired by travelers' tales of Brazil when he dreamed up his *Utopia*. And the historians could be right, because this land of the exhilarating samba and superb cuisine will probably inspire you, too.

COUNTRY BRIEFING

Size: 3,286,344 square miles   **Population:** 119,024,000
Capital: Brasilia   **Capital Population:** 1,777,000
Rio de Janeiro: 9,018,961   **São Paulo:** 12,578,045
   Climate: Generally mild in Rio with plenty of sunshine; summer

months December to February can be warm, especially further north. Best time to visit is March–November when weather is cooler and off-season rates prevail.

Weather in Rio de Janeiro: Lat S22°55′; Sea level

Temp (°F)	Jan	Feb	Mar	Apr	May	Jun	Jul	Aug	Sep	Oct	Nov	Dec
Av Low	73°	73°	73°	69°	66°	64°	63°	64°	65°	66°	68°	71°
Av High	84°	85°	83°	80°	77°	76°	75°	76°	75°	77°	79°	82°
Days no rain	18	17	19	20	21	23	24	24	19	18	17	17

Government: A federation of some 27 states and territories with the federal district of Brasilia.

Language: Portuguese, but English and French understood in better hotels and restaurants. Spanish is generally understood, but outside the major cities language can be a problem.

Religion: Roman Catholic, but many places of worship of all denominations in Rio and São Paulo.

Currency: Cruzeiro. 100 centavos = 1 cruzeiro.

	c	Cr	Cr	Cr	Cr	Cr	Cr	Cr
	50	1	5	10	50	100	200	300
US (dollars, cents)	—	.01	.05	.12	.60	1.21	2.42	3.63
UK (pounds, pence)		—	.02	.06	.29	.58	1.16	1.74

Public Holidays:

New Year's Day, 1 Jan
Carnival, 4 days before Ash
    Wednesday
Good Friday
Tiradentes, 21 Apr
Labor Day, 1 May

Corpus Christi, 10 June
Independence Day, 7 Sep
All Souls Day, 2 Nov
Proclamation of the Republic,
    15 Nov
Christmas Day, 25 Dec

HOW TO GET THERE

Flying time to Rio de Janeiro International Airport from New York is 9½ hours; from Los Angeles, 13 hours; from Caracas, 5¾ hours; from Buenos Aires, 2¾ hours. Flying time between Rio de Janeiro and Congonhas Airport in São Paulo is ¾ hours. Time in Rio de Janeiro and São Paulo: GMT−3.

REQUIREMENTS FOR ENTRY AND CUSTOMS REGULATIONS

A passport, a round-trip ticket to the country of origin; a tourist visa (which can be obtained from any Brazilian embassy or consulate—free of charge, one passport 2″ × 3″ photo needed). You may take in as much currency as you wish, but cannot take out more money than you brought in. Departing visitors wishing to cash Brazilian currency for other currencies may do so at a bank only (including the airport bank) and only if a receipt is shown to prove the original exchange of money at a bank into cruzeiros. The bank will then exchange up to 30% of the cruzeiros shown on this receipt. Remember to keep your exchange

BRAZIL

receipts; they are necessary to cash in cruzeiros. A point to remember is that from time to time it is worth purchasing cruzeiros before you leave for Brazil, depending on the market rate obtaining. Duty-free allowance: 400 cigarettes, half-pound pipe tobacco, or 25 cigars; 3 quarts wine, 2 quarts champagne, 2 quarts liquor; small amount of cosmetics and food for personal use; articles of personal use valued up to US$100; used portable radio, movie camera, typewriter, tape recorder, and binoculars.

AIRPORT INFORMATION

The Rio de Janeiro International Airport is conveniently located. Airport for São Paulo is Viracopos. Domestic flights land at Santos Dumont Airport in Rio and at Congonhas in São Paulo. There is bus service from Rio International and taxis are plentiful. Taxi fares are Cr600 (about $9) to the heart of Rio, and Cr1,000 (about $14) to Copacabana. Taxi fares are set and paid for in advance at one of the taxi booths. Passenger merely shows driver the receipt and nothing else is paid except a tip. Porters are tipped Cr35 (about 50¢) per bag. Duty-free goods can be bought at the airport. For international flights departing from Rio de Janeiro, the embarkation tax is Cr280, for domestic flights Cr50 and must be paid in cruzeiros.

ACCOMMODATIONS

Hotel rates are readjusted to the domestic inflation rate from time to time. Use the following price list as a guide only. If you want a good view from your window, you will have to pay more. Rio is extremely noisy. An inside room is less expensive and much quieter. Rates in Rio are much higher during Carnival. Service charge of 10-15% (20% in Petrópolis) and a hotel tax of 10% will be added to the bill. All hotels on Avenida Atlântica are directly across the street from the Copacabana beach. Other hotels are in the downtown district unless otherwise indicated. Hotels in Rio:

Rates are in US$ for a double/twin room with bath or shower

Aeroporto, Avenida Beira Mar 280 (from $61)
Ambassador, Rua Senador Dantas 25 (from $40)
California, Avenida Atlântica 2616 (from $70)
Caesar Park, Viera Souto 460 (Ipanema), (from $95)
Castro Alves, Avenida Copacabana 522 (from $40)
Copacabana Miramar Palace, Avenida Atlântica 3668 (from $55)
Copacabana Palace, Avenida Atlântica 1702 (from $55)
Everest Rio, Rua Prudente de Morais 1117, Ipanema Beach (from $60)
Excelsior Copacabana, Avenida Atlântica 1800 (from $60)
Gloria, 632 Rua do Russel (from $60)
Grande Hotel Sao Francisco, Rua Visconde de Inhauma (from $47)
Guanabara Palace, Avenue Pres Vargas 392 (from $30)
INTER·CONTINENTAL RIO, Gavea Beach, 13 miles from city center (from $116)
Lancaster, Avenida Atlântica 1470 (from $60), on Copacabana beach
Leme Palace, Avenida Atlântica 656 (from $61)

Luxor Hotel Continental, Rua Gustavo Sampaio 320, one half block from Copacabana (from $70)

Méridien, Avenida Atlântica 1020 (from $115)

Nacional Rio, Avenida Niemeyer 769, Gavea Beach, 13 miles from city center (from $95)

Novo Mundo, Rua Silveiva Martins 10 (from $40)

Ouro Verde, Avenida Atlântica 1456 (from $69)

Regente, Avenida Atlântica 3716 (from $71)

Rio Othon Palace, Avenida Atlântica 3264 (from $85)

Rio Palace, Avenida Atlântica 4240 (from $105), Copacabana beach

Savoy Othon, Avenida NS Copacabana 995 (from $60)

Sheraton, Avenida Niemeyer 121, Gavea Beach (from $120)

Trocadero, Avenida Atlântica 2064 (from $71)

USEFUL INFORMATION

Banks: Most are open 10-4:30 Mon-Fri, though some vary hours. You can also change currency or travelers' checks at shops marked Cambio. Exchange rates are the same at hotels.

Mail: Buy stamps and mail letters only at post offices (look for the sign *Correio*); there are street mailboxes. Many hotels sell stamps and mail letters, but the post office is quicker.

Telephone Tips: In many shops, restaurants, cafés, bars, and street booths. Token-operated, and can be used only for local calls with a *Ficha* (token) which can be bought at newspaper stands, drugstores, and some bars at a cost of Cr4. Useful numbers in Rio:

Pan Am 240-2322/398-3307	**Emergencies** 232-1234
Airport Information Galeao Airport	**Fire Department** 234-2020
393-3450	**Police** 243-6716
Tourist Information 263-9122	**Directories** 102
Operator 100 (local calls)	
101 (long distance)	

For long-distance telephone calls other than from your hotel, look for the sign *Cia Telefònica*.

Newspapers: You can get *Time* and *Newsweek* from almost any large newsstand in Rio and São Paulo, but newspapers are harder to come by. The local English-language newspaper is *The Latin American Daily Post.* The *Miami Herald* and *Business Week* are sold at São Paulo Hilton newsstand.

Tipping: A service charge is already included in most restaurant checks, but a tip of 5% or extra is still customary. Tip porters Cr25 per piece of luggage; hairdressers, Cr75; cloakroom attendants, Cr50; museum guides, Cr80.

Electricity: Rio and São Paulo—110 volts 60 cycles AC; Brasilia—220 volts 60 cycles AC; Salvador, Manaus, and Curitiba—127 volts 60 cycles AC. Check locally elsewhere. Some hotels have converters.

Laundry: Dry-cleaning and laundry services are of a very high standard in major cities; 24-hour dry-cleaning service available, mainly in hotels (dry-cleaning a suit Cr220, laundering a shirt Cr65).

Hairdressing: Most first-class hotels have good salons. (Shampoo and set about Cr500; man's haircut Cr200.)

Photography: Good selection of equipment in cities, but very expensive. Black and white film costs about Cr350 and color film Cr470. Developing services quite reliable: black and white film takes 2-3 days, color, 4-5 days.

Clubs: Rotary, Lions, and Kiwanis.

Babysitting: Most hotels have a service.

Rest Rooms: In hotels, restaurants, bus and ferry terminals. No charge and no tip expected; women, *Senhoras* or *Damas;* men, *Cavalheiros* or *Homens.*

Health: Many doctors have trained in the US or Britain and speak English. Pharmaceuticals available. Drink only bottled water. Outside main cities, mosquitoes can be a nuisance.

Car Rental: Hertz (275-4795), Nobre (275-5297).

TRANSPORTATION

In Rio, the buses are excellent and inexpensive: Cr15 to see most attractions. Both Rio and São Paulo are extensively covered by bus services, but during rush hours they can be crowded, uncomfortable, and noisy. Metered taxis are the quickest form of city transport. Taxi drivers receive about 45% more than is marked on the meter. A chart calculating the additional amount is posted inside the cab. You can hail one in the street almost any time, day or night, but finding one in the rush hour is difficult; tip 5-10% or round off to the next highest cruzeiro. For longer journeys and excursions, agree on the price with the driver. Extra charge of 25% for night fares and on Sundays. Heavy trunks will cost you Cr40 each. Drivers in São Paulo are generally courteous, but in Rio they can be quite the opposite. You can rent a small car for about Cr1,330 per day, plus Cr6.60 per km, a larger car for Cr2,370, plus Cr6.60 per km. A chauffeur adds Cr1,200 to the price (for 8 hours); (Cr1,500 for an English-speaking driver). An international driver's license is required, available from American Automobile Association offices. Traffic lights are high over the middle of the roads and go from green to red surprisingly fast. Driving is not recommended. It can be dangerous for the uninitiated, since traffic signals are confusing.

Train services connecting Rio, São Paulo, and Belo Horizonte are quite reasonable, with sleepers and food available. Express bus services link most Brazilian cities. By bus from Rio to São Paulo and Belo Horizonte is 7½ hours (fare Cr465). A luxury bus service between Rio and Brasilia takes 20 hours.

Air travel is the most convenient form of transportation. Brazil has one of the largest domestic networks in the world. Main internal airlines are Varig, Vasp, and Transbrasil. Air taxis are available between main metropolitan centers. Advance reservations between Rio and São Paulo are not required (Ponte Aerea), but are required for Rio to Brasilia. Flights leave every 20 to 30 minutes between Rio and São Paulo and cost Cr2,970 ($42); flight time is 45 minutes. Reservations are to be recommended for all weekend and holiday flights since space is at a premium. Flights out of Brasilia on Thursday and Friday nights are impossible to obtain at short notice, and advance booking is essential. (Round trip from São Paulo to Brasília is about $170, or Cr12,000; cab fare to downtown is about $6, by air-conditioned bus $1.50).

FOOD AND RESTAURANTS

Brazilians are natural gourmets; the native food is very spicy and strongly influenced by their Portuguese and African origins. A good introduction to the local diet is the *feijoada*—the ingredients vary but include rice, black beans cooked with dried beef, smoked bacon, pork sausage and other meats, manioc meal, and slices of orange. It is not too rich and is traditionally served at most restaurants on Saturdays. *Frango com arroz* is boned chicken and rice mixed with green peas and other vegetables, chopped olives, and hard boiled eggs. Then move on to *Vatapá*—a porridge-like stew with fish and shrimps as the main ingredients; *caruru*—a traditional dish—a stew of minced herbs and spices in oil—from Bahia; *cosido*—an enormous meat and vegetable stew. Simpler fish and shrimp dishes are numerous. Try *Camarões a bahiana*—shrimps in a thick spiced tomato sauce, served with rice. The quality of meat is excellent, and beef dishes are superb. Even a simple steak with french fries *(bife com batatas fritas)* tastes good as does the slightly different *bife de panela* where the steak is grilled with onion and tomatoes. But *churrasco gaucho*—barbecued steak, pork, and sausages, served with peppers, onions, and manioc meal—is a must. Sip *cafezinho,* a demitasse of rich Brazilian coffee. Desserts are very sweet; try *goiaba,* a sweet made from guavas, delicious light coconut *quindins* and *dôce de leite,* which looks like fudge. And remember to try a chocolate popsicle *(Chio, Bom de Chocolate).*

There are many counter service eating places for quick snacks and beverages in Rio. Relaxing outdoor cafés are plentiful. International cuisine is available in all good hotels. There are also numerous French, Italian, Hungarian, and Chinese restaurants. The following is a small selection of restaurants in the Rio area. Downtown, **A Cabaça Grande** (Rua do Ouvidor 12) serves Portuguese food and is one of Rio's finest restaurants. Also downtown, try the **Restaurant Mesbla** (Rua do Passeio 42, 11th floor) for *frango a Indiana* (chicken curry), or the house specialty *brochette de camarao a grega* (barbecued shrimp), and **Museu de Arte Moderna** (Avenida Beira Mar) for international cuisine. **The Ouro Verde Restaurant** in the Ouro Verde Hotel is also recommended for its international cuisine. The **Vendôme** (Avenida Franklin Roosevelt 194-A) is a first-class French restaurant, closed on Saturdays and Sundays. **Vergel** (Rua da Alfândega 176) is good for vegetarian meals and the **Leieria Mineira** (Rua São José 82) for business lunches and prompt service. Particularly good is their *tutu a mineira* (beans with manioc flour served with pork chops) and *camarao com arroz* (shrimp with rice). In Copacabana, **Flag** (Rua Xavier do Silveria 13) is outstanding for its international cuisine, **La Fiorentina** (Avenida Atlântica 458-A) for Italian food—very popular with theater and movie stars. **Le Bec Fin** (Avenida Copacabana 178) and **Le Bistro** (R. Fernando Mendes 7) are good French restaurants but expensive and **A Poloneza** serves the best *boeuf Strogonoff* in town (Rua Helário de Gouvêia 116). **Churrascaria Jardim** (Rua Republica do Peru 225, near Copacabana) features reasonably priced native food of grilled beef, pork, sausage, or chicken; worth noting is the *cordeira* (lamb) and *maminha de alcatra* (baby beef), while the *churrasco mixto a Jardim* (the house mixed grill of steak, liver, and sausage) is enough for two; informal. In Ipanema, **Le Relais** (Rua General Venâncio Flores 365) is known for excellent French cuisine, as is **Les Templiers** (Av Borges de Medeiros 3207). Recommended lunch bars are **Bob's** (scattered all over town); **Kid's** (Praca Mahatma Gandhi); and **Zig-Zag** (Rua Santa Clara). Try *Kibon* ice creams, sold in the streets. For a European tea, try **Confeitaria Colombó** (Rua Goncalves Dias 32). In Botafogo, you must go to **Chalé** (Rua da Matriz 54) or almost nextdoor to **Tabefe** (at number 62) with its Bahian decor, for traditional Brazilian cooking. Try the *muqueca de piexe* with either shrimp *(camarao)* or *mixta* (fish and shrimp). For dessert, *doce de leite com coco*. Also in Botafogo is **Aurora** (Rua Visconde de Caravellas), and the churrascaria **Estrela do Sul**. In Tijuca, just outside town, there is **Churrascaria Rincão Gaúcho** (Rua Marquês de Valença 83/85), and excellent *churrascaria*. If you like Japanese food, try **Akasaka** (Avenida Copacabana 1142). For Chinese fare, **China Town** (Barrao da Torre 450, Ipanema) is good, as are **Restaurant Pequim** (Barata Ribeiro), **Restaurante Chinesa** (Av Atlântica 2334-B), and **Restaurante Oriente** (Av Copacabana at Rua Bolivar). **Le Chalet Suisse** (Rua Xavier da Silveira 112) is an attractive Swiss restaurant, and very popular with Cariocas. Its sister restaurant **Le Mazot** (Rua Paula Freitas 31) is equally popular, with slightly more emphasis on French rather than Swiss cuisine. The *fondue bourguignon* at the latter is as popular as the *fondue du fromage* at the former. For German food try **Bierklause** (Rua Ronald de Carvalho 55), also a nightspot, or **Alpino Restaurant** (Av Epitacio Pessoa 40), for Polish cuisine, and excellent beef stroganoff; the **Restaurante a Poloneza** (Rua Hilario de Gouveia 116) is a family-run business. **La Tour,** Rio's revolving restaurant, is to be found in the tower at Rua Santa Luzia 651. Excellent fare.

Breakfast is usually served from 7-10, lunch from 12-2, dinner from 7 to the early hours of the morning. A dinner for one in an expensive restaurant costs Cr1,200; medium-priced Cr700; and inexpensive, about Cr350.

DRINKING TIPS

Beer, bottled or draft, is superb; favorite brands are Pilsner, Brahma, and Antarctica. Draft beer is called Chopp. Malzbier is a good Brazilian stout. Beer is cheap, Cr40 for a large bottle. *Cachaca,* the local sugarcane brandy, is delicious and very potent. Mixed with lime and sugar and ice, it is called *caipirinha* or *caipirissimo,* and somewhat similar to a margarita. Local wines include Precioso (white), Granja Uniao (red), Forestier (red), Chateau, and Chateau Duvalier. A bottle of ordinary red wine will cost about Cr160. Imported liquor is expensive. Average price of a whisky and soda varies from Cr150 (for local Scotch) to Cr300 (for imported Scotch). There are no liquor restrictions, but no alcoholic drinks for those under 21. Bars open from 7am to the early hours of the next morning.

Local bottled soft drinks are worth a try, and most bars and cafés serve fresh fruit drinks. *Mate*, a strong Brazilian tea, is very refreshing; it is served along the beaches in Rio by barefooted boys carrying large drums on their backs and shouting *"mate gelado"* (iced bitter form of tea, usually heavily sugared to counter the bitterness). Drinking coffee is a national custom (served black in tiny cups with lots of sugar).

ENTERTAINMENT

Most large cities are very lively, but Rio and São Paulo most of all. There are always plenty of good theater shows to be seen, from lavish musicals to small experimental groups—all performed in Portuguese. Opera, concerts, and ballet are performed at the **Teatro Municipal** and music recitals at the **Sala Cecilia Meireles**. **Hotel Nacional** presents lavish shows. Movies are very popular in Brazil; tickets are inexpensive (around Cr180) and lines are long, so get there early. International films are shown with original sound tracks. Nightclubs are plentiful and many top performers appear regularly. In Rio try **Number One** (Rua Maria Quitéria 19), which has a first-class show; **Zum-Zum Club** (Rua Barata Ribeiro), a psychedelic disco; **Sacha's** (Avenida Atlântica 928), which shows silent movies, closed-circuit TV, and slides; **Canecao** (Rua Lauro Muller, Botafogo), a wild, stadium-sized club very popular with the local people; **Le Bateau** (Praça Serzeldo Corrêa), a cozy "in" spot; **Crazy Rabbit** (Avenida Princesa Isable 185), designed for the sophisticated and good for the single person; **Sucata** (Avenida Borges Medeiros 1426), which is very good for Brazilian music; also good are the tiny **Kilt Club** (Rua Carvalho de Mendonca 35), **Ponto Final** (Barata Ribeiro 90), live music, and **Lord Jim** (Rua Paul Redfern 63), a British pub with authentic fish and chips and usually crowded. For the single man **Big Al's** (Rua Francisco Sa 35) while **Bolero** (Avenida Atlântica 1910) and **Holiday** (Atlântica and Carvalho) feature attractive dance hostesses. **Assyrius** (Av Rio Branco 277) is also popular. A trip to the suburbs to watch an *Escola de Samba* rehearse for the Carnival is unforgettable—inquire at the Tourist Office first, however, as sometimes there are only band rehearsals.

SHOPPING

Stores are open weekdays from 9-6 or 6:30, closed Saturday afternoons. There are many large department stores, shopping arcades, thousands of boutiques, record stores, and jewelry and gift shops. At **Importadoras** chain stores you can buy an assortment of imported goods, usually very expensive. It is not advisable to buy ready-made clothing, as the workmanship may be poor. Cottons and silks are of excellent quality, and fabrics are colorful. Buy a *figa*, symbolic clenched hand said to bring good luck. Best buys are leather goods (shoes are highly fashionable and well made), wallets, cigarette cases, antique silver (the delicate coffee spoons with semiprecious stones set in the handles make beautiful gifts), wood carvings, and above all, precious and semiprecious gems, pendants, necklaces, and bracelets. Topaz, amethyst, opal, aquamarine, and tourmaline, cut or uncut, are very popular and inexpensive. Brazilian handicraft shops are well stocked with unique native goods; examples are rosewood (jacaranda) bowls and trays, unusual beads, wooden dolls and latex figures from the Amazon Indians, clay sculptures and miniature balsa rafts from the northeast, native musical instruments, framed butterflies and tarantula spiders, soapstone carvings, tapestries, and stuffed baby alligators. Children will love the Papagaio kites, which are lightweight and easy to pack; records make excellent souvenirs. It is not customary to bargain in shops, but you will usually get a 10% discount if you ask for it. Main department stores in Rio are **Mesbla** (off Praça Mahatma Gandhi), **Sears** (Praia de Botafogo), and **Sloper** (Rua do Ouvidor). For jewelry **Maximino** (Rua Santa Clara), **H Stern** (Avenida Rio Branco 173), and **Burle Marx** (near Copacabana Palace Hotel); for handicrafts and souvenirs **Casa Hugo** (Rua Buenos Aires) and **Caso do Folclore** (Avenida Rio Branco); for Macumba artifacts, the **Casa Sucena** just across from Hugo's is well spoken of; for perfumes **Perfumarias Carneiro** (Rua do Ouvidor) and **Casa Hermanny** (Rua Gonçalves Bias). An open-air market known as the **Hippie Fair** is open every Sunday 9am to sunset at the Praça General Osório (Ipanema)—artists display paintings, wood carvings and handicrafts, leather and metal work.

SPORTS

Soccer is the Brazilian national sport. There are fierce league championships, and the **Maracanã Stadium** is the world's largest, holding 200,000 people. The amateur soccer championships are held on the spotlighted beaches of Copacabana, Ipanema, and Flamengo. Watch them from the mosaic sidewalks, free of charge. There are also boxing, volleyball, and basketball matches at the **Maracanãzinho Stadium,** and horse racing at the **Jockey Club** on Thursdays and Sundays (pari-mutuel betting), admission charges about Cr80. The biggest race is the **Grande Premio Brasil,** held on the first Sunday in August. On Sunday mornings, spectators gather on Gávea beach to watch the brilliant colored hang gliders leap off a nearby mountain cliff and sail gracefully down to the shore.

There are innumerable sports and social clubs in Rio, all with first-class facilities. Most offer temporary membership to visitors at reasonable rates but require introductions from current members. English-speaking residents in Rio belong to the **Payssandú Tenis Clube** (tennis, bowling, swimming); **Rio Country Club** (tennis, swimming); **Gávea Golf and Country Club** (golf and polo) or the **Yacht Clube do Rio de Janeiro** (sailing and water-skiing). Visiting cards can be obtained for the **Itanhangá Golf and Country Club** from the Avenida Rio Branco 26, 16th floor (tel: 243-2175). Across the Guanabara Bay, in the city of Niterói, there are the **Rio Cricket Club** (swimming, soccer, cricket, rugby) and the **Rio Sailing Club** (swimming and yachting).

WHAT TO SEE

Rio De Janeiro

Tourist agencies offer tours of the city. If you would rather explore on your own, include in your itinerary a trip by funicular to the **Corcovado Mountain**, which is crowned by the 1,200-ton, 130-foot statue of *Christ the Redeemer*. By cable car (you can also take the tram) from the station on Av Chile (next to Petrobras) travel up the mountain to the tiny town of Santa Teresa overlooking Rio and Guanabara Bay. This is what the old Rio is all about. Also by cable car from Praça General Tiburcio on Praia Vermelha, to the top of **Pao de Acucar** (Sugarloaf Mountain) for one of the most spectacular views of Rio. There's a restaurant, nightclub plus gift shops at the summit, and a marionette show for children, every hour on the hour during the day. There are lines at the weekend, so go early or be prepared for long waits. Rio is known for its nine magnificent beaches, home of the string bikini or *tanga*. A stroll you will not easily forget is along the world-famous mosaic walks of **Copacabana Beach.** Rio's gardens and parks are luxurious. The **Jardim Botanico** (Botanical Gardens) has over 7,000 varieties of exotic plants and 600 types of orchids in season—open every day from 8-5. The **Quinta da Bôa Vista** is the largest park in Rio and houses the **National Museum**, the **Zoo**, and a tropical aquarium. Open from 12-4:30—closed on Mondays. Among the many churches, be sure to see the **Candelária**, on Praça Pio X, which has beautiful interior decorations and paintings: the **Convent of Santo Antonio** on the Largo da Carioca has a magnificent sacristy; the church of **Nossa Senhora de Gloria do Outeiro** (on Glória Hill) has fine examples of Brazilian blue-facing tiling. The **Museum of Modern Art and War Memorial**, Avenida Beira Mar, is virtually all glass—open 12-7 Mon to Sat, 2-7 Sundays and holidays. The **Museum of Fine Art**, on the Avenida Rio Branco opposite the Teatro Municipal, has exhibitions by contemporary artists and many old masters; open Tues-Fri, 12:30-6:30. **The National Historical Museum**, Praca Marechal Ancora, has a collection of historical treasures, colonial sculptures, armor, and silver—open Tues-Fri 11-5, weekends and holidays 2-5. The **Museum of the Indian,** Rua das Palmeiras 55 in Botafogo, illustrates the life of the Brazilian Indian, open weekdays 10-5. A trip to **Flamengo Park** is worthwhile. It includes a lovely beach within sight of Sugarloaf. A short walking distance away is a new government museum dedicated to Carmen Miranda, Brazil's famous actress and dancer of the 1950s.

On New Year's Eve, go down to the beaches to watch the *Macumbeiros* making offerings to Iemanejá, the goddess of the sea (Macumba is a relatively mild form of Brazilian voodoo). **Carnival** in Rio is zany. For the four days preceding Ash Wednesday (late February, early March) the city goes festive. There are all-night costume balls in hotels and clubs, processions by the *Escolas de Samba* in their traditional colors, *Mascarados* (hooded clowns), floats, and communal dancing in the streets. Everybody joins in. In September and October, Rio holds an **International Song Festival** that is very popular.

Petrópolis, Teresopolis, and Nova Friburgo are mountain resorts not far from Rio. In Petrópolis, see the Hotel Quintandinha, which used to be a gambling casino and is now a private club—there are 20-foot bird cages, indoor Roman pools, a theater, a marble entrance hall, and a restaurant which is open to visitors. The Imperial Museum houses the old Empire's Crown Jewels—open 12-5 Tues-Sun. The Cathedral houses the tombs of the Emperor and the Empress. Buses leave the Nova Rio bus station every 30 minutes, and the journey takes 90 minutes. Hotels are Casablanca (Avenida 7 de Setembro 286) and the Casablanca Palace (Rua 16 de Marco 123). In Teresopolis the hotel is Hotel São Moritz, Nova Friburgo station, 35 Kilometer road mark, $75. Hotels in Friburgo are Hotel Sans Souci, Jardim Sans Souci, $60 and Hotel Bucksy, Estrada Rio-Friburgo, 76 Kilometer road mark, $55.

Ferries leave from the Praça XV de Novembro in Rio every 20 minutes for Niterói, a quiet residential city across Guanabara Bay, much preferred by the British and American communities. Beyond Niterói you can reach the deserted beaches of Saquarema, Marciá, and Cabo Frio. Ferries (Cr15) also leave the Praça XV for the island of Paquetá. Cars are not allowed on the island, but you can rent horse-driven carriages and bicycles. It is a traditional meeting place for lovers. There are also full-day and half-day boat tours around Guanabara Bay, operated by Bateau Mouche, in the Botafogo section of Rio. Fares include lunch on board.

South of Rio

Traveling south of Rio, the weather gets cool; severe frosts in winter are not unknown and bother the large coffee plantations. This region has been very much in favor with settlers from Italy (São Paulo), Germany, Austria and Switzerland (Santa Catarina), Poland, Russia, and the Ukraine (Paraná). São Paulo also has the largest Japanese colony outside Japan. In the deep south, bordering Argentina, Paraguay, and Uruguay, you find the gauchos, handling the largest cattle herds in the world.

São Paulo, lying on the Tropic of Capricorn, is South America's leading industrial center, the fastest growing city in the world. *Paulistas,* as they are called, pride themselves on their cosmopolitan way of life, their splendid skyscrapers, highways, and modern shopping arcades. You get a superb view of the city from the 41-story Edificio Italia, the highest building in the city and right in the heart of São Paulo. You can dine at the Terraco Italia restaurant at the top of the building where the view of São Paulo seems to extend to the horizon. Visit the new Catholic Cathedral, the Municipal Stadium of Pacaembú, the Jockey Club (races on Saturdays and Sundays), the Teatro Municipal and the Museum Paulista, in the suburb of Ipiranga (open daily 12-5, closed Monday). The São Paulo Art Museum (open Tues-Fri 1-5, weekends 2-6, closed Monday) is considered by many to be one of the best in South America. Located on Avenida Paulista, it has regularly changing exhibits of Brazilian and foreign artists in addition to an extensive collection of European impressionists. The famous Butantã Snake Farm and Museum is just outside the suburb of Pinheiros, open Tues-Sun 9-5, Monday 1-5. Take a bus

or taxi to **Ibirapuera Park;** there is an up-to-date **Planetarium,** a velodrome for bicycle and motorcycle racing, the new **Legislative Assembly,** and the **Museum of Contemporary Art** (open Tues-Sun 2-6, closed Monday), where the São Paulo Biennial Exhibition is held, the most important show of paintings and art in South America.

On Sundays, the popular handicrafts fair at **Praca Republica** in city center lasts from 8am to 1pm, featuring leather and wood handicrafts, basketry, paintings, fossils and semiprecious stones. In **Liberdade,** the equivalent of Chinatown, the Sunday fair lasts until early evening and includes Japanese food. There's another **Feira** held every Tuesday, Thursday, and Saturday near the old stadium, while at Embú, about 20 miles outside the city there's a Sunday market at which soapstone objects are among the handicrafts offered for sale. In Liberdade handicrafts have an Oriental flavor, as do the many restaurants specializing in Japanese, Chinese, and Korean cuisines. For international cuisine try **Paddock** (Rua São Luiz 258); **A Baiuca** (Praça Roosevelt 256); and **Terraćo Italia** (Avenida Ipiranga 344). For first-class French cooking go to **La Casserole** (Largo do Arouche 346), and try **Maria Fulô** (Rua São José 563) for Brazilian dishes. **Bolinha** (Avenida Cidade Jardim 53) serves an excellent *feijoada* Saturdays at noon. **Eduardo's** Restaurant (Rua Nestor Pestana, 80) offers the traditional barbecue or *churrascaria*—all you can eat for Cr480. In the Japanese section of Liberdade, try **Enomoto** (Rua Galvao Bueno 54). Cab drivers know the area.

Entertainment in São Paulo is thriving. For good shows (in Portuguese) there are many modern comfortable theaters, among them **Teatro Oficina, Teatro Cacilda Becker, Teatro Maria Della Costa,** and **Teatro Brasileiro de Comedia.** Nightclubs are first-class. There are **Baiuca, Michel's** (very expensive), **Stardust,** and **Captain's Bar,** all highly recommended. For a lively evening **Sargentelli's Oba Oba** club features a Samba show and dancing. It's one of São Paulo's best clubs. Also good, with Samba show, dancing, and dinner is **O Beco** (Rua Bela Cintra 306); **Opera Cabaret** (Rua Rui Barbosa); **Moustache** (Rua Sergipe); and **Cafe Societe** (Rua 13 de Maio). For the single man, **Merival** (Rua Guriva) is a popular disco. **La Licorne** has live music and floor shows for men only. And there are hundreds of movie houses all over town. If you enjoy auto racing, the magnificent course at Interlagos is a must; the 500-kilometer race is held in September and the 1000 in November. Hotels in downtown São Paulo:
Rates are in US$ for a double/twin room with bath or shower

Alvear, Avenida Cáspar Libéro 65 (from $40)
Brasilton São Paulo, Rua Martins Fontes (from $80)
Caesar Park, Rua Augusta 1508 (from $90)
Comodoro, Rua Duque de Caxias 525 (from $38)
Danúbio, Avenida Brig Luiz Antonio 1099 (from $39)
Eldorado, Avenida São Luiz 234 (from $82)
Excelsior, Avenida Ipiranga 770 (from $40)
Grand Ca' d'Oro, Rua Avanhandava 308 (from $65)
Jaraguá, Rua Major Quedinho 40 (from $46)
Maksoud Plaza, Alameda Campinas (from $100)

Normandie, Avenida Ipiranga 1187 (from $45)
Novotel São Paulo, Avenida Ministro Nelson Hungria 450 (from $60)
Othon Palace, Rua Libero Badaro 190 (from $41)
Planalto, Av Casper Libero 117 (from $45)
Samambaia, Rua 7 de April 422 (from $50)
San Raphael, Avenida Sao Joao 1173 (from $64)
São Paulo, Praca das Bandeira 15 (from $54)
São Paulo Hilton, Avenida Ipirango 165 (from $90)
Vila Rica, Avenida Vieira de Carvalho 167 (from $45)

Santos can be reached in a leisurely way by ocean steamer from Rio in 12 to 15 hours or by car from São Paulo in less than two hours. This is one of Brazil's largest ports. The best resort is **Guarujá,** with luxurious apartment homes, good hotels, and a pleasant beach. More deserted and cleaner beaches are to be found about two hours up the coast from Santos. Try the fresh oysters, sprinkled with lemon juice, sold from little stalls along the beach. **Iguaçu Falls** is one of the marvels of the world and Brazil's second major tourist attraction after Rio. Fly there in two hours, using one of the four Brazilian airlines serving the city of Foz de Iguacu. The **Hotel das Cataratas,** with a spectacular view overlooking the falls, is one of Latin America's finest. Several other less expensive hotels lie on the 15-mile road joining the falls with Foz de Iguacu. Skilled guides can take you for a stunning close-up view of the falls by boat. A few miles upstream on the Paraná River, **Itaipu** is the world's largest hydroelectric installation.

Blumenau (Santa Catarina) is a prosperous agricultural and manufacturing district settled mainly by Germans. **Florianópolis,** on the island of Santa Catarina, is joined to the mainland by Brazil's largest steel suspension bridge; **Campos de Jordão,** with its European and New England ambiance, is one of São Paulo's leading resort areas. **Porto Alegre** is a busy river port on the **Lagôa dos Patos,** the most important commercial center south of São Paulo; **Vila Velha** in the state of Paraná has the "old village built by nature"—an enormous extension of rocks carved by wind and rain.

West of Rio

To the west of Rio lies the state of **Minās Gerais,** with its beautiful colonial towns and spa centers and the dense forests of the **Mato Grosso,** where hunting is superb. In the state of Goiás, in the Federal District, lies **Brasilia,** the new capital of Brazil, about 4,000 feet above sea level and 758 miles from Rio. It was inaugurated on 21 April 1960. André Malraux once called it "the capital of hope." The buildings were designed by architect Oscar Niemeyer. They include the **Presidential Palace,** 100 yards from a huge artificial lake; the **Praça dos Tres Poderes** (housing the three powers of the government); the **Catholic Cathedral;** the **National Theater;** the **Acoustic Bowl;** and vast residential blocks. From the observation deck of the **Television Tower** you will see that the city is shaped like a large aircraft or cross. There is an international airport, and domestic flights from Rio to Brasilia (fare US$97) take 1½ hours.

An interregional system of highways links Brasilia to **Belém** and **Porto Alegre.** There are many first-class hotels serving international cuisine. Try the restaurant in the Eron Brasilia Hotel. Hotels in Brasilia include **Nacional** (from US$65); **Hotel das Nações,** SHS 4 Bloco I (from US$47); and the **Eron Brasilia Hotel,** SHS Av/W-3 Blocos EFHJ (from US$54).

Belo Horizonte, the capital of the state of Minãs Gerais, is the center of the mining and steel industries and has mysterious caves and grottoes; **Maquiné** cave near Cordisburgo, a suburb of Belo Horizonte, was once occupied by prehistoric Indians. There are fine museums to be visited, **Museu da Cidade,** in town, and **Museu de Arte Moderna,** facing Lake Pampulha, in a fashionable district. The **Igreja de São Francisco de Assiã** was designed by Niemeyer and has blue tile murals by Portinari, a leading Brazilian exponent of modern art. From Belo Horizonte you must take a day tour to **Ouro Preto,** a beautiful colonial town, 60 miles away. Its cobblestone streets, charming houses, and 13 churches are preserved as a national monument. The historic town of **Congonhas do Campo** is also a must. Here Aleijadinho ("the little Cripple"), a leprosy-stricken genius of the 18th century, ringed the **Church of Bom Jesus** with incredible life-sized soapstone figures of the twelve prophets (you can get miniature replicas, also in soapstone, from good handicraft stores). South of the city lie the quiet spa towns of **Sao Lourenço, Pocos de Caldas,** and **Caxambú.** Hotels in Belo Horizonte: **Del Rey,** Praca Alfonso Arinos 60 (from US$60); **Excelsior,** Rua Caetis 753 (from US$53), and the **Normandy,** Rua Tamoios 212 (from US$52).

North and Northeast

Northwards towards the Equator lies the basin of the great São Francisco River, the **Sertão,** the dry region where the earth is burned dry by an implacable sun, and the Amazon jungle. **Salvador** is a dream city, famous for its 365 colonial churches, its rainbow-tinted houses, and colorful markets. It is divided in two: **Cidade Baixa** (lower city), with the **Mercado Modelo** near the Praca Cairú and the old port, and **Cidade Alta** (higher city), 200 feet above, which can be reached by steep roads, and by four public elevators. Here are the **Government Palace,** the **Custom House,** and many other buildings. Scattered through the city are about 640 *Terreiros,* where the rites of the Candomblé worship are conducted by Afro-Brazilian priests and priestesses. An important local festival is the **Festa do Bonfim,** in January. See the *Copoeira,* a dance developed by the blacks to practice fighting with their legs, and look for the *Berimbau,* a musical instrument resembling a bow with a coconut attached to it. Hotels in Salvador include **Bahia Othon Palace,** Av Presidente Vargas 2456 (from US$75); **Hotel Meridien Bahia,** Rua Fonte de Boi 216 (from US$85); **Hotel Plaza,** Av 7 de Setembro 1839 (from US$69) and **Salvador Praia Hotel,** Av Presidente Vargas 2032 (from US$73).

Recife, "the Venice of America," is laced with waterways crossed by numerous graceful bridges. The city is famous for its primitive balsawood fishing fleet (*Jangadas*—you can go out to sea with a fisherman for Cr80). Look for the *Frêvo,* an athletic native dance. At the **Museu do Acucar**

(Sugar Museum) see models of colonial mills and devices for torturing slaves. Hotels in Recife include **Grande Hotel do Recife,** Avenida Martins de Barros, 593 (from US$50); **Hotel Guararapes,** Rua da Palma 57 (from US$40), centrally located; **Miramar Hotel,** Rua des Navegentes 363 (from US$69), beach location; **Olinda Quatro Rodas,** Av Sao Luis still under construction, (reopening soon); and **Vila Rica Hotel,** Avenida Boa Viagem, 4308, (from US$62). Recife is three days from Rio by mail steamer, or it can be reached by main national airlines.

Belém, at the mouth of the Amazon, 90 miles from the open sea, is just south of the Equator. It has an 18th-century **Cathedral,** a beautiful theater, and one of the most moving and remarkable popular festivals, **Festival of the Candles** in October. Accommodations at the **Excelsior Grão Para,** Praca da República 718 (from US$52) or **Novotel Belem,** Av Bernardo Sayao (from US$43).

Manáus, where the mean temperature is 80 degrees, is 1,000 miles up the Amazon, in the heart of the jungle. From this river port, with its Opera House where Caruso and Bernhardt appeared, you can charter small river boats to take you into "the last page of the Book of Genesis," as writer Euclides da Cunha described this mysterious region. Parrots, exotic birds, and athletic monkeys chatter in the forest. You can hunt the fierce jungle cat, the onça; the giant relative of the pig, the tapir; or fish for a 500-pound piracuru, the largest freshwater fish in the world. A swim in the warm waters of the Amazon, however, is not advisable; there are schools of piranha, small vicious fish with razor-sharp teeth. The **Hotel Amazonas** organizes inexpensive fishing and hunting expeditions. Air services from most Brazilian cities. Hotels in Mánaus include **Amazonas,** Praca Dalberto Valle, S/N (from US$67); **Lord,** Rua Quintino Bociauva/Marcilio Dias (from US$50); **Novotel Mánaus,** Av Mandii (from US$60). **Tropical Hotel Mánaus,** Estrada de Ponta Negra, and just outside of Mánaus, is one of Brazil's most luxurious hotels (from US$87).

SOURCES OF FURTHER INFORMATION

Pan Am offices: Nacional Brasilia Hotel, Loja 56, Brasilia; Avenida São Luis 50, São Paulo; Avenida Presidente Wilson 165-A, Rio de Janeiro, and any Pan Am office around the world; **Secretaria de Turismo,** Rua Real Grandeza 293, Rio de Janeiro; **Secretaria de Turismo,** Praca da Republica 154, São Paulo; **Departamento de Turismo,** Amexco Patacio do Buriti—3rd floor, Brasilia; **Brazilian Consulate General,** 630 Fifth Avenue, New York, NY 10020; 6 Deanery Street, London W1.

Chile

WHAT'S SPECIAL

The Andes mountains run the entire length of the country and occupy more than half its width, rising to an average altitude of 10,000 feet. The country stretches some 2,630 miles south from its Peruvian borders to the tip of the continent at Cape Horn. Despite its length its width only averages 110 miles, and is a bare 56 miles at its narrowest point. One half of the territory is occupied by the beautiful snow-capped Andes Mountains, and because of its north-south location a wide range of soils and climates is to be found.

Chile is a land of contrasts, with five distinctly different natural regions, from the arid north (some 600 miles long and one of the driest areas on earth) down to the bitterly chilling, stormy and windswept south. The far north is the site of copper mines and nitrate deposits, while iron ore is extracted immediately south. The middle region is a fertile valley that has been called the Switzerland of South America. It is here that the three principal cities (and the bulk of the population) are found. Immediately south to Puerto Montt is a forest region, rich with bright lakes and tumbling rivers, and where the rains can oppress during fall and winter. The southernmost region has been compared to the fjords and glaciers of Norway. One of the interesting features of rural life is the *huasos*, Chilean cowboys, who appear at rodeos (September-March) in typical garb, playing guitars and singing traditional Chilean songs. Some 300,000 pure-blooded Mapuche (from the Indian words *mapu*, meaning earth, and *che*, people) Indians survive among the population, which is predominantly of Spanish descent with a generous sprinkling of other Europeans and Asians.

COUNTRY BRIEFING
Size: 292,257   **Population:** 12,214,000
Capital: Santiago   **Capital Population:** 4,276,132
Climate: North Chile is dry, central Chile temperate, and south Chile wet all year. Summer is October-March.

Weather in Santiago: Lat S33°27'; Alt 1,706 ft

Temp (°F)	Jan	Feb	Mar	Apr	May	Jun	Jul	Aug	Sep	Oct	Nov	Dec
Av Low	53°	52°	49°	45°	41°	37°	37°	39°	42°	45°	48°	51°
Av High	85°	84°	80°	74°	65°	58°	59°	62°	66°	72°	78°	83°
Days no rain	31	28	30	29	26	24	25	26	27	28	29	31

Government: Chile is a republic. A constitution was approved by plebiscite in September, 1980, electing General Augusto Pinochet president for an 8-year term.
Language: Spanish. English spoken in major cities.
Religion: Predominantly Roman Catholic.
Currency: Pesos. 100 centavos = 1 peso (sign: $).

	1 peso	5 peso	10 peso	50 peso	100 peso	200 peso	500 peso	600 peso
US (dollars, cents)	.03	.13	.26	1.28	2.56	5.13	12.82	15.38
UK (pounds, pence)	.01	.06	.12	.61	1.22	2.45	6.12	7.34

Public Holidays:

New Year's Day, 1 Jan
Good Friday
Labor Day, 1 May
Battle of Iquique Day, 21 May
Assumption Day, 15 Aug
Independence Day, 18-19 Sep
Columbus Day, 12 Oct
All Saints' Day, 1 Nov
Immaculate Conception, 8 Dec
Christmas Day, 25 Dec

HOW TO GET THERE
Flying time to Santiago's Aeropuerto Internacional Comodoro Arturo Merino Benitez (formally Pudahuel Airport) from Miami ½ hours, from Rio de Janeiro, 6 hours; from Buenos Aires, 2 hours. Time in Chile: GMT–4.

REQUIREMENTS FOR ENTRY AND CUSTOMS REGULATIONS
Passport. Vaccination certificates are not necessary for visitors from most Western-hemisphere countries, including the US and Canada. Ninety-day renewable (for a further ninety days) tourist cards are given to visitors who enter Chile by land or air. Best rate of exchange to pesos is in Chile but convert back before leaving. Duty-free allowance: 400 grams of pipe tobacco, 400 cigarettes, 50 cigars, 2.5 liters liquor allowance.

AIRPORT INFORMATION
The Internacional Comodoro Arturo Merino Benitez Airport (13½ miles from Santiago) is connected to the capital by a half-hourly public bus

service (about US75¢) and special tourist buses which go to the Hotel Carrera (about US$2). Taxis to downtown Santiago cost about US$12 in the daytime and US$19 at night and on Sundays. A departure tax for international flights is about US$5. There are three hotel reservation counters.

ACCOMMODATIONS

Hotels in Santiago:

Rates are in US$ for a double/twin room with bath or shower

Acacias de Vitacura, El Manantial 1781 (from $66)

City, Compania 1063 (from $35)

El Conquistador, Miguel Cruchaga 920 (from $66)

Foresta, Ave Subercaseaux 353 (from $35)

Gran Palace, Huérfanos, esquina Morande 1175 (from $35)

Holiday Inn Cordillera, 136 Avenida Bernardo O'Higgins (from approximately $76)

Hotel Carrera, Teatinos 180-Casilla 2272 (from $66)

Kent, Huérfanos 878 (from $35)

Panamericano, Teatinos/Huérfanos (from $35)

Posada del Salvador, Avenida Elidoro Yánez 893 (from $30)

Ritz, Estado 248 (from $35)

Santa Lucia, Huérfanos 779, esquina San Antonio (from $35)

Santiago Galerias, 65 San Antonio Street (from approximately $72)

Sao Paulo, San Antonio 357 (from $30)

Sheraton San Cristóbal, Avenida Santa Maria 1472 (from $66); 10 minutes from downtown

Hotel Splendid, Estado 360 (from $30)

Tupahue, San Antonio 477 (from $66)

All hotels centrally located unless otherwise indicated.

USEFUL INFORMATION

Helpful Hints: Tea customary at 5pm, which makes dinner a late meal.

Banks: Open 9-2 Mon-Fri in all major cities.

Telephone Tips: Phones are operated by tokens, which are sold at stores and hotels that have phones. A local call costs 4 pesos.

Newspapers: Foreign newspapers are hard to find, but a wide variety of Spanish papers and magazines are available. English-language magazines and books available, and *The New York Times* is available in the Hotel Carrera.

Tipping: Taxi drivers not usually tipped; porters 25 pesos per bag, hotel porters 10%; chambermaids 5%; hairdressers 10%.

Electricity: 220 volts 50 cycles AC.

Laundry: Good dry-cleaners in main towns. Laundromats everywhere in Santiago.

Hairdressing: Good barbers and hairdressers in the larger cities.

Photography: Film is available but expensive.

Clubs: Several branches of Rotary and Lions clubs.

Rest Rooms: No charge, but a small tip is customary.

Health: Many doctors and dentists speak English. Day and night medical and dental service available through the Asistencia Publica, Av Portugal 125 (tel: 224422). Imported pharmaceutical goods scarce and expensive. Stick to bottled water.

TRANSPORTATION

State and private companies operate public transportation in the main cities and towns. The capital is served by buses and *liebres,* minibuses seating 17, all of which are inexpensive. Taxis (black and yellow) in Santiago have meters, and private automobiles (with and without meters) can be hailed. Taxis are at a premium in the rush hours 12:30-1:30 and 6:30-7:30; there is a 50% night and Sunday surcharge. Rental cars are available. A regular intercity express bus serves the north-south Pan American Highway, and a fast and efficient train service (sleeper and restaurant cars) reaches from Santiago to Puerto Montt in the south. A number of bus companies offer luxury double-decker service to the cities of the south, complete with meals, drinks, and reclining chair/beds. Regular Linea Aerea Nacional (LAN) flights go to all main cities and to Easter Island. LADECO airline flies to some northern cities. All coastal towns can be reached by sea, and TAXPA Airlines has flights to outlying Pacific islands, including **Juan Fernández,** where a famous castaway, Alexander Selkirk, provided Daniel Defoe with the model for Robinson Crusoe.

FOOD AND RESTAURANTS

Seafood is excellent, particularly lobsters and oysters (May-August). *Caldillo de Congrio* is an eel broth, and *chupe de mariscos* is a shellfish dish. Meat and poultry are good quality. *Cazuela de ave* is a chicken and vegetable broth, usually with corn, potatoes, squash, and spices. Chilean bullfrog is a delicacy. *Empanadas* are turnovers filled with meat, onions, eggs, olives, and whatever the cook fancies. *Pastel de choclo* is a summertime green corn pie with ground meat and vegetables. *Humitas* are Chilean tamales. For one-course meals and snacks try *tallarines con lomito,* steak and noodle casserole; *bife lomo,* steak with rice; and *vienesas,* a type of hot dog with tomato and onion relish. Fruit and vegetables in season are abundant, inexpensive, and delicious. An expensive dinner can run from US$30 and an expensive lunch from US$15, while a moderately priced dinner will cost US$20 (without wine), and lunch (again without wine) will run from US$10. Quick sandwich or hamburger lunches cost about US$1.60-2. Good international cuisine can be sampled at the **Maistral** (Mosqueto 485); the **Arlequin,** General Holley 2322; the **International** at the Hotel Carrera; **Jacaranda** (Huérfanos 612), with delightful open-air dining in summer. The **ENOTECA,** a vintner (plus restaurant) within the grounds of the Parque Metropolitano offers wine tastings, and while the view from this San Cristóbal restaurant is superb, the food is priced high. For Italian food try the **San Marco Trattoria** (Huerfanos 612) and **Da Carla** (McIver 577); seafood at moderate to expensive prices is to be found at **Aqui Esta Coco** (La Concepcion 236) while **La Estancia**—a new, large restaurant—places an emphasis on steak, plus a popular floor show (Las Condes 13810). A moderately priced *prix fixe* chicken menu is to be found at **Lo Barnechea:** try the *Pollo al Cognac.* Steaks are a specialty at **El Parrón** (Providencia 1184). The **Munchen** (Providencia 2601) serves good Bavarian food at moderate prices. French cuisine with a fine reputation is found at the **Cascade** (Francisco Bilbao 1947) and the **Bric à Brac** (Abadia 25). About 30 minutes from downtown Santiago is the **Alero de los Ramon** (Las Condes 9889), expensive but with an exuberant atmosphere in a Spanish-colonial-style house. **La Pension no me Olvides** (San Enrique 14880) is a typical Chilean restaurant in the lovely town of El Arrayan, about half an hour from downtown. The most pleasant fast-food spot downtown is the **Burger Inn** (Estado 236), a clean, cafeteria-style hamburger den. A favorite luncheon spot of Chilean businessmen is the **Pinpilinpausha** (Matias Cousiño 62), which serves Spanish and Basque dishes at moderate prices.

DRINKING TIPS

Bars and clubs are open between 6pm and 1am. Local wine is excellent and inexpensive. Try Santa Carolina and Cousiño-Macul (white) and Tarapaca ex-Zavala (burgundy-type). The native drink is the potent *Pisco,* a grape distillation best drunk as a Pisco sour cocktail or as a *Pichuncho,* mixed with sweet vermouth. *Aguardiente* is the brandy equivalent and is also very alcoholic. The delicious Christmastime punch, *cola de mono,* is sold in many downtown bars. Escudo is the most popular beer. Tea parlors are crowded for the five o'clock ritual, and most popular are the **Waldorf,** the **Paula,** and the **Colonia.** Customers stand at the counter for hours at the **Haiti Coffee House** (Ahumada Street) and at the **Do Brasil** on Bandera, which serves a refreshing fruit milkshake called *leche con fruta* and unusual varieties of coffee.

ENTERTAINMENT

There are many lavish movie houses in the cities showing recent American and English films with subtitles. Matinees generally begin at 3:30 and evening performances at 7 and 10. During the winter season there are weekly symphony concerts and occasional ballet and opera presentations. The capital has many theaters, among them the **Teatro Municipal, Teatro "La Comedia,"** and **Teatro del Angel.** Musicals, including popular US classics, are played at the **Casino Las Vegas** (Rosas 1531), and drinks are served at your seat. Two nightclubs worth noting are **Crazy Horse** (Avenida Providencia 1,100) and **Maxim** (Avenida Matta 533). **Mon Bijou** (Bulnes 475) and **Tap Room** (Bulnes 135) both offer popular revues and occasionally feature international performers. Popular nightspots are **La Châtelaine** (Plaza Pedro de Valdiria 1718), with Latin-American music, and **El Pollo Dorado** (Estado 215), where you can see Chile's national folk dance, the *cueca.* Popular discothèques are **Le Moustache** (Nueva Costanera 2905) and **Boite Domus** (Bandera, off Agustinas), usually crowded on weekends. Also offering a show, plus dancing, is **Night and Day** (Agustinas 1022).

SHOPPING

Stores open late (about 10am) and close at 7pm during the week and 2pm Saturday. Some stores on the Avenida Providencia stay open as late as 8pm weekdays. Summer hours are generally shorter. Best buys are copperware, Chilean wine, wooden carvings from Easter Island, and leather goods, including saddles made in Rancagua and Chillán. Chile is noted for its black pottery, and the town of **Pomaire** near Melipilla (37 miles from Santiago) produces attractive handmade ceramics. **Chilean Art** has a wide range of copperware. **Chile Lindo** handles black pottery and **Chile Tipico** a variety of souvenir items, including ponchos. All three are on Agustinas, and on the same street is **José Sánchez**, with fine-quality Chilean woolens and worsteds. **El Arte** (Merced 673) specializes in jewelry made from locally mined lapis lazuli. Pottery, baskets, dolls, and other typical souvenirs can be found at Santiago's **Central Market.** Typical Chilean artisan goods, from carved bone figures to handwoven Indian rugs, can be viewed and bought at a government-sponsored store, at Portugal 351 and another at Providencia 1652. Good clothing for men and women can be bought at **Flaño** downtown, Huerfanos 964, and Flaño uptown, Providencia 2202. Clothing for men can also be found at **Juven's** (Huerfanos 1034 and Providencia 2360) and **Le Monde Pierre Cardin** (Huerfanos 1033). Fashionable Chilean women shop at the numerous boutiques along the Avenida Providencia. Among the best are **Privilege** (Providencia 1968), **Via Veneto** (Providencia 2382), and for leather goods, **Maria Ines Matte's** (Galvarino Gallardo 1917). The municipality of Santiago recently completed the facelift of the central downtown area, creating an attractive shopping center. The **Paseo Ahumada**, with its fountains and benches, now boasts some of the better shops in the capital, among them **Shopping Group** for men's and women's clothes, while **Gucci** has its complete line of products. Paseo Ahumada crosses **Paseo Huerfanos,** forming the heart of downtown Santiago. Huerfanos boasts numerous shoe emporia, while for electric and electronic goods—at prices lower than in most of South America (though still higher than the US)—stores on Estado, from Agustinas south to Alameda, provide a large selection. A best buy in Chile is *lapis lazuli,* the sapphire of the ancients, with its rich azure blue. Numerous jewelers on McIver between Merced and the Alameda stock this stone. The *lapis lazuli* jewelry is also available at the **H. Stern** stores located at the Cristobal-Sheraton, Carrera Hotels and at the International Airport.

SPORTS

The most popular spectator sport is soccer, closely followed by horse racing. There are race tracks in Santiago with meetings every Saturday, Sunday, and feast-day. The annual social event, **The Derby,** is held at the Viña del Mar Track in October. The most famous ski resorts in South America are only a few hours by train from the capital, and there is ample scope year round for the novice as well as the experienced skier. At the nearer ski centers of **Farellones** and **Lagunillas** accommodations are *refugios* or private lodges. **Portillo,** the largest of the resorts, has top instructors, chairlifts, wonderful trails, ski runs up to 6 miles long, and a luxury hotel. A day trip to the peace memorial, **Christ of the Andes,** affords uninterrupted skiing all the way back. Portillo is 2½ hours from Santiago by car or four hours on a scenic train ride. The southern lake area, rich in river trout and salmon, offers excellent opportunities for fishing, and there are good beach resorts on the Pacific Coast. Game fishers can try for tuna and swordfish in the waters of the north. A permit to fish must be obtained from **SAG** (Servicio Agricola y Ganadero) with offices in Santiago and most important cities and towns throughout the country. Most visitors will find the 30-day permit sufficient, though season licenses are available. In addition to the modest fee, you are expected to be familiar with Chilean regulations regarding weight limits, protected species, and minimum size that may be taken. Deep sea and coastal fishing is a sport, while inland freshwater fishing rules vary by area and species, though generally from November 16 through April 15. The SAG office in Santiago is at Pedro de Valdivia 942 (tel: 460378) and can advise of current rules. Skin-diving, yachting, and water-skiing can all be practiced at **Algarrobo** and **Zapallar,** which is one of the most exclusive of the coastal resorts. Tennis and riding are to be found in most centers. Tennis courts at **Rancho Mellink,** Camino Las Flores 11020, cost around US$6 per hour during the day, higher at night, and equipment can also be hired.

WHAT TO SEE

Santiago: Set on a plateau 1,706 feet high with the snow-clad Andes as a clearly visible backdrop, Santiago, the fourth largest city in South America, has the added attraction of spacious streets, lovely gardens, and a sunny Mediterranean climate. It is the focus of the commercial, industrial, and cultural life of Chile, and tall modern structures rise alongside more venerable monuments. The hub of the city is the **Plaza de Armas,** on which stands the **Cathedral,** which houses a fine painting of the Last Supper and a 17th-century silver lamp weighing 50 pounds. In **Quinta Normal** park are the **Modern Art Museum** and the **National History Museum,** with Chilean Indian mummies and a perfectly preserved body of a pre-Inca boy. The **Historical Museum,** next to the National Library on Miraflores, contains Indian, colonial, and folklore exhibits. (All Santiago museums are closed Mondays.) Visit the castle and gardens on the picturesque central **Santa Lucia Hill,** delightfully laid out with ornamental and pleasure gardens. Santiago city was founded in this place. A funicular climbs the 1,000-foot **Cerro San Cristóbal** to the observatory and restaurant. The views from this hill are particularly impressive at night. A few miles south is **Maipu,** with a monument to commemorate the battle here in 1818, an outstanding museum open Saturday and Sunday, and a temple to the Virgin of Carmen. The **San Francisco Church** on central Alameda Boulevard dates from 1572 and houses a colonial museum with religious relics. Guided tours of the city are available and arrangements can be made at your hotel. Cost is around US$8 for an excursion including the **Club Hipico, Santa Lucia Hill, Fine Arts Museum, Cathedral,** the

Congress building and other points of interest. Similar tours and excursions to other places can be easily arranged.

Valparaiso, founded in 1536, is Chile's principal port, 115 miles from the capital by rail and some 90 miles by road. The old town and business section is built on a low terrace on land reclaimed from the sea, and the residential part of the city rises in tiers on hills surrounding the crescent-shaped **Bay of Valparaiso.** Winding roads and cliff railways *(ascensores)* lead to the upper town. The cathedral, parks, theaters, and the few remaining colonial buildings, such as the church of **La Matriz,** are in the lower town. **Plaza Sotomayor** is the shipping front, **Calle Esmeralda** the main shopping center, and **Avenida Pedro Montt,** with cafés and theaters, is the social hub.

Viña del Mar: Coastal resorts stretch all the way from La Serena to San Antonio, but the most fashionable is the elegant Viña del Mar (high season January-March). An attractive city of flowers and trees, with the president's **Summer Palace** on Castle Hill (Cerro Castillo), its parks include the central **Plaza Vergara, Plaza Mexico** with illuminated fountains, and the **Quinta Vergara,** an estate (the palace is now a **Museum of Fine Arts**) with large gardens where concerts and other events are held in summer. Drama and ballet are performed in the **Municipal Theater.** The famous **Casino** offers roulette, baccarat, a nightclub with excellent cabaret and floor shows, and a restaurant with orchestra. Good restaurants are **Chez Gerald, Cap Ducal, Parrillada Armandita,** and **Curia Nurin,** on the lovely road to the seaside resort of **Concón** (about 20 miles). Hotels in Viña del Mar:

Rates are in US$ for a double/twin room with bath or shower

    Alcazar, Alvarez 646 (from $35)

    Miramar, Caleta Abarca (from $66)

    O'Higgins, Plaza Vergarra (from $66)

    San Martin, Casilla 568 (from $35)

All hotels are on or convenient to oceanfront.

Chilean Lake Country: A region of mountain and lake scenery offering top-rate fishing (rainbow and brown trout) in little-fished waters, the Chilean Lake Country extends from Los Angeles, 320 miles south of Santiago, to Puerto Montt. See the 200-foot **Laja Falls,** just north of Los Angeles. Fishing competitions are held in Laja Lake. Further south is **Lake Villarrica.** Hotels here are the **Ciervo** (from US$35) and the **Yachting Club** (from US$35). Approximately 15 miles from Villarrica is the best-known lake resort in Chile, **Pucon.** There can be found excellent fishing, golf, and winter skiing. Hotels are the **Gran Hotel** (from US$66) and the **Antumalal** (from US$66). The **Puyehue Lake,** with many islands and waterfalls, has abundant bird life. Nearby is the **Antillanca** volcano, with good ski slopes. **Osorno** is near lakes **Puyehue** and **Rupanco** (hot springs). This old-fashioned city was colonized by Germans, and their language is still as commonly used here as Spanish. Hotels here are **Granhotel** (from US$35); **Waeger** (from US$35), and **Termas de Puyehue** (from US$35). Another German town is **Puerto Varas** on **Lake Llanquihue,** largest of the lakes (320 square miles) and ringed with snow-capped volcanoes. **Puerto Montt** is a seaport, and excellent seafood plays a major role in its cuisine. Stay at the **Hotel Vicente Pérez Rosales** (from US$35). Ten-day boat trips are organized from here through a region criss-crossed with canals and inhabited mainly by fishing folk.

Punta Arenas is the most southerly city in the world, the last stop for Tierra del Fuego and Cape Horn. The center of an area rich both in oil and produce such as sheep, fish, and shellfish, the city is also a whaling town. There are racing, tennis, and golf and, close by, one low ski run with a view of the Straits of Magellan. You can take a cruise to **Tierra del Fuego** or visit the local ranches.

Antofagasta: In northern Chile, in a province of desert and mountain ranges, is the unique city of Antofagasta. Although earth for its main square had to be brought as ballast in sailing ships and water has to be piped from the Andes, a city of lovely parks and plazas has sprung from the barren soil. Stay at the **Antofagasta Hotel** (from US$66) or the **Diego de Almargro** (from US$66). The province of Antofagasta is rich in archeological remains, and there is a pre-Columbian museum at **San Pedro de Atacama.** Other tourist attractions are the **Tatio** geysers and **Chuquicamata,** the world's largest open-pit copper mine, near Calama. You need authorization for this particular trip; inquire at your travel agent or airline before departure.

Easter Island: Located 2,300 miles west of Santiago in the Pacific is the 45 square mile Easter Island, population 1,300. Discovered in 1722 by the Dutch navigator Jacob Roggeveen; he was followed by the Spanish and English who used the same island as a port stop. In September of 1888, it became a Chilean colony and in 1966 the residents became Chilean citizens. Easter Island is best noted for its archeological discoveries as well as its pleasant climate and deserted beaches. Most famous in **Aku Akivi** are the seven stone statues that were unearthed by archeologist Dr. Mulloy. Also of interest is the 30,000 pound statue at **Ahu Tahai** facing the Pacific with a stone ring on its head. Tours can be made to the island's over 1,000 statues and 300 ancient villages as well as to the Rano Raraku volcano. Accommodations on Easter Island include the **Hosteria Hangaroa,** S38/D$60 or the **Hotua Matu,** S/D$30.

SOURCES OF FURTHER INFORMATION

Pan Am agents: Temco, Huerfanos 1160, Office 1213, Santiago, or any Pan Am office around the world; **Servicio Nacional de Turismo,** Catedral 1165, Santiago (tel: 60474); and the **Chilean Consulate General,** 360 Madison Ave, NY, NY 10017, and 12 Devonshire St, London W1.

Colombia

WHAT'S SPECIAL

Placed astride the land routes to the South American continent from the isthmus that is Central America, Colombia appears to have started life as a looseknit federation of city states, resulting largely from the geophysical nature of its terrain. The land was inhabited by Amerindian tribes as early as 5,000 BC from whom descended the Barrancoid, Arawak, and Carib colonizers of the Lesser Antilles. The first Spanish settlement to be founded was at Santa Marta, while Bogotá, the capital, was originally founded in 1538, following the defeat of the Chibcha Indians by General Gonzalo Jimenez de Quesada and the area became the nucleus of New Grenada, following other Spanish successes to the north by Cortes. The Chibchas were an agricultural tribe whose mines of copper, emeralds, and gold were in the mountainous interior. The Spanish imposed their autocratic colonial rule, which lasted until news of the French Revolution triggered the flame of a movement towards independence. Once Napoleon had seized control of Spain a revolutionary junta was able to proclaim July 20, 1810 as Independence Day. The arrival of Simón Bolívar just two years later (from Venezuela) meant the start of a series of wars against the royalist faction. By 1819, Simón Bolívar—the Liberator—had secured independence for the new republic of Greater Colombia. Today, the memory of this national hero has secured the nation as the largest working democracy in South America, while preserving the best of its Spanish heritage. The nation's traditional export has for years been coffee (the best in the world, it is claimed, though Costa Ricans disagree), and there has been the recent encouragement—

and development—of petrochemicals, textiles, and other industry. For the bona fide tourist, Colombia has an incredible range of experience to offer: some of the finest beaches in the world; the beauty of the triple range of Andean mountains; lushly green valleys, torrential streams, dense jungle. Every variety of tropical flower is to be found, and wild jaguars and pumas, armadillos, and tapirs still lurk in the bush. It is said of Colombia that in no other country in the world are so many varieties of birds to be found.

COUNTRY BRIEFING

Size: 440,000 square miles   **Population:** 29,100,000
Capital: Bogotá   **Capital Population:** 4,900,000
    Climate: On the Caribbean coast, the average temperature is 83°. Cities in the temperate zone (3,000 to 6,500 feet) have an average temperature of 65-70°; Bogotá (8,669 feet above sea level) is usually cool. Rainy season March-April and October-November. Best time to go: December-February.

Weather in Bogotá: Lat N5°36'; Alt 8,678 ft

Temp (°F)	Jan	Feb	Mar	Apr	May	Jun	Jul	Aug	Sep	Oct	Nov	Dec
Av Low	48°	49°	50°	51°	51°	51°	50°	50°	49°	50°	50°	49°
Av High	67°	68°	67°	67°	66°	65°	64°	65°	66°	66°	66°	66°
Days no rain	25	21	18	10	14	14	13	15	17	11	14	16

Government: A republic.
Language: Spanish. English widely spoken.
Religion: Roman Catholic.
Currency: Peso. 100 centavos = 1 peso.

	1 peso	5 peso	10 peso	20 peso	50 peso	100 peso	500 peso	1,000 peso
US (dollars, cents)	.02	.09	.19	.38	.94	1.88	9.42	18.84
UK (pounds, pence)	.01	.04	.09	.18	.45	.90	4.50	9.00

Public Holidays:

New Year's Day, 1 Jan
Epiphany, 6 Jan
St Joseph, 19 Mar
Holy Week
Labor Day, 1 May
Ascension Day
Sacred Heart—varies each year, June
Corpus Christi, late June
Peter and Paul, 29 June

Independence Day, 20 July
Battle of Boyaca, 7 Aug
Assumption, 15 Aug
Columbus Day, 12 Oct
All Saints Day, 1 Nov
Independence Day—
  Cartagena, 11 Nov
Immaculate Conception, 8 Dec
Christmas Day, 25 Dec

HOW TO GET THERE

Flying time to El Dorado Airport in Bogotá from New York is 5½ hours; from London, 13 hours; from Guatemala City, 2¾ hours; from Mexico City, 5 hours. Time in Colombia: GMT−5.

REQUIREMENTS FOR ENTRY AND CUSTOMS REGULATIONS

Passport and tourist card. To obtain the latter, a valid passport, plus two passport size photographs, plus roundtrip ticket must be presented at any Colombia consulate. It's issued free of charge and is valid for one entry with a stay limitation of 90 days. Duty-free allowance: 200 cigarettes or 50 cigars or 200 grams of tobacco; ½ bottle liquor, opened; perfume for personal use; and gifts to the total value of US$10. A typewriter, radio, binoculars, movie camera and equipment are allowed, provided these are not new. Permit needed for guns and ammunition: apply in advance to the Ministry of Defense.

AIRPORT INFORMATION

El Dorado Airport is 8 miles from Bogotá. From 6am-8pm, buses run every 10 minutes, fare 10 pesos. Tip the porter about 10 pesos per bag. Taxis available at all times. Fare to the center of town between 175-200 pesos, additional costs for Sunday and holidays. Hotel reservation center and duty-free shop at the airport. Departure tax is US$10. Ernesto Cortissoz Airport is 6 miles from Barranquilla. The taxi fare is about 200 pesos.

ACCOMMODATIONS

Throughout Colombia there is a 5% hotel tax, but no service charge. There are also motels, *hosterias* (inns), and cottages. For assistance in finding accommodations in Bogotá go to the **Corporación Nacional de Turismo de Colombia,** Calle 28 #13A-15 pisco 16 (tel: 2839-466). Hotels in Bogotá, centrally located:

Rates are in US$ for a double/twin room with bath or shower

  Bacatá, Calle 19, 5-32 (from $36)
  Bogotá Hilton, Carrera 7, 32-16 (from $68)
  Bogotá Plaza, Calle 100, 18A-30 (from $58)
  Comendador, Carrera 18, 38-41 (from $21)
  Continental, Avenida Jiménez, 4-16 (from $45)
  Cordillera, Carrera 8a, 16-89 (from $31)
  Dann, Avenida 19, 5-72 (from $26)
  El Presidente, Calle 23, 9-45 (from $44)
  Tequendama, Calle 26, 10-42 (from $47)

USEFUL INFORMATION

  Helpful Hints: Carry travelers' checks instead of cash, and leave valuables in hotel safe. Women should hold pocketbooks securely. Do not wear jewelry, and be careful of your wristwatch.

  Banks: Open Mon-Thurs 9-3 in Bogotá and most other cities, and last day of month 9-12.

  Mail: Most good stores sell stamps. Internal surface mail is unreliable; send all letters airmail. Main post office in Bogotá is on Carrera 7, number 16-36.

Telephone Tips: Booths on main streets and in hotels, restaurants, and cafés. Useful numbers in Bogotá:

Pan Am agent 2420-720	Directories 13 and 14
Airport Information 2669-200	Time 17
Tourist Offices 2810-510	Fire 19
Accommodations Offices 2669-200	Police 12
	Red Cross 2453-333

Newspapers: Foreign magazines and newspapers available. Local English-language newspaper is *The Chronicle.*

Tipping: Customary, but some exceptions—neither taxi drivers nor museum guides are tipped. In restaurants, 10%—if a service charge of 10% has been included in the check, a tip of 5% is still expected. Airport porter, 10 pesos per bag; porters and hotel porters, 10 pesos per bag; rest-room attendant, 5 pesos.

Electricity: Bogotá—150 volts 60 cycles AC, but in most first-class hotels 110 volts 60 cycles AC; same in other parts of the country.

Laundry: Dry-cleaning and laundry services quick, efficient, and inexpensive. First-class hotels have a 24-hour service (dry-cleaning a suit, from 145 pesos; laundering a shirt, from 45 pesos).

Hairdressing: First-class hotels have good salons (shampoo and set from 300 pesos; man's haircut, from 100 pesos).

Photography: Equipment and film easily found in major cities, but expensive. Developing times: 2-3 days for black and white, from 4-5 days for color.

Clubs: Rotary, Lions, and Kiwanis.

Babysitting: Most hotels have services—ask the hotel clerk. Services include Guarderia Infantil La Porciuncula (tel: 2497-484) Nenelandia (tel: 2566-695) and Mi Pequeno Mundo (tel: 2365-482).

Health: Many doctors are US-trained and speak English. Except in large hotels, drink only bottled water. Eat only fruit and vegetables which have been peeled. Most pharmaceuticals and toiletries available but expensive.

TRANSPORTATION

Bogotá has a bus service with reasonable fares, but taxis are the most convenient form of city transport and are a must after nightfall. Taxis are metered, with a minimum charge of 50 pesos; extra charges after 9pm and on Sundays and holidays. You can hail one in the street or phone Taxi Real (tel: 2430-580). You can rent a car from Hertz, which has branches at the airport and at the Tequendama Hotel arcade (tel: 2347-961). Daily rates start at 2,100 pesos, with an additional 18 pesos per kilometer. Traffic in cities is disorganized and difficult, and cross-country roads are poorly marked. Best bet is to rent a chauffeur-driven car. Rates are $6 per hour within the city.

Railroad services are interesting but rustic and not recommended. Long-distance bus services also connect main cities, but they, too, are not very comfortable. Airways are the best way to travel. Avianca, SAM,

Aerotal, TAC, are the domestic airlines. Helicopter services are also available through Helicol (Helicópteros Nacionales de Colombia, an Avianca affiliate). Avianca has a "See Colombia" ticket for $200, valid for unlimited travel within the country, except to San Andrés in the Caribbean and Leticia on the Amazon ($290 with San Andrés and Leticia included). Flying times from Bogotá are: Barranquilla—1 hour 10 minutes; Cartagena—1 hour 5 minutes; Santa Marta—1 hour 10 minutes; Cali—40 minutes; and Medellín—35 minutes.

FOOD AND RESTAURANTS

Colombians are specialists in soups and stews. Native dishes well worth trying are *ajiaco*, a delicious chicken and potato soup, served with avocados or corn on the cob and *cuchuco* and *sopa de indios* (a vegetable and meat stew with ground maize); *puchero santafereño*, boiled chicken, brisket of beef, and pork, with pumpkin and vegetables; *lechona*, stuffed pork; *arroz con pollo*, traditional chicken with rice; *viudu de pescado*, a fish stew; and *sancocho*, which could be compared with bouillabaisse. *Tamales*, spicy meat pies steamed in banana leaves, are extremely tasty and nutritious. But if you prefer international cuisine, good restaurants are plentiful. In Bogotá are the **Monserrate Dining Room,** on the 17th floor of the Tequendama (tel: 2812-080), and **La Hacienda** and **Le Toit Supper Club** (tel: 2325-020) at the Bogotá Hilton. **La Reserve** (Carrera 15, 37-15—tel: 2459-659), **Eduardo** (Carrera 11, 89-43—tel: 2364-387), **Salinas** (Calle 21, 6-43—tel: 2437-755), and the **Unicorn Club** (Calle 94, 7-75—tel: 2362-641) are also first-class international restaurants. For excellent fish and steaks, try **La Fragata** (Calle 15, 9-30—tel: 2410176) in a sophisticated atmosphere, or try the trout specialties at **Lighthouse** (Calle 93B, 15-34, tel: 2579-686). The *paella* and other Spanish dishes at **La Zambra** (Carrera 3, 74-32) are delicious, and **Giuseppe Verdi** (Calle 58, 5-35—tel: 495368) specializes in Italian food. There's a great view and international fare at **La Casa de San Isidro** 2496-855 and German dishes at **Pimm's** (Carrera 15, 87-46). For native Colombian meals go to the **Casa Vieja** (3-73, Avenida Jiménez—tel: 2346-171), one of the oldest houses in town and a must to visit, and **Los Arrayanes** (tel: 2348-908) in the same building famed for highland crab soup and casseroled *capitan,* a rare, eel-type fish from the nearby plateau country. **La Pola** (Calle 19, 1-85—tel: 2411-343), **Mesón de Indias** (Calle 13, 3-53—tel: 2438-651), and **Zaguan de Las Aguas** (Carrera 3, 74-32). In Cali, the Hotel Inter • Continental's **Los Farallones** is well known, excellent both for international and local dishes, lavish buffets Thursdays, and two bands for dinner dancing. **Cali Viejo** has splendid atmosphere with local food and strolling musicians, while **Don Carlos** is one of the oldest and best in the area. At Jauchito, a small port on the Rio Cauca, there's a lively atmosphere Sundays, where staple fare is the national regional *sancocho de gallina* (a robust chicken stew) washed down with aguardiente, a very strong local drink (80% alcohol). In Medellín, the **Hotel Bolívar** (Carrera 53, 45-99), **Hotel Veracruz** (Carrera 50, 54-22), and the **Inter • Continental Medellín,** 5 miles out of town, also have international cui-

sine. **Fondas Antioqueñas,** Carabobo (Carrera 52, 51-62), specializes in excellent Colombian food. Excellent French cuisine at **La Bella Epoca,** Carre Tera al Poblado Envigada (Calle 4 Sur, 45-37), regional specialties at **Posada de la Montana** (a restored hacienda), a spectacular view and continental cuisine at **El Mirador de Anburra,** (Calle 5 Sur, Carrera 43A). **Las Res** serves succulent Argentine-style steak. In Cartagena, go to **Capilla del Mar** (Avenida del Chile) for splendid lobster and fish. The **Club de Pesca,** at the Fuerte del Pastelillo, has superb seafood. **Bodegor de la Candelarin** in the center of town is worth a visit for its sumptuous ambiance, while **Chez Julian** offers excellent Spanish dishes. **Marcel's** for French food.

Breakfast is from 8 to 10, lunch from 12 to 2:30, and dinner from 8 to 10. A meal for one in an expensive restaurant will cost about 500 pesos, in a medium-priced restaurant about 200 pesos, and in an inexpensive one about 125 pesos. For low-priced meals and snacks **Le Chalet Suizo** (Carrera 7, 21-51—tel: 341721), **Monte Blanco** (throughout the city), **Club Sandwich** (between Carrera 9 and 7), and **Crem Helado** (Carrera 14, 31-49) are recommended—you can get hamburgers, sandwiches, *empanadas* (two layers of corn dough with filling), and hot *chile con carne.* For late-afternoon tea and pastries go to **La Suiza** (Calle 25, 9-41) or **Belalcázar** (Carrera 7). Most restaurants close on Sunday. Some can be fussy about dress; men may need a jacket and tie. Eating from street stalls is not recommended.

DRINKING TIPS

The best beer is Club Colombia, which is now exported to the US, while Medellín brews an attractive pilsentype ale. Local rums are good, too, and inexpensive. Ron Caldas is similar to Jamaican rum, Ron Medellín is lighter. But try *guarapo* and the potent *aguardiente* ("firewater"), both made from sugarcane. The latter is the Colombian equivalent of tequila, the *Nectar Diamente* being somewhat sweet, the *Onix* dry. There are some local wines, but most are imported, the best being wine from Chile. The average price of a whisky and soda is 100 pesos; of a bottle of wine, 500 pesos. There are no liquor restrictions, but women are not welcome in bars and cafés, except in top hotels. Visitors find alcohol has a much more immediate effect here than at lower altitudes. Colombian coffee is perhaps the best in the world. At the **El Dorado Airport** there is a free coffee bar in the International Passengers Section.

ENTERTAINMENT

Concerts and ballets are held at the **Teatro Colón** on Calle 10 in the old quarter in Bogotá and at the **Teatro Municipal Jorge Eliécer Gaitan** on Carrera 7 between Calles 22 and 23. Usually there is one performance per evening. Concerts (and art exhibitions) are given at the **Luis Angel Arango** library, and musicals, plays, and native dances at **La Media Torta,** an open-air theater near Quinta de Bolívar. Movie-going is very popular. The best movie houses are on Carrera 7. There are also several theater groups, including the Spanish-language **TPB** (Teatro Popular de Bogotá),

Carrera 5 Avenida Jiménez, performances Wednesday through Sunday; the **Teatro La Candelaria** (Antigua Casa de la Cultura), Calle 12, 2-59; and the **Bogotá Community Players,** who perform wherever the group can rent a theater. Most performances are in favor of a charity organization.

The most sophisticated nightspots in Bogotá are the **Monserrate Room** at the Tequendama Hotel and **Le Toit** on the 41st floor of the Bogotá Hilton. The **As de Copas** (Carrera 13, 59-24) features flamenco dancing and classical Spanish cuisine; **El Unicornio** (Calle 94, 7-75) is a swinging private club, where tourists are welcome, with an attractive restaurant, bar, and disco; also good is **La Pampa,** with a midnight show to complement its fine beef, and **La Zambra** (Cr. 3, 74-32) where kegs serve for tables, fine Spanish fare, guitar music, and dancing to the morning hours. **Bar Santa Fé,** at the Tequendama Hotel, has a "western" atmosphere, and **Candilejas** (off Carrera 13) is a Spanish nightclub. Discothèques include **Topsi** (also a nightclub), **Disco, Studio 54,** and **Escondite.** Women should not walk alone in the streets at night.

SHOPPING

One of the best buys are emeralds, since most of the world's supply is mined here, while there's an abundance of attractive gold jewelry, and intriguing antiques from Spanish colonial days. The main shopping areas of Bogotá are on Calles 18 and 15 (downtown); Carrera 15 (between Calles 72 and 100—El Lago); Carrera 13—between Calles 55 and 65, and Unicentro. Shops and stores are open from 8:30 or 9 to 6:30, including Saturdays. Very fashionable and warm are the native *ruanas,* woolen ponchos in brilliant colors worn by both men and women over their street clothes. Good jewelers are in the **Tequendama** and **Hilton** hotels, in the nearby **Bavaria** shopping complex, and on Carreras 6, 12, and 13, where you'll find the **Jewelry Center.** A delightful gift is an 18-carat gold charm—a little basket enclosing an uncut emerald—which you can get for about 1,300 pesos. For silver and leather goods or handicraft antiques the best store is the government-controlled **Artesanias de Colombia** (Carrera 10, 26-50), where you can get leather duffel bags, calfskin rugs, woven mats, heavy copper paella pans, and many delightful pieces. For pre-Columbian artifacts go to **Galeria Cano** in the Hilton Hotel or **Galeria Bogotá** (Carrera 13, 44-54). For antiques, brass, and copperware try **La Toma de Agua** (Calle 10, 2-7) or a delightful three-story shop called simply **Antiques,** on Plaza Bolívar. Try bargaining, except in the large department stores.

SPORTS

Tejo, played by throwing a metal disc at a "cap" which explodes (similar to pitching horseshoes), is the only native Colombian sport. You can watch this game at the **Campo Colombia** (Calle 32, 6-23). Soccer, tennis, and basketball are popular. There is horse racing on Sundays and Wednesdays at the **Hipódromo de Techo;** at the **Hipodromo de los Andes,** Autopista Norte, Thurs, Sat and Sun in Bogotá. During the winter the best Spanish bullfighters are in South America; you can see them at **Plaza de Toros de Santamaria.** Among the many golf courses are **Bogotá Country Club** (two 18-hole courses), **Los Lagartos,** and **San Andrés.** Baseball is played in **Barranquilla** and **Cartagena,** polo in **Medellín.** There is marlin fishing off **Barranquilla** and trout fishing in the lakes near Bogotá, water-skiing in **Santa Marta,** and skin-diving in **San Andrés.** There are bear, jaguar, panther, tapir for the hunter; you need a license. Partridge, duck, and goose are plentiful. Hunting and fishing licenses may be obtained from the Instituto Nacional De Recursa Naturales Y Renovables, Inderena, Carrera 14, 25A-66, Bogotá (tel: 281-3311).

WHAT TO SEE

Bogotá

An absolute must is the **Museo del Oro** (Gold Museum) on Carrera 6, Calle 16, where a collection of 15,000 pre-Colombian gold pieces is displayed. Nearby are the churches of **San Francisco, La Tercera** (distinguished for its fine wood carvings), and **Veracruz,** which contains the remains of the heroes of the War of Independence with Spain. A few blocks away, across busy Avenida Jiménez de Quesada, you will find **La Candelaria,** one of the largest and best-preserved colonial districts in South America. Among the treasures of Colombia's colonial past are the **Palace of San Carlos,** where Simón Bolívar once lived; the new **Palace of Narino** is the president's home (go at 5pm and you will see the changing of the guard); the **Cathedral** in Plaza Bolívar, originally built in 1573, which holds a very fine collection of paintings from the colonial period; **La Toma de Agua,** one of the finest old buildings in the city; and the **Teatro Colón.** Some former mansions have been converted into museums, and you will enjoy the colonnaded balconies and romantic patios as much as the displays. The **Colonial Art Museum** and **Archaeology Museum** are on Carrera 6; the **20 of July Museum** is on Carrera 7; the **Museum of Native Handicrafts and Traditions** (with an excellent shop) is on Carrera 8. The **National Museum,** between the Hilton and Tequendama hotels (Carrera 7, 28-66), is in an old prison and has collections of anthropology, fine arts, and historic mementos. Museums are open 10-6 Tuesday to Saturday and 10-2 Sundays and holidays. Bogotá also has a modern **Planetarium** and **Museum of Natural History.**

Another must is the **Quinta de Bolívar,** the Liberator's villa and gardens, at the edge of town. Nearby, you can go by cable car *(teleférico)* to the top of Monserrate for a spectacular view of Bogotá. Only 35 miles from the heart of the town is one of the wonders of South America, the **Salt Cathedral of Zipaquirá,** carved by the Chibcha Indians, and half a mile below ground. It can hold 10,000 people, and you can walk three miles into the mine, almost to the altar. But don't forget your coat—it's chilly.

The Caribbean Coast

Barranquilla: On the mouth of the Magdalena River, this modern industrial city of 690,471 is the main port of the country. The **Caujanal Country**

Club has golf, tennis, bowling, billiards, and swimming facilities, and you can rent a boat from the Yacht Club for a day's deep-sea fishing. For international cuisine try the **Steak House** and **Taberna Aleman;** for Spanish, **Gran Paella;** for Chinese, **El Gran Chop Suey.** Hotels in Barranquilla, centrally located:

Rates are in US$ for a double/twin room with bath or shower

Caribana, Carrera 41, 40-42 (from $27)

Central, Calle 38, 41-122 (from $34)

El Prado, Carrera 54, 70-10 (from $36)

Genova, Calle 44, 44-66 (from $15)

Royal Lebolo, Carrera 54, 68-129 (from $29)

Cartagena: The "golden gate to South America" is the most perfectly preserved example of a walled city in the *New World.* See the historic castles of **San Felipe** and **San Fernando** and the imposing fortress of **San Sebastián** and **Bocachica.** Visit the **Vaults,** the **Clock Tower,** the **Inquisition Palace.** Hotels in Cartagena, centrally located unless indicated:

Rates are in US$ for a double/twin room with bath or shower

Capilla del Mar, Carrera 1 (from $78), on the beach

Del Caribe, Carrera 1 (from $34), on the beach

Flamingo, Bocagrande (from $21)

Hotel Cartagena Hilton, El Loguito (from $29)

Hotel Cartagena Real, on the beach (from $51)

Las Velas, Calle Las Velas 1-60 (from $45), at the beach and about 15 minutes from the city center

Santa Marta: Reckoned to be the first Spanish settlement in South America (1525), Santa Marta today is an attractive and relatively unspoiled resort with a couple of fine beaches just south of town. There's good game fishing both up and down the coast, with bonito, dolphin, jack crevalle, snook, snapper, and tarpon for surfcasting or boating with light gear, while for deep-sea game there's relatively good sport after marlin, sailfish, and wahoo. There's snorkeling and scuba-diving. Both the **Hotel Irotoma** (from US$38) and **Hotel La Sierra** (from US$30) are popular with visitors. Just south of town is the **Hacienda de San Pedro Alejandrino,** a national shrine and museum, with the room where Simón Bolívar died in 1830.

San Andrés: Just off the coast of Nicaragua and some 600 miles south of Miami is a free port, about seven miles long and a mile and a half wide. Morgan is supposed to have buried treasure here, and it has never been found. The offshore reefs provide some of the most exciting underwater scenery anywhere, while protecting the miles of sandy shores. **Old Town,** the capital, has more style than its cousin Key West off the Florida shore, and most people speak with a Jamaican lilt to their English (and a Caribbean twang to their Spanish). **New Town** is busy, bustling, and usually thronged with Colombians buying duty-free bargains—including American, Chinese, English and Japanese imports, French crystal, European porcelains and china, much jewelry, and watches. Good day excursions to nearby **Alburquerque** and **Bolívar Keys.** Treasure hunting has many devotees and full scuba equipment is available on island. Two casinos at **Hotel Royal Abaco** (from US$39) and **Hotel El Dorado** (from US$34) while the **Hotel El Isleno** (from US$40) has been building a following. **Providencia,** an island that Henry Morgan captured from Spain, lies about 45 miles north.

The Western (Pacific) Coast

Medellín, the second city of Colombia, is an industrial center in a beautiful Andean valley 4,500 feet above sea level. Its **Cathedral** is said to be the largest brick building in the world, and Medellín is also known as the "Orchid Capital of the World." Do visit the orchid plantation at **La Finca El Ranchito,** just outside the city, and the estate owned by Señor Mariano Ospina Pérez, which has 70,000 orchid plants of more than 300 varieties. The city's Orchid Show takes place in August. Hotels are **Europa-Normandie,** Calle Maracaibo 53, 49-100 (from US$24 double); **INTER·CONTINENTAL MEDELLIN** (from US$68), (interestingly the only such hotel in South America with its own bullring); **Variante Las Palmas** (from US$32 double); **Nutibara** (from US$32 double); **Vera Cruz,** Carrera 50, 54-18 (from US$27 double).

Cali: It is said that the most beautiful women in Colombia come from Cali. It has an ideal climate. It has fine universities, good sports facilities, and many social clubs. Among hotels is the **INTER·CONTINENTAL CALI,** Avenida Colombia 2-72 (from US$72 double). Big event of the year is the Feria, a weeklong celebration to the art of the bullfight, with masked balls, street parades, much dancing and singing in the streets. Center of the event is the 16,000-seat **Canaveraejo Ring** where the world's best matadors assemble for the occasion. Advance reservations absolutely essential.

Manizales: Here on the peaks of **El Nevado dei Ruiz** you can go skiing and tobogganing the year round. There's great fishing in the mountain streams where rainbow trout are said to go to 30 pounds, good hunting (duck especially), and a fine collection of Quibaya Indian artifacts at the local **Museum of Anthropology.**

San Agustin: The most important archaeological zone in Colombia, with gigantic stone statues, pre-Colombian tombs, and burial mounds.

North and East of Bogotá

Tunja: In the Departamento of Boyacá, "the birthplace of Colombia," on the site of the citadel of the ancient Chibcha Indians, Tunja is another colonial city. Many of the Spanish conquistadores settled here, and their coats of arms, carved in stone, still adorn the facades of ancient mansions.

Llanos Orientales: A plain of 110,000 square miles, where with a jeep and a tent you can enjoy a really inexpensive and adventurous vacation fishing and hunting—there are cougar, deer, alligator, and crocodile.

The Amazon:

Deep in the south on a splinter of territory that divides Peru from Brazil lies **Leticia,** typical of the many upcountry settlements to be found in this intriguing continent. From here the adventurous traveller can move in to the remote regions of the Icotee and Putumayo rivers (both tributaries of the Amazon) or more comfortably make the two-day excursion to **Sta. Sofia** and **Puerto Narino** and the **Tarapoto Lakes.** (You visit the Yaguas and get to overnight in a hammock). Comfortable accommodations at the **Parador Ticuna,** Leticia (from US$35 double).

SOURCES OF FURTHER INFORMATION

Pan Am agents: Valco SA, Carrera 7, 17-01, Office 903, Bogotá, or any Pan Am office around the world; **Corporación Nacional de Turismo,** Calle 28, 13A-15, Piso 16 Bogotá, and in main cities; **Colombian Government Tourist Office,** 140 East 57th Street, New York, NY 10022; the **Colombian Consulate General,** 140 Park Lane, London W1.

Costa Rica

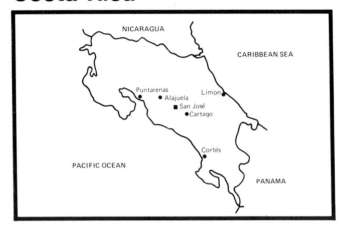

WHAT'S SPECIAL

Bananas, coffee, tobacco, and honey all come out of Costa Rica, a country with compulsory education and no army. Here orchids bloom all year round, and there are forests of rosewood, cedar, and mahogany. Visitors can climb volcanoes and view two oceans; hunt jaguar, tapir, ocelot, and deer; go mining for remnants of legendary gold that led to the country's name of "Rich Coast"; and fish for black marlin, tarpon, sawfish, and lobster. Some visitors are also interested in Costa Rica as a retirement haven, since it is possible for foreigners to own property here, and there are fair incentives to those who would like to start a business.

COUNTRY BRIEFING

Size: 19,652 square miles   **Population:** 2,184,000
Capital: San José   **Capital Population:** 812,184
   Climate: The dry season, December-May, is the best time to visit, but the climate is agreeable all year round, making air-conditioning unnecessary and virtually nonexistent.

Weather in San José: Lat N9°56'; Alt 3,760 ft

Temp (°F)	Jan	Feb	Mar	Apr	May	Jun	Jul	Aug	Sep	Oct	Nov	Dec
Av Low	58°	58°	59°	62°	62°	62°	62°	61°	61°	60°	60°	58°
Av High	75°	76°	79°	79°	80°	79°	77°	78°	79°	77°	77°	75°
Days no rain	28	27	29	23	12	8	8	7	6	6	16	15

   Government: A republic.
   Language: Spanish is the official language.

Religion: Roman Catholic, but other denominations represented.
Currency: Colón. 100 céntimos = 1 colón.

	50 cent	1 Col.	5 Col.	10 Col.	20 Col.	50 Col.	100 Col.	400 Col.
US (dollars, cents)	.06	.12	.58	1.17	2.33	5.83	11.67	46.67
UK (pounds, pence)	.03	.06	.28	.56	1.11	2.78	5.57	22.26

Public Holidays:

New Year's Day, 1 Jan
Feast of St Joseph, 19 Mar
Anniversary of the Battle of Rivas, 11 Apr
Labor Day, 1 May
Corpus Christi, June
St Peter and St Paul, 29 June
Anniversary of the Annexation of Guanacaste Province, 5 July

Our Lady of the Angels, 2 Aug
Assumption and Mother's Day, 15 Aug
Independence Day, 15 Sep
Columbus Day, 12 Oct
Immaculate Conception, 8 Dec
December Day, 25 Dec

HOW TO GET THERE

Flying time to San José's Juan Santa Maria Airport from New York is 6¼ hours; from Los Angeles, 6¼ hours; from Guatemala City, 1½ hours. Time in Costa Rica: GMT−6.

REQUIREMENTS FOR ENTRY AND CUSTOMS REGULATIONS

Tourist card (costing $2 and valid for 30 days), available from Costa Rican Consulates or at US Pan Am offices, plus means of identification and tickets for onward travel. A US passport can be extended. A smallpox vaccination certificate is required for all but US and Canadian citizens. No currency restrictions and no customs declaration necessary for passengers carrying only personal effects. Duty-free allowance: 1 pound tobacco in any form; up to 3 liters wine or liquor; other items not exceeding US$100 as a taxable amount.

AIRPORT INFORMATION

Juan Santa Maria Airport is 11 miles from San José. Buses are frequent and cost 2.50Cs. Taxis are plentiful and cost about 55Cs. Airport departure tax, US$8. Duty-free shop and hotel reservation counter.

ACCOMMODATIONS

For help in finding accommodations there is the **Instituto Costarricense de Turismo,** Calle Central, Avenidas 4 y 6, Apartado 777, San José (tel: 23-1733). Open from 8am-4pm. There are also tourism representatives at frontiers and airport, Mon-Fri 8am-4pm. Inexpensive *pensiones* available from about 30Cs (US$3.60). New resort-type hotels with gardens outside San José provide free minibus service to and from the city. Hotels in San José:
Rates are in US$ for a double/twin room with bath or shower
  Ambassador, Paseo Colon, Calles 26-28 (from $52.94)

Amstel, Calle, 7, Avenidas 10/12 (from $18)
Balmoral, Avenida Central, Calles 7/9 (from $40)
Canada Pension, Calle 9, Avenida 7 & 9 (from $20.50)
Cariari, Autopista General Cañas, seven miles from downtown (from $54)
Chorotega Tower, Calle 29, Avenidas 0/2 (from $23.60)
Europa, Calle Central, 5a Avenida (from $32.94)
Gran Hotel Costa Rica, 3a Calle, Avenidas Central/2 (from $35.41)
Herradura Americano Hotel & Club, 10 mins to downtown (from $47)
Irazú, Autopista General Cañas, about 10 min from downtown (from $43)
Playboy Hotel & Club, San José (from $65)
President, Avenida Central, Calles 7/9 (from $25)
Royal Dutch, Calle Central, Avenida Central (from $35)
Tennis Club, Sabana Sur (from $30)
Torremolinos, C. 40Av 5 Bis, San José (from $35)

Unless otherwise indicated, all the above hotels are centrally located.

USEFUL INFORMATION

When giving directions, the Costa Rican will give distances not in blocks or yards, but in *varas*—a *vara* is approximately 33 inches, and about 100 *varas* is a block. They tend not to direct you by street names and numbers but advise you to look for a landmark, such as a movie theater, pharmacy, or *pulperia* (corner grocery).

Banks: Open 8-11 and 1:30-3 Mon-Fri, 8-11am Sat. Change currency and travelers' checks at hotels and stores.

Mail: Stamps at post offices, newsstands, bookshops. Minimum airmail postage to the US is 1.50C.

Telephone Tips: Phones in streets, cafés, and restaurants. Useful numbers in San José:

Pan Am 21-8877	**Police** 117
Airport Information 41-1488	**Weather** 22-5616
Operator 113	**Fire** 118
Time 112	**Ambulance** 21-5888

Newspapers: English-language newspapers available. Local English-language publications are the *Tico Times,* the *San José News,* and *La Prensa,* the most important paper published, lists daily events.

Tipping: A 10% charge is either included in the check (if cost is over 10Cs) or expected in restaurants. Porters 2C per piece of luggage, hotel porters and chambermaids, 1C; taxi drivers do not expect tips.

Electricity: 110 volts 60 cycles AC throughout the country.

Laundry: Good laundry and dry-cleaning services (dry-cleaning a suit, from 15Cs; laundering a shirt, from 8Cs).

Hairdressing: First-class hotels have salons (shampoo and set from 20-40Cs, man's haircut, from 15Cs).

Photography: Good suppliers in main cities. Black and white film costs about US$4.50 and color about US$7. Developing, 2-3 days for black and white, 4-8 for color.

Clubs: Rotary, Lions, Kiwanis, Jaycees.

Babysitting: None.

Rest Rooms: No public facilities, but rest rooms are located in restaurants, bars, hotels, and gas stations. Women, *Damas* or *Señoras;* men, *Caballeros* or *Hombres.*

Health: Many English-speaking doctors and dentists. Imported pharmaceuticals are expensive. Tap water is drinkable in San José; wash fruit. Antimalarial drugs should be taken when visiting some coastal regions.

TRANSPORTATION

Flying is not too expensive within the country, and there is a fascinating (albeit slow) railroad, called the "Jungle Train," between San José and Puerto Limon, which passes through the coffee and banana plantations and through the mountains and the Meseta Central. The roads in Costa Rica are not very good, and buses are slow, but inexpensive. There are 232 local and private airports, the main ones served by LACSA, APSA, AVE, and ALPA, among internal airlines. Virtually all places are within 45 minutes' flight of San José. Flights tend to leave in the morning only. Taxis in San José are abundant and can be hailed on the street. A taxi ride will usually cost not more than US$2 in San José, within the metropolitan area. Radio taxis can be reached at 21-2552 and 21-8466. Rented cars cost 200Cs a day, plus 5Cs per kilometer and 30Cs insurance, and another 200Cs a day if you want a chauffeur. There are a few good highways, but most surfaces are fair. The ferry across the Nicoya Gulf from Puntarenas to Nicoya cuts the 3-hour road time in half.

FOOD AND RESTAURANTS

Local dishes tend to be rather starchy, but there are a number of tasty Central American standbys. Try *tamales*—made from meat, rice, and corn with chili on top, wrapped in a banana leaf; *ceviche*, raw fish marinated in spices and lemon juice; *mondongo*, tripe in different sauces, and soups—*olla de carne* and *pozol*. You can enjoy avocados, shrimp, lobster tails, and delicious local fish, including *corvino* and *robalo molinera*, otherwise known as snook. Breakfast is from 6-9, lunch 12-2, dinner 6-8. You can get continental food at the **Royal Dutch Hotel** (Calle Central, Avenida Central—tel: 22-1414) and the **Gran Hotel Costa Rica** (Calle 3, Avenida Central 2—tel: 21-4000); French food at **La Bastille** (Paseo Colón, Calle 22—tel: 22-0243), **L'Escargot** (Avenida 5, #136—tel: 22-4728), and **Le Mirage,** across from the National Theater. Fondues are a specialty at **Chalet Suizo** (Calle 5/7, Avenida 1—tel: 22-3118). Indonesian dishes are served buffet-style at **Van Gogh** (Calle 3, Avenida 1/3—tel: 22:9444). For national dishes try **Balcón de Europa** (Avenida Central, Calle 7/9—tel: 21-9547); for seafood, **The Lobster Inn** (Calle 24, Paseo Colon—tel: 23-85-94); **Marisqueria Piscis** (Sabana Oeste—tel: 32-07-37). For barbecues, **La Cascada** (at Escazu) or **Bonanza Steak House** (midway to airport). There are several good restaurants in the El Pueblo commercial center.

DRINKING TIPS

Rum is the national drink. Beer is popular and good. A whisky and soda costs 15-20Cs. **Arturo's Bar** (Calle 7 and Av Central) is a pleasant transplanted New York style bar, while **Ye Pub** (Avenida 7 and Calle Central) speaks for itself. It is generally inadvisable for women to go into bars unaccompanied.

ENTERTAINMENT

At the **National Theater** in San José there is drama, opera, and ballet, and often concerts are given by international companies. Movie houses show English and American movies with original soundtracks. San José has several nightclubs, including **Boite Bocaccio, La Giuaría** in the Irazú Hotel, and the **Dolphin Club** at the President Hotel. For disco dancing there's **Barroco,** in front of the National Stadium in Sabana Norte, **Coco Loco** at El Pueblo Mall, or the **Aquarius** on Calle Central (Avenida 2). A popular local spot is in San Sebastian, a taxi ride of around 18Cs from San José, called **A Bailar Carino.** Also pleasant in El Pueblo are **Infinito** and **La Choza del Recuado.**

SHOPPING

Stores open 8-12 and 2-6, Mon-Sat. The best shops: **La Gloria, La Galeria, Chantelle, El Ibis, El Siglo Nuevo,** and **Mil Colores** on Avenida Central, and others around the Central Market. Jewelry stores have copies of gold artifacts in the Banco Central. The best souvenirs to buy are articles made from wood. Bargain in stores and markets.

SPORTS

Soccer is the national sport, but there is also basketball, boxing, and baseball; you can see bullfights in the last week of every year. You can play tennis or golf or go horseback riding, yachting, or fishing. The annual **Holy Week Tarpon Tournament** attracts many North American sportsmen, who come for the marlin, sharks, sawfish, snook, and tarpon. Guided safaris are arranged for big-game hunting in the **Sarapiqui** region for jaguar, tapir, deer, and alligator.

WHAT TO SEE

In San José the 19th-century **National Theater** has a lavish interior with murals, gold decorations, and fine marble staircases. Other interesting buildings are the **Supreme Court,** the **Metropolitan Cathedral,** and the **National University** in the remarkable University City. The **Museo Nacional** (Calle 15/17, Avenida 2) has collections of pre-Columbian artifacts displayed in an old fort (closed Monday), and the **Banco Central's Gold Museum** houses pre-Columbian gold ornaments. (Open Monday, Wednesday, and Saturday mornings; check hours locally.)

Sugar mills, cocoa plantations, and coffee and banana processing plants are all interesting, and at **Sarchi's** ox-cart factory wagons are still painted by hand. Not very far from San José is the oldest church in Costa Rica, the **Orosi Mission,** built by the Spanish in 1743. On the Pacific coast are the white sand beaches of **Playas del Coco** and **Bahia de Culebra** (Coconut Beach and Snake Bay). The resort of **Ojo de Agua** is famous for its pure mountain spring.

Two-and-a-half hours' drive from the capital is the 11,000-foot volcano **Irazú**, still active. From the top, on a clear day, both the Atlantic and Pacific oceans can be seen. **Poas Volcano** is also active, and in the same direction is **Alajuela**, a good summer resort. Further west—15 minutes by air or 4 hours by train from the capital—is **Puntarenas**, a resort and center for great fishing. There are some good hotels here, including the **Tioga** (from US$36 double) and the **Hotel Colonial** (from US$43 double). At **Jaco Beach** there's the complete resort of Jaco Beach **Resort Hotel**, (from US$37) with numerous sports, including fishing, horseback riding, water skiing, and so forth. On an excursion north of San José, the **Mountain Resort Hotel** on the Guacalillo Road is a good place to stop for international and Costa Rican food.

Two hundred miles offshore is **Cocos Island**, whose legendary buried treasure has drawn hundreds of expeditions. Eastward from San José, a short trip by air, or a scenically exciting 6 hour train ride, is the port of **Limón**, where Columbus landed on his fourth voyage. From here, bananas, coffee, honey, and other goods are shipped. Hotels are the **Acon** (from US$18.81 double), **Getsemani** (from US$23.52 double), **Humac** (from US$26.30 double), and **Puerto** (from US$18.82 double). **The American Bar** near the local park is popular with American tourists.

SOURCES OF FURTHER INFORMATION

Pan Am, Avenida 3a, Calle 5a, San José, and any Pan Am office around the world; **Instituto Costarricense de Turismo**, Calle Central, Avenidas 4 y 6, Apartado 777, San José; **Costa Rica Consulate General**, 211 East 43rd Street, New York, NY 10017; **Costa Rican Embassy**, 8 Braemar Mansions, Cornwall Gardens, London SW7; **Costa Rican Tourist Board**, 200 SE First Street, Room 400, Miami, Fla 33131.

Ecuador

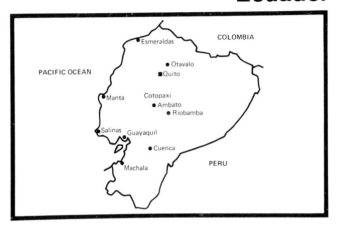

WHAT'S SPECIAL

Tiny Ecuador is full of natural beauty. From the north to the south run two imposing Andean cordilleras, the backbone of the country, with magnificent volcanoes, some extinct but some only dormant. Between these two mountain ranges, at an altitude of 7,000 to 9,000 feet, lies the Central Valley, where over half the Ecuadorians live. Nearly 40% of all Ecuadorians are Indians, and their life has changed little since their land was invaded by the Spanish conquistadores. Between the Andes and the Pacific Ocean lie the sprawling plantations and the coastal plains of the Guayas River. Guayaquil, largest city in Ecuador, is the commercial capital of the region. Quito, a well-preserved treasury of colonial art and architecture, has been proclaimed a World Heritage Site by UNESCO. To the east of the cordilleras lies the sparsely inhabited Oriente—the Amazonian jungles, where the recently discovered oil deposits have made Ecuador the second-largest oil-exporting country in Latin America.

COUNTRY BRIEFING

Size: 109,483 square miles
Capital: Quito
Population: 7,763,000
Capital Population: 742,858

Climate: Sharp contrasts according to altitude. On the coastal lowlands, the climate is equatorial, with average temperature 83°, a hot rainy season from November-May, and a dry season for the rest of the year. Quito, in the Central Valley, has a cool spring climate throughout the year, with average temperature 55°. The Oriente, in the eastern section of the country, is a tropical rainforest.

Weather in Quito: Lat SO°13′; Alt 9,446 ft

Temp (°F)	Jan	Feb	Mar	Apr	May	Jun	Jul	Aug	Sep	Oct	Nov	Dec
Av Low	46°	47°	47°	47°	47°	45°	44°	45°	45°	46°	45°	46°
Av High	72°	71°	71°	70°	70°	71°	72°	73°	73°	72°	72°	72°
Days no rain	15	11	11	8	10	18	24	22	16	13	16	15

Government: A republic.

Language: Spanish. English spoken only in hotels, tourist centers, and major shops.

Religion: Predominantly Roman Catholic.

Currency: Sucre. 100 centavos = 1 sucre.

	1	5	10	20	50	100	500	1,000
	Sucre	Sucre	Sucre	Sucre	Sucre	Sucre	Sucre	Sucre
US (dollars, cents)	.03	.17	.33	.66	1.66	3.32	16.60	33.20
UK (pounds, pence)	.01	.08	.16	.32	.79	1.58	7.93	15.87

Public Holidays

New Year's Day, 1 Jan
2-day carnival on Mon and Tues
  preceding Lent
Maundy Thursday and Good Friday
Easter Sunday
Labor Day, 1 May
Battle of Pichincha, 24 May
Bolívar's Birthday, 24 July
Independence Day, 10 Aug

Anniversary of Guayaquil, 9 Oct
Columbus Day, 12 Oct
All Saints Day, 1 Nov
All Souls Day, 2 Nov
Independence of Cuenca, 3 Nov
Foundation of Quito, 6 Dec
Christmas Day, 25 Dec

HOW TO GET THERE

Flying time to Quito's Mariscal Sucre Airport from New York is 6 hours; from Miami, 4 hours; from Caracas, 3 hours; from Panamá City, 1½ hours. Time in Ecuador: GMT−5.

REQUIREMENTS FOR ENTRY AND CUSTOMS REGULATIONS

A valid passport plus an onward ticket are required, for stays of up to 90 days. Departure tax of approximately US$5. Duty-free allowance: 300 cigarettes or 50 cigars or 7 ounces of tobacco, 1 liter liquor, personal effects. No restrictions on currency.

AIRPORT INFORMATION

The International Airport for Quito is Mariscal Sucre, 5 miles from downtown. Taxis available at all times. The fare to the city is 100 sucres. At the airport there is a duty-free shop, exchange office, and a tourist information desk. Tip airport porter 10-20 sucres. Simón Bolívar Airport is 3 miles from Guayaquil. A taxi to the city center costs 75 sucres.

ACCOMMODATIONS

Quito has luxurious first-class hotels; the **Hotel Inter · Continental Quito** is perhaps the most famous. But you will not have any difficulty in finding

accommodations at very reasonable prices. Pensions and *residencias* are comfortable and clean; most offer full board as an option. If there is no central heating, make sure you have enough blankets, as nights are quite chilly. The hotel reservation counter at the airport is open daily from 7am to 6. For help in finding accommodations write to the **Tourist Directorate**, PO Box 24-54, Calle Reina Victoria 514 & Roca Quito. All hotel bills are subject to 10% service charge and 10% tax. Hotels in Quito:
Rates are in US$ for a double/twin room with bath or shower

Chalet Suisse, Calle Reina Victoria y Calama Esquinaz Quito (from $34.50)

Colón Internacional, Amazonas and Patria (from $24.50)

Humboldt Capitol, Espejo Street 931 (from $19.50)

Inca Imperial, 219 Bogotá Street (from $29.50)

INTER · CONTINENTAL QUITO, PO Box 2201 (from $45), 10 minutes from center city

Santa Maria, Inglaterra 993 (from $32)

Savoy Inn, Yasuni Street, El Inca (from $20) near the airport

Waldorf, Calle Tamayo 233 (from $17)

All hotels centrally located unless otherwise indicated.

USEFUL INFORMATION

Banks: Open 9-1:30 Mon-Fri. Take travelers' checks in dollars; you can cash them in good hotels and major stores.

Mail: Stamps are available in post offices and hotels.

Telephone Tips: Phones in restaurants, hotels, shops. Useful numbers: **Tourist Information** 527 702; **Ecuadorian Tours** (agency of American Express) 219 000 and **Metropolitan Touring** 524 400.

Newspapers: The weekly *Ecuadorian Times* is published in English. The *Miami Herald* is flown in daily.

Tipping: Restaurants generally include a 10% service charge in checks, but a 5-10% tip is still expected. If service charge is not included, leave a tip of 15%. Porters, 10-15 sucres per bag; hairdressers, 20% of the bill; cloak-room attendants, 15 sucres. Taxi drivers not tipped.

Electricity: 110 volts 60 cycles AC.

Laundry: Dry-cleaning and laundry service excellent and speedy in luxury hotels (dry-cleaning a suit, from 70 sucres; laundering a shirt, from 15 sucres).

Hairdressing: First-class hotels have good salons (shampoo and set, from 270 sucres plus 20% tip). A man's haircut is 150 sucres.

Photography: Equipment and film available in Quito and Guayaquil, but prices high. Developing not very reliable.

Clubs: Lions, Rotary, Jaycees, and Kiwanis.

Babysitting: Services can be arranged in good hotels.

Rest Rooms: Rely on hotels and good restaurants. Women, *Damas;* men, *Caballeros;* unisex, *Banos.*

Health: Good hospitals in Quito and Guayaquil, where some doctors speak English. Pharmaceuticals and toiletries available in major cities, but expensive. Avoid fresh fruit and vegetables, except in good hotels and first-class restaurants. Inoculation against typhoid and hepatitis advisable. Remember the high altitude, and take it easy.

TRANSPORTATION

Buses and *colectivos* (smaller buses seating up to 20) are available and the names on the front indicate the first and last stop, but taxis are more convenient; you will find them at stands in the main plazas, or you can hail one on the street. Average fare in the city for a 15 minute ride is around US$1.50. For a self-drive car the daily rate starts at around US$14 plus 10¢ per kilometer (a cash deposit is usually required when a credit card is not used for payment). Roads on the whole are good. If you have time to spare, the rail journey from Quito to Guayaquil is exciting; it takes 12 hours to cover 288 miles, so do not forget to take sandwiches. Perhaps the most exciting part of the journey is the climb up the **Nariz del Diablo** (Devil's Nose), via a series of switchbacks, to a perpendicular ridge, 1000 feet above the river's gorge.

You can also travel from Quito to Guayaquil in comfortable air-conditioned buses via Transandina. The journey takes 8 hours (reserve in advance). CFA (Compania Ecuatoriana de Aviación), SAETA, SAN, and TAME (Ecuadorian Military Air Transports) have flights to Guayaquil and other cities and to the Galápagos Islands. Flying time from Quito to Guayaquil, 45 minutes.

FOOD AND RESTAURANTS

It is possible to eat very well and relatively inexpensively in Quito and there are some native specialties that you ought to try. Favorites are *lorco,* a potato soup with cheese and avocado; *humitas,* sweet corn tamales; *llapingachos,* fried potato cakes with onion and cheese, served on a bed of salad with a fried egg; and *hornado,* roast pig. If you fancy something really typical try *cuy,* which is baked guinea pig, and (if you like fish), *ceviche de corvina,* white fish in marinaded lemon sauce, and *fanesca,* made from pumpkin and peas. **La Choza** (12 of Octubre and Cordero) where the *morocho empanada* is appetizing and **La Taberna Quiteina** (Amazonas and Cordero) serve good native fare. On the seventh floor of the Hotel Inter · Continental Quito you will find **El Techo del Mundo,** with first-class international cuisine, organ music, and strolling guitarists and singers. Some 10 blocks north of the Intercontinental is **Calle Calama,** as Restaurant Row is called in Quito, a small street between Amazones and 6 de Diciembre. For native food try **El Companaric,** Juan Sebastian Bar for *marisco* dishes, **Jet Set** and **Le Chalet Suisse,** all good. For French cooking, go to **Le Bistrot,** across from the Inter · Continental Quito, **Flandes** (Robles Street), **La Marmita** (Calle Pradera), **Rincon de Francia** (Noca 779 and 9 de Octubre), **El Limonar** (Calle 1 Rodriguez), and **Castel Ross** (Amazona and Beintimilla). You can have a delicious pizza at the friendly **La Vieja Europa** (Amazonas and Calama 458). **La Cueva de Luiz Candelas** (Benalcázar 709) is a Spanish-style restaurant with excellent food as are **Los Faroles** (9 de Octubre 354) and **La Jaiba**

(Reina Victoria & Colon). **Chifa China** (Carrion Street and Versalles), **Pekin** (Bello Horizonte and 6 de Diciembre), **La Terraza del Tartaro** (Roca 779), and **Rolls Royce** (Amazonas and Orellana) are all good. Hotel food can be very good as at the Hotel Colon, and the **Inti Raymi Cafe** at the Humboldt Hotel.

Four courses usually make up an average meal: soup, entrée, salad, and dessert. Breakfast is usually 7-9, lunch 12:30-2:30, and dinner 7:30-9:30. A meal in an expensive restaurant costs 300 to 400 sucres.

DRINKING TIPS

Best beers in Ecuador are Pilsner, Club, and Lowenbrau. Pisco sour is the national cocktail. A whisky and soda (or a glass of red wine) will cost 50 sucres. Popular drinking spots are **El Techo del Mundo** (Inter · Continental Quito), **El Conquistador Bar** (Hotel Colón), and an authentic English **Pub** across the street from the Inter · Continental Quito.

ENTERTAINMENT

Movies are inexpensive and popular. The most lively nightclubs in Quito are **La Llama** in the Hotel Inter · Continental Quito, **Le Toucan** (Camino al Inca), the **Rolls Royce** discothèque (Amazonas and Orellana), and **La Licorne** discothèque at the Colón Hotel where there is often live entertainment. The top two discos are **Snobismo** and **Piano Teca**. The **Inter · Continental Quito, Humboldt,** and **Colón** hotels have small and sophisticated casinos. In Guayaquil there are nightclubs and restaurants at the **Continental, Atahualpa, Grand** and **Humboldt** hotels, and **El Terminal,** at the airport, has a casino, dancing, and floor shows.

SHOPPING

Elegant boutiques are to be found along **Amazonas Avenue** and **6 de Diciembre Avenue** in Quito. Many tourist shops are located all over the city, and among the best are **Ocepa, Folklore-Olga Fisch, Arte y Folclor Dalmau, Paipaco** (Colón Hotel), and **Akios Industries** and for local jewelry, **H. Stern.** Good, low priced gold and silver items are to be found at **Hamilton,** Avenida Amazonas, just across from the Colón Hotel. Stores are open on weekdays 8:30-12:30 and 2:30-6:30 and on Saturdays 8:30-12. For the best Panama hats (which are really made from **toquilla** straw in Ecuador) go to **Donat's** (Calle Chile 1060), where you can pick one up for 700 sucres—there are some very pretty ones for women, too. For thick, handwoven woolen ponchos and rugs in brilliant colors and stripes, go to **Folklore-Olga Fisch** (Av Colón 260—there are also branches at the Inter · Continental Quito and Colón hotels), where you will also find embroidered blouses, silver work, balsa wood items, straw baskets, and pottery. A handicraft store with a wide range of goods is **Ocepa-Artesanias del Ecuador** (Calle Carrion 1336), where prices are reasonable. For pre-Colombian and colonial antiques, go to the better shops like **Antiquedades** (Chile 1035) or **El Poncho Artesanias** (6 de Diciembre 1138), or **La Botega** (614 Com Carrion). There is a thriving trade in fake antiques and fake *tsanzas* (shrunken heads, which are the trophies of the Jivaro headhunters) made out of goatskin. For silver and gold, shop along **Venezuela Street,** known to *quiteños as la calle de los joyeros,* the street of the jewelers or go to **H. Stern** in the Hotel Inter · Continental Quito. In the old section of town, **La Ronda Street** has some nice tourist shops. At No 954 you can buy woven rugs. Except in the larger stores, bargaining is customary, and haggling over prices is a must at the Indian markets. In Quito there is an open-air furniture market on 24 de Mayo Avenue, every Tuesday and Saturday.

SPORTS

Soccer is very popular with Ecuadorians, and there are matches throughout the year. The main stadium is the **Atahualpa.** Basketball and indoor sports can be seen at the **Coliseo.** There is a local sport called *pelota de guante* (glove ball); watch it at the **Estadio Mejía,** in Mejía High School, on Saturdays and Sundays—no admission charge. Quito has one of the more famous bullfighting seasons, held in December with the best *toreros* from Spain, Mexico, and South America. Cockfighting is also very popular. You can see horse racing on Sundays at **La Carolina** racetrack in Quito and at the **Hipódromo Santa Cecilia** in Guayaquil. Guayaquil and Quito have golf and tennis clubs and horseback riding; ask at your hotel desk for guest cards. **Hotel Inter · Continental Quito** has a heated outdoor swimming pool. There is good pigeon shooting near Quito—partridges and deer are found in the *páramos* (highlands), while jaguars, tapirs, and alligators roam the **Oriente.** There is excellent trout fishing in the rivers and brooks of **Mount Cotopaxi** and **Chimborazo;** you will need a license and should apply to the Ministry of Industry. If you like mountaineering, this is the place to be. There is year-round swimming, yachting, and other sea sports along the Pacific coast, and deep-sea fishing off **Playas, Salinas,** and **Manta.** Best time to go is January-May: boats can be chartered for US$275.

WHAT TO SEE

Quito is a city of white houses with balconies and woodwork painted blue (the colors of the Virgin). The **Plaza de Independencia** lies in the shadow of the **Cathedral,** where the national hero Sucre is buried. Nearby are the **Municipal Palace** and the **Government Palace.** Do not miss **La Compañia,** the Jesuit church whose facade is so delicately carved it resembles lacework, and whose high altar is made of solid gold. The **Church of San Francisco** has magnificent art treasures and cloisters, and the **Church of Santo Domingo** has rich wood carvings and a remarkable Chapel of the Rosary. The **Museum of the Monastery of Santo Domingo** and the **Franciscan Museum** next to the Church of San Francisco have splendid collections of colonial religious art. The Museum in the **Banco Central** (Avenida 10 de Agosto) houses 5,000 years of Ecuadorian culture, including a fabulous gold collection on the fifth floor and colonial art on the sixth floor, while the **Casa de la Cultura Ecuatoriana** has a unique collection of musical instruments. The **Municipal Museum of Art** (Calle Espejo) and **Casa Benalcázar** have fine collections of Ecuadorian paintings from the last four centuries. There are dozens of art galleries in Quito, among the most famous are those of Oswaldo Guayasamin, the world-renowned Indian painter, and **La Galeria** (Juan Rodrigues 168). The latter exhibits the work of Oswaldo Viteri, famous for his Indian doll collages.

Take a tour to the top of **El Panecillo,** the little Breadloaf Hill, 600 feet above the city. If you like to swim, there are thermal pools at **Alaugasi** and **Tingo** in the Valley of Chillos, half an hour out of Quito. Very popular is a trip to the Equator, 15 miles north of Quito. You can have your photograph taken with one foot in each hemisphere.

A must for the visitor to Ecuador is a trip to one of the Indian markets in the neighboring townships; **Saquisili** (Thursday is market day) is the nearest one to Quito, (about 35 miles south), where you can buy decorative fabrics with birds, cats, and war gods woven into the design. On the way you will pass by **Cotopaxi,** the largest active volcano in the world. **Otavalo,** 180 miles from Quito and the only major market to the north has a colorful market very early on Saturday mornings. Lunch at a picturesque hacienda, such as **Hotel Cusin in San Pablo del Lago.** At **Santo Domingo** (market day on Sundays), three hours from Quito, the native Colorado Indians comb their hair into a helmet shape and paint their bodies red to ward off evil spirits. **Riobamba** has its market on Saturdays. **Ambato,** known as the "Garden City of Ecuador," holds a **Festival of Flowers and Fruits** from the 6th to the 10th of February and the **Indian Market** on Mondays is the largest in Ecuador. A short drive to the east of Ambato lies **Baños,** a summer resort and a natural health spa. Stay in the **Palace Hotel** (from US$24 double). There is a cattle ranch, **Tambo Mulalo,** on the Pan American Highway from Quito where you can rent an arena, if you would like to try your luck with a baby bull.

Guayaquil, the largest city in Ecuador, is its most important seaport. Well worth seeing are the **Cathedral of San Francisco,** the **Church of Santo Domingo** (built in 1548), **Palacio Municipal, Casa de la Cultura** (gold collection), "white city" cemetery, and **Barrio Las Penas** (colonial section). There are tennis, golf, and yachting clubs, many first-class movie houses, and the **Bogotá Theater,** with open-air performances and excellent restaurants. Recommended restaurants are those at the **Hotel Atahualpa Internacional,** which also has a casino and a nightclub, and at the **Hotel Continental.** The **Trocadero Restaurant,** on Calle P Ycaza, is good. Best time to go to Guayaquil is during the dry season from May to November. Hotels here are: **Hotel Apartamentos Boulevard,** 9 de Octubre 432 (from US$52 double); **Humboldt International,** Malecon 2309 (from US$38); **Continental,** Ballen 319 (from US$55); the **Atahualpa Internacional** (from US$38) and **Grand Hotel Guayaquil** (from US$50). From Guayaquil you can go on an excursion up the Guayas river into the tropical jungle, with its exotic birds and large plantations, or to the popular seaside resorts of **Playas.** Stay at the **Humboldt Hotel Playas,** on Balneario Victoria beach (from US$25). **At Salinas** the deep-sea fishing in the Humboldt current is superb. **Punta Carnero,** the newest of the coastal resorts, has a luxurious hotel, the **Punta Carnero Inn** (from US$36 double). There is a fleet of cruisers for deep-sea fishing which can be rented near the hotels. Black marlin, striped marlin, and tuna are found in these waters.

Cuenca is the third-largest city in Ecuador and is famous for its Panama hat industry (also known as Montecristi hats). There is a nightclub at the El Dorado Hotel (from US$33 double); or stay at the Crospo International (from US$18.50 double). Visit the old and new cathedrals, Crespo Toral municipal museum, Salesian Museum, and the Thursday and Sunday markets.

The Galápagos Islands, 650 miles off the coast of Ecuador, form one of the most extraordinary regions in the world. The 12 islands, only five of which are inhabited, are peaks of gigantic underwater volcanoes, rising 7,000 to 10,000 feet above the sea bed. It was the flora and fauna of this wildlife sanctuary that inspired Charles Darwin to formulate his theory of evolution in *The Origin of Species*. The Ecuadorian government has declared the entire region to be a natural sanctuary, and visits are carefully regulated. The Darwin Station on Santa Cruz is well worth the visit for the conservation work they undertake, which includes the removal of feral animals from the out-islands and the protection of turtles after whom the islands were named. Metropolitan Touring of Quito offers a selection of all-inclusive packages to the islands with accommodations based at the Hotel Delfin on Santa Cruz. The tours include the service of scientists who brief visitors on the habitat and actual flora and fauna. Metropolitan is represented in the US by Adventure Associates, Dallas, TX 75235, tel: 800-527-2500. You can fly from Quito to Baltra Island (TAME has flights every Friday and Tuesday) and then go on an excursion of the islands. The Flotel Orellana offers a 4-5 day cruise down the Napa River through the Amazon Jungle. Fly from Quito to Coca, a thatched roof settlement, to visit a Yumbo Indian village, Monkey Island, and Lake Taracoa.

SOURCES OF FURTHER INFORMATION

Any Pan Am office around the world; Ecuadorian Tourist Commission, PO Box 2454, Quito, Ecuador; Ecuadorian Embassy, 2535 15th Street NW, Washington, DC 20009; the Ecuadorian Consulate General, 1270 Avenue of the Americas, New York, NY 10020; the Ecuadorian Embassy and Consulate, 3 Hans Crescent, London SW1.

Note: Because of the political situation in El Salvador, it has not been possible to provide complete information for this chapter.

El Salvador

WHAT'S SPECIAL

The country itself has great natural beauty with numerous beaches, six inland lakes and nearly two hundred extinct volcanoes. Some of the most beautiful churches in the world are to be found here, and the local people spend a full 12 days each year honoring their various saints. Mayan ruins have produced a wealth of material for archeologists, giving a better idea of what pre-Columbian civilizations existed here. Indeed, El Salvador remains one of the foremost places for discovering the lives of earlier human ancestors in the world.

COUNTRY BRIEFING

Size: 8,260 square miles
Capital: San Salvador
Population: 4,450,000
Capital Population: 461,000

Climate: Temperature varies according to altitude, but it is generally warm all year round. There is a warm, rainy season ("summer") May-November and a dry season November-May. Evenings are cool.

Weather in San Salvador: Lat N13°42′; Alt 2,238 ft

Temp (°F)	Jan	Feb	Mar	Apr	May	Jun	Jul	Aug	Sep	Oct	Nov	Dec
Av Low	60°	60°	62°	65°	67°	66°	65°	66°	66°	65°	63°	61°
Av High	90°	92°	94°	93°	91°	87°	89°	89°	87°	87°	87°	89°
Days no rain	30	27	30	27	18	11	12	12	10	15	26	29

Government: A republic.
Language: Spanish.
Currency: Colón. 100 centavos = 1 colón.

SOURCES OF FURTHER INFORMATION

Instituto Salvadoreño de Turismo, Calle Rubén Dario 619, San Salvador; **El Salvador Tourist Information Office,** 200 West 58th Street, NY, NY 10019; **El Salvador Consulate General,** 46 Park Avenue, NY, NY 10016; **Embassy of El Salvador,** Flat 16, Edinburgh House, 96 Portland Place, London W1.

French Guiana

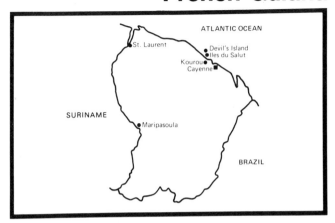

WHAT'S SPECIAL

The land that makes up French Guiana—actually an overseas *departement* of France—has had a somewhat checkered history, having been British, Dutch, and Anglo-Portuguese until it became French again in 1817. The discovery of gold in the mid-19th-century led to disputes with both Surinam and Brazil, which were finally settled in 1915. And it is probably best remembered for being the site of the notorious French penal colony at Devil's Island, some six miles off shore. Devil's Island was just one of several penal colonies in French Guiana; France began sending prisoners to the country during the French Revolution and closed the penal colonies in 1945. It is a wild and primitive land, with fertile soils, considerable resources of timber, and coastal waters teeming with fish and shrimp. The removal of the French space research headquarters from Algeria to French Guiana in the late 60s sparked a new interest in the territory in France, and also led to the extensive modernization of the city of Kourou. However, the local government has opposed a resettlement plan that would have brought in some 10,000 settlers to develop a wood pulp and lumber industry.

The result is that much of the country remains undeveloped, much virgin jungle. For the adventuresome it is truly an explorer's paradise, and wilderness excursions are little more than a few miles upriver. Indeed, rivers are the principal means of travel into the interior. For those who want to stalk wild animals, there are haka tigers, ocelots, jaguars, and tapirs, not to mention the piranhas in the water, and the *moving vines*—as the waterloving anacondas are called. The population is predominantly Creole, descendants of Africans, Asians, and Europeans. There is still a small population of indigenous Indians, including a small tribe of Arawaks, who live in picturesque settlements. The main exports are gold, shrimp, rum, and wood.

COUNTRY BRIEFING

Size: 35,135 square miles **Population:** 50,000
Capital: Cayenne **Capital Population:** 30,000
Climate: Hot and humid, with temperatures averaging 80°. Heavy rainfall from April to July. Best time to visit is August to December.

Weather in Cayenne: Lat N4°56'; Alt 20 ft

Temp (°F)	Jan	Feb	Mar	Apr	May	Jun	Jul	Aug	Sep	Oct	Nov	Dec
Av Low	74°	74°	74°	75°	74°	73°	73°	73°	74°	74°	74°	74°
Av High	84°	85°	85°	86°	85°	87°	88°	90°	91°	91°	89°	86°
Days no rain	11	22	9	9	5	7	13	22	26	27	19	13

Government: French Overseas Department.
Language: French. Very little English spoken.
Religion: Roman Catholic.
Currency: French franc. 100 centimes = 1 franc.

	5c	10c	50c	1F	10F	50F	100F	250F
US (dollars, cents)	.02	.04	.19	.39	3.90	19.50	39.00	97.50
UK (pounds, pence)	.01	.02	.09	.19	1.86	9.30	18.60	46.51

Public Holidays:

New Year's Day, 1 Jan
Mardi Gras
Mi-Carême
Good Friday
Easter Monday
Labor Day, 1 May
Ascension

Whit Monday
Bastille Day, 14 July
Assumption, 15 Aug
All Saints Day, 1 Nov
All Souls Day, 2 Nov
Armistice Day, 11 Nov
Christmas Day, 25 Dec

HOW TO GET THERE

Flying time to Cayenne, Rochambeau Airport from New York is about 7 hours; from Miami, 5 hours; from Georgetown, 1½ hours. Time in French Guiana: GMT−3.

REQUIREMENTS FOR ENTRY AND CUSTOMS REGULATIONS

Passport and round-trip ticket required, and smallpox vaccination certificate and yellow-fever inoculation if staying more than 15 days, and cholera inoculation if coming from an infected area. No visa is necessary for stays of up to 3 months. No currency regulations; currency may be freely exchanged at local banks. Duty-free allowance: 400 cigarettes or 100 cigars; 1 liter alcohol; perfume for personal use.

AIRPORT INFORMATION

Rochambeau Airport is about 10 miles from Cayenne. Airport buses meet planes and are free, except for excessive luggage. Taxi fare to the center of Cayenne, about 50 francs. No duty-free shop.

ACCOMMODATIONS

Two miles outside Cayenne is the excellent **Hotel du Montabo** (part of the chain PLM), on Montabo Hill, overlooking the ocean with a view of Devil's Island to the northwest (from 120 francs double); in Cayenne are the **Hotel Neptima** (from 120 francs double) and **Chez Matilde** (from 50 francs double). At Kourou, site of the sophisticated French space center, is the **Hotel des Roches** (from 110 francs double), considered by many to be one of the best hotels in the country. The **Syndicat d'Initiative** (tel: 919) will help with finding accommodations.

USEFUL INFORMATION

Banks: Open 7:30-11:30 and 3-5:30 Mon-Fri, and mornings on Sat. You can change currency and travelers' checks at hotels. It is a good idea to buy French francs before arriving in the country.

Mail: Stamps at post offices and in hotels.

Telephone Tips: There are phones in the post office, street booths, hotels, and restaurants. Useful numbers in Cayenne:

Tourist Information 919	**Airport Information** 20
Operator 453	**Police** 18
Directories 477	

Newspapers: English-language publications available.

Tipping: Service charge is not usually included in restaurant checks, so tip about 12½%; porters, 1 franc per piece of luggage; taxi drivers, hotel staff, museum guides do not expect tips.

Electricity: 220 and 110 volts 50 cycles AC.

Laundry: Major hotels have good services (dry-cleaning a suit, from 12F; laundering a shirt, from 2F).

Hairdressing: No facilities in hotels (shampoo and set, from 16F; man's haircut, from 8F).

Photography: Good selection of black and white and color film in main cities. Developing takes a week for black and white, 2 months for color.

Clubs: Rotary and Lions.

Babysitting: None.

Rest Rooms: In hotels, restaurants, cafés. Women, *Dames;* men, *Hommes.*

Health: Many doctors and dentists speak English. Imported pharmaceuticals available at reasonable prices. Drink bottled water.

TRANSPORTATION

There is a bus service connecting Cayenne, Kourou, and the main cities, but otherwise one cannot rely on public transportation. Taxis are readily available by phone (tel: 307/357 or 770) but are expensive. A complete taxi tour of the city and island of Cayenne costs about 100F. Rented cars are available from Hertz. New roads have been built outside Cayenne. There are jitneys in the city, automobiles or canoes in the interior. Internal airlines serve Cayenne, Saint-Laurent, and Maripasoula.

FOOD AND RESTAURANTS

French Guiana does not produce enough food for its population and must import, so in general meals are expensive. Breakfast is from 7:30 to 8:30, lunch from 12 to 2, and dinner from 7:30 to 9. Best international food is at the **Hotel du Montabo** and at **Guilbaud's** and **Montjoly** bar-restaurants in Cayenne. Creole specialties include *bouillon d' Awaras,* Colombo curry, and several dishes with kidney beans. These can be tried in Cayenne at **Felix** (18 Rue C. Colomb—tel: 45), **Le Tatou** (Rue Chausée Sartines), **Le Snack Créole** (Rue Félix Eboué), and **La Bonne Cervoise** (Route de Gallion). Chinese restaurants in Cayenne include **Chen Teng You** (Cité Mirza—tel: 292), **Coq d'Or** (Avenue Général de Gaulle—tel: 183), and **Kim Lone** (Rue Lallouette—tel: 90). **La Baie d'Along** (Rue Francois Arago), **Le Viet Nam** (16 Rue Felix Eboue), and **Dragon D'Or** have Vietnamese specialties. For continental cuisine try **Les Amandiers** (Place A. Hort), and go to **Les Palmistes** (12 Avenue Général de Gaulle—tel: 50) if you just want a snack. In Kourou some good restaurants are **Guinguette Pim-Pum, Le Cactus,** and **Au Bon Accueil.**

DRINKING TIPS

Rum is the national drink. Bars are open all day, women welcome. Minimum drinking age is 21.

ENTERTAINMENT

Cayenne has four movie houses. There is dancing at most hotels in the evenings. The **Hotel du Montabo** has a discothèque and nightclub. Other night spots in the Cayenne area are **Le 106** and **Le Cric Crac.** In Kourou there is a jazz club at the **Hotel des Roches,** and **Le Cachin** has a Creole band.

SHOPPING

Best buys are jewelry, ceramics, and Indian arts and crafts such as woodcarvings and dolls. Good stores in Cayenne are mostly around the **Avenue Général de Gaulle.**

SPORTS

Most popular spectator sports are basketball, soccer, tennis, and cockfighting. For visitors there is swimming, river fishing, yachting, golf (at Cayenne), tennis (clubs at Cayenne and Kourou), riding, and hunting. Canoes can be rented for hunting waterfowl. Guns must be declared and require a permit.

WHAT TO SEE

Cayenne has a **Museum** and **Botanical Gardens.** To the north is the official residence of the Prefect which was built by the Jesuits, the hospital, and government offices. Nearby is the sports stadium. From **Fort Ceperou** there is a good view of the city, the countryside, and the sea. Excursions to the space center can be organized from **Kourou,** which lies less than 5° north of the Equator and is thus an ideal place for rocket launching. The **Hotel des Roches** at Kourou also organizes trips to the **Iles du Salut,** including **Devil's Island,** which contained France's political prisoners. Other prisoners were held in Kourou and in **St-Laurent,** a little town on the Maroni River bordering Surinam. The **Quartier Special,** the old prison in St-Laurent, can be seen.

Jungle tours are available from Cayenne—ask at the Hotel du Montabo. On these you can visit remote Indian villages, bivouac in the forest, or fish in the lakes and rivers and walk over the orchid-studded mountains. On river trips you "rough it" overnight in primitive jungle shelters. It is also interesting to fly right across country for a weekend in **Maripasoula,** a remote town amid the waterfalls and lakes of true Indian country.

SOURCES OF FURTHER INFORMATION

Any **Pan Am** office around the world; inquire at **Hotel du Montabo,** Cayenne, or **Hotel des Roches,** Kourou, for trips and excursions; **Air France,** 5 Place de Grenoble, Cayenne; **Cie. Le Transatlantique,** 80 Place de Grenoble, Cayenne; **French Government Tourist Office,** 610 Fifth Avenue, New York, NY 10020, and 178 Piccadilly, London W1.

Guatemala

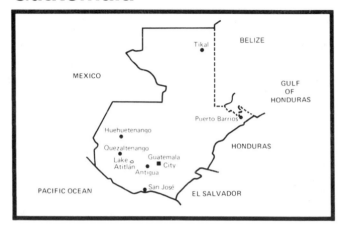

WHAT'S SPECIAL

One of the most unusual of the Central American republics, Guatemala is noteworthy for its large population of indigenous Indians—direct descendants of the former Mayans. For archaeologists, or anyone with a sense of history, Guatemala has unique attractions. The northern part of the country was the home of the Mayan civilization, one of the most sophisticated in the ancient world. Some idea of their staggering art and architecture can be had at Tikal. Here is one of the world's greatest archaeological sites—miles of great pyramids, temples, palaces—still only a fraction of it unearthed. The Maya-Quiché Indians, descendants of those great temple builders, are a friendly, dignified people whose way of life has changed little in centuries. For the most part they retained their independence from the colonial Spanish, and still maintain a distance to this day.

The climate is another attraction; the country is called "the land of eternal spring." While the weather is subtropical, it is never oppressively humid or hot in the highlands. There is wildlife in plenty—ocelot, puma, wild boar, and alligator—and rare birds, one of which, the quetzal, is the national bird and gives the currency its name. Guatemala survived a serious earthquake in February 1976.

COUNTRY BRIEFING

Size: 42,031 square miles

Capital: Guatemala City

Population: 6,849,000

Capital Population: 1,400,000 (metropolitan area)

Climate: Ranges from hot and humid on the coastal plains to cool and dry in the highlands.

Weather in Guatemala City: Lat N14°37'; Alt 4,855 ft

Temp (°F)	Jan	Feb	Mar	Apr	May	Jun	Jul	Aug	Sep	Oct	Nov	Dec
Av Low	53°	54°	57°	58°	60°	61°	60°	60°	60°	60°	57°	55°
Av High	73°	77°	81°	82°	84°	81°	78°	79°	79°	76°	74°	72°
Days no rain	26	26	28	25	16	17	10	10	8	13	23	27

Government: An independent republic.

Language: Spanish. The Indians speak over 20 Mayan dialects. English is understood in hotels and shops in larger centers.

Religion: Roman Catholic predominates.

Currency: Quetzal. 100 centavos = 1 quetzal. The quetzal is on a par with the US$.

	5¢	10¢	25¢	1Q	5Q	10Q	20Q	50Q
US (dollars, cents)	.05	.10	.25	1.00	5.00	10.00	20.00	50.00
UK (pounds, pence)	.02	.05	.12	.48	2.39	4.77	9.54	23.85

Public Holidays:

New Year's Day, 1 Jan
Easter, 8-20 Apr
Labor Day, 1 May
Army Day, 30 June
Bank Employees' Day, 1 July
Independence Day, 15 Sept

Columbus Day, 12 Oct
Revolution Day, 20 Oct
All Saints' Day, 1 Nov
Christmas Eve, 24 Dec
Christmas, 25 Dec
New Year's Eve, 31 Dec

HOW TO GET THERE

Flying time to Guatemala City, La Aurora Airport from New York is 4 ¾ hours; from Miami, 2½ hours; from San Francisco 5¼ hours; from Panama City, 2 hours. Time in Guatemala: GMT−6.

REQUIREMENTS FOR ENTRY AND CUSTOMS REGULATIONS

US citizens require proof of citizenship plus tourist card or visa, obtainable from Guatemalan Consulates or your Pan Am office. All other nationals require a passport, tourist card (which costs US$1), and sometimes, a visa. A cholera vaccination is required if coming from an infected area. US dollars readily accepted, so no need to convert into local currency. A permit is needed for firearms and ammunition: inquire through a Consulate well in advance of departure. Duty-free allowance: 80 cigarettes, 1 bottle liquor. Archaeological relics and jade are prohibited exports.

AIRPORT INFORMATION

La Aurora International Airport is about 5 miles south of Guatemala City center. You can take a local bus—uncomfortable but adequate— into town for 15 centavos or, easier, a taxi, available at all times. Taxi fare is Q10 to the center of town, Q8 to the Conquistador and Plaza Hotels, and Q5 to the Camino Real Hotel. There is a departure tax of Q5. The Guatemalan Tourist Commission has two information desks at the airport, one at the gate area for departing passengers and the other near the immigration and customs desks downstairs for those arriving. Tip porters Q.25 per bag, Q.50 for a large piece.

ACCOMMODATIONS

The range is from luxury hotels to inexpensive (but clean and comfortable) pensions. For advice ask the Tourist Information Bureau at the airport. Guest houses cost about Q7-8 a day each for a room; and mostly operate on European Plan. Hotels are crowded at the peak of the two tourist seasons (June-August and January-March), so it's best to reserve ahead. Hotels in Guatemala City:

Rates are in US$ for a double/twin room with bath or shower

   Best Western Jardin Louisiana, Carretera 2 El Salvador (from $51), 3 miles from airport

   Camino Real, Biltmore, Zona 10 (from $50), 5 minutes from airport

   Centenario, 6a Calle 5-33, Zona 1 (from $14)

   Conquistador Sheraton, Via 5, 4-68, Zona 4 (from $53), 5 minutes from center city and airport

   Cortijo Reforma, Avenida La Reforma 2-18, Zona 9 (from $40)

   Del Centro, 13a Calle 4-55, Zona 1 (from $28)

   El Dorado Americana, 7a Avenida 15-45, Zona 9 (from $36)

   Hotel Embajador, 19 Calle 11-31 Zona 1 (from $36)

   Guatemala Fiesta, 1a Avenida 13-22, Zona 10 (from $38)

   Maya Excelsior, 7a Avenida 12-46, Zona 1 (from $18)

   Motel Plaza, Via 7, 6-16, Zona 4 (from $20), in residential section

   Pan American, 9a Calle 5-63, Zona 1 (from $30)

   Hotel Paris Plaza, 6a Avenida 9-62, Zona 1 (from $15)

   Ritz Continental, 6a Avenida (A) 10-13, Zona 1 (from $32)

All hotels in center city unless otherwise indicated.

USEFUL INFORMATION

   Banks: Open 9-3, Mon-Fri. First-class hotels change travelers' checks.

   Mail: Stamps at post offices and hotels.

   Telephone Tips: Phones in public booths, hotels, and cafés. Useful numbers:

Pan Am 82181	**Information** (how to dial international calls) 174
Airport Information 63227	
Tourist Information 311333	**National Long Distance Service** 121
International Operator (Mexico, Nicaragua, Panama) 177	**International Radiograms** 127
International Operator (rest of world) 171	Time 126
Red Cross 125	Fire 122

   Newspapers: English-language papers available. There is also a weekly newspaper in English called *The Guatemala News,* with regular features of interest to tourists.

   Tipping: Luggage porters, Q.25 per bag, or more for a large item; taxi drivers, 10%; hotel porters, cloakroom attendants, museum guides, Q1.00; hotel chambermaids, 5% of the bill; hairdressers, 10% of the bill. In restaurants service charges are not generally included, so leave about 10% of the bill.

Electricity: 110 volts 60 cycles AC.

Laundry: Guatemala City has reliable and prompt laundry and dry-cleaning services, and luxury hotels can provide express service (dry-cleaning a suit, Q2.50; laundering a shirt, Q1).

Hairdressing: Facilities in salons and major hotels (shampoo and set, Q8; man's haircut, Q3).

Photography: Black and white film available in most places, but color film hard to find outside the capital. Processing of color takes 1-2 days.

Clubs: Rotary, Lions, and Jaycees.

Babysitting: Larger hotels can arrange.

Rest Rooms: Only in good hotels, cafés, and restaurants. Women, *Damas* or *Señoras;* men, *Caballeros, Hombres,* or *Señores.*

Health: There are good doctors and dentists, and many speak English. The Medical Center (tel: 65061/2) and the Herrera Llerandi Hospital (tel: 66771/5) give emergency treatment—both are private, and medical charges can be quite high. Imported medicines and toiletries expensive. Immunizations against typhoid and tetanus are recommended. Precautions should be taken against diarrhea and dysentery. If going to the interior, take Chloroquine tablets for malaria prevention. Wash all fruit and vegetables bought in markets. Tap water is chlorinated and considered safe in Guatemala City, but elsewhere bottled water is best.

TRANSPORTATION

There is a comprehensive bus service in Guatemala City (fare 5 centavos). Buses are not crowded, except during morning, noon, and evening rush hours. Unmetered taxis are numerous and relatively expensive. It is easy to rent a car. For a Hertz Toyota Starlett the cost would be Q20 per day, plus Q.15 per kilometer. Hertz and Avis are at the airport. On mountain roads use the horn. Buses for all points in the interior leave from the Bus Terminal in Zone 4; fares are reasonable. First-class buses for Quezaltenango and the Mexican border, connecting with Mexican bus lines: Auto Pullmans Galgos, 7a Avenida 19-44, Zona 1 (tel: 539943/23661); Rutas Lima, 8a Calle 3-63, Zona 1 (tel: 531828/531851). Bus service to all of Central America: Tica Bus, 14a Calle 4-10, Zona 1 (tel: 514325/24184). Trains are inadequate and not recommended. The best way to visit Tikal is by air: Aviateca, the internal airline, will fly you there in 45 minutes.

FOOD AND RESTAURANTS

National cuisine may be savored in many colorful restaurants in the capital and interior. Try *tamales* (banana leaves stuffed with meat and corn), *rellenitos de platano* (fried bananas stuffed with black beans), *chiles rellenos* (green and red peppers stuffed with meat), and *gallo en chicha* (chicken cooked in cider). Guatemalan coffee is among the best in the world. International cuisine is available in all the tourist centers. In the capital try **Estro Armonico** (Via 4 4-36, Zona 4—tel: 319240) for excellent *haute cuisine,* reservations essential, and the **Petit Suisse** (Avenida La Reforma 6-67, Zona 10—tel: 316804)—both relatively expensive, around Q12. Also **Safari** (3 Av 11-65, Zona 10—tel: 67386), interesting jungle atmosphere. The food is also excellent. **La Ronda** (tel: 681271), in the Camino Real Hotel, is fun for an evening's entertainment and also has music, dancing, and a floor show. Also in the Camino Real is **El Cafetal** for continental cuisine. The Ritz Continental Hotel also has a good medium-priced restaurant, **La Taberna de Don Pedro** (tel: 81671). Try **La Parrillita** (Plazuela España, 12a Calle 6-45, Zona 9—tel: 61485), **El Fogón** (12a Calle 4-23, Zona 9—tel: 316351), **La Estancia** (Avenida La Reforma and 7 Calle, Zona 9—tel: 316607), and **La Hacienda** (16a Calle 7-19, Zona 9—tel: 314909) for steaks. If you like seafood go to **Delicias del Mar** (Ruta 44-33, Zona 4), across from the Conquistador Sheraton Hotel, or **Automariscos** (Via 9, 5-04, Zona 4—tel: 316657) for charcoal-broiled lobster and shrimp. **Mar y Flores** (1 Av 13-42, Zona 10—tel: 680663) is also good for seafood. **El Parador** (12a Calle 4-09, Zona 9), and **Ranchón Antigueño** (13a Calle 3-50, Zona 1—tel: 28358) offer typical Guatemalan food and for authentic local atmosphere try **Roca Negra** (18 Av 40-76, Zona 8), somewhat tricky to find, or **Rincon Salvadoreno** (9a Calle 4-49, Zona 1). There are several places for quick, inexpensive meals and snacks in the main shopping district, around 6th Avenida. Other restaurants that offer international food are **Puerto Chico** (Avenida La Reforma 13-70, Zona 9), **Costa Brava** (11a Calle 7-44, Zona 9—tel: 316509), and **Martin's** (Ruta 5, 7-69, Zona 4—tel: 316949). If you are looking for Chinese food, try **Canton** (6a Avenida 14-20, Zona 1—tel: 537851) and **Palacio Royal** (7a Avenida 11-00, Zona 9—tel: 314273). For Italian food, try **Il Focolare** (10a Calle 6-20, Zona 1—tel: 538454) and **Bologna** (10a Calle, near 6th Avenue). The restaurant of the **Pan American Hotel** (9a Calle 5-63, Zona I) offers some of the best food in town at very reasonable prices, as does **Los Arcos** in the El Dorado Americana Hotel (7a Avenida 15-45, Zona 9).

DRINKING TIPS

Bars are open from noon till late—some to 5am. Women should be accompanied. Imported liquor is expensive, especially wines, so try the local product. Best local beers are Gallo and Monte Carlo. Guatemalan rum has a high reputation, and the adventurous can sample *aguardiente* (sugarcane liquor). It is one of the ingredients, with grenadine and Kümmel liqueurs, of an *El Jaguar* cocktail (fiery red and garnished with lime) at the **El Jaguar** bar in the Hotel Camino Real. The Ritz Continental, Conquistador Sheraton, and the Pan American hotels also have popular bars. **El Mostachon,** in the Plaza Montúfar shopping center on 12 Calle near 6 Avenida, Zona 9, is a favorite drinking spot with young business people. Next door is **J-J,** a plush lounge featuring good guitar music. **Las Sillas** (in La Cupula, 7 Av and 13 Calle, Zona 9) has a very pleasant ambiance plus good music, while **El Establo** (El Patio Building, 7 Av, between Calle 6 and 7, Zona 4) is highly popular with the younger set with numerous discothèques nearby.

ENTERTAINMENT

The **National Symphony Orchestra** gives concerts from May to October, and the ballet season starts in August. There are theater performances all year round in Spanish and English, and several movie houses. The Ritz Continental Hotel has a nightclub, **The Brasilia**, as does the Conquistador Sheraton. **La Cancilleria** in the Hotel Embajador offers a floor show as well as dining and dancing. For marimba music and dancing there is **El Gallito** (9a Calle between 8 and 9 Avenidas, Zona 1). Mariachi bands play all night at the Avenida La Liberacion near "El Trebol." There are now a number of first rate discos, with **Greenery** on La Reforma (between Calle 6 and 7, Zona 9) considered the best. Others include **Le Pont** (13 Calle 0-48, Zona 10), **Las Parejas** (in the El Patio Building, 7 Av between Calle 6 and 7, Zona 4), plus **La Manzana** (edificio Maya, Zona 4); **Tijuana** (Avenida Las Americas, Zona 13); **El Gato Pardo** (20a Calle 0-76, Zona 10); and **La Andromeda,** which resembles a flying saucer (Avenida Las Americas, Zona 13). **After Dark** (6 Avenida and 10 Calle, Zona 9), and **El Gitanillo,** next door to After Dark, have a Spanish atmosphere and live entertainment.

SHOPPING

Stores generally open 8am-12 and 2-6 Mon-Fri and 8-12 Sat. Best buys are handwoven Indian textiles (sold by the meter and made up into dresses, jackets, ponchos, purses, etc.), wood carvings, silver jewelry, leather goods, and ceramics. You'll find a wide choice of attractive handicrafts for under Q12. The best bargains are at the **18th Street** (Zona 1) **Market** and also on 12th Street from 4th to 6th Avenues. The old Central Market was torn down after the earthquake, but the activity continues at the **Plazuela Barrios** near the railroad station. The best selection of traditional Indian weaving at reasonable prices can be found at 4 Ahua, 11 Calle 3-76, Zona 1. **El Patio**, across the street, is full of colonial antiques and furniture. Other good places for native crafts are **El Dzunan** (1 Av 13-29, Zona 10) across the street from the Guatemala Fiesta hotel, **Sombol** (Avenida La Reforma 14-14, Zona 9), textiles, dresses, furniture; **Mayatex** (12a Calle 4-56, Zona 1), textiles and silver jewelry; **San Antonio** (6a Avenida 11-58, Zona 1), silver jewelry; **La Regional** (8a Avenida 6-75, Zona 1), textiles and leather goods. **La Dama** (Avenida La Reforma 13-70, Zona 9) specializes in handmade wooden furniture. For general shopping, main department stores are **Almacenes Paiz** (Centro Comercial, Zona 4) and **Sears Department Store** (6 Av between Calle 12 and 13). Bargaining is customary in markets but not in stores. You should visit the **National Handcraft Market** in La Aurora Park.

SPORTS

Golf is popular, and you can play at the **Country Club** or the **Mayan Golf Club.** Both also offer tennis and swimming facilities. Hotels can arrange temporary membership for their guests. Several other clubs have squash, tennis, and swimming all the year round. The **Squash Club** (6

Av 7-19—tel: 316406) has 4 indoor courts. There is swimming on the coasts, and you can try waterskiing and skin-diving on **Lakes Atitlán** and **Amatitlán.** There is some freshwater fishing on the lakes and rivers, but deep-sea fishing is better. Mountaineers can try the volcanoes: **Agua, Fuego,** and **Pacaya** are the most popular. The many beautiful trails on the outskirts of the capital make horseback riding a rewarding way to explore the countryside, and you can hire horses from the stable of the **Association Hipica de Guatemala.** Wild game is abundant in the forests, and hunting is excellent; travel agents in the capital can arrange expeditions, or ask the Caza, Tiro y Pesca (hunting, shooting, and fishing club), 3a Avenida 8-35, Zona 2, for advice. As for spectator sports, there are soccer games at the **Mateo Flores Stadium;** baseball at the **Parque Minerva;** boxing, tennis tournaments, swimming events, wrestling, and basketball at the **Ciudad Olímpica.**

WHAT TO SEE

In Guatemala City, there is a magnificent collection of Mayan art at the **Museum of Archaeology and Ethnology** (Building 5, La Aurora, Zone 13). The **Museum of Natural History** (5a Avenida and 8a Calle Esquina) and the **Museum of Popular Arts and Crafts** (10a Avenida 10-72, Zona 1) have interesting exhibits of Indian handicrafts. There are two excellent private collections now open, the **Ixchel Museum** of Indian costumes and handwoven textiles, open daily except Monday (4a Avenida 16-27, Zona 10), and **Museo Popul-Vuh** (16 Calle 0-55, Zona 10 on La Reforma), a collection of archaeological and colonial art. The country's colonial past has left a heritage of fine churches, such as the **Cathedral** and **La Merced Church,** though the latter was severely damaged by the earthquake. The **National Palace,** in pale green stone, and the **Torre del Reformador** (like an illuminated Eiffel Tower at night) are prominent landmarks. In the **Hipódromo del Norte** a relief map displays the contours of the country. Children will enjoy the zoo at Aurora Park.

Antigua is the former capital. Severely damaged by an earthquake in 1773, it still preserves something of its colonial grandeur, and you can see the ruins of once ornate churches and other fine 16th-century buildings. The **Colonial Museum** is housed in the former university, one of the first to be founded in the Americas. Try to go on market days—Saturday, Monday, or Thursday—when you can bargain for hand-wrought silver, pottery, and Indian textiles. Antigua is about half an hour by car from the capital; you can also go by bus, or take one of the tours organized by local travel agents. The high point of the year is Holy Week, when processions take place in the main streets over intricate carpets made of colored sawdust. Stay at the **Hotel Antigua** (from US$37), the **Aurora,** 4a Calle Oriente (from US$13), the **Santa Isabel,** Barrio Santa Isabel (from US$32 double) or **Ramada Antigua,** 9a Calle y Carretera Ciudad (from US$32). There are a number of good restaurants in town including **Restaurant Internacional** (1 Av Norte #2—tel: 032566), excellent pastries and good native fare, **Zen Restaurant,** serving Japanese food on 5 Av beneath the Arc, while **La Olla Azul** (5 Av #21) offers good delicatessen fare. For souvenirs, try the local jade jewelry at **La Casa de Jade** (4a Calle #3, off the park) or **Jades, SA** (4a Calle Oriente #34).

Chichicastenango, the central market town for the Indians in the surrounding highland villages, is well known for its markets held on Thursdays and Sundays. The **Mayan Inn** (tel: 60213 in Guatemala City for reservations, from US$21) is a pleasant place to stay—and a good base for trips by car or on horseback into the surrounding hills.

Lake Atitlán must not be missed: one mile high, deep turquoise water with cascading waterfalls, it must be one of the most spectacularly beautiful lakes in the world. Around it are 12 Indian villages named after the 12 apostles. The new **Hotel Atitlán** (from US$20) is recommended for its fine position on the lake. The **Tzanjuyu** (from US$20) and **Regis** (from US$14) can also be recommended. The **Posada Camino Real Atitlán** (from US$24) is located along the lake between Santa Catarina Palopó and San Antonio Palopó and is quiet and isolated. The **Hotel del Lago** (from US$30) is a small, secluded resort facing the lake.

The second city of Guatemala is **Quezaltenango,** meaning "place of the quetzal," a cool, highland town with spring waters said to be medicinal. Another center for visiting Indian villages, its market is held every day, and the week of 15 September is fiesta time. You can stay at the **Pension x—Bonifax,** 4a Calle 10-50, Zona 1—tel: 061-2959 (from US$20).

Undoubtedly, Guatemala's greatest treasures are the ruins of the Mayan city of **Tikal,** one of the world's most fascinating archaeological sites. The Mayan people, whose ancestors are thought to have come from Asia some 10,000 years ago, developed an astonishingly advanced civilization and independently invented sciences of astronomy and mathematics. Tikal has only recently begun to be excavated, and only a fraction of its huge extent has been uncovered from the jungle growth of centuries. But you will see miles of massive pyramids and temples, plazas, and intricately carved pillars. Its treasures—carvings, painted vases, jade ornaments—are on show at the archaeological museum. You can go to Tikal and return in one day by air, but to make the most of your visit it is worth staying a day or so. Stay at the **Mayan International** (from US$18) near Flores or **Posada de la Selva** (from US$28), or **Jaguar Inn** (from US$30 MAP), both in Tikal itself.

In the northeast, toward the Mexican border, is **Huehuetenango,** another rewarding place for ruin hunters, with the temples, forts, and ball courts of **Zaculeu** ("white land") just outside the city. Stay at the **Hotel Zaculeu,** 5a Avenida 1-14, Zona 1 (from US$20). On the Atlantic coast **Puerto Barrios** is the major port, about 5 hours by road through the jungle on the new Atlantic Highway or 30 minutes by air. The **Hotel del Norte** (from US$18) is recommended. From here you can take a pleasant trip by boat on the Rio Dulce to **Lake Izabal,** famous for its flora and fauna, and the castle of **San Felipe de Lara,** built as a defense against English pirates. In **Livingston,** a charming Caribe community which can be reached by ferry from Puerto Barrios, there is the **Casa Rosada** (from US$12). Hotels upriver from Livingston to the San Felipe castle are **Hotel Catamaran,** on an island with marina and swimming pool (from US$20—tel: 60279 in Guatemala City), and **Turicentro Marimonte** (from US$25).

The Pacific coast at **San José,** 2 hours by car from the capital on the first-class highway, is popular for deep-sea fishing. Nearby you can stay at **Turicentro Likin** in Iztapa (bungalows from US$28-45), where there is a private beach and swimming pool. There are special buses from the capital, or you might take a day tour arranged by one of the travel agencies.

SOURCES OF FURTHER INFORMATION

Pan Am, 6a Avenida 11-43, Zona 1, Guatemala City, or any Pan Am office around the world; **Guatemala Tourist Commission,** 7a Avenida 1-17, Centrp Civico (tel: 311333/47), Guatemala City; **American Chamber of Commerce,** Edificio Etisa, 5 Nivel Of. 5-B, Zona 9 (tel: 61882) Guatemala City; **Guatemala Tourist Commission,** 929 Sunrise Lane, Fort Lauderdale, FL 33304; and **Consulate General of Guatemala,** 1270 Avenue of the Americas, New York, NY 10020.

Guyana

WHAT'S SPECIAL

Little is known of the early history of this nation before the arrival of Europeans in the late 1500s, save that it was known as the "land of the waters" by its indigenous Amerindian population. The resourceful Dutch who originally colonized the region put in a sophisticated system of dykes and drainage canals which—300 years later—still keeps the coastal area, below sea-level for the most part, dry.

For the visitor, Guyana offers numerous possibilities for adventure in the interior, excellent fishing, and the opportunity to study at first hand the only Marxist republic in South America. Some of the finest scenery in the world is to be found up country, and includes the breathtaking Kaieteur Falls, five times higher than the Niagara, and one of the natural wonders of the world.

There are tropical forests, cattle-ranching savannahs and vast sugar plantations, bauxite mines, and many picturesque towns inhabited by people of Amerindian, African, East Indian, Chinese, and European origins.

COUNTRY BRIEFING

Size: 83,000 square miles   **Population:** 780,000
Capital: Georgetown   **Capital Population:** 183,000
    Climate: Mild tropical. Best time to visit is from July to September.

Weather in Georgetown: Lat N6°50'; Alt 6 ft

Temp (°F)	Jan	Feb	Mar	Apr	May	Jun	Jul	Aug	Sep	Oct	Nov	Dec
Av Low	74°	74°	75°	76°	75°	75°	75°	75°	76°	76°	76°	75°
Av High	84°	84°	84°	85°	85°	85°	85°	86°	87°	87°	86°	84°
Days no rain	14	15	19	19	11	6	10	15	23	22	20	11

Government: A cooperative republic.

Language: Only English-speaking country in South America.

Religion: Christian (57%); Hindu (33%); and Muslim (9%).

Currency: Guyanese dollar. 100 Guyanese cents = 1 Guyanese dollar.

	G 25¢	G 50¢	G $1	G $5	G $10	G $20	G $50	G $100
US (dollars, cents)	.10	.20	.39	1.96	3.92	7.84	19.61	39.22
UK (pounds, pence)	.05	.10	.19	.93	1.87	3.74	9.35	18.71

Public Holidays:

New Year's Day, 1 Jan
Youman Nabi
Republic Day, 23 Feb
Good Friday
Easter Monday
Labor Day, 1 May
Caribbean Community Day, first
   Mon in July

Freedom Day, first Mon in
   Aug
Deepavali
Eid-ul-Ahza
Christmas Day, 25 Dec
Boxing Day, 26 Dec

The dates of Eid-ul-Ahza, Youman Nabi, and Deepavali vary annually according to the lunar calendar.

HOW TO GET THERE

Flying time to Timehri International Airport from New York is 5¼ hours; from Port of Spain, 1 hour, from Caracas, 1½ hours. Time in Guyana: GMT−3 hours 45 minutes.

REQUIREMENTS FOR ENTRY AND CUSTOMS REGULATIONS

Passport, onward ticket, and a smallpox vaccination certificate are required. Visas not required of US and Commonwealth visitors. Cholera and yellow-fever immunization needed if coming from an infected area. Duty-free allowance: 200 cigarettes, or 50 cigars, or 8 ounces tobacco, 32 ounces of liquor for personal use; perfume for personal use. Firearms must be licensed by the Ministry of Home Affairs, Georgetown. Information on exchange control regulations available from the Bank of Guyana in Georgetown.

AIRPORT INFORMATION

The International Airport for Georgetown is Timehri, 25 miles from the city center. There are buses into town, and the taxi fare is about G$25 per person in a shared taxi. Departure tax: G$10. Timehri Airport has a duty-free shop and a hotel reservation counter. Tip the porter about G$1 per suitcase.

ACCOMMODATIONS

Belvedere Hotel, 234 Camp Street (from US$20 double); the **Guyana Pegasus,** Sea Wall Road (from US$114 double); **Park,** 38 Main Street (from US$18 double); **Tower** 74/75 Main Street (from US$24.80 double).

USEFUL INFORMATION

Banks: Open 8-12 Mon-Sat.

Mail: Stamps must be obtained from post offices. For overseas telegrams and radio telephone services go to Guyana International Telecommunication Corporation at the Bank of Guyana Building.

Telephone Tips: Booths available in restaurants and cafés. Useful numbers in Georgetown:

Tourist Information, Guyana   Time 95
    Overland Tours 66741   Emergencies 999
Directories 91   Operator 009
International Operator 94

Newspapers: *The Guyana Chronicle, New Nation, Catholic Standard, The Sunday Chronicle* and *Mirror.*

Tipping: In restaurants, 10%; porters, G70¢ per piece of luggage; hotel chambermaids and porters, G$1.50; taxi drivers, 10%.

Electricity: 110 volts, 60 cycles AC.

Laundry: Dry-cleaning and laundry services available and inexpensive.

Hairdressing: In Georgetown there is **Dave's Salon** in the Pegasus Hotel (shampoo and set G$18, haircut G$10, no tip) and **Noreen's Salon,** Church Street.

Photography: Equipment and film imported and expensive. Black and white and color film developed within a week at the photographic department of Guyana Stores Limited, Water Street.

Babysitting: Services arranged through your hotel.

Rest Rooms: It is best to use your hotel.

Health: Good general practitioners and some specialists in Guyana, also good dentists. Imported pharmaceuticals available and expensive. Water in Georgetown and elsewhere is unsafe to drink without boiling. Milk other than canned milk should be boiled. Malaria has been eliminated, but mosquitoes can be a nuisance. Cooked food from street vendors not recommended.

TRANSPORTATION

Bus services in the city are fairly good, but crowded; taxis are scarce in rush hours and at night. There are taxi stands in the main centers. Fares in Georgetown generally average G$3-6, but check with the driver before setting off. The average daily rate for a rented car is US$15. Contact **Gee-Tee Self Drive Car Service,** First Federal Life Building, Croal Street and Manget Place (tel: 61519). Traffic drives on the left; watch out for bicycles, donkey carts, and animals. Long-distance bus services are good, especially along the coast. Guyana Airways Corporation operates scheduled services within the country, including flights to Kaieteur

Falls and Orinduik Falls. There are ferries across the Demerara, Berbice, and Essequibo rivers and steamer services from Georgetown to towns on the coastal strip. There is also a bridge over the Demerara River, the toll being G$5 per car.

FOOD AND RESTAURANTS

International cuisine is available in hotel restaurants; the **El Dorado** in the Pegasus Hotel and the **Cactus Club** in the Tower Hotel. The **Palm Court** has atmosphere and good food, as do the dining rooms in the Belvedere and Park Hotels. Creole food at **Green Shrimp** and **Grub Inn** and French food at the **Club Diabolique.** The **Rendezvous** serves excellent chicken, and **Qik-Serv Restaurant** is recommended for the take-out chicken, prawns, pizza, curry and roti, fish in batter, and good desserts. **Demico** is popular for its ice cream. Try the **Rice Bowl,** the **Chinese Dragon,** and **Kwang Chow** for Chinese meals. If you wish to sample local dishes, try *metamgee,* a concoction of yams, plantains, and cassava cooked in coconut milk, or *pepperpot,* a sort of perpetual stew. Garlic pork is a tasty Portuguese dish. Food is generally inexpensive, and even in an expensive restaurant dinner for one will not cost more than G$25-28. Breakfast is served from 6:30-7:30, lunch 11:30-12:30, and dinner 6 onwards.

DRINKING TIPS

Local beers and rums are very good; D'Augiar's X.M., Demerara, and Eldora rum are excellent. Gin and vodka are produced locally. Diamond Club is a Guyanese whisky. Women are welcome in bars but may feel more comfortable with an escort. Best places to go for a drink are the hotel bars.

ENTERTAINMENT

For evening entertainment there are occasional concerts and theater performances: the **Theater Guild,** which has a high reputation, stages about eight plays a year. The **National Cultural Centre** provides international entertainment, and local folk groups perform regularly. There are several movie houses in Georgetown and one drive-in movie 6 miles east of the city. There is dancing on weekends in most restaurants. It is inadvisable to wander the streets at night.

SHOPPING

Stores are open 8-12 and 2-4 Mon-Fri, and 8-1 Sat. Best buys are Amerindian wares and curios, bead aprons, blowpipes, basketwork, and pottery. Recommended are the **Amerindian Handicrafts Centre** (Water Street), **Guyana Crafts Co-op** (Avenue of the Republic and Brickdam), **Margarita Gift Shop** (92 Middle Street), **Scandinavian Shop** and **Oleander Boutique. Enachu Diamond Traders Ltd** (24 Howes Street) and **Correia's** jewelry establishment (159 Charlotte Street) specialize in Guyanese diamonds and other jewelry. The best place in Georgetown to bargain for local arts and crafts is the **Stabroek Market.**

SPORTS

There are dozens of cricket grounds in and around the city, but the **Georgetown Cricket Club** is one of the finest in the tropics. Soccer, tennis, hockey, boxing, and golf are also very popular. There is a nine-hole golf course at **Lusignan,** 9 miles from Georgetown, and another at **Linden,** 40 miles from Georgetown. Motor racing at the **South Dakota** circuit in Atkinson Fields attracts big crowds. There is swimming at the municipal pools at **Fort Groyne** and **Luckhoo Park.** Riding horses are available at **Manari Ranch** in the Rupununi Savannahs. The annual rodeo, held during Easter on cattle ranches of the Rupununi River savannahs in the southwest, is a big tourist attraction. Freshwater fishing is marvelous.

WHAT TO SEE

Georgetown is a pleasant and attractive city. Of its many beautiful Georgian-style wooden buildings, the Anglican **St George's Cathedral** is said to be the second highest wooden building in the world. The **City Hall,** painted bright blue, is a Gothic extravaganza, and other attractions are the **Law Courts** and the Gothic tower over the colorful and lively **Stabroek Market.** Miniature diamond and gold mines are displayed at the **Guyana Museum,** and there is an important collection relating to the history of the Amerindians at the **Carnegie Free Library.** The **Benab** building, made of leaves and bamboo by the Wai-Wai Amerindians, is an interesting site located opposite the Pegasus Hotel. The **National History Museum** is also worth seeing. A must is a visit to the 180-acre **Botanical Gardens,** which has one of the best collections of palms in the world. Here, too, you can see the giant Victoria Regia and lotus lilies, experimental rice fields, and tropical flowers such as the cannonball flower; and in the Gardens' **Zoo** there are manatees (Guyanese sea cows), tapirs, and many other animals including the world's rarest parrot in captivity. Georgetown is 5 feet below sea level, and the **Sea Wall** that protects the city from flooding is a promenade for its residents. The **National Park** is also a good place to relax. Outside the capital, there are huge cane plantations and sugar factories, the bauxite mines of **Linden,** and the ruins of a 300-year-old Dutch fort at **Kyk-over-al,** near **Bartica.** Hotels in Bartica are the **Moderne** (from US$23 double) and the **Marin** (from US$24 double). Guyana's main tourist attraction is the almost incredible 741-foot-high, 300-foot-wide **Kaieteur Falls** on the Potaro River. There are Sunday excursion flights from Georgetown by Guyana Airways Corporation to this magnificent fall, one of the highest in the world. Interestingly, the noise of the falling waters is so loud that it can be heard above the engine noise in the cockpit of the aircraft. The excursion leaves at 10:30am and returns at 2:30pm. Try to see the **Timehri rock paintings** in the River Mazaruni area, the **Mazpuri Falls** and the **Tramen cliff paintings** in the Imbaimadai area, and the **Rupununi Savannahs,** where you can go fishing for the arapaima, the largest freshwater fish in the world. **Manari Guest House,** 6 miles from **Lethem** in southwestern Guyana and 250 miles from Georgetown, is Rupununi's holiday ranch, with horseback riding and creek bathing. Guyana Airways offers 3-day package tours including air fare, accommodations, and meals to the Lethem area (G$350) and the Imbaimadai area (G$350). Contact Guyana Airways Corporation (tel: 64011) or Guyana Overland Tours (38 Main Street, Georgetown—tel: 66741). Reserve tours and excursions well in advance.

SOURCES OF FURTHER INFORMATION

Pan Am: Guyana Airways Corporation (G.S.A.), Bank of Guyana Building, Georgetown, and any Pan Am office around the world; **Guyana Overland Tours,** Park Hotel Building, 37-42 Main Street, Georgetown; the **Guyana Consulate General,** 622 Third Avenue, New York, NY 10017; **Guyana High Commission,** 3 Palace Court, Bayswater, London W2.

Honduras

WHAT'S SPECIAL

Second largest of the Central American republics, Honduras is also one of the most sparsely populated. There are many mountains in the east, south and west, while an irregular plateau in the southwest near Tegucigalpa and La Esperanza has peaks of nearly 8,000 ft. Columbus reached Honduras in 1502 and named it for the waters in which his ships anchored—the word means "deep." Spanish seekers of gold began formal colonization in 1524, and the coastal area was untouched until the 19th century when US corporations began their banana plantations. Honduras is one of the most mountainous, beautiful, and fascinating countries in Central America, with forests, fine beaches, coffee and cotton plantations, tobacco, and, of course, bananas. The remains of the Mayan civilization at Copan show that Honduras was highly developed about the time the Vikings were tentatively beginning to sail out of sight of land.

COUNTRY BRIEFING

Size: 43,277 square miles   **Population:** 4,000,000
Capital: Tegucigalpa   **Capital Population:** 323,000
   Climate: Tropical, with clearly defined wet and dry seasons. Heaviest rains from end of August to end of December. Tegucigalpa has pleasant temperatures year-round.

Weather in Tegucigalpa: Lat N14°03'; Alt 3,294 ft

Temp (°F)	Jan	Feb	Mar	Apr	May	Jun	Jul	Aug	Sep	Oct	Nov	Dec
Av Low	43°	40°	41°	50°	54°	58°	52°	51°	53°	53°	66°	48°
Av High	78°	81°	82°	88°	91°	85°	85°	87°	87°	86°	84°	84°
Days no rain	30	26	30	27	21	18	23	22	19	23	27	30

Government: Independent republic.

Language: Spanish. Many business people speak English.

Religion: Predominantly Roman Catholic.

Currency: Lempira. 100 centavos = 1 lempira.

	10¢	50¢	1 lemp	5 lemp	10 lemp	20 lemp	50 lemp	100 lemp
US (dollars, cents)	.05	.25	.50	2.50	5.00	10.00	25.00	50.00
UK (pounds, pence)	.02	.12	.24	1.19	2.39	4.77	11.93	23.85

Public Holidays:

New Year's Day, 1 Jan

Patron Saint's Day: Virgen de Suya, 3 Feb

Pan American Day, 14 Apr

Easter Thursday

Good Friday

Easter Sunday

Labor Day, 1 May

Independence Day, 15 Sep

Francisco Morazán Day, 3 Oct

Discovery Day, 12 Oct

Christmas Day, 25 Dec

HOW TO GET THERE

Flying time to Tegucigalpa Airport from New York is 6 hours; from Mexico City, 2¾ hours; from Guatemala City, 1 hour. Time in Honduras: GMT—6.

REQUIREMENTS FOR ENTRY AND CUSTOMS REGULATIONS

Valid passport and roundtrip ticket required. Visas and tourist cards are required by US and Canadian citizens—other nationalities should check with nearest Honduran consulate for latest rules. Visas are obtainable from any Honduran consulate and are free of charge. A tourist card is obtainable at point of departure, cost $2. Business visas require a covering letter from company stating nature and purpose of visit and 4 passport photographs. Cholera vaccination required only if coming from an infected area. Apply to the Immigration Office in Honduras for a permit to stay beyond 90 days. Citizens of Cuba or the Arab countries must obtain a special entry permit through Honduran consulates. No currency restrictions. Duty-free allowance: 200 cigarettes or 1 pound of tobacco; 2 quarts liquor or wine.

AIRPORT INFORMATION

Honduras has three international airports. Toncontin Airport is 3 miles from Tegucigalpa; Ramón Villeda Morales Airport is 11 miles from San Pedro Sula; Golozón Airport is 5 miles from La Ceiba. Taxis are available in all airports and cost upwards of 12 Lps. There are some buses, but they are small and not recommended for travelers with a lot of luggage;

they cost 15 centavos for adults and children. No airport arrival tax. There are duty-free shops. Tip airport porters 50 centavos.

ACCOMMODATIONS

The Honduran government is backing efforts in the private sector for the development of tourism, with the result that there are new hotels in Tegucigalpa, San Pedro Sula, Puerto Cortes, Tela, La Ceiba and the Bay Islands. It is expected that the number of existing rooms—approximately 1,000 first class and deluxe—will triple. The most recent hotel listing is available from the offices of the **Instituto Hondureño de Turismo** which has offices in Tegucigalpa and principal airports. Because of inflation, visitors should expect to pay a slightly higher rate than indicated here. There is a 3% tax on all prices shown.

Rates are in US$ for a double/twin room with bath or shower.

Hotels in Tegucigalpa:

Hotel Alameda, Boulevard Suyepa (from $35)

Gran Hotel Lincoln, 4a Av. 4a Calle (from $45)

Hotel Honduras Maya, Colonia Palmire (from $55)

Hotel La Ronda, 6a Calle (from $40)

Hotel Istmania, 5a., 8a Calle (from $35)

Hotels in San Pedro Sula: (First Class and Deluxe)

Copantl Sula, Colonia Las Mesetas (from $44)

Gran Hotel Sula, Facing Central Park (from $44)

Hotel Bolivar, 2a Calle NO. + 2a. Av. (from $50)

Hotel Palmira, 6a Calle S.O. ± 6a Av. (from $12)

Hotel Terraza, 6a Av. + 4a Calle (from $12)

Hotels in Omoa:

Vitanza Omoa, Omoa (from $30)

Hotels in Tela:

Hotel Atlantico, on the beach (from $20)

Hotel Marabu Inn, Calle Dionisio de Herrera (from $10)

Hotel Paradise, Bo. El Paraiso (from $30)

Villas Telamar, Tela Nuevo (from $50)

Hotels in La Ceiba:

Gran Hotel La Ceiba, Av. San Isidro (from $25)

Hotel Paris, facing Parque Morazan (from $25)

Hotels on Lake Yoja:

Hotel Agua Azul (from $20)

Hotel Brisas del Lago (from $50)

Hotel Los Remos (from $19)

Hotels in Choluteca:

Imperio Maya, Carretera de Emergencia (from $18)

Hotel La Fuente, Carretera Panamericana (from $24)

Motel Camino Real, Carretera a Guasaule (from $15)

Hotels in Jicaro Galan:

Hotel Oasis Colonial, Carretera Panamericana (from $32)

Hotels in Copan Ruinas:

Hotel Marian (from $12)

Hotel **Posadas de Copan** (soon to open)
Hotels in Sana Rosa de Copan:
   Hotel **Elvir**, Barrio El Calvario (from $12)
   Hotel **Maya Land**, Colonia Miraflores (from $8)
Hotels in Amapala:
   Villas Tina, Isla del Tigre (from $25)
Hotels on the Bay Islands: Rates quoted represent MAP or AP:
Roatan Island:
   Anthony's Key Resort, Sandy Bay (from $95)
   Caribinn, French Harbour (from $35)
   Hotel Pirates' Den, San Bay (from $60)
   Lost Paradise of West End, West End (from $45)
   Buccaneer Inn, French Harbour, (from $90)
   Reef House Resort, Oakridge (from $90)
   Hotel Brick Bay, French Harbour (from $100)
   French Harbour Yacht Club, French Harbour (from $25)
   Horizon End, Honesville, (from $100)
   Port Royal Villas, Port Royal Harbour (from $35)
   Caribbean Sailing Yachts, French Harbour (from $35)
   Pirates Den, Sandy Bay (from $55)
   Spyglass Hill, Punta Gorda (from $90)
   Roatan Lodge, Port Royal Harbour (from $120)
(Many of the higher priced hotels include scuba diving, snorkeling, boating, guides, and equipment for diving).
Guanaja Island:
   Bayman Bay Club, Piedras Nuevas (from $150 AP)
   Hotel Posada del Sol (from $150)
   Hotel Miller (from $44)
Utila Island:
   Trudy's Hotel (from $25)
   Sony's Villa Utila (from $12)

USEFUL INFORMATION

Banks: Open Mon-Fri 9-3. Currency and travelers' checks can be changed at hotels and some stores.

Mail: Stamps only at post offices. Mail is very slow, often unreliable. To ensure delivery of letters it's best to register them Lp.0.90 (about 45¢).

Telephone: Service is extremely poor both locally and for long distance, and there are no booths in the streets. A new telephone system is being installed in Tegucigalpa and San Pedro Sula.

Useful numbers: Tourist Office, Tegucigalpa 228934.

Newspapers: No local English-language publications, but English-language newspapers and magazines from abroad on sale.

Tipping: Service charge not generally included in checks, so tip 10%. Taxi drivers and chambermaids are tipped; give porters 50 centavos.

Electricity: 110 or 220 volts 60 cycles AC.

Laundry: Dry-cleaning available and not expensive (dry-cleaning a suit, 2-4 lempiras; laundering a shirt, 60 centavos-1 lempira) but may take longer than anticipated.

Hairdressing: Numerous excellent salons available in major cities at very low rates (US$2-4) and all first class hotels have salons, (shampoo and set, 4-8 lempiras; man's haircut, 1 lempira).

Photography: All types of film available. Black and white developed within a week; color takes longer, less reliable.

Clubs: Rotary and Lions.

Babysitting: None.

Rest Rooms: No public facilities in streets; try hotels and restaurants. Women, *Servicio de Damas;* men, *Servicio de Caballeros.*

Health: Many doctors and dentists speak English. Hospital services are satisfactory. Imported pharmaceuticals available, but expensive. Take precautions against malaria in coastal areas. Do not drink tap water or eat fruits or vegetables that *cannot* be peeled, unless thoroughly washed. It is suggested to take a dysentery preventive before arrival, and a good insect repellant for sandflies in the Bay Islands. Avoid unbottled drinks.

TRANSPORTATION

Both air and land transportation is good, while sea transport between the Bay Islands and mainland is improving. Minibuses in Tegucigalpa cost a standard fare of 15 centavos. There are good bus services between major cities at very moderate prices throughout the day. Intercity service between Tegucigalpa and San Pedro Sula is first-class; roads are paved and in excellent condition, and the drive past Lake Yojoa and through pine covered mountains is spectacular. The trip takes 3½ hours and costs 8 lempiras (US$4) one way. San Pedro Sula to Puerto Cortes: buses leave every 20 minutes for the 45 minute ride through tropical country-side on well paved roads, fare less than US$1. San Pedro Sula to Tela: buses leave every 10 minutes to Progreso where transfers are made for the bus to Tela, journey about two hours, fare about US$2. San Pedro Sula to La Ceiba: three express buses daily, fare about US$4 for the 2½ hour ride through tropical country on well paved highway. On Bay Islands there are no regular bus services, but buses and taxis have fixed rates between points on Roatan and charge for either an "express" or a "collective" ride. Buses usually leave when full or when it appears no more passengers will arrive. Taxis in major cities are available at taxi stands or can be called by phone or hailed in the street. Tegucigalpa has cruising taxis, which are less expensive because they are shared. Car rental is available in all major cities and a US or International driver's license is accepted everywhere in Honduras. When renting, be sure there are no additional charges, such as a surcharge for inter-city journeys. The Honduran government has undertaken a vast roadbuilding program which is enabling visitors to see much more of the country. Although 700 miles of railroad have been constructed in the north, these are used to carry banana freight, and passenger services are few. Tegucigalpa is the only Central American capital without a railroad station. But it is the hub of Central American air services, with daily flights to and from the other capitals and good service to the US. Internal air services are excellent with flights from Tegucigalpa to 28 other airports within the country.

FOOD AND RESTAURANTS

Tortillas are a popular native food—anything from meat or cheese to red beans can be inside these pancakes. *Tapado* is a stew of local vegetables and grated coconut, and you can try the unusual taste of *mondongo* soup, made from vegetables, bananas, and yuca root. Snack meals include *curiles*, a seafood cocktail, and *yuca con chicharrón*, pieces of fried pork and boiled yuca root. There are inexpensive restaurants in the capital.

Mealtimes are: breakfast 6:30-8:30, lunch 12-2, dinner 5:30-7 or 8. International cuisine is available in the major cities, especially Tegucigalpa; **La Ronda** is an expensive international restaurant, and **El Prado** is medium-priced. Good food is served at a number of Italian restaurants, notably **Roma** and **Dino's**, and Spanish cooking can be tried at **El Chico Club**. **Boca del Mar**, near the airport, specializes in seafood, and **La Barbacoa**, also near the airport, specializes in meat dishes—try the *carne asada*. In San Pedro Sula, **Gran Hotel Sula** and **Hotel Bolivar** have an international menu, and **Motel Vitanza, Touche, Vicente's,** and **El Rincó Gaucho** are also recommended.

DRINKING TIPS

Bars are open all the time. Good spots for a leisurely drink in Tegucigalpa are **Jardin de Italia** and **Le Papillon**. The **Honduras Maya Hotel** has a pleasant coffee shop, and there are two drive-ins near the airport, the **Riviera** and **El Pinguino**. Imported wines, liquor, and beers available; a whisky and soda costs about 2 lempiras and a bottle of ordinary red wine 8 lempiras. Avoid mixed drinks and stay with bottled types.

ENTERTAINMENT

Both Tegucigalpa and San Pedro Sula have excellent nonprofessional theater groups which give weekly performances in Spanish and English. The number of art galleries has burgeoned recently and there has been a steady growth of modern movie houses where first run US and European films may be seen. Classical music societies have been instrumental in bringing international performers. Further details about cultural activities available from Instituto Hondureño de Turismo office, plus listings in local newspapers. There is a **Museum of History and Anthropology,** and the **Banco Atlantida** has excellent collections of Mayan artifacts and such famous Honduran painters as the primitive Jose Antonio Velazquez and Carlos Garay, both at their head office in Tegucigalpa and in San Pedro Sula. Discothèques are fast increasing in number, while most major hotels have nightclubs with excellent shows. Among them are **La Belle Epoque** at the Honduras Maya hotel and one at La Ronda, both in Tegucigalpa. The Gran Hotel Sula in San Pedro Sula and the Hotel Paris in

La Ceiba also have nightclubs. Gambling casinos are to be found at the Honduras Maya hotel and at the Hotel Paris in La Ceiba. Others are soon to open.

SHOPPING

Stores are open 8:30-5:30 Mon-Fri, closed Sat afternoons, all day Sunday. Best places for buying local souvenirs are stores run by the Centro Cooperativo Tecnico Industrial (CCTI), a government sponsored operation which promotes local handicrafts. Best buys include hand carved wooden plaques for wall hanging, bowls for fruit and salad, tables, chairs, even doors, with exquisitely wrought Mayan motifs. **Valle de Angeles,** about a 45-minute drive from the capital, is the national handicraft center. **San Pedro Sula**—home of many factories—produces excellent men's shirts, attractive children's clothing and low priced women's lingerie. One of the best places in Tegucigalpa to go for these is the **Los Dolores** market or the handicraft market, open Saturdays and Sundays, at **Comayaguela.** Bargaining is customary. Better-class shops are to be found on **Avenida Paz Barahona** in Tegucigalpa and on **Calle Comercio** in San Pedro Sula.

SPORTS

Soccer and basketball are the most popular spectator sports. There is also baseball and cockfighting. There are several golf clubs, and the **Tegucigalpa Country Club** has bowling alleys as well as facilities for golf, tennis, and swimming. The **Bay Islands,** off the Caribbean coast, are excellent for swimming and fishing, and **Lake Yojoa** is good for freshwater fishing. There is some horseback riding in the mountains, and hunting is popular. You need a permit to import guns.

WHAT TO SEE

The two major tourist attractions of Honduras are the incredible **Maya Ruins of Copan** and the **Bay Islands** off the north coast. Reaching both can occasionally be difficult, though the service from La Ceiba to the island has much improved. Honduras is not sophisticated. The pace of life is easy-going; the people are friendly, the country unspoiled, and the towns not highly developed. The capital, originally a Spanish silver mining town, is built mainly in the Spanish colonial style on the slopes of **Mount El Picacho,** 3,200 feet above sea level. The **Cathedral** has elaborate wood carvings and a pulpit covered in pure gold. The **President's Palace** faces the river and the **Palace of the Congress** is on stilts. Atop Mount Picacho is the **United Nations Park.** The fascinating ruins of **Copan,** once a city of the Mayans and lost for eight centuries, and reachable from San Pedro Sula overland, via a beautiful highway in 3 hours, or from Tegucigalpa overland in 8 hours, cover 12 square miles. English speaking tourist guides available with tours will explain the history of the ruins and the pyramids. Copan may be reached by air by chartering a small airplane, or by bus from San Pedro Sula, a journey of 4 hours. Guided tours start at $90 for a full day excursion, including lunch and entrance to the Archaeological Park, and transportation from San Pedro Sula.

Comayagua, once the capital of the country, is a 16th-century town remaining almost as it was at the time of the Spanish conquest. Its beautiful **Cathedral** and churches have altars of solid gold, and the **Padres Franciscanos Museum** at the Casa Cultural is quite interesting. It has a clock brought by the Spaniards from the Alhambra. A drive up Mount El Picacho gives a series of breathtaking views of the former capital. Half and full day tours available from Tegucigalpa, and also to the **Pan American School of Agriculture** at Zamorano, where tropical plants, flowers and orchids abound, to **Santa Lucia, Valle de Angeles** and **Ojojona**—all 17th-century Spanish colonial towns. From San Pedro Sula, excursions include those to Copan (above), the **Spanish Fortress of Omoa** near Puerto Cortes, to banana plantations (a must for those who want to understand the meaning of *banana republic*), the **Lancetilla Botanical Gardens** near Tela, where more than 3,000 species of plants, flowers and trees from all over the world are to be found, in addition to the largest orchid collection in Honduras. There are beautiful beaches near **Puerto Cortes, Tela, La Ceiba** and **Trujillo** on the north coast. Another popular excursion is fishing for bass—or just plain boating—at beautiful Lake Yojoa.

There are frequent flights between the capital and **San Pedro Sula,** the country's biggest industrial town and port. The **Semana Sanpedrana,** a fair in honor of the patron saint of Honduras, takes place here the last week of June. It includes a cattle exhibit that draws visitors from all over Central America. In addition to being a departure point for excursions to the Mayan ruins of Copan and to Lake Yojoa, San Pedro Sula has daily flights to the Bay Islands, major Honduran cities, and international points. The Bay Islands lie some 30 miles off the north coast and are an ideal spot to "get away from it all." A former British colony, the islands retain much of their heritage in that English is more widely spoken than Spanish and many islanders identify themselves with England. In addition to the ferry service, the islands can be reached by air, with either SAHSA Airlines or LANSA Airways from San Pedro Sula and La Ceiba.

SOURCES OF FURTHER INFORMATION

Any **Pan Am** office around the world. **Instituto Hondureño de Turismo,** PO Box 154-C, Tegucigalpa; **Honduras Information Service,** 501 Fifth Avenue, New York, NY 10017; **Honduran Consulate,** 18 East 41st Street, New York, NY, 10017, and 48 George Street, London W1.

Mexico

WHAT'S SPECIAL

Mexico offers the delights of long beaches, a temperate climate, beautiful countryside, and charming people. It's a land of striking differences. Here you will find luxurious resort areas—such as Acapulco, with its famous cliff-divers—and, not far away, picturesque Indian villages with simple adobe dwellings. Grand colonial mansions are juxtaposed with modern skyscrapers. And you will discover a rich archaeological heritage in the ancient stone pyramids dating back to the splendor of the pre-Hispanic civilizations. There is, of course, Mexico City itself, the oldest city in North America, situated on the site of an Aztec community discovered by the great Cortés in 1519, and today a great modern capital city as sophisticated as any in Europe.

Mexico is a forward-looking and progressive country, and the instinctive charms of its people and their culture is as welcoming today as always.

COUNTRY BRIEFING

Size: 759,528 square miles   **Population:** 79,000,000
Capital: Mexico City   **Capital Population:** 18,000,000
  Climate: Tropical in the south, coastal resorts temperate, mountains cool. Rainy season is from June to September.

Weather in Mexico City: Lat N19°24'; Alt 7,575 ft

Temp (°F)	Jan	Feb	Mar	Apr	May	Jun	Jul	Aug	Sep	Oct	Nov	Dec
Av Low	42°	43°	47°	51°	54°	55°	53°	54°	53°	50°	46°	43°
Av High	66°	69°	75°	77°	78°	76°	73°	73°	74°	70°	68°	66°
Days no rain	27	23	22	16	14	9	4	4	7	18	24	27

Government: A republic (known as the United States of Mexico).
Language: Spanish. Some English spoken.
Religion: Roman Catholic.
Currency: Peso. 100 centavos = 1 peso.

	50¢	1 peso	5 peso	10 peso	20 peso	50 peso	100 peso	500 peso
US (dollars, cents)	.02	.04	.21	.42	.83	2.08	4.15	20.75
UK (pounds, pence)	.01	.02	.10	.20	.40	.99	1.98	9.92

Public Holidays:

New Year's Day, 1 Jan
Day of the Kings, 6 Jan
Constitution Day, 5 Feb
Flag Day, 24 Feb
Birthday of Benito Juárez, 21 Mar
Easter
Labor Day, 1 May
Battle of Puebla, 5 May

National Holiday (El Diadel Informe), 1 Sep
Independence Day, 16 Sep
Columbus Day (El Dia de la Raza), 12 Oct
Revolution Anniversary, 20 Nov
Guadalupe Day (optional), 12 Dec
Christmas Day, 25 Dec

HOW TO GET THERE

Flying time to Benito Juárez International Airport from New York is 5¾ hours; from San Juan, 5 hours; from Tampa, 2¾ hours. Time in Mexico City: GMT–6.

REQUIREMENTS FOR ENTRY AND CUSTOMS REGULATIONS

Passport (except for US and Canadian citizens, who require only proof of citizenship); cholera and yellow-fever immunization certificates if coming from an infected area; and a tourist card in duplicate. The tourist card may be obtained (free) from a Mexican Consulate, Mexican Government Tourist Office, or your Pan Am office. If you get the card from the Mexican Consulate or the Department of Tourism, it is valid for 6 months. Multiple-entry cards can be obtained only from consulates and require photographs and proof of identification. To take such items as radios or televisions into Mexico it is necessary to obtain a temporary permit, and the goods must be taken out of the country by the person who obtained the permit. Duty-free allowances are: four cartons of cigarettes and 50 cigars; two fifths of liquor; quarter liter of perfume for personal use; 12 rolls of film; gifts up to US$120. No currency restrictions. No gold or archaeological antiquities may be exported.

907

AIRPORT INFORMATION

Benito Juárez International Airport is 8 miles from the Mexico City center. Taxis are plentiful and cost up to 250 pesos, or only 80 pesos if you share with others. The airport has its own hotel reservations counter. Airport departure tax is 100 pesos for international flights and 20 pesos for domestic flights. Crescencio Rejón airport is 5 miles from Mérida; the taxi fare is 140 pesos, or there is a local bus into town. A duty-free shop, car rental agency, and hotel reservations counter are available.

ACCOMMODATIONS

The range is from air-conditioned skyscrapers to inns and *haciendas*, with plenty of motels, too. You pay more in Acapulco and other resorts during the high season (November-March), and less in the country. Resort hotels will often give a 30% discount in the off season. Budget travelers should look for *pensiones* and *casas de huéspedes*, where you can arrange bed and breakfast by the month for about 8,000 pesos. A 4% tax is added to all hotel bills. For help and information go to the **Tourism Ministry**, Presidente Masaryk 172, Colonia Polanco, Mexico City (tel: 250-8555). Reserve well in advance at resorts in the high season, everywhere at Christmas and Easter. Hotels in Mexico City, centrally located:

Rates are in US$ for a double/twin room with bath or shower

Alameda, Avenida Juárez 50 (from $92)

Aristos, Paseo de la Reforma 276 (from $83)

Camino Real, Mariano Escobedo 700 (from $116)

Continental, Paseo de la Reforma 166 (from $65)

De Carlo, Plaza de la Republica 35 (from $37)

Del Prado, Avenida Juárez 70 (from $53)

El Presidente, Hamburgo 134 (from $65)

El Presidente Chapultepec, Campos Eliseos 218 (from $83) 10 minutes by taxi from city center

Fiesta Palace, Paseo de la Reforma 80 (from $109)

Galeria Plaza, Hamburgo 195 (from $100)

Maria Isabel-Sheraton, Paseo de la Reforma 325 (from $83)

Metropol, Luis Moya 39 (from $30)

Plaza Florencia, Florencia 61 (from $58)

Reforma, Paseo de la Reforma and Paris (from $33)

Ritz, Avenida Madero 30 (from $50)

USEFUL INFORMATION

Banks: Open from 9-1:30pm Mon-Fri. Big hotels, restaurants, and some shops will change money and traveler's checks, but watch the rate.

Mail: Stamps available from post offices and hotels.

Telephone Tips: Phones in shops, restaurants, and, in all towns, public booths. Useful numbers in Mexico City:

Pan Am 566 26 DD or 395 0077

Airport 571 3279

Tourism Ministry 250 8555

Directory 04 (local) 01 (outside capital)

International 09

Long Distance 02

Newspapers: English-language paper is *The News.*

Tipping: Luggage porters 20 pesos per bag, with a minimum of 15 pesos; taxi driver, 20 pesos; hotel porter, 20 pesos for getting a taxi; chambermaid, 30-50 pesos a day; cloakroom attendants, 20 pesos; waiter 15%—8% of the 15% tax will usually be removed if you show the waiter your tourist card; museum guides, 20 pesos; sightseeing guides, 50 pesos per person per trip.

Electricity: 110 volts 60 cycles AC.

Laundry: Readily available, and standards are high (dry-cleaning a suit, from 110 pesos; laundering a shirt, from 35 pesos).

Hairdressing: Major hotels have salons (shampoo and set, from 370 pesos; man's haircut, from 180 pesos).

Photography: Film and equipment readily available in cities, and film can be developed quickly. Black and white film costs about 80 pesos, color 146 pesos.

Clubs: Lions, Rotary, Freemasons, and Jaycees.

Babysitting: Arranged by good hotels.

Rest Rooms: In hotels, restaurants, and major stores. Women, *Damas* or *Mujeres;* men, *Caballeros* or *Hombres.*

Health: Doctors and dentists generally speak English. Drink bottled water and wash fruit. Imported pharmaceuticals available, but Mexican equivalents are good, and less expensive. Remember the altitude and take it easy at first.

TRANSPORTATION

In Mexico City, try to avoid riding the subway (open 6am-midnight) during rush hours. Stations are decorative works of art; at Pino Suárez station there is a complete Aztec altar. Books of tickets can be bought at stations and some tobacco shops. Buses are frequent and inexpensive. Shared cruising taxis cost 7-20 pesos; ordinary taxis, 40-80 pesos for rides in the city center. In the country buses are inexpensive, and there is a first-class long distance service to all major cities. Most cities can also be reached by railroad, but air is the most convenient form of travel. There are several internal airlines, including Aero-Mexico and Mexicana. Cars can be rented in major cities, with or without driver, from about 445 pesos (US$20) a day (plus mileage charge), about 180 pesos an hour (US$8) if chauffeur-driven; double for English-speaking driver.

FOOD AND RESTAURANTS

Lunch is the heavy meal, and it can go until 4:30pm; dinner is about 9pm. In all the big cities there is international cuisine, but Mexico has unique and unforgettable dishes including *mole de guajalote,* which is turkey in a chocolate and spice sauce; *ceviche,* raw finely sliced fish marinated in lime juice with tomatoes; *tamales,* thin steamed pancakes with a filling that varies from state to state; and, of course, *tortillas* thin, flat, corn pancakes in a hundred different guises—as *tacos,* filled with shredded meat, cheese, eggs, or vegetables and fried; as *enchiladas,* cooked in tomato sauce with a filling of meat or cheese; or just as a sort of edible spoon to scoop up stews like *guisados*. They turn up again in *chalupas*, with chicken, tomatoes, and lettuce, and in *quesadillas*, wrapped around cheese and green peppers or beans, and under *huevos rancheros*, which are fried eggs with tomato and chili sauce. The sauces, too, are of a kind you're not likely to meet elsewhere—such as *Pipián*, made of green tomatoes, chili, and pumpkin seeds, and *mole verde*, a green vegetable sauce. Look for fish specialties: *pescado blanco*—delicate white lake fish, and *huachinango*—red snapper. Mexican cooks have an imaginative way with vegetables as well. Try *chiles rellenos* (stuffed peppers) and *frijoles refritos* (fried mashed beans), or *guacamole* (avocado mashed with onion and tomato). Other dishes to look for are *cabrito* (kid) and all the tropical fruits—papaya, pineapples, limes, *higos rebandos* (sliced fresh figs), mangoes, pomegranates, guavas, and *zapote*. The price of a meal can be as low as 35 pesos, but a four-course meal costs about 230 pesos in a medium-priced restaurant and 450 pesos in the best places.

For restaurants with Mexican atmosphere and food as well as international cuisine, there are two *haciendas* in Mexico City: **Hacienda Los Morales** (Vásquez de Mella 525) and **San Angel Inn** (Palmas 50), both expensive. In the same class are **Ambassadeurs** (Paseo de la Reforma 12); **Mirabel** (Reforma 509); **Anderson's** (Reforma 400); **del Lago** (Nuevo Bosque de Chapultepec); **Jena** (Morelos 110); **Rivoli** (Hamburgo 123); **Sir Winston Churchill** (Blvd Avila Camacho 64); **Cazadores de Guadalajara** (Insurgentes Sur 643); **Loredo** (Hamburgo 29), for regional Mexican dishes; and **Passy** (Amberes 10). Specialty restaurants include **La Lorraine** (San Luis Potosi 132), **Normandie** (Niza 5), **Fouquet's** (Camino Real), all French; **Picadilly** (Copenhague 23), English; **Párador** (Calle de Niza 177), Spanish; **Mauna Loa** (San Jeronimo 240), Polynesian; **Focolare** (Hamburgo 87), Italian; **Acapulco** (López 8), seafood; **Chalet Suizo** (Niza 37), German-Swiss, very popular with tourists; **Bellinghausen** (Londres 595), German; **La Mansion** (Insurgentes 778) and **La Troje Pepe's** (Insurgentes and Millet), Argentinian; **Shirley's Restaurant** (Sullivan 166), American. Recommended moderately priced places are **La Cava** (Insurgentes 2465), French; **El 77** (Londres 77); and all the 31 branches of **VIP's**. Try, too, **Sanborn's** restaurants (a dozen or so of them) and **Woolworth's** blue-plate specials. Look for inexpensive meals in the Arizpe area, opposite Frontón.

DRINKING TIPS

Mexico's own drinks are made from the agave plant. Most famous is *tequila*, drunk as an apéritif or in cocktails like the tequila sour, the Margarita (with lime juice and Cointreau), or the sunrise (grenadine and lime juice). Other drinks are *mescal* and *pulque*—less popular with the tourist. Imported drinks are expensive; whisky costs about 60 pesos, and a bottle of imported wine in a restaurant will rarely go below 280 pesos; choice vintages can cost several thousand. But there are good cheap local wines, beers, and liqueurs. Mexican men drink in *cantinas* or *salones de cerveza*, which are open from noon to 1am but closed on Sundays

and on the days before public holidays. Women never enter these places. Women may go to other drinking bars but should be escorted.

ENTERTAINMENT

The most important center in Mexico City is the **Palacio de Bellas Artes,** where visiting companies appear; this is the home of the **Ballet Folklórico,** presented on Sundays at 9:30am, 12 noon, and 9:00pm and on Wednesdays at 9:00pm. Theater is in Spanish, but an English performance of *son et lumière* at the pyramids of **Teotihuacan** takes place at 7pm except during the rainy season, May through September. Films are usually shown in their original language. There are frequent musical concerts both in halls and in the open air, and you can choose from several musical comedies, vaudeville shows, and a burlesque theater. Nightlife is plentiful and imaginative. Most big hotels have their own cabarets and discothèques, including the **Barbarella** at the **Fiesta Palace** hotel and those at the **Maria Isabel Sheraton Hotel,** the **Aristos,** the **Camino Real,** and the **Alameda** hotels. Other places with music until 4am include the **El Patio** (Atenas 5), **El Senorial** (Hamburgo and Florencia), and restaurants and clubs around **Garibaldi Square.**

SHOPPING

Stores open 10-7 and until 8 on Wednesdays and Saturdays. The best shops are in the **Niza** district (known as Zona Rosa or the Pink Zone), off Reforma. No bargaining there, but do haggle in markets and small shops. The obvious bargain is silver, sometimes a setting for amethysts and opals. But look for the official hallmark, a spread eagle. There is also basketwork, pottery, and tiles, carved onyx, tin and copper work, lacquerware, and hand-blown glass. The blankets are thick and brilliantly colored, the blouses beautifully embroidered, and the long-fringed shawls a specialty. For under 450 pesos you can also get hand-worked leather and dolls. Good places to buy are the **Museum of Popular Arts and Crafts,** government-run and housed in an old colonial church (Avenida Juárez 44), the **Monte de Piedad** (Zócalo), which is a pawnshop also run by the government, and the **Bazaar Sábado** in the San Angel suburb. This opens only on Saturdays. For basketwork go to the **San Juan Market,** and on Sunday morning at 11 you can find the **Flea Market** at La Lagunilla. Also go to the **Handicraft Market** at Revillagigedo 29 and to branches of **Sanborns'.** There is also a handicrafts market at **La Ciudadela.** Other markets: **Xochimilco, Teotihuacán, Chalco** (open every day), **Amecameca, Cuernavaca** (open on Sunday only). On Friday there is the fabulous market at **Toluca,** an hour's drive from the city.

SPORTS

The great spectacles are the bullfight and the *charreada*—a Mexican rodeo. The proper season for bullfights is from November to April, but it varies and they start at 4:30pm on Sundays. Tickets cost between 12 and 480 pesos. At 7:30 every night except Mondays and Fridays there is *jai lai* at **Frontón Mexico**; horse racing takes place at the **Hipodrómo de Las Américas** on Tuesday, Thursday, Saturday, and Sunday afternoons. Admission is free to tourists with their tourist cards, except for a small tax. There is also limited auto racing, soccer, golf, tennis, horseback riding, polo, bowling, swimming, and water sports of all kinds. The island of **Cozumel** off the Yucatán coast, 20 minutes by air from Mérida, is one of the world's best places for fishing and skin-diving. For surfing, go to **Mazatlán**. The fisherman can choose from countless lakes and rivers, and the hunter has every kind of terrain from mountains to jungle where the animals still roam free. Fishing and hunting permits have to be obtained, as well as a license to bring a gun into the country.

WHAT TO SEE

Mexico City

From the **Zócalo**, the main square in the center of Mexico City, you can see the imposing **National Palace**, the **Cathedral**, the **Town Hall**, and the **Supreme Courts**, the **Aztec Ruins**, the **Monte de Piedad** (official pawnshop), and the **Latin-American Tower**. Walk toward it to find the **House of Tiles**, the baroque church of **San Francisco**, and the **Alameda Gardens**. Go to the top of the Tower for a superb view over the city and its site, then visit the **Palacio de Bellas Artes**, with exhibitions of Mexican art and a glass Tiffany curtain. You also get a wonderful view from the still higher **Hotel Mexico** on Avenida Insurgentes Sur. At **Chapultepec Park** you will find the whole of Mexico's history vividly set out. The **National Museum of Anthropology** (open Tuesday to Sunday 10-6, closed Monday) should be at the top of your list. Next go to **El Castillo de Chapultepec**, the **Palace of Maximilian**, and the **National Museum of History** (open Wednesdays to Monday, closed Tuesdays). In the same park are a zoo, botanical gardens, a fun fair, an elaborate playground for children, two additional museums, and an underwater mural by Diego Rivera. His collection of Aztec sculpture is to be seen at the **Anahuacalli Museum** (in the suburb of San Pablo Tepetlapa). You may also want to see the **Museum of Religious Art** (open Tuesdays to Sundays 10-6, closed Mondays), for its vestments and altar furniture; the **San Carlos Museum**, with its paintings by El Greco, Titian, Bosch, and Van Dyck; the **National Museum of Popular Arts** (open Tuesday to Sunday 10-6, closed Monday), where you can buy the crafts on display; the **Museum of Mexico City**, in a palace of pink stone at Pino Suárez 30 (open Tuesday to Sunday 10-6, closed Monday); the **Square of Three Cultures** in Nonoalco Tlatelolco; and the **Plaza de Santo Domingo**, where the Inquisition once sat. In the suburb of **Tlalpán** is the oldest building on the American continents—the **Pyramid of Cuicuilco**.

Outside Mexico City: Two trips are musts—go to the **Floating Gardens of Xochimilco**, to be poled in bright boats *(trajineros)* through the canals to the sound of *mariachi* music, and to the great pyramids of **Teotihuacán**, from a civilization older than the Aztecs. A more ambitious day trip is to **Cuernavaca** and **Taxco.** The first has been a fashionable resort since Aztec times; see **Cortés' palace** with its Rivera murals, the **Cathedral,** the **Teopanzolso double pyramid,** and the beautiful **Borda Gardens.** Then on to Taxco, "Silver City," a good place to buy sterling silver, to sit and listen to music, to see **Santa Prisca,** an outstanding baroque church, or to enjoy a fiesta. Dates of festivals in the area are: 18 January, Santa Prisca; 2 February, Candelaria; 4 March, Holy Week, when children dance; 3 May, Santa Cruz (fireworks); and 24 September. Hotels in Taxco are **Posada de la Misión,** Cerro Cruz de la Misión 32 (from US$27), and **Holiday Inn,** 3 miles from downtown (from US$36). From Mexico City you can drive out to the **Toluca** district and explore Indian villages, drive into the crater of a volcano called the **Nevado,** bargain in Toluca's famous market, and see the great ruins at **Calixtlahuaca** and **Malinalco,** one of the most beautiful of ancient buildings. To the southeast about 86 miles is **Puebla,** city of ceramics. Homes, fountains, churches are covered with brilliant local tiles. You can buy the pottery in the market. Accommodations are available at the **Hotel Posada San Pedro,** 2 Oriente 202 (from US$26). From here go to visit the richly decorated church of **San Francisco Acatepec,** 5 miles southwest, and do not miss **Cholula,** holy city of the Aztecs, with its vast pyramid. Fiestas are held here on 2 February, 25 July, 15 August, 6-9 September (Indian dances), 2 November. On your way see the ancient frescoes at **Tizatlán.**

The North

North lies **Tula,** long-lost city of the Toltecs, with its majestic stone figures and 16th-century church. On the same trip you can go to **Tepotzlán,** a village famous for its baroque seminary, and **Pachuca.** Beyond is the flower garden of Mexico, where orchids are grown, and the towns of **Huauchinango** and **Xocotepec de Juárez.**

To the northwest is the great sea-sport area. **La Paz, Guaymas,** and **Mazatlán** are the famous resorts, where the hunting is so good. You can get to Mazatlán by air from Mexico City or Los Angeles. Nearer the capital is Mexico's second city, **Guadalajara.** A gracious colonial town, it is famous for its mild, healthy climate and the paintings of Orozco. Hotels in Guadalajara centrally located unless otherwise indicated:
Rates are in US$ for a double/twin room with bath or shower
> **Camino Real,** Avenida Vallarta 5005, ½ mile from center (from $80)
> **De Mendoza,** Via Carranza 64 (from $38)
> **Guadalajara Sheraton,** Ninos Heroes y 16 de Septiembre, at entrance to Guadalajara from the airport (from $69)
> **Holiday Inn,** Lopez Mateos and Mariano Otero, 6 miles from center (from $64)

Near here is **Tequila,** home of the well-known liquor, where a celebrated fiesta is held on 12 December. Also north of the capital are **Guanajuato** and **San Miguel Allende,** where there is the **Hotel Posada de San Francisco,** Plaza Principal (from US$48). Worth a visit is the enigmatic but strangely preserved city of **La Quemada.**

The Southeast

This is the richest route for travelers. First, go south to **Oaxaca**, City of Jade, by plane or train. This is the center for exploring the fabulous cities of **Monte Alban** and **Mitla**, holy ground of the Zapotecs and Mixtecs. The ruins of these sacred cities contain huge palace buildings, pyramids, walls, tombs, and sculptures. Gold and jade jewelry, along with crystal and alabaster carved vessels found at Monte Alban, can be seen in the museum of Oaxaca. Oaxaca also has a market worth waiting for, on Saturday, and spectacular fiestas at the end of July. The **Hotel Victoria**, Pan American Highway 190 KM545 (from US$32), is on the outskirts of the city. **Villahermosa** is best approached via the lively city of **Veracruz**, famous for its Mardi Gras celebrations, or you can fly the 500 miles direct. Here is the great **La Venta Museum** of Olmec carvings—old as Tyre. From here you should visit **Palenque**, 89 miles south. Trips are easily organized by car, train, or air taxi; you can stay in a small hotel next to the ruins. This is the center of a great complex of ancient ruins—palaces—extending over 20 square miles. Next site is **Bonampak**, where the final leg must be done on horseback. Even more hidden by the jungle is **Yaxchilán**, reachable only by the determined. To discover the great Maya culture you must go to **Mérida** in the Yucatán, a thousand miles from Mexico City. Here you will be at the center of a vast area of deserted cites of the Mayans, most prolific of builders and sculptors. Many of the sites are choked by the jungle, still to be discovered, or reachable only by long jeep rides. Hotels in Mérida include the **Maya Excelsior**, Calle 58, 483 (from US$25), **Hacienda Inn**, Avenida Aviacion (from US$27), and **Montejo Palace**, Paseo de Montejo 483C (from US$27). From the White City, Mérida, you can go for a day to spectacular **Chichén Itzá**. In the shadow of the great pyramid lie the **Red Jaguar Throne**, the **ball court**, a round **observatory**, and the complex **Temple of the Warriors**. Go first, though, to the **Institute** to learn about what has been found here. To the south is **Uxmal**, which has perhaps the finest of the Mayan buildings: the remarkable **House of the Governor**. Here the graceful Mayan work is seen beside later grim Toltec carvings. By contrast, just off the coast are the holiday islands of **Cozumel** and **Isla Mujeres**, where the fishing, sailing, and swimming are superb and there is the resort paradise of **Cancun**, with its beaches of fine, white sand.

Acapulco: Then there is the great Mexican resort of **Acapulco**, said to have the best beach, best hotels and nightclubs in the Americas. Hotels in Acapulco:

Rates are in US$ for a double/twin room with bath or shower

Acapulco Imperial, Costera Miguel Alemán 251 (from $57)

Acapulco Princess, Guerrero (from $56)

Condesa del Mar, Costera Miguel Alemán overlooking the bay (from $45)

Continental, Costera Miguel Alemán (from $63)

El Presidente, Costera Miguel Alemán (from $58)

Fiesta Tortuga, Costera Miguel Alemán (from $49)

Holiday Inn, Costera Miguel Alemán 1260 (from $62)

Hyatt Regency Acapulco, Costera Miguel Alemán 666 (from $75)
La Palapa, Fragute Yucatán (from $69)
La Brisas, Carretera Escenica, overlooking the bay (from $67)
Paraiso Marriott, Los Hornos Beach (from $57)
Pierre Marques, Playa Revolcadero (from $53)
Ritz, Los Hornos Beach (from $51)

Unless otherwise indicated, hotels are located on the beach. Low and high season rates are shown where applicable. During high season some hotels offer MAP rates only. Low season runs from 15 April to 15 December, and 4% tax is added to all hotel bills.

Not far away along the coast are other beautiful spots such as **Puerto Vallarta** and **Zihuatenejo.** All around here the hunting is marvelous, and you will have no difficulty renting horses or equipment for any sport you like.

SOURCES OF FURTHER INFORMATION

Pan Am: Paseo de la Reforma 35, Mexico City IDF; Edificio Condominio Acero, Despacho 410 Zaragoza Sur 1000, Monterrey; Edificio La Nacional, Avenida Vallarta No. 1390-501, Guadalajara; Avenida Revolución 1232, Tijuana; and any Pan Am office around the world; **Mexican Government Tourist Ministry,** Pres. Masaryk 172, Colonia Polanco, Mexico City; **Mexican National Tourist Council,** 405 Park Avenue, New York, NY 10022; **Mexican Tourist Office,** 52 Grosvenor Gardens, London SWI.

Nicaragua

WHAT'S SPECIAL

Nicaragua has deep blue oceans on either side (both Atlantic and Pacific coasts are over 200 miles long), winding tropical rivers, huge lakes with freshwater sharks, and little tropical islands with coconut trees. Jungle cats stalk the wild Cordillera Mountains that extend through the center of the country from the northwest to the southeast. There are ancient Spanish cities, even older Mayan ruins, an English pirate's settlement with houses on stilts, and even a few gold mines. It has a long tradition of culture and learning, with a long-established university and a private one run by Jesuit priests. The capital, Managua, was almost devastated by an earthquake in December 1972, the second time in this century. Many new tourist facilities have been built, however, and this beautiful, historic, and friendly country still has much to offer.

COUNTRY BRIEFING
Size: 57,143 square miles   **Population:** 2,365,000
Capital: Managua   **Capital Population:** 622,759
  Climate: Tropical. Cooler in the northern mountainous regions. The year is divided into two seasons: dry, which is summer (December to May) and the best time to visit; and wet, winter.
  Weather in Managua: Lat N12°8′; Alt 180 ft

Temp (°F)	Jan	Feb	Mar	Apr	May	Jun	Jul	Aug	Sep	Oct	Nov	Dec
Av Low	69°	70°	72°	73°	74°	73°	73°	73°	73°	72°	71°	70°
Av High	88°	89°	91°	94°	93°	88°	88°	89°	89°	88°	88°	87°
Days no rain	31	28	31	29	25	17	20	21	19	21	27	30

Government: The country is a republic of 16 departments and one district.

Currency: Cordoba. 10 cordobas = US$1

Public Holidays:

New Year's Day, Jan 1	Battle of San Jancinto, Sept 14
Holy Week, Apr 4-12	Independence Day, Sept 15
Labor Day, May 1	Columbus Day, Oct 12
Army Day, May 27	All Saints' Day, Nov 1
Abrogation of Chamorro-Bryan	Immaculate Conception, Dec 8
Treaty, July	Christmas, Dec 25-26

HOW TO GET THERE

Flying time to Managua's Augusto Cesar Sandino Airport from New York is about 7 hours; from Miami, 4½ hours; from Guatemala City, 1 hour. Time in Nicaragua: GMT−6.

REQUIREMENTS FOR ENTRY AND CUSTOMS REGULATIONS

US and Canadian citizens require a passport, photocopies of roundtrip ticket, two black-and-white photographs to be presented with free visa application form. Business visa requirements are the same, plus a letter of intent, stating length and purpose of stay. Other nationalities should check with nearest Nicaraguan Consulate for requirements. Travelers may bring into the country duty-free 200 cigarettes or 1 lb 1 oz tobacco, 1 fifth liquor or wine; 1 bottle perfume. Archeological artifacts may not be taken from the country without a certificate from the Ministry of the Interior.

AIRPORT INFORMATION

Augusto Cesar Sandino Airport is 7 miles east of Managua. Bus fare to city center is Cor 1.05; taxi fare is Cor 80. Airport departure tax, Cor 50. There is a duty-free shop.

ACCOMMODATIONS

Hotels in Managua include:

Rates are in US$ for a double/twin room with bath or shower

Carlos V, 4a Av SE No 605 (from $25)

Colon Hotel, Colonia Los Robles (from $18)

Dilido Hotel, 21A Avemie SO, 13A Calle (from $18)

Embassy Hotel, Av Bolivar Sur y 10 Calle SO (from $25)

Estrella Hotel, Av del Ejercito (from $18)

USEFUL INFORMATION

Banks: Open from 8:30 to 12 and 3 to 5:30 Mon-Fri, and from 8:30 to 11:30 Sat.

Tipping: Service charge is not included in bills; about 10% is customary. It is not customary to tip taxi drivers, but Cor 1.50 per bag for porters.

Electricity: 110 volts 60 cycles AC.

Rest Rooms: Facilities are provided in restaurants, hotels, and some stores. They are marked *Caballeros* for men, *Damas* for women, and are free.

Health: Most doctors and some dentists are English-speaking. Malarial precautions are recommended. Fruits and vegetables should be cooked before they are eaten. Drink bottled water and avoid eating food from street stalls.

TRANSPORTATION

Crowded micro-buses are the cheapest form of public transportation. Cars may be rented for about US$25 a day. Taxis can be hailed on the street, but agree on the fare before starting the trip. Local airlines fly to Puerto Cabezas, Bluefields, Corn Islands, and Bonanza. The Pacific Railway has service to the Port of Corinto via Leon and Chinandega, and to El Sauce and Granada.

SPORTS

Nicaragua's geography makes it ideal for the outdoor sportsman and those who enjoy the water. There is year-round swimming, and a choice of the beautiful sandy beaches of the Pacific, and in the Atlantic there is surfing on the Corn Islands. The yachtsman also has the Atlantic and Pacific to choose from; San Juan del Sur, Bluefields, and the Corn Islands, as well as the crystal-like waters of Ziloa and Apoyo Lagoons and Lake Nicaragua.

Hunting is the popular sport in the mountains around Matagalpa and Jinotega where there is an abundance of wild boar, deer, birds, and other game.

FOOD AND RESTAURANTS

You will not want to leave Nicaragua without sampling the local specialties. The staples of the native diet are rice and beans. *Sopa de mondongo* is the national dish. There is a soup made of tripe, vegetables, and yucca root; usually it is eaten with tortillas. But perhaps the native fare with the greatest appeal is charcoal-barbecued steak. For gourmet meals try the restaurants in the good hotels, **El Rincon Espanol** in old Managua, **La Marseillaise** (Colonia los Robles), and **Peppers**, in the Drefus Center, for good fast-food service.

DRINKING TIPS

The national soft drink of the country is **Tiste,** made from corn and cocoa; there are also various tropical fruit drinks. **Pozol** is made from corn and sugar and is drunk mid-morning. There are several native rums that are popular and not expensive. A whisky and soda is US$1.50-2.50, and a bottle of wine is US$15 and up.

SHOPPING

Stores are open Mon-Sat 8-12 and 3-5:30. Some handmade articles are available in the **Centro Commercial de Managua;** leatherwork, embroidered shirts and dresses, and woven hammocks. **Casa del Lagarto** sells alligator handbags and shoes at reasonable prices. (US citizens check import restrictions.)

WHAT TO SEE

Masaya, near Managua, has a large Indian population and thriving handicrafts. **Granada,** 30 miles from the capital on Lake Nicaragua, is the oldest "European" city. Founded by the Conquistadors in 1524, it has fine examples of Spanish architecture. There is also a fine residential section. **Leon** is another Spanish colonial city, with churches of remarkable beauty. One of the oldest churches in the New World is here, as well as superb religious artifacts. Nearby is **Leon Viejo,** the ancient capital of Nicaragua, founded by Hernandez Cordoba in 1524 and destroyed by a volcanic eruption 85 years later. Excavations have revealed the main street and important buildings, including the Cathedral. Lake Nicaragua, also known as Colcibolga, is one of the largest lakes in the world and one of the most fascinating. Rich in tropical vegetation, dotted with islands, and marked by volcanoes, its sweet fresh water is stocked with voracious shark, sawfish, and tarpon. **Matagalpa,** a two-hour drive north of Managua, is in an alpine setting of misty pine forests and wild orchids. The wildlife here includes the rare quetzal, jaguar, and mountain lion. There is good fishing and good hunting. A short flight from the capital is the old English colonial town and port of Bluefields. Here old houses, built on stilts and surrounded by coconut palms, present a great contrast to the rest of Nicaragua. Fifty miles offshore and also linked by air to the mainland are the fabulous Corn Islands, where you can stay at **Lundy's Island Inn** (from US$65 double). These are the essence of the Caribbean Islands—crystal-clear waters, dazzling white sand, and coconut palms.

SOURCES OF FURTHER INFORMATION

National Tourist Office, DNT, Avenida Bolivar, PO Box 122, Managua, Nicaragua. tel: 22498; **Consulate General of Nicaragua,** 1270 Avenue of the Americas, New York, NY 10020.

Panama

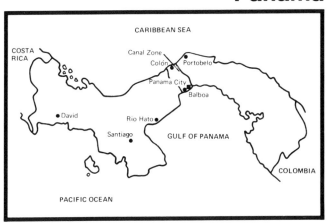

WHAT'S SPECIAL

Panama's land mass divides the waters of the Pacific and the Caribbean, and the 31-mile distance between the two has made it a natural short cut for centuries. Little is known of the early history of Panama and its Indians, for in those days the *quipu* (a device consisting of cords variously colored and knotted) and oral tradition served to inform of their past. The secrets of reading the quipu were never transmitted to the Spanish and they have yet to be unravelled.

In modern times, the area was discovered by the Spanish explorer Rodrigo de Bastidas in 1502, though the area soon fell into the control of Balboa who in 1513 made his famous journey over the isthmus to discover the Pacific Ocean. Because it could be serviced from both shores, Panama became a key transhipment point for Indian gold to Spain. In those days, gold was transported across the isthmus by mule to Portobelo from Panama City, which was then located a little further east in an area now called Panama Viejo, or Old Panama.

The activities of Harry Morgan, an English privateer in the area of Panama, have been the subject of calumnies since soon after they occurred. What brought Morgan to Portobelo was not merely treasure; he was seeking the release of shipmates, prisoners-of-war whom the Spanish had left to starve in the dungeons of Fort San Geronimo. When he discovered that only 11 men survived out of the 50 who'd been captured, he determined to ransom the city. The English took 250,000 pieces of eight, together with treasure worth half as much again. As for the so-called later "sacking" of Panama, the truth is elsewhere, as dispatches from Don Juan Perez de Guzman to authorities in Madrid affirm; he boasts how clever he was to burn it. The Spanish were, in fact, so panic-stricken in their haste to blow up the city that they not only killed more than 40 of their own men, but scattered burning fragments for a mile all about that set the roofs afire.

The '49 California gold rush brought Panama to the notice of the US, with many travelers choosing to go south and cross the isthmus rather than to go directly west. Then the French company that pioneered the Suez Canal in 1869 (under Ferdinand de Lesseps) arrived for a stay in 1881. By 1889, disease among the workers and a cash flow shortage drove the company into bankruptcy. Ten years later, with considerable help from US President Teddy Roosevelt, Panama declared its independence from Colombia and the US went ahead with the canal's completion. Panama granted the right of the US to a narrow strip—called the Canal Zone, now the Area del Canal de Panama—in return for rent. The treaty was renegotiated in 1979 and Panama obtains complete control of the waterway in the year 2000.

While the canal provides nearly 40% of the nation's revenue in the form of lease payments, dues, and labor services, there is significant export of agricultural products including rice, bananas, and shrimp, plus processed foods. There is some refining, and petroleum feedstocks are also exported. Major copper and molybdenum deposits have been located in recent years, and await development. Tourism is important, and there are many low-duty stores that offer a shopper's paradise of the world's goods, such as brass-trimmed furniture from China, Siamese bronzes, Swedish crystal, fruitwood from Guatemala, Scottish cashmere, German and Japanese cameras and electronic equipment. The population is a mingling of races. Over 60% are of mixed blood, owing their ancestry to the Spanish, Indians, Jamaicans, and other Latin Americans. In the jungles of Darien are long-haired Choco Indians living in river huts of woven reeds and lashed palm fronds. In the San Blas islands are the picturesque, closely knit Cuna Indian tribes, whose women make artistic *molas* in reverse appliqué.

COUNTRY BRIEFING

Size: 29,856 square miles   **Population:** 1,881,000
Capital: Panama City   **Capital Population:** 452,000
    Climate: Tropical, but trade winds keep the temperature down. Mid-December through March is "summer," or the dry season. But there are only about 14 days a year when the sun doesn't shine.

Weather in Balboa Heights: Lat N8°57′; Alt 40 ft

Temp (°F)	Jan	Feb	Mar	Apr	May	Jun	Jul	Aug	Sep	Oct	Nov	Dec
Av Low	71°	71°	72°	74°	74°	74°	74°	74°	74°	73°	73°	74°
Av High	88°	89°	90°	90°	87°	83°	87°	87°	86°	85°	85°	87°
Days no rain	26	26	30	24	16	14	16	16	14	13	13	19

Government: A republic.
Language: Spanish. English is the required second language in the

schools, and is widely spoken. The indigenous Indians speak their own languages and know little Spanish.

Religion: Predominantly Roman Catholic.

Currency: Balboa. 100 centesimos = 1 balboa. The balboa is on a par with the US dollar. US and Panamanian coins under $1 are interchangeable; otherwise, US paper currency is the medium of exchange.

	5¢	10¢	25¢	B1	B5	B10	B20	B50
US (dollars, cents)	.05	.10	.25	1.00	5.00	10.00	20.00	50.00
UK (pounds, pence)	.02	.05	.12	.48	2.39	4.77	9.54	23.85

Public Holidays:

New Year's Day, 1 Jan
Day of the Martyrs, 9 Jan
Carnival Tuesday (day before Lent)
Good Friday
Easter Saturday
Labor Day, 1 May
Day of the Revolution, 11 Oct
Memorial Day, 2 Nov

Independence from Colombia, 3 Nov
Flag Day, 4 Nov*
Independence from Spain, 28 Nov
Mother's Day, 8 Dec
Christmas Day, 25 Dec
*Observed only by government offices, banks

HOW TO GET THERE

Flying time to Panama City, Tocumen Airport from New York is 5½ hours; from Miami, 2¾ hours, from San Francisco, 7½ hours. Time in Panama: GMT−5.

REQUIREMENTS FOR ENTRY AND CUSTOMS REGULATIONS

All nationalities require a passport, visa or tourist card ($2 plus proof of onward transportation, available from airlines or at entry) for stays of 30 days. No currency regulations, and duty-free import allowance is 3 bottles of liquor, 500 cigarettes or 1 pound of tobacco.

AIRPORT INFORMATION

Tocumen Airport is 15 miles from Panama City. There is no airport bus, but taxis ($12 per car, or $4 per person in a shared ride) are always available, and there is a slightly more expensive limousine service; car rentals also available. Airport departure tax, $8. Duty-free shop.

ACCOMMODATIONS

The tourist season in Panama is January to April, and this is when hotel prices are at their highest. Rooms are 10%-20% less expensive out of season. Government hotel tax is 10% but no service charge is added. Pension and boarding-house rates start at B5. Hotel apartments also available. Hotels in Panama City, air conditioned and centrally located unless otherwise indicated:

Rates are in US$ for a double/twin room with bath or shower
  Bella Vista, Vía España 30 (from $18)
  Branca Plaza, Vía Bolivar, Federico Clement (from $26.50)

Caribe, Avenida Peru & Calle 28 (from $36)

El Conquistador, 51st Street East, No. 36 (from $43)

El Continental, Vía España & Calle Ricardo Arias (from $56)

El Ejecutivo, Calle Aquilino de la Guardia & Calle 52 (from $49)

El Panamá, Vía España 111 at Augusto Boyd (from $45)

Europa, Vía España (from $22)

Granada, Avenida Eusebio A. Morales, Cangrejo (from $42)

Holiday Inn, Winston Churchill at Vía Italia, Punta Paitilla (from $60) on the waterfront, one mile from downtown

Ideal, West 17th Street (from $14)

Internacional, Plaza 5 de Mayo (from $32)

La Siesta Hotel, International Airport (from $44) near Tocumen International Airport

Monteserin, Calle Monteserin (from $28)

Premier, Avenida Central, 18-105 (from $16)

Roma, Avenida Justo Arosemena & Calle 33 (from $36)

USEFUL INFORMATION

Banks: Open 8am-1pm Mon-Fri. Some banks are open on Saturday. Stores will change currency and will accept credit cards and travelers' checks.

Mail: Some drugstores and magazine stands sell stamps. Area del Canal (formerly CZ) post office open 8am-5:30pm Mon-Fri and it's cheaper to mail packages as you pay domestic US rates.

Telephone Tips: Phones in booths, restaurants, cafés, and drugstores. Useful numbers in Panama City:

Pan Am 25-6500	**Airport Information** 66-7222
Tourist Office 64-4000	**Operator, Directories** 102

Newspapers: English-language newspapers and magazines available. Local publications are the *Star Herald* and Panamanian daily *La Republica,* also *Critica, La Estrella de Panama,* and *Matatino.*

Tipping: Taxi drivers are not usually tipped; restaurants do not have service charge, so leave 10-15% of the check; airport and hotel porters, 25 centesimos per bag; hairdressers, 25-50 centesimos; cloakroom attendants, 25 centesimos; movie ushers, nothing.

Electricity: 110 volts 60 cycles AC.

Laundry: First class hotels have their own services (dry-cleaning a suit, from B3; laundering a shirt, from 75-80 centesimos).

Hairdressing: First class hotels have salons (shampoo and set, from B7; man's haircut, from B4).

Photography: Low duty on German and Japanese cameras encourages the buying and selling of equipment in the major cities. Black and white film costs B2 or more and usually takes one day to be developed. Color film costs from B3 and takes 3-5 days for developing.

Clubs: Lions, Kiwanis, Rotary, Knights of Columbus, Skal.

Rest Rooms: In hotels, cafés, restaurants. Women, *Damas;* men, *Caballeros.*

Health: Doctors and dentists speak English. Imported pharmaceuticals at reasonable prices. Water safe to drink.

TRANSPORTATION

Panama City has an ample supply of buses. Taxis are easily called by phone and have a fixed tariff for distance (by city zone) and number of passengers. Microtaxis charge B1 for the first zone and 25 centesimos per additional zone; large taxis charge B1.75 for the first zone. Green taxis (limousines) have a meter and are slightly more expensive. Limousines with bilingual drivers can be rented by the hour for B8 (within city limits) and cost B100 per day. The only railroad service is from Panama City to Colón (90 minutes), but it is comfortable. Buses link most cities, ranging from the open wooden-framed buses and small vans (holding 8 to 10 passengers) to the air-conditioned Tica Bus, which serves all Central America. The island of Taboga has a regular launch connection with the mainland, and on the Pacific Coast boats are for rent from B80-250 per day. Several airlines fly to David, San Blas, Chitré, Chiriquí, and Contadora.

FOOD AND RESTAURANTS

Panamanians are very fond of small delicacies before a meal. *Carimañolas* are yuca puffs filled with meat and shrimp. *Patacones de plátano verde* are fried plantain. *Sancocho* is a tasty chicken and vegetable soup, and *ceviche* is corvina fish marinated in lime juice, onions, and pepper. Panamanian *tamales* served in banana leaves are very good. Seafood is excellent, and there are a variety of Spanish, French, Italian, Chinese, and American restaurants. Breakfast is 7-9, lunch 12-3, dinner 6-11. A meal in an expensive restaurant costs about B12, in a medium-priced restaurant about B7, and in a less expensive one, B2. A Panamanian meal consists of four courses: hors d'oeuvres, soup, meat with rice or beans and vegetables or salad, and dessert.

Typical Panamanian food served in an authentic thatched roof setting is to be found at **La Tablita** on the Transisthmian Highway, and typical offerings are *ceviche* (fish), *churrasco* (steak), and *pollo ahumado* (smoked chicken); for an attractive seaside setting, **Club Panamar** (Calle 50 Final & San Francisco de la Caleta) offers fine seafood (shrimp, lobster, filet of corvina, red snapper) in an indoor/outdoor restaurant where you can dine in air-conditioned style or in the pleasant garden overlooking Panama Bay; upstairs one flight at **Dorado** (Calle 51, corner of Calle Colombia) is first class style and fine fare in an attractive villa setting; specialties include *corvina ajillo* and *mariscos* (shellfish), and *arroz marinara*. Expensive and good. For seafood and Spanish cuisine, the **Casa del Marisco,** Avenida Balboa, is excellent. For a bistro atmosphere, there's **El Joran** (Vía Fernando de Cordova) while **Pez de Oro** (Calle J near Plaza Einstein) is well spoken of as a seafood-Peruvian style restaurant. For Italian fare try **Sarti** (Calle Ricardo Arias 5, just behind El Continental) or **Sorrento** (Vía España); for Chinese both **Lung Fung** (Barriado Los Angeles) and the red-lanterned **Pana-China** have their followers, as does **La Gran China. Cafe Kyoto** (Vía España 117) offers a variety of Japanese fare including *tempura, shabushabu,* and *sukiyaki.* For good Spanish food try **Marbella** (Calle 39 & Ave. Balboa), informal, or for more style, **El Patio Andaluz** (Calle 52 & Calle Elvira Mendez) with a pleasing hacienda-style setting and such offerings as *cazuela marinara,* and authentic *paella valenciana,* and *rinones al jerez.* The **Boulevard Balboa, Vía España,** and **Avenida Perú** are all well supplied with restaurants of all classes. Snack foods are sold in cafeterias and on the street. Two popular snacks are *empanadas,* fried ground corn filled with meat or cheese, and *pastelitos,* baked pastry with meat or cheese. **Kentucky Fried Chicken** and **McDonald's** have outlets here. **Pizzeria Italiana** (Av. Balboa 8) sells good pizza and ice cream, while the major hotels offer good international fare, with the **Portobelo Room** (Hotel El Panamá) one of the several local favorites.

DRINKING TIPS

Many different types of rum are widely drunk, and rum punch is popular, particularly in Taboga. There is no shortage of imported wines, liquor, or beers, and local brews are Balboa, Atlas, Panamá, and Cristal beers and the liquor Seco Herrerano. Whisky and soda costs about B2.50, while wine can be expensive—anywhere from B4.50-B20 in a restaurant. Liquor is usually sold until the early hours of the morning. Coffee or soft drinks (*chicha de naranja* is a delicious fresh-fruit drink) can be enjoyed in boulevard cafés; two of the most popular are **Manolo** and the **Del Prado,** both on Vía Argentina.

ENTERTAINMENT

The **Teatro Nacional** puts on opera, ballet, and music (concert season May to December). There is national folk music and dancing every Saturday (10am) in February and March in the ruins of Old Panama. Films are shown with their original soundtrack and Spanish subtitles. Drive-in movies can be seen at **Autocino No. 1** and **Autocine Pacifico.** For full movie listings check the English language *Star Herald.* Major hotels have dancing, and there are floor shows at the **El Panamá** and **El Continental** hotels. **La Siesta Hotel** has a supper club. The principal nightclubs in Panama City are **Maxims, El Sombrero,** and **Playboy de Panama,** with three shows nightly. Best discos are **Number One** (Calle 50, corner of Calle Ricardo Arias) and **El Oasis** (Vía Brasil Este at 3a. Sur). Others are **Las Molas, Club Windsor, Zebra,** and **El Ancla.** Dozens of small *boîtes* have music and dancing, and pop music is played at **Llave-Dorado** (Calle 1) by two American bands. Gambling has widespread appeal in Panama, and if you forgo the lottery (Wednesday and Sunday at noon in Santa Ana Plaza), try the casinos at hotels **El Panamá, La Siesta, Granada, El Continental,** and **Gran Lux.** There are casinos also in Colón, at the **Washington-Hyatt** and the **Hotel Sotelo,** and a new one on **Contadora Island.** Panama is famous for its colorful festivals, spread liberally throughout the year. The biggest event of all is the **Pan-**

ama Carnival, lasting for 4 days. *La pollera*, 10 yards of embroidered flounced dress, is traditionally worn by the female revelers, and troupes of dancers close the streets to traffic. Decorated floats, fireworks, and bands brighten the streets until dawn of Ash Wednesday, when the mock-solemn "burial of the sardine" closes the festival.

SHOPPING

Stores open 9-12 and 2-6 Mon-Sat. Goods from all over the world are to be found in Panama, very many of them duty free. Some best buys include pearls, camera equipment, radios, tape recorders, fine linen, silk, cashmere, jewelry, and Far Eastern jade, ivory, porcelain, china, and crystal. *Molas*, cloth panels of hand-stitched reverse appliqué made by Cuna Indians to decorate the fronts and backs of their blouses, start at B15, and *chaquiras*, necklaces of tiny beads, make good gifts for less than B10. *Tembleques* are attractive hair ornaments worn with the national dress; there is also a delicious and distinctive dessert by the same name, made with rosewater, coconut, and gelatin. Where prices are not marked in stores, it is usual to bargain. Major stores will pack and ship purchases.

Avenida Central is the main shopping center, with several large department stores, two of which are **Dante** and **Felix B. Maduro,** and the superb Oriental store **Salomón** (branch at the El Continental Hotel). The **Avenida Tivoli** in suburban Panama City has the best merchandise at good prices, and **P Jhangimal,** at 18-68, is clean and spacious, with fine jewelry, inlaid furniture, carved ivory, and other imports. **Shaw's** (Campo Alegre) specializes in china and old coins. **Avenida Ricardo Arias,** near the El Continental and El Panamá Hotels, is the chic shopping area. **Artesania Panameña** (Calle 55) is good for handicrafts. **Ben Betesh** (137 Vía España) imports French couture and perfume, wool, and cashmere from the US, silk and shoes from Italy, and shirts from Australia. There is a duty-free branch at the airport. **Salsipuedes** off Avenida Central is a colorful waterfront market area, selling anything from fresh fish to souvenirs, food, clothing, and household and fancy goods. **Artesania Nacional** at Panamá Viejo has a large variety of Panamanian handicrafts.

SPORTS

Fishing can go on all year in Panama, which holds more than 40 world records and is considered the "black marlin capital of the world." Mackerel, kingfish, snook, and tarpon are there for the catching in the blue waters of the Caribbean, and marlin, sailfish, dolphin, tuna, amberjack, and others are next door in the Pacific. There is freshwater fishing in the **Chagres** and **Chiriquí** rivers and in **Gatún** and **Gamboa** lakes. Horse racing is highly popular, and takes place at the **Hipodromo Presidente Remón** racetrack Thursday, Saturday, Sunday, and holidays. Tourists admitted free (show your tourist card), bets win and place only, minimum B2. Cockfights are held Sunday and Monday at the **Club Gallistico de Panama.** Admission 50 centesimos, betting gets wild with the regulars. Boxing, soccer, basketball, baseball (Dec-Feb), car racing (Feb-Apr), and speedboat racing are all popular. Visitors are welcome to play at the **Panama Golf Club,** Panama City, where an **Open Tournament** is held in February. There is an 18-hole professional course at the **Coronado Golf Club,** on the Pacific 50 miles west of Panama City. Swimming is particularly good at the **Olimpico Pool** and the Pacific beaches.

WHAT TO SEE

Panama City divides into three distinct areas: the downtown area of the "new" city built by the Spanish in the 17th century, with narrow streets and overhead balconies; the beautiful residential suburbs, with gracious villas, modern hotels, gardens, and pools; and Old Panama, destroyed by fire as mentioned. **King's Bridge** marks the boundary of the old city, whose scattered ruins lie beneath the looming tower of the former cathedral. The **National Museum,** 5 de Mayo Plaza (9-12 and 2-5, closed Mon), has collections of pre-Columbian artifacts, Incan and Spanish treasures, ethnology, natural history, and colonial life. Spanish colonial architecture at its best can be seen in the **Palace of Justice** facing the Promenade Las Bovedas, with fascinating old dungeons. Also worth seeing are the **Cathedral** (mother-of-pearl towers) and the churches of **San José,** with a golden altar saved from the original church in Old Panama, and **Santo Domingo** (Calle 3a), with an unusual flat arch. In the **Presidencia,** home of the president, plumed herons wander freely through the patios.

  Panama Canal: The canal is an irresistible attraction to all visitors to Panama, and the Panama Canal Administration provides a guide service at **Miraflores Locks,** where there is also a theater showing historical and documentary films. The famous "ditch" is about 50 miles long, took 10 years to complete (following De Lesseps's attempts) at a cost of $525 million. Tolls are levied on a net-tonnage basis, averging $7,175; this is still ten times cheaper than the alternate route around Cape Horn. The headquarters of the 10-mile-wide Area del Canal de Panama is **Balboa,** with beautiful orchid gardens. At the Atlantic end of the canal, the port of **Cristóbal** is one of the busiest in Latin America. **Colón,** a few hundred yards away in front of Cristobal, is a free zone area, and this typical Panamanian town is alive with tourists and sailors, in bazaars and bars. The most impressive building is the ornate **Hotel Washington-Hyatt,** which has a casino (from US$44 double); the **Sotelo Hotel** (from $25 double), also has a casino. Restaurants are **Alhambra, VIP Club,** and **El Trópico.** The **Club 61** and **Club Florida** have floor shows and slot machines. Twenty miles from Colón are the extensive ruins of the Spanish gold city of **Portobelo,** captured by Morgan.

  Pacific Beaches: Miles of sandy beaches, for 75 miles along the scenic Interamerican Highway, line the Pacific coast—**Gorgona, Coronado, San Carlos,** and **Santa Clara.** Coronado is a luxury resort with condominiums, villas, and a golf club. San Carlos has a new tourist center with beach facilities for the budget traveler. **El Valle,** across the mountains, is a cool resort famous for its "golden" frogs, square trees, and picturesque Sunday market with excellent handicrafts. **Taboga:** The clear sea and the silvery beaches are the main attractions of the Island of Flowers. Scuba-diving, glass-bottomed boats, fishing, water-skiing, and parasailing (parachutes drawn by speedboat) are all popular. There are no cars on the island, and even taxis take to the water *(pangas)*. The only other means of transportation are the electric trolleys and bicycles. During the **July Saints' Day** festival there is a marine procession. **Taboga Hotel** has double rooms priced from US$23.

The **San Blas Archipelago Islands** in the Caribbean—an air trip from Panama City—are the homes of the Cuna Indians, who live in bamboo huts. These people have changed little since pre-Columbian days, and although Panamanians, they live by their own tribal laws. The women favor ear disks, arm and leg bands, and nose rings, and they wear beaten gold around their necks. Some experts claim to see similarities in the designs of the traditional cloth *molas*, fashioned by the Cuna women, and the designs found on coinage dedicated variously to Ishtar and Astoroth around 2,500 BC, in the Middle East. **Pidertupo Village** (thatched-cottage accommodations with modern facilities) costs US$125 for two, including meals, trips, and snorkeling equipment. Other San Blas hotels, operated by the Cuna Indians, are **Las Palmeras,** on Ailigandi (from $10 per person); **El Porvenir,** on Porvenir (from $28 per person); and the **Anai,** on Wichub Wala ($50 double). San Blas rates include meals and sightseeing trips. Bring your camera by all means, but be prepared to pay the local people for taking their pictures. *Molas* can be purchased on the mainland, but if you go to the San Blas, shopping directly from the Indians can be an unforgettable experience. Sometimes if you admire a *mola* on the blouse a Cuna woman is wearing, she will literally sell you the shirt off her back. *Molas* are collected as artwork, and their prices go only up. Some of the carved wooden objects are nice.

Contadora: Only 17 minutes by air from Panama City (fare is US$35 round trip), this island has 13 beautiful, secluded white sand beaches. Skin-diving equipment, sailboats, and Mini-Mokes are available, also tennis, golf, and a casino. Accommodations are at the **Hotel Casino Contadora,** with double rooms from $85 and cabanas from $55 EP. Nearby are many small uninhabited islands easily reached by motorboat; 14 of these will be eventually included in a fabulous resort development of which Contadora is the base.

The Chiriquí Province: The mountains in the province bordering on Costa Rica are famous for their Easter lilies, blue jacaranda, orchids, and wild strawberries. The coffee-growing areas of **Boquete** and **El Hato del Volcán** are excellent centers for all-year-round wild-game hunting and rainbow trout fishing in the mountain streams. The Guaymí Indians who live in the mountains are noted for *chaquiras*, beaded collars used by women for evening wear. The **Fundadores Hotel** in Boquete has double rooms from US$20. **David,** the capital of the province, is a pleasant, quiet city, with an airport. The biggest hotels are the **Nacional,** with swimming pool and air conditioning (from $18 double), and the new **Palacio Imperial** (from $14 double).

Bocas del Toro on the Caribbean coast can be reached only by air or boat from Colón. Some of the beaches in this area, although underdeveloped, are among the most beautiful in the Caribbean.

SOURCES OF FURTHER INFORMATION

Pan Am: Edificio Hatillo, Avenida Justo Arosemena, Panama City, and any Pan Am office around the world; **Instituto Panameño de Turismo** (Panama Government Tourist Office), El Panamá Hotel Grounds, Vía España, Panama City; 630 Fifth Avenue, New York, NY 10020; Suite #1304, 150 SE 2nd Ave., Miami, FL 33131; 3900 W Third St, Los Angeles, CA 90020; 404 King Street East, Toronto, Ontario M5A 1L4; **Panamanian Embassy**, 16 The Boltons, London SW10.

Paraguay

WHAT'S SPECIAL

Paraguay is a beautiful, subtropical land, still largely undiscovered and unspoiled. Although the country was conquered by the Spanish in the 16th century, the native Guaraní retained their national identity. Since that time the two cultures have blended together and created the intriguing country that is Paraguay today.

The country is cut in half by the Paraguay River, which is also its main access to the ocean, 900 miles away. To the west lies the Gran Chaco—95,300 square miles of cattle country and scrub forest. To the east of the river is Paraguay proper, where most of the population lives, with wooded hills and flat plains stretching toward the rich lands and forests of the Paraná Plateau.

COUNTRY BRIEFING

Size: 157,047 square miles
Capital: Asunción
Population: 2,973,526
Capital Population: 600,000

Climate: Subtropical. Summer (December-March) can be oppressively hot; winters are much cooler, with occasional frosts at night. Best time to go is May-September.

Weather in Asunción: Lat S25° 17′; Alt 456 ft

Temp (°F)	Jan	Feb	Mar	Apr	May	Jun	Jul	Aug	Sep	Oct	Nov	Dec
Av Low	71°	71°	69°	65°	58°	53°	53°	57°	60°	62°	65°	70°
Av High	95°	94°	92°	84°	77°	72°	74°	78°	83°	86°	90°	94°
Days no rain	23	22	25	23	25	24	26	27	23	23	22	24

Government: A dictatorship.

Language: Bilingual: Spanish and Guaraní. Both are recognized as national languages. Spanish is used for commerce and in the schools, for the most part, while Guaraní is the preferred tongue for general communication.

Religion: Roman Catholic.

Currency: Guaraní. 100 centimos = 1 guaraní.

	5 G	10 G	50 G	100 G	500 G	1,000 G	2,000 G	5,000 G
US (dollars, cents)	.04	.08	.40	.79	3.97	7.94	15.87	39.68
UK (pounds, pence)	.02	.04	.19	.38	1.89	3.79	7.57	18.93

Public Holidays:

New Year's Day, 1 Jan
San Blas, 3 Feb
Heroes' Day, 1 Mar
Maundy Thursday
Good Friday
Labor Day, 1 May
National Independence Days, 14 and 15 May
Chaco Peace Day, 12 June
Corpus Christi
Foundation of Asunción Day, 15 Aug
Constitution Day, 25 Aug
Battle of Boquerón, 29 Sep
Dia de la Raza (Columbus Day), 12 Oct
All Saints Day, 1 Nov
Virgin of the Miracles of Caacupé, 8 Dec
Christmas Day, 25 Dec

HOW TO GET THERE

Flying time to Asunción's Presidente General Stroessner Airport from New York is 9½ hours; from São Paulo, 1¾ hours; from Buenos Aires, 1½ hours; from Montevideo, 2 hours. Time in Paraguay: GMT—4.

REQUIREMENTS FOR ENTRY AND CUSTOMS REGULATIONS

A passport and a tourist card. The latter you can buy for US$1 from airline offices or on arrival in the country. Vaccinations advisable if coming from infected areas. No restrictions on amount of currency you can take in or out. 200 cigarettes, or 50 cigars or 1lb of tobacco, plus 1 bottle of liquor admitted duty free. Visitors will be asked to open their suitcases. Colonial antiques may not be taken out of the country.

AIRPORT INFORMATION

The international airport for Paraguay is Presidente General Stroessner, 8 miles from Asunción. Bus No 30 runs every 10 minutes between the airport and the city (fare 35G). Taxis available at all times (fare to city center, 1,600G). No airport arrival tax. Duty-free shop in the airport for departing passengers on international flights. Tip porters 50G per suitcase.

ACCOMMODATIONS

A *pensión* or *residencia* has rooms from US$5, all meals included. It is not easy to find hotel rooms at the last minute in Paraguay; if possible, book in advance. For help in finding accommodations go to the **Dirección de Turismo**, Alberdi esquina Oliva—tel: 47865. Hotels in Asunción:

Rates are in US$ for a double/twin room with bath or shower

Armele, Palma and Colon (from $41)

Casino Ita Enramada, Lambare & Ribera del Rio (from $62) about 4 miles south of Asunción

Chaco, Caballero & Mariscal Estigarribia (from $60)

Del Paraguay, Presidentes & Triunvirato (from $49)

Husa, Estrella & 15 de Agosto (from $60)

Paraná, Caballero & 25 de Mayo (from $58)

Plaza, Eligio Ayala & Paraguarí (from $37)

Premier, 25 de Mayo & Curupayty (from $45) just out of town

Senorial del Paraguay, Av Mariscal Lopez (from $38)

Unless otherwise indicated, the above hotels are centrally located.

USEFUL INFORMATION

Banks: Open only 7:30-11am. *Casas de Cambios* are legal exchange dealers.

Mail: Stamps at post offices only. No mailboxes in use.

Telephone Tips: Phone booths in public places and in cafés and restaurants. Useful numbers in Asunción:

Pan Am's Agent 4.4171	Long Distance Operator 00
Airport Information 2.2012/3	Time 15
Tourist Office and Information 41	Weather 19
530	First Aid 21 000
Operator and Directories 12	Police 49 116

Newspapers: *The Buenos Aires Herald* and other English-language magazines are regularly flown into Asunción. There are no local English-language newspapers. Libreria Universal, Palma 519, has a good supply of English-language books.

Tipping: Customary. In restaurants, leave 10% (no service charge included); porters, 30-50G; taxi drivers, 10G or 5%; hairdressers, about 12%.

Electricity: 220 volts 50 cycles AC.

Laundry: Dry-cleaning and laundry services good and inexpensive (dry-cleaning a suit, from 150G; laundering a shirt, from 30G).

Hairdressing: Some better hotels have salons (shampoo and set from 300G; man's haircut from 120G).

Photography: Equipment and films available in Asunción only. Black and white film costs about 165G and color film 1000G.

Clubs: Lions, Rotary.

Babysitting: Can be arranged through major hotels.

Rest Rooms: In cafés and restaurants. Women, *Damas;* men, *Caballeros.*

Health: Many doctors and dentists speak English. Fees are high, and pharmaceuticals expensive. Tap water safe only in Asunción. Peel all fruit and vegetables.

TRANSPORTATION

Asunción has a streetcar service, except on Sundays, and buses and micro-buses; fares inexpensive. Metered taxis readily available but expensive. It is usually better to hire a car with chauffeur by the day. Rates average about $25-45 without chauffeur; add about 2000G for a chauffeur. You pay for the gas. Or look into hiring a taxi with driver by the hour.

Railroad services outside Asunción are limited and not recommended, except for the train to Encarnación. The trip to Encarnación is very dusty so go first class, unless you really want to rough it. Long-distance bus services are better. There is a paved highway between Asunción and Puerto Presidente Stroessner, near Iguazú Falls (227 miles), and fairly good roads to Encarnación, Villarica, through the Chaco to Filadelfia, etc. There are also ferry and boat services from Asunción: north toward Rosario and Concepción (in the Chaco) and south toward Pilar and Buenos Aires. Boats leave for Buenos Aires every 10 days (journey takes 2½ days) except during heavy rains. There are scheduled air services to most parts of the country by TAM (Transportes Aéreos Militares) and LATN (Lineas Aéreas de Transporte Nacional). Planes can also be chartered. Flying times from Asunción: Concepción (335 miles), 1 hour; Pilar (229 miles), 50 minutes; Filadelfia (285 miles), 1 hour 40 minutes; Encarnación (222 miles), 1 hour.

FOOD AND RESTAURANTS

The basic meal is *soo-yosopy,* a soup with a base of cornmeal and ground beef. *Sopa Paraguaya* is a stiff soufflé of mashed corn, cheese, milk, eggs, and onions. If you like meat, try *asados,* beef grilled over an open pit. The *surubí* fish, served in a number of ways, is a great delicacy. International cuisine is readily available at the Hotels **Chaco, Ita Enramada,** and **Del Paraguay**—the last serves an excellent curry dinner Wednesday evenings. For the real flavor of Paraguay enjoy good Paraguayan beef, and the unforgettable music at one of the several *parrillados* in the suburbs of Asunción. The harp, accompanied by guitars, seems to become a new instrument. Try **Yguazu** (Choferes del Chaco, closed Sun) or **Hermitage** (15 de Agosto & 2a, closed Sundays) or **Jardin de la Cerveza** (Rca Argentina & Castillo, evenings only). **La Preferida** (Estados Unidos & 25 de Mayo) offers good international cuisine as well as local specialties in a pleasant atmosphere. **El Bosque** and **La Carreta,** both at Aviavores del Chaco & General Genes, are very fine restaurants offering international food accompanied by a floor show. Other restaurants include **Los Canibales** (Colon & Oliva), the **Munich** (Calle Ayala 163), the **Bolsi** (Estrella & Alberdi) and **El Hostal** (Yegros & Independencia) for excellent steaks. The **Amstel** has a pleasant atmosphere reminiscent of Holland (in Villamorra), while for Italian fare, **La Piccola Gondola** (Av 5a & Caballero) is good. **Hosteria El Caballito Blanco** (Alberdi, Haedo & Gral Diaz), and **La Pergola** (Estrella & Alberdi) are also worthy of note.

Breakfast is usually from 6:30-8:30; lunch, 11:30-1:30; dinner, 8:30-10:30. A meal for one in an expensive restaurant will cost about 850G;

in a medium-priced restaurant, 600G, and in an inexpensive restaurant, about 400G. You can also get a snack meal for about 150G in a cafeteria.

DRINKING TIPS

The national drink is *Caña*, a potent Paraguayan rum made from sugarcane or honey. Imported wines and liquor are available; a large whisky and soda or a bottle of wine will cost about 180G. No liquor restrictions; some bars stay open until 3am.

ENTERTAINMENT

There are few night spots in Asunción outside of the parrilladas, though there is dinner dancing and entertainment at **Yguazu**, and the casino at the **Hotel Ita Enramada** is impressive. (There's also gambling at the Gran Hotel Casino Acaray, in Puerto Stroessner.) Have a drink in one of the sidewalk *whiskerías* (bars) at the Main Plaza, in front of the river. **Capri** (Palma 479 & Calle Alberdi) and **San Marino** (Palmas y Independencia Nacional) are also very popular with young people, especially after dinner. Concerts and recitals are held in the Auditorium at the **Centro Cultural Paraguayo-Americano** (Avenida España c/Brazil). Movies are very popular, too. For nightclubs, the **Hotel Guaraní** has a rooftop club on weekends. You can also try **Zafari** (Avenida San Martin y General Genes), **Elite** (22 de Septiembre). **Coracol Discotec** (Avenida José Felix Bogado), and, for bowling, **Boliche** (Villa Morra).

SHOPPING

Stores open 7:30-11:30 and 3-7 Mon-Fri (the siesta at lunchtime is observed, especially in summer), 7:30-12 Sat. Government offices open only 6:30-11:30am in summer and 7:30-noon in winter. Best buys include dresses or shirts of *aho-poi* cloth (linen woven by the people of Yataity) or tablecloths, mantillas, quilts, or pleated capes tied at the waist by a wide sash. Most items will cost under 1,420G. **La Recova del Puerto** is a shopping street that caters to tourists, as is **Calle Colón**, starting at the port, and **Calle Palma**. **Casa Arnaldo** (Calle Palma 640) is a good store, and **La Riojana** is a favorite department store. For local crafts, including carvings made from the rare Paraguayan wood *lapacho*, go to the shop formerly run by the Society of Brothers located in the **Calle Independencia Nacional**, behind the Hotel Guaraní. You can also get leather goods, basketry, bright ceramics, and woven rugs, silver *bombillas* (straws for drinking *yerba maté*), and *maté* gourds, handmade guitars, and harps. Gifts include puzzle rings or multilooped bracelets that uncoil to great lengths. No bargaining in larger stores, but do your best in street markets—**Petti Rossi Avenue** is the largest one in the city. And don't leave Paraguay without a record of that enchanting music. You can find an ample selection at **Discos Folkloricos** (at Mariscal Estigarribia 323, Independencia Nacional & 25 de Mayo and at Estrella & Alberdi).

SPORTS

Soccer is the national sport; in Asunción alone there are 30 clubs. You can try golf at the nine-hole course at the **Botanical Gardens** (Artigas y

Primer Presidente); tennis at the **Paraguay Lawn Tennis Club;** boxing at the **Comuñeros Stadium.** Basketball, volleyball, horseback riding, polo, and horse-racing facilities are available. There are two rowing and swimming clubs, a motor boat club, and the **Paraguayan Aviation Club.** For hunting and fishing go out on safari after jaguar, puma, tapir, armadillos, large barking *cururu chini* toads, alligator, the 150-pound *surubí*, and the lungfish. Book a safari through **Tiger Hill** (Independencia Nacional 225, PO Box 934, Asunción) or **Hugo Pesce** (Finantur), at 14 de Mayo y Presidente Franco, PO Box 762A.

WHAT TO SEE

Asunción: Guaraní women in colorful dresses and smoking big cigars sell local merchandise throughout the city. Interesting buildings are the **Government Palace** (El Paraguayo Independente), the **Cathedral** (Plaza Constitución), the **Pantheon of Heroes,** a replica of Les Invalides, which contains the body of Francisco Solano López, the **Congressional Palace** (Plaza Constitución), and the **Casa de la Independencia** (14 de Mayo y Presidente Franco). Museums are open 8:30-11:30 and 1:30-6:30, closed Saturday afternoons and Sundays. The **Museum of Natural Sciences** of the Colegio Internacional (Mayor Fleitas y Rio de Janeiro) is probably the best; the museum in **La Casa de la Independencia** has recently been modernized. Children will enjoy the very pleasant parks in Asunción: **Parque Carlos Antonio López** (not very well maintained), **Parque Caballero** (which has a swimming pool and waterfalls), and **Parque Gaspar Rodriquez de Francia.** The **Botanical Gardens,** with a **Zoo** and the **Museum of Natural History,** are 4 miles out of town; microbus No 23 or a taxi will get you there. From the gardens, you can go by open motorboat to an island in the Paraguay River where a group of several hundred former-warrior Maca Indians live. A popular trip is to the resort of **San Bernardino** on the shore of Lake Ypacarai, 35 miles from Asunción.

Other places of interest: Along the paved highway to Puerto Presidente Stroessner you will pass **Capiatá,** where there is a fine cathedral and a 16th century carving made by Indians under the tutelage of the Jesuit Fathers; **Itagua,** where you can watch women weaving the *ñandutí* lace, and **Caacupé,** with the beautiful **Church of the Blue Virgin of the Miracles.**

The other main road out of Asunción goes toward **Encarnación,** a port on the Alto Paraná River. On the way pass **Yaguarón,** which has one of the most exciting churches in South America, completed in 1729. The altars, pulpits, and images were worked by native Guaraní Indians under the supervision of the Franciscan friars. The paints, made from local plants, are as vivid now as they were almost three centuries ago.

SOURCES OF FURTHER INFORMATION

Pan Am's agent, A.y.C. Abente Haedo, Calle Independencia Nacional 571, Asunción, and any other Pan Am office around the world; the **Dirección General de Turismo,** Alberdi y Oliva, Asunción; **Paraguay Mission to the UN,** 211 East 43rd Street, New York, NY 10017; the **Paraguayan Consulate,** Braemar Lodge, Cornwall Gardens, London SW7.

Peru

WHAT'S SPECIAL

Peru, a land of many fascinations, is the site of fabled Machu Picchu—one of the most spectacular places in the world. Situated high in the Andes, it is constructed with stones fitted together without mortar so surely that the centuries and earthquakes have not tumbled them. Cuzco is the city of gold where Spain melds with Inca. When the Indians embraced Christianity, they incorporated it into their lives: a wonderful illustration of this can be seen in the painting of the Last Supper in the church in Cuzco. Christ and his disciples are shown feasting on *kwi*, a small guinea pig still regarded as a delicacy by the Indians (and available in restaurants). Peru is the home of the ill-tempered llama, the alpaca, and the vicuna, whose wool has been transformed into the clothing and blankets that are among Peru's most distinctive exports. The highest lake in the world is here, Lake Titicaca, and in its center is the Island of the Sun, which legend says is the birthplace of man. Recent archaeological activity has now established that human settlement dates back 10,000 years. The mystery of Nazca is here, the huge drawings on land that predate airplanes by many centuries, yet can only be seen from the air. The high Inca culture flourished here in Cuzco, unifying the land as far north as Ecuador and as far south as Chile.

When the Spanish conquistadores came, they were not interested in the finer points of civilization—it was gold that they were after. At the time of their arrival a division had split the Incan empire—which had 100 years earlier under the skilled leadership of Pachacutec, expanded to its greatest size.

Peru did not become free from Spanish rule until 1824 when her troops were defeated by the revolutionary armies of Bolivar and Colombian General Jose de Sucre.

Tourism is important to Peru and for the traveller, Lima is one of the most attractive of all South American capital cities and certainly one of the world's most interesting, with its unique combination of old and new.

COUNTRY BRIEFING

Size: 496,222 square miles   **Population:** 17,164,000
Capital: Lima   **Capital Population:** 3,500,000

Climate: Peru, the third largest country in South America, has several very different climates. Temperatures along the coast are cooled by the Humboldt Current—the thermometer rarely rises above 80° or falls below 55°. Lima sits under a massive low cloudbank much of the time, and while sunshine is rather rare, so is rain. There is considerable mist and dampness during the winter (June-September). Summer lasts from December to April. The jungle region is humid and warm. The mountain areas are generally cooler than the coast, becoming quite cold at high altitudes when the sun goes down, with a rainy season lasting throughout the summer. Best time to visit Lima is January-April; the mountain and jungle regions are at their best June-October. Lima lies in an earthquake zone, but earthquakes aren't very frequent.

Weather in Lima: Lat S12°05′; Alt 394 ft

Temp (°F)	Jan	Feb	Mar	Apr	May	Jun	Jul	Aug	Sep	Oct	Nov	Dec
Av Low	66°	67°	66°	63°	60°	58°	57°	56°	57°	58°	60°	62°
Av High	82°	83°	82°	80°	74°	68°	67°	66°	68°	71°	74°	78°
Days no rain	30	27	31	29	30	29	30	29	29	31	30	31

Government: A republic.

Language: Spanish, but about half the population speaks only the Indian tongues of Quechua or Aymará. English is spoken in hotels, restaurants, and some shops.

Religion: Roman Catholic. Other denominations are represented in Lima.

Currency: Sol. 100 centavos = 1 sol.

	5 sol	10 sol	50 sol	100 sol	200 sol	500 sol	1,000 sol	2,000 sol
US (dollars, cents)	.01	.02	.12	.25	.49	1.23	2.46	4.91
UK (pounds, pence)	—	.01	.06	.12	.23	.59	1.18	2.35

Public Holidays:

New Year's Day, 1 Jan
Maundy Thursday (half day)
Good Friday
Labor Day, 1 May
Indian Day, 24 June (half day)
St Peter and St Paul, 29 June
Independence Day Celebrations, 28 & 29 July

Santa Rosa, 30 Aug
National Dignity Day, 9 Oct
All Saints Day, 1 Nov
Immaculate Conception, 8 Dec
December 24 (half day)
Christmas Day, 25 Dec

HOW TO GET THERE
Flying time to Lima, Jorge Chavez International Airport from Panamá City, 3 hours; Caracas, 3½ hours; Miami, 6 hours; and New York, 7½ hours. Time in Peru: GMT−5.

REQUIREMENTS FOR ENTRY AND CUSTOMS REGULATIONS
Passport, onward or round-trip ticket, an embarkation/disembarkation card issued by airline offices for stays of 90 days or less, and an international certificate of vaccination against smallpox. Immunization against yellow fever, typhoid, tetanus, poliomyelitis, and typhus also recommended if coming from an infected area. Duty-free allowance: 200 cigarettes or 25 cigars or ½ pound pipe tobacco; 2 bottles liquor; a reasonable amount of camera film; and a reasonable amount of perfume for personal use. No currency restrictions.

AIRPORT INFORMATION
The international airport for Lima is Jorge Chavez, about 8 miles from the city center. Large hotels have buses waiting at the airport. Taxis also available; fare to the city center (maximum five passengers), about US$1.50. Tip porters 15 soles per suitcase. Duty-free shop, information and hotel reservation counters at airport. There is a departure tax of about US$8.50.

ACCOMMODATIONS
There are many excellent hotels in Lima, with high standards of service. In most towns there are government-controlled hotels called *Turista;* for information about these contact the **Empress Nacional de Turismo** (ENTURPERU), Junin 455, Lima–tel: 28-7450. Hotels in Lima:
Rates are in US$ for a double/twin room with bath or shower (add 28% tax and service unless otherwise indicated)
    Alcázar, Camana 564 (from $26)
    Claridge, Jirón Cailloma (from $15 tax included)
    Columbus, Avenida Arequipa 421 (from $24)
    Continental, Esquina Puno & Carabya (from $22 tax included)
    Country Club de Lima, Avenida Golf, San Isidro (from $27.50), 10 minutes from center
    Crillón, Nicholas de Piérola 589 (from $56)
    El Pardo Hotel, Av Pardo 420 (from $40)
    El Pueblo Hyatt Hotel, 30 minutes from downtown (from $39)
    Hotel Gran Bolivar, Plaza San Martin (from $50)
    Lima-Sheraton, Paseo de la Republica 170 (from $65)
    Maury, Ucayali 201 (from $25)
    Miraflores Cesar's Hotel, 10 minutes from downtown (from $65)
    Riviera, Avenida Garcilaso de la Vega 981 (from $39 tax included)
    Savoy, Cailloma 224 (from $29 tax included)
    All hotels in center of city unless otherwise indicated.

USEFUL INFORMATION

Banks: Open Apr-Dec, 9:15-12:45 Mon-Fri; Jan-Mar, 8:30-11:30 Mon-Fri. Change currency and travelers' checks at hotels, travel agencies, and exchange bureaus.

Telephone Tips: Booths available and phones in restaurants and cafés. Useful numbers in Lima:

Pan Am agents 28-9999	Aeroperu 28-7825
Airport Information 52-3135	Emergency 05
Tourist Office 27-4077/28-7457	Operator 08
Tourist Information 28-2742/28-7815	Directories 03
	British American Hospital 40-3570

Newspapers: *The Lima Times* is the local English-language weekly. *The New York Times* (a day or so after publication), the *Miami Herald* (on day of issue), *Time, Newsweek,* and other American magazines are available.

Tipping: A 10% service charge and a 5-11% tax is added to checks in restaurants and hotels, but you should leave the waiter an extra 5%, and give the hotel porter 15 soles per bag; taxi drivers are not tipped.

Electricity: 220 volts 60 cycles AC. To use US 110-volt appliances, ask at the hotel for a *transformador* (transformer).

Laundry: Services in first-class hotels are good and fast.

Hairdressing: Salons available in first-class hotels.

Photography: All main brands of film and camera equipment available in Lima, but generally expensive. Take your film home for developing.

Clubs: Lions, Rotary, Jaycees.

Babysitting: Large hotels may be able to arrange.

Rest Rooms: In restaurants, bars, and hotels. Women, *Damas;* men, *Caballeros.*

Health: English-speaking doctors and dentists available. There is a British-American Hospital in the San Isidro residential suburb; some of the staff of the Clinica San Borja speak English. Few imported pharmaceuticals are on sale in Lima; however, the local equivalents with imported ingredients are available. Toiletries can be expensive. In the Andes you may suffer from altitude sickness (symptoms similar to seasickness, but watch for feelings of faintness); hotels have oxygen supplies. Move slowly and don't try to do too much for the first few days. Taxis have altimeters, which are interesting to see as you drive around in altitudes you are probably unaccustomed to. Machu Picchu is lower than Cuzco; some people can feel the difference. On board trains crossing the mountains there is a man in white overalls whose duty is to assist passengers who are affected by the altitude. Drink only bottled water, except in principal hotels. Fruit and raw vegetables should be washed thoroughly.

TRANSPORTATION

Lima has a local bus service as well as a fleet of *colectivos* (shared taxis), which travel along fixed routes. Normal taxis are also readily available; there are stands in the main plazas, or you can hail one on the street—

wave your arm up and down and hiss loudly! Fares average 400 soles in the city, double at night. Car rental rates average about US$22 to US$30 per day, plus 30¢- 50¢ per kilometer—weekly rates US$140-200. Leading car rental agencies represented here are Hertz at Ocoña 262 (tel: 28-633); Avis at the Sheraton Hotel (tel: 32-7146) and in Cuzco, Arequipa, and Iquitos; also Budget, National, Satary, ABC, and Nova. Most have offices at the airport. Lima has four traffic jams a day; as well as normal morning and evening rush hours, there is also chaos before and after the siesta period at about noon and 1:30. You must leave your left window open, as signaling has to be done by hand. **Receptour** at Rufino Torrico 889 (tel: 31-2022) will arrange excursions with chauffeur, bilingual guides, etc.

There are two main railways, one in central Peru starting from Lima and the other in southern Peru going from the Port of Matarani to Arequipa, Lake Titicaca, and Cuzco. The journey along the highest normal-gauge railroad in the world, from Lima to Huancayo across the Andes, will take you from sea level to 15,688 feet in 4 hours 48 minutes. Trains leave daily, Monday-Saturday, from the station at Desamparados. If you are going by train from Cuzco to Machu Picchu, you would be well advised to take the tourist train, as the local service seems interminable. Food is usually available on trains, and there is a sleeping car service between Arequipa and Puno. There are regular bus and *colectivo* services from Lima to most important centers on the coast and the sierras. *Colectivos* carry up to five passengers and charge higher fares than buses. There are two internal airlines, AeroPeru and Faucett, with jet and prop-jet services to key cities such as Cuzco, Arequipa, Tacna, Chiclayo, and Piura. AeroPeru, Av Nicolás de Piérola 914, Plaza San Martin, Lima—tel: 31-7620, operates jet services to the principal Peruvian cities. You can also travel by lake steamer across Lake Titicaca, then by train to La Paz in Bolivia, and there are speedboat trips to Yanamono Island. A hydrofoil service operates between Copacabana and Huatajata via the Sun Islands on the lake also, while you can travel by helicopter from Cuzco to Machu Picchu, roundtrip about US$175 for the 35 min ride each way.

FOOD AND RESTAURANTS

Peruvian cuisine is imaginative and rich, but unless you like your food very spicy, make sure you say *"No muy picante, por favor"* to the waiter; *aji* (pepper) seems to be used with almost reckless abandon. Try *ceviche de corvina*, uncooked sea bass marinated in lemon juice, hot peppers, onions, corn, and sweet potatoes. Or you might prefer *chupe de camarones*, a soup made of potatoes, milk, shrimp, eggs, and pepper while *sopa a la criolla* is pleasantly spicy. *Anticuchos* are a must; beef hearts, beef, fish, or chicken livers, skewered and broiled and dipped in a piquant sauce, a sort of Peruvian version of shish kebab. If you feel like a feast, order a *pachamanca*, which consists of chicken, pork, sweet potatoes, and yuca cooked in a pit over hot stones. Local delicacies include *rocoto relleno* (stuffed peppers), *palta rellena* (avocado stuffed with salad of chicken) and *tomate relleno* (stuffed tomato)—**Las Trece Monedas** (536

Ancash) is one of the loveliest restaurants on the continent: a charming, well-furnished colonial mansion, with a cobblestone courtyard where you will find some of the city's smartest shops. Have a drink in the sitting room before going in to enjoy the cuisine. French-Swiss and Creole specialties. Another fine creole restaurant is **Jose Antonio** (Monteagudo 200) in San Isidro. Also, **La Chasse a la Licorne,** done with mirrors and featuring excellent cuisine—very expensive. **Tambo de Oro** (Belén 1066) is the fanciest restaurant in town; a magnificently converted hacienda; there are five elegant dining rooms and a cocktail lounge, very expensive. The moderately priced **Chalet Suisse** (Colmena 560), across from the Hotel Crillón, is casual and fun; it serves Swiss specialties and first-class Peruvian dishes. Their cheese fondue is especially good—also reasonably priced. Opposite the Hotel Gran Bolivar, on Plaza San Martin, you will find **El Cortijo,** which is highly recommended for steaks and chicken Argentinian style, while **La Caleta** (Dionisio Derteano 126), in the San Isidro district, specializes in seafood. Also in San Isidro, the **Acquarium Room** of the Country Club has excellent cuisine and a dance orchestra. Downstairs at **Giannino** (R Torrico 899) there is a café-style restaurant where a meal for four, including wine, will not cost more than 8,000 sol. Start off with the *fondo alcachofas con camarones*—artichoke hearts stuffed with fresh shrimp and covered in tomato sauce. Upstairs, the menu is far more expansive and the prices higher. You might like **Raymondi** (Avenida Miro Quesda 110), which is reasonable for *churrasco* (steak), *corvina* and chicken. There are many good restaurants in the suburbs of San Isidro and Miraflores. **Carlin** (Avenida La Paz 644, Miraflores) has quality food and is located in a converted old house. **Periple** (Malecon de la Marina 450) is excellent and expensive, as is the **Ebony 56** at the Todos Shopping Center (Las Begonias 730) in San Isidro. **Cafe de Paris** (Colmena 722) offers good French (and Peruvian) fare. There are also many good Chinese restaurants in Lima—all prefaced by the word *Chifa:* the **Chifa Lung Fung** (Avenida Pan-americana, San Isidro) is a Chinese pagoda complete with quiet gardens and ponds. **La Granja Azul,** at the El Pueblo Hyatt 10 miles from the center of town along the Central Highway, is the most famous restaurant in Peru; make sure that you rent a taxi for the round trip, or you may find yourself stranded.

Dinner for one in an expensive restaurant will cost about 4,200 soles; in a medium-priced one, 3,000 soles, and in an inexpensive one, about 1,200 soles. If you fancy a snack, very popular are the **Goyesca,** a café-confitería on Plaza San Martin; **Rucaray,** a sandwich and soda-fountain-type restaurant on Jirón de la Unión; the **Café Continental, Café Europa,** and **Willy's Soda Fountain,** all on Unión; and the **Todos** snack bar in the San Isidro Shopping Center. If you are in a more sophisticated mood, go to the tea rooms under the stained-glass dome at the **Hotel Gran Bolivar.**

DRINKING TIPS

The *pisco sour* looks innocent, but is potent. Made from the local grape brandy with the white of an egg, lemon juice, and crushed ice, and served with a sprinkling of cinnamon, it will take you by surprise. Other *pisco* concoctions are the *chilcano* (*pisco* and ginger ale), *capitán* (*pisco* and Vermouth), and *algarrobina* (*pisco* and *algarrobina* syrup). Peruvian wines will remind you of a very ordinary French table wine, about 1,800 soles and up per bottle. Imported wines and liquor are also available. *Chicha morada* is a soft drink made from purple corn, whereas *chicha de jora* is a kind of beer made from fermented but not distilled corn. Women should keep to hotel bars and cocktail lounges; they are not usually welcome in street bars.

ENTERTAINMENT

Movie-going is by far the most popular form of evening entertainment in Lima; there are many excellent movie houses, including the Tacna, Metro, City Hall, Le Paris, Teatro Central, El Pacifico, Alcázar, and Roma, where first-run English language movies are shown with original soundtracks. The **National Symphony Orchestra** gives concerts with visiting conductors and soloists (also ballet) at the Teatro Municipal (Jirón Ica 323), and during the summer there are open-air concerts at the **Campo de Marte,** with free seats for 10,000 people. Opera, drama, and ballet are performed at the **Teatro Municipal** (Ica 355) and the **Teatro Segura** (Plazuela del Teatro). The **Amauta Arena** (Chacra Rios, Avenida Venezuela) offers programs ranging from Peruvian festivals to circuses and even the Moscow Ballet. There are several small, and usually good, Peruvian theatrical groups in Lima and especially in the suburb of Miraflores where theater-cafés abound.

Although many Limeños prefer to entertain lavishly at home, there are several night spots. The **Lima-Sheraton** has several orchestras and a floor show along with dinner and dancing, and both the **Grill Room** at the Hotel Gran Bolívar and the **Sky Room** of the Hotel Crillón are attractive and expensive society haunts. You can also enjoy dinner and dancing at the **Country Club Acquarium. The Unicorn** (Paseo de la República 3030) is the best discothèque in Lima, but many young people also go to the **Sunset Club** in San Isidro, which is dark, romantic, and usually crowded; **Percy's, Jumbo 747, La Miel,** and **Johann Sebastian Bar.** Also popular is the intimate **Le Popol** (Avenida Canaval 198, San Isidro). **Negro-Negro,** on Nicolás de Piérola 955, is small and intimate, and there are Peruvian floor shows at the **Embassy Club** (Carabaya 815) and at **El Chalán** (Avenida Limatambo).

SHOPPING

Store hours are usually 10am to 1pm and 3pm to 7pm, Mon-Sat. Best buys are alpaca fluffy hats, slippers, mufflers, and stoles in natural brown and beige—beautifully soft and costing about 1,200 soles; inexpensive handwoven wool fabrics; heavy wool ponchos in oranges and deep reds, which look marvelous in midi length; and fur rugs and heavy handloomed wool rugs in brilliant colors which can be used as bed covers or wall hangings, depending on size and quality.

You will find many tourist shops along **Jirón Unión,** between Plaza de Armas and Plaza San Martin, and you must go to **Casa Tahuantinsuyo** (Colmena 661), and to **Casa Inca** (Colmena 714). For fine gems, silver, and gold shop at **H Stern** in the Hotel Bolivar. **Vierlinger,** on Plaza de Armas, has unusual modern designs in Peruvian silver. **Casa Mas** has some inexpensive and attractively designed silver items, while **La Gran Via** has a number of attractive boutiques including **Mabex,** especially good for sweaters. There are high-quality cotton and linen goods with Inca and pre-Inca designs at **Silvania Prints** (Colmena 727); objets d'art of Indian inspiration at **Graceila Laffi** (Plaza Mexico); and leather goods at **Pedro P Diaz** (Unión 415). If you enjoy browsing around for antiques and reproductions, **Galeria Pitta** (Miraflores, Pasaje Porvenir) and **Casa Paracas** (Jirón Unión 713) are the places to go. For handicrafts, the best shop in Lima is **Huamanqaqa** (Jirón Unión 1041), just off Plaza San Martin—expensive, but worth it for its quality and taste. Or you might try the **EPPA,** Empresa Peruana de Promoción Artesanal (Avenida Orrantia 610, San Isidro), a handicraft-marketing cooperative or the **Art Center** (Avenida Ricardo Parma 246) in the suburb of Miraflores. Some of the best shopping values are to be found at the **Centro Artesanal de Pueblo Libre,** where Indian families offer a variety of alpaca, copper, silver and gold jewelry, leatherware, handicraft items, mostly handmade. The best market in the capital is the **Mercado Central** (Huallaga 650). Bargain hard: even in shops with fixed prices bargaining is expected, and the price will almost always be dropped by at least 10%, maybe as much as 30%. In markets keep an eye out for pickpockets.

SPORTS

Horse races are held at the **Hipódromo de Monterrico** on Saturday and Sunday afternoons and on Tuesday and Thursday evenings. Bullfights can be seen at the **Acho Bull Ring** on Sunday afternoons from January to March; during the **October Fair,** from 15 October to 30 November, there are bullfights on both Saturdays and Sundays with top Spanish and Mexican *toreros.* There is cockfighting at the **Coliseo de Gallos Sandia** (Sandia 150), soccer at the **Estadio Naciónal,** polo at the **Club Villa** and the **Lima Polo and Hunt Club,** boxing at **Luna Park.** There are facilities for tennis and golf; the finest courses in Lima are at the **Lima Golf Course** and the **Los Inkas Club**—you must obtain a guest card from a member. Miraflores has a bowling club. There are pools at the mountain resort of **Chaclacayo** (20 miles east of Lima) where you can swim during the winter, while during the summer the Pacific Ocean is inviting. Little *cabañas* can be rented by the hour at beach resorts like **Lobo de Mar** and **Herradura,** among others. Surfing on the beaches of Lima ranks along with the best in Hawaii—boards are for rent from the **Waikiki Club** (invitation necessary). The **International Surfing Championships** are held every February. Deep-sea fishing is incomparable off **Chorrillos, Pucusana, Ancón,** and especially off **Cabo Blanco** (Talara). Riding is popular, particularly for sightseeing trips, in the mountain valleys near Huancayo in Central Peru. The charge for several hours horseback riding is about US$20. Lake Titicaca and the rivers flowing into it abound with

945

salmon and trout, but facilities are limited, and information should be obtained in advance of a trip. Partridge, wild duck, pigeon, small deer, and hare are to be found in regions not too far from Lima. If you are a keen mountaineer, you will find the **Andean Cordilleras** irresistible; there are a number of clubs for enthusiasts, including the **Club Andino Peruano, Club Andinista Cordillera Blanca,** and the **Club Peruano de Alta Montana.**

WHAT TO SEE

Lima and Nearby

Lima was named **City of the Kings** and constructed deliberately to exclude all Inca influence. The result today is that juxtaposed against the skyscrapers of the 20th-century is the old quarter, still rich in all its Spanish colonial architecture. The adjacent port town of Callao was developed for the transhipment of gold and silver.

As with many other countries in South America, the main points of interest lie outside the capital, though there are sights in Lima which you should not miss. In the heart of the old town lies the **Plaza de Armas;** although most of the buildings surrounding the historic sight are of modern construction, their facades have kept the intricately carved wooden balconies and arcades of Spanish colonial architecture. On one side of the Plaza is the impressive white **Palacio de Gobierno,** the official residence and office of the President. Every day at 12:45 and about 6pm you can see the **Changing of the Guard**—red-and-black-uniformed guards with gleaming Roman-style helmets doing a slow, unaccompanied goosestep around the Palace courtyard. In a glass coffin within the **Cathedral** lie the remains of Francisco Pizarro, the great conquistador, who founded the city in 1535 and was murdered in 1541. Next to the Cathedral you will see the **Archbishop's Palace** with its latticework balcony. You must also visit the **Torre Tagle Palace,** a beautiful colonial mansion built in 1735, which now houses the Ministry of Foreign Affairs; the building nearby where the Court of Inquisition sat until 1820; **San Marcos,** the oldest university in the Americas, founded in 1551; the **Puente de Piedra** (Bridge of Stone), 530 feet long, built in the early 17th century; and the churches of **Santo Domingo** and **San Pedro.** The most beautiful church in Lima is the baroque **San Francisco Church,** on Jirón Lampa, with its hand-carved ceilings, gold-leaf altar, and mysterious catacombs; the adjoining monastery, which admits male visitors only, is famous for its tilework and paneled ceiling. Then take a stroll through **Chinatown** on Avenida Abancay.

Also worth a visit are the **Museum of Anthropology and Archeology,** which details much of the art and history of the earlier civilizations and where you can see mummies and over 80,000 other archeological finds; the **National Museum of Art** (Paseo Colón), covering 5,000 years of Peruvian culture from the Paracas civilization to the present day; the **Peruvian Gold Collection;** the **Museum of the Republic;** the **Institute of Contemporary Art;** the **Archeological Museum;** and the **Natural History Museum.**

Also worth the visit is the **Rafael Larco Herrera Museum** (Av. Bolívar 1515) with its famous collection of pre-Columbian artifacts dating to 2,000 BC and including more modern items up to the Inca era. The building housing the collection makes this definitely worth the detour.

The **October Fair** is a colorful traditional holiday lasting well into November. There are fiestas and street processions (the largest of which is that of **El Señor de los Milagros,** on 17, 18, and 28 October), and after nightfall thousands of candles flicker in the darkness. During the fiesta, street stalls sell a specialty known as the *Turrón de Doña Pepa,* an almond nougat candy.

Pacahacámac lies 20 miles south of Lima in the Lurín Valley. Here you will see the ruins of a sacred city dating back almost to 900 BC; the immense **Temple of the Sun,** built by the Inca Pachacutec in the 14th century; the reconstructed **Temple of the Virgins;** and the remains of the extraordinary Inca irrigation works and reservoirs. **Puruchuco,** 5 miles east, is where an authentically reconstructed village depicts early Peruvian life; don't miss it. And if you want to take a picture of a llama, here is your chance—there is a special corral of llamas. During the summer, Indian dance festivals are held after nightfall.

Huallamarca: Right in the heart of the exclusive San Isidro residential suburb stands a remarkable pyramid nearly 100 feet high and dating back to 100 BC. **Cajamarquilla,** 10 miles east of the capital, is a mysterious fortified city, abandoned even before the Incas' arrival. **Chosica,** 25 miles east of Lima, is a delightful winter resort where the **Fiesta de la Cruz** is held in May. **Ancón** is now an elegant beach resort, half-an-hour's drive from Lima. **Callao,** the main port of Lima, lies 7 miles from the city. Here you must see the star-shaped masonry stronghold of **Real Felipe,** built between 1747 and 1772 as a defense against the English and Dutch pirates. Early in the morning or late in the afternoon the pier is busy with fishing boats; you must have at least one meal in a dockside fish restaurant there.

South and East of Lima

Huancayo lies at an altitude of 10,690 feet. No planes fly here, but the rail journey over the Andes is really exciting—round trip about $12. If you go over the weekend, which you should, you will see the **Sunday Fair;** at dawn the Indians come in from the surrounding countryside, laden with alpaca rugs, hats and slippers, food, pottery, woven basket gourds, and jewelry. A tremendous amount of serious bargaining goes on, most of it almost in silence. Other local points of interest are the **Convent of Santa Rosa de Ocopa** and the **Lagoon of Paca.**

Cuzco is one of the prettiest and most fascinating cities of South America, a self-contained little place with an air of friendliness. This was the capital of Tahuantinsuyo, the Inca Empire, when the Spaniards arrived, and is now one of Peru's leading tourist attractions and the center of an important archeological region. The city is a mixture of Spanish and Inca civilizations; many of its streets and buildings are constructed over old Inca stone walls of remarkable craftsmanship—the large stones are so perfectly joined, without the use of mortar, that not even the thinnest object can be slipped in between them. The **Church of Santo Domingo** was built by the Spanish over the walls of Coricancha, the great Inca Temple of the Sun, while the **Cathedral** on the **Plaza de Armas,** with its exquisite altar of silver, rests over the Palace of Inca Viracocha. The Great Monstrance of the Cathedral is a jeweled masterpiece of pearls and emeralds. You must also see the church of **La Merced,** built in 1534; the **Archeological Museum,** with its Inca and pre-Inca metalwork, pottery, weaving, mummies, and successfully trepanned skulls; the new **Museum of Art** at the Archbishop's Palace; and the curious and imposing fortress amphitheater of **Saqsayhuaman,** standing guard over the city. Cuzco is 332 miles and only 55 minutes by air from Lima. Stay at the **El Libertador** (from US$52 double), or the **Picoaga,** a converted monastery (from US$43 double) or **Savoy Hotel,** Avenida de Sol 954 (from US$50 double). You can also stay at a number of smaller pensions. But make sure you reserve well in advance—and take things easy when you first arrive; Cuzco lies at an altitude of 11,444 feet.

Machu Picchu, the "Lost City of the Incas," lies 70 miles from Cuzco. Very little is known about this mountain redoubt, save that it was built by the Incas, though whether for ceremonial reasons, or as a military stronghold, no one knows. The Spanish never found it, for it is so ingeniously located on a narrow saddle of almost inaccessible mountains that it remained virtually invisible from the valley floor. In the middle of a semitropical jungle and at an altitude of 8,200 feet, there are more than 200 buildings, including baths, temples, altars, and houses, all intact except for the straw roofs, which have rotted, and all connected by endless stairways carved out of solid rock. For centuries it was hidden under fern and bush until it was discovered in 1911 by Hiram Bingham, onetime senator from Connecticut. If you want to see Machu Picchu at its finest, get off the train at the first hydroelectric dam, walk up the steep hillside to the ruins of **Huiñay-Huayna,** and camp the night there. Very early next morning, walk along the old Inca road which will bring you to the military lookout over the city; the ruins of Machu Picchu in the dawn mists, surrounded by the beautiful Urubamba gorge and the snow-capped mountains in the distance, have an almost mystical effect which is never to be forgotten. Stay at the **Machu Picchu Hotel,** Conde de Superunda 298 (from US$19 double); reservations should be made well in advance. Visits to Cuzco and Machu Picchu are in themselves worth a trip to Peru.

Southeast of Cuzco by road or rail through the Andes (journey time about 12 hours) are the Peruvian *altiplano* and **Puno,** on Lake Titicaca, the highest navigable lake in the world. The streets of Puno are full of colorfully dressed Indian people—the women wear long skirts and bowler hats. During fiesta time (4 November to 2 February), the town is alive with music and dancing. From here you can visit the pre-Inca stone tower-tombs of **Sillustani;** the beautiful churches of **Juli** and **Pomata;** and the floating reed islands of **Los Uros.** The famous steamer trip across the lake, at an elevation of 12,664 feet, is made only at night, but there are daytime trips by hydrofoil for 8,499 sol across the lake to **Huatajata,** Bolivia, via the Island of the Sun. In Puno stay at the **Puno Tourista Hotel** (from US$15 double) or the new **Tambo Titicaca** on the shores of the lake; make sure you have reservations before leaving Lima.

Arequipa is the second city of Peru, in the shadow of the perfectly shaped El Misti volcano (19,200 feet). This picturesque city of white volcanic stone buildings lies in beautiful countryside. The air is clean and dry. The many churches, with their exceptionally fine carvings in baroque style, will delight you: **San Agustín, Santo Domingo, San Francisco,** the **Compañia,** and the **Monastery of Santa Teresa.** The **Convent of Santa Catalina,** with its lovely church, is one of Arequipa's main tourist attractions: a miniature city inhabited only by cloistered nuns and their attendants for 400 years, it is now open to the public. The Convent's museum houses one of the finest collections of religious art on the continent. You must also see the mineral springs of **Jesús, Yura,** and **Socosani** and the **Museum of Arequipa.** This city is only 70 minutes by air south of Lima, but if you want to see the barren coastal desert and its green valley oasis, then you should take the 12- to 16-hour journey by road along the Pan American Highway. Hotels: the **Crismar** (from US$18 double); **El Presidente** (from US$21 double); **Turistas Arequipa** (from US$12 double).

North of Lima

Huaraz is the chief town in the valley of Callejón de Huaylas, one of the beauty spots of Peru; it will take you about six hours over the highway to reach the valley by car. Badly damaged in the 1970 earthquake, extensive rebuilding has taken place. The former picturesque old churches and buildings have been replaced by modern homes, but the beauty of this valley has been untouched. From here you can visit the pre-Columbian ruins of **Chavin** and **Paramonga** and the springs of **Monterrey** and **Chancos.**

Trujillo, the third largest city in Peru, lies 343 miles from Lima. A quiet, dignified Spanish colonial town, its main attraction is the nearby ruins of the Chimu city of **Chan Chan,** covering an area of 14 square miles and once the center of a great pre-Incan civilization. While in Trujillo you must go to the **Archeological Museum** of the University, and take a swim at the **Huanchaco Beach.** Hotels: **Hotel El Golf** (from US$32 double), the newest, and **Turista** (doubles from US$11). **Cajamarca** is the town where Pizarro, the Spanish conquistador, waited to meet Atahualpa, the Inca ruler of the north, supposedly to become allies. When the Inca refused to swear allegiance to the King of Spain, many of his followers were slaughtered and he was captured alive and imprisoned. See the **Cuarto del Rescate,** a room said to have been filled with gold from floor to ceiling for Atahualpa's ransom and the place where he was traitorously garroted under orders from the Spaniards after the ransom was paid. See also the **Plaza** where the Incas were massacred by the Spaniards. Other sights include the **Temple of Belén,** the ruins of **Otuzco,** and the Inca Baths.

Iquitos is a thriving commercial city and a busy port in the heart of the Amazon jungle. The great Amazon itself is formed nearby by the merging of the Marañon and Ucayali Rivers. Expeditions are organized daily into the tropical jungle (contact the Pan Am office in Lima for tour operators). Yagua tribesmen still use curare-tipped darts, blown through a long *cerbatana*, to capture wild monkeys, which taste like delicately smoked turkey. Hunting expeditions can be arranged through local agencies, and you can go on a boat trip to the tributaries of the Amazon, visiting Indian villages and orchid farms, or take a ship down the Amazon on your way back home to Europe or the USA. It will take you about 1 hour 40 minutes to fly from Lima to Iquitos. In Iquitos, accommodations are to be found at the **Holiday Inn** (from US$35 double) and **Turistas Iquitos** (from US$20 double). And then there are the various excursions into the jungle including **Amazon Safari Camp** (one night from $85, two nights from $115), **Explorama Lodge** (3-day package including 50 mile boat ride, from US$150 pp) and **Explornapo Camp** (5-day package with 95 mile boat excursion, from US$400 pp).

SOURCES OF FURTHER INFORMATION

Pan Am agents: Aero Rep, Rufino Torrico 889, Lima, or any Pan Am office around the world; official Government Tourist Office, **Dirección General de Turismo**, Santo Toribio 250, San Isidro; **The Peruvian Consulate General**, 10 Rockefeller Plaza, New York, NY 10020; 52 Sloane Street, London SWI.

Suriname

WHAT'S SPECIAL

Just slightly smaller than the state of Wisconsin, Suriname is one of the more unusual nations of South America in that it shares—along with Guyana and French Guiana—the distinction of being one of the three lands formerly colonized by northern Europeans. In the case of Suriname it was the Dutch.

What makes Suriname doubly interesting is the fact that it is only here that the West African tribal practices can be seen in their pristine state. The customs, religious worship of ancestors and jungle spirits, tribal lore and laws—extremely strict, concerning marriage—together with the matrilinear descent of tribal chief and priest, all these are still to be found as practiced by the Bushnegroes.

Separated from neighboring Guyana and French Guiana by large rivers, Suriname is on the northeast coast of the South American continent with some 230 miles of coastline. The western section of the coast contains an extensive land reclamation project, with the kind of dykes and canals for which the Dutch are famous. An independent republic since 1975, Suriname maintains close ties with the Netherlands, which obtained the territory from England in 1667 in exchange for the island of New Amsterdam (Manhattan). The population mix includes Javanese, Chinese, European, Middle Easterners, Hindu, and Creole, plus the Bushnegroes and Amerindians. Suriname is a major exporter of bauxite and timber, and the 600-square-mile Van Blommenstein Meer (or lake) provides hydroelectric power for industry.

COUNTRY BRIEFING

Size: 62,500 square miles   **Population:** 350,000
Capital: Paramaribo   **Capital Population:** 100,000

Climate: Tropical, rains from mid-May through mid-August, lesser rains from November through February. September hottest, January coolest. Average temperature = 80°F.

Weather in Paramaribo: Lat N5°49′; Alt 12 ft

Temp (°F)	Jan	Feb	Mar	Apr	May	Jun	Jul	Aug	Sep	Oct	Nov	Dec
Av Low	70°	71°	72°	73°	73°	73°	73°	73°	73°	73°	72°	71°
Av High	85°	85°	85°	86°	86°	86°	87°	89°	91°	91°	89°	86°
Days no rain	13	15	17	14	18	17	11	17	21	22	18	12

Government: Independent republic. The parliament, consisting of 39 members, is elected by universal suffrage.

Language: The official language is Dutch. English is widely spoken. Spanish, Javanese, Hindi, and Chinese are spoken by people of those origins. Surinamese, or *taki-taki*, is the native, unofficial language.

Religion: Mixed: 27% Hindus, 20% Muslims, 22% Roman Catholics. Also Moravians, Lutherans, and others.

Currency: Suriname guilder (or florin). 100 cents = 1 guilder.

	10¢	25¢	SG 1	SG 5	SG 10	SG 25	SG 50	SG 100
US (dollars, cents)	.06	.14	.56	2.80	5.60	14.01	28.01	56.02
UK (pounds, pence)	.03	.07	.27	1.34	2.67	6.68	13.36	26.72

Public Holidays:

New Year's Day, 1 Jan	Labor Day, 1 May
Day of the Revolution, 25 Feb	Freedom Day, 1 July
Pre-Lenten Carnival	Independence Day, 25 Nov
Good Friday	Christmas, 25/26 Dec
Easter Monday	

Hindu and Muslim holy days also observed.

HOW TO GET THERE

Flying time to Paramaribo's Zanderij Airport from Miami is 4½ hours; from Caracas, 2 hours; from Georgetown, ¾ hour. Time in Suriname: GMT−3 hours 30 minutes.

REQUIREMENTS FOR ENTRY AND CUSTOMS REGULATIONS

Valid passport; round-trip ticket; smallpox and cholera vaccination certificates if coming from an infected area. Duty-free allowance: 400 cigarettes or 100 cigars or 200 cigarillos or 500 grams of tobacco; 2 liters spirits and 4 liters wine; 50 grams perfume and 1 liter eau de cologne. No limitations on the amount of foreign currency taken into the country. A permit is required for taking out certain antiques.

AIRPORT INFORMATION

The International Airport for Paramaribo is Zanderij, 30 miles from the city center. Buses are available (fare SF10.), but you may have difficulty in finding a taxi. The taxi fare to the city center is SF35-40. Porters are tipped SF0.50 per piece of baggage. There is a departure tax of SF10. The airport has a duty-free shop.

ACCOMMODATIONS

Hotel bills include a 10-15% service charge. If you need help in finding accommodations, get in touch with the **Tourist Development Board** (Kerkplein 10—tel: 73733). Hotels in Paramaribo:

Rates are in US$ for a double/twin room with bath or shower

Ambassador, Plaza de la Independencia (from $40)

Krasnapolsky Paramaribo, Dominestraat (from $48)

Lashley Hotel, Watermolenstrasse (from $28)

Riverclub, 5 miles from city at Leonsberg (from $28)

Torarica, Rietbergplein 1 (from $51)

All hotels centrally located, except as indicated.

USEFUL INFORMATION

Banks: Open from 8-12 Mon-Fri, 8-11 Sat.

Mail: Stamps available from post offices, hotel porters.

Telephone Tips: Few public telephones. Useful numbers:

Tourist Information 73733	**Police** 71111 or 77777
Operator 000	**Fire Department** 99999 or
Directories 008	73333
	Accidents 99933

Newspapers: English-language magazines and newspapers are available, and there are complimentary ANP tourist bulletins in hotels.

Tipping: In restaurants it is customary to leave a tip of 10% unless a service charge of 10% has already been included in the check. Porters are tipped SF0.50 per suitcase. No need to tip taxi drivers, hotel porters, or chambermaids.

Electricity: 110-115 volts 60 cycles AC. Plug prongs are round instead of flat, so a converter is necessary.

Laundry: 24-hour dry-cleaning service available.

Hairdressing: There are salons in Paramaribo; man's haircut from SF4, shampoo from SF7, and set from SF15.

Photography: Equipment and film are available in major towns. Black and white film will cost SF3 (20 exposures) and will take 2 days to develop; color film, SF5.50 (20 exposures) and 7 days to develop.

Clubs: Rotary, Lions, Round Table, Jaycees.

Rest Rooms: Not easy to find and can be rather substandard. Women, *Dames;* men, *Heren.*

Health: English-speaking doctors are plentiful. Good selection of pharmaceutical goods in drugstores, but these and toiletries are expensive. Water safe to drink.

TRANSPORTATION

There is a bus service in the city and its suburbs, and unmetered taxis are readily available, but agree about the fare in advance. For a rental car, go to City Taxi, Hoge Straat 39. Traffic drives on the left, and conditions are chaotic; beware of mopeds and dogs. Chauffeur-driven cars with English-speaking drivers are available. For private or group tours, contact Ram's Tour & Travel Service, Neumanpad 30; STINASU, C. Jongbawstraat 10; or De heer Nijon, Boni Tours, Wagenwegstraat 10.

Railroad enthusiasts will enjoy the old-fashioned train service, but there is a good long-distance bus service along the east-west highway from Paramaribo to Moengo, Albina, and Nickerie. Suriname Airways (SLM) is the domestic airline. Ferries are used to cross main rivers, and you might enjoy traveling upstream across the rapids in a canoe with an outboard motor.

FOOD AND RESTAURANTS

International cuisine is available at the larger hotels, often with a Dutch flavor. The local cuisine is principally Dutch and Dutch Indonesian, Creole and Chinese. Local specialties include *pom* (a chicken pastry), *moksi alesi* (a rice dish with chicken or steak), *soto* (a soup of peas and potato with shredded chicken) plus *pindasoep met Tom Tom* (peanut soup with mashed plantain). A number of these are available at the hotels, or at the charming **Park Club** which overlooks Independence Square and the river, the **Hola Cafe** in the Krasnapolsky Hotel building, and at **Roline's** restaurant. **Yvonne's** is excellent for international and Surinamese food. Because the nation is rich in agricultural produce—Suriname has the largest automated rice farm in the world—there are plenty of vegetables and fruit, including oranges, varieties of plantain and banana, plus fish and fat sweet shrimp. Quality beef is still imported.

In Suriname it's possible to experience the glory of colonial Holland in the banquet-style *rijsttafel* (literally, rice table), the 64-dish Indonesian buffet. According to old hands, the hotter the day, the hotter the condiments and food should be. It's widely served. For Indonesian specialties, there's *Sarinah,* and the local Parbo pilsen beer goes well, as does the local water which is surprisingly good. There are several good Indian *roti* shops which serve this specialty, a spicy paratha-like bread with which vegetables and meats are eaten. For Chinese food **Iwan** is a perennial favorite, while **Roline's** serves authentic Surinamese food. Other places to eat in Paramaribo include **Chindy's Soda Fountain,** the **Deli, Orlando**—good for lunch, **Njoeksang,** while the **Coconut Club**—an authentic pub—is open in the evening. People rise early and breakfast is served from about 6:30am until 10, lunch from 11:45 and 3:15pm, while dinner is from 6:30-11:30pm.

DRINKING TIPS

There are a number of refreshing soft drinks, including tamarind syrup, *orgeade* (extract of almonds), and cool root beer called *gemberbier.* Two locally made alcoholic drinks well worth a try are Black Cat rum and Mang Bai, derived from sugar cane. A whisky and soda will cost you SF2. Popular drinking spots, especially with young people, are the **Spanhoek Cafeteria, Chindy's Soda Fountain,** and **Orlando's Coffee Shop.**

ENTERTAINMENT

As in many slightly-off-the-beaten-track places around the world, much of the best evening entertainment takes place around the better local hotels. Paramaribo is no exception. There are casinos at both the **Ambassador** (formerly Suriname Palace) and **Torarica,** plus nightclubs with entertainers and shows. **Riverclub** also has shows, music and dancing, the **Blue Bell** disco, and a new dance-nightclub called the **Odysee. The Royal** is also a nightclub. Other discos, of which there are many, include **Eximium, Numero Uno.** Javanese dancing is also available. There are a number of theatrical groups including the venerable Thalia group, founded in 1839. Several cinemas show English language movies. Check the weekly list of local events published by the Suriname Tourist Board for details, available at all hotels and tourist offices.

SHOPPING

Stores in Paramaribo are open Mon-Thurs from 7-4:30; Fri 7-1, 5-8; Sat 7-1. Best buys are dress fabrics (you can have a custom-made suit delivered within 48 hours or even less)—go to **Het Manifakturen Paleis** on Sivaplein, or **Brokopondo** or **Ramaker's,** both on Zwartenhovenburgstraat. Also good are the wood carvings made by the Bushnegroes. Other souvenirs are wooden figurines, Amerindian seed necklaces, weapons, hammocks, trays. You can browse for these at **Michely's, Ruby's,** or **Sjiem Fat** on Maagdenstraat and at many other shops. For Javanese-style bamboo and wickerwork, go to **Surindo** on Ladesmastraat. Large department stores are **Kersten's, Kirpalani's,** and on Maagdenstraat, **J. Nassief & Co.** Bargaining is not customary in stores but a must in markets.

SPORTS

Soccer and basketball are the most popular sports, but there are also facilities for cricket, volleyball, tennis, and cycling. Golf is available at the **Paramaribo Golf Club.** All sports clubs welcome visitors when introduced by a member.

WHAT TO SEE

Twelve miles up the Suriname river from the Atlantic Ocean, Paramaribo is another of the more unusual capital cities of the world. It enjoys an incredible mix of cultures and people, and some incredibly colorful costumes—including the koto-missie dress and headgear of the black women—are still worn. The kerchiefs are tied quipulike to express information.

For just watching people, early morning at the **Central Market** is as good a place to start as any, or the ferry at the waterfront as people come to town. **Independence Square** (or **Plaza de la Independencia**) is incongruously European in style, save for the reminders of the tropics in trees and birds. The government offices are here.

The restored Palm Gardens and **Fort Zeelandia** (which now houses the **Suriname Museum**) have excellent early prints, drawings, plus numerous local artifacts, and the **Botanical Gardens** are worth noting. Adjacent the gardens is a Javanese-style village, and experimental sections where cocoa, citrus, and coffee are being grown.

One of the more exciting adventures to be found in Suriname is a journey back in time, taken by making the trip up river into the bush. Here one can find virtual facsimile copies of the culture and people of the West African villages, once ravaged by slavers. These are the settlements of the Bushnegro, descendants of early slaves who escaped to the jungle. The people themselves are under government protection, and have adjusted to field anthropologists and to tourism.

It is possible to make a full day excursion to **Albina** and **Bigiston** by car and dugout canoe, which also includes a ferry ride across the Suriname river, and the Commewijne river too. Bigiston actually means Big Stone and in addition to the Bushnegroes there are also native Indians. En route a voodoo Fire Dance may sometimes be seen at Neger Kreek, near Albina. For the more adventurous a number of safari arrangements are available, including the three day (two night) jungle trip up the Saramacca River which includes a visit to an old gold mining town—you can pan for gold—and piranha fishing with overnights at the Jungle Plaza resthouse. There's a four day trip to **Raleigh Falls**, itself a photographer's paradise, where there's some excellent tarpon fishing to be had. Another adventure is the journey to **Stoelman's Island**, and the 'Apoema and Granhola Falls. **Brownsberg Nature Park** is 2½ hours by car from Paramaribo, or 6 scenic hours by colorful antique wood-burning steam train. In this pristine rain forest is an extraordinary bird sanctuary, where ornithologists have documented and identified some 600 species of birds. Trails lead to waterfalls, creeks where gold can be panned, and lookouts offering panoramic views of the interior. Accommodations are available at the **Mazaroni Lodge** with its sweeping view of **Afobaka,** supposedly the largest manmade lake in the world. There are numerous opportunities for scientific study, for Suriname is the only nation in South America with a comprehensive national program of conservation and research. Of particular interest is the project to save the turtles, including the rare Karet, the hawksbill and green, plus the legendary Bigisanti beach turtle (also known as the 8-sided leatherback).

Other excursions include the visit to the open-air museum at **Nieuw Amsterdam,** half an hour from Paramaribo; to the ruins of the **Beracha Ve Shalom Synagogue** and its cemetery at Joden Savanna; or the bauxite mines and the port of **Moengo.** In the neighboring settlements you can see Bushnegroes working on their beautiful carvings (they charge SF0.50 for each photo you take of them).

SOURCES OF FURTHER INFORMATION

Any **Pan Am** office around the world; **Suriname Tourist Development Board,** Kerkplein 10, Paramaribo; **Consulate General of Suriname,** One United Nations Plaza, New York, NY 10017.

Uruguay

WHAT'S SPECIAL

Uruguay is notable for its delightful capital, with beautiful beaches only 20 minutes from the central business district, and its 200 miles of coastal resorts. Vacationers from all over the continent, even from far-off Rio de Janeiro, flock to the "Riviera of South America" to enjoy comfortable hotels and casinos and dazzling sandy beaches where you can go yachting, surfing, water-skiing, and swimming or simply mingle with the "beautiful people" at Punta del Este. In the *estancias* in the interior of the country, the romantic and legendary gauchos roam the countryside rounding up cattle, or gallop after South American ñandúes with their *boleadoras*—heavy stone balls wrapped in leather—or relax against the *estancia* bar sipping the potent *grappa* or drinking *yerba mate* through a silver straw.

COUNTRY BRIEFING

Size: 68,536 square miles   **Population:** 3,100,000
Capital: Montevideo   **Capital Population:** 1,230,000
    Climate: Ideal. Summer days (from December to March) are beautifully warm, with cooling breezes from the sea. Temperatures hover around 80 degrees. Nights are mild and pleasant, with temperatures between 60° and 65°. Winters (June to September) are cool, but rarely does the thermometer fall below 40°, and there is rarely any snow. Best times to go are springtime, October-November, or January-February at the seaside.

Weather in Montevideo: Lat S34°33′; Alt 30 ft

Temp (°F)	Jan	Feb	Mar	Apr	May	Jun	Jul	Aug	Sep	Oct	Nov	Dec
Av Low	62°	61°	59°	53°	48°	43°	43°	43°	46°	49°	54°	59°
Av High	83°	82°	78°	71°	64°	59°	58°	59°	63°	68°	74°	79°
Days no rain	25	23	26	24	25	25	25	24	24	25	24	24

Government: Civil-Military government.

Language: Spanish. Some English, French, and German.

Religion: Roman Catholic. Other denominations represented.

Currency: New peso. 100 centesimos = 1 NP.

	5 NP	10 NP	50 NP	100 NP	500 NP	1,000 NP	5,000 NP	10,000 NP
US (dollars, cents	.47	.94	4.70	9.40	47.00	94.00	470.00	940.00
UK (pounds, pence)	.22	.45	2.25	4.49	22.46	44.92	224.61	449.23

Public Holidays:

New Years, 1 Jan

Epiphany, 6 Jan

Carnival, Mon & Tue preceding Ash Wednesday

Landing of the 33 Orientales, 19 Apr

Labor Day, 1 May

Battle of Las Piedras, 18 May

Birth of the hero Don José Gervasio Artigas, 19 June

Signing of the 1st Constitution, 18 July

Independence Day, 25 Aug

Discovery of America, 12 Oct

All Souls Day, 2 Nov

Immaculate Conception, 8 Dec

Christmas Day, 25 Dec

HOW TO GET THERE

Flying time to Montevideo, Carrasco Airport, from New York, is 11¼ hours, Buenos Aires, ¾ hour; Miami, 12 hours; Rio de Janeiro, 3¾ hours; and Caracas, 7¼ hours. Time in Uruguay: GMT−3.

REQUIREMENTS FOR ENTRY AND CUSTOMS REGULATIONS

Passport. A visa is not required of citizens of the US, the UK, Canada, and many European countries for stays of less than 3 months. An international vaccination certificate against smallpox is not required unless having visited an infected area within 14 days of arrival in Uruguay. It is advisable to carry passport for identification. If coming from an infected area, a vaccination certificate against cholera is required. Duty-free allowance: 400 cigarettes or 50 cigars, 2 liters of liquor. There are no restrictions on the amount of currency which may be brought in or taken out. Firearms, drugs, subversive or pornographic literature, and pork products cannot be brought into the country. Pets are allowed, but check with consulate for required forms.

AIRPORT INFORMATION

The International Airport for Montevideo is Carrasco, 13 miles from the city center. Only the airlines flying between Montevideo and Buenos

Aires, such as Pluna, have buses to downtown—buses run all day, and the fare is about US$2. Taxis are regularly available up to 11pm, and the fare to the heart of town is NP50. Airport departure tax is NP2 to LAFTA (Latin American Free Trade Association) nations, and NP4 elsewhere. There is a duty-free shop (not open to passengers in transit). Allow NP2 per piece of luggage at the airport.

ACCOMMODATIONS

Hotel rates in Uruguay are very reasonable, though higher in the summer months. Some hotels close down after 1 April. Hotels in Punta del Este charge 20% more than those in the capital, especially during Carnival Week (beginning on the Monday preceding Ash Wednesday) and the Semana de Turismo (which replaces Holy Week, the week preceding Easter Sunday). The Government Tourist Office is near the Hotel Lancaster in the Plaza Libertad and can help usually. Open weekdays 8am-8pm, Sat 9am-5pm, Sun 9am-12. Advance reservation is advisable throughout the year and absolutely essential for the summer months. Hotels in Montevideo, centrally located unless otherwise noted:

Rates are in US$ for a double/twin room with bath or shower

California, San José 1237/99 (from $42)

Casino Carrasco, Rep. Mejico s/n (from $44) 20 mins from downtown at beach

Columbia Palace, Reconquista 468 (from $46)

Cottage, Miraflores 1360 (from $80) Carrasco, 20 mins from downtown at beach

Crillón, Andes 1318 (from $43)

Gran Hotel America, Rio Negro 1330 (from $46)

Hotel Parque Casino, Rambla Wilson (from $44)

Iguazu, Ibicuy 1296 (from $42)

Lancaster, Plaza Libertad 1334 (from $43)

Libertador, Florida 1128 (from $43)

London Palace, Rio Negro 1278 (from $43)

Oxford, Paraguay 1286 (from $46)

Presidente, Avenida 18 de Julio 1038 (from $43)

Victoria Plaza, Plaza Independencia 759 (from $57)

USEFUL INFORMATION

Banks: Open 1-5 Mon-Fri. Foreign currency can be exchanged only at banks.

Mail: Stamps obtainable only in post offices or from *concierges*. For cables, go to Western Telegraph Co (Mercury House, Calle Cerrito 449) or All American Cables & Radio (Victoria Plaza Hotel).

Telephone Tips: Phones available in restaurants and cafés. You must deposit a 10-centavo coin to get a dial tone. Useful numbers in Montevideo:

Pan Am 980613

Airport Information 502261, extension 247

Special Information (weather, communications, etc) 214

First Aid 401111

Tourist Offices 916773 and 80509	British Hospital 409011
Tourist Information 905216 and 917394	Long Distance (International) Operator 218
Directory Inquiries 212	
Police 890	Time 6

Newspapers: The English-language *Buenos Aires Herald* is flown in each day.

Tipping: A tax and service charge of 10% upwards is included by hotels and restaurants supposedly as tips, but actually as wages for service employees. Therefore a further 10% tip is expected. Tip porters NP2 for each piece of luggage; taxi drivers, 10% of the fare or a minimum of NP1; hairdressers, 10% of the bill or a minimum of NP1; hotel porters, NP2 per suitcase; chambermaids, NP3 for each day spent at the hotel; museum guides, NP2 (except at Parliament House, where a tip will not be accepted). In cafés, tip about 15% of the bill. Movie ushers get a small tip—about NP.30.

Electricity: 220 volts 50 cycles AC throughout the country.

Laundry: Dry-cleaning and laundry services are readily available, and in Montevideo you can count on 24-hour service (dry-cleaning a suit, from NP8-10; laundering a shirt, from NP2).

Hairdressing: The Victoria Plaza Hotel has a very good salon, and you will not have any difficulty in finding a salon in Montevideo or Punta del Este (shampoo and set, from US$4-7; man's haircut, from US$2).

Photography: Equipment and film will be found only in Montevideo, Punta del Este, Salto, Paysandu, and Rivera though color film is in short supply. Black and white film takes 24 hours to be developed, color 3-5 days. Prices are moderate. (Color film, 20 exposures US$6.)

Clubs: Lions, Rotary, Junior Chamber of Commerce. The Golf Club, Automobile Club, and Yacht Club are open to visitors.

Babysitting: Services can be arranged through your hotel.

Rest Rooms: Can be difficult to find, but tea rooms *(confiterías)*, bars, and gas stations often have facilities. Women, *Ellas* or *Damas;* men, *Ellos* or *Caballeros.* There is no charge, but a tip is expected in ladies' rooms.

Health: Medical services are of a very high standard, and many doctors speak English. The British Hospital at Avenida Italia 2402 has a British matron and nurses. Most pharmaceutical goods are produced locally; neither these nor toiletries are expensive. Water and milk are safe in Montevideo, and you can enjoy fresh fruit and salads without fear. *Salus* and *Matutina* are excellent. If you do not want it carbonated, ask for *Agua sin gas.* For night-duty pharmacist call 214.

TRANSPORTATION

Bus and trolley-bus services cover the city and suburbs. Buses numbered 116, 117, 121, and 122 will get you to the beaches. Taxis are also readily available; hail one in the street—they have meters and there is an extra charge depending on the number of passengers. Taxis are still a good bargain. Night fares are 30% higher. You can rent a car from Sudamcar at Mercedes 908 for about $23 a day plus 12¢ a kilometer (Volkswagens,

US$18 daily plus 10¢ per kilometer). Gasoline is about US$4 a gallon, and a deposit of around US$90 will be required (plus gas), but you will probably find traffic conditions in Montevideo absolutely hair-raising— vehicles will stop suddenly, and there is no right of way at uncontrolled crossroads and intersections. If you want to play it safe, hire a chauffeur-driven car. A US$100 deposit is required, plus cost of gasoline, US$35 a day for driver, plus 12¢ per kilometer, and the driver's meals. English-speaking drivers are not easily available—best thing is to take an English-speaking guide with you, at an extra cost of about NP170-210 a day. Long-distance travel by rail is not recommended since trains are slower than buses (but far cheaper), though the new cars on the service to Punta del Este are very comfortable in first class, with good food available on board. The 85-mile journey takes just over two hours. Bus services, on the other hand, are first-class; Onda (Plaza Libertad—tel: 912333) and Cot are reliable companies, with a fleet of comfortable air-conditioned buses operating to most Uruguayan cities. Tamu (Transportes Aéreos Militaires) and Pluna (on Colonia, near Agraciada—tel: 91-65-91) are domestic airlines, with flights to most major cities. There are 775 miles of navigable waterways. There are buses connecting Montevideo to Mercedes, Fray Bentos, and Salto. Boats leave from Paysandu to Colón in Argentina, and from Salto to Concordia, also in Argentina. A ferry, the General Artigas, travels the Buenos Aires-Montevideo route in 8 hours.

FOOD AND RESTAURANTS

Uruguay is one of the largest consumers of beef in the world; the average inhabitant will not usually consider a meal complete without a steak *churrasco*. 90-percent of the land area is devoted to the raising of cattle and agriculture, and the local beef and lamb inexpensive and delicious. Uruguayans are therefore expert at providing, at astonishingly low prices, a wide variety of delicious broiled dishes, barbecues, and stew, each more succulent than the next. *Parrillada* is both a style of dish as well as the name of the type of restaurant that serves this tasty mixed grilled dish, the term deriving from *parrilla*—meaning the grill upon which the meats are cooked. Typically *parrillada* will be made up of steak and chunks of beef, chicken and sausage. Other local specialties include *puchero*, a shredded beef stew served with vegetables and beans, bacon and sausage. *Carbonada*, another beef stew, contains rice, peaches, pears and raisins. *Carne asado*, spit-roasted steak, and *churrasco*, broiled steak, are often eaten with the spicy *salsa criolla*. Uruguay also has an excellent local *chorizo*, a pleasantly spicy sausage often used to flavor stews. For dessert, *dulce de leche* is a great favorite (made with boiled milk and sugar), or try a *torta* (cake) with whipped cream. And though an average meal will have three courses, you'll find that your check, even in an expensive restaurant, will rarely exceed US$5-6 for one. In a medium-priced restaurant you can expect to pay about US$4-5, and in an inexpensive one as little as US$3. Good snack foods are pizzas and delicious beef called *chivitos*. As dinner is served late, from 9-11, you will probably enjoy an afternoon tea at a *confitería*—there are many of these attractive tea rooms around the Avenida 18 de Julio, where you can have a *mate* (tea) and really light pastry or a strawberry tart. In Punta del Este meals are served even later; lunch is from 2-4pm.

There are some splendid restaurants in Montevideo: **Restaurant del Aguila** (Plazoleta del Teatro Solis) where house specialties include *arroz valenciana* (rice with seafood), *brochette de lomo* (spit-broiled lamb), *entrecot parrilla* (beef), while for dessert there are the *guayaba* (guava) fruit, delicious peaches or the house *gâteau águila*. The Grill Room—**La Rôtisserie**—at the Victoria Plaza is not merely elegant (a strolling violinist entertains) but the food is excellent, including both local and international dishes. Not quite so plush is the **Short Horn Grill Room** at the Columbia Palace where the chateaubriand rivals only that of **Morini's** (Ciudadela 1229), which is decorated in the manner of a ship's dining salon. There are a number of *parrilladas* including **La Azotea** and **El Entrevero** in the Pocitos area, **El Fogon** (San Jose 1080) where the lower level dining room is quieter and more intimate, and **Las Brasas** (San Jose 909) where one *parrillada* is almost sufficient for two. **Forte di Makalé**, in the Parque Rodo (Rambla Wilson), serves typical local cuisine in a warm, informal setting; dining on the terrace is particularly delightful. Other restaurants include **Tahiti** (Boulevard Artigas) and **Mi Tio** (Rivera 2697), where the *parrilladas* and other typical dishes will certainly not disappoint you. For chicken and fish, **El Galeón** (Leyenda Patria 3096, in Playa Pocitos) is unbeatable. If you fancy fondue and pork chops, go to **El Bungalow Suizo** (Sol 150, in Playa Carrasco), and you must try the *smörgåsbord* at the **Bristol Hotel** (Rambla R de Mexico 6995), or **Club Alemán** (Paysandu 935) for good German and local food. **Hong Kong Restaurant** (8 de Octubre 2691) is the place for a Chinese meal. **Catari** (Colonia 971) and **Portofino** (Belastiqui 1325) are good Italian restaurants. For a bit of real local color, try the **Mercado del Puerto,** a large warehouse-like market on the docks of the port of Montevideo. It has numerous eating spots and is rustic and fun.

DRINKING TIPS

Uruguayan light beers are called *rubia;* darker beers are called *negra.* Made of barley, they have plenty of body and a delicious flavor. Local wines are very good and very inexpensive; you will not be let down by a bottle of Santa Rosa Cabernet with your Chateaubriand steak, or by a bottle of Mil Botellas Chablis with your filet of sole. Local champagnes worthy of respect are Faraut and Fond De Cave. *Grappa*, a delicious and very potent brandy made from the residue of grapes, is excellent as an apéritif, but you should also try *caña,* an equally potent brandy made from sugarcane. *Mate,* a strong tea made of yerba leaves, is very popular, especially between meals; the gaucho seems to carry his silver-edged gourd and silver straw for *mate* drinking wherever he goes. Women are welcome in bars, except in the harbor area. You can enjoy a good drink at the bar of the **Hotel Columbia Palace** overlooking the River Plate, or the sophisticated **Roof Garden** at the Victoria Plaza Hotel, with a fine view of the city.

ENTERTAINMENT

The Government of Uruguay runs its own ballet, opera, and theater companies and subsidizes individual artists and theaters; it also engages, on a nonprofit basis, international touring companies while in Uruguay. The result is that tickets are surprisingly inexpensive (an orchestra seat ticket for opera, ballet, or symphony ranges from US$2-8), and there is a lively interest in the performing arts. **Solis Theater** (Buenos Aires at Plaza Independencia) houses most visiting international companies, and it is also the home of the excellent **Comedia Nacional.** (Ch 5 of the local television station frequently screens both opera and ballet.) There are also experimental and exciting theater groups in Montevideo, performing in Spanish; if you are a lover of the theater, you should certainly not miss a performance at the **Teatro del Centro** or at the **Teatro Circular,** both theaters-in-the-round. There is an imaginative children's theater at the Hotel Victoria Plaza on Saturday and Sunday afternoons. The opera season here is in August and September. During the summer, you can enjoy a fine open-air concert at the **Rodó Theater** in Parque Rodó or in the Parque Rivera, where the *pericón,* a stately and lovely old Uruguayan dance, is performed for the public. Movie-going is a great favorite with Uruguayans. There are good movie houses, and films are shown with original soundtracks. Tickets are available three days before the performance at the movie box office, so there is no need to line up. Matinees are at 3, evening performances at 6 and 9. Current programs are listed in *The Montevidian.* For late-night entertainment, go to the **Parador del Cerro,** at El Cerro, for dinner, music, and floor shows nightly, at 12:30 am. **Bonanza Lancelot, Scrum 5, Tom-Tom,** (near airport) and **El Mar de la Tranquilidad** at Carrasco are pleasant nightclubs. **Anacapri** (Mercedes 871), where the waiters and customers sing along with the show, is great fun. **Zum Zum** (Edificio Panamericano) is a lively disco always packed on weekends, while **Baiuca** (Benito Blanco and Juan Maria Pérez) is dark and intimate—but the music is wild! If you like tango or gaucho songs, you must go to **La Cumparsita** (Carlos Gardel and Cuareim) or the **Teluria** (Cuareim), which are very popular with older people. **Las Grutas,** near Punta del Este, is a popular disco; as is **Papa Charlie.** If you want to try your luck at a baccarat or roulette before going to Punta del Este, there are casinos at the **Hotel Parque Casino** (Rambla Wilson) and the **Hotel Casino Carrasco,** near the airport. Clubs for men only include **Cubilete,** (Gabriel A Pereira 3106) in Pocitos.

SHOPPING

The main shopping area in Montevideo is from **Plaza Libertad** to **Plaza Independencia** on **Avenidas 18 de Julio** and **8 de Octubre.** Stores are open from 9-12 and 2:30-7 Mon-Fri; on Saturdays they close at 12:30pm. Best buys are leather goods and furs. Antelope, sealskin, pony, nutria (the best in the world, with thick, long, soft fur and good color), *nonato* (the soft skin of unborn calf), sea-wolf, leather and suede jackets, handbags, gloves, stoles, even ostrich bags are all incredibly good buys. The best furriers in town are **Paris-New York** (18 de Julio 1114) and **Revillon** (18 de Julio 853). At **Los Renos** (18 de Julio 915) or at the **Montevideo Leather Factory** (Plaza Independencia 832) you can pick a ready-made suede or leather jacket, or have one made to order in 24 hours. For the best antelope, suede and leather goods, try **Express Leather Factory** (Plaza Independencia 1327), also handbags, wallets, belts, and other goods; **Kings** (Plaza Independencia 729), good for suede coats (men and women); also **Taborelli** (Galeria Madrilena). Also very good values are jewelry and precious stones. For amethysts try **Amatistas Uruguayas** (Sarandi 604) and **Uruguay Piedras** (Galeria Florida). **Brela** and **Freccero** are also recommended for pearls and gold jewelry. Sweaters made from a cashmere-like wool called Burma (from NP50), woolen skirts, and ponchos are good buys too; look for these goods in the large department stores like **Soler** (Avenida 18 de Julio 952) and **La Opera** (Calle Sarandi 672). There are some shops selling handicrafts, typical gift items, and souvenirs. Visit **Ene** at the Victoria Plaza Hotel for paintings, gaucho dolls, and carvings in wood and horn; **Schiavo** for *mates* and gaucho knives; and **Manos del Uruguay** for ponchos, rugs, and *boleadoras,* the stone or metal balls wrapped in leather used by the gauchos to catch ostriches. There are branches of several Montevideo stores in Punta del Este. Purchases may be shipped back to the US, but this is not recommended. Don't be shy about bargaining for purchases. Two very interesting markets are the **Mercado del Puerto** (in front of the harbor) and the **Feria de Tristan Navaja,** in the open air on Sundays—ask about this flea market at the Government Tourist Office—held most Sunday mornings near Av 18 de Julio.

SPORTS

Soccer and basketball are very popular. In Montevideo the **Estadio Centenario** in Parque Batlle y Ordoñez is an 80,000-seat stadium where important soccer matches are played. There are also a bicycle race track and grounds for athletic sports in this park. Look for horse racing at two tracks, the **Hipódromo de Maroñas** and **Las Piedras;** polo at **Carrasco Polo Club;** golf at the **Club del Uruguay** and the **Cerro Golf Club.** Hotel guests of the Victoria Plaza, Lancaster, Carrasco, and Parque Hotels are granted guest cards for the **Montevideo Golf Clubs.** Punta del Este has the **Golf Club of Cantegril.** There are several tennis clubs in Montevideo and the beach resorts, and there is a yearly rugby football championship. Montevideo has a cricket club. Water sports are very popular in summer, and there are year-round swimming clubs in Montevideo, the best of which is the **Neptuno.** You can go surfing in Montevideo, Punta del Este, Maldonado, and Rocha from November to May, and yachting in Montevideo and Punta del Este from October to May (**Uruguayo, Nautilus,** and **Punta del Este Yacht Clubs**). Deep-sea fishing is excellent throughout the year, and there is superb fishing for the freshwater dorado at **Salto** and **Paysandú.** The hunting season opens December 1 and ends on March 31. Duck, armadillo, partridge, hare, pigeon, snipe, and wild boar are popular game. An exciting event during the Easter holidays is the **Domas Rodeo.**

WHAT TO SEE

Montevideo: One of the first things that will strike you about Monte (as the local English residents affectionately call the capital) is a marvelous feeling of openness. There are many wide avenues and tree-lined streets, parks, gardens, and plazas surrounded by pleasant flat-roofed houses and taller buildings. The heart of the city is the **Plaza Independencia,** with a statue of Jose Gervasio Artigas, a national hero who helped Uruguay gain independence in the early 19th century. The **Palacio Legislativo,** with its pink granite pillars, mosaic floors, and historical murals. The **Teatro Solis** and the **Museum of Natural History** (open 2-5pm Tues, Thurs, Sun) are there. A short distance from the **Plaza Independencia** is the oldest square in the city, the **Plaza Constitucion.** Here is the Cathedral, built between 1790 and 1804, and the Town Hall, completed in 1810. Walk along the busy avenida 18 de Julio and see the statue of the gaucho by Zorrilla de San Martin. At the end of the avenue is the **Parque Batlle y Ordoñez,** a delightful spot for a picnic. Here you will find *La Carreta* (The Oxcart), a monument by the sculptor Belloni in honor of the early Uruguayan settlers; it shows three yoke of oxen pulling a covered wagon. Not far from this park is the zoo and the modern **Planetarium.** Then go to **El Prado,** a glorious park along the Avenida Agraciada; there are lakes, grottoes, impeccable lawns, and a rose garden that would do an Englishman proud—there are no less than 850 varieties! During the **Semana de Turismo** (Tourist Week), horse-breaking competitions are held in El Prado. Most beautiful of the parks is **Parque Rodó,** on Rambla Presidente Wilson, with a lake where you can go canoeing around delightful little islands; if you're feeling particularly romantic, you can rent a gondola. Take a stroll around the open-air theater while the kids enjoy themselves in the children's playground. Take them to the amusement center, too. In Parque Rodó you will find the **National Museum of Fine Arts** (open 1-5 every day except Monday), where you can see paintings by Juan Manuel Blanes, Pedro Figari, and other Uruguayan artists. Also of interest for contemporary sculpture and painting is the **Joaquin Torres Garcia Museum** (Constituyente 1467). (Reconfirm museum schedules before visiting.)

Half an hour from the center of town is the **Tablada,** which is a must. Very early in the morning gauchos on horseback bring their cattle to market. In his baggy trousers, tight-fitting shirt, and hand-embroidered jacket, with the traditional black broad-brimmed hat and black boots, and carrying a silver-handled rawhide whip, the legendary gaucho is held in great respect—he is also the backbone of the country's economy. Make sure you see him by arriving at the Tablada before 8am.

At the western end of Horseshoe Bay and rising 388 feet above Montevideo is the **Cerro.** Legend has it that during Magellan's historic voyage around South America, the lookout on board his ship sighted this isolated hill and shouted to his comrades *"Monte videu!"* (meaning "I saw a hill" in Portuguese)—hence the name of the city. At the top of the Cerro stands the oldest lighthouse in the country (1804), and from the fort, which is a military museum, you'll get an unforgettable view of the **River Plate Estuary** and the surrounding countryside. Tours of Montevideo can be arranged through **COT** (Sarandi 669); **Tudet** (Julio Herrera ȳ Obes 1338—tel: 987921); **Viajes Cynsa** (18 de Julio 1120—tel: 984121); and **Onda.** There are also half-day tours to nearby *estancias,* working ranches, where you can see the gaucho on his own ground—rounding up steers, drinking grappa at the *estancia,* or just riding through the plains.

Eastward along the Coast: Uruguay is famous for its "Riviera"—over 200 miles of glorious beaches with clear sands and unpolluted waters, a major attraction for the 3 million tourists who visit the country every year. Montevideo itself boasts eight delightful beaches along the **Rambla Naciones Unidas.** Among them are **Playa Ramirez,** the nearest to the city center and the most crowded; the more fashionable **Playa Pocitos,** with smart apartment houses and restaurants and the **Ermitage Hotel; Puerto Buceo,** where there is a yacht club and the **Oceanographic Museum; Playa de Los Ingleses,** beneath the pleasant Virgilio Park; and the most beautiful of them all, **Playa Carrasco,** which is backed by the heavily wooded **Franklin D. Roosevelt National Park.** Here you will find the imposing **Hotel Casino Carrasco.**

Further east, along the "Interbalnearea" road, lie the pretty resorts of **Atlantida, La Floresta, Solís,** where the fishing is superb (**Hotel Chajá**), and **Piriápolis,** a very popular resort with a yacht club and many fine hotels (**Argentino,** with a casino, **Embassy,** and **Rex** are recommended). Behind the town, volcanic hills rise 1,000 feet above the sea—there are mineral springs, and at the top of Cerro San Antonio is an attractive restaurant and tea room. In **Punta Ballena** is a cluster of white buildings called **Casapueblo.** The work of artist-sculptor Carlos Paez Vilaro, the complex has swimming pools, apartments, gorgeous vistas from many levels. The town of **Maldonado** has some very interesting colonial structures.

Punta del Este, 90 miles from Montevideo, is the most famous and dazzling of Uruguayan beach resorts. Laguna del Sauce is the airport for this international pleasure spot. There are direct flights from Montevideo and Buenos Aires. Onda (Plaza Libertad—tel: 912333) has several buses a day from the capital; round trip fare is about US$25. Situated on a peninsula, it has miles of stunning beaches, including the calm **Playa Mansa** facing the bay and **Playa Brava** on the other side of the peninsula, with large breakers often fine for surfing. There is a yacht club, and the many sports facilities include excellent fishing in three nearby lakes and on the river Maldonado. **Lobos Island,** within sight of the town, is home for nearly 400,000 seals and can be reached by launch. Nightlife revolves around the casinos, and there are some very pleasant nightclubs: **Mau Mau, El Carousel, My Drink, Club de las Grutas.** First-class restaurants are the **Marisconea** (Calle 26), **Catari** (Avenida Gorlero), **Bungalow Suizo** (Avenida Roosevelt), and the restaurant at the **San Rafael Hotel** (Rambla Lorenzo Batlle—tel: 82161). An ideal place to stay is the **Cantegril Country Club,** which is beautifully situated in wooded grounds. You can rent a cottage complete with kitchen, living room with fireplace, bedrooms, and bath. You can also rent apartments at the **Edificio Santos Dumont** and the **Edificio Lafayette;** or you can stay at the luxurious Tudor-style **San Rafael Casino Hotel** (from US$196 AP double), or the less expensive **Playa** (from US$60 double), the **Auberge du Cap** (US$170 double EP), **La Capilla** (from US$75 double EP), the **Suizo Palace** (from US$52 double), and the **Peninsula** (from US$51 double). At **Punta Ballena** the **Solana del Mar y Punta Ballena** is luxurious (from US$196 double AP), while the **Playa Portezuelo** (US$68 double EP) provides excellent accommodations. The season is from December to March, and it is essential that you book reservations in advance.

Further east lie **Rocha,** near the colonial fort of **Santa Teresa; La Paloma,** another popular beach resort; **La Coronilla,** where ocean fishing is superb (shark, skate, black corvina); and **Chuy,** through the middle of which runs the border with Brazil.

Other places of interest in Uruguay are **Colonia,** on the River Plate, a pleasure resort with appealing colonial buildings (**Hotel Esperanza**), and the beautiful **Colonia Suiza,** a Swiss settlement ideal for autumn vacations. In nearby **Nueva Helvecia,** you can buy Swiss-style music boxes—made locally. Perhaps the prettiest town in Uruguay is **Mercedes,** 170 miles from Montevideo, a livestock center and resort. **Salto** (population 60,000) is a center for oranges and citrus fruits and mines, set in a most delightful countryside with wooded hills which supply the granite and marble used to construct the Legislative Palace in Montevideo. You can stay at the **Parador Salus,** 8 miles out of town.

SOURCES OF FURTHER INFORMATION

Pan Am, Avenida 18 de Julio 945, Montevideo, and any Pan Am office around the world; **The National Tourist Commission Information Bureau,** Avenida 18 de Julio 845, Montevideo; **The Uruguayan Consulate,** 301 East 47th Street, New York, NY 10017; and the **Embassy of Uruguay,** 48 Lennox Gardens, London SW1.

Venezuela

WHAT'S SPECIAL

Venezuela is the third-largest exporter of oil in the world and the richest country in South America. Venezuelans enjoy the highest standard of living, the highest income per capita, and the finest highway system on the continent. They also enjoy a country with superb beaches backed by lovely mountains and forests that hide, among other delights, gold, great game hunting, and the world's highest waterfall. Caracas, the capital, is a modern cosmopolitan city with superb hotels and restaurants, excellent shopping centers, and lively nightclubs. Visitors are welcomed not only by the people themselves but also by the government, which publishes maximum excursion and transportation rates and solicits complaints in case of noncompliance.

COUNTRY BRIEFING

Size: 352,143 square miles

Capital: Caracas

Population: 14,529,000

Capital Population
Metropolitan Area: 3,300,000

Climate: Venezuela is a tropical country, but climate is largely a matter of altitude. Caracas, 3,164 feet above sea level, has summer temperatures in the 80s, with cool evenings. In winter, when temperatures fall to about 55°, the weather is mild and pleasant. In Maracaibo, on the coast, the average temperature is 83°. The rainy season is May-November, the dry season December-April.

Weather in Caracas: Lat N10°30′; Alt 3,418 ft

Temp (°F)	Jan	Feb	Mar	Apr	May	Jun	Jul	Aug	Sep	Oct	Nov	Dec
Av Low	56°	56°	57°	60°	62°	62°	61°	61°	61°	61°	60°	58°
Av High	75°	77°	78°	80°	80°	78°	77°	78°	79°	79°	77°	75°
Days No rain	24	26	28	26	22	16	16	16	17	19	17	21

Government: A constitutional democratic republic.

Language: The official language is Spanish, but many people can speak English, especially in Caracas and Maracaibo.

Religion: 90% of the population is Roman Catholic.

Currency: Bolivar. 100 centimos = 1 bolivar.

	50¢	Bs 1	Bs 10	Bs 20	Bs 50	Bs 100	Bs 200	Bs 300
US (dollars, cents)	.12	.23	2.32	4.64	11.61	23.22	46.44	69.66
UK (pounds, pence)	.06	.11	1.11	2.22	5.55	11.10	22.19	33.29

Public Holidays:

New Year's Day, 1 Jan
Feast of the Magi, 6 Jan
Carnival, 2 days
St Joseph's Day, 19 Mar
Easter Thursday
Good Friday
Easter Saturday
Declaration of National Independence, 19 Apr
Labor Day, 1 May
Battle of Carabobo, 24 June
Independence Day, 5 July
Birth of Simón Bolívar, 24 July
Discovery of America, 12 Oct
All Saints Day, 1 Nov
Anniversary of the Death of the Liberator, 17 Dec
Christmas Day, 25 Dec

HOW TO GET THERE

Flying time to Caracas' Maiquetia Airport from New York is 4½ hours; from Miami, 3 hours; from Los Angeles, 7 hours; from Guatemala City, 3½ hours. Time in Venezuela: GMT−4.

REQUIREMENTS FOR ENTRY AND CUSTOMS REGULATIONS

Entry cards are issued by the airline or steamship company on which travelers will arrive in Venezuela, to citizens of the US, Australia, Austria, Barbados, Belgium, Brazil, the British Antilles, Canada, Costa Rica, Denmark, France, French Antilles, French Guyana, Great Britain, Ireland, Iceland, Italy, Liechtenstein, Mexico, Monaco, the Netherlands, the Netherlands Antilles, Norway, New Zealand, Panama, Surinam, Sweden, Switzerland, Trinidad & Tobago and West Germany. All other nationalities require a visa from a Venezuelan consulate. Entry cards are issued free and are valid for 45 days from day of entry into Venezuela. Visitors may bring in duty free all personal belongings, plus a carton of cigarettes and liquor for personal use.

AIRPORT INFORMATION

The International Airport for Caracas is Maiquetia, 17 miles from the city center, on the coast. There is coach service every 10 mins to downtown Caracas; fare is Bs11. Buses are scheduled every 45 mins; fare, Bs2.20. Taxi fare is Bs53 per person. You will find a hotel reservation counter at the airport; tip the porter Bs17 per piece of luggage. There is no arrival tax, but departure tax is Bs80.

ACCOMMODATIONS

There are a number of international hotels in many Venezuelan cities with luxurious accommodations and many extra facilities, but even the less expensive guesthouses have comfortable, clean rooms. At most hotels a 10% service charge will be added to your bill, but a tip is still expected. If you need help finding accommodations, ring the **Hotel Reservation Center** at the airport (tel: 0313605). Hotels in Caracas are centrally located, save for those at Caracas/Macuto Beach, about forty minutes from downtown, and so indicated:

Rates are in US$ for a double/twin room with bath or shower:

   Avila, Av. George Washington, San Bernardino (from $43)

   Bahia Del Mar, Av. La Playa, Los Corales, Macuto Beach (from $30)

   Caracas Hilton, Urb. El Conde, Caracas (from $65)

   Coliseo, Av. Casanova, Bello Monte, Caracas (from $22)

   Continental Altamira, Av. San Juan Bosco, Altamira, Caracas (from $44.20)

   Crillon, Av. Libertador, Esq. Acacias, Caracas (from $25)

   El Conde, Conde a Principal, Caracas (from $12.50)

   Holiday Inn, Av. Principal Las Mercedes, Caracas (from $64.44)

   Kursal, Av. Casanova, Calle El Colegio, Caracas (from $26)

   La Floresta, Av. Avila, Altamira, Caracas (from $29)

   Las Americas, Calle Los Cerritos, Bello Monte, Caracas (from $24.40)

   Las 15 Letras, Av. La Playa, Macuto Beach (from $19)

   Macuto Sheraton, Urb. Tanaguarena, Caraballeda (from $54.14)

   Melia Caribe, Urb. Tanaguarena, Caraballeda (from $69.95)

   Monserrat, Plaza Sur Altamira, Caracas (from $16.75)

   Palm Beach, Urb. Tanaguarena, Caraballeda (from $20.95)

   Residencias Anauco Hilton, Parque Central, Caracas (from $62.80)

   TAMANACO INTER · CONTINENTAL, Avenida Principal Las Mercedes (from $82), 10 minutes from center

   Tampa, Calle La Iglesia, Sabana Grande, Caracas (from $29.75)

USEFUL INFORMATION

Banks: Open 8:30-11:30 and 2-4:30. There are branches in major cities and many towns. You can also change foreign currency at *casas de cambio* and hotels; restaurants and shops will take travelers' checks. Citibank of New York has a branch in the Edificio Torre del Este (Avenida Francisco de Miranda).

Mail: Stamps are obtainable from post offices *(estación de correos);* the main one is on Avenida Urdaneta, corner of Carmelitas; stamps can also be obtained from the desk in some hotels. Mailboxes are blue and are marked *Correos.*

Telephone Tips: There are phones in restaurants and cafés, as well as public booths; lift the receiver, wait for dial tone, deposit a *medio* (25-centimos coin), then make call. Useful numbers in Caracas:

Pan Am 55 81 01	**Police** 169 or 160
Airport Information 031 50 84	**Fire Department** 166
Directories 103	**Long Distance Operator**
Weather 41 02 79	**(Venezuela)** 100
Time 19	**Overseas Operator** 122
	Tourist Office 781 83 11

Newspapers: The English-language newspaper is the *Caracas Daily Journal,* the best in Latin America and a must for the visitor. You can also get the *Wall Street Journal* and *New York Times* (a day after publication). *Time* magazine and other English-language publications are also available, while *Radio Liberator* broadcasts in English for several hours a day.

Tipping: At restaurants, 10% service charge will be added to your bill (as well as an extra Bs1-5 for the *cubierto*—bread, rolls, and butter), but another 10% is expected. Give porters Bs2; hairdressers, 10% or more of check. Taxi drivers are not tipped (unless they carry suitcases—then Bs4.50 for two bags); neither are museum guides.

Electricity: 110 volts 60 cycles AC.

Laundry: Dry-cleaning and laundry services are excellent and reliable; there is good 24-hour service in *lavanderias* (laundries) in major cities. Hotels also have good express services (dry-cleaning a suit, from Bs5.25; laundering a shirt, from 60 centimos).

Hairdressing: Most first-class hotels have excellent salons (shampoo and set from Bs54, man's haircut from Bs10-11).

Photography: Equipment and film are readily available throughout the country, and prices are reasonable. Black and white film costs Bs12, and you can have it developed in 24 hours. Color film costs Bs17 and will take 36 hours to process.

Clubs: Lions, Rotary, Kiwanis, and Junior Chamber of Commerce.

Babysitting: Most hotels have services. US baby foods and disposable diapers available in Caracas.

Rest Rooms: Can be found in hotels, restaurants, and nightclubs. Women, *Damas;* men, *Caballeros.*

Health: Many Venezuelan doctors have studied abroad and speak English, though fees are high. You will find some advertised in the *Daily Journal.* Toiletries, pharmaceuticals, and medicines are easily available. On Sundays there is always one pharmacy open in each district of Caracas. Water in all main towns is chlorinated and safe to drink, but in rural areas drink only bottled water. If you are going to Orinoco Valley, you should be inoculated against typhoid and yellow fever.

TRANSPORTATION

Although there is a bus service with very reasonable fares (50 centimos), the most popular form of city transportation is *por puesto* (collective taxis). Look for the *por puesto* sign and destination, and simply raise your hand. They're rather like independent cabs and charge around

50 centimos. Regular taxis are also readily available; you can hail one on the street or phone a taxi stand. Initial charge is Bs4 when the flag goes down; thereafter about Bs1 per kilometer. Fares double after 10pm. Because Venezuela is an oil exporter, rental cars are inexpensive, about US$9.36 per day plus 9¢ per mi, and the highways are good, making it a simple matter to drive around on your own. Either ask your hotel to make arrangements, or call at the several rental firms available in most cities. Chauffeur-driven cars are also available, and no extra charge is made for English-speaking drivers.

There is no railroad service as such, but long-distance buses are air-conditioned and very comfortable. Buses leave for all the main towns in Venezuela from the Nuevo Circo Terminal on Avenida Bolívar Esteb, off Avenida Fuerzas Armadas. AVENSA (Esquina El Chorro, Edificio 29—tel: 81 52 54) is the largest domestic airline, with excursions and regular flights to all parts of the country. Aerotaxis are also available. Flying times from Caracas: Mérida, ¾ hour; Maracaibo, 45 minutes (by jet); Isla Margarita, 1 hour. There are ferry services from Puerto la Cruz and Cumana to Isla Margarita.

FOOD AND RESTAURANTS

The people of Venezuela enjoy their food and have developed their own inimitable style of cooking. In Caracas, there are restaurants offering just about every world variety of cooking, ranging from the haute cuisine of France, through Austro-Hungarian, Swiss, Italian, Spanish, Middle Eastern, Indian, to Japanese and Chinese. Perhaps best known of all Venezuelan dishes is *pabellon criollo*, a delicious simplicity of black beans and rice, served with fried plantain (a cooking banana), shredded meat, and often garnished with lettuce, tomato and sliced avocado. Since it is still possible to eat turtle here, try real turtle soup as a starter, or turtle steak as an entree—both delicious. Shrimp-stuffed avocado is another popular starter here. Then order the *hallacas*—small pieces of chicken, pork, or beef seasoned with olives, raisins, and onions, rolled into a layer of corn dough, wrapped in plantain leaves, and boiled for several hours. Or try the *sancocho*, a thick chicken, beef, or fish broth with vegetables. *Mondongo* will make you change your mind about tripe; it is made of cowheel and tripe, plus lots of vegetables. If you like steak, order a *punta trasera*, served very tender, with hot red pepper and cool green pepper relishes. And if you enjoy seafood, you will not forget the *cazuela de mariscos:* baked clams, mussels, lobster, shrimp, and squid served with hot creole sauce. For dessert, try *huevos chimbos*, egg yolks boiled and bottled in sugar syrup, or *cascos de guayaba con queso crema*—guavas in syrup with cream cheese. With your meal, instead of bread have *arepa*, a round corn cake, also sold as a snack with ham, pork, cheese, or fish filling at *areperas* all over town. You can dine extremely well in Caracas, and save money by looking for those restaurants which offer fixed price meals—look for the word *cubierto*.

For authentic Venezuelan fare, try **El Porton** (Av Pinchincha, El Rosal—tel: 71.60.71), **El Jardin II** (Av Alameda/Av Boyaca, San Bernar-

dino—tel: 52.08.21 & 52.07.57), **Tarzilandia** (Decima Transversal/Final
Av San Juan Bosco—tel: 33.28.80) and **La Atarraya** (San Jacinto a Plaza
El Venezolano—tel: 45.82.35 & 45.78.59). Also worth noting is **Rancho
Tranquilino II** (Av Principal at Av Londres, Las Mercedes—tel: 91.32.94),
El Submarino, very popular with government officials at lunch time,
and located in the basement of the south tower of the Centro Simón
Bolívar (Pasaje Caroni, Centro Simón Bolívar—tel: 41.30.58) and **La Po-
sada del Angel** (Calle Alameda at Calle Boyaca, El Rosal—tel: 33.44.70).
Efe and *Tio Rico* are brands of excellent ice cream; on the beach, oysters
and clams with lemon juice are a must.

The comparison between Venezuelan fare and that of Spain can be
made at **Gallegos** (Esquina El Muerto No 125—tel: 441.03.57, 45.05.17
& 45.87.63), **La Caleta** (Prolongacion Sur Las Acacias, Sabana Grande—
tel: 872.72.43), **Camilos** (Av Francisco Solano, Sabana Grande), **Las Cane-
las** (2a Calle de Bello Monte, Edif Campero, Sabana Grande), or **La Casbah** (Alcalbala a Puente Anauco, La Candelaria—tel: 572.63.87), the last
two for delicious seafood. Mexican fare can be enjoyed at **El Chalet de
Mexico** (Av Venezuela, El Rosal—tel: 33.42.72) which also has a musical
show, or at **Mexico Tipico** (Av Libertador, Chacao—tel: 31.48.08), while
authentic and fine tasting Argentinian *parrilladas*—skewered mixed
grill—can be enjoyed at **Martin Fierro's** (Calle Herrero Toro, Seccion
Los Naranjos, Las Mercedes—tel: 92.57.79). Try also **La Estancia** (Av
Principal, La Castellana—tel: 33.19.37) and if not in the mood for parrillada, the *bistec de churrasco* is excellent as is the boned chicken—*pollo
a la parrilla*—which is served on a wooden board. Then there's a wide
range of first-rate French restaurants. For a special treat try **Lasserre**
(Tercera Av Los Palos Grandes—tel: 283.45.58 & 283.30.79), **La Belle
Epoque** (Av Leonardo da Vinci, Colinas Bello Monte—tel: 76.13.42),
Aventino (Av San Felipe/Av Los Chaguaramos, La Castellana—tel:
32.26.40) or **Chic Ambassador** (Cuarta Transversal, Los Palos Grandes—
tel: 284.68.01 & 284.17.90). And for one of the best restaurants in South
America, go to **Toni's '65** (Av Miranda near Cine Lido). **Amadeo** (Torre
"La Primera" Av Fco. de Miranda—by the Cine Lido—tel: 33.01.30)
offers both French and international cuisine to the tuneful sounds of
music. Less expensive are **Le Coq d'Or** (Av Francisco Solano, Sabanada
Grande—tel: 71.08.91), **L'Inferno** (Av La Trinidad, Las Mercedes—tel:
92.15.02 & 92.45.02) and **Le Perigord** (Av Francisco de Miranda, Los
Palos Grandes—tel: 284.70.65 & 284.49.34). **Henry IV** (Av Los Jabillos
No 35, La Florida—tel: 74.32.42 & 74.30.29), **La Bastille** (Calle Madrid,
between Orinoco & New York, Las Mercedes—tel: 91.51.19) and **La
Cigogne** (Calle Garcilazo, Colinas Bello Monte—tel: 751.33.13) continue
to enjoy their excellent reputation. Lovers of fine Italian fare need look
no further than **Il Romanaccio** (Centro Comercial Pasco Las Mercedes—
tel: 92.86.08 & 92.79.20) which also serves French food, **Il Padrino** (Ed.
"Teatro Altimira" Plaza Sur Altimira—tel: 31.47.39), **Franco's** (Av Los
Jabillos/Av Francisco Solano, Sabana Grande—tel: 72.09.96) and **Caruso**
(Av Tamanaco, El Rosal—tel: 33.13.58), closed Mondays. Austrian food
is to be found at **El Tirol** (Callejon Pedroza, La Florida), while Austro-

Hungarian fare is to be found at both **Barrilito** (Final Av Tamanaco, El Rosal—tel: 33.07.06) and **La Choza** (Av Mohedano/Av Tamanaco, El Rosal—tel: 71.02.15) which also serves a number of Balkans' delicacies. Steaks are to be found at the **Rotisserie** at the Hilton hotel, **La Mansion** (Av Tamanaca, El Rosal—tel: 33.34.55), the **Lee Hamilton Steak House** (Av San Felipe, La Castellana—tel: 32.52.27) and the **Shorthorn Grill** (Av Libertador, El Bosque—tel: 33.19.37).

For lovers of Japanese food, there's **Avila Tei** (Calle Guaicaipuro, between Avs Casanova & Pinchincha, El Rosal—tel: 71.05.84) and **Kamon** (Av Casanova/ Av Pinchincha, Chacaito—tel: 71.81.62). There are a number of good Chinese restaurants, including **El Dragon Verde** (Av Maturin, Los Cedros—tel: 71.84.04 & 72.59.11) and **Mee Nam** (Av Luis Roche, Altimira—tel: 32.18.38). International fare is to be found at **Le Gourmet** in the Hotel Tamanaco, Las Mercedes, **Bagatelle** (Av Principal de Las Mercedes—tel: 92.51.75—also French), **Da Emore** (Centro Comercial "Concresa" Prados del Este—tel: 978.48.73—also Italian) and **El Chalet** (Av Libertador Esq. Av Las Acacias in the Hotel Crillon—also Swiss). For mideastern and Arabic specialties try **Baalabeck** (Av Rio de Janeiro, Las Mercedes—tel: 91.66.19) or **El Rincon del Medio Oriente** (Calle El Retiro, El Rosal—tel: 33.40.64). For hamburger lovers, try **Tropiburger** at Av Las Mercedes and at the Los Palos Grandes shopping center.

DRINKING TIPS

Cardenal and Solera are probably the best Venezuelan beers, but Polar and Zulia are more popular. Local rums and gin are also excellent and inexpensive. Try a *ponche crema* (made with milk, eggs, sugar, and rum), or a rum punch before dinner. You might also sample an assortment of nonalcoholic brews like the *chicha* (made from milk and rice), or the *chicha andina* (made from fermented rice), or *guarapos* of cane or pineapple and other fermented tropical fruit. Your whisky and soda will cost at least Bs15 (much more in a nightclub), and a bottle of ordinary red wine will cost about Bs57. Bars and cafés are open from 10am to the small hours of the morning, and though women are welcome, young people under 18 cannot be served alcoholic drinks. Bars are closed on Sundays in the Federal District, but drinks may be served in restaurants with meals.

Popular drinking spots are the *automercados,* in all the big cities, the open-air cafés, and the *cervecerias,* where you can also dance. However, the **La Cota** rooftop bar at the Hilton is one of the nicer places to enjoy a drink, while **Petronio's** on Av Las Mercedes is one of the more popular "in" places to spend time. **El Papagayo** (Centro Comercial Chacaito) and the **Café Piccolo** (Calle Real de Sabana Grande) are also very popular. **Juan Sebastian Bar** (Av Venezuela, El Rosal) is a favorite of the younger set.

ENTERTAINMENT

Like any large cosmopolitan city, Caracas comes to life after dark. There are concerts, recitals, and ballets at the **Teatro Municipal,** where interna-

tional stars often appear. The opera season is in June. Concerts, too, are given at the **Sala Metropolitan de Conciertos.** Exciting live (Spanish-speaking) theater can be seen at the **Teatro Municipal,** the **Ateneo de Caracas,** the **Teatro Alberto de Paz y Mateo,** and the **Aula Magna,** in the Ciudad Universitaria. If you would rather go to a movie house, recent films are shown with their original soundtracks all over town; programs start at 5:30, 7:30, and 10. For a complete guide to the social and cultural life of the city, with current programs and reviews, look in the *Caracas Daily Journal.*

Late at night your choice of entertainment is vast. A safe starting point is the **Hipocampo** (Centro Comercial Chacaito 25—tel: 72.50.96), with three of the best dance orchestras—Latin, rock and pop—or try **Eva** (lowest level of the same building—tel: 72.91.38), which is somewhat wild, with statues of women occupying velvet red couches, while **Labyrinth** (Av Pincipal de la Castellana in La Castellana—good if you're dining at La Estancia, just across the street) has an incredible maze effect which can confuse. **El Hipopotamo** (Centro Comercial El Parque) has a large dance floor and loud music. **La Conga** (Av Blandin, La Castellana) has stunning decor and good live music. **La Cota 880** at the Hilton is perhaps one of the most romantic spots in town, though **Blow Up** (Av Avila, Altamira—tel: 33.50.86) is the fashionable disco at which to be seen. **La Haya** (Av Estrella, San Bernardino—tel: 55.09.22) is a disco where *creole* specialties are served, and black leather booths flank the two tiny dance floors. **Number Two** is a couples only disco—no singles—and men must wear jackets. Across the street is **Zebra,** and **Menfhis. La Jungla** (same neighborhood as Labyrinth at Plaza La Castellana, near La Estancia—tel: 32.23.36) has incredible Tarzanlike films flashing on the wall. **Mon Petit** (Edificio Autocomercial, Plaza Sur Altamira—tel: 33 00 06) dark and intimate; **Mi Vaca y Yo**—"My Cow and I"—(Antigua Carretera de Baruto—tel: 91 86 51) is a French spot with an outdoor farm setting while **La Cueva de Monterrey** (Avenida Humboldt) is a flamenco club. The **Salon Naiquata** (at the Hotel Tamanaco) has a good floor show, and **La Scala Supper Club** (Centro Plaza) is also recommended. Most places will let you in only if you are accompanied by one of the opposite sex, and men should wear a jacket and tie. A student spot with good folk music during the week is **Underground** (Centro Comercial del Este). A note of warning: At some of these nightclubs drinks are very expensive, and your check could be quite staggering.

SHOPPING

Stores open 9-1 and 3-7, Mon-Sat. The main shopping areas in Caracas are the **Sabana Grande** along the Avenida Lincoln, the **Centro Comercial Chacaito,** Sabana Grande, and the **Centro Comercial Beco,** near the Tamanaco Hotel. Shopping in Caracas is on a par with that in other major cities of the world, but prices are quite high. Good buys are shoes and clothing—you can have a suit made to order, and it will be ready in a few days. Handicraft items and souvenirs are plentiful, some of them exquisite: rugs, ceramics, Indian masks, bead necklaces. Chocano gold is used to make delightful trinkets for charm bracelets. A beautiful gift is the Hand of Fatima, in ebony and gold or silver; it is said to ward off evil spirits. The Cacique coins honor the Indians who fought the conquistadors. Best buys include pearls from Isla Margarita, and it's best to have them only temporarily strung. The local Venezuelan soft gold *(cochano)* is used to make some stunning jewelry, also another good buy, though less so with the price of gold soaring. Good stores for jewelry include **Walter Peter** (Edif. Marco, Av Fco. Liranda, Chacaito), **Arte Suiza** (Edif. Easo. Patek Phillipe, Av Francisco de Miranda), **El Arte** (Centro Comercial, Chacaito and Calle Real, Sabana Grande), **Panchita Labady** (Calle Real de Sabana Grande, 98), and **Retzignac** (Plaza Chacaito, El Rosal) which also stocks Piaget watches.

The best handicraft stores in Caracas are the **Casa de las Artisanias** (Calle Real, Sabana Grande), **Arte Folklórico** (Conde and Principal) and **Artesania Venozolano** (Palacio de las Industrias, Sabana Grande). **Yakera** (Av Andres Bello between 1 and 2 Trans, Los Palos, Grandes) has colorful handwoven cotton hammocks. Other shopping areas include **Ciudad Comercial Tamanaco**, Las Mercedes; **Centro Comercio Concresa**, Prados del Este; **Centro Comercial Paseo Las Mercedes**, Las Mercedes; **Centro Comercial**, Bella Vista; **Centro Comercial**, Los Ruices; and **Centro Comercial**, La Florida. There are street markets in all Venezuelan cities and good shopping centers in Maracaibo, Valencia, Maracay, Ciudad Bolívar, and Mérida.

SPORTS

Baseball is a year-round sport; during the winter months major league stars from the US play with Venezuelan teams. There are bullfights every Sunday during the winter—you will find bull rings all over the country. **La Rinconada** is the most lavish racetrack in South America; races are on Saturdays and Sundays. Golf can be played at the **El Junko** and the **Lagunita Golf Clubs**, just outside the city, or at **Valle Arriba Club** in Caracas. Special arrangements can also be made for visitors to use club facilities at the **Altamira** and **Tamanaco** clubs (tennis and swimming) and at the luxurious **Country Club**, which has an 18-hole golf course.

There is swimming, surfing and yachting all year round on the Caribbean and marvelous water-skiing and snorkeling off **Isla Margarita.** You can arrange to go deep-sea fishing at one of the coastal boating clubs or at the **Macuto Sheraton Hotel;** cabin cruisers with a captain and *marinero* can be rented for approximately US$370 for a full day at sea, US$265 for half a day. Rates include tackle, bait, ice, and soft drinks for four to six people. For fishing along the coast you can hire a boat with inboard motor (including tackle and guide) by the hour.

Inland there is splendid mountaineering, game hunting, and freshwater fishing (season from 17 March to 30 September) and skiing from May to October. The cockfighting tournament of San Juan de los Moros, 70 miles from Caracas, is well worth the trip.

WHAT TO SEE

Caracas and Nearby

Known as the "City of Eternal Spring" Caracas has wide avenues and highways and modern architecture. The finest examples are the **Centro Simón Bolívar,** the **Military Academy,** and the **Ciudad Universitaria,** with its 174-acre Botanical Gardens (open daily 8-12 and 2-6) right in the heart of town. But the city also harbors treasures from the colonial past; it was here that Simón Bolívar was born—you can see the **Casa Natal**—a 1920s reproduction of the adobe home in which Bolívar was born—the original was destroyed in an earthquake—in Esquina Traposos (open 9-12 and 3-5 Tues-Sun). The **Cathedral,** with its beautiful facade, was originally built in 1595, and has twice been rebuilt following earthquakes. Here are the family vaults of the Bolívar family, and a number of important paintings, including a Rubens and a Murillo. It is on the east side of the peaceful and spotless **Plaza Bolívar,** which has its stone walks scrubbed every day. (The equestrian statue of Simón Bolívar has a copy in New York City on Central Park South.) On Sundays there are concerts here, and the changing of the guard (also on holidays) in front of the statue. Don't be worried about the monkeys. They're harmless. Beautiful churches are the **Iglesia de San Francisco,** where Bolívar was given the title of Liberator in 1813, and **La Basilica de Santa Teresa** containing a miraculous image of the Nazareno de San Pueblo. Museums are usually open 9-12 and 3-5:30 Tues-Sun. A must for the visitor is the **Museo Bolívar** (San Jacinto and Traposos), where fascinating relics of the revolution against Spain are kept. The **Museo del Arte Colonial** is a delightful replica of an 18th-century villa, while the **Museo de Bellas Artes** (Avenida Mexico) has works by important international and Venezuelan artists. Opposite the Bellas Artes is the **Museo de Ciencias Naturales,** which has among its many precious items fine specimens of pre-Columbian ceramics. Go to the **Parque del Este,** with its beautifully landscaped acres of exotic plants and an artificial lake where you will see a replica of Columbus's ship, the *Santa María.* This is a beautiful spot for picnics, and children will love boating on the lake. Here, too, is the modern **Humboldt Planetarium. Parque El Pinar** is famous for its zoo.

From the top of **Mount Avila,** which lies between Caracas and the sea, the view is breathtaking. From here you can go down the 1,267-foot drop to **El Litoral**—the Riviera of Venezuela. Have a swim at one of the many beach resorts—**Macuto, Niaguatá, Catia La Mar,** or the exclusive **Caraballeda Beach** (closed on Mondays). In addition to a number of good hotels, listed earlier, there are several restaurants, including the beach restaurant **Timotes** in the town of Maiquetia (Caalejon Libertador—take the bus from the Macuto Sheraton), **Las Quince Letras** (Av La Playa, Macuto) and **Hong Kong Chef.** For Italian fare, the restaurants at the hotels Fioremar and Royal Atlantic are popular. There's also a **Tropiburger** here too.

Maracay: An important agricultural and military center, 70 miles to the west of Caracas, Maracay was first put on the map by the dictator

Juan Vincente Gomez (1909-1935), who built **Las Delicias,** a beautiful estate, now a public park with an adjoining zoo. Gomez also built the magnificent **Maestranza Bull Ring,** an exact replica of the one in Seville. Just outside the city is the idyllic **Lake Valencia,** the second largest in Venezuela. With its 22 islands, this lake is superb for boating—but swimming here is not recommended. Twelve miles from Maracay is the **Henri Pittier National Park,** a lush tropical forest where Pittier and C W Beebe spent many years studying the fauna and flora of the country. The **Hotel Maracay** (Av Las Delicias, from US$21.40) is extraordinary, with its own movie theater, tennis courts, an 18-hole golf course, an enormous swimming pool, and horseback riding stables. It's a good place to stay if you want to inspect the **Museo Aeronautico** (open weekends only) where there's an interesting collection of antique aircraft, or if you want to make the drive through exotic rain forest to one of South America's most beautiful *plage*—the fabled **Playa Cata,** little more than 90 minutes' drive over the Andes from Maracay.

Valencia is an old colonial city, 31 miles from Maracay. It is now the fourth-largest city in Venezuela and an important industrial and commercial center; at 1,600 feet above sea level, the climate is ideal (average temperature 76°), and many Europeans and Americans live there. Worth seeing are the 18th-century **Cathedral,** the **Capitol** and **Cellis House,** an architectural jewel from colonial days. Eighteen miles from Valencia, on the site of the decisive battle for independence, is the bronze **Monumento de Carabobo,** in honor of Bolívar. **Safari Carabobo,** located about 20 minutes from Valencia, is an African wildlife preserve worth a visit. In Valencia stay at the **INTER · CONTINENTAL VALENCIA,** Calle Juan Uslar (from US$56).

Mérida: The capital of Mérida State is known as *el techo de Venezuela* (Venezuela's rooftop); 76 mountain peaks are crowded into this state, not one of them under 13,000 feet. The city, which is 45 minutes by plane from Caracas, lies at an altitude of 5,397 feet and has a mean temperature of 66°. There are tree-lined streets, quiet plazas, and colonial buildings. High point of your visit will be an awe-inspiring ride on the cable car to **Pico Espejo** (15,640 feet)—the highest and longest cable car in the world, which goes up in four stages. Best time to go is from October-June; cars run from 7-12 noon Thursday to Sunday, and the round trip, which takes 3 hours, costs Bs30. Watch out for sunburn at the top. One hour's walk from the last station you can see a magnificent ice cave with crystal ice stalactites, and, if you like mountaineering, you can make your way to the **Glacier of Timoncito,** with its dazzling ice caves and steaming springs. Electric storms in the mountains are not uncommon. And from one of the intermediate stations on the cable car you can walk to **Los Nevados,** a village which is higher than Lhasa in Tibet. For further information write to **Club Andino** (PO Box 66). Another good excursion from Mérida is a visit to Jaji, a colonial village of great charm not quite 30 miles from Mérida. Accommodations in Mérida include **Hotel Belensate** (from US$28), **Moruco** (from US$20), and **Prado Rio** (from US$25).

Maracaibo: On the shores of the lake—45 minutes by jet from Caracas— lies the oil city of Maracaibo, enriched by two million barrels of "black gold" taken daily from the wells on the lake. The mean temperature here is 83°, and the average humidity is 78%—but you will find air conditioning everywhere, except in the old part of town near the docks, which has changed hardly at all for 100 years in spite of the prosperity. The city has a completely international population, fine theaters, and first-class restaurants (**Mi Vaquita, Ranco Grande,** and **El Pescadito** are recommended). The **INTER · CONTINENTAL HOTEL DEL LAGO** has a fine restaurant, a pleasant bar, an outstanding nightclub, and an excellent swimming pool (from US$56). A trip across the lake through the oil derricks is an unforgettable experience; also worthwhile is an excursion to **Rio Limón,** where you can rent a boat and see Indians living in houses made of woven reed mats built on stilts.

East of Caracas

Isla Margarita: In just over one hour's flying time from Caracas by **Avensa** or **Aeropostal** (about US$117 roundtrip) you can get to the "pearl is- land"—a 42-mile long Caribbean beachcomber's paradise of magnificent unspoiled sands, sheltered bays, and peaceful lagoons, where pearl fishing has been carried out for centuries. There are no mosquitos, and practically no other insects or flies. It's inexpensive by most Caribbean standards, and there's a continuous breeze on shore and save for December and January—and occasionally November—there's hardly any rain at all. The capital is Porlamar, with a population of around 30,000 and headquarters of tourism and the pearl industry. There is superb underwater fishing, snorkeling, and scuba-diving. You can rent a craft and go sailing on **La Arestinga Lagoon,** one of the few places in the world where the ibis escarlata (a heron with red plumage) can be found. Or rent a launch to see the ruins of **New Cadiz,** on Cubagua Island, which was destroyed by a tidal wave in 1541. Best time to visit is during the pearl-fishing season from December to March. **Porlamar,** on the east coast, is the island's major resort. On Margarita Island stay at **Club Puerto Esmeralda,** Porlamar (from US$23.25) or the New **Margarita Concorde** (Bahia El Morro, from US$65) with a beachfront location. A free port has been established in Margarita, and commerce is booming with sales of US and European goods. Requirements for duty-free shopping are a mini- mum 3-day stay, plus a $1 permit to purchase up to $150 in merchandise. Each purchase must be entered on the permit, and you'll need duplicate bills. Before leaving, visit the Customs Office where your packages will be waiting. Do not break the official seals before leaving the island. Check current regulations locally.

The Orinoco

Ciudad Bolívar: This romantic city lies 400 miles from Caracas and 250 miles from the sprawling delta of the Orinoco. It has an average tempera- ture of 85° and is the best place to buy anything made of gold: handmade charms and earrings and the exquisite Venezuelan orchid made of red, yellow, and green chocano gold. From here you can go into the jungle to see diamond prospectors and Indian villages, or take an excursion to the **Caroni Falls,** one of the tourist treasures of the country. There are also excursions to the magnificent **Angel Falls,** the highest in the world; the waters cascade down 3,212 feet from **Auyantepuy** (Devil Mountain), whose flat top was the locale for W H Hudson's *Green Mansions.* Farther south, near the Brazilian border, is **Roraima,** the setting for Conan Doyle's *Lost World.* Interestingly, it was to CB—as the locals call Ciudad Bolívar—that Bolívar came following a defeat, and he was declared President of Gran Colombia in this same town, then known as Angostura—and the true place of birth of Angostura bitters.

Canaima is a tourist camp where you can spend the night in a thatched cabaña, on the edge of a pink lagoon surrounded by orchid-filled jungles, then go in a dugout canoe to the **Hacha Falls.** In Ciudad Bolívar stay at the **Gran Hotel Bolivar,** Paseo Orinoco 88 (from US$25). Avensa Airlines has inclusive tours to Angel Falls and Canaima from Maiquetia Airport in Caracas, and Aerotaxis Tanca has day trips from Ciudad Bolívar. There is big-game hunting, superb fishing, and water-skiing.

Ciudad Guayana (Puerto Ordaz): Sixty-seven miles downstream from Ciudad Bolívar is an entirely new metropolis, where you will find the famous **Cerro Bolívar** open cast-iron mine, the government steel works of Matanzas, and the **Guri Dam,** site of one of the world's largest hydroelectric plants. From here you can hire a dugout canoe and go downriver to **Los Castillos;** there are two old forts where children will sell you cannonballs and old Spanish coins which they find in the river. It was here probably that Sir Walter Raleigh's son was killed in the disastrous expedition of 1618. In Ciudad Guayana, stay at the **INTER · CONTINENTAL GUAYANA,** Apartado Postal 293, Puerto Ordaz (from US$58).

SOURCES OF FURTHER INFORMATION

Pan Am: Central Plaza Torre C., Pisas 16 Y 17, Avenida Francisco de Miranda, Caracas; and any Pan Am office around the world; **Venezuela National Tourist Board,** Centro Capriles, 7th Floor, Plaza Venezuela, Caracas; **Venezuelan Government Tourist Bureau,** 485 Madison Ave, New York, NY 10022 (tel: (212) 335-1101); **Venezuelan Consulate-General,** 71A Park Mansions, Knightsbridge, London SW1.

THE CARIBBEAN

ATLANTIC OCEAN

Tropic of Cancer

DOMINICAN
REPUBLIC
San
Juan
VIRGIN IS.
ANGUILLA
St.
Thomas
SABA
ST. MAARTEN
ito
omingo
PUERTO RICO
ST. EUSTATIUS
NEVIS
ST. KITTS
ANTIGUA
MONTSERRAT
GUADELOUPE
Pointe-a-Pitre
DOMINICA
Fort de France
MARTINIQUE
ST. LUCIA
ST. VINCENT
BARBADOS
THE GRENADINES
CURAÇAO
BONAIRE
GRENADA
TOBAGO
TRINIDAD
Port of Spain
Caracas
VENEZUELA

CARIBBEAN CURRENCY CONVERSION

Country	United States $				United Kingdom £			
	5¢	10¢	50¢	$1	5p	10p	50p	£1
Antigua dollars α cents	.14	.27	1.35	2.70	.29	.57	2.83	5.66
Aruba, Bonaire, Curacao florins • cents	.03	.06	.29	.57	.06	.13	.61	1.19
Bahamas dollars • cents	.05	.10	.50	1.00	.10	.21	1.05	2.10
Barbados dollars • cents	.10	.20	1.00	2.01	.21	.42	2.10	4.21
Bermuda dollars • cents	.05	.10	.50	1.00	.10	.21	1.05	2.10
Cayman Islands dollars • cents	.04	.08	.41	.83	.08	.17	.86	1.74
Cuba pesos • centavos	.04	.07	.37	.73	.08	.15	.78	1.53
Dominica dollars • cents	.14	.27	1.35	2.70	.29	.57	2.83	5.66
Dominican Republic pesos • cents	.05	.10	.50	1.00	.10	.21	1.05	2.10
Grenada dollars • cents	.14	.27	1.35	2.70	.29	.57	2.83	5.66
Guadeloupe francs • centimes	.28	.56	2.78	5.56	.59	1.17	5.83	11.66
Haiti gourdes • centimes	.25	.50	2.50	5.00	.52	1.05	5.24	10.48
Jamaica dollars • cents	.03	.06	.28	.56	.06	.13	.59	1.17
Martinique francs • centimes	.28	.56	2.78	5.56	.59	1.17	5.83	11.66
Montserrat dollars • cents	.14	.27	1.35	2.70	.29	.57	2.83	5.66
Puerto Rico dollars • cents	.05	.10	.50	1.00	.10	.21	1.05	2.10
St. Kitts—Nevis— Anguilla dollars • cents	.14	.27	1.35	2.70	.29	.57	2.83	5.66
St. Lucia dollars • cents	.14	.27	1.35	2.70	.29	.57	2.83	5.66
St. Maarten florins • cents	.03	.06	.29	.57	.06	.13	.61	1.19
St. Martin francs • centimes	.27	.55	2.75	5.49	.57	1.15	5.77	11.51

CARIBBEAN CURRENCY CONVERSION

Country	United States $				United Kingdom £			
	5¢	10¢	50¢	1$	5p	10p	50p	£1
St. Vincent dollars • cents	.14	.27	1.35	2.70	.29	.57	2.83	5.66
Trinidad & Tobago dollars • cents	.12	.24	1.20	2.40	.25	.50	2.52	5.03
Virgin Islands dollars • cents	.05	.10	.50	1.00	.10	.21	1.05	2.10

Antigua

WHAT'S SPECIAL

A holiday island with a beach for every day of the year, luxurious resort hotels, and facilities for sailing, swimming, and all water sports—that is Antigua, once an important British naval base (Admiral Nelson was stationed there for a couple of years) and the key to the Caribbean. Today the forts and gun emplacements of the 18th century are in ruins, and what was Nelson's dockyard is now one of the Caribbean's finest yachting harbors. Forty miles north is the island of Barbuda, part of the state of Antigua, which again is a paradise for the vacationer.

COUNTRY BRIEFING

Size: 108 square miles   **Population:** 80,000
Capital: St John's   **Capital Population:** 35,000
   Climate: Dry and pleasant all year round; September and October are the hottest months.

Weather in St John's: Lat N17°07'; Alt 62 ft

Temp (°F)	Jan	Feb	Mar	Apr	May	Jun	Jul	Aug	Sep	Oct	Nov	Dec
Av Low	72°	72°	72°	74°	75°	77°	77°	77°	76°	75°	75°	73°
Av High	81°	81°	82°	83°	84°	85°	86°	86°	86°	86°	84°	83°
Days no rain	24	24	28	27	25	23	24	22	23	22	22	24

Government: An associated state within the British Commonwealth.
Language: English.
Religion: Most Protestant denominations represented.

Currency: East Caribbean dollar. 100 cents = EC$1.

	EC 10¢	EC 50¢	EC $1	EC $5	EC $10	EC $20	EC $50	EC $100
US (dollars, cents)	.05	.19	.37	1.85	3.70	7.41	18.52	37.04
UK (pounds, pence)	.02	.09	.18	.88	1.76	3.53	8.83	17.67

Public Holidays:

New Year's Day, 1 Jan
Valentine's Day, 14 Feb
Good Friday
Easter Monday
Labor Day, 1st Monday in May
Queen's Official Birthday

Whit Monday
Carnival (first Mon and Tues in Aug)
State Day, 1 Nov
Christmas Day, 25 Dec
Boxing Day, 26 Dec

HOW TO GET THERE

Flying time to Antigua, Coolidge Field Airport from New York is 3½ hours; from Miami, 3 hours; from San Juan, 1 hour. Time in Antigua: GMT−4.

REQUIREMENTS FOR ENTRY AND CUSTOMS REGULATIONS

Citizens of the USA, Canada, and the UK need only show proof of identity and nationality (not necessarily a passport) and a round-trip ticket. Other nationalities need a passport and round-trip ticket. A visa is not required for entry for vacation purposes. Smallpox vaccination certificates are required, except for US citizens or Canadians arriving direct from the USA or Canada; cholera and yellow-fever vaccination certificates are needed when arriving from an infected area. Duty-free allowance: 200 cigarettes or ½ pound tobacco or 50 cigars; 1 quart bottle of liquor; perfume for personal use. No currency restrictions. Firearms or drugs may not be imported.

AIRPORT INFORMATION

Coolidge Airport is 6 miles from St John's. There is no bus service, but taxis are plentiful; fare to St John's is about EC$9. Airport departure tax is EC$5 to Eastern Caribbean states, EC$8 to other places. The airport has a duty-free shop and hotel reservation counter.

ACCOMMODATIONS

There are good hotels in the most attractive spots, and they are centers of social life. There is a limited number of small guesthouses and boarding-houses, where accommodations may cost as little as US$8 per night. Rates are lower from April to December, and there is a 5% hotel tax and 10% service charge. Hotels in Antigua include:

Rates are in US$ for a double/twin room with bath or shower
   Admiral's Inn, English Harbor (from $42)
   Anchorage, Dickenson Bay (from $110 MAP)
   Antigua Beach, Hodges Bay (from $65)
   Antigua Horizons, Long Bay (from $138 MAP)
   Atlantic Beach, Crosbies (from $58)

Blue Waters Beach, Soldier Bay (from $72)
Castle Harbour Club, St John's (from $50)
Cortsland, Upper Gambles (from $48 MAP)
Curtain Bluff, Morris Bay (from $165 MAP)
Galley Bay Surf Club, Five Islands (from $84)
Halcyon Reef, St John's (from $156 MAP)
Halcyon Cove, Dickenson Bay (from $103 MAP)
Half Moon Bay, Half Moon Bay (from $120 MAP)
Hawksbill, Five Islands (from $120 MAP)
The Inn, English Harbor (from $73)
Jolly Beach, Jolly Beach (from $68)
Long Bay, Long Bay (from $110 MAP)
Runaway Beach Club, Runaway Bay (from $42)
White Sands, Hodges Bay (from $40)

USEFUL INFORMATION

Banks: Open 8-12 Mon-Thurs, 1-5 Fri. Travelers' checks are accepted.

Mail: Main St John's Post Office, on High Street, is open 8:15-3:30 Mon-Fri, 8:15-11:30 Sat. Mailboxes are red.

Telephone Tips: There are public phone booths and a new efficient telephone system now operates throughout the island. The Tourist Bureau advises patience when using the system. Useful numbers:

Harbor Master 20050	Operator and Directories 0
Airport Information 23000	Overseas 890
Airport Reservations 20241	Hospital 20251
Tourist Office & Information	Police 20045 & 20125
20029 & 20480	Emergencies 999
Hotel Association 20374	

Newspapers: There are two local newspapers, the *Worker's Voice* and the *Lantern,* in addition to English and US newspapers.

Tipping: Restaurants add a 10% service charge; staff are not tipped beyond this. Baggage porters, US$.50 for each piece.

Electricity: 110 volts 60 cycles AC in most hotels; 220 volts 60 cycles AC elsewhere.

Laundry: Major hotels have an express service; prices vary greatly.

Hairdressing: Some hotels have salons—others will arrange for a hairdresser (shampoo and set, from EC$11; man's haircut, from EC$4.50). There are a number of beauty salons in St John's.

Photography: There are photographic shops in St John's. Black and white film takes 2-3 days to develop; color is processed abroad, taking around 2 weeks. If possible, buy and develop film at home.

Clubs: Lions, Rotary, Jaycees.

Babysitting: Services can usually be obtained through hotels.

Rest Rooms: No public facilities, hotels and restaurants have rest rooms.

Health: All doctors speak English and good hospital and medical services are available.

TRANSPORTATION

Taxis are readily available by phone or by hailing in the street. They charge a fixed rate for an agreed trip—the Tourist Board booklet lists the prices of the most popular journeys—or they can be rented by the hour. Cars can be rented for about US$25 a day during the season (US$100 a week in summer). A local driving license can be obtained at the airport for US$5 with a valid US license. Gasoline prices are about the same as in the US. Drive on the left, and go slowly—40 mph on open road, 20 mph in towns. There are many unpaved roads, and these are worth exploring as many of them lead to beautiful deserted beaches. LIAT flies from Coolidge Airport to nearby islands. Boats of all kinds may be rented for cruises.

FOOD AND RESTAURANTS

The food is varied, colorful, and spicy—a mixture of Caribbean ingredients influenced by English traditions. Visitors usually eat in the hotels, which are well situated and have good restaurants. The **Admiral's Inn** at the Dockyard provides a relaxed lunch, with club sandwiches and lobster. **Maurice's Restaurant** on Market Street serves good local food at reasonable prices in a pleasant atmosphere. **The Yard** features atmosphere and good food (corner of Upper Long and East Sts), and **Darcy's** specializes in hamburgers, as well as West Indian cuisine (Kensington Court). The **Spanish Main Inn** (East Street), **The Kensington** (St Mary's Street), **Brother B's** (Long Street), **Maurice's** (Market Street), and the **China Garden** (Newgate Street) are among other restaurants which provide interesting local dishes. Worth noting for seafood is **The Cockleshell** (Fort Road).

DRINKING TIPS

Rum, the local drink of the Caribbean, has a special taste here found nowhere else in the world. Try a rum punch or a cool daiquiri, made with banana or pineapple. Imported liquor is sold at low duty-free prices. A Scotch costs from EC$1.75. Bars are open from 9am to midnight. Women are not expected to go into public bars unaccompanied. Besides the hotel bars there are some other delightful drinking spots—visit the **Admiral's Inn** at the Dockyard or **Darcy's Restaurant and Bar** at the **Kensington** on St Mary's Street for rum drinks and fruit punches—steel bands play at noontime. The **Spanish Main** (East Street) is also a popular drinking spot.

ENTERTAINMENT

Carnival is a Caribbean institution—a week of intense gaiety and excitement. Antigua's **Carnival** is held the last week of July through the first Tuesday in August, with a **Calypso Competition** in which the island's new Calypso king is chosen and steel bands compete to become top band. Like eating out, entertainment and nightlife centers in the hotels—each has its special night with bands, dancing, and entertainment. The **Castle Harbour Club and Casino** is open late in the evening and includes a casino, restaurant, and nightclub. The *Tourist Guide,* or your hotel, will give details of all forms of entertainment. There are three movie houses, one of them a drive-in, where British and American movies are shown.

SHOPPING

Stores are open 8:30-12 and 1-4 Mon-Sat (8:30-12 on Thurs). The range is good—it varies from wooden carvings imported from Haiti and fine bone china and cosmetics from England to elegantly printed fabrics made locally and other arts and crafts. Most of the best shops in St John's are in **Kensington Court** and on nearby **St Mary's Street** and **High Street.** The **Shipwreck Shop** has a collection of local handwork on display, and more arts and crafts of the Caribbean can be found at the **Pink Mongoose,** St Mary's Street, and the **Handicraft Center** on High Street. **Kelprint,** St Mary's Street, has a display of silk-screened fabrics and printed Sea Island cottons, which can also be found made up attractively in dozens of smaller shops. **Coco Shop,** St Mary's Street, and the **Bay Boutique,** in Kensington Court, are the right places for fashion, and **Y de Lima,** on High Street, sells jewelry and watches. Pictures by local artists can be viewed and bought at two galleries—**Pamela Wright's Art Gallery,** Kensington Court, and **Jacqueline La Fauve's Gallery** on Church Street. **The Specialty Shop,** Kensington Court, is good for bone china, crystal, gold and silver jewelry. Duty-free shops in St John's sell imported liquors and perfumes at real bargain prices. A visit to the **Golden Peanut Shopping Plaza,** High Street, with its range of shops and garden bar, is a pleasant way of finding good bargains.

SPORTS

Visitors come to Antigua for the sun and water sports. The beaches are dominated by the luxury hotels and the long deserted stretches of sand (all beaches are public) that seem like another world.

Go to **Antigua Water Sports,** Dickenson Bay, to learn snorkeling and scuba-diving. Equipment can be rented on the spot. Boats at English Harbor, Antigua Water Sports, and the Long Bay and Curtain Bluff hotels will take you out after big game fish—or if you are a serious angler, you can sail from St John's Wharf to **Barbuda** on the local fishing boats. Rent a yacht for sailing yourself, or for a luxury cruise; **VEB Nicholson's** office at English Harbor will give details and prices. Antigua Water Sports has a 30-foot catamaran sailing daily out of Dickenson Bay, and other boats too. The high spot of the year for boat owners and visitors is **Antigua Sailing Week** in the spring—a regatta with sailing- and power-boat races, fishing contests, and diving competitions, with the **Lord Nelson Costume Ball** as a climax.

Antigua provides an 18-hole golf course at the **Cedar Valley Golf Club** near St John's and 9-hole courses at the Half Moon Bay and the Antigua Beach hotels. Soccer and cricket are popular local sports, but interest in tennis continues to grow. Many hotels have their own tennis courts, and horseback riding can be arranged through the Antigua Beach or Atlantic Beach hotels and the **Galley Bay Surf Club.**

WHAT TO SEE

For the best picture of the island's social life drive across from St John's through the villages of All Saints, Sweets, and Liberta to the **English Harbor,** once the headquarters of the British fleet. **Nelson's House** is a museum of island life. **Clarence House,** once occupied by the sailor Duke of Clarence, who became King William IV, is now a country residence of the Governor of the island. Above the harbor, **Shirley Heights,** with the ruins of Fort Shirley, provides a magnificent view of the scene. If you climb higher, you reach the ruins of **Fort Berkeley.** Drive back to St John's along **Fig Tree Drive** in the evening for the glories of the Caribbean sunset.

In St John's, visit the **Anglican Cathedral;** go to **Rat Island** near St John's deep-water harbor and see the distillery where rum is made. **Sea View Farm** is the site of one of Antigua's potteries—see the potters at work and buy a barbecue pot for less than a dollar. Great estate houses of plantation days still stand all over the island—**Montpellier Great House, Harmon's House, Coconut Hall,** and many others. A glass-bottomed boat leaves Dickenson Bay every afternoon at 2:30 for a cruise of **Paradise Reef,** with its underwater life.

If you would like a glimpse of other islands, LIAT Airlines runs day trips to 24 nearby islands, including **St Kitts, St Lucia,** and **St Vincent.**

SOURCES OF FURTHER INFORMATION

Any **Pan Am** office round the world; **Antigua Tourist Board,** PO Box 363, St John's, Antigua, WI; **Antigua Department of Tourism,** 610 Fifth Avenue, New York, NY 10020, and 21 St Clair Avenue East, Toronto M4T 1L9, Ontario, Canada; **Eastern Caribbean Tourist Association,** 220 East 42nd Street, New York, NY 10017, and Rooms 238-240, 200 Buckingham Palace Road, London SW1.

Aruba, Bonaire, Curaçao

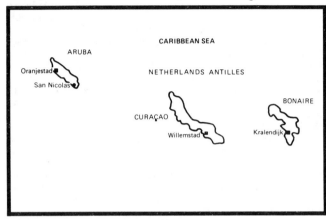

WHAT'S SPECIAL

The "ABC islands," or Holland-in-the-Caribbean, are off the coast of Venezuela, and together with Sint Maarten, Saba, and St. Eustatius, they form the Netherlands Antilles. The life-style is a blend of Low Country and Creole. The brightly painted towns are as neat and trim as any on the canals of Holland, while the landscape, unusually arid for the Caribbean, is a blend of cactus brush and hardy, windswept trees running down to good beaches. The population is cosmopolitan, and the shops are well stocked with merchandise from Europe and Latin America; there are of course ample stocks of the liqueur which has made Curaçao a household word.

COUNTRY BRIEFING

Size: 363 square miles   **Population:** 240,000

Capitals: Willemstad (Curaçao)
Kralendijk (Bonaire)
Oranjestad (Aruba)

Climate: Sunny and exceptionally dry. Trade winds blow throughout the year, even during hot summers.

Weather in Curaçao: Lat N12°06'; Alt 75 ft

Temp (°F)	Jan	Feb	Mar	Apr	May	Jun	Jul	Aug	Sep	Oct	Nov	Dec
Av Low	75°	74°	74°	76°	77°	78°	77°	78°	78°	78°	76°	75°
Av High	83°	84°	84°	86°	86°	87°	87°	88°	89°	88°	86°	84°
Days no rain	17	20	24	26	27	23	22	23	24	22	25	15

Government: Autonomous Dutch territory.

Language: Papiamento is the native language, and Dutch the official language. English and Spanish are widely spoken.

Religion: Roman Catholic (70%); Protestant (30%).

Currency: Netherlands Antilles florin. 100 cents = NAF1.

	10¢	50¢	NA F1	NA F5	NA F10	NA F25	NA F50	NA F100
US (dollars, cents)	.18	.88	1.75	8.75	17.50	43.75	87.50	175.00
UK (pounds, pence)	.09	.42	.83	4.17	8.35	20.87	41.74	83.48

Public Holidays:

New Year's Day, 1 Jan
Carnival Monday
Good Friday
Easter Monday
Queen Beatrix Birthday
    Celebration, 30 April

Labor Day, 1 May
Ascension Day
Kingdom Day, 15 Dec
Christmas Day, 25 Dec
Boxing Day, 26 Dec

HOW TO GET THERE

Flying time from New York to Aruba and Curaçao is 4 hours; from Caracas to both Aruba and Curaçao, ¾ hour; from San Juan to both Aruba and Curaçao, 1¼ hours; from Port of Spain to Curaçao, 1¼ hours; from Aruba to Bonaire, ½ hour; and from Curaçao to Bonaire, 20 minutes. Time in Aruba, Bonaire, and Curaçao: GMT−4.

REQUIREMENTS FOR ENTRY AND CUSTOMS REGULATIONS

US and Canadian citizens require only proof of citizenship (e.g. birth certificate, voter's registration card) and an onward ticket. All others require passport and onward ticket. Smallpox, cholera, and yellow-fever inoculations required if arriving from an infected area. Duty-free allowance: tobacco, liquor, and perfume in reasonable quantities. There are no currency regulations.

AIRPORT INFORMATION

Plesman Airport in Curaçao is 5 miles from Willemstad. Taxis are available, and the trip into town costs about US$7-8. There is a 10% increase in rates after 8pm and 50% after 11pm. The airport has a duty-free shop and hotel reservation bureau. Departure tax is NAF6 or US$3.50. In Aruba the Queen Beatrix International Airport is about 2 miles from Oranjestad and 6 miles from the Palm Beach resort area. Taxi fare from the airport to Oranjestad is about US$5 and to the resort area about US$9. Departure tax, NAF10 or US$5.75. Duty-free shops (for liquor and cigarettes) are in the departure hall.

ACCOMMODATIONS

There are both hotels and guest rooms in Aruba, Bonaire, and Curaçao. Rates are lower April to December, and there is a 10-15% service charge and 5% accommodation tax. Hotels in Curaçao:

Rates are in US$ for a double/twin room with bath or shower
Arthur Frommer, Piscadera Bay (from $48)
Avila Beach, Penstraat, Willemstad (from $26)
Curaçao Hilton, Piscadera Bay, Willemstad (from $61)
Curaçao Plaza, Plaza Piar, Willemstad (from $58)
Holiday Beach, Pater Euwensweg (from $72)

USEFUL INFORMATION

Banks: Open 8-12 and 1:30-4 in Aruba, 8:30-12 and 2-4 in Bonaire, 8:30-12 and 1:30-4:30 in Curaçao, Mon-Fri. Currency also changed in hotels, restaurants, and stores.

Mail: Mailboxes are red.

Telephone Tips: Local calls are free. Useful numbers: **Tourist Board** (Aruba) 3777, (Bonaire) 8322-8649, (Curaçao) 13397-11967.

Newspapers: English-language newspapers and magazines available; English publications in Aruba are *The News* (daily) and *The Local* (weekly).

Tipping: At your discretion. In hotels and restaurants, 10-15% of the bill if no service charge included.

Electricity: 110-130 volts 50 cycles AC in Curaçao, Bonaire; 120 volts 60 cycles AC in Aruba.

Laundry: Hotels have laundry and dry-cleaning services.

Hairdressing: Salons in leading hotels (shampoo and set from NAF16; man's haircut from NAF10).

Photography: Photo departments in leading shops. Color film developed in 48 hours at El Louvre in Curaçao and in Oranjestad, Aruba.

Health: All doctors and dentists speak English. Water is safe to drink.

TRANSPORTATION

Taxis can be phoned for or hailed in the streets. Cars can be rented from about US$20 a day (US drivers license needed).

FOOD AND RESTAURANTS

Holland's famous *rijsttafel* is an integral part of these islands' cuisine. Here, as in Holland or Indonesia, it consists of rice and as many as 40 different garnishes—meat, shrimp, pickles, fried foods, and hot relishes. *Keshi yena*, or stuffed Edam cheese, is another ABC speciality. You can also have European, American, or Chinese food, as well as fresh fish in a variety of styles. Breakfast is from 7 to 9, lunch from 12 to 2, and dinner from 7 to 10. Dinner for one in an expensive restaurant will cost about US$15 and up, in a medium-priced one, US$9-10, and in an inexpensive eating place, US$5-6.

In Aruba you will have your pick of international restaurants including one housed in a genuine old Dutch windmill, Chinese and Indonesian restaurants. The windmill was built in Holland in 1804, shipped piece by piece to Aruba, and is now located in the Palm Beach area as **De Olde Molen** (tel: 22060), where continental food is served. Another choice for international meals is the gourmet cuisine of the **Talk of the Town**

(Talk of the Town Hotel—tel: 23380). In the same hotel, the **Moonlight Grill** specializes in charcoal-broiled meats. Across the street, the **Surfside Restaurant** (tel: 23380) serves Creole dishes. The French food at **Le Petit Bistro** (Aruba Caribbean Hotel—tel: 22250) is also outstanding as are the **French Steak House** at the Manchebo Beach Hotel (tel: 23444) and the **Red Parrot** dining room at the Divi Divi Beach (tel: 23300), also featuring a Gallic menu. The **Astoria Hotel** at San Nicolas has an excellent Chinese and American menu. Other excellent restaurants for Chinese food are the **Hong Kong** (tel: 22966), the **Oriental** (tel: 1008), and the **Dragon-Phoenix Bar and Restaurant** (tel: 21928), all in Oranjestad. The **Trocadero** on Nassaustraat (tel: 21210, 1756) serves delicious seafood, Dutch, and Aruban specialties. The **Bali Floating Restaurant** (tel: 2131), in a houseboat in Oranjestad Harbor, brings a touch of exotic Indonesia to its own *rijsttafel.*

Bonaire's hotels provide excellent eating places, especially the **Bonaire** (tel: 8448) and **Flamingo Beach** (tel: 8285). The **Beefeater** on Breedestraat (tel: 8081) serves steaks, chops, and local fish. At both the **China Garden** (tel: 8480) and **Great China** (tel: 8666) on Breedestraat, and at **Zeezicht** (tel: 8434) on Bernhardweg, there is Indonesian food as well as Chinese.

Gourmet restaurants abound in Curaçao's hotels, from the luxurious **Penthouse** at the Curaçao Plaza (tel: 12500) through the dining rooms at the **Avila Beach** (tel: 53160), **Hilton** (tel: 25000), and **Holiday Beach** (tel: 25400), not forgetting that stronghold of Dutch food, the **Bianca** at the Airport Hotel (tel: 81084). Outside the hotels there is international cooking at **Fort Nassau Restaurant** (tel: 13450), Italian cuisine at the **San Marco** (tel: 12988) in the Columbusstraat shopping district (near the Synagogue), and superb seafood at **Jaanchie's** (tel: 88126), on the road to Weat Point. Try the **Playa Forti Restaurant,** Westpoint Bay, 25 miles out of town. For Indonesian dishes, try the **Lido** (tel: 11800) on Gomezplein, the **Peach Garden** (tel: 36108) at Schottegatweg Oost 177, and the **Rijsttafel Restaurant Indonesia** (tel: 12915) on Windstraat, overlooking Santa Ana Bay. **La Parrillada Steakhouse** (tel: 78865), Cas Coraweg 78, offers Argentinian barbecues and Spanish *paella.* Sample French cuisine at **Bistro Le Clochard,** on the Otrabanda side of the Pontoon Bridge (tel: 25666) and at **La Bastille,** on the outskirts of town at Sint Michielweg. **La Bastille** (tel: 38643), near the end of Caracas Bay Road, just outside Willemstad. The **Chateau Swiss** (tel: 55418), Penstraat 5, offers tournedos Swiss and excellent scampi (jacket and tie suggested for dinner).

DRINKING TIPS

Apart from the obvious Curaçao, rum drinks are popular, among them the *bon bini* cocktail made of rum, vodka, and pineapple juice. Imported wines, liquors, and beers are all available. The price of a whisky and soda is around US$2.50. A bottle of ordinary red wine costs approximately US$6. Drinking hours are from 11am to midnight; in nightclubs from 7pm to 3am.

ENTERTAINMENT

In Aruba, the **Americana Aruba,** the **Aruba Caribbean,** the **Holiday Inn Aruba,** the **Aruba Concorde,** and the **Aruba Sheraton** all have casinos, and there is music for dancing at these and other hotels. Bonaire has a casino at the **Hotel Bonaire,** cocktail lounges at the **Bonaire, Flamingo, Rochaline,** and **Habitat** hotels, and the **EWoWo** and **Limelight,** both discothèques. In Curaçao, there is the **Cave of Neptune** nightclub at the Curaçao Plaza Hotel, and the **Kini-Kini Bar** and a casino in the same establishment. The **Curaçao Hilton,** the **Holiday Beach,** and the **Princess Isles** hotels also have nightclub entertainment and casinos. Many of the hotels in the islands have a weekly folklore night with steel bands, dancers, and other local entertainment.

There are movies every evening using original soundtracks with either Dutch or Spanish subtitles, and there are midnight shows on Fridays and Saturdays.

SHOPPING

Stores are open 8-12 and 2-6 Mon-Sat. Bargaining is not customary. In Aruba, there is the **Aruba Trading Company,** the largest of the island's several department stores, for low-priced French perfumes, women's dresses, shoes from Switzerland, cashmeres, and many gift items. The ATC-run **Le Gourmet** sells liquor, cheese, and chocolates (ATC also has a liquor shop at the airport). **Spritzer & Fuhrmann,** one of the leading chains in the Netherlands Antilles for good buys in jewelry, watches, crystal, china, and other luxury items, is a cluster of four stores in the heart of downtown. Other imported goods are at the **New Amsterdam Store.** Curaçao's **Photo El Globo** has cameras and photo equipment in its shop on Nassaustraat. At the same location is the **Aruba Peasant Shop** with souvenirs, gifts, and handicrafts from Aruba and elsewhere. The **Casa del Mimbre** (or Wickerwork House) has Latin American handicrafts and Spanish-style *alpargatas* (espadrilles). **La Linda** features Spanish and Italian shoes in its main emporium but sells many other things as well. The **Boulevard** on L G Smith Boulevard is a covered mall with a variety of shops.

In Curaçao, **Heerenstraat**—a pedestrian mall, **Breedestraat,** and **Madurostraat** are the shopping streets. As in Aruba, **Spritzer & Fuhrmann** is a leader of china, crystal, watches, and jewelry. The main store is on Breedestraat but there are many branches elsewhere on the island. **J L Pehna & Sons,** on Heerenstraat in the oldest building in town (1708), sells just about every French perfume, cashmeres, handbags, Italian sports shirts for men, and porcelain. The **Yellow House** has perfumes, colognes, and cosmetics from France, cashmeres from Vienna, English figurines, Spanish children's wear, Belgian linens, and French and Italian ties. **The New Amsterdam Store,** at three locations, has gloves, bags, and perfumes from Europe, French lingerie, Mallorca and Mikimoto pearls, and men's wear. The **Beehive** makes its own jewelry and has unmounted gems which can be set on the spot. Other shops are **Kan Jewelers** (one of several branches throughout the Netherlands Antilles); **Photo El Globo,** here, too, with cameras and photo equipment; the **Wooden Shoe,** with china, pewter, silver, and clogs. The five **Obra di Man** shops sell locally-made handicrafts. Buy the famous Curaçao liqueur from its maker, **Senior and Co,** at Chobolobo, or from liquor stores and supermarkets elsewhere.

In Bonaire, **Casa Pana** has fishing equipment, film, and souvenir beach towels; **Jenny's** carries women's wear as well as cosmetics and costume jewelry. **Spritzer & Fuhrmann** has two stores, and **Berlinsky's** also features fine jewelry and china. Both the **Bonaire** and **Flamingo Beach** hotels have interesting and well-stocked boutiques.

SPORTS
Water sports rank highest among tourist attractions. Swimming, snorkeling, scuba-diving, fishing, and sailing are year-round activities. In Curaçao, the tennis clubs and 9-hole golf course of the **Shell Refinery** may be used if a previous appointment is made (tel: 92664).

WHAT TO SEE
Aruba: The town of **Oranjestad,** with colorful Dutch-style houses, busy shops along **Nassaustraat,** its main street, and the fruit and vegetable stalls and fishing boats in its harbor, is the focus of urban sightseeing on the island. Out-of-town sights include the beaches, especially the beautiful three-mile-long **Palm Beach** northwest of Oranjestad, and the windswept countryside, known as the *koenoekoe* or *cunucu.* Here the trade winds have sculpted unusual rock formations and made the *divi-divi* tree one of the world's great natural rarities—its branches bend completely in one direction. Hotels in Aruba (rates are in US$ for a double/twin room with bath or shower; summer rates are lower; government tax of 5% and service charge of 10-15% not included):

Americana Aruba, Palm Beach (from $95)
Aruba Beach Club, Druif Beach (from $110)
Aruba Caribbean, Palm Beach (from $85)
Aruba Concorde, Palm Beach (from $100)
Aruba Sheraton, Palm Beach (from $110)
Divi Divi Beach, Druif Beach (from $88)
Holiday Inn Aruba, Palm Beach (from $90)
Manchebo Beach, Manchebo Beach (from $85)
Talk of the Town, Oranjestad (from $70)
Tamarijn Beach, Druif Beach (from $78)

Bonaire stands for beaches and offers some of the best swimming, snorkeling, and scuba-diving in the Caribbean. There is excellent fishing, with a great variety of tropical fish—bonito, red snapper, wahoo, and tuna; spearfishing is outlawed, however, to protect underwater life. The Bonaire, Habitat, and Flamingo Beach hotels will help with sports equipment. Bonaire also has one of the best flamingo colonies in the Americas; at nesting time, in May or June, the old salt flats where the birds have settled are a mass of chicks. At **Pekelmeer** by the salt pans themselves are the old slave huts where the salt workers were housed in the 19th century, when this was the island's most thriving industry. Try to see the ancient Indian cave inscriptions at **Boca Onima**. When the island was discovered, Bonaire's Arawak Indians were still living in Stone Age conditions. See also **Cai Beach**, covered with pink conch shells. Hotels in Bonaire: **Bonaire Hotel & Casino**, Kralendijk (from US$55 double); **Flamingo Beach Hotel**, Kralendijk (from US$45 double); **Hotel Rochaline**, Kralendijk (from US$26 double).

Curaçao: **The Queen Emma Pontoon Bridge** opens about 20 times a day, and each time there is much scrambling to get across before it swings aside. The bridge divides the city into the Punda side on its east and the Otrabanda, literally the "other side" on the west. **Fort Amsterdam**, on the Punda side of Queen Emma's, is an 18th-century stronghold which houses the **Governor's Palace**. The other architectural attraction in Willemstad is the **Mikve Israel Synagogue**, the oldest Jewish house of worship in continuous use in the Western hemisphere, dating from 1732. Its floor is strewn with sand in memory of the Israelites' years of wandering in the desert. On the outskirts of town is the **Jewish Cemetery**, which is one of the oldest Caucasian burial places in the New World. There are over 2,500 graves, some dating back to the 17th century. Many of the funeral sculptures are very impressive. You should also visit the **Curaçao Museum** for a glimpse of antiques and handicrafts out of the island's past. The museum's garden has a fine collection of the varieties of flowers and trees growing on the island.

The floating market, held inside the harbor along De Ruyterkade on Waaigat, on scores of small boats from Venezuela, should not be missed. The **Shell Refinery**, mainstay of the economy, is one of the world's largest, and the world in itself. Tours of the **Amstel Brewery** are also available. Curaçao liqueur is made at **Chobolobo** (from locally grown oranges) and sold in attractive Delft jugs; you can sample it at the distillery.

SOURCES OF FURTHER INFORMATION

Any **Pan Am** office around the world; **Aruba Tourist Bureau**, L G Smith Boulevard, Aruba, and 1270 Avenue of the Americas, New York, NY 10020; **Bonaire Tourist Bureau**, Kralendijk, Bonaire, and **Bonaire Tourist Information Office**, 685 Fifth Avenue, New York, NY 10022; **Curaçao Tourist Board**, Plaza Piar, Willemstad, Curaçao, and 685 Fifth Avenue, New York, NY 10022.

Bahamas

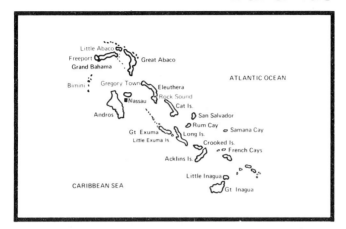

WHAT'S SPECIAL

The Bahamas is a vacation playground located just 50 miles off the coast of Florida. Fringed with palm trees, beautiful beaches, and bright resorts, The Bahamas seem almost as much part of the sea as of the land. The name "Bahama" comes, in fact, from the phrase *baja-mar*, meaning underwater or shallows, used to describe the islands by the 16th-century Spanish explorer Ponce de Léon. Of all the buccaneers, gun-runners, speculators, cotton traders, and rum smugglers who visited the islands during their strange, piratical history, most were just passing through, though some stayed to give The Bahamas their unique cosmopolitan flavor.

Today the islands' economy is still based on tourism, and one of the pleasures of visiting The Bahamas is their wide-open friendliness, the tremendous effort that goes into making visitors feel welcome and providing for their comfort. The islands and their towns have separate characters; Freeport provides modern glitter, Nassau traditional dignity, and the hundreds of resorts of the Out Islands give unrivaled opportunities for fishing, swimming, diving, sailing, or sunning lazily on a long white beach. There are casinos, clubs, restaurants—entertainment both indoor and outdoor, both simple and sophisticated. But remember that it is also a decorous country: do not appear on the street in beach clothes.

COUNTRY BRIEFING

Size: 5,353 square miles   **Population:** 215,090

Capital: Nassau, New Provi-   **Capital Population:** 131,342
dence

Climate: Subtropical. June through October is the wettest period, but for most of the year the sun shines and overcast days are rare.

Weather in Nassau: Lat N25°05′; alt 12 ft

Temp (°F)	Jan	Feb	Mar	Apr	May	Jun	Jul	Aug	Sep	Oct	Nov	Dec
Av Low	65°	64°	66°	69°	71°	74°	75°	76°	75°	73°	70°	67°
Av High	77°	77°	79°	81°	84°	87°	88°	89°	88°	85°	81°	79°
Days no rain	25	23	26	24	22	18	17	17	15	18	21	25

Government: An independent democracy within the British Commonwealth of Nations.

Language: English.

Religion: Christian, with many sects represented.

Currency: Bahamian dollar. 100 cents = B$1. The Bahamian dollar is at par with the US dollar and US coins and bills are accepted currency in the Bahamas.

	10¢	50¢	B$1	B$5	B$10	B$15	B$20	B$50
US (dollars, cents)	.10	.50	1.00	5.00	10.00	15.00	20.00	50.00
UK (pounds, pence)	.05	.24	.48	2.39	4.77	7.16	9.54	23.85

Public Holidays:

New Year's Day, 1 Jan   Independence Day, 10 July
Good Friday   Emancipation Day, 1st Mon in Aug
Easter Monday   Discovery Day, 12 Oct
Whit Monday   Christmas Day, 25 Dec
Labor Day, 1st Fri in June   Boxing Day, 26 Dec

HOW TO GET THERE

Flying time to Nassau International Airport from New York is 2½ hours; from Paris, 9½ hours; from Caracas, 3½ hours; from Tokyo, 14½ hours. Time in the Bahamas: GMT—5. Daylight Saving Time observed.

REQUIREMENTS FOR ENTRY AND CUSTOMS REGULATIONS

Citizens of the US, Canada, and the UK do not require passports provided they have some other proof of citizenship (e.g. voter's registration card or birth certificate). Passports, and in some cases, visas, required of others. All travelers should have a round-trip or onward ticket. Smallpox or cholera certificates may be required if arriving from an infected area. No currency restrictions, but convert all local currency before leaving because it may be difficult to convert elsewhere. Duty-free allowances: 200 cigarettes or 50 cigars, or 2 pounds tobacco; 40 ounces liquor. Tropical fish may not be taken out.

AIRPORT INFORMATION

Nassau International Airport (10 miles from city center) is the usual point of entry. There is no downtown terminal, and you reach Nassau by taxi (about $10 to downtown Nassau, $11.50 to Paradise Island, plus $2 for the Paradise Island Bridge toll). No airport arrival tax; departure tax of $4 for adults, $2 for children. There are two information desks at the airport. Also liquor and airport shops.

ACCOMMODATIONS

As a popular vacation center The Bahamas offer an immense variety of hotels. Rates are lowest May to December, although in many of the Out Islands there is little difference between winter and summer prices.

It is also possible on some islands to rent a holiday apartment for $30 and up a night. For more information contact your travel agent or The Bahamas Tourist office nearest you. There is a 6% hotel tax, and some hotels include a 10-15% service charge in the bill. Hotels in Nassau, and Paradise Island:

Winter (high season) rates are in US$ for a double/twin room with bath or shower

Ambassador Beach, West Bay Street, Cable Beach area (from $105)

Atlantis, West Bay Street, within 5 minutes walking distance of downtown Nassau (from $52)

Balmoral Beach, West Bay Street, Cable Beach area (from $92)

Beach Inn, Paradise Island (from $75)

Britannia Beach, Paradise Island (from $98)

Club Land'Or, Paradise Island (from $98)

Dolphin, West Bay Street, 5 minutes from downtown Nassau (from $62 CP)

Emerald Beach Hotel, Cable Beach area (from $75)

Holiday Inn, Paradise Island (from $98)

Loews Harbour Cove, Paradise Island (from $89)

Mayfair, West Bay Street, 5 minutes from downtown Nassau (from $58)

Nassau Beach, West Bay Street, Cable Beach area (from $115)

Nassau Harbour Club, East Bay Street, within 10 minutes by car from downtown Nassau (from $65)

New Olympia, West Bay Street, edge of downtown Nassau (from $48)

Ocean Club, Paradise Island (from $130)

Ocean Spray, West Bay Street, 5 minutes from downtown Nassau (from $46)

Parthenon, West Street, 5 minutes from downtown Nassau (from $30)

Pilot House, East Bay Street, within 10 minutes by car from downtown Nassau (from $75)

Sheraton British Colonial, Bay & Marlborough Streets, edge of downtown Nassau (from $77)

South Ocean Beach, South West Road, near airport and Lyford Cay, 30 minutes from Nassau (from $73)

Towne, George Street, edge of downtown Nassau (from $46)

West Bay Street extends west from downtown Nassau along the northern coast of New Providence Island. Hotels on West Bay Street in the Cable Beach area are located 3 to 5 miles from downtown Nassau. Paradise Island is reached by bridge (toll $2) from Mackey and East Bay Streets, at the eastern end of town.

USEFUL INFORMATION

Banks: Open 9:30-3 Mon-Thurs, 9:30-5 Fri in Nassau; 9-3 Mon-Thur, 9:30-5 Fri in Freeport. There is a nominal government tax for cashing travelers' checks.

Mail: Stamps sold in hotels and post offices.

Telephone Tips: There are booths in public places, restaurants, cafés, and hotels. The prefix for New Providence Island and Paradise Island is 32, and for Grand Bahama Island 34, 35, and 37. Do not use the prefixes when calling from within those areas. Useful numbers:

Tourist Office	**Police** Nassau 32-24444
Nassau 32-59171	Freeport 35-28333
Freeport 35-28044	**Fire** 919
Operator 0	**Hospital** 32-22861
Directories 916	**Ambulance** 32-22221
Time Nassau 917	**Bahamas Air & Sea Rescue**
Freeport 35-28111	Nassau 32-23877
Weather 915	Freeport 37-32264

Newspapers: Overseas newspapers are easily obtainable. The two local English-language newspapers are *The Guardian* (morning) and the *Tribune* (evening).

Tipping: It is customary to tip those who perform personal services, though normally a service charge is included in hotel and restaurant bills. Tip taxi drivers 15% of fare; luggage porters and hotel porters, 50 cents a bag; chambermaids, $1 a day; restaurants, 15% of check (if not included).

Electricity: 120 volts 60 cycles AC.

Laundry: Excellent services, with guaranteed 24-hour return from the larger companies and most hotels (dry-cleaning a suit, from $5, laundering a shirt, from $1.50). Principal cities also have laundromats.

Hairdressing: First-class hotels have salons (shampoo and set, from $12.50; man's haircut, from $10).

Photography: Good selection of equipment; all types of film in big cities, though not on the smaller islands; 24-hour developing service. Black and white film costs $5, color $8.50.

Clubs: Rotary, Kiwanis, Lions, Toastmasters International.

Babysitting: Can be arranged through your hotel.

Rest Rooms: Usually on the ground floor of downtown hotels and in most major department stores. Signs are in English.

Health: Excellent doctors and dentists. Top-flight hospitals, the Princess Margaret in Nassau and the Rand Memorial in Freeport. Imported pharmaceuticals and toiletries available but expensive. Local water safe to drink, but has high salt and chloride content.

TRANSPORTATION

There is a small local bus (Jitney) service from downtown Nassau to the outskirts of the city. Cable Beach hotels provide scheduled bus service to downtown Nassau on a complimentary basis or at a nominal cost. Taxis can be quickly found, either in the street or (in Nassau) by calling 35111. Cost for two passengers is $1.20 for the first ¼ mile and 20 cents for each additional ¼ mile. (Rates higher in the Out Islands.) A chauffeur-driven car for five people costs $12 plus $6 for each additional half hour; car rentals, about $35-45 a day, $205-16 a week plus gas; bicycle, $6 a day; motor scooter, about $18 a day. Drive on the left. Speed limits are 25 mph through residential areas and 45 mph on highways. Flying is the usual way of getting from island to island, and there are 52 or more airstrips. Bahamasair provides quick airhop services from Nassau to the other islands (the longest flight takes 1 hour 10 minutes), as does Chalk Airlines via sea plane to Bimini. Boats are not often used for transportation, though there are some local mail boat services taking passengers at a nominal fare. Some have no meal service or sleeping accommodations, so check details with the Tourist Office (tel: 32-59171).

FOOD AND RESTAURANTS

The most distinctively Bahamian dishes are, of course, those that come from the sea. A great favorite is the conch, a shelled mollusc caught in local waters, and there are numerous variations on this theme, such as cracked conch (rolled in batter and deep fried), conch chowder (stewed with vegetables) and conch salad. Other local specialties are boiled crawfish and green turtle pie (turtle meat baked in a shell with vegetables). Favorite desserts are coconut pit and guava duff. Mealtimes are fairly flexible: breakfast 7-11, lunch 12-3, and dinner 6:30-10.

Nassau has restaurants to suit all tastes and pockets, and dinner could cost anywhere from $5 to $20 per person. **Café Martinique (Britannia Beach Hotel,** Paradise Island—tel: 57366), the **Sun and . . .** (Lakeview Avenue—tel: 31205), and **Buena Vista** (Delancy Street—tel: 22811) are all excellent and expensive ($15 and up). Less expensive restaurants are in the Bay Street area and the streets adjoining it—such as **Bridge Inn** (East Bay Street—tel: 32077) and the **King and Knights Club** (West Bay Street—tel: 24758). For authentic and inexpensive Bahamian cooking, go to **Three Queens' Restaurant** (Wulff Road—tel: 56203) and **Travellers' Rest** (West Bay Street—tel: 77633). Another restaurant well worth trying is the **Cafe de la Mer** (tel: 52070), moderate, on West Bay Street in the Cable Beach area. **Green Shutters** (48 Parliament Street—tel: 55702), English pub-style, is popular at lunch but also open for dinner. For a quick snack, there are branches of American chains such as **Kentucky Fried Chicken, Burger King,** and **Lum's** on Bay Street.

DRINKING TIPS

Sale of liquor is unrestricted, and hotels usually serve drinks throughout the day. Most drinking is done in hotel bars, clubs, and nightspots, and many of these have developed a special atmosphere of their own. *Planter's Punch*, a fresh fruit punch with plenty of rum, is the great local drink, closely followed by *Goombay Smash* (rum, lemon and pineapple juice, coconut rum, and sugar). Imported wines, liquors, and beers are also available (a whisky and soda costs about $2.50). For a bottle of ordinary red wine expect to pay about $10 in a restaurant, $4 in a store.

Especially nice places for a casual drink are **No. 20** (Cumberland Street), **Marlborough Arms** (Marlborough Street), and the **Trade Winds Lounge** at the Paradise Island Hotel. There is native entertainment and dancing at **Pino's**, Prince George Hotel, and **Dirty Dick's** (Bay Street), one of the oldest nightspots in Nassau for native shows and atmosphere.

ENTERTAINMENT

Native folk music (goombays and calypsos) and cabaret with a lively, local flavor is the most typically Bahamian form of entertainment. Highlight of the year is Junkanoo, the Bahamian version of Mardi Gras. On both 26 December and 1 January there are colorful, carnival-like parades with singing and dancing in Nassau, Freeport, and some of the Out Islands. The revelry starts at 4am and is liveliest along Bay Street. All year round you can hear good native bands in Nassau at the **Sugar Mill Pub**, Ambassador Beach Hotel; **Blackbeard's Tavern**, Bay Street; the **King and Knights Club**, West Bay Street; or **Ronnie's Rebel Room**, West Bay Street. International artists appear regularly in cabaret at the **Trade Winds Lounge** at the Paradise Island Hotel and **Le Cabaret** at the Paradise Island Casino. There are plenty of recent English and American movies showing in Nassau. For gamblers there is the smart **Casino** on Paradise Island, the **Playboy Casino** in the Ambassador Beach Hotel, and **El Casino** in Freeport, Grand Bahama.

SHOPPING

Stores open 9-5 Mon-Fri, 9-6 Sat. Nassau is an international marketplace, and some of the best buys are imported goods: cameras and binoculars from Japan and Germany, Swiss watches, Scottish tweed, French perfume, and British china, crystal, and leather goods. Bahamian craftsmen also produce handmade straw goods and shell jewelry (conch shell cameos, coral jewelry, and tortoiseshell items can all be bought for under US$10—but US visitors should beware: tortoise is an endangered species and tortoiseshell cannot be brought back into the United States).

Bargain in the **Straw Market** on Rawson Square (open seven days a week), but not in stores. Stores include: **John Bull,** on Bay Street and also at Charbay Plaza on Charlotte Street North (watches, clocks, jewelry, cameras); **Nassau Shop,** Bay Street (fine crystal and china); **Bernard's China & Gifts,** Bay Street (china, crystal, jewelry); **Scottish Shop,** Charlotte Street (tweeds and woolens); the **Brass & Leather Shop,** Charlotte Street (English leather); **Johnson Brothers,** Bay Street (tortoiseshell jewelry); **Lightbourn's Perfume Center,** Bay and George Streets (French perfumes); **Xanadu** and **The Carib Shop,** both on Bay Street (gifts and cosmetics); and **The Linen Shop,** Parliament Street (English linens). Some major stores will order directly from the factory for visitors, and the saving can be as much as 30%. **Ambrosine,** a fashionable boutique for women, and the **Distinctive Shop,** for menswear, both carry imported lines and are both on Marlborough Street. The **Nassau International Bazaar** on Bay Street is a collection of shops selling items from around the world.

SPORTS

Nearly every hotel in Nassau can arrange facilities all year for fishing, water-skiing, snorkeling, scuba-diving, spearfishing, sailing, para-sailing, and windsurfing. There are regular fishing contests all over the islands; visitors are welcome to take part. **Playtours** runs daily catamaran tours around Paradise Island. Golf clubs welcoming visitors include, on New Providence Island, the **Ambassador Beach Golf Glub,** and the **South Ocean Beach Golf Club;** on Paradise Island, the **Paradise Island Golf Club;** and on Grand Bahama Island, the **Bahama Reef Golf and Country Club,** the **Lucayan Golf and Country Club,** and the **Bahamas Princess Golf Club.** There are open tennis courts at the **Balmoral Club** and at hotels, and tennis and squash courts at the new **Nassau Squash and Racquets Club.** There are regattas, both large and small, as well as championship and standard golf and tennis tournaments. Boxing and wrestling take place at Nassau Stadium.

WHAT TO SEE

Nassau on New Providence Island is full of color and small enough for a few pleasant rambles. **Rawson Square,** almost on the waterfront, is the heart of the city. At **Woodes Rogers Walk,** west of the square, you can see Bahamians unloading catches of conch, crabs, and other fish, which are on sale at the streetside stalls. See the **Flamingo Show** at **Ardastra Gardens,** and the **Sea Floor Aquarium.** Up on the hill there is **Government House,** where the guard is changed in the English manner on alternate Saturdays at 10am. The **Bahamas Antiquity Museum** on the corner of East and Shirley Streets gives an excellent picture of the Bahamian way of life and its crafts. Do not miss reminders of the islands' past—**Queen's Staircase; Forts Montagu, Charlotte,** and **Fincastle;** or the beautiful **French Cloister** and **Versailles Gardens** on Paradise Island.

Abaco is a group of smaller islands or cays, clustered round the major islands of Great Abaco and Little Abaco, on the northern edge of the Bahamian archipelago. The mainland is dotted with lakes, great pine forests, and groves of cedar and cypress. **Marsh Harbour** is the main shopping area and **Treasure Cay** a large tourist development. Hotels in Abaco, winter (high season) rates:

Bluff House Club, Green Turtle Cay (from $67 double)
Conch Inn, Marsh Harbour (from $45 double)
Elbow Cay Club, Hope Town (from $44 double)
Green Turtle Club, Green Turtle Cay (from $75 double)
Hopetown Harbour Lodge, Hope Town (from $46 double)

Treasure Cay Beach Hotel & Villas, Treasure Cay (from $82 double)
Walker's Cay Club, Walker's Cay (from $80 double)
Andros: The largest of the Bahama islands, 104 miles long and 40 miles wide, much of Andros is still quite undeveloped and covered with forests of pine, mahogany, and hardwood. Along the east coast a number of attractive and sophisticated resorts have sprung up beside the broad white beaches, and there are now four airports. Yachting and fishing are excellent. Hotels in Andros (high season):

Andros Beach, Nicoll's Town, North Andros (from $65 double)

Chickcharnie, Fresh Creek, Andros Town (from $40 double)

Small Hope Bay Lodge, Fresh Creek, Andros Town (from $110 double AP)

Berry Islands: This chain of tiny islands is a magnet for yachtsmen. Stay at the **Chub Cay Club,** Chub Cay (from $70 double).

Bimini: Only 50 miles from Miami, Bimini is often the first Bahamas landfall for the thousands of yachtsmen who enter the Bahamas each year. Famous for the marine life which congregates around its coast, it is a great center for big-game fishing. Information on fishing can be obtained from the executive secretary of the **Bimini Big Game Fishing Clubs** and from the local paper, the *Bimini Bugle.* Hotels here (year-round rates) are:

Bimini Big Game Fishing Club & Hotel, Alice Town (from $60 double)

Brown's, North Bimini (from $30 double)

Compleat Angler, North Bimini (from $40 double)

Eleuthera: Over 100 miles long and only 2 miles wide, hook-shaped Eleuthera is the orchard and farm of the Bahamas, supplying the islands with fruit, eggs, milk, and poultry. Some of the Bahamas' most pleasant resorts have sprung up along its pink sand beaches, and it has lovely old towns like Governor's Harbour. There are good shops and a small airport. **Rock Sound** is an old settlement, mainly known for the **Cotton Bay Club,** a self-contained community with pool, tennis courts, skin- and scuba-diving facilities, sailing, fishing, and excellent food. **Current** takes it name from the tide which whirls through the cay separating Eleuthera from Current Island. Hotels on Eleuthera (high season) include:

Buccaneer Club, Governor's Harbour (from $41 double)

Cotton Bay Club, Rock Sound (from $140 double MAP)

Current Yacht & Diving Club, The Current (from $110 double AP)

Sea Raider Cottages, The Current (from $35 double)

Winding Bay Beach Cottages, Rock Sound (from $125 double MAP)

Harbour Island: A tiny island off the northeast tip of Eleuthera, this is the oldest and one of the loveliest resort islands in the Bahamas. **Dunmore Town,** a 17th-century village circling a harbor, is separated by a high green ridge from a beautiful pinkish beach. Hotels here (high season) include:

Coral Sands Hotel, Harbour Island (from $70 double)

Valentine's Yacht Club, Harbour Island (from $45 double)

Spanish Wells: A charming old fishing village on **St George's Cay** off the northwest tip of Eleuthera. It is a town in miniature, with narrow streets and pastel-painted houses. Local residents have a reputation as fishermen, pilots, and fishing guides, and the town has become a well-known fishing center. Hotels (high season, winter) are **Spanish Wells Harbour Club** (from $55 double) and **Sawyer's Marina** (from $37.50 double).

The Exumas is a chain of 350 or more islands and cays, the principal ones being **Great** and **Little Exuma.** Near the northern end is a 22-mile stretch, the **Exuma Cays Land and Sea Park,** accessible only by boat and set aside as a protected reserve for land and sea life. It is a fascinating area for naturalists and underwater explorers. Hotels are **Hotel Peace and Plenty,** George Town (from $88 double MAP), and **Out Island Inn,** George Town (from $109 double AP).

Grand Bahama: After centuries of neglect, the last 20 years have seen the opening up of the island as one of the great international playgrounds of the Western world. **Freeport** is a modern city with a busy international airport, an immense Moorish gambling casino, smart nightclubs, and an international bazaar selling goods from all over the world. Add to this six 18-hole golf courses and every imaginable facility for water-skiing, skin- and scuba-diving, fishing, sailing, championship tennis, skeet and trap shooting, riding, shuffleboard, bowling, and badminton. Definitely a place for the energetic. Hotels are:

Winter (high season) rates are in US$ for a double/twin room with bath or shower

Bahamas Princess Hotel, downtown Freeport (from $68)

Bahamas Princess Tower, downtown Freeport (from $78)

Castaways, downtown Freeport (from $75)

Coral Beach, Lucaya (from $77)

Freeport Inn, downtown Freeport (from $49)

Grand Bahama, West End, at western tip of island, about 32 miles from Freeport (from $80)

Holiday Inn, Lucaya (from $72)

Shalimar, downtown Freeport (from $56)

Silver Sands, midway between downtown Freeport and Lucayan Beach (from $80)

Xanadu Beach, on beach south of downtown Freeport (from $87)

Lucaya is a residential and hotel section of Freeport, approximately 3 miles from downtown Freeport.

Cat Island: The highest and scenically the most magnificent of the islands, a fisherman's paradise. The summit is topped by a miniature monastery, **The Hermitage.** Hotels are the **Cutlass Bay Yacht Club,** Cutlass Bay (from US$80 double AP year round) and **Hawk's Nest Club,** Hawk's Nest Creek (from US$90 double AP year round).

San Salvador: The site of Columbus's first landing in the New World in 1492 (the exact spot has been marked in four different places), now reached by regular flights from Nassau. Stay at the **Riding Rock Inn,** from $58 double AP all year.

There are other "Out Islands" with romantic names: **Ragged Island, Crooked Island, Inagua,** and **Long Island.** The latter is renowned for its scenic beauty and supplies the rest of the Bahamas with fruit and vegetables, grown by the unusual "pot hole" method of farming—raising crops in holes blasted out of the rock. The **Stella Maris Inn** (cottages) has a yachting marina and private landing strip; rates are from $53 double AP.

SOURCES OF FURTHER INFORMATION

Any **Pan Am** office around the world; the **Bahamas Ministry of Tourism,** Nassau International Airport and Rawson Square, Nassau, and in the International Bazaar, Freeport; **Bahamas Tourist Office,** 30 Rockefeller Plaza, New York, NY 10020, and other offices in Atlanta, Boston, Chicago, Dallas, Los Angeles and San Francisco, Miami, Philadelphia, and Washington, DC, and in Montreal, Toronto and Vancouver, and Frankfurt, London, and Paris.

Barbados

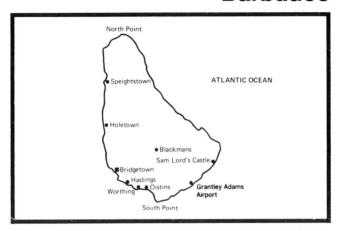

WHAT'S SPECIAL

The easternmost of the Lesser Antilles, Barbados has for more than 400 years been—and still is—the landfall of choice among transatlantic sailors, despite the hedging of reefs that protects its windward side from the ever turbulent Atlantic rollers. One reason is that during the day, soft clouds build up over the ocean and reflect the silvery green of the land. For the long-distance navigator, this shimmer confirms a soon to be successful landfall, for from those distances the island itself lies too low to be seen beyond the horizon.

The first inhabitants of Barbados were very probably members of the Barrancoid culture, the precursors of the Arawak immigration which proceeded from South America. There is some evidence that the area still known as The Potteries was used by the earlier inhabitants for its fine clays. In 1536, Pedro a Campos—on his way to Brazil—landed for water and wild pig and reported the island deserted. He supposedly marked it on his chart as **Los Barbados** for the beardlike hangings which clung to fig trees. The name remained ever since, while not quite one hundred years later a group of British privateers landed (also for water) near Holetown on the west coast and thereupon claimed the island in the name of good King James. Reports reaching London were sufficiently enthusiastic that a new expedition was quickly funded, and under the directorship of Sir William Courteen set sail. Its objective: a self-sustaining settlement to be constructed, with the name of Jamestown. By 1631 more than 5,000 new settlers were involved in agriculture, mostly maize and tobacco, and by 1640 population had jumped to more than 30,000 and a system of local government had been established. Indeed, Barbados leads all Third World nations in that it enjoyed the first parliamentary democracy, older indeed, than that of the United States.

The very quantity of successfully grown Virginian tobacco had its effect upon the market, tending to drive out the smaller amounts of Caribbean-grown product, which was held to be inferior by the merchants of the northern colonies. So the Bajan farmers looked around for another product, as easy to grow and market, and found it in sugar.

The results came quickly. Just 500 acres could produce a profit of $40,000 in an economy where sugar was worth 1¢ a pound, 18¢ for a suit of clothes (labor, maybe 5¢ more to make it), while a pair of shoes would cost 16¢. That there was never a slave uprising in Barbados is generally thought to show that the sugar barons cared for their people, working their white indentured laborers far harder than they did their slaves.

While Barbados has inherited a number of British traditions—including cricket, soccer, lawn tennis, and even the habit of afternoon tea—it is very much its own nation, providing happy experience in the fields of entertainment and relaxation for the entire family. You'll enjoy a very cordial welcome in Barbados.

COUNTRY BRIEFING

Size: 166 square miles **Population:** 280,000
Capital: Bridgetown **Capital Population:** 113,000
Climate: A glorious climate; 3,000 hours of sunshine annually.

Weather in Bridgetown: Lat N13°08'; Alt 181 ft

Temp (°F)	Jan	Feb	Mar	Apr	May	Jun	Jul	Aug	Sep	Oct	Nov	Dec
Av Low	70°	69°	70°	72°	73°	74°	74°	74°	74°	73°	73°	71°
Av High	83°	83°	85°	86°	87°	87°	86°	87°	87°	86°	85°	83°
Days no rain	18	20	23	23	22	16	13	15	15	16	14	17

Government: An independent nation within the British Commonwealth. It has 11 subdivisions called parishes.
Language: English.
Religion: Protestant.
Currency: Barbados dollar. 100 cents = 1 Barbados dollar.

	B10¢	B50¢	B$1	B$5	B$10	B$20	B$50	B$100
US (dollars, cents)	.05	.25	.50	2.50	5.00	10.00	25.00	50.00
UK (pounds, pence)	.02	.12	.23	1.16	2.33	4.65	11.63	23.26

Public Holidays:

New Year's Day, 1 Jan
Good Friday
Easter Monday
May Day, 1 May
Whit Monday
Kadooment Day, 3 Aug

Caricom Day, 6 Aug
United Nations Day, first Mon in Oct
Independence Day, 30 Nov
Christmas Day, 25 Dec
Boxing Day, 26 Dec

HOW TO GET THERE

Flying time to Barbados from New York is 4¼ hours; from Miami, 2½ hours; from Toronto, 5½ hours; from Port of Spain, ¾ hours. Time in Barbados: GMT−4.

REQUIREMENTS FOR ENTRY AND CUSTOMS REGULATIONS

US, UK, and Canadian citizens do not require passports, but must show proof of citizenship, if staying less than 6 months and holding round-trip tickets. All others need passports. Visas are not necessary for citizens of other Commonwealth countries, of the US, or of countries with mutual visa abolition agreements. International smallpox vaccination certificate required of all visitors except those arriving directly from the US, Canada, and UK; also, cholera and yellow-fever certificates if coming from an infected area. Duty-free allowance: 200 cigarettes or 50 cigars or ½ pound tobacco; 26 ounces liquor or wine; reasonable amount of perfume for personal use.

AIRPORT INFORMATION

Grantley Adams International (recently modernized) Airport is 11 miles from Bridgetown. Buses connecting with the city run about every 15 minutes (fare B45¢). Some hotels provide their own minibus service. Taxis are available day and night (fare about B$25 to Bridgetown area, slightly more, further north). Airport departure tax is B$10. There is a duty-free shop and hotel reservation counter at the airport.

ACCOMMODATIONS

Extensive accommodations are available for visitors. Information can be obtained from the **Barbados Hotel Association** or the **Barbados Board of Tourism** (PO Box 242, Bridgetown). Guesthouses and apartments are also available at lower prices. There are hotels in the international luxury class, but there is a wide range, and all accommodations offer from 25-50% reduction in the off season, 15 April to 15 December. Some hotels and guesthouses add 10% for gratuities, and there is an 8% government tax. Hotels in Barbados (all rates high season):

Rates are in US$ for a double/twin room with bath or shower
  Atlantis Hotel, St Joseph (from $40), 13 miles from Bridgetown
  Barbados Beach Village, St James (from $140 MAP)
  Barbados Hilton, St Michael (from $99), 1 mile
  Caribbee, Hastings (from $52), 2 miles
  Cobbler's Cove, St Peter (from $110), 11 miles
  Coconut Creek, St James (from $134 MAP), 6 miles
  Colony Club, St James (from $160 MAP), 6 miles
  Coral Reef, St James (from $198 AP), 8 miles
  Crane Beach, St Philip (from $75), 12 miles
  Discovery Bay Inn, St James (from $155 MAP), 6 miles
  Holiday Inn, St Michael (from $103), 1½ miles

Marriott's Barbados Resort/Sam Lord's Castle, St Philip (from $112), 15 miles

Miramar Beach, St James (from $130 MAP), 8 miles

Ocean View, Hastings (from $69 MAP), 2 miles

Paradise Beach, St Michael (from $150), 5 miles

Rainbow Reef Hotel, St Lawrence (from $60), 5 miles

Rockley Resort, Christchurch (from $125), 3 miles

Sandpiper Inn, St James (from $175 MAP), 10 miles

Sandy Lane, St James (from $310 MAP), 7 miles

Settlers Beach, St James (from $175), 7 miles

South Winds, St Lawrence (from $65), 3 miles

Southern Palms, St Lawrence (from US$91), 4 miles

USEFUL INFORMATION

Banks: Open 8-1pm Mon-Thurs, 8-1pm and 3-5:30 Fri; closed Sat.

Mail: Many post offices in the capital. Stamps can also be bought from stationers' shops and licensed stamp dealers.

Telephone Tips: Public booths, automatic and coin operated. Useful numbers:

Airport 87101	**Police** 112 and 60800
Board of Tourism 72623	**Queen Elizabeth Hospital**
Hotel Association 65041	60930
Directories 119	**Weather** 87101
Overseas Operator 118	

Newspapers: English and American newspapers and periodicals available. Local newspapers include *Advocate-News, The Nation,* and *The Bajan* (monthly).

Tipping: In hotels and restaurants tip 10%, if it is not already added to bill; taxi drivers, 10%; airport and other porters, B35¢ per piece of baggage; hairdressers and chambermaids are tipped only for special services.

Electricity: 110 volts 50 cycles AC throughout the country.

Laundry: Laundries and laundromats available, and some hotels have 24-hour service. Dry-cleaners have 24-hour service (dry-cleaning a suit, from B$5; laundering a shirt, from B65¢).

Hairdressing: Some hotels have salons, and there are some in Bridgetown (shampoo and set, from B$12; man's haircut, from B$10).

Photography: Equipment (including Polaroid film) is widely available. Color film costs from B$7.50, black and white from B$5.00. To process color takes one week; black and white, 1-5 days.

Clubs: Rotary, Lions, Jaycees, Kiwanis

Babysitting: No listed agencies, but hotel staff may oblige.

Rest Rooms: Found in the usual places and at beaches with changing facilities.

Health: Imported toiletries and pharmaceuticals available. Drinking water is pure and safe everywhere.

BARBADOS

TRANSPORTATION

There are buses at a flat rate of 45¢, pay cash on entry. Taxis are readily available, whether by phoning, hailing one on the street, or going to a stand. Some are metered. Fares are B$1 per mile, with 25% increase at night. Chauffeur-driven cars are available at about B$24 for the first hour and B$16 thereafter, and rented cars cost from B$50. Motorcycles and scooters can also be rented from about B$18 per day. Traffic drives on the left; speed limits are strictly enforced. There are 850 miles of good roads, but they are narrow, and traffic is heavy—particularly in early morning and evening. **LIAT** (Leeward Islands Air Transport, 1974) is the principal inter-island carrier in the Lesser Antilles.

FOOD AND RESTAURANTS

Barbados offers a wide choice of good food. International and continental cuisine of high standard is available, and outdoor barbecues provide hearty steaks and roast lamb, but the great charm of Barbadian cooking is the exciting use of local foods—fish, meat, fruit, and vegetables. The flying fish, emblem of the island, is eaten baked, steamed, fried, or in a pie. Crane chubb and kingfish are other delicious fish. Roast suckling pig, sea urchins, green turtle steak, crab soup, and coconut bread are other exotic specialties. You can sample this exotic fare at the **Brown Sugar Inn** and several other indigenous local restaurants, or at the buffets provided at most hotels. *Coucou* (cornmeal pudding) and *jug-jug* (peas, guinea corn, and ground meat—a traditional Christmas dish) are worth trying. Local fruit includes sweet potatoes, yams, breadfruit, okras, plantains, paw-paws, mangoes, bananas, avocados, nutmeg, and coconut—their scent and flavor seem to float on the warm Caribbean breeze. Hotel restaurants are good, and arrangements can be made for visitors to dine at other hotels at no extra cost. It is advisable to make reservations.

Recommended are **Bagatelle Great House** in St Thomas, once the residence of the Governor of the West Indies (tel: 02072), for continental and Bajan dishes; **Chateau Creole,** St James (tel: 24116), local and continental specialities; **da Luciano,** Hastings, Christchurch (tel: 75518), traditional Italian cuisine; **Pisces,** St Lawrence Gap (tel: 86558), seafood; **Greensleeves,** St Peter (tel: 22275), haute cuisine in elegant setting; and the **Steak House,** St Lawrence Gap, Christchurch (tel: 87152). Good places to eat in and around Bridgetown include **The Flying Fish Club** (Bay Street—tel: 64537), the **Windmill** (Swan & Prince Willian Henry Streets—tel: 65481), the **Fort Charles Grill** at the Barbados Hilton (tel: 60200), the **Net & Trident** (Broad Street—tel: 64756), **Pebbles** (Hilton Drive—tel: 64668), and **Luigi's** (Dover—tel: 89218).

DRINKING TIPS

After the introduction of sugar cane on the island, a refreshing drink resulted—rum; it has been made and drunk in Barbados ever since and is the outstanding local beverage. Tours of both the Mount Gay distillery and the Banks brewery (local beer) can be arranged. Try all the concoctions: rum punch, planter's punch, rum on the rocks, egg flip, and *san-*

garee (with Madeira and Curaçao). Try *Bentley* too, a fruit punch named after the bishop who invented it in an effort to stop his parishioners drinking rum. The attempt failed, but *Bentley* is still worth trying. Another traditional refreshment is the Caribbean *mauby* (Spanish, *mavi*), a bittersweet beverage made from boiled tree bark extract. Imported liquors are sold at low duty-free prices—a whisky costs about B$1.25-4.50. There are no controls on drinking hours, and hotel bars are open to all. Better restaurants (including those in hotels) have wine lists, but wines tend to be expensive.

ENTERTAINMENT

Music and dancing are the big features of the entertainment scene. Concerts are given by the **Royal Barbados Police Band** and by the **Barbados Folk Singers**. "1627 and all that . . ." is an evening of feasting and entertainment offered on Thursday and Sunday at the Barbados Museum. The cost is B$50 per person, including dinner with wine and liquors and transportation to and from your hotel. Hotels and nightclubs have bands for dancing on different evenings, and they often feature floor shows with limbo dancers and calypso singers who compose impromptu verses. Steel bands flourish at local dances and hotels, as well as at nightspots. Most of the nightlife centers on the hotels, but the **Pepperpot** (St Lawrence Road) features Barbados' top floor shows and bands including **The Merrymen**, which has quite a following in Canada and USA. There are various discothèques—the **Hippo Disco** at the Barbados Beach Hotel and **Alexandra's** are good for singles. Other nightspots include the **Banana Boat, Tamarind Tree Club,** and **Bel Air.** On Mondays, **Island Inn** is jumping to the music of the steel bands. The annual **Crop-Over Festival** is celebrated with numerous sporting, artistic, and cultural events, ending with Kadooment Day, August 3. There are five movie houses in Bridgetown and two drive-ins showing British and American films.

SHOPPING

Stores are open 8-4 Mon-Fri, 8-12 noon Sat; closed Sun. Duty-free goods are available at low prices, and the range includes fine British woolens, tweed, Irish linen, Liberty silks, English bone china, French perfume, European glass, Swiss watches, Danish figurines, gold jewelry, and Japanese cameras.

The main stores are in the **Broad Street** area of Bridgetown, and many of the hotels run specialty and gift shops. Along the **St James Coast Road** stores sell Thai silks and Indian cottons made up into attractive clothing. In **Pelican Village** (on the Princess Alice Highway leading from Bridgetown to the Deep Water Harbor), sponsored by the Barbados Industrial Development Corporation, 30 shops sell Barbados arts and crafts—craftsmen can be seen as they work. You can buy tortoiseshell (some countries forbid this item to be brought back) and coral jewelry, mahogany articles, silverware, handwoven straw baskets, and tablemats.

Potters use primitive wheels to shape mugs, vases, and flowerpots at **Chalky Mount** in St Andrew. The largest selection of locally made batik is at the **Crane Beach Hotel.**

SPORTS

With its sun, coral reefs, and clear sea, water sports are one of the greatest attractions of Barbados. There is skin-diving and spearfishing, and the adventurous diver can explore the old ships that lie wrecked in **Carlisle Bay.** All equipment for water sports can be rented, and experts are available to give instruction if required. The hotels and Tourist Board offices will give information. The waters around Barbados are a happy hunting ground for all manner of fishermen, and a fantastic range of fish is waiting to challenge their skill—there are blue marlin, dolphin, tuna, barracuda, bonito, mackerel, wahoo, snapper, yellowtail, and many more, as well as the champion fighter of them all, the tarpon. Here too, hotels will give information. More water sports are covered by the **Barbados Yacht Club,** the **Barbados Sailing & Cruising Club,** and the **Water Ski Association.** There are three good 18-hole golf courses, the **Sandy Lane** (tel: 21493), the **Rockley Golf & Country Club** (tel: 77974), and the **Barbados Golf and Country Club** (tel: 86528)—all arrange for temporary membership and green fees are reasonably priced for visitors. The national game is cricket, played from June to January. A Barbados cricket match is a lively and colorful affair, well worth seeing. Soccer is another favorite pastime. Horseback riding along the coast by the Atlantic surf is exhilarating and very popular—the cost is B$18 an hour, with a guide; hotels will give details. There are tennis clubs, government tennis courts, and courts at the hotels. Horse racing, goat racing, crab racing, rugby, polo, bridge, croquet, badminton, and cycling are all available.

WHAT TO SEE

Bridgetown: Stroll along the **Wharf** and the **Careenage** and watch the busy harbor scene, where shrimp boats and flying-fish boats unload their catch; then go through **Trafalgar Square,** once the Green, center of island life, then renamed after the Battle of Trafalgar. A statue of Nelson presides over this Trafalgar Square, just as it does in London, but the Barbados statue was erected 27 years earlier. The **Barbados Museum** is a record of the island's history (open 10-6pm Mon-Sat, 2:30-6 Sun). The **Barbados Arts Council,** founded in 1957, arranges exhibitions of the work of local artists at the museum and elsewhere. The **Henry Bayley Observatory,** Clapham Street, gives demonstrations and lectures. Visit the island's churches; **St Michael's Cathedral** in Bridgetown, **St John's,** where you see the tomb of Ferdinando Paleologous, a descendant of Constantine the Great, and **St George's** church—built in 1784, but a church has stood here since 1641.

Around the island do your sightseeing by boat—there are boat trips with day picnics, sunset cocktail cruises, expeditions to the sunken ships wrecked off the lovely rugged coast, and trips in glass-bottomed boats to gaze at myriad fish. Visit a sugar factory and watch the way a stick of green sugarcane becomes the delectable Barbados rum. **Speightstown** in St Peter, once known as Little Bristol, was the original center of the busy sugar trade. **Morgan Lewis Windmill** at St Andrew is one of the last relics of early methods of sugar cultivation.

Barbados is dotted with plantation houses and old mansions, relics of the British colonial life of long ago and the lives of the wealthy planters— the "plantocracy," as they have been called. Many of these stately homes are open to the public from January to June, through the good work of the Barbados National Trust. These include **Villa nova,** St John, which has trees planted by Queen Elizabeth II and Prince Philip; **Porters,** St James; **Mullins Mill,** St Peters; **Bay Mansion,** St Michael; and **Drax Hall** and **Nicholas Abbey. Sam Lord's Castle** was built by a notorious pirate and wrecker out of his ill-gotten gains and furnished with his plunder. It is part of the Marriott Hotel now, and well worth a visit. Barbados abounds in old forts and signal towers, relics of 17th-century fortifications. See the house where George Washington is said to have stayed with his half-brother Lawrence—Barbados is the only place outside the United States George Washington ever visited—at the junction of Bay Street and Chelsea Road, in Bridgetown.

Cherry Tree Hill, reached through an avenue of casuarina and mahogany trees, gives a marvelous view of the fields of vivid green sugarcane and the Scotland District. **Cole's Cave** is a large cavern crossed by a river full of crayfish with stalagmites and stalactites. **Welchman's Hall Gully** in St Thomas is a garden of fruit, spice-bearing trees, and natural caves. Nearby is **Harrison Crystal Caves,** one of the world's most spectacular caves that can be visited by regular tram excursions (B$5).

Turner's Hall Woods in St Andrew is 45 acres of forest, as dense as that which once covered the island. There is a boiling spring of natural gas, and monkeys swing and scuffle in the trees. In **Holetown** there is a monument to the first landing of the British (1625). **Bathsheba** is a beautiful seaside resort on the east coast. The **Ashford Bird Park** is 12 miles from Bridgetown. Barbados would not be complete without reference to one of the most popular seagoing excursions—the **Jolly Roger Pirate Cruise** and **Cap'n Patch Cruises.** These are half-day (or day) excursions in island schooners converted to pirate ships. The two put out from the Careenage daily for a ride up the west coast (depending on wind and sea) to Discovery Bay, offering non-stop music, a West Indian style buffet lunch, plus an open bar. At the stop, water-skiing and parasailing are available, as is swimming. The excursions are sold at hotels and include the cost of transfer from hotel to Bridgetown and return.

SOURCES OF FURTHER INFORMATION

Any **Pan Am** office round the world; **Barbados Board of Tourism,** PO Box 242, Bridgetown, Barbados, WI; 800 2nd Avenue, New York, NY 10017; **Barbados High Commission,** 6 Upper Belgrave Street, London SWI.

Bermuda

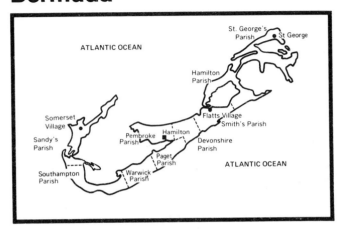

WHAT'S SPECIAL

Bermuda enjoys a temperate climate and is renowned for its pink sand beaches, so it should come as no surprise that tourism is the chief industry of these subtropical islands. Apart from the luxury hotels there are guest houses, cottage colonies, and apartments. And the islands have something for everyone most of the year—golf, fishing, water-skiing, sailing, swimming, or lying on the beach soaking up the sun. At night there is a wide choice of delicious food and entertainment—and you can dance until the small hours.

COUNTRY BRIEFING

Size: 21 square miles

Population: 54,000

Capital: Hamilton

Capital Population: 3,784

Climate: Mild, with an annual average temperature of 70° and lots of sunshine. Warmest months are May to mid-November; the rest of the year is slightly cooler. Average rainfall is 55" spread evenly through the year.

Weather in Hamilton: Lat N18°32'; Alt 150 ft

Temp (°F)	Jan	Feb	Mar	Apr	May	Jun	Jul	Aug	Sep	Oct	Nov	Dec
Av Low	58°	57°	57°	59°	64°	69°	72°	74°	72°	69°	63°	60°
Av High	68°	68°	68°	71°	76°	81°	85°	86°	84°	79°	74°	70°
Days no rain	17	15	19	21	22	21	21	18	20	19	17	16

Government: A self-governing British Colony.

Language: English.

Religion: Church of England. Other denominations are represented.

Currency: Bermuda dollar. 100 cents = 1 Bermuda dollar. The Bermuda dollar is on a par with the US dollar and is freely accepted everywhere. Canadian currency is accepted in most places but may be discounted. Sterling and all other foreign currencies are not accepted anywhere.

	B10¢	B50¢	B75¢	B$1	B$5	B$10	B$20	B$50
UK (pounds, pence)	.05	.24	.36	.48	2.39	4.77	9.54	23.85

Public Holidays:

New Year's Day, 1 Jan
Good Friday
Bermuda Day, 24 May
Queen's Birthday,
    13 June

Cup Match Day, Last Thur
    and Fri in July
Remembrance Day, 11 Nov
Christmas Day, 25 Dec
Boxing Day, 26 Dec

HOW TO GET THERE

Flying time to Bermuda from New York is 2 hours; from Toronto, 2½ hours; from London, 8½ hours. Time in Bermuda: GMT−4.

REQUIREMENTS FOR ENTRY AND CUSTOMS REGULATIONS

Round-trip ticket and one of the following items: passport, birth certificate, or for Americans US Naturalization Certificate, US Alien Registration Card, US Re-entry permit, or US Voter's Registration Card. Smallpox vaccination certificates required only of travelers who have been in an infected country within the preceding 14 days. Visitors may stay in Bermuda for 3 weeks; for longer stays, apply to the Chief Immigration Officer. No restrictions on foreign currency. Duty-free allowance: 200 cigarettes or 50 cigars or 1 pound tobacco; 1 quart liquor or wine; perfume for personal use; no allowance for gifts.

AIRPORT INFORMATION

The Civil Air Terminal is 8½ miles from Hamilton. Hotel pick-up buses meet all flights; fare into Hamilton is B$6. By taxi the fare is approximately B$7. No airport arrival tax, but departure of B$5.

ACCOMMODATIONS

The range is from luxury hotels to guest houses, cottage colonies, and housekeeping apartments and cottages. In Bermuda prices are generally lower during the winter months (December-March). There is a 5% hotel tax and an automatic service charge at most hotels of either B$4 per person per day or about 10%. Hotels in Bermuda:

Rates are in US$ for a double/twin room with bath or shower

Belmont, Warwick Parish (from $134 MAP), 3¼ miles from Hamilton

Bermudiana, Pembroke Parish (from $136 MAP), ¼ mile from center of Hamilton

Castle Harbour, Hamilton Parish (from $126 MAP), 7 miles from Hamilton

Elbow Beach, Paget Parish (from $126 MAP), 2½ miles from Hamilton

Glencoe, Paget Parish (from $105 MAP), 2¾ miles from Hamilton

Grotto Bay, Hamilton Parish (from $152 MAP), 7½ miles from Hamilton

Harmony Hall, Paget Parish (from $120 MAP), 2 miles from Hamilton

Holiday Inn, St George's Parish (from $130 MAP), 11¾ miles from Hamilton

Inverurie, Paget Parish (from $134 MAP), 3 miles from Hamilton

Mermaid Beach, Warwick Parish (from $106 MAP), 4¼ miles from Hamilton

Palmetto Bay, Smith's Parish (from $95 MAP), 4¼ miles from Hamilton

Pompano, Southampton Parish (from $98 MAP), 9 miles from Hamilton

Princess, Pembroke Parish (from $130 MAP), ½ mile from center of Hamilton

Reefs, Southampton Parish (from $108 MAP), 6¾ miles from Hamilton

Sonesta Beach, Southampton Parish (from $165 MAP), 6½ miles from Hamilton

Southampton Princess, Southampton Parish (from $142 MAP), 5¾ miles from Hamilton

Stonington, Paget Parish (from $82 BP), 2 miles from Hamilton

Waterloo House, Pembroke Parish (from $100 MAP), ¼ mile from center of Hamilton

White Sands, Paget Parish (from $90 MAP), 2 miles from Hamilton

USEFUL INFORMATION

The wearing of abbreviated costumes anywhere in public is actively discouraged; it is wiser to dress on the conservative side. Better restaurants are apt to be formal; wear a jacket and tie for dinner. Visitors are not allowed to rent cars, only motor bikes—and crash helmets are compulsory for riders. Traffic is on the left-hand side of the road.

Credit cards are accepted by most hotels which are members of the Bermuda Hotel Association (except the Holiday Inn). They are accepted by many stores and restaurants.

Banks: Open 9:30-3 Mon-Thurs, 9:30-3 and 4:30-6 Fri, closed Sat. No need to change US or Canadian currency.

Mail: Hotels usually sell stamps. In Hamilton the post office is on the corner of Church Street and Parliament Street.

Telephone Tips: Available in street booths and in hotels. Useful numbers:

Visitors' Service Bureau 5-1480	**Weather** 077
Air Sea Rescue 7-1010	**Police** 2-2222 (emergency only)
Directories & Operator 02	**Hospital** 5-2345
Time 09	**Current Events** 074

Newspapers: Local daily paper is *The Royal Gazette*. US, Canadian, and UK papers available.

Tipping: Customary. Where not included in the bill, 10-15% is the accepted amount. Taxi drivers, 15% of the fare; porters B50 cents for each piece of baggage; hotel porters B$1, at your discretion. At large hotels this is included in the bill.

Electricity: 110 volts 60 cycles AC.

Laundry: Facilities are excellent; all large hotels have good services (dry-cleaning a suit, from B$6; laundering a shirt from B$1.50).

Hairdressing: At major hotels and in Hamilton (shampoo and set, from B$8.50; man's haircut, from B$6).

Photography: Equipment available in Hamilton. Black and white film costs from about B$3.50 for a roll of 20; color from about B$4 for a roll of 12 prints, or from about B$5 for a roll of 24 prints, but prices vary. For developing either color or black and white, allow 24 hours.

Clubs: Rotary, Lions, Kiwanis, and Leopards.

Babysitting: Hotels help to find babysitters.

Rest Rooms: Public toilets in parks and at the ferry docks, also in hotels and restaurants.

Health: All doctors and dentists speak English. Pharmaceuticals available.

TRANSPORTATION

You can rent a bicycle for about B$4 a day, B$21 a week, and there are small motor bikes from B$11 a day, B$42 for 5 days. Metered taxis are available; those with a blue flag have earned the status of "qualified tour guide," and it is worth renting a taxi at B$11 an hour or B$66 a day to be shown the sights. Horse-drawn carriages are also available in Hamilton; a single carriage (for two) costs B$7.50 for 30 minutes; a double carriage (for four) costs B$10 for 30 minutes. The ferries, used by residents as well for transportation, are an inexpensive means of travel and a pleasant way to see Hamilton Harbor. Cost is B60 cents to B$1. The island also has a network of public buses with set timetables. Exact change in coin is required and fares are B60 cents to B$1. Schedule information obtainable from the Visitor's Service Bureau in Hamilton, by the ferry docks.

FOOD AND RESTAURANTS

Bermuda lobster is perhaps the most popular of the local foods. Other seafood dishes include Bermuda rockfish, red snapper, delicious fish chowder, turtle soup, and codfish. *Cassava pie*, made of pork, chicken, or beef filling surrounded by cassava crust, is another local dish, but hard to find—it's served only at Christmas. For seafood, go along to the **Lobster Pot** (tel: 2-6898) and the **Waterfront** (tel: 2-6122). For a more elegant atmosphere try the **Penthouse** (tel: 2-3414) or **Tom Moore's Tavern** (Bailey's Bay—tel: 3-1166). **The Harbourfront** (tel: 5-4207) has an open terrace with good harbor views; the specialty is charcoal-broiled entrées. The **Hog Penny** (tel: 2-2534) is a Bermudian pub with a warm atmosphere and good food. The **Horse and Buggy** is publike too. At **Rum Runners** or at **Longtail Bar and Restaurant** you can have a casual lunch on a balcony overlooking Hamilton Harbor. **The Four Ways** is in the center of Hamilton and offers good food at a medium price. Nearby is the **Penthouse** for steaks. For pleasant atmosphere, try **Waterlot Inn** in Southampton; **King Henry VIII**, also in Southampton, has good food in an English-pub setting. **The Holiday Inn** (tel: 7-8222) on a cliff overlooking historic Fort St Catherine, houses the **Mid-Atlantic Supper Club,** with good food and entertainment. **Little Venice,** on Bermudiana Road, is a good Italian restaurant, and **Ding Ho,** on Pitts Bay Road, serves Chinese and Polynesian specialties.

DRINKING TIPS

Drinking laws are very much the same as in the US. Liquor is available in bars and restaurants after 10am. A whisky and soda will cost from about B$2.50, a bottle of red wine from about $9. Try **Ye Olde Clock & Feather, The Waterlot Inn, The King Henry VIII,** the **Somerset Country Squire,** or **The White Horse Tavern.** The **Ram's Head** (Pitt's Bay Road, Pembroke) has a good pub atmosphere. **Pub on the Square** (King's Square—tel: 7-1522) is one of the oldest buildings in St George's; they will sell you a pint of British draught and a pub lunch, as will the **Carriage House** (tel: 7-1730) on Water Street, St George's.

ENTERTAINMENT

All large hotels provide dancing and entertainment. Examples are the **Princess** (Pitt's Bay Road), **Le Cabaret** nightclub at the Inverurie, and the famous **Elbow Beach Hotel.** Apart from the hotels, there is **Disco 40** (Hamilton), **The Clay House Inn** (Devonshire Parish), the **Half & Half** (Southampton Princess), and the **Hoop-a-loo Disco** at the Bermudiana Hotel (Hamilton). There are four movie houses in Bermuda, two in Hamilton, one in St George's, and one in Sandy's. The local newspaper will provide information on concerts and plays.

SHOPPING

Principal shopping areas are along Front Street in Hamilton, in St George, and in Somerset. Most hotels also have small shops. English imports are widely sold. There is genuine Wedgwood china from **A S Cooper** on Front Street and cashmere and wool sweaters, tweeds, and doeskin from **Trimingham's** and **H A & E Smith.** These two stores also stock Bermuda scarves, bags, and shorts. Boutiques selling sports and casual wear made in Bermuda are **Calypso** and the **English Sports Shop,** both on Front Street. English antiques can be bought at **H A & E Smith** and **Trimingham's** (open 9-5).

SPORTS

There are nine golf courses, and championships are held throughout the year, open to visitors. According to season there is cricket, rugby, or soccer. The **Royal Bermuda Yacht Club** welcomes visitors and races all classes of yachts. The **Newport-Bermuda Yacht Race** takes place every two years, and every April/May there is **International Race Week.** Bermuda is excellent fishing territory; best season is May through November.

Hire a ketch with a group of friends (from the **Bermuda Charter Booking Service** at Shed 6, Front Street, Hamilton—tel: 2-6246), and go out and catch yourself some wahoo, bonefish, yellowtail, amberjack, marlin, tuna, or mackerel. An annual **Game Fishing Tournament** is held, with trophies for the top catches in 17 different species of fish. If diving for fish is more appealing, you can rent equipment or take lessons at one of the several diving schools. However, spearfishing is prohibited within one mile of shore. You can also water-ski, swim at any of the many beaches or hotel pools, or play tennis.

WHAT TO SEE

St George's is the most enchanting part of the island. It was founded in 1612, and its old-world charm has been preserved. **St Peter's Church,** the oldest Anglican church site in the Western hemisphere, houses a set of communion silver which was a gift from King William III. **Gates Fort** and **St Catherine** are old rambling forts guarding the ancient town. Visit the **Confederate Museum, Carriage Museum,** or **St George's Historical Society Museum.** At Paget, visit the lovely **Botanical Gardens, Camden Museum,** and 17th-century **Verdmont House,** which has been restored by the Bermuda National Trust. Other attractions of the island are **Devil's Hole,** a tidal pond full of fish and turtles, the **Leamington** and **Crystal Caves,** and the **Blue Grotto** for delightful entertainment by performing dolphins. You can cruise in a glass-bottomed boat and see ancient shipwrecks, coral reefs, and marine life. Or you may prefer to visit the smaller islands for a picnic, taking one of the many cruise boats. Take a ferryboat trip from Hamilton Harbor to Paget, Warwick, or Somerset Island, and don't miss a 3-hour sail from the Bermudiana Waterfront, given by **Bermuda Water Tours** (from B$14 per person). There are limited sailings from June-September; make reservations in advance.

SOURCES OF FURTHER INFORMATION

Any **Pan Am** office around the world; **Bermuda Department of Tourism,** PO Box 465, Hamilton 5-23, Bermuda; 630 5th Avenue, New York, NY 10111; Suite 1010, 44 School Street, Boston, MA 02108; Suite 1150, Marina Towers Building, 300 North State Street, Chicago, IL 60610; 235 Peachtree Street, NE Atlanta, Georgia 30303; 9/10 Savile Row, London XIX 2BL; Suite 510, 1075 Bay Street, Toronto, Canada, M5S2B1.

British Virgin Islands

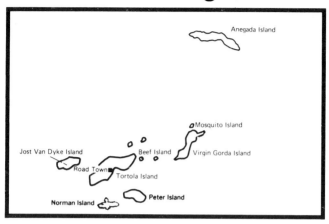

WHAT'S SPECIAL

The 16 inhabited islands in the group are favored by yachtsmen, divers, and nature lovers—there is no golf, no gambling, and no big-time entertainment. Norman Island is "Treasure Island," after which R L Stevenson named his famous novel; treasure was found there in the late 19th century.

COUNTRY BRIEFING

Size: 59 square miles
Population: 11,000
Capital: Road Town on Tortola
Capital Population: 8,500

Climate: Subtropical, with very little variation in temperature—78°-85° year round.

Government: UK territory; elected legislative council.

Religion: Protestant

Currency: The US dollar; some credit cards, such as American Express, are accepted.

Public Holidays:

New Year's Day, 1 Jan
Commemoration of Visit of HM The
  Queen, 23 Feb
Good Friday
Easter Monday Festival, Virgin Gorda
Commonwealth Day, 24 May

Whit Monday
Sovereign's Birthday, June
Territory Day, 1 July
August Weekend Festival
  (first Mon in Aug), Tortola
St Ursula's Day, 21 Oct

Prince of Wales's Birthday,
14 Nov

Christmas Day, 25 Dec
Boxing Day, 26 Dec

HOW TO GET THERE

Flying time to Beef Island Airport, Tortola from New York is 3¾ hours; from Miami 2½ hours; from San Juan, ¾ hour. Flying time from San Juan to Virgin Gorda is 50 minutes. Time in the British Virgin Islands: GMT−4.

REQUIREMENTS FOR ENTRY AND CUSTOMS REGULATIONS

US and Canadian citizens can enter on proof of citizenship and possession of an onward ticket. Because of tight immigration controls, American visitors are advised to travel with proper proof of citizenship other than a social security card or driver's license. A valid passport is preferred but not mandatory. Other nationals require an onward ticket, passport, and, in some cases, a visa. A smallpox vaccination certificate is required (except for US citizens), as are cholera and yellow-fever inoculations if coming from an infected area. No customs allowances on tobacco, liquor, perfume, and gifts. Not a duty-free port.

AIRPORT INFORMATION

No airport buses, but taxis readily available. Fare from Beef Island Airport into Road Town is about US$8. No arrival tax; departure tax of $2.50 by air, or $1.50 if by sea.

ACCOMMODATIONS

Accommodations in the British Virgin Islands range from luxury hotels to the much smaller guest-houses. Rates are lower from April 15 to December 15. There is a 10% service charge and 5% hotel tax. Hotels in the British Virgin Islands:

Rates are in US$ for a double/twin room with bath or shower
  Anegada Reefs, Anegada (from $65 AP)
  Biras Creek, Virgin Gorda (from $95)
  Bitter End Yacht Club, Virgin Gorda (from $115)
  Blackbeard's Tavern, Virgin Gorda (from $60 AP)
  CSY Yacht Club, Tortola (from $35 EP)
  Fischers Cove Beach, Virgin Gorda (from $50 EP)
  Guavaberry Spring Bay, Virgin Gorda (from $70 EP)
  Last Resort, Tortola (from $50 MAP)
  Little Dix Bay, Virgin Gorda (from $250)
  Long Bay, Tortola (from $24 EP)
  Marina Cay, Road Town, Tortola (from $80 MAP)
  Moorings/Mariner Inn, Tortola (from $40 EP)
  Ocean View, Virgin Gorda (from $50 MAP)
  Olde Yard Inn, Virgin Gorda (from $60 MAP)
  Peter Island Yacht Club, Peter Island (from $160 AP)
  Prospect Reef Resort, Tortola (from $90 EP)
  Sea View, Tortola (from $17 EP)

Smuggler's Cove, Tortola (from $43 EP)
Sugar Mill Estate, Tortola (from $62 EP)
Treasure Isle, Tortola (from $55 EP)
Village Cay Marina, Tortola (from $44 EP)
White Bay Sand Castle, Jost Van Dyke (from $112 MAP)

USEFUL INFORMATION

Banks are open 9-2 weekdays, and stay open late 4-6 Fri. **Stamps** are available from hotels and post offices. **Public telephones** few and far between. Useful numbers: **Tourist Office,** 4-3134; **Operator,** 0; and **Overseas Operator,** 7. English-language **newspapers** available; local *Island Sun* appears weekly. **Tipping:** a service charge of 10-15% is generally included in restaurant checks; it is customary to leave a little extra. **Electricity** is variable between 115 and 210 volts 60 cycles AC (no adaptors therefore necessary). Only the larger hotels have express **laundry** and **dry-cleaning.** Few hotels have **hairdressing** salons. Limited selection of film and **photographic** equipment; developing and processing take minimum of a week. Hotels will arrange **babysitting** services. No charge for **rest rooms,** which you will find in hotels, bars, and restaurants. **Health:** imported pharmaceuticals available at reasonable prices.

TRANSPORTATION

Beef Island Airport (Tortola) is 15 minutes by air from St Thomas, 30 minutes from St Croix and about 40 minutes from San Juan. The trip from downtown Charlotte Amalie, St Thomas, to West End Tortola by air-conditioned ferry (the Bomba Charger) takes 45 minutes. No public land transport, but taxis are available. Cars, preferably 4-wheel-drive jeeps, Land Rovers or Mini-Mokes, can be rented for about US$20 a day (US driver's license and locally purchased permit—US$2.50—are required). Drive on the left. Roads are narrow and many unsurfaced. There are regular ferry services between some islands.

FOOD AND RESTAURANTS

On Tortola is **Upstairs** (tel: 42175), which specializes in continental cuisine and has a panoramic view of Road Harbor. **Sea View** (tel: 42595) serves local West Indian dishes. Another recommended restaurant is **Fischers Cove** on Virgin Gorda (tel: 55252). Popular dining spots in Road Town are **Caribe Casseroles,** and the **Sir Francis Drake Pub** (tel: 42608). **Jill's Beach Bar** is an attractive, informal spot at Cane Garden Bay. Next door is **Stanley's,** where the hamburgers are remarkable. Hotels have their own generally excellent restaurants for guests and "outsiders." Reservations are required.

SHOPPING

Some good handicraft and gift stores in Road Town are **Caribbean Handprints,** the **Handcraft Centre, Past & Presents, Little Denmark, Cockle Shop, Bonkers Gallery, Landfall, Turtle Dove,** and **Esme's Shop** for cashmere sweaters, Liberty fabrics, etc.

SPORTS

Yachts, with or without crew, can be chartered from **Caribbean Sailing Yachts, Tortola Yacht Charters,** and **Moorings,** all on Road Harbor, Tortola. Diving is popular, and there are hundreds of wrecks along **Horseshoe Reef,** off Anegada Island. **Dive BVI** and **Kilbride's Underwater Tours** on Virgin Gorda, and **Aquatic Centers,** and the **Moorings** on Tortola have instructors and equipment. One of the best dives is to the wreck of the *Rhône*, which sank off Salt Island in 1867. Game fishing for marlin, sailfish, wahoo, and tuna is excellent everywhere.

WHAT TO SEE

Mount Healthy and Mount Sage—a primeval rain forest—are superb areas for walking tours on Tortola. **The Baths** at Virgin Gorda is a strange coastal area where boulders as big as houses are tumbled together forming grottoes, caverns, and pools. The copper mine on Virgin Gorda was worked by the Spaniards in the early 18th century.

SOURCES OF FURTHER INFORMATION

Any **Pan Am** office around the world; The BVI **Tourist Board,** PO Box 134, Road Town, Tortola; **British Virgin Islands Information Office,** 515 Madison Avenue, New York, NY 10022; **West India Committee,** 48 Albemarle Street, London WIX 4AR England.

Cayman Islands

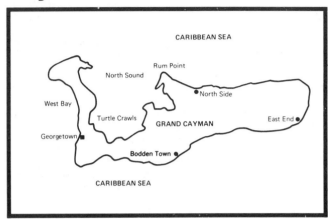

WHAT'S SPECIAL

The Cayman Islands were first sighted by Christopher Columbus in 1503 on his last voyage to the New World. He called them Las Tortugas, or the "islands of the turtles," after all the tortoises he saw there—and though that name was not to last, turtle soup and turtle steaks are still the specialty of local chefs. These charming little islands, with their lovely beaches, open bays, and ragged coastlines, are almost surrounded by a treacherous ring of coral reefs, the graveyard for over 300 ships. Lying all around the islands are the hulls of old sailing ships and not-so-old steamers. The notorious "Wreck of the Ten Sails" was in 1788—ten ships went down at Gun Bay on Grand Cayman. These sunken vessels are now an attraction for underwater divers. Tales of buried treasure and buccaneers add romance to the history of the Cayman Islands.

COUNTRY BRIEFING

Size: Grand Cayman, 76 square miles

Cayman Brac, 14 square miles

Little Cayman, 10 square miles

Population: 17,000

Capital Population: 7,617

Capital: George Town

Climate: The average winter temperature is 75°, and the average summer temperature 85°.

Weather in George Town: Lat N19°20′; Alt sea level

Temp (°F)	Jan	Feb	Mar	Apr	May	Jun	Jul	Aug	Sep	Oct	Nov	Dec
Av Low	69°	69°	69°	69°	72°	75°	75°	75°	74°	74°	72°	70°
Av High	82°	83°	84°	86°	87°	88°	89°	89°	89°	87°	84°	83°
Days no rain	21	19	18	26	14	20	7	13	8	12	13	15

Government: British Crown Colony.

Language: English.

Religion: Presbyterian.

Currency: Cayman Islands dollar. CI$.83 = US$1. US, Canadian, and UK currencies are widely accepted, but it is probably easier to carry travelers' checks and convert into the local currency.

Public Holidays:

New Year's Day, 1 Jan	Constitution Day, 1st Mon in
Ash Wednesday	July
Good Friday	Mon after Remembrance Sun,
Easter Monday	Nov
Discovery Day, 3rd Mon in May	Christmas Day, 25 Dec
Queen's Birthday	Boxing Day, 26 Dec

HOW TO GET THERE

Flying time to Grand Cayman's Owen Roberts Airport from New York is 3½ hours; from Miami, 1¼ hours; from Mexico City, 2 hours. Time in the Cayman Islands: GMT−5.

REQUIREMENTS FOR ENTRY AND CUSTOMS REGULATIONS

For citizens of the US and Canada, no passport or visa required—only proof of citizenship and round-trip ticket. For British or other Commonwealth citizens, passports but not visas required. Smallpox vaccination certificate not needed if arriving from US, Canada, or UK. No currency regulations. Duty-free allowances: 200 cigarettes or 50 cigars or ½ pound tobacco; 1 quart liquor or wine; perfume for personal use.

AIRPORT INFORMATION

Owen Roberts International Airport, George Town, is 2 miles from the city center; taxi fare is about CI$5. The departure tax is CI$3.28 (US$4). There is a duty-free shop at the airport and a hotel reservations counter.

ACCOMMODATIONS

Hotels are comfortable and well appointed, and in many it is possible to rent cottages or apartments. Rates are highest December-April. Most hotels include a 15% service charge in the rates and there is a 5% government tax added to bills at departure. Cayman Island Hotels:

Rates are in US$ for a double/twin room with bath or shower

 Beach Club Colony, PO Box 903, West Bay Beach (from $80)

 Brac Reef Hotel, Cayman Brac (from $65 EP)

 Buccaneer's Inn, PO Box 68, Cayman Brac (from $95 AP)

 Caribbean Club, PO Box 504, West Bay Beach (from $110 EP)

 Cayman Kai, PO Box 1112, North Side (from $79)

 Dillon Cottage, Little Cayman (from $250 weekly)

 Galleon Beach, PO Box 71, West Bay Beach (from $85)

 Grand Caymanian Holiday Inn, PO Box 904, West Bay Beach (from $88)

Royal Palms, PO Box 490, West Bay Beach (from $79)
Sea View, PO Box 260, George Town (from $48)
Sunset House, PO Box 479, George Town (from $63)
Tortuga Club, PO Box 496, East End (from $139 MAP)
West Indian Club, PO Box 703, West Bay Beach (from $110)
Kingston Bight Lodge, Little Cayman (from $90 EP)

USEFUL INFORMATION

Banks: Open from 9-2:30 Mon-Thurs.; 9-4:30 Fri.

Telephone Tips: Telephone booths are coin operated. Useful numbers:

Airport Information 9-2811	Operator, Time, Directory
Tourist Office 9-4844 ext. 175	Enquiries 10
Hotel Association 9-4341	Hospital 9-2121

Newspapers: Foreign newspapers are available; local papers are the *Caymanian Compass* and the *Cayman Times* (both twice weekly). The *Nor'wester* magazine comes out monthly.

Tipping: Not customary. Hotels and restaurants charge 10-15%.

Electricity: 110 volts 60 cycles AC.

Laundry: Good facilities in George Town (dry-cleaning a suit, from CI$3; laundering a shirt, from CI50 cents).

Hairdressing: There are hairdressers in the town but not at hotels (shampoo and set from CI$5.00, man's haircut from CI$2).

Photography: A good selection of equipment is available at duty-free prices in George Town. Take film home to be developed.

Clubs: Rotary, Lions, Jaycees, Kiwanis, Inner Wheel, and Freemasons.

Health: Imported pharmaceuticals and toiletries available.

TRANSPORTATION

Taxis are available, their rates fixed by the Taxi Cab Association. You can rent a car from about CI$20 per day, bicycles from CI$4 a day, mopeds and motorcycles from CI$8.50-11 a day. Drive on the left.

FOOD AND RESTAURANTS

The specialties of the island are turtle soup and turtle steaks. The seafoods—including lobster, conch pie, and snapper—are superb. If you make a good catch while out fishing, ask your hotel to cook it for you. If you rent a local boat, the boathands will assist you in preparing a cookout on the beach. Many other foods in the Caymans are imported, and continental cuisine is available. For a native-style lunch, the **Lighthouse Club** at **Breakers,** beyond Bodden Town, is delightful, and for Cayman and Jamaican dishes go along to **Welly's Cool Spot** (North Sound Road—tel: 9-2541). For excellent food and service and the charm of eating on the Victorian veranda of a gracious old plantation mansion, go to the **Grand Old House** (South Church Street—tel: 9-2020). Also elegant and recommended is **Ports of Call** (North Church Street—tel:

9-2231). At the **Lobster Pot** (North Church Street—tel: 9-2736) the specialty is obvious, as it is **Cap'n Morgan's Steak Gallery** at the Galleon Beach Hotel (tel: 9-2692). The **Man o'War Room** in the same hotel is another excellent place for seafood. Seafood and beef are also served at the popular **Yorkshire Pudding** at West Bay Beach (tel: 9-5575). For a sophisticated lunch or dinner, drive out to the East End of Grand Cayman to the **Tortuga Club** (tel: 7-2488). **The Cayman Arms** on the waterfront (Harbour Drive—tel: 9-2661) is a popular place with good food and **Corita's Copper Kettle,** on Edward Street in downtown George Town, is the place for light lunches, snacks and carry outs, plus Caymanian cooking on Friday and Saturday evenings (tel: 9-2695).

DRINKING TIPS

Imported liquors are available. Fresh fruit and rum punches are specialties. Bars generally have an intimate English-pub-like atmosphere.

ENTERTAINMENT

The islands are quiet at night, a good place for those who want to go to bed early for an early start at the sun and sea the next day. During the high season there is nightly entertainment at the **Royal Palms Hotel,** the **Holiday Inn,** the **Galleon Beach Hotel, Pedro's Castle,** and the **Apollo Eleven,** a native bar and restaurant. There are also two open-air movie theaters, a drive-in, and movies shown by the Hotel Association.

SHOPPING

The Caymans are a duty-free port, and imports are available—watches, perfume, china, jewelry, cameras, cashmere, and electrical goods. Some specialist stores in George Town are **Kirk Freeport** at two locations and at the airport, the **Treasure Cove,** and the **English Shoppe.** Good local crafts include hats, bags, and articles made of caymanite and black coral. Best shops for these and other crafts by local artisans are **Black Coral And. . .,** **Caribe Island Jewellery, The Jewellery Factory, Caymandicraft,** the **Cayman Curio Shop, Cayman ARTVentures,** and the **Grand Cayman Craft Market,** all in George Town. Turtleshell products are sold at the **Cayman Turtle Farm Jewellery Shop** in town and the **Turtle Gift Shop** at the farm at North West Point. Be aware, however, that though items are sold with a certificate attesting their origins as farmed turtles, even the products of farmed turtles are prohibited in the United States and in many other countries that prohibit trade in endangered species. It is not customary to bargain.

SPORTS

Conditions are ideal and world famous for water sports and fishing. The flats around Little Cayman are said to be the best bone-fishing area in the world. You can hire a boat and go out after giant bluefin, wahoo, marlin, bonito, amberjack, and barracuda. Coral reefs and submerged shipwrecks provide a superlative environment for snorkelers and scuba divers. Most hotels rent equipment. Many hotels have tennis courts and the **Cayman Racquet Club** has facilities for tennis and squash.

WHAT TO SEE

On Grand Cayman, the **Seven Mile Beach,** sometimes known as the West Bay Beach, stretches north of George Town and is considered one of the best in the Caribbean. The **Cayman Turtle Farm,** the world's first such commercial green turtle farming project, makes a fascinating visit at **North West Point.** Go up to **Pedro's Castle,** a romantic old castle built by Pedro the Terrible and said to have been the headquarters of Henry Morgan and his pirates. In the fall, the islands' buccaneering background is celebrated during **Pirates' Week** with a parade, treasure hunts, a mock invasion and a ball. **Rum Point** has a beautiful garden of orchids and colorful parrots. Visit the **Kiemanus Museum** in George Town, with treasures from the ancient shipwrecks, or take a boat trip over to **Cayman Brac,** about 90 miles northeast of Grand Cayman. Cayman Brac has a precipitous bluff running the entire length of the island and is honeycombed with caverns reputed to contain pirate treasure. Nests of a very rare bird, the booby, can be found here. Stay at the **Brac Reef Hotel,** Cayman Brac (from US$65 double EP) or the **Buccaneer's Inn,** PO Box 68, Cayman Brac (from US$95 double AP). **Little Cayman,** practically undeveloped, is a low-lying island of lovely beaches and coral reefs.

SOURCES OF FURTHER INFORMATION

Any **Pan Am** office around the world; **Cayman Islands Department of Tourism,** PO Box 67, George Town, Grand Cayman, BWI; 250 Catalonia Avenue, Coral Gables, FL 33134; 420 Lexington Avenue, Room 2312, New York, NY 10017, and in Chicago, Houston and Los Angeles; **Earl B. Smith, Travel Marketing Consultants,** 11 Adelaide Street W., Suite 406, Toronto, Ontario; Canada M5H 1L9; 48 Albermarle Street, London W1X 4AR; Goethestrasse 21, D-8000 Munchen 2, Germany; **Cayman Islands News Bureau Inc.,** PO Box 330106, Coconut Grove, Miami, FL 33133.

Cuba

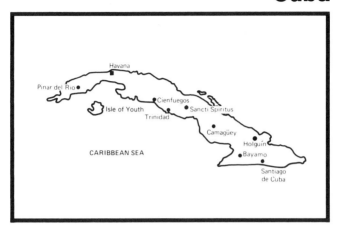

WHAT'S SPECIAL

At different periods in her history Cuba has been dominated by Spain, Britain, and the United States, until an intensely nationalistic movement established Cuban independence in 1902. Another revolution in 1959, led by Fidel Castro and involving the now legendary Che Guevara, established a socialist government. Visitors to Cuba today not only enjoy tropical beaches but can observe a changing society as well.

COUNTRY BRIEFING

Size: 44,218 square miles
Capital: Havana

Population: 9,825,000
Capital Population: 1,900,240

Climate: Semitropical or temperate except in the mountains. Rainy season from mid-May to October; dry season November to April. Cuba is a Spanish-speaking socialist republic. The **currency** is the peso; 100 centavos = 1 peso; .73 pesos = US$1. The only travelers' checks accepted are American Express, Barclay's and Cook's. (Leave "payee" and "date" blank when cashing travelers' checks.) Exchange currency at local banks and hotels. Currency control sheets are issued and purchases made in foreign currency shops are deducted from the sheets. Surplus pesos may be reconverted at departure only on presentation of currency control sheets. Only Cuban currency is accepted in hotels and shops so be sure to exchange it as soon as you arrive at the hotel. **Public Holidays:** Liberation Holidays, 1-2 Jan; Labor Day, 1 May; Revolution Day, 26 July.

HOW TO GET THERE

Flying time to José Marti Airport, Havana from Toronto is 4¼ hours; from Panama City, 3¼; from Mexico City, 2 hours. From the US, direct flights are via charter only. Time in Cuba: GMT−5. Daylight Saving Time observed.

REQUIREMENTS FOR ENTRY AND CUSTOMS REGULATIONS

US and Canadian citizens require a valid passport and a visa obtained in the United States from the Cuban Interests Section of the Czechoslovak Embassy in Washington, DC, or in Canada from the Cuban Embassy in Ottawa. At the time of writing, citizens of France, Sweden, Switzerland, Italy, the USSR, Poland, and Czechoslovakia do not require visas, but it is best to check locally for the latest information. Tour operators usually secure visas for tourists. Both cultural-historical and beach holiday tours are available.

At present, US citizens visiting Cuba as tourists may do so on a tour, or on an individual basis. Most tours include airfare from the home country. The daily rate is approximately US$75 per day, including all meals.

US citizens visiting Cuba on business or for professional reasons as individuals must have a visa sponsor in Cuba who either extends a formal invitation or assumes visa responsibility on specific request. Sponsors are usually institutions or ministries of government.

For visa information and names of travel agencies that arrange visits to Cuba, contact: Cuban Interests Section, Embassy of Czechoslovakia, 2639 16th Street NW, Washington, DC 20009.

No Cuban pesos may be brought into Cuba. Jewelry and other valuables including electrical appliances should be declared upon entering. Smallpox, yellow-fever, and cholera certificates are needed if entering from an infected region. Duty-free allowance: 200 cigarettes or 100 cigars, 1 bottle liquor. There is a $100 limit on departing with duty-free purchases.

ACCOMMODATIONS

Hotels are operated by **INTUR** (National Institute of Tourism), and reservations are made through **Cubatur**, its service division. Deluxe accommodation costs about US$34 per person in a double/twin room. First class, approximately US$29 per person in a double/twin room. Deluxe hotels in Havana are the **Riviera,** the **Habana Libre,** the **Capri,** and the **Nacional.** Less expensive hotels can be reserved. In Santiago de Cuba, **Hotel Versalles** and **Balcon de Caribe** are first class. Other comfortable hotels around the country are the **Marazul Hotel** in Santa Maria del Mar; **Pasacaballos** in Cienfuegos; **Hotel Guardalavaca** at Guardalavaca; the **Colony** on the Isle of Youth; and the **International Hotel,** Varadero Beach.

Group tourists have hotel rooms pre-booked but individuals must reserve well in advance since accommodations are in great demand. Hotels are assigned by Cubatur.

USEFUL INFORMATION

There is no tipping. Electricity is 110 volts 60 cycles, 2-prong system. Take with you camera film, extra batteries for any battery-operated apparatus, and all items of a personal nature, including pharmaceuticals and toiletries. You will be issued an identification card when you check into any hotel; it must be presented whenever you wish to pay or sign a bill or to exchange money. A 40-50% discount on liquor and wine is granted holders of foreign currency control sheets in hotels and deluxe restaurants. At present, MasterCard is the only credit card accepted.

TRANSPORTATION

Cubana, the national airline, has flights to all major points on the island. A modern bus service also serves major centers along good-quality main roads. Public transportation in larger cities is inexpensive but crowded. Taxis are metered, but difficult to hail on the street. It's easier to request a cab from the dispatcher at any hotel, where taxis are assigned on a first-come, first-served basis. A car and driver can be hired in Havana for $7 dollars per hour, through the Cubatur desk in deluxe hotels. Self-drive cars are not yet available. Cars and drivers outside of Havana can also be booked through Cubatur at varying rates.

FOOD AND ENTERTAINMENT

Restaurant menus are limited, and the cost of food is rather high— US$15-$25 in a first-class restaurant and US$12 in an average one. Members of group tours have all meals included, usually in hotel dining rooms. However, tour members are free to eat elsewhere—though meals consumed off the tour plan are at the tourist's expense as no refund is made for unconsumed tour meals. Among Havana's better known restaurants are: **La Bodeguita del Medio,** a bohemian-style restaurant serving typically Cuban dishes and once favored by Hemingway; **Floridita,** another old Hemingway haunt with French romantic decor; **Las Ruinas** in Lenin Park; **Las Andes,** South American dishes; **La Torre,** on the rooftop of the Focsa apartment building; **Conejito,** specializing in rabbit. In Santiago de Cuba, try **Santiago 1900,** a beautifully restored Spanish mansion; in Camagüey, **La Volanta,** and in Cienfuegos, **La Verja,** both also restored mansions.

About 12 theater halls provide varied entertainment, including symphony concerts and folkloric music and dance performances. There are performances by the **National Ballet** throughout the year. At night, see the colorful floor show at the **Tropicana** and the shows at the **Parisien** (Nacional Hotel), the **Salon Rojo** (Capri Hotel), and the **Copa Room** (Riviera Hotel). At Varadero Beach, the floor show at the **International Hotel** is very well-known, as is **Las Americas,** a restaurant on the grounds of the former mansion of Irene Du Pont. There are movie houses all around the country, charging not more than one peso admission and showing both Cuban and foreign films, including the occasional US import.

SPORTS

Cuba has many lovely beaches ideal for swimming and underwater diving. Small boats and fishing and scuba equipment are available. Sport fishing is gaining prominence and the **Barlovento Marina** near Havana is frequent host to tournaments. **Treasure Lake** is also famous for its plentiful lake bass. Tennis is available at some hotels or at local tennis clubs. Baseball is the most popular spectator sport, although bicycle racing is also popular, and soccer and basketball are often played. There is a 9-hole golf course at **Varadero Beach.** There is horseback riding at Havana's **Lenin Park.**

WHAT TO SEE

Modern Havana is a cosmopolitan city with very distinct sections: **Vedado** and **Central Havana** are residential and commercial areas; the **Plaza de la Revolucion** is the focal point of major government buildings; **Old Havana,** partially restored, has scenic, narrow cobblestoned streets and Spanish colonial architecture. In Old Havana, see the **Cathedral** and the **Cathedral Plaza,** the **Museum of Colonial Art,** the **Castillo del Morro,** the **Castillo de la Fuerza** now housing the **Arms Museum,** and the **Captains and Generals Palace,** housing the **Museum of the City of Havana** on the lovely **Plaza de Armas.** The **National Museum of Art** contains both classical and modern Cuban art, as well as excellent Greek and Egyptian collections. The **Hemingway Museum** is the American writer's former home, with books, furniture, and memorabilia as they were when he lived there. (Actual entry is not permitted—the house is seen through its windows.) Other interesting museums are the **Museum of Decorative Arts,** with objects from all over the world; the **Numismatic Museum,** with a collection from colonial times to the present; and the **Napoleonic Museum,** with 18th- and 19th-century period furniture, clothing, and paintings.

Other towns often visited by groups are **Trinidad,** virtually a museum city of 18th- and 19th-century buildings; **Cienfuegos, Camagüey,** and **Santiago de Cuba,** the latter at the island's extreme eastern end. Other sites of interest include **Gran Piedra National Park, Treasure Lake,** the **Viñales Valley** with beautiful and unusual geological formations, the mountain resort of **Soroa.**

The best beaches can be found just east of Havana at **Santa Maria del Mar,** where hotel and private villa accommodation, plus recreational facilities and public bus service into the city are available. **Varadero Beach,** Cuba's most famous, is located 84 miles east of Havana. The beach itself is some 10 miles long and in the town there are hotel and villa accommodations ranging from deluxe and first class to budget, numerous restaurants, and many recreational options including tandem bicycling, costing about $1.30 per hour.

Situated 60 miles off the southern coast of Cuba is the **Isle of Youth** (formerly called the Isle of Pines), well known as the site of Cuba's first schools in the countryside. Today the island is a major producer of citrus fruits. There are fine beaches and excellent snorkeling and diving.

SOURCES OF FURTHER INFORMATION

Cubatur, Calle 23 #156, Vedado, Havana, 4; **Cuban Interests Section,** Embassy of Czechoslovakia, 2639 16th Street NW, Washington, DC 20009; **Cuban Embassy,** 282 Main Street, Ottawa, Ontario K1S 1E3; 57 Kensington Court, London W8.

Dominica

WHAT'S SPECIAL

Dominica is one of the largest of the Windward Islands, yet, apart from its capital and a few other settlements, it is one of the least "developed." Its landscape must be very much as it was when Columbus discovered it in 1493, on a Sunday, and named it in honor of the Sabbath. It is mountainous and rugged, with a tropical jungle, whose rich soil yields bumper crops of bananas, vanilla, and citrus; according to popular legend, it has as many rivers as days of the year. It is the inaccessibility of the island that made it unconquerable for most of its history. Fortunately, it still remains isolated enough to provide a refuge for the tourist who seeks beauty, solitude, and peaceful surroundings. The island was badly damaged by Hurricane David in 1979 but tourist facilities are being reconstructed.

COUNTRY BRIEFING

Size: 290 square miles   **Population:** 81,300
Capital: Roseau   **Capital Population:** 18,000
   Climate: Temperature varies according to the altitude. Rainfall is 60-70 inches on the coast and as much as 300 inches in the mountainous interior. The driest and best time to visit is November-June.
   Weather in Roseau: Lat N15°18'; Alt 60 ft

Temp (°F)	Jan	Feb	Mar	Apr	May	Jun	Jul	Aug	Sep	Oct	Nov	Dec
Av Low	68°	67°	68°	69°	71°	73°	72°	73°	73°	72°	71°	69°
Av High	84°	85°	87°	88°	90°	90°	89°	89°	90°	89°	87°	86°
Days no rain	15	18	18	20	20	15	9	9	14	15	12	15

Government: Formerly a British Colony, Dominica gained its independence within the British Commonwealth in 1978 and is now fully self-governing.

Language: English, a French patois, and Creole.

Religion: Roman Catholic and Protestant.

Currency: Eastern Caribbean dollar. $2.70 EC=US$1.00

Public Holidays:

New Year's Day, 1 Jan	Whit Monday, 31 May
Carnival, 20-21 Feb	Queen's Birthday, 3 June
Good Friday, 9 Apr	Bank Holiday, 2 Aug
Easter Monday, 12 Apr	Christmas, 25 Dec
Labor Day, 1 May	Boxing Day, 26 Dec

HOW TO GET THERE

There is no jetport in Dominica. Flying time to Melville Hall Airport from New York via connecting flight in Puerto Rico is about 4½ hours; from Miami, 2 hours, from Puerto Rico 1¼ hours. Time in Dominica: GMT−4.

REQUIREMENTS FOR ENTRY AND CUSTOMS REGULATIONS

Citizens of the USA, Canada, and the UK need only show proof of citizenship (not necessarily a passport) and a round-trip ticket. Other nationalities need a passport and round-trip ticket and some need visas. Check your Consulate before leaving. Cholera and yellow-fever vaccination certificates are needed when arriving from an infected area. Duty-free allowance: 200 cigarettes or 4 oz tobacco or 50 cigars; 40 oz liquor.

AIRPORT INFORMATION

Melville Hall Airport is 36 miles northeast of Roseau. There is no bus service other than pickup service by specific hotels, but taxis are available; fare to Roseau is EC$30, or about US$11.50. Airport departure tax is EC$8. There is no duty-free shop.

ACCOMMODATIONS

There are good hotels in attractive spots, and they are centers of social life. There are a limited number of small guesthouses where accommodations may cost no more than US$12 per night. Rates are lower from April to December, and there is a 10% hotel tax and 10% service charge. Hotels in Dominica include:

Rates are in US$ for a double/twin room with bath or shower

Anchorage Hotel (from $45 EP)

Reigate Hall, Reigate (from $65 MAP)

Sisserou, Castle Comfort (from $53 CP)

Springfield Plantation, 2 miles from National Park (from $70 MAP)

USEFUL INFORMATION

Banks: Open 8-12 Mon-Fri.

Tipping: A 10% service charge is added by most hotels and restaurants.

Electricity: 220–240 volts, AC, 50 cycles. American appliances require a converter.

TRANSPORTATION

Taxis are available. Rates are set by law and are about 40¢ per mile. Cars can be rented for US$20 for one day; US$15 for a longer period. Ask for a jeep or Land Rover; the roads are poor. Drive on the left. A local driver's permit is available for a small fee.

FOOD AND RESTAURANTS

Island food is spicy—Bello Hot Pepper sauce, a local product, is served with or on almost everything except desserts. Expect to enjoy Creole, Continental, and American styles of cooking. Among local delicacies are smoked agouti, wild pigeon, pork, frog legs, and smoked stuffed crabs. For well-prepared native dishes, try **Calabash Inn** in Roseau. **Green Parrot,** open for lunch only, features cold soups. **La Robe Creole Tavern Lounge** is a popular choice for ambience, salads, and sandwiches. Outside Roseau, near the Trafalgar Falls, is the **Papillote Rain Forest Restaurant,** specializing in health foods—homemade bread and yogurt, bean sprout salad, and the like. **Seamoon Club,** north of Roseau on the coast, serves wonderful fried chicken and rum punch. Most hotels have restaurants and will accept reservations from nonguests.

DRINKING TIPS

The island fruit juices are remarkable, and so are the rum punches. An outstanding local drink is the nonalcoholic seamoss, made from seamoss or seaweed, with a minty taste. Rum and liquor are not expensive, but wines are costly.

ENTERTAINMENT

Most hotel lounges close at 10. There are two discos in Roseau, **The Green Grotto** and the **Night Pot**—both are popular locally on weekends.

SHOPPING

Shops are open 8-12 and 1:30-4pm Mon-Sat. **Tropicrafts** features local handicrafts of vetiver grass joined with wild banana fronds, creating rugs, hats, bags. Prices are reasonable and the products are attractive. Two clothing factories on the island produce french-cut blue jeans that sell for US$12.

SPORTS

Snorkeling is popular. Equipment and an instructor are available for about US$10 an hour for a party of four. It's possible to rent a motorboat for four for about US$20 an hour. Check with your hotel for specifics. For about US$8 (per person) an hour, a party of four can charter a boat and a guide for deep-sea fishing.

WHAT TO SEE

Roseau's Botanical Garden houses a collection of the plants of the island. This is the place for an overview of what to see in the mountains, and to recognize such exotic local fauna as ginger plant, lobster claw, and halaconia. **Scott's Head,** at the southern tip of the island, is easy to reach by motor boat. Climb to the top for an incredible view of the Atlantic on one side, and the Caribbean on the other. **Trafalgar Falls,** not far from Roseau, can be reached by car and a 15-minute climb up a fairly steep slope. However, the struggle is worthwhile. Three sets of falls spill into a large pool bordered by huge black rocks where orchids bloom and breadfruit trees grow. **Trois Pitons National Park** is a rain forest that is still in a primitive state; many acres have never been explored. Palm, cedar, mahogany, ferns, and bamboo grow in profusion.

SOURCES OF FURTHER INFORMATION

Caribbean Tourism Association, 20 E 46th St, New York, NY, 10017. **National Tourist Office**—Dominica Tourist Board, PO Box 73, Roseau.

Dominican Republic

WHAT'S SPECIAL

The Dominican Republic covers two-thirds of the island known as Hispanola and shares with its western neighbor, Haiti. Columbus discovered and named the island in 1492. Santo Domingo, the capital, is the oldest city in the New World, and here, too, are the oldest street, the oldest cathedral, the oldest house, the oldest university, and the first hospital (San Nicolas de Bari Ruins, 1503) in the Americas. Many fine examples of 16th-century Spanish architecture remain in Old Santo Domingo, and the history of the country is fascinating. The national dance is the maranque. The economy is based on sugar, bananas, coffee (good souvenir to bring home), tobacco, and cocoa. In early times Italian marble was imported from Italy for construction; now Dominican Republic exports marble to Italy. The Dominican Republic is the perfect place for a relaxing vacation: the weather is good, the country beautiful and unspoiled, and the beaches stretch for about 1,000 miles. At this time the beaches are unusable, due to the devastation of hurricane David in 1979. From 1930 until 1961 the Dominican Republic was ruled by dictator Trujillo and many atlases still show Santo Domingo as the "City of Trujillo."

COUNTRY BRIEFING

Size: 19,120 square miles
Capital: Santo Domingo

Population: 5,002,000
Capital Population: 1,200,000

Climate: Tropical along the coast, not so humid in the mountains. Warm all year round; rainy in May-June, September-October.

Weather in Santo Domingo: Lat N18°29′; Alt 57 ft

Temp (°F)	Jan	Feb	Mar	Apr	May	Jun	Jul	Aug	Sep	Oct	Nov	Dec
Av Low	66°	66°	67°	69°	71°	72°	72°	73°	72°	72°	70°	67°
Av High	84°	85°	84°	85°	86°	87°	88°	88°	88°	86°	86°	85°
Days no rain	24	22	26	23	20	18	20	20	19	20	20	23

Government: A republic.
Language: Spanish.
Religion: 94% Roman Catholic.
Currency: Peso. 100 cents = 1 peso.

	10¢	50¢	75¢	1 peso	5 pesos	10 pesos	20 pesos	50 pesos
US (dollars, cents)	.10	.50	.75	1.00	5.00	10.00	20.00	50.00
UK (pounds, pence)	.05	.24	.36	.48	2.39	4.77	9.54	23.85

Public Holidays:

New Year's Day, 1 Jan
Epiphany, 6 Jan
Nuestra Señora de la Altagracia, 21 Jan
Duarte's Day (National Hero), 26 Jan
Independence Day, 27 Feb
Good Friday
Labor Day, 1 May

Corpus Christi
Restoration of Independence, 16 Aug
Nuestra Señora de las Mercedes, 24 Sep
Columbus Day, 12 Oct
Christmas Day, 25 Dec

HOW TO GET THERE

Flying time to Santo Domingo, Las Americas Airport from New York is 3¾ hours, from Miami 1½ hours, San Juan ¾ hour; from Caracas, 2¼ hours. Time in the Dominican Republic: GMT−5.

REQUIREMENTS FOR ENTRY AND CUSTOMS REGULATIONS

US and Canadian citizens need proof of citizenship (passport, birth certificate, or voter registration card) and a Tourist Card obtainable through airlines for US$5 or equivalent. Citizens of most other countries, including the UK, need passports, and visas are required of some. Round-trip or onward ticket required. Duty-free allowance: one carton cigarettes; 1 quart of liquor; a reasonable amount of other items. Pre-Columbian art objects are not allowed out of the country. Keep all exchange receipts in order to convert, at departure, up to 60% of the amount of currency originally exchanged for pesos.

AIRPORT INFORMATION

Las Americas is Santo Domingo's international airport, 20 miles from the city center. There is no airport bus service, but some hotels provide their own bus transportation. Taxis cost about US$12-15 into Santo Domingo. Departure tax is $5. The tourist office has a counter at the airport.

ACCOMMODATIONS

Highest rates apply during the winter season, December-April. A 5% hotel tax and 10% service charge are added to bills. Hotels in Santo Domingo:

Rates are in US$ for a double/twin room with bath or shower

Comodoro, Avenida Bolívar 193 (from US$27)

Continental, Avenida Máximo Gómez 16 (from US$35)

Embajador, Avenida Sarasota 65 (from US$32), 10 minutes from center

Hostal Nicolas de Ovando, Calle Las Damas 53 (from US$40)

Jaragua, Avenida Independencia 62 (from US$30)

Plaza Dominicana Holiday Inn, Avenida Anacaona, Mirador del Sur (from US$65), 15 minutes from center

San Geronimo, Avenida Independencia 205 (from US$27)

Santo Domingo, Avenida Independencia (from US$56)

Santo Domingo Norte, Avenida Independencia (from US$50)

Santo Domingo Sheraton, Avenida George Washington 355 (from US$70)

USEFUL INFORMATION

Note: It is illegal to buy pesos from street vendors; it is black market and you can be arrested.

Banks: Open 7:30-1:30 Mon-Fri (a few from 2:30-5:30). Exchange only what you think you will need and keep all exchange receipts. Without them unused pesos cannot be reconverted at departure; with them up to 60% of the amount exchanged can be reconverted to foreign currency. US dollars are widely accepted. Duty-free shops accept US and Canadian dollars only, in cash, travelers' checks, or payment by credit card.

Mail: Stamps at post offices, some hotels, and drugstores.

Telephone Tips: There are some phone booths, and phones are in hotels, restaurants, cafés. Useful numbers in Santo Domingo:

Airport Information 687 0421	Time 544 1111
National Tourist Bureau 688 5537	Long Distance 0
Tourist Information Center 685 3282 or 687 8038	Police 682 3000

Tipping: Customary. A 10% service charge is generally included in hotel and restaurant bills, in addition to which 5-10% is expected. If service has been included, one should leave 15%. Porters get 50¢ per bag; chambermaids 1 peso per day. Taxi drivers, optional, but do so if they have provided some extra service. Standard tips for others is 10-15%.

Newspapers: English-language newspapers and magazines are available. Local English-language publication is the *Santo Domingo News.*

Electricity: 110 volts 60 cycles AC.

Laundry: 24-hour and express service at most hotels.

Hairdressing: First-class hotels have salons (shampoo and set from 15 pesos in hotels; man's haircut from 7 pesos in hotels).

Photography: There is a good selection of equipment as well as black and white and color film in Santo Domingo and Santiago. Processing of color film takes 7-10 days, black and white 3-5 days.

Clubs: Lions and Rotary.

Babysitting: Hotels can make arrangements.

Rest Rooms: In hotels, restaurants, museums, etc. Women, *Damas;* men, *Caballeros.*

Health: Some doctors and dentists speak English. Imported pharmaceuticals are available but expensive. In a few hotels water is drinkable but, as a rule, drink bottled water.

TRANSPORTATION

Buses and taxis are available. However, the local buses do not have fixed routes and may wander off to drop passengers at their homes. In Santiago there are horse-drawn carriages, and some cities have *publicos,* or taxis which travel certain specific routes. You can get a taxi at a stand, outside a nightclub, or at hotels. Taxis have a fixed rate of 10 pesos an hour or about 80 pesos per day for sightseeing; minimum taxi charge is 1.50 pesos. Make sure you establish taxi rate before hiring, even though rates are fixed. It is possible to rent a car from about US$15 a day plus 10¢ or more per kilometer (a valid driver's license from one's country of residence is required). There are no trains, but good bus services link all cities. The internal airline is **Servicio Aereos Dominicanos,** which flies both scheduled and charter flights to most cities in the country.

FOOD AND RESTAURANTS

Food is quite reasonable in price, and there are many first-rate restaurants, especially along the principal avenue, George Washington. The basic cooking is Spanish, with American-international in the major hotels and a number of "foreign" restaurants such as Italian, Chinese, and French. One of the best-known local dishes is *sancocho,* a thick heavy soup-cum-stew of pork, yams, sausages, onions, pumpkins, tomatoes—18 ingredients in all; another is *arroz con pollo,* which is chicken and rice. *Pastelitos,* small pastries filled with chicken or other meats, are Dominican specialties to be found in small bistros or at street stalls. Some other snack foods are *empanadas* (meat patties); *fritos* (assorted fritters); and coconut milk in the shell. Fruit from street vendors is always peeled as a service. An expensive restaurant will generally cost from US$15-30 per person, a medium-priced one about US$10-15, and an inexpensive one US$5-10. **Lina** (Hotel Lina, Avenida Máximo Gómez and 27 de Febrero—tel: 689-5185) specializes in Spanish fare and is an island institution. For steaks, **Mesón de la Cava** (Mirador del Sur—tel: 533-2818), in the interior of an underground cave, is the place to go. **Fonda de la Atarazana** (tel: 689-2900), in a restored building with a view of the Alcázar, serves international and Dominican dishes. Less expensive Dominican restaurants are **Blanquini** (Avenida Independencia and Osvaldo Baez), **La Bahia** (Avenida Independencia and Pte Billini), and **El Lechón** (Paseo Presidente Billini). There are many inexpensive restaurants along Avenida George Washington, with every nationality represented. **Karin's** (tel: 688-8334) serves German cuisine; **Vesuvio** (tel: 682-2766) and **Vesuvio II** (tel: 565-9797), Italian.

DRINKING TIPS
The locally made rum and Dominican beer are both very good. Of the beers, Presidente and Criolla are the best brands. *Mabi* (a fermented sweet drink) and *cocoloco*, a combination of rum and coconut milk, are popular drinks. Reasonably priced imported wines, liquors, and beers are available. A whisky and soda costs about 2 pesos. No licensing restrictions, although some bars may close part of the afternoon. Popular drinking spots are **Rincon Argentino,** Cazerio, **Karin's** on Avenida George Washington, and **Lucky Seven** on Avenida Pasteur.

ENTERTAINMENT
There are occasional theatrical and ballet performances at the **National Theater** which has the world's fourth largest stage, and a **National Symphony Orchestra** which performs several times during the year. **Las Palmas** is a piano bar at the Hotel Santo Domingo. There are also a number of nightclubs, including **El Castillo** at Hotel San Geronimo, **La Fuente** at Hotel Jaragua, and the **Embassy** at the Embajador Hotel. Popular discos are the **Omni** at Santo Domingo Sheraton, **La Azotea** at Plaza Dominicana Holiday Inn, **Neon 2002** at Hotel Hispaniola, and **Waldo's** at Hotel Jaragua. There are gambling casinos at the **Santo Domingo Sheraton, Plaza Dominicana Holiday Inn, Embajador, Jaragua,** and **Naco** hotels; the **Maunaloa** (Centro de los Héroes—tel: 533-9718) is a nightclub and casino.

SHOPPING
Stores open 8:30-12 and 2:30-6, Mon-Sat. The Dominican Republic is noted particularly for its reasonably-priced amber. Another local stone is *larimar,* blue in color. Other good buys are mahogany carvings, pottery, ceramics, straw articles, embroidery, and paintings. Tortoiseshell objects are plentiful but cannot be returned to countries that prohibit trade in endangered species. In Santo Domingo, **Calle El Conde** and **Avenida Mella** are the main shopping streets and there are duty-free shops at Centro de los Héroes where you can find inexpensive non-Dominican items such as Swiss watches and French perfumes. A high spot for shoppers is the **Mercado Modelo** (Avenida Mella), a model native market selling fruits and vegetables, mahogany, woven goods, handicrafts, and island artifacts. Bargaining is expected here, open until noon on Sunday. Crafts are also to be found at the **Plaza Criolla** (Avenida 27 de Febrero) shopping center. **Monika** is a popular crafts and souvenir shop on Calle El Conde, and **Mendez** (Calle Arzobispo Nouel) is a jewelry shop specializing in *larimar.* For art galleries, boutiques, other souvenir shops, and more duty-free shopping, visit **La Atarazana,** a restored area in Old Santo Domingo. Clothing and gifts are in the fashionable stores of the **Naco Shopping Center** (Avenida Tiradentes).

SPORTS

Baseball, basketball, horse racing (once a week in Santo Domingo), polo, soccer, and cockfights are all popular spectator sports. The two **Cajuiles** golf courses at La Romana are of international renown and there is tennis at hotel courts. Surfing is becoming popular near Santo Domingo; boating and sailing are available at Santo Domingo, La Romana, and along the northern shore; deep-sea fishing throughout the island. Beach swimming is particularly fine at **Boca Chica,** east of Santo Domingo. Visitors are welcome at the **Santo Domingo Country Club.**

WHAT TO SEE

The centerpiece of Old Santo Domingo is the **Cathedral of Santa Maria La Menor,** the oldest cathedral in the Americas, founded in 1540. Part Gothic and part baroque, it still holds many treasures brought to this part of the world by the early Spanish settlers—a *Madonna* by Murillo, a silver carillon by Cellini, the crown of Isabella of Spain, and numerous jewels. The remains of Christopher Columbus are buried here, by his decree, in a marble sarcophagus. Shorts are not permitted dress inside the cathedral. Another great palace is the **Alcázar of Diego Columbus,** built for Columbus's son Diego, the second governor, in 1514 and recently restored. This castle-fortress has been beautifully furnished and provides an accurate image of life here at the time of Spain's great power on the island. Nearby is the 16th-century **House of the Cord** (Casa del Cordón), the Western Hemisphere's oldest standing house. **Calle Las Damas** is its oldest street, and on it is the **Museum of the Royal Houses** (Museo de las Casas Reales) which traces the history of the island. Many old buildings are made of coral limestone, held together by position, rather than mortar or wire. The **Museum of the Viceroys** (Museo Virreinal), next to the Alcázar, has paintings and furniture of the colonial period. **La Atarazana,** a collection of restored buildings that once housed ships' supplies, is now a block of shops and restaurants. The **University of Santo Tomas de Aquino,** founded in 1538, is the oldest university in the Americas. The **Gallery of Modern Art** with works by native artists and others, the **Museum of Dominican Man,** the **Museum of Natural History and Science** and the **Museum of National History and Geography** are in the Plaza de la Cultura complex in New Santo Domingo, along with the **National Theater** and the **National Library.** The **National Museum** (Centro de los Héroes) has artifacts of the Taino and Arawak Indians. In the northern section of Santo Domingo are the **Dr. Moscoso National Botanical Gardens,** with large displays of orchids in season, and the **National Zoo,** both in the Plaza de la Cultura. **Los Tres Ojos** (The Three Springs), on the road to the airport, are open, water-filled caverns with stalactites and stalagmites and are worth a visit.

Nineteen miles from Santo Domingo is **Boca Chica,** considered to be the finest lagoon and beach on the whole of the island. The fishing and swimming are very good, and en route to Boca Chica it is possible to visit **La Caleta Park,** which has Tainus works of art, ceramics, and artifacts.

San Cristobál, some 18 miles from Santo Domingo, is one of the most interesting towns along the Sanchez Highway. It is Trujillo's birthplace and the site of his **Mahogany House.**

Santiago is the second city of the Dominican Republic, and its location commands a magnificent view of the **Cibao Plain** and the **Yaque del Norte River.** This is the Republic's "aristocratic" city, a place of wide, tree-lined avenues with many churches and parks. Stay at **El Caimino** (from US$30), the **Hotel Don Diego** (from US$28 double), or the **Matum Hotel** (from US$26 double), which overlooks all of Santiago and the surrounding countryside.

Jarabacoa, about 2 hours drive northwest of Santo Domingo, is a highland resort in the center of a valley, famous for its pine forest. Many Dominicans come here for a spectacular view of the **Duarte Pico Peak.** There is also the **Constanza** mountain resort below sea level, known for fruit and flowers.

Seaside resorts include **Puerto Plata** on the northern coast, the third largest city. It is surrounded by mountains on one side and boasts fine beaches on the other. There are pristine gingerbread houses, a lovely botanical garden, and mountain **Isabel de Torres,** which commands an outstanding view of the city. The major hotels include **Castilla** (from US$8), **Jack Tar Village** (from US$170), and **Montemar** (from US$30). In the east are **El Macao, Punta Cana,** and **Club Mediterranee.** On the southeast coast is the beautiful resort town of **La Romana,** with its new village of **Chavon,** an artists' colony built in the old medieval style. Major resort hotels are **Casa de Campo** (from US$140 double), and **Club Dominicus** (from US$65 MAP for a cabana).

On Columbus' second voyage he founded **Isabella** (after the Queen) on the western side of the island. It was only on his third voyage that he founded **Nouella Isabella,** now known as **Santa Domingo.**

SOURCES OF FURTHER INFORMATION

Dirección Nacional de Turismo, César Nicolás Pensón 59, Santo Domingo; **Centro Dominicano de Información Turística,** Arzobispo Meriño 156, Santo Domingo; **Dominican Tourist Information Center, Inc,** 485 Madison Avenue, New York, NY 10022; **Dominican Republic Tourist Office,** 1038 Brickwell Avenue, Miami, Florida 33131; **Dominican Republic Embassy,** 4 Braemar Mansions, Cornwall Gardens, London SW7. Dominikanisches Fremdenverkehrsamt, Grosse Bockenheimer Strasse, 6, D-6000 Frankfurt am Main 1.

Grenada & Grenadines

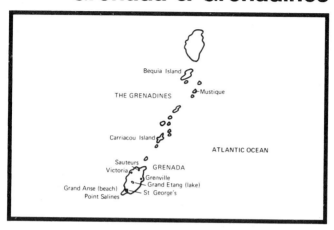

THE GRENADINES

Bequia Island

Mustique

Carriacou Island

ATLANTIC OCEAN

Sauteurs
Victoria   GRENADA
Grenville
Grand Etang (lake)
Grand Anse (beach)
Point Salines   St George's

WHAT'S SPECIAL

Grenada (pronounced Grenăda) is truly "Spice Island," for it produces cloves, mace, and nutmeg in abundance and even has the nutmeg on its flag. Grenada is a volcanic, mountainous island with crater lakes, a beautiful tropical landscape, lovely beaches, and friendly people.

COUNTRY BRIEFING

Size: 133 square miles (with Grenadine Dependencies: Carriacou and Petit Martinique)

Population: 105,000
Capital Population: 30,000

Capital: St George's

Climate: Year-round average temperature of 80°. Dry season is January-May, but even in the wet season there is rarely more than an hour of rain a day.

Weather in St George's: Lat N12°03'; Alt approx. sea level

Temp (°F)	Jan	Feb	Mar	Apr	May	Jun	Jul	Aug	Sep	Oct	Nov	Dec
Av Low	73°	73°	74°	74°	76°	76°	76°	77°	77°	76°	76°	75°
Av High	84°	85°	85°	86°	87°	87°	86°	87°	88°	88°	87°	85°
Days no rain	17	20	23	23	21	13	11	10	12	15	13	15

Language: English.

Government: Independent nation, with a prime minister.

Religion: Anglican, Methodist, Presbyterian, Roman Catholic, Seventh Day Adventist and others.

Currency: East Caribbean dollar. 100 cents = EC$1.

	EC 10¢	EC 50¢	EC $1	EC $5	EC $10	EC $20	EC $50	EC $100
US (dollars, cents)	.04	.19	.37	1.85	3.70	7.41	18.52	37.04
UK (pounds, pence)	.02	.09	.18	.88	1.76	3.53	8.83	17.67

Public Holidays:

New Year's Fiesta, 1-2 Jan
Peoples' Independence Day, 7 Feb
Revolution Day, 13 March
Whit Monday
Queen's Birthday
Corpus Christi
Carnival, Mon and Tues prior to Ash Wed

Easter Monday
Easter Tuesday
Labor Day, 1 May
Emancipation Holidays, first Mon and Tues in Aug
National Day, 15 Aug
Christmas Day, 25 Dec
Boxing Day, 26 Dec

HOW TO GET THERE

Flying time to Pearls Airport, Grenada from New York is 4½ hours; from Miami 3 hours; from Barbados, ¼ hour. Time in Grenada and the Grenadines: GMT−4.

REQUIREMENTS FOR ENTRY AND CUSTOMS REGULATIONS

Proof of citizenship and round-trip ticket required of US, Canadian, and UK citizens for stays up to 3 months. Smallpox vaccination certificate required if coming from an infected area. Duty-free allowance: 200 cigarettes or 50 cigars or ½ pound tobacco; 1 quart liquor. No currency restrictions.

AIRPORT INFORMATION

Pearls Airport is 16 miles from St George's. Taxis from the airport to towns and resorts cost EC$50. Departure tax EC$5. Duty-free shop.

ACCOMMODATIONS

There are luxurious hotels, guesthouses, and apartments to rent. Rates are considerably lower from mid-April to mid-December as bargain hunting travellers have discovered. A 7½% tax and 10% service charge are added to published rates, which are shown in US dollars and are for a double/twin room with bath or shower except where noted.

Rates are in US$ for a double/twin room with bath or shower

Adam's Guest House, St. George's (from $14 EP)
Blue Horizons, Grand Anse Beach, 4 miles from St George's (from $55 EP)
Calabash, L'Anse aux Epines, 5 miles from St George's (from $150 MAP)
Cinnamon Hill, Grand Anse Beach (from $46 MAP)
Holiday Inn, Grand Anse Beach (from $82 MAP)
Horse Shoe Bay, L'Anse aux Epines (from $120 MAP)

Mermaid Inn, Carriacou, Grenadine Islands (from $46 MAP), at beach

Riviera Cottage Hotel, Grand Anse (from $34.50 EP)

Ross Point Inn, Belmont, about 3 miles from St George's (from $85 MAP)

Sam's Inn, ½ mile from Pearls Airport (from $36 MAP)

Secret Harbour, L'Anse aux Epines (from $175 MAP)

Silver Sands, Grand Anse Beach (from $40 EP)

Skyline, Grand Anse Beach (from $28 MAP)

South Winds, Grand Anse Beach (from $150 EP)

Spice Island Inn, Grand Anse Beach (from $140 MAP)

St Ann's Guest House, St George's (from $24 MAP)

St James Hotel, St. George's (from $47 AP)

USEFUL INFORMATION

Banks are open 8-12 Mon-Fri, 8-12 and 2:30-5 Fri. **Tipping:** There is no need to tip anywhere, as service charges and tax are included in most checks and bills. **Laundry and babysitting** can usually be arranged through hotels. **Hairdressing:** shampoo and set from US$6; man's haircut from US$2.50. **Health:** avoid the Manchineel trees—the apples are poisonous.

TRANSPORTATION

The tourist will find the bus service more picturesque than practical. Your hotel will help you get a taxi. Rented cars are about US$30 a day and US$175 a week. Chauffeur-driven cars are available.

FOOD AND RESTAURANTS

Try conch *(lambi),* crab-backs, turtle, lobster; and local fruits like paw paw, guava, mangoes. Avocado ice cream is a specialty. Try the **Nutmeg** (St George's—tel: 2539) on the Carenage; **Rudolph's, The Turtle Back** and **The Cubby Hole** all by St George's Harbor; the **Bamboo Lunch Basket** in Esplanade Plaza, and **Casa Mia** at Grand Anse shopping center. At L'Anse aux Epines is the **Red Crab,** an English pub specializing in barbecued chicken and steaks. Also in the resort area: **Ross Point Inn,** for some of the finest West Indian fare anywhere, **The Hill, La Belle Creole** and **Yin Wo** (the Bird's Nest) for Chinese food.

DRINKING TIPS

Try the rum punch topped with the native nutmeg. Other liquors and a local beer are inexpensive. Gin and coconut milk is a favorite local drink.

ENTERTAINMENT

Nightlife in Grenada revolves around the hotels; there are discothèques at the **Silver Sands Hotel, Blanco's Beach Club** (known locally as the BBC), the **Hibiscus,** and the **Sugarmill Inn** at Grand Anse, the **Red Crab** at L'Anse aux Epines, and the **Rock Gardens** at Tanteen. The week before Ash Wednesday is Carnival time.

SHOPPING

Goods from all over the world are duty free. Shops on **Melville Street** and **Granby Street** in St George's sell cameras, watches, perfume, china, and jewelry, as well as local crafts and black coral. **Dinah's Originals** (Granby Street, St George's) sells ready-made and made-to-order women's clothes. Paintings and sculpture are the specialty of **Yellow Poui Art Gallery** (Melville Street). **Tikal** (Young Street) features exotic objets d'art. The **Straw Mart** is opposite Market Square. Along the harbor docks are rows of vendors selling spices (a good souvenir) and local crafts.

SPORTS

Cricket and soccer are major spectator sports. All ocean sports are popular—swimming, sailing, water-skiing, snorkeling, and scuba-diving. In January there is a fishing tournament. **Richmond Hills Tennis Club, Tanteen Tennis Club,** and **Grenada Golf Club** all welcome temporary members. Yachts can be chartered from **Grenada Yacht Service** or **Spice Island Charters,** both in St George's.

WHAT TO SEE

The crater lake **Grand Etang,** 2,000 feet high, is a beautiful sight, as is **Pointe Saline** at the southern tip of the island. It has two beaches, one with white sand and one with black sand. Take a trip to **Annadale Falls** for a swim in a tropical pool beneath the 50-foot waterfall. The spice town of **Grenville,** just south of Pearls Airport, is well worth a visit, as is the smaller spice town of **Gouyave,** located along a scenic drive from where you will see the picturesque harbor of St George's with its pink and white Colonial buildings. Fascinating varieties of tropical trees and plants can be seen in the **Botanical Gardens** in St George's, and the **Bay Gardens,** St Paul. There are no poisonous creatures on the islands. The **Grenada National Museum** is of historical interest.

ABOUT THE GRENADINES

The Grenadines are a sunny chain of almost 100 beautiful, tiny, sandy islands which lie between St Vincent and Grenada. The total population is about 10,000. The islands are administered by St Vincent, except for Carriacou and Petit Martinique in the south, which belong to Grenada. Comfortable and reasonable accommodations are available in Carriacou, largest of the Grenadines, with an area of 13 square miles. **Petit St Vincent,** one of the smallest, is one resort.

There are flights to Carriacou, Palm Island, and Mustique from Grenada and St Vincent, but the usual mode of transport in the Grenadines is by boat. With the trade winds, the beautiful clear waters, and their location south of the hurricane belt, the Grenadines seem to have been designed for sailing. The area is regarded as a sailors paradise, rivalled only by the waters of the British Virgin Islands.

On shore, the main attractions of the islands are their wonderful sandy beaches and the warm sunshine. There are some good hotels, such as the **Friendship Bay** (from US$120 double MAP) on Bequia, or the **Palm**

Island Beach Club (from US$160 double MAP) on Palm Island, specializing in water sports. Carriacou has the **Mermaid Inn** (from US$46 double MAP).

The islands have a variety of sea-related occupations; on Carriacou and Petit Martinique, the descendants of the 19th-century Scottish shipbuilders carry on the craft. In the lagoons of Carriacou, there are oyster beds. On Bequia, there is whaling—and spear-fishing for barracuda or kingfish.

SOURCES OF FURTHER INFORMATION

Any **Pan Am** office around the world; the **Grenada Tourist Board,** PO Box 293, St George's, Grenada; **Grenada Mission to the UN,** 141 East 44th Street (between Lexington and 3rd Ave), Suite #905, New York, NY 10017. For the Grenadines, **St Vincent Tourist Board,** PO Box 834, Kingstown, St Vincent; **Eastern Caribbean Tourist Association,** 220 East 42nd Street, New York, NY 10017, 200 Buckingham Palace Road, London SWIW 9SP, and Place de Ville, Tower B, suite 701, 112 Kent Street, Ottawa, Ontario.

Guadeloupe

WHAT'S SPECIAL

Columbus named Guadeloupe after a Spanish monastery. The two islands were settled by the Spanish and became a center for buccaneers. It was occupied by the French in 1635, and the Carib Indian population was gradually replaced by French settlers and African slaves. The French and English changed control four times. Today it remains strongly French. To this day, many people on Guadeloupe's island dependencies of Les Saintes still speak old Norman French and dress in the traditional style of Brittany or Normandy. Marie-Galante, Désirade, and French St Martin are Guadeloupe's other island dependencies.

Although a Caribbean island, Guadeloupe is, in fact, a part of metropolitan France and the traveler is well aware of the French influence.

Over the past ten years a series of new programs for these overseas Caribbean territories and the steady increase of tourism has meant the creation of new local wealth, a substantial decrease in unemployment and a homegrown stimulus to agriculture and fishing. Financial allowances for children encourage large families.

The island, seen from the air, is shaped like a giant butterfly, the "wings," separated by the Salt River, forming two islands. Grand-Terre (the eastern wing) is actually flat with Pointe-à-Petre being the principal commercial port city and the smaller of the two and good for sugar cane and tourists. The raw sugar is sent to France for refining. Basse-Terre is mountainous and crowned by La Soufrire (4,813 ft, the word actually means sulfur mine). The scenery is spectacular, volcanic peaks over vivid green forest, lakes, waterfalls and the dazzling tropical flowers.

This area is good for growing bananas. Basse-Terre is the capital. Basse and Grand were names given in seafaring days of sail vessels and are unrelated to their island's topography.

COUNTRY BRIEFING

Size: 687 square miles

Population: 330,000

Capital: Basse-Terre

Capital Population: 15,457

Climate: Pleasantly tropical, tempered by trade winds. Rainy season, August-November. Best time to go, November-May.

Weather in Pointe-à-Pitre: Lat 16°01'; Alt 1,750 ft

Temp (°F)	Jan	Feb	Mar	Apr	May	Jun	Jul	Aug	Sep	Oct	Nov	Dec
Av Low	64°	63°	63°	65°	67°	69°	68°	69°	69°	68°	67°	65°
Av High	77°	76°	77°	79°	80°	80°	81°	82°	82°	81°	80°	78°
Days no rain	8	10	11	10	8	5	4	5	7	7	8	8

Government: French Overseas Department with three representatives and two senators to the French parliament. The governor is sent by France.

Language: French and Creole. Very little English spoken.

Religion: Roman Catholic.

Currency: The franc; 100 centimes = 1 franc.

	10C	50C	1F	5F	10F	50F	100F	300F
US (dollars, cents)	.02	.09	.18	.90	1.81	9.03	18.05	54.15
UK (pounds, pence)	.01	.04	.09	.43	.86	4.31	8.61	25.83

Public Holidays:

New Year's Day, 1 Jan	Bastille Day, 14 July
Mardi Gras, Feb	Schoelcher Day, 21 July
Easter Monday	Assumption Day, 15 Aug
Labor Day, 1 May	All Saints Day, 1 Nov
Ascension Day	Armistice Day, 11 Nov
Pentecost Monday	Christmas Day, 25 Dec

HOW TO GET THERE

Flying time to Pointe-à-Pitre, Le Raizet Airport from New York is 4 hours, from Miami, 1¾ hours; from Paris, 11 hours. Time in Guadeloupe: GMT−4.

REQUIREMENTS FOR ENTRY AND CUSTOMS REGULATIONS

Proof of citizenship is required for visits up to 21 days, passport for visits up to 3 months, visas for longer stays—plus return-trip or onward ticket in all cases. Duty-free allowance: 200 cigarettes for visitors from non-EEC European countries, 300 from EEC states, 400 for those coming from elsewhere; 1 bottle liquor or 3 bottles wine; 2 still cameras plus 20 rolls film, 1 movie camera plus 10 rolls.

AIRPORT INFORMATION

Le Raizet Airport is 2 miles from Pointe-à-Pitre. Taxi fare from airport to city center is 15 francs, to Gosier resorts 30 francs. Night fares are increased by 33%. Tip baggage porter 2 francs per bag. No arrival or departure tax for regularly scheduled flights. Duty-free shop and hotel reservation counter, car rental desks.

ACCOMMODATIONS

As a result of recent hotel development, there is a varied choice of good accommodations. Prices of hotel rooms are generally reduced by one third during low season (mid-April to mid-December). There are a number of good little inexpensive hotels on the smaller islands. Most hotels have 10-15% service charge. Help in finding accommodations can be obtained from the **French West Indies Tourist Board,** 628 Fifth Ave., NY, NY 10020—tel: (212) 757-1125 or the **Office du Tourisme,** Pointe-à-Pitre—tel: 82 09 30. Hotels in Guadeloupe:

Rates are in US$ for a double/twin room with bath or shower

Auberge de la Vieille Tour, Gosier, Grande-Terre (from $124 CP), 5 miles

Callinago Hotel & Village, Gosier (from $73 EP), 5 miles

Club Mediterranee Caravelle, Ste Anne (from $460 weekly), 12 miles

Club Mediterranee Fort Royal, Deshaies (from $460 weekly), 22 miles

Ecotel Guadeloupe, Gosier (from $63), 5 miles

Frantel Guadeloupe, Bas du Fort, (from $86), 3 miles

Hamak Village, St François (from $200), 23 miles

Holiday Inn, Gosier (from $103), 5 miles

Hotel Caraibe Copatel, Baie du Moule (from $85 EP), 18 miles

Le Bougainville, Pointe-à-Pitre, Grande-Terre (from $49 EP), 2 miles

Les Alizes, Le Moule (from $85 EP), 17 miles

Méridien, St François, Grande-Terre (from $85 EP), 23 miles

Novotel Fleur D'Epee Caraïbe, Bas du Fort (from $100 CP), 3 miles

PLM Arawak, Gosier, Grande-Terre (from $74 CP), 5 miles

PLM Sun Village, Bas du Fort (from $52 EP), 3 miles

Realais Du Moulin (from $55 CP), 20 miles

Salako, Gosier, Grande-Terre (from $104 CP), 5 miles

Trois Mats, St François, Grand-Terre (from $84 CP), 22 miles

USEFUL INFORMATION

Banks: Open 8-12 and 2-4, Mon-Fri. Hotels change money; most shops accept dollars and travelers' checks.

Mail: Mailboxes at post offices and hotels.

Telephone Tips: There are booths in post offices, restaurants, and cafés and on streets. Useful numbers:

Airport Information 82 11 81

Tourist Office
for emergencies
82-99-99 and for
information 82-09-30

Newspapers: English-language newspapers obtainable.

Tipping: In restaurants 10-15%, if no service charge included in check. Porters, 2 francs per piece of luggage; cloakroom attendants, 1 franc per coat.

Electricity: 220 volts 50 cycles AC.

Laundry: Good services in hotels; dry-cleaning expensive.

Hairdressing: Most major hotels have salons.

Photography: Black and white and color film available. Developing takes about 2 days.

Clubs: Rotary, Lions, and Soroptomists.

Rest Rooms: In restaurants, hotels, cafés (give attendant 50 centimes). Women, *Toilette dames;* Men, *Toilette hommes.*

Health: French-speaking doctors and dentists. Imported pharmaceuticals available.

Tourist Office: In downtown Pointe-à-Pitre near open-air market by the docks. Pick up a free copy of "Guadeloupe Bou Jour," a useful guide in English to shopping, sports, restaurants, and hotels.

TRANSPORTATION

Town Mercedi bus services are not expensive and charge by the distance. It is easy to pick up a bus; in the country they stop anywhere at the wave of a hand. The spectacular ride from Pointe-à-Pitre through the mountains to Basse-Terre takes 2½ hours and costs about 10 francs. Taxis are plentiful but fairly expensive. Rented cars are available from $25 plus 7½% tax. Note: the residents are very fast drivers. Antilles Air Service links Guadeloupe to its dependent islands, which all have airports, and Air Guadeloupe runs daily round trips. Boats can also be hired in Pointe-à-Pitre to visit the islands.

FOOD AND RESTAURANTS

You have a choice of French or Creole cooking. Many hotels, such as the **Auberge de la Vieille Tour** in Gosier and the **Relais de la Grande Soufrière** at Saint-Claude on the slopes of the volcano, serve both French and Creole. Excellent French dishes *(haute cuisine)* are to be found at **Le Grenier** in Pointe-à-Pitre. **Le Bistrot,** off the Ste Anne road at Petit Havre serves French specialties in its delightful open air dining room overlooking the sea. For "nouvelle cuisine" try **Le Barokko** (formerly **La Ciboulette**), a deluxe restaurant in the St François resort area.

Creole specialties which should not be missed are *crab farcis* (stuffed land crab), *accras* (deep fried seafood seasoned with herbs), *colombo* (local curries), and the local lobsters, baby clams and lambi (conch). Scattered around the island are a number of good Creole restaurants, most notably **La Créole-Chez Violetta, La Chaubette, Le Sud Americain,** and **Chez Rosette** in Gosier. Also worth the visit for Creole and seafood specialties is **La Pecherie,** a 200-year-old stone house on the waterfront, or **Chez Jerco,** both at St François. On the other side of the island, south of the western terminus of La Traversee, try **Chez Vaneau.** Near Deshaies don't miss **Le Karacoli.**

DRINKING TIPS

Rum is the local drink, and Guadeloupe rum punch is inexpensive, as is imported and local beer. The sale of drink is restricted to those over 21.

ENTERTAINMENT

Obtain the "Guadeloupe Bon Jour" from the Tourist Bureau. Discothèques and cabarets at many hotels and nightclubs. There are casinos in Gosier and at St François. Local bands play native music at two Gosier nightspots: **Club 97-1,** and **Le Boukarou.**

Like all West Indians the people of Guadeloupe love carnivals, and their big event, with costume parades, singing, and dancing in the streets, is on the days leading up to Ash Wednesday. At other times of the year try to see Aimée Adeline's folklore group, **La Brisquante,** entertain at the major resort hotels. They perform traditional dances like the *béguine* (the national dance was created in Guadeloupe) in colorful Creole costumes. Movies are French, American, and English, with original soundtracks.

SHOPPING

Stores are open 8-12 and 2:30-5 Mon-Fri, closed Sat afternoons and Sun. French perfumes, lingerie, and wines are sold at prices often lower than in France. Fashionable shops in Pointe-à-Pitre are on **rue Frébault, rue de Nozières,** and **Schoelcher.** For one with a French flavor try **Champs-Elysées.** Go to the open air markets in the center of town at **Place de la Victoire.** Good local buys are native wood and straw crafts, including the bamboo hats worn by the fishing folk of the Iles des Saintes "Salacos," dou-dou dolls, baskets, and also bracelets and carvings made of aromatic *vetivert* roots. Some shops give a discount of 20% on luxury items bought with travelers' checks.

SPORTS

Good beaches for swimming are **Sainte Anne** (8 miles past Gosier) and **Gosier** (15 minutes from town by taxi). Sailing boats and motorboats can be rented from **Guadeloupe Chartaire** or **Guadeloupe Yachting** in Pointe-à-Pitre: King Farouk's former pleasure boat, *Diogène II,* is available for charter. Snorkeling, scuba-diving, windsurfing, and deep-sea fishing are available at most hotels. Best areas for snorkeling and scuba-diving are at **Grande Cul-de-Sac Narin** and **Port Louis.** Both 16 miles from town. There is an 18-hole golf course in the St François resort area, and visitors can play tennis at major hotels and **Amical Tennis Club** at Gosier. Cycling, hiking, and mountain-climbing are also popular. Horseback riding at **Societe Hippique del la Guadalope** and **LeCriollo Riding School** at Gosier. A chief spectator sport is cockfighting, held every Sunday at cockpits throughout the island.

WHAT TO SEE

The style of old Pointe-à-Pitre is Creole, like New Orleans in the USA. The **Plaza** in the city center has royal palms planted in 1848 in honor of slavery abolition. Some homes in the area are built on spring-like platforms to sway in earthquakes. There are three museums in Pointe-à-Pitre: **Centre Culturel Rémy Nainsouta, Pavillon d'Exposition de Ber-**

gevin and **The Basilica of St Peter and St Paul.** Drive from Pointe-à-Pitre to **Fort Fleur d'Epée** and explore the underground dungeons and passageways of the 18th-century fort, overlooking the city that was the scene of fierce struggle between the French and the English. Ten miles on is **Sainte Anne,** a little sugar town with a good beach. The old cemetery at **Moule,** with petrified skulls unearthed by the sea, is a reminder of past battles between the French and British. Moule was a principal harbor town in the 18th century.

On Basse-Terre principal historic sights include **Sainte-Marie de Capesterre,** where Columbus landed, and **Trois Rivières,** with Carib relics and rocks with Indian inscriptions.

The inland drive from Pointe-à-Pitre to Basse-Terre passes through the **Guadeloupe Natural Park**—74,100 acres of tropical forest brilliant with hibiscus flowers, mahogany trees and giant ferns. **Corbet Falls,** a 20-minute trail walk, is a magnificent 350-ft water fall. Some parts of this region are still unexplored, and it is marvelous for hiking, with marked trails and picnic sites in some areas. The Tourist Office in Pointe-à-Pitre or the Maison de la Foret in the Park can provide maps and details. Rent a car and explore on your own, or make arrangements at your hotel to join a sightseeing excursion. Lava spills from the volcano **Soufriere** have changed much of the environment. The mountain is difficult to see, except on a clear day. The Tourist Office prefers that visitors check with them first, and have excellent maps for the intrepid.

Basse-Terre lies between the volcano and the sea, with well-laid-out parks, handsome administrative buildings, and a 17th-century **Cathedral.** Nearby is **Matouba,** an East Indian village where the people still live much as they did in the East.

Do not miss a visit to the offshore islands. The **Iles des Saintes** consist of eight islands; the two main ones are **Terre de Haut** and **Terre de Bas.** Many of their inhabitants are the descendants of Breton and Norman sailors, and they have the reputation of being the best seamen in the Caribbean. Round trip on the ferry from Trois Rivières is a bargain at about $7. The main town on Terre de Haut is **Bourg,** an attractive little fishing village with white-painted houses. One house is built in the shape of a steamship, and you will see lots of donkeys everywhere. Hotels on Terre de Haut include the **Bois Joli** (from US$33 CP), **Saintoise** (from US$30 CP), **Jeanne D'Arc** (from US$30 EP), **Le Foyal** (from US$30 EP), and **Kanoa** (from US$30 EP). As might be expected in an island for fishing, seafood heads most menus with grilled conch, stuffed crabs, Blaf (fish in court bouillon), and steamed clams among many delicious offerings. Children selling "Tourment d'amour" (delicious coconut tart), the dessert specialty of this island, meet all incoming boats in a gesture of hospitality. **Le Mouillage,** on the main street and **Le Coq d'Or** and l'**Abordage**— both in the village—join the hotel restaurants in providing good, attractive surroundings in which to try the local fare. **Marie-Galante,** named after Columbus's ship, is a sugar island where the women wear "Sunday" dress with turbans and long dresses with layers of underskirts. The capital is **Grand Bourg.** The island of **Désirade,** a former leper colony, is 6 miles east of Grande-Terre; it is now a quiet retreat with good beaches and many iguanas.

SOURCES OF FURTHER INFORMATION

Any **Pan Am** office around the world: **Office du Tourisme,** 5 Sq de la Banque, 97181 Pointe-à-Pitre; **French Government Tourist Office,** 628 Fifth Avenue, New York, NY 10020; and Beverly Hills and San Francisco, CA; **French Tourist Office,** 178 Piccadilly, London W1. **French Government Tourist Offices** also in Montreal & Toronto, Canada; Sydney, Australia; Madrid, Spain; Caracas, Venezuela; Mexico City, Mexico.

Haiti

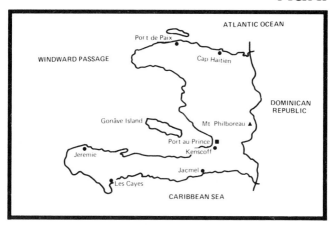

WHAT'S SPECIAL

Haiti occupies the western two-thirds of the island it shares with its neighbor, the Dominican Republic. It is a country that was once one of the most productive in the West Indies, and there are lovely architectural reminders of its glorious era. Its complicated and turbulent political history is fascinating. Coffee is the main export, although light industry is growing. Haiti is a crowded, less than prosperous country, but the climate is pleasant all year round and the scenery is spectacular.

Most of the population is Roman Catholic, but voodoo, a ritual based on African belief, plays an important part in Haitian life too. There is a commercial version for the tourist, but the real thing is hidden away.

COUNTRY BRIEFING

Size: 10,714 square miles   **Population:** 5,670,000
Capital: Port-au-Prince   **Capital Population:** 1,000,000

   Climate: Tropical, with little variation summer or winter. Temperatures range 70°-85°. The annual average temperature is 81°F in the western portion of the country and 76°F in the elevated interior.

Weather in Port-au-Prince: Lat N18°33'; Alt 121 ft

Temp (°F)	Jan	Feb	Mar	Apr	May	Jun	Jul	Aug	Sep	Oct	Nov	Dec
Av Low	68°	68°	69°	71°	72°	73°	74°	73°	73°	72°	71°	69°
Av High	87°	88°	89°	89°	90°	93°	94°	93°	91°	90°	88°	87°
Days no rain	28	23	24	19	18	22	24	20	18	19	23	28

Government: A republic.
Language: French is the official language, but most Haitians speak

Creole. Most hotels, restaurants, and airline offices have English-speaking personnel.

Religion: Roman Catholic; Protestant faiths represented.

Currency: Gourde. 100 centimes = 1 gourde.

	10c	50c	G1	G5	G10	G50	G100	G300
US (dollars, cents)	.02	.10	.20	1.00	2.00	10.00	20.00	60.00
UK (pounds, pence)	.01	.05	.10	.48	.95	4.77	9.54	28.62

Public Holidays:

Independence Day and
  New Year's Day, 1 Jan
Forefathers' Day, 2 Jan
Mardi Gras, 3 days before
  Ash Wednesday
Good Friday
Pan American Day, 14 Apr
Labor Day, 1 May
Flag Day and University
  Day, 18 May
Sovereignty Day, 22 May

Presidency-for-Life Day, 22
  June
Assumption Day, 15 Aug
Dessaline's Death
  Anniversary,
  17 Oct
United Nations Day, 24 Oct
All Saints Day, 1 Nov
Armed Forces Day, 18 Nov
Discovery Day, 5 Dec
Christmas Day, 25 Dec

HOW TO GET THERE

Flying time to Port-au-Prince's Duvalier International Airport from New York is 3¾ hours; from Miami, 1½ hours; from San Juan, 1½ hours. Time in Haiti: GMT−5.

REQUIREMENTS FOR ENTRY AND CUSTOMS REGULATIONS

Proof of citizenship (birth certificate, voters registration card, naturalization papers) or a valid passport, and a round-trip ticket for a stay of up to 30 days are required. Smallpox, cholera, and yellow-fever certificates are required if coming from an infected area. For US$4 or its equivalent, a visitor's card is issued on arrival, valid for 3 months. For trips taking you out of the capital province, a *Laissez Passer* is required, obtained from the National Office of Tourism and Public Relations (ONTPR) in Port-au-Prince. Sporting guns brought into the country must be registered. Duty-free allowance: 200 cigarettes or 50 cigars or 2.2 pounds of tobacco; 1 liter liquor.

AIRPORT INFORMATION

François Duvalier Airport is 8 miles from the city center. The taxi fare is US$10 for up to five passengers. Airport departure tax is US$4.

ACCOMMODATIONS

Haiti is one of the few Caribbean islands which offer a full range of accommodations from luxury hotels to less costly pensions and guesthouses. The best hotels are located in the cooler heights of Pétionville, a mountain village above Port-au-Prince. Prices in the summer season are reduced by 10-40%. There is a 5% tax and 10% service charge added upon departure. Hotels in Port-au-Prince:

Rates are in US$ for a double/twin room with bath or shower

Beau Rivage, Boulevard Harry Truman (from $38)

Castel Haiti, Avenue Christophe (from $36)

Grand Hotel Oloffson, Avenue Christophe (from $70)

Habitation Leclerc, PO Box 2263 (from $110), on grounds of Habitation Leclerc estate

Ibo Beach Cacique Island, on an island in Port-au-Prince Bay (from $60)

Prince, Rue 3 (from $34)

Royal Haitian, PO Box 2075 (from $55)

Sans Souci, Avenue Charles Summer (from $48)

Splendid, PO Box 1214 (from $45)

USEFUL INFORMATION

Do not take pictures of people unless you have their permission. Never try to attend an authentic voodoo service on your own. The Haitian dress is conservative.

Banks: Open 9-1 Mon-Fri.

Mail: Mailboxes are in the post office and some stores.

Telephone Tips: Local calls cost 10 centimes. Useful numbers in Port-au-Prince:

Airport Information 2-3913

Tourist Office 2-1729

Operator, Directories, and Emergencies 0

Overseas Operator 09

Newspapers: *News of Haiti* is a monthly English-language paper.

Tipping: Not customary. Hotels and restaurants charge 10% service and 5% tax. Porters, 50 centimes for each piece of luggage.

Electricity: 110 volts 60 cycles AC.

Laundry: 24-hour service is available (dry-cleaning a suit, from G10; laundering a shirt, from G3).

Hairdressing: Some hotels have salons.

Photography: Film and equipment are expensive. It takes 3 days to develop color, 1 day for black and white.

Clubs: Rotary, Lions, Skal.

Health: Many doctors and dentists speak English. New hospitals have been built. There is purified drinking water in hotels and restaurants; otherwise, boil water before drinking.

TRANSPORTATION

Taxi rates are standardized, although your driver will try to convince you they are not. Within the city limits of Port-au-Prince, Pétionville, and Carrefour, taxis cost US$5 per person. A ride from Port-au-Prince to Pétionville or from Port-au-Prince to Carrefour costs US$10 per car. City and intercity rates are US$10 per hour and US$5 each half-hour thereafter. For longer hours, taxis can be rented for US$30 for a half-day, US$40 for a full 8-hour day. The *publique,* or public cars, cost 90 centimes to anywhere within the city, and you ride with as many people as will fit into the car. *Camionnettes* are open trucks (fare 50 centimes). Car rentals are about US$25 per day plus mileage. An internal air service links Port-au-Prince with Port de Paix and Cap Haïtien.

FOOD AND RESTAURANTS

Authentic French cuisine can be enjoyed in fine restaurants in Port-au-Prince and Pétionville. Creole cooking—part French and part African in its approach to local, tropical ingredients—is equally delicious. You can try it at **Le Rond Point** (Avenue Marie-Jeanne—tel: 2-0621), which has *tassot de dinde* (dried turkey), *grillot* (fried pork), *diri et djondjon* (rice and black mushrooms), and *langouste flambée* (flaming rock lobster). Also in Port-au-Prince, **Le Tiffany** has Haitian and French specialties. Go to **Le Recif** (Route de Delmas—tel: 6-2605) for seafood. In Pétionville, **Le Belvedère** (tel: 7-1115) has a menu that is mainly French and a wonderful view over Port-au-Prince. **Chez Gérard** (17 Rue Pinchinat—tel: 7-1949) and **La Lanterne** (41 Rue Borno—tel: 7-0479) are both French with Creole and international selections. Haiti has numerous sidewalk cooks: you might sample *cassave* with hot fish or vegetable, cashew candies, meat pies, or charbroiled pork.

DRINKING TIPS

Barbancourt is the famous local rum. Barbancourt Liqueurs (28 varieties of spice, flower, and fruit liqueurs), *Clairin,* and *Sellebride* are also excellent. Imported wines and liquor are available. No local restrictions exist on the sale of liquor, and bars are closed only on election day.

ENTERTAINMENT

Your nightlife will be lively if you follow the social calendar and the crowd. The major hotels in Port-au-Prince take turns in putting on the show for the night. There will be dining, dancing, cabaret, folklore shows, voodoo shows, barbecues, gambling, whatever takes your fancy. The **Grand Hotel Oloffson,** the **Sans Souci, Castel Haiti,** the **Villa Créole, El Rancho,** the **Ibo Beach,** and the **Choucoune** are the centers of this whirlwind Haitian nightlife. Generally you have to pay a cover charge of about G15. Dress according to place and event.

The **Cabane Choucoune** is of special interest as a nightclub in the shape of an African tribal house. Another nightspot is the **Peristyle,** where you can see the closest thing to authentic voodoo. The **Casino** at the Royal Haitian Hotel is open every night from 9pm until 3am and dress is informal. The **Théâtre de Verdure** has regular performances of native dancing.

SHOPPING

The **Iron Market,** distinctive with its twin minarets, sells everything from peanuts to turtles. It is a colorful sight, with hundreds of women sitting around smoking their pipes and gossiping. Good buys are wooden statuettes, inlaid trays and jewelry boxes, oil paintings, embroidered clothes, copper jewelry, heavy bedspreads, and draperies. Remember to bargain for everything everywhere. The **Red Carpet Gallery** and the **Rainbow Art Display** in Pétionville and **Nader's Gallery, Issa's,** and **Claire's Gallery** in Port-au-Prince represent the nation's top artists. For clothing try **Jacqueline's, Hanotte,** and **Madam Célestin.** Tailors line the **Rue Dr Dehoux. Carlos Shop,** Avenue Pie XII, sells Haitian handicrafts including men's and women's clothing. Cameras, watches, perfume, and electrical goods can be found at the **Versailles, Le Continental,** and **Little Europe.** Stores are open 8-4 Monday through Friday, 9-12 Saturday.

SPORTS

Most hotels have swimming pools, and there is good spear-fishing and snorkeling. For fun with a difference, go out to **Sandy Cay Reef** and allow a small boat to tow you over the reefs while floating on an inner tube wearing goggles. The **Pétionville Club** has tennis courts. Soccer is the national sport and is played everywhere. Cockfighting is popular, and anyone will tell you where the Saturday afternoon match is. Hunting for wild boar, guinea hen, ducks, and crocodile is popular with visitors. Migratory ducks favor the island in the winter and provide excellent sport.

WHAT TO SEE

Port-au-Prince rises from the rambling wooden structures of its waterfront business center to the cooler, greener, beflowered residential sections of the city. Visit the **Arts Center** (17 Rue de la Révolution), where the Haitian school of primitive painting was started by the American, Dewitt Peters. Haitian art has an increasing international reputation, and the works of famous artists may be seen here, at the **Museum of Haitian Art** (Place des Héros), and in the **Foyer des Arts Plastiques.** Primitive murals done by Haitians can also be seen on the wall of the **Cathedral of Ste Trinité.** The **National Museum** is a hilltop mansion with relics of Haitian history including the anchor of Columbus' ship the *Santa Maria.* The **Ethnographical Museum** houses interesting relics of voodoo. Visit the lovely old distillery, reminiscent of a romantic old castle, where Jane Barbancourt liqueurs are made. Also see the tomb of **Le Grand Disparu** (the late President Duvalier), marked by a perpetual flame. Reminiscent of Napoleon and his era is the mansion which belonged to Pauline Bonaparte, **Habitation Leclerc,** still elegant and gracious. The **Presidential Palace,** or White House, is striking against a rich green background. **Pétionville** is the elegant suburb of Port-au-Prince and is set in beautifully shaded hills. The houses are superb. Hotels in Pétionville:

Rates are in US$ for a double/twin room with bath or shower

    Choucoune, Rue Lamare (from $70)
    El Rancho, Rue Panaméricaine (from $60)
    Ibo Lélé, Ibo Lélé (from $50)
    Montana, Route Montana (from $27)

Regent, Rue Panaméricaine (from $38)
Villa Creole, Pétionville (from $45)

Jacmel, on the southern coast of Haiti, is a gem of an old French colonial town. Until recently, it was reachable only after an 8-hour jeep ride from Port-au-Prince, but with the completion of a new highway, the trip is 2 hours by bus or 1½ hours by car. A small, new resort hotel, **Le Jacmelienne,** has been built amid palm trees on a black sand beach, and in the Jacmel area are the popular white sand beaches of **Cyvadier, Raymond-les-Bains,** and **Ti Mouillage.**

Cap Haïtien, 175 miles from Port-au-Prince, was the lavish and splendid capital during the heyday of Haitian pomp and luxury. The old French architecture still predominates, and the nearby ruins of the **Palace of Sans Souci** and **La Citadelle** are awe-inspiring sights not to be missed by anyone who visits Haiti. The Palace of Sans Souci, built by Henry Christophe when he proclaimed himself King Henry I in 1811, is at **Milot,** 12 miles from the city. It is set at the head of grand staircases, an exact replica of Frederick the Great's Sans Souci at Potsdam. Today the palace is empty and eerie, though its great marble-flooded rooms with mahogany paneling were once bedecked with lavish tapestries and furnishings, and streams were diverted underneath to cool them. From Sans Souci climb by horse or mule to the top of the 3,100-foot Pic de Laferrière where Christophe's Citadelle stands, an impressive feat of military architecture. The fort took the entire island 10 years to build and cost countless lives in the mammoth effort. The fortress could hold 15,000 men, contained provisions for a year's siege, and had catchments leading to underground water supplies; it was totally impregnable, but was never attacked. The King shot himself in 1829, and his remains were buried on the ramparts. Hotels in Cap Haïtien are the **Hostellerie du Roi Christophe** (from $45 double MAP) and the **Mont-Joli** (from US$60 double MAP). One-day tours to Cap Haïtien, Sans Souci, and La Citadelle can be arranged in Port-au-Prince; the trip is 4 hours by car or 45 minutes by air.

Port-de-Paix, located in the northwest, is protected from gales by the **Ile de La Tortue.** Columbus, thrilled by the scenery, called the place **Valparaiso** (valley of delights). Port-de-Paix's coastline has many beautiful beaches and seaside resorts.

Jérémie, in the south, has been called the "City of the Poets." It was the birthplace of Alexandre de la Pailleterie, who gave up his father's name to adopt that of his black mother, Césette Dumas. He was the father of Alexandre Dumas, author of *The Three Musketeers.*

SOURCES OF FURTHER INFORMATION

Any **Pan Am** office around the world; **National Office of Tourism & Public Relations,** Avenue Marie-Jeanne, Port-au-Prince; **Haiti Government Tourist Bureau,** 1270 Avenue of the Americas, New York, 10020.

Jamaica

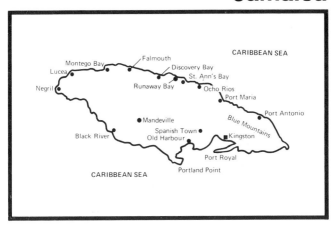

WHAT'S SPECIAL

The original inhabitants of this island called it *Xamayca*, meaning "land of woods and streams"; the Arawak word is still descriptive, for Jamaica has dense, intensely green, forested mountains rising above 7,000 feet, deeply indented by countless streams pouring down their sides. Jamaica is close to being the ideal place for a vacation, as the number of tourists and hotels there will show. The weather is just about perfect, the beaches are long and white, and there are brilliantly colored birds and flowers, many of which you will never have seen before.

COUNTRY BRIEFING

Size: 4,411 square miles   **Population:** 2,215,000
Capital: Kingston   **Capital Population:** 705,000

   Climate: Warm and sunny all year round; little seasonal variation in temperature. Inland mountainous regions cooler and much wetter than the coast. Normally, wettest months are May and October.

Weather in Kingston: Lat N11°58'; Alt 110 ft

Temp (°F)	Jan	Feb	Mar	Apr	May	Jun	Jul	Aug	Sep	Oct	Nov	Dec
Av Low	67°	67°	68°	70°	72°	74°	73°	73°	73°	73°	71°	69°
Av High	86°	86°	86°	87°	87°	89°	90°	90°	89°	88°	87°	87°
Days no rain	28	25	29	27	27	25	27	24	24	22	25	27

   Government: An independent dominion in the British Commonwealth.

   Language: English.

Religion: Anglican church predominant; other sects represented.
Currency: Jamaican dollar. 100 cents = 1 Jamaican dollar.

	J1¢	J10¢	J50¢	J$1	J$5	J$10	J$20	J$50
US (dollars, cents)	.02	.18	.89	1.78	8.91	17.82	35.63	89.08
UK (pounds, pence)	.01	.09	.42	.85	4.25	8.50	17.00	42.49

Public Holidays:

New Year's Day, 1 Jan	Independence Day, first Mon in Aug
Ash Wednesday	
Good Friday	National Heroes' Day, third Mon in Oct
Easter Monday	
National Labor Day, 23 May	Christmas Day, 25 Dec
	Boxing Day, 26 Dec

HOW TO GET THERE

Flying time to Kingston and/or Montego Bay from New York is 3½ hours; from Miami, 1½ hours; from Caracas, 3 hours. Time in Jamaica: GMT−5.

REQUIREMENTS FOR ENTRY AND CUSTOMS REGULATIONS

Proof of citizenship (valid or expired passport, birth certificate, or voter registration card) plus a return or onward ticket for US or Canadian citizens. A drivers license alone is not considered proof of citizenship. British citizens and others must have a passport to enter Jamaica. Visitors get a disembarkation or tourist card on arrival, which is handed back to the immigration authorities on leaving. There is no limit on the amount of foreign currency you can bring in and you can take out up to the amount you brought in. You may not import or export any Jamaican currency. Forbidden imports are guns and explosives, fresh fruit, flowers, vegetables and meat, seeds, and rum. Duty-free allowance: 250 cigarettes; ¾ pound of tobacco or 50 cigars; 1 quart liquor or wine; a reasonable amount of perfume.

AIRPORT INFORMATION

Jamaica has two international airports. Norman Manley Airport, 11 miles from the center of Kingston, and Sangster, 3 miles out of Montego Bay. There are no special buses; local ones are crowded, so take a taxi into town. The fare into Montego Bay is about US$5 and into Kingston US$10. Some hotels in Montego Bay meet guests at the airport. **Martin's Jamaica, JUTA,** and **Blue Danube** operate car transfer services between the airports and hotels in limousines that take up to four passengers. From Norman Manley Airport into Kingston is US$28 per car (US$7 each if four riders, US$14 each if two riders, etc.). It costs US$3-6 per person (in a full car and depending on location of hotel) from Sangster into Montego Bay; US$15-17.50 per person to the Ocho Rios area; US$12.50 per person to Negril. Airports have duty-free shops and tourist information desks which can help to find accommodations. Airport tax is J$8 (US$4.50).

ACCOMMODATIONS

Many hotels are expensive, for Jamaica has some of the most exclusive in the Caribbean, but there are plenty of more moderate establishments. Good, inexpensive accommodations are available in many guesthouses—small but clean and friendly. Hotel rates are lower between April and December, although some offer restricted facilities during that time. Reserve accommodations as far ahead as possible. For help ask the **Jamaica Tourist Board,** New Kingston Hotel Complex, 78 Knutsford Boulevard, New Kingston (tel: 929-8070) or at Cornwall Beach in Montego Bay (tel: 952-4425) or the **Jamaica Hotel and Tourist Association** (2 Ardenne Road, Kingston, tel: 926-3635; Montego Bay, tel: 952-2784). There are also apartments and villas to rent in Jamaica: for information write or call the **Jamaica Association of Villas and Apartments,** Ocho Rios PO (tel: 974-2508). A 5% government room tax is added, and a 10% service charge is usually included. During the Dec-Apr high season there is a US$2 per night occupancy tax. All hotel bills must be paid in foreign currency in the form of cash, travelers' checks, or credit cards. Hotels in Kingston:
Rates are in US$ for a double/twin room with bath or shower

> INTER · CONTINENTAL KINGSTON, Kingston Mall (from $60), downtown Kingston
>
> **Jamaica Pegasus,** New Kingston (from $60), 10 minutes from downtown
> **Morgan's Harbour,** Port Royal (from $30), near airport
>
> **New Kingston,** New Kingston (from $60), 10 minutes from downtown
> **Terra Nova,** 17 Waterloo Road (from $40), 15 minutes from downtown

USEFUL INFORMATION

Banks: Open 9-2 Mon-Thurs, 9-12 and 2:30-5 Fri in Kingston. Also change travelers' checks at airport exchange desks and hotel front desks. Keep all exchange receipts in order to reconvert Jamaican currency into foreign currency at departure. It is illegal to change money in the street or from unauthorized dealers. Be careful about accepting J$10 or J$20 bills except those bearing the signature of H S Walker, Governor, and dated 1 October 1978. There have been counterfeit bills in these denominations. Remember that hotel bills, car rentals, and duty-free shopping must be paid for in foreign currency.

Telephone Tips: Phones coin operated. When calling locally, drop the first two digits of seven-digit numbers. The last five are all that's required. Useful numbers:

Tourist Board Kingston 929-8070	**Time** 117
Operator 112	**Fire** 110
Directories 114	**Ambulance** 110
International operator 113	**Police** 119

Newspapers: Good selection of foreign newspapers and magazines. The local *Gleaner* and the *Daily News* have useful information on current events. The *Gleaner* publishes a twice monthly *Tourist Guide to Jamaica,* distributed free, and *The Visitor* comes out weekly in Montego Bay, also free. They're found at hotels, airports, and Jamaica Tourist Board offices.

Tipping: Taxis, 15% of fare; airport porters and hotel bellboys, J50 cents per piece of luggage; chambermaids J$1 per person per day. Service charge is generally included in restaurants, but leave 10-15% if it is not. Cloakroom and beach attendants expect around J50 cents; museum guides, the same, but optional; hairdressers, 15-20%.

Electricity: 110 volts 50 cycles AC. American flat-pin plugs in general use.

Laundry: High standards of laundry and dry-cleaning; good hotels have 24-hour service.

Hairdressing: There are several salons, and major hotels have facilities (shampoo and set from J$15; man's haircut from J$6).

Photography: Bring your own film, especially color, as it is scarce in areas outside of Kingston and Montego Bay. Black and white developed in about a week; color may take a little longer.

Clubs: Rotary, Kiwanis, Lions.

Babysitting: Nursemaid service is available through the Tourist Board, travel agents, hotels.

Rest Rooms: In hotels and restaurants.

Health: Good doctors, dentists, and hospitals. A limited range of pharmaceuticals and toiletries is available, but expensive. Water is drinkable in tourist resorts.

TRANSPORTATION

City buses tend to be overcrowded; it is best to take a taxi, but if it is unmetered, agree on the fare in advance and try to bargain, or ask a hotel clerk the standard point to point rate and verify this when the taxi arrives. For long distances trains are an adequate but slow link. International car rental companies are represented, and there are several local firms. Rates are from US$30 per day, including mileage. You must be over 21 years of age, and if between 21-25, a deposit of US$400 is required. A US$100 deposit is required of others. Drive on the left, but do not count on other people doing the same in country districts; use your horn and great caution. Trans-Jamaican Airlines flies between the main resorts; Kingston to Montego Bay takes 25 minutes.

FOOD AND RESTAURANTS

Hotels and many excellent restaurants provide standard international cuisine, but sample the Jamaican specialties with names like *jerk pork, run-down, stamp-and-go,* and *pepperpot soup.* Salt fish and *ackee* is the national dish—a combination of cod and a uniquely flavored yellow fruit. There are all sorts of exotic fruits and vegetables—tamarinds, rose apples, soursops, ortaniques, jackfruit, callaloo, yampies, tannias, susumbers. Try Bombay mango in coconut cream for dessert. For a snack, there is guava cheese, a plantain tart, or the Jamaicans' own favorite, a *patty* (pastry filled with spicy ground meat).

Restaurants in Kingston: for dinner, **The Mill** (Manor Park Plaza—tel: 924-1163) offers a wide range of European and Jamaican cooking. Others, such as the **Kohinoor Indian Restaurant** (11 Holborn Road—tel:

926-0301), offer varied exotic dishes. Reservations necessary; closed Sundays, as are many restaurants on the island. The **Terra Nova Hotel** (17 Waterloo Road—tel: 926-2211) has elegant food and service; expensive, and reservations are essential. In the same New Kingston area the **Devon House** (26 Old Hope Road—tel: 926-3580) in which the Jamaican National Trust has recreated the atmosphere of a colonial mansion serves unusual Jamaican specialties at moderate prices—the drinks, from the legendary *Devon Duppy*, a fine-flavored, head kicking, rum-based drink to fruit juices such as tamarind fizz and mango walk, are unique. The **Blue Mountain Inn** (Gordon Town—tel: 937-7400) is Jamaica's most famous restaurant, housed in an 18th-century residence on the banks of the Mammee River (reserve as far ahead as you can; dinner only; expensive; dress formal). For a much fuller guide, consult *Eating Out in Jamaica* by Dr Alex D Hawkes, obtainable through the Tourist Board.

DRINKING TIPS

Jamaica is the place for rum and coffee. The rum, varying from rich and dark to pale and smooth, is an ingredient of many powerful punches. Blue Mountain coffee flavors the world-renowned Tia Maria liqueur and the award-winning Old Jamaica liqueurs (try old Jamaica Coffee or Wild Orange) which make delicious after-dinner drinks. Red Stripe is a good local beer, and there are also unusual fruit juices. Imported wines are expensive. In Kingston the **Jonkanoo Lounge** in the New Kingston Hotel is popular at cocktail time, or try the **Surrey Tavern** in the Jamaica Pegasus Hotel or the terrace of the **Blue Mountain Inn.**

ENTERTAINMENT

Jamaica is a great place for music, from calypsos to the compulsive beat of *reggae*. Most hotels have good bands and singers. Try the **Jonkanoo Lounge** at the New Kingston Hotel or other nightspots such as **Turn Table Discothèque** or **Epiphany. Cloud 9** (Half Way Tree Road) is open late, and you can have a pizza with your beer. In Kingston it is unwise to wander around after dark without an escort who is familiar with the area.

Movies are shown in the larger hotels; avoid public movie houses, which can be noisy. Local theater is, however, recommended: the **Ward Theater** puts on pantomimes in the winter; **The Way Out** (Jamaica Pegasus Hotel); **Stage One** (New Kingston Hotel), **The Barn,** and the **Little Theater** on Tom Redcam Drive are other small, comfortable theaters in Kingston. There are good modern dance companies.

SHOPPING

There are tremendous bargains to be had at the duty-free shops in Kingston, Montego Bay, and Ocho Rios. Called in-bond shopping, you can take the items with you except for liquor or cigarettes, which are delivered to the in-bond counter at the airport and picked up at departure. Payment for in-bond shopping is in foreign currency only, and you can save 30-40% on cameras, Swiss watches, English china, and cashmere, and, of course, liquor, perfume, and tobacco. Best local buys are clothes and textiles in vivid cotton prints, embroidery, native paintings, and wood carvings. There are many art galleries in Kingston, including the **National Gallery** at Devon House or **Bolivar Gallery** at Old Oxford Road, near Half Way Tree Road. For crafts go to the **Jamaica Crafts Market,** on the waterfront, or to **Devon House,** where, in addition to a restaurant, there is a shopping arcade (and a museum). The main shopping centers in Kingston are **Tropical Plaza, Liguanea Plaza,** and **Premier Plaza.** The area round the New Kingston Hotel is best for clothes boutiques, etc., but you will find a wider choice in Montego Bay than in Kingston.

SPORTS

There are 9 golf courses; the top ones are **Tryall, Half Moon, Eden,** and **Rose Hall** in the Montego area, and **Runaway** at Runaway Bay, 18 miles from Ocho Rios. (The Tourist Board has a special brochure detailing all courses.) There is tennis at clubs and hotels all over the island, including the famous **Montego Bay Racquet Club.** There is horseback riding at several Montego Bay hotels and at the Tryall Golf and Beach Club, also at the **Double AA Ranch** near Rose Hall, Montego Bay. Polo is played at the **Drax Hall** and **Hanover Clubs,** and there is racing at the **Caymanas Park** track near Kingston on Wednesdays, Saturdays, and public holidays. For water sports there is snorkeling, yachting, water-skiing, and sea and river fishing. Most sports clubs provide temporary membership for visitors, and hotels or Tourist Board offices can arrange this. Jamaica's best beaches tend to be on the northern coast. If you are not staying at a beachfront hotel, go to the public beaches, the long and wide **Turtle Beach** at Ocho Rios or the seven miles of sand at **Negril.** Public beaches equipped with changing rooms for a small fee are **Doctor's Cave Beach** and **Cornwall Beach** at Montego Bay, and **Puerto Seco** and **Dunn's River Falls and Beach** in the Ocho Rios area.

WHAT TO SEE

Montego Bay on the north shore is one of the world's great resorts. Its phenomenal growth began at the turn of the century at the "Doctor's Cave," where the beach was thought to be fed by spring waters of therapeutic value. The **Doctor's Cave Beach Club** is still a social center.

In the Montego Bay area some of the best food and night-time entertainment is to be had in the hotels, including the **Bay Roc, Round Hill,** and **Montego Bay Racquet Club;** all these are expensive—advance reservations and formal dress are required (jacket and tie for men, black tie in some). Other recommended restaurants are the **Diplomat** (Queen's Drive—tel: 952-3353); the **Rum Barrel Inn** (Market Street—tel: 952-2688); the **Admiral's Inn** (Upper Deck Hotel off Queen's Road—tel: 952-3732), with well-trained staff and unusual dishes at moderate prices; also **Au Refuge** (37 Gloucester Avenue—tel: 952-3840), where the wine list is above average. More elegant, though very expensive, is the **Georgian House** (Orange Street and Union Street—tel: 952-5705). The **Town House** (16 Church Street—tel: 952-2660) is a handsomely restored 18th-century house with excellent Jamaican specialties. At a more moderate price level are the **Front Porch** for Jamaican cooking (Wexford Court Hotel), the **Toby Inn** (Kent Avenue), the **Reef Club**, next to the Holiday Inn, and the **Calabash** (Queen's Drive), where vegetable dishes are unusual and delicious. For lunch, the **Pelican Grill** (Gloucester Avenue) is very popular, or try the **China Doll** (St James Street).

For nightlife, the **Witch's Hideaway** and the **Hummingbird Lounge** are popular spots in the Holiday Inn. There are steel bands and calypsos, and rock music, local or imported, is played at discothèques such as **Ipso Facto** (Casa Montego Hotel), **Playpen** (Rosemount Hotel), **Banana Boat** (Union Street), the **Cave** (Seawind Beach Resort), and **Carousel** (Parkway Plaza). The **Disco Inferno,** opposite the Holiday Inn, claims to be the largest discothèque in the Caribbean. As in Kingston, it is wise to be wary of downtown streets at night; take a taxi. Montego Bay is the best place to shop for clothes, especially exclusive locally made beach and evening wear. **Ruth Clarage, Elizabeth Jean,** and the **Poupée Rouge** are names for women to look for; men should pay a visit to **Beard's & Co** and **Buckley's.** For worthwhile, inexpensive presents, choose something from the **Straw Market** on Harbour Street and Howard Cooke Boulevard. At the **Blue Mountain Gem Shop,** across from the Holiday Inn, you can watch the jewelers at work as you buy. **Negril,** Jamaica's most up-and-coming resort area, is 50 miles west of Montego Bay, at the western end of the island, where the sunsets are almost as famous as its marvelous 7-mile strip of white sand. Eat and drink at the **Negril Sands Beach Club** or enjoy the free-style living of the **Negril Beach Village.** The **Sundowner Hotel** is pleasant and moderately priced, and cottages can be rented very cheaply. Hotels in the Montego Bay area:

Rates are in US$ for a double/twin room with bath or shower

Bay Roc, PO Box 100 (from $60EP)
Beach View, PO Box 86 (from $30)
Buccaneer Inn, PO Box 469 (from $39)
Carlyle Beach, PO Box 412 (from $40)
Casa Montego, PO Box 161 (from $52)
Coral Cliff, PO Box 201 (from $39)
Doctor's Cave, PO Box 94 (from $42)
Half Moon, PO Box 80 (from $159)
Holiday Inn, PO Box 480 (from $58)
Montego Bay Racquet Club, PO Box 245 (from $50)
Montego Beach, PO Box 144 (from $59)
ROSE HALL INTER · CONTINENTAL, PO Box 999 (from $77)
Round Hill, PO Box 64 (from $135)
Royal Caribbean, PO Box 167 (from $78)
Seawind Beach Resort, PO Box 1168 (from $38)
Sign Great House, Sign PO (from $32)
Tryall Golf & Beach Club, Sandy Bay PO (from $110 MAP)
Upper Deck, PO Box 16 (from $58)

Falmouth, 22 miles along the coast from Montego Bay, dates from the end of the 18th century, when the sugar planters' prosperity was at its height. Its gracefully decaying Georgian buildings preserve something of the atmosphere of those leisured days. On the way there you can visit **Rose Hall Great House,** once the grandest mansion on the island. In Falmouth there is the **Trelawny Beach Club** (from US$685 per person per week MAP all inclusive package). For a complete contrast to 20th-century sophistication, you might venture into the wild and primitive **Cockpit Country,** home of the Maroons, descendants of runaway slaves who took refuge here from the British in the 17th century and fought a guerrilla war so successfully that the British were obliged to negotiate a treaty guaranteeing the rebels exemption from taxation and government interference. The Maroons still live under the terms of this 1739 treaty and are governed by an elected "Colonel." For wildlife lovers there is the **Paradise Jungle Park** and the **Rocklands Feeding Station** at Anchovy near Montego Bay, where hummingbirds will eat out of your hand.

Ocho Rios is fast becoming a rival resort center to Montego Bay, and it offers similar luxury facilities. It is an area of great scenic beauty which you will best appreciate if you arrive by road from Kingston, over **Mount Diablo** and through **Fern Gully,** a deep green, 3-mile valley shaded by giant ferns, finally emerging at Ocho Rios Bay. Between here and **St Ann's Bay, Dunn's River Falls** are deservedly famous, and you can climb the rapids. Hotels in the Ocho Rios area:

Rates are in US$ for a double/twin room with bath or shower
   Berkley Beach, PO Box 20, Runaway Bay (from $58)
   INTER · CONTINENTAL OCHO RIOS, PO Box 100 (from $74)
   Jamaica Hilton, PO Box 51, Ocho Rios (from $86)
   Jamaica Inn, PO Box 1, Ocho Rios (from $130AP)
   Plantation Inn, PO Box 2, Ocho Rios (from $100MAP)
   Runaway Bay, PO Box 58, Runaway Bay (from $75)
   Shaw Park Beach, PO Box 17, Ocho Rios (from $114 CP)
   Turtle Beach Towers, PO Box 73, Ocho Rios (from $58)

For eating out in Ocho Rios, the **Casanova** at Sans Souci, with imported chefs from the best hotel in Venice, sets a very high standard and is expensive. The **Plantation Inn** (tel: 974–2501) offers excellent service in a beautiful setting; the **Hilton** has a good reputation for its food, as have the **Silver Spray Club** at Runaway Bay and **The Jamaica Inn** (tel: 974-2514). In the moderate category, the **Hibiscus Lodge** has authentic Jamaican cooking, and the **Little Pub** (tel: 974-2324) is popular after dark. Nightlife is concentrated in the **Ocho Rios Inter · Continental, the Hilton, Silks** discothèque at the Shaw Park Hotel, and the **Footprints in the Ceiling** discothèque. For shopping Ocho Rios has branches of the best stores and boutiques; of special interest are the **Galleries,** a workshop for handmade furniture, and the **Little Pub/Celia Byass Center** for local crafts. **Pineapple Place** (Main Street) and **Coconut Grove,** near the Plantation Inn, are two shopping centers where you'll find imported articles at duty-free prices and the boutiques of native fashion designers. Also visit the **Crafts Market,** near the Inn on the Beach. If you come to Ocho Rios along the coast from Montego Bay, you will have passed

Discovery Bay, the spectacular **Runaway Caves,** and the **Seville Estate,** St. Ann's Bay, where Columbus first landed in 1494.

Port Antonio is the chief banana port of Jamaica and the third major tourist resort. Deep-sea fishing is the great attraction of this beautiful harbor town. Then there is the famous **Blue Lagoon.** Everybody comes here to raft down the Rio Grande—a pleasant drift through lovely tropical scenery, punctuated (if you like) by dips in the cool clear water. Hotels at Port Antonio are the **Bonnie View,** PO Box 82 (from US$32 double), **Dragon Bay,** PO Box 176 (from US$67CP), the luxurious **Frenchman's Cove,** PO Box 101 (from US$90 double), **Jamaica Hill Estates,** PO Box 26 (from US$250 double MAP). **Trident Villas,** PO Box 119 (from US$95 double), is a modern resort hotel designed as a Jamaican village. The **De Montevin Lodge,** 21 Fort George Street (tel: 993-2604), has excellent Jamaican cooking at moderate cost. In the hills is the pleasantly cool and peaceful town of **Mandeville** in the uplands above Kingston. Its tidy village green and slightly sedate ex-colonial atmosphere give it a very English feeling. You can play golf and tennis here and stay at the **Mandeville Hotel,** PO Box 78 (from US$20 double).

Kingston, the capital, is a good base for trips to the **Blue Mountains, Port Royal,** and **Spanish Town. Port Royal,** once the "wickedest city in the world" when Henry Morgan's buccaneers caroused in its taverns and brothels, was duly punished when in 1692 an earthquake caused it to sink into the sea. You can get there by ferry across the harbor and skin-dive to see the ruins. **Spanish Town,** 13 miles west of Kingston, has a fine square and cathedral, and its **Folk Museum** is worth a visit. To the north of the capital are the **Royal Botanical Gardens** at **Hope.** In the town there is the Straw Market for handicrafts, and, if you are interested in the history of the island, you can see relics of the Arawak people in the **Arawak Museum,** run by the Jamaica Institute on the road between Kingston and Spanish Town.

SOURCES OF FURTHER INFORMATION

Any **Pan Am** office around the world; **Jamaica Tourist Board,** 77-83 Knutsford Blvd., Kingston; 866 Second Avenue, New York, NY 10017, and 50 St James Street, London SW1A IJT.

Martinique

WHAT'S SPECIAL

Martinique is the most exotic of the West Indian Islands. Overshadowed
by a volcano, the country ranges from lush rain forests to a desert of
petrified wood. Her people are distinctly French and delightfully Creole.
The former capital, St. Pierre, once the most cultured city in these seas
until a volcanic eruption laid it to waste. Tourism has come late, and
the old life makes few concessions to it. Martinique is a ready-made
vacation island, and you can eat as only the French know how, or shop
as you would in Paris—for perfume, jewelry, lingerie, and fashions. Then
there is the music—the *béguine,* the *mazurka,* and, on Ash Wednesday,
the frenzy of Carnival.

COUNTRY BRIEFING

Size: 425 square miles   **Population:** 350,000

Capital: Fort-de-France   **Capital Population:** 100,000

   Climate: Tropical, tempered by trade winds. Rainy season in September and October.

Weather in Fort-de-France: Lat N14°36′; Alt 13 ft

Temp (°F)	Jan	Feb	Mar	Apr	May	Jun	Jul	Aug	Sep	Oct	Nov	Dec
Av Low	69°	69°	69°	71°	73°	74°	74°	74°	74°	73°	72°	71°
Av High	83°	84°	85°	86°	87°	86°	86°	87°	88°	87°	86°	84°
Days no rain	12	13	16	17	13	9	9	9	10	12	10	12

   Government: An overseas *departement* of the Republic of France
since 1946.

Language: French and Creole.
Religion: Roman Catholic.
Currency: French franc. 100 centimes = 1F.

	10c	50c	1F	5F	10F	50F	100F	300F
US (dollars, cents)	.02	.09	.18	.90	1.81	9.03	18.05	54.15
UK (pounds, pence)	.01	.04	.09	.43	.86	4.31	8.61	25.83

Public Holidays:

New Year's Day, 1 Jan
Mardi Gras (Feb)
Good Friday
Easter Monday
Labor Day, 1 May
Ascension Day

Pentecost Monday
Bastille Day, 14 July
Assumption Day, 15 Aug
All Saints Day, 1 Nov
Armistice Day, 11 Nov
Christmas Day, 25 Dec

HOW TO GET THERE

Flying time to Lamentin Airport, Fort-de-France from New York is 5½ hours, from London, 13 hours, from Miami, 3 hours, from San Juan, 1¼ hours. Time in Martinique: GMT−4.

REQUIREMENTS FOR ENTRY AND CUSTOMS REGULATIONS

The following are needed: proof of identity for stays up to 21 days, a passport for stays up to 3 months, and a visa for stays over 3 months; round-trip or onward ticket. Duty-free allowance: 200 cigarettes for visitors from non-EEC European countries, 300 from EEC countries, 400 from elsewhere; 1 bottle liquor, 3 bottles wine; 2 still cameras and 20 rolls of film; 1 movie camera and 10 rolls.

AIRPORT INFORMATION

Lamentin Airport is about 5 miles from Fort-de-France. Tip porters 2F. Departure tax for charter passengers only. Duty-free shop. Car rental desks.

ACCOMMODATIONS

In general, there is not the enormous variety of hotel accommodations here that you expect to find on other West Indian Islands. It is not developed in the same way—which is a large part of its charm. But the serious traveler will find what he wants. Go first to the **Tourist Bureau** at the airport or on Boulevard Alfassa by the harbor. Ask for a free copy of "Ici Martinique," a useful directory in English to hotels, restaurants, shopping, touring, and sports. For off-season discounts make arrangements with the hotel in advance. Hotels in Martinique (high-season rates):
Rates are in US$ for a double/twin room with bath or shower
  Auberge de L'Anse Mitan, Trois Ilets (from US$45 EP) 20 miles
  Bakoua, Pointe du Bout (from $150 CP), 20 miles from Fort-de-France
  Buccaneer's Creek Club Mediterranee, Ste Anne (from $460 weekly) 31 miles
  Frantel, Pointe du Bout (from $100 CP)

Latitude, Carbet (from $95 CP) 20 miles
L'Imperatrice, Fort-de-France (from $45)
Leyritz Plantation, Basse-Pointe (from $100 CP) 40 miles
Meridien Martinique, Pointe du Bout (from $50 MAP)
PLM La Bataliere, Schoelcher (from $110 CP) 1 mile
PLM La Marina, Pointe du Bout (from $110 EP)
PLM Manoir de Beauregard, Ste Anne (from $69 CP) 31 miles
Victoria, Fort-de-France (from $40 EP)

USEFUL INFORMATION

Helpful Hints: Men may need jackets and ties to eat in the top restaurants; women should avoid wearing shorts in the shopping district. Women are welcome in bars and nightclubs. Sunglasses, a lightweight sweater, and a pocket raincoat, are recommended.

Banks: Open 8-12 and 2:30-4 Mon-Fri, closed Sat. Hotels will change currency and travelers' checks; a 20% discount is offered on luxury items when paid for with travelers' checks.

Mail: Stamps at post offices and hotels.

Telephone Tips: Some booths and phones in cafés and restaurants. Useful numbers:

Airport Information: 71-12-34

Tourist Office 74-18-55 (airport)

71-79-60 (Fort-de-France)

Newspapers: English-language newspapers imported.

Tipping: In general, if a service charge is not included, about 10-15%; porters about 2F; taxis, optional.

Electricity: 220 volts 50 cycles AC almost everywhere.

Laundry: Good hotels have 24-hour service; dry-cleaning is not, however, readily available.

Hairdressing: Some good salons in town and at resort hotels (shampoo and set, from 25F; man's haircut, from 10F).

Photography: Black and white and color film and equipment available. Color processing takes 10 days.

Clubs: Rotary, Lions, and Kiwanis.

Babysitting: Ask at your hotel or the Martinique Tourist Office.

Rest Rooms: In cafés, etc, look for *toilettes.* Women, *Dames:* men, *Messieurs or Hommes.*

Health: Doctors and dentists are good but may not speak English. Medical standards are high, and there are good hospitals. Well-known pharmaceuticals imported. Tap water is safe to drink; bottled water is also available.

TRANSPORTATION

There are plenty of taxis, which charge 33% extra at night. Rented cars are available from US$18 a day, plus mileage, or from US$195 weekly with unlimited mileage. There is a bus service, but just as inexpensive and more convenient are the shared or collective taxis which go all over the island. There is a regular ferry service from Fort-de-France to Pointe du Bout across the bay (20 minutes, 5F) and to the beach at **Anse Mitan** (30 minutes, 5F).

FOOD AND RESTAURANTS

This could be the reason you chose to come here in the first place, since Martinique is a part of France and pays homage to the cult of *haute cuisine*. But cooking here is not merely sophisticated and subtle; it is made exciting by Creole inventiveness—especially with seafoods. There are dozens of restaurants, large and small, plain and fancy, in hotels and privately operated. *Crabes Farcis* (stuffed land crabs in their own shells), for example, are a specialty, as are *oursins* (sea urchin), *lambi* (conch), *soudons* (baby clams), and *langoustines* (crayfish). Try *calalou*, a green herb soup, and *colombo* (the creole version of curry). Gourmets, and Martinique is full of them, award top honors to **La Grand' Voile** (Pointe Simon, Fort-de-France—tel: 71-29-29), *"le plus chic"* and also the most expensive, but worth every sou. Other good possibilities in Fort-de-France: **L'escalier** (tel: 71-25-22), **Le Bitaco** (tel: 71-35-16), **Typic Bellevue** (tel: 71-68-87), **D'Esnambuc** (tel: 71-46-51), and **Le Tiffany** (tel: 71-23-82). Across the bay at Pointe du Bout try **Chez Sidonie** (tel: 76-30-54), or to the south at Sainte Anne, **Manois de Beauregard** (tel: 76-73-40), or 10 minutes away in Schoelcher, **Le Foulard** (tel: 71-05-72). For a longer expedition go to **Plantation de Leyritz** in Basse Pointe (tel: 75-53-08). Reservations are recommended.

DRINKING TIPS

Bars are almost always open. The wine and champagne come from France without import duty, and the rum is famous. Bally and Clement are two excellent, and inexpensive, local brands. Liquor is expensive—roughly double the cost of a bottle of wine. A specialty is *petit punch* or *punch martiniquais*, made with rum, cane syrup, and lime and drunk as an apéritif (not with meals). A good place to drink and to watch the evening crowds is in **La Savane**, the park in the center of Fort-de-France.

ENTERTAINMENT

Movies and television are in French, but there are better pastimes—such as dancing a *béguine* or a *merengue*, or watching the graceful swoon of the Creole girls at the end of a *mazurka*. At the resort hotels the **Ballets Martiniquais** folkloric dance troupe performs traditional dances in colorful Creole costumes. The music on Martinique is very special and should not be missed. There are also several discothèques, including **Sweety** (rue Capitaine Rose), **Latin Club** (rue Francois Arago), and **Club Bernard, The Rive Gauche,** and **Hippopotamus,** all on Boulevard Allegre. There are casinos at the **PLM La Batalière** and at the **Meridien.** An exciting time to be in Martinique is Carnival time. Beginning in January, the celebrations come to a climax in the week of **Mardi Gras** and on Ash Wednesday. On the fourth day in particular, great images of deities are burned in La Savane, and the dancing reaches a pitch of hysterical

frenzy. Another uniquely Martinican fête is **La Toussaint** (All Saints, 1 Nov), when candles are lit on all the graves—a sight no one forgets.

SHOPPING

Specialties of the island are appliquéd hangings—works of art in multi-colored cloth. These you will find in the **Art Center** on the harbor front, along with other native products: basketwork, and dolls. You can bargain for paintings at the covered market in the **rue Isambert.** Enormous savings can be made when buying world-famous perfumes and other luxury goods by using travelers' checks in Fort-de-France. Swiss watches, Hermès scarves, Lalique and Baccarat glass, Limoges china, and beautiful jewelry can all be bought at virtually free-port prices at **Roger Albert's** in rue Victor Hugo. Other shops to try are **Thomas Derogatis, La Chamade, Beaufrand,** and **Au Printemps.** For bargains in ordinary French goods, especially kitchenware, go to **La Licorne.**

SPORTS

Water sports of all kinds are available—diving, fishing, water-skiing, and sailing. To rent a boat contact one of the agencies at the Pointe du Bout marina area; **Martinique Charter and Services** (tel: 76-30-33), or **Roger Albert Voyages,** 7 rue Victor Hugo, Fort-de-France. Swimmers will prefer the beaches in the south of the island, especially at **Diamant Roc;** and **Les Salines.** Those near Fort-de-France are not so good. Soccer is played on Sundays. The most typical "sports" of the island are cockfighting and contests between snakes and mongooses. Tennis is available at most large hotels. Many courts are lighted for night play. There is also golf, horseback riding, and cycling.

WHAT TO SEE

The most important sight of the island is the town of **St Pierre,** once the most cultured city in these seas and enjoying the title of "P'tit Paris des Caraibes"; only 77 years ago its 30,000 inhabitants were obliterated in minutes the morning of May 8, 1902 when two shattering explosions rocked **Mont Pelée.** Reportedly there was but one survivor to this incredible disaster—a prisoner in an underground jail cell. The ruins today are a poignant sight, and the **Dr. Franck Perret Musee Volcanologique** houses numerous objects found after the disaster, and chronicles the occasion with pictures and news accounts, evoking thoughts of a Caribbean Pompeii. The drive there and back (excursions are easily arranged) is a *circuit touristique* in itself, revealing the extensive savannahs, the slopes of the dormant volcano, and the tropical rain forest of the interior. To the south of the island are the good beaches, the dry savannah with its prehistoric **Petrified Wood,** and **Diamant Roc,** where British sailors from Nelson's fleet once created a miniature Gibraltar. You may also want to visit the childhood home of the Empress Joséphine, a ruin with a small museum in **Trois Ilets,** only a short distance from the resort area of Pointe du Bout. In Fort-de-France, her statue dominates La Savane park. Also in the capital you should go to the **Centre des Arts,** and to the museum with its Carib and Arawak artifacts. The library is an interesting building to the memory of Schoelcher, the man who freed the slaves and who, in doing so, probably freed the creative spirit of Martinique.

SOURCES OF FURTHER INFORMATION

Any **Pan Am** office around the world; **Office du Tourisme,** B.P. 520, 97206 Fort-de-France; **French West Indies Tourist Board,** 610 Fifth Avenue, New York, NY 10020; also in Beverly Hills and San Francisco, CA; **French Government Tourist Board,** 1840 Sherbrooke Ouest, Montreal, Quebec; 178 Piccadilly, London W1. Offices in Sydney, Australia, Mexico City, Mexico and Caracas, Venezuela.

Montserrat

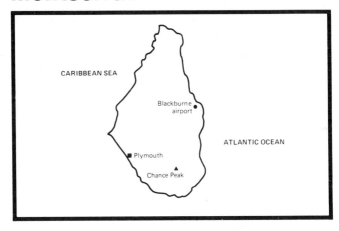

CARIBBEAN SEA

Blackburne
airport

ATLANTIC OCEAN

Plymouth

▲
Chance Peak

WHAT'S SPECIAL

Save in the minds of poets and copywriters—and despite the tiny shamrock that nestles atop the Governor's mansion—the island of Montserrat
has long since lost its connections with Ireland, though there are still
plenty of Malones, Mahoneys and Ryans around, and a touch of Blarney
in the Irish lilt of the locals speech may still be heard. The island was
originally settled by Sir Thomas Warner, though like most Caribbean
islands it was originally sighted by Christopher Columbus in 1493. (He
named it Montserrat from its silhouette, which supposedly reminded
him of a mountain in Spain.)

The Irish connection came about when Oliver Cromwell sent an
army—which included an Irish battalion—to defend the island against
attacks by the French in the 1650s. The French successfully took Montserrat in 1644, but it was finally ceded to Britain in 1783. And for those
who prefer a vacation just slightly off the beaten track, Montserrat is
hard to beat. Once an important exporter of limes and Sea Island cotton,
Montserrat is known today for Perks Rum Punch, a cordial made to a
recipe of Mr. J. W. R. Perkins.

COUNTRY BRIEFING

Size: 39.5 square miles   **Population:** 13,000
Capital: Plymouth   **Capital Population:** 3,000
  Climate: Even temperature all year round, with low humidity.

Weather in Plymouth: Lat N26°43'; Alt 130 ft

Temp (°F)	Jan	Feb	Mar	Apr	May	Jun	Jul	Aug	Sep	Oct	Nov	Dec
Av Low	70°	70°	70°	72°	74°	75°	75°	75°	74°	74°	73°	72°
Av High	82°	83°	85°	86°	88°	88°	87°	88°	89°	87°	85°	83°
Days no rain	19	19	22	22	21	17	17	15	17	17	14	18

Government: A British Crown Colony.

Language: English.

Religion: Roman Catholic and Protestant denominations.

Currency: East Caribbean dollar. 100 cents = EC$1.

	EC 10¢	EC 50¢	EC $1	EC $5	EC $10	EC $20	EC $50	EC $100
US (dollars, cents)	.05	.19	.37	1.85	3.70	7.41	18.52	37.04
UK (pounds, pence)	.02	.09	.18	.88	1.76	3.53	8.83	17.67

Public Holidays:

New Year's Day, 1 Jan
Good Friday
Easter Monday
Whit Monday
Labor Day, (1st Mon in May)
Queen's Birthday (2nd Sat in June)

August Bank Holiday (1st Mon in Aug)
Christmas Day, 25 Dec
Boxing Day, 26 Dec

HOW TO GET THERE

Flying time to Montserrat from New York is about 5 hours; from Miami, 3 hours; from Antigua, ¼ hour. Time in Montserrat: GMT−4.

REQUIREMENTS FOR ENTRY AND CUSTOMS REGULATIONS

Passport and round-trip ticket are needed (US and Canadian citizens need only proof of citizenship); also smallpox vaccination certificate, plus cholera and yellow-fever certificates if coming from an infected area. There is a 1% tax charged on all foreign exchange. Duty-free allowance: 200 cigarettes or 50 cigars or ½ pound tobacco; 1 opened quart bottle of liquor or 1 bottle wine; perfume for personal use. Import of firearms is forbidden without an import license from the Plymouth Chief of Police.

AIRPORT INFORMATION

No international airport, but arrival airport from Antigua is Blackburne, 10 miles from capital. No bus service to Plymouth, but taxis always available; fare to city center is EC$10 (US$4.80). Departure tax of EC$6.

ACCOMMODATIONS

Hotel rates vary in peak and off seasons; off season in April-December. For help in finding accommodations contact the **Montserrat Tourist Board,** Plymouth, PO Box 7 (tel: 2230) or Eastern Caribbean Tourist Association, 220 East 42nd Street #411, New York, N.Y. 10017—tel: (212) 986-9370. Most hotels add a 10% service charge, and there is a hotel tax of 7%. Winter rates are given; summer rates are generally lower. Hotels in Montserrat:

Rates in US$ for a double/twin room with bath or shower
  Caribelle Inn, Plymouth (from $93 MAP)
  Coconut Hill, Plymouth (from $58 MAP), ½ mile from Plymouth
  Emerald Isle, Richmond Hill ($90 MAP), 1 mile
  Hideaway Hotel, Rocklands (from $55 MAP), 7 miles
  Vue Pointe, Old Towne (from $115 MAP), 5 miles

USEFUL INFORMATION

Always ask permission before taking pictures of the people. Women should not wear shorts away from the beach and are not expected to drink in the local "rumshops." Beware of "seed beans," often made into necklaces—they can be poisonous. And do not touch Manchineel apples—smallish yellow-green fruit about the size of crab apples—or sit under the tree if it is raining, as they are also highly poisonous and the rain drops can burn the skin.

Banks: Open 8-12 Mon-Fri and 3-5 Fri. Most hotels change currency.

Mail: Stamps obtainable from post office, hotels, and many stores.

Telephone Tips: There are public booths and phones in hotels and cafés. Useful numbers:

Airport Information 4200   **Emergencies** 99
Tourist Information 2230

Newspapers: The local paper is the *Montserrat Mirror.*

Tipping: In hotels tip 10% for all services; elsewhere (taxis, hairdressers, etc.) 10% or less.

Electricity: 230 volts 60 cycles AC.

Laundry: Services through hotels.

Hairdressing: Professional hairdressing is available at the "House of Beauty" in Plymouth.

Photography: Color and black and white film available. Developing takes 24 hours for black and white; take color film home.

Clubs: Rotary, Jaycees.

Babysitting: Service can be arranged.

Rest Rooms: In hotels, restaurants, and bars. Signs in English.

Health: Doctors and dentists speak English. Imported pharmaceuticals available and not expensive. Water safe to drink.

TRANSPORTATION

The roads are good—taxis and car rentals are expensive. Taxi fares from airport to hotels are from EC$13-25 (fares are standardized and controlled by law); the average daily rate for a rented car is from US$15-20 per day. Drive on the left.

FOOD AND RESTAURANTS

Meal times are breakfast 7:30-9:30, lunch 12-2, dinner 7-9. Local specialties are fruit, mangoes, avocados; also try the boiled rice and pigeon peas; a highly seasoned goat stew called goat water; and mountain chicken, a type of frog found only in Montserrat and Dominica. American and English dishes are available at all hotels. A meal in an expensive restaurant will cost just over US$15, at a medium-priced one about US$9, and at an inexpensive place, US$5. It is usual to eat at your hotel, but if you prefer to go out try **Cynthy's** in Plymouth, or the **Mariner's Club,** Wapping (tel: 2774). For West Indian dishes try **The Wade Inn,** Plymouth (tel: 2304), where the specialty is the native "goat water" and an exceptional *callalloo*—a soup made of crabs and *dasheen,* a spinach-like vegetable that grows on the island. West Indian food is also found at **The Hideaway.** The **Belham Valley** restaurant has international cuisine.

DRINKING TIPS

Rum is the local drink, and of all the rum punches the most famous is *Perks Punch,* made to the special recipe of Mr J. W. R. Perkins and drunk as a liqueur. Imported wines, beers, and Scotch are available; average price of a whisky and soda is EC$10, and a bottle of wine costs about EC$23. Bars are generally open 9am-2am. The **Agouti** in Plymouth, the **Hideaway Hotel,** 7 miles from Plymouth, and the **Nep-Co-Den,** 2 miles from Plymouth, are popular night spots.

ENTERTAINMENT

Nightlife mainly revolves around the hotels during the winter season.

SHOPPING

Stores are open 8-12 Mon-Sat and until 12:30 Wed. Best buys are the clothes made of Sea Island cotton or the fabric itself. Buy them from the **John Bull Shop.** Local souvenir items include scatter rugs made from calico, cord bags, and hammocks; go to the **Cottage Crafts Shop** and **Montserrat Crafts. Gifts of Quality** has luxury imported items; **The Sugar Mill** has imported clothes, jewelry, and furniture; **Etcera** has imported clothing and locally made souvenir items.

SPORTS

The **Belham River Valley Golf Course** of the Montserrat Gulf Club runs from the coast into the mountains, with a Club House built almost 200 years ago by a British plantation owner. Its 11 holes were designed by Edmund Ault to be played as two 9-hole courses. Greens fees are US$6 per day or US$30 per week. There are two lawn tennis courts at the **Vue Pointe Hotel.** Try climbing **Chance Peak,** 3,000 feet, or any of the other mountains. There is also horseback riding, yachting, and swimming.

WHAT TO SEE

A small museum situated in an old sugar mill tower at **Richmond Hill** contains relics of the island's past. **St. Anthony's** church in Plymouth, though rebuilt several times as a result of earthquake and hurricane damage, was originally consecrated in the early 17th century. Take a picnic to the ruins of the 18th-century fort at **St George's Hill.** In Plymouth, visit **Government House,** a Victorian-tropic building decorated with an Irish shamrock. Climb up to **Galway's Soufrière,** an open crater spewing out molten sulphur, or picnic beside the **Great Alps Waterfall,** though if you're not feeling energetic it can easily be reached by road. There is also a thermal spa within easy reach.

SOURCES OF FURTHER INFORMATION

Any **Pan Am** office around the world; **The Montserrat Tourist Board,** PO Box 7, Plymouth, Montserrat; the **Eastern Caribbean Tourist Association,** 220 East 42nd Street, Room 411, New York, NY 10017, and 200 Buckingham Palace Road, London. SWI; government representatives: Mr. D. W. Currie, Station A, Toronto M5W1E4, Canada; Mr. K. A. Knaack, Broicher Strasse 94, D-5060 Bergisch Gladbach 1, W Germany; and Mr. M. J. Gillis, Suite 650, 444 Brickwell Avenue, Miami, Florida 33131.

Puerto Rico

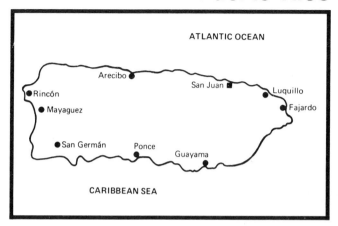

WHAT'S SPECIAL

The island enjoys a pleasant climate, and for the tourist the profusion of beaches and brilliant sunshine has made Puerto Rico a year round resort. The cultural background is Spanish, dating from 1508 when Juan Ponce de León—whose name was adopted for the second city of the island—established his first settlement here. He is buried in San Juan Cathedral. The Spanish settlement was contested over the centuries—both Sir Francis Drake and the Earl of Cumberland attempted to change its status—but Spain held grimly on. Finally, Luis Muñoz Rivera (popularly known as the George Washington of PR) obtained a Charter of Autonomy from the Imperial Court of Spain in 1897, which provided dominion status and effective local self-government. A year later, following its policy of Manifest Destiny, the US went to war with Spain, landing troops on the south coast on 25 July 1898. The Treaty of Paris the following year ceded the island to the USA. Puerto Ricans were finally granted US citizenship nearly 20 years later.

In recent times the debate continues on whether the island should opt for independence, statehood, or continue the current so-called commonwealth status. Under commonwealth status, the island pays no federal income tax and local taxes are used locally. As a result of the success of Operation Bootstrap, new industry has been established by the granting of tax exemptions and deferral, and income from manufacturing today is worth nearly four times that from farming, though sugar, rum, and tobacco are still exported. Tourism is an extremely important industry, and the traveler, whether arriving by sea or air, is generally well served by the wide range of facilities available. Marketing and general supervision are provided by a quasi-governmental organization known as The Tourism Company.

For the traveler, Puerto Rico offers many different faces, from rain forest and wild orchids, golf courses and casinos, all of it sufficiently "foreign" and yet familiar enough to make you feel at home.

COUNTRY BRIEFING
Size: 3,435 square miles   **Population:** 3,187,566
Capital: San Juan   **Capital Population:** 432,973
   Climate: Marine tropical, warm and sunny most of the year. Mountain regions are cooler.

   Weather in San Juan: Lat N18°29'; Alt 82 ft

Temp (°F)	Jan	Feb	Mar	Apr	May	Jun	Jul	Aug	Sep	Oct	Nov	Dec
Av Low	70°	69°	70°	71°	73°	73°	73°	76°	75°	74°	73°	71°
Av High	80°	80°	81°	82°	84°	85°	85°	85°	86°	86°	84°	81°
Days no rain	11	13	16	16	15	13	12	10	12	13	11	10

   Government: A quasi-autonomous commonwealth voluntarily associated with the US.
   Language: Spanish; English widely spoken.
   Religion: 80% of population Roman Catholic.
   Currency: US dollar.

Public Holidays:
In addition to US holidays:
Epiphany, 6 Jan
Hostos' Birthday, 11 Jan
Abolition of Slavery, 22 Mar
Good Friday
De Diego's Birthday, 16 Apr

Muñoz Rivera's Birthday, 17 July
Constitution Day, 25 July
Barbosa's Birthday, 27 July
Columbus Day, 12 Oct
Discovery of Puerto Rico, 19 Nov

HOW TO GET THERE
Flying time to San Juan, Isla Verde International Airport from New York is 4 hours; from Miami 2¼ hours; from Caracas 1½ hours. Time in Puerto Rico: GMT−4.

REQUIREMENTS FOR ENTRY AND CUSTOMS REGULATIONS
No passports or visas required for US citizens, but foreign nationals must have passports and pass through customs before entering. Vaccination certificates are necessary only if arriving from an infected area. You are allowed to bring in anything necessary for personal use. No customs duty is charged on purchases made in Puerto Rico and taken into the United States. However, tobacco and Puerto Rican rums are subject to US taxes.

AIRPORT INFORMATION
The airport is Isla Verde International, about 9 miles from Old San Juan. A pick-up bus carries travelers free Mon-Fri from the terminal to the

highway at the airport entrance 6am-7pm; there travelers can take the
T-1 bus to Old San Juan; 7-11pm T-1 bus enters airport directly, boarding
and discharging passengers. On Sat-Sun service ends about 10:10pm.
The airport limousine costs from US$1-2. Car rentals available. Taxis
into Isla Verde cost about US$3, to the Condado about US$6, to Old
San Juan about US$10; tip airport porters 50¢ per bag. The airport has
a hotel reservations counter and a duty-free shop for passengers of international flights.

ACCOMMODATIONS

It is wise to reserve in advance, particularly for the period of January
to May. Rates tend to be lower in the off or summer season, May to
December. The least expensive accommodations are guest houses, which
in the winter season average about US$17-25 single. There is a 6% accom-
modation tax. Hotels in San Juan:

Rates in US$ for a double/twin room with bath or shower

    Best Western Pierre Hotel, 105 de Diego Ave., Santurce (from $55)
    Carib Inn, Isla Verde (from $64)
    Caribe Hilton, PO Box 1872, Puerta de Tierra (from $99)
    Condado Beach, (Convention Center), Condado (from $80)
    Condado Holiday Inn, Ashford Ave., Condado (from $90)
    Da Vinci, PO Box 12038, Condado (from $90)
    DuPont Plaza, Ashford Ave., Condado (from $85)
    El Convento, Cristo Street, Old San Juan (from $70)
    Holiday Inn on the Beach, PO Box 6888, Isla Verde (from $75)
    La Concha, Ashford Ave., Condado (from $80)
    La Gran Bahia, Fernandez Juncos Ave, Miramar (from $48)

The city of San Juan stretches eastward along the Atlantic Ocean from
Old San Juan at its westernmost tip almost to the Isla Verde International
Airport, a distance of approximately 9 miles. Hotels in the Puerta de
Tierra section are east of Old San Juan; the Condado section is just east
of that. Miramar and Santurce are south of the Condado, and the Isla
Verde section is adjacent to the airport.

USEFUL INFORMATION

    Banks: Open 9-2:30 Mon-Fri. Many local, Spanish and US banks oper-
ate here. Money and checks can also be changed at hotels and main
stores.
    Mail: Post offices in metropolitan area and most interior towns. Mail-
boxes red and blue, as in the US.
    Telephone Tips: Phones in hotels, cafés, or restaurants and coin-oper-
ated booth phones. Useful numbers in San Juan:

Pan Am 754-7470	**Weather** 791-0320
Airport 791-4845	**Time** 728-9595
Traveler's Aid 791-1054	**Police** 343-2020
Accommodations office 791-1853 or	**Bus Information** 765-0330
791-3443	

Newspapers: The *San Juan Star* is published daily in English.
Tipping: 15% of any check is acceptable.
Electricity: Same as in the US.
Laundry: Hotels provide laundry and dry-cleaning services and a 24-hour service (dry-cleaning a suit, from US$3; laundering a shirt, from 75¢).
Hairdressing: First-class hotels have good salons.
Photography: Equipment and film available in cities.
Clubs: Rotary, Kiwanis, Lions, Elks, Jaycees, and Exchange.
Babysitting: No service available, but most hotels can refer you to responsible sitters.
Health: Many English-speaking doctors and dentists. Imported pharmaceuticals available. Water is safe to drink, and pasteurized milk is available.

TRANSPORTATION

Good public service, with bus or *guaguas* serving San Juan and the metropolitan area (fare 25¢; most are air conditioned). Exact fare or token is necessary on all buses. Five-passenger cars *(publicos)* serve the rest of the island; they will collect you from your hotel if you phone 722-0234. Lineas de Carro (tel: 725-2460) provides scheduled bus service to north-coast towns and Mayagüez. In Old San Juan there is a cab stand along the waterfront. Most taxis are metered; the initial charge is 80¢, then 10¢ for each additional ⅛ mile; 50¢ extra if you phone for the cab. Cars are also available for rental. **Boriquen Tours,** or **Gray Line** provide limousine tours of the island; their cars carry a shield for identification. Children can be sent on **Uncle Sam's Kiddie Tours,** with special 1-day tours. Ferryboats leave twice daily for Vieques and once daily for Culebra (single fare US$2 and US$2.25). There are two sailings to Vieques, one to Culebra. Both are small islands off Puerto Rico's east coast. Air BVI, Coral Air, Sun International Airways, Aero Virgin Islands, and Prinair provide service to the Virgin Islands, while Aero Caribe and Prinair provide domestic flights to Ponce and Mayagüez.

FOOD AND RESTAURANTS

Puerto Rico presents a wide range of food, from Oriental to Italian, French, and even English. Not surprisingly, there is more than a suggestion of old Spain about Puerto Rican cooking, and also a strong Cuban influence. The basic staples are rice and beans, and one of the best-known dishes is *arroz con pollo,* chicken and rice. Paella is available with a wide variety of seafood and Spanish sausage called *chorizos.* There is also a soupy version of the paella called *asopao,* combining chicken, seafood, and rice, but it is wetter than paella or *arroz con pollo.* Cuban black bean soup is popular, as are snacks such as *tostones,* which are plantains (a taste between a banana and a potato) fried in deep fat. Other snack foods to try are *hallacas* and *pasteles,* similar to *tamales.*

In Old San Juan, **La Mallorquina** (207 San Justo—tel: 722-3261) is the capital's oldest restaurant and a fine place to sample seafood; **El Callejón**

de la Capilla (317 Fortaleza—tel: 725-8529) serves *calamares en su tinta,* squid in their own ink, and Spanish and Puerto Rican specialties. The restaurant is housed in an old restored building. Other restaurants in Old San Juan include **Mago's Saxony Steak House** (257 Tanca—tel: 723-3339); **La Chaumière** (367 Tetuan—tel: 722-3330); **Sam's Patio** (102 San Sebastian—tel: 723-1149); **La Gallega** (tel: 725-8018), for Spanish dishes; **La Danza** and **Tetuan 20** for Puerto Rican specialties.

In numerous restaurants in and around metropolitan San Juan—in Puerta de Tierra, Condado, Isla Verde, and Santurce—you will find such diverse items as *lechón asado* (barbecued pig), *jueyes* (fresh land crabs), excellent paella, at the **Valencia Restaurant,** delicious pasta at **El Consulado** or **Mama's Little Italy,** or good Chinese fare at **Cathay** (410 Ponce de León Ave, Puerta de Tierra—tel: 723-5738).

In Isla Verde try **Mario's** (2 Rosa Street), serving Puerto Rican dishes, **Cecilia's Place** (Calle Rosa 8) for fish, and generally some of the best seafood in San Juan. While at **Che's** (corner of Caoba and Laurel) you can dine on authentic Argentinian style food. In Condado, there is **Scotch 'N' Sirloin** (1020 Ashford, La Rada Building) for good steaks. The **Swiss Chalet** on Avenida de Diego serves Swiss specialties—very popular and quite expensive.

DRINKING TIPS

Puerto Rico is the rum capital of the world. Some brands are Bacardi; Rum Superior Puerto Rico; Don Q; Ron Rico; Llave; Granado. A favorite rum drink is the *piña colada,* made with pineapple juice, coconut milk, and whipped egg white.

ENTERTAINMENT

Nightclubs in Puerto Rico are part of the international circuit, with high-quality entertainment and many well-known stars often appearing there. Dress appropriately. Particularly good are the **Club Caribe** in the Caribe Hilton and the **Fiesta Room** at the Condado Beach. Hotels with casinos are the Gran Bahia, Caribe Hilton, Carib Inn, DuPont Plaza, **Palace, El San Juan, Holiday Inn on the Beach,** Holiday Inn of the Condado, and La Concha, all in San Juan; **Cerromar Beach** and **Dorado Beach** at **Dorado,** about 22 miles west of San Juan. The smaller, more intimate places are found in Old San Juan and include **Monólogo, The Place, Los Balcones,** and **Sam's Patio.** There are now a number of first class discothèques including **Pier One, Juliana's** (Caribe Hilton), **Isadora** (Condado Holiday Inn), and **The Flying Saucer,** at Isla Verde.

There are also cultural attractions—the **Casals Festival** is an annual festival, usually the first two weeks in June; it is composed of concerts organized around the late Pablo Casals and his work. San Juan has a ballet company, and there is also a symphony orchestra, which can be heard either in San Juan or in other parts of the island during its touring season (Jan-May). There are also two theater festivals and a number of Cultural Activities Programs provided by the University of Puerto Rico. San Juan has a new **Performing Arts Center.**

SHOPPING

The best place to shop is in Old San Juan, where some 400 stores are crowded into an area of 15 to 16 blocks. San Juan has become a major jewelry center in the Caribbean. Prominent among dozens of jewelry shops that crowd Old San Juan are **Barquets** (205 Fortaleza), **Riviera** (205 Cruz), and **Jewels of the World** (150 Fortaleza). The last is also known for fine porcelain. The government-sponsored **Folk Arts Center** in the Dominican Convent sells native crafts and arranges visits to artisans' workshops, where you might see hammocks being made or baskets woven. You can also watch craftsmen at work at the **Craft Market** at **Hornos Militares,** not far from the **Tourism Pier,** and buy if you wish. Cigars are made and sold at several shops. Puerto Rican painting is developing into a serious movement, and paintings are for sale in numerous galleries around town. **Galeria Antillas** on Cristo Street is one that takes an active role in exhibiting and selling contemporary Puerto Rican art. Older, more traditional art forms include Puerto Rican *Santos,* small religious figures carved by local craftsmen; hand-carved tortoiseshell; handwoven straw; hand-screened fabrics; Spanish furniture; hand-embroidered clothing and ceramics. San Juan is also noted as a Caribbean fashion center, and you can buy locally designed clothes here at **Crazy Alice,** 106 Fortaleza, or at **Barbara Ann** on the Tourism Pier. **Timi's** is a good place for tortoiseshell creations; try **Don Roberto's** at Calle Cristo 205 for copper jewelry, and **Los Muchachos,** a large hardware store, for Spanish tiles. Some of the more interesting boutiques include **Fernando Pena** (Condado), **Carlota Alfaro** (1750 Loiza Street), and **Edith Tress** (1604 Loiza Street).

SPORTS

Foremost among spectator sports is cockfighting, which takes place from November through August in the **Coliseo Gallistico** in Isla Verde. There is also horse racing at **El Comandante** three times a week, and tennis tournaments are played at the Dorado Beach Hotel, and at the **Carib Inn,** Isla Verde. There is baseball at the **Estadio Municipal Hiram Bithorn** and boxing, wrestling, and basketball at **Roberto Clemente Coliseum.** Swimming is an all-year sport, and there are a number of beaches, including **Luquillo,** one of the most beautiful, as well as pools at many hotels. Deep-sea fishing is also popular; blue and white marlin, sailfish, wahoo, Allison tuna, dolphin, mackerel, tarpon, and snook are all available in great quantity. Boats are available from $65 per person, minimum two people, for four hours. A 38-ft deep-sea fishing boat runs $190 half day to $325 full day from the **San Juan Marina,** Tourism Fishing Pier, Fernández Juncos Ave, Stop 10, Miramar (tel: 725-0139), or **Captain Mike Benitez,** San Juan Yacht Club, charters the 53-foot *Sea Born* at $240 half day, $400 full day. Good beaches for surfing are around the north and west coasts, particularly at **Punta Rincón.** Skin-diving and snorkeling can be arranged through your hotel. Hotels with tennis courts include the **Carib Inn, La Concha, Caribe Hilton, Dupont Plaza San Juan,** and **El San Juan.** Courts are also available at the **University of Puerto Rico** at Rio Piedras and in **Hato Rey** by the WIPR studios, and at the **Parque Central** courts, near the Constitution Bridge. There are two 18-hole golf courses at the Cerromar Beach Hotel and two at the Dorado Beach Hotel in Dorado. There is skeet and trap shooting at the **Club Metropolitano de Tiro** in Rio Piedras. Yachtsmen should head for the **Isleta Marina** off Fajardo for comprehensive facilities, including repair and rental.

WHAT TO SEE

Metropolitan San Juan is a fast-growing commercial center composed of a number of municipalities whose major attraction, from a tourist's point of view, is **Old San Juan,** a 62-acre, 35-block-square city which is now more than 450 years old. The area of the old city itself is defined by the two forts, **El Morro** (completed 1785) and **San Cristóbal** (completed 1772), and the **Great City Wall.** Both forts are open daily 8-5, and there are tours at 11 and 2. Pan Am has Tours on Tape for El Morro Castle and for a trip around the island by car. Within the small enclosed structure of the city are numerous shops and restaurants, two ancient step streets, the old San Juan cemetery with its circular chapel, and a number of parks and plazas, some of the most pleasant of which are **Plaza de Armas, Plaza de San José,** and **Parque de las Palomas.** Otherwise the city is composed of a large number of buildings which go back to the days when Old San Juan was the commercial, financial, and governmental center of the city as well as the major residential area. Dozens of homes have been privately restored, while the Institute of Puerto Rican Culture has restored the impressive Dominican Convent and converted several residences into museums. Many of the pastel-colored buildings have elegant latticework windows of wrought-iron bars.

Particularly worth seeing is **San José Church,** one of the most beautiful in this part of the world; it is claimed to be the oldest functioning place of Christian worship in the Western hemisphere. Also, **La Fortaleza,** the old executive mansion, completed in 1540 and "refined" in the 19th century, makes for a memorable visit. There are tours of La Fortaleza, 9, 10, 11:30, 2, and 3:30 Monday to Friday. Other old buildings worth a visit include the **San Juan Cathedral,** the **Dominican Convent,** the **Tapia Theater,** and the **Casa Blanca,** which was the house lived in by the descendants of Ponce de León for 250 years. Museums include the **Casa de las Contrafuertes,** reckoned to be the oldest house in the old city (now a **Pharmacy Museum** on the ground floor and a **Graphic Arts Museum** and **Santos Museum** on the second floor); the **Museum of Puerto Rican Art; La Casa del Callejon,** an 18th-century house which contains the **Museum of Colonial Architecture;** the **Museum of the Puerto Rican Family;** and the new **Pablo Casals Museum,** which contains memorabilia of the famed cellist and tapes of his work.

The Metropolitan area itself has a number of "sights," among them **El Capitolio,** seat of the Puerto Rican Legislature; **Fort San Jerónimo** (1788), which houses a **Military Museum** (open 9-5, free on Sundays). At the edge of the city is the relaxing **Botanical Garden,** part of the University of Puerto Rico's ongoing experimental station in agriculture which supervises the operation. Across San Juan Bay, in Catano, is the big Bacardi rum distillery (open Mon-Sat). The 10¢ ferry ride linking Catano to San Juan is one of the better bargains of the island. But for a full cruise of the Bay and a seaborne view of the Forts, take the San Juan Bay Cruise. It lasts 1½ hours, costs $1.50, and leaves from the Ferry Terminal adjacent to Pier Three in Old San Juan at 2:30 and 4:30pm, Sundays and holidays. A tour of the **Bacardi Rum plant,** a visit to the **Ponce de León Museum,** and the 1½-hour cruise around **San Juan Bay** provide excuses to explore Metropolitan San Juan.

Outside San Juan one is said to be "out on the island," with a wide range of scenery, from cactus-covered desert to green mountains. Worth visiting is **El Yunque,** the beautiful tropical rainforest and bird sanctuary which is 25 miles from San Juan on route 191.

Areas of the island well worth visiting include **La Parguera,** a fishing village which is relatively unspoiled; nearby **Phosphorescent Bay,** where the slightest movement sets the night water sparkling; and **Ponce** and **Mayagüez.** Ponce, second-largest city of the island, is an important industrial center. The **Melia Hotel** (from US$40) is located downtown, and the **Holiday Inn** (from US$70) is at El Tuque Public Beach, 4 miles west of the city. In Ponce, see **Our Lady of Guadalupe Cathedral,** the **Parque de Bombas** firehouse, the market and the waterfront, and the superb **Ponce Museum of Art.** Designed by Edward Durell Stone, it has one of the finest collections of any museum in Latin America, including works by Gainsborough, Van Dyke, Velazquez, Reynolds, and more.

Mayagüez has the largest collection of tropical plants in the New World here at the Mayagüez Institute of Tropical Agriculture. Stay at the **Mayagüez Hilton Hotel,** PO Box 3629—tel: 832-7575 (from US$62 double).

Finally, see **San Germán,** perhaps the loveliest town on the island. Although it once rivaled San Juan for supremacy, it is now only a small town. Founded in 1573, it still retains the aura of its Spanish Mediterranean origins. **Porta Coeli,** now closed for restoration, is the chapel of the town and stands on a knoll at the end of a long plaza.

SOURCES OF FURTHER INFORMATION

Pan Am, 255 Ponce de León Ave, Hato Rey, and any other **Pan Am** office around the world; **Puerto Rico Tourism Company,** Calle San Justo, corner Recinto Sur, Old San Juan, PR, and 1290 Avenue of the Americas, New York, NY 10019; **United States Embassy,** 24 Grosvenor Square, London W1.

St Kitts-Nevis-Anguilla

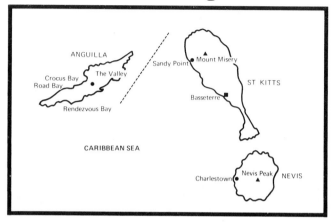

WHAT'S SPECIAL

From the upper reaches of the mountains where traces of the former rain forest are still to be found, down the slopes and to the cane fields and to its sea-swept shores, St. Kitts lives up to the name *Liamuiga*— the fertile isle—as the Caribs, who formerly lived here used to call it. Growing sugarcane and agricultural produce and catering to tourists are the main preoccupations of these islanders today, and the tourists grow in number as they recommend their friends.

St. Kitts is the oldest former British settlement in the West Indies, originally settled by Sir Thomas Warner and his wife and a party of fourteen, in 1623, intent on farming. They were joined by a group of Frenchmen, and from this base the British and French went about settling the other islands that because of their size were of no interest to Spain. These new arrivals caused the indigenous Caribs to get restless, and they planned an attack. One of the Carib women, it's said, forewarned the settlers who set about a defense. Copying the Caribs' own practice, they killed the men and male children, sparing the womenfolk, though whether to work as slaves or to join their clan, history is silent.

These early settlers grew cotton and indigo, tobacco and ginger. But as experience was gained in the growing of sugar and its distillation into rum and molasses towards the end of the 17th century, the earlier favored products dropped out. Today, cane is still the number one export crop of the territory, outside of tourism.

Nevis, less than a couple of miles south across The Narrows, enjoyed fame as a most fashionable spa during the 18th century, thanks to its sulphur springs. It was here that Lord Nelson married the attractive (and rich) young widow Franny Nesbit. Also the birthplace of Alexander Hamilton. Much of the charm of the former era remains and there are long, long stretches of palm-shaded beach—and of course, the 19th century Bath House still stands.

Anguilla, some 70 miles north of the islands, while legally part of the associated state, is now a self-governing British colony, and St. Kitts-Nevis is in fact, St. Kitts-Nevis-Sombrero. Anguilla is known for its beaches, lobster, and splendid water for scuba-diving and snorkeling.

COUNTRY BRIEFING

Size: 120 square miles   **Population:** 48,000
Capital: Basseterre (St Kitts)   **Capital Population:** 14,133
    Climate: The islands are in the path of the northeast trades, so cooling winds keep the temperature between 73°-84°.

Weather in Basseterre: Lat N17°20'; Alt 157 ft

Temp (°F)	Jan	Feb	Mar	Apr	May	Jun	Jul	Aug	Sep	Oct	Nov	Dec
Av Low	71°	70°	71°	73°	75°	76°	76°	76°	76°	75°	74°	73°
Av High	80°	81°	82°	83°	84°	85°	86°	86°	86°	85°	84°	82°
Days no rain	14	17	20	20	19	18	15	15	14	16	13	15

Government: Associated state within the British Commonwealth.
Language: English.
Religion: Protestant and Catholic.
Currency: East Caribbean dollar. 100 cents = EC$1.

	EC 10¢	EC 50¢	EC $1	EC $5	EC $10	EC $20	EC $50	EC $100
US (dollars, cents)	.04	.19	.37	1.85	3.70	7.41	18.52	37.04
UK (pounds, pence)	.02	.09	.18	.88	1.76	3.53	8.83	17.67

Public Holidays:

New Year's Day, 1 Jan
National Carnival, 26 Dec-2 Jan
Statehood Day, 27 Feb
Good Friday
Labor Day (1st Mon in May)
Whit Monday
Queen's Birthday (2nd Sat in June)

Easter Monday
August Bank Holiday (1st Mon in Aug)
Prince of Wales' Birthday, 14 Nov
Christmas Day, 25 Dec
Boxing Day, 26 Dec

HOW TO GET THERE

Flying time to St Kitts, Golden Rock Airport from New York is about 4 hours, from Miami 1¾ hours, from Paris 11½ hours. Fly to Nevis from St Kitts; flying time, 10 minutes. Time in St Kitts-Nevis-Anguilla: GMT−4.

REQUIREMENTS FOR ENTRY AND CUSTOMS REGULATIONS

Passports not needed for US, Canadian, or UK citizens (on visit of less than 6 months)—only proof of citizenship and a round-trip ticket. Smallpox vaccination required if coming from an infected area. Currency used is the Eastern Caribbean dollar and there are no currency regulations. All dutiable articles should be declared at point of entry. Duty-free allowance: 200 cigarettes, 50 cigars, or ¾ pound of tobacco; 1 bottle liquor; 1 bottle wine, and a reasonable amount of perfume for private use.

AIRPORT INFORMATION

Golden Rock Airport, Basseterre, is 1¾ miles from the city, or an EC$6 taxi ride. Newcastle Airport is 8 miles out of Charlestown. Departure tax, EC$5.

ACCOMMODATIONS

There are very good hotels on both St Kitts and Nevis. During the summer rates are reduced by about 15%-20%. Inexpensive guesthouse accommodations are available. A 10% service charge is added to your bill. Hotels on St Kitts (high-season rates):

Rates are in US$ for a double/twin room with bath or shower
Banana Bay Beach, Banana Bay (from $120 MAP)
Cockleshell, Cockleshell Bay (from $100 MAP)
Fairview Inn, Basseterre (from $50 EP)
Golden Lemon, Dieppe Bay (from $160 AP)
Fort Thomas, Basseterre (from $126 MAP)
Ocean Terrace Inn, Basseterre (from $65 MAP)
Rawlins Plantation, Mt Pleasant (from $120 MAP)
Royal St Kitts, Frigate Bay (from $156 MAP)

USEFUL INFORMATION

Banks: Open 8-12 Mon-Fri, also 3:30-5:30 Fri; National Bank Limited open 8:30-11 Sat.

Mail: Mailboxes, in concrete pillars, are red. Post Office open 8am-3pm daily except Thursday when closes at 11:30am.

Telephone Tips: Cost of local call EC15¢. Useful numbers on St Kitts:
Airport Information 2019 or 2470   **Emergencies** 999
Tourist Office 2620   **Operator** 0
Hospital 2551

Newspapers: Local publications in English are *Labor Spokesman* and *The Democrat.*

Tipping: At guest's discretion.

Electricity: 230 volts 60 cycles AC.

Laundry: Two-day service (dry-cleaning a suit costs from EC$20).

Hairdressing: Salons in town rather than hotels (shampoo and set from EC$15; man's haircut from EC$5).

Photography: All equipment available in St Kitts. Black and white film from EC$5; color from EC$10. Black and white, 1-2 days to develop; color developing not handled.

Clubs: Rotary, Lions.

Health: Tap water safe on St Kitts; it should be boiled on Nevis and Anguilla.

TRANSPORTATION

Taxis can be found on all three islands. You can rent a car from US$25 per day, or US$160 weekly. Remember that the islands are British, and driving is on the left. There is a ferry service to Nevis Mon-Wed, Fri, and Sat and at least one motorized schooner leaves for Anguilla weekly. You can fly with LIAT.

FOOD AND RESTAURANTS

The fertile land of St Kitts produces a bonus for the traveller in the form of tasty local crops, which has led to careful attention to good food. You'll find roast suckling pig, and even turtle steak at some places, while seafood is an island specialty. Some restaurants to sample in St Kitts are the **Blakeney Hotel, Golden Lemon** at Dieppe Bay, **Ocean Terrace Inn** [authentic "goat water" (mutton stew)], **The Palms, Rawlins Plantation, Anchorage** at Frigate Bay, and **Fairview Inn.**

DRINKING TIPS

Hours for the sale of liquor are 7am-9pm. For local products try *sorrel,* a drink made from sorrel pods and flavored with liquor, or *Duke,* a locally made liqueur, or a very passable local beer.

ENTERTAINMENT

All nightlife centers on the hotels. There is a casino at the **Royal St Kitts Hotel.** Discos include **Royal Disco** and **City Gate,** both on Fort Street, Basseterre, St Kitts.

SHOPPING

Basseterre is the shopping center of the islands. Most stores are in the **Circus** or on **Fort Street.** Best buys are English imports, perfume, china, linens, clothing, and cosmetics. Island handicrafts such as straw and raffia work, embroidery, and wood carvings are bargains. Shops to try are **Losada's Boutique** for silver and china, **American House** for Indian goods, the **Lotus Gift Shop,** the **Curio Shop,** the **Reliance Store** for linen and sea island cotton, and the **Crafthouse** and the **Tourist Bureau** for local crafts. Some of the Caribbean's finest batik is produced by **Caribelle** at Romney Manor, to the north and west of Basseterre, worth a stop on your way to Brimstone Hill Fort.

SPORTS

There is an 18-hole championship golf course surrounding the **Royal St Kitts Hotel** at Frigate Bay, St Kitts. There is also a 9-hole golf course at **Golden Rock,** on St Kitts and tennis clubs which welcome visitors on St Kitts and Nevis. Fishing from the shore is always successful, and deep-sea fishing trips can be arranged. There is good hunting for migratory birds from July to September, when the birds settle on a narrow neck of land called the **Great Salt Pond** at one end of the island, an area which can be reached only by jeep. For climbers, the full day ascent of **Mt Misery** (3,792 ft) is an exciting tropical adventure through virgin rain forest, alive with hummingbirds and the shrill chatter of green-backed monkeys, culminating in a strenuous descent into the crater. **Nevis Peak** is more akin to hill walking, though there are some steep pitches to be found towards the summit (3,232 ft). The beaches on Nevis and Anguilla are some of the best in the Caribbean.

WHAT TO SEE

You can drive around St Kitts in slightly more than four hours. **Brimstone Hill Fort** started life as a battery in 1689, following a successful skirmish by the British against the French. Completed in 1694, this former **Gibraltar of the West Indies** was developed into a fortress in the following century, and remained undefeated until 1782, when the French overpowered a small battalion of regulars and militia, Scots and English. In recognition of their bravery, the defenders were permitted to march out in full regalia. The following year a similar courtesy was extended to the French. The building is being actively restored and the refurbished Prince of Wales Bastion was reopened by HRH Prince Charles, June 1, 1973. The views are incredible—to the northwest are **Statia** and **Saba**, **Nevis** and **Montserrat** to the south. Northerly lie **St Barths** and **St Maarten**. Motor to the **Belmont** or **Harris Estates** for a closer look at **Mount Misery**. At **West Farm** and **Wingfield Estate** are large stones with Carib—or earlier—petroglyphs, and the more recent pre-Columbian discoveries at **Pond Pasture. Guy Fawkes Day** is celebrated by islanders on 5 November each year at **Black Rocks**, a scenic seascape on the Atlantic shore where prehistoric lava meets the ceaseless turbulent flow of winds and waves. **Basseterre** has a number of interesting colonial-style buildings. **Pall Mall Square** is lined with old English homes. The **Treasury Building** is distinctive, as is the **Customs Building.** The **Circus,** the center of town, has a Victorian clock tower, a fountain, and tall royal palms.

Nevis rises from the sea up to a perfect cone at Nevis Peak. The volcano is live, and clouds continually wreathe the summit. Sulphuric springs on the island made it a fashionable health resort in the 18th century, and the **Old Bath House Hotel,** built 1807, still stands amid the center of the gardens. A plaque on a stone wall marks the ruins of the house where Alexander Hamilton was born. One mile north of Charlestown is **Pinney's Beach,** probably the prettiest beach in the Caribbean. Snorkelers will love the coral reefs around **Newcastle Bay. Jamestown,** which slid into the sea in an earthquake of 1680, is still standing in the clear waters and makes a fascinating snorkeling expedition. Hotels on Nevis (high-season rates):

Cliffdwellers, Tamarind Bay (from US$120 MAP)
Croney's Old Manor Estate (from US$108 MAP)
Golden Rock Estate, St George (from US$120 MAP)
Nisbett Plantation, Beachlands (from US$130 MAP)
Pinney's Beach, Charlestown (from US$48 MAP)
Rest Haven Inn, Charlestown (from US$45 MAP)
Zetlands Plantation (from US$110 MAP)
Anguilla, 70 miles from St Kitts, but only 7 miles from St Martin, is

a small flat island, with mile upon mile of beautiful coral sands. The waters are clear and excellent for water sports, but take your own equipment. The superb beaches and relaxed atmosphere have led to recent increases in hotel facilities. Check latest listings before you go, or try **Lloyd's** in The Valley, **Rendezvous**, Rendezvous Bay, **Cul de Sac Hotel**, Blowing Point, **Maunday's Bay Beach Hotel** and a number of cottagestyle accommodations. Day boat trips to tiny, romantic **Sandy Island,** and deepsea fishing trips can be arranged through your hotel.

SOURCES OF FURTHER INFORMATION

Any **Pan Am** office around the world; **St Kitts-Nevis-Anguilla Tourist Board,** PO Box 132, Basseterre, St Kitts, WI; **Caribbean Tourism Association,** 20 East 46th Street, New York, NY 10017; **Eastern Caribbean Commission,** 10 Haymarket, London SW1 and 8 Frontenac Street, Place Bonaventure, Montreal 114 Canada; **Eastern Caribbean Tourism Association,** PO Box 146, St John's, Antigua, WI; 200 Buckingham Palace Road, London SW 1W 9SP, England; 220 East 42 Street, New York, NY 10017; **Nevis Tourist Committee,** Charleston, Nevis.

St Lucia

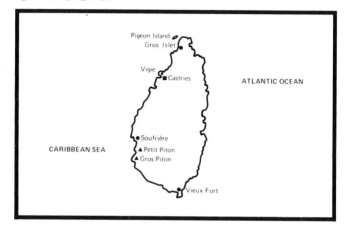

WHAT'S SPECIAL

One of the more delightful islands of the Eastern Caribbean, it's said that the islanders sing and cook in French while they use English for speaking, as a direct result of the Franco-British background they enjoy. Certainly the patois spoken has a melodious lilt, and in Castries, a Caribbean freeport, you'll find fine bargains in French perfumes, English porcelain and silks, plus the usual international items that are cheaper away from home.

Interestingly, the Castries City Council is the oldest democratically elected civic organization in the entire West Indies, while another claim to fame is the unusual "drive-in volcano"—at Soufrière—where Napoleon's troops made a *spa* of simple military fashion that may be enjoyed to this day. If you're planning on spending any length of time here, a self-drive car is inexpensive and worth the extra effort of weaving your way through fallen coconut-palm fronds and potholes. Also, of the more than 100 beaches, despite the interest of the sailing people, many are deserted and ideal for just getting away from it all.

St Lucia is scenically beautiful; it has picturesque harbor towns, white sandy beaches and clear blue sea, orchids, fruit trees, vast banana plantations, and volcanic peaks. It is a real vacation island, which annually celebrates the Feast of St Lucia (13 December); according to legend, St Lucia was discovered by shipwrecked French sailors in 1502, and after that was ruled seven times by the French and seven times by the English.

COUNTRY BRIEFING
Size: 238 square miles   **Population:** 120,000
Capital: Castries   **Capital Population:** 50,000
Climate: Temperature range is 76-90. Winter is dry, sunny, and not too hot. July is the wettest month.

Weather in St Lucia: Lat N14°; Alt 10 ft

Temp (°F)	Jan	Feb	Mar	Apr	May	Jun	Jul	Aug	Sep	Oct	Nov	Dec
Av Low	69°	69°	69°	71°	73°	74°	74°	74°	73°	72°	71°	70°
Av High	82°	83°	84°	87°	88°	88°	87°	88°	88°	87°	85°	83°
Days no rain	13	15	18	20	15	9	8	9	9	12	10	12

Government: An independent state and member of the British Commonwealth.
Language: English; a French *patois* also spoken.
Religion: Roman Catholic.
Currency: East Caribbean dollar. 100 cents = EC$1.

	10¢	50¢	EC $1	EC $5	EC $10	EC $20	EC $50	EC $100
US (dollars, cents)	.04	.19	.37	1.85	3.70	7.41	18.52	37.04
UK (pounds, pence)	.02	.09	.18	.88	1.76	3.53	8.83	17.67

Public Holidays:

New Year, 1 & 2 Jan
Independence Day, 22 Feb
Good Friday
Easter Monday
Labor Day, 1st Mon in May
Whit Monday

Corpus Christi
First Mon in Aug
Thanksgiving Day
Feast of St Lucia, 13 Dec
Christmas Day, 25 Dec
Boxing Day, 26 Dec

HOW TO GET THERE
Flying time to St Lucia, Vigie Airport from New York is 5½ hours; from Miami, 3 hours; from San Juan, 1¼ hours. Time in St Lucia: GMT−4.

REQUIREMENTS FOR ENTRY AND CUSTOMS REGULATIONS
Passport, or for US and UK citizens proof of citizenship plus round-trip or onward ticket. Smallpox, cholera, and yellow-fever vaccinations required if coming from an infected area. You can take as much currency as you like into the country. Imported flowers or plants have to be certified disease-free. Duty-free allowance: 200 cigarettes or 50 cigars or ½ pound tobacco; 1 quart liquor (including wine). Perfume for personal use.

AIRPORT INFORMATION
The International Airport is Hewanorra, 45 miles south of Castries. Interconnecting flights from Barbados, Antigua, or Martinique by LIAT (Leeward Islands Air Transport) fly into Vigie Airport, 2 miles outside Castries. LIAT links island to island and stops at St Lucia daily. Airport departure

tax is US$4. No airport bus. Taxis from Vigie to Castries cost US$5 and shared taxis cost US$35 from Hewanorra to Castries.

ACCOMMODATIONS

The central information bureau is the **St Lucia Tourist Bureau** (PO Box 221, Jeremie Street, Castries—tel: 4094). In the summer (April-December) rates are almost halved. Hotels in Castries:

Rates are in US$ for a double/twin room with bath or shower

Anse Chastenet, Soufrière (from $148 MAP)
Bois d'Orang, Choc Bay (from $80 EP)
Cariblue, Cap (from $134 MAP)
East Winds Inn, La Brelotte Bay (from $58 EP)
Halcyon Beach Club, Choc Beach (from $122 EP)
Halcyon Days, Vieux Fort (from $85 EP)
Halcyon Sands, Vigie Beach (from $36 EP)
Hurricane Hole, Marigot Bay (from $45 EP)
La Toc, La Toc (from $80 EP)
Malabar Beach, Vigie Beach (from $160 EP)
St Lucian, Reduit Beach (from $118 EP)
Villa Cottages, Vigie Beach (from $112 EP)
Villa, The Morne (from $80 EP)

USEFUL INFORMATION

Banks: Open 8-12:30pm and 1:30-4:00pm Mon-Fri; Sat 8:00-12:30pm.
Telephone Tips: Phones in public booths, restaurants, and cafés. Useful numbers:

Airport Information	**Tourist Office &**
(Castries) 6335	**Accommodation** 4094
(Hewanorra) 6335	**Directories and Operator** 0
Airport Tourist Office	**Ambulance** 95
(Castries) 2596	**Fire** 97
(Hewanorra) 6644	**Police** 99

Newspapers: English-language newspapers and magazines available. Local papers are *The Crusader, Voice of St Lucia, Herald, Standard,* and *Castries Catholic Chronicle.*
Tipping: Customary. Hotels usually add a service charge of 10% and a 5% occupancy tax; tip 10% in restaurants and same for taxis.
Electricity: 220 volts 50 cycles AC.
Laundry: Arrange through hotels. Dry-cleaning available.
Hairdressing: First-class hotels have salons (shampoo and set from EC$18-20; man's haircut from EC$10).
Photography: Color film is available in the island, but better bring your own and have it processed on your return; black and white film is available.
Clubs: Rotary, Lions, Jaycees.
Rest Rooms: In all stores. Signs in English.
Health: Doctors and dentists speak English. Imported pharmaceuticals not expensive.

TRANSPORTATION

Taxis are easy to get by phoning or at stands; fixed rates. Rate for renting a car is US$27-30 a day. Drive on the left. Boats are an important part of the interisland communications network. There is a ferry from Castries to Soufrière in the southwest, traveling to Soufrière Tuesdays and Thursdays and back to Castries Wednesdays and Fridays.

FOOD AND RESTAURANTS

The outstanding local dish is lobster, prepared in Creole style. There is also a rich soup-cum-stew, *callaloo*. International food is available in all hotels. The average cost of dinner for one in an expensive restaurant is US$15, in a medium-priced one US$8-10, and in an inexpensive one US$5-6. Good places to eat in Castries (remember to reserve in advance) are **The Coal Pot** of Lunar Park for *callaloo* and duck, and **Rain** (13 Brazil Street) in the Town Square for baked dolphin and banana flambée. Just outside Castries try the **East Winds Inn,** good for curries and sweet-and-sour pork, and the **Cloud's Nest Hotel** at Vieux Fort, for genuine West Indian food. Go to the **Green Parrot,** on Morne Fortuné, for local delicacies. Also worth noting are **Nick's Place,** for steak and seafood, and the **Calabash** (creole) both in Castries, while **Dolittle's,** seafood, Marigot Bay and **The Still,** (creole), Soufrière, have a following.

DRINKING TIPS

Rum is the local drink, and you have it in every kind of punch. Imported wines, liquors, and beers are on sale at reasonable prices. Average cost of a whisky and soda is US$2.50. Bars are open 6am to 10pm. A popular spot for drinks is **The Calabash** in the center of town.

ENTERTAINMENT

There are two movie houses showing films with original soundtracks. The most popular night life is dancing to calypso and soul music. In the high season, all the hotels have an active schedule of night life.

SHOPPING

St Lucia is now a free port, so shopping is good and inexpensive. All goods normally carrying a heavy duty are tax free. Best buys are crystal, jewelry, cameras, watches, perfumes, and, of course, liquor. Shops close early on Saturday afternoons. All main stores are downtown and easy to find. For West Indian crafts go to **The Shipwreck Shop** on Columbus Square, and for local pottery try the **Market.** In **Bagshaw's Studio** you will find original silk-screen prints on every kind of fabric. Buy the material by the yard or made up as table linen, placemats, cushions, etc. **Noah's Arcade** has a plentiful selection of handicrafts, sandals and dress, while you can stock up on locally made fragrances at St Lucia Perfumerie. The **West Indian Sea Island Shop** offers a selection of tropical wear, American, and locally designed clothing. **Noah's Arcade** is a good port of call for souvenirs, including some fine turtle shell items and local art. Bargain in street markets, but not in stores.

SPORTS

Golf or tennis can be arranged through your hotel. For scuba, the best place is **Anse Chastenet,** Soufrière, where a complete arrangement including gear is available. Go deep-sea fishing from the west coast; all equipment can be rented. The best beaches are **Vigie, Reduit,** and **Choc.** To see the island you can charter a **Carib Cruise** for just a day or for a week or two. They are luxury yachts; contact Carib at Vigie Cove, Castries (tel: 3184). Alternatively, arrangements can be made with Steven Yachts at Rodney Bay (tel: 8648).

WHAT TO SEE

Castries has one of the most magnificent landlocked harbors in the world, flanked by the impressive hills of **Vigie** and **Morne Fortuné.** At Morne Fortuné visitors can still see the military **Fort Charlotte** barracks, commanding a magnificent view of the coastline and the nearby islands. Drive to **Gros Islet** and take a boat to **Pigeon Point,** or drive to **Soufrière,** the second largest town on the island, named after the live volcano nearby. You can drive to within 50 yards of the sulphur springs. Soufrière is shadowed by the famous twin peaks of the **Pitons,** which can be scaled by semi-experienced climbers.

SOURCES OF FURTHER INFORMATION

Any **Pan Am** office around the world; **St Lucia Tourist Board,** PO Box 221, Castries, St Lucia; 41 East 42nd Street, Room 315, New York, NY 10017; St Lucia Tourist Board, 151 Bloor Street West, Toronto, Ontario M5SIP, Canada; **Eastern Caribbean Tourist Association,** 200 Buckingham Palace Road, London SWIW 9TJ.

St Maarten

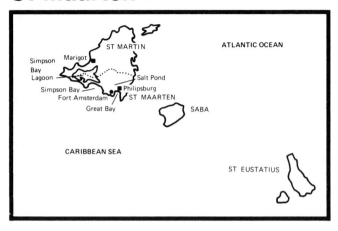

WHAT'S SPECIAL

The island enjoys the joint sovereignty of France and Holland. The island's name was originally Italian—San Martino, so named for St. Martin of Tours on whose saint's day Columbus sighted it back in 1493. Carib artifacts and the ruins of earlier primitive dwellings confirm its earlier habitations by this tribe of Amerindians.

In 1627 the Dutch discovered natural salt lakes on the island and settled there in 1631. Salt was a scarce commodity in Europe and the Spanish tried, without success, to regain control. It was during the battle in 1644 that the Dutchman Peter Stuyvesant (the governor of New Amsterdam, later renamed New York by the British) lost his leg. The Spanish left in 1648 and the Dutch found the French well established on the island. Legend has it that on March 23, 1648 one Frenchman and one Dutchman divided the island between their respective forces by means of a pace off and their descendants have lived harmoniously together ever since. The Frenchman was apparently the faster walker, and the French side is the larger, about 21 square miles. The Dutch part—16 square miles—turned out to be the more valuable over the years, on account of its salt pond. Wages were paid in salt, establishing the word salary.

Today there are two ways to spell the name, two different currencies (though the US dollar is acceptable throughout the island), two distinctive styles of architecture, and two distinctive ways of life. Perhaps more importantly, from the visitor's point of view, is that there are two distinct ways of cooking food, and the possibility exists of enjoying the best of both.

There are no customs, no immigration, no bureaucracy at the mutual frontier. Just a simple sign welcoming you to the French (or Dutch) side of the island. Everybody mingles. Tourism is the only economy. New hotels, restaurants, and beachside apartments plus such amenities as golf, deep-sea fishing, and scuba make this an increasingly popular destination.

COUNTRY BRIEFING

Size: 38 square miles

Capital: (Dutch) Philipsburg
(French) Marigot

Population: 17,000 St Martin
11,000 Sint Maarten

Climate: Temperatures, which range from 71-86°, vary very little. Rainfall scant and mainly in the fall.

Weather in Philipsburg: Lat N18°3′; Alt 13 ft

Temp (°F)	Jan	Feb	Mar	Apr	May	Jun	Jul	Aug	Sep	Oct	Nov	Dec
Av Low	71°	70°	71°	73°	75°	76°	76°	76°	76°	75°	74°	73°
Av High	80°	81°	82°	83°	84°	85°	86°	86°	86°	85°	84°	82°
Days no rain	14	17	20	20	19	18	15	15	14	16	13	15

Government: Sint Maarten is part of the Netherlands Antilles; St Martin is a dependency of Guadeloupe in the French Antilles.

Language: Dutch and French; English is widely spoken.

Religion: Protestant and Roman Catholic; other denominations represented.

Currency: St Maarten uses the Netherland Antilles florin (NAF96 = US$1); St Martin uses the new franc (4.20NF = $1). Dollars will be accepted almost everywhere.

Public Holidays: **Sint Maarten:** Christian holidays at Easter, Ascension Day, Whit Monday, and Christmas; Dutch Queen's Birthday, 30 Apr; Labor Day, 1 May; Concordia Day, 11 Nov; Kingdom Day, 15 Dec; New Year's Day.

St Martin: French national holidays and Catholic feast days.

HOW TO GET THERE

Flying time to St Maarten from New York is 3½ hours, from Miami, 1¼ hours, from London, 11½ hours. Flying time from St Maarten to Saba, St Barthélémy, or St Eustatius is about ¼ hour. Time in St Maarten: GMT−4.

REQUIREMENTS FOR ENTRY AND CUSTOMS REGULATIONS

Proof of US or Canadian citizenship is needed, and a round-trip ticket; all others require passports. St Maarten is a free port, and there are no currency regulations and no customs.

AIRPORT INFORMATION

Juliana Airport is 6 miles from the center of Philipsburg. Taxi fare downtown is about US$4.50. Departure tax is US$3.

ACCOMMODATIONS

Most tourist hotels are on the Dutch side of the island. There is a 5% accommodations tax and a 10% service charge. Hotels on Sint Maarten (high season rates):

Rates are in US$ for a double/twin room with bath or shower

Caravanserai, PO Box 113, Philipsburg (from $132 EP)

Castle Cove, Pointe Blanche (from $45 CP)

Coralita Beach (from $51 EP) 5 miles

Great Bay Beach, PO Box 310, Philipsburg (from $130 MAP)

Little Bay Beach, PO Box 61, Philipsburg (from $115 EP)

Mary's Boon, Juliana Beach (from $75 EP)

Mullet Bay Beach, PO Box 309, Philipsburg ($120 EP)

Oyster Pond Yacht Club, PO Box 239, Philipsburg (from $120 EP)

Pasanggrahan, PO Box 151, Philipsburg (from $88 MAP)

Seaview, PO Box 65, Philipsburg (from $80 MAP)

Simson Bay Beach, PO Box 34, Philipsburg (from $90 MAP) (note: there's a minimum of 5 nites, here)

Summit Hotel, Simson Bay Lagoon (from $74 EP)

Hotels on St Martin:

Beau Sejour (from $43 CP)

Holland House Beach Hotel, PO Box 393, Philipsburg (from $85 EP)

La Samanna, Baie Longue (from $200) 6 miles from Marigot

Le Galion, Baie de l'Embouchure (from $100 EP) 7 miles

Le Pirate, Marigot (from $90 MAP)

PLM St Tropez, Marigot (from $70 CP)

USEFUL INFORMATION

Banks: 8:30 to 1, Mon-Fri, 4pm-5pm Fri.

Mail: Mail should be taken to the post offices in Philipsburg and at the airport, or left at the hotel desk.

Newspapers: The local English-language newspapers are *The Clarion, Windward Island's Newsday, Morning Mirror* and the *New Age.*

Electricity: 110 volts 60 cycles AC (Dutch); 220 volts 50 cycles AC (French).

Laundry: Hotels have 24-hour service, there are two laundromats.

Hairdressing: Salons in hotels.

Photography: Good selection of film, but 3 weeks to develop.

Health: Doctors and dentists speak English. Toiletries expensive.

TRANSPORTATION

No airport limos. Local taxis are unmetered and may be expensive. Be sure to negotiate fare before starting out. Mopeds are inexpensive. Daily rate for rented cars from $25, or $160 weekly. The prices are fixed by the government.

FOOD AND RESTAURANTS

The island offers Dutch, French, Continental American and Caribbean cuisine. Seafood is the specialty. There is nothing tastier than lobster boiled in butter served the French way, with green salad and white wine. Conch is delicious. Reservations are suggested for dinner where phone number is included. In Philipsburg, good fare is to be found at **Restaurant Antoine** (2964), **La Grenouille** (2269), **L'Escargo** (2483), and **West Indian Tavern** (2965), with its slow turning ceiling fans, a parrot called Long John Silver, first rate piña coladas, plus daily backgammon. The French side has finer restaurants. At Marigot, dine at **L'Aventure** (87-53-58), an attractively restored house with an open air terrace overlooking the harbor, or try the duck in banana sauce at **La Calanque** (87-50-82) on the quay and **Chez Lolott** (Creole). A 10-minute taxi ride from Marigot is the rustic but elegant **La Nacelle** (87-50-42). At Grand Case, the ever popular **Chez Christophine** serves lobster crepes and duck with banana sauce, while bouillabaisse and seafood top the menu at **Le Fish Pot** (87-50-88). Then there's good French cooking at **Bilboquet** (reservations must be made in person), or **Le Panoramique** (2260), both in Point Blanche near Philipsburg on the Dutch side of the island, both overlooking the sea; at **La Bouillabaisse** on Front Street in Philipsburg or at **Le Filibustier**, which serves everything from Chateaubriand to pastry, also on Front Street. **Le Nosh,** off Front Street, combines the best in French cuisine with New York delicacies. Other popular restaurants are **Gianni's** (Italian), in Mary's Fancy Hotel, **Sam's Place,** and **Rusty Pelican.** In St Eustatius, go to **The Tea Shop** for snacks or to **L'Etoile** for West Indian fare.

DRINKING TIPS

No liquor restrictions. As this is a duty-free port, liquor is not expensive. For a local drink with a kick, try a guava berry punch. For drinks, there is the **West Indian Tavern** in Philipsburg (at the top end of Front Street).

ENTERTAINMENT

Little organized activity at night, though many hotels have dancing and steel band entertainment, and there is the disco at **L'Escargot.** Casinos are at the **Little Bay Beach Hotel, Great Bay Resort Hotel, Mullet Bay Beach Hotel,** and **Concord Hotel.**

SHOPPING

Shops in Philipsburg offer a wide range of purchases from Dutch silver and pewter and Delft china—at **Windmill,** perfume at **Yellow House,** West Indian crafts and souvenirs at the **Shipwreck Shop,** imported linens at **New Amsterdam** and **Carib House.** For fashion, try **Windward Islanders, La Romanna, St Trop' Boutique,** or **Penha;** for fine jewelry, china and crystal, try **Spritzer & Fuhrmann,** and for the unusual, **Around The Bend, Sea Urchin,** and **"C" Shell Shop.** There are plenty of island fashions, straw hats, baskets, tortoiseshell, and carved wood items to be found, and Marigot offers good buys in French cognac, champagne, liquors, and perfumes. See a good selection at **Vendome.** The new European high fashion shop is **La Ronada.** See **Little Switzerland** for china, crystal and jewelry.

SPORTS

Countless sandy beaches for swimming. The Dutch side has better beaches; **Great Bay** is a public beach and **Little Bay** is a popular hotel beach. You can rent snorkels and scuba-diving equipment, go water-skiing, and rent sailboats and fishing equipment. Then there's tennis at most of the large hotels, water-skiing at Mullet Bay, and golf. Best fishing months are March-July. **Island Water World,** in Philipsburg, can arrange equipment rental.

WHAT TO SEE

A drive around the island will take you past sandy beaches, and rolling hills. The main feature is the old 17th-century **Fort Amsterdam,** which recalls days of buccaneering. Cassette tape tours of the island are available at the **Shipwreck Shop.** Windward Islands Airways can take you to nearby Saba and St Eustatius. **Saba** is a 20-minute flight away. It is an extinct volcano rising 3,000 feet above the sea. You can fly over in the morning, take a chauffeur-driven tour across the island, lunch at **Ye Olde Inn** in **Bottom,** the principal village, and buy some Saba lace or fabric and clothing made by the Saba Artisans Foundation, then return to Sint Maarten in the afternoon. Accommodations on Saba include **Captain's Quarters,** Windwardside (from $60 MAP), **Cranston's Antique Inn** (from $50 AP), The Bottom, and **Scout's Place,** also Windwardside (from $45 AP). **St Eustatius** was long ago called The Gold Rock because of the opportunities for wealth that accrued to its earliest settlers. Its most unusual claim to fame is in being the first territory to recognize the United States as a sovereign nation, for which temerity it was razed by a British squadron under the command of Admiral Lord Bridges Rodney. Tourism is being steadily if slowly developed and accommodations include **Golden Rock Resort,** Zeelandia (from US$60 MAP) on two miles of beach, **Mooshay Bay Publick House** (from $72 EP), in the historic Lower Town of Oranjestad and **The Old Gin House,** Oranje Bay (from $92 EP).

Near the island of St Maarten is **St Bartélémy,** 8 square miles, 100 miles north of Guadeloupe, population 2,200; it has fine white sandy beaches and has developed as a tourist destination. Commonly called St Barts. The people here are of Swedish and French origin, as France sold the island to Sweden in the 18th century. It became French again in 1878 and remains a French possession. Some of its inhabitants still speak old Norman French and wear Norman provincial dress on feast days. The principal feast days are 15 and 24 August. They provide a glimpse of a way of life now extinct in mainland France. The port of **Gustavia** is one of the few naturally protected harbors which still offers refuge for sailing vessels. Quiet area for swimming and water sports. Gustavia has a Swedish atmosphere. Hotels on St Barts include **Baie des Flamands,** Anse des Flamands (from US$74 CP) 3 miles from Gustavia;

Hotel Castelets, Mount Lurin (from US$85 MAP) 1 mile; **PLM Jean Bart,** St Jean (from US$110 EP) 3 miles; and **St Barth Beach,** Grand Cul de Sac (from US$82 CP) 4 miles. Only 150 cars have been registered since before World War II and there are only three large estates—Rockefellers, Rothschilds, and Biddles.

SOURCES OF FURTHER INFORMATION

Any **Pan Am** office around the world; **St Maarten Tourist Bureau,** Philipsburg, St Maarten; 243 Ellerslie Avenue, Willowdale, Toronto: **St Maarten Tourist Information Office,** 445 Park Avenue, New York, NY 10022; **French West Indies Tourist Board,** 610 Fifth Avenue, New York, NY 10020.

St Vincent

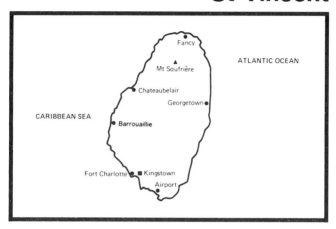

WHAT'S SPECIAL

St Vincent and its constellation of green islets, known as the St Vincent Grenadines, constitute one of the healthiest and most relaxing tourist spots in the Caribbean. The people are friendly, the climate radiant, the scenery a delight. Originally claimed by the French, the islands were ceded to Britain in the 18th century. From St Vincent to Petit St Vincent at the far end of the archipelago, the islands appear as a collage of emerald hills and glistening beaches.

COUNTRY BRIEFING

Size: 150 square miles **Population:** 75,000

Capital: Kingstown **Capital Population:** 23,000

   Climate: Sunny and warm, with an average temperature of 78°F and rainy spells in the summer and fall. Though the dry or showerless period runs from December to April, St Vincent's sun knows no seasons, making the island a year-round resort.

   Weather in Kingstown: Lat N13°13'; Alt approx. sea level

Temp (°F)	Jan	Feb	Mar	Apr	May	Jun	Jul	Aug	Sep	Oct	Nov	Dec
Av Low	73°	73°	74°	74°	76°	76°	76°	77°	77°	76°	76°	75°
Av High	84°	85°	85°	86°	87°	87°	86°	87°	88°	88°	87°	85°
Days no rain	30	28	31	30	31	30	29	26	27	28	29	29

   Government: St Vincent is an independent nation and a member of the British Commonwealth.

   Language: English.

Religion: Anglican, Methodist, Roman Catholic
Currency: East Caribbean dollar, 100 cents = EC$1.

	10¢	50¢	EC $1	EC $5	EC $10	EC $20	EC $50	EC $100
US (dollars, cents)	.04	.19	.37	1.85	3.70	7.41	18.52	37.04
UK (pounds, pence)	.02	.09	.18	.88	1.76	3.53	8.83	17.67

Public Holidays:

New Year's Day, 1 Jan
Discovery Day, 22 Jan
Good Friday
Easter Monday
May Day, first day in May

Whit Monday
Carnival, first Mon and Tues in July
August First Monday
Statehood Day, last Mon in Oct
Christmas Day, 25 Dec
Boxing Day, 26 Dec

HOW TO GET THERE

Flying time to St Vincent, Arnos Vale Airport from New York is 4¾ hours; from Miami, 3¼ hours; from Barbados, 35 minutes. Time in St Vincent: GMT−4.

REQUIREMENTS FOR ENTRY AND CUSTOMS REGULATIONS

US, Canadian, and UK citizens need only a passport or proof of identity (such as birth certificate) plus a round-trip or onward ticket for stays up to 6 months. Passports and, in some cases, visas are required of nationals of other countries. Cholera, smallpox, and yellow-fever certificates are required if arriving from an infected area. Duty-free allowance: 200 cigarettes or 1 box cigars or ½ pound tobacco; 1 quart wine or liquor; reasonable amount of perfume for personal use. There are no currency restrictions.

AIRPORT INFORMATION

Arnos Vale Airport is 3 miles from Kingstown. Taxis are available, the fare into town averaging EC$12-18. The airport has a duty-free shop and tourist information counter. No arrival fee; a departure tax of EC$10.

ACCOMMODATIONS

There are about 32 hotels in St Vincent and the neighboring islands. Summer season (May-November) rates can be lower by one-half or two-thirds, especially in the out-of-town hotels. The **St Vincent Tourist Board** can arrange accommodations at its two bureaus—one at the airport (tel: 84685) and the other in town (tel: 61224). There are also branches on the islands: Bequia (tel: 83286), Union (tel: 88350). Hotels in St. Vincent:

Rates are in US$ for a double/twin room with bath or shower

Cobblestone Inn, Kingstown (from $48 MAP)
Coconut Beach, Indian Bay (from $40 MAP)
Grand View Beach, Indian Bay (from $72 MAP)
Haddon, Kingstown (from $31.60 MAP)

Heron, Kingstown (from $125 MAP)
Sunset Shores, Villa (from $72 MAP)
Villa Lodge, Indian Bay (from $50 EP)
Young Island, Young Island (from $198 MAP)

USEFUL INFORMATION

Helpful Hints: Women should refrain from wearing shorts or other scanty attire in town. Men should pack a sports jacket or suit for evening wear, though the trend is toward increasing informality.

Banks: Open 8-12 Mon-Fri and 3-5 Fri. US currency accepted almost everywhere.

Mail: Stamps may be bought in most gift shops and at the Tourist Bureau. Mailboxes are red.

Telephone Tips: There are booths in town and phones in cafés and restaurants. Useful numbers:

Airport Information 84841
Tourist Bureaus 61224 (Kingstown), 83286 (Bequia), 88350 (Union)
Tourist Information 84685 (Airport)
Hospital 61185

Fire 999
Accommodations Offices St Vincent Hotel Association 71072
Police 71121
Operator, Information, Overseas Operator 0

Newspapers: English-language newspapers and magazines are on sale in St Vincent. In addition, the island has its own publications, *The Vincentian, The Star, Voice of St Vincent,* and *Tree.*

Tipping: 10% is customary where a service charge is not included in the bill. Porters, EC75 cents per piece handled; taxi drivers no less than 15%.

Electricity: 230 volts 50 cycles AC. A transformer is needed.

Laundry: Dry-cleaning and laundry can be arranged through the hotels (dry-cleaning a suit, from EC$5; laundering a shirt, from EC$2.50).

Hairdressing: There are salons in hotels in Kingstown. Shampoo and set, from EC$18; man's haircut, from EC$5.

Photography: Film and photographic equipment are available. Black and white can be developed overnight; color is not processed locally. Black and white costs from EC$10, color from EC$14.

Clubs: Rotary, Lions, and Jaycees.

Babysitting: Arrange through hotels.

Rest Rooms: In hotels and bars. English signs.

Health: Doctors and dentists speak English. Imported pharmaceuticals are sold at moderate prices.

TRANSPORTATION

Taxis are best obtained by phone. They charge fixed rates—for example, EC$20 for the trip between Kingstown and Fort Charlotte. Rented cars are about EC$60 daily, about EC$20 an hour if chauffeur driven. Drive on the left; a local license is needed, obtainable on presentation of your own license and payment of EC$5.

FOOD AND RESTAURANTS

Restaurants in St Vincent's hotels offer American and European food with local specialties, especially Caribbean fish dishes. In an expensive restaurant dinner will come to about EC$40 per person; at a medium-priced one about EC$25, and about EC$10 in an inexpensive eating place. An excellent hotel restaurant in Kingstown is the **Cobblestone Inn** (lobster flambe, callalou soup, dolphin Caribbean style). Seafood is also a favorite at the **Caribbean Sailing Yacht Club.** At the **Young Island** you can get a variety of dishes, while curry is a specialty of **Tropic Breeze.**

DRINKING TIPS

As in many other corners of the Caribbean, rum is *the* drink. Try the excellent local punch and the banana daiquiri. Imported liquor is relatively inexpensive, with a whisky and soda costing EC$3-3.50 and a bottle of red wine EC$25. There are no restrictions on the sale of liquor, and bars are open from 7am to 4am the next morning. The best and most popular spots for drinking are the hotel bars and the Aquatic Club.

ENTERTAINMENT

The nightlife is put on by the local hotels on a kind of rotating basis. On Friday the **Mariners Inn** has its own barbecue and steel band. Saturday is the **Villa Lodge's** turn, while simultaneously a combo is played at **Sunset Shores Hotel.** The **Aquatic Club** has music for dancing on Tuesday, Wednesday, Friday and Saturday. In addition, there are two movie houses which show recent films with original soundtrack at 8:30pm and a drive-in which opens at 7pm.

SHOPPING

Stores are open from 8-12 and 1-4 Mon-Fri, 8-noon Sat. Local handicrafts such as woven straw items, tortoiseshell products, and pottery are good buys. So are batik and tie-dyed materials, as well as cameras, perfumes, and other duty-free merchandise. Gifts under US$10 might be mahogany bowls, local straw and shell work, or imported china. The main stores at Kingstown are **Laynes Department Store, Y De Lima** (St Vincent) **Ltd., Traders Ltd, Trotman's Local Industries,** the **St Vincent Craftsmen Center, Noah's Arcade** (gifts), and **Stecher's** (jewelry, glassware and perfume), plus several boutiques—**Norma's, Batik Caribe, Dan Dan's, Charmaine's, Giggles,** and **Ashanti.** When in Bequia, go the the **Crab Hole** for cotton prints and for Javanese and Malaysian batiks.

SPORTS

Swimmers, snorkelers, and fishermen can enjoy superb sport in St Vincent and adjoining islands. In addition, complete facilities are now available for scuba diving, including courses and certification. **Villa Beach** and **Indian Bay** are only two of the sparkling beaches on the "mainland." Snorkelers will find vast new worlds to explore in the crystalline waters around **Bequia** and **Petit Nevis.** Spear-fishing expeditions can be arranged through hotels, with deep-sea fishing especially good in April and May,

when the blackfish abound. Cruises around the islands are increasingly popular with yachting and sailing enthusiasts. Those who enjoy mountaineering can tackle the summit of **Mount Soufrière,** a still-active volcano in the north of St Vincent. Golfers will find a 9-hole course at the **Aquaduct Golf Club** in the **Buccament Valley** about 20 minutes north of Kingstown. Tennis also is available there and at the **Kingstown Tennis Club,** both of which welcome visitors.

WHAT TO SEE

Kingstown's two cathedrals are examples of Colonial architecture at its best. **St George's Cathedral** has beautiful stained-glass windows and an interesting churchyard. The Roman Catholic **Cathedral of St Mary's** (built in 1877) is a mixture of Gothic, Romanesque, and Baroque styles. **Fort Charlotte,** overlooking the capital, is a typical 18th-century stronghold with the moat, walls, and original cannons still intact.

Rounding off the capital's attractions are its **Botanic Gardens,** established in 1765, and probably the oldest in the "New World." A new museum which showcases Caribbean and Arawak artifacts is now established within the garden grounds. Out of town the visitor should not miss the exquisite **Marriaqua Valley,** surrounded by towering mountains and dotted with banana, nutmeg, cocoa, coconut, and breadfruit plantations. Another must, especially for addicts of archaeology and folk art, is a trip to the **Carib Picture Rocks** at Layou and Barrouaillie. These are large human faces carved by the Indians in prehistoric times; the one at Barrouaillie is in fact an altar and was probably used for worshiping the Spirit of the Sun.

Perhaps the most spectacular excursion is to the summit of **Mount Soufrière,** which rises to over 4,000 feet. It last erupted April 13, 1979. Those who are fit enough to make the climb will find the crater lake and desolate slopes an unforgettable sight.

SOURCES OF FURTHER INFORMATION

Any **Pan Am** office around the world; **St Vincent Tourist Board,** PO Box 834, Kingstown; **Eastern Caribbean Tourist Association,** 220 East 42nd Street, New York, NY 10017; **Carribbean Tourism Association,** 20 E. 46 Street, New York NY 10017; 200 Buckingham Palace Road, London SWIW 9SP; **Eastern Caribbean Commission,** Place de Ville, Tower B, Suite 701, 112 Kent Street, Ottawa, Ontario.

Trinidad & Tobago

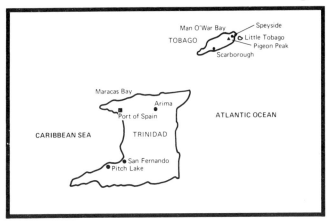

WHAT'S SPECIAL

Trinidad with its petroleum-based economy is still the home of gaiety and great humor, the birthplace of the calypso and the steel band, the home of the limbo dance, and a place where "carnival" is almost a way of life. And there is more to Trinidad than just people and atmosphere; it has sugar, cocoa, rum, coffee, citrus fruits, Angostura bitters, and the asphalt lake that has helped to pave half the world's highways. You may want to settle for the scenery: jungle, mountains, and the sort of beaches you would expect of the Caribbean. There is a good climate, too. Tobago was once the "in" place for pirates; you may not find any treasure left, but there are good beaches, breadfruit, mango and banana trees, a great coral reef to explore, the only bird-of-paradise sanctuary outside New Guinea, a cave where Robinson Crusoe probably did not live, and goat and crab racing.

COUNTRY BRIEFING

Size: 1980 square miles   **Population:** 1,150,000
Capital: Port-of-Spain, Trinidad   **Capital Population:** 250,000
   Climate: Temperatures range from 68°F to 89°F. Best time to go is in the cool dry season, January to May.

Weather in Port-of-Spain: Lat N10°37′; Alt 41 ft

Temp (°F)	Jan	Feb	Mar	Apr	May	Jun	Jul	Aug	Sep	Oct	Nov	Dec
Av Low	68°	69°	69°	71°	73°	73°	73°	72°	73°	72°	71°	70°
Av High	86°	86°	88°	89°	89°	87°	87°	88°	89°	89°	88°	86°
Days no rain	13	13	18	19	10	4	5	7	12	11	18	10

Government: An independent republic.

Language: English. Some French, Spanish, Hindi, and Chinese also spoken.

Religion: Mainly Christian, Hindu, and Muslim.

Currency: Trinidad dollar. 100 cents = TT$1.

	10¢	50¢	TT $1	TT $5	TT $10	TT $25	TT $50	TT $100
US (dollars, cents)	.04	.21	.42	2.08	4.17	10.42	20.83	41.67
UK (pounds, pence)	.02	.10	.20	.99	1.99	4.97	9.94	19.88

Public Holidays:

New Year's Day, 1 Jan
Eid-ul-Fitr
Good Friday
Easter Monday
Whit Monday
Corpus Christi
Labor Day, 19 June

Discovery Day (1st Mon in Aug)
Independence Day, 31 Aug
Republic Day, 24 Sep
Divali (Hindu Festival of
    Light), Oct or Nov
Christmas Day, 25 Dec
Boxing Day, 26 Dec

HOW TO GET THERE

Flying time to Port-of-Spain's Piarco Airport from New York is 4¾ hours; from Miami, 2¾ hours; from Caracas, 1 hour. Fly to Tobago, Crown Point Airport, from Piarco (20 minutes). Time in Trinidad and Tobago: GMT−4.

REQUIREMENTS FOR ENTRY AND CUSTOMS REGULATIONS

Citizens of the US or UK and nationals of most European countries do not need visas, except for stays exceeding 6 months—providing they have sufficient funds for their stay and a return or onward ticket. However, a birth certificate and/or driver's permit is no longer valid for entry and a current passport is mandatory. A smallpox vaccination is required of all except US citizens arriving direct from the US, British citizens arriving from the UK, and nationals arriving from certain Caribbean islands. Cholera and yellow-fever vaccination required only if arriving from an infected area. No more foreign currency may be taken out than was brought in. Duty-free allowance: 200 cigarettes or 50 cigars or 1 pound tobacco; 1 quart of wine or liquor.

AIRPORT INFORMATION

Piarco Airport, Trinidad, is 17 miles from Port-of-Spain; Crown Point Airfield is on Tobago. There is no airport bus service, but taxis are available at airports. Departure tax is TT$3. There are duty-free shops at the airports.

ACCOMMODATIONS

The **Trinidad** and **Tobago Tourist Board,** 56 Frederick Street, Port-of-Spain (and offices in New York, Miami, Toronto, and London) publishes a twice-yearly index of hotel rates. It will also help you to find somewhere to stay. Accommodations range from luxury hotels to modest guest houses. On both islands rates are reduced considerably out of season. There is a 3% accommodation tax and 10% service charge. Hotels in Port-of-Spain:

Rates are in US$ for a double/twin room with bath or shower

Bagshot House, 9 Saddle Road, Maraval (from $25)

Bel Air, Piarco Airport (from $30), at airport

Chaconia Inn, 106 Saddle Road, Maraval (from $30)

Chagacabana, Chaguaramas (from $22), 12 miles from city

Holiday Inn, Wrightson Road (from $50 MAP)

Kapok, 16-18 Cotton Hill, St Clair (from $27)

Normandie, 10 Nook Avenue, St Ann's (from $29)

Pan American Guest House, Piarco Airport (from $24), at airport

Trinidad Hilton, Belmont Hill (from $65 MAP)

Tropical, 6 Rookery Nook, Maraval (from $19)

USEFUL INFORMATION

Banks: Open 8-12:30 Mon-Thurs, 8-12 and 3-5 Fri.

Mail: Stamps at post offices.

Newspapers: Local English-language newspapers are the *Trinidad Guardian, Express, Evening News, Punch, The Bomb, The Sun,* and *National Target.*

Tipping: When a service charge is not included, tip 10% of the restaurant check. Tip taxi drivers 10-15%.

Electricity: 110 volts 60 cycles AC.

Laundry: Services at most hotels (dry-cleaning a suit, from TT$9; laundering a shirt, from TT$3).

Hairdressing: Shampoo and set from TT$20; man's haircut from TT$6.

Clubs: Rotary, Lions, Jaycees, and Kiwanis.

Babysitting: Arrange through hotel.

Health: Doctors and dentists are English-trained. Pharmaceuticals are available; water is safe to drink.

TRANSPORTATION

There are good bus services in major towns and long-distance buses to all parts of Trinidad and in Tobago. An express service runs every hour between Port-of-Spain and San Fernando. Taxis are readily available from stands or taxi firms. They have no meters, so arrange the charge in advance. Car rentals are available on production of a driver's license. Drive on the left. Trinidad & Tobago Air Services (T&TAS) runs services between Trinidad and Tobago, flying time 15-20 minutes. Two government coastal steamers do the 7-hour boat trip between the two islands four times a week.

FOOD AND RESTAURANTS

Cooking is cosmopolitan; you can choose standard English, American, or French food, Indian curries, or Chinese chop suey, but it is more fun to sample a Creole dish such as *callaloo soup, stewed tatoo* (the West Indian name for armadillo), crab backs (crab meat and stuffing served in the shell), fried plantain, or *tum tum,* which is mashed green plantains. Seafood is excellent and includes tiny bean-sized oysters, one of the specialties of the local seas, and *chip-chip,* small shellfish which taste like clams. The *cascadura* is a freshwater shellfish which is delicious stuffed. Do not miss the local-grown avocados, mangoes, and paw paw. The Tropical Hotel, Maraval, Port-of-Spain, is noted for the West Indian cuisine in its **Bamboo Room,** and **La Boucan** restaurant in the Hilton Hotel combines French and Creole cooking. The **Errol J Lau Hotel** also serves good Creole food. If you want to eat American-style, try the **Pan American Guest House,** where the steaks are flown in daily from the States and the ice cream is delicious. Port-of-Spain has two Italian restaurants—**Luciano's** on Prince Street and **Luciano's** in the suburban valley of St. Ann's. **Mangal's Indo-China** at 13 Queen's Park East, Port of Spain is a popular Indian restaurant. Chinese restaurants are plentiful and include **Shay Shay Tien, Ling Nam, Kapok,** and the **Golden Dragon.** Try **Kam's** for seafood, and for snacks try **Big Daddy, G's,** or the **Big L** cafeterias. In Tobago the **Hotel Robinson Crusoe,** a mile from Scarborough, is a good spot for Creole food.

DRINKING TIPS

Rum is the national drink, and Trinidadians mix the biggest planters' punch imaginable. Gin and coconut milk, sipped from the shell in the shade of a palm tree, is exotic and refreshing. Because this is the home of Angostura bitters, pink cocktails are popular. Bars are usually open, and women are welcome.

ENTERTAINMENT

The most exciting time to go to Trinidad is during the famous **Carnival** on the two days before Ash Wednesday. In **Port-of-Spain** calypso singers and steel bands rehearse nightly during the month preceding Carnival before enthusiastic audiences. Themes based on both local and international incidents are selected, and everyone starts making elaborate and colorful costumes months before Carnival begins.

But calypso is a big element all year round. The steel band as we know it was born on VE Day, 1945, so it is generally believed, when the population of Trinidad grabbed garbage can lids, saucepans, oil drums, anything to beat out a victory march in the streets of Port-of-Spain. Since then the steel band has reached a refinement which enables it to range from calypso to Bach.

Port-of-Spain nightclubs resound with calypso and steel band rhythm nearly every night. The **Penthouse Bar** and lounge at Independence Square is a popular spot; **La Boucan** at the Hilton has dancing mostly on weekends; and there is also dancing and a floor show nightly at the **Miramar Night Club** on South Quay and at the **Bagshot Hotel** in Maraval just outside Port-of-Spain. The **Club La Tropicale** at the Della Mira guest house in Tobago has floor shows on Saturdays. Of the discos, **JayBee's Discotheque** at Valsayn is tops. The **Little Carib Theatre** on White Street, Woodbrook, Port-of-Spain offers dramatic productions. Movie houses in Trinidad and Tobago show English and American movies with original soundtrack. There are plays and concerts at **Queens Hall,** Port-of-Spain. On Thursday evenings there is a dinner theater at the **Hotel Normandie,** Port-of-Spain.

SHOPPING

Shops are open 8-4 weekdays, closed half-day Saturday, and closed all day Sunday. Liquor and food stores close at 12 pm on Thursdays. Port-of-Spain is one of the big bazaars of the West Indies. Tourist shopping can be done by the "in bond" system, whereby luxury items such as Swiss watches, English woollens and bone china, French perfumes, Japanese cameras, Indian silks, Irish linens, and Trinidad rum are purchased at below duty-free prices and sent direct to the departing ship or plane. **Stechers** (the main shop on Frederick Street) is good for jewelry and perfumes. **Stephens & Johnsons,** Frederick Street, is a department store with a good china department.

Local handicrafts include straw and sisal goods, woodwork, bamboo trinket boxes, gold and silver jewelry, and dolls dressed as calypso singers, Hindu beauties, limbo dancers, or steel band players. The **Trinidad and Tobago Handicraft Co-operative** on King's Wharf and at the Hilton Hotel is a good place to go for these. They also have large steel drums and the smaller variety known as ping pongs. A good selection of calypso and steel band records can be found at **Sa Gomes Ltd** on Upper Frederick Street, **Rhyner's** on Prince Street and at **Sports & Games Ltd,** Chacon Street. Indian souvenirs are available at the **Bombay Bazaar,** Frederick Street, and **Y de Lima** nearby at no. 23. Fine handmade leather goods are to be found at **Drag Brothers** on Independence Square.

The prices in the shops in Scarborough (Tobago) are lower than in Port-of-Spain, though there is a smaller selection. East Indian fabrics and jewelry are good buys here, and there are good shops in the Market Square.

SPORTS

Favorite sports are cricket, soccer, hockey, tennis, and horse racing. There are race meetings virtually year around at **Queen's Park Savannah** in Port-of-Spain, at **Santa Rosa Park** in Arima and at **Shirvan Park** in San Fernando. At **Buccoo Village** on Tobago, goat and crab races are held once a year at Easter. Hunting is popular, the prey being armadillo, deer, alligator, mongoose, wild duck, and the wild hog known as *quenk.* The **Tourist Board** can give particulars about guns and hunting licenses.

Visitors are admitted to several tennis clubs. Tobago has an 18-hole championship golf course at **Mount Irvine Bay,** and in Trinidad there is the **St Andrew's Golf Course** at Moka Estate in Maraval. Snorkeling and scuba-diving are also excellent on Tobago, especially at **Buccoo Reef.**

In Trinidad, **Maracas** and **Las Cuevas** bays are good for water-skiing and sometimes surfing, and there are plenty of beaches on both islands which are excellent for bathing. Arrangements can be made at hotels for deep-sea, inshore, or inland-water fishing.

WHAT TO SEE

Trinidad has high mountains, tropical jungles, sweeping beaches, and sugar and cocoa plantations. Sightseeing tour operators in Port-of-Spain, such as **Hub Travel Ltd** (44 New Street), **Bacchus Taxi Service** (37 Tragarete Road), and **Battoo Bros** (67B Tragarete Road), run trips to such spots as the **Caroni Bird Sanctuary,** where there are about 6,000 scarlet ibis. There are also moonlight tours, the most spectacular being along "**Skyline Highway**" to beautiful Maracas beach. The **Pitch Lake,** a plain black lake of asphalt, which has provided asphalt for roads all over the world, should not be missed.

Port-of-Spain is set between high hills and has one of the busiest ports in the West Indies. You can see the shore of the Spanish Main from here, across the strip of water known as **Dragon's Mouth.** In the center of the town is **Woodford Square,** with the Parliament building (called **Red House**) and the Anglican **Cathedral.** Like Speakers' Corner in London, Woodford Square is famous for its open-air orators. In Independence Square is the **Roman Catholic Cathedral,** built in 1832. There is a large **Muslim mosque** on Queen Street and another, built as a memorial to Jinnah, in the village of St Joseph. The **National Museum and Art Gallery** on Frederick Street contains historical relics and a display of carnival costumes. Works by contemporary artists can be seen at **Fine Art,** 109 Frederick Street. The fashionable promenade of Port-of-Spain is the **Queen's Park Savannah,** a tropical park with racecourses and cricket grounds. North of the park are the **Botanical Gardens,** laid out in 1818.

Tobago, once a big sugar- and rum-producing island, is now a quiet holiday retreat. **Scarborough** has a colorful native market, and there is a good view across the ocean toward Trinidad from **Fort George.** Hotels are:

Arnos Vale, Plymouth (from US$55 MAP)
Mount Irvine Bay, Mount Irvine (from US$156 MAP)
Radisson Crown Reef, Store Bay (from US$108 MAP)
Turtle Beach, Great Courtland Bay (from US$120 MAP)

From the fishing village of **Speyside,** under Pigeon Peak, Tobago's highest mountain, boat trips are run to **Little Tobago,** also known as "Bird of Paradise Island"; this 450-acre bird sanctuary is the only place outside New Guinea where these gold-plumed birds can be seen in their wild state. The birds were introduced by Sir Thomas Ingram in 1909. Just round the headland is **Man O'War Bay,** one of the finest natural harbors in the Caribbean.

Buccoo Reef is the place to see marine life in the underwater coral gardens, and the **Nylon Pool,** hollowed out from a coral reef, is a good place to swim. "**Robinson Crusoe's cave**" is a mile-and-a-half walk from Store Bay at the western end of the island.

SOURCES OF FURTHER INFORMATION

Any **Pan Am** office around the world; **Trinidad and Tobago Tourist Board,** 56 Frederick Street, Port-of-Spain, and Administration Building, Scarborough; 400 Madison Avenue, New York, NY 10017; 20 Lower Regent Street, London SW1Y 4PH.

US Virgin Islands

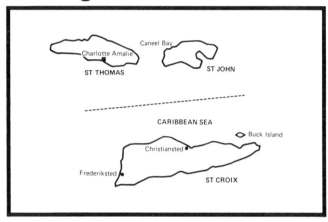

WHAT'S SPECIAL

The United States bought the Virgin Islands from Denmark in 1917 and acquired an excellent vacation area. Among dozens of islets are St Croix, the largest, St Thomas, the liveliest, and St John, the most beautiful. The climate and the beaches are both superb, and as almost everything is duty-free, imports from all over the world often can be bought at a fraction of their usual cost. Old merchants' warehouses have been made into smart shops, and there are new luxury hotels.

COUNTRY BRIEFING

Islands' Size: 133 square miles

Population: 97,000

Capital Population: 48,916

Capital: Charlotte Amalie (St Thomas)

Climate: The temperature averages about 80°, with low humidity.

Weather in St Thomas & St Croix: Lat N18°20′; Alt approximately sea level.

Temp (°F)	Jan	Feb	Mar	Apr	May	Jun	Jul	Aug	Sep	Oct	Nov	Dec
Av Low	69°	70°	70°	71°	74°	75°	76°	75°	74°	74°	73°	70°
Av High	84°	84°	84°	85°	86°	87°	88°	89°	88°	87°	85°	84°
Days no rain	24	23	27	24	24	23	24	23	21	23	22	24

Government: Unincorporated Territory of the United States.

Language: English. Some Spanish and Creole.

Religion: Roman Catholic and Protestant denominations.

Currency: The US dollar.

Public Holidays in addition to US holidays:

Three Kings' Day, 6 Jan

Martin Luther King's Birthday, 15 Jan

Lincoln's Birthday, 12 Feb

Transfer Day, last Mon in Mar

Carnival, Apr

Holy Thursday

Good Friday

Easter Monday

Organic Act Day, third Mon in June

Emancipation Day, 3 July

Supplication Day, third week in July

Local Thanksgiving Day, third Mon in Oct

Liberty Day, first Mon in Nov

Christmas Second Day, 26 Dec

HOW TO GET THERE

Flying time to Harry Truman Field, St Thomas from New York is about 3¼ hours, from Miami, 2 hours. Flying time between St Thomas and St Croix is ¾ hour. St John Island can be reached by air from St Croix in ¾ hour. Time in the US Virgin Islands: GMT−4.

REQUIREMENTS FOR ENTRY AND CUSTOMS REGULATIONS

Same as the United States. Returning US citizens are allowed $600 duty-free, including the cost of 1 gallon liquor and unlimited cigarettes. All other visitors are guided by their local customs regulations.

AIRPORT INFORMATION

Harry Truman Field Airport is 2 miles from Charlotte Amalie. No airport bus; taxis always available, costing $3 for one person plus $1 each additional passenger, suitcases 40¢ each. There is no departure tax. The airport has a tourist information booth.

Hamilton Airport, St Croix, is about 5 miles from Christiansted and taxis are always available for $4 a person. At the baggage counter there is a list of taxi rates. There is no departure tax.

ACCOMMODATIONS

Most hotel rates are 25-35% lower 1 May-15 December. Less expensive guesthouse accommodations available. Hotels in St Thomas (high season rates):

Rates are in US$ for a double/twin room with bath or shower

Bluebeard's Castle, PO Box 7480, in Charlotte Amalie, overlooking harbor (from $98)

Bolongo Bay Beach, PO Box 7337, on beach southeast of Charlotte Amalie (from $120)

Carib Beach, PO Box 340, on beach southwest of Charlotte Amalie (from $68)

Frenchman's Reef, PO Box 7100, on beach southeast of Charlotte Amalie (from $120)

Harbor View, PO Box 1975, overlooking Charlotte Amalie (from $60)

Hotel 1829, PO Box 1579, downtown Charlotte Amalie (from $50)

Island Beachcomber, PO Box 1689, on beach west of town near airport (from $60)

Limetree Beach, PO Box 7307, on beach southeast of Charlotte Amalie (from $94)

Mafolie, on hill overlooking harbor (from $48)

Magens Point, Magens Bay Road, on a hillside overlooking Magens Bay on north shore of St Thomas (from $90)

Mahogany Run Golf and Tennis Resort, on the north shore of St Thomas (from $108)

Morningstar Beach Resort, PO Box 8328, on beach southeast of Charlotte Amalie (from $60)

The Pavilions & Pools, Sapphire Bay (from $114)

Pineapple Beach Resort, PO Box 2516, on beach on eastern coast of St Thomas (from $96)

Sapphire Beach, Box 8088, on beach at Sapphire Bay (from $81)

Scott, PO Box 127, in hills above Charlotte Amalie (from $45)

Sea Horse Cottages, Nazareth Bay at beach (from $37)

Secret Harbour, PO Box 7576, on beach at southeast corner of St Thomas (from $85)

St Thomas Sheraton, PO Box 7970, walking distance from Charlotte Amalie (from $78)

Sugar Bird Beach, PO Box 570, on an island, 7 minutes by launch from Charlotte Amalie (from $85)

Virgin Isle Hotel, on hill overlooking harbor (from $83)

Windward Passage, PO Box 639, downtown Charlotte Amalie (from $70)

USEFUL INFORMATION

Dress is casual, but bathing suits should not be worn in towns; men should wear shirts.

Banks: Open 9-2:30 Mon-Thurs, also 9-2 and 3:30-5 Fri; closed Sat. Outside towns, banks are in shopping centers. Travelers' checks accepted everywhere.

Mail: Mailboxes are blue.

Telephone Tips: Public booths; phones rarely in restaurants and cafés. Useful numbers in St Thomas and St Croix:

Police 915	**Directory** 922
Ambulance 922	**Fire** 921

St Thomas **Emergency Hospital** 774-1212; St Croix 773-1212.

St Thomas **Tourist Information** 774-2566; St Croix 773-0495.

Newspapers: Local publications are *The Daily News, The Daily Post, The Weekly Journal,* and, for visitors, *St Thomas This Week* (also covers St John) and *This Week in St Croix,* both free.

Tipping: Service charge not usually included in restaurant checks, so tip 15%. Taxi drivers, 10%; porters, 50¢ per bag.

Electricity: 120 volts 60 cycles AC.

Laundry: 24-hour service available in the cities, and hotels have express facilities (dry-cleaning a suit, from $3.50; laundering a shirt, from 75 cents).

Hairdressing: Some large hotels have salons (shampoo and set from $10, man's haircut from $5).

Photography: Excellent selection of equipment. Two days to develop black and white; new 1-hour service for color at Bakery Square, St Thomas.

Babysitting: Check with hotel.

Health: Good medical facilities. Pharmaceuticals more expensive generally than on US mainland.

TRANSPORTATION

On St Thomas, Mannassah Bus Line vehicles stop in Charlotte Amalie (Market Place and along the Waterfront Highway) on their route between the College of the Virgin Islands to the west and Red Hook at the southeast tip of the island. A 2-hour tour by surrey bus covers most sights and costs $7.50. Taxis can be hailed in the street and have a fixed rate, with $1 per additional passenger. Suitcases in excess of one per passenger are 40¢ and after-midnight fares 50 cents extra in towns, $1 in the country. Taxi drivers will sometimes ask for more. A taxitour for one or two is $15 per hour; three or more, $6 per passenger. Water taxis begin at about $12 during the day, and there are frequent ferry services between St Thomas and St John. Antilles Airboats and other airlines operate island flights. A seaplane and launch service connects St Thomas with St John and St Croix with Buck Island. Traffic drives on the left; speed limits are 20 mph in town, 35 mph in the country. Car rental begins at $28 per day for a compact, and motorbikes are also for rent at $22. A temporary driver's license is required, obtainable from the car rental agency for $1. A US driving license is valid in the Virgin Islands for 90 days.

FOOD AND RESTAURANTS

Local delicacies are fish soups, *fungi* (spiced cornmeal paste), turtle, *kalaloo* (a spinach-type soup or stew), *souse* (spicy pig's feet stew), and *soursop* (a local fruit) ice cream. Mealtimes are as in the US, and prices are about $15 for an expensive meal, $7 for a medium-priced one, and $4-5 for an inexpensive one.

On St Thomas try **Bluebeard's Castle** on Bluebeard's Hill (tel: 774-1600) and **Daddy's** (tel: 775-1787). In Charlotte Amalie **Harbor View** (tel: 774-2651) has enjoyed a reputation for good fare with island gourmets for some time, while **Frenchman's Reef** (tel: 774-8500) has no less than three restaurants (Friday night is West Indian buffet dinner). **Magens Point Hotel** (tel: 774-2790) overlooking Magens Bay and the downtown **Hotel 1829** in Charlotte Amalie both have island dishes. **L'Escargot,** just outside of Charlotte Amalie (tel: 774-6565) is an excellent French restaurant; it has a downtown branch (774-8880). Chinese food is at its best in **China Gardens,** 10 Norre Gade (tel: 774-3256), and **Kum Wah** in St Thomas Gardens (tel: 774-5575), while Italian cuisine is represented by **Driftwood Inn** (tel: 774-2390), up in the hills. **Mafolie** (tel: 774-2790), on Mafolie Mountain 800 feet above Charlotte Amalie, specializes in charcoal-broiled steak and lobster. **Bartolino's** (tel: 774-8554) is a favorite spot in Frenchtown. At Compass Point, try **Fisherman's Wharf** (tel: 775-3755).

DRINKING TIPS

Although imported liquor is inexpensive (Scotch and soda, $1), islanders remain loyal to their locally distilled rum, used in drinks with names like *Virgin Me Eye* and *Shy Virgin*. There are no liquor restrictions for adults; cafés and bars are always open late. Popular bar/restaurants in St Thomas: **Sebastian's** (with calypso singers), the **Carousel** (fun for daiquiris and watching the world go by), the **Crazy Cow,** a downtown soda fountain, **Sparky's Waterfront Saloon,** and the **Greenhouse,** a Trader Vic-type bar-restaurant.

ENTERTAINMENT

In St Thomas most hotels and restaurants have dancing and entertainment, usually steel bands and limbo dancers. Nightclubs stay open until the small hours. Some of the best in St Thomas include **Limetree, Waiter's Living Room, Top of the Reef** at Frenchman's Reef Hotel, and the **Carib Beach Hotel,** featuring limbo and native steel bands on Saturday nights. **Studio 54** is a popular disco at the Virgin Isle Hotel. A big annual event is the **St Thomas Carnival** at the end of April, a week of parades, fireworks, costumes, and nonstop calypso. St John has a similar **Fourth of July Carnival,** while St Croix has an annual **Christmas Festival.**

SHOPPING

In St Thomas, cameras, watches, perfume, liquor, jewelry (in fact all luxury goods) are at near duty-free prices. **Main Street** (Dronningens Gade) is lined with stores, many in old warehouses, open from 8:45-5, closed Sunday (except when cruise ships are in port). You do not need to bargain. The **Continental** is a large department store, and **Bolero** stocks most things from a handkerchief to a Picasso lithograph. Try some island scents at **Tropicana Perfume Shoppes.** The **Mahogany Center of the Virgin Isles** displays carvings and lovely tortoiseshell jewelry. The **Jewel Box** prides itself on the low price of its rubies, sapphires, and pearls. **H Stern** is known around the world for jewelry. **Little Switzerland** is the place for cameras, and **Lion in the Sun** and **Caron's** are luxury boutiques with fashions and perfume from France and Italy. Many new shops have opened at Bakery Square on **Back Street.** The old **Market** on Main Street is busy on Saturday mornings, when local farmers bring in produce.

SPORTS

The islands are perfect for anything that takes place on, in, and under the sea—swimming, sailing, snorkeling, scuba-diving, deep-sea fishing, and water-skiing. At **Harm's Marina,** the lagoon Undersea Center offers beginners' training programs, wreck exploration, and underwater safaris. There is the 18-hole **Fountain Valley Golf Course** at Davis Bay Beach on St Croix, the new 18-hole **Mahogany Run Golf Course** on St Thomas, and tennis courts on St Croix, St Thomas, and St John. Horse racing, horseback riding, baseball, basketball, and cricket are other activities.

WHAT TO SEE

St Thomas: The capital, **Charlotte Amalie,** a pirate rendezvous in the 17th and 18th centuries, is still a lively town of narrow cobbled streets and steps, villas, and a lovely harbor. The oldest building is the 17th-century **Fort Christian,** with a small museum in its cells, and the most attractive is **Crown House** on top of the 99 Steps, an 18th-century colonial residence on **Blackbeard's Hill.** The reception rooms of **Government House** have a collection of paintings, including two by the Impressionist painter Pissarro, a native of St Thomas. A "must" on St Thomas is a trip to **Coral World,** with its underwater observation tower and marine park. The **Orchidarium,** off Harwood Highway, has tropical plants and hundreds of orchids. Explorer Sir Francis Drake is said to have reviewed his fleet from **Drake's Seat,** high above Magens Bay. Near the bay is the **Indies House** luxury hotel, with a popular children's zoo. Take a ride on a glass-bottomed boat for a tour of the harbor (from the dock near the coastguard station). Along the eastern coast of the island are the hotel resorts of **Pelican Beach Club, Pineapple Beach Club, Pavilions and Pools** (each cottage unit has its own swimming pool), **Sapphire Beach Club,** and **Mahogany Run Golf and Tennis Resort.**

St Croix: With its delightfully named sugar plantations (Jealousy, Hope, Love), windmills, and crumbling ruins of grand old estates, this is the most historic of the islands. It also has, at **Buck Island,** the only US national monument that is partially underwater—with a superb underwater trail. In **Christiansted,** Danish architecture is preserved among the pastel-colored houses, and many old colonial buildings have been converted to modern use. **Government House** was originally a wealthy merchant's house, taken over in 1771. The old **Custom House** is now the public library, and the Danish West Indian and Guinea Company Warehouse is occupied by the telegraph office. **Fort Christiansvaern** is the best preserved of the five remaining forts on the islands. In **Steeple Building,** a Lutheran church, is the **St Croix Museum,** with interesting pre-Columbian artifacts. On the waterfront by the picturesque wharf area (a national historic site) are the **King Christian** and **King's Alley** hotels and the **Club Comanche,** with a popular bar. On a tiny island in the harbor is the first-class **Hotel on the Cay.** The **Island Center** is the cultural heart of St Croix; there are programs of ballet and drama, concerts, and musicals, sometimes free but always inexpensive. **Frederiksted** on the west coast is another charming old Danish city; like Christiansted, it has a good shopping center. The **Frederiksted Hotel** is downtown. **Sprat Hall,** a mile away, has good food and lots of sports, especially horseback riding. **Cottages-by-the-Sea** and **Waves at Cane Bay** are informal family accommodations. The estate of **Whim's Greathouse,** 4 miles east, has a lovely old mansion with period furnishings which is open to the public. Good restaurants include the **Persian Virgin** and the **Smithfield Mill** in Frederiksted. In Christiansted try **Dick Boehm's Comanche Restaurant,** which serves steak and seafood; **Top Hat,** where you can sample Danish dishes; **Frank's, Eccentric Egret, Tivoli Gardens,** or **Café de Paris.** Nightclubs in the Christiansted area are **Cruzan Moon, Buccaneer, St Croix-by-the-Sea,** the **Moonraker,** the **Grandstand Play, Kips,** and **Grapetree Bay.** In Frederiksted: **Belardo's,** the **Brandy Snifter,** and **Seven Flags.** Hotels in St Croix (high season rates):

Rates are in US$ for a double/twin room with bath or shower

Anchor Inn of St Croix, 58-A King Street, on the waterfront of Christiansted (from $69)

Buccaneer, PO Box 218, on beach northeast of Christiansted (from $100)

Cane Bay Plantation, Kingshill, on beach west of Christiansted, near golf course (from $85)

Caravelle, Queen Cross Street, downtown Christiansted (from $48)

Cane Bay Reef Club, PO Box 1407, suites, on beach west of Christiansted (from $295 weekly)

Club Comanche, 1 Strand Street, downtown Christiansted (from $53)

Gentle Winds, PO Box 3000, on North Shore Beach, west of Christiansted (from $65)

Grapetree Beach Hotel, Grapetree Bay, on beach at southeastern corner of St Croix (from $90)

Holger Danske, 1 King Cross Street, downtown Christiansted (from $55)

King Christian, 59 King Street, downtown Christiansted (from $43)

King's Alley, 55-57 King's Alley, downtown Christiansted (from $45)

St Croix-by-the-Sea, PO Box 248, on beach west of Christiansted (from $110)

St John, most of which is in the **Virgin Islands National Park,** is an unspoiled island of deserted beaches, wooded mountains, and 18th-century sugar plantations. At **Petroglyph Falls** there are rock carvings made by Arawak and Carib Indians. At Trunk Bay the famous **Underwater Trail** to Buck Island (off St Croix) has fish, coral formations, and seaplants, identified with plaques. **Caneel Bay Plantation,** PO Box 120 (from US$180 MAP) has some top names on its hotel register. Rates in the island's resort cottages range from $250-$1,000 per week. Campsites and cabins in the Park should be reserved well in advance. A scheduled taxi-bus ($1) leaves **Cruz Bay** for **Caneel, Trunk,** and **Cinnamon Bays** several times daily. Full day tours of St John may be arranged from St Thomas ($25).

SOURCES OF FURTHER INFORMATION

Any **Pan Am** office around the world; **Virgin Islands Government Tourist Office,** Department of Commerce, St Croix 00820; 1270 Avenue of the Americas, New York, NY 10020.

Index